THE BRITISH BOXING BOARD OF CONTROL

BOXING YEARBOOK 2010

Edited by
Barry J. Hugman

MAINSTREAM
PUBLISHING

EDINBURGH AND LONDON

First published in Great Britain in 2009 by
MAINSTREAM PUBLISHING COMPANY
(EDINBURGH) LTD
7 Albany Street
Edinburgh EH1 3UG

ISBN 9781845964863

A catalogue record for this book is available
from the British Library

Typeset and designed by
Aeshna Ltd

Printed and bound in Great Britain by
CPI Mackays of Chatham Ltd, Chatham, ME5 8TD

Contents

TARA BOXING PROMOTIONS & MANAGEMENT

Doughty's Gym
Princess Road, Shaw, Oldham OL2 7AZ
Tel/Fax: 01706-845753 (Office)
Mobile: 07932-085865
Tel: 01706-846762 (Gym)

Trainers: JACK DOUGHTY & GARY FORD
Matchmakers: JOHN INGLE
MC: MICHAEL PASS / MIKE GOODALL

Acknowledgements

Now in its 26th year this publication has always been very much a team effort, with many of the original members still participating, and I would like to thank all those who continue to help establish the *British Boxing Yearbook* as the 'Wisden' of British boxing.

As in previous years, I am indebted to the new BBBoC's General Secretary, Robert Smith, along with Lynne Conway, Helen Oakley, Donna Streeter and Sarah Aldridge, for their help and support in placing information at my disposal and being of assistance when required. Other Board members to be of help were Les Potts, who now looks after the Midlands, Southern and Western Areas, and Simon Block, who now handles Commonwealth matters. John Carey was also most helpful. I also appreciated the fact that Charles Giles, the Board's Chairman, took time out to produce an interesting insight into his involvement in boxing.

On a business front, I would like to thank the BBBoC for their support and Bernard Hart, the Managing Director of the Lonsdale International Sporting Club, for his efforts in helping to organise the annual British Boxing Board of Control Awards Luncheon where the book will be officially launched. The Awards Luncheon or Dinner has been an ongoing function since 1984, when it was established as a vehicle to launch the first *Yearbook*. Following that, Bernard, ably backed up by Kymberley and Chas Taylor, helps to make sure that the standard remains top class. At the same time, I would like to thank all of those who advertised within these pages for their support.

Members of the *Yearbook* 'team' who wrote articles for this year's edition and who have recently been published, or are in the process of publishing their own books are: the Northern Area Secretary, John Jarrett (currently working on a book about Mickey Walker, 'The Toy Bulldog'); Ralph Oates (as a boxing quiz book specialist, having published The Muhammad Ali Boxing Quiz Book last year, Ralph is in the process of publishing *The Ultimate Boxing Quiz Book*); Keith Robinson (has recently published *Lanky Bob: The Life, Times and Contemporaries of Bob Fitzsimmons*); Bob Lonkhurst (the author of excellent biographies on Tommy Farr, Jack Petersen, Terry Spinks and Dave 'Boy' Green, is well on the way to finalising the life story of Eric Boon); and Patrick Myler (who has recently published *Dan Donnelly, 1788-1820, Pugilist, Publican, Playboy*). Others who have written articles for the Yearbook and in the process of publishing are Melanie Lloyd (who is due to produce another *Sweet Fighting Man*) and Tony Gee (who has published the acclaimed *Up to Scratch* and is working on a book about the Scottish prize-ring).

Once again, Wynford Jones, a Class 'A' referee and a big supporter of boxing, came to my aid when travelling to the Board's offices on a regular basis in order to collate vital data required for this publication. Other members of the *Yearbook* 'team' are Bob Yalen, who has covered boxing with ABC across the world and looks after the 'World Title Bouts" section; Harold Alderman MBE, an unsung hero who has spent over 40 years researching the early days of boxing through to modern times, Eric Armit, the Chairman of the Commonwealth Boxing Council and a leading authority on boxers' records throughout the world, who is responsible for the 'A-Z of Current World Champions'; Derek O'Dell, a former amateur boxer and the former Chairman of Croydon EBA, produces the 'Obituaries" section; and Ray Caulfield, who is one of the leading lights of the London EBA and a driving force of the EBA movement as a whole, keeps the 'Directory of Ex-Boxers' Associations' up to date. I would also like to thank Brian Donald, an old friend of mine, and Anton Shapiro for kindly producing articles for this edition.

Regarding photographs, With Les Clark still mainly incapacitated following the loss of a leg, Philip Sharkey again came to the aid of the *Yearbook* when getting to as many shows as he could to make sure that the complement of illustrations was up to its normal standard. Philip also produced 'Glove Story', which reviews boxing books published during the season. As in previous years, Les, who has possibly the largest library of both action shots and poses from British rings over the last 20 years or more, continued to visit shows whenever he could. If anyone requires a copy of a photo that has appeared in the *Yearbook* credited to Les, or requires a list, he can be reached at 352 Trelawney Avenue, Langley, Berks SL3 7TS. Les bravely struggles on and is determined to get back at ringside as quickly as possible. We wish him well. Other photos were supplied by my good friend Larry Braysher, a well-known collector, who provided several illustrations for the 'Tommy Milligan', 'Dai Corp' and 'I'll Knock You Out Inside Four Rounds' articles, as well as for the 'Obituaries' and 'World Champions Since Gloves" sections.

Also, additional input came from Michael Featherstone (who is always available to help out on birth/death details); Mrs Enza Jacoponi, the Secretary of the European Boxing Union (EBU Championship data covering the past 12 months); Malcolm Collins (Welsh amateur boxing); Brian Donald (Scottish amateur boxing); Steve Brooks, Dave Cockell, John Donnelly, Stuart Gill and Kevin Williams (English Amateur Boxing). I must also make mention of John Sheppard, of BoxRec.Com, who kindly delivered the update for the 'Active British-Based Boxers: Career Records" section in the correct order for me to start my audit. John and his contributors also kept me informed of many old fighters who passed away during the season.

Almost last, but not least, my thanks go to Paul Bastin, who took over the typesetting from his mother, Jean, who sadly passed away before work on the Yearbook got underway last year and stayed on this time round. As in previous years, my wife, Jennifer, looked after the proof reading. It goes without saying that without their input the book would not be the product it is.

Joe Calzaghe, who has now retired, was a worthy winner of the BBBoC 'Fighter if the Year' award last November. Having beaten Roy Jones in his final contest, Joe had nothing left to prove
Philip Sharkey

Introduction

By Barry J Hugman

It gives me great pleasure to welcome you to the 26th edition of the *British Boxing Yearbook*. The format has not changed too much over the years, certainly not since the 1993 edition, as myself and the team continue to monitor and update the current goings on, while also continuing to research the past and pass on our findings.

Beginning with the modern era, once again we have decided to stay with the way we produce 'Active British Based-Boxers: Complete Records'. The decision to have one alphabet, instead of separating champions, being taken on the grounds that because there are so many champions these days – British, Commonwealth, European, IBF, WBA, WBC, WBO, and more recently WBU, IBO, WBF, etc, etc, and a whole host of Inter-Continental and International titles – it would cause confusion rather than what was really intended. If you wish to quickly locate whether or not a boxer fought during the past season (1 July 2008 to 30 June 2009) then the 'Boxers' Record Index' at the back of the book is the place to look. Also, as in the very first edition, we chart the promotions in Britain throughout the season, thus enabling one to refer to the exact venue within a boxer's record.

Regarding our records, if a fighter is counted out standing up we have continued to show it as a stoppage rather than that of a kayo or technical kayo, as in fights where the referee dispenses with the count. Thus fights are recorded as count outs (the count being tolled with the fighter still on the canvas), retirements (where a fighter is retired on his stool) and referee stopped contest. Of course, other types of decisions would take in draws, no contests, and no decisions. In these days of health and safety fears, more and more boxers are being counted out either standing up or when initially floored, especially when a referee feels that the man on the receiving end is unable to defend himself adequately or requires immediate medical attention. One of the reasons that we have yet to discriminate between cut-eye stoppages and other types of finishes, is because a fighter who is stopped because of cuts is often on his way to a defeat in the first place. Thus, if you want to get a true reflection on the fight it is probably better to consult the trade paper, *Boxing News*, rather than rely on a referee's decision to tell you all you want to know; the recorded result merely being a guide.

Continuing the trend, there are always new articles to match the old favourites. Regular features such as 'Home and Away with British Boxers' (John Jarrett), 'World Title Bouts During the Season' (Bob Yalen), 'A-Z of Current World Champions' (Eric Armit), 'Directory of Ex-Boxers' Associations' (Ray Caulfield), 'Glove Story: A Review of British Boxing Books' (Philip Sharkey) and 'Obituaries' (Derek O'Dell) being supported this year with interesting articles such as 'My Love of Boxing' (Charles Giles), 'East-End Landmark: The History of the Peacock Gym' (Bob Lonkhurst), 'Britain's Horizontal Heavyweights: Justified or Unfair' (Patrick Myler), 'Dai Corp: A Passion for Boxing' (Ralph Oates), 'Tommy Milligan: The Lanarkshire Lionheart' (Brian Donald), 'Will The Real Jack Dempsey Stand Up?' (Anton Shapiro), 'I'll Knock You Out Inside Four Rounds Or You Win: Jem Mace, John L Sullivan, and the Remarkable Ted Pablo Fanque' (K R Robinson) and 'Dai Dower: The Wizard from Abercynon' (Wynford Jones).

Elsewhere, hopefully, you will find all you want to know about British Area, English, Celtic, British, Commonwealth, European and world title bouts that took place in 2008-2009, along with the amateur championships that were held in England, Scotland, Wales and Ireland, as well as being able to access details on champions from the past, both amateur and professional.

Historically, what was started several years ago under the heading of 'Early Gloved Championship Boxing', is still being researched for new material and we hope to present further offerings once we have something to share with you. Much of this earlier work was due to Harold Alderman MBE painstakingly piecing together results for the pre-Lonsdale Belt and named-weight division period. There are still many who believe as gospel much of what was reported down the ages by 'respected' men such as Nat Fleischer, the owner of *The Ring* magazine and the *Ring Record Book*, and then copied by numerous historians who failed to grasp what the sport was really like before the First World War. Basically, boxing prior to the period in question was a shambles, following bare fists with an assortment of driving gloves, knuckle gloves, and two-ounce gloves, etc, until it arrived at what we recognise today. There were no commissions, with newspapermen becoming all-powerful by naming their own champions at all kinds of weights, and in much of America the sport was illegal, no-decision contests rescuing it from being abolished. If you thought today was dire, then boxing prior to that period was almost impossible in all divisions bar the heavyweights. Because movement was difficult and news travelled slowly, fighters were able to move from town to town proclaiming themselves to be the best and 'ringers' constantly prevailed. With today's research being aided by access to early newspapers, and the use of computers, it is becoming clear that men like Fleischer 'took' the best fighters of the day and then 'fitted' them into the named-weight divisions we now know so well. As not to confuse anybody any further we continue to list world champions from 1889 through to 1909 despite the weights for named weight divisions not being agreed to universally, apart from the heavyweights.

Abbreviations and Definitions used in the record sections of the Yearbook:

PTS (Points), CO (Count Out), RSC (Referee Stopped Contest), RTD (Retired), DIS (Disqualification), NC (No Contest), ND (No Decision).

British Boxing Board of Control Ltd: Structure

(Members of the Commonwealth Boxing Council and European Boxing Union)

PRESIDENT	Lord Brooks of Tremorfa DL
CHAIRMAN	Charles Giles
VICE CHAIRMAN	John Handelaar
GENERAL SECRETARY	Robert W. Smith
ADMINISTRATIVE STEWARDS	Baroness Golding* John Rees QC Dave Roden Andrew Vanzie* John Williamson
REPRESENTATIVE STEWARDS	Geoff Boulter Bernard Connolly Martin Florey Ken Honniball Phil Lundgren Ron Pavett Fred Potter
STEWARDS OF APPEAL*	Robin Simpson QC Geoffrey Finn William Tudor John Robert Kidby Prof. Andrew Lees Timothy Langdale QC John Mathew QC Ian Mill QC Colin Ross-Munro QC Peter Richards FRCS Nicholas Valios QC
HONORARY STEWARDS*	Sir Henry Cooper OBE, KSG Mary Peters DBE Leonard Read QPM Bill Sheeran Billy Walker
HONORARY MEDICAL CONSULTANT*	Dr Roger C. Evans FRCP
HONORARY PARLIAMENTARY CONSULTANT*	Ian Stewart MP
LEGAL CONSULTANT	Michael Boyce DL
MARKETING CONSULTANT	Nicky Piper MBE
HEAD OFFICE	14 North Road Cardiff CF10 3DY Tel: 02920 367000 Fax: 02920 367019 E-mail: rsmith@bbbofc.com Website: www.bbbofc.com

* Not directors of the company

AREA COUNCILS - AREA SECRETARIES

AREA NO 1 (SCOTLAND)
Brian McAllister
11 Woodside Crescent, Glasgow G3 7UL
Telephone 0141 3320392. Fax 0141 3312029
E-Mail bmacallister@mcallisters-ca.com

AREA NO 2 (NORTHERN IRELAND)
John Campbell
8 Mount Eden Park, Belfast, Northern Ireland BT9 6RA
Telephone 02890 299 652. Fax 02890 382 906
Mobile 07715 044061

AREA NO 3 (WALES)
Mark Warner
14 North Road
Cardiff CF10 3DY
Telephone 01792 390239
Mobile 07890 867397

AREA NO 4 (NORTHERN)
(Northumberland, Cumbria, Durham, Cleveland, Tyne and Wear, North Yorkshire [north of a line drawn from Whitby to Northallerton to Richmond, including these towns].)
John Jarrett
5 Beechwood Avenue, Gosforth, Newcastle upon Tyne NE3 5DH
Telephone/Fax 01912 856556
E-Mail john.jarrettl@tesco.net

AREA NO 5 (CENTRAL)
(North Yorkshire [with the exception of the part included in the Northern Area - see above], Lancashire, West and South Yorkshire, Greater Manchester, Merseyside and Cheshire, Isle of Man, North Humberside.)
Richard Jones
1 Churchfields, Croft, Warrington, Cheshire WA3 7JR
Telephone/Fax 01925 768132
E-Mail richardjones@mjones88.freeserve.co.uk

AREA NO 6 (SOUTHERN)
(Bedfordshire, Berkshire, Buckinghamshire, Cambridgeshire, Channel Islands, Isle of Wight, Essex, Hampshire, Kent, Hertfordshire, Greater London, Norfolk, Suffolk, Oxfordshire, East and West Sussex.)
Les Potts
1 Sunnyside Villas, Gnosall, Staffordshire
Telephone 01785 823641. Mobile 07973 533835
E-Mail lezpotts@hotmail .com

AREA NO 7 (WESTERN)
(Cornwall, Devon, Somerset, Dorset, Wiltshire, Avon, Gloucestershire.)
Les Potts
1 Sunnyside Villas, Gnosall, Staffordshire
Telephone 01785 823641. Mobile 07973 533835
E-Mail lezpotts@hotmail .com

AREA NO 8 (MIDLANDS)
(Derbyshire, Nottinghamshire, Lincolnshire, Salop, Staffordshire, Herefordshire and Worcestershire, Warwickshire, West Midlands, Leicestershire, South Humberside, Northamptonshire.)
Les Potts
1 Sunnyside Villas, Gnosall, Staffordshire
Telephone 01785 823641. Mobile 07973 533835
E-Mail lezpotts@hotmail.com

Foreword

by Robert Smith (General Secretary, British Boxing Board of Control)

The 2008-2009 season has been a successful year for British boxing with some excellent performances from our boxers overseas, at home and, as always, competitive British championship contests in all divisions.

Carl Froch has established himself very much a world champion while Amir Khan, after a disastrous end to last year, has brushed himself off and shown great maturity in winning the World Boxing Association light-welterweight title.

Unfortunately, Ricky Hatton's brave attempt to be considered pound for pound champion against modern great, Manny Pacquiao, failed, but Ricky is still one of the world-class operators in a very competitive light-welterweight division.

Britain has some outstanding opportunities for further world honours with the likes of Jamie Moore, Rendall Munroe and David Haye, all looking to challenge for world championships in the coming year. Both Junior Witter and Clinton Woods will be looking to re-establish themselves on the world scene.

The domestic scene has seen some wonderful dustups with some of the contests being considered for 'Fight of the Year'. In addition, some very good contests involving European and Commonwealth championships have taken place and the English, Celtic and Area championships always remain competitive.

ITV's decision to consider pulling out of boxing at the end of the year is worrying, especially as the contests they have broadcast have been excellent value for money. It was obviously disappointing that Setanta have been unable to continue with their boxing programme but I am always grateful to Sky for their excellent coverage and I am sure the contests that take place next year will be ample reward for their continued commitment to the sport.

This has also been a year of great change for the Board. From 1 January 2009, the introduction of the new purpose built Training Course for applicant trainers and seconds, hosting the first European Medical Conference and organising the first National Board Inspectors Meeting which takes place in September, shows the Stewards of the Board's commitment in ensuring the highest possible standards are achieved for the safety of our boxers.

Also, I am grateful to my staff at the Board's head office for their help throughout my first year as General Secretary following the retirement of Simon Block. Thanks are also extended to all Area Secretaries, Council members, Inspectors and Medical Officers who provide invaluable support to the Board.

Finally, congratulations to Barry and his team for producing this year's edition of the Yearbook, which contains just about everything you need to know about boxing over the last season.

I look forward to a successful boxing season.

British Boxing Board of Control Awards

Now in its 26th year, the BBBoC Awards Ceremony will be held in London later this year and will once again be co-hosted by the Lonsdale International Sporting Club's Bernard Hart. The winners of these prestigious statuettes, designed in the form of a boxer, are selected by a well-informed panel of judges who make a judgement on the season as a whole at an annual meeting.

British Boxer of the Year: The outstanding British Boxer at any weight. 1984: Barrry McGuigan. 1985: Barry McGuigan. 1986: Dennis Andries. 1987: Lloyd Honeyghan. 1988: Lloyd Honeyghan. 1989: Dennis Andries. 1990: Dennis Andries. 1991: Dave McAuley. 1992: Colin McMillan. 1993: Lennox Lewis. 1994: Steve Robinson. 1995: Nigel Benn. 1996: Prince Naseem Hamed. 1997: Robin Reid. 1998: Carl Thompson. 1999: Billy Schwer. 2000: Glenn Catley. 2001: Joe Calzaghe. 2002: Lennox Lewis. 2003: Ricky Hatton. 2004: Scott Harrison. 2005: Ricky Hatton. 2006: Joe Calzaghe. 2007: Ricky Hatton. 2008: Joe Calzaghe.

British Contest of the Year: Although a fight that took place in Europe won the 1984 Award, since that date, the Award, presented to both participants, has applied to the best all-action contest featuring a British boxer in a British ring. 1984: Jimmy Cable v Said Skouma. 1985: Barry McGuigan v Eusebio Pedroza. 1986: Mark Kaylor v Errol Christie. 1987: Dave McAuley v Fidel Bassa. 1988: Tom Collins v Mark Kaylor. 1989: Michael Watson v Nigel Benn. 1990: Orlando Canizales v Billy Hardy. 1991: Chris Eubank v Nigel Benn. 1992: Dennis Andries v Jeff Harding. 1993: Andy Till v Wally Swift Jnr. 1994: Steve Robinson v Paul Hodkinson. 1995: Steve Collins v Chris Eubank. 1996: P. J. Gallagher v Charles Shepherd. 1997: Spencer Oliver v Patrick Mullings. 1998: Carl Thompson v Chris Eubank. 1999: Shea Neary v Naas Scheepers. 2000: Simon Ramoni v Patrick Mullings. 2001: Colin Dunne v Billy Schwer. 2002: Ezra Sellers v Carl Thompson. 2003: David Barnes v Jimmy Vincent. 2004: Michael Gomez v Alex Arthur. 2005: Jamie Moore v Michael Jones. 2006: Kevin Anderson v Young Muttley. 2007: Jamie Moore v Matthew Macklin. 2008: Kevin Mitchell v Carl Johanneson.

Overseas Boxer of the Year: For the best performance by an overseas boxer in a British ring. 1984: Buster Drayton. 1985: Don Curry. 1986: Azumah Nelson. 1987: Maurice Blocker. 1988: Fidel Bassa. 1989: Brian Mitchell. 1990: Mike McCallum. 1991: Donovan Boucher. 1992: Jeff Harding. 1993: Crisanto Espana. 1994: Juan Molina. 1995: Mike McCallum. 1996: Jacob Matlala. 1997: Ronald Wright. 1998: Tim Austin. 1999: Vitali Klitschko. 2000: Keith Holmes. 2001: Harry Simon. 2002: Jacob Matlala. 2003: Manuel Medina. 2004: In-Jin Chi. 2005: Joshua Okine. 2006: Tshifhiwa Munyai. 2007: Steve Molitor. 2008: Tim Bradley.

Special Award: Covers a wide spectrum, and is an appreciation for services to boxing. 1984: Doctor Adrian Whiteson. 1985: Harry Gibbs. 1986: Ray Clarke. 1987: Hon. Colin Moynihan. 1988: Tom Powell. 1989: Winston Burnett. 1990: Frank Bruno. 1991: Muhammad Ali. 1992: Doctor Oswald Ross. 1993: Phil Martin. 1994: Ron Olver. 1995: Gary Davidson. 1996: Reg Gutteridge and Harry Carpenter. 1997: Miguel Matthews and Pete Buckley. 1998: Mickey Duff and Tommy Miller. 1999: Jim Evans and Jack Lindsay. 2000: Henry Cooper. 2001: John Morris and Leonard 'Nipper' Read. 2002: Roy Francis and Richie Woodhall. 2003: Michael Watson. 2004: Dennie Mancini and Bob Paget. 2005: Barry McGuigan. 2006: Jack Bishop. 2007: James Cook MBE and Enzo Calzaghe. 2008: John Coyle and Larry O'Connell.

Sportsmanship Award: This Award recognises boxers who set a fine example, both in and out of the ring. 1986: Frank Bruno. 1987: Terry Marsh. 1988: Pat Cowdell. 1989: Horace Notice. 1990: Rocky Kelly. 1991: Wally Swift Jnr. 1992: Duke McKenzie. 1993: Nicky Piper. 1994: Francis Ampofo. 1995: Paul Wesley. 1996: Frank Bruno. 1997: Lennox Lewis. 1998: Johnny Williams. 1999: Brian Coleman. 2000: Michael Ayers and Wayne Rigby. 2001: Billy Schwer. 2002: Mickey Cantwell. 2003: Francis Ampofo. 2004: Dale Robinson and Jason Booth. 2005: Ricky Hatton and Kostya Tszyu. 2006: Enzo Maccarinelli and Mark Hobson. 2007: Mark Thompson. 2008: Martin Rogan, David Dolan, Billy Bessey, Dave Ferguson, Paul Butlin, Colin Kenna, Alex Ibbs and Darren Morgan.

Joe Calzaghe, the 2008 'British Boxer of the Year'
Philip Sharkey

"The Future"
Hatton Promotions

Ricky Hatton MBE - Promoter
Gareth Williams – CEO
Telephone: 0161 366 2657
Email: info@brandhatton.com

Hatton Health & Fitness
Telephone: 0161 366 0000
Email: info@brandhatton.com

Hatton Boxing TV
Telephone: 0117 972 2215
Email: tv@brandhatton.com

Hatton Merchandise
Telephone: 01204 863240
Email: sales@hattonboxing.com

Hatton Promotions
Hatton House
Market Street
Hyde
Cheshire
SK14 1HE

13

My Love of Boxing

by Charles Giles (Chairman, British Boxing Board of Control)

I was used to 'boxing talk' in the household, with Joe Louis, Tommy Farr, Freddie Mills, Len Harvey, etc, being on the agenda and there would always be excitement in the air when the usual crew turned up to set off to some sporting event, usually boxing or football. On one occasion, my uncles Joey, Teddy, Walter and Bernard arrived carrying small cases that meant they were staying overnight somewhere, leaving my mother noticeably quiet and subdued as she never liked dad staying out all night. This time, however, it turned into two nights, but that is another story. The conversation was intense in anticipation of the forthcoming event that they were travelling to London to attend - one of the biggest boxing tournaments ever to take place in Great Britain at that time - the middleweight championship of the world between the great Sugar Ray Robinson and local favourite Randolph Turpin. Randolph was to win this first encounter.

All this and more had whet my appetite for the fabulous sport of boxing. Some 18 months later, in 1953, my father took me to see the man that I had heard so much about. I was two months short of my ninth birthday and was not prepared for what I was about to witness in the Embassy Sportsdrome, Birmingham on that cold January night. The first thing to hit me was the thick cloud of smoke that made my eyes water the whole evening. Everywhere I looked men were puffing on some form of tobacco. I had to wait around with my glass of lemonade while the men had a drink at the bar, but I enjoyed listening to the banter. When we took our seats I realised that I could not see so dad took off his crombie and

folded it up so I could sit on it and view the boxing that was taking place. There were not too many televisions around at that time so I had no previous perception of what I was about to witness. Then, suddenly, there was a noticeable increase in the excitement of the onlookers as the main event was about to take place. When Turpin was announced my ears hurt with the applause of this packed house, the atmosphere being electric. Turpin stopped his opponent in six rounds to the delight of the crowd.

It was then that the greatest thing happened to me. My father had boxing friends and I was escorted to the dressing room of this great British middleweight. Randolph sat me on his lap and signed my programme 'To My Best Pal Charlie from Champ Randolph Turpin'. What more could a young fan wish for.

All of this is to explain my initiation into the sport that has dominated my life and had me hooked from that night on. Whilst still at school I travelled on my own to shows and aged 17 years, having acquired a driving licence, I was able to travel all over the country, sometimes to the big tournaments. It was not long before I was on the mailing list of Jack Solomons, Harry Levene, Mickey Duff, Alex Griffiths and others. Since those days I have attended more than 3000 shows, including many championship contests.

It was in 1984, having reached the ripe old age of 40, that I was invited to represent the Midlands Area of the British Boxing Board of Control at the Board's headquarters at Vauxhall Bridge Road in London. I was flattered and

Charles seen here flanked by Enzo Maccarinelli (left) and Joe Calzaghe, one of Britain's greatest ever boxers

felt privileged to be asked to hold such a position in the governing body of my chosen sport. Never would I have guessed that 20 years later I would become the Chairman of the Board, with such eminent people around the table. A lot is owed to the great contributions made by all the previous custodians be it Chairmen, Stewards, General Secretaries and others who have built the reputation that the BBB of C enjoys today.

Like me, most Stewards of the Board have some life-long connection with the sport and they are able to bring the benefit of their vast experience to the table for the interests of the boxers, the licenceholders, and the sport of professional boxing in general. Indeed, some Stewards are involved on a daily basis in their regional areas, giving much of their time for the love of the sport.

Each decade has had its outstanding British boxers. The '60s had a competitive domestic heavyweight scene, with Henry Cooper, Brian London, Joe Erskine, Dick Richardson, Billy Walker, Johnny Prescott and Jack Bodell, boxing each other. I was there for Muhammad Ali v Cooper and Ali v London. It was in 1964, at the Terry Downes v Willie Pastrano world light-heavyweight title fight in Manchester, that I had the pleasure of first meeting Harry Carpenter, the 'Voice" of Boxing' at that time. The '70s saw me in America for the first time, at Madison Square Garden for the Ali v Joe Frazier world heavyweight title in 1971, and just one week later I was at Wembley for the Cooper v Joe Bugner fight. Then it was back to the States again in 1973 to see Bugner challenge Ali. On the undercard at the Hilton, Las Vegas were two of Britain's best, John Conteh and John H. Stracey, who both won. The '80s saw me back in Las Vegas when Alan Minter took the world title from Vito Antuofermo. Alan then successfully defended the title against Antuofermo before losing it on that memorable occasion at Wembley against the great Marvin Hagler. Next came popular big Frank Bruno in big encounters with the likes of Tim Witherspoon and the great Mike Tyson, with Jim Watt and Charlie Magri picking up titles during the period. In the '90s I witnessed those two epic battles between Chris Eubank and Nigel Benn, and later Richie Woodhall won the prized WBC green belt. During this time, Lennox Lewis proved himself to be arguably the best British heavyweight of all time. More successes followed, with outstanding champions such as Prince Naseem Hamed, Carl Froch, super champs Joe Calzaghe and Ricky Hatton, and many others too numerous to mention.

Listen, I could write a book about my experiences in boxing. However, I hope this has given you an insight into some of my personal involvement and also the support that I currently receive from the Board members and the excellent working relationship I enjoy with the current General Secretary, Robert Smith, in jointly carrying out the necessary duties of the British Boxing Board of Control.

Boxing has always had its gloomy predictions for the future and the last few decades have been no exception. Television is not immune to the ravages of the current credit crunch and the budget has been affected, but time shows that these situations do not last for ever. The British Isles has always managed to produce a steady stream of world-class fighters, competing and often winning the honours, and I believe that we will continue to be as successful in the future with the help of our licensed promotors, managers and trainers. I look forward to a promising future for our beloved sport of Boxing.

Charles Giles with Ali

East-End Landmark: The History of the Peacock Gym

by Bob Lonkhurst

Adjacent to the old London docks, Canning Town in the east end of the capital has, for generations, been one of the most deprived regions of the United Kingdom. With exceptionally high rates of crime and unemployment, countless rundown and unoccupied buildings, and graffiti splashed across endless square feet of wall space, the area has always been a haven for fighting. Consequently, thousands of young men have turned to boxing for recreation or as a means to supplement their meagre incomes. Many have become champions.

Three decades ago the prestigious Royal Oak Gym situated at Barking Road, turned out a string of champions. Yet in many ways it was a closed shop, open only to young prospects trained and managed by the leading promotional team of the day. There was no time for boys whose limited ability meant they would only ever compete in supporting contests.

During the same period, however, a new operation that would eventually become an essential part of the community was in its infancy. From humble beginnings as a small activities centre based in a squalid room at the bottom of a block of flats, sheer hard work and determination by its founders led to its progression into one of the finest gyms in the country. The Peacock is now an established east-end landmark and a point for potential London black cab drivers doing 'the knowledge'.

With former boxers Frank Bruno, George and Billy Walker among its patrons, there is probably no other gym which offers the range of activities the Peacock does. Currently located at Caxton Street North, a quiet side road off the busy Silvertown Way, it has become a hugely successful operation. The founders and operators are brothers Tony and Martin Bowers from a family who have been involved in boxing for over three centuries and seven generations. The knowledge passed down over the years has been immense. The first fighting Bowers was Sam who was born in the early 1800s and became a rugged bare-knuckle fighter whose ring career lasted until 1867. His son, Tim Bowers, had many fights in the late 1890s and he was followed by two of his seven sons, William and Dan. Apart from being a stylish fighter, Dan became well known for organizing prize fights at horse stables in and around the City of London.

Dan had three sons who boxed, but it was George who was the most successful. A member of Fairbairn House ABC, he won many schoolboy championships and a National Association of Boys Clubs championship (Class B) in 1953. He went on to become one of the most successful amateur trainers in the country, spending over 20 years coaching juniors at the Repton Club. He also worked with St George's, Poplar and West Ham clubs, and more recently at the Peacock ABC when it was in its infancy.

George produced over 200 junior champions and was recently honoured with an MBE for his services to the sport. His sons Kevin, Barry and Graham all boxed as youngsters.

Kevin won National Schoolboy Championships in 1971 and 1972, and became a professional footballer with Coventry City before following in his father's footsteps by becoming a trainer at Repton for ten years.

William (Bill) Bowers had three sons all of whom were born during the 1930s. Charles had over 70 contests between 1946 and 1957 and became an Army Southern Command champion. Walter boxed from 1946 to 1956, had over 60 bouts and was a BOAR finalist in 1951. He was the father of Tony and Martin.

The most successful of Bill's sons, however, was Jackie who boxed amateur and professional between 1946 and 1960. He won five West Ham schoolboy championships, two Essex County championships and, representing Pretoria School, won a National Schoolboy championship (Junior Class A for boys aged 13-14 years at five stone, four pounds at Wembley in 1952 before a crowd of nearly 10,000. Testimony of his skill was the fact that he beat Terry Spinks on two occasions.

One of Jackie's professional contests was at Cardiff in 1959 against Howard Winstone and although he lost on points he left the ring to great applause. The crowd loved his value for money display in what Boxing News described as a "sparkling, all-action six-rounder".

After retiring from the ring in 1960, Jackie concentrated on training boxers of all levels, among them John H. Stracey, Maurice Hope and Johnny Waldron to name just a few. Fifty years later he is still active on the London scene.

With the long family involvement in boxing, Tony and Martin were destined to follow in that tradition, yet it was more to do with social troubles of the deprived area that first sucked them in. With vandalism and petty crime rife in the tower blocks throughout the Borough of Newham, particularly the Barnwood Court area where they lived, they realised that some form of impetus was needed to keep kids off the streets. Still at school, but with maturity beyond their years, they decided to try and do something about it.

During early 1973, and after some close brushes with the local Police, the brothers approached Julie Stockbridge, a strong-minded 60 year old local Councillor, who also lived at Barnwood Court. She was a highly respected community figurehead and, being a stickler for law and order, was impressed with what they told her.

Tony and Martin asked if she could help them acquire the use of a disused building known as 'The Rumpus Room' at the bottom of a local tower block. If successful they would clean, paint, decorate and turn it into an activities room that they would run themselves. They maintained that the project would help keep youngsters from Barnwood Court occupied and away from vandalism and street crime.

With Julie's influence, the council and local Tenant's Association agreed that the project was worth pursuing. New toilets, doors and windows were installed by the council, and through sheer hard work by Tony and Martin, aided by generous donations from local residents of furniture, DIY accessories, TV and audio equipment, the centre was up and running in no time. Despite their tender years, the Bowers brothers were the proud tenants of 'The Rumpus Room', and in reality the first steps had been taken towards creating what would eventually become the highly regarded Peacock Gym.

Although 'The Rumpus Room' was used mainly as a keep-fit and activities centre, outdoor interests such as football matches and camping were also on the agenda. Equipment, utilities and events were funded mainly from the proceeds of weekly raffles. The club became an instant success because youth of the area were brought together to take part and enjoy themselves thus relieving boredom that inevitably led to mischief.

The development of the project attracted great media interest and Tony and Martin appeared on the ITN programme, Today, and featured in the local press on a regular basis. As vandalism and youth crime reduced considerably they became recognised as important and respected members of the community. Both enjoyed boxing as a recreation, but during the mid-1970s became aware that there was a serious lack of facilities within Newham for like-minded youngsters. It was something else they were keen to try and address.

Coming from a family heavily steeped in boxing, and encouraged by the success of their first project, they persuaded youngsters to train and box at 'The Rumpus Room'. With growing membership, however, the room soon became too small so they set up a small gym in an empty room at nearby Drew Road School Youth Club. All monies raised went back into the gym for the purchase of equipment. It was hugely successful, but again an increase in membership meant the room was too small to meet demand. Undeterred, the brothers had a meeting with youth leaders and a larger room was made available to them at a weekly rent of £10.

Although Tony and Martin both had full time jobs they devoted their spare time to the gym four nights a week. Activities included boxing, weight-training, and fitness training, but on Tuesdays and Thursdays they spent one hour giving younger members of the youth club boxing tuition. Two boys, Terry Abbott and Lee Baker, became particularly successful, Lee eventually moving on to become a trainer at West Ham for a number of years.

Considering their ages the success of the brothers was incredible, and with the passing of time their contribution to the community became more widely appreciated. With help from the landlords of the Jubilee Public House at Barnwood Court they were able to organise fun-runs during the summers of 1978 and 1979. Entry fees and sponsorship donations were divided equally between the gym for purchase of new equipment, and local worthy causes chosen by patrons of The Jubilee.

By 1981 the gym had outgrown itself and the hours of availability were too limited as the school was closed at weekends and during holiday periods. In January that year, Jackie Bowers, an uncle of Tony and Martin, took over the tenancy of the Railway Tavern, at Silvertown known locally as Cundy's. It had a large unused function room and, having been involved in boxing all his life, Jackie was happy to allow his nephews to have it rent free to set up as a gym. Once equipped it operated from 9 am to 9 pm seven days a week. The usage fee was 50p and although there were occasions when individuals could not pay, they were never turned away. No liberties were taken because there was a great deal of trust. With Tony and Martin working during the daytime, subs were left in a jar, a regular practice that was generally treated with honesty and respect.

Despite Cundy's changing hands a couple of times the gym remained there until 1986 when it returned to Drew Road School until 1989. By this time Tony and Martin were the tenants of three Canning Town pubs, the Pits Head, Flying Sand, and the Peacock at Freemasons Road. As the Peacock was a trouble pub the brewery allowed them to have it rent free because they needed it open so as to eventually sell on as a going concern. It was an arrangement that suited both parties because the Peacock, being a large old pub, had a massive unused function hall at the rear. It was the ideal setting for a new gym.

Transformation was quick, and with them being on site Tony and Martin were able to devote more time to its development. They entered charitable events and raised money for a wide range of local organisations. Two teams were entered for the annual PARAS Assault Course competition and came first and third of 12 good quality outfits. They also raised £500 for the then Spastics Society.

Although boxing, both amateur and professional, became the backbone of the gym, there was also an ever-increasing number of weight-lifting and keep-fit fanatics using it on a regular basis. Wrestling was another activity to gain momentum and played a large part in developing the Peacock relationship with the local community. Through the medium of its amateur and professional members, countless numbers of visits were made to schools where talks were given about social dangers, including bullying, under age drinking and the misuse of drugs. At the request of Police, talks were also given to young offenders who found it easier to relate to a sporting personality than a member of the authority.

In 1992 the brewery sold the Peacock, but the new owner retained Tony and Martin as caretakers because there were no immediate plans to reopen it for business. At the time the brothers were actively searching for new premises in order to expand what was becoming an essential part of the community. Although membership continued to rise at a rapid rate, the gym was in reality a health hazard and not the most salubrious place to spend leisure hours. There were holes in the walls and during winter months strong winds blew rain and snow into the building. At times it was so cold that boxers trained wearing duffle coats and a propane bottle was used to warm it up. Yet even this had to be turned off because the gas it emitted affected the boxers. Water had to be got from the cellar, but as there were no lights, there were a few tumbles. This was the old Peacock and this was Canning Town in the early 1990s.

Realising that they would eventually lose the pub, Tony and Martin decided to approach the Charity Commission to see if they could get any help. During a subsequent meeting it was explained to them that the Peacock in fact already had the skeleton of its own charity and that an approved charity would qualify for a substantial reduction in rates. This really opened the door for them because it made their expansion plans a viable proposition. New premises, originally a canvas-making factory, were eventually found at Caxton Street North, and the lease was signed in August 1993. After a 12-month probationary period, during which activities were monitored, the Peacock was granted full charity status.

Following 18 months of intense planning and development a much larger and more modern gym was opened. Every square foot of space was accounted for and over the past 15 years it has developed into an attractive and extremely professional set-up, catering for the needs of all

sections of the local community.

Inside the main entrance is a restaurant, its walls crammed with photographs of boxers of all levels and teams of youngsters representing the Peacock at other sports. Adjacent is a large weight-training section packed with modern equipment including the latest in free and fixed weights. The main boxing gym, situated at the back of the building, has two rings, punch bags, running machines and everything needed by the professionals. A quiet side room houses an Olympic sized ring and more bags for exclusive use of amateur members of the Peacock ABC, which was formed in 1998. Upstairs is a superb wooden floored hall with old-fashioned wall bars and mirrored along two walls. It is used by boxers for sprint training and also by a variety of martial arts competitors, fitness and dance clubs. A fully matted wrestling room and furnished living quarters round

Tony Bowers (left) and his brother Martin pose with Richie Wenton's Lonsdale Belt in front of the Bradley Stone Memorial, situated outside the Peacock Gym

Richard Barber

off an impressive establishment.

As word spread around the East End so membership of the new Peacock continued to rise, thus providing the opportunity for further expansion. Tony, who boxed briefly as a professional with Joe Lucy as his manager, was granted British Boxing Board of Control manager and promoter licences whilst his brother obtained those as trainer and second. Martin, an avid keep fit fanatic, is also a registered coach with the British Amateur Wrestling Association and has trained competitors for Olympic wrestling. He is a dedicated triathlete who has competed in numerous Dockland triathlons, the London Marathon and the Montague Wailers Class, a 25-mile endurance rowing race.

They quickly built a small stable of boxers and the first Peacock Promotions professional boxing show took place in October 1994 at the Brittania Hotel, Docklands, where they would stage numerous successful charity dinner shows. Further promotions were staged at Ilford, Poplar, Mayfair, York Hall, Hove Town Hall, Newmarket and Norwich over a nine-year period.

With continued expansion, the Peacock rapidly developed into a fully-fledged community-based organisation and an essential part of an area where people still struggle in a difficult multi-cultural and often violent environment. Apart from boxing, other sporting facilities and activities include amateur and professional kick-boxing, karate for juniors and seniors, all forms of aerobics, fitness and circuit training. Qualified trainers are on hand to facilitate all requirements. There is a therapy clinic covering osteopathy, acupuncture, reiki, back and sports injuries, stress and headaches. The Peacock also has its own appointed medical officer.

The aims of the organisation are, and have always been, to improve the quality of life through sport, improve health and well being of local people through the provision of sport and leisure, and through education and training skills. It works constantly with private and public sectors, including the local police and probation service, and is run as a social type enterprise privately funded by income generated by use of the gym and entry fees. It also benefits from time to time by small grants that are spent largely on new equipment programmes.

The gym has been involved in many national charity events by sponsoring competitors for marathons, cycle rides, rowing across the channel and anything that can raise money for good causes. Being a registered charity the Peacock also stages its own events, including golf days, cricket matches and football competitions. Two such events in 2009 raised almost £5,000 for the Peacock youth trip to Centre Parcs. In 2008, £15,000 was raised for Newbridge School, which caters for youngsters with learning difficulties.

A wonderful camaraderie abounds within the Peacock founded on respect for anyone willing to accept the risks and step into the boxing ring. It has always had the reputation of being a home for quality boxing and this has been borne out by the men who have used it as a base. Yet no matter what level participants reach they have time for everyone and each other. A world champion and a non-boxing youngster there on a training course are absolutely equal. In an interview with Combat Magazine in 2003, Tony Bowers adequately summed up what the Peacock is all about when he remarked. "When you come here you leave all your prejudices at the door. This is a family run gym with a family atmosphere inside. When you come here everyone is equal".

Despite the massive commitment to the community, the Peacock remains primarily a boxing gym used by fighters of all levels. Since obtaining his Board of Control licences, Martin Bowers has coached many good men including champions Gary Delaney, Scott Dixon, Ali Forbes, Mark Baker, Richie Wenton, Elvis Michailenko, Julius Francis, Paul 'Silky' Jones, Lester Jacobs, John 'Boy' Humphrey, Danny James, Erik Teymour, and Justin Juuko. Graham Townsend became his first champion when he won the Southern Area super-middleweight title in 1996. Many other good fighters have been trained by Martin, including Rocky Dean who has been at the Peacock since turning professional in 1999.

The gym has attracted many top boxers, including some from other parts of the world. The Klitschko brothers both worked out there during the early part of their careers. Johnny Tapia, John Ruiz, Marco Antonio Barrera, Mike McCallum, Eddy Smulders, Jeff Fenech, Brian Mitchell, Gerald McClennan and Zelco Mavrovic have also sparred in Peacock rings, as have top British fighters including Lennox Lewis, Chris Eubank, Naseem Hamed, Danny Williams, Steve Collins, Ricky Hatton, Paul Lloyd and Amir Khan. Some of the world's top trainers including Angelo Dundee, Eddie Futch, Emmanuel Steward and Freddie Roach have also recognised the value of the Peacock and consequently used it from time to time.

Celebrities from many walks of life have also been to the Peacock over the years on social or official visits. They include retired boxers Sir Henry Cooper, Sugar Ray Leonard in 2005, and John Conteh, Members of Parliament, Kate Hoey and Tony Banks, both former sports ministers, and Jim Fitzpatrick. From show business have come Sir Michael Caine, Shane Ritchie, Billy Murray, Bradley Walsh, Glen Murphy and Orlando Bloom. The gym has also been used in the making of six films including Shiner starring Caine, and Matthew Marsden, who was given extensive boxing tuition there for his role as Golden Boy.

A number of retired boxers often visit the Peacock for social purposes or to use the facilities to keep fit. They include former Central Area light-heavyweight champion, Pat Thompson, a veteran of over 70 fights who, although now turned 60, works out there daily. Another regular is Dean Hollington, a promising lightweight in the 1990s who was trained by Jimmy Tibbs and in the later stages of his career by present Board of Control General Secretary, Robert Smith. Dean is now a member of the Southern Area Council. Former British featherweight champion, Sammy McCarthy, and his close friends, Olympians Ronnie Cooper and Terry Spinks, MBE, have been frequent visitors to the gym since its opening.

Periodically, crowds have packed the gym to watch the stars in action, but the highlight must surely be the public workout by Floyd Mayweather in 2009. Hundreds crammed inside whilst an estimated further 2000 filled the street outside bringing traffic to a standstill. I had the good fortune to meet Floyd privately later that day and asked him why he had chosen the Peacock for the workout. He said that he had been told it was the finest gym in England. "Is it?", I asked. "Sure", he replied, "it was like being back home. The place is top class, the people there know boxing and those fans were fantastic".

One attribute of the Peacock is that it combines the old with the new. Modern equipment has been moulded into old-fashioned training methods while the easily recognizable smell of stale sweat identifies it as a real fighter's workplace. There have always been solid, knowledgeable boxing people working at the gym. Apart from Martin Bowers, resident trainers have included Olympian, John Boscoe, Jackie Bowers, Frank Black, who taught Martin everything about cuts, and the late John Humphrey.

Currently on hand are former British super-middleweight champion Ali Forbes and Mark Tibbs, who as a professional lost only two of 25 contests, and Babatunde Ajayi, a former professional who currently trains former WBO light-middle and middleweight champion, Harry Simon, amongst others. Former Commonwealth light-middleweight champion, Mickey Hughes, runs the gym nursery for six to ten year olds on Saturday mornings, but the stalwart is Jimmy Tibbs, regarded by many people in the sport as one of the finest trainers Britain has had.

After years at the Royal Oak, Jimmy took a small group of young professionals under his wing at West Ham, but later became the first established professional trainer to use the old Peacock at Freemasons Road. When that closed, he moved his stable to the present gym where he has trained a host of top men including Michael Watson, Chris Pyatt, Gary Stretch, Garry Delaney, Maurice Core and Neville Brown. He now works there daily with former amateur star and Olympic representative, Billie Jo Saunders.

On the amateur front the Peacock club has made giant steps in just 11 years, producing about 20 champions at different weights and levels. Although the club has a number of good prospects there are particularly high hopes for heavyweight, Wadi Camacho, from Ilford. A winner of three north-east London Divisional Championships and a Three Nations competition silver medal, he has recently been with the England squad at Sheffield for assessment towards the 2012 Olympic Games.

Despite its considerable success, the Peacock has suffered setbacks along the way, but always had the ability and determination to overcome them. The worst was undoubtedly in April 1994 when Canning Town youngster, Bradley Stone, died 48 hours after his contest with Richie Wenton for the inaugural British super-bantamweight championship at York Hall. Originally trained and managed by Jimmy Tibbs, he was a huge favourite at the Peacock where he prepared for the fight. Consequently, Tony and Martin organised a series of events and raised over £10,000 to commission a sculpture of him which local artist Anne Downey created in bronze. It was set on a stone weighing three tonnes that had been transported from Scotland. Appropriately, it stands at the main entrance to the gym bearing the inscription: "He died in pursuit of his dreams".

Apart from being a lasting memory to Bradley, Tony and Martin also wanted it to serve as a warning to people that boxing is a dangerous sport and not just a game. It was a moving gesture and inside the gym on the restaurant wall hangs a small plaque presented by Bradley's girlfriend Donna and her family inscribed: "With heartfelt thanks for the way you honoured Bradley".

In April 2009, the Stone-Wenton story took a moving twist, one that demonstrates the respect and compassion that exists between boxers and youngsters they seek to influence. Wenton, who won the super-bantamweight Lonsdale Belt outright in 1996, telephoned Tony and Martin asking if they would display it at the Peacock. Having been trained by Martin during the last three years of his career, he wanted the belt to be recognised as a trophy of respect and remembrance for Bradley and also as an inspiration to youngsters using the gym.

Much of the success of the Peacock is due to solid support from colleagues and family. Tony and Martin have had that in abundance. Stalwarts include former Vice-President, Roy Hilder, matchmaker, Neil Bowers, and Jackie Bowers, long time trainer and manager. All have moved on with Roy and Neil now acting as matchmakers for other promoters and Jackie still training his own boxers, albeit to a lesser degree.

The Peacock continues to move from strength to strength both in sport and community involvement. In 2004 membership stood at 6,000, but five years later it was in excess of 14,000. Courses have been designed in education, first aid, health and safety in the workplace and training is available for youths with learning difficulties. The activity and commitment is immense and it would take a book to document the extent of everything under the Peacock umbrella.

Affiliated to the ABA and London Federation of Boys Clubs, certificates are also displayed on the gym walls from the Phillip Lawrence Trust, Newham Education Business Partnership and Newham Trident. Another confirms that the Peacock appears in the official London 2012 pre-Olympic Games training camp guide. More recently, the British Boxing Board of Control trainer and second suitability courses have been held at the venue and will hopefully continue there for the foreseeable future.

Whilst essentially a boxing story the development of the Peacock is one of spiralling success achieved by the foresight and determination of two ambitious teenagers who convinced local councillors to consider their proposals. From those humble beginnings at the 'Rumpus Room', Tony and Martin Bowers have developed into astute businessmen who are widely respected in their community. Assisted by a faithful band of associates they now operate what is arguably the finest establishment of its kind in the country.

Everyone in boxing knows about the Peacock and where it is located. Regulars at the gym wear the training tops, tee-shirts and vests with pride and feel important to belong to such a fine organisation. It has become an east-end landmark and both the community and the sport of boxing are better for its existence.

JIM EVANS PROMOTIONS

Licensed to the British Boxing Board of Control
88 Windsor Road, Maidenhead, Berks SL6 2DJ
Tel: 01628 623640 : Fax: 01628 684633
Mobile: 07768 954643
e-mail: boxevans@yahoo.co.uk

Heavyweight	-	Rounds	Middleweight	-	Rounds
Roman Greenberg	-	10 – 12	Stuart Barr	-	4 – 6
Michael Sprott	-	10 – 12	Carl Drake	-	6 – 8 - 10
Cruiserweight			Osumanu Adama	-	8 – 10 - 12
Nick Okoth	-	6 – 8	**Light-Middleweight**		
Shane Massey	-	Debut	Danny Maka	-	4 - 6
Joe St John	-	Debut	George Katsimpas	-	6 – 8 - 10
Light-Heavyweight			**Welterweight**		
Michael Banbula	-	4 – 6	Mark Douglas	-	8 – 10
Marco Stevenson	-	Debut	Gary Young	-	6 - 8
Stefan Hughes	-	Debut	**Light-Welterweight**		
Super-Middleweight			Shane Watson	-	6 – 8 - 10
Matthew Barr	-	4 – 6	**Lightweight**		
Patrick Mendy	-	6 – 8	Mark McCullough	-	6 – 8 - 10
Gary Boulden	-	4 – 6	**Super-Featherweight**		
Patrick J Maxwell	-	6 - 8	Ibrar Riyaz	-	6 – 8 - 10
			Super-Bantamweight		
			Najah Ali	-	6 - 8

Trainers: Jim Evans: Dave Laxen: Darren Whitman: Steve Bernath: Graham Stevenson: Andy Edge
JIM EVANS PROMOTIONS is a member of the P.B.P.A

Glove Story: A Review of British Boxing Books in 2008-2009

by Philip Sharkey

After last year's bumper crop of British boxing books, I have found less than half the amount to review this year. I have heard that books being worked on presently include Eric Boon, Brian London, a book on Cardiff boxers, Shaun Cummings, Duke McKenzie and the third Sweet Fighting Man. I also spoke to Brendan Ingle after he had received an award from the London Ex Boxers Association and suggested it was about time he got on with his autobiography, so whilst we have those to look forward to lets start this year's review.

We begin with LEN JOHNSON AND THE COLOUR BAR by Rob Howard. This is quite fortuitous, as it is also the 100th anniversary of the Lonsdale Belt and the 80th anniversary of the British Boxing Board of Control. Had not a ban on 'coloured' fighters contesting British titles, Len may well have won the prestigious strap. Len was considered one of the leading British middleweights of the late 1920s and defeated many champions and top contenders of the time, men like Johnny Bee, Joe Bloomfield, Harry Collins, the great but over the hill Ted 'Kid' Lewis and future great, Len Harvey. Harvey got his revenge five years later in a fight promoter Jeff Dickson advertised for the British Middleweight Title, but it was not recognised by the BBBoC, who also forbade the Lonsdale Belt from being contested. Johnson even outpointed future British heavyweight champ, Jack London, flooring him twice in what would be his last win before retiring. Eye problems and rheumatism persuading him to quit at 32 years of age. He was also famous for his boxing booth, travelling all over the North of England, attracting future world champions, Peter Kane and Benny Lynch. Len always regarded the booth as not only great entertainment, but also a great learning ground for young fighters. He credits the booths for giving him the real start to his fistic education, perfecting the defensive skills that were to become a trademark throughout his career. Rob Howard's main source of reference for the text is from Len's unfinished autobiography and the Topical Times articles from the 1930s. Thus, the book is as authoritative as it can be and touches on his politics and friendships, but it is regulation 24, paragraph 27 that forms the focus of the book, stating that:"Contestants must be legally British subjects and born of white parents". At long last, on the 28 June 1948, Dick Turpin outpointed Vince Hawkins for the British middleweight title and the 'colour bar' finally ended. Many of the photographs have not been previously published and of great interest are the reproductions of fight posters from some of his biggest bouts. The book is available from Rob Howard, 42 Avondale Road, Edgeley, Stockport, Cheshire SK3 9NY. Telephone 0161 480 8858 or email robaccord5@hotmail.com.

A book a long time in the making is K. R. Robinson's LANKY BOB: THE LIFE AND TIMES AND CONTEMPORARIES OF BOB FITZSIMMONS (Trafford publishing). Befitting a heavyweight champion, this book weighs in at almost 500 pages and is the result of over 12 years painstaking research that has taken Keith around the world and back. He even had help from David Jack, Fitzsimmons' great-great nephew in Timaru, New Zealand. Searching through acres of newspaper cuttings and fight reports, Keith has separated the fact from the fiction of the oft repeated tales of Bobs exploits in and out of the ring. Reading the book, however, the truth is sometimes less believable than the fiction! 'Fitz', who was born in Helston, Cornwall and raised in New Zealand, boxed in Australia for seven years and arrived in San Francisco in 1890. After only three fights there he won the world middleweight title from 'Nonpareil' Jack Dempsey with a 13th round knock-out. Then, at the age of 34, he knocked out Peter Maher to capture a disputed heavyweight title, before making it official when knocking out James J. Corbett in Carson City, Nevada on 17 March 1897 to become the undisputed heavyweight champion of the world. Great Britain had to wait almost 100 years for London-born Lennox Lewis to once again claim the biggest prize in sport. After losing the title to James J Jeffries in 1902, Bob dropped down to light-heavyweight to claim the crown from George Gardner on points over 20 rounds, just over a year later. He was married four times (all his wives being actresses) and he fathered six children, dying at just 54 years of age. He

Tony Booth turns his hands to writing   Philip Sharkey

did a lot of living in those 54 years and this book seems to have recorded it all in intricate detail. A quick glance at the quotes on the back of the book show how Jeffries, Corbett, Gene Tunney and Jack Dempsey all considered him to be the hardest-punching, toughest champion of his time, so it is essential that such a thoroughly researched book on him is now available.

When Tony Booth stepped into the ring on 8 March 1990, weighing just over 11 stone, to take on Paul Lynch of Swansea, I wonder if he, or any of the crowd knew it was the start of one of the longest and most colourful careers in recent times? BOXING BOOTH (Riverhead Publishing), Tony's autobiography, tells us he will quit after his appointment with Howard Daley at the City Hall in his hometown of Hull on 11 October 2008. However, Tony could not resist one more fight before his medicals ran out. Quite fittingly he went out with a win, beating debutant, Raz Parnez, on a fourth-round retirement. Maybe a pro debut against a 161 fight veteran was a little ambitious and one must remember that when fully focused, fit and ready, Tony was a match for the highest echelon of fistic contenders and champions that included Neville Brown, Eddy Smulders, James Cook, Franco Wanyama, Tony Wilson, Ralf Rocchigiani, Victor Cordoba, Ole Klemetsen, Dean Francis, Montell Griffin, Johnny Nelson, Bruce Scott, Crawford Ashley, Omar Sheika, Bash Ali, Enzo Maccarinelli, Martin Rogan, champions all. And, soon to be fighting for the world heavyweight title, ex world cruiserweight kingpin, David Haye, also turns up on Tony's record. If that list is not impressive enough it is worth noting that he beat Sheika when the American was an unbeaten prospect and the draw against a six-pound heavier Rocchigiani was not in Hull but in Germany! Tony writes candidly about his boxing life, and although he often took fights when not properly prepared, he always tried to entertain the crowd, the 'Boothy shuffle being his speciality! Sometimes the crowd can be quite partisan in cheering on their man and this could spur Tony on to try and silence them. This he did on a show at the Guild Hall in Southampton, but you will have to read his book to see what the crowd chanted and how he reacted ! Looking past the tales of fun and games with friends such as poker maestro, Dave 'Devilfish' Ulliott, the real Tony seems to be a devoted family man supported by his sometimes long suffering wife Jane. Now his time in the ring has ended, he has started promoting dinner evenings with celebrity boxing speakers and I am sure if you contact him on www.boothyspromotions.co.uk he will sign your book.

TEDDY BALDOCK: THE PRIDE OF POPLAR is a powerful glory and tears story of an East-End boxing idol who went from national hero to fallen star. Written by Brian Belton, in complete contrast to Tony Booth's 18-year career that ended when he was 38, Britain's youngest world champion was finished at just 24 years of age. These were different days, Teddy debuted two months short of his 14th birthday and was unbeaten (save for a disqualification from a low blow to Kid Nicholson at Premierland in 1926) until he lost his world title recognition following a contest against South Africa's Willie Smith at the Royal Albert Hall on 6 October 1927. Teddy bounced back, notching four

wins in front of huge crowds, before capturing the British and Commonwealth titles from Johnny Brown at Clapham Orient football ground with 32,000 cheering spectators watching the action. He defended his titles against Alf 'Kid' Pattenden, winning on points over 15 rounds. His fight with Dick Corbett on 7 September 1931 would be his last, Corbett going on to win the British bantamweight title in his next bout. And so, after 81 recorded contests and aged only 24, Alfred Stephen Baldock's boxing career was over. As the book's title suggests the adulation and the money soon disappeared, and with his marriage unable to stand the strain Teddy's life spiralled out of control until, living rough on the street, it hit rock bottom. He died in March 1971 a largely forgotten man. For me the most moving and poignant tale in the story of the great champ is one that is not covered in the book. It is that of his young grandson, Martin Sax, discovering some cuttings and scrap books in his mother's loft and realising the grandfather whose name was rarely mentioned, and who had died when he was two, was Britain's youngest world champion! What an extraordinary piece of family history to uncover. To his family, Teddy had become an embarrassment, but the more Martin delved, the more forgiveness and understanding came Teddy's way, albeit posthumously. By coincidence, Martin is very interested in the noble art himself, having boxed as an amateur. And as a serving Royal Marine, having seen active service in Iraq and Afghanistan, he is someone all the boxing world can be very proud of as well. He has certainly done his grandfather proud by getting his life story written and published.

Most people write their autobiographies to show themselves in a better light or right some wrongs, so, I suppose, you have to credit Herbie for not hiding from some of the more unpleasant aspects of his colourful life in HERBIE HIDE: NOTHING BUT TROUBLE. The only people he seems to have any praise for is Matchroom supreme, Barry Hearn, and his younger brother Alan, who sadly died from leukaemia in 1997. Nearly everyone else gets the same brutal treatment that Herbie dished out in the ring. Trouble seems to follow Herbie around. After losing the ABA final to Henry Akinwande at just 17 years of age, Herbie was snapped up by Barry Hearn's Matchroom stable and was soon training hard under the expert eye of trainer, Freddie King. He quickly gobbled up his diet of journeymen, weighing just 13 stone, eight pounds on his debut, and remained unbeaten until meeting 'Big Daddy' Riddick Bowe. Bowe weighed just over 17 stone and had reached his peak of desire and fitness, while Herbie had grown to just 15 stone, two pounds. He put up a brave fight, getting up from the canvas numerous times. Unfortunately I think most people's memory of Herbie in a world title scrap was when he and Michael Bentt had a spot of fisticuffs at their press conference and he once again made the headlines for all the wrong reasons. At least, with a couple of million in the bank he could build his dream mansion and take a couple of years off following his loss to Vitaly Klitschko. Herbie is now back down to cruiserweight and campaigning in Germany, looking to land a world title shot and, who knows, he might just pull it off.

Always good value and great fun, fellow yearbook contributor Ralph Oates' MUHAMMAD ALI QUIZ BOOK is a knockout! Thirty rounds of tricky questions should rope a few dopes! As boxing expert George Zeleny says on the back cover: "answer all the questions and call yourself the greatest too". The book is available from Pitch Publishing. Boxing historian, Board of Control official and acclaimed boxing biographer, Bob Lonkhurst, is currently working on the life story of Eric Boon, but, due to popular demand, has reprinted his book on TOMMY FARR: MAN OF COURAGE first published in 1997. Like his previous books on British legends, Jack Petersen, 'East End Idol' Terry Spinks MBE and 'Fen Tiger' Dave 'Boy' Green, it is meticulously researched and written with great warmth. All Bob's books are available by post from 6 Drayton Avenue, Potters Bar, Herts EN6 2LF.

Prior to this, my yearly reviews have been confined to books on or about British boxers, but a fascinating new book by former boxing promoter and New York State Athletic Commission inspector, Mike Silver, is well worth mentioning. THE ARC OF BOXING: THE RISE AND DECLINE OF THE SWEET SCIENCE was not written to add fuel to the old school versus the new school boxing debate. "I wrote it to end the debate", says Mike, and he has interviewed over a dozen experts old enough to have personally witnessed the best fighters of the last 70 years. Three of the worlds most renowned current teacher-trainers, Teddy Atlas, Emanuel Steward and Freddie Roach also add their two cents worth. Roy Jones, Bernard Hopkins and Floyd Mayweather are some of the contemporary fighters compared with the champions from the golden era of boxing, generally recognised as stretching from the 1920s to the 1950s.Even Roberto Duran, trained by Ray Arcel, is not considered by some as good enough to beat Billy Petrolle or Sid Terris, neither of whom were champions in the 1930s. Arcel himself only has Duran scrapping into his top-ten lightweights of all time. Although the book talks almost exclusively about fighters from the United States one cannot help thinking of modern-day British champions facing 'Golden Era' fighters. Jack 'Kid' Berg versus Ricky Hatton, Randolph Turpin versus Joe Calzaghe or Naseem Hamed up against Nel Tarleton, would, I am sure, provide British boxing fans with the same level of debate. It is a thought provoking book, other sports of course can be measured in heights jumped or distances ran or swam, but boxing is a far subtler science; the sweet science in fact! For those who wish to order a copy, the book is published by McFarland.

The launch of the Teddy Baldock book: left to right: Brian Belton (author), James Cook, Martin Sax (Teddy Baldock's grandson), Nicky Cook, Jimmy Batten, Joe Egan, Paul Cook, Chas Taylor, Sammy McCarthy   Philip Sharkey

Britain's Horizontal Heavyweights: Justified or Unfair?

by Patrick Myler

Remember when American boxers dominated the heavyweight division, when a world champion born outside the United States was as rare as a bald-headed beauty queen? In the 100 years from the time James J. Corbett became the first Queensberry Rules' titleholder to the end of the Muhammad Ali era, only five undisputed heavyweight champions – Bob Fitzsimmons (England), Tommy Burns (Canada), Max Schmeling (Germany), Primo Carnera (Italy) and Ingemar Johansson (Sweden) – were non-Americans. Such was the American supremacy that, in the early part of the last century, many US writers adopted a dismissive, often sneering, attitude to contenders from abroad, especially the British, who were slotted into a special category labelled 'Horizontal Heavyweights'. How justified was their criticism? Well, let us examine the facts.

The first Briton since Fitzsimmons (who was an American citizen when he took the title from Corbett) to get British fans excited about the prospect of breaking the American domination of world heavyweight boxing was Bombardier Billy Wells. A handsome, blond-haired Londoner of six foot, three inches and weighing around 13½ stone, he attracted plenty of female attention as well as male support as a potential world champion. Wells was admired as a gentleman, inside and outside of the ring, but unfortunately he lacked the killer instinct and allowed too many tottering opponents off the hook. In several important fights, he had his rivals on the floor, but still finished up on the losing end. The possessor of a stiff, accurate jab (or straight left as it was known in his time) and a strong right cross, Wells revealed his weaknesses when it came to taking solid punches to the body or chin.

Bombardier Billy Wells

On the credit side, Wells held the British heavyweight title from 1911 to 1919, a record tenure that stood until Henry Cooper's reign some 60 years later. He defended the title successfully 13 times and was the first outright winner of a Lord Lonsdale Belt in the heavyweight division. For all his domestic success, however, Billy failed lamentably in international competition. Touted as one of the numerous 'White Hopes' lined up to knock the arrogant black American, Jack Johnson, off the title throne, his limitations were ruthlessly exposed when he met Al Palzer for the ridiculously labelled 'White Heavyweight Championship of the World' at New York's Madison Square Garden on 28 June 1912. Wells, giving away three stone to the tough farmer from Iowa, dropped Palzer for seven in the first round, but it was his turn to hit the canvas in the next. He was down three more times before his corner threw in the towel in the fifth round.

Wells knocked out another American, Tom Kennedy, in three rounds a few weeks later, but his world title ambitions were finally extinguished when Gunboat Smith sank him in two rounds. Now concentrating his ambitions towards winning the European title, even that proved too lofty a goal when he faced Georges Carpentier in Ghent, Belgium, on 1 June 1913. Wells was the favourite to beat the 19-year-old Frenchman, who was four inches shorter and weighed 12 stone to the Bombardier's 13¼ stone. Once again, the Englishman opened brightly and countered Carpentier's rush with a powerful right to send Georges slumping to the floor. Up at nine, but groggy, he managed to survive by holding on for dear life as the crowd called for the referee to save the teenager from execution. Wells had lost his chance. Carpentier, now fully recovered from his first-round nightmare, found the Londoner's body a soft target. At the start of the fourth round, the confident Frenchman feinted with a left and sank a right into his distressed opponent's body. Wells dropped his hands, exposing his jaw to Carpentier's lethal right hand, and it was all over for Billy.

Wells defeated three challengers for his British title and someone thought it was a good idea to challenge Carpentier again for the European crown, six months after their initial encounter. This time Billy had home advantage, the bout taking place at the National Sporting Club in London, but it made no difference. Wells looked scared as he answered the opening bell and it proved justified. Carpentier had him in agony from a body assault and a left and right to the jaw sent him sprawling for the full count. The fight had lasted just 73 seconds.

Wells continued to dominate the domestic scene, but was knocked out in two rounds when he took on another American, Frank Moran, whose powerful right hand, nicknamed 'Mary Ann', caressed him to sleep in the tenth round. He lost his British title to Joe Beckett on a fifth-round knockout and was dispatched in three in a return. The Bombardier retired in 1925 with a record of 47 wins, 32 by knockout, and seven defeats, all of them by knockouts.

Bye-bye Billy, hello Joe. The new British heavyweight champion, Joe Beckett, having looked impressive in his two defeats of Wells, was then lumbered with the responsibility of restoring British pride on the world scene. Short and thick-set with a lethal left hook, he looked altogether a better prospect for higher honours than the unfortunate Wells. Beckett, from Wickham, outside Southampton, knocked out American Eddie McGoorty in 17 rounds, thus encouraging promoter Charles B. Cochran to invite Georges Carpentier to defend his European prize against Joe at Holborn Stadium on 4 December 1919. The Frenchman ducked through the ropes, waving to his friends and blowing kisses to the selected few women at ringside, while Beckett looked dour, with not a smile for anyone. With just 73 seconds gone, Beckett was counted out after collecting a tremendous right to the jaw.

Joe Beckett

Joe got his career back on track with a few worthy wins, including a seventh- round stoppage of former world champion Tommy Burns, but he then suffered the same fate as Wells when he ran into Frank Moran's 'Mary Ann' right and was put away in two rounds. Beckett gained revenge over Moran a year later and announced that he aimed to avenge the one blot on his record in a rematch with Carpentier. The Frenchman had just lost in four rounds in a bid to take the world title from Jack Dempsey, but he could not miss Beckett's inviting chin with his flashing right hand and the Englishman was counted out inside 48 seconds. That was 25 seconds less than he had lasted in their first clash. Joe never fought again and, years later, he lamented: "I beat all the British heavyweights of my time, but all everyone talked about was my two defeats by Carpentier".

Hope springs eternal, it is said, and by 1927 British fight fans were pinning their faith in Phil Scott, a six foot, three inch Londoner with decent boxing skills and knockout power in his right hand. Unfortunately, like his predecessors, he had his weaknesses, particularly around the body, and a questionable temperament. Scott's first fight in America proved disastrous, when he was knocked down six times and counted out in the first round against Knute Hansen, from Denmark. Though he notched up a home win against Tom Heeney, who had unsuccessfully challenged Gene Tunney for the world title, Scott's American prestige hit rock bottom following his defeats by Hansen and Johnny Risko, and he was given little hope against Victorio Campolo, who was pressing his claim, along with Max Schmeling and Jack Sharkey, to contest the vacant title after Tunney's retirement. Scott was a revelation as he outboxed and outfought the Argentinian for a comprehensive points victory. The win put the Englishman into the world's top four and even the hard-to-please Americans were behind him when he took on Otto Von Porat, another leading contender. Regrettably, it was the old Phil Scott who had disappointed in winning on fouls in previous US appearances. Von Porat sank a right into Scott's body in the second round and the Briton went down in apparent agony, kicking his legs and claiming a foul. The referee, ex-champion Jack Dempsey, appealed to him to get up and make a fight of it. Scott would have none of it, so Dempsey disqualified Von Porat.

Despite the unsatisfactory result, Phil landed a shot at Sharkey in a final eliminator, the winner to meet Schmeling for the vacant title. The fight was held in Miami in February 1930 and Scott held his own in the opening round, but went down in the next from a punch that looked below the belt. He rose to his feet and was immediately struck down with another punch to the body. The referee sent Sharkey to his corner as Scott was taken back to his corner to be examined by the ringside doctor, who declared him fit to continue. The Englishman reluctantly squared up to Sharkey again, only to be subjected to another body assault. He held up his hand in surrender, to the disgust of many Americans, who called him a quitter and a coward. Among the derogatory nicknames he picked up were 'Phaintin' Phil' and 'The Swooning Swan of Soho', as well as the latest British 'Horizontal Heavyweight'. Ironically, when Sharkey went on to contest the world title with Schmeling, he was disqualified for a foul blow in the fourth round. Any hope Scott had of re-establishing himself as a world title challenger vanished when another American, Young Stribling, flattened him in two rounds at Wimbledon Greyhound Stadium.

Britain's next heavyweight hope was Jack Petersen, who packed power in his right hand and certainly did not lack courage. His big weakness was his susceptibility to cut eyes. The Welshman's nemesis was Germany's Walter Neusel, who beat him three times. Promoter Sydney Hulls was hoping to lure Max Baer, who had won the world title from Primo Carnera, to London to defend it against Petersen, and matched Jack with Neusel in 1935 to prove his worthiness to the big fight. In a hugely exciting encounter, Petersen slammed home countless right-handers, but the sturdy German took them all. Though hurt from Neusel's body punches, Petersen was ahead on points in the 11th round when a vicious right worsened a cut over his eye. 'Pa' Petersen, the Welshman's father and manager, threw in the towel.

Convinced he could do better in a return, Petersen looked a certain winner in the rematch after punishing Neusel so badly that the German wanted to quit after nine rounds. His manager, Paul Damski, reminded him that Petersen had been bleeding from early on, and angrily pushed him out for the next round. Petersen, aware that the injuries could cause his defeat, went all out to stop his rival, but it proved to be unwise. Neusel struck back forcibly, hurting the Welshman with body digs, and causing further damage to his eyes. Once again, 'Pa' Petersen was forced to signal his son's surrender at the end of the tenth round. After a six-months rest, Petersen returned to outscore Len Harvey and Jock McAvoy in British title fights, but his cut eye bogey let him down again when he lost his British title to Ben Foord in three rounds. Warned of the danger to his sight if he kept boxing, Petersen decided to have one more fight – a third encounter with Walter Neusel. Promoter Hulls promised the winner a shot at Max Baer, even though the American had lost the world title to Jim Braddock. Petersen gave it a go, but he was beaten by the strength and body punching of the German, and was bearing a cut over his eye when his corner once more made the decision that he would not make for himself, to quit after ten rounds. He hung up his gloves at the age of 25.

It took a hardy Welshman named Tommy Farr to finally erase the 'Horizontal Heavyweights' stigma when, on the unforgettable night of 30 August 1937, at Yankee Stadium, New York, he took the great Joe Louis the full 15 rounds in a brave bid for the world heavyweight title. Farr, not a heavy puncher, but a crafty boxer with a solid chin, took everything the Brown Bomber threw at him without going down once and, though he finished with multiple cuts and bruises, he gave Louis one of the toughest fights of his illustrious career. The American was a unanimous points winner – referee Arthur Donovan only gave Farr one round, with one round even, while the two judges scored it 9-6 and 8-5 with two rounds even – but Louis admitted that the Welshman was one of the toughest men he ever fought. The world champion's trainer, Jack Blackburn, said: "Louis hit Farr with shots that would have dropped, yeah, flattened most other fighters in the world. Farr is a real tough man and he has an awkward style".

It was 18 years before another Briton got the chance to capture boxing's biggest prize, and Londoner Don Cockell bravely took Rocky Marciano's lethal brand of punishment – not all of it strictly within the rules – for nine rounds until he was rescued by the referee. Even the Americans lauded Cockell for his plucky stand. Those old enough to remember the era of Britain's 'Horizontal Heavyweights' accepted that the charge no longer held any validity.

Phil Scott

Dan Donnelly, 1788-1820, Pugilist, Publican, Playboy

By Patrick Myler

In his latest book, Patrick Myler tells the remarkable story of an Irishman whose exploits in the bare-knuckle ring made him into an early 19th-century folk hero. His victories over highly regarded English opponents won him countless fans, including the Prince Regent (later King George the 4th), who was said to be so impressed by Donnelly's performances that he awarded him a knighthood.

'Sir' Dan's famous victory over George Cooper on the Curragh of Kildare in December 1815 is commemorated with a monument at the spot known as Donnelly's Hollow, and visitors still delight in being able to walk in the Irish champion's preserved footprints.

Even after his sudden death at 32, Donnelly continued to make news. His body was stolen from the grave and his right arm was cut off and preserved. For almost 200 years, the grisly relic has fascinated viewers as it travelled the world and is currently on display at The Fighting Irishmen Exhibition at the Ulster American Folk Park in Omagh, County Tyrone.

'Myler's story on the life and myths of Dan Donnelly is possibly one of the best written about a bare-knuckle fighter' – Ron Jackson, Superboxing website, South Africa.

Dan Donnelly, 1788-1820, Pugilist, Publican, Playboy, by Patrick Myler, is published in paperback by the Lilliput Press, 62 Sitric Road, Arbour Hill, Dublin 7, Republic of Ireland (HYPERLINK "http://www.lilliputpress.ie" www.lilliputpress.ie) at a cost of £10.

Dai Corp: A Passion for Boxing

by Ralph Oates

To make the decision to box, to take that first vital step into the world of fighting men, is often made for various reasons. Often kids are introduced to the sport by concerned parents who want to keep the young off the streets, and the local boxing gym is the answer to their problem. Sometimes it is the individual who wants to put on the gloves because he quite simply wants to fight and at the same time keep fit. The reasons for fighting are indeed numerous.

One thing is for certain, once you step into the ring for your first contest, no matter what level, your life will never really be the same whether you win or lose your respective bout. From the moment you hear the bell to start the first round – it really is exciting. The supporters, both yours and your opponent's, will stir you in to action and within seconds you will realise just why you had to work so hard at your training. The memory of this momentous occasion will be with you for the rest of your life. There is no doubt that from the moment that bell rang to start your contest you duly embark upon a journey of discovery whereupon you will find many answers to questions about your character.

The ring can be a place of education where you will be given problems to solve, and awkward situations to overcome. During the contest you will often find that things will not go your way; just as in life you have to take the rough with the smooth and battle on. The jab of your opponent can often be sickening, especially if you cannot find an answer to it, etc. The first time you have to take a count will truly test your character to the full. Boxing is not easy, but then again neither is life. The lesson is to fight on, sometimes against the odds, sometimes in pain, and not to give up without a battle, even when it seems all is lost. Once again, as in life, there are winners and losers. We cannot all be boxing champions, but we can be champions of dignity and class and thus make our efforts count. Many boxers, both amateurs and professionals, do not win a title during their time in the ring, but that does not belittle their efforts in any way whatsoever. During their respective careers they have given the best they could and no one can ask or indeed expect more than that.

Such is the nature of the sport of boxing, that when many boxers decide that their activities inside the square ring are over they find that it is not easy to walk away from. They still want to be part of the sport in some shape or form. This is of course great for the game because these men have experience that can be passed on to others who are starting out in the sport. Experience is a commodity of great value and such a man with a great deal of that vital commodity is Dai Corp. Dai is one of those men who has served boxing well over the years without any fuss and attention and he continues to play a role in a sport which he loves so well. Confirmation, if indeed any was needed, that the game turns out men of fine character who prove to be a credit to boxing.

On behalf of the yearbook I contacted Dai to ask about his time in both the amateur and professional ranks, and his opinions about the sport in general.

(Ralph Oates) When were you born?

(Dai Corp) I was born on the 15th August 1940.

(RO) Where were you born?

Dai (left) seen here with the legendary Howard Winstone in their amateur days

(DC) Fairwater in Cardiff

(RO) How tall are you?

(DC) 5'5".

(RO) How old were you when you started to box?

(DC) I started boxing at ten years of age.

(RO) Have any other members of your family ever boxed?

(DC) Yes, my brother Gordon, who was born in 1941.

(RO) What made you take up boxing?

(DC) My brother and I were always fighting at school, and on numerous occasions we were sent home. It was then that our father took the two of us to the local boxing club, St Clare's, where we learned about 'Behaviour'. Then having failed the Eleven Plus exams, I went to Radnor Road Secondary Modern school in Canton, Cardiff. This is where I met Arthur Floyd, who used to train the Boxing Class, and he asked me if I would like to join his club, Victoria Park ABC, which was also situated in Canton. I was really impressed when I saw the number of Welsh and Army Cadet champions that were training there, which included Joe Erskine.

(RO) Was Arthur Floyd your only trainer at the club?

(DC) No. Sadly, when Arthur passed on, Ernie Davies, a very good amateur flyweight whose career had been interrupted by the war, took over.

(RO) Approximately how many amateur bouts did you have?

(DC) I had 98 amateur contests.

(RO) Can you remember how many you actually won?

(DC) I won approximately 76 and lost 22. I also boxed a number of exhibitions.

(RO) In which weight division did you box?

(DC) I boxed in the flyweight division and then later moved up to bantamweight when boxing as a senior.

(RO) Did you win any titles in the amateur ranks?

(DC) Yes, I won Schoolboy, Junior, and Youth titles in the respective Welsh Championships. I also won a Cardiff Schoolboy's title.

(RO) In which stance did you box?

(DC) I started off as a southpaw but later turned orthodox.

(RO) Many boxers do not like fighting southpaws. How did you feel about meeting them in the ring?

(DC) Awful, the style was very difficult to deal with.

(RO) Who was your most difficult opponent in the amateur ranks?

(DC) Tony Wynn (a southpaw). I won on points in what was a terrible contest.

(RO) Who was your most difficult opponent in the professional ranks?

(DC) A fighter by the name of Jon-Jo Donaghy.

(RO) What would you say was your proudest moment when boxing in the amateur ranks?

(DC) Winning three consecutive Welsh championships, Schoolboy, Junior and Youth.

(RO) Did you ever box abroad with the amateurs?

(DC) Yes. I boxed in Switzerland twice (Lucerne and Zurich). I won one bout and lost the other.

(RO) Why did you turn professional?

(DC) I became very disappointed with the amateurs, so turning to the paid ranks was the next logical step.

(RO) How many professional contests did you have?

(DC) I had 14 contests of which I won nine and lost four, with one bout being a draw.

(RO) Did you ever box abroad when in the professional ranks?

(DC) I boxed abroad on just the one occasion and that was in Israel. I lost on points over eight rounds to a French opponent.

(RO) In which year did you retire from boxing?

(DC) 1963.

(RO) What made you decide to retire when you did?

(DC) I caught a thumb in the eye when sparring. I later had an examination, whereby the Doctor informed me that I had the start of a cataract and it would only get worse with the passage of time. This left me with no alternative but to retire from boxing. It was of course a shock at the time, because it was not something I was expecting, but you have to get over these setbacks and get on with life.

(RO) Where you ever superstitious before a fight?

(DC) No, I cannot say that I was.

(RO) Did you ever consider becoming a manager?

(DC) No, but I always wanted to be a matchmaker, so I took out a licence and did just one tournament in Cardiff. It was a very good show, but the promoter lost money and although he wanted to run another promotion I did not want to be involved.

(RO) I understand you were a trainer for some time.

(DC) Yes, I had a trainer's licence from 1 September 1977 to October 1982.

(RO) Can you remember some of the fighters you trained during that period of time?

(DC) This was of course a number of years ago, but I can remember some of the fighters I trained and worked with, men such as Billy Waith, Ronnie Hough, Carl Thomas, Dick Duffy, Terry Gale, Terry Phillips, Gerry Maxwell, Tony Burnett, Rodney Parkinson, Clive Cook and Des Rea. Des became the first fighter to win the British light-welterweight title, which was then called the junior light-welterweight title. All the said fighters were managed by Mac Williams and I really enjoyed training the boxers in question. We had some great moments, which I often think about. Happy thoughts are a treasure to behold and I have many of them.

(RO) I understand that you had a great regard for Howard Winstone, the former WBC world, British and European featherweight champion.

(DC) I had always respected Howard as a friend and a brilliant boxer; his three epic battles for the world featherweight title against Vicente Saldivar will long be remembered. Saldivar, who boxed in the southpaw stance, was one of the true greats in the division and Howard really ran him close for the crown. It was only justice when Howard took the vacant WBC crown in his fourth attempt at the championship in 1968, stopping Mitsunori Seki in round nine. A very fond memory I have is when I was due to box at the National Sporting Club. My trainer, Mac Williams, suggested having a public workout for me, with the gym being open to all who wanted to come. He invited Howard to come down and spar a number of rounds with me, which he did. I can remember when we got into a clinch he would say to me: "Come on Dai, double the jab, keep the pressure on", etc and hence made me look a lot better than I really was. As it turned out it was a good evening's boxing. Howard of course won two Lonsdale Belts outright and had one notch on a third belt during his career. The only title he did not hold in the professional ranks was the Empire crown.

(RO) Do you believe that boxing instils discipline and respect into those who participate?

(DC) Yes, it makes men out of boys, as the saying goes. I think that when some of the 'Hard' cases go to the gym and try to start skipping, hitting the bags, and doing some real exercises it comes as a bit of a shock to them. Especially when they look around and see other boys doing it and making it look so simple.

(RO) How do you feel about female involvement in the sport?

(DC) Not a lot personally, however the world changes and we have to accept it.

(RO) Who is your favourite old-time fighter?

(DC) Joe Louis. He was what the sport needed after some of his predecessors. Joe really showed his strength of character when he fought the former world heavyweight champion, Max Schmeling of Germany, on the 19 June 1936. The American went into the bout with an undefeated record and was a firm favourite to increase his run of victories. However, Max, a very experienced fighter who knew his craft, overcame the odds and knocked Joe out in round 12. This was of course a devastating defeat for the then young Louis, but he later fought his way back to become world heavyweight champion by knocking out holder James J. Braddock in eight rounds on 22 June 1937. He then went on to gain sweet revenge over Schmeling by knocking him out in round one, in the fourth defence of his title on the 22 June 1938. Louis was a true great in every sense of the word. Joe made 25 defences of the world heavyweight title, a record which still holds good today and will take some beating, in that division.

(RO) How do you feel about title fights being held over the duration of 12 rounds rather than 15?

(DC) I have mixed feelings about this. From the 'Health and Safety' point of view, it keeps the anti-boxing brigade at bay. The Board's medical team are always discussing ways and means to ensure the health and safety of today's boxers. So, in the light of that, you could say that 12-round title fights are a good thing.

(RO) Who is your favourite modern day fighter?

(DC) I would say Marco Antonio Barrera. The Mexicans have a long tradition of producing great fighters in the lighter divisions and Barrera's name can without doubt join the elite group. Marco, of course, became the first and only man to defeat Prince Naseem Hamed when he outpointed him over 12 rounds in Las Vegas in 2001. The Mexican fighter has also scored many other notable victories over the years when matched with highly rated fighters. However, at this stage I feel that time is clearly not on his side and he is a little past his best.

(RO) Which is your favourite weight division?

(DC) Super-featherweight. We have seen many marvellous fights in this weight division, both in Britain and in various parts of the world.

(RO) Who in your opinion was the best professional heavyweight champion in the history of the sport?

(DC) I would have to say three-times world heavyweight champ Muhammad Ali. The man certainly drew a great deal of attention to the sport during his time and gave the sport a much-needed boost. Ali may have upset a few people with some comments during his career, but he was more than able to deliver on the night when called upon to do so.

(RO) Which is your favourite world heavyweight title fight?

(DC) The 'Rumble In The Jungle' which took place on the 30th October 1974 in Kinshasa, Zaire. It was the occasion when Ali became only the second man in the history of the sport to regain the world heavyweight crown. The first man to do so was of course Floyd Patterson, who lost and then regained the championship from Ingemar Johansson of Sweden. Few, if any, gave Ali a chance against the then undefeated George Foreman, whom Ali knocked out in round eight, to secure his place amongst the greats. You could not really write Ali off in these fights and it was such a great shame that he continued to fight on long after he should have retired from the sport. A mistake so many fighters seem to sadly make.

RO) Who is your favourite British fighter?

(DC) I would have to say Sammy McCarthy, who won the British featherweight title in 1954 when defending champion Ronnie Clayton retired in round eight. Sammy had previously outpointed Ronnie over ten rounds in 1952. However, going into this contest, Clayton was a former European and Empire titleholder, and a winner of two Lonsdale Belts outright. So McCarthy took the crown from a good champion. However, the bout with McCarthy proved to be Clayton's last professional contest since he retired soon after. To his credit, Sammy always came to fight. I know that it is a well-used phrase but it is true in Sammy's case. He always gave value to the fans when in the ring. His reign did not last for long, losing his title in the first defence of the crown to Billy Spider Kelly in 1955, when outpointed over 15 rounds. An eventual move up in weight to challenge Joe Lucy for the British lightweight title in 1956 saw McCarthy stopped in round 13, a defeat that ended his quest for further titles. However, he can look back at a good career that saw him meet fighters like Jackie Turpin, Hogan Kid Bassy, Ray Famechon, Guy Garcia and Dave Charnley, and put together a record of 53 bouts, with 44 wins, one draw and eight defeats.

(RO) How do you feel about fighters who continue to box on even when middle aged?

(DC) To be honest, a little disappointed. However, it is difficult to stop this from happening, what with the 'Restraint of Trade' and the politically correct brigade. However the Board is cautious and very careful about the situation.

(RO) What changes, if any, would you like to see made in the professional ranks?

(DC) Difficult one, this. However, one of the changes I would like to see is the referees becoming more 'aware' of the shouting from the corners when a contest has just started because the corner men take very little notice of an inspector to the annoyance of spectators and officials at the ringside.

Also, corner men should in some cases show a little more compassion for their boxers, particularly when they have little chance of winning or are taking a beating. Be it in a championship fight or non-title bout.

(RO) Out of all the boxers in recent years who would you say was an excellent role model for the sport?

(DC) Nicky Piper, Johnny Nelson, Ricky Hatton, Joe Calzaghe, Ian Napa and many, many more. The majority of boxers are well behaved in general and prove to be a real credit to the sport they represent.

(RO) What annoys you most in professional boxing?

(DC) I would have to give the same answer that I gave to the 'what changes would I like to see made in the professional ranks' and it would be the shouting from the corner during a contest.

(RO) What annoys you most in amateur boxing?

(DC) The self-righteous attitude of some of the referees.

(RO) What was your most disappointing moment in boxing?

(DC) When I was disqualified in the Welsh championship finals. This was my year to win it, after being beaten in past attempts by Terry Crimmins and then Howard Winstone, both these defeats coming about by way of a points verdict. I had no complaints about those, but I was not too happy about my disqualification defeat, particularly as it prevented me from going into the quarter-finals of the ABA Championships.

(RO) What do you think about computer scoring that is now used in amateur bouts?

(DC) To be truthful, I have not spoken to anyone who has had a good word to say about this system. In fact, I think it is doing more harm than good. With all due respect, how can three elderly gentlemen sitting on different sides of the ring press a button simultaneously? Hence the diabolical decisions we often see.

(RO) How do you feel about the vast number of world governing bodies in the sport at the moment?

(DC) There are far too many, in my opinion, and to be honest I think that boxing will eventually lose its credibility, as we know it. Having too many world champions devalues the term 'World Champion'. It is so much better for the sport if one is able to name the world champion in each weight division without too much thought. These days many cannot even name one world champion in any respective division. Now that cannot be good for the game.

(RO) How do you feel about there being so many weight divisions in the sport today?

(DC) I am not too happy with this situation. I think this trend of adding new weight divisions will also help boxing to lose its credibility if it continues. I would also say that I am not sure that it stops boxers from dehydrating.

(RO) What would you say to those who would like to ban boxing?

(DC) Take a long, hard look at the charts for injuries in sport and see just how far down the list boxing is.

(RO) There have been a number of films made about boxing over the years, do you have a particular favourite?

(DC) No, I really cannot stand watching films about boxing.

(RO) What was the best advice you were given when boxing?

(DC) Chin down and hands up.

(RO) Looking at the domestic scene at the moment, who do you tip for the top in the amateur ranks?

(DC) I do not really follow amateur boxing enough to give a comment.

(RO) Who do you tip for the top in the professional ranks?

(DC) At this time I would say Nathan Cleverly, he really does have a great deal of potential. Nathan did very well when defeating Tony Oakey for the vacant Commonwealth light-heavyweight title in just his 13th professional fight. Some say 13 is unlucky, but not for Cleverly who, shall we say, boxed cleverly to outpoint Oakey over 12 rounds for the crown and thus became the first Welsh holder of this Championship since Nicky Piper. Tony was a good test for Cleverly, bringing a wealth of experience to the fight, having been a former British, Commonwealth, WBU and Southern Area light-heavyweight titleholder. He had also shared the ring with Neil Simpson, Matthew Barney, Peter Haymer, Steven Spartacus, Brian Magee and Dean Francis, and let us not forget that soon after his defeat by Nathan he won the 'Prize-Fighter' light-heavyweight title. Which further confirmed just what a good win it was. Nathan also had an excellent win when in just his seventh professional bout he stopped the then-undefeated Tony Quigley in round five. Quigley later went to capture the vacant British super-middleweight title, stopping Tony Dodson in round 12 in a hard-hitting, relentless contest. A great deal can happen in boxing to change the course of a fighter's direction, but at the moment Cleverly looks to have the desire, ambition and tools to go a very long way in the sport.

(RO) How long have you been married?

(DC) I have been married for 37 years.

(RO) Do you have any children?

(DC) Yes, I have a son, Michael, who is aged 33, and a daughter, Nicola, who is 36 years of age.

(RO) Do you have any grandchildren?

(DC) Yes, two, both boys, Bradley and Morgan Rees.

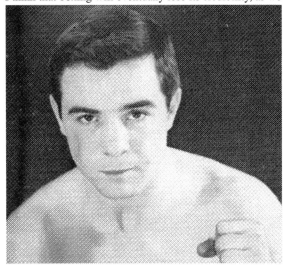

Dai in fighting pose

(RO) Do you discuss boxing much at home?

(DC) No, I cannot say that I do in general.

(RO) How does your wife feel about your involvement in boxing?

(DC) Well, I think that my wife, Heulwen, is glad to get me out of the house. Although, to be honest, I could not have got so involved in boxing without her help in my capacity as (Welsh and Western Area secretary) and (Council Member). I have also taken out an Inspector's badge, which keeps me in touch with the sport.

(RO) How long have you been a Welsh Area Inspector?

(DC) At this moment in time, I would say three years.

(RO) Do you have a hobby?

(DC) No, not really, but I do find that my time is often taken by doing odd jobs at home.

(RO) Do you still keep fit?

(DC) I go to Ronnie Rush's gym twice a week to keep the old ticker going. I must confess that I like the atmosphere of the boxing gym.

(RO) What advice would you give to anyone embarking on a career in boxing?

(DC) To seek advice before signing a boxing/manager's contract. Train at a gym where there are a number of boxers and facilities and to appreciate the importance of working out in between contests. It is vital to keep fit and sharp, particularly if you are offered any substitute contests.

(RO) Looking back at your boxing career to date, would you do anything different if you had your time over again?

(DC) No, not really. I have really enjoyed my time, which indeed equates to years being connected with boxing, and will hopefully enjoy a few more years yet with the sport.

(RO) Apart from boxing, do you follow any other sport?

(DC) No, I cannot say that I do.

(RO) What did you do when you first retired from boxing?

(DC) I had a clean break for some months before making the decision to go back to the gym. I have been going ever since.

(RO) You were for a number of years the Welsh Area Secretary, did you find this role rewarding?

(DC) Yes, very much so once I had settled in. When I first took over the position of Welsh Area Secretary it was a financially interested council with plenty of characters like Benny Jacobs, Mac Williams, Eddie Thomas, and Joe Morgan, etc. Unfortunately, there were some very heated discussions and after some considerable time a decision was reached that the council would be non-financial, remaining that way ever since. I have to say that I thoroughly enjoyed being 'someone' in boxing, in this capacity.

(RO) I understand that you have received a number of awards for your services to boxing over the years.

(DC) Yes, several. The Welsh Hall of Fame for services to boxing and Welsh Area Council services to boxing. Also awards from promoters, Chris Sanigar and Paul Boyce, for my contribution to boxing. They all came as a very big surprise and made me feel very proud that my efforts over the years have been appreciated.

(RO) Do you still attend boxing promotions?

(DC) Yes, I do. Although we do not have regular tournaments as such here in Wales, we have had several shows promoted by Frank Warren, Barry Hearn and Chris Sanigar. I often attend these promotions in my role as Welsh Area Inspector.

(RO) What are your ambitions for the future?

(DC) To keep going to the gym as often as I can, and to continue to work in boxing. I formerly worked in the office of The British Boxing Board of Control, helping out where required. This kept my finger on the pulse of the sport, so to speak.

Over the years Wales has contributed greatly to British boxing, producing many fine fighters, indeed some great fighters in both the amateur and professional ranks whose names will be long remembered in the sport's rich history. Dai Corp did not win a professional title, due to an injury to his left eye that sadly cut short his career in the ring, so we will never know if his name would have been put into the record books as a British champion. However, this blow to his career did not get Dai down, since he does not complain about what might have been or what could have been. He showed a true fighter's spirit and accepted the fact that his boxing career inside the ring was over and got on with his life. You could say that Dai was floored but got up and beat the count. Dai duly found another outlet in the sport he loved and hence continued in boxing, taking part in other aspects of the game and bringing his vast experience into play. During my interview with Dai it became very clear that the man really knows his sport. Dai is a man who is modest about his own achievements, but is indeed quick to praise others for theirs.

Today Dai is a very happy family man, a father and a grandfather who still serves boxing to a high degree. The critics who often knock boxing should take account of men like Dai Corp who are indeed a credit. I, on behalf of the Boxing Yearbook, wish Dai, his wife Heulwen and family, all the very best for the future.

Tommy Milligan: The Lanarkshire Lionheart

by Brian Donald

The only Scot to cleanly knock out an American world champion in ring battle; the only Scot to fight with two Scottish Peers in attendance, as MC and timekeeper, respectively; the first Scot to win a British and European welterweight title; the first and last Scot to contest a world middleweight crown and the Scottish boxer who figured in two Scottish record attendances-outdoor and indoor-in Scotland in the 20th century. Without a doubt, the Lanarkshire born fighter has many claims to fame.

Born on 2 March 1904 into the social realities of the Lanarkshire coalfields in the Craigneuk and Wishaw area that has produced so many outstanding Caledonian ringmen, Tommy was one of a family of 11 and the son of a miner who had no interest in boxing and never saw his son box. Right from the start, Tommy's father was determined that his son would not follow him underground.

Incidentally, Craigneuk was also the birthplace of top world-rated British 1960s southpaw lightweight ace, Dave Charnley's parents and Chic Calderwood, the first Scottish light-heavyweight to win a British title and Lonsdale Belt.

However, Tommy's Dad's indifference to boxing meant it was Tommy's mother who was the driving force behind his boxing career. Not for Ma Milligan the movie stereotypical Mum who does not want her boy to box, while the young Milligan worked as a steel mill engineering apprentice. In fact, so determined was Ma Milligan that her son would box that it was she who provided Tommy with his first sidestake money. She also arranged for her son to train -aged just 14-in 1918 at Tommy Murphy's Glasgow gym where the shrewd Murphy soon spotted that this 14-year-old lightweight was a bit special and rapidly took him under his wing.

Similarly, nothing illustrates the eagerness of the budding pugilist to take up the sport than the story he himself recounted in later years of how he had once walked six miles to get a loan of some boxing gloves from a pal!.

Meanwhile, Murphy ensured Tommy was well schooled in all the skills of boxing, from slipping to punching, while sparring with the 1919 Scottish amateur bantamweight champion, John Fleming, who became a British pro welterweight champion as Hamilton Johnny Brown in the 1920s. Fleming had won Scottish and British amateur featherweight titles in 1909 when Tommy was just five years old and he soon developed a feeling that Tommy Murphy was spending too much time with Milligan thus creating a jealousy-fuelled rivalry which Tommy later claimed had the positive benefit of ensuring that he learned a great deal from the needle inspired no holds barred sparring sessions the pair had.

So by 1921, when he won a novice Miners championship boxing bout, young Milligan not only gradually built up a reputation as a skilful lightweight but

more importantly had attracted the attention of the shrewd manager and promoter, Pat McGreechan. A wily bookmaker, McGreechan's business smarts merged with the ring smarts of Milligan to mutually beneficial effect. So much so, that according to McGreechan in a 1935 newspaper article, the £4,858 ring purse that Milligan received for challenging America's Mickey Walker for the world middleweight title (worth £1.2 million at today's values) was a Scottish record.

However, that was all that was in the future when Tommy launched his ring pro career in 1921 by knocking out Duncan Starke and then outpointing the Glaswegian, Johnny Connors. Wins that made the gifted Lanarkshire ring technician a firm favourite with the fans.

Milligan's first ring defeat was no disgrace as his 1922 conqueror, Jim Cater, would end the boxing career of future top British referee, Eugene Henderson. Indeed, in an 1986 interview with this author ex-referee Henderson recalled:

Tommy posing for the camera before his meeting with the great Mickey Walker

"Cater could hit like a mule and I did not come to until I was standing in the shower...". Revenge came to the 18-year-old Milligan in November 1922, when he outpointed Cater over 15 hard rounds, prompting a ringside journalist to call Tommy 'The Wishaw Wonderman'' when Tommy was actually from Craigneuk.

By now a rising star, Tommy also became a firm favourite with leading Glasgow boxing promoters like Jim Gilmour, Bill Strelly and George Aitchison because he proved time and again that he could box boxers and slug with sluggers in a crowd-pleasing style.

But 1923, despite being knocked out for the first time by one Billy Mattick in Newcastle in 11 rounds, was to prove a significant year for Milligan. Of the 11 wins that Paddy McGreechan's rising middleweight star had in 1923, two of them - one in London and the other in Edinburgh - had a major significance in progressing Tommy's ring career. Ironically, however, it was a losing 15-round points decision to tough Bob Jackson on a Nat Dresener promotion in Edinburgh's cavernous Waverley Market in Princes Street that alerted Dresner to Tommy's talents. Dresner, then Scotland's number-one promoter, became a big fan and mentor of the Craigneuk man. Besides, even in losing to Jackson, Milligan had demonstrated his full mastery of all the classic punches, plus evasive skills and ring smarts that won for Milligan the admiration of Dresner's regular ring MC, Sir Ian Colquhoun of Luss, who would become the very Chairman of the then newly set up BBBoC Scottish Area Council. A former Scottish amateur welterweight champion in 1913 and a highly decorated World War One hero, Sir Ian also took to Tommy Milligan's above average intelligence and gentlemanly ways that made a mockery of crude 1920s stereotypes of boxers. Thus, a life-long friendship terminated only by Sir Ian's death in 1948 was formed.

Again, not content with having Scotland's number-one promoter in the 1930s and an influential ex-boxing Baronet on his side, Tommy Milligan also took London's National Sporting Club by storm in 1923, when outpointing the tough Englishman, Jack Kirk, over 15 rounds. It was a win that prompted famous English 20th century boxing writer, Gilbert Odd, to write in 1948: "I well remember Tommy Milligan when he made his first appearance at the National Sporting club...he (Milligan) pleased everyone by the way that he tore out of his corner and hammered into his opponent, Jack Kirk, in non-stop, two-fisted fashion to gain a decisive victory". On another occasion, Odd noted of Tommy's NSC appearances: "Each time that he (Milligan) appeared at the NSC he seemed to fight fiercer and fiercer". Meanwhile, Pat McGreechan and Nat Dresner struck a deal in 1924 that highlighted that year as being the year when Lanarkshire's Tommy Milligan was going to become a champion.

Enter Alex Ireland from Leith, who had won a welterweight silver medal in the Antwerp Olympics of 1920 and was widely tipped for the highest pro-game honours. True, Milligan had been aided by the fact that clever Ireland

lacked a big punch, a deficiency that would cost the man from Leith his British middleweight title against Len Harvey, but the victory over Ireland put the "Wishaw Wonder' firmly on the road to getting, with Dresner's support, a crack at the British welterweight title. To this end, Milligan went south again to the London-based National Sporting Club to kayo a Welsh tough guy, Tom Thomas, inside two rounds. Tommy followed this up at the same venue when stopping his hard as nails English rival, Joe Rolfe, with a barrage of punches in the ninth round.

These impressive ring performances in the English capital led to Tommy notching up another boxing first for Scotland, for when he outpointed the leading English contender, Johnny Sullivan, over 20 rounds he did so at the recently opened Wembley.

To reward this hat-trick of London victories, Nat Dresner told Tommy that if he could beat his old sparring partner, Hamilton Johnny Brown, in Edinburgh then the promoter would get him a British and European welterweight title fight with England's legendary Ted Kid Lewis. Brown had recently taken the world-rated Bronx American, Augie Ratner, to a 20-round draw in Edinburgh in 1923, but before 10,000 ringside fans in the Waverley Market, the man from Hamilton was well beaten over 20 rounds on points.

Tommy was clearly fired up by the prospect of winning what was a an eliminator for the British title and finally settling, once and for all as to who was the best between himself and his old gym antagonist, Johnny Brown. Although now a veteran, Brown had twice triumphed over a former Milligan foe in Alex Ireland, yet the *Edinburgh Evening News*' headline on this all-Lanarkshire clash the next day said it all as far as Tommy's performance was concerned: "Brown loses to former pupil Milligan...". After 20 rounds a sore, weary and defeated Brown could only look on as Milligan's many fans lifted him aloft in the Waverley Market.

The wily Nat Dresner, having read of reigning British and European welterweight champion, Ted Kid Lewis' impending bankruptcy hearing in the press, offered the legendary but cash strapped a large purse to defend against Tommy at Edinburgh's Industrial Hall. Incidentally, just two years later the London heavyweight, Phil Scott, would win the British Empire heavyweight crown by a 17th-round disqualification in January 1926 when beating Australian George Cook.

As the Edinburgh police battled constantly in Annandale Street to stop 10,000 disappointed fans who made repeated assaults on the venue gates the 20,000 fans inside in this record indoor attendance for a Scottish boxing match watched enthralled as the *Edinburgh Evening News* reported: "Milligan carried the fight to Lewis from the start...". Meanwhile, a fired up Milligan sank left hooks into weight-weakened Lewis' ribs, whose effects could be gleaned from the fact that referee Joe Palmer continually cautioned the Londoner for holding.

The *Evening News*' reporter further observed: "Milligan was always superior in clean hitting and by the

15th round the fight was clearly his...". Yet proof positive that Lewis still had some of the old venom, that had seen him knockout over 70 opponents, came in the 17th round when Tommy was shaken up by a heavy right to the chin. The reporter further observed: "Lewis had the reserve strength that Milligan lacked...and when the 20th round ended with Joe Palmer raising of Milligan's hand in victory there was much cheering...".

So, remarkably, aged just 20, Tommy Milligan was a British and European champion. Again, in 1925, having beaten Lewis on a disqualification for holding in London's

Albert Hall on 19 March, Tommy was matched with Italy's Bruno Frattini at London's Holland Park Arena for the European middleweight title.

A former art college student who had learned to box in the Italian Army during World War One, Frattini had been knocked out previously in 17 rounds by Lewis in 1922, but the tough Italian had also beaten the current British middles champion, Roland Todd, and would prove a tough handful for Milligan. One Scottish newspaper reported: "In the fifth round the Italian was very clever and crafty and covered up well", adding, "In round six Frattini scored with several

Tommy (right) and his trainer inspecting the guard at Windsor Castle, while in training for the fight against Maxie Rosenbloom

well directed right crosses over Milligan's left". However, a magnificent 20th round by Tommy prompted the same ringside scribe to write: "Milligan quite outclassed his opponent at this stage". Certainly, British NSC boxing Czar 'Peggy' Bettinson concurred, making a point of telling Tommy, post-fight: "You're a fine fighter Milligan, you have the makings of a world beater".

Equally impressed was London-based boxing impresario, Charles B. Cochran, who now planned to match Scotland's Tommy with the American world middleweight champion, Mickey 'Toy Bulldog' Walker, managed by Jack 'Doc' Kearns. Walker had used two defeats in the USA when Tommy had campaigned there as an excuse not to defend his welter crown against Milligan but money, then as now, talks and Cochrane persuaded Walker to defend his world middlweight title against the Craigneuk clouter in June 1927 at London's Olympia. Tommy, meantime, had beaten the English ex-Guardsman, George West, at the NSC for the British title, vacated by Roland Todd, in July 1926.This was soon followed by the two 14th-round stoppage wins by Tommy over Plymouth's world-rated Ted Moore in October 1926 and January 1927 that clinched the Walker bout. At this stage of his career, Milligan also acquired a new trainer in 'Puggy' Morgan, who would later play a key role in Scottish flyweight legend, Benny Lynch's rise to greatness.

Cochran had originally intended to stage Tommy's world middleweight title challenge in the Northern seaside resort of Blackpool, but eventually this idea was abandoned and London's Olympia arena chosen with a date of June 30 1927 agreed. Future Star 'A' Class referee, Eugene Henderson, helped world title contender Milligan prepare for his quest for world title glory at Walker's expense and he recounted: "Tommy Milligan was trained to the minute by 'Puggy' Morgan at Shieldmiur, near Glasgow. I know because during a sparring session with Tommy I received a tremendous dig just below the heart and despite his fists being encased in 16-ounce gloves he put me down". Henderson also noted that for the Walker fight Milligan was the fittest, fastest specimen of physical perfection that he had ever come across.

Remarkably, when Milligan arrived in London's Euston station in June 1927 a press picture shows Tommy receiving what is arguably the most tumultuous welcome given to any Scottish boxer by a London crowd when at least 30,000 people turned up in that London rail terminus to welcome him for his epic world title clash with Mickey Walker.

To the fight itself, Eugene Henderson, who was a ringside witness to what happened, said: "For the first six rounds the smack of Milligan's gloves against Walker's chin and ribs were music to my ears, but unfortunately coming up for the seventh round Milligan took a wicked left hook to the chin which forced him to take a count of nine". This blow was the turning point as Milligan was further decked, twice in round eight and twice more in the ninth before another big Walker left hook, which split the gallant Scottish

challenger's mouth, brought the bout to a halt.

Then followed a miserable period for Tommy. After outpointing Kid Nitram in London in November 1927, even though he attracted 10,000 fans to Wavereley Market in March 1928, Tommy lost his British title on a controversial disqualification to Leith's Alex Ireland, despite having had the latter on the verge of a knockout several times. However, a ringside press witness at the Ireland v Milligan title joust observed some slippage in Milligan skills, writing: "Time and time again the challenger (Ireland) appeared to be on the verge of being knocked out but Milligan's timing was out".

Yet fistic fame was not yet finished with Tommy Milligan. In June 1928 Tommy accepted the chance to fight American 'Slapsie' Maxie Rosenbloom at London's Albert Hall. This was the same Rosenbloom who would, post-ring career, go on to star with Hollywood screen legends, James Cagney and George Raft, in the 1939 gangster movie "Each Dawn I Die" and partner ex-heavyweight champion, Max Baer, in a comedy night club act. Rosenbloom was also just two years away from becoming world light-heavyweight champion.

Putting up a great performance, Tommy became the first and only Scottish boxing champion to knock out - cleanly - an American world champion, future or otherwise, when he stopped Rosenbloom in the ninth with a solar plexus punch. Afterwards, the American showed that it was not just British heavyweights like Phil Scott who cried 'foul', when he claimed that Tommy's perfectly good body shot was below the belt. Tommy told the *Edinburgh Evening News*: "I knew that Rosenbloom, who had six-inch reach advantage, was noted for a left hook so I let him get confident then I delivered the same punch that Bob Fitzsimmons used to take Jim Corbett's title in 1897".

Yet, just two month's later, Tommy's old sparring partner, Frank Moody, knocked him out in one minute, 45 seconds of round one with the very same punch. This would be Milligan's last fight. The *Edinburgh Evening News*, noting Moody's devastating body shot to the solar plexus, reported: "There was no question of a fluke about it...and the blow which laid Milligan low was a masterpiece of timing and precision as well as power ...it would have felled an ox". But even then, the 35,000 reported to be present in the open-air Cartyne Dog Track that August Monday in 1928, was a Scottish attendance record beaten only in 1937 when Benny Lynch defeated Goldborne's Peter Kane in defence of his world flyweight crown.

And that was it. Astute and naturally articulate and intelligent, Tommy Milligan never became one of Scottish championship boxing's sob stories. When he died in 1970 Tommy lived in the upmarket Glasgow suburb of King's Park, adored by his wife, son, Tommy junior, and his daughter who had gone to live in Spain. He left behind several Scottish boxing firsts, having trained for the Moody fight by invitation at the Duke of Hamilton's palace. Never has a Scottish boxing champion been so royally served, but then as man and boxer Craigneuk's Tommy Milligan was truly a Prince among men.

Will The Real Jack Dempsey Stand Up?

by Anton Shapiro

A short time ago, *The Ring* magazine printed a few lines on an old-timer who remembered the great John L. Sullivan and harked back to the good old days, where there was only one recognised champion at eight given weights. By comparison, he loathed the fact that boxing has become a fringe sport, with at least four champions at as many weights as different Boxing Associations can dream up.

If that was not bad enough, under the umbrella of a twisted interpretation of the phrase 'Political Correctness', many so-called boxing historians have distorted the history of the game almost beyond recognition. More than most, one of the true immortals of the game who has suffered from the mindless slander is Jack Dempsey. They have imposed a twisted image of him on an unsuspecting generation and written things they would not have dared have said to his face, hence the title chosen for this piece. Some historians, who should have known better, have taken Dempsey's five fights with 'Fat' Willie Meehan as a yardstick as if to prove that those who had actually seen him fight had got it wrong, and he was not the great master he was cracked up to be. Fine, so let us start with that assumption.

All Dempsey's five fights with Meehan were limited to four rounds. If we impose that same time limit on other great fights, the whole history of boxing would be turned on its head. To give some prime examples, had a four-round limit been imposed on the Sullivan v Corbett fight, John L. never would have lost the title. He literally chased Corbett for at least four rounds. Corbett, one of the greatest fighters in the history of the game, knocked out Sullivan in 21 rounds and he needed every round to accomplish that. Equally, over four rounds, Corbett never would have lost the title fight to Fitzsimmons. Corbett gave Fitz the thrashing of his life for 13 rounds before being knocked out in the 14th. Joe Louis would certainly have lost the title to Billy Conn over four rounds and been beaten twice over that distance by Jersey Joe Walcott. In their first fight Walcott decked Louis in the first round, outboxed him in the second and third, then decked him again in the fourth. Reasonably, it might be doubted if Louis could ever have beaten Walcott over four rounds, yet no one doubts that Louis was by far the greater fighter. And finally Muhammad Ali's perfect record going into his fight with Sonny Liston would have been shattered by a four round time limit. A nifty boxer named Daniels outboxed and outsmarted Ali for six rounds before being stopped on cuts in the seventh and Henry Cooper more than had an edge on Ali in their first fight at the end of four rounds. This list could go on endlessly, yet some 'experts' say that 'Fat' Willie had Dempsey's number.

Nigel Benn once stated that there are some fighters you simply cannot go tearing in against. 'Fat' Willie Meehan was probably one of them. However, this should take nothing away from Meehan. He took on Dempsey when the 'Manassa Mauler' was knocking out more world-class heavyweights in the first round than any other heavyweight in the history of the game. His four-round battles against Dempsey were all very close; Willie winning the first,

Dempsey the second, followed by two draws. Dempsey claimed he was surprised at the verdict when he lost their final encounter in 1918. Dempsey, at his peak, needed more than four rounds to defeat 'Fat' Willie and Meehan had every right to be proud of that.

The race riots that followed the showing of the films of Jack Johnson's title defeat against Stanley Ketchel and Jim Jefferies, cost the lives of almost 40 people and the repercussions were a disaster for the next generation of fighters, both black and white. The civil authorities put heavy pressure on fight promoters to avoid mixed race title fights, although their attitude was not that different from any mixed race fights. When Joe Choynski fought Jack Johnson in 1902 they both ended up in jail. The pressure was not only disastrous for black contenders, but soiled the reputations of white champions who never drew the colour line. Where did the real Jack Dempsey fit into all this? It is known that the promoter Tex Rickard pressurised Dempsey as soon as he won the title, to appease the authorities by stating in the *New York Times* that he would not defend the crown against a black fighter. Dempsey did this very reluctantly. Indeed, to counteract this he hired the best black fighters in the weight division as his sparring partners. These fighters were highly paid professionals who were not afraid to lose their jobs. If anything, it was an opportunity to embarrass, if not shame the champion into giving them a shot at the title. All they had to do was get the better of him. Nat Fleischer, the founder and editor of *The Ring* magazine commented that before winning the title, Dempsey was not an outstanding gymnasium fighter. Following some quirk, he even allowed some sparring partners to slap him around. All that changed after he won the title. Fleischer attended many of Dempsey's training sessions after he was champion and stated no sparring partner, black or white, ever got the better of him, with the exception of one session with the great Harry Greb.

In 1923 Dempsey finally defied the authorities by stating in the *Wisconsin Times* that he was open to any challenge from black contenders. This was about the time that Harry Wills emerged as his chief challenger. Many writers claim that Wills being black was the only reason he was unable to fight for the title. Dempsey himself agreed with that, blaming racism, yet Nat Fleischer, who did so much to champion Wills' cause, admitted privately that the fight would not have drawn peanuts. It is more than likely the promoters thought so too, as there was never a rush to put up the fight. The belief to this day remains that in that era no black man had a hope of a crack at the heavyweight title. Actually, this is not true. This is not to deny that racialism did not exist in its extreme form, it did, but when it came to money, promoters, then as now, were colour blind. And to prove it, they did come up with a black challenger, and promised him very handsome rewards at that. It is understandable if this has escaped the researchers of most boxing writers, because the man in question was not a professional fighter. Yet this was not a gimmick but a genuine offer.

It started after a football game ended in a fist fight between the ageing Olympic, football and baseball legend, Jim Thorpe, and the great actor, singer, all-American football player and Civil Rights champion, Paul Robeson. Robeson was one of the great Americans of his time and, ironically, in a more subtle way, far more dangerous to the barbaric racial system than even Jack Johnson was. Thorpe may have been past his best as an athlete, but he was still one of the toughest men around and Robeson's performance in standing up to him was enough for the promoters. The next day he was flooded with offers to fight Dempsey. He turned them all down due to the race riots that had followed Johnson's title defences. Robeson did not think that boxing at the time, was a suitable platform for the Civil Rights movement.

So in 1923, carrying two year's ring rust Dempsey pounded out an ungainly 12-3 victory over Tom Gibbons before destroying Luis Firpo in what was arguably the most exciting title fight in the history of the game. Dempsey signed a contract to fight Harry Wills in 1924, but the fight fell through. He then returned to Hollywood, married, then broke up with his overbearing manager and, finally, after three years inactivity he returned to the ring wars. Wills was still waiting for him and the New York Athletic Commission insisted Dempsey fight him, but still no promoter came forward to sanction the fight, and no offers were made. In fact, Dempsey was in no condition to fight anyone. Harry Greb, out of friendship, turned down Dempsey's offer as a sparring partner at a thousand dollars a round. He felt no amount of training could get Dempsey in shape enough against the contender the promoter Tex Rickard came up with - Gene Tunney. He was right. Dempsey practically handed Tunney the title on a silver platter with a 10-0 points loss. Nevertheless, the fight drew a million dollar gate.

Then a new star burst onto the horizon. Jack Sharkey, a brilliant but temperamental fighter, defeated George Godfrey and then Harry Wills in quick succession. Rickard persuaded Dempsey to fight him and it brought another million dollars at the turnstyles. The ex-champ was clearly not the fighter he used to be and was struggling when he landed a controversial blow to Sharkey's midriff in the seventh. When Sharkey took his eyes off his opponent to complain to the referee, all Dempsey could see was Sharkey's exposed chin and as he explained later: "What was I supposed to do, write him a letter". A poor correspondent, Jack never wrote the letter, laying Sharkey out with a left hook instead. Opinion is still divided as to whether the body blow was a foul or not. Tunney, sitting at ringside, stated it depended on where one was sitting and from where he was sitting the blow seemed a fair one.

Dempsey was now signed up to meet Tunney again. This time the fight drew over two million dollars. The notorious gangster Al Capone, was one of Dempsey's greatest fans, and to prove it he is said to have offered to fix the forthcoming fight in the ex-champion's favour. Supposedly, Dempsey quickly responded, saying he wanted to win fair and square. Capone sent him a large bouquet of flowers with the note: "To A Real Sportsman". Yet if Dempsey felt he had no need of Capone, Tunney was to be in need of a friendly referee, and in Dave Barry he found one, although Gene himself had nothing to do with it.

A new rule was introduced, in that in the event of a knockdown the fighter who scored that knockdown must retreat to a neutral corner before the count could begin. The referee strictly enforced this new rule, but only on Dempsey. Ironically, this fact was not acknowledged until the latter part of the 20th century. At first the fight was a carbon copy of their previous bout, but in the sixth Dempsey seemed to have regained a little of his old form and took the round. In the seventh, he knocked Tunney out, but by force of habit stood over him. Barry bravely frog-marched him to a neutral corner, then returned to the stricken champion, who was still unconscious. The timekeeper, seeing Barry now in the counting position called out 'five', but Barry ignored him and giving Tunney an extra second started his own count. At the timekeeper's count of six, Barry called out 'one'. Tunney claimed he first heard the count of 'two' and later admitted he could have got up any time after the count of 'five'. However, lining that up with the timekeeper's count it was another way of saying that he could have got up after the count of 'ten'. The controversy will remain.

There have been eyewitnesses with stop-watches, who claimed that Barry slowed down the count. The boxing legend, Abe Attell, stopped his watch at 22 seconds before Gene was ready to continue. During the excitement, five men died of heart attacks listening to the fight on the radio. In the eighth round a vengeful Tunney dropped Dempsey but did not retreat to a neutral corner, nor did Barry make any effort to send him there. Instead, he quickly rushed in and started the count. Dempsey however, sprang to his feet and Gene jumped back on his bicycle to retain the title with a clear points win.

Dempsey retired and with that came the end of a golden era. Despite his age he saw action in the Second World War, redeeming himself from the charge of 'slacker' that had caused the fans to hate him during his tenure as champion, and became an idolised legend until his death in 1987.

Since then, he has been vilified by second-rate boxing historians and falsely aligned to a racial ticket. Dempsey never claimed to be a social reformer, but he was a fair-minded man and a once-proud champion who feared no one. Moreover, during his peak years he did make some effort to break the colour bar in boxing and should be remembered for that. He was also a generous man. Many fighters, both black and white, had reason to be grateful to him. Perhaps that should not be forgotten either.

Jack Dempsey

Born William Harrison Dempsey in Manassa, Colorado, USA on 24 June 1895. Died 31 May 1983, aged 87.

83 Contests, won 62 (51 inside), lost six (one inside), drew nine, no decision distance six. Apart from his two ten-round points losses at the hands of Gene Tunney, men who outscored him over four rounds were Jack Downey and Willie Meehan (twice). Although Jim Flynn stopped him in the first round, Jack put that behind him a year later when winning inside a round. His first recorded contest was on 17 August 1914 and he announced his retirement in February 1928.

I'll Knock You Out Inside Four Rounds Or You Win: Jem Mace, John L Sullivan and the Remarkable Ted Pablo Fanque

by K R Robinson

An undertaking to stop an opponent within a given number of rounds was a common and popular 'entertainment' in the far off days of transition from the knuckles of the prize-ring to the gloves of the Queensberry code. The old prize-ring champions travelled the country with boxing booths, visiting towns and villages with a challenge to the local champion or hard man to last three or four rounds for a prize of a few shillings or pounds. The use of gloves or 'mufflers' were invariably the order of the day. Prize-ring champion Jem Mace claimed to be one of the originators of the form offering a prize of five pounds to any who could stand up before him for three three-minute rounds. People thought that Jem would lose many a fiver, but the English champion believed that no ordinary boxer could possibly stand up against a trained prize-fighter who had won his way to championship form for that length of time. If he felt that it was safe he would let a man stay into the second round before applying the quietus - but not a moment longer. Jem's favourite finisher was a blow to 'the mark' – solar plexus – followed, if required, by a couple of left-handers to the throat. Pride was just as great a motivation as saving a fiver.

The early use of the Queensberry rules amongst amateur fighters in clubs and sparring saloons played a role in bringing boxing in from the cold as the prize-ring declined under the weight of legislation and the general lawlessness of some of the sport's supporters. Early professional gloved championship contests were of unlimited rounds 'endurance' bouts; a well known example being that between Fred Johnson and Bill Baxter held in London on 21 December 1888 when Johnson won the English bantamweight title on a 42-rounds retirement.

The majority of bouts took place in public houses and small clubs frequented by working men. The most famous venues of this nature were probably Bill Richardson's Blue Anchor at Shoreditch and Bob Habbijam's West End School of Arms in Marylebone. Both former fighters, they trained aspiring young boxers and offered small purses for bouts, often on a winner-take-all basis. Young fighters might face old pros or former champions in exhibitions, thus being given the chance to impress a likely backer who could arrange a match or entry into a competition in one of the gentleman's clubs. The Pelican Club and later the National Sporting Club sat at the top of the game in the capital. A similar system operated in other sporting centres such as Birmingham, Manchester and Newcastle. The organization of boxing in America, South Africa and Australasia followed a similar pattern, the saloons and clubs often being run by transplanted Brits.

A driving force behind professional – and much amateur – sport was betting. However much of a mismatch a bout might seem betting opportunities abounded. Bets were laid on not only who would win, but who scored first blood, first knock down, or how many rounds a bout might last. An undertaking to stop an opponent within an agreed distance or forfeit the purse and verdict was a popular arrangement not least with top US professionals, who often undertook barnstorming tours across the States.

John L Sullivan, the 'Boston Strongboy' and American prize-ring champion, is credited as an early advocate of the Queensberry code. He did not relish the training required to prepare for a championship defence but was in constant need of cash to maintain his expensive life style. He made many sparring tours throughout his career, offering a cash prize to any who could last the agreed distance and gaining his income from ticket sales. In winning his championship with a nine-round knockout of Paddy Ryan at Mississippi City on 7 February 1882, Sullivan also gained the status of an outlaw for having taken part in an illegal prizefight. By July various alcoholic and fistic indiscretions, which may have added to his 'manly' reputation amongst the rougher elements of his supporters, had further stained his character. He was in need of a means of salvaging his popularity and of filling his empty coffers.

Sullivan's arch detractor, Richard K Fox, proprietor of the *Police Gazette*, had discovered, through the agency of an English friend, a fighter who might stand against Sullivan in a four-round contest – Joe Collins aka Tug Wilson. A 35-year-old veteran of the prize-ring, Wilson was fresher than it might seem, having taken a ten-year rest from combat between 1868 and 1878. Tug had taken part in five bare-knuckle contests, none lasting less than 70 minutes nor 21 rounds. He claimed the English heavyweight prize-ring title on the strength of a draw with the retired champion Alf Greenfield. Though recognized as American bare-knuckle

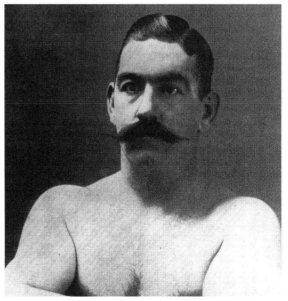

John L. Sullivan

champion, Sullivan had only engaged in two such bouts lasting a total of 26 minutes, 30 seconds.

Sullivan was undoubtedly a major attraction but few boxing fans of the day could ever see their hero in serious action in an environment where they were safe from being robbed or assaulted. However, this bout was to be no side show. Madison Square Garden was the venue and the international nature of the contest, particularly a match against a limey, ensured a big gate.

Sullivan first met his opponent on 28 June 1882 at transplanted cockney Harry Hill's theatre in New York to sign an agreement, the first condition of which began: 'John L. Sullivan, champion of America, agrees to give Joseph Collins (Tug Wilson) 1,000 dollars and half the gate receipts if he spars four three-minute rounds at Madison Square Garden, New York, on Monday evening 17 July'. The discrepancy in size between Sullivan and Wilson, who was giving away two and a half inches in height and 30lb in weight, was discounted in the odds, which outside of Boston, were even. Though not specifically mentioned in the arrangement, the Queensberry rules were generally understood to be the order of the day. However, ringside reports clearly show that both men used prize-ring tactics. Jem Mace claimed to have been at ringside and later recorded in his autobiography his impressions of the contest: 'Tug Wilson managed to stay out the allotted time with J. L. Sullivan, much to that champion's disgust. But then Tug was a very clever boxer, indeed, a prize-fighter of the old school, and he adopted every device known to the expert in ring strategy in order to avoid punishment, going down as soon as he was touched, sparring for wind, ducking, feinting and so on. In this way he just managed to last out the specified number of rounds and win the prize, which in this case amounted to over £1,000. But it was not so much a boxing match as a carpet-crawling contest. I know, for I was there and saw it. Had 'Tug' stood up to JL fair and square, he would have been knocked out in no time'.

When under pressure, Wilson went to the canvas – 27 times in all – with Sullivan often falling on top of him. John L. was not above punching Tug when he was in the act of rising from a 'knockdown', nor the referee from ignoring such fouls. Heavy blows were exchanged in the early rounds until poor conditioning and exhaustion over took the pair. Wilson's corner stool disappeared early in the contest leaving him to stand between rounds, which he cheerfully accepted as part of the game. After four rounds Wilson was declared the winner, received $8,000 and cheekily claimed the heavyweight championship. A rather chastened Sullivan, nursing his wounded pride, put it down to experience - mostly Wilson's.

Far from being at the Sullivan v Wilson contest, Jem Mace was half the world away in New Zealand. He had first passed through the land of the Kiwi in 1877 on passage from San Francisco to Sydney, Australia. During a four-year stay in Australia Mace is credited with establishing the Queensberry code on the island continent. His willing accomplice was Larry Foley, a prizefighter with intelligence and business acumen far beyond that normally expected in a fighter of the day. A fine, courageous boxer, Foley quickly

assimilated the lessons which Jem taught and through his skills as a trainer developed the 'Australian style' of boxing which was exemplified by Peter Jackson, Mick Dooley and Jim Hall. The more individual styles of Bob Fitzsimmons, Frank Slavin, Billy McCarthy, Young Griffo and 'Torpedo' Billy Murphy, though not from the classic Foley/Mace mould, gained greatly by association with Foley.

By 1882 Mace was becoming bored with the settled domestic life that he was living as a hotelier in Melbourne and decided on an expedition to New Zealand. Jem put together a touring theatrical-sporting combination of singers, musicians, boxers and wrestlers headed by Professor William Miller, a world-class wrestler who was also an outstanding boxer. Having toured the North Island the combination crossed over to Christchurch, then to Temuka and then to Timaru, where they appeared at the Theatre Royal for two performances on 13 and 14 June. Three amateur boxing matches took place, with lightweight Bob Fitzsimmons winning them all.

The top attraction proved to be a local South Canterbury champion wrestler, Herbert Slade, who tackled Miller, losing by the only fall. Slade, a local butcher born of an Irish father and a Maori mother in 1855, had already won a £100 wrestling challenge match and excelled as a runner. Sturdily built, at six feet tall and 14 stones in weight, Herbert impressed Mace who took him along for the remainder of the tour. Mace introduced his discovery to the noble art and began to spar with him on the public shows. Before returning to Timaru for shows on 13 and 14 September, the young Fitzsimmons again winning the boxing competition, Jem had got the news from New York of Tug Wilson's win over Sullivan. Well acquainted with Richard Fox and his search for a challenger for Sullivan, Mace placed Slade under contract and declared his intention of taking him to the US. They arrived in San Francisco on Christmas Day and proceeded to box exhibitions together in California before touring the east coast then crossing over to Liverpool for an English tour. Mace puffed his 'champion' to all who would listen, sparred lightly with Herbert, allowing himself to be outpointed, and never told that Slade's only serious encounter with one George Robinson in San Francisco had ended with the bout being stopped to avoid Herbert's defeat.

Sullivan fought a serious challenger in Charlie Mitchell, of Birmingham, at the Garden on 14 May 1883. Mitchell was contracted to last four rounds as had Wilson. He was a very skilled and knowledgeable prize-fighter and could have matched Wilson's performance with ease but that was not Charlie's style. Though three inches shorter and almost 50lb lighter, Mitchell was confident and fearless and wanted to fight Sullivan punch for punch and win on merit.

At the first bell, Mitchell advanced and landed a good solid blow on Sullivan's face. The champion retaliated with a punch to the head that turned Charlie completely over. Quickly on his feet, after a clinch the Englishman backed off before stepping forward and landing a fast blow to John's head that knocked him over backwards. Jumping up without a count Sullivan bulled Mitchell into the ropes where Charlie wrestled with the champion until the bell sounded. Mitchell landed only one solid punch, to the ribs, in the second round. Overwhelmed by Sullivan, Charlie was knocked out of the ring and was seen to be limping when he returned. The third was a nightmare for the Birmingham man, four times he was floored but each time he sprung up and engaged Sullivan. The fifth knockdown saw Charlie dazed on rising and seemingly beaten. Police Captain 'Clubber' Williams stepped between the two men and asked Mitchell if he was satisfied. Charlie indicated that he was and Sullivan was declared the winner.

Sullivan's fights against Wilson and Mitchell showed a fast, strong, big-punching heavyweight being out-foxed by one aging English middleweight and floored by a younger one. The New York crowds were with Sullivan all the way but, exciting as he was, his form left a lot to be desired. Against a real heavyweight who could give and take a punch he might be in trouble. Jem Mace was trying to convince the American public that Herbert Slade was that heavyweight. "He was a magnificent athlete, and a quick and skilful boxer. His weight in fighting trim was 236 pounds, and he stood six feet one and three-quarter inches in height" Mace recalled.

The Maori looked an impressive figure when entering to ring at the Garden on 7 August 1883 to face Sullivan. When stripped for action it was noted that neither man was trained to a nicety, though John L. was the more streamlined when compared to the fleshy Herbert. Both men appeared calm and controlled waiting for the start.

Sullivan commenced in his usual rushing manner driving Slade to the ropes, but Herbert extricated himself and the pair exchanged blows before clinching. The referee, Barney Aaron, broke them and on parting Sullivan was seen to be bleeding from the mouth. "First blood for Slade!" cried ringsider Harry Hill. An angry Sullivan leapt on Slade and knocked him over backwards to the floor from which Herbert rose just before the ten. Backed against the ropes, a hard right knocked Herbert out of the ring. He quickly got back but the bell sounded before they could get to grips.

The second round was more even. Sullivan rained blows at his adversary who countered strongly and got himself off the ropes. In clinches they exchanged head and body punches until Slade was again floored. Quickly back on his feet and with John L. breathing heavily from his exertions, Herbert seemed to be at an advantage as he easily avoided the champion's ponderous blows. "Now's your time Slade! Go in and punish him!" shouted Hill, but Herbert was wary and missed his only chance. Sullivan rallied and drove Herbert to the ropes but he survived to the bell.

The third round opened with an exchange of heavy blows and ended with a heavy Sullivan right to Herbert's face that turned him around. Slade was powerless to withstand the champion's onslaught, which ended with another right-hander that sent him to the floor, hanging half out of the ring, and provoked his corner to sky the sponge.

Sullivan, as always, was full of praise for his defeated opponent, saying: "as good a man as Mitchell and better than Tug Wilson. I thought that I was going to meet a man stronger than myself, but then it is no disgrace to be whipped, for he is a plucky fellow. He showed his spirit in coming back on the stage, after I knocked him off. Some men would not have come back".

To describe Edward Charles Pablo as a colourful character would be a gross understatement. He was the grandson of John Darby, a former African slave. His father William, born at Norwich in 1796, was apprenticed to a circus at an early age as an acrobat and rope-walker before becoming an outstanding equine trainer. He established his own circus under the name of Pablo Fanque, becoming Britain's first black circus proprietor. He was a formidable character. Deeply religious, he attracted the support of the local clergy and police forces and the animosity of publicans. So popular was his circus that consumption of alcohol fell and public order improved when he was in town.

Darby legally changed his surname to Pablo and after the death of his first wife in a circus accident in 1848 he married Elizabeth Corker. Ted Pablo was his second son with Elizabeth, being born in Manchester on 20 October 1855. He trained in the circus under his father, becoming an accomplished equine clown, acrobat, rider, vaulter and juggler.

Always on the lookout for fresh attractions, Fanque presented Jem Mace in his circus ring, sparring Wolf, also known as Mace's Black, and displaying his belts and trophies. Mace toured the northern counties for six weeks, receiving £70 a week. Ted remembered meeting Mace in early 1861 and the champion taking a shine to him, awarding him three-penny pieces for bopping him on the nose or beating him in foot races. Mace was in training to face Sam Hurst for the English championship and, Ted claimed, insisted that he and his father witness the encounter. This they did travelling by train to Sittingbourne, then by carriage and ferry to the site on

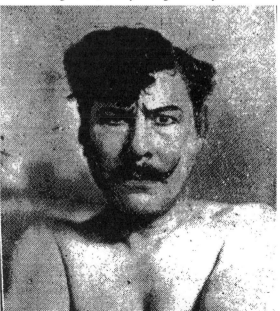

Charles Edward Pablo

the marshes where Ted sat close to the ring and watched his hero become champion.

After the death of his father in 1871, Ted travelled with many of the leading circuses around the country. He visited Egypt during 1876, appearing for six weeks at Cairo, was said to have toured New Zealand with Mace in 1882, though evidence has yet to be presented, and the Belgium Congo in 1885 where he was awarded the Order of King Leopold for his part in the rescue of a white family from a dangerous situation.

By 1886, Ted was in Australia where he had family connections. No doubt through those connections he gained the acquaintance of Larry Foley and made regular appearances at Foley's Athletic Hall in Sydney as a boxer. Billed as Pablo Fanques he was often reported as Pablo Frank or Fank. What previous experience he had is not clear, though some instruction by Mace is not out of the question – but he was very fit and impressively built and as the year progressed his improvement was noted in the sports pages. Fanques' first two bouts were probably against the young Bob Fitzsimmons, himself a newcomer on the Sydney scene. Bob claimed to have won the first on a second- round knockout and the second was probably a four-round no-decision bout at Foley's Hall both in February.

Foley's Hall was in fact the rear yard of his pub, the White Horse Hotel, which had been roofed over with corrugated iron sheeting to provide seating for two thousand spectators and was known in boxing circles as the Iron Pot. Larry Foley was the greatest fighter that Australia had produced to date and though then in his late 30s he was still a match for any but the very top class. He had a gym in the cellar beneath the pub where his stable of fighters and visiting boxers trained. Regular twice weekly promotions were staged, which ensured a steady stream of customers passing through the bars of the hotel.

Foley's promotions followed the same pattern week by week. Top of the bill was usually a fight to the finish, or a quality fighter undertaking to knock out a lesser fighter within six or eight rounds, for a small purse put up by Larry, or a larger purse put up by a local sport. The remainder of the bill was made up of four round no-decision bouts or exhibitions between semi-professionals or amateurs with the occasional demonstration of wrestling or gymnastics. Though Foley trained and managed some of the greatest Australasian fighters of the time, he did not invest his money to progress their careers but occupied the role of a kind of 'enabler', happy to let out the Iron Pot for matches financed by his boys' backers or to allow them to stage their own benefits.

Pablo, just under five feet eight tall and probably fighting as a middleweight, was matched with Jim Fogerty over four rounds at Foley's on 6 March, gaining an enthusiastic write-up in the *Sydney Bulletin*. The paper reported that "an impromptu meeting between Pablo Frank and Fogerty fully made up for [a] deficiency in the programme. Both powerful, well-built men they made a splendid set-to. For though either of them with a cleverer man, would, perhaps, have been a 'chopping block', they were so evenly matched that the contest proved of more than passing interest. For four rounds they fought so equally that no decision could be given. Then a fifth, and

sixth, and it was not until a seventh round had been completed that Foley told them to shake hands as it was impossible to decide between them'.

Having sparred four fast rounds with 'a friend' at Foley's on 20 March, Ted took on Jim Nolan. Nolan and Frank, two old antagonists, sparred a couple of lively rounds and, the latter, by way of showing his satisfaction with the sport, threw a few active somersaults round the ring. This innovation may be the dawning of a new era in boxing, the precursor of a general game of ground and lofty sparring, with the free use of the trapeze as a get-away from fast fighting.

Pablo won a four-round match with Paddy Gorman before facing Fogarty again, fighting a pretty battle, and surprising his bulky opponent into an activity of which he was not usually guilty. The Maori had the best of it all the way. Obviously the most acceptable explanation of Pablo's dusky complexion was to cast him as a native Kiwi.

On 17 April Ted was matched with Larry Foley himself over three rounds. The *Bulletin* reported the affair thus: "Larry Foley then had a bit of fun with Pablo Franks. Though anything but a star in the boxing firmament, a sight of Pablo always 'takes a trick' when he exhibits his magnificent form in gladiatorial costume. He is certainly a splendid specimen of a muscular man, not artificial stuff piled on with heavy-weight lifting and gymnastic exercises, but natural bone and muscle".

The following Saturday, Pablo headed the bill against Larry's pride and joy, Mick Dooley, for a £25 purse. Dooley at this time was at his magnificent best, being a skinny, six foot, hard-punching, fast-boxing middleweight. Mick Dooley and Pablo Fanques wound up the programme with a real good set-to, in which Dooley had the better of his acrobatic opponent.'

On 15 May slick Londoner Jack Hall was scheduled to meet Jim Fogerty but failed to show. Pablo was elevated to top of the bill against an American visitor in a fight to the finish at catchweights that only made sense as a betting opportunity. It was reported that the choicest morsel of the evening came in the shape of a Queensberry contest, as arranged for endurance between Pablo Frank and a San Franciscan recently arrived from the Pacific Coast (Dowling?). Pablo had a big lump the better of the American in avoirdupois and the American played into the big'un's hands by rushing like a bull at his opponent, who either met him with a smashing left hander or a knockdown cross counter. The visitor was as plucky as they make 'em for Foley had to hard work to persuade him he had had enough. Whatever faults might be found with Larry Foley he could never be found wanting in mercy. Some old fighters were slow to stop bouts, but Larry never allowed men on his shows to take a beating.

Pablo's reward was to top the bill on 22 May when Professor Peter Jackson undertook to knock him out in four rounds or forfeit £25 and the verdict. Jackson was at the beginning of his illustrious career. Six feet one and a half inches tall and 190lb in weight, he had failed in an attempt to win the Australian heavyweight championship but this was all part of the learning process. Along with Dooley, Peter was the epitome of the straight punching Australian style developed by Foley and Jem Mace. The title 'Professor' was bestowed on the leading teachers of boxing, gymnastics and similar activities in the late Victorian period.

The *Sydney Evening News* reported: "Professor Jackson then set to work with Pablo Fanques. Jackson had a great advantage in the way of height, but Pablo is a very powerfully built man. The Professor at once went for his man, but Pablo got out of his way in the best manner he could, which mainly consisted in falling down. This exasperated the Professor to such an extent that he lost his temper. The third round was a merry one, but in the fourth Pablo acted all on the defensive, and not being knocked out the verdict was given in his favour". The *Sydney Bulletin* commented: "To the surprise of most present Pablo made a first-rate show and turned up the winner. Pablo is a very dodgy sort of boxer, and accordingly very hard to knockout in a given time". This was a remarkable performance by Pablo. Using the same tactics as Tug Wilson he succeeded in frustrating Jackson in the early rounds, making his opponent lose his temper allowing him to adopt a more positive attitude in the later rounds. *The Sydney Evening News* noted that he had plenty of fight left in him at the end.

The following Saturday, Pablo was again matched with Foley, who agreed to knock Pablo out in four rounds for a trophy given by one of the leading sporting gentlemen. The bout was a terrible anti-climax as reported by the *Evening News*. "With Pablo Fanque, having been matched to box Tom Taylor, it was not considered good policy to allow him to face the champion Lawrence Foley in the match made that the latter could not knock him out inside four rounds. They both, however, appeared in a friendly spar, in which some heavy hitting was done. In the second round, though, Pablo accidentally butted Foley, breaking the skin on his forehead. This brought the bout to an end". This rather strange encounter was reported in the *Telegraph* as such: "Lawrence Foley and Pablo Fanque came next in what was announced as a friendly engagement, but the opening round brought with it anything but light exchanges. In the second one, and when the pair were at close quarters, an accidental butt by Pablo Fanque split the champion's forehead just above the right eye, and the set-to was ended". The *Bulletin* had a different view. "Foley was on the card for a four-round knockout with Pablo Frank, but for some reason or other Pablo could not exactly see it in the same light, and a friendly set-to took the place of the knockout. However, it was doomed, blood was to flow as Pablo accidentally butted Foley on the forehead and drew blood when the curtain was rung down". We are used to varying reports from ringsiders on the same bout. These reports agreed as to who were fighting and that Foley was stopped with a cut forehead; where they disagree is how they were to fight. A friendly spar is one thing and one man attempting to knock out his opponent is quite another.

In Sydney at this time there were three fighters who were solid press favourites who, could in essence, do no wrong. They were Peter Jackson, Larry Foley and George Seale. Though records vary, Foley engaged in around 60 bouts, including exhibitions. In the only bout that he ever seriously faced defeat, the ring was broken into by the crowd and the fight stopped. In later negotiations Foley agreed that his opponent, Professor William Miller, should receive

the whole of the purse monies on condition that the bout be declared a draw, thus preserving his unbeaten record. My suspicion is that against Pablo Fanques, Foley's unbeaten record was again preserved aided and abetted by an adoring press. Pablo's proposed bout against Tom Taylor went unrecorded.

On 5 June Pablo faced Jim Fogerty over six rounds for £25 aside. They had clashed twice previously and were pretty well evenly matched. The *Bulletin* reported the bout at length. 'The six-round bout between Pablo Frank and Fogerty on Saturday night was looked upon as the best morsel at Foley's show, but it resulted in a very tame affair of the one afraid and the other not game order. Fogerty was livelier than usual, took a lead from the start, and in the third round Pablo came down all of a heap, and was up only in time to save the fight being given to Fogerty. The men sparred very cautiously till the termination of the sixth round when the referee declared a draw, but had we been in the unthankful post, we should not have hesitated in at once declaring Fogerty the winner. Whatever fighting was done Fogerty did it. We did not see the terrible blow struck which laid Pablo out for more than his ten seconds and we thought at the time he was 'playing possum'... Fogerty should have been awarded the battle".

George Seale was an amateur, a middleweight, a southpaw and a draftsman by trade. His manner of employment was then a very important consideration in amateur boxing. Seale was a 'clerical amateur'. Bricklayers, blacksmiths and such like were 'manual labour amateurs'. It was considered in Australia in the 1880s that manual labourers had an unfair advantage over a desk worker such as Seale and a few hours training could not instil the same toughness and resilience in him as a man who had spent years as a manual labourer. Bob Fitzsimmons claimed that he was an amateur until he went to America, and so were most of the local boxers who fought at the Iron Pot. Boxing was a very popular spectator sport in Sydney at this period not least due to Larry Foley, who ruled his promotions with an iron hand, thus ensuring that his patrons were safe from harassment. There was however little money in the sport and to gain a reputation as a boxer, even if you were a manual labourer, was to risk becoming unemployable. Jackson, Dooley and Billy McCarthy, who acted as professors at Foley's Hall, and such as 'Torpedo' Billy Murphy, Frank Slavin or Tom Lees, who were busy top-liners, were probably among the few who could afford to be full time pros. Forming 'combinations', taking on all-comers in the gold or opal mining areas, often in partnership with touring foreign pros such as Jack Burke, 'The Irish Lad', was a popular and profitable enterprise.

George Seale's main 'amateur' rival was butcher Dick Sandal of New Zealand. Few of his 'amateur' opponents were named, they being usually billed as the 'amateur champion of wherever'. Seale did not need protection from anyone in the ring, fighting his labouring rivals for trophies, prizes and often money purses and winning. He faced top professionals in Jackson, Dooley, Hall, Buffalo Costello, Jack Burke and Foley and was rarely bested. Retaining his job and amateur status by his personal demeanour and sporting connections, Seale was often billed unnamed or as 'the amateur champion' or the 'amateur champion of the colonies'. He rowed, played cricket and Australian rules football, all as an amateur. With Larry Foley acting as his trainer and manager and a steady stream of Sydney sportsmen willing to back him, Seale probably made as good a living from the ring as all but the top professionals.

Pablo was matched against Seale on 12 June at Foley's. The amateur champion undertook to knock out Fanque in six rounds or forfeit the verdict. All three local newspaper carried reports which, as often happens, were at some variance. The *Evening News'* reporter failed to see any knockdowns so can perhaps be ignored, while the *Telegraph* reported: "The champion amateur and Pablo Fanque then mounted the stage, the former to try his hand at knocking his opponent out in six rounds; but the task was too heavy, and he, like Professor Jackson, failed in his attempt. Pablo fought awkwardly, varying his style occasional, and though he was the recipient of many 'hard knocks', his opponent's left frequently visiting his head very heavily, he went smiling to work and several times got home. The champion amateur, however, had a good deal the best of the encounter, and when he floored Pablo in the third round with a stinging left-hander the latter's supporters lost a share of their confidence. But he was soon on his feet again and, acting on the defensive, was enabled with his extra weight to hold out for the stipulated number of rounds". The *Bulletin* had a little more to say about the sixth round: "Pablo hit him a couple of hard knocks, one in the sixth round taking him off his feet. So Pablo, much the less experienced man though bigger, scored a third victory over top-ranked opposition.

Seven days later Pablo was matched against Jim Hall, then an 18-year-old at the very start of his career. Hall was tall, smart and tricky, and gained the referee's decision after six rounds.

George Seale, no doubt smarting at his 'defeat' at the hands of an acrobat, occupied the opposite corner when Pablo next entered the ring at Foley's Hall on 26 June. The terms were as before – last six rounds and take the verdict. The newspapers hailed the contest, predicting, along with the betting fraternity, that Pablo would last. The only report was short and to the point: "All eagerly watched the six rounds between the amateur champion and Pablo Fanque, in which the amateur showed to great advantage; completely smothering his burly opponent upon many occasions.' Pablo was not stopped so gained the victory.

Between 6 March and 31 July 1886, Ted Pablo appeared on no less than 21 occasions at Foley's Hall. Of those contests in which a decision was rendered he gained six victories, was defeated twice and fought two draws. His four wins against Peter Jackson, Larry Foley and George Seal do not appear as such on their records though the evidence is clearly reported in the newspapers of the time. Pablo was undoubtedly a popular performer at Foley's. His circus background was well known, he appeared in costume as a gladiator, did acrobatics – shades of Prince Naseem – flexed his muscles and generally put on a performance.

Pablo again appeared at Foleys on 2 April 1887 when he faced Frank Slavin in a four-rounds no-decision affair, giving the 'Sydney Cornstalk' a run for his money. His last recorded bout in Australia was a five-round knockout defeat at the fists of Jim Hall on 14 December 1889. Hall was reaching his peak

and when fighting on the level few could match him at that time. The abrupt end to Ted's ring appearances on 31 July 1886 suggests that he may have come under contract with a circus or theatrical company and gone on tour. He is known to have been active in Ireland during 1888, so the encounter with Hall, if it was indeed Ted who was beaten, must have been during a return visit down under.

Pablo is known to have appeared in the ring billed as 'The Terrible Turk', however there were a number of fighters using that nom de guerre in Europe and America at various times, most usually wrestlers. It is likely that Pablo confined his boxing exploits in the UK to the boxing booths, which then accompanied most fun fairs and circuses. He toured Ireland in 1888 in company with booth owner Billy Congo. Whether Ted was employed in the circus or the booth is not known. Ted was a tough, talented and resourceful man, steeped in the traditions of the more robust end of show business where one was expected to turn his hands to whatever work required doing. One would imagine that taking a turn in the boxing booth was a task that he found much to his liking.

Partnered by his wife, Ted was active in the music halls with a patter and juggling act and as a circus performer in England in the 1890s. Returning to Africa again in 1899, he visited what is now Namibia and Kimberly in South Africa.

Remarkably well preserved for his age at 59, Pablo was determined to enlist in the army at the beginning of World War One. He joined a battalion of 'decrepit old men' organized in 1915 who were rejected by the War Office despite the support of a thousand doctors who declared their fitness to campaign. By deducting 13 years from his age he gained enlistment into the Army Service Corps and served in France until being discharged as unfit for service after suffering fractured ribs, concussion, a damaged spine, crushed chest, and an internal rupture in 1916. After a long convalescence he gained employment as stage-door keeper at the Finsbury Park Empire until his retirement 1928. Pablo maintained his interest in the circus, was an enthusiastic contributer of letters to the circus and funfair 'trade' magazine *World's Fair* and attended circus reunions, eventually dying in 1936, aged 81, at the Entertainment Artistes' Home, Brinsworth House, Twickenham.

Dai Dower: The Wizard From Abercynon

by Wynford Jones

Dai Dower was born on 20 June 1933 and was brought up in the family home at Herbert Street, Abercynon, a small mining community north of Pontypridd in the heart of the South Wales valleys.

As a youngster he contracted diphtheria and missed about two years of his schooling. He actually suffered two bouts of the illness and spent time in isolation, as was customary at the time, and could only be seen through the window by visiting relatives at Mountain Ash Hospital. Attending school at Carnetown and later, Abercynon, when the time came to leave he worked for a time at a factory in Treforest, but like so many young men in these communities he then entered the mining industry, working on the surface at Abercynon Colliery. Here he enjoyed the comradeship that is so characteristic of mining but boxing as well, and the latter was already an important part of his life.

Boxing out of Roath Youth Amateur Boxing Club he was eventually chosen to represent Wales, thought Dai felt this particular honour should have come sooner than it did. He lost in the final of the Welsh ABA championships in 1951 to Richie Jenkins, but in 1952 he captured both the Welsh and ABA flyweight championships and represented Britain at the Olympic Games in Helsinki. His team-mates at the Olympics included Peter Waterman, Henry Cooper and Terry Gooding of Cardiff, who boxed in the middleweight division where future world champion Floyd Patterson took

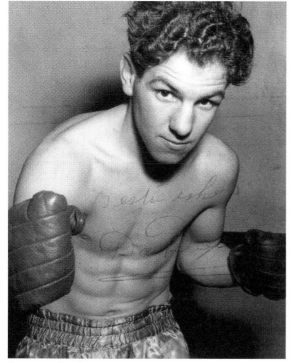

Dai poses for the camera

the gold medal.

The stage was now set for a successful professional career and he made his eagerly awaited debut on a Sid Evans promotion at Sophia Gardens, Cardiff on 16 February 1953. On a bill topped by Roy Agland and Wally Beckett, Dai faced Vernon John of Neath. He weighed in at 113lbs with John one pound heavier and the contest was scheduled for six rounds. Dower had his opponent reeling for much of the fourth round and even though he was unable to find a finishing blow, John wisely retired at the end of the session.

Five weeks later Dai was back in action, this time at the Empress Hall, Earls Court, where his opponent was Ron Hughes of Romford. This was an impressive first showing in London. Hughes was floored for a count of seven from a terrific right to the jaw, perfectly timed by Dower as Hughes moved in to attack. He took several more hard punches and looked badly shaken as he returned to his corner at the end of the second round. He was followed by referee Harry Paulding, who, on closer observation, stopped the contest. Dai moved beautifully in this contest and hit with precision. His left leads were superb and he showed the ability to draw his opponent on to his punches.

On 20 April, Dai beat Colin Clitheroe on points over six rounds at the Colston Hall, Bristol and a week later he faced Peter Halberg at Sophia Gardens on a bill which marked the comeback of Eddie Thomas. Eddie, who had been out of action for 18 months, returned to beat George Roe, the Midlands Area middleweight champion, on points. Dai once more showed good movement and also showed the ability to slip punches in stopping the man from Grimsby.

In his next contest, on 18 May, Dai knocked out Alf Smith in the first round at the Empress Hall and on 1 June he was back in action at the Drill Hall, Newport. Once again, Eddie Thomas topped the bill with an overwhelming points win over Kit Pompey, but the fight of the night was that between Dai and Dublin's Micky Roche. There was toe to toe action throughout all six rounds with Dai`s ringcraft eventually carrying the day. Less than three weeks later Dai faced Roche in a return at Sophia Gardens on a bill staged by promoter Stan Cottle to mark the Queen`s coronation. This turned out to be one of the best shows staged in Wales for many years, with Richie Jenkins, Phil Edwards and Dai Dower all keeping their unbeaten records, Dai taking a points decision from referee Ike Powell.

He was back in action at Sophia Gardens on 27 July to inflict a first stoppage defeat on Colin Clitheroe, who was floored briefly in the first round. He went down again in the second and took three counts in the third round and had little to offer, having to defend desperately in the fifth round when the referee decided he had seen enough. Once again, Eddie Thomas topped the bill and celebrated his 27th birthday by stopping Roy Baird in the seventh.

Next up was Scottish flyweight champion, Jimmy Quinn, in what was to have been Dai`s first eight-rounder.

The Abercynon man was at his best, both in defence and attack, while his footwork and balance were virtually perfect. Improving in every contest, a crowd of about 5,000 at Coney Beach Arena, Porthcawl saw Dai stop his man in the seventh round. When the referee stepped between them, Dai was scoring freely and Quinn insisted after the fight that Dai was the fastest opponent he had ever faced. In October, he beat Henry Carpenter at Earls Court and rounded off the year with wins over Joe Cairney and Joe Murphy. In all, he had boxed 12 times in his first year as a professional and this level of activity represented the ideal apprenticeship.

Dai began 1954 with a points win over Ogli Tettey at Nottingham Ice Rink and in March he faced former world flyweight champion Terry Allen at Earls Court. Allen was knocked out in the second round, giving the Welshman a rare knockout victory. Allen, from Islington, was coming to the end of a long career that had started in September, 1942. In 1949 he drew with Rinty Monaghan in Belfast with the British, European and world flyweight titles at stake and following the Irishman`s subsequent retirement he was matched with Honore Pratesi in London in 1950 for the vacant title, which he won on points over 15 rounds. He lost the title in his first defence, but later captured the British title though by now his record was becoming patchy. In all, Allen had taken part in nine championship contests while, for Dai, this was fight number 14.

Terry Allen was a wily boxer who excelled at in-fighting and was well capable of 'spoiling, when faced with a comparatively inexperienced opponent. He was warned twice for holding in the opening seconds but Dai showed from the first bell that he was able to keep Allen on the retreat and he dictated the pattern of the fight. In the second round, Dower, moving superbly, fired in a string of rapid lefts and then stepped in with a short right-cross to the chin, thus paving the way for the finishing blow which landed a few seconds later. Allen tried to crowd Dower and as he moved in he was floored by another superb right. The Londoner dropped to his knees and was clearly in a daze as he just failed to beat the count of referee Jack Hart.

Dai was still three months short of his 21st birthday and not old enough to challenge for the British title, but he had clearly established himself as the outstanding challenger for Allen's title. Dai`s manager, Nat Seller, insisted after the contest that his man would not be rushed into a championship fight. He felt sure that Eric Marsden would challenge Allen for the title and was happy for Dai to continue gaining experience with a view to meeting the winner of this match at some stage in the future.

On 11 May, Dai clearly outpointed Holland's Hein van der Zee over ten rounds at the Empress Hall, being watched by his mother, father and sister and a crowd of about 100 mining friends who had turned out to support him. Many of them had worked an extra shift, known in the valleys as 'a doubler', in order to travel to see him and this was part of a long tradition amongst fight fans in mining communities who travelled to London to support their heroes. Dai gave another superb display and won every round with ease. Van der Zee had given the South African, Jake Tuli, considerable trouble before losing to the Empire champion on a cut in the sixth round, but he was not in the same class as Dower. The Welshman delighted the crowd with his evasive tactics and his ring generalship and van der Zee chased Dai vainly in his attempts to land his power punches.

After four more wins over continental opposition Dai was matched with the Zulu, Jake Tuli, for the Empire title at Harringay Arena. The eagerly awaited clash was set for 19 October 1954 and the promoter, Jack Solomons, was delighted that the show had sold out well before fight time. Dai`s rise through the professional ranks had been quite amazing but some critics feared that his opportunity had come too early and that he would not be able to cope with the power of the champion. Tommy Farr offered the opinion that if Dai went eight rounds he would earn his corn, but the Abercynon man had other ideas and gave Tuli a boxing lesson. Dower weighed in at 113lbs, 12 ounces, with Tuli coming in two ounces heavier. His plan was to make Tuli miss and he did this for 15 gruelling rounds as the champion tried desperately to land his wicked hooks. Dai`s left eye was cut in the sixth round, but from the ninth onwards it was all Dower, with Tuli on the defensive for much of the time. As he saw his title slipping away, Tuli put everything into landing the knockout blow but, in truth, he was outboxed and outclassed. Dai claimed at the end that Tuli was the toughest opponent he had faced and paid tribute to his manager for preparing him for 15 rounds.

At the final bell, the singing of the Welsh National Anthem echoed around the arena with the crowd sporting red and white rosettes and many wearing huge leeks. Dai then took the microphone to thank his mother, father and the fans for their support. He was presented with the Empire trophy by J. Onslow Fane and was mobbed by his fans all the way back to his dressing room. Dai claimed that apart from one punch in the second round he had not been hurt, but that large blisters under the ball of each foot were extremely painful. He was congratulated by Jimmy Wilde in his changing room, with the former world champion stating: "I said if Dai boxed him and did not fight him he would win. That is what he did, exactly". Ultimately, the boxer triumphed over the fighter and it was only in the last couple of rounds that Tuli was able to land any telling punches on Dower`s body. Tuli was warned four times for his body punches and twice for misuse of the head, but it was not a dirty fight and referee Andrew Smythe had no hesitation in raising the Welshman`s hand at the end of an epic battle.

The following morning, Dai was pictured on the front page of the Western Mail together with his mother, father and fiancé, Evelyn Trapp. Such was the level of interest in the fight, while manager Nat Seller said he would now discuss with promoter Jack Solomons the possibility of a world title fight against the Japanese Yoshio Shirai, a contest against Eric Marsden for the British title was already within Dai's sights.

The new Empire Champion secretly married Evelyn on 6 January 1955 at Pontypridd Register Office, with manager Nat Seller as his best man, and on 10 January he was back in action in Cardiff, knocking out Willibald Koch in the third round. Barely a month later he was matched with Eric Marsden for the vacant British flyweight title, with his own Empire title also at stake. Once again promoter Jack Solomons was delighted with his sell-out crowd at Harringay and it was predicted that millions would be listening to the radio broadcast. Previewing the contest in the Western Mail, Alan Wood wrote: "Not since the days of Jim Driscoll have we seen a boxer who does everything perfectly and moves so beautifully in the execution of the noble art".

Marsden, from St Helens, held all the advantages going into this contest, being six inches taller than Dai and enjoying a four-inch reach advantage. Dai led all the way, but it was his toughest contest to date. His speed, coupled with exceptional ringcraft, were crucial elements but he also showed himself to be a great fighter and had answers for every move made by Marsden. He made Eric miss early on and by the third round he had worked his opponent out. Dai scored freely with his left during the fourth round and was beating Marsden to the punch but the St Helens man rocked Dai with solid lefts during the fifth though caught flush with a left and right as the round ended. By round six, Dai`s speed was beginning to tell and he had Marsden rocking in the seventh. Marsden looked determined at the start of round eight but was soon having to defend and Dai had the crowd on their feet in the ninth when he had his man in trouble. The tenth was one of the best rounds of the fight as Dai, well ahead on points, tried to press home his advantage. The tempo slowed a little in round 11 and the 12th was a good round for Marsden. Over the last three rounds Marsden showed great courage and strength, but Dai was always able to keep him at bay with his immaculate left hand.

When the radio commentary ended crowds rushed out into the streets of Abercynon and customers at the Richards

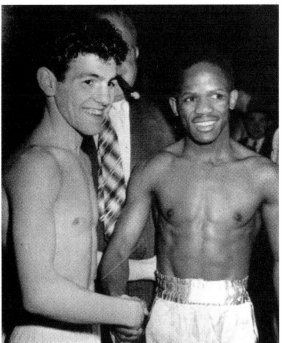

Dai (left) and Jake Tuli at the weigh-in for their British Empire title fight at Harringay Arena on 19 October 1954

Arms in Cilfynydd, where Dai trained, sang outside. It was only as the fight ended that the announcement finally came that Dai and Evelyn had been married since January. The fact that Dai trained at the pub brought about a huge increase in beer sales and it was not unusual for coaches to turn up with up to 200 people watching his training sessions. Sadly, it was decided to increase Dai`s gym rental to an unacceptable level and he left. The resulting dip in beer sales brought about the closure of the pub in a short time!

Exactly a month later, Dai faced Italy's Nazzareno Giannelli for the European title at Earls Court. Dai was comfortably down to eight stone a week before the contest and success would bring him his third title in just five months. There was an early shock when Dai slipped to the canvas in the opening round as Giannelli attacked at speed and though he jabbed well in the second, Dai, blocking and countering, soon began to score heavily with his own left. Dower landed a beautiful left hook in round three but he was made to miss by the Italian though the tables were turned in the next session. The Welshman continued to box beautifully but it was clear he could not take chances against Giannelli, who was giving him more trouble than either Tuli or Marsden. However, by round eight, Dai was dictating the pattern of the fight and the ninth saw him at his best. Giannelli looked worried as he returned to his corner at the end of the tenth and for the remainder of the contest he was on the receiving end of Dai`s left hand. There seemed to be nothing he could do to change the pattern of the contest and despite coming out strongly for the final round he was having to hold on as the bell rang.

Dai was a worthy winner and his brilliant exhibition of boxing was one for the purists. The following night he was honoured by the Boxing Writers` Club, having been voted the best young boxer of 1954, and he was presented with the Geoffrey Simpson award by Mr Alexander Elliott, vice-chairman of the British Boxing Board of Control. Tom Phillips of the Daily Herald maintained that within two years Dai had become the greatest box-office draw in the country and that he had saved boxing from one of the greatest slumps ever known.

Dai kept busy with three wins over European bantamweights of questionable quality and on 3 October he faced the tough Spanish southpaw, Young Martin, in defence of his European crown at Nottingham Ice Rink. The Spaniard was an experienced fighter who had boxed several times outside Spain and it is interesting to note that he and Dai shared several common opponents, with Martin seemingly able to deal with them rather more quickly than the Abercynon man.

From the start it was clear that Dai was having trouble with the southpaw stance of his opponent and his own lack of punching power meant that he was not able to keep Martin away. Dai was being caught by the Spaniard`s right leads which were invariably followed by vicious left hooks to the body and from the ninth onwards he was on the canvas no less than a dozen times, though on one occasion he was thrown to the boards and still received a count! The end came in the 12th round. Dai had been floored for a count of nine by a left to the stomach and another left to the body, followed by a right, put him down for the full count. Dai was upset at losing his title but realised his preparation had been less than ideal and vowed that these things would be put right when he returned to action.

On 6 December 1955 he faced Jake Tuli in a return at Harringay Arena and once again every ticket had been snapped up. It was an important contest for both men, as Tuli was also coming back after being knocked out in the 14th round of his contest with Peter Keenan for the Empire bantamweight title. Dai gave a brilliant exhibition of boxing showing that he was back to his very best. Once more he was troubled by blisters and was suffering from cramp in his right leg during the final round but all in all he outboxed and outfought Tuli, who was bewildered by Dai`s left hand and his brilliant defence.

Between January and July 1956, Dai engaged in five contests against continental opposition, winning each one on points, before being called upon to complete his National Service.

In March 1957 he received a telephone call offering him an opportunity to challenge Pascual Perez for the flyweight championship of the world. Dai immediately accepted, but shortly afterwards he stepped on the scales and found his weight to be 142lbs. This meant that he would have just three weeks to reduce to eight stone and in recent years Dai has admitted that he should have turned down the opportunity, given the difficulty of reducing so much weight in such a short space of time. It is also worth remembering that the pressure from Jack Solomons, the most powerful figure on the British fight scene at the time, would have been difficult to resist.

It took three days to reach Buenos Aires and the champion turned out to greet Dai on his arrival. This gave Dai confidence because for once, he was much the bigger man! The temperatures were up in the 80s and initially there were no sparring partners available. By fight time, the odds were 5-1 against Dai and it was revealed that he had engaged in just ten rounds of sparring in preparation for a contest against a man who had held the title since November, 1954. The fight was staged at the San Lorenzo Stadium in front of a crowd of 85,000 with Dai weighing in at 7st. 13lbs. 10oz and Perez coming in five pounds lighter at 7st. 8lbs. 7oz. At this weight, and at 4ft 11.1/2ins the Argentinian was both the lightest and the shortest champion since Jimmy Wilde.

His attempts to make weight had seriously weakened Dai and, sadly, he was knocked out in the first round. Perez had been quick to notice that Dai dropped his left hand slightly after leading and after coming in with a left hook to the body, followed by a right cross, Dai was sent to the canvas. He was still motionless as the count reached nine and it was all over as he slowly raised his head. Perez was a formidable opponent and just had too much for a man who had not boxed for eight months. At 31, he was unbeaten in 37 contests and Dai could not cope with the sheer forcefulness of the Argentinian. Dai was still groggy some ten minutes later and, significantly, manager Nat Seller stated that he would not fight again while in the Army.

In January, 1958 Dai returned to the ring as a bantamweight and took on Eric Brett, winning on points over eight rounds, but it would be another nine months before his next appearance.

Jack Solomons planned a spectacular show for his final night at Harringay Arena and he invited many former champions who had appeared on his promotions. These included Max Baer and Gus Lesnevich and Wales was represented by Jack Petersen, Tommy Farr, Johnny Williams, Joe Erskine and Phil Edwards. Topping the bill was Dave Charnley in an international ten-round contest against Carlos Ortiz, a man who went on to establish himself as one of the greats of the lightweight division. Charnley was beaten on points while Dick Richardson won a rough fight on points against America's Garvin Sawyer. Dai made what turned out to be his final ring appearance when he took on the Canadian bantamweight champion, Pat Supple. Pat had given Peter Keenan a good fight for the Empire title and was a tough opponent given Dai`s lack of activity because of his time in the Army. It was a case of pure boxer against a fighter and the verdict of referee Jack Hart in favour of the Canadian caused uproar. In truth, Dai, despite his nose being grazed in the second round, was never in serious trouble. Regardless of that, he went down twice without taking a count and the decision seemed to be a case of referee Hart favouring the power of Supple over the skill of Dower. Dai thought he had won, being supported by several ringside critics who had the Welshman winning seven rounds, and he was bitterly disappointed to say the least. The crowd erupted into a storm of booing as Jack Hart lifted the Canadian`s arm and they were still booing as J. Onslow Fane introduced the parade of champions on this historic night.

By now, Dai had taken up a post as a PE teacher at Ringwood Grammar School in Bournemouth and had promised the head teacher that this would be his last fight. Dai still recalls the anger of Jack Solomons at this defeat, but with ringside opinion so strongly in Dai`s favour he could hardly be blamed for the result. However, had Dai emerged as the winner the promise to his head teacher may have been more difficult to keep. After retiring from the ring his teaching career went from strength to strength. He stayed at Ringwood for 18 years and the school enjoyed great success in swimming, athletics and rugby before he moved on to Bournemouth College of Education, which was eventually granted University status. In all, he was there for 21 years, with 19 of them as head of sport, and there were great celebrations in 1998 when he was awarded the MBE for services to education. Held in high regard by his colleagues and his students, Dai has fond memories of his retirement do when Sir Henry Cooper was one of the principal guests.

Dai has always enjoyed the love and support of his family and still looks remarkably fit, no doubt helped by regular visits to the golf course, and he continues to be involved in boxing. As President of the Bournemouth Ex-Boxers` Association he attends functions around the country and it is fair to say that even with the passage of time the popularity of this most unassuming of men remains undiminished. In the ring, his speed of hand and foot, coupled with superb balance, bordered on magic and these qualities will live long in the memory of all those who saw him box.

Home and Away with British Boxers, 2008-2009

by John Jarrett

JULY

Having won a Lonsdale Belt outright as British welterweight champion in 2004, David Barnes carved a second notch on another belt when retaining his British light-welterweight title against former champion Barry Morrison at Everton Park Sports Centre in Liverpool. The Manchester southpaw was always one punch ahead of his Motherwell rival to come out with a unanimous decision. The Scot roused his supporters in the early rounds as he took the fight to the champion and after four rounds Barnes was bleeding from a facial cut. But David began to draw away at the half way mark and his class told in the homestretch. "Morrison is good, but I knew I could beat him," David told the press afterwards, adding: "I need a challenge and am looking for a European title". Still only 27, Barnes took his pro log to 24-1-1 as Morrison slipped to 16-3.

Brixton's former European light-welterweight champion, Ted Bami, swinging back into action since losing to Barnes in their bout for the vacant British title in March, had too much stuff for the Walsall southpaw, Stuart Elwell, and a heavy body attack brought a seventh-round stoppage, Elwell being rescued after taking a count. At 30, Bami could still do something, his record is now 24-3.

After mixing with the big boys and suffering his first defeat, to Martin Rogan in the Prizefighter heavyweight final, Sunderland's David Dolan dropped into the cruiserweight division and celebrated with a cracking fourth-round knockout of Brazil's Elvecio Sobral, taking his pro record to 10-1.

Making his second challenge for the British heavyweight title at Dagenham's Goresbrook Leisure Centre, you had to figure big John McDermott would do better than his initial foray into the champion's domain. That one lasted only 79 seconds as champion Matt Skelton had McDermott down three times and on his way to an early shower. The memory stayed with the big fellow a lot longer, 13 months in fact, before he ventured back into the ring. Six wins later he was in with three-time champion Danny Williams and he was ready, with good victories over former champ Scott Gammer and Pele Reid. He almost made it too, as Williams survived a punishing fifth round and needed a majority decision to hang on to his laurels. Danny also risked disqualification as he was three times docked a point for various rule infractions.

County Durham's English light-welterweight champion, Nigel Wright, needed the luck of the Irish if he was going to dent the unbeaten 17-fight run of Derry's Paul McCloskey in an all-southpaw clash at the University Sports Arena in Limerick. But Nigel came away empty-handed as McCloskey took a rather generous 97-93 decision from Referee David Irving. "I thought I did enough to win", said the rueful loser. "Perhaps a draw might have been a fairer result".

Salford southpaw Jamie Moore fared better on his trip to Dublin where he picked up the Irish light-middleweight title when champion, Ciaran Healy, surrendered in the third round after sampling Moore's vicious body shots. Jamie, a former British and Commonwealth champion, qualified for the Irish trinket as his mother was from Tullarone, County Kilkenny, but there were better things in the offing with a possible clash with John Duddy for a world title, the Derryman being lined up for either IBF or WBA honours in the near future. Moore also had a European championship fight on his dance card, so he was not going hungry! On the Dublin bill, local Paul Hyland scored a runaway points victory over Barking's Marc Callaghan to win the vacant Irish super-bantamweight title and complete a Hyland family hat-trick, brothers Patrick (featherweight) and Edward (super-feather) having already become champions.

Manchester's John Murray had not lost a fight going in 24-0 and there was no way he was going to lose this one. Fighting pal and former sparring partner, Lee Meager, for the vacant British lightweight championship, recently held by Lee, in an atmospheric Robin Park Arena in Wigan, Murray was unstoppable as he hammered the Salford man to a punishing fifth-round stoppage to claim the title. Meager, now 21-3-2, was cut on both eyes in round three and by the fifth had nothing left. But he and John were still pals after the fight!

Cwmbran's Jamie Arthur won a Commonwealth Games gold medal before turning pro and racking up nine straight wins. Then he was stopped twice inside the distance, and he stopped fighting…for three years. Now he was back and at the Newport Centre he crushed defending Welsh super-featherweight champion, Dai Davies, inside two rounds. Still only 28, good things could happen for Jamie.

Liverpool featherweight Derry Matthews had it all; unbeaten in 20 contests, WBU champion at the weight and successful defences against John Simpson and Matthew Marsh. Then Choi Tseveenpurev happened. The Mongol marauder took Derry's title with a brutal fifth-round knockout. Now, three months later, Derry was back and beating undefeated Kenya's John Gicheru over eight rounds in Liverpool.

The globetrotters had mixed fortunes this month, as ever. London light-welterweight Ashley Theophane set his stall up in New York City and was ready when a call came in from upstate Rochester, former WBO world champ DeMarcus 'Chop Chop' Corley no less! Corley still had some of the nice moves that gave him 31 wins in a 40-fight pro career, but Ashley was full of juice and outpunched the ex-champ over eight rounds to cop the unanimous decision. Over in Ankara, veteran heavyweights Herbie Hide and Henry Akinwande put the gloves on again. Former champion Hide, now at cruiserweight, defended his WBC International title against Switzerland's Nuri Seferi and had to come off the deck in the first round before taking his log to 43-4. Former WBO champion Akinwande was rusty after a year out and blew the six-rounds decision to Ondrezj Pala, a Czech with a big punch but not much more. It was not much of a fight and when the lights failed in the last round most of the customers wished it had happened in the first round! At Campeone D'Italia, Liverpool super-middleweight, Tony Dodson, got back in the ring after almost a year out with medical problems. The Scouser was fit enough to take every one of the six rounds over the Frenchman, Mounir Sahli, and go off and celebrate his 28th birthday the next day. Former undefeated British, English, and Central Area super-middleweight champion and former WBF Inter-Continental title-holder, Dodson took his record to 23-1-4. Battles still to be won! This is a nice month to go to Spain; sunshine, sand and sangria. But Dewsbury light-middleweight, Steve Conway, did not head for the beach. He went to Leon in the north and he was not wearing his swimming trunks, he was wearing his boxing trunks and he was having it out with a fellow whose name he could not even pronounce. Gennady Martirosyan was an Armenian with a not very nice disposition. He knocked the canny Yorkshireman down in the third round and twice more in the seventh and at the final bell when the referee looked at the judges they all pointed to Gennady whatshisname! Next time Steve head for Benidorm.

AUGUST

Talk about anti-climax! The stage was all set for the 100th and final professional fight of Ojay Abrahams at his local venue, Watford Town Hall, now grandly transformed into the Colosseum, the perfect arena for this gloved gladiator. The place was packed and the crowd was ready to turn thumbs down for the intended sacrifice, Jamie Ambler, brought in from Wales for the event. Ring the bell! Well, the stellar attraction of the evening lasted just two minutes. Just over two minutes actually. The Welshman threw a punch as the bell sounded ending round one. Ojay, somewhat incensed at this cavalier treatment, replied with a left hook and referee Bob Williams waved his arms to signal the end of the fight and a career. Abrahams was disqualified, much to his disgust, and that of his trainer, Billy Graham, also making his swansong, and the 1,000 fans packing the hall. More than a journeyman despite losing 76 of his 100 fights spread over 17 years, the 43-year-old Abrahams deserved a fitting finale and this was not it, but he had no one to blame but himself. His final punch was thrown in anger, and out of time. This was truly a night to remember, but for all the wrong reasons.

Barnet's Commonwealth middleweight champion, Darren Barker, looking to broaden his horizons, landed in Alberta for a non-title fight with Canadian veteran, Larry 'Razor' Sharpe, at River Cree. Darren's unbeaten run of 17 fights did not look in danger as Sharpe's previous crack at a Commonwealth champion had ended in a stoppage defeat by Scott Dann in Plymouth a couple of years previously. Well, Darren won his fight all right, but he could have done without the medical mix-up that preceded it. The examining doctor was not happy with Barker's resting heart beat and he was in the hospital until 3.30am the morning of the contest. Darren's promoter, Mick Hennessy, wanted a second

opinion, the original doctor wanted to be there, so our hero was back in hospital for a further three hours. Given the all-clear, poor Darren was roused from his few hours sleep when the fire alarm was tested. He was glad to get into the ring when he was able to run things his own way, cruising to a ten-rounds decision. What time is the flight home?

The American campaign of London-based Israeli heavyweight, Roman Greenberg, ground to a shuddering halt against the Detroit veteran, Cedric Boswell, in Atlanta, Georgia, when a superb right hand sat Roman on the ropes, an open target that Boswell did not ignore. A follow-up combination landed and the referee dived in to halt matters at 2.05 of round two. Greenberg suffered his first pro loss, now 27-1. Cedric came out with a very similar record, 28-1, but he came out a winner!

Another British big fellow to lose abroad was former British champion, Scott Gammer, going against the German-based Italian southpaw, Francesco Pianeta, for the vacant EU heavyweight title on the Valuev-Ruiz bill in Berlin. Pianeta was 16-0 going in and he did not lose this one, leading on the scorecards when the Pembroke man pulled out after eight rounds, claiming a broken right hand. Scott saw his pro log slip to 18-3-1. The music was not so nice for former WBO featherweight champion Scott Harrison. He received a two-month jail sentence for assaulting his girlfriend, and was charged with alleged drunk driving. This after a two-year period that saw him stripped of his title, lose his boxing licence, and become involved in several brushes with the law.

SEPTEMBER

Whichever way you looked at it, Amir Khan was on a hiding to nothing. Starring on the big MEN bill in Manchester, the Bolton boy wonder was facing a virtual unknown in Breidas Prescott, a Columbian lightweight who was not even a household name in his own household. Like Khan, Prescott was unbeaten, winning 17 of his 19 fights inside the distance, so the guy could punch. Promoter Frank Warren was gambling on this one because for the first time Khan was on pay-per-view television, at £14.95 a pop. "Is He Worth It?" asked the front page of *Boxing News*. The short answer was No! Everything about this fight was short. Try 54 seconds! Amir's ring walk was longer than the fight. As I said, Khan was on a hiding to nothing. He got the hiding, being smashed to the canvas twice before referee Terry O'Connor completed his count. There was even criticism of Mr O'Connor for letting Khan resume after the first knockdown, as the Bolton boy was badly shaken and a sitting duck for the Colombian's follow-up attack. For the record, Khan's WBO Inter-Continental title was on the line. Having suffered his first defeat in 19 professional fights, could Khan bounce back from this devastating defeat? History has shown the unknown conqueror usually drops out of sight again and the home favourite carries on topping the bill. Amir is only 21, still a dazzling talent, and will have to be carefully matched in the future. Frank Warren will see to that. "He has still got a lot to give", he told the press afterwards, "and I'm sure he will get back on the road and go on to achieve everything we always hoped he would".

If Amir Khan was shocked at his devastating defeat, Alex Arthur was even more so when losing his WBO super-featherweight championship to Nicky Cook on the same bill. "In my heart I feel as if I won", the Edinburgh man told the press after it was all over. Yet the three judges and the majority of ringsiders saw Cook a clear winner. Losing for only the second time in 28 contests, the Scot has nevertheless been something of an under-achiever. He was actually proclaimed world champion when Joan Guzman handed in the title due to weight problems rather than defend against Arthur. Alex himself does not make 130lbs easily which could account for his performance, prompting Mr Warren to suggest a move to lightweight. Whatever, on the night, Cook, the former British, Commonwealth and European featherweight title holder, outboxed and outpunched the Scot to become a world champion and take his record to 29-1. His only defeat came in a world title challenge to American Steve Luevano down at feather.

Defending his European super-bantamweight title against Arsen Martirosyan at Nottingham, Leicester's Rendall Munroe did enough to win but failed to impress against a limited foe. Martirosyan is an Armenian based in France with a 12-1 pro log and he stormed out in the early rounds. It was round five before the champion got into his stride and began to put things together, turning it on through rounds seven and eight and the stocky challenger was found wanting at this level. But he was still there at the final bell as Munroe moved to 16-1 and looked forward to a big fight with Irishman Bernard Dunne.

Last time in the UK, New Jersey's Freddy Curiel stopped Ross Minter in a thriller. Now Freddy was back and moving up to light-middleweight to box Anthony Small on Frank Warren's charity show in London. Small put on a virtuoso performance to stop Curiel in round ten to win the WBA International championship.

Barry Hearn's second heavyweight Prizefighter competition brought a decent crowd into the Metro Radio Arena in Newcastle to support north-east rivals David Ferguson of North Shields and Darlington's Chris Burton. Ferguson lost a split decision to Luke Simpkin while Burton punched his way into the final with victories over Dave Ingleby and Lee Swaby. In the final fight for the £25,000 prize, Burton was looking good against Sam Sexton for two rounds. But the Norwich man opened up in the last session and Burton was in trouble when Mickey Vann stopped it with 50 seconds left in the last round of the last fight.

Ryan Rhodes seems to have been around forever. He has actually been a pro since 1995, and after retaining his British light-middleweight title against Scotland's Jamie Coyle at the Hillsborough Leisure Centre in Sheffield, Ryan took his record to 40-4. After two attempts at world titles against Otis Grant and Jason Mathews, the 31-year-old local man was confident he could make it third time lucky. Derby's Scott Haywood was due to fight Nigel Wright for the County Durham southpaw's English light-welterweight title at Nottingham, but when the first bell rang, Wright was sitting in a ringside seat and on the stool opposite Haywood was Dean Hickman. Nigel, down with flu, sportingly agreed to give up the title and the unbeaten Wolverhampton man

happily stepped into the breach. He gave it a good try and took an early lead, but Haywood finished strong taking the decision and the title. Former WBU featherweight champion, Derry Matthews, was trying to get back after a devastating knockout by Choi Tseveenpurev stripped him of his crown. But when he clashed with Belfast's Martin Lindsay at Nottingham, his career prospects went into freefall. The Liverpool man had floored his opponent early on but Lindsay boxed his way back in and in the ninth threw one of those punches that have KO written all over it. Matthews was out before he hit the deck.

OCTOBER
When a fighter gets to be 36, he thinks what have I done, what have I won, have I made my mark, is it time to hang them up? Stourbridge cruiserweight Robert Norton had not done too badly, losing only four of his 35 fights in a 15-year career and winning the minor league WBU, English and British Masters titles. But he had come up empty when going for the big ones, losing in challenges for the Commonwealth title to Darren Corbett and to Mark Hobson, the latter fight also being for the British belt. Well, what goes around comes around. At the Meadowside Leisure Centre in Burton-on-Trent, southpaw Robert found himself facing Micky Steeds for the vacant British title and the Lonsdale Belt. Could be your last chance, son! Steeds, 11 years younger, had been campaigning at heavyweight, losing to Scott Gammer for the British title. Now he wanted the cruiserweight crown. So did Robert Norton and he wanted it more. And at the final bell he had it, a unanimous decision over Steeds after a so-so fight that saw Robert use his height and reach advantages to control the Londoner and almost send him through the ropes in the sixth round. Winner, and new British cruiserweight champion, Robert Norton.

Twenty-four hours later, another British 15-year veteran, Jonathan Thaxton, sent his supporters wild at The Showgrounds in hometown Norwich when he smashed a right hook against the Spanish jaw of Juan Carlos Diaz Melero in round three to win the vacant European lightweight championship. A former British champion, Thaxton had lost to then-champion Yuri Romanov for this title six months previously, but there was no way he was losing this one. The Spaniard was never in with a chance and when that big punch landed in round three it was Adios Senor!

On a night when one British fighter took a major step toward possible world title glory, another lay on an operating table in a London hospital as surgeons fought to relieve a blood clot on his brain. For little Ian Napa the world was a wonderful place as another championship dream was realised, but for Gilbert Eastman his world had become a nightmare place he did not want to be in. That night in a crowded York Hall, Napa fought out of his skin to win the European bantamweight title with a thrilling decision victory over Belgiium's Carmelo Ballone. Earlier in the evening, in an eight-round contest down the bill, Eastman was stopped by Sam Webb, the referee calling a halt in the last second of the last round. The London-based Guyanese left the ring only to collapse while dressing. Gilbert was rushed to hospital where an operation was performed and fortunately he was able to leave hospital a week later. He will fight no more. The fight game is a misnomer. It is not a game. You do not play boxing. The boxers know that their next fight could well be their last and every time one of them is taken from the ring on a stretcher we, who are seated around the ring, question our enthusiasm for this sport. But we also know that we will be back in our seats the next time these guys climb into the ring to entertain us with their skills and their bravery.

Watch Birmingham super-flyweight Don Broadhurst in action and you know why you love this sport. A clean-cut 24-year-old, his skills have seen him triumph as ABA champion, Commonwealth Games gold medallist, and now on a night at the Aston Events Centre in only his ninth professional contest, as Commonwealth champion. In 12 one-sided rounds, Don showed Ghana's Isaac Quaye what boxing was all about, with one ringside observer writing: "His speed, combination punching, evasion of counters and variety were, at times, breathtaking".

Fight number 13 was anything but unlucky for Nathan Cleverly as the young Welshman outfought Portsmouth's tough Tony Oakey to win the vacant Commonwealth light-heavyweight title at Liverpool. Accidental head clashes left both men bleeding but they were still there at the finish, with the 21-year-old winning over the 32-year-old former Southern Area, British, Commonwealth and WBU champion.

Off the scene for eight years or so, as a guest of Her Majesty, London cruiserweight Terry Dunstan came back with a predictable four-rounds decision win over durable warhorse, Paul Bonson. Dunstan was in superb condition, but with his 40th birthday just days away his fight future did not look promising.

Promoter Barry Hearn is on a roll with his Prizefighter shows. This time it was a welterweight shoot-out with Chingford southpaw, Michael Lomax, claiming the £25,000 jackpot after winning over Craig Dickson, Nigel Wright, and Ted Bami in the final. From TV, I thought Wright outboxed Lomax, who had suffered two cuts in his opening bout yet was allowed to box on. Wright had gashed his shin on the ring steps when entering the ring to outbox Ross Minter yet still moved well enough to give Lomax problems. However, to the victor the spoils.

At Newport, Abercarn tree surgeon Jamie Way chopped away at Ali Wyatt for ten rounds but could not bring him down and had to be content with the decision that gave him the International Masters light-welterweight title. Wyatt, Iranian-born but from Torquay, could not match Jamie's workrate and finished a poor second. Heavyweight Herbie Hide, back in the UK after four years campaigning on the continent, was on the Norwich show matched with his pal and former sparmate, Aleksejs Kosobokovs. It was all business, rough and sometimes dirty business, when they squared up for an eight rounder. It went three before the Latvian baled out, claiming a knee injury.

Robert Norton (right) won the vacant British cruiserweight title when comfortably outscoring the game Micky Steeds

Philip Sharkey

NOVEMBER

If this was to be Joe Calzaghe's last fight, he went out in style, beating an American legend in Roy Jones junior at the famous Madison Square Garden in New York City to cap his unbeaten pro career, now an incredible 46-0, that included an 11-year reign as world super-middleweight champion with 21 successful defences. The fight also completed a fine hat-trick, with victories over Mikkel Kessler and Bernard Hopkins preceding the Jones victory. Retirement looked more than an option, it looked mandatory for the man from Newport. There were no more mountains to climb, nothing to prove. Granted that both Hopkins (43) and Jones (39) were over their peak years, but Joe himself was pushing 37 and had been fighting since he was in short pants. As in the Hopkins fight, Joe had to climb off the deck after a first-round knockdown to storm his way to victory and earn the grudging respect of the American fight crowd. Jones finished with blood streaming down his face from his left eye, cut in the seventh round. Once the pound-for-pound champion, winner of world titles at four weights, the puncher from Pensacola lost for the fifth time in 57 fights and, like Calzaghe, he has nothing more to prove. His name is in the book.

A couple of weeks later, in Las Vegas, Ricky Hatton turned in a terrific performance to stop Paulie Malignaggi inside 11 rounds to retain his IBO light-welterweight title and show he was back on top of his game. In superb condition, with new trainer Floyd Mayweather senior in his corner, Hatton chased the cocky New Yorker out of the ring and set tongues wagging over a fight with the winner of the upcoming contest between Oscar de la Hoya and Manny Pacquiao. Either one would be considerably tougher than Malignaggi. Billed as the 'Magic Man' he had few tricks up his sleeve that Hatton had not seen before. Ring down the curtain.

David Haye nails America's Monte Barrett immediately prior to scoring a fifth-round stoppage win   Philip Sharkey

While Calzaghe and Hatton were flying the flag in America, David Haye was making a heavyweight statement in London. At the O2 Arena, the former world cruiserweight champion (WBC, WBA, WBO) looked good in a thrilling, five-knockdown, fifth-round stoppage win over American Monte Barrett and called for a shoot-out with either or both of the Klitschko brothers. The Barrett fight was an eliminator for Vitali's WBC title, but Haye needs to build on his 22-1 pro record before that happens. The big Londoner has the charisma and the punch to draw the fans in and the fact that he sometimes gets hit and knocked down makes him a viable attraction for TV. In previous fights, admittedly at cruiser, Haye was stopped by Carl Thompson (his only defeat) and floored by Lolenga Mock and Jean-Marc Mormeck. He was down against Barrett but decked the American five times before it was stopped in round five. The time is right for a new heavyweight to carry the division.

Certainly, the British champion, Danny Williams, looked ready for retirement as he suffered a punishing eighth-round stoppage at the rough hands of Albert Sosnowski at the York Hall. The UK-based Polish heavyweight came in with impressive stats, 43-2 with 26 inside wins, but he had not faced anyone of Danny's class and Williams was ahead when the bombs fell in round eight, suddenly coming apart at the seams. At 35, with a pro log of 40-7, maybe it was time for Danny to make his exit.

A new star is rising in the welterweight division by the name of Kell Brook. The kid from Sheffield, who says he just loves beating people up, defended his British title against the former champion, Kevin McIntyre, in Glasgow and in no time at all (two minutes) had the Paisley southpaw on his way back to the dressing room. Just 22, Brook took his pro record to 18-0 with 11 inside. As McIntyre hit the canvas for the third time in the opening round, the referee waved hostilities over and those who had booed Brook's ring entrance knew that they had seen something special.

A couple of weeks later, Glasgow fans did have something to shout about as their new British featherweight champion, Paul Appleby, retained his title with a shutout decision over a former champion in Esham Pickering. It was a frustrating but rewarding experience for the young Scot who stayed undefeated at 13-0. Pickering won the race but Appleby won the fight, and that is what counts in this business.

Sleaford lightweight Amir Unsworth drew a sellout crowd to the local Northgate Leisure Centre for his challenge against the International Masters champion, Paul Holborn, only for the Sunderland southpaw to run out a convincing winner on points when turning in an impressive performance to take his log to 9-1-1.

It was Prizefighter time again with the middleweights taking the floor at York Hall. Emerging as the winner over Joe Rea, Danny Butler and Cello Renda to grab the £25,000 jackpot was Martin Murray, a former ABA champion from St Helens, who had to fight all the way to claim his prize.

The Café Royal in London's Piccadilly, scene of countless gloved encounters through the years and featuring many a champion, finally closed its doors to boxing with a charity tournament that starred Dudley super-middleweight,

Sam Horton, winning for the 11th time over Georgia's Vepkhis Tchilaia. Hull's veteran heavyweight Tony Booth had second thoughts about his recently announced retirement and was delighted with his fourth-round victory over Raz Parnez in Glasgow, in what was Tony's 166th professional bout. Well, maybe just one more, eh? One fighter who did hang up his gloves was Barking's Marc Callaghan, who had won English and Southern Area titles in his 19-5-1 record. Callaghan was knocked out in round two of a contest for the vacant Southern Area featherweight title by Akaash Bhatia, his fifth straight defeat. Enough was enough.

DECEMBER

It was the moment of truth for Carl Froch and he came through with a superb performance to beat Jean Pascal over 12 thrilling rounds to win the vacant WBC super-middleweight title in front of a packed Trent FM Arena in Nottingham. Both men were undefeated; Froch on 23-0 (19) and Pascal 21-0 (14), so somebody's O had to go. The local favourite was 31 to 26 for the man from Haiti via Canada, but youth was not going to be served this night. Carl's granite chin was tested in the early rounds as Pascal let both hands go and there was nothing in it after five rounds. Then Froch began to take charge from round six, using his superior boxing and fighting when he had to. Why not? This guy loves a fight! And at the final bell he had won his greatest fight, champion of the world! It does not get any better than this.

When going to Italy for a fight, they used to say you have got to knock the local man out to get a draw. Maybe Matt Skelton had heard that one around the gym when he was training for his challenge to Paolo Vidoz in Milan for the vacant European heavyweight championship. Well, the 'Bedford Bear' did not take any chances on a dodgy decision as he mauled the Italian from the opening bell and Paolo seemed lucky to still be there after four rounds. He hung in there until the ninth round and Skelton was even easing up on his punches when Vidoz suddenly lost his appetite for boxing. He refused to leave his corner for round ten, saying: "I had no more energy". Skelton had enough for both of them as he racked up a stunning upset victory to take his record to 22-2 (19). On the way home, Matt was already dreaming of world title fights, while Paolo Vidoz was telling friends: "After 20 years, I have developed a sort of nausea for the ring. Maybe one more and then I will hang them up". Think no more, Paolo, and hang them up now!

Three months after crashing to a first-round defeat at the destructive fists of Columbia's Breidis Prescott, Amir Khan started his comeback in fine style with a two-round blow-out of Dublin's Oisin Fagan at the ExCel Arena in London. Khan was as sharp as a tack after training under Freddie Roach in Los Angeles, where he sparred with Manny Pacquiao and held his own with the Filipino who went on to destroy Oscar de la Hoya. A decent opponent who had taken former IBF champion Paul Spadafora to a split decision in his 27-fight record 12 months previously, the Irishman barely laid a glove on Khan, who overwhelmed him from the opening bell. Fagan suffered two knockdowns in the first round and was stopped in round two as he went down again. Amir Khan, 19-1, was back in business.

The Irish light-welterweight, Paul McCloskey, was on the bill at the Goresbrook Leisure Centre in Dagenham,

It was the body shots that eventually paid dividends for Brian Magee (left) when knocking out the unbeaten Steve McGuire to win the vacant British super-middleweight title

Philip Sharkey

topped by Colin Lynes v David Barnes for the vacant British title. A few days before the fight, Barnes dropped out with injury and McCloskey found himself in the ring with the former British and European champion. Paul seized his opportunity to outbox and outpunch Lynes, who retired on his stool after nine rounds. The delighted Irishman, still undefeated at 18-0, was the new champion.

Barnet's Commonwealth middleweight champion, Darren Barker, kept his unbeaten record (19-0) when he forced Northern Ireland's Jason McKay to retire after six rounds at Brentwood and set his sights on a European title in the New Year. On the same bill, Jason's fellow countryman, Brian Magee, had better luck when he captured the vacant British super-middleweight title with an eighth-round knockout over Scotland's Steve McGuire. The Belfast southpaw, in his third crack at a British title, made no mistake this time as his body attack paid off big time.

At Widnes, Nathan Cleverly's first defence of his Commonwealth light-heavyweight title saw the Welshman stop Kenya's Douglas Otieno in round four, the referee waving it over with Otieno flat on his back. Nathan retained his unbeaten record at 14-0 and looked forward to a British title challenge against Dean Francis.

Italy's Fabrizio Trotta went to Dublin City University hoping to get his degree, but the test paper set by 'Professor' Rendall Munroe was too hard and the Leicester southpaw retained his European super-bantamweight title for the third time, stopping his man in round five to set up talk of a fight with former champion, Bernard Dunne. On the Dublin bill, the Commonwealth bantamweight champion, Jason Booth, saw off the challenge of Pontefract's Sean Hughes, a southpaw, who retired after ten painful rounds. Also retiring with that fight was referee Mickey Vann, 65 and out!

Hanging up the gloves for the last time was Middlesbrough super-middleweight, Dave Pearson, a serving soldier at Chilwell Barracks in Nottingham. Dave went out with a draw against Lee Nicholson at Humberston, a record of 6-25-2, and the words of manager Mike Shinfield ringing in his ears: "A credit to the sport and a pleasure to work with". Another fighter hopefully thinking retirement was Audley Harrison, run over by Belfast taxi driver Martin Rogan, who was a clear winner in only his 11th fight, now 11-0. The former Olympic super-heavyweight champion (2000) once again failed to deliver and, at 37, with a record of 23-4, is going nowhere. So what does the future hold for former ABA super-heavyweight champion, Tyson Fury? A towering six feet, nine inches and bouncing the scales at nearly 19 stone, Manchester's Fury took just over two minutes of his pro debut at Nottingham to blow away the Hungarian, Bela Gyongyosi. Maybe there is a case for a dreadnought division after all.

JANUARY

Sheffield's British welterweight champion, Kell Brook, is the face of the future, one of our best bets for super stardom, perhaps even world class. Still only 22, he has racked up 19 straight victories, 12 inside schedule, and put three notches on the Lonsdale belt that looks certain to become a permanent fixture on his mantelpiece. His latest victim,

Darlaston's Stuart Elwell, was a former unbeaten Midlands Area champion who had boxed for English and WBA Inter-Continental titles. However, Elwell was not at the races when meeting Brook for his title at a packed York Hall in London. Elwell had trained for two months for this one and was in peak condition. If he had not done his homework, he might not have made it out of the first round! As it was, he lasted 89 seconds of round two before the referee called a halt, saving Stuart for another day. The young man from Sheffield was cool, calm, collected, and utterly ruthless as he picked his punches, flooring Elwell twice in the opening round before moving up a gear in the second to punish his man and bring about the referee's intervention. Kell Brook is on his way!

The future is also bright for the British lightweight champion, John Murray, who held on to his unbeaten 26-0 record with a testing defence against lively Scot, Lee McAllister, at Wigan's Robin Park Centre. Lee, unorthodox but a winner in all but one of his 28 pro fights, did not lack support in the packed hall as his fans had followed him south, and they were encouraged by his bright start. But Manchester's Murray picked the pace up after three rounds and McAllister began shipping more punishment than he cared for. Thudding body shots took the spring out of Lee's legs and in round eight a vicious left dropped the Scot. He managed to get to his feet as the count reached eight but the referee looked into his eyes and decided he was through for this evening.

A little man making big news was Stoke flyweight, Chris Edwards. A former holder of the super-flyweight title, Chris was fighting for the vacant British and Commonwealth flyweight championships in his hometown with Grimsby's Wayne Bloy in the opposite corner. Edwards is a good fighter with a poor record, 11 wins in 27 pro fights (3 draws), but he was too good for Bloy. The Grimsby lad had boxed just nine times for a 5-3-1 log, but most fellows his size are riding horses. There is more work and more money for jockeys than flyweight boxers in Britain today, but you go where your heart is and on this night Wayne and Chris were climbing into a boxing ring seeking championship honours. From the opening bell it was soon apparent that the experience of Edwards would win the day. He had too much of everything and was outboxing and outpunching Bloy for the best part of four rounds when Wayne indicated a hand injury. The referee followed him to his corner and accepted his retirement, leaving Edwards once again a British champion with the Commonwealth title sweetening the pot.

I was ringside at the Eston Sports Academy in Middlesbrough to share the bitter disappointment of local youngster, Paul Truscott, when a nasty cut by his right eye brought a summary conclusion to his Commonwealth featherweight title defence against former British champion, John Simpson, in round eight. I had Paul ahead but once the blood appeared the Scot stepped up his attack and referee Howard Foster rightly decided it could not go on. Truscott will come again.

The big boys were in action again, with Manchester giant Tyson Fury racking up his second pro win against a kilt-wearing German heavyweight (Scottish father), who was stopped in three rounds at Wigan, and the former ABA champion, Derek Chisora, moved to 9-0 but had to travel the eight rounds to take a decision over Daniel Peret, a Russian-born Norwegian at York Hall.

At Glasgow, as usual it was a packed house for the St Andrew's Sporting Club annual Burns Night show with a ten rounds contest for the Scottish lightweight title following the haggis, a tasty titbit between Newarthill's Charles Paul King and Stuart Green from Glenrothes. The fight lived up to the occasion, King winning a narrow decision in an all-action thriller that could have gone either way. On the same bill, the Birmingham journeyman, Jason Nesbitt, lost a lopsided decision to the former British light-welterweight champion, Barry Morrison, over six rounds.

Southern Area championships had an airing this month as Gosport's Steve Ede took the vacant middleweight title with his second victory over Crawley's Anthony Young, who was stopped in the dying seconds of the eighth round. With his stats now 4-15, Young was retired by manager Jim Evans before he left the ring. In a bout for the vacant super-middleweight title at York Hall, Finchley's Tony Salam, a southpaw, came out a winner when Romford's Richard Horton was taken out by the referee in round four when suffering a badly cut left eyelid. Salam was now on 8-1.

A professional fight record of 24-1 is excellent, but transpose those figures to 1-24 and you are thinking about alternative employment. But the East Ham light-welterweight, Johnny Greaves, keeps plugging on, his latest defeat coming at the talented fists of the English lightweight champion, Scott Lawton, in a six-rounder at Stoke. Scott's title was not at stake as he took his figures to 26-4-1. There are winners and there are losers. That is boxing! The English light-welterweight champion, Lenny Daws, was having difficulty making the weight for his defence against Dean Harrison at Wigan, so the fight was put on the back burner. Lenny came in seven pounds heavier, a full welter, for his re-arranged ten rounds bout with Latvia's Sergej Savrinovics, and was in command all the way until it was halted in the sixth round.

FEBRUARY

Belfast taxi driver Martin Rogan has driven right through the British heavyweight scene and after his brutal demolition of the Commonwealth champion, Matt Skelton, at Birmingham was hungry for more. Skelton had hammered Paolo Vidoz into submission in Italy to grab the European title but elected not to defend that belt against Rogan. The Irishman's victory meant the title was now vacant so he looks a good bet to add that one to his collection. At 37, Rogan is still fresh, Skelton being only his 12th victim in a pro career that started in 2004. He hit the £25,000 jackpot when winning the first Prizefighter competition in April 2008 and had since upset Audley Harrison's ambitions, beating the former Olympic gold medallist and convincing him to retire. Martin was in superb condition for the Skelton fight and it paid off as he was able to stand up to Matt's power shots and take command, putting the 'Bedford Bear' on his backside for the first time. Matt got up from that 11th round knockdown but Rogan steamed in and the referee had to call a halt.

Heavyweight championship fights were always boxing's biggest crowd pullers. With more fights like Rogan versus Skelton, those days could well come back.

Clinton Woods was back in business almost a year after losing his IBF light-heavyweight title to Antonio Tarver in America. The former champion was giving the dice one more roll, facing Elvir Muriqi in an eliminator, with 'Lady Luck' riding on his shoulder in the unlikely setting of the Hotel de France in Jersey. The Albanian had also lost to Tarver for the IBO title and was looking for a way back. But this night, the Sheffield man showed him the way out, taking a unanimous decision as well as taking a number of low blows from a frustrated opponent. Clinton gradually gained control and was a good winner at the final bell.

Those fans who stayed away from the Aston Events Centre in Birmingham missed a helluva fight when Sunderland's David Dolan went after Robert Norton's British cruiserweight title, with the vacant Commonwealth belt added for good measure. The 37-year-old southpaw champion looked ripe for a younger fellow to come along and take over and the former amateur star fitted the bill. Especially when he dumped Norton on the deck twice in the fourth round and again in the eighth. But Robert had come to fight for his titles and he had Dolan down twice in what turned out to be a thriller, with the champion wanting it more as Dolan played it safe. At the final bell old man Norton was a double champion.

Away from the ring Rendall Munroe is a bin man, or refuse technician if you like. But inside the ring there is no rubbish from this Leicester southpaw, especially when his European super-bantamweight title is on the line, as it was at Barnsley against a former victim, Kiko Martinez, himself a former champion. The Spaniard was in it up to halfway, but then Munroe took over to finish a unanimous points winner, retaining his title for the fourth time. The way Munroe is

Peter McDonagh (right) smashes in a right to the jaw of Lee Purdy on his way to winning the vacant Southern Area light-welter title   Philip Sharkey

going, it may well take a surgical operation to remove that belt from his steely mitts. He can empty my bin any time!

Commonwealth light-welterweight champion, Ajose Olusegun, kept his title and his unbeaten record, now 26-0, against the challenge of Derby's Scott Haywood, who gave it a good try before the London-based Nigerian took all the fight out of him with a steaming right to the body in the seventh. Scott beat the count but the referee took one look at him and waved it over.

It was a big night for Olympic bronze medallist, Tony Jeffries, when making his professional debut. A light-heavy in Beijing six months earlier, the Sunderland man was boxing at super-middle and stopping Aliaksandr Vayavoda at 2.42 of round one. Bring it on! Jeffries was the first Olympian to hit the pro circuit, quickly followed one night later by team-mates Frankie Gavin, Billy Joe Saunders and James DeGale. All three came out winners on the Birmingham bill. Middleweight Saunders got rid of Attila Molnar in round two; Gavin, cut on the nose, stopped George Kadaria in the fourth; DeGale, our only gold medal winner in Beijing, boxed his way carefully to a four-rounds decision over Vepkhia Tchilaia. So far, so good.

With a world title shot in his sights, Jonathan Thaxton put his European lightweight title on the line in hometown Norwich against the unheralded Frenchman, Anthony Mezaache, only to see his dream come apart with the visitor winning the title on a unanimous decision. It looked odds on for Thaxton when he dropped the Parisian in the opening round, but Mezaache fought back and edged a thrilling bout that sent Jonathan's fans home disappointed but happy.

The Prizefighter tournament moved into York Hall, this time for light-heavyweights, and the seven-fight format kept the fans happy all night. Portsmouth veteran and former champion, Tony Oakey, was the happiest of all as he won the £25,000 jackpot and title with victories over Billy Boyle, Courtney Fry and Darren Stubbs in his final bout.

I have always liked Michael Jennings, a former British welterweight champion. A good boxer with nice moves, only one defeat in 35 fights and a role model. But when the news came that he was to fight Miguel Cotto for the vacant WBO championship in New York, I thought mismatch. I thought Gary Locket against Kelly Pavlik.

Jennings, like Lockett, was just not in that league and had done nothing to justify such a fight. Good purse, yes, so long as you can count it afterwards. Michael made the trip to Madison Square Garden where he was sacrificed to the mighty Cotto for the delight of his Puerto Rican fans. The game British boy was smashed to the canvas three times before it was stopped in round five.

MARCH

Fighting Mexican legend Marco Antonio Barrera at the MEN Arena in Manchester, Amir Khan desperately wanted to win. Victory would wipe out the devastating one-round defeat by Breidis Prescott two fights earlier. It would also put the Bolton boy wonder into the 'senior bracket, and herald his arrival in the big time. A crack at one of the world lightweight titles would be a question of when rather than if. Well, Amir got his victory, Barrera being pulled out of the

fight in round five, his swarthy face a mask of blood spilling from a laceration on his scalp that took 33 stitches to close. An accidental head clash in the very first round put the seven-time, three-weight champion on the road to a bloody defeat. Barrera looked like he had been in a car wreck! So, not the way Khan wanted to beat this great fighter, or what was left of him at 35 after 71 fights (65-6). It definitely would have been a harder fight for Amir had the Mexican not been blinded by his own blood. Yet the way the 22-year-old Bolton lad did his job made you wonder if he would still have beaten Barrera, cut or no cut. Khan was on top all the way, boxed when he had to, fought when he had to, and came out with credit. And the victory. Well done.

Dagenham's Nicky Cook had a bad night when defending his WBO super-featherweight title against unbeaten Puerto Rican, Roman Martinez. He got away to a good start and looked to edge the opening three rounds. But in the fourth, Martinez set up a savage attack and Cook was floored twice by wicked left hooks before the referee called a halt, much to Nicky's disgust. He had almost decked the Puerto Rican in the second round with his own left hook, but the visitor did not go down and two rounds later Cook did. With another eight rounds still to go, the stoppage was probably justified.

It was not a good night for either Enzo Maccarinelli or Bradley Pryce as they tried to shake off ring rust. In fact Enzo admitted that he had done no sparring for the match, which may or may not have made any difference once Ola Afolabi opened up with his big guns. The Welshman had tasted Ola's right hand in round three and seemed to get his act together. But the Kent-born, US-based Nigerian dropped another right-hand bomb in the eighth round, and when Enzo staggered to his feet it was stopped. The Commonwealth light-middleweight champion, Pryce, fared no better against Manchester's Matthew Hall, who was looking for another knockout. He got it in round two after dumping Pryce three times on the floor to take away his title.

Irish eyes were smiling over in Dublin where Bernard Dunne smashed his way to a sensational 11th-round victory over the Panama southpaw, Ricardo Cordoba, to take his WBA super-bantamweight title. Bernard, egged on by a capacity 9,000 crowd, sent Cordoba to the floor in round three. While Cordoba got up to weather the storm, Dunne finished the fourth with a bad cut over his left eye. It looked worse in the fifth when two thudding rights decked the Irishman for two counts and he was under pressure at the bell. He survived and over the second half was giving the champion all he could handle, but going into round 11 Dunne needed a knockout. He got it! A savage left hook poleaxed the Panamanian and it was all over at 2.52 of the round. Cordoba went to hospital but happily was released after several hours with the all-clear.

Making the first defence of his European bantamweight title at Newham Leisure Centre against Malik Bouziane, Ian Napa failed to solve this French box of tricks and the unsung visitor went back home with the unanimous decision and the belt. Now the Londoner was left with the task of fighting his way back and would be targeting the British title that he had previously relinquished.

When the former British super-middleweight champion, Tony Dodson, hooked up with his fellow Merseysider, Tony Quigley, in the first fight show at Liverpool's Echo Arena, his old title (now vacant) was on the line and you had to fancy Dodson to rule again. At 28, with 29 fights behind him, he had it over Quigley, just 24 and 12-1 as a pro. But the kid prevailed in a classic encounter, a fight that rightly took its place in Liverpool's rich boxing history. Dodson reached the final round but was running on empty and two knockdowns brought about the referee's intervention. It was a fight the fans will remember, but it was also a fight a boxer does not want too many of in his career.

It was the kind of fight Michael Gomez has experienced many times in a 14-year pro career and it was a fight, against Ricky Burns in Glasgow for the Scot's Commonwealth super-featherweight title, that ended in a punishing seventh-round stoppage, that finally convinced Gomez it was time to listen to wife Alison and hang them up. At 31, after 47 fights, the former British and WBU super-feather champ has earned his place in the sun.

Former British and Commonwealth light-middleweight champion, Jamie Moore, finally got a crack at the (vacant) European title, putting everything into his fight with Italy's Michele Piccirillo at Wigan, and it was more than enough for the Salford southpaw to drop his man three times in three rounds for the finish.

Finally getting out from under brother Ricky's shadow,

Matthew Hatton won himself a shot at the IBO welterweight title with a devastating left hook in round six that sent the former European light-welterweight champion, Ted Bami, off to the showers for an early night. Hatton took his record to an impressive 36-4-1 and looks ready for bigger things.

APRIL

When Carl Froch finally got his act together over there in Connecticut and hammered the resistance out of Jermain Taylor to retain his WBC super-middleweight championship with just 14 seconds remaining in the fight, it reminded me of Jake LaMotta saving his world middleweight title in the dying seconds of his defence against Laurent Dauthuille in 1950, knocking the Frenchman out with 13 seconds left in the 15th round. Like LaMotta, Froch was trailing on the scorecards going into that final round against the challenger, and like the Bronx Bull he knew what he had to do. And he did it! As those last three minutes ticked away, Carl hunted his man down, hurting him with heavy punches, and finally dropped Taylor in a corner. It looked all over, but, with the crowd going crazy, the former world middleweight champ hauled himself off the deck and stood by the ropes, waiting. Froch moved in, smashing in lefts and rights, and as Taylor sagged the referee moved in and called a halt. Froch had won a sensational victory against the ex-champion, still a top fighter, in front of his own people, people who just the day before the fight were asking who the hell is this guy Carl Froch? Well, now they know. He calls himself The Cobra,

Steve Ede (left), seen here ploughing in to Anthony Young, the man he stopped in the eighth round to win the vacant Southern Area middleweight title

Les Clark

comes from Nottingham, and was still undefeated in the professional ring after 25 fights, 20 of them finishing inside the distance. Jermain Taylor knows who Carl Froch is. The American boxed one of his best fights and only had to stay out of trouble for that final three minutes to win another world title. But over those last few rounds, Taylor was tiring as Carl was coming on strong and when the referee stopped the fight he was still the WBC super-middleweight champion of the world. And the American fight crowd finally knew just who the hell this guy Carl Froch was! He was a fighter! A champion fighter!

Back home, the little guys were making a big noise. At the venerable York Hall, Gary Davies, a 26-year-old from St Helens, won the vacant British bantamweight title with a seventh-round stoppage of Matthew Edmonds. The Newport man had failed in a previous challenge for the vacant Commonwealth title, being stopped in nine rounds by Jason Booth, and he failed this time when a big right hand took everything out of him. The new champion is now 9-2-1 with seven of those wins inside.

Three weeks later, Birmingham's Don Broadhurst defended his Commonwealth super-flyweight title against Ghana's Asamoah Wilson and had to take a few stiff belts along the way before bringing the referee's intervention in round six to stay undefeated at 11-0.

At Leigh, the Commonwealth super-bantamweight champion, Jason Booth, added the vacant British title to his collection with a sixth-round cut eye stoppage over Liverpool southpaw, Mark Moran. The form line proved a good guide. Booth, a former British flyweight champion, was 31-5 going in against the 11-0-1 stats of Moran and it was a fight too far for the man from the Mersey.

It was fight night in Belfast, at the Ulster Hall, a hometown boy fighting a Scot for his British featherweight championship, and their supporters were out in force, ready to fight anybody after a few pints of Guinness. Fortunately, security kept the lid on it and the fighting inside the ring was enough to keep everybody happy as Martin Lindsay forced a sixth-round stoppage over Paul Appleby to take away his unbeaten record and his title. New champ Lindsay took his log to 14-0.

In an all-southpaw battle at York Hall, London's John O'Donnell squeaked home against Manchester's Craig Watson to take a split decision and the Commonwealth welterweight title in a fight many thought the champion had done enough to hang on to his title. Would make a good return.

The championship hopes of the Derry middleweight, John Duddy, took a knock when he was beaten by Billy Lyell at Newark, New Jersey. The split-decision loss was the first for the Irishman after 26 straight wins, mostly in the States. A worrying aspect of the fight was the ease with which Lyell, a non-puncher, landed his right hand. It left Duddy still a work in progress.

Blackpool's Matthew Ellis had a few big names on his 29-fight record but he probably had not met anyone as big as Tyson Fury (what a name for a fighter!) who stood 6`7" in his socks against 5`11 ½" for Ellis. Matthew could not reach the big heavyweight, who had no trouble reaching him, and

it was all over after 48 seconds of round one as Fury picked up his fifth win in a row. Sheffield's Ryan Rhodes, after giving up his British light-middleweight title for personal reasons, was on the Belfast bill to work out the rust with a seventh-round stoppage win over the reluctant Hungarian, Janos Petrovics. Rhodes was still looking at an EU title bout with Lukas Konecny. At York Hall, Lenny Daws, the former British light-welterweight champion, went in with the Southern Area titleholder, Peter McDonagh, for the vacant English title (are you following this?) and Lenny was too strong and forceful over the ten rounds, coming out with the decision. At Leigh, the Heywood welterweight, Mark Thompson, upped his record to 19-1 with a six-rounds decision over Johannes Fabrizius, a late sub hailing from Germany…The launch of the St George's Sporting Club at Limehouse, appropriately on St George's Day, saw serving soldier Ross Burkinshaw march to victory over Liverpool's Mike Robinson, who was dropped twice in round seven to bring the third man's intervention and give Burkinshaw the first ever English super-flyweight championship.

MAY

The disturbing sight of Ricky Hatton stretched out unconscious in the ring at the MGM Grand Garden in Las Vegas will hopefully be the last time this brave Manchester warrior is seen inside a boxing ring wearing short pants. Ricky was destroyed by Manny Pacquiao in just five minutes, 59 seconds, barely surviving two knockdowns in the opening round before being brutally crushed in round two by surely the best pound-for-pound fighter in the business. It was only Hatton's second defeat in 47 professional fights, but, at 30, he does not want another one.

Promoter Frank Maloney brought big time boxing back to Sunderland with three championship bouts on a mammoth bill, but it was Tony Jeffries, the local hero, who accounted for most of the 1,600 capacity crowd in the Crowtree Leisure Centre. The Olympic bronze medal winner at Beijing, super-middleweight 'Jaffa' sent his delirious fans home happy after seeing him stop Germany's hapless Roy Meissner in round two.

Championship action saw Jamie Moore retain his European light-middleweight title against Ukraine's Roman Dzhuman with a second-round stoppage…Danny Williams hung on to his British heavyweight title after a disappointing decision win over John McDermott…Busy Rendall Munroe, the Leicester refuse collector, added the vacant Commonwealth super-bantamweight title to his European belt following a points win over Isaac Nettey of Ghana.

They had themselves a fight in Belfast that Friday night when the Commonwealth heavyweight champion, Martin Rogan, put his title on the line against Sam Sexton at a jam-packed Odyssey Arena. Both men had been winners of the Prizefighter competitions, with the Belfast cabbie going on to turn over Audley Harrison and take Matt Skelton's parking space and his title in a brutal battle. Sexton had to be the underdog with his 11-1 pro record but he was the younger man by 14 years, at 24. Well, youth carried the day when referee Dave Parris, on the advice of the ringside doctor, stopped the action in round eight due to Rogan's badly swollen left eye. Yet Rogan had almost stopped his man earlier in the round, rocking the Norwich man with big punches as the crowd went crazy. This one could go on again. On the undercard, former Olympians James DeGale, Billy Joe Saunders, and Frankie Gavin all came out winners in their second pro fights. Southpaw Saunders forced a second- round stoppage over Germany's Ronny Gabel; Gavin took three rounds to see off France's Mourad Frarema and DeGale wasted no time getting rid of the Czech Republic's Jindrich Kubin in the opening round. It was a far cry for Chorley's former British and WBU welterweight champion, Michael Jennings, coming from his world title defeat by Miguel Cotto in Madison Square Garden to boxing seven-fight novice Willie Thompson on the Belfast bill. He got back to winning ways and looked good in stopping the Ballyclare boxer in four rounds. Former British welterweight champion, Neil Sinclair, is getting on a bit, 35, but his old punches still had the sting in them that gave him 24 stoppage wins in his 31 victories. Henry Coyle felt their power in this fight for the vacant Irish light-middle-weight title and it was Neil's title inside three rounds.

On paper, the latest of Matchroom's Prizefighter competitions, for cruiserweights, looked to be possibly the best, with all eight contestants having won a title of one sort or another. With six of the fighters on the wrong side of 30, it was perhaps fitting that the winner was a mere stripling of 29. Yet late substitute Ovill McKenzie had been out for 18 months before a losing fight to Bob Ajisafe. Well, Mac made no mistake this night as he beat Terry Dunstan, Darren Corbett and John (Buster) Keeton to cop the trophy and the £25,000 cheque.

Commonwealth middleweight champion Darren Barker is a class act, and getting better. He was too good for his challenger, Darren McDermott, in the Watford Colosseum, retaining his title with a fourth-round stoppage, but the decision of referee Dave Parris to call a halt as the Dudley man regained his feet after his first ever knockdown was controversial and hotly disputed by McDermott and his manager, Dean Powell. But it would be Barker who would be looking to challenge British champion, Matthew Macklin, hoping to become a double titleholder. At 20-0, he can do it.

At the venerable York Hall, the Commonwealth light-heavyweight champion, Nathan Cleverly, eased to a second-round stoppage over Sheffield's Billy Boyle to retain his title and line up a fight against Danny McIntosh for the vacant British championship. The tall Welshman took his undefeated record to 16-0. On the same bill, the British super-featherweight champion, Kevin Mitchell, came back to the ring after hand injuries had kept him idle for best part of a year. Kevin stopped Ghana's Lanquaye Wilson in the third round to take his pro log to 28-0, with 21 stoppages.

Thirty-year-old Glasgow lightweight, Willie Limond, picked up the vacant WBU title with a one-sided decision over English champion, Ryan Barrett, at the city's Thistle Hotel. With just two losses, to Alex Arthur and Amir Khan,

Nathan Cleverly, defending his Commonwealth light-heavyweight title, was far too good for Kenya's Samson Onyango who was stopped after just 135 seconds

Philip Sharkey

Back in action after a long layoff, Kevin Mitchell (right) took just three rounds to see off Ghana's Lanquaye Wilson at the York Hall last May

Philip Sharkey

on his 34-fight record, Willie was looking for bigger things to happen. With 48 pro fights behind him, Lincoln's Lee Swaby thought it was about time he fought in his own hometown, so he promoted his fight with Paul Butlin for the vacant Midlands Area heavyweight championship, and to cap a perfect night at the local Showground Lee came out with the decision and the title. At nearby Sleaford, the former British, Commonwealth and European super-bantamweight champion, Esham Pickering, came back after six months out to take the points over Birmingham's Sid Razak in a comfortable six rounder.

JUNE

Heading for Wigan for his fight with the English champion, Scott Lawton, at the Robin Park Sports Complex, John Murray, the British lightweight champion, was quietly confident of beating his former sparring partner. Heading home to Manchester two nights later, Murray was no longer British lightweight champion and Lawton was still just the English titleholder. So what happened? Things started going pear-shaped on the way to the official weigh-in. Heavy traffic delayed Murray and trainer Joe Gallagher and they arrived 50 minutes late for their date with the scales. It got worse!

When John stepped on the scales, he was three ounces over the 135lbs class limit. With a mere ten minutes left to sweat off the surplus, the already-finely tuned champion kissed his title goodbye. When they climbed into the ring the following night, the only way Lawton could win the championship, now officially vacant, was by winning the fight. Murray had lost enough already. He was not about to lose the fight. He did not. He almost won it in the first round, a left hook and two rights sending Lawton to the floor. Scott was up at 'six' to be saved by the bell. He had to be saved by the referee halfway through round six as Murray took his frustration out on his unfortunate opponent. No longer the champion, he still looked like the best lightweight in the country.

When Barry Morrison was knocked out by a virus a week before his fight with Commonwealth light-welterweight champion, Ajose Olusegun, County Durham's Nigel Wright jumped at the chance of a rematch with the Nigerian, now a London resident, thus making him eligible for the British title which was added to the pot. In their first encounter, Olusegun had retained on a decision and he did the same this night in Liverpool, only more so. The now-double champion is a very good fighter as his undefeated record of 27 straight wins bears out. He is ready for a bigger stage.

65

The age-old Scots-Irish rivalry had another outing at the Bellahouston Leisure Centre in Glasgow, where the Commonwealth super-featherweight champion, Ricky Burns, turned back the spirited challenge of Belfast's Kevin O'Hara when taking a unanimous decision. But the Coatbridge man had a tough job on his hands and never looked like knocking out his rival as he had predicted. The Belfast banger never stopped trying and he was still pitching leather at the final bell. In the chief support, the former WBO super-featherweight champion, Alex Arthur, made his lightweight debut with a devastating destruction of France's Mohamed Benbiou. Three counts and 92 seconds into the fight it was all over, with the Edinburgh man predicting big things for the 'new, dynamic Alex Arthur'. We'll see! One man Arthur could be looking at is his fellow Scot, Lee McAllister, who won the vacant Commonwealth title in hometown Aberdeen with a devastating three-rounds victory over Ghana's Godfriend Sowah. Although the opposition was weak, it was a strong performance from the former WBU champion as he took his pro log to 29-2.

In his patchy 14-10-2 pro record, Thetford's Rocky Dean could never win the big ones, and his luck was not about to change on a night at York Hall when going in against the British super-bantamweight champion, Jason Booth. The Nottingham man turned in a flawless performance to take the unanimous decision but Rocky, in true Balboa fashion, fought all the way to the final bell. Booth could reckon on a tougher assignment in his next defence when he would face Hartlepool's former triple champion, Michael Hunter.

Dublin super-middleweight, Darren Sutherland, the Olympic bronze medallist, won his fourth pro fight and his first in London when the tough Ukrainian, Gennady Rasalev, was sent to his corner in round four with a cut by his left eye. Up to then it had been a rough fight with Darren wondering if he had made the right career choice.

I think it was Norman Mailer who wrote: "Tough Guys Don't Dance". Portsmouth light-heavyweight Tony Oakey does not dance when he gets through those ropes, so you do not hold your arms out to him when the bell rings, you put them up in front of you and wait for the next bell so you can sit down. At his local Mountbatten Centre, the former British champion engaged Wales' Shon Davies in

With the International Masters light-heavyweight title at stake, Shon Davies (left) was no match for Tony Oakey and was rescued by the referee in round four

Les Clark

Challenging for the British super-featherweight title for the second time in eight months, Thetford's Rocky Dean (left) was again outpointed, this time by Jason Booth

Philip Sharkey

hand-to-hand combat for the best part of four rounds before the lad from Llanelli had taken enough. Hammered back into his own corner, Shon dropped to a knee and the third man stopped it. Thirty-three-year-old Oakey, at 29-4-1, was looking to get back on top again.

In hometown of Luton, the former British and Commonwealth lightweight champion, Graham Earl, worked the kinks out with a predictable six-rounds decision win over veteran loser Karl Taylor, but after 12 years in the business and aged 30, Earl was still working things out as to his future. Meanwhile, Herbie Hide was still pondering his fistic future as he faced up to Gabor Halasz in the German town of Volklingen. The former WBO heavyweight champion's WBC cruiserweight eliminator against Matt Godfrey had twice fallen through, which was bad luck for Mr Halasz as Herbie released his pent-up energy in round three and a sweeping left and right sent Halasz off for an early shower. The ladies, God bless 'em, are still battling away. At Wolverhampton Civic Hall the local lass, Lyndsay Scragg, outboxed and outfought

Kristine Shergold over ten rounds to win the vacant GBC female super-featherweight title, finishing with an egg on her forehead and a diagonal cut above her left eye. More importantly to Lyndsay, she finished up holding the belt. At the York Hall in Bethnal Green, Martin Power, the former British bantamweight champion, eased himself back into the business with a six-rounds decision win over the Birmingham journeyman, Sid Razak, taking his log to 20-4.

Facts and Figures, 2008-2009

There were 722 (665 in 2006-2007) British-based boxers who were active between 1 July 2008 and 30 June 2009, spread over 193 (203 in 2007-2008) promotions held in Britain, not including the Republic of Ireland, during the same period. Those who were either already holding licenses or had been re-licensed amounted to 541, while there were 164 (142 in 2007-2008) new professionals, plus eight non-nationals who began their careers elsewhere, and nine women.

Unbeaten During Season (Minimum Qualification: 6 Contests)

7: Chris Lewis, Martin Murray, Tyrone Nurse, Ashley Sexton. 6: Tom Dallas, Tyson Fury, Chris Goodwin (1 draw), Steve O'Meara, Scott Quigg, Stephen Smith.

Longest Unbeaten Sequence (Minimum Qualification: 10 Contests)

46: Joe Calzaghe. 28: Kevin Mitchell. 27: John Murray, Ajose Olusegun. 25: Carl Froch. 20: Darren Barker. 19: Kell Brook, Paul McCloskey. 16: Nathan Cleverly. 15: Andrew Murray. 14: Gareth Couch, Martin Lindsay, Martin Murray. 13: Ryan Brawley, Michael Grant (1 draw), Sam Horton, Rob Hunt (1 draw), Scott Quigg, Brian Rose (1 draw). 12: Ricky Burns, Chris Goodwin (1 draw), David Haye, Jamie Moore, Gary Sykes. 11: Don Broadhurst, Jamie Cox, Ricky Owen, Denton Vassell. 10: Kenny Anderson, Jack Arnfield, Derek Chisora, Karl Chiverton (1 draw), Danny McIntosh, Gary McMillan (1 draw), Jack Perry (1 draw), John Watson.

Most Wins During Season (Minimum Qualification: 6 Contests)

7: Chris Lewis, Martin Murray, Tyrone Nurse, Ashley Sexton. 6: Danny Butler, Tom Dallas, Tyson Fury, Steve O'Meara, Scott Quigg, Stephen Smith.

Most Contests During Season (Minimum Qualification 10 Contests)

20: Johnny Greaves, Sid Razak. 19: Delroy Spencer. 17: Jason Nesbitt. 16: Matt Scriven. 16: Karl Taylor. 15: Jamie Ambler. 13: Paul Royston, Matt Seawright, James Tucker, Shaun Watson. 12: Carl Allen, Michael Banbula, Chris Brophy, Anthony Hanna, Kristian Laight, Kevin McCauley, Daniel Thorpe. 11: Youssef Al Hamidi, Howard Daley, Robin Deakin, Geraint Harvey, Ernie Smith, Alexander Spitjo. 10: Steve Gethin.

Most Contests During Career (Minimum Qualification: 50 Contests)

300: Pete Buckley. 166: Tony Booth. 159: Ernie Smith. 49: Karl Taylor. 134: Paul Bonson. 121: Peter Dunn. 112: Anthony Hanna. 107: Daniel Thorpe. 106: Carl Allen. 100: Ojay Abrahams, Jason Nesbitt, Delroy Spencer. 90: Billy Smith. 89: David Kirk. 72: Kristian Laight. 69: Mark Phillips. 68: Chris Woollas. 66: Matt Scriven. 64: Hastings Rasani. 60: Baz Carey, Simeon Cover, Steve Gethin. 56: Duncan Cottier. 54: Shaun Walton.

Stop Press: Results for July/August 2009 (British-Based Boxers' Results Only)

Levallois-Perret, France – 3 July
Souleymane Mbaye w pts 12 Colin Lynes, Julien Marie-Sainte w co 2 Darren Rhodes.

Tower Ballroom, Edgbaston – 5 July (Promoter: Rowson)
Eddie McIntosh w pts 6 Jamie Norkett, Nasser El Harbi w pts 4 Martyn King, Dee Mitchell w pts Martin Concepcion, Quinton Hillocks w pts 4 Adam Wilcox, Richie Wyatt w pts 4 Craig Dyer.

Seaburn Leisure Centre, Sunderland – 10 July (Promoter: Maloney)
Lee Haskins w rsc 4 Ross Burkinshaw (British S.Flyweight Title Defence), Tony Jeffries w rsc 1 Ilya Shakuro, Brian Rose w pts 8 Francis Tchoffo, Dave Ferguson w pts 4 Daniel Peret, Kyle King w pts 4 Delroy Spencer, Trevor Crewe w rsc 1 Danny Dontchev, Travis Dickinson w rsc 2 Hamed Jamali, Jon-Lewis Dickinson w pts 4 Hastings Rasani, Chris Mullen w pts 4 Kristian Laight.

The Leisure Centre, Altrincham – 11 July (Promoter: Hatton)
Mark Thompson w co 5 Serjei Savrinovics, Scott Quigg w co 1 Ricardo Tanase, James Barker drew 6 Pavels Senkovs, Matty Askin w rsc 4 Mark Nilsen, Adrian Gonzalez w pts 4 Jason Thomas, Alfonso Vieyra w pts 4 Sid Razak, Martin Robins w pts 6 Chris Brophy.

Town Hall, Kensington – 11 July (Promoter: Fearon)
Kreshnik Qato w rsc 3 Zoltan Surman, Choi Tseveenpurev w rsc 3 Lubos Priehradnik, Nathan Graham w rsc 3 Tomas Grublys, Mene Edwards w pts 4 Jamie Ambler, Junior Saeed w pts 4 Yanis Lakrout.

Redondo Beach, California, USA – 17 July
Matthew Ellis drew 4 David Johnson.

Civic Hall, Wolverhampton – 17 July (Promoter: Rowson)
Jamie Ball w pts 4 Ernie Smith, Troy James w rsc 4 Anthony Hanna, Chris Truman w pts 4 Karl Taylor, Chris Male w pts 4 Steve Gethin, Rob Doody w pts 6 Jason Nesbitt.

The Racecourse, Doncaster – 18 July (Promoter: Hobson)
Jezz Wilson w pts 8 Patrick Mendy, Joe Elfidh w pts 6 Daniel Thorpe.

MEN Arena, Manchester – 18 July (Promoter: Warren)

Amir Khan w pts 12 Andreas Kotelnik (WBA L.Welterweight Title Challenge), Anthony Small w rsc 8 Matthew Hall (Commonwealth L.Middleweight Title Challenge. Vacant British Middleweight Title), Kell Brook w rsc 3 Michael Lomax (British Welterweight Title Defence), Denis Lebedev w rsc 3 Enzo Maccarinelli (Vacant WBO Inter-Continental Title), Kevin Mitchell w rsc 8 Rudy Encarnacion, Paul Smith w pts 8 Michal Bilak, Frankie Gavin w rsc 2 Graham Fearn, James DeGale w rsc 1 Ciaran Healy, Billy Joe Saunders w rsc 2 Matt Scriven, Richard Towers w pts 4 Howard Daley.

York Hall, Bethnal Green – 18 July (Promoter: Hennessy)

Nathan Cleverly w rsc 7 Danny McIntosh (Commonwealth L.Heavyweight Title Defence. Vacant British L.Heavyweight Title), Tom Glover w pts 8 Jonathan Thaxton, Tyson Fury w rsc 3 Aleksandrs Selezens, Andrew Murray w rtd 3 Adam Kelly, Steve O'Meara w pts 6 Lee Noble, Bobby Ward w pts 4 Sid Razak, Lee Purdy w rsc 2 Kevin McCauley, Del Rogers drew 4 Mo Khaled, Angel McKenzie w pts 4 Lana Cooper.

Leisure Centre, Newport – 24 July (Promoter: Hatton)

Garry Buckland w pts 10 Henry Castle (British Lightweight Title Eliminator), Danny Butler w pts 10 Paul Samuels (Vacant British Masters Middleweight Title), Henry Janes w pts 6 Pete Leworthy, Justyn Hugh w pts 6 Adam Wilcox, Damian Owen w rsc 4 Chris Long, Lee Churcher w pts 4 Gary Cooper, Wayne Brooks drew 4 Hastings Rasani.

Oasis Leisure Centre, Swindon – 24 July (Promoter: Mayo)

Jamie Cox w pts 8 Janos Petrovics, Marlon Reid w rsc 1 Ernie Smith, Danny Stewart w pts 6 Andrew Patterson, Jamie Speight w pts 4 Asamoah Wilson, Chris Higgs w pts 4 Kark Taylor, Adam Cummings w pts 4 Johnny Greaves, Lewis Browning w pts 4 Anwar Alfadi.

Liquid & Envy Nightclub, Redhill – 25 July (Promoter: Alldis)

Ben Jones w pts 10 Ibrar Riyaz (Vacant International Masters Featherweight Tuitle), Pat McAleese w rsc 4 Lewis Byrne, Tony Owen w pts 4 Daniel Thorpe, Daryl Setterfield w pts 4 Duncan Cottier.

Sutton Sports Centre, St Helens – 25 July (Promoter: Harrison)

Martin Murray w pts 8 Thomas Awinbono, Craig Lyon w pts 6 Isaac Owusu, Tom Doran w pts 6 Craig Tomes, Martyn Grainger w pts 6 Howard Daley, Scott Mitchell w pts 6 Chris Woollas, Steve Harkin w pts 4 Jason Smith, Rob Beech w pts 4 Mark Lewis, Justin Jones w pts 4 Jamie Norkett.

Dublin, Ireland – 25 July

Paul Hyland w pts 8 Robert Nelson, Anthony Fitzgerald w rsc 3 Peter Cannon,

Rancho Mirage, California, USA – 1 August

Devon Alexander w rtd 8 Junior Witter (Vacant WBC L.Welterweight Title).

Municipal Hall, Colne – 1 August (Promoter: Wood)

Chris O'Brien drew 6 William Warburton, Alastair Warren w pts 6 Davey Jones, Shayne Singleton w rsc 5 Jason Thompson, Stephen Jennings w pts 4 Carl Allen, Terry Flanagan w pts 4 Michael O'Gara, Yassine El Maachi w pts 4 Alexander Spitjo, Stuart McFadyen w pts 4 Sid Razak.

Floral Hall, Southport – 8 August (Promoter: Wood)

Rick Godding w pts 6 Darren Askew, Geraint Harvey w rsc 3 Chris Johnson, Carl Dilks w pts 6 Michael Banbula, Lee Jennings w pts 4 Ibrar Riyaz, Nick Quigley w pts 4 Jason Nesbitt, Mike Stafford w pts 4 Hastings Rasani.

Jumeirah Carlton Tower Hotel, Knightsbridge – 10 August (Promoter: Sanigar)

Johnny Greaves w pts 6 Ali Wyatt, Lee Selby w pts 6 Ian Bailey, Eisa Al Dah w pts 6 Matt Seawright, Rocky Chakir w pts 4 Jimmy Briggs.

Redondo Beach, California, USA – 21 August

Lance Whitaker w rsc 1 Matthew Ellis.

The Velodrome, Manchester – 21 August (Promoter: Hatton)

Craig Watson w pts 6 Matt Scriven, Andy Morris w rsc 1 Jesus Garcia Simon, Michael Brodie w rsc 4 Mark Alexander, Graeme Higginson w pts 6 Kristian Laight, Alex Dilmaghani w pts 4 Daniel Thorpe, Kieran Maher w pts 4 Jason Nesbitt, Joe Murray w pts 4 Steve Gethin.

Leisure Centre, Newport – 21 August (Promoter: Calzaghe)

Bradley Pryce w pts 10 Michael Monaghan, Gavin Rees w rtd 4 Johnny Greaves, Harry Miles w rtd 4 Michael Banbula, Wayne Brooks w pts 4 Mark Lewis, Jeff Evans w pts 4 Jamie Norkett.

Diary of British Boxing Tournaments, 2008-2009

Tournaments are listed by date, town and BBBoC licensed promoter, covering the period 1 July 2008 to 30 June 2009.

Code: SC + Sporting Club

Date	Town	Venue	Promoters
04.07.08	Liverpool	Everton Park Sports Centre	Hearn
11.07.08	Wigan	Robin Park Leisure Centre	Hennessy
12.07.08	Newport	Leisure Centre	J & C Sanigar
18.07.08	Dagenham	Goresbrook Leisure Centre	Maloney
19.07.08	Liverpool	Olympia	Greaves
24.07.08	Wolverhampton	Civic Hall	Rowson
25.07.08	Houghton le Spring	Rainton Meadows Arena	Jeffries
01.08.08	Watford	The Colosseum	Feld
04.09.08	Edgbaston	Tower Ballroom	Hatton
05.09.08	Nottingham	Harvey Hadden Leisure Centre	Maloney
06.09.08	Manchester	MEN Arena	Warren
12.09.08	Sheffield	Don Valley Stadium	Rhodes
12.09.08	Wolverhampton	Civic Hall	Rowson
12.09.08	Newcastle	Metro Radio Arena	Hearn
12.09.08	Mayfair	Grosvenor House Hotel	Warren
13.09.08	Stoke	Kings Hall	Carney
13.09.08	Bethnal Green	York Hall	Maloney
14.09.08	Edgbaston	Tower Ballroom	Pegg
14.09.08	Wigan	Robin Park Leisure Centre	Wood
19.09.08	Doncaster	The Dome	Hobson
20.09.08	Sheffield	Hillsborough Leisure Centre	Booth
20.09.08	Newark	Grove Leisure Centre	Greaves
22.09.08	Glasgow	Radisson Hotel	Gilmour
26.09.08	Wolverhampton	Civic Hall	Rowson
26.09.08	Bethnal Green	York Hall	Warren
27.09.08	Bethnal Green	York Hall	Carter
27.09.08	Bracknell	Leisure Centre	Evans
28.09.08	Colne	Municipal Hall	Wood
02.10.08	Piccadilly	Café Royal	Helliet
03.10.08	Sunderland	Tavistock Roker Hotel	Conroy
03.10.08	Burton	Meadowside Leisure Centre	Hearn
04.10.08	Norwich	The Showground	Hennessy
05.10.08	Nottingham	Victoria Leisure Centre	Scriven
05.10.08	Watford	Town Hall	Helliet
06.10.08	Birmingham	Holiday Inn	Cowdell
10.10.08	Sheffield	Don Valley Stadium	Rhodes
10.10.08	Motherwell	Dalziel Park Hotel	Rea
10.10.08	Liverpool	Everton Park Sports Centre	Warren
11.10.08	Hull	City Hall	Greaves
12.10.08	Leigh	Indoor Sports Centre	Wood
12.10.08	Bristol	Marriott Hotel	Couch/Hodges
17.10.08	Swindon	Oasis Sports Centre	Mayo
17.10.08	Bethnal Green	York Hall	Maloney
18.10.08	Paisley	Lagoon Leisure Centre	Hughes
20.10.08	Glasgow	Radisson Hotel	Gilmour
24.10.08	Newport	Leisure Centre	J & C Sanigar
24.10.08	Bethnal Green	York Hall	Hearn
25.10.08	Aberdeen	Beach Ballroom	Gilmour/McAllister
25.10.08	St Helier	Hotel de France	Hobson
31.10.08	Birmingham	Aston Villa Leisure Centre	Warren
01.11.08	Glasgow	Thistle Hotel	Morrison

07.11.08	Wigan	Robin Park Leisure Centre	Maloney
08.11.08	Bethnal Green	York Hall	Hennessy
08.11.08	Wigan	Robin Park Leisure Centre	Harrison
09.11.08	Wolverhampton	Civic Hall	Rowson
10.11.08	Glasgow	Radisson Hotel	Gilmour
14.11.08	Birmingham	Holiday Inn	Pegg
14.11.08	Glasgow	Kelvin Hall	Warren
15.11.08	Greenwich	O2 Arena	Booth
15.11.08	Bethnal Green	York Hall	Maloney
15.11.08	Plymouth	The Guildhall	J & C Sanigar
16.11.08	Shaw	Tara Sports & Leisure Centre	Doughty
16.11.08	Southampton	Civic Hall	Bishop
16.11.08	Derby	Heritage Hotel	Mitchell
19.11.08	Bayswater	Royal Lancaster Hotel	Evans/Waterman
21.11.08	Bethnal Green	York Hall	Warren
22.11.08	Bethnal Green	York Hall	Hearn
22.11.08	Blackpool	Tower Ballroom	Wood
26.11.08	Piccadilly	Cafe Royal	Helliet
27.11.08	Leeds	Elland Road Conference & Leisure Centre	Spratt/Bateson
28.11.08	Glasgow	Bellahouston Leisure Centre	Gilmour/Hearn
29.11.08	Sleaford	Northgate Leisure Centre	Greaves
30.11.08	Rotherham	Consort Hotel	Booth
04.12.08	Bradford	Hilton Hotel	Garber
04.12.08	Sunderland	Tavistock Roker Hotel	Conroy
05.12.08	Sheffield	Don Valley Stadium	Rhodes
05.12.08	Dagenham	Goresbrook Leisure Centre	Hearn
06.12.08	Nottingham	The Arena	Hennessy
06.12.08	Canning Town	Excel Arena	Warren
06.12.08	Bethnal Green	York Hall	Carter
06.12.08	Wigan	Robin Park Leisure Centre	Harrison
08.12.08	Birmingham	Holiday Inn	Cowdell
08.12.08	Cleethorpes	Beachholme Holiday Park	Frater
12.12.08	Widnes	Kingsway Sports Centre	Warren
13.12.08	Brentwood	International Centre	Hennessy
14.12.08	Bristol	Thistle Hotel	Feld
20.12.08	Bristol	Marriott City Centre Hotel	Hatton
21.12.08	Coventry	Hilton Hotel	Coventry SC
21.12.08	Motherwell	Dalziel Park Hotel	Rea
21.12.08	Bolton	De Vere White's Hotel	Wood
16.01.09	Middlesbrough	Eston Sports Academy	Hearn
17.01.09	Wigan	Robin Park Leisure Centre	Hennessy
19.01.09	Glasgow	Radisson Hotel	Gilmour
19.01.09	Mayfair	Park Lane Hilton Hotel	Evans/Waterman
23.01.09	Stoke	Fenton Manor	Maloney/Carney
24.01.09	Blackpool	Tower Ballroom	Wood
29.01.09	Holborn	Connaught Rooms	Helliet
30.01.09	Bethnal Green	York Hall	Warren
01.02.09	Edgbaston	Tower Ballroom	Rowson/Pegg
01.02.09	Bethnal Green	York Hall	Booth
06.02.09	Birmingham	Aston Villa Leisure Centre	Hearn/Rowson
07.02.09	Craigavon	Leisure Centre	Peters
13.02.09	Swindon	Oasis Sports Centre	Warren/Mayo
13.02.09	Wigan	Robin Park Leisure Centre	Harrison
14.02.09	St Helier	Hotel de France	Hobson
16.02.09	Glasgow	Radisson Hotel	Gilmour
20.02.09	Bethnal Green	York Hall	Hearn
21.02.09	Hull	KC Stadium	Greaves
21.02.09	Merthyr Tydfil	Rhydycar Leisure Centre	Calzaghe
23.02.09	Birmingham	Holiday Inn	Cowdell

27.02.09	Barnsley	The Metrodome	Maloney
27.02.09	Wolverhampton	Civic Hall	Rowson
27.02.09	Paisley	Lagoon Leisure Centre	Morrison
28.02.09	Birmingham	National Indoor Arena	Warren
28.02.09	Newcastle	Lightfoot Centre	Hyde
28.02.09	Norwich	The Showground	Hennessy
05.03.09	Limehouse	The Troxy	Helliet
06.03.09	Glasgow	Thistle Hotel	Morrison
06.03.09	Wigan	Robin Park Leisure Centre	Maloney
07.03.09	Birmingham	New Bingley Hall	Hobson (senior)
07.03.09	Chester	Northgate Arena	Greaves/Harrison
08.03.09	Sheffield	Grosvenor Hotel	Rhodes
13.03.09	Newport	Leisure Centre	J & C Sanigar
13.03.09	Widnes	Kingsway Leisure Centre	Hearn
14.03.09	Birmingham	Aston Arena	Hennessy
14.03.09	Aberdeen	Beach Ballroom	McAllister
14.03.09	Manchester	MEN Arena	Warren
14.03.09	Bristol	Marriot City Centre Hotel	Hatton
16.03.09	Glasgow	Radisson Hotel	Gilmour
20.03.09	Newham	Leisure Centre	Maloney
20.03.09	Bethnal Green	York Hall	Evans/Waterman
22.03.09	Bethnal Green	York Hall	Carter
24.03.09	Glasgow	Kelvin Hall	Hearn
27.03.09	Glasgow	Bellahouston Leisure Centre	Warren
27.03.09	Kensington	Town Hall	Fearon
28.03.09	Liverpool	Echo Arena	Booth
28.03.09	Lincoln	North Kesteven Leisure Centre	Greaves
28.03.09	Altrincham	Leisure Centre	Hatton
29.03.09	Sheffield	Bramall Lane Platinum Suite	Booth
29.03.09	Bolton	De Vere White's Hotel	Wood
03.04.09	Wolverhampton	Civic Hall	Rowson
03.04.09	Bethnal Green	York Hall	Hearn
03.04.09	Leigh	Indoor Sports Centre	Harrison
04.04.09	Coventry	Hilton Hotel	Allen
10.04.09	Birmingham	Holiday Inn	Pegg
10.04.09	Cheltenham	Town Hall	Mayo
11.04.09	Bethnal Green	York Hall	Hennessy
17.04.09	Leigh	Indoor Sports Centre	Maloney
17.04.09	Bristol	Thistle Hotel	Feld
23.04.09	Mayfair	Millenium Hotel	Helliet
23.04.09	Limehouse	The Troxy	Maloney
24.04.09	Sheffield	Don Valley Stadium	Rhodes
24.04.09	Wolverhampton	Civic Hall	Warren
25.04.09	Belfast	Ulster Hall	Booth
27.04.09	Glasgow	Radisson Hotel	Gilmour
01.05.09	Hartlepool	Seaton Carew Mayfair Suite	Garside
02.05.09	Sunderland	Crowtree Leisure Centre	Maloney
09.05.09	Lincoln	The Showground	Waterman
10.05.09	Derby	Heritage Hotel	Mitchell
14.05.09	Leeds	Elland Road Conference & Leisure Centre	Spratt/Bateson
15.05.09	Belfast	Odyssey Arena	Warren
17.05.09	Bolton	De Vere White's Hotel	Wood
18.05.09	Birmingham	Holiday Inn	Cowdell
19.05.09	Kensington	Earls Court Arena	Hearn
22.05.09	Bethnal Green	York Hall	Warren
23.05.09	Queensferry	Deeside Leisure Centre	Harrison
23.05.09	Sleaford	Northgate Leisure Centre	Greaves
23.05.09	Watford	The Colosseum	Hennessy
24.05.09	Bradford	Rio Grande Banqueting Hall	Margel

DIARY OF BRITISH BOXING TOURNAMENTS, 2008-2009

24.05.09	Shaw	Tara Sports & Leisure Centre	Doughty
29.05.09	Dudley	The Venue	Rowson
29.05.09	Stoke	Fenton Manor	Maloney
29.05.09	Glasgow	Thistle Hotel	Morrison
31.05.09	Burton	Meadowside Leisure Centre	Rowson
05.06.09	Newport	Leisure Centre	J & C Sanigar
06.06.09	Beverley	Leisure Complex	Greaves
08.06.09	Glasgow	Radisson Hotel	Gilmour
12.06.09	Wolverhampton	Civic Hall	Rowson
12.06.09	Clydebank	The Playdrome	Gilmour
12.06.09	Liverpool	Olympia	Hearn
12.06.09	Bethnal Green	York Hall	Helliet
13.06.09	Wigan	Robin Park Leisure Centre	Hennessy
13.06.09	Bristol	Marriott City Centre Hotel	Hatton
19.06.09	Glasgow	Bellahouston Leisure Centre	Warren
19.06.09	Aberdeen	Beach Ballroom	McAllister
21.06.09	Bethnal Green	York Hall	Carter
23.06.09	Longford	Heathrow Thistle Hotel	Carman
25.06.09	Glenrothes	Gilvanbank Hotel	C Gilmour
25.06.09	Mayfair	Millenium Hotel	Hobson
26.06.09	Melksham	Leisure Centre	Rowson
27.06.09	Portsmouth	Mountbatten Centre	Hatton
28.06.09	Luton	Liquid Envy Nightclub	Rowson
30.06.09	Bethnal Green	York Hall	Maloney

Active British-Based Boxers: Career Records

Shows the complete record for all British-based boxers who have been active between 1 July 2008 and 30 June 2009. Names in brackets are real names, where they differ from ring names, and the first place name given is the boxer's domicile. The given weight class for each boxer is based on the weights made for their last three contests and boxers are either shown as being self-managed or with a named manager, the information being supplied by the BBBoC shortly before going to press. Also included are foreign-born fighters who made their pro debuts in Britain, along with others like Shinny Bayaar (Mongolia), Yassine El Maachi (Morocco), Ayitey Powers (Ghana), Hastings Rasani (Zimbabwe), Harry Ramogoadi (South Africa), Sergei Rozhakmens (Latvia), Michal Skierniewski (Poland) and Albert Sosnowski (Poland), who, although starting their careers elsewhere, now hold BBBoC licenses. Former champions, such as Howard Eastman, Herbie Hide and Neil Sinclair, who continue their careers elsewhere, are also included.

Ojay Abrahams
Watford. *Born* Lambeth, 17 December, 1964
L.Heavyweight. Former British Masters Middleweight Champion. *Ht* 5' 8"
Manager Self
21.09.91 Gordon Webster W RSC 3 Tottenham
26.10.91 Mike Reed W RSC 5 Brentwood
26.11.91 John Corcoran W PTS 6 Bethnal Green
21.01.92 Dave Andrews DREW 6 Norwich
31.03.92 Marty Duke W RSC 2 Norwich
19.05.92 Michael Smyth L PTS 6 Cardiff
16.06.92 Ricky Mabbett W PTS 6 Dagenham
13.10.92 Vince Rose L RSC 3 Mayfair
30.01.93 Vince Rose DREW 6 Brentwood
19.05.93 Ricky Mabbett L RSC 4 Leicester
18.09.93 Ricky Mabbett L PTS 6 Leicester
09.12.93 Nick Appiah W PTS 6 Watford
24.01.94 Errol McDonald W RSC 2 Glasgow
09.02.94 Vince Rose W PTS 6 Brentwood
23.05.94 Spencer McCracken L PTS 6 Walsall
11.06.94 Darren Dyer W RSC 1 Bethnal Green
29.09.94 Gary Logan L PTS 10 Bethnal Green
(Southern Area Welterweight Title Challenge)
13.12.94 Geoff McCreesh L PTS 6 Potters Bar

Ojay Abrahams   Philip Sharkey

11.02.95 Gary Murray L PTS 8 Hammanskraal, South Africa
17.07.95 Andreas Panayi L PTS 8 Mayfair
02.10.95 Larbi Mohammed L RSC 5 Mayfair
08.12.95 Jason Beard W CO 2 Bethnal Green
09.04.96 Kevin Thompson W RSC 3 Stevenage
07.05.96 Harry Dhami L RSC 5 Mayfair
(Vacant Southern Area Welterweight Title)
12.11.96 Spencer McCracken L PTS 8 Dudley
22.04.97 Paul King W RSC 4 Bethnal Green
29.05.97 Paul Ryan L RSC 3 Mayfair
30.06.97 Ahmet Dottuev L RSC 4 Bethnal Green
08.11.97 Anthony McFadden L PTS 8 Southwark
24.03.98 Leigh Wicks W PTS 6 Bethnal Green
28.04.98 Jim Webb W RSC 2 Belfast
10.09.98 Delroy Leslie L PTS 10 Acton
(Vacant Southern Area L.Middleweight Title)
19.12.98 Michael Jones L PTS 6 Liverpool
23.01.99 Wayne Alexander L DIS 1 Cheshunt
(Vacant Southern Area L.Middleweight Title)
01.05.99 Wayne Alexander L RSC 3 Crystal Palace
26.06.99 Geoff McCreesh L PTS 8 Millwall
05.10.99 Hussain Osman L PTS 4 Bloomsbury
23.10.99 Paul Samuels L PTS 8 Telford
18.01.00 Howard Eastman L RSC 2 Mansfield
23.03.00 Pedro Thompson DREW 6 Bloomsbury
08.04.00 Anthony Farnell L PTS 8 Bethnal Green
16.05.00 Ryan Rhodes L PTS 6 Warrington
23.05.00 Alexandru Andrei L PTS 6 Levallois-Perret, France
04.07.00 Lester Jacobs L PTS 4 Tooting
21.09.00 Harry Butler W PTS 6 Bloomsbury
07.10.00 Kofi Jantuah L RSC 3 Doncaster
25.11.00 Donovan Smillie W RSC 2 Manchester
16.12.00 Marlon Hayes L PTS 6 Sheffield
15.01.01 Gordon Behan DREW 6 Manchester
24.02.01 Ruben Groenewald L PTS 6 Bethnal Green
22.04.01 Harry Butler W PTS 6 Streatham
17.05.01 Lee Murtagh W RSC 2 Leeds
(Vacant British Masters L. Middleweight Title)
21.06.01 Charden Ansoula L PTS 4 Kensington
28.07.01 Gary Logan L RSC 4 Wembley
10.12.01 Jimmy Vincent L PTS 10 Birmingham
(British Masters L. Middleweight Title Challenge)
28.01.02 Ian Cooper W PTS 6 Barnsley
16.03.02 John Humphrey L PTS 10 Bethnal Green
(Vacant Southern Area L.Middleweight Title)
13.04.02 Mihaly Kotai L PTS 6 Liverpool

20.04.02 Freeman Barr L PTS 8 Cardiff
10.05.02 Carl Froch L CO 1 Bethnal Green
15.06.02 Sam Soliman L PTS 4 Tottenham
17.08.02 Wayne Elcock L PTS 4 Cardiff
17.09.02 David Starie L RSC 4 Bethnal Green
25.10.02 Gilbert Eastman L PTS 4 Bethnal Green
12.12.02 Allan Gray L PTS 10 Leicester Square
(Vacant WBF Inter-Continental Middleweight Title. Southern Area Middleweight Title Challenge)
05.03.03 David Walker L PTS 6 Bethnal Green
19.04.03 Geard Ajetovic L PTS 4 Liverpool
12.05.03 Jason Collins L PTS 10 Birmingham
(Vacant British Masters S. Middleweight Title)
05.07.03 Allan Foster L PTS 4 Brentwood
18.09.03 Steve Roache W CO 2 Mayfair
18.10.03 Michael Jones L PTS 6 Manchester
22.11.03 Jason McKay L PTS 4 Belfast
01.12.03 Omar Gumati L PTS 6 Leeds
10.02.04 Daniel Teasdale L PTS 6 Barnsley
23.02.04 Matt Galer L PTS 6 Nottingham
08.03.04 Hamed Jamali L PTS 8 Birmingham
02.04.04 Scott Dann L RSC 6 Plymouth
06.05.04 Daniel Teasdale L PTS 4 Barnsley
13.05.04 Conroy McIntosh L RSC 2 Bethnal Green
12.06.04 Matthew Macklin L PTS 4 Manchester
10.09.04 Paul Smith L PTS 4 Liverpool
29.10.04 Tommy Cannon L PTS 4 Renfrew
12.11.04 Matthew Hall L CO 1 Halifax
27.01.05 Eder Kurti L PTS 6 Piccadilly
27.05.05 Paul Buchanan L PTS 6 Spennymoor
04.06.05 Ricardo Samms L PTS 4 Manchester
18.06.05 Jon Ibbotson L PTS 4 Barnsley
25.10.05 Ricardo Samms L PTS 4 Preston
24.11.05 Jason McKay L PTS 4 Lurgan
04.03.06 Tony Quigley L PTS 4 Manchester
20.03.06 Danny Thornton L PTS 6 Leeds
01.04.06 Richard Horton L PTS 4 Bethnal Green
14.05.06 Rod Anderton L PTS 6 Derby
27.05.06 Andrew Facey L PTS 6 Aberdeen
09.10.06 Neil Tidman L PTS 4 Bedworth
27.10.06 Ali Mateen L PTS 6 Glasgow
11.11.06 Adie Whitmore L PTS 6 Sutton in Ashfield
24.11.06 Darren Barker L RTD 1 Nottingham
02.03.07 Grzegorz Proksa L RTD 2 Neath
01.08.08 Jamie Ambler L DIS 1 Watford
Career: 100 contests, won 20, drew 4, lost 76.

Ali Adams
Chelsea. *Born* Baghdad, Iraq, 1 November, 1980
Heavyweight. *Ht* 6'4"
Manager Self

19.10.07 Tony Booth W PTS 4 Mayfair
01.12.07 Radcliffe Green L CO 4 Bethnal Green
16.05.08 Gareth Hearns L PTS 4 Holborn
07.10.08 Valentin Milosh W RSC 1 Minsk, Belarus
19.11.08 Lee Mountford W RSC 3 Bayswater
19.01.09 Jason Callum W PTS 4 Mayfair
20.03.09 Stas Belokon W PTS 4 Bethnal Green
25.06.09 Chris Woollas W PTS 6 Mayfair
Career: 8 contests, won 6, lost 2.

Rizza Ahmad

Leeds. *Born* Leeds, 18 November, 1981
Middleweight. *Ht* 6' 0"
Manager M.Bateson
14.05.09 Nathan Brook L RSC 1 Leeds
Career: 1 contest, lost 1.

Usman Ahmed

Derby. *Born* Derby, 21 November, 1981
Flyweight. *Ht* 5'6"
Manager M.Shinfield
30.09.06 Chris Edwards L PTS 6 Stoke
11.12.06 Delroy Spencer DREW 6 Cleethorpes
03.03.07 Gary Sheil W PTS 6 Alfreton
16.09.07 Gary Sheil W PTS 6 Derby
16.11.08 David Keogan W PTS 6 Derby
18.12.08 Luke Wilton W PTS 4 Dublin
17.04.09 Francis Croes W PTS 6 Leigh
29.05.09 Chris Edwards L PTS 12 Stoke
(Vacant British & Commonwealth Flyweight Titles)
Career: 8 contests, won 5, drew 1, lost 2.

Joey Ainscough

Liverpool. *Born* Liverpool, 16 August, 1979
L.Heavyweight. *Ht* 6'0"
Manager D. Hobson
27.11.99 Mark Dawson W PTS 4 Liverpool
05.02.00 Hussain Osman L PTS 4 Bethnal Green
25.03.00 Chris Crook W PTS 4 Liverpool
06.05.07 Mark Phillips W PTS 6 Altrincham
11.08.07 Ernie Smith W PTS 6 Liverpool
03.12.07 Paulino Da Silva L PTS 10 Manchester
(Vacant Central Area S.Middleweight Title)
23.02.08 Mark Nilsen W PTS 4 Liverpool
19.07.08 Robert Burton W PTS 4 Liverpool
29.03.09 Carl Wild DREW 4 Bolton
Career: 9 contests, won 6, drew 1, lost 2.

Tony Aitcheson

Dewsbury. Born Fife, 15 April, 1989
L.Welterweight. *Ht* 5' 7"
Manager S. Wood/C. Aston
17.05.09 Karl Taylor W PTS 6 Bolton
Career: 1 contest, won 1

Geard Ajetovic

Liverpool. *Born* Beocin, Yugoslavia, 28 February, 1981
S.Middleweight. *Ht* 5'8½"
Manager Self
19.04.03 Ojay Abrahams W PTS 4 Liverpool
17.05.03 Jason Samuels W PTS 4 Liverpool
26.09.03 Gary Beardsley W RSC 3 Reading
07.11.03 Joel Ani W RTD 1 Sheffield

06.02.04 Tomas da Silva W RSC 4 Sheffield
12.05.04 Dmitry Donetskiy W PTS 6 Reading
10.12.04 Conroy McIntosh W PTS 6 Sheffield
21.01.05 Dmitry Yanushevich W RSC 4 Brentford
24.07.05 Conroy McIntosh W PTS 6 Sheffield
14.10.05 Jason Collins W RSC 6 Huddersfield
26.11.05 Magid Ben Driss W PTS 8 Sheffield
18.03.06 Christophe Canclaux L PTS 8 Monte Carlo, Monaco
13.05.06 Manoocha Salari W RSC 4 Sheffield
27.04.07 Patrick J. Maxwell DREW 6 Wembley
29.05.07 Robert Roselia W PTS 10 Pont Audemer, France
13.07.07 Patrick J. Maxwell W RSC 3 Barnsley
14.11.07 Joey Vegas W RSC 4 Bethnal Green
08.02.08 Francis Cheka W PTS 8 Peterlee
27.06.08 Daniel Geale L PTS 12 Sydney, Australia
(Vacant IBO Middleweight Title)
19.07.08 Dmitry Pirog L PTS 10 Chekhov, Russia
31.10.08 Matthew Macklin L PTS 10 Birmingham
Career: 21 contests, won 16, drew 1, lost 4.

Bob Ajisafe

Darlington. *Born* Nottingham,13 April, 1985
L.Heavyweight. *Ht* 6'2¼"
Manager M. Marsden
18.11.07 Tom Owens W RSC 2 Birmingham
22.02.08 Victor Smith W PTS 4 Bethnal Green
26.04.08 Jamie Norkett W PTS 4 Darlington
09.05.08 Yanko Pavlov W PTS 4 Middlesbrough
25.07.08 Jamie Norkett W PTS 4 Houghton le Spring
05.09.08 Adie Whitmore W RSC 4 Nottingham
20.02.09 Carl Dilks L PTS 3 Bethnal Green
17.04.09 Ovill McKenzie W PTS 8 Leigh
Career: 8 contests, won 7, lost 1.

Eisa Al Dah

Bristol. *Born* Dubai, United Arab Emirates, 31 December, 1978
L.Welterweight. *Ht* 5' 6"
Manager C. Sanigar
24.03.07 Larry Foster W RSC 1 Dubai, United Arab Emirates
08.02.08 David Love W CO 1 Dubai, United Arab Emirates
24.10.08 Karl Taylor W PTS 6 Newport
23.01.09 Alfredo Valdes L RSC 2 Polanco, Mexico
21.02.09 Wayne Downing W PTS 6 Merthyr Tydfil
13.03.09 Steve Cooper W CO 2 Newport
Career: 6 contests, won 5, lost 1.

Mark Alexander

Hackney. *Born* Hackney, 18 November, 1975
Lightweight. *Ht* 5' 9"
Manager P. Fondu
10.04.01 Steve Hanley W PTS 4 Wembley
31.07.01 Damien Dunnion W PTS 4 Bethnal Green
19.12.01 Dazzo Williams L PTS 6 Coventry
15.05.03 Buster Dennis W PTS 4 Mayfair
01.08.03 Arv Mittoo W PTS 4 Bethnal Green
25.09.03 Henry Castle L PTS 6 Bethnal Green

01.11.03 John Simpson L PTS 4 Glasgow
19.11.05 Graeme Higginson W PTS 4 Southwark
21.05.06 Steve Gethin W PTS 4 Bethnal Green
21.10.06 Shaun Walton W PTS 6 Southwark
27.03.09 Robin Deakin W PTS 4 Kensington
Career: 11 contests, won 8, lost 3.

Mark Alexander   Philip Sharkey

Anwar Alfadi

Sheffield. *Born* Kuwait, 18 October, 1987
Bantamweight. *Ht* 5' 3"
Manager J. Ingle
14.03.09 Craig Lyon L PTS 4 Manchester
15.05.09 Luke Wilton DREW 6 Belfast
24.05.09 Tasif Khan DREW 4 Bradford
12.06.09 John Donnelly L PTS 6 Liverpool
Career: 4 contests, drew 2, lost 2.

Youssef Al Hamidi

Dewsbury. *Born* Syria, 16 December, 1977
Lightweight. *Ht* 5'5"
Manager C.Aston
05.10.06 Paul Holborn L PTS 6 Sunderland
28.10.06 Dwayne Hill W RSC 3 Sheffield
17.11.06 Akaash Bhatia L PTS 4 Bethnal Green
03.12.06 Paul Halpin W PTS 4 Bethnal Green
26.01.07 Clifford Smith DREW 4 Dagenham
09.03.07 Lee Cook L PTS 6 Dagenham
24.06.07 Michael Gomez L RTD 3 Wigan
03.11.07 Ricky Burns L PTS 6 Cardiff
25.11.07 Carl Allen W PTS 6 Colne
15.12.07 John Simpson L PTS 8 Edinburgh
08.02.08 Michael Hunter L PTS 6 Peterlee
20.03.08 George Watson L PTS 6 South Shields
05.04.08 Anthony Crolla W PTS 8 Bolton
10.05.08 John Murray L PTS 8 Nottingham
17.05.08 Scott Lawton L PTS 5 Stoke
26.09.08 Anthony Crolla L PTS 6 Bethnal Green
07.11.08 Mark Moran L PTS 6 Wigan
06.12.08 Liam Walsh L PTS 4 Canning Town
21.12.08 Lee Jennings W PTS 6 Bolton
21.02.09 Jamie Arthur L PTS 6 Merthyr Tydfil
14.03.09 Steve Bell L PTS 6 Manchester
27.03.09 Andy Morris L PTS 4 Glasgow
02.05.09 Paul Holborn L PTS 6 Sunderland

22.05.09 Vinny Mitchell L PTS 4 Bethnal Green
29.05.09 Chris Riley L PTS 4 Stoke
12.06.09 Tony Owen L PTS 4 Bethnal Green
Career: 26 contests, won 5, drew 1, lost 20.

Nasser Al Harbi

Birmingham. *Born* Birmingham, 20 June, 1989
Middleweight. *Ht* 5'11¼"
Manager P. Rowson
13.04.08 Ernie Smith W PTS 4 Edgbaston
30.05.08 Paul Royston W PTS 6 Birmingham
14.09.08 Matt Scriven W PTS 4 Birmingham
17.10.08 Lloyd Creighton W PTS 6 Swindon
14.11.08 Davey Jones W PTS 6 Birmingham
07.03.09 Danny Maka W PTS 6 Birmingham
29.05.09 Kevin McCauley W PTS 6 Dudley
Career: 7 contests, won 7.

Nasser Al Harbi   Philip Sharkey

Najah Ali

London. *Born* Baghdad, Iraq, 9 May, 1980
Flyweight. *Ht* 5'2¼"
Manager F. Joseph
15.06.08 David Keogan W RSC 1 Bethnal Green
19.01.09 Delroy Spencer W PTS 4 Mayfair
20.03.09 Shaun Walton W PTS 4 Bethnal Green
Career: 3 contests, won 3.

Syed Ali

Bristol. *Born* India, 3 July, 1980
L.Middleweight. *Ht* 5' 11"
Manager C. Sanigar
05.09.08 Liam Anthony L PTS 4 Nottingham
20.09.08 Mark Walsh DREW 6 Newark
16.11.08 Johnny Creamer L PTS 4 Southampton
Career: 3 contests, drew 1, lost 2.

Carl Allen

Wolverhampton. *Born* Wolverhampton, 20 November, 1969
L.Welterweight. Former Undefeated Midlands Area S. Bantamweight Champion.
Ht 5'7¼"
Manager P. Bowen

26.11.95 Gary Jenkinson W PTS 6 Birmingham
29.11.95 Jason Squire L PTS 6 Solihull
17.01.96 Andy Robinson L PTS 6 Solihull
13.02.96 Ervine Blake W RSC 5 Wolverhampton
21.02.96 Ady Benton L PTS 6 Batley
29.02.96 Chris Jickells W PTS 6 Scunthorpe
27.03.96 Jason Squire DREW 6 Whitwick
26.04.96 Paul Griffin L RSC 3 Cardiff
30.05.96 Roger Brotherhood W RSC 5 Lincoln
26.09.96 Matthew Harris W PTS 10 Walsall
          (Midlands Area S. Bantamweight Title Challenge)
07.10.96 Emmanuel Clottey L RTD 3 Lewisham
21.11.96 Miguel Matthews W PTS 8 Solihull
30.11.96 Floyd Havard L RTD 3 Tylorstown
29.01.97 Pete Buckley W PTS 8 Stoke
11.02.97 David Morris DREW 8 Wolverhampton
28.02.97 Ian McLeod L RTD 3 Kilmarnock
21.05.97 David Burke L PTS 4 Liverpool
30.06.97 Duke McKenzie L PTS 8 Bethnal Green
12.09.97 Brian Carr L PTS 8 Glasgow
04.10.97 Sergei Devakov L PTS 6 Muswell Hill
03.12.97 Chris Lyons W PTS 8 Stoke
21.05.98 Roy Rutherford L PTS 6 Solihull
09.06.98 Scott Harrison L RSC 6 Hull
30.11.98 Gary Hibbert L PTS 4 Manchester
09.12.98 Chris Jickells W RSC 3 Stoke
04.02.99 Mat Zegan L PTS 4 Lewisham
17.03.99 Craig Spacie W PTS 8 Stoke
08.05.99 Philip Ndou L RSC 2 Bethnal Green
14.06.99 Pete Buckley W PTS 6 Birmingham
22.06.99 David Lowry L PTS 4 Ipswich
11.10.99 Lee Williamson L PTS 6 Birmingham
19.10.99 Tontcho Tontchev L CO 2 Bethnal Green
20.12.99 Nicky Cook L CO 3 Bethnal Green
08.02.00 Lee Williamson W PTS 8 Wolverhampton
29.02.00 Bradley Pryce L PTS 4 Widnes
28.03.00 Lee Williamson W PTS 8 Wolverhampton
16.05.00 Bradley Pryce L RSC 3 Warrington
24.06.00 Michael Gomez L CO 2 Glasgow
10.10.00 Steve Hanley W PTS 8 Brierley Hill
05.02.01 Lee Meager DREW 6 Hull
12.03.01 Pete Buckley W PTS 6 Birmingham
27.03.01 Pete Buckley W PTS 8 Brierley Hill
15.09.01 Esham Pickering L PTS 6 Derby
17.11.01 Steve Conway L PTS 8 Dewsbury
08.12.01 Esham Pickering L PTS 8 Chesterfield

Syed Ali   Philip Sharkey

07.02.02 Mark Bowen L PTS 6 Stoke
20.04.02 Esham Pickering L PTS 6 Derby
21.07.02 Eddie Nevins L PTS 4 Salford
07.09.02 Colin Toohey DREW 6 Liverpool
26.10.02 Dazzo Williams W RSC 2 Maesteg
02.12.02 Esham Pickering L PTS 6 Leicester
28.01.03 Lee Meager L PTS 8 Nottingham
09.05.03 Jeff Thomas DREW 6 Doncaster
08.11.03 Baz Carey W RSC 2 Coventry
28.11.03 Carl Greaves L PTS 4 Derby
28.02.04 Michael Kelly L PTS 4 Bridgend
03.04.04 Andy Morris L PTS 4 Manchester
16.04.04 Dave Stewart L PTS 6 Bradford
17.06.04 Scott Lawton L PTS 10 Sheffield
          (Vacant Midlands Area Lightweight Title)
03.09.04 Gavin Rees L PTS 6 Newport
22.10.04 Craig Johnson L PTS 6 Mansfield
12.11.04 Billy Corcoran L RSC 5 Wembley
13.12.04 Jonathan Thaxton L RSC 1 Birmingham
05.03.05 Ryan Barrett L PTS 4 Dagenham
15.05.05 Scott Lawton L PTS 6 Sheffield
18.06.05 Joe McCluskey L PTS 6 Coventry
16.09.05 Stefy Bull L PTS 10 Doncaster
          (Vacant WBF Inter-Continental Lightweight Title)
13.11.05 Carl Johanneson L RTD 2 Leeds
17.02.06 Dwayne Hill L PTS 6 Sheffield
25.02.06 Damian Owen L PTS 6 Bristol
10.03.06 Martin Gethin L PTS 4 Walsall
25.03.06 Haider Ali DREW 4 Burton
21.05.06 Andrew Murray L PTS 4 Bethnal Green
01.06.06 Tristan Davies L PTS 6 Birmingham
22.09.06 Ben Jones L PTS 4 Bethnal Green
13.10.06 Stefy Bull L PTS 6 Doncaster
10.11.06 Tristan Davies L PTS 10 Telford
          (Vacant Midlands Area Lightweight Title)
09.02.07 Henry Castle L RSC 4 Leeds
20.04.07 Martin Gethin DREW 6 Dudley
27.05.07 Femi Fehintola L PTS 6 Bradford
16.06.07 Garry Buckland L PTS 6 Newport
15.07.07 Mark Dawes L PTS 4 Hartlepool
15.09.07 Billy Smith L PTS 10 Birmingham
          (Vacant Midlands Area L.Welterweight Title)
17.11.07 Scott Lawton L PTS 6 Stoke
25.11.07 Youssef Al Hamidi L PTS 6 Colne
08.12.07 Gary Sykes L PTS 6 Wigan
25.01.08 Martin Gethin L PTS 6 Dagenham
15.02.08 Dwayne Hill L PTS 6 Sheffield
23.02.08 Amir Unsworth L PTS 4 Newark
14.03.08 Steve Bell L PTS 6 Manchester
10.05.08 Dave Ryan L PTS 4 Nottingham
06.06.08 Chris Goodwin L PTS 4 Stoke
15.06.08 Rick Godding L PTS 6 St Helens
22.06.08 Dave Ryan L PTS 8 Derby
05.09.08 Tyrone Nurse L PTS 4 Nottingham
28.09.08 Tyrone Nurse L PTS 4 Colne
10.10.08 Anthony Crolla L PTS 6 Liverpool
07.11.08 Karl Place L PTS 4 Wigan
24.01.09 Scott Quigg L PTS 4 Blackpool
06.02.09 Rob Hunt L PTS 4 Birmingham
14.03.09 Anthony Crolla L PTS 6 Manchester
28.03.09 Ben Lawler L PTS 4 Lincoln
17.05.09 Rick Godding L PTS 4 Bolton
24.05.09 Graeme Higginson L PTS 6 Shaw
31.05.09 Jack Perry L PTS 4 Burton
12.06.09 Chris Lewis L PTS 4 Wolverhampton
Career: 106 contests, won 18, drew 7, lost 81.

77

Peter Allen

Birkenhead. *Born* Birkenhead, 13 August, 1978
Lightweight. *Ht* 5'5½"
Manager Self
30.04.98 Sean Grant L PTS 6 Pentre Halkyn
21.06.98 Garry Burrell W PTS 6 Liverpool
20.09.98 Simon Chambers L PTS 6 Sheffield
16.11.98 Stevie Kane W PTS 6 Glasgow
07.12.98 Simon Chambers L PTS 6 Bradford
28.02.99 Amjid Mahmood L PTS 6 Shaw
12.03.99 Marc Callaghan L PTS 4 Bethnal Green
15.09.99 Steve Brook L PTS 6 Harrogate
07.10.99 Nicky Wilders L PTS 6 Sunderland
18.10.99 Mark Hudson L PTS 6 Bradford
15.11.99 Craig Docherty L RSC 1 Glasgow
09.12.01 Jeff Thomas L PTS 6 Blackpool
01.03.02 Andrew Ferrans L PTS 8 Irvine
15.03.02 Ricky Burns L PTS 6 Glasgow
17.04.02 Andrew Smith W PTS 6 Stoke
24.06.02 Tasawar Khan L PTS 6 Bradford
14.09.02 Carl Greaves L PTS 6 Newark
08.10.02 Andrew Ferrans L PTS 8 Glasgow
21.10.02 Tony McPake L PTS 6 Glasgow
17.11.02 Choi Tseveenpurev L RSC 4 Shaw
16.02.03 Darryn Walton L PTS 6 Salford
31.05.03 Mally McIver L PTS 6 Barnsley
29.08.03 Steve Mullin L PTS 6 Liverpool
25.04.04 Craig Johnson L PTS 6 Nottingham
08.05.04 Michael Graydon L PTS 6 Bristol
30.05.04 Willie Valentine W PTS 4 Dublin
10.09.04 Steve Mullin L PTS 4 Liverpool
05.11.04 Damian Owen L RSC 1 Hereford
04.03.05 Isaac Ward DREW 6 Hartlepool
10.04.05 Lloyd Otte L PTS 6 Brentwood
30.04.05 Eddie Nevins W PTS 6 Wigan
25.09.05 Carl Johanneson L RTD 9 Leeds
     (Vacant Central Area S.Featherweight Title)
16.06.06 David Appleby DREW 4 Liverpool
21.07.06 Chris Pacy L RSC 2 Altrincham
24.09.06 Henry Castle L RSC 6 Southampton
07.03.08 Barrington Brown L PTS 4 Nottingham
28.03.08 Gary Sykes L PTS 6 Barnsley
18.04.08 Akaash Bhatia L PTS 6 Bethnal Green
19.07.08 Scott Quigg L RSC 1 Liverpool
Career: 39 contests, won 5, drew 2, lost 32.

Peter Allen   Philip Sharkey

Sherman Alleyne

Bedford. *Born* London, 3 October, 1976
Middleweight. *Ht* 5'5"
Manager Self
24.09.06 Greg Barton L RSC 3 Bethnal Green
17.03.07 Max Maxwell L PTS 6 Birmingham
15.04.07 Jon Musgrave L PTS 6 Barnsley
26.04.07 Prince Arron L PTS 6 Manchester
01.06.07 Rocky Muscas W PTS 6 Peterborough
21.07.07 Kerry Hope L PTS 6 Cardiff
07.09.07 Denton Vassell L RSC 1 Mayfair
19.10.07 Danny Goode L PTS 4 Mayfair
02.03.08 Steve Ede L PTS 6 Portsmouth
22.03.08 Stuart Brookes L PTS 6 Sheffield
16.05.08 Gokhan Kazaz L PTS 4 Holborn
02.10.08 Sam Horton L RSC 4 Piccadilly
13.12.08 Matthew Thirlwall L RSC 4 Brentwood
13.02.09 Marlon Reid L RSC 3 Swindon
Career: 14 contests, won 1, lost 13.

Luke Allon

Hull. *Born* Plymouth, 8 March, 1986
Middleweight. *Ht* 6' 1"
Manager J. Phelan
11.10.08 Dave Pearson W RTD 2 Hull
21.02.09 James Tucker W PTS 6 Hull
06.06.09 Patrick Mendy L PTS 6 Beverley
Career: 3 contests, won 2, lost 1.

Wayne Alwan Arab   Philip Sharkey

Wayne Alwan Arab

Hackney. *Born* Zimbabwe, 28 February, 1982
Middleweight. *Ht* 5'10"
Manager M. Helliet
01.02.07 Peter Dunn W PTS 6 Piccadilly
04.10.07 Peter Dunn W PTS 6 Piccadilly
28.11.07 Mark Phillips W PTS 4 Piccadilly
10.04.08 Steve Cooper W PTS 6 Piccadilly
02.10.08 Matt Scriven W PTS 6 Piccadilly
29.01.09 Tye Williams W RSC 4 Holborn
05.03.09 Jason Nesbitt W PTS 6 Limehouse
23.04.09 Paul Royston W PTS 6 Mayfair
12.06.09 Chris Thompson W PTS 6 Bethnal Green
Career: 9 contests, won 9.

Jamie Ambler

Aberystwyth. *Born* Aberystwyth, 16 January 1985
L.Heavyweight. *Ht* 6'2½"
Manager N. Hodges
12.11.05 Liam Stinchcombe W RTD 3 Bristol
12.12.05 Jason Welborn L RSC 1 Birmingham
10.02.06 Jon Harrison L PTS 4 Plymouth
07.04.06 Danny Goode L PTS 4 Longford
21.04.06 Scott Jordan L PTS 4 Belfast
16.09.06 Jonjo Finnegan L PTS 6 Burton
24.09.06 Paul Morby L PTS 4 Southampton
03.11.06 Kenny Davidson W PTS 6 Glasgow
10.12.06 Stuart Brookes L RSC 1 Sheffield
16.02.07 Shon Davies L PTS 6 Merthyr Tydfil
26.03.07 Ricky Strike W CO 6 Glasgow
07.04.07 Kerry Hope L PTS 6 Cardiff
22.09.07 Martin Murray L PTS 6 Wigan
06.10.07 Tony Bellew L RSC 2 Nottingham
28.11.07 Matthew Hough DREW 4 Walsall
08.12.07 Alex Matvienko L PTS 4 Wigan
23.12.07 Nigel Travis W PTS 6 Bolton
03.02.08 Robert Boardman L PTS 6 Bristol
15.02.08 Jezz Wilson L PTS 6 Sheffield
29.02.08 Steve McGuire L PTS 6 Glasgow
30.03.08 David Gentles L PTS 6 Port Talbot
13.04.08 Joe Rea L PTS 4 Edgbaston
02.05.08 Danny Butler L CO 2 Bristol
27.06.08 Dwayne Lewis L RSC 2 Bethnal Green
01.08.08 Ojay Abrahams W DIS 1 Watford
28.09.08 Ally Morrison L PTS 6 Colne
12.10.08 Carl Dilks L PTS 4 Leigh
31.10.08 Tariq Quaddas L PTS 4 Birmingham
05.12.08 Mike Stanton L PTS 4 Dagenham
21.12.08 Yassine El Maachi L RSC 3 Motherwell
01.02.09 Llewellyn Davies L PTS 4 Birmingham
21.02.09 Paul Samuels L PTS 4 Merthyr Tydfil
14.03.09 Danny Gwilym L PTS 4 Bristol
03.04.09 Sam Horton L PTS 6 Wolverhampton
10.04.09 Joe Skeldon W PTS 4 Cheltenham
24.04.09 Darren McDermott L PTS 6 Wolverhampton
17.05.09 Mick Jenno L PTS 4 Bolton
12.06.09 Jack Morris L PTS 4 Bethnal Green
25.06.09 Gordon Brennan DREW 6 Glenrothes
Career: 39 contests, won 6, drew 2, lost 31.

James Ancliff

Fettercairn. *Born* Perth, 26 February, 1984
Featherweight. *Ht* 5'5"
Manager A. Morrison/F. Warren
22.04.06 Mickey Coveney L PTS 6 Glasgow
28.10.06 John Baguley W PTS 6 Aberdeen
10.12.06 Neil Marston W PTS 6 Glasgow
26.05.07 John Baguley W PTS 6 Aberdeen
01.12.07 Mark Bett DREW 6 Liverpool
09.12.07 Michael Crossan W RSC 1 Glasgow
14.03.08 Buster Dennis L RSC 3 Glasgow
17.05.08 Cristian Nicolae W PTS 6 Glasgow
26.09.08 Rocky Dean L PTS 4 Bethnal Green
25.10.08 Shaun Walton W PTS 6 Aberdeen
27.03.09 Kris Hughes L PTS 4 Glasgow
03.04.09 Ricky Owen L PTS 6 Bethnal Green
25.04.09 Michael Maguire L PTS 4 Belfast
29.05.09 Santino Caruana L PTS 4 Glasgow
19.06.09 Kris Hughes L PTS 6 Glasgow
Career: 15 contests, won 6, drew 1, lost 8.

James Ancliff   Philip Sharkey

Kenny Anderson

Edinburgh. *Born* 5 January, 1983
L.Heavyweight. *Ht* 5'11½"
Manager Self
14.10.06 Nick Okoth W RSC 4 Manchester
07.04.07 Jorge Gomez W RSC 3 Cardiff
21.07.07 Dean Walker W RSC 2 Cardiff
17.11.07 Shon Davies W RSC 3 Glasgow
15.12.07 Simeon Cover W CO 6 Edinburgh
29.03.08 Dean Walker W RTD 4 Glasgow
12.09.08 Roman Vanicky W PTS 6 Mayfair
18.10.08 Jevgenijs Andrejevs W PTS 6 Paisley
14.11.08 Hastings Rasani W RSC 3 Glasgow
27.03.09 Nathan King W PTS 10 Glasgow
           (Vacant Celtic S.Middleweight Title)
Career: 10 contests, won 10.

Rod Anderton

Nottingham. *Born* Nottingham, 17 August,
1978
Former Undefeated International Masters
L.Heavyweight Champion. *Ht* 5'11¾"
Manager M. Shinfield
22.04.05 Michael Pinnock W PTS 6 Barnsley
18.06.05 Nicki Taylor W RSC 4 Barnsley
02.09.05 Paul Billington W RTD 1 Derby
08.12.05 Gary Thompson W PTS 6 Derby
28.01.06 Nick Okoth W PTS 4 Nottingham
14.05.06 Ojay Abrahams W PTS 6 Derby
06.10.06 Richard Turba L RSC 2 Mansfield
24.11.06 Philip Callaghan W RSC 4 Nottingham
03.03.07 Michael Monaghan L PTS 10 Alfreton
           *(Vacant Midlands Area L.Heavyweight
           Title)*
23.03.07 Philip Callaghan DREW 4 Nottingham
13.07.07 Carl Wild W PTS 4 Barnsley
21.09.07 Dean Walker W PTS 6 Burton
07.03.08 Mark Nilsen W PTS 4 Nottingham
16.05.08 Hamed Jamali W PTS 10 Burton
           *(Vacant International Masters
           L.Heavyweight Title)*
06.12.08 Danny McIntosh L RSC 1 Nottingham
           (English L.Heavyweight Title Challenge)
Career: 15 contests, won 11, drew 1, lost 3.

John Anthony

Doncaster. *Born* Doncaster, 16 October,
1974
Cruiserweight. *Ht* 5'11½"
Manager D. Coldwell
22.04.05 Gary Thompson W PTS 4 Barnsley
18.06.05 Lee Mountford W RSC 5 Barnsley
04.11.05 Sandy Robb L PTS 6 Glasgow
12.02.06 Lee Kellett W RSC 1 Manchester
03.06.06 Andrew Lowe L PTS 6 Chigwell
01.10.06 Clint Johnson W PTS 6 Rotherham
02.03.07 Andrew Young W RSC 1 Irvine
17.03.07 Alexander Alexeev L RSC 5 Stuttgart,
           Germany
15.04.07 JJ Ojuederie L PTS 6 Barnsley
27.04.07 Tony Salam L PTS 4 Wembley
18.05.07 Micky Steeds L PTS 6 Canning
           Town
31.10.07 Vadim Usenko L PTS 6 Bayswater
09.11.07 Kelly Oliver W RSC 5 Nottingham
01.12.07 Neil Simpson L PTS 4 Coventry
23.02.08 Santander Silgado L RSC 2 Halle,
           Germany
23.01.09 Jon-Lewis Dickinson L PTS 4 Stoke
Career: 16 contests, won 6, lost 10.

Liam Anthony

Derby. *Born* Derby, 5 March, 1985
L.Middleweight. *Ht* 5'10"
Manager M. Shinfield
28.06.08 Billy Smith W PTS 6 Leicester
05.09.08 Syed Ali W PTS 4 Nottingham
Career: 2 contests, won 2.

Adil Anwar

Leeds. *Born* Leeds, 6 July, 1987
L.Welterweight. *Ht* 5'9¾"
Manager M. Bateson
14.06.07 Craig Tomes W PTS 6 Leeds
15.11.07 Graeme Higginson L PTS 6 Leeds
21.02.08 Steve Cooper W PTS 6 Leeds
05.06.08 Scott Sandmann W RSC 1 Leeds
27.11.08 Ernie Smith W PTS 6 Leeds
14.05.09 Johnny Greaves W RSC 4 Leeds
Career: 6 contests, won 5, lost 1.

Paul Appleby

Edinburgh. *Born* Edinburgh, 22 July, 1987
Former British Featherweight Champion.
Ht 5'9"
Manager T. Gilmour
23.01.06 Graeme Higginson W RTD 3 Glasgow
17.03.06 Ian Reid W RSC 3 Kirkcaldy
28.04.06 Andy Davis W RSC 1 Hartlepool
01.06.06 Graeme Higginson W RSC 2
           Birmingham
22.09.06 Mickey Coveney W PTS 6 Bethnal
           Green
15.12.06 Rakhim Mingaleev W PTS 4 Bethnal
           Green
16.02.07 Buster Dennis W PTS 8 Kirkcaldy
11.05.07 Istvan Nagy W RSC 5 Motherwell
12.10.07 Riaz Durgahed W RSC 3 Peterlee
02.11.07 Ben Odamattey W RSC 6 Irvine
29.02.08 Ferenc Szabo W RSC 3 Glasgow
06.06.08 John Simpson W PTS 12 Glasgow
           (British Featherweight Title Challenge)

28.11.08 Esham Pickering W PTS 12 Glasgow
           (British Featherweight Title Defence)
13.03.09 Juan Garcia Martin W RSC 1 Widnes
25.04.09 Martin Lindsay L RSC 6 Belfast
           (British Featherweight Title Defence)
Career: 15 contests, won 14, lost 1.

Callum Archer

Birmingham. *Born* Solihull, 14 September,
1989
Welterweight. *Ht* 5'9¼"
Manager P. Lynch
12.05.08 Russell Pearce DREW 6 Birmingham
06.10.08 Danny Coyle W RSC 1 Birmingham
08.12.08 Byron Vince W RSC 1 Birmingham
23.02.09 JJ Bird L PTS 8 Birmingham
14.03.09 Jason Nesbitt W PTS 4 Birmingham
18.05.09 Kevin McCauley W PTS 8 Birmingham
Career: 6 contests, won 4, drew 1, lost 1.

Jack Arnfield

Blackpool. *Born* Buxton, 22 May, 1989
L.Middleweight. *Ht* 6'2¼"
Manager S. Wood
26.10.07 Lewis Byrne W RSC 1 Wigan
25.11.07 Lance Verallo W RSC 4 Colne
08.12.07 Ben Hudson W PTS 4 Wigan
16.02.08 David Kirk W PTS 6 Blackpool
30.03.08 Billy Smith W PTS 6 Colne
23.05.08 Terry Adams W RSC 3 Wigan
14.09.08 Jon Harrison W PTS 4 Wigan
22.11.08 Paul Royston W PTS 4 Blackpool
06.03.09 Dee Mitchell W PTS 4 Wigan
17.04.09 Paul Morby W PTS 4 Leigh
Career: 10 contests, won 10.

Dean Arnold

Wednesbury. *Born* Sandwell, 10 March,
1990
L.Welterweight. *Ht* 5'7¼"
Manager E. Johnson
12.05.08 Kristian Laight W PTS 6 Birmingham
26.09.08 Pete Buckley W PTS 4 Wolverhampton
26.11.08 Bheki Moyo W PTS 6 Piccadilly
Career: 3 contests, won 3.

Dean Arnold   Philip Sharkey

79

Prince Arron

Droylsden. *Born* Crumpsall, 27 December, 1987
Former Undefeated British Masters Middleweight Champion. *Ht* 6'3"
Manager T. Gilmour
28.04.06 Tommy Jones W PTS 6 Manchester
18.06.06 Karl Taylor W PTS 6 Manchester
10.07.06 Geraint Harvey W PTS 6 Manchester
11.09.06 Martin Marshall W PTS 6 Manchester
21.10.06 Anthony Small L RSC 2 Southwark
23.11.06 Rocky Muscas W PTS 6 Manchester
03.12.06 Danny Reynolds L PTS 6 Wakefield
18.02.07 George Katsimpas W PTS 8 Bethnal Green
26.04.07 Sherman Alleyne W PTS 6 Manchester
29.06.07 Cello Renda W PTS 10 Manchester
  (Vacant British Masters Middleweight Title)
22.09.07 Olufemi Moses W PTS 6 Coventry
12.10.07 Martin Marshall W PTS 4 Peterlee
20.10.07 John Duddy L RSC 2 Dublin
03.10.08 Tony Randell W RSC 4 Burton
06.02.09 Dee Mitchell W PTS 6 Birmingham
28.03.09 Danny Gwilym W PTS 4 Altrincham
Career: 16 contests, won 13, lost 3.

Alex Arthur

Edinburgh. *Born* Edinburgh, 26 June, 1978
Former WBO S.Featherweight Champion. Former Undefeated British, Commonwealth, European, WBO Inter-Continental, WBA Inter-Continental & IBF Inter-Continental S.Featherweight Champion. Former British S.Featherweight Champion. *Ht* 5'9"
Manager F Warren
25.11.00 Richmond Asante W RSC 1 Manchester
10.02.01 Eddie Nevins W RSC 1 Widnes
26.03.01 Woody Greenaway W RTD 2 Wembley
28.04.01 Dafydd Carlin W PTS 4 Cardiff
21.07.01 Rakhim Mingaleev W PTS 4 Sheffield
15.09.01 Dimitri Gorodetsky W RSC 1 Manchester
27.10.01 Alexei Slyautchin W RSC 1 Manchester
17.11.01 Laszlo Bognar W RSC 3 Glasgow
19.01.02 Vladimir Borov W RSC 2 Bethnal Green
11.03.02 Dariusz Snarski W RSC 10 Glasgow
  (Vacant IBF Inter-Continental S.Featherweight Title)
08.06.02 Nikolai Eremeev W RTD 5 Renfrew
  (Vacant WBO Inter-Continental S.Featherweight Title)
17.08.02 Pavel Potipko W CO 1 Cardiff
19.10.02 Steve Conway W CO 4 Renfrew
  (Vacant British S. Featherweight Title)
14.12.02 Carl Greaves W RSC 6 Newcastle
  (British S.Featherweight Title Defence)
22.03.03 Patrick Malinga W RSC 6 Renfrew
  (Vacant WBA Inter-Continental S.Featherweight Title)
12.07.03 Willie Limond W RSC 8 Renfrew
  (British S.Featherweight Title Defence)
25.10.03 Michael Gomez L RSC 5 Edinburgh
  (British S.Featherweight Title Defence)
27.03.04 Michael Kizza W CO 1 Edinburgh
  (Vacant IBF Inter-Continental S.Featherweight Title)
22.10.04 Eric Odumasi W RSC 6 Edinburgh *(IBF Inter-Continental S.Featherweight Title Defence)*
03.12.04 Nazareno Ruiz W PTS 12 Edinburgh
  (IBF Inter-Continental S.Featherweight Title Defence)
08.04.05 Craig Docherty W CO 9 Edinburgh
  (Vacant British S.Featherweight Title. Commonwealth S.Featherweight Title Challenge)
23.07.05 Boris Sinitsin W PTS 12 Edinburgh
  (European S.Featherweight Title Challenge)
18.02.06 Ricky Burns W PTS 12 Edinburgh
  (British, Commonwealth & European S.Featherweight Title Defences)
29.04.06 Sergey Gulyakevich W TD 7 Edinburgh
  (European S.Featherweight Title Defence)
04.11.06 Sergio Palomo W RSC 5 Glasgow
  (European S.Featherweight Title Defence)
21.07.07 Koba Gogoladze W RSC 10 Cardiff
  (Vacant WBO Interim S.Featherweight Title)
15.12.07 Steve Foster W PTS 12 Edinburgh
  (WBO Interim S.Featherweight Title Defence)
06.09.08 Nicky Cook L PTS 12 Manchester
  (WBO S.Featherweight Title Defence)
19.06.09 Mohamed Benbiou W RSC 1 Glasgow
Career: 29 contests, won 27, lost 2.

Jamie Arthur

Cwmbran. *Born* Aberdeen, 17 December, 1979
Welsh Area S.Featherweight Champion. *Ht* 5'9¼"
Manager C. Sanigar
22.03.03 Daniel Thorpe W PTS 4 Renfrew
28.06.03 James Gorman W PTS 4 Cardiff
13.09.03 Dave Hinds W RTD 1 Newport
11.10.03 Dafydd Carlin W RSC 4 Portsmouth
15.11.03 Andrei Mircea W RSC 3 Bayreuth, Germany
06.12.03 Jus Wallie W PTS 4 Cardiff
27.03.04 Karl Taylor W PTS 4 Edinburgh
03.07.04 Frederic Bonifai W PTS 6 Newport
03.09.04 Buster Dennis W PTS 6 Newport
21.01.05 Haider Ali L RSC 3 Bridgend
23.07.05 Harry Ramogoadi L RSC 5 Edinburgh
05.04.08 Ayittey Mettle W PTS 6 Newport
12.07.08 Dai Davies W CO 2 Newport
  (Welsh Area S.Featherweight Title Challenge)
26.11.08 Steve Gethin W PTS 4 Piccadilly
21.02.09 Youssef Al Hamidi W PTS 6 Merthyr Tydfil
13.03.09 Andrey Kostin W PTS 6 Newport
30.06.09 Akaash Bhatia W PTS 10 Bethnal Green
  (Elim. British Featherweight Title)
Career: 17 contests, won 15, lost 2.

Jamie Arthur   Philip Sharkey

Darren Askew

Manchester. *Born* Whiehaven, 15 November, 1984
Welterweight. *Ht* 5'9¼"
Manager J. Pennington
07.10.07 Pete Buckley W PTS 6 Shaw
10.11.07 Amir Nadi W PTS 6 Stalybridge
23.11.07 Joe Elfidh L PTS 6 Rotherham
20.04.08 Kristian Laight W PTS 6 Shaw
11.07.08 Graham Fearn W PTS 4 Wigan
03.04.09 Daniel Thorpe W PTS 6 Leigh
Career: 6 contests, won 5, lost 1.

Matty Askin

Blackpool. *Born* Barnsley, 24 December, 1988
Cruiserweight. *Ht* 6'2"
Manager B. Hughes
22.11.08 Paul Bonson W PTS 4 Blackpool
24.01.09 Nick Okoth W PTS 4 Blackpool
Career: 2 contests, won 2.

Matty Askin   Philip Sharkey

John Baguley

Sheffield. *Born* Rotherham, 13 March, 1988
Central Area Lightweight Champion. *Ht*
5'9"

Manager J. Ingle
13.10.06 Wez Miller W PTS 4 Doncaster
28.10.06 James Ancliff L PTS 6 Aberdeen
07.11.06 Matthew Martin Lewis L PTS 6 Leeds
01.12.06 Deniss Sirjatovs W PTS 4 Doncaster
17.12.06 James Brown W PTS 6 Bolton
09.02.07 Stuart McFadyen L PTS 4 Leeds
27.04.07 Chris Hooper W RSC 1 Hull
26.05.07 James Ancliff L PTS 6 Aberdeen
10.06.07 Henry Jones W RSC 4 Neath
01.07.07 Tom Glover L PTS 10 Colchester
　　　　 (Vacant British Masters Lightweight
　　　　 Title)
15.07.07 James McElvaney L PTS 6 Hartlepool
22.09.07 Mark Moran L PTS 4 Wigan
05.11.07 Furhan Rafiq W PTS 6 Glasgow
17.11.07 Kevin Buckley L PTS 6 Stoke
23.02.08 Danny Stewart W RSC 2 Crawley
08.03.08 Vinny Mitchell L PTS 4 Greenwich
22.03.08 Femi Fehintola L PTS 6 Sheffield
07.06.08 John Watson L PTS 4 Wigan
12.09.08 Dwayne Hill W RSC 3 Sheffield
　　　　 (Vacant Central Area Lightweight Title)
14.11.08 George Watson DREW 4 Glasgow
12.12.08 Anthony Crolla L PTS 4 Widnes
17.01.09 Chris Goodwin L PTS 4 Wigan
15.05.09 Kevin O'Hara L PTS 6 Belfast
Career: 23 contests, won 8, drew 1, lost 14.

Ian Bailey

Slough. *Born* Taplow, 18 April, 1984
S.Bantamweight. *Ht* 5'4¼"
Manager J. Eames
15.06.08 Delroy Spencer W PTS 6 Bethnal
　　　　 Green
27.09.08 Ibrar Riyaz W PTS 6 Bracknell
06.12.08 John Gicharu W PTS 4 Bethnal Green
13.03.09 Nick MacDonald L RTD 3 Widnes
Career: 4 contests, won 3, lost 1.

Mariusz Bak

Brentford. *Born* Poland, 23 June, 1980
Lightweight. *Ht* 5'8½"
Manager M. Stone
12.10.07 James McElvaney L PTS 4 Peterlee
11.04.09 Del Rogers L PTS 4 Bethnal Green
Career: 2 contests, lost 2.

Carl Baker

Sheffield. *Born* Sheffield, 3 January, 1982
Former Undefeated British Masters
Heavyweight Champion. *Ht* 6'4"
Manager C. Mitchell
06.09.03 Dave Clark W RSC 1 Aberdeen
15.09.03 Billy Wilson W RSC 2 Leeds
28.11.03 Alvin Miller W CO 1 Hull
03.04.04 Paul King L PTS 6 Sheffield

17.09.04 Scott Gammer L PTS 4 Plymouth
04.03.05 Paul King W RSC 2 Rotherham
26.04.05 Luke Simpkin L RSC 4 Leeds
25.06.05 Scott Lansdowne W RSC 8 Melton
　　　　 Mowbray
　　　　 (Vacant British Masters Heavyweight
　　　　 Title)
11.09.05 Luke Simpkin W PTS 10 Kirkby in
　　　　 Ashfield
　　　　 (British Masters Heavyweight Title
　　　　 Defence)
13.05.06 David Ingleby W RSC 4 Sheffield
09.05.09 Chris Woollas W PTS 6 Lincoln
Career: 11 contests, won 8, lost 3.

Vince Baldassara

Clydebank. *Born* Clydebank, 6 November,
1978
Scottish Middleweight Champion. *Ht* 5'11"
Manager T. Gilmour
14.03.03 George Telfer L PTS 4 Glasgow
28.02.04 Rob McDonald W PTS 6 Manchester
08.10.04 Barrie Lee DREW 6 Glasgow
09.12.04 Eddie Haley W PTS 6 Sunderland
21.02.05 Cafu Santos W CO 2 Glasgow
08.04.05 Barrie Lee L PTS 4 Edinburgh
25.04.05 Ciaran Healy W RSC 4 Glasgow
20.05.05 Mark Wall W PTS 6 Glasgow
17.06.05 Jack Hibbert W CO 1 Glasgow
12.11.05 Craig Lynch W PTS 10 Glasgow
　　　　 (Vacant Scottish Area Middleweight
　　　　 Title)
09.03.06 Ryan Kerr DREW 6 Sunderland
08.09.06 Wayne Elcock L RSC 6 Birmingham
　　　　 (Vacant WBF Inter-Continental
　　　　 Middleweight Title)
23.02.07 Cello Renda L CO 3 Birmingham
19.01.09 Kevin McCauley W PTS 6 Glasgow
16.03.09 Ernie Smith W RSC 2 Glasgow
12.06.09 Darren Gethin W RSC 4 Clydebank
Career: 16 contests, won 10, drew 2, lost 4.

Jamie Ball

Coseley. *Born* Wordsley, 5 June, 1984
Middleweight. *Ht* 5'10¾"
Manager P. Rowson
20.06.08 Paul Royston W PTS 4 Wolverhampton
24.07.08 Peter Dunn W PTS 4 Wolverhampton
26.09.08 Ernie Smith W PTS 6 Wolverhampton
09.11.08 Tye Williams W PTS 4 Bethnal Green
06.02.09 Arturs Selaves W RSC 3 Birmingham
24.04.09 Matt Scriven W PTS 4 Wolverhampton
Career: 6 contests, won 6.

Ted Bami (Minsende)

Brixton. *Born* Zaire, 2 March, 1978
Former Undefeated European
L.Welterweight Champion. Former WBF
L.Welterweight Champion. *Ht* 5'7"
Manager B. Hearn
26.09.98 Des Sowden W RSC 1 Southwark
11.02.99 Gary Reid W RSC 2 Dudley
10.03.00 David Kehoe W PTS 4 Bethnal Green
08.09.00 Jacek Bielski L RSC 4 Hammersmith
29.03.01 Keith Jones W PTS 4 Hammersmith
05.05.01 Francis Barrett W PTS 6 Edmonton
31.07.01 Lance Crosby W PTS 6 Bethnal Green
19.03.02 Michael Smyth W CO 4 Slough

23.06.02 Keith Jones W RSC 4 Southwark
17.08.02 Bradley Pryce W RSC 6 Cardiff
26.10.02 Adam Zadworny W PTS 4 Maesteg
07.12.02 Sergei Starkov W PTS 4 Brentwood
08.03.03 Andrei Devyataykin W RSC 1 Bethnal
　　　　 Green
12.04.03 Laszlo Herczeg W RSC 9 Bethnal Green
　　　　 (Vacant WBF L.Welterweight Title)
26.07.03 Samuel Malinga L RSC 3 Plymouth
　　　　 (WBF L.Welterweight Title Defence)
09.10.03 Zoltan Surman W RSC 3 Bristol
31.01.04 Jozsef Matolcsi W PTS 6 Bethnal Green
08.05.04 Viktor Baranov W RSC 2 Dagenham
08.10.04 Rafal Jackiewicz W PTS 8 Brentwood
13.02.05 Ricardo Daniel Silva W CO 2
　　　　 Brentwood
21.10.05 Silence Saheed W PTS 6 Bethnal Green
24.02.06 Maurycy Gojko W CO 4 Dagenham
22.09.06 Giuseppe Lauri W PTS 12 Bethnal
　　　　 Green *(Vacant European L.Welterweight*
　　　　 Title)
30.03.07 Giuseppe Lauri W PTS 12 Crawley
　　　　 (European L.Welterweight Title Defence)
25.01.08 Nicolas Guisset W PTS 8 Dagenham
14.03.08 David Barnes L PTS 12 Manchester
　　　　 (Vacant British L.Welterweight Title)
04.07.08 Stuart Elwell W RSC 7 Liverpool
24.10.08 Andrew Ferrans W RSC 1 Bethnal Green
24.10.08 Mark Lloyd W PTS 3 Bethnal Green
24.10.08 Michael Lomax L PTS 3 Bethnal Green
28.03.09 Matthew Hatton L RSC 6 Altrincham
　　　　 (Elim. IBO Welterweight Title)
Career: 31 contests, won 26, lost 5

Michael Banbula

Staines. *Born* Poland, 26 December, 1980
L.Heavyweight. *Ht* 5'11¼"
Manager Self
30.04.05 Gareth Lawrence L PTS 6 Dagenham
14.05.05 Tommy Tolan L PTS 4 Dublin
02.06.05 Cello Renda DREW 6 Peterborough
01.07.05 Gareth Lawrence L PTS 4 Fulham
16.07.05 Daniel Cadman L PTS 6 Chigwell
06.10.05 Danny McIntosh L PTS 6 Longford
22.10.05 Neil Tidman L PTS 6 Coventry
19.11.05 Danny Tombs L RSC 2 Southwark
21.09.07 Dwayne Lewis L PTS 4 Bethnal Green
28.09.07 Carl Dilks L PTS 6 Preston
09.10.07 Jack Morris W PTS 6 Tower Hamlets
18.11.07 Leon Senior L PTS 4 Tooting
01.12.07 Richard Horton L PTS 4 Bethnal Green
16.02.08 Kevin Concepcion L PTS 6 Leicester
02.03.08 Danny Couzens L PTS 6 Portsmouth
16.03.08 Martin Murray L PTS 6 Liverpool
28.03.08 James Tucker W PTS 4 Piccadilly
04.04.08 Victor Smith W PTS 4 Bethnal Green
01.05.08 Pawel Trebinski L PTS 6 Piccadilly
14.06.08 Tommy Saunders L RSC 1 Bethnal
　　　　 Green
25.07.08 John Robinson W PTS 6 Houghton le
　　　　 Spring
27.09.08 Sammy Couzens L PTS 6 Bracknell
04.10.08 Paul Davis DREW 4 Norwich
24.10.08 Justyn Hugh L PTS 6 Newport
08.11.08 Paulino Da Silva DREW 6 Wigan
06.12.08 Paulino Da Silva W PTS 4 Wigan
07.03.09 Mark Regan L PTS 4 Birmingham
24.04.09 Carl Wild W PTS 4 Sheffield
05.06.09 Justyn Hugh L PTS 6 Newport
12.06.09 Rhys Davies L PTS 6 Wolverhampton

19.06.09 Tobias Webb L PTS 4 Glasgow
27.06.09 Sammy Couzens W PTS 4 Portsmouth
Career: 32 contests, won 7, drew 3, lost 22.

Richard Barclay

Glasgow. *Born* Milngavie, 22 October, 1987
Lightweight. *Ht* 5' 4"
Manager T. Gilmour
16.02.09 Steve Gethin W PTS 6 Glasgow
12.06.09 Scott Slater L CO 1 Clydebank
Career: 2 contests, won 1, lost 1.

Darren Barker

Barnet. *Born* Harrow, 19 May, 1982
Commonwealth Middleweight Champion.
Former Undefeated Southern Area
Middleweight Champion. *Ht* 6'0½"
Manager Self
24.09.04 Howard Clarke W PTS 6 Nottingham
12.11.04 David White W RSC 2 Wembley
26.03.05 Leigh Wicks W RTD 4 Hackney
10.04.05 Andrei Sherel W RSC 3 Brentwood
09.07.05 Ernie Smith W PTS 6 Nottingham
16.07.05 Dean Walker W PTS 6 Chigwell
02.12.05 John-Paul Temple W RSC 6 Nottingham
20.01.06 Richard Mazurek W PTS 8 Bethnal Green
17.02.06 Louis Mimoune W RSC 2 Bethanl Green
12.05.06 Danny Thornton W RSC 6 Bethnal Green
12.07.06 Conroy McIntosh W RSC 7 Bethnal Green
15.09.06 Hussain Osman W PTS 10 Muswell Hill
(Vacant Southern Area Middleweight Title)
24.11.06 Ojay Abrahams W RTD 1 Nottingham
08.12.06 Paul Samuels W RSC 1 Dagenham
05.10.07 Greg Barton W RSC 3 Bethnal Green
14.11.07 Ben Crampton W PTS 12 Bethnal Green
(Vacant Commonwealth Middleweight Title)
22.02.08 Steven Bendall W RSC 7 Bethnal Green
(Commonwealth Middleweight Title Defence)
15.08.08 Larry Sharpe W PTS 10 Enoch, Canada
13.12.08 Jason McKay W RTD 6 Brentwood
(Commonwealth Middleweight Title Defence)
23.05.09 Darren McDermott W RSC 4 Watford
(Commonwealth Middleweight Title Defence)
Career: 20 contests, won 20.

James Barker

Droylsden. *Born* Salford, 17 July, 1985
Welterweight. *Ht* 5'9"
Manager W. Barker
23.02.07 Ali Hussain W PTS 6 Manchester
06.10.07 Muhsen Nasser L RSC 1 Aberdeen
Career: 2 contests, won 1, lost 1.

David Barnes (Smith)

Manchester. *Born* Manchester, 16 January, 1981
Former Undefeated British L. Welterweight
Champion. Former Undefeated British

Welterweight Champion. *Ht* 5'8½"
Manager J. Trickett
07.07.01 Trevor Smith W RSC 2 Manchester
15.09.01 Karl Taylor W PTS 4 Manchester
27.10.01 Mark Sawyers W RSC 2 Manchester
15.12.01 James Paisley W RTD 2 Wembley
09.02.02 David Kirk W RTD 1 Manchester
04.05.02 David Baptiste W CO 3 Bethnal Green
01.06.02 Dimitri Protkunas W RSC 1 Manchester
28.09.02 Sergei Starkov W PTS 6 Manchester
12.10.02 Rusian Ashirov W PTS 6 Bethnal Green
14.12.02 Rozalin Nasibulin W RSC 3 Newcastle
18.01.03 Brice Faradji W PTS 6 Preston
05.04.03 Viktor Fesetchko W PTS 8 Manchester
17.07.03 Jimmy Vincent W PTS 12 Dagenham
(Vacant British Welterweight Title)
13.12.03 Kevin McIntyre W RTD 8 Manchester
(British Welterweight Title Defence)
03.04.04 Glenn McClarnon W PTS 12 Manchester
(British Welterweight Title Defence)
12.11.04 James Hare W RSC 6 Halifax
(British Welterweight Title Defence)
28.01.05 Juho Tolppola W PTS 10 Renfrew
22.04.05 Ali Nuumbembe DREW 12 Barnsley
(Vacant WBO Inter-Continental Welterweight Title)
04.06.05 Joshua Okine L RSC 12 Manchester
(Commonwealth Welterweight Title Challenge)
28.01.06 Fabrice Colombel W RSC 4 Nottingham
04.03.06 Silence Saheed W PTS 4 Manchester
10.12.06 Vadzim Astapuk W PTS 6 Sheffield
03.05.07 Jay Morris W RSC 1 Sheffield
02.11.07 Arek Malek W PTS 6 Irvine
14.03.08 Ted Bami W PTS 12 Manchester
(British L.Welterweight Title Defence)
04.07.08 Barry Morrison W PTS 12 Liverpool
(British L.Welterweight Title Defence)
Career: 26 contests, won 24, drew 1, lost 1.

Steve Barnes

Sheffield. *Born* Sheffield, 24 April, 1991
S.Featherweight. *Ht* 5'6"
Manager J. Ingle
15.11.08 Piotr Niesporek W PTS 4 Castlebar
23.05.09 Nick Seager W RSC 1 Watford
13.06.09 Jevgenijs Kirillovs W PTS 4 Wigan
Career: 3 contests, won 3.

Matthew Barney

Southampton. *Born* Fareham, 25 June, 1974
Cruiserweight. Former Undefeated WBU
L.Heavyweight Champion. Former
Undefeated British, IBO Inter-Continental,
Southern Area & British Masters
S.Middleweight Champion. *Ht* 5'10¾"
Manager J. Bishop
04.06.98 Adam Cale W PTS 6 Barking
23.07.98 Adam Cale W PTS 6 Barking
02.10.98 Dennis Doyley W PTS 4 Cheshunt
22.10.98 Kevin Burton W PTS 6 Barking
07.12.98 Freddie Yemofio W PTS 4 Acton
17.03.99 Simon Andrews W RTD 4 Kensington
09.05.99 Gareth Hogg W PTS 4 Bracknell
20.05.99 Bobby Banghar W RSC 5 Kensington
(British Masters S. Middleweight Final)
05.06.99 Paul Bowen DREW 10 Cardiff
(Southern Area S. Middleweight Title Challenge)

20.08.99 Adam Cale W PTS 4 Bloomsbury
05.10.99 Delroy Leslie L PTS 10 Bloomsbury
(Vacant Southern Area Middleweight Title)
15.04.00 Mark Dawson W PTS 6 Bethnal Green
06.05.00 Jason Hart W PTS 10 Southwark
(Vacant Southern Area S. Middleweight Title)
30.09.00 Neil Linford L PTS 10 Peterborough
(Elim. British S. Middleweight Title)
02.02.01 Darren Covill W PTS 6 Portsmouth
16.03.01 Matt Mowatt W RSC 1 Portsmouth
(British Masters S. Middleweight Title Defence)
14.07.01 Robert Milewics W PTS 8 Wembley
20.10.01 Jon Penn W RSC 4 Portsmouth
26.01.02 Hussain Osman L RTD 9 Dagenham
(Vacant IBO Inter-Continental S.Middleweight Title. Southern Area S.Middleweight Title Defence)
08.04.02 Hussain Osman W PTS 12 Southampton
(IBO Inter-Continental & Southern Area S. Middleweight Title Challenges)
22.09.02 Paul Owen W CO 7 Southwark
(Vacant British Masters S.Middleweight Title)
20.10.02 Chris Nembhard W PTS 10 Southwark
(Southern Area S. Middleweight Title Defence)
29.03.03 Dean Francis W PTS 12 Wembley
(Vacant British S.Middleweight Title)
01.08.03 Charles Adamu L PTS 12 Bethnal Green
(Vacant Commonwealth S.Middleweight Title)
11.10.03 Tony Oakey W PTS 12 Portsmouth
(WBU L.Heavyweight Title Challenge)
10.09.04 Simeon Cover W PTS 4 Wembley
26.03.05 Thomas Ulrich L PTS 12 Riesa, Germany
(European L.Heavyweight Title Challenge)
09.07.05 Carl Froch L PTS 12 Nottingham
(British & Commonwealth S.Middleweight Title Challenges)
01.12.06 Varuzhan Davtyan W PTS 4 Tower Hill
23.02.07 Ayitey Powers W PTS 6 Peterborough
23.02.08 Kim Jenssen W PTS 6 Crawley
16.05.08 Ayitey Powers W PTS 6 Holborn
28.02.09 Danny McIntosh L DIS 5 Norwich
(English L.Heavyweight Title Challenge)
Career: 33 contests, won 25, drew 1, lost 7.

Matthew Barr

Walton England. *Born* Kingston, 22 May, 1977
Middleweight. *Ht* 5' 11"
Manager J. Evans
02.12.97 Keith Palmer L RSC 3 Windsor
23.02.98 Martin Cavey W RSC 1 Windsor
14.05.98 Gerard Lawrence L RSC 1 Acton
29.10.98 Sonny Thind W RSC 2 Mayfair
20.05.99 Paul Knights L RSC 1 Barking
31.10.99 Allan Gray W PTS 4 Raynes Park
25.02.00 John Humphrey W RSC 1 Newmarket
06.05.00 Ernie Smith W PTS 4 Southwark
22.10.00 Ernie Smith W PTS 4 Streatham
23.11.00 Harry Butler W PTS 4 Mayfair
23.11.01 John Humphrey L RSC 2 Bethnal Green
13.09.02 Brian Knudsen W PTS 6 Randers, Denmark

Matthew Barr   Philip Sharkey

29.03.03 Lee Hodgson W RSC 1 Wembley
29.10.03 Domvill Hendrix W RSC 4 Leicester
Square
27.11.03 Leigh Wicks W PTS 4 Longford
21.01.05 Gareth Lawrence W RSC 2 Brentford
16.12.05 Howard Clarke W PTS 4 Bracknell
25.06.09 Nick Okoth W PTS 4 Mayfair
Career: 18 contests, won 14, lost 4.

Stuart Barr

Walton on Thames. *Born* Ashford, 6 July,
1980
Middleweight. *Ht* 6' 3"
Manager J. Evans
23.06.09 Chris Brophy W PTS 4 Heathrow
Career: 1 contest, won 1.

Coleman Barrett

London. *Born* Galway, 10 November, 1982
Heavyweight. *Ht* 6' 1"
Manager K. Walker
11.12.03 Marcus Lee W PTS 4 Bethnal Green
12.03.04 Dave Clarke W PTS 4 Nottingham
02.06.04 Terry Morrill W PTS 6 Nottingham
05.03.05 Valery Semishkur W PTS 6 Durres,
Albania
12.06.05 Czaba Andras W RSC 1 Leicester
Square
24.07.05 Tony Booth W PTS 4 Leicester Square
18.04.09 Vlado Szabo W RSC 3 Galway
23.06.09 David Ingleby W PTS 6 Longford
Career: 8 contests, won 8.

Ryan Barrett

Thamesmead. *Born* London, 27 December,
1982
English S. Featherweight Champion.
Former Undefeated British Masters
Featherweight Champion. *Ht* 5'10"
Manager Self
13.06.02 Gareth Wiltshaw W PTS 4 Leicester
Square
06.09.02 Jason Gonzales W PTS 4 Bethnal Green
12.12.02 Martin Turner W RSC 1 Leicester
Square

08.03.03 David Vaughan DREW 4 Bethnal Green
04.10.03 Dafydd Carlin L PTS 4 Belfast
01.05.04 Marty Kayes W RSC 2 Gravesend
19.06.04 Kristian Laight W PTS 4 Muswell Hill
16.10.04 Daniel Thorpe W PTS 4 Dagenham
19.12.04 James Paisley W DIS 5 Bethnal Green
21.01.05 Peter McDonagh W PTS 8 Brentford
05.03.05 Carl Allen W PTS 4 Dagenham
23.03.05 Pete Buckley W PTS 6 Leicester Square
20.06.05 Anthony Christopher W RSC 1
Longford
01.04.06 Martin Watson L PTS 10 Bethnal Green
(Elim. British Lightweight Title)
23.07.06 Baz Carey W PTS 6 Dagenham
02.09.06 Amir Khan L RSC 1 Bolton
21.10.06 Steve Gethin W PTS 6 Southwark
03.12.06 Riaz Durgahed W PTS 6 Bethnal Green
18.02.07 Jamie McKeever W PTS 10 Bethnal
Green
*(Vacant British Masters Featherweight
Title)*
08.06.07 John Simpson L CO 5 Mayfair
(British Featherweight Title Challenge)
18.04.08 Henry Castle L RSC 3 Bethnal Green
13.09.08 Michael Frontin DREW 4 Bethnal Green
25.10.08 Femi Fehintola W CO 3 St Helier
*(English S.Featherweight Title
Challenge)*
22.03.09 Gheorghe Ghiompirica W PTS 6 Bethnal
Green
29.05.09 Willie Limond L PTS 12 Glasgow
(Vacant WBU Lightweight Title)
Career: 25 contests, won 17, drew 2, lost 6.

(Alex) Sandy Bartlett

Inverness. *Born* Dingwall, 20 April, 1976
S.Featherweight. *Ht* 5'7"
Manager Self
15.03.04 Marty Kayes W PTS 6 Glasgow
19.04.04 Abdul Mougharbel L PTS 6 Glasgow
11.10.04 Abdul Mougharbel W PTS 6 Glasgow
05.11.04 Ricky Owen L RSC 2 Hereford
19.09.05 Neil Marston W PTS 6 Glasgow
04.11.05 Craig Bromley L RSC 2 Glasgow
20.02.06 Kevin Townsley L PTS 4 Glasgow
25.03.06 John Bothwell L PTS 4 Glasgow
02.12.06 Brian Murphy W RSC 5 Clydebank
02.03.07 Furhan Rafiq L PTS 6 Irvine
28.09.07 Scott Quigg L RSC 3 Preston
18.02.08 Furhan Rafiq L RSC 10 Glasgow
*(Vacant Scottish Area Featherweight
Title)*
25.10.08 Anthony Hanna L CO 4 Aberdeen
*(British Masters Featherweight Title
Challenge)*
Career: 13 contests, won 4, lost 9.

(Shinebayer) Shinny Bayaar (Sukhbaatar)

Oldham/Mongolia. *Born* Mongolia, 27
August, 1977
International Masters S. Flyweight
Champion. *Ht* 5'5½"
Manager J. Doughty
25.02.00 Yura Dima DREW 10 Erdene, Mongolia
28.06.00 Manny Melchor L PTS 12 Manila,
Philippines
*(WBC International M.Flyweight Title
Challenge)*

10.10.01 Damien Dunnion L PTS 8 Stoke
09.12.01 Delroy Spencer W PTS 4 Shaw
17.11.02 Anthony Hanna W PTS 6 Shaw
20.03.03 Sunkanmi Ogunbiyi L PTS 4 Queensway
08.06.03 Darren Cleary W RSC 2 Shaw
19.10.03 Delroy Spencer W PTS 6 Shaw
21.02.04 Reidar Walstad W RSC 1 Cardiff
31.10.04 Delroy Spencer W PTS 6 Shaw
11.12.04 Martin Power L PTS 10 Canning Town
20.11.05 Abdul Mougharbel W PTS 4 Shaw
02.04.06 Delroy Spencer W PTS 6 Shaw
15.09.06 Andrew Kooner W RSC 3 Muswell Hill
11.03.07 Pete Buckley W PTS 6 Shaw
20.04.08 Sumaila Badu W RSC 2 Shaw
16.11.08 Jordi Gallart W PTS 10 Shaw
*(Vacant International Masters S.
Flyweight Title)*
24.05.09 Daniel Thorpe W PTS 4 Shaw
Career: 18 contests, won 13, drew 1, lost 4.

Jimmy Beech

Walsall. *Born* Walsall, 19 January, 1979
Welterweight. *Ht* 5'7¼"
Manager E. Johnson
23.06.99 Ike Halls W RTD 2 West Bromwich
03.09.99 Tom Wood W PTS 6 West Bromwich
07.04.00 Willie Limond L RSC 2 Glasgow
28.01.01 Lenny Hodgkins W PTS 6
Wolverhampton
16.11.01 Pete Buckley W PTS 6 West Bromwich
23.11.01 Henry Castle L PTS 4 Bethnal Green
07.02.02 Dave Cotterill W PTS 6 Stoke
25.02.02 Mickey Bowden W PTS 4 Slough
09.03.02 Tony Mulholland L PTS 6 Manchester
05.05.02 James Rooney W RSC 5 Hartlepool
25.05.02 Henry Castle L PTS 4 Portsmouth
07.09.02 Ricky Eccleston W RSC 3 Liverpool
28.09.02 Michael Gomez L RSC 4 Manchester
14.12.02 Gavin Rees L PTS 4 Newcastle
22.03.03 Willie Limond L CO 4 Renfrew
28.04.03 Tony McPake L PTS 6 Nottingham
27.05.03 Billy Corcoran W PTS 6 Dagenham
26.09.03 Dave Stewart L RTD 2 Reading
14.11.03 Scott Lawton L RSC 5 Bethnal Green
24.01.04 Steve Murray L RSC 4 Wembley
28.01.05 Martin Watson L PTS 4 Renfrew
26.02.05 Scott Haywood L PTS 6 Burton

Jimmy Beech   Philip Sharkey

11.03.05 Stefy Bull L PTS 4 Doncaster
08.05.05 Carl Johanneson L CO 2 Bradford
30.03.08 Shaun Horsfall L PTS 6 Colne
10.04.08 Peter Dunn W PTS 6 Piccadilly
20.04.08 Muhsen Nasser L PTS 6 Shaw
17.05.08 Scott Miller L RTD 2 Stoke
18.07.08 Scott Woolford L PTS 4 Dagenham
06.09.08 Denton Vassell L PTS 6 Manchester
20.09.08 Curtis Woodhouse L PTS 4 Sheffield
Career: 31 contests, won 10, lost 21.

Rob Beech

Liverpool. *Born* St Helens, 8 June, 1982
Heavyweight. *Ht* 6' 2"
Manager O. Harrison
08.11.08 Howard Daley W PTS 4 Wigan
13.02.09 Lee Mountford W PTS 4 Wigan
Career: 2 contests, won 2.

Andy Bell (Langley)

Nottingham. *Born* Doncaster, 16 July, 1985
Former British S.Flyweight Champion.
Former Undefeated English S.Flyweight
Champion. Former Undefeated Midlands
Area & British Masters Bantamweight
Champion. *Ht* 5'8"
Manager M. Scriven
22.10.04 Steve Gethin W RSC 5 Mansfield
10.12.04 Dean Ward W PTS 6 Mansfield
06.03.05 Abdul Mougharbel W PTS 4 Mansfield
24.04.05 Wayne Bloy L PTS 4 Askern
13.05.06 Steve Gethin L RSC 2 Sutton in Ashfield
06.10.06 Shaun Walton W PTS 6 Mansfield
01.12.06 Jamie McDonnell L RSC 3 Doncaster
01.04.07 Neil Marston W RSC 8 Shrewsbury
  (*Vacant Midlands Area Bantamweight Title*)
19.05.07 Delroy Spencer W PTS 4 Nottingham
17.06.07 Mo Khaled W PTS 10 Mansfield
  (*Vacant British Masters Bantamweight Title*)
22.07.07 Delroy Spencer W PTS 6 Mansfield
07.09.07 Robert Nelson W RSC 7 Doncaster
  (*Vacant English S.Flyweight Title*)
01.12.07 Wayne Bloy W PTS 10 Nottingham
  (*English S.Flyweight Title Defence*)
28.03.08 Chris Edwards W PTS 12 Barnsley
  (*British S.Flyweight Title Challenge*)
07.11.08 Lee Haskins L PTS 12 Wigan
  (*British S.Flyweight Title Defence*)
Career: 15 contests, won 11, lost 4.

Billy Bell

South Shields, *Born* Westminster, 13 May, 1986
Featherweight. *Ht* 5'6"
Manager M. Gates
20.03.08 Duane Cumberbatch W PTS 6 South Shields
18.04.08 Dean Mills L PTS 6 Houghton le Spring
13.06.08 Tony McQuade W PTS 6 Sunderland
28.11.08 Davey Savage L RSC 1 Glasgow
Career: 4 contests, won 2, lost 2.

Steve Bell

Manchester. *Born* Manchester, 11 June, 1975
Central Area S.Featherweight Champion.
Ht 5'10"
Manager Self
08.05.03 Jus Wallie DREW 4 Widnes
27.09.03 Jaz Virdee W RSC 1 Manchester
13.12.03 Fred Janes W PTS 4 Manchester
03.04.04 Pete Buckley W PTS 4 Manchester
22.05.04 Haider Ali W PTS 6 Widnes
01.10.04 Daniel Thorpe W PTS 6 Manchester
11.02.05 Henry Janes W RTD 3 Manchester
03.06.05 Buster Dennis DREW 6 Manchester
04.03.06 Pete Buckley W PTS 4 Manchester
01.04.06 Jason Nesbitt W PTS 6 Bethnal Green
02.09.06 Daniel Thorpe W RTD 4 Bolton
28.10.06 Steve Gethin W RTD 5 Bethnal Green
10.03.07 Jamie McKeever W RSC 7 Liverpool
  (*Vacant Central Area S.Featherweight Title*)
31.05.07 Rom Krauklis W PTS 6 Manchester
06.10.07 Femi Fehintola L PTS 10 Nottingham
  (*Vacant English S.Featherweight Title*)
14.03.08 Carl Allen W PTS 6 Manchester
05.04.08 Baz Carey W PTS 6 Bolton
06.09.08 Anthony Hanna W PTS 8 Manchester
12.12.08 Shaun Walton W PTS 6 Widnes
14.03.09 Youssef Al Hamidi W PTS 6 Manchester
Career: 20 contests, won 17, drew 2, lost 1.

Tony Bellew

Liverpool. *Born* Liverpool, 30 November, 1982
L.Heavyweight. *Ht* 6'2½"
Manager F. Warren
06.10.07 Jamie Ambler W RSC 2 Nottingham
03.11.07 Adam Wilcox W RSC 3 Cardiff
08.12.07 Wayne Brooks W CO 3 Bolton
05.04.08 Paul Bonson W PTS 4 Bolton
18.07.08 Ayitey Powers W PTS 4 Dagenham
06.09.08 Hastings Rasani W RSC 1 Manchester
10.10.08 Jevgenijs Andrejevs W PTS 4 Liverpool
12.12.08 Phil Goodwin W CO 2 Widnes
15.05.09 Matthew Ellis W RSC 4 Belfast
Career: 9 contests, won 9.

Scott Belshaw

Lisburn N.Ireland. *Born* Aghalee, N.Ireland, 8 July, 1985
Heavyweight. *Ht* 6'7¼"
Manager A. Wilton
07.10.06 Lee Webb W RSC 1 Belfast
11.11.06 Anatoliy Kusenko W RSC 1 Dublin
25.11.06 Alexander Subin W RSC 2 Belfast
26.01.07 Makhmud Otazhanov W RSC 2 Dagenham
09.03.07 Paul King W PTS 4 Dagenham
30.06.07 Chris Woollas W CO 1 Belfast
26.01.08 Aleksandre Borhovs W RSC 3 Cork
07.03.08 Daniel Peret L PTS 6 Nottingham
31.05.08 Edgar Kalnars W RSC 4 Belfast
18.07.08 Daniil Peretyatko W PTS 6 Dagenham
13.09.08 Pavol Polakovic W PTS 8 Bethnal Green
23.05.09 Tyson Fury L RSC 2 Watford
Career: 12 contests, won 10, lost 2.

Steven Bendall

Coventry. *Born* Coventry, 1 December, 1973
Former English Middleweight Champion.
Former Undefeated IBO Inter-Continental
&WBU Inter-Continental Middleweight
Champion. *Ht* 6'0"
Manager Self
15.05.97 Dennis Doyley W RSC 2 Reading
13.09.97 Gary Reyniers W PTS 4 Millwall
27.02.99 Israel Khumalo W PTS 4 Oldham
02.07.99 Darren Covill W RTD 3 Bristol
24.09.99 Sean Pritchard W PTS 6 Merthyr
03.12.99 Ian Toby W PTS 6 Peterborough
07.04.00 Des Sowden W RSC 3 Bristol
02.06.00 Simon Andrews W RSC 5 Ashford
08.09.00 Jason Barker W PTS 6 Bristol
03.11.00 Eddie Haley W RSC 1 Ebbw Vale
01.12.00 Peter Mitchell W PTS 8 Peterborough
22.08.01 Bert Bado W RSC 1 Hammanskraal, South Africa
29.09.01 Alan Gilbert W RTD 3 Southwark
08.12.01 Jason Collins W PTS 12 Dagenham
  (*Vacant WBU Inter-Continental Middleweight Title*)
02.03.02 Ahmet Dottouev W RTD 4 Brakpan, South Africa
  (*WBU Inter-Continental Middleweight Title Defence*)
26.04.02 Viktor Fesetchko W RSC 10 Coventry
  (*Vacant IBO Inter-Continental Middleweight Title*)
13.07.02 Philip Bystrikov W RSC 5 Coventry
06.09.02 Tomas da Silva W RSC 8 Bethnal Green
24.01.03 Lee Blundell W RSC 2 Sheffield
  (*IBO Inter-Continental Middleweight Title Defence*)
26.04.03 Mike Algoet W PTS 12 Brentford
  (*IBO Inter-Continental Middleweight Title Defence*)
14.11.03 Kreshnik Qato W PTS 8 Bethnal Green
17.09.04 Scott Dann L RSC 6 Plymouth
  (*Vacant British Middleweight Title*)
18.06.05 Ismael Kerzazi W PTS 8 Coventry
22.10.05 Magid Ben Driss W PTS 6 Coventry
15.12.05 Donovan Smillie W RSC 5 Coventry
  (*English Middleweight Title Challenge*)
22.04.06 Sebastian Sylvester L RSC 3 Mannheim, Germany
  (*European Middleweight Title Challenge*)
07.10.06 Conroy McIntosh W PTS 6 Weston super Mare
01.12.06 Wayne Elcock L RSC 8 Birmingham
  (*English Middleweight Title Defence*)
20.07.07 Davey Jones W RTD 2 Wolverhampton
28.09.07 Andrzej Butowicz W RSC 8 Coventry
28.11.07 Alexander Matviechuk W PTS 6 Walsall
22.02.08 Darren Barker L RSC 7 Bethnal Green
  (*Commonwealth Middleweight Title Challenge*)
21.06.08 Paul Smith W PTS 10 Birmingham
  (*English Middleweight Title Challenge*)
28.02.09 Darren McDermott L PTS 10 Birmingham
  (*English Middleweight Title Defence*)
Career: 34 contests, won 29, lost 5.

Mark Bett

Larkhall. *Born* Lanark, 30 September, 1982
Welterweight. *Ht* 5'7"
Manager A. Morrison
22.04.06 Marco Cittadini DREW 6 Glasgow
27.05.06 Colin Bain DREW 6 Glasgow
21.10.06 Marco Cittadini W PTS 6 Glasgow
10.12.06 Colin Bain L PTS 6 Glasgow
16.02.07 Ali Hussain DREW 6 Sunderland
16.03.07 Ali Hussain W RSC 3 Glasgow
24.06.07 Davey Watson L RTD 5 Sunderland
11.08.07 Amir Unsworth L RSC 4 Liverpool
06.10.07 Adam Kelly W RTD 3 Aberdeen
26.10.07 Paddy Pollock DREW 6 Glasgow
01.12.07 Peter Allen DREW 6 Liverpool
09.12.07 Gary McMillan L RSC 1 Glasgow
14.03.08 David Kehoe W PTS 6 Glasgow
29.03.08 Adam Kelly L PTS 6 Aberdeen
16.05.08 Charles Paul King L PTS 6 Motherwell
09.06.08 Matt Seawright W RSC 5 Glasgow
11.07.08 Steve Saville L RSC 4 Wigan
18.10.08 Jason Hastie L PTS 4 Paisley
14.11.08 Ryan Scott L RSC 1 Glasgow
Career: 19 contests, won 5, drew 5, lost 9.

Akaash Bhatia   Philip Sharkey

Akaash Bhatia

Harrow. *Born* Loughborough, 1 May, 1983
Southern Area Featherweight Champion.
Ht 5'7"
Manager F. Maloney
30.05.06 Kristian Laight W PTS 4 Bethnal Green
29.06.06 Nikita Lukin W PTS 4 Bethnal Green
06.10.06 Rakhim Mingaleev W PTS 4 Bethnal Green
17.11.06 Youssef Al Hamidi W PTS 4 Bethnal Green
26.01.07 Sergii Tertii W RSC 2 Dagenham
27.04.07 Dai Davies W PTS 4 Wembley
13.07.07 Steve Gethin W RSC 5 Barnsley
21.09.07 Frederic Gosset W PTS 6 Bethnal Green
30.11.07 Riaz Durgahed W PTS 6 Newham
01.02.08 Wladimir Borov W PTS 8 Bethnal Green
18.04.08 Peter Allen W PTS 6 Bethnal Green
18.07.08 John Vanemmenis W RSC 3 Dagenham
07.11.08 Marc Callaghan W CO 2 Wigan
  *(Vacant Southern Area Featherweight
  Title)*

20.03.09 Elemir Rafael W RSC 1 Newham
30.06.09 Jamie Arthur L PTS 10 Bethnal Green
  (Elim. British Featherweight Title)
Career: 15 contests, won 14, lost 1.

Willie Bilan

Fife. *Born* Kirkcaldy, 17 April, 1986
Welterweight. *Ht* 5'11¼"
Manager T. Gilmour
23.10.06 Steve Cooper W PTS 6 Glasgow
16.02.07 David Kehoe W RSC 1 Kirkcaldy
11.05.07 Steve Anning W PTS 4 Motherwell
14.09.07 Alexander Spitjo L CO 1 Kirkcaldy
10.10.08 Matt Seawright W PTS 6 Motherwell
10.11.08 Gavin Deacon W PTS 6 Glasgow
14.03.09 Paul Royston L PTS 6 Aberdeen
25.06.09 William Warburton W PTS 6 Glenrothes
Career: 8 contests, won 6, lost 2.

Stephen Birch

St Helens. *Born* Whiston, 25 September,
1981
L.Heavyweight. *Ht* 6'0"
Manager O. Harrison
09.09.05 Nick Okoth L PTS 4 Sheffield
08.11.08 Lee Nicholson W CO 1 Wigan
Career: 2 contests, won 1, lost 1.

JJ Bird   Philip Sharkey

(Joe John) JJ Bird

Peterborough. *Born* Peterborough, 9
September, 1986
Middleweight. *Ht* 6'1½"
Manager D. Powell
23.02.07 Frank Celebi W PTS 4 Peterborough
01.06.07 Duncan Cottier W PTS 4 Peterborough
21.09.07 Lance Verallo W PTS 6 Peterborough
10.11.07 Paul Morby L PTS 6 Portsmouth
02.12.07 Tommy Heffron DREW 6 Oldham
27.06.08 David Walker W PTS 4 Bethnal Green
20.09.08 Dale Miles L PTS 4 Newark
08.11.08 Steve O'Meara L PTS 4 Bethnal Green
21.11.08 Grant Skehill L PTS 4 Bethnal Green
23.02.09 Callum Archer W PTS 8 Birmingham
27.03.09 Nathan Graham L PTS 4 Kensington
24.04.09 Rob Kenney DREW 4 Wolverhampton
Career: 12 contests, won 5, drew 2, lost 5.

Chris Black

Coatbridge. *Born* Bellshill, 19 November,
1979
Middleweight. *Ht* 5'7½"
Manager T. Gilmour
22.10.04 Brian Coleman W PTS 4 Edinburgh
12.12.04 Jak Hibbert W RSC 2 Glasgow
28.01.05 Geraint Harvey W PTS 4 Renfrew
01.04.05 Tony Randell W PTS 6 Glasgow
17.06.05 Ciaran Healy DREW 4 Glasgow
22.04.06 Barrie Lee L PTS 10 Glasgow
  *(Scottish L.Middleweight Title
  Challenge)*
28.10.06 Tyan Booth L PTS 6 Aberdeen
19.10.07 Shaun Farmer W CO 1 Motherwell
24.11.07 Tyan Booth W PTS 6 Clydebank
22.02.08 Tony Randell W PTS 6 Motherwell
16.05.08 Darren Gethin W PTS 6 Motherwell
22.09.08 Paul Royston W PTS 6 Glasgow
16.02.09 Max Maxwell DREW 6 Glasgow
08.06.09 Alex Spitjo L PTS 6 Glasgow
Career: 14 contests, won 9, drew 2, lost 3.

Nick Blackwell

Trowbridge. *Born* Bath, 27 October, 1990
Middleweight. *Ht* 5'10"
Manager P. Rowson
26.06.09 Dave Sadler W RSC 3 Melksham
Career: 1 contest, won 1.

Wayne Bloy

Grimsby. *Born* Grimsby, 30 November,
1982
Bantamweight. *Ht* 5'5"
Manager C. Greaves
14.06.04 Neil Read DREW 6 Cleethorpes
20.09.04 Gary Ford W PTS 6 Cleethorpes
24.04.05 Andy Bell W PTS 4 Askern
23.05.05 Neil Marston W PTS 6 Cleethorpes
24.02.06 Abdul Mougharbel W PTS 6
  Scarborough
13.10.06 Jamie McDonnell L PTS 4 Doncaster
23.02.07 Jamie McDonnell L RSC 3 Doncaster
  (Vacant English Bantamweight Title)
08.09.07 Delroy Spencer W PTS 4 Sutton in
  Ashfield
01.12.07 Andy Bell L PTS 10 Nottingham
  (English S.Flyweight Title Challenge)
23.01.09 Chris Edwards L RTD 4 Stoke
  *(Vacant British & Commonwealth
  Flyweight Titles)*
Career: 10 contests, won 5, drew 1, lost 4.

Steve Bodger

Blackburn. *Born* Hannover, Germany, 29
August, 1981
Heavyweight. *Ht* 6'3"
Manager T.Schofield
15.05.08 Danny Hughes L PTS 6 Sunderland
23.01.09 Alex Ibbs L PTS 4 Stoke
Career: 2 contests, lost 2.

Jamie Boness

Luton. *Born* Luton, 17 October, 1983
L.Middleweight. *Ht* 6'0"
Manager G. Earl
28.06.09 Ryan Clark DREW 6 Luton
Career: 1 contest, drew 1.

Jamie Boness   Philip Sharkey

Paul Bonson

Featherstone. *Born* Castleford, 18 October, 1971
Cruiserweight. Former Central Area L.Heavyweight Champion. *Ht* 5'10¼"
Manager M. Marsden
04.10.96 Michael Pinnock W PTS 6 Wakefield
14.11.96 Michael Pinnock DREW 6 Sheffield
22.12.96 Pele Lawrence DREW 6 Salford
20.04.97 Shamus Casey W PTS 6 Leeds
26.06.97 Andy Manning L PTS 6 Sheffield
19.09.97 Mike Gormley W PTS 6 Salford
03.10.97 Rudi Marcussen L PTS 4 Copenhagen, Denmark
03.12.97 Alex Mason DREW 6 Stoke
14.12.97 Willie Quinn L RSC 4 Glasgow
15.01.98 Alex Mason L PTS 6 Solihull
13.02.98 Peter Mason L PTS 4 Seaham
23.02.98 Martin McDonough W PTS 6 Windsor
07.03.98 Michael Bowen L PTS 6 Reading
14.03.98 Alain Simon L PTS 6 Pont Saint Maxence, France
08.04.98 Tim Brown DREW 4 Liverpool
21.05.98 Mark Hobson L PTS 6 Bradford
21.06.98 Kenny Rainford L PTS 6 Liverpool
01.09.98 Roberto Dominguez L PTS 8 Vigo, Spain
23.10.98 Rob Galloway W PTS 6 Wakefield
16.11.98 Chris P. Bacon L PTS 8 Glasgow
11.12.98 Robert Zlotkowski L PTS 4 Prestwick
20.12.98 Glenn Williams L PTS 6 Salford
24.04.99 Kenny Gayle DREW 4 Peterborough
29.05.99 Dave Johnson L PTS 6 South Shields
19.06.99 Sebastiaan Rothmann L PTS 8 Dublin
12.07.99 Jim Twite L PTS 4 Coventry
07.08.99 Juan Perez Nelongo L PTS 8 Tenerife, Spain
11.09.99 Mark Hobson L PTS 4 Sheffield
02.10.99 Enzo Maccarinelli L PTS 4 Cardiff
16.10.99 Robert Zlotkowski L PTS 6 Bethnal Green
27.10.99 Peter McCormack W PTS 6 Birmingham
04.12.99 Glenn Williams W PTS 4 Manchester
11.12.99 Chris Davies L PTS 4 Merthyr Tydfil
05.02.00 Paul Maskell L PTS 4 Bethnal Green

11.03.00 Tony Dodson L PTS 4 Kensington
26.03.00 Wayne Buck L PTS 8 Nottingham
29.04.00 Cathal O'Grady L PTS 4 Wembley
13.05.00 Mark Hobson L PTS 4 Barnsley
25.06.00 Andy Manning W PTS 10 Wakefield
        (*Vacant Central Area L.Heavyweight Title*)
08.09.00 Robert Milewicz L PTS 4 Hammersmith
21.10.00 Jon Penn L PTS 6 Sheffield
12.11.00 Glenn Williams L PTS 10 Manchester
        (*Central Area L.Heavyweight Title Defence*)
24.11.00 Alex Mason L PTS 6 Darlington
09.12.00 Mark Baker L PTS 6 Southwark
23.01.01 Calvin Stonestreet W PTS 4 Crawley
03.02.01 Tony Dodson L PTS 4 Manchester
18.02.01 Butch Lesley L PTS 6 Southwark
13.03.01 Konstantin Schvets L PTS 6 Plymouth
07.04.01 Bobby Scott L PTS 4 Wembley
26.04.01 Mike White L PTS 6 Gateshead
17.05.01 Clint Johnson W PTS 6 Leeds
24.05.01 Sven Hamer L PTS 4 Kensington
04.06.01 Joe Gillon DREW 6 Glasgow
11.06.01 Darren Chubbs L PTS 4 Nottingham
21.06.01 Michael Pinnock W PTS 6 Sheffield
27.07.01 Clinton Woods L PTS 6 Sheffield
09.09.01 Eamonn Glennon W PTS 6 Hartlepool
28.09.01 Elvis Michailenko L PTS 6 Millwall
13.11.01 Tony Moran W PTS 6 Leeds
23.11.01 Elvis Michailenko L PTS 6 Bethnal Green
06.12.01 Shaun Bowes W RSC 5 Sunderland
16.12.01 Tommy Eastwood L PTS 4 Southwark
26.01.02 Dominic Negus L PTS 4 Bethnal Green
10.02.02 Butch Lesley L PTS 4 Southwark
25.02.02 Roman Greenberg L PTS 6 Slough
15.03.02 Michael Thompson L PTS 6 Spennymoor
22.03.02 Mark Smallwood L PTS 6 Coventry
19.04.02 Michael Thompson L PTS 6 Darlington
11.05.02 Mark Brookes L PTS 4 Chesterfield
15.06.02 Peter Haymer L PTS 4 Tottenham
23.06.02 Scott Lansdowne W PTS 6 Southwark
13.07.02 Jason Brewster W PTS 6 Wolverhampton
27.07.02 Albert Sosnowski L PTS 4 Nottingham
08.09.02 Varuzhan Davtyan L PTS 4 Wolverhampton
22.09.02 Neil Linford L PTS 6 Southwark
29.09.02 Tony Dowling L PTS 6 Shrewsbury
12.10.02 Andrew Lowe L PTS 4 Bethnal Green
25.10.02 Carl Froch L PTS 6 Bethnal Green
30.11.02 Robert Norton L PTS 6 Coventry
14.12.02 Nathan King W PTS 4 Newcastle
18.01.03 Enzo Maccarinelli L PTS 4 Preston
08.02.03 Steven Spartacus L PTS 6 Norwich
05.03.03 Marcus Lee W PTS 4 Bethnal Green
18.03.03 Mark Krence L PTS 4 Reading
28.03.03 Eric Teymour L PTS 6 Millwall
19.04.03 Tony Moran L PTS 4 Liverpool
12.05.03 Colin Kenna L PTS 6 Southampton
10.06.03 Lee Swaby L PTS 4 Sheffield
26.09.03 Garry Delaney L PTS 6 Reading
06.10.03 Pinky Burton L PTS 6 Barnsley
07.11.03 Carl Thompson L PTS 6 Sheffield
14.11.03 Tony Booth L PTS 6 Hull
01.12.03 David Ingleby W PTS 6 Leeds
20.02.04 Colin Kenna L PTS 6 Southampton
13.03.04 Neil Dawson L PTS 4 Huddersfield
16.04.04 John Keeton L PTS 4 Bradford
01.05.04 Carl Wright L PTS 6 Coventry

26.11.04 Tony Booth L PTS 6 Hull
06.12.04 Robert Norton L CO 6 Leicester
        (*Vacant British Masters Cruiserweight Title*)
06.02.05 Ovill McKenzie L PTS 4 Southampton
30.04.05 Tony Moran L PTS 6 Wigan
14.05.05 John Keeton L PTS 4 Aberdeen
18.06.05 Neil Simpson L PTS 6 Coventry
09.07.05 Dean Francis L PTS 6 Bristol
24.07.05 Toks Owoh L PTS 4 Leicester Square
03.09.05 Sam Sexton L PTS 6 Norwich
23.09.05 Gyorgy Hidvegi L PTS 4 Manchester
07.10.05 Junior MacDonald L PTS 4 Bethnal Green
20.11.05 Darren Stubbs L PTS 6 Shaw
10.12.05 Bruce Scott L PTS 4 Canning Town
24.02.06 Gyorgy Hidvegi DREW 8 Dagenham
05.03.06 Amer Khan L PTS 6 Sheffield
23.03.06 Ovill McKenzie L PTS 6 The Strand
30.03.06 Ovill McKenzie L RSC 3 Bloomsbury
06.05.06 Billy McClung L PTS 6 Irvine
09.06.06 Dean Cockburn L PTS 6 Doncaster
26.01.08 Jonathan O'Brien L PTS 4 Cork
02.03.08 Billy Bessey W PTS 6 Portsmouth
16.03.08 Paul Keir L PTS 4 Liverpool
05.04.08 Tony Bellew L PTS 4 Bolton
18.04.08 Micky Steeds L PTS 8 Bethnal Green
30.04.08 Neil Perkins L PTS 6 Wolverhampton
23.05.08 Scott Mitchell L PTS 6 Wigan
07.06.08 Mike Stafford L PTS 4 Wigan
21.06.08 Mark Krence L PTS 4 Sheffield
04.07.08 Joe Smyth L PTS 4 Liverpool
19.07.08 Mike Stafford L PTS 4 Liverpool
19.09.08 Jon Ibbotson L PTS 4 Doncaster
03.10.08 Neil Simpson DREW 4 Burton
10.10.08 Terry Dunstan L PTS 4 Sheffield
07.11.08 Jon-Lewis Dickinson L PTS 4 Wigan
22.11.08 Matty Askin L PTS 4 Blackpool
06.12.08 Martyn Grainger W RSC 3 Wigan
14.12.08 Henry Smith L PTS 4 Bristol
Career: 134 contests, won 21, drew 8, lost 105.

Jason Booth

Nottingham. *Born* Nottingham, 7 November, 1977
British S. Bantamweight Champion. Commonwealth Bantamweight Champion. Former IBO S.Flyweight Champion. Former Undefeated British & Commonwealth Flyweight Champion. Former Undefeated Commonwealth Flyweight Champion.
Ht 5'4"
Manager J. Gill/T. Harris
13.06.96 Darren Noble W RSC 3 Sheffield
24.10.96 Marty Chestnut W PTS 6 Lincoln
27.11.96 Jason Thomas W PTS 4 Swansea
18.01.97 David Coldwell W PTS 4 Swadlincote
07.03.97 Pete Buckley W PTS 6 Northampton
20.03.97 Danny Lawson W RSC 3 Newark
10.05.97 Anthony Hanna W PTS 6 Nottingham
19.05.97 Chris Lyons W PTS 6 Cleethorpes
31.10.97 Mark Reynolds W PTS 6 Ilkeston
31.01.98 Anthony Hanna W PTS 6 Edmonton
20.03.98 Louis Veitch W CO 2 Ilkeston
        (*Elim. British Flyweight Title*)
09.06.98 Dimitar Alipiev W RSC 2 Hull
17.10.98 Graham McGrath W RSC 4 Manchester
07.12.98 Louis Veitch W RSC 5 Cleethorpes

08.05.99 David Guerault L PTS 12 Grande Synthe, France
(European Flyweight Title Challenge)
12.07.99 Mark Reynolds W RSC 3 Coventry
16.10.99 Keith Knox W RSC 10 Belfast
(British & Commonwealth Flyweight Title Challenges)
22.01.00 Abie Mnisi W PTS 12 Birmingham
(Commonwealth Flyweight Title Defence)
01.07.00 John Barnes W PTS 6 Manchester
13.11.00 Ian Napa W PTS 12 Bethnal Green
(British & Commonwealth Flyweight Title Defences)
26.02.01 Nokuthula Tshabangu W CO 2 Nottingham
(Commonwealth Flyweight Title Defence)
30.06.01 Alexander Mahmutov L PTS 12 Madrid, Spain
(European Flyweight Title Challenge)
23.02.02 Jason Thomas W PTS 6 Nottingham
01.06.02 Mimoun Chent L TD 8 Le Havre, France
(Vacant European Flyweight Title)
16.11.02 Kakhar Sabitov W RSC 6 Nottingham
28.04.03 Lindi Memani W PTS 8 Nottingham
20.09.03 Lunga Ntontela W PTS 12 Nottingham
(IBO S.Flyweight Title Challenge)
13.03.04 Dale Robinson W PTS 12 Huddersfield
(IBO S.Flyweight Title Defence)
17.12.04 Damaen Kelly L PTS 12 Huddersfield
(IBO S.Flyweight Title Defence)
03.11.06 Abdul Mougharbel W PTS 6 Barnsley
09.02.07 Jamil Hussain W PTS 6 Leeds
06.07.07 Ian Napa L PTS 12 Wigan
(Vacant British Bantamweight Title)
08.12.07 Matthew Edmonds W RSC 9 Wigan
(Vacant Commonwealth Bantamweight Title)
07.03.08 Lante Addy W PTS 12 Nottingham
(Commonwealth Bantamweight Title Defence)
13.06.08 Dai Davies W PTS 6 Portsmouth
18.12.08 Sean Hughes W RTD 10 Dublin
(Commonwealth Bantamweight Title Defence)
17.04.09 Mark Moran W RSC 6 Leigh
(Vacant British S.Bantamweight Title)
30.06.09 Rocky Dean W PTS 12 Bethnal Green
(British S.Bantamweight Title Defence)
Career: 38 contests, won 33, lost 5.

Tony Booth
Hull. *Born* Hull, 30 January, 1970
Heavyweight. Former Undefeated British Masters L.Heavyweight Champion. Former Undefeated British Masters & Central Area Cruiserweight Champion. *Ht* 5'11½"
Manager Self
08.03.90 Paul Lynch L PTS 6 Watford
11.04.90 Mick Duncan W PTS 6 Dewsbury
26.04.90 Colin Manners W PTS 6 Halifax
16.05.90 Tommy Warde W PTS 6 Hull
05.06.90 Gary Dyson W PTS 6 Liverpool
05.09.90 Shaun McCrory L PTS 6 Stoke
08.10.90 Bullit Andrews W RSC 3 Cleethorpes
23.01.91 Darron Griffiths DREW 6 Stoke
06.02.91 Shaun McCrory L PTS 6 Liverpool
06.03.91 Billy Brough L PTS 6 Glasgow
18.03.91 Billy Brough W PTS 6 Glasgow

28.03.91 Neville Brown L PTS 6 Alfreton
17.05.91 Glenn Campbell L RSC 2 Bury
(Central Area S. Middleweight Title Challenge)
25.07.91 Paul Murray W PTS 6 Dudley
01.08.91 Nick Manners DREW 8 Dewsbury
11.09.91 Jim Peters L PTS 8 Hammersmith
28.10.91 Eddie Smulders L RSC 6 Arnhem, Holland
09.12.91 Steve Lewsam L PTS 8 Cleethorpes
30.01.92 Serg Fame W PTS 6 Southampton
12.02.92 Tenko Ernie W PTS 4 Wembley
05.03.92 John Beckles W RSC 6 Battersea
26.03.92 Dave Owens W PTS 6 Hull
08.04.92 Michael Gale L PTS 8 Leeds
13.05.92 Phil Soundy W PTS 6 Kensington
02.06.92 Eddie Smulders L RSC 1 Rotterdam, Holland
18.07.92 Maurice Core L PTS 6 Manchester
07.09.92 James Cook L PTS 8 Bethnal Green
30.10.92 Roy Richie DREW 6 Istrees, France
18.11.92 Tony Wilson DREW 8 Solihull
25.12.92 Francis Wanyama L PTS 6 Izegem, Belgium
09.02.93 Tony Wilson W PTS 8 Wolverhampton
01.05.93 Ralf Rocchigiani DREW 8 Berlin, Germany
03.06.93 Victor Cordoba L PTS 8 Marseille, France
23.06.93 Tony Behan W PTS 6 Gorleston
01.07.93 Michael Gale L PTS 8 York
17.09.93 Ole Klemetsen L PTS 8 Copenhagen, Denmark
07.10.93 Denzil Browne DREW 8 York
02.11.93 James Cook L PTS 8 Southwark
12.11.93 Carlos Christie W PTS 6 Hull
28.01.94 Francis Wanyama L RSC 2 Waregem, Belgium
(Vacant Commonwealth Cruiserweight Title)
26.03.94 Torsten May L PTS 6 Dortmund, Germany
21.07.94 Mark Prince L RSC 3 Battersea
24.09.94 Johnny Held L PTS 8 Rotterdam, Holland
07.10.94 Dirk Wallyn L PTS 6 Waregem, Belgium
27.10.94 Dean Francis L CO 1 Bayswater
23.01.95 Jan Lefeber L PTS 8 Rotterdam, Holland
07.03.95 John Foreman L PTS 6 Edgbaston
27.04.95 Art Stacey W PTS 10 Hull
(Vacant Central Area Cruiserweight Title)
04.06.95 Montell Griffin L RSC 2 Bethnal Green
06.07.95 Nigel Rafferty W RSC 7 Hull
22.07.95 Mark Prince L RSC 2 Millwall
06.09.95 Leif Keiski L PTS 8 Helsinki, Finland
25.09.95 Neil Simpson W PTS 8 Cleethorpes
06.10.95 Don Diego Poeder L RSC 2 Waregem, Belgium
11.11.95 Bruce Scott L RSC 3 Halifax
16.12.95 John Marceta L RSC 2 Cardiff
20.01.96 Johnny Nelson L RSC 2 Mansfield
15.03.96 Slick Miller W PTS 6 Hull
27.03.96 Neil Simpson L PTS 6 Whitwick
17.05.96 Mark Richardson W RSC 2 Hull
13.07.96 Bruce Scott L PTS 8 Bethnal Green
03.09.96 Paul Douglas L PTS 4 Belfast
14.09.96 Kelly Oliver L RSC 2 Sheffield
06.11.96 Martin Jolley W PTS 4 Hull
22.11.96 Slick Miller W RSC 5 Hull
11.12.96 Crawford Ashley L RSC 1 Southwark

18.01.97 Kelly Oliver L RSC 4 Swadlincote
27.02.97 Kevin Morton L PTS 6 Hull
25.03.97 Nigel Rafferty DREW 8 Wolverhampton
04.04.97 John Wilson L PTS 6 Glasgow
16.04.97 Robert Norton L RSC 4 Bethnal Green
15.05.97 Phill Day W PTS 4 Reading
11.09.97 Steve Bristow L PTS 4 Widnes
22.09.97 Martin Langtry W PTS 6 Cleethorpes
04.10.97 Bruce Scott W PTS 8 Muswell Hill
28.11.97 Martin Jolley W PTS 6 Hull
15.12.97 Nigel Rafferty W PTS 6 Cleethorpes
06.03.98 Peter Mason W RSC 3 Hull
09.06.98 Crawford Ashley L RSC 6 Hull
(British L. Heavyweight Title Challenge. Vacant Commonwealth L. Heavyweight Title)
18.07.98 Omar Sheika W PTS 8 Sheffield
26.09.98 Toks Owoh L PTS 6 Norwich
29.10.98 Nigel Rafferty W PTS 8 Bayswater
14.12.98 Sven Hamer W PTS 6 Cleethorpes
05.01.99 Ali Saidi W RSC 4 Epernay, France
17.05.99 Darren Ashton W PTS 6 Cleethorpes
12.07.99 Neil Simpson L PTS 10 Coventry
(Elim. British L. Heavyweight Title)
27.09.99 Adam Cale W PTS 6 Cleethorpes
16.10.99 Cathal O'Grady L CO 4 Belfast
18.01.00 Michael Sprott L PTS 6 Mansfield
12.02.00 Thomas Hansvoll L PTS 6 Sheffield
29.02.00 John Keeton L RSC 2 Widnes
09.04.00 Greg Scott-Briggs W PTS 10 Alfreton
(Vacant British Masters L. Heavyweight Title)
15.05.00 Michael Pinnock W PTS 6 Cleethorpes
19.06.00 Toks Owoh L RSC 3 Burton
08.09.00 Dominic Negus W PTS 6 Bristol
30.09.00 Robert Norton L RSC 3 Peterborough
31.10.00 Firat Aslan L RSC 2 Hammersmith
11.12.00 Mark Krence L PTS 6 Sheffield
05.02.01 Denzil Browne L RSC 5 Hull
(Vacant Central Area Cruiserweight Title)
01.04.01 Kenny Gayle DREW 4 Southwark
10.04.01 Mark Baker L PTS 4 Wembley
16.06.01 Butch Lesley L RSC 3 Dagenham
09.09.01 Tommy Eastwood L PTS 4 Southwark
22.09.01 Peter Haymer L PTS 4 Bethnal Green
15.10.01 Colin Kenna L PTS 6 Southampton
01.11.01 Terry Morrill W RSC 7 Hull
24.11.01 Matt Legg L PTS 4 Bethnal Green
16.12.01 Blue Stevens L PTS 4 Southwark
19.01.02 John McDermott L RSC 1 Bethnal Green
20.04.02 Enzo Maccarinelli L PTS 4 Cardiff
28.04.02 Scott Lansdowne W RSC 4 Southwark
10.05.02 Paul Buttery L PTS 4 Preston
23.06.02 Neil Linford L RSC 5 Southwark
03.08.02 Mark Krence L PTS 4 Derby
17.08.02 Enzo Maccarinelli L RTD 2 Cardiff
23.09.02 Slick Miller W PTS 6 Cleethorpes
05.10.02 Phill Day W PTS 4 Coventry
19.10.02 James Zikic L PTS 4 Norwich
27.10.02 Hughie Doherty L PTS 4 Southwark
21.11.02 Jamie Warters L PTS 8 Hull
28.11.02 Roman Greenberg L PTS 4 Finchley
08.12.02 David Haye L RTD 2 Bethnal Green
30.01.03 Mohammed Benguesmia L RTD 4 Algiers, Algeria
05.04.03 Jason Callum L PTS 6 Coventry
17.05.03 Tony Moran L PTS 6 Liverpool
26.07.03 Kelly Oliver L PTS 4 Plymouth
26.09.03 Radcliffe Green W PTS 6 Millwall

14.11.03 Paul Bonson W PTS 6 Hull
14.02.04 Oneal Murray W PTS 8 Holborn
01.05.04 Elvis Michailenko L RTD 4 Gravesend
15.08.04 Bash Ali L RSC 4 Lagos, Nigeria
(*WBF Cruiserweight Title Challenge*)
26.11.04 Paul Bonson W PTS 6 Hull
11.12.04 Hovik Keuchkerian L CO 1 Madrid,
Spain
05.03.05 Junior MacDonald L PTS 4 Southwark
15.04.05 Johny Jensen L PTS 6 Copenhagen,
Denmark
04.06.05 Martin Rogan L RSC 2 Manchester
24.07.05 Coleman Barrett L PTS 4 Leicester
Square
10.09.05 Darren Morgan L PTS 4 Cardiff
24.09.05 Carl Wright L PTS 4 Coventry
06.10.05 Tommy Eastwood L PTS 4 Longford
25.11.05 Dave Clarke DREW 6 Hull
26.02.06 Ovill McKenzie L PTS 4 Dagenham
05.03.06 Jon Ibbotson L PTS 4 Sheffield
30.03.06 Ervis Jegeni L RSC 1 Piccadilly
13.05.06 Paul Souter L PTS 4 Bethnal Green
26.05.06 Lee Mountford W PTS 6 Hull
12.07.06 Ervis Jegeni L PTS 4 Bethnal Green
23.07.06 Tommy Eastwood L PTS 4 Dagenham
24.09.06 Mervyn Langdale W RSC 1
Southampton
09.10.06 Oneal Murray W PTS 4 Bedworth
21.10.06 Danny Tombs W PTS 4 Southwark
03.11.06 Leigh Alliss L PTS 4 Bristol
03.12.06 JJ Ojuederie L PTS 4 Bethnal Green
23.02.07 Billy Wilson W RSC 5 Doncaster
07.04.07 Derek Chisora L PTS 4 Cardiff
21.04.07 Paulino Da Silva L PTS 6 Manchester
18.05.07 Troy Ross L RSC 2 Canning Town
13.07.07 Tom Owens L PTS 4 Birmingham
25.09.07 Neil Simpson L PTS 10 Hull
(*Vacant British Masters Cruiserweight
Title*)
19.10.07 Ali Adams L PTS 4 Mayfair
09.11.07 Ben Harding L PTS 4 Plymouth
23.11.07 David Dolan L RSC 3 Houghton le
Spring
01.03.08 Neil Simpson L PTS 4 Coventry
14.03.08 Howard Daley L RTD 2 Manchester
11.10.08 Howard Daley W PTS 6 Hull
01.11.08 Raz Parnez W RTD 4 Glasgow
Career: 166 contests, won 52, drew 9, lost 105.

Tyan Booth

Sheffield. *Born* Nottingham, 20 March,
1983
Welterweight. *Ht* 6'2½"
Manager D. Ingle
29.10.05 Jimi Hendricks W PTS 6 Aberdeen
08.11.05 Jimi Hendricks W PTS 6 Leeds
27.02.06 Jason Welborn W CO 4 Birmingham
06.05.06 Richard Turba W PTS 6 Blackpool
17.05.06 Alexis Callero LPTS 6 Lanzarote,
Canary Islands, Spain
22.09.06 George Hillyard W PTS 6 Bethnal Green
13.10.06 Karl David W PTS 6 Aberavon
28.10.06 Chris Black W PTS 6 Aberdeen
24.11.06 Peter Dunn W PTS 4 Nottingham
02.12.06 Nathan Graham W PTS 6 Southwark
23.03.07 Darren Gethin L RSC 10 Nottingham
(*Vacant Midlands Area Welterweight
Title*)
24.11.07 Chris Black L PTS 6 Clydebank
03.12.07 Matthew Hall L PTS 8 Manchester

29.03.08 Colin McNeil W CO 1 Aberdeen
28.06.08 Kevin Concepcion L PTS 10 Leicester
(*Vacant British Masters Middleweight
Title*)
07.03.09 Julien Marie Sainte W PTS 8 Montreal,
Canada
Career: 16 contests, won 11, lost 5.

Gary Boulden

Shepperton *Born* Ashford, 11 February,
1986
L.Middleweight. *Ht* 5' 9"
Manager J. Evans
16.08.08 Oliver Tchinda L RSC 3 Arona, Spain
20.03.09 Paul Brown W PTS 4 Bethnal Green
Career: 2 contests, won 1, lost 1.

Billy Boyle   Philip Sharkey

Billy Boyle

Sheffield. *Born* Sheffield, 8 July, 1976
Former Undefeated International Masters L.
Heavyweight Champion. *Ht* 5'11½"
Manager G. Rhodes
20.04.07 David Ingleby W PTS 4 Sheffield
02.06.07 John Smith W RSC 3 Bristol
16.09.07 James Swindells W RSC 4 Sheffield
19.10.07 Lee Mountford W PTS 6 Doncaster
23.11.07 Clint Johnson W RSC 2 Sheffield
15.02.08 Nick Okoth W PTS 4 Sheffield
28.03.08 Mark Nilsen W RTD 1 Barnsley
21.06.08 Paul Davis W CO 5 Sheffield
12.09.08 Simeon Cover W RSC 5 Sheffield
10.10.08 Martins Kukuls W RSC 3 Sheffield
05.12.08 Jevgenijs Andrejevs W PTS 6 Sheffield
20.02.09 Tony Oakey L PTS 3 Bethnal Green
24.04.09 Shon Davies W PTS 10 Sheffield
(*Vacant International Masters
L.Heavyweight Title*)
22.05.09 Nathan Cleverly L RSC 2 Bethnal Green
(*Commonwealth L.Heavyweight Title
Challenge*)
Career: 14 contests, won 12, lost 2.

Ryan Brawley

Irvine. *Born* Irvine, 2 February, 1986
Lightweight. *Ht* 5'10½"
Manager T. Gilmour

19.09.05 Pete Buckley W PTS 6 Glasgow
14.10.05 Lance Verallo W PTS 6 Motherwell
20.02.06 Gavin Deacon W PTS 4 Glasgow
25.03.06 Chris Long W PTS 8 Irvine
06.05.06 Dariusz Snarski W PTS 6 Irvine
28.04.07 Rom Krauklis W PTS 8 Clydebank
11.05.07 Zsolt Jonas W PTS 6 Motherwell
02.11.07 George Watson W PTS 6 Irvine
06.06.08 Jamie McKeever W RSC 7 Glasgow
24.03.09 Stephen Burke W PTS 3 Glasgow
24.03.09 Paul Holborn W PTS 3 Glasgow
24.03.09 Ben Murphy W PTS 3 Glasgow
12.06.09 Daniel Thorpe W PTS 6 Clydebank
Career: 13 contests, won 13.

Gordon Brennan

Dunfermline. *Born* Dunfermline, 1 August,
1982
L.Heavyweight. *Ht* 5'11"
Manager Self
31.03.06 Jimi Hendricks W PTS 6 Inverurie
11.11.06 Tyrone Wright L PTS 6 Sutton in
Ashfield
16.02.07 Simon Wood W PTS 4 Kirkcaldy
11.05.07 Leon Owen W PTS 4 Motherwell
14.09.07 Nick Okoth L PTS 4 Kirkcaldy
05.12.08 Joe Smyth L RSC 2 Dagenham
25.06.09 Jamie Ambler DREW 6 Glenrothes
Career: 7 contests, won 3, drew 1, lost 3.

Jimmy Briggs

Plymouth. *Born* Fareham, 17 December,
1987
Welterweight. *Ht* 5'8¼"
Manager N. Christian
09.11.07 Ben Wakeham L PTS 6 Plymouth
02.03.08 Lloyd Smith W PTS 6 Portsmouth
05.04.08 Jamie Way L PTS 6 Newport
20.06.08 Bheki Moyo L PTS 6 Plymouth
27.09.08 Mark Douglas L PTS 4 Bracknell
11.10.08 Glen Matsell L PTS 6 Hull
08.11.08 Thomas Mazurkiewicz L PTS 6 Wigan
29.11.08 Mark Walsh L PTS 6 Sleaford
08.12.08 Billy Graham L PTS 6 Cleethorpes
24.01.09 Nick Quigley L PTS 6 Blackpool

Jimmy Briggs   Philip Sharkey

07.03.09 Chris Goodwin L PTS 6 Chester
14.05.09 Tommy Broadbent L PTS 6 Leeds
12.06.09 Peter McDonagh L PTS 4 Bethnal Green
Career: 13 contests, won 2, lost 11.

Tommy Broadbent

Leeds. *Born* Leeds, 13 July, 1987
Welterweight. *Ht* 5'10"
Manager M. Bateson
07.11.06 Steve Cooper W PTS 6 Leeds
27.11.08 Janos Fidel W RSC 2 Leeds
14.05.09 Jimmy Briggs W PTS 6 Leeds
Career: 3 contests, won 3.

Don Broadhurst

Birmingham. *Born* Birmingham, 2
February, 1984
Commonwealth S. Flyweight Champion.
Ht 5'2½"
Manager F. Warren
02.09.06 Delroy Spencer W PTS 4 Bolton
18.11.06 Kemal Plavci W PTS 4 Newport
17.02.07 Ravil Mukhamadiarov W PTS 4
Wembley
07.04.07 Delroy Spencer W PTS 4 Cardiff
21.07.07 Kakha Toklikishvili W PTS 4 Cardiff
06.10.07 Gary Sheil W PTS 6 Nottingham
08.12.07 Kakhaber Avetisian W RSC 3 Bolton
21.06.08 Alain Bonnel W PTS 6 Birmingham
31.10.08 Isaac Quaye W PTS 12 Birmingham
*(Vacant Commonwealth S.Flyweight
Title)*
28.02.09 Isaac Owusu W RSC 11 Birmingham
*(Commonwealth S.Flyweight Title
Defence)*
24.04.09 Asamoah Wilson W RSC 6
Wolverhampton
*(Commonwealth S.Flyweight Title
Defence)*
Career: 11 contests, won 11.

Caine Brodie

London. *Born* Rinteln, Germany, 8 April,
1982
Heavyweight. *Ht* 5'11¼"
Manager J. Rooney
08.12.07 Andrei Tolstihs W PTS 4 Belfast
01.08.08 Jamie Norkett W PTS 4 Watford
01.02.09 Lee Nicholson W RSC 1 Bethnal Green
Career: 3 contests, won 3.

Kurt Bromberg

Leeds. *Born* Leeds, 16 January, 1985
Middleweight. *Ht* 5'11¼"
Manager M. Bateson
21.02.08 Jason Smith W PTS 6 Leeds
05.06.08 Gavin Brook W PTS 6 Leeds
14.05.09 Wayne Reed L PTS 6 Leeds
12.06.09 Mike Stanton W RSC 3 Liverpool
Career: 4 contests, won 3, lost 1.

Craig Bromley

Sheffield. *Born* Sheffield, 28 June, 1986
S.Featherweight. *Ht* 5' 5"
Manager D. Coldwell
10.12.04 Darren Broomhall L PTS 6 Mansfield
19.12.04 Paddy Folan DREW 6 Bolton

13.02.05 Paddy Folan W PTS 6 Bradford
15.04.05 Neil Marston W CO 1 Shrewsbury
24.07.05 Neil Read W PTS 4 Sheffield
16.09.05 Dave Hinds W PTS 4 Doncaster
14.10.05 Shaun Walton W PTS 4 Huddersfield
04.11.05 Sandy Bartlett W RSC 2 Glasgow
14.12.06 Eduards Krauklis W PTS 6 Leicester
12.09.08 Sid Razak W PTS 4 Sheffield
Career: 10 contests, won 8, drew 1, lost 1.

Gavin Brook

Plymouth. *Born* Plymouth, 24 November,
1984
Middleweight. *Ht* 5'9¼"
Manager N. Christian
05.04.08 James Evans DREW 6 Newport
02.05.08 Kevin Hammond L RTD 1 Nottingham
05.06.08 Kurt Bromberg L PTS 6 Leeds
15.11.08 Geraint Harvey L RSC 1 Plymouth
03.04.09 Bobby Wood L PTS 4 Wolverhampton
Career: 5 contests, drew 1, lost 4.

Kell Brook   Philip Sharkey

(Ezekiel) Kell Brook

Sheffield. *Born* Sheffield, 3 May, 1986
British Welterweight Champion. *Ht* 5'9"
Manager F. Warren
17.09.04 Pete Buckley W PTS 6 Sheffield
29.10.04 Andy Cosnett W CO 1 Worksop
09.11.04 Lee Williamson W RSC 2 Leeds
10.12.04 Brian Coleman W RSC 1 Sheffield
19.12.04 Karl Taylor W PTS 6 Bolton
04.03.05 Lea Handley W PTS 6 Rotherham
15.05.05 Ernie Smith W PTS 6 Sheffield
09.07.05 Jonathan Whiteman W RSC 2
Nottingham
10.09.05 Ernie Smith W PTS 4 Cardiff
29.04.06 Ernie Smith W PTS 6 Edinburgh
01.06.06 Geraint Harvey W RSC 3 Barnsley
14.10.06 Duncan Cottier W RSC 3 Manchester
09.12.06 David Kirk W RSC 1 Canning Town
07.04.07 Karl David W RSC 3 Cardiff
06.10.07 Alex Stoda W PTS 6 Nottingham
22.03.08 Darren Gethin W RTD 3 Cardiff

14.06.08 Barrie Jones W RSC 7 Bethnal Green
(Vacant British Welterweight Title)
14.11.08 Kevin McIntyre W RSC 1 Glasgow
(British Welterweight Title Defence)
30.01.09 Stuart Elwell W RSC 2 Bethnal Green
(British Welterweight Title Defence)
Career: 19 contests, won 19.

Nathan Brook

Plymouth. *Born* Plymouth, 17 March, 1983
L.Heavyweight. *Ht* 5' 8"
Manager N. Christian
14.05.09 Rizza Ahmad W RSC 1 Leeds
Career: 1 contest, won 1.

Wayne Brooks

Cardiff. *Born* Cardiff, 13 October, 1986
Cruiserweight. *Ht* 6'1"
Manager B. Coleman
13.10.06 Marko Doknic W RSC 3 Aberavon
15.12.06 Simon Wood W RSC 1 Bethnal Green
02.03.07 Nick Okoth DREW 4 Neath
10.06.07 Danny Couzens W PTS 4 Neath
08.12.07 Tony Bellew L CO 3 Bolton
30.03.08 Shon Davies L RSC 7 Port Talbot
(Vacant Welsh Area L.Heavyweight Title)
05.06.09 Harry Miles W PTS 4 Newport
Career: 7 contests, won 4, drew 1, lost 2.

Chris Brophy

Swansea. *Born* Preston, 28 January, 1979
L.Middleweight. *Ht* 5'10"
Manager Self
29.10.03 Aidan Mooney L RSC 5 Leicester
Square
30.11.03 Casey Brooke W PTS 6 Swansea
21.12.03 Gary O'Connor L PTS 6 Bolton
21.02.04 Tony Doherty L RSC 2 Cardiff
02.04.04 Tommy Marshall DREW 6 Plymouth
26.04.04 Scott Haywood L RSC 5 Cleethorpes
05.06.04 Ashley Theophane L RSC 3 Bethnal
Green
17.09.04 Tommy Marshall W PTS 6 Plymouth
21.11.04 Jay Morris L RSC 1 Bracknell
31.01.05 George McIlroy L RSC 6 Glasgow
16.09.05 Garry Buckland L PTS 4 Plymouth
24.10.05 Mike Reid L RSC 2 Glasgow
26.02.06 Freddie Luke L PTS 4 Dagenham
11.03.06 Stephen Burke L PTS 4 Newport
08.09.06 Dee Mitchell L PTS 4 Birmingham
03.12.06 Danny Butler L PTS 4 Bristol
16.02.07 Barrie Jones L PTS 4 Merthyr Tydfil
24.02.07 Jimmy Doherty L PTS 6 Stoke
18.03.07 Chris Long DREW 6 Bristol
07.06.07 Patrick Doherty L CO 4 Kensington
15.09.07 Lewis Byrne L CO 5 Bristol
21.10.07 James Lilley L PTS 4 Swansea
02.12.07 Steve Cooper W PTS 6 Bristol
18.02.08 Stuart Elwell L PTS 6 Glasgow
14.03.08 Jonathan Hussey L RSC 6 Manchester
31.05.08 Andrew Alan Lowe L RSC 4 Newark
12.09.08 Russ Colley L PTS 6 Wolverhampton
28.09.08 Michael Gomez L RSC 2 Colne
16.11.08 Lloyd Smith L PTS 6 Southampton
04.12.08 Martyn King L PTS 6 Bradford
23.02.09 Duane Parker L PTS 6 Birmingham
07.03.09 Tristan Davies L PTS 6 Birmingham
29.03.09 Chris O'Brien L PTS 6 Bolton
27.04.09 Jamie McLevy L PTS 8 Glasgow

24.05.09 Peter Cannon L PTS 6 Bradford
31.05.09 Nathan McIntosh L PTS 6 Burton
13.06.09 Martin Robins L PTS 6 Bristol
23.06.09 Stuart Barr L PTS 4 Longford
Career: 38 contests, won 3, drew 2, lost 33.

Nathan Brough

Liverpool. *Born* Liverpool, 18 May, 1984
Welterweight. *Ht* 6'0"
Manager T. Gilmour
08.06.07 Billy Smith W PTS 4 Motherwell
14.09.07 Alex Stoda W DIS 2 Kirkcaldy
01.12.07 Baz Carey W RSC 3 Liverpool
14.03.08 Leonard Lothian W PTS 6 Manchester
09.05.08 Arek Malek W PTS 6 Middlesbrough
28.11.08 Russell Pearce W RSC 1 Glasgow
12.06.09 Michael Frontin W PTS 6 Liverpool
Career: 7 contests, won 7.

Barrington Brown

Nottingham. *Born* Nottingham, 11 May,
1982
S.Featherweight. *Ht* 5'7"
Manager J. Gill
06.03.05 Paddy Folan W RSC 6 Shaw
30.09.05 Craig Morgan L PTS 6 Carmarthen
09.10.05 Vinesh Rungea W PTS 6 Hammersmith
18.02.06 Mick Abbott W PTS 6 Stoke
24.04.06 Kevin Townsley L PTS 6 Glasgow
30.05.06 Lloyd Otte W RSC 1 Bethnal Green
30.09.06 Gary Davies DREW 6 Stoke
03.11.06 Danny Wallace L PTS 4 Barnsley
07.03.08 Peter Allen W PTS 4 Nottingham
02.05.08 Dean Mills DREW 4 Nottingham
06.03.09 Jon Kays L PTS 6 Wigan
Career: 11 contests, won 5, drew 2, lost 4.

Paul Brown

Plymouth. *Born* Plymouth, 29 October,
1978
Middleweight. *Ht* 6'0¼"
Manager N. Christian
09.11.07 Jason Smith W PTS 6 Plymouth
29.02.08 Kenroy Lambert W RSC 6 Plymouth
02.05.08 Ollie Newham L RSC 4 Nottingham
15.11.08 Gatis Skuja L PTS 6 Plymouth
20.03.09 Gary Boulden L PTS 4 Bethnal Green
23.05.09 Kevin Hammond L RSC 2 Sleaford
Career: 6 contests, won 2, lost 4.

Garry Buckland

Cardiff. *Born* Cardiff, 12 June 1986
Celtic Lightweight Champion. Former
Undefeated Welsh L.Welterweight
Champion. *Ht* 5'7"
Manager B. Powell
05.03.05 Warren Dunkley W PTS 4 Dagenham
24.07.05 Danny Gwilym W RSC 2 Leicester
Square
16.09.05 Chris Brophy W PTS 4 Plymouth
17.11.05 Bheki Moyo W RSC 3 Bristol
10.02.06 Anthony Christopher W RSC 4
Plymouth
07.04.06 Judex Meemea W RSC 5 Bristol
14.07.06 Ubadel Soto W PTS 4 Alicante, Spain
15.09.06 Karl Taylor W PTS 6 Newport
10.11.06 Judex Meemea W PTS 6 Newport

03.03.07 Stuart Philips W PTS 10 Newport
(Vacant Welsh Area L.Welterweight Title)
16.06.07 Carl Allen W PTS 6 Newport
05.10.07 Martin Watson W PTS 10 Newport
(Celtic Lightweight Title Challenge)
07.03.08 Alexander Spitjo W RSC 3 Nottingham
05.04.08 Ali Wyatt W PTS 6 Newport
13.06.08 Ben Murphy L PTS 6 Portsmouth
27.02.09 Craig Docherty W PTS 10 Barnsley
(Celtic Lightweight Title Defence)
Career: 16 contests, won 15, lost 1.

Kevin Buckley

Chester. *Born* Chester, 20 April, 1986
Lightweight. *Ht* 5'7½"
Manager Self
03.03.07 Shaun Walton W PTS 6 Burton
20.04.07 Pete Buckley W PTS 4 Dudley
20.07.07 Tony McQuade W PTS 4
Wolverhampton
17.11.07 John Baguley W PTS 6 Stoke
01.03.08 Dwayne Hill W PTS 6 Stoke
17.01.09 Mo Khaled W PTS 4 Wigan
07.03.09 Dean Mills DREW 4 Chester
Career: 7 contests, won 6, drew 1.

Pete Buckley

Birmingham. *Born* Birmingham, 9 March,
1969
Welterweight. Former Undefeated Midlands
Area S. Featherweight Champion. Former
Midlands Area S. Bantamweight Champion.
Ht 5'8"
Manager Self
04.10.89 Alan Baldwin DREW 6 Stafford
10.10.89 Ronnie Stephenson L PTS 6
Wolverhampton
30.10.89 Robert Braddock W PTS 6 Birmingham
14.11.89 Neil Leitch W PTS 6 Evesham
22.11.89 Peter Judson W PTS 6 Stafford
11.12.89 Stevie Woods W PTS 6 Bradford
21.12.89 Wayne Taylor W PTS 6 Kings Heath
10.01.90 John O'Meara W PTS 6 Kensington
19.02.90 Ian McGirr L PTS 6 Birmingham
27.02.90 Miguel Matthews DREW 6 Evesham
14.03.90 Ronnie Stephenson DREW 6 Stoke
04.04.90 Ronnie Stephenson L PTS 8 Stafford
23.04.90 Ronnie Stephenson W PTS 6
Birmingham
30.04.90 Chris Clarkson L PTS 8 Mayfair
17.05.90 Johnny Bredahl L PTS 6 Aars, Denmark
04.06.90 Ronnie Stephenson W PTS 8
Birmingham
28.06.90 Robert Braddock W RSC 5 Birmingham
01.10.90 Miguel Matthews W PTS 8 Cleethorpes
09.10.90 Miguel Matthews L PTS 8
Wolverhampton
17.10.90 Tony Smith W PTS 6 Stoke
29.10.90 Miguel Matthews W PTS 8 Birmingham
21.11.90 Drew Docherty L PTS 8 Solihull
10.12.90 Neil Leitch W PTS 8 Birmingham
10.01.91 Duke McKenzie L RSC 5 Wandsworth
18.02.91 Jamie McBride L PTS 8 Glasgow
04.03.91 Brian Robb W RSC 7 Birmingham
26.03.91 Neil Leitch DREW 8 Wolverhampton
01.05.91 Mark Geraghty W PTS 8 Solihull
05.06.91 Brian Robb W PTS 10 Wolverhampton
*(Vacant Midlands Area S. Featherweight
Title)*

09.09.91 Mike Deveney L PTS 8 Glasgow
24.09.91 Mark Bates W RTD 5 Basildon
29.10.91 John Armour L PTS 6 Kensington
14.11.91 Mike Deveney L PTS 6 Edinburgh
28.11.91 Craig Dermody L PTS 6 Liverpool
19.12.91 Craig Dermody L PTS 6 Oldham
18.01.92 Alan McKay DREW 6 Kensington
20.02.92 Brian Robb W RSC 10 Oakengates
*(Midlands Area S. Featherweight Title
Defence)*
27.04.92 Drew Docherty L PTS 8 Glasgow
15.05.92 Ruben Condori L PTS 10 Augsburg,
Germany
29.05.92 Donnie Hood L PTS 8 Glasgow
07.09.92 Duke McKenzie L RTD 3 Bethnal Green
12.11.92 Prince Naseem Hamed L PTS 6
Liverpool
19.02.93 Harald Geier L PTS 12 Vienna, Austria
*(Vacant WBA Penta-Continental S.
Bantamweight Title)*
26.04.93 Bradley Stone L PTS 8 Lewisham
18.06.93 Eamonn McAuley L PTS 6 Belfast
01.07.93 Tony Silkstone L PTS 8 York
06.10.93 Jonjo Irwin L PTS 8 Solihull
25.10.93 Drew Docherty L PTS 8 Glasgow
06.11.93 Michael Alldis L PTS 8 Bethnal Green
30.11.93 Barry Jones L PTS 4 Cardiff
19.12.93 Shaun Anderson L PTS 6 Glasgow
22.01.94 Barry Jones L PTS 6 Cardiff
29.01.94 Prince Naseem Hamed L RSC 4 Cardiff
10.03.94 Tony Falcone L PTS 4 Bristol
29.03.94 Conn McMullen W PTS 6 Bethnal
Green
05.04.94 Mark Bowers L PTS 6 Bethnal Green
13.04.94 James Murray L PTS 6 Glasgow
06.05.94 Paul Lloyd L RTD 4 Liverpool
03.08.94 Greg Upton L PTS 6 Bristol
26.09.94 John Sillo L PTS 6 Liverpool
05.10.94 Matthew Harris L PTS 6 Wolverhampton
07.11.94 Marlon Ward L PTS 4 Piccadilly
23.11.94 Justin Murphy L PTS 4 Piccadilly
29.11.94 Neil Swain L PTS 4 Cardiff
13.12.94 Michael Brodie L PTS 6 Potters Bar
20.12.94 Michael Alldis L PTS 6 Bethnal Green
10.02.95 Matthew Harris W RSC 6 Birmingham
*(Midlands Area S. Bantamweight Title
Challenge)*
23.02.95 Paul Ingle L PTS 8 Southwark
20.04.95 John Sillo L PTS 6 Liverpool
27.04.95 Paul Ingle L PTS 8 Bethnal Green
09.05.95 Ady Lewis L PTS 4 Basildon
23.05.95 Spencer Oliver L PTS 4 Potters Bar
01.07.95 Dean Pithie L PTS 4 Kensington
21.09.95 Patrick Mullings L PTS 6 Battersea
29.09.95 Marlon Ward L PTS 4 Bethnal Green
25.10.95 Matthew Harris L PTS 10 Telford
*(Midlands Area S. Bantamweight Title
Defence)*
08.11.95 Vince Feeney L PTS 8 Bethnal Green
28.11.95 Barry Jones L PTS 6 Cardiff
15.12.95 Patrick Mullings L PTS 4 Bethnal Green
05.02.96 Patrick Mullings L PTS 8 Bexleyheath
09.03.96 Paul Griffin L PTS 4 Millstreet
21.03.96 Colin McMillan L RSC 3 Southwark
14.05.96 Venkatesan Deverajan L PTS 4
Dagenham
29.06.96 Matt Brown W RSC 1 Erith
03.09.96 Vince Feeney L PTS 4 Bethnal Green
28.09.96 Fabrice Benichou L PTS 8 Barking
09.10.96 Gary Marston DREW 8 Stoke
06.11.96 Neil Swain L PTS 4 Tylorstown

29.11.96 Alston Buchanan L PTS 8 Glasgow
22.12.96 Brian Carr L PTS 6 Glasgow
11.01.97 Scott Harrison L PTS 4 Bethnal Green
29.01.97 Carl Allen L PTS 8 Stoke
12.02.97 Ronnie McPhee L PTS 6 Glasgow
25.02.97 Dean Pithie L PTS 4 Sheffield
07.03.97 Jason Booth L PTS 6 Northampton
20.03.97 Thomas Bradley W PTS 6 Newark
08.04.97 Sergei Devakov L PTS 6 Bethnal Green
25.04.97 Matthew Harris L PTS 6 Cleethorpes
08.05.97 Gregorio Medina L RTD 2 Mansfield
13.06.97 Mike Deveney L PTS 6 Paisley
19.07.97 Richard Evatt L PTS 4 Wembley
30.08.97 Michael Brodie L PTS 8 Cheshunt
06.10.97 Brendan Bryce W PTS 6 Piccadilly
20.10.97 Kelton McKenzie L PTS 6 Leicester
20.11.97 Ervine Blake L PTS 8 Solihull
06.12.97 Danny Adams L PTS 4 Wembley
13.12.97 Gary Thornhill L PTS 6 Sheffield
31.01.98 Scott Harrison L PTS 4 Edmonton
05.03.98 Steve Conway L PTS 6 Leeds
18.03.98 Ervine Blake L PTS 8 Stoke
26.03.98 Graham McGrath W RTD 4 Solihull
11.04.98 Salim Medjkoune L PTS 6 Southwark
18.04.98 Tony Mulholland L PTS 4 Manchester
27.04.98 Alston Buchanan L PTS 8 Glasgow
11.05.98 Jason Squire W RTD 2 Leicester
21.05.98 Lee Armstrong L PTS 6 Bradford
06.06.98 Tony Mulholland L PTS 6 Liverpool
14.06.98 Lee Armstrong L PTS 6 Shaw
21.07.98 David Burke L PTS 6 Widnes
05.09.98 Michael Gomez L PTS 6 Telford
17.09.98 Brian Carr L PTS 6 Glasgow
03.10.98 Justin Murphy L PTS 6 Crawley
05.12.98 Lehlohonolo Ledwaba L PTS 8 Bristol
19.12.98 Acelino Freitas L RTD 3 Liverpool
09.02.99 Chris Jickells L PTS 6 Wolverhampton
16.02.99 Franny Hogg L PTS 6 Leeds
26.02.99 Richard Evatt L RSC 5 Coventry
17.04.99 Martin O'Malley L RSC 3 Dublin
29.05.99 Richie Wenton L PTS 6 Halifax
14.06.99 Carl Allen L PTS 8 Birmingham
26.06.99 Paul Halpin L PTS 4 Millwall
15.07.99 Salim Medjkoune L PTS 6 Peterborough
07.08.99 Steve Murray L PTS 6 Dagenham
12.09.99 Kevin Gerowski L PTS 6 Nottingham
20.09.99 Mat Zegan L PTS 6 Peterborough
02.10.99 Jason Cook L PTS 4 Cardiff
09.10.99 Brian Carr L PTS 6 Manchester
19.10.99 Gary Steadman L PTS 4 Bethnal Green
27.10.99 Miguel Matthews W PTS 8 Birmingham
20.11.99 Carl Greaves L PTS 10 Grantham
(British Masters S. Featherweight Title Challenge)
11.12.99 Gary Thornhill L PTS 6 Liverpool
29.01.00 Bradley Pryce L PTS 4 Manchester
19.02.00 Gavin Rees L PTS 4 Dagenham
29.02.00 Tony Mulholland L PTS 4 Widnes
20.03.00 Carl Greaves L PTS 4 Mansfield
27.03.00 James Rooney L PTS 4 Barnsley
08.04.00 Delroy Pryce L PTS 4 Bethnal Green
17.04.00 Franny Hogg L PTS 8 Glasgow
11.05.00 Craig Spacie L PTS 4 Newark
25.05.00 Jimmy Phelan DREW 6 Hull
19.06.00 Delroy Pryce L PTS 4 Burton
01.07.00 Richard Evatt L PTS 4 Manchester
16.09.00 Lee Meager L PTS 4 Bethnal Green
23.09.00 Gavin Rees L PTS 4 Bethnal Green
02.10.00 Brian Carr L PTS 4 Glasgow
14.10.00 Gareth Jordan L PTS 4 Wembley
13.11.00 Kevin Lear L PTS 6 Bethnal Green

24.11.00 Lee Williamson L PTS 6 Hull
09.12.00 Leo O'Reilly L PTS 4 Southwark
15.01.01 Eddie Nevins L PTS 4 Manchester
23.01.01 David Burke L PTS 4 Crawley
31.01.01 Tony Montana L PTS 6 Piccadilly
19.02.01 Kevin England W PTS 6 Glasgow
12.03.01 Carl Allen L PTS 6 Birmingham
19.03.01 Duncan Armstrong L PTS 6 Glasgow
27.03.01 Carl Allen L PTS 8 Brierley Hill
05.05.01 Danny Hunt L PTS 4 Edmonton
09.06.01 Gary Thornhill L PTS 4 Bethnal Green
21.07.01 Scott Miller L PTS 4 Sheffield
28.07.01 Kevin Lear L PTS 4 Wembley
25.09.01 Ricky Eccleston L PTS 4 Liverpool
07.10.01 Nigel Senior L PTS 6 Wolverhampton
31.10.01 Woody Greenaway L PTS 6 Birmingham
16.11.01 Jimmy Beech L PTS 6 West Bromwich
01.12.01 Chill John L PTS 4 Bethnal Green
09.12.01 Nigel Senior W PTS 6 Shaw
26.01.02 Scott Lawton L PTS 4 Bethnal Green
09.02.02 Sam Gorman L PTS 6 Coventry
23.02.02 Alex Moon L PTS 4 Nottingham
04.03.02 Leo Turner L PTS 6 Bradford
11.03.02 Martin Watson L PTS 4 Glasgow
26.04.02 Scott Lawton L PTS 4 Coventry
10.05.02 Lee Meager L PTS 6 Bethnal Green
08.06.02 Bradley Pryce L RSC 1 Renfrew
20.07.02 Jeff Thomas L PTS 4 Bethnal Green
23.08.02 Ben Hudson DREW 4 Bethnal Green
06.09.02 Dave Stewart L PTS 6 Bethnal Green
14.09.02 Peter McDonagh L PTS 4 Bethnal Green
20.10.02 James Paisley L PTS 4 Southwark
12.11.02 Martin Hardcastle DREW 6 Leeds
29.11.02 Daniel Thorpe L PTS 6 Hull
09.12.02 Nicky Leech L PTS 6 Nottingham
16.12.02 Joel Viney L PTS 6 Cleethorpes
28.01.03 Billy Corcoran L PTS 6 Nottingham
08.02.03 Colin Toohey L PTS 6 Liverpool
15.02.03 Terry Fletcher L PTS 4 Wembley
22.02.03 Dean Lambert L PTS 4 Huddersfield
05.03.03 Billy Corcoran L PTS 6 Bethnal Green
18.03.03 Nathan Ward L PTS 4 Reading
05.04.03 Baz Carey L PTS 4 Manchester
15.05.03 Mike Harrington W PTS 4 Clevedon
27.05.03 Dave Stewart L PTS 4 Dagenham
07.06.03 Rimell Taylor DREW 6 Coventry
12.07.03 George Telfer L PTS 4 Renfrew
22.07.03 Chas Symonds L PTS 6 Bethnal Green
01.08.03 Jas Malik W PTS 4 Bethnal Green
06.09.03 John Murray L PTS 4 Huddersfield
13.09.03 Isaac Ward L PTS 6 Wakefield
25.09.03 Gary Woolcombe L PTS 6 Bethnal Green
06.10.03 Scott Haywood L PTS 6 Barnsley
20.10.03 Joel Viney W PTS 6 Bradford
29.10.03 David Kehoe L PTS 6 Leicester Square
07.11.03 Femi Fehintola L PTS 6 Sheffield
14.11.03 Dave Stewart L PTS 4 Bethnal Green
21.11.03 Henry Castle L PTS 4 Millwall
28.11.03 Lee Meager L PTS 4 Derby
13.12.03 Derry Matthews L PTS 4 Manchester
21.12.03 Daniel Thorpe L PTS 6 Bolton
16.01.04 Nadeem Siddique L PTS 4 Bradford
16.02.04 Scott Haywood L PTS 6 Scunthorpe
29.02.04 Gary O'Connor L PTS 6 Shaw
03.04.04 Steve Bell L PTS 4 Manchester
16.04.04 Isaac Ward L PTS 6 Hartlepool
23.04.04 Colin Bain L PTS 6 Glasgow
06.05.04 Amir Ali L PTS 4 Barnsley
13.05.04 Lee Beavis L PTS 4 Bethnal Green
04.06.04 Tristan Davies L PTS 6 Dudley

03.07.04 Barrie Jones L PTS 4 Newport
03.09.04 Stefy Bull L PTS 6 Doncaster
10.09.04 Tiger Matthews L PTS 4 Liverpool
17.09.04 Kell Brook L PTS 6 Sheffield
24.09.04 Ceri Hall L PTS 6 Dublin
11.10.04 Darren Johnstone L PTS 6 Glasgow
22.10.04 Jonathan Whiteman L PTS 6 Mansfield
29.10.04 Colin Bain L PTS 4 Renfrew
09.11.04 Tom Hogan L PTS 6 Leeds
21.11.04 Chris McDonagh L PTS 4 Bracknell
10.12.04 Craig Johnson L PTS 6 Mansfield
17.12.04 Steve Mullin L PTS 4 Liverpool
12.02.05 Jay Morris L PTS 6 Portsmouth
21.02.05 Stuart Green L PTS 6 Glasgow
05.03.05 Paul Buckley L PTS 6 Southwark
23.03.05 Ryan Barrett L PTS 6 Leicester Square
09.04.05 Nadeem Siddique L PTS 6 Norwich
25.04.05 Jimmy Gilhaney L PTS 6 Glasgow
14.05.05 James Gorman L PTS 6 Dublin
27.05.05 Alan Temple L PTS 4 Spennymoor
04.06.05 Patrick Hyland L PTS 4 Dublin
25.06.05 Sean Hughes DREW 6 Wakefield
24.07.05 Scott Lawton L PTS 6 Sheffield
03.09.05 Jackson Williams L PTS 6 Norwich
19.09.05 Ryan Brawley L PTS 6 Glasgow
14.10.05 Jimmy Gilhaney L PTS 6 Motherwell
23.11.05 Shane Watson L PTS 6 Mayfair
02.12.05 Billy Corcoran L PTS 6 Nottingham
14.12.05 Stephen Burke L PTS 4 Blackpool
23.01.06 David Appleby L PTS 6 Glasgow
02.02.06 Michael Grant L PTS 4 Holborn
18.02.06 Jimmy Doherty L PTS 6 Stoke
04.03.06 Steve Bell L PTS 4 Manchester
13.03.06 Gary McArthur L PTS 6 Glasgow
25.03.06 Brian Murphy L PTS 6 Irvine
02.04.06 Barry Downes L PTS 6 Shaw
13.04.06 Paul Newby L PTS 4 Leeds
28.04.06 Gary O'Connor L PTS 6 Manchester
06.05.06 Ian Clyde L PTS 6 Stoke
20.05.06 Stephen Haughian L PTS 4 Belfast
09.06.06 Wez Miller L PTS 6 Doncaster
18.06.06 James Brown L PTS 6 Manchester
29.06.06 Rob Hunt L PTS 6 Dudley
10.07.06 Calvin White L PTS 6 Manchester
09.09.06 Stuart Green L PTS 8 Inverurie
18.09.06 Stuart Green L PTS 6 Glasgow
29.09.06 Mitch Prince L PTS 6 Motherwell
03.11.06 Mitch Prince L PTS 6 Glasgow
12.11.06 Danny Harding L PTS 6 Manchester
24.11.06 Adam Kelly L PTS 6 Hull
06.12.06 Daniel Thorpe L PTS 6 Rotherham
19.02.07 Mark Hastie L PTS 6 Glasgow
03.03.07 Wayne Downing L PTS 4 Burton
11.03.07 Shinny Bayaar L PTS 6 Shaw
26.03.07 Charles Paul King L PTS 6 Glasgow
20.04.07 Kevin Buckley L PTS 4 Dudley
28.04.07 Furhan Rafiq L PTS 6 Clydebank
03.06.07 Andrew Ward L PTS 4 Barnsley
24.06.07 Jon Kays L PTS 6 Wigan
23.09.07 Shane Watson L PTS 6 Longford
07.10.07 Darren Askew L PTS 6 Shaw
17.11.07 Chris Goodwin L PTS 4 Stoke
28.11.07 Kim Poulsen L PTS 6 Piccadilly
10.12.07 Leonard Lothian L PTS 6 Leicester
11.07.08 Ali Shah L PTS 4 Wigan
24.07.08 Scott Evans L PTS 4 Wolverhampton
12.09.08 Chris Lewis L PTS 4 Wolverhampton
19.09.08 Joe Elfidh L PTS 6 Doncaster
26.09.08 Dean Arnold L PTS 4 Wolverhampton
05.10.08 Matin Mohammed DREW 4 Nottingham
12.10.08 Pete Leworthy L PTS 6 Bristol

91

24.10.08 Lee Selby L PTS 6 Newport
31.10.08 Matin Mohammed W PTS 4 Birmingham
Career: 300 contests, won 32, drew 12, lost 256.

(Andrew) Stefy Bull (Bullcroft)

Doncaster. *Born* Doncaster, 10 May, 1977
Former Undefeated Central Area & WBF Inter-Continental Lightweight Champion. Former Undefeated WBF Inter-Continental Lightweight Champion. Former Undefeated Central Area Featherweight Champion.
Ht 5'10"
Manager C. Greaves
30.06.95 Andy Roberts W PTS 4 Doncaster
11.10.95 Michael Edwards W PTS 6 Stoke
18.10.95 Alan Hagan W RSC 1 Batley
28.11.95 Kevin Sheil W PTS 6 Wolverhampton
26.01.96 Robert Grubb W PTS 6 Doncaster
12.09.96 Benny Jones W PTS 6 Doncaster
15.10.96 Kevin Sheil DREW 6 Wolverhampton
24.10.96 Graham McGrath W PTS 6 Birmingham
17.12.96 Robert Braddock W RSC 4 Doncaster
    (*Vacant Central Area Featherweight Title*)
10.07.97 Carl Greaves W PTS 6 Doncaster
11.10.97 Dean Pithie L RSC 11 Sheffield
    (*Vacant WBO Inter-Continental S. Featherweight Title*)
19.03.98 Chris Lyons W RSC 4 Doncaster
08.04.98 Alex Moon L RSC 3 Liverpool
31.07.99 Jason Dee L RSC 4 Carlisle
09.05.03 Joel Viney W RTD 3 Doncaster
02.06.03 Jason Nesbitt W PTS 6 Cleethorpes
05.09.03 Dave Hinds W PTS 6 Doncaster
20.02.04 Anthony Christopher W PTS 6 Doncaster
07.05.04 Daniel Thorpe W PTS 10 Doncaster
    (*Central Area Lightweight Title Challenge*)
03.09.04 Pete Buckley W PTS 6 Doncaster
29.10.04 Haroon Din W RSC 2 Doncaster
    (*Central Area Lightweight Title Defence*)
04.02.05 Gwyn Wale W PTS 10 Doncaster
    (*Central Area Lightweight Title Defence*)
11.03.05 Jimmy Beech W PTS 4 Doncaster
20.05.05 Billy Smith W PTS 6 Doncaster
16.09.05 Carl Allen W PTS 10 Doncaster
    (*Vacant WBF Inter-Continental Lightweight Title*)
02.12.05 David Kehoe W PTS 6 Doncaster
03.03.06 Baz Carey W PTS 10 Doncaster
    (*WBF Inter-Continental Lightweight Title Defence*)
09.06.06 Scott Lawton L RSC 8 Doncaster
    (*Vacant English Lightweight Title*)
13.10.06 Carl Allen W PTS 6 Doncaster
07.04.07 Amir Khan L RSC 3 Cardiff
19.10.07 Kristian Laight W PTS 4 Doncaster
19.09.08 Graeme Higginson L PTS 10 Doncaster
    (*British Masters L. Welterweight Title Challenge*)
28.03.09 Baz Carey W PTS 6 Lincoln
Career: 33 contests, won 26, drew 1, lost 6.

Stephen Burke

Liverpool. *Born* Liverpool, 18 March, 1979
Welterweight. *Ht* 5'8"
Manager Self

13.05.05 Imad Khamis W RSC 3 Liverpool
14.12.05 Pete Buckley W PTS 4 Blackpool
11.03.06 Chris Brophy W PTS 4 Newport
02.09.06 Billy Smith W PTS 4 Bolton
10.03.07 Daniel Thorpe W PTS 4 Liverpool
11.08.07 Craig Tomes W RSC 1 Liverpool
01.12.07 Billy Smith W PTS 6 Liverpool
19.07.08 Baz Carey W PTS 4 Liverpool
24.03.09 Stuart Green W PTS 3 Glasgow
24.03.09 Gary McArthur W RSC 1 Glasgow
24.03.09 Ryan Brawley L PTS 3 Glasgow
Career: 11 contests, won 10, lost 1.

Ross Burkinshaw

Sheffield. *Born* Sheffield, 10 August, 1986
English S. Flyweight Champion. *Ht* 5'8"
Manager G. Rhodes
03.11.06 Robert Bunford W CO 1 Barnsley
09.02.07 Delroy Spencer W PTS 4 Leeds
13.07.07 Iordan Vasilev W CO 3 Barnsley
16.09.07 Faycal Messaoudene W PTS 4 Sheffield
19.10.07 Shaun Doherty DREW 6 Doncaster
15.02.08 Abdul Mougharbel L RSC 2 Sheffield
10.10.08 Mike Holloway W RSC 1 Sheffield
27.02.09 Mike Robinson DREW 4 Barnsley
23.04.09 Mike Robinson W RSC 7 Limehouse
    (*Vacant English S.Flyweight Title*)
Career: 9 contests, won 6, drew 2, lost 1.

Paul Burns

Uddingston. *Born* Rutherglen, 5 January, 1983
Former Undefeated International Masters Welterweight Champion. *Ht* 6'2"
Manager T. Gilmour
06.06.05 Terry Carruthers DREW 6 Glasgow
14.10.05 Surinder Sekhon W PTS 6 Motherwell
21.11.05 Malik Khan W RTD 2 Glasgow
13.03.06 David Kehoe W PTS 6 Glasgow
29.09.06 Peter Dunn W PTS 6 Motherwell
20.11.06 Steve Cooper DREW 6 Glasgow
28.04.07 Danny Gwilym W PTS 6 Clydebank
10.09.07 Steve Cooper W PTS 6 Glasgow
21.01.08 Andrew Butlin DREW 6 Glasgow
22.02.08 Matt Scriven W PTS 6 Motherwell
16.05.08 Gavin Tait W PTS 10 Motherwell
    (*Vacant International Masters Welterweight Title*)
28.11.08 Stuart Elwell L PTS 6 Glasgow
Career: 12 contests, won 8, drew 3, lost 1.

Ricky Burns

Coatbridge. *Born* Bellshill, 13 April, 1983
Commonwealth S.Featherweight Champion. Former Undefeated International Masters S. Featherweight Champion. *Ht* 5'10"
Manager F. Warren/A. Morrison
20.10.01 Woody Greenaway W PTS 4 Glasgow
15.03.02 Peter Allen W PTS 6 Glasgow
08.06.02 Gary Harrison W RSC 1 Renfrew
06.09.02 Ernie Smith W PTS 6 Glasgow
19.10.02 Neil Murray W RSC 2 Renfrew
08.12.02 No No Junior W PTS 8 Glasgow
08.10.04 Daniel Thorpe W PTS 6 Glasgow
29.10.04 Jeff Thomas W PTS 4 Renfrew
12.12.04 Colin Bain W PTS 6 Glasgow

25.02.05 Graham Earl W PTS 8 Wembley
08.04.05 Buster Dennis W PTS 6 Edinburgh
17.06.05 Haider Ali W PTS 8 Glasgow
23.07.05 Alan Temple W PTS 4 Edinburgh
18.02.06 Alex Arthur L PTS 12 Edinburgh
    (*British, Commonwealth & European S.Featherweight Title Challenges*)
01.04.06 Adolph Avadja W RSC 5 Bethnal Green
04.11.06 Wladimir Borov W PTS 8 Glasgow
09.02.07 Carl Johanneson L PTS 12 Leeds
    (*British S.Featherweight Title Challenge*)
15.09.07 Ernie Smith W PTS 6 Paisley
13.10.07 Frederic Bonifai W RSC 5 Bethnal Green
26.10.07 Ben Odamattey W PTS 8 Glasgow
03.11.07 Youssef Al Hamidi W PTS 6 Cardiff
15.12.07 Billy Smith W PTS 6 Edinburgh
22.02.08 Silence Saheed W RSC 3 Motherwell
22.03.08 Billy Smith W PTS 4 Cardiff
17.05.08 Gheorghe Ghiompirica W PTS 10 Glasgow
    (*Vacant International Masters S.Featherweight Title*)
26.09.08 Osumanu Akaba W PTS 12 Bethnal Green
    (*Vacant Commonwealth S.Featherweight Title*)
14.11.08 Yakubu Amidu W RSC 7 Glasgow
    (*Commonwealth S.Featherweight Title Defence*)
27.03.09 Michael Gomez W RSC 7 Glasgow
    (*Commonwealth S.Featherweight Title Defence*)
19.06.09 Kevin O'Hara W PTS 12 Glasgow
    (*Commonwealth S.Featherweight Title Defence*)
Career: 29 contests, won 27, lost 2.

Chris Burton

Darlington. *Born* Darlington, 27 February, 1981
Heavyweight. *Ht* 6'5"
Manager Self
02.06.05 David Ingleby W RSC 3 Yarm
03.03.06 Istvan Kecskes W PTS 4 Hartlepool
28.04.06 Istvan Kecskes W PTS 4 Hartlepool
23.06.06 Simon Goodwin W RSC 3 Blackpool
30.09.06 Istvan Kecskes W RSC 5 Middlesbrough
05.12.06 Paul Butlin W RSC 4 Wolverhampton
28.01.07 Chris Woollas W RSC 3 Yarm
06.05.07 Paul King W PTS 4 Darlington
18.11.07 Franklin Egobi W PTS 6 Tooting
08.02.08 Matthew Ellis W RTD 2 Peterlee
09.05.08 Lee Swaby W PTS 8 Middlesbrough
12.09.08 David Ingleby W PTS 3 Newcastle
12.09.08 Lee Swaby W RSC 3 Newcastle
12.09.08 Sam Sexton L RSC 3 Newcastle
16.01.09 Yavor Marinchev W PTS 8 Middlesbrough
Career: 15 contests, won 14, lost 1.

Robert Burton

Barnsley. *Born* Barnsley, 1 April, 1971
L.Heavyweight. Former Central Area L.Middleweight Champion. Former Central Area Welterweight Champion. *Ht* 5'9"
Manager Self
05.02.01 Gavin Pearson W RSC 3 Bradford

23.02.01 Scott Millar W CO 5 Irvine
20.03.01 Peter Dunn W PTS 6 Leeds
08.05.01 Arv Mittoo W PTS 4 Barnsley
10.06.01 Martyn Bailey DREW 6 Ellesmere Port
08.10.01 Gavin Pearson W RSC 2 Barnsley
16.11.01 Martyn Bailey DREW 4 Preston
24.11.01 Peter Dunn L PTS 6 Wakefield
28.01.02 Peter Dunn W RSC 8 Barnsley
    (*Vacant Central Area Welterweight Title*)
23.08.02 David Walker L RSC 2 Bethnal Green
19.10.02 John Humphrey L RTD 4 Norwich
09.02.03 Donovan Smillie L PTS 6 Bradford
24.03.03 Andy Halder L PTS 6 Barnsley
31.05.03 David Keir W RSC 9 Barnsley
    (*Central Area Welterweight Title
    Defence*)
01.11.03 Scott Dixon L PTS 6 Glasgow
08.12.03 Jed Tytler W PTS 6 Barnsley
10.02.04 Paul Lomax W PTS 6 Barnsley
06.05.04 Matthew Hatton L PTS 10 Barnsley
    (*Central Area Welterweight Title
    Defence*)
08.06.04 Lee Murtagh W CO 3 Sheffield
    (*Vacant Central Area L.Middleweight
    Title*)
12.11.04 Matthew Hatton L PTS 10 Halifax
    (*Central Area L.Middleweight Title
    Defence*)
11.02.05 Paul Smith L CO 1 Manchester
22.04.05 John Marshall L RTD 4 Barnsley
23.07.05 Craig Lynch L PTS 4 Edinburgh
30.09.05 Jonjo Finnegan DREW 4 Burton
22.10.05 Richard Mazurek W PTS 6 Coventry
25.11.05 Matthew Hough L PTS 4 Walsall
12.12.05 Cello Renda L CO 1 Peterborough
11.03.06 Matthew Hall L CO 1 Newport
13.04.06 Donovan Smillie DREW 6 Leeds
29.04.06 Craig Lynch L PTS 4 Edinburgh
01.06.06 Ryan Rowlinson W PTS 4 Barnsley
22.06.06 Jon Ibbotson DREW 6 Sheffield
15.09.06 Daniel Cadman L RSC 5 Muswell Hill
20.10.06 Jon Ibbotson L CO 2 Sheffield
24.11.06 Ricardo Samms L PTS 4 Nottingham
03.12.06 Darren Rhodes L PTS 6 Wakefield
16.03.07 Danny McIntosh L PTS 4 Norwich
15.04.07 Dean Walker W PTS 6 Barnsley
21.09.07 Adie Whitmore L PTS 6 Burton
25.05.08 Craig Denton L RSC 3 Hartlepool
19.07.08 Joey Ainscough L PTS 4 Liverpool
14.09.08 Eddie McIntosh L PTS 4 Birmingham
11.10.08 Phil Goodwin L PTS 6 Hull
14.11.08 Mark Regan L RSC 5 Birmingham
Career: 44 contests, won 13, drew 5, lost 26.

Danny Butler

Bristol. *Born* Bristol, 10 November, 1987
Western Area Middleweight Champion.
Former Undefeated British Masters
S. Middleweight Champion. Former
Undefeated British Masters L.Middleweight
Champion. *Ht* 5'10½"
Manager T. Woodward
25.02.06 Magic Kidem W PTS 6 Bristol
07.04.06 Tommy Jones W PTS 4 Bristol
21.05.06 Martin Sweeney W PTS 6 Bristol
03.12.06 Chris Brophy W PTS 4 Bristol

24.02.07 Rocky Chakir W PTS 6 Bristol
18.03.07 Pawel Jas W PTS 6 Bristol
01.06.07 Surinder Sekhon W PTS 6 Birmingham
15.09.07 Carl Drake W PTS 6 Bristol
02.12.07 Terry Adams W PTS 10 Bristol
    (*Vacant British Masters L.Middleweight
    Title*)
03.02.08 Dave Wakefield W RTD 7 Bristol
    (*British Masters L.Middleweight Title
    Defence*)
02.05.08 Jamie Ambler W CO 2 Bristol
    (*British Masters L.Middleweight Title
    Defence*)
04.09.08 Matthew Hough W RSC 5 Birmingham
    (*Vacant British Masters S.Middleweight
    Title*)
12.10.08 Mark Phillips W PTS 4 Bristol
22.11.08 Paul Samuels W PTS 3 Bethnal Green
22.11.08 Martin Murray L PTS 3 Bethnal Green
20.12.08 Tony Randell W PTS 6 Bristol
14.03.09 Carl Drake W PTS 10 Bristol
    (*Vacant Western Area Middleweight
    Title*)
13.06.09 Matt Scriven W PTS 4 Bristol
Career: 18 contests, won 17, lost 1.

Andrew Butlin

Huddersfield. *Born* Huddersfield, 31
January, 1982
Middleweight. *Ht* 5'10"
Manager C. Aston
12.11.04 Martin Concepcion L RSC 1 Halifax
22.02.07 Steve Cooper W PTS 6 Leeds
14.04.07 Rocky Muscas W PTS 6 Wakefield
21.01.08 Paul Burns DREW 6 Glasgow
22.02.08 David Walker L PTS 6 Bethnal Green
16.03.08 Ben Hudson W PTS 6 Sheffield
24.04.08 Duncan Cottier W PTS 6 Piccadilly
06.06.08 Jamie Coyle L RTD 3 Glasgow
04.12.08 Geraint Harvey W PTS 6 Bradford
17.05.09 Simon Fleck W PTS 4 Bolton
Career: 10 contests, won 6, drew 1, lost 3.

Paul Butlin   Philip Sharkey

Paul Butlin

Oakham. *Born* Oakham, 16 March, 1976
Heavyweight. *Ht* 6'1½"
Manager Self
05.10.02 Dave Clarke W PTS 4 Coventry
16.11.02 Gary Williams W RSC 1 Coventry
09.12.02 Slick Miller W PTS 6 Nottingham
08.03.03 Dave Clarke W PTS 6 Coventry
19.04.03 Paul Buttery L RSC 3 Liverpool
27.04.04 Ebrima Secka W PTS 6 Leeds
26.09.04 Lee Mountford W PTS 6 Stoke
06.12.04 David Ingleby W CO 5 Leicester
30.04.05 David Ingleby L PTS 6 Coventry
25.06.05 Mal Rice W PTS 4 Melton Mowbray
22.10.05 Jason Callum W PTS 4 Coventry
18.03.06 David Ingleby W PTS 6 Coventry
05.12.06 Chris Burton L RSC 4 Wolverhampton
03.03.07 Luke Simpkin W PTS 4 Burton
12.01.08 Derek Chisora L PTS 4 Bethnal Green
29.02.08 Sebastian Koeber L PTS 6 Alsterdorf,
    Germany
11.04.08 David Dolan L PTS 3 Bethnal Green
11.04.08 Colin Kenna W RSC 2 Bethnal Green
16.05.08 Paolo Vidoz L CO 2 Turin, Italy
09.05.09 Lee Swaby L PTS 10 Lincoln
    (*Vacant Midlands Area Heavyweight
    Title*)
22.05.09 Derek Chisora L PTS 8 Y, Bethnal Green
20.06.09 Johnathon Banks L CO 7 Gelsenkirchen,
    Germany
Career: 22 contests, won 12, lost 10.

Lewis Byrne   Philip Sharkey

Lewis Byrne

Cambridge. *Born* Gravesend, 28 December,
1984
L.Middleweight. *Ht* 5'11¼"
Manager G. Everett
16.06.07 Robbie James L PTS 4 Newport
15.09.07 Chris Brophy W CO 5 Bristol
05.10.07 Jamie Way L PTS 4 Newport
26.10.07 Jack Arnfield L RSC 1 Wigan
01.12.07 Brett Flournoy L RSC 2 Liverpool
22.03.09 Nathan Weise L PTS 4 Bethnal Green
11.04.09 Steve O'Meara L RTD 2 Bethnal Green
23.05.09 Phil Fury L PTS 4 Watford
Career: 8 contests, won 1, lost 7.

Marc Callaghan

Barking. *Born* Barking, 13 November, 1978
Former English S.Bantamweight
Champion. Former Undefeated Southern
Area S.Bantamweight Champion. *Ht* 5'6"
Manager Self
08.09.98 Kevin Sheil W PTS 4 Bethnal Green
31.10.98 Nicky Wilders W RSC 1 Southend
12.01.99 Nicky Wilders W RTD 2 Bethnal Green
12.03.99 Peter Allen W PTS 4 Bethnal Green
25.05.99 Simon Chambers L RSC 1 Mayfair
16.10.99 Nigel Leake W PTS 4 Bethnal Green
20.12.99 Marc Smith W PTS 4 Bethnal Green
05.02.00 Steve Brook W RSC 2 Bethnal Green
01.04.00 John Barnes W PTS 4 Bethnal Green
19.08.00 Anthony Hanna W PTS 4 Brentwood
09.10.00 Jamie McKeever L PTS 6 Liverpool
04.11.00 Nigel Senior W RSC 4 Bethnal Green
03.03.01 Anthony Hanna W PTS 6 Wembley
26.05.01 Roy Rutherford L RSC 3 Bethnal Green
01.12.01 Nigel Senior L CO 1 Bethnal Green
26.01.02 Richmond Asante W PTS 4 Dagenham
18.03.02 Michael Hunter DREW 4 Crawley
11.05.02 Andrew Ferrans W PTS 6 Dagenham
21.09.02 Steve Gethin W PTS 6 Brentwood
07.12.02 Stevie Quinn L PTS 4 Brentwood
08.03.03 Dazzo Williams L PTS 8 Bethnal Green
05.07.03 Mark Payne L PTS 6 Brentwood
08.05.04 Baz Carey W PTS 6 Dagenham
27.05.04 Steve Gethin W PTS 6 Huddersfield
20.09.04 John Simpson L PTS 8 Glasgow
19.11.04 Michael Hunter L RSC 10 Hartlepool
*(British S.Bantamweight Title
Challenge)*
16.06.05 Ian Napa W PTS 10 Dagenham
*(Vacant Southern Area S.Bantamweight
Title)*
18.11.05 Jackson Asiku L RSC 1 Dagenham
*(Vacant Commonwealth Featherweight
Title)*
03.03.06 Sean Hughes W PTS 10 Hartlepool
(Vacant English S.Bantamweight Title)
15.12.06 Dariusz Snarski W PTS 4 Bethnal Green
16.03.07 Esham Pickering L PTS 12 Norwich
(Vacant British S.Bantamweight Title)
12.10.07 Rendall Munroe L RTD 6 Peterlee
(English S.Bantamweight Title Defence)
16.05.08 Martin Lindsay L PTS 8 Turin, Italy
05.07.08 Paul Hyland L PTS 10 Dublin
(Vacant Irish S.Bantamweight Title)
07.11.08 Akaash Bhatia L CO 2 Wigan
*(Vacant Southern Area Featherweight
Title)*
22.05.09 Ryan Walsh L RTD 3 Bethnal Green
Career: 36 contests, won 19, drew 1, lost 16.

Jason Callum

Coventry. *Born* Coventry, 5 April, 1977
Heavyweight. *Ht* 6' 3"
Manager E. Johnson
05.04.03 Tony Booth W PTS 6 Coventry
15.11.03 Alvin Miller W PTS 4 Coventry
01.05.04 David Ingleby W PTS 6 Coventry

06.12.04 Scott Lansdowne L RSC 1 Leicester
22.10.05 Paul Butlin L PTS 4 Coventry
11.12.05 Sam Sexton L PTS 6 Norwich
17.03.06 Ian Millarvie L CO 3 Kirkcaldy
19.01.09 Ali Adams L PTS 4 Mayfair
13.02.09 Martyn Grainger L PTS 4 Wigan
20.03.09 Ian Lewison L PTS 6 Bethnal Green
03.04.09 Lee Kellett DREW 6 Leigh
12.06.09 Neil Perkins L RSC 3 Wolverhampton
Career: 12 contests, won 3, drew 1, lost 8.

Phillip Callaghan

Leeds. *Born* Leeds, 16 May, 1973
L.Heavyweight. Ht 5'11"
Manager Self
15.10.06 Paul Davis L RSC 4 Norwich
24.11.06 Rod Anderton L RSC 4 Nottingham
23.02.07 Lee Jones L PTS 4 Birmingham
23.03.07 Rod Anderton DREW 4 Nottingham
20.04.07 Carl Wild L RSC 1 Sheffield
25.09.07 Phil Goodwin L PTS 6 Hull
26.10.07 Martin Murray L RSC 1 Wigan
25.01.08 Eddie McIntosh L PTS 4 Birmingham
Career: 8 contests, drew 1, lost 7.

Joe Calzaghe

Newbridge. *Born* Hammersmith, 23 March,
1972
Former Undefeated WBO, WBA, WBC,
British & IBF S.Middleweight Champion.
Ht 5'11"
Manager Self
01.10.93 Paul Hanlon W RSC 1 Cardiff
10.11.93 Stinger Mason W RSC 1 Watford
16.12.93 Spencer Alton W RSC 2 Newport
22.01.94 Martin Rosamond W RSC 1 Cardiff
01.03.94 Darren Littlewood W RSC 1 Dudley
04.06.94 Karl Barwise W RSC 1 Cardiff
01.10.94 Mark Dawson W RSC 1 Cardiff
30.11.94 Trevor Ambrose W RSC 2
Wolverhampton
14.02.95 Frank Minton W CO 1 Bethnal Green
22.02.95 Bobbi Joe Edwards W PTS 8 Telford
19.05.95 Robert Curry W RSC 1 Southwark
08.07.95 Tyrone Jackson W RSC 4 York
30.09.95 Nick Manners W RSC 4 Basildon
28.10.95 Stephen Wilson W RSC 8 Kensington
(Vacant British S. Middleweight Title)
13.02.96 Guy Stanford W RSC 1 Cardiff
13.03.96 Anthony Brooks W RSC 2 Wembley
20.04.96 Mark Delaney W RSC 5 Brentwood
(British S. Middleweight Title Defence)
04.05.96 Warren Stowe W RTD 2 Dagenham
15.05.96 Pat Lawlor W RSC 2 Cardiff
21.01.97 Carlos Christie W CO 2 Bristol
22.03.97 Tyler Hughes W CO 1 Wythenshawe
05.06.97 Luciano Torres W RSC 3 Bristol
11.10.97 Chris Eubank W PTS 12 Sheffield
(Vacant WBO S. Middleweight Title)
24.01.98 Branco Sobot W RSC 3 Cardiff
(WBO S. Middleweight Title Defence)
25.04.98 Juan Carlos Gimenez W RTD 9 Cardiff
(WBO S. Middleweight Title Defence)
13.02.99 Robin Reid W PTS 12 Newcastle
(WBO S. Middleweight Title Defence)
05.06.99 Rick Thornberry W PTS 12 Cardiff
(WBO S. Middleweight Title Defence)
29.01.00 David Starie W PTS 12 Manchester
(WBO S, Middleweight Title Defence)
12.08.00 Omar Sheika W RSC 5 Wembley
(WBO S.Middleweight Title Defence)

16.12.00 Richie Woodhall W RSC 10 Sheffield
(WBO S. Middleweight Title Defence)
28.04.01 Mario Veit W RSC 1 Cardiff
(WBO S. Middleweight Title Defence)
13.10.01 Will McIntyre W RSC 4 Copenhagen,
Denmark
(WBO S. Middleweight Title Defence)
20.04.02 Charles Brewer W PTS 12 Cardiff
(WBO S. Middleweight Title Defence)
17.08.02 Miguel Jimenez W PTS 12 Cardiff
(WBO S.Middleweight Title Defence)
14.12.02 Tocker Pudwill W RSC 2 Newcastle
(WBO S. Middleweight Title Defence)
28.06.03 Byron Mitchell W RSC 2 Cardiff
(WBO S.Middleweight Title Defence)
21.02.04 Mger Mkrtchian W RSC 7 Cardiff
(WBO S.Middleweight Title Defence)
22.10.04 Kabary Salem W PTS 12 Edinburgh
(WBO S.Middleweight Title Defence)
07.05.05 Mario Veit W RSC 6 Braunschweig,
Germany
(WBO S.Middleweight Title Defence)
10.09.05 Evans Ashira W PTS 12 Cardiff
(WBO S.Middleweight Title Defence)
04.03.06 Jeff Lacy W PTS 12 Manchester
*(IBF S.Middleweight Title Challenge.
BO S.Middleweight Title Defence)*
14.10.06 Sakio Bika W PTS 12 Manchester
*(IBF& WBO S.Middleweight Title
Defences)*
07.04.07 Peter Manfredo W RSC 3 Cardiff
(WBO S.Middleweight Title Defence)
03.11.07 Mikkel Kessler W PTS 12 Cardiff
*(WBA & WBC S.Middleweight Title
Challenge. WBO S.Middleweight Title
Defence)*
19.04.08 Bernard Hopkins W PTS 12 Las Vegas,
Nevada, USA
08.11.08 Roy Jones W PTS 12 NYC, New York,
USA
Career: 46 contests, won 46.

Darryl Campbell

Fife. *Born* Kirkcaldy, 18 June, 1983
L.Middleweight. *Ht* 6' 0"
Manager T. Gilmour
27.04.09 Ernie Smith W RSC 5 Glasgow
25.06.09 Simon Fleck W RTD 2 Glenrothes
Career: 2 contests, won 2.

Drew Campbell

Colchester. *Born* Elgin, 30 September, 1980
L.Middleweight. *Ht* 5'9¼"
Manager T. Sims
22.09.07 Kevin Concepcion L PTS 4 Coventry
25.11.07 Rocky Muscus W PTS 6 Colchester
02.12.07 Lee Noble L PTS 6 Oldham
23.02.08 Joe McNally L PTS 4 Liverpool
22.03.08 Gavin Smith L PTS 6 Sheffield
26.04.08 Alex Matvienko L RSC 4 Wigan
20.06.08 Rob Kenney L PTS 4 Wolverhampton
28.02.09 Steve O'Meara L PTS 4 Norwich
11.04.09 Stephen Haughian L RSC 1 Bethnal Green
23.05.09 Steve O'Meara L PTS 6 Watford
Career: 10 contests, won 1, lost 9.

Peter Cannon

Bradford. *Born* Bradford, 20 January, 1981
S.Middleweight. *Ht* 6'1"
Manager M. Marsden

20.04.07 Jezz Wilson L RSC 5 Sheffield
29.11.07 Tony Stones DREW 6 Bradford
24.05.09 Chris Brophy W PTS 6 Bradford
Career: 3 contests, won 1, drew 1, lost 1.

(Barry) Baz Carey

Coventry. *Born* Coventry, 11 March, 1971
L.Welterweight. *Ht* 5'4½"
Manager P. Carpenter
19.12.01 J.J. Moore L PTS 4 Coventry
18.01.02 J.J. Moore DREW 4 Coventry
25.02.02 Chris McDonagh L PTS 6 Slough
19.03.02 Ilias Miah W PTS 6 Slough
21.09.02 Jackson Williams L PTS 6 Norwich
10.10.02 Dean Scott W RSC 2 Stoke
19.10.02 Lee McAllister L PTS 4 Renfrew
21.11.02 Chris Hooper L RTD 3 Hull
22.03.03 Dave Hinds W PTS 6 Coventry
05.04.03 Pete Buckley W PTS 4 Manchester
12.05.03 Matthew Marshall L PTS 6 Southampton
07.06.03 Joel Viney W PTS 6 Coventry
26.07.03 Andrew Ferrans DREW 4 Plymouth
13.09.03 Paul McIlwaine W RTD 2 Coventry
12.10.03 Daniel Thorpe DREW 6 Sheffield
08.11.03 Carl Allen L RSC 2 Coventry
15.03.04 Andrew Ferrans L PTS 10 Glasgow
(Vacant British Masters S.Featherweight Title)
17.04.04 Michael Kelly L PTS 4 Belfast
26.04.04 Rendall Munroe L PTS 6 Cleethorpes
08.05.04 Marc Callaghan L PTS 6 Dagenham
06.11.04 Daniel Thorpe L PTS 6 Coventry
20.11.04 Dave Hinds W RSC 4 Coventry
17.12.04 Kristian Laight W PTS 6 Coventry
30.04.05 Billy Smith W PTS 6 Coventry
26.05.05 Daniel Thorpe L PTS 6 Mayfair
10.09.05 Amir Khan L PTS 4 Cardiff
24.09.05 Billy Smith NC 5 Coventry
03.12.05 Billy Smith W PTS 6 Coventry
14.12.05 Jeff Thomas W PTS 6 Blackpool
03.03.06 Stefy Bull L PTS 10 Doncaster
(WBF Inter-Continental Lightweight Title Challenge)
06.05.06 Scott Lawton L PTS 10 Stoke
(Midlands Area Lightweight Title Challenge)
01.06.06 Martin Gethin L PTS 4 Birmingham
23.07.06 Ryan Barrett L PTS 6 Dagenham
09.10.06 Kristian Laight DREW 6 Bedworth
04.11.06 Barry Hughes L PTS 4 Glasgow
05.12.06 Dean Harrison L PTS 4 Wolverhampton
09.02.07 Chris Pacy L PTS 4 Leeds
23.02.07 Lewis Smith L PTS 6 Manchester
24.03.07 Billy Smith L PTS 10 Coventry
(Vacant Midlands Area L.Welterweight Title)
13.10.07 Paul Newby L PTS 6 Barnsley
03.11.07 Dave Ryan L PTS 6 Derby
01.12.07 Nathan Brough L RSC 3 Liverpool
22.02.08 Jamie Spence L PTS 4 Bethnal Green
16.03.08 John Watson L PTS 4 Liverpool
29.03.08 Michael Gomez L PTS 6 Glasgow
05.04.08 Steve Bell L PTS 6 Bolton
30.04.08 Rob Hunt L PTS 6 Wolverhampton
17.05.08 Chris Goodwin L PTS 4 Stoke
31.05.08 Amir Unsworth L PTS 4 Newark
20.06.08 Steve Williams L PTS 4 Wolverhampton
27.06.08 Gareth Couch L PTS 4 Bethnal Green
19.07.08 Stephen Burke L PTS 4 Liverpool
13.09.08 Gavin Tait L PTS 4 Bethnal Green

10.10.08 Michael Gomez L PTS 6 Motherwell
09.11.08 Steve Saville L RSC 7 Wolverhampton
(Vacant Midlands Area Lightweight Title)
27.02.09 Tyrone Nurse L PTS 4 Barnsley
06.03.09 Karl Place L PTS 4 Wigan
28.03.09 Stefy Bull L PTS 6 Lincoln
23.04.09 Alex Dilmagahmi L PTS 4 Limehouse
22.05.09 Liam Walsh L RSC 3 Bethnal Green
Career: 60 contests, won 11, drew 4, lost 44, no contest 1.

Jason Carr

Sheffield. *Born* Kirkcaldy, 29 June 1986
L.Heavyweight. *Ht* 5' 11"
Manager G. Rhodes
05.12.08 Craig Dyer W PTS 6 Sheffield
08.03.09 Jason Thompson DREW 4 Sheffield
24.04.09 Tim Witherspoon Jr L PTS 4 Sheffield
Career: 3 contests, won 1, drew 1, lost 1.

Kris Carslaw

Paisley. *Born* Paisley, 1 September, 1984
L.Middleweight. *Ht* 5'9¼"
Manager Self
15.09.07 Surinder Sekhon W PTS 4 Paisley
17.11.07 David Kehoe W PTS 4 Glasgow
15.12.07 Paul Royston W PTS 4 Edinburgh
29.03.08 Dave Wakefield W PTS 4 Glasgow
18.10.08 Ernie Smith W PTS 4 Paisley
27.02.09 Duncan Cottier W RTD 2 Paisley
Career: 6 contests, won 6.

Santino Caruana

Glasgow. *Born* Glasgow, 30 November, 1988
Lightweight. *Ht* 5' 5"
Manager A. Morrison
29.05.09 James Ancliff W PTS 4 Glasgow
19.06.09 Johnny Greaves W PTS 4 Glasgow
Career: 2 contests, won 2.

Henry Castle

Salisbury. *Born* Southampton, 7 February, 1979
Lightweight. *Ht* 5'6¾"
Manager R. Davies/F. Maloney
29.01.01 Jason Nesbitt W CO 6 Peterborough
26.03.01 Eddie Nevins W RSC 2 Peterborough
23.11.01 Jimmy Beech W PTS 4 Bethnal Green
11.03.02 David Lowry W RSC 1 Glasgow
20.04.02 Jason Nesbitt W PTS 4 Cardiff
25.05.02 Jimmy Beech W PTS 4 Portsmouth
17.08.02 Joel Viney W RSC 1 Cardiff
23.11.02 John Mackay L RTD 8 Derby
29.03.03 Jus Wallie L RSC 2 Portsmouth
25.09.03 Mark Alexander W PTS 6 Bethnal Green
21.11.03 Pete Buckley W PTS 4 Millwall
20.02.04 Daleboy Rees W RSC 4 Bethnal Green
26.06.05 Karl Taylor W PTS 6 Southampton
04.12.05 Gareth Couch L PTS 6 Portsmouth
24.09.06 Peter Allen W RSC 6 Southampton
03.12.06 Wladimir Borov W RSC 4 Bethnal Green
09.02.07 Carl Allen W RSC 4 Leeds
09.03.07 Ian Wilson L RSC 5 Dagenham
30.11.07 Kevin O'Hara W PTS 8 Newham

01.02.08 Frederic Gosset W PTS 6 Bethnal Green
18.04.08 Ryan Barrett W RSC 3 Bethnal Green
13.06.08 Lee Cook W RSC 5 Portsmouth
17.10.08 Graham Earl W RSC 1 Bethnal Green
20.03.09 Kristian Laight W PTS 6 Newham
Career: 24 contests, won 20, lost 4.

Henry Castle   Philip Sharkey

Brock Cato

Dolgellau. *Born* Wrexham, 19 August, 1987
Welterweight. *Ht* 5'10¼"
Manager N. Hodges
30.03.08 Gary Cooper W RSC 2 Port Talbot
02.05.08 Lance Verallo W PTS 6 Bristol
04.09.08 Steve Cooper W RSC 3 Birmingham
12.10.08 Steve Cooper W PTS 6 Bristol
14.03.09 Matt Scriven W PTS 6 Bristol
13.06.09 Kevin McCauley L PTS 6 Bristol
Career: 6 contests, won 5, lost 1.

(Yuvuzer) Rocky Chakir (Cakir)

Bristol. *Born* Trabzon, Turkey, 12 April, 1982
L.Middleweight. *Ht* 5'7¼"
Manager C. Sanigar
03.11.06 Pawel Jas W PTS 6 Bristol
10.11.06 Steve Anning W PTS 6 Newport
03.12.06 Chris Long L PTS 6 Bristol
24.02.07 Danny Butler L PTS 6 Bristol
23.09.07 Paul Porter W RSC 1 Longford
01.12.07 Lester Walsh W PTS 6 Coventry
25.02.08 Richard Mazurek W RSC 2 Birmingham
24.05.08 Jamie Way L PTS 6 Cardiff
05.06.09 James Lilley L PTS 6 Newport
Career: 9 contests, won 4, lost 5.

Derek Chisora

Finchley. *Born* Zimbabwe, 29 December, 1983
Heavyweight. *Ht* 6' 1¼"
Manager F. Warren
17.02.07 Istvan Kecskes W RSC 2 Wembley
07.04.07 Tony Booth W PTS 4 Cardiff

13.10.07 Darren Morgan W PTS 4 Bethnal
Green
12.01.08 Paul Butlin W PTS 4 Bethnal Green
14.06.08 Sam Sexton W RSC 6 Bethnal Green
12.09.08 Shawn McLean W RSC 6 Mayfair
26.09.08 Lee Swaby W RSC 3 Bethnal Green
06.12.08 Neil Simpson W RTD 2 Canning Town
30.01.09 Daniil Peretyatko W PTS 8 Bethnal
Green
22.05.09 Paul Butlin W PTS 8 Bethnal Green
Career: 10 contests, won 10.

Derek Chisora   Philip Sharkey

Karl Chiverton

Mansfield. *Born* Sutton in Ashfield, 1
March, 1986
Middleweight. *Ht* 5' 9¾"
Manager M. Shinfield
18.09.04 Karl Taylor W PTS 6 Newark
10.12.04 Cafu Santos L RSC 4 Mansfield
13.05.06 Mark Wall W PTS 6 Sutton in Ashfield
16.09.06 Tony Randell W PTS 6 Burton
11.11.06 Ernie Smith W PTS 6 Sutton in Ashfield
19.05.07 Peter Dunn W PTS 4 Nottingham
22.07.07 Lance Verallo W PTS 6 Mansfield
26.10.07 Peter Dunn W PTS 6 Birmingham
10.12.07 Sean McKervey W PTS 6 Birmingham
28.03.08 Martin Sweeney W PTS 4 Barnsley
05.09.08 Billy Smith W PTS 4 Nottingham
18.12.08 Willie Thompson DREW 4 Dublin
Career: 12 contests, won 10, drew 1, lost 1.

Lee Churcher

Newport. *Born* Newport, 28 November,
1980
Middleweight. *Ht* 5' 10"
Manager C. Sanigar
05.06.09 Luke Osman W PTS 6 Newport
Career: 1 contest, won 1.

Ryan Clark

Lincoln. *Born* Lincoln, 18 August, 1989
L.Middleweight. *Ht* 6' 2"
Manager C. Greaves
28.06.09 Jamie Boness DREW 6 Luton
Career: 1 contest, drew 1.

Mark Clauzel

Newcastle. *Born* Newcastle, 11 December,
1982
L.Middleweight. *Ht* 5' 10"
Manager T. Gilmour
16.01.09 Geraint Harvey W PTS 4 Middlesbrough
Career: 1 contest, won 1.

Nathan Cleverly

Cefn Forest. *Born* Caerphilly, 17 February,
1987
Commonwealth L.Heavyweight Champion.
Ht 6'1½"
Manager F. Warren
23.07.05 Ernie Smith W PTS 4 Edinburgh
10.09.05 Darren Gethin W PTS 4 Cardiff
04.12.05 Lance Hall W RSC 3 Telford
04.03.06 Jon Foster W PTS 4 Manchester
01.06.06 Brendan Halford W PTS 4 Barnsley
08.07.06 Mark Phillips W PTS 4 Cardiff
14.10.06 Tony Quigley W RSC 5 Manchester
18.11.06 Varuzhan Davtyan W PTS 4 Newport
07.04.07 Nick Okoth W PTS 8 Cardiff
21.07.07 Ayitey Powers W CO 6 Cardiff
03.11.07 Joey Vegas W PTS 8 Cardiff
19.04.08 Antonio Baker W PTS 8 Las Vegas,
Nevada, USA
10.10.08 Tony Oakey W PTS 12 Liverpool
*(Vacant Commonwealth L.Heavyweight
Title)*
12.12.08 Douglas Otieno W CO 4 Widnes
*(Commonwealth L.Heavyweight Title
Defence)*
13.02.09 Samson Onyango W RSC 1 Swindon
*(Commonwealth L.Heavyweight Title
Defence)*
22.05.09 Billy Boyle W RSC 2 Bethnal Green
*(Commonwealth L.Heavyweight Title
Defence)*
Career: 16 contests, won 16.

Nathan Cleverly   Philip Sharkey

Kevin Coglan

Darlington. *Born* Darlington, 25 October,
1990
Flyweight. *Ht* 5' 3"
Manager M. Marsden
01.05.09 Francis Croes W PTS 4 Hartlepool
Career: 1 contest, won 1.

Russ Colley

Wolverhampton. *Born* Wolverhampton, 9
December, 1983
L. Middleweight. *Ht* 5' 9¼"
Manager E. Johnson
30.04.08 Peter Dunn W PTS 4 Wolverhampton
20.06.08 Ricky Strike W PTS 4 Wolverhampton
12.09.08 Chris Brophy W PTS 6 Wolverhampton
26.09.08 Tye Williams W PTS 4 Wolverhampton
27.02.09 Ernie Smith W PTS 4 Wolverhampton
Career: 5 contests, won 5.

Kevin Concepcion

Leicester. *Born* Leicester, 22 February,
1980
Former Undefeated British Masters
Middleweight Champion. *Ht* 5'10¾"
Manager Self
23.09.06 Ben Hudson W PTS 6 Coventry
09.10.06 Ryan Rowlinson W PTS 6 Bedworth
02.12.06 Rocky Muscas W PTS 6 Coventry
24.03.07 Davey Jones W RSC 1 Coventry
13.05.07 Mark Phillips W PTS 6 Birmingham
22.09.07 Drew Campbell W PTS 4 Coventry
06.10.07 David Kirk W PTS 6 Leicester
01.12.07 Darren Rhodes W RSC 5 Coventry
16.02.08 Michael Banbula W PTS 6 Leicester
28.03.08 Darren Rhodes W CO 4 Barnsley
02.05.08 Billy Smith W PTS 6 Nottingham
28.06.08 Tyan Booth W PTS 10 Leicester
*(Vacant British Masters Middleweight
Title)*
05.09.08 Vepkhia Tchilaia W PTS 6 Nottingham
15.11.08 Yassine El Maachi L RSC 2 Bethnal
Green
21.12.08 Paul Dyer W PTS 4 Coventry
17.04.09 Martin Murray L RSC 3 Leigh
Career: 16 contests, won 14, lost 2.

Scott Conway

Derby. *Born* Derby, 27 October, 1979
L.Middleweight. *Ht* 6' 0"
Manager M. Shinfield
27.09.04 Rocky Flanagan W RSC 2 Cleethorpes
16.12.04 Tony Randell L PTS 6 Cleethorpes
20.02.05 Sujad Elahi DREW 6 Sheffield
24.04.05 Casey Brooks W PTS 6 Derby
18.06.05 Joe Mitchell L RSC 5 Barnsley
02.09.05 Darren Gethin L CO 1 Derby
08.12.05 Lance Verallo W PTS 6 Derby
25.03.06 Tye Williams DREW 4 Burton
14.05.06 Tye Williams L RSC 5 Derby
10.05.09 Karl Taylor W PTS 6 Derby
31.05.09 Wayne Downing L RSC 2 Burton
Career: 11 contests, won 4, drew 2, lost 5.

Steve Conway

Dewsbury. *Born* Hartlepool, 6 October,
1977
L.Middleweight. Former IBO
L.Middleweight Champion. *Ht* 5'8"
Manager Self
21.02.96 Robert Grubb W PTS 6 Batley
24.04.96 Ervine Blake W PTS 6 Solihull
20.05.96 Chris Lyons W PTS 6 Cleethorpes
30.05.96 Ram Singh W PTS 6 Lincoln
03.02.97 Jason Squire W PTS 6 Leicester

11.04.97 Marc Smith W PTS 4 Barnsley
22.09.97 Arv Mittoo W PTS 6 Cleethorpes
09.10.97 Arv Mittoo W PTS 6 Leeds
01.11.97 Brian Carr L PTS 6 Glasgow
14.11.97 Brendan Bryce W PTS 6 Mere
04.12.97 Kid McAuley W RSC 5 Doncaster
15.12.97 Nicky Wilders W PTS 6 Cleethorpes
05.03.98 Pete Buckley W PTS 6 Leeds
25.04.98 Dean Philips W PTS 6 Cardiff
09.05.98 Gary Flear W PTS 4 Sheffield
18.05.98 Brian Coleman W PTS 6 Cleethorpes
05.09.98 Benny Jones W PTS 4 Telford
19.12.98 Gary Thornhill L RSC 9 Liverpool
(WBO Inter-Continental
S. Featherweight Title Challenge)
04.06.99 Brian Coleman W PTS 6 Hull
27.09.99 Brian Coleman W PTS 6 Leeds
27.02.00 Chris Price W RTD 3 Leeds
21.03.00 Pedro Miranda L RSC 3 Telde, Gran
Canaria
15.07.00 Arv Mittoo W PTS 6 Norwich
20.10.00 Junior Witter L RTD 4 Belfast
25.02.01 Ram Singh W RSC 2 Derby
02.06.01 Jimmy Phelan W PTS 4 Wakefield
18.08.01 Keith Jones W PTS 8 Dewsbury
17.11.01 Carl Allen W PTS 8 Dewsbury
27.04.02 Steve Robinson W PTS 8 Huddersfield
05.10.02 Rakhim Mingaleev W RSC 4
Huddersfield
19.10.02 Alex Arthur L CO 4 Renfrew
(Vacant British S. Featherweight Title)
05.07.03 Dariusz Snarski W RSC 4 Brentwood
05.10.03 Brian Coleman W PTS 6 Bradford
06.11.03 Yuri Romanov L PTS 8 Dagenham
23.11.03 Gareth Wiltshaw W RSC 5 Rotherham
16.04.04 Norman Dhalie W CO 3 Hartlepool
23.10.04 Ernie Smith W PTS 6 Wakefield
25.09.05 Lee Williamson W PTS 6 Leeds
02.12.05 Mihaly Kotai W PTS 10 Nottingham
03.03.06 Mihaly Kotai W PTS 12 Hartlepool
(IBO L.Middleweight Title Challenge)
03.06.06 Attila Kovacs L PTS 12 Szolnok,
Hungary
(IBO L.Middleweight Title Defence)
15.12.06 Grzegorz Proksa L PTS 6 Bethnal Green
10.11.07 Christophe Canclaux L RSC 3 Paris,
France
05.07.08 Gennady Martirosyan L PTS 8 Leon,
Spain
24.10.08 Mark Lloyd L PTS 3 Bethnal Green
06.12.08 Anthony Small L RSC 2 Canning Town
Career: 46 contests, won 34, lost 12.

Lee Cook   Philip Sharkey

Lee Cook

Morden. *Born* London, 26 June, 1981
Southern Area Lightweight Champion. *Ht*
5'8"
Manager D. Powell
24.09.04 Jus Wallie W RSC 2 Bethnal Green
26.11.04 Willie Valentine W PTS 4 Bethnal Green
05.03.05 Billy Smith W PTS 4 Southwark
29.04.05 Eddie Anderson W RSC 2 Southwark
20.05.05 Ian Reid W PTS 4 Southwark
04.11.05 Buster Dennis DREW 4 Bethnal Green
11.02.06 David Kehoe W RTD 2 Bethnal Green
02.04.06 Rakhim Mingaleev W PTS 4 Bethnal
Green
09.03.07 Youssef Al Hamidi W PTS 6 Dagenham
15.06.07 Rom Krauklis W PTS 4 Crystal Palace
13.06.08 Henry Castle L RSC 5 Portsmouth
01.02.09 Daniel Thorpe W PTS 4 Bethnal Green
20.03.09 Shane Watson W PTS 10 Bethnal Green
(Vacant Southern Area Lightweight
Title)
21.06.09 Mark McCullough W PTS 6 Bethnal
Green
Career: 14 contests, won 12, drew 1, lost 1.

Nicky Cook

Dagenham. *Born* Stepney, 13 September,
1979
Former WBO S. Featherweight Champion.
Former Undefeated British, European &
Commonwealth Featherweight Champion.
Former Undefeated WBF Inter-Continental
S. Featherweight Champion. *Ht* 5'6½"
Manager Self
11.12.98 Sean Grant W CO 1 Cheshunt
26.02.99 Graham McGrath W CO 2 Coventry
27.04.99 Vasil Paskelev W CO 1 Bethnal Green
25.05.99 Wilson Acuna W PTS 4 Mayfair
12.07.99 Igor Sakhatarov W PTS 4 Coventry
20.08.99 Vlado Varhegyi W PTS 4 Bloomsbury
27.11.99 John Barnes W PTS 6 Liverpool
20.12.99 Carl Allen W CO 3 Bethnal Green
10.03.00 Chris Jickells W RSC 1 Bethnal Green
27.05.00 Anthony Hanna W PTS 6 Mayfair
16.06.00 Salem Bouaita W PTS 6 Bloomsbury
04.11.00 Vladimir Borov W RSC 1 Bethnal
Green
08.12.00 Rakhim Mingaleev W PTS 8 Crystal
Palace
19.05.01 Foudil Madani W RSC 1 Wembley
28.11.01 Woody Greenaway W RSC 3 Bethnal
Green
19.12.01 Marcelo Ackermann W RSC 3 Coventry
(Vacant WBF Inter-Continental
S.Featherweight Title)
20.04.02 Jackie Gunguluza W RTD 4 Wembley
(WBF Inter-Continental S.Featherweight
Title Defence)
10.07.02 Andrei Devyataykin W PTS 8 Wembley
05.10.02 Gary Thornhill W RSC 7 Liverpool
(WBF Inter-Continental S.Featherweight
Title Defence)
08.02.03 Mishek Kondwani W RSC 12 Brentford
(Vacant Commonwealth Featherweight
Title)
31.05.03 David Kiilu W CO 2 Bethnal Green
(Commonwealth Featherweight Title
Defence)
24.10.03 Anyetei Laryea W PTS 12 Bethnal
Green

(Commonwealth Featherweight Title)
20.03.04 Cyril Thomas W CO 9 Wembley
(European Featherweight Title
Challenge)
08.10.04 Johny Begue W PTS 12 Brentwood
(European Featherweight Title Defence)
16.06.05 Dazzo Williams W CO 2 Dagenham
(European &Commonwealth
Featherweight Title Defences. British
Featherweight Title Challenge)
24.02.06 Yuri Voronin W PTS 12 Dagenham
(European Featherweight Title Defence)
09.12.06 Harry Ramogoadi W PTS 8 Canning
Town
14.07.07 Steven Luevano L CO 11 Greenwich
(Vacant WBO Featherweight Title)
02.02.08 Kirkor Kirkorov W RSC 2 Canning
Town
06.09.08 Alex Arthur W PTS 12 Manchester
(WBO S.Featherweight Title Challenge)
14.03.09 Roman Martinez L RSC 4 Manchester
(WBO S.Featherweight Title Defence)
Career: 31 contests, won 29, lost 2.

Gary Cooper

Bargoed. *Born* Cardiff, 5 November, 1988
Middleweight. *Ht* 5'9¼"
Manager D. Gardiner
01.12.07 Mick Jenno L PTS 4 Liverpool
30.03.08 Brock Cato L RSC 2 Port Talbot
17.10.08 Marlon Reid L PTS 4 Swindon
26.06.09 Myles Holder L PTS 6 Melksham
Career: 4 contests, lost 4.

Lana Cooper

Bargoed. *Born* Caerphilly, 2 April, 1987
Lightweight. *Ht* 5' 5"
Manager D. Gardiner
17.10.08 Kristine Shergold L PTS 4 Swindon
16.11.08 Suzanne Hemsley L PTS 4 Derby
27.02.09 Lyndsey Scragg L PTS 6
Wolverhampton
26.06.09 Kristine Shergold L PTS 6 Melksham
Career: 4 contests, lost 4.

Steve Cooper   Philip Sharkey

Steve Cooper

Worcester. *Born* Worcester, 19 November,
1977
L.Middleweight. *Ht* 5'8½"
Manager E. Johnson

09.12.02 Darren Goode W CO 3 Birmingham
16.09.06 Dale Miles L PTS 6 Burton
29.09.06 Mark Hastie L PTS 6 Motherwell
09.10.06 Sean McKervey DREW 6 Birmingham
23.10.06 Willie Bilan L PTS 6 Glasgow
07.11.06 Tommy Broadbent L PTS 6 Leeds
20.11.06 Paul Burns DREW 6 Glasgow
11.12.06 Sean McKervey L PTS 6 Birmingham
22.02.07 Andrew Butlin L PTS 6 Leeds
03.03.07 Steve Anning L PTS 6 Newport
10.03.07 Denton Vassell L RSC 2 Liverpool
28.04.07 Andrew Alan Lowe L PTS 6 Newark
12.05.07 Jimmy Doherty L PTS 6 Stoke
25.05.07 Eamonn Goodbrand L PTS 6 Glasgow
03.06.07 Paul Royston W PTS 6 Barnsley
16.06.07 Jamie Way L PTS 6 Newport
10.09.07 Paul Burns L PTS 6 Glasgow
22.09.07 Sean McKervey L PTS 6 Coventry
05.10.07 Robbie James L PTS 6 Newport
13.10.07 Jon Musgrave L PTS 6 Barnsley
21.10.07 Russell Pearce L PTS 4 Swansea
02.12.07 Chris Brophy L PTS 6 Bristol
23.12.07 Chris Johnson L RSC 4 Bolton
31.01.08 Chris Thompson W RSC 2 Piccadilly
21.02.08 Adil Anwar L PTS 6 Leeds
01.03.08 Danny Coyle L PTS 6 Coventry
17.03.08 Steve Williams L PTS 6 Glasgow
10.04.08 Wayne Alwan Arab L PTS 6 Piccadilly
16.05.08 Simon Ivekich DREW 6 Burton
25.05.08 Ryan Ashworth L PTS 6 Hartlepool
15.06.08 Pat McAleese L RSC 4 Bethnal Green
24.07.08 Kevin McCauley L PTS 4
            Wolverhampton
04.09.08 Brock Cato L RSC 3 Birmingham
12.10.08 Brock Cato L PTS 6 Bristol
20.10.08 Jamie McLevy L PTS 6 Glasgow
13.03.09 Eisa Al Dah L CO 2 Newport
Career: 36 contests, won 3, drew 3, lost 30.

Darren Corbett

Belfast. *Born* Belfast, 9 July, 1972
Cruiserweight. Former Undefeated
IBO Inter-Continental L. Heavyweight
Champion. Former Commonwealth,
IBO Inter-Continental & All-Ireland
Cruiserweight Champion. *Ht* 5' 11"
Manager Self
10.12.94 David Jules W RSC 1 Manchester
13.12.94 Carl Gaffney W RSC 1 Potters Bar
21.02.95 Steve Garber W PTS 6 Sunderland
18.03.95 Gary Williams DREW 6 Millstreet
14.04.95 Dennis Bailey W CO 2 Belfast
27.05.95 Roger McKenzie L PTS 6 Belfast
26.08.95 Nigel Rafferty W PTS 6 Belfast
07.10.95 Nigel Rafferty W PTS 6 Belfast
02.12.95 Bobbie Joe Edwards W PTS 6 Belfast
07.05.96 Cliff Elden W CO 1 Mayfair
28.05.96 Darren Fearn W CO 1 Belfast
03.09.96 Chris Woollas W CO 7 Belfast
05.11.96 Ray Kane W RSC 5 Belfast
            (Vacant All-Ireland Cruiserweight Title)
17.12.96 Chris Woollas W RSC 1 Doncaster
28.01.97 Nigel Rafferty W PTS 10 Belfast
            *(All-Ireland Cruiserweight
            Title Defence)*
29.04.97 Noel Magee W CO 2 Belfast
            *(All-Ireland Cruiserweight
            Title Defence)*
02.06.97 Chris Okoh W CO 3 Belfast

*(Commonwealth Cruiserweight Title
Challenge)*
17.10.97 Hector Sanjurjo W PTS 10
            Mashantucket, Connecticut, USA
20.12.97 Robert Norton W PTS 12 Belfast
            *(Commonwealth Cruiserweight Title
            Defence)*
21.02.98 Dirk Wallyn W PTS 10 Belfast
28.04.98 Konstantin Okhrey W CO 4 Belfast
            *(Vacant IBO Inter-Continental
            Cruiserweight Title)*
26.05.98 Roberto Dominguez Perez W CO 1
            Mayfair
            *(IBO Inter-Continental Cruiserweight
            Title Defence)*
28.11.98 Bruce Scott L RSC 10 Belfast
            *(Commonwealth Cruiserweight Title
            Defence. Vacant British Cruiserweight
            Title)*
10.04.99 Stephane Allouane L RSC 9 Manchester
            *(Vacant IBO Inter-Continental
            Cruiserweight Title)*
31.07.99 Darren Ashton W RSC 2 Carlisle
14.12.99 Neil Simpson W PTS 12 Coventry
            *(Vacant IBO Inter-Continental
            L.Heavyweight Title)*
25.03.00 John Lennox Lewis W RSC 2 Liverpool
            *(IBO Inter-Continental L.Heavyweight
            Title Defence)*
16.06.01 Tyler Hughes W CO 1 Yonkers, New
            York, USA
16.11.01 Radcliffe Green W PTS 8 Dublin
05.04.03 Clint Johnson W RSC 4 Belfast
17.04.04 Karim Bennama L RSC 6 Belfast
12.07.08 Remigijus Ziausys W PTS 6 Dublin
19.05.09 Ovill McKenzie L RSC 2 Kensington
19.05.09 Micky Steeds W PTS 3 Kensington
Career: 34 contests, won 28, drew 1, lost 5.

Eddie Corcoran

Neasden. *Born* Manchester, 5 October, 1985
L.Welterweight. *Ht* 5'11½"
Manager J. Eames/F. Warren
09.12.06 David Kehoe W RSC 3 Canning Town
17.02.07 Karl Taylor W PTS 4 Wembley
13.10.07 Billy Smith W PTS 4 Bethnal Green
08.03.08 Johnny Greaves W PTS 4 Greenwich
14.06.08 Dave Wakefield W PTS 6 Bethnal
            Green
21.11.08 Jay Morris W RTD 4 Bethnal Green
14.03.09 Denton Vassell L RSC 6 Manchester
Career: 7 contests, won 6, lost 1.

Eddie Corcoran   Philip Sharkey

Nick Coret

Cleethorpes. *Born* Mauritius, 8 May, 1981
L.Middleweight. *Ht* 5' 10"
Manager C. Sanigar
13.09.08 Tomas Grublys L RSC 2 Bethnal Green
08.12.08 Luke Gallear DREW 6 Cleethorpes
Career: 2 contests, drew 1, lost 1.

Dennis Corpe

Nottingham. *Born* Nottingham, 6 May,
1976
L.Middleweight. *Ht* 5'9¾"
Manager M. Scriven
22.10.04 Joe Mitchell L PTS 6 Mansfield
16.09.05 Mark Lloyd L PTS 6 Telford
01.10.05 Tiger Matthews L PTS 4 Wigan
19.05.07 Wayne Downing W PTS 4 Nottingham
20.07.07 Wayne Downing W RSC 3
            Wolverhampton
05.10.08 Nicky Furness L PTS 4 Nottingham
Career: 6 contests, won 2, lost 4.

Thomas Costello

Chelmsley Wood. *Born* Birmingham, 9
January, 1989
L.Middleweight. *Ht* 5'11"
Manager J. Costello
29.04.07 Deniss Sirjatovs W RSC 1 Birmingham
13.07.07 Jason Nesbitt W PTS 4 Birmingham
18.11.07 Duncan Cottier W PTS 4 Birmingham
02.02.08 David Kehoe W RSC 2 Canning Town
05.04.08 David Kirk W PTS 4 Bolton
21.06.08 Duncan Cottier W PTS 4 Birmingham
31.10.08 Geraint Harvey W PTS 4 Birmingham
28.02.09 Matt Scriven W PTS 4 Birmingham
Career: 8 contests, won 8.

Duncan Cottier

Woodford. *Born* Isleworth, 10 October,
1977
Welterweight. *Ht* 5'7½"
Manager Self
05.03.05 Geraint Harvey W PTS 4 Dagenham
10.04.05 John O'Donnell L PTS 4 Brentwood
28.04.05 Stuart Philips DREW 4 Clydach
13.05.05 David Burke L PTS 6 Liverpool
20.05.05 Colin McNeil L PTS 6 Glasgow
16.06.05 Robert Lloyd-Taylor L RSC 1 Mayfair
30.10.05 Aaron Balmer L PTS 4 Bethnal Green
19.11.05 Ashley Theophane L PTS 6 Southwark
04.12.05 Shane Watson L PTS 4 Portsmouth
19.12.05 Gilbert Eastman L RTD 3 Longford
28.01.06 Stephen Haughian L PTS 4 Dublin
18.02.06 Paul McCloskey L PTS 6 Edinburgh
26.02.06 Nathan Graham L PTS 4 Dagenham
05.03.06 Jay Morris W RSC 2 Southampton
30.03.06 Jamal Morrison DREW 4 Bloomsbury
06.04.06 Ben Hudson W PTS 4 Piccadilly
22.04.06 Paddy Pollock L PTS 6 Glasgow
12.05.06 John O'Donnell L RTD 3 Bethnal Green
08.07.06 Ross Minter L PTS 6 Cardiff
24.09.06 Jay Morris L PTS 4 Southampton
14.10.06 Kell Brook L RSC 3 Manchester
23.11.06 Lewis Smith L PTS 6 Manchester
02.12.06 Joe McCluskey L PTS 6 Coventry
09.12.06 Denton Vassell L PTS 4 Canning Town
17.02.07 Grant Skehill L PTS 4 Wembley
25.02.07 Danny Goode L PTS 6 Southampton
16.03.07 Eamonn Goodbrand L PTS 6 Glasgow

25.03.07 Scott Jordan L PTS 6 Dublin
15.04.07 Curtis Woodhouse L PTS 4 Barnsley
26.04.07 Olufemi Moses L PTS 4 Manchester
11.05.07 Tibor Dudas L PTS 4 Motherwell
01.06.07 JJ Bird L PTS 4 Peterborough
16.06.07 Lee Purdy L PTS 4 Chigwell
28.09.07 Max Maxwell L PTS 6 Birmingham
05.10.07 Peter McDonagh L PTS 4 Bethnal
Green
13.10.07 Jamie Cox L PTS 4 Bethnal Green
10.11.07 Paul Dyer L PTS 6 Portsmouth
18.11.07 Thomas Costello L PTS 4 Birmingham
08.12.07 Willie Thompson L PTS 4 Belfast
12.01.08 Sam Webb L PTS 4 Bethnal Green
14.03.08 Gary McMillan L PTS 6 Glasgow
28.03.08 Paul Porter DREW 6 Piccadilly
04.04.08 Daniel Herdman L PTS 4 Bethnal
Green
24.04.08 Andrew Butlin L PTS 6 Piccadilly
17.05.08 Paddy Pollock L PTS 6 Glasgow
14.06.08 Grant Skehill L PTS 4 Bethnal Green
21.06.08 Thomas Costello L PTS 4 Birmingham
27.09.08 Kevin Lilley L PTS 4 Bethnal Green
10.10.08 Liam Smith L PTS 4 Liverpool
18.10.08 Stevie Weir L PTS 4 Paisley
01.11.08 Ciaran Duffy L PTS 6 Glasgow
19.11.08 Danny Maka L PTS 6 Bayswater
29.11.08 Kevin Hammond L PTS 4 Sleaford
06.12.08 Pat McAleese L PTS 4 Bethnal Green
27.02.09 Kris Carslaw L RTD 2 Paisley
27.06.09 Steve Ede L PTS 6 Portsmouth
Career: 56 contests, won 3, drew 3, lost 50.

Gareth Couch
High Wycombe. *Born* High Wycombe, 11
September, 1982
L.Welterweight. *Ht* 5'7½"
Manager Self
19.12.04 Oscar Milkitas W PTS 6 Bethnal Green
23.03.05 Ian Reid W RSC 6 Leicester Square
16.06.05 David Pereira W PTS 4 Mayfair
01.07.05 Silence Saheed W PTS 4 Fulham
23.11.05 Kyle Taylor W PTS 6 Mayfair
04.12.05 Henry Castle W PTS 6 Portsmouth
18.03.06 Martino Ciano W PTS 6 Monaco
18.10.06 Daniel Thorpe W PTS 4 Bayswater
04.11.06 Tony Jourda W PTS 6 Monaco
07.06.07 Rom Krauklis W PTS 8 Kensington
04.04.08 Tom Glover W PTS 6 Bethnal Green
27.06.08 Baz Carey W PTS 4 Bethnal Green
08.11.08 Shaun Walton W RSC 1 Bethnal Green
13.12.08 Steve Gethin W PTS 4 Brentwood
Career: 14 contests, won 14.

Blaine Courtney　　　　　Philip Sharkey

Blaine Courtney
Luton. *Born* Luton, 25 June, 1989
Featherweight. *Ht* 5'6"
Manager G. Earl
28.06.09 Pavels Senkovs W PTS 6 Luton
Career: 1 contest, won 1.

Danny Couzens
Titchfield. *Born* Portsmouth, 29 August,
1984
Cruiserweight. *Ht* 6'0¾"
Manager J. Bishop
24.09.06 Csaba Andras L PTS 6 Southampton
10.06.07 Wayne Brooks L PTS 4 Neath
10.11.07 Shpetim Hoti W PTS 6 Portsmouth
02.03.08 Michael Banbula W PTS 6 Portsmouth
27.09.08 Anthony Young W PTS 4 Bracknell
06.12.08 Bobby Scott DREW 4 Bethnal Green
18.04.09 John Waldron W DIS 4 Galway
27.06.09 Peter Haymer DREW 4 Portsmouth
Career: 8 contests, won 4, drew 2, lost 2.

Sammy Couzens
Fareham. *Born* Portsmouth, 5 May, 1986
L.Heavyweight. *Ht* 6'1"
Manager J. Bishop
27.09.08 Michael Banbula W PTS 6 Bracknell
16.11.08 Daniel Roberts W PTS 4 Southampton
27.06.09 Michael Banbula L PTS 4 Portsmouth
Career: 3 contests, won 2, lost 1.

Simeon Cover
Worksop. *Born* Clapton, 12 March, 1978
S.Middleweight. Former British Masters
S.Middleweight Champion. *Ht* 5'11"
Manager D. Ingle
28.03.01 Danny Smith L PTS 6 Piccadilly
18.08.01 Rob Stevenson W PTS 6 Dewsbury
24.09.01 Colin McCash L PTS 6 Cleethorpes
01.11.01 Rob Stevenson L PTS 6 Hull
16.11.01 Jon O'Brien L PTS 6 Dublin
24.11.01 Darren Rhodes L RSC 5 Wakefield
31.01.02 Shpetim Hoti W PTS 6 Piccadilly
13.04.02 Earl Ling L CO 4 Norwich
13.05.02 Roddy Doran DREW 8 Birmingham
02.06.02 Gary Dixon W PTS 6 Shaw
03.08.02 Mike Duffield W RSC 2 Derby
14.09.02 Ivan Botton L PTS 6 Newark
05.12.02 Mark Brookes L RSC 3 Sheffield
15.02.03 Peter Jackson W RSC 2 Wolverhampton
23.02.03 Roddy Doran L PTS 10 Shrewsbury
*(Vacant British Masters S.Middleweight
Title)*
22.03.03 Barry Connell L PTS 4 Renfrew
12.04.03 Danny Smith L CO 5 Norwich
08.06.03 Ivan Botton W PTS 6 Nottingham
25.07.03 Steven Spartacus L CO 3 Norwich
*(Vacant British Masters L.Heavyweight
Title)*
06.10.03 Hamed Jamali L PTS 6 Birmingham
17.10.03 Barry Connell L PTS 6 Glasgow
14.11.03 Terry Morrill W PTS 6 Hull
01.12.03 Clint Johnson L PTS 6 Leeds
15.12.03 Lee Nicholson W RSC 4 Cleethorpes

06.02.04 Mark Brookes L RSC 4 Sheffield
12.03.04 Hastings Rasani L CO 6 Irvine
07.05.04 Dean Cockburn L PTS 6 Doncaster
15.05.04 Gary Thompson W PTS 6 Aberdeen
04.06.04 Danny Norton L RSC 3 Dudley
10.09.04 Matthew Barney L PTS 4 Wembley
05.10.04 Andrew Flute W PTS 4 Dudley
04.11.04 Gary Thompson W PTS 6 Piccadilly
13.12.04 Hamed Jamali W PTS 10 Birmingham
*(Vacant British Masters S.Middleweight
Title)*
21.01.05 Jamie Hearn L PTS 4 Brentford
23.03.05 Jamie Hearn W CO 7 Leicester Square
*(Vacant British Masters S.Middleweight
Title)*
30.04.05 Lee Blundell L PTS 10 Wigan
*(Vacant British Masters Middleweight
Title)*
14.05.05 Danny Thornton DREW 6 Aberdeen
03.06.05 Paul Smith L PTS 6 Manchester
20.06.05 Ryan Walls L RSC 8 Longford
16.09.05 Dean Cockburn W PTS 10 Doncaster
*(British Masters S.Middleweight Title
Defence)*
25.09.05 Danny Thornton L PTS 6 Leeds
03.11.05 Ryan Kerr L PTS 10 Sunderland
*(English S.Middleweight Title
Challenge)*
02.02.06 Jimi Hendricks W PTS 4 Holborn
26.02.06 JJ Ojuederie L PTS 4 Dagenham
30.03.06 Joey Vegas L PTS 10 Piccadilly
*(British Masters S.Middleweight Title
Defence)*
01.06.06 Tony Quigley L PTS 4 Barnsley
16.06.06 Steve McGuire L PTS 6 Liverpool
12.07.06 Joey Vegas L PTS 4 Bethnal Green
15.09.06 Kreshnik Qato L PTS 6 Muswell Hill
06.10.06 Michael Monaghan W PTS 6 Mansfield
28.10.06 Tony Oakey L PTS 6 Bethnal Green
08.12.06 Kreshnik Qato L PTS 10 Dagenham
*(Vacant Southern Area S.Middleweight
Title)*
28.09.07 Neil Tidman L RSC 2 Coventry
09.11.07 Tyrone Wright L PTS 4 Nottingham
02.12.07 Darren Stubbs L PTS 6 Oldham
15.12.07 Kenny Anderson L CO 6 Edinburgh
20.04.08 Darren Stubbs L RTD 7 Shaw
*(Vacant British Masters L.Heavyweight
Title)*
21.06.08 Jon Ibbotson L PTS 6 Sheffield
11.07.08 Brian Magee L RSC 4 Wigan
12.09.08 Billy Boyle L RSC 5 Sheffield
Career: 60 contests, won 16, drew 2, lost 42.

Jamie Cox
Swindon. *Born* Swindon, 24 August, 1986
Welterweight. *Ht* 5'11"
Manager F. Warren
14.07.07 Johnny Greaves W PTS 4 Greenwich
13.10.07 Duncan Cottier W PTS 4 Bethnal
Green
03.11.07 David Kirk W PTS 4 Cardiff
08.12.07 Surinder Sekhon W RSC 3 Bolton
22.03.08 David Kehoe W RSC 1 Cardiff
21.06.08 Billy Smith W PTS 6 Birmingham
12.09.08 Steve Conkin W CO 3 Mayfair

17.10.08 Billy Smith W RSC 5 Swindon
06.12.08 Ernie Smith W CO 1 Canning Town
13.02.09 Jason Rushton W RSC 1 Swindon
24.04.09 Mark Lloyd W RSC 8 Wolverhampton
Career: 11 contests, won 11.

Danny Coyle

Atherstone. *Born* Nuneaton, 1 December, 1982
Welterweight. *Ht* 5'9¼"
Manager Self
01.03.08 Steve Cooper W PTS 6 Coventry
13.04.08 Craig Tomes W PTS 6 Edgbaston
14.09.08 Keith Sheen L PTS 6 Birmingham
06.10.08 Callum Archer L RSC 1 Birmingham
21.12.08 Kristian Laight L PTS 6 Coventry
Career: 5 contests, won 2, lost 3.

Jamie Coyle

Bannockburn. *Born* Stirling, 24 August, 1976
L. Middleweight. *Ht* 6'0"
Manager T. Gilmour
02.06.03 Richard Inquieti W RSC 2 Glasgow
20.10.03 Jed Tytler W RSC 2 Glasgow
04.12.03 George Robshaw DREW 6 Huddersfield
28.02.04 Geraint Harvey W PTS 4 Bridgend
22.04.04 Peter Dunn W PTS 6 Glasgow
15.10.04 Terry Adams W RSC 5 Glasgow
17.12.04 Arv Mittoo W RSC 5 Huddersfield
25.04.05 Tony Montana W RSC 3 Glasgow
16.06.05 Michael Lomax L PTS 6 Dagenham
30.09.05 Arek Malek W PTS 6 Kirkcaldy
04.11.05 Arek Malek W PTS 6 Glasgow
17.03.06 Karl David L RSC 1 Kirkcaldy
23.06.06 Ben Hudson W PTS 6 Blackpool
10.11.06 Franny Jones L RSC 2 Hartlepool
23.04.07 Rocky Muscas W PTS 8 Glasgow
08.06.07 Graham Delehedy W RSC 4 Motherwell
24.11.07 Ernie Smith W PTS 6 Clydebank
29.02.08 Tye Williams W RSC 2 Glasgow
28.04.08 Tony Randell W PTS 8 Glasgow
06.06.08 Andrew Butlin W RTD 3 Glasgow
20.09.08 Ryan Rhodes L PTS 12 Sheffield
  (British L.Middleweight Title Challenge)
28.11.08 Paddy Pollock W RSC 3 Glasgow
12.06.09 Grzegorz Proksa L RSC 3 Liverpool
Career: 23 contests, won 17, drew 1, lost 5.

Johnny Creamer

Portsmouth. *Born* Portsmouth, 11 August 1987
Welterweight. *Ht* 5' 11"
Manager J. Bishop
16.11.08 Syed Ali W PTS 4 Southampton
06.12.08 Karol Ozimkowski W PTS 4 Bethnal Green
27.06.09 Jay Morris L PTS 4 Portsmouth
Career: 3 contests, won 2, lost 1.

Lloyd Creighton

Darlington. *Born* Darlington, 11 May, 1977
Middleweight. *Ht* 5' 9¼"
Manager M. Marsden
26.04.08 Ricky Strike W PTS 6 Darlington

17.10.08 Nasser Al Harbi L PTS 6 Swindon
19.01.09 Mark Douglas L CO 1 Mayfair
Career: 3 contests, won 1, lost 2.

Lloyd Creighton   Philip Sharkey

Trevor Crewe

Dene. *Born* Sunderland, 22 June, 1986
L.Middleweight. *Ht* 5' 8"
Manager S. Wood
17.05.09 Geraint Harvey W RSC 4 Bolton
Career: 1 contest, won 1.

Francis Croes

Middlesbrough. *Born* Middlesbrough, 7 May, 1988
Flyweight. *Ht* 5' 4"
Manager P. Fondu
07.10.08 Dmitry Agafonov L PTS 6 Minsk, Belarus
29.03.09 Kieran Farrell L PTS 4 Bolton
17.04.09 Usman Ahmed L PTS 6 Leigh
01.05.09 Kevin Coglan L PTS 4 Hartlepool
29.05.09 Paul Edwards L PTS 6 Stoke
12.06.09 James Mulhern L PTS 4 Wolverhampton
Career: 6 contests, lost 6.

Anthony Crolla

Manchester. *Born* Manchester, 16 November, 1986
S. Featherweight. *Ht* 5'8¾"
Manager T. Jones/F. Warren
14.10.06 Abdul Rashid W PTS 4 Manchester
09.12.06 Arial Krasnopolski W RSC 3 Canning Town
10.03.07 Rom Krauklis W PTS 4 Liverpool
31.05.07 Neal McQuade W RSC 1 Manchester
06.10.07 Johnny Greaves W RSC 3 Nottingham
08.12.07 Daniel Thorpe W RTD 2 Bolton
19.01.08 Tomasz Kwiecien W CO 5 Dusseldorf, Germany
14.03.08 Steve Gethin W PTS 6 Manchester
05.04.08 Youssef Al Hamidi L PTS 8 Bolton

06.09.08 Robin Deakin W PTS 4 Manchester
26.09.08 Youssef Al Hamidi W PTS 6 Bethnal Green
10.10.08 Carl Allen W PTS 6 Liverpool
12.12.08 Jon Baguley W PTS 4 Widnes
14.03.09 Carl Allen W PTS 6 Manchester
29.05.09 Gary Sykes L PTS 10 Stoke
  (Elim. British S. Featherweight Title)
Career: 15 contests, won 13, lost 2.

Michael Crossan

Glasgow. *Born* Glasgow, 21 June, 1975
Featherweight. *Ht* 5'5¼"
Manager A. Morrison
17.10.03 Hussain Nasser W PTS 6 Glasgow
07.12.03 Rocky Dean W PTS 6 Glasgow
23.04.04 Dean Ward W PTS 6 Glasgow
19.06.04 Colin Moffett DREW 4 Renfrew
01.04.05 John Bothwell W PTS 6 Glasgow
17.11.07 Jason Hastie L PTS 4 Glasgow
09.12.07 James Ancliff L RSC 1 Glasgow
29.05.09 Kris Hughes L PTS 6 Glasgow
Career: 8 contests, won 4, drew 1, lost 3.

Adam Cummings   Philip Sharkey

Adam Cummings

Bristol. *Born* Bristol, 8 June, 1979
L.Welterweight. *Ht* 5' 8"
Manager J. Feld
14.12.08 James Todd DREW 4 Bristol
13.02.09 Karl Taylor DREW 4 Swindon
10.04.09 Karl Taylor W PTS 4 Cheltenham
17.04.09 Matt Seawright W PTS 6 Bristol
Career: 4 contests, won 2, drew 2.

Dougie Curran

Newcastle. *Born* Newcastle, 15 June, 1988
S.Featherweight. *Ht* 5' 7"
Manager T. Gilmour
16.01.09 Sid Razak W PTS 4 Middlesbrough
Career: 1 contest, won 1.

Howard Daley

Preston. *Born* Preston, 4 July, 1976
Heavyweight. *Ht* 6'1¼"
Manager O. Harrison
28.09.07 David Ingleby W PTS 6 Preston
12.10.07 David Dolan L RSC 2 Peterlee
02.12.07 Billy Bessey L PTS 6 Oldham
29.02.08 Ben Harding DREW 4 Plymouth
14.03.08 Tony Booth W RTD 2 Manchester
12.04.08 Mike Perez L RSC 1 Castlebar
13.06.08 Dave Ferguson L PTS 4 Sunderland
21.06.08 Dean O'Loughlin L PTS 6 Hull
24.07.08 Neil Perkins L PTS 4 Wolverhampton
01.08.08 Matt Legg L RSC 2 Watford
12.09.08 Dave Howe L RSC 1 Sheffield
11.10.08 Tony Booth L PTS 6 Hull
08.11.08 Rob Beech L PTS 4 Wigan
15.11.08 Tom Dallas L RSC 2 Bethnal Green
17.01.09 Zahid Kahut L PTS 4 Wigan
13.02.09 Ben Harding L PTS 4 Swindon
28.02.09 Dave Ferguson L RSC 2 Newcastle
02.05.09 Danny Hughes L PTS 6 Sunderland
24.05.09 Zahid Kahut L PTS 6 Bradford
Career: 19 contests, won 2, drew 1, lost 16.

Howard Daley   Philip Sharkey

Tom Dallas

Gillingham. *Born* Chatham, 23 April, 1985
Heavyweight. *Ht* 6' 6"
Manager M. Roe
13.09.08 Vlado Szabo W PTS 4 Bethnal Green
17.10.08 Aleksandrs Selezens W PTS 4 Bethnal Green
15.11.08 Howard Daley W RSC 2 Bethnal Green
20.03.09 Ben Harding W RSC 1 Newham
23.04.09 Slavomir Selicky W RSC 1 Limehouse
30.06.09 Stas Belokon W RSC 2 Bethnal Green
Career: 6 contests, won 6.

Paulino Da Silva

Manchester. *Born* Almada Portugal, 29
April, 1978
Central Area S.Middleweight Champion.

Ht 5' 10"
Manager Self
28.02.04 Nick Okoth W PTS 6 Manchester
02.04.04 Courtney Fry L PTS 4 Plymouth
24.10.04 Amer Khan L PTS 6 Sheffield
16.09.05 Dan Guthrie W RSC 2 Plymouth
21.04.07 Tony Booth W PTS 6 Manchester
30.06.07 Lee Jones W PTS 6 Manchester
03.12.07 Joey Ainscough W PTS 10 Manchester
            (Vacant Central Area S.Middleweight
            Title)
08.11.08 Michael Banbula DREW 6 Wigan
06.12.08 Michael Banbula L PTS 4 Wigan
03.04.09 James Tucker W PTS 6 Leigh
Career: 10 contests, won 6, drew 1, lost 3.

Paul David

Sheffield. *Born* Northampton, 2 September,
1984
English S. Middleweight Champion,
Former Undefeated Midlands Area
S.Middleweight Champion. *Ht* 6'0½"
Manager D. Ingle
27.02.06 Peter McCormack W RTD 2
            Birmingham
17.03.06 Steve McGuire L PTS 6 Kirkcaldy
25.03.06 Duane Reid W RSC 3 Burton
12.05.06 Daniel Cadman W RSC 6 Bethnal Green
23.06.06 Richard Turba W PTS 6 Blackpool
21.10.06 Gary Thompson W PTS 6 Glasgow
03.11.06 Brian Magee L PTS 6 Barnsley
26.01.07 Tony Salam L PTS 4 Dagenham
18.05.07 Peter Haymer W PTS 8 Canning Town
05.10.07 Andrew Lowe W PTS 8 Bethnal Green
09.11.07 Michael Monaghan W PTS 10
            Nottingham
            (Vacant Midlands Area S.Middleweight
            Title)
29.03.08 Ayitey Powers W PTS 6 Aberdeen
10.05.08 Tyrone Wright L PTS 10 Nottingham
            (Midlands Area L.Heavyweight
            Title Challenge)
06.12.08 Tyrone Wright W CO 7 Nottingham
            (Vacant English S.Middleweight Title)
Career: 14 contests, won 10, lost 4.

Tom Dallas   Philip Sharkey

Kenny Davidson

Wishaw. *Born* Motherwell, 11 September,
1981
S.Middleweight. *Ht* 6' 0"
Manager T. Gilmour
03.11.06 Jamie Ambler L PTS 6 Glasgow
23.04.07 Mark Phillips W PTS 6 Glasgow
10.11.08 James Tucker DREW 6 Glasgow
Career: 3 contests, won 1, drew 1, lost 1.

Dai Davies

Merthyr Tydfil. *Born* Merthyr Tydfil, 20
April, 1983
Welsh Area Featherweight Champion,
Former Welsh Area S.Featherweight
Champion. *Ht* 5'6"
Manager D. Gardiner
08.07.04 Neil Marston W PTS 6 Birmingham
01.10.04 Riaz Durgahed W PTS 4 Bristol
02.12.04 Martin Lindsay L RSC 1 Crystal Palace
25.02.05 Matthew Marsh L PTS 4 Wembley
16.07.05 Derry Matthews L RSC 2 Bolton
12.12.05 Riaz Durgahed L PTS 6 Peterborough
13.04.06 Gary Sykes L CO 3 Leeds
09.06.06 Jamie McDonnell DREW 4 Doncaster
29.06.06 Jed Syger W PTS 6 Bethnal Green
08.10.06 Henry Jones W PTS 10 Swansea
            (Vacant Welsh Area S.Featherweight
            Title)
16.02.07 Riaz Durgahed W PTS 8 Merthyr Tydfil
27.04.07 Akaash Bhatia L PTS 4 Wembley
13.07.07 Rendall Munroe L RSC 5 Barnsley
30.03.08 Ricky Owen L CO 5 Port Talbot
13.06.08 Jason Booth L PTS 6 Portsmouth
12.07.08 Jamie Arthur L CO 2 Newport
            (Welsh Area S.Featherweight Title
            Defence)
05.06.09 Rob Turley W RSC 9 Newport
            (Vacant Welsh Area Featherweight Title)
Career: 17 contests, won 6, drew 1, lost 10.

Gary Davies (Harding)

St Helens. *Born* Liverpool, 17 October,
1982
British Bantamweight Champion. Former
Undefeated Central Area & British Masters
S.Bantamweight Champion. *Ht* 5'6"
Manager Self
01.06.02 Steve Gethin L RSC 2 Manchester
05.10.02 Jason Thomas W RSC 5 Liverpool
29.11.02 Simon Chambers W RSC 2 Liverpool
15.11.04 Furhan Rafiq W PTS 6 Glasgow
18.09.05 Rocky Dean L RSC 4 Bethnal Green
24.02.06 Chris Hooper W RSC 1 Scarborough
            (Vacant Central Area S.Bantamweight
            Title. Vacant British Masters
            S.Bantamweight Title)
30.09.06 Barrington Brown DREW 6 Stoke
24.02.07 Abdul Mougharbel W PTS 6 Stoke
15.06.08 Sumaila Badu W RSC 2 St Helens
14.09.08 Sumaila Badu W RSC 5 Wigan
18.12.08 Martin Power W RSC 2 Dublin
03.04.09 Matthew Edmonds W RSC 7 Bethnal
            Green
            (Vacant British Bantamweight Title)
Career: 12 contests, won 9, drew 1, lost 2.

Llewellyn Davies

Stoke. *Born* Coventry, 20 September 1983
S.Middleweight. *Ht* 6' 0"
Manager E. Johnson/O. Harrison
01.02.09 Jamie Ambler W PTS 4 Birmingham
29.05.09 Mark Phillips W PTS 4 Dudley
Career: 2 contests, won 2.

Rhys Davies

Stoke. *Born* Coventry, 20 September, 1983
L.Heavyweight. *Ht* 6' 1"
Manager E. Johnson/O. Harrison
14.09.08 Andrejs Tolstihs W PTS 4 Birmingham
01.02.09 Hastings Rasani DREW 4 Birmingham
12.06.09 Michael Banbula W PTS 6
      Wolverhampton
Career: 3 contests, won 2, drew 1.

Shon Davies

Llanelli. *Born* Carmarthen, 6 September, 1986
Welsh Area L.Heavyweight Champion. *Ht* 5' 1½"
Manager D. Davies
23.07.06 Richard Horton W RSC 1 Dagenham
08.10.06 Mark Phillips W PTS 4 Swansea
26.10.06 Nicki Taylor W RSC 1 Wolverhampton
16.02.07 Jamie Ambler W PTS 6 Merthyr Tydfil
03.03.07 Tyrone Wright L PTS 6 Alfreton
21.10.07 Leon Owen W PTS 6 Swansea
17.11.07 Kenny Anderson L RSC 3 Glasgow
30.03.08 Wayne Brooks W RSC 7 Port Talbot
      (Vacant Welsh Area L.Heavyweight
      Title)
27.09.08 Peter Haymer W PTS 6 Bethnal Green
20.02.09 Courtney Fry L PTS 3 Bethnal Green
24.04.09 Billy Boyle L PTS 10 Sheffield
      (Vacant International Masters L.
      Heavyweight Title)
27.06.09 Tony Oakey L RSC 4 Portsmouth
      (Vacant International Masters L.
      Heavyweight Title)
Career: 12 contests, won 7, lost 5.

Shon Davies   Philip Sharkey

Tristan Davies

Telford. *Born* Shrewsbury, 13 October, 1978
Welterweight. Former Undefeated Midlands Area Lightweight Champion. *Ht* 5' 10"
Manager E. Johnson
04.06.04 Pete Buckley W PTS 6 Dudley
05.10.04 Gavin Tait W PTS 6 Dudley
17.02.05 Stuart Philips W PTS 6 Dudley
16.09.05 Karl Taylor W PTS 4 Telford
04.12.05 Jonathan Whiteman W PTS 4 Telford
14.04.06 Kristian Laight W PTS 6 Telford
01.06.06 Carl Allen W PTS 6 Birmingham
09.10.06 Peter Dunn W PTS 6 Birmingham
10.11.06 Carl Allen W PTS 10 Telford
      (Vacant Midlands Area Lightweight
      Title)
01.04.07 Peter Dunn W PTS 6 Shrewsbury
25.10.07 Billy Smith W PTS 4 Wolverhampton
01.12.07 Graeme Higginson L RSC 5 Telford
      (Vacant British Masters L.Welterweight
      Title)
03.10.08 Tom Glover W PTS 6 Burton
07.03.09 Chris Brophy W PTS 6 Birmingham
03.04.09 Jason Nesbitt W PTS 4 Wolverhampton
Career: 15 contests, won 14, lost 1.

Paul Davis

Lowestoft. *Born* Dublin, 10 August, 1979
L.Heavyweight. *Ht* 6' 1"
Manager G. Everett
15.10.06 Philip Callaghan W RSC 4 Norwich
16.03.07 Omid Bourzo W RSC 4 Norwich
21.06.08 Billy Boyle L CO 5 Sheffield
04.10.08 Michael Banbula DREW 4 Norwich
Career: 4 contests, won 2, drew 1, lost 1.

Sara Davis

Nottingham. *Born* Ontairo Canada, 24 August, 1971
L.Middleweight. *Ht* 5' 8"
Manager C. Mitchell
31.03.07 Borislava Goranova W PTS 4 Derby
03.11.07 Angel McKenzie W PTS 4 Derby
16.11.08 Angel McKenzie W PTS 6 Derby
05.06.09 Anna Ingman L PTS 6 Sedavi, Spain
Career: 4 contests, won 3, lost 1.

Mark Dawes

Sedgefield. *Born* Stockton, 9 April, 1981
L.Welterweight. *Ht* 5' 9"
Manager Self
06.05.07 Peter Dunn W PTS 6 Darlington
09.06.07 Karl Taylor W PTS 6 Middlesbrough
15.07.07 Carl Allen W PTS 6 Hartlepool
23.09.07 Sergei Rozhakmens W PTS 6
      Hartlepool
25.07.08 Karl Taylor W PTS 6 Houghton le
      Spring
Career: 5 contests, won 5.

Lenny Daws

Morden. *Born* Carshalton, 29 December, 1978
English L.Welterweight Champion. Former British L.Welterweight Champion. Former Undefeated Southern Area L.Welterweight

Champion. *Ht* 5' 10½"
Manager R. McCracken
16.04.03 Danny Gwilym W RSC 2 Nottingham
27.05.03 Ben Hudson W RSC 2 Dagenham
25.07.03 Karl Taylor W RTD 2 Norwich
04.10.03 Ernie Smith W PTS 4 Muswell Hill
28.11.03 Tony Montana W PTS 6 Derby
11.12.03 Keith Jones W PTS 6 Bethnal Green
30.01.04 Denis Alekseev W CO 3 Dagenham
24.09.04 Ernie Smith W PTS 6 Nottingham
12.11.04 Keith Jones W PTS 8 Wembley
10.04.05 Silence Saheed W PTS 6 Brentwood
09.07.05 Ivor Bonavic W PTS 6 Nottingham
28.10.05 Oscar Hall W RTD 7 Hartlepool
      (Elim. English L.Welterweight Title)
20.01.06 Colin Lynes W RTD 9 Bethnal Green
      (Elim. British L.Welterweight Title.
      Vacant Southern Area L.Welterweight
      Title)
12.05.06 Nigel Wright W PTS 12 Bethnal Green
      (Vacant British L.Welterweight Title)
20.01.07 Barry Morrison L PTS 12 Muswell Hill
      (British L.Welterweight Title Defence)
18.05.07 Billy Smith W PTS 6 Canning Town
14.11.07 Nigel Wright DREW 10 Bethnal Green
      (English L.Welterweight Title
      Challenge)
27.06.08 Mihaita Mutu W PTS 10 Bethnal Green
08.11.08 Jay Morris W PTS 6 Bethnal Green
17.01.09 Sergej Savrinovics W RSC 6 Wigan
11.04.09 Peter McDonagh W PTS 10 Bethnal
      Green
      (Vacant English L.Welterweight Title)
Career: 21 contests, won 19, drew 1, lost 1.

Gavin Deacon   Philip Sharkey

Gavin Deacon

Northampton. *Born* Northampton, 5 June, 1982
Midlands Area L. Welterweight Champion. *Ht* 5' 9¼"
Manager J. Cox
12.11.05 Colin Bain L PTS 6 Glasgow
12.02.06 Danny Harding L PTS 6 Manchester
20.02.06 Ryan Brawley L PTS 4 Glasgow
03.03.06 Wez Miller L PTS 4 Doncaster
17.03.06 David Appleby L PTS 4 Kirkcaldy
15.10.06 Neal McQuade W PTS 6 Norwich

07.12.06 Tony McQuade DREW 6 Peterborough
14.12.06 Daniel Thorpe L PTS 6 Leicester
23.02.07 Waz Hussain W PTS 4 Birmingham
03.03.07 Deniss Sirjatovs W PTS 4 Alfreton
30.03.07 Neal McQuade W PTS 6 Peterborough
13.04.07 Rendall Munroe L PTS 6 Altrincham
11.05.07 George Watson L PTS 6 Sunderland
08.06.07 Charles Paul King L PTS 4 Motherwell
13.10.07 Andrew Ward W PTS 6 Barnsley
25.11.07 Tom Glover L PTS 6 Colchester
10.12.07 Craig Johnson L PTS 6 Cleethorpes
13.09.08 Vinny Woolford L RTD 2 Bethnal Green
10.11.08 Willie Bilan L PTS 6 Glasgow
28.11.08 Jamie McLevy L RSC 2 Glasgow
07.03.09 Amir Unsworth L PTS 6 Chester
23.05.09 Amir Unsworth W PTS 10 Sleaford
  (Vacant Midlands Area L.Welterweight Title)
Career: 22 contests, won 6, drew 1, lost 15.

Robin Deakin

Crawley. *Born* Crawley, 19 April, 1986
Lightweight. *Ht* 5'8½"
Manager G. Earl
28.10.06 Shaun Walton W PTS 4 Bethnal Green
17.02.07 Rom Krauklis L PTS 4 Wembley
13.10.07 Eddie Hyland L PTS 4 Belfast
02.11.07 Ricky Owen L RSC 2 Irvine
12.01.08 Vinny Mitchell L PTS 4 Bethnal Green
23.02.08 Steve Gethin L PTS 4 Crawley
08.03.08 Ryan Walsh L PTS 4 Greenwich
16.03.08 Josh Wale L PTS 6 Sheffield
29.03.08 Jason Hastie L PTS 4 Glasgow
26.04.08 Jon Kays L PTS 4 Wigan
31.05.08 Patrick Hyland L RSC 5 Belfast
06.09.08 Anthony Crolla L PTS 4 Manchester
13.09.08 Liam Shinkwin L PTS 4 Bethnal Green
26.09.08 Ryan Walsh L PTS 4 Bethnal Green
10.10.08 Stephen Smith L RSC 2 Liverpool
08.11.08 Kevin O'Hara L RSC 1 Bethnal Green
14.12.08 Danny Stewart L RSC 3 Bristol
30.01.09 Vinny Mitchell L PTS 4 Bethnal Green
27.02.09 Jason Hastie L PTS 4 Paisley
13.03.09 Rob Turley L PTS 6 Newport
27.03.09 Mark Alexander L PTS 4 Kensington
10.04.09 Chris Higgs L RSC 3 Cheltenham
Career: 22 contests, won 1, lost 21.

Rocky Dean

Thetford. *Born* Bury St Edmonds, 17 June, 1978
Featherweight. Former Southern Area Featherweight Champion. *Ht* 5'5"
Manager Self
14.10.99 Lennie Hodgkins W PTS 6 Bloomsbury
30.10.99 Lennie Hodgkins W PTS 6 Southwark
18.05.00 Danny Lawson W RSC 1 Bethnal Green
29.09.00 Anthony Hanna W PTS 4 Bethnal Green
10.11.00 Chris Jickells L RSC 1 Mayfair
19.04.02 Peter Svendsen W PTS 6 Aarhus, Denmark
19.10.02 Sean Grant W RSC 3 Norwich
21.12.02 Darren Cleary W PTS 4 Millwall
08.02.03 Steve Gethin DREW 4 Norwich
11.07.03 Isaac Ward DREW 4 Darlington
26.07.03 Michael Hunter L RSC 1 Plymouth
10.10.03 Isaac Ward L PTS 6 Darlington
06.11.03 Martin Power L PTS 6 Dagenham
07.12.03 Michael Crossan L PTS 6 Glasgow

24.09.04 Simon Wilson W PTS 4 Millwall
19.12.04 Jim Betts W PTS 8 Bethnal Green
05.03.05 Mickey Coveney W PTS 10 Dagenham
  (Vacant Southern Area Featherweight Title)
20.05.05 Andy Morris L PTS 10 Southwark
  (Vacant English Featherweight Title)
18.09.05 Gary Davies W RSC 4 Bethnal Green
21.10.05 Andrey Isaev L RSC 12 Ukraine
  (Vacant WBF Inter-Continental Featherweight Title)
26.02.06 Vinesh Rungea W PTS 6 Dagenham
09.12.06 Matthew Marsh L PTS 10 Canning Town
  (Southern Area Featherweight Title Defence)
14.07.07 Matthew Marsh L PTS 10 Greenwich
  (Vacant Southern Area S.Bantamweight Title)
01.12.07 Steve Gethin W RSC 5 Bethnal Green
26.09.08 James Ancliff W PTS 4 Bethnal Green
21.11.08 Matthew Marsh L PTS 12 Bethnal Green
  (British S.Bantamweight Title Challenge)
30.06.09 Jason Booth L PTS 12 Bethnal Green
  (British S.Bantamweight Title Challenge)
Career: 27 contests, won 14, drew 2, lost 11.

Leon Dean

Ilkeston. *Born* Nottingham, 20 January, 1986
Lightweight. *Ht* 5'10"
Manager M. Shinfield
19.06.09 Joe Kelso W RSC 2 Aberdeen
Career: 1 contest, won 1.

James DeGale

London. *Born* Hammersmith, 3 February, 1986
Middleweight. *Ht* 6'0"
Manager F. Warren
28.02.09 Vepkhia Tchilaia W PTS 4 Birmingham
15.05.09 Jindrich Kubin W RSC 1 Belfast
Career: 2 contests, won 2.

James DeGale　　　　　Philip Sharkey

Ben Deghani

Glasgow. *Born* Iran, 16 September, 1986
L.Middleweight. *Ht* 5'11"
Manager A. Morrison
01.11.08 Paddy Pollock L CO 1 Glasgow
06.03.09 Craig Windsor L RSC 3 Glasgow
29.05.09 Mike Reid W RSC 2 Glasgow
19.06.09 Craig Windsor L RSC 3 Glasgow
Career: 4 contests, won 1, lost 3.

Graham Delehedy

Liverpool. *Born* Liverpool, 7 October, 1978
L.Middleweight. *Ht* 5'8"
Manager T. Gilmour
17.05.03 Joel Ani W RSC 4 Liverpool
27.10.03 Rocky Muscus W RSC 2 Glasgow
01.12.03 Gary Cummings W RSC 1 Bradford
27.05.04 Ernie Smith W RSC 3 Huddersfield
08.10.04 David Kehoe W RSC 2 Brentwood
26.11.04 Tony Montana W PTS 6 Altrincham
30.04.05 Cafu Santos W RSC 1 Wigan
23.09.05 Arek Malek W PTS 6 Manchester
28.04.06 Taz Jones L CO 6 Hartlepool
30.03.07 Martin Marshall W CO 2 Crawley
08.06.07 Jamie Coyle L RSC 4 Motherwell
11.08.07 Lee Murtagh L PTS 6 Liverpool
08.10.07 Tony Randell L PTS 10 Glasgow
  (Vacant International Masters Middleweight Title)
09.06.08 James Tucker DREW 6 Glasgow
28.03.09 Joe McNally L RTD 3 Liverpool
Career: 15 contests, won 9, drew 1, lost 5.

Senol Dervis

Salford. *Born* Hammersmith, 1 February, 1969
L.Welterweight. *Ht* 5'6¼"
Manager O. Harrison
23.11.07 Chris Kitson L PTS 6 Sheffield
16.02.08 Rick Godding L PTS 6 Blackpool
28.02.08 Rob Hunt L PTS 4 Wolverhampton
26.04.08 Tamao Dwyer L RTD 2 Wigan
31.05.08 Eddie O'Rourke L PTS 6 Newark
15.06.08 Stuart McFadyen L PTS 6 St Helens
19.07.08 Amir Unsworth L PTS 4 Liverpool
Career: 7 contests, lost 7.

Michael Devine

Luton. *Born* Luton, 24 April, 1959
Lightweight. *Ht* 5'8"
Manager G. Earl
28.06.09 Michael Harvey W RSC 3 Luton
Career: 1 contest, won 1.

Jon-Lewis Dickinson

Edmondsley. *Born* Durham, 3 May, 1986
Cruiserweight. *Ht* 6'4"
Manager F. Maloney
07.11.08 Paul Bonson W PTS 4 Wigan
23.01.09 John Anthony W PTS 4 Stoke
02.05.09 Nick Okoth W PTS 4 Sunderland
Career: 3 contests, won 3.

Travis Dickinson

Edmondsley. *Born* Durham, 19 March, 1988
L.Heavyweight. *Ht* 6'3"
Manager F. Maloney

06.03.09 Patrick Mendy W PTS 4 Wigan
02.05.09 Pawel Trebinski W RSC 1 Sunderland
Career: 2 contests, won 2.

Craig Dickson

Glasgow. *Born* Glasgow, 6 March, 1979
L.Middleweight. *Ht* 5'11"
Manager T. Gilmour
21.10.02 Paul Rushton W RSC 2 Glasgow
18.11.02 Ernie Smith W PTS 6 Glasgow
17.02.03 Jon Hilton W RSC 2 Glasgow
14.04.03 Richard Inquieti W PTS 4 Glasgow
20.10.03 Danny Moir W RSC 3 Glasgow
19.01.04 Dean Nicholas W RSC 5 Glasgow
19.04.04 Ernie Smith W PTS 6 Glasgow
30.09.04 Taz Jones DREW 6 Glasgow
15.11.04 Tony Montana W PTS 8 Glasgow
21.03.05 David Keir W RTD 3 Glasgow
30.09.05 Vadzim Astapuk W RSC 4 Kirkcaldy
21.11.05 David Kehoe W PTS 8 Glasgow
20.02.06 Arek Malek W RSC 5 Glasgow
17.03.06 Kevin Anderson L RSC 7 Kirkcaldy
    (Commonwealth Welterweight Title
    Challenge)
01.06.06 Darren Gethin L PTS 6 Birmingham
23.10.06 Martin Marshall W RTD 4 Glasgow
02.12.06 Franny Jones L RSC 6 Clydebank
10.09.07 Darren Gethin W PTS 6 Glasgow
24.11.07 Billy Smith W PTS 6 Clydebank
25.01.08 Michael Lomax L PTS 6 Dagenham
24.10.08 Michael Lomax L PTS 3 Bethnal Green
07.11.08 Mark Thompson L RSC 7 Wigan
Career: 22 contests, won 15, drew 1, lost 6.

Carl Dilks   Philip Sharkey

Carl Dilks

Liverpool. *Born* Liverpool, 29 September,
1983
L.Heavyweight. *Ht* 5'11"
Manager S. Wood
06.05.07 Carl Wild W PTS 6 Altrincham
16.06.07 Carl Wild W PTS 6 Bolton
28.09.07 Michael Banbula W PTS 6 Preston
26.10.07 Lee Nicholson W RSC 4 Wigan
01.12.07 Brian Wood W RSC 1 Liverpool
16.03.08 Dean Walker W PTS 6 Liverpool

15.06.08 Adam Wilcox W RSC 3 St Helens
12.10.08 Jamie Ambler W PTS 4 Leigh
24.01.09 Mark Nilsen W RSC 4 Blackpool
20.02.09 Darren Stubbs L PTS 3 Bethnal Green
20.02.09 Bob Ajisafe W PTS 3 Bethnal Green
17.04.09 James Tucker W PTS 4 Leigh
Career: 12 contests, won 11, lost 1.

Alex Dilmagahmi

Worthing. *Born* Redhill, 29 July 1990
L.Welterweight. *Ht* 5' 8"
Manager R. Davies
23.04.09 Baz Carey W PTS 4 Limehouse
Career: 1 contest, won 1.

Craig Docherty

Glasgow. *Born* Glasgow, 27 September,
1979
Lightweight. Former Commonwealth
S.Featherweight Champion. *Ht* 5'7"
Manager A. Morrison
16.11.98 Kevin Gerowski W PTS 6 Glasgow
22.02.99 Des Gargano W PTS 6 Glasgow
19.04.99 Paul Quarmby W RSC 4 Glasgow
07.06.99 Simon Chambers W PTS 6 Glasgow
20.09.99 John Barnes W PTS 6 Glasgow
15.11.99 Peter Allen W RSC 1 Glasgow
24.01.00 Lee Williamson W PTS 6 Glasgow
19.02.00 Steve Hanley W PTS 6 Prestwick
05.06.00 Sebastian Hart W RSC 1 Glasgow
23.10.00 Lee Armstrong DREW 8 Glasgow
22.01.01 Nigel Senior W RSC 4 Glasgow
20.03.01 Jamie McKeever W RSC 3 Glasgow
11.06.01 Rakhim Mingaleev W PTS 8
    Nottingham
27.10.01 Michael Gomez L RSC 2 Manchester
    (British S.Featherweight Title
    Challenge)
18.03.02 Joel Viney W CO 1 Glasgow
13.07.02 Dariusz Snarski W PTS 6 Coventry
25.01.03 Nikolai Eremeev W PTS 6 Bridgend
12.04.03 Dean Pithie W CO 8 Bethnal Green
    (Commonwealth S. Featherweight Title
    Challenge)
01.11.03 Abdul Malik Jabir W PTS 12 Glasgow
    (Commonwealth S.Featherweight Title
    Defence)
22.04.04 Kpakpo Allotey W RSC 6 Glasgow
    (Commonwealth S.Featherweight Title
    Defence)
15.10.04 Boris Sinitsin L PTS 12 Glasgow
    (European S.Featherweight Title
    Challenge)
08.04.05 Alex Arthur L CO 9 Edinburgh
    (Vacant British S.Featherweight Title.
    Commonwealth S.Featherweight Title
    Defence)
30.09.05 John Mackay W RSC 7 Kirkcaldy
25.05.07 Billy Smith W PTS 6 Glasgow
06.10.07 Lee McAllister L RSC 9 Aberdeen
    (Vacant WBU Lightweight Title)
09.12.07 Silence Saheed W PTS 6 Glasgow
14.03.08 Jay Morris W PTS 6 Glasgow
27.02.09 Garry Buckland L PTS 10 Barnsley
    (Celtic Lightweight Title Challenge)
22.03.09 Ashley Theophane L PTS 6 Bethnal
    Green
Career: 29 contests, won 22, drew 1, lost 6.

Craig Docherty   Philip Sharkey

Tony Dodson

Liverpool. *Born* Liverpool, 2 July, 1980
Former Undefeated British, English &
Central Area S.Middleweight Champion.
Former WBF Inter-Continental
S.Middleweight Champion. *Ht* 6'0½"
Manager Self
31.07.99 Michael McDermott W RTD 1 Carlisle
02.10.99 Sean Pritchard W RSC 3 Cardiff
22.01.00 Mark Dawson W PTS 4 Birmingham
11.03.00 Paul Bonson W PTS 4 Kensington
19.08.00 Jimmy Steel W RSC 3 Brentwood
09.09.00 Danny Southam W RSC 2 Manchester
09.10.00 Elvis Michailenko DREW 6 Liverpool
03.02.01 Paul Bonson W PTS 4 Manchester
25.09.01 Paul Wesley W PTS 6 Liverpool
13.10.01 Roman Divisek W CO 1 Budapest,
    Hungary
10.11.01 Valery Odin W RSC 4 Wembley
10.12.01 Jon Penn W RSC 2 Liverpool
    (Vacant Central Area S.Middleweight
    Title)
23.02.02 Jason Hart W RSC 2 Nottingham
09.03.02 Varuzhan Davtyan L PTS 6 Manchester
13.04.02 Brian Barbosa W PTS 8 Liverpool
07.09.02 Mike Algoet W PTS 10 Liverpool
    (Vacant WBF Inter-Continental
    S.Middleweight Title)
26.10.02 Albert Rybacki L RSC 9 Maesteg
    (WBF Inter-Continental S.Middleweight
    Title Defence)
19.04.03 Pierre Moreno L RSC 9 Liverpool
    (Vacant WBF Inter-Continental
    S.Middleweight Title)
26.07.03 Varuzhan Davtyan W RTD 3 Plymouth
22.11.03 Allan Foster W RSC 11 Belfast
    (Vacant British S.Middleweight Title)
23.09.05 Varuzhan Davtyan W PTS 4 Manchester
25.11.05 Szabolcs Rimovszky W RSC 3
    Liverpool
03.03.06 Dmitry Adamovich W PTS 4 Hartlepool
16.06.06 Jamie Hearn W RSC 4 Liverpool
    (Vacant English S.Middleweight Title)
24.11.06 Carl Froch L CO 3 Nottingham
    (British & Commonwealth
    S.Middleweight Title Challenges)

06.07.07 Nick Okoth W PTS 4 Wigan
29.09.07 Yuri Tsarenko W PTS 6 Sheffield
01.07.08 Mounir Sahli W PTS 6 Campione
     d'Italia, Italy
20.09.08 Nathan King W PTS 6 Sheffield
28.03.09 Tony Quigley L RSC 12 Liverpool
(Vacant British S.Middleweight Title)
Career: 30 contests, won 24, drew 1, lost 5.

Tony Dodson   Philip Sharkey

Jimmy Doherty

Stoke. *Born* Stafford, 15 August, 1985
L.Middleweight. *Ht* 5'11"
Manager M. Carney
12.11.05 Surinder Sekhon W PTS 6 Stoke
18.02.06 Pete Buckley W PTS 6 Stoke
06.05.06 Jason Nesbitt W PTS 6 Stoke
30.09.06 Aldon Stewart W PTS 6 Stoke
24.02.07 Chris Brophy W PTS 6 Stoke
12.05.07 Steve Cooper W PTS 6 Stoke
17.11.07 Matt Seawright W PTS 4 Stoke
17.05.08 Dale Miles L PTS 6 Stoke
13.09.08 Tye Williams W PTS 6 Stoke
23.01.09 Kevin Hammond L PTS 8 Stoke
Career: 10 contests, won 8, lost 2.

David Dolan

Sunderland. *Born* Sunderland, 7 October,
1979
Heavyweight. *Ht* 6'2"
Manager D. Garside
13.05.06 Nabil Haciani W PTS 4 Sheffield
03.11.06 Paul King W PTS 4 Barnsley
13.04.07 Paul King W PTS 4 Houghton le Spring
27.07.07 Luke Simpkin W RSC 6 Houghton le
     Spring
12.10.07 Howard Daley W RSC 2 Peterlee
23.11.07 Tony Booth W RSC 3 Houghton le
     Spring
08.02.08 Lee Swaby W PTS 6 Peterlee
11.04.08 Darren Morgan W PTS 3 Bethnal
     Green
11.04.08 Paul Butlin W PTS 3 Bethnal Green
11.04.08 Martin Rogan L PTS 3 Bethnal Green
04.07.08 Elvecio Sobral W CO 4 Liverpool
03.10.08 Rachid El Hadak W PTS 6 Burton

06.02.09 Robert Norton L PTS 12 Birmingham
(British Cruiserweight Title Challenge.
Vacant Commonwealth Cruiserweight
Title)
01.05.09 Ferenc Zsalek W CO 1 Hartlepool
Career: 14 contests, won 12, lost 2.

John Donnelly

Croxteth. *Born* Liverpool, 15 July, 1984
Featherweight. *Ht* 5'4½"
Manager T. Gilmour
05.06.07 Shaun Walton W PTS 6 Glasgow
14.09.07 Sergei Rozhakmens W PTS 4
     Kirkcaldy
05.11.07 Delroy Spencer W PTS 6 Glasgow
01.12.07 David Keogan W RSC 1 Liverpool
23.02.08 Gheorghe Ghiompirica W PTS 6
     Liverpool
14.03.08 Tony McQuade W PTS 6 Manchester
09.05.08 Gavin Reid L CO 4 Middlesbrough
07.06.08 Gheorghe Ghiompirica W PTS 6 Wigan
04.07.08 Faycal Messaoudene W PTS 6 Liverpool
06.02.09 Carlos Ruiz W PTS 6 Birmingham
12.06.09 Anwar Alfadi W PTS 6 Liverpool
Career: 11 contests, won 10, lost 1.

(Robert) Rob Doody (Shinn)

Tipton. *Born* Tipton, 9 October, 1981
L.Welterweight. *Ht* 5' 9"
Manager E. Johnson
03.04.09 Kristian Light W PTS 6
     Wolverhampton
12.06.09 Karl Taylor W PTS 6 Wolverhampton
Career: 2 contests, won 2.

Tom Doran

Connah's Quay. *Born* St Asaph, 7 August,
1987
L.Middleweight. *Ht* 5' 11"
Manager O. Harrison
23.05.09 Alex Spitjo W PTS 4 Queensferry
Career: 1 contest, won 1.

Mark Douglas   Philip Sharkey

Mark Douglas

Wokingham. *Born* Reading, 28 December,
1984
Welterweight. *Ht* 5'9¼"
Manager J. Evans
15.06.08 Nathan Weise W PTS 4 Bethnal Green
27.09.08 Jimmy Briggs W PTS 4 Bracknell
06.12.08 Alex Spitjo L RSC 1 Bethnal Green
19.01.09 Lloyd Creighton W CO 1 Mayfair
20.03.09 Scott Woolford W RSC 3 Bethnal Green
21.06.09 Ashley Theophane L PTS 8 Bethnal
     Green
Career: 6 contests, won 4, lost 2.

Scott Douglas   Philip Sharkey

Scott Douglas

Dagenham. *Born* Orsett, 25 November,
1978
L.Heavyweight. *Ht* 5' 10"
Manager C. Okoh
21.06.09 Jamie Norkett W PTS 4 Bethnal Green
Career: 1 contest, won 1.

Wayne Downing

West Bromwich. *Born* Sandwell, 30
December, 1979
L.Middleweight. *Ht* 5'9"
Manager Self
16.02.06 Peter Dunn L PTS 4 Dudley
18.05.06 Malik Khan L RSC 3 Walsall
18.09.06 Tye Williams L RSC 2 Glasgow
17.11.06 Peter Dunn W PTS 6 Brierley Hill
06.12.06 Martin Gordon W PTS 6 Stoke
03.03.07 Pete Buckley W PTS 4 Burton
19.05.07 Dennis Corpe L PTS 4 Nottingham
20.07.07 Dennis Corpe L RSC 3 Wolverhampton
28.11.07 Martin Gordon W PTS 4 Walsall
21.06.08 Curtis Woodhouse L CO 1 Birmingham
21.02.09 Eisa Al Dah L PTS 6 Merthyr Tydfil
05.03.09 Tony Randell L RSC 2 Limehouse
31.05.09 Scott Conway W RSC 2 Burton
Career: 13 contests, won 5, lost 8.

Philip Dowse

Aberystwyth. *Born* Aberystwyth, 31 March, 1984
Middleweight. *Ht* 5' 10"
Manager N. Hodges
16.02.07 Ernie Smith W PTS 6 Merthyr Tydfil
10.06.07 Paul Morby W RSC 4 Neath
04.09.08 Davey Jones DREW 6 Birmingham
Career: 3 contests, won 2, drew 1.

Eddie Doyle

Coatbridge. *Born* Coatbridge, 26 February, 1985
Welterweight. *Ht* 5' 8"
Manager T. Gilmour
21.12.08 Matt Seawright W PTS 6 Motherwell
14.03.09 Daniel Thorpe W PTS 6 Aberdeen
08.06.09 Peter Jones W PTS 6 Glasgow
Career: 3 contests, won 3.

Carl Drake

Plymouth. *Born* Plymouth, 22 February, 1975
Western Area L.Middleweight Champion.
Ht 5'8"
Manager J. Evans
02.06.07 Tommy Marshall W RSC 4 Bristol
15.09.07 Danny Butler L PTS 6 Bristol
06.10.07 Simon Fleck DREW 8 Leicester
01.12.07 Ryan Mahoney W PTS 4 Chigwell
29.02.08 Jon Harrison W RSC 7 Plymouth
(Vacant Western Area L.Middleweight Title)
20.06.08 Taz Jones L RSC 1 Plymouth
(Vacant International Masters L.Middleweight Title)
15.11.08 Simon Fleck W RSC 3 Plymouth
14.03.09 Danny Butler L PTS 10 Bristol
(Vacant Western Area Middleweight Title)
18.04.09 Lee Murtagh L PTS 6 Galway
Career: 9 contests, won 4, drew 1, lost 4.

Elvis Dube

Derby. *Born* Swaziland, 25 July, 1978
L.Heavyweight. *Ht* 5' 7"
Manager M. Shinfield
04.12.08 Jason Smith L PTS 6 Sunderland
13.03.09 Daniel Roberts L CO 6 Newport
Career: 2 contests, lost 2.

Ciaran Duffy

Glasgow. *Born* Donegal, 11 September, 1980
Scottish Area L. Middleweight Champion.
Ht 5'11"
Manager Self
03.11.01 Wayne Shepherd W PTS 6 Glasgow
03.12.01 Pedro Thompson W PTS 6 Leeds
22.04.02 Richard Inquieti W PTS 6 Glasgow
20.11.02 Gavin Pearson DREW 6 Leeds
17.03.03 Danny Moir W PTS 6 Glasgow
10.12.06 Paddy Pollock L PTS 6 Glasgow
10.02.07 Rocky Muscas W PTS 4 Letterkenny
26.10.07 Martin Sweeney L RSC 4 Glasgow
01.11.08 Duncan Cottier W PTS 6 Glasgow

14.11.08 Ernie Smith W PTS 4 Glasgow
06.03.09 Paddy Pollock W PTS 10 Glasgow
(Vacant Scottish Area L.Middleweight Title)
Career: 11 contests, won 8, drew 1, lost 2.

Lee Duncan

Sheffield. *Born* Barnsley, 14 November, 1988
Middleweight. *Ht* 6'1¼"
Manager J. Ingle
10.05.08 Keiron Gray L RSC 3 Nottingham
14.03.09 Quinton Hillocks L PTS 4 Birmingham
Career: 2 contests, lost 2.

Peter Dunn

Pontefract. *Born* Doncaster, 15 February, 1975
Middleweight. *Ht* 5'8"
Manager Self
08.12.97 Leigh Daniels W PTS 6 Bradford
15.05.98 Peter Lennon W PTS 6 Nottingham
18.09.98 Jan Cree L RSC 5 Belfast
23.10.98 Bobby Lyndon W PTS 6 Wakefield
03.12.98 Craig Smith L RSC 3 Sunderland
17.03.99 Des Sowden W PTS 6 Kensington
15.05.99 Ray Wood DREW 4 Blackpool
29.05.99 Dean Nicholas L PTS 6 South Shields
01.10.99 Jon Honney L PTS 4 Bethnal Green
18.10.99 Jan Cree W PTS 6 Glasgow
26.11.99 Gavin Pearson DREW 6 Wakefield
18.02.00 John T. Kelly L PTS 6 Pentre Halkyn
11.03.00 Iain Eldridge L RSC 2 Kensington
18.09.00 Joe Miller L PTS 6 Glasgow
26.10.00 Ram Singh W PTS 6 Stoke
27.11.00 Young Muttley L RSC 3 Birmingham
22.02.01 Darren Spencer W PTS 6 Sunderland
03.03.01 Glenn McClarnon L PTS 4 Wembley
20.03.01 Robert Burton L PTS 6 Leeds
08.04.01 Martyn Bailey L PTS 6 Wrexham
17.05.01 Gavin Pearson L PTS 6 Leeds
25.09.01 Darren Spencer L PTS 4 Liverpool
06.10.01 Lee Byrne L RSC 4 Manchester
13.11.01 Richard Inquieti DREW 6 Leeds
24.11.01 Robert Burton W PTS 6 Wakefield
28.01.02 Robert Burton L RSC 8 Barnsley
(Vacant Central Area Welterweight Title)
23.03.02 Colin Lynes L PTS 4 Southwark
19.04.02 Oscar Hall L PTS 6 Darlington
28.05.02 Matt Scriven L PTS 8 Leeds
29.06.02 Darren Bruce L PTS 6 Brentwood
28.09.02 Surinder Sekhon L PTS 6 Wakefield
13.09.03 Wayne Shepherd W PTS 6 Wakefield
20.09.03 Michael Lomax L PTS 4 Nottingham
04.10.03 Andy Gibson L PTS 6 Belfast
25.10.03 Gary Young L PTS 6 Edinburgh
13.12.03 Michael Jennings L PTS 6 Manchester
19.02.04 Young Muttley L PTS 4 Dudley
26.02.04 Matthew Hatton L PTS 6 Widnes
06.03.04 Jason Rushton L PTS 6 Renfrew
10.04.04 Ali Nuumembe L PTS 6 Manchester
22.04.04 Jamie Coyle L PTS 6 Glasgow
06.05.04 Jason Rushton L PTS 4 Barnsley
19.06.04 Chris Saunders L PTS 4 Muswell Hill
03.07.04 Oscar Hall L PTS 6 Blackpool
10.09.04 Tony Doherty L RSC 2 Bethnal Green
09.10.04 Steve Russell W PTS 6 Norwich
23.10.04 Geraint Harvey L PTS 6 Wakefield
11.12.04 Gary Woolcombe L PTS 4 Canning Town

19.12.04 Freddie Luke L PTS 4 Bethnal Green
25.02.05 Chas Symonds L PTS 4 Wembley
07.04.05 Jonjo Finnegan L PTS 6 Birmingham
26.04.05 Tyrone McInerney L RSC 6 Leeds
03.06.05 Oscar Hall L PTS 6 Hull
19.06.05 Gary Woolcombe L RSC 6 Bethnal Green
21.09.05 Danny Moir L PTS 6 Bradford
30.09.05 Paul McInnes L PTS 6 Burton
10.10.05 Joe Mitchell L PTS 6 Birmingham
13.11.05 Khurram Hussain L PTS 4 Leeds
21.11.05 Muhsen Nasser L RSC 4 Glasgow
16.02.06 Wayne Downing W PTS 4 Dudley
23.02.06 Darren Rhodes L PTS 6 Leeds
05.03.06 Muhsen Nasser L PTS 4 Sheffield
30.03.06 Oscar Milkitas L PTS 6 Bloomsbury
14.04.06 Gary Round L PTS 4 Telford
21.04.06 Jason Rushton L PTS 6 Doncaster
29.04.06 Lee McAllister L PTS 6 Edinburgh
09.05.06 Ryan Ashworth L PTS 6 Leeds
18.05.06 Stuart Elwell L PTS 6 Walsall
29.06.06 Marcus Portman L PTS 6 Dudley
18.09.06 Marcus Portman L PTS 6 Glasgow
29.09.06 Paul Burns L PTS 6 Motherwell
09.10.06 Tristan Davies L PTS 6 Birmingham
27.10.06 Lee Noble L PTS 6 Glasgow
04.11.06 Matt Scriven L PTS 6 Mansfield
17.11.06 Wayne Downing L PTS 6 Brierley Hill
24.11.06 Tyan Booth L PTS 4 Nottingham
05.12.06 Rob Kenney DREW 4 Wolverhampton
14.12.06 Simon Fleck L PTS 6 Leicester
22.12.06 Abul Taher L PTS 6 Coventry
01.02.07 Wayne Alwan Arab L PTS 6 Piccadilly
15.02.07 Rob Kenney L PTS 4 Dudley
23.02.07 Max Maxwell L PTS 6 Birmingham
02.03.07 Mark Hastie L PTS 6 Irvine
17.03.07 James McKinley L PTS 6 Birmingham
24.03.07 Sean McKervey L PTS 6 Coventry
01.04.07 Tristan Davies L PTS 6 Shrewsbury
14.04.07 Rob Kenney L PTS 4 Wakefield
06.05.07 Mark Dawes L PTS 6 Darlington
19.05.07 Karl Chiverton L PTS 4 Nottingham
27.05.07 Khurram Hussain L PTS 4 Bradford
03.06.07 Curtis Woodhouse L PTS 4 Barnsley
21.06.07 Clint Smith L PTS 6 Peterborough
30.06.07 Lee Murtagh L PTS 6 Belfast
27.07.07 Muhsen Nasser L PTS 6 Houghton le Spring
08.09.07 Ollie Newham L PTS 6 Sutton in Ashfield
21.09.07 Duane Parker L PTS 6 Burton
04.10.07 Wayne Alwan Arab L PTS 6 Piccadilly
13.10.07 Willie Thompson L PTS 6 Belfast
26.10.07 Karl Chiverton L PTS 6 Birmingham
03.11.07 Jack Perry L PTS 6 Derby
18.11.07 Dee Mitchell L PTS 6 Birmingham
25.11.07 Chris Johnson L PTS 6 Colne
08.12.07 Damian Taggart L PTS 4 Belfast
26.01.08 Gary O'Sullivan L RSC 6 Cork
02.03.08 Paul Dyer L PTS 6 Portsmouth
17.03.08 Charles Paul King L PTS 6 Glasgow
30.03.08 Paul Royston W PTS 4 Colne
10.04.08 Jimmy Beech L PTS 6 Piccadilly
20.04.08 Dave Murray L PTS 6 Shaw
30.04.08 Russ Colley L PTS 4 Wolverhampton
16.05.08 Duane Parker L PTS 6 Burton
13.06.08 Stuart Kennedy L PTS 6 Sunderland
28.06.08 Joe Hockenhull L PTS 6 Leicester
24.07.08 Jamie Ball L PTS 4 Wolverhampton
13.09.08 Omar Gumati L PTS 6 Stoke
26.09.08 Scott Evans L PTS 4 Wolverhampton

05.10.08 Nathan McIntosh L PTS 4 Nottingham
25.10.08 Danny Maka L PTS 6 St Helier
15.11.08 Mark Stupple L PTS 6 Bethnal Green
22.11.08 Chris O'Brien L PTS 6 Blackpool
30.11.08 Curtis Woodhouse L RSC 6 Rotherham
Career: 121 contests, won 12, drew 4, lost 105.

Terry Dunstan

Vauxhall. *Born* Vauxhall, 28 October, 1968
Former Undefeated British & European
Cruiserweight Champion. *Ht* 6' 3"
Manager G. Rhodes
12.11.92 Steve Osborne W PTS 6 Bayswater
25.11.92 Steve Yorath W PTS 8 Mayfair
31.03.93 Lee Prudden W PTS 6 Barking
15.09.93 Paul McCarthy W RSC 3 Ashford
02.12.93 Devon Rhooms W CO 2 Sheffield
30.09.94 Michael Murray W PTS 8 Bethnal Green
20.12.94 Trevor Small W RSC 4 Bethnal Green
04.03.95 Art Stacey W CO 1 Livingston
13.05.95 Dennis Andries W PTS 12 Glasgow
　　　　 (British Cruiserweight Title Challenge)
09.09.95 David Robinson W RSC 5 Cork
25.11.95 Jimmy Bills W RSC 7 Dublin
13.02.96 Dennis Andries W PTS 12 Bethnal
　　　　 Green
　　　　 (British Cruiserweight Title Defence)
11.05.96 John Keeton W RSC 1 Bethnal Green
　　　　 (British Cruiserweight Title Defence)
09.11.96 Sergio Daniel Merani W CO 3
　　　　 Manchester
12.04.97 Art Jimmerson W RSC 1 Sheffield
19.07.97 Nigel Rafferty W RSC 4 Wembley
14.02.98 Alexander Gurov W CO 1 Southwark
　　　　 (Vacant European Cruiserweight Title)
28.03.98 Imamu Mayfield L CO 11 Hull
　　　　 (IBF Cruiserweight Title Challenge)
21.11.98 Peter Oboh W PTS 8 Southwark
30.10.99 Chris Woollas W RSC 1 Southwark
03.12.99 Carl Thompson L CO 12 Peterborough
　　　　 (Vacant British Cruiserweight Title)
10.10.08 Paul Bonson W PTS 4 Sheffield
19.05.09 Ovill McKenzie L PTS 3 Kensington
Career: 23 contests, won 20, lost 3.

Terry Dunstan　　　　　Philip Sharkey

Riaz Durgahed　　　　　Philip Sharkey

Riaz Durgahed

Bristol. *Born* Mauritius, 4 May, 1977
S.Featherweight. *Ht* 5'6"
Manager C. Sanigar
29.02.04 Jason Thomas W RSC 1 Bristol
19.06.04 Buster Dennis W PTS 4 Muswell Hill
01.10.04 Dai Davies L PTS 4 Bristol
02.12.04 Lloyd Otte L PTS 6 Crystal Palace
08.04.05 Scott Flynn L PTS 4 Edinburgh
02.06.05 Jason Nesbitt W PTS 6 Peterborough
02.09.05 Rendall Munroe L PTS 6 Derby
16.10.05 Dave Hinds W PTS 6 Peterborough
18.11.05 Lloyd Otte DREW 4 Dagenham
12.12.05 Dai Davies W PTS 6 Peterborough
03.03.06 Jamie McKeever L PTS 6 Hartlepool
15.09.06 Billy Corcoran L CO 3 Muswell Hill
10.11.06 Sean Hughes W PTS 6 Hartlepool
03.12.06 Ryan Barrett L PTS 6 Bethnal Green
16.02.07 Dai Davies L PTS 8 Merthyr Tydfil
20.04.07 Paul Truscott L PTS 4 Dudley
12.10.07 Paul Appleby L RSC 3 Peterlee
30.11.07 Akaash Bhatia L PTS 6 Newham
02.02.08 Ryan Walsh L CO 1 Canning Town
24.05.08 Rob Turley W PTS 6 Cardiff
21.11.08 Vinny Mitchell L RSC 1 Bethnal Green
03.04.09 Ben Jones L PTS 6 Bethnal Green
Career: 22 contests, won 7, drew 1, lost 14.

Craig Dyer

Swansea. *Born* Swansea, 23 August, 1986
L.Welterweight. *Ht* 5'7¼"
Manager N. Hodges
21.09.07 Jamie Spence L PTS 6 Peterborough
10.11.07 Darryl Still L PTS 6 Portsmouth
25.01.08 Lee Purdy L RSC 1 Dagenham
30.03.08 Danny Stewart L PTS 4 Port Talbot
16.11.08 Shane Watson L PTS 4 Southampton
28.11.08 Charles Paul King L PTS 4 Glasgow
05.12.08 Jason Carr L PTS 6 Sheffield
27.02.09 Richard Ghent L PTS 4 Wolverhampton
14.03.09 Pete Leworthy L PTS 4 Bristol
28.03.09 Samir Mouneimne L PTS 4 Lincoln
12.06.09 Phil Gill L PTS 4 Bethnal Green
Career: 11 contests, lost 11.

Paul Dyer

Portsmouth. *Born* Portsmouth, 11 July,
1970
L.Middleweight. Former Southern Area
Welterweight Champion. *Ht* 5'11¼"
Manager J. Bishop
24.09.91 Mike Reed W PTS 6 Basildon
19.11.91 Dave Andrews W PTS 6 Norwich
23.02.93 Kevin Mabbutt L PTS 6 Kettering
17.06.94 Dewi Roberts W PTS 6 Plymouth
27.10.94 George Wilson W PTS 4 Bayswater
25.01.95 John Janes W PTS 6 Cardiff
08.03.95 Anthony Huw Williams W PTS 6
　　　　 Cardiff
06.05.95 Wahid Fats W PTS 4 Shepton Mallet
15.09.95 Mark Ramsey W PTS 6 Mansfield
16.12.95 Dennis Gardner W RSC 1 Cardiff
26.01.96 Danny Quacoe W PTS 6 Brighton
30.11.96 Mark Winters L PTS 6 Tylorstown
09.12.96 Paul Miles W PTS 6 Bristol
08.02.97 Michael Carruth W PTS 6 Millwall
14.03.97 Harry Dhami L PTS 10 Reading
　　　　 (Southern Area Welterweight Title
　　　　 Challenge)
24.03.99 Steve Brumant W PTS 4 Bayswater
16.10.99 Neil Sinclair L RSC 8 Belfast
16.05.00 Neil Sinclair L RSC 6 Warrington
01.12.00 Paul Denton W PTS 4 Peterborough
02.02.01 David Baptiste W PTS 10 Portsmouth
　　　　 (Vacant Southern Area Welterweight
　　　　 Title)
16.03.01 Peter Nightingale W PTS 6 Portsmouth
01.12.01 Paul Knights L PTS 10 Bethnal Green
　　　　 (Southern Area Welterweight Title
　　　　 Defence)
16.03.02 David Walker L RSC 6 Bethnal Green
　　　　 (Vacant Southern Area Welterweight
　　　　 Title)
16.09.07 Kenroy Lambert W PTS 6
　　　　 Southampton
10.11.07 Duncan Cottier W PTS 6 Portsmouth
02.03.08 Peter Dunn W PTS 6 Portsmouth
13.06.08 Sam Webb L PTS 6 Portsmouth
21.12.08 Kevin Concepcion L PTS 4 Coventry
20.03.09 Tomas Grublys L RSC 4 Newham
Career: 29 contests, won 18, lost 11.

Paul Dyer　　　　　Philip Sharkey

107

Graham Earl

Luton. *Born* Luton, 26 August, 1978
Lightweight. Former Undefeated WBU,
British, Commonwealth & Southern Area
Lightweight Champion. Former Undefeated
Southern Area Lightweight Champion. *Ht*
5'5¾"
Manager F. Warren
02.09.97 Mark O'Callaghan W RSC 2 Southwark
06.12.97 Mark McGowan W PTS 4 Wembley
11.04.98 Danny Lutaaya W RSC 2 Southwark
23.05.98 David Kirk W PTS 4 Bethnal Green
12.09.98 Brian Coleman W PTS 4 Bethnal Green
10.12.98 Marc Smith W RSC 1 Barking
16.01.99 Lee Williamson W RSC 4 Bethnal
Green
08.05.99 Benny Jones W PTS 6 Bethnal Green
15.07.99 Simon Chambers W CO 6 Peterborough
04.03.00 Ivo Golakov W RSC 1 Peterborough
29.04.00 Marco Fattore W PTS 6 Wembley
21.10.00 Lee Williamson W RSC 3 Wembley
10.03.01 Brian Gentry W RSC 8 Bethnal Green
*(Vacant Southern Area Lightweight
Title)*
22.09.01 Liam Maltby W CO 1 Bethnal Green
*(Southern Area Lightweight Title
Defence)*
15.12.01 Mark Winters W PTS 10 Wembley
(Elim. British Lightweight Title)
12.10.02 Chill John W PTS 10 Bethnal Green
*(Southern Area Lightweight Title
Defence)*
15.02.03 Steve Murray W RSC 2 Wembley
*(Southern Area Lightweight Title
Defence. Final Elim. British Lightweight
Title)*
24.05.03 Nikolai Eremeev W PTS 8 Bethnal
Green
17.07.03 Bobby Vanzie W PTS 12 Dagenham
(British Lightweight Title Challenge)
11.10.03 Jon Honney W PTS 8 Portsmouth
05.06.04 Bobby Vanzie W PTS 12 Bethnal Green
(Vacant British Lightweight Title)
30.07.04 Steve Murray W RSC 6 Bethnal Green
(British Lightweight Title Defence)
25.02.05 Ricky Burns L PTS 8 Wembley
19.06.05 Kevin Bennett W RSC 9 Bethnal Green
*(Commonwealth Lightweight Title
Challenge. British Lightweight Title
Defence)*
27.01.06 Yuri Romanov W PTS 12 Dagenham
28.10.06 Angel Hugo Ramirez W PTS 12 Bethnal
Green
(Vacant WBU Lightweight Title)
17.02.07 Michael Katsidis L RTD 5 Wembley
(Vacant Interim WBO Lightweight Title)
08.12.07 Amir Khan L RSC 1 Bolton
*(Commonwealth Lightweight Title
Challenge)*
17.10.08 Henry Castle L RSC 1 Bethnal Green
28.06.09 Karl Taylor W PTS 6 Luton
Career: 30 contests, won 26, lost 4.

Gilbert Eastman

Balham. *Born* Guyana, 16 November, 1972
L.Middleweight. Former Southern Area
L.Middleweight Champion. *Ht* 5'10¼"
Manager Self
22.04.96 Wayne Shepherd W PTS 4 Crystal
Palace
09.07.96 Costas Katsantonis W RSC 1 Bethnal
Green
11.01.97 Mike Watson W RSC 1 Bethnal Green
25.03.97 Danny Quacoe W RSC 3 Lewisham
30.08.97 Karl Taylor W PTS 4 Cheshunt
08.11.97 Ray Newby W PTS 6 Southwark
14.02.98 Cam Raeside W RSC 5 Southwark
21.04.98 Dennis Berry W RSC 6 Edmonton
23.05.98 Shaun O'Neill W RSC 1 Bethnal Green
12.09.98 Everald Williams W RTD 5 Bethnal
Green
21.11.98 Lindon Scarlett W RTD 3 Southwark
06.03.99 Kofi Jantuah L RSC 11 Southwark
*(Commonwealth Welterweight Title
Challenge)*
25.10.02 Ojay Abrahams W PTS 4 Bethnal
Green
21.12.02 Pedro Thompson W RSC 2 Dagenham
05.03.03 Howard Clarke W PTS 6 Bethnal
Green
16.04.03 Andrew Facey L RSC 3 Nottingham
25.07.03 Jason Collins W RSC 1 Norwich
04.10.03 Spencer Fearon W RSC 4 Muswell Hill
*(Vacant Southern Area L.Middleweight
Title)*
28.11.03 Eugenio Monteiro L PTS 8 Derby
30.01.04 Craig Lynch W PTS 6 Dagenham
16.04.04 Delroy Mellis W RSC 5 Bradford
*(Southern Area L.Middleweight Title
Defence)*
24.09.04 Clive Johnson W PTS 6 Nottingham
19.12.05 Duncan Cottier W RTD 3 Longford
11.03.06 Gary Lockett L RSC 1 (12) Newport
(Vacant WBU Middleweight Title)
26.05.06 Gary Woolcombe L RSC 7 Bethnal
Green
*(Southern Area L.Middleweight Title
Defence)*
23.02.08 George Katsimpas L PTS 6 Crawley
17.10.08 Sam Webb L RSC 8 Bethnal Green
Career: 27 contests, won 20, lost 7.

Howard Eastman

Battersea. *Born* New Amsterdam, Guyana,
8 December, 1970
Guyanese Middleweight Champion. Former
British Middleweight Champion. Former
Undefeated Commonwealth & European,
IBO Inter-Continental, WBA Inter-
Continental & Southern Area Middleweight
Champion. *Ht* 5'11"
Manager Self
06.03.94 John Rice W RSC 1 Southwark
14.03.94 Andy Peach W PTS 6 Mayfair
22.03.94 Steve Philips W RSC 5 Bethnal Green
17.10.94 Barry Thorogood W RSC 6 Mayfair
06.03.95 Marty Duke W RSC 1 Mayfair
20.04.95 Stuart Dunn W RSC 2 Mayfair
23.06.95 Peter Vosper W RSC 1 Bethnal Green
16.10.95 Carlo Colarusso W RSC 1 Mayfair
29.11.95 Brendan Ryan W RSC 2 Bethnal Green
31.01.96 Paul Wesley W RSC 1 Birmingham
13.03.96 Steve Goodwin W RSC 5 Wembley
29.04.96 John Duckworth W RSC 5 Mayfair
11.12.96 Sven Hamer W RSC 10 Southwark
*(Vacant Southern Area Middleweight
Title)*
18.02.97 John Duckworth W CO 7 Cheshunt
25.03.97 Rachid Serdjane W RSC 7 Lewisham
14.02.98 Vitali Kopitko W PTS 8 Southwark
28.03.98 Terry Morrill W RTD 4 Hull
23.05.98 Darren Ashton W RSC 4 Bethnal Green
30.11.98 Steve Foster W RSC 7 Manchester
(Vacant British Middleweight Title)
04.02.99 Jason Barker W RSC 6 Lewisham
06.03.99 Jon Penn W RSC 3 Southwark
*(Vacant IBO Inter-Continental
S. Middleweight Title)*
22.05.99 Roman Babaev W RSC 6 Belfast
*(WBA Inter-Continental Middleweight
Title Challenge)*
10.07.99 Teimouraz Kikelidze W RSC 6
Southwark
*(WBA Inter-Continental Middleweight
Title Defence)*
13.09.99 Derek Wormald W RSC 3 Bethnal
Green
(British Middleweight Title Defence)
13.11.99 Mike Algoet W RSC 8 Hull
*(WBA Inter-Continental Middleweight
Title Defence)*
18.01.00 Ojay Abrahams W RSC 2 Mansfield
04.03.00 Viktor Fesetchko W RTD 4
Peterborough
29.04.00 Anthony Ivory W RTD 6 Wembley
25.07.00 Ahmet Dottouev W RTD 5 Southwark
*(WBA Inter-Continental Middleweight
Title Defence)*
16.09.00 Sam Soliman W PTS 12 Bethnal Green
*(Commonwealth Middleweight Title
Challenge)*
05.02.01 Mark Baker W RTD 5 Hull
10.04.01 Robert McCracken W RSC 10 Wembley
*(British & Commonwealth Middleweight
Title Defences. Vacant European
Middleweight Title)*
17.11.01 William Joppy L PTS 12 Las Vegas,
Nevada, USA
*(Vacant WBA Interim Middleweight
Title)*
25.10.02 Chardan Ansoula W RSC 1 Bethnal
Green
21.12.02 Hussain Osman W RTD 4 Dagenham
28.01.03 Christophe Tendil W RTD 4 Nottingham
(Vacant European Middleweight Title)
05.03.03 Gary Beardsley W RSC 2 Bethnal Green
16.04.03 Scott Dann W RSC 3 Nottingham
*(British, Commonwealth & European
Middleweight Title Defences)*
25.07.03 Hacine Cherifi W RTD 8 Norwich
(European Middleweight Title Defence)
30.01.04 Sergei Tatevosyan W PTS 12 Dagenham
(European Middleweight Title Defence)
24.09.04 Jerry Elliott W PTS 10 Nottingham
19.02.05 Bernard Hopkins L PTS 12 Los Angeles,
California, USA
*(WBC, WBA, IBF & WBO Middleweight
Title Challenges)*
16.07.05 Arthur Abraham L PTS 12 Nuremburg,
Germany
*(WBA Inter-Continental Middleweight
Title Challenge)*

24.03.06 Edison Miranda L RSC 7 Hollywood, Florida, USA
(Final Elim. IBF Middleweight Title)
15.12.06 Richard Williams W CO 12 Bethnal Green
(Vacant British Middleweight Title)
20.04.07 Evans Ashira W PTS 12 Dudley
(Vacant Commonwealth Middleweight Title)
28.09.07 Wayne Elcock L PTS 12 Coventry
(British Middleweight Title Defence)
08.12.07 John Duddy L PTS 10 Belfast
05.07.08 Denny Dalton W PTS 12 Georgetown, Guyana
(Vacant Guyanese Middleweight Title)
25.10.08 Andrew Lewis W PTS 12 Georgetown, Guyana
(Guyanese Middleweight Title Defence)
28.02.09 Leon Gilkes W PTS 10 Georgetown, Guyana
Career: 51 contests, won 45, lost 6..

Paul Economides

Connah's Quay. *Born* Chester, 19 November, 1986
S.Bantamweight. *Ht* 5'5¼"
Manager S. Goodwin
01.03.08 Duane Cumberbatch W PTS 6 Stoke
17.05.08 Delroy Spencer W PTS 6 Stoke
13.09.08 Tony McQuade W PTS 6 Stoke
06.12.08 Tony McQuade W PTS 4 Wigan
13.02.09 Delroy Spencer W PTS 4 Wigan
07.03.09 John Vanemmenis W PTS 4 Chester
23.05.09 Pavels Senkovs W PTS 6 Queensferry
Career: 7 contests, won 7.

Steve Ede

Gosport. *Born* Southampton, 22 June,1976
Southern Area Middleweight Champion.
Former Undefeated British Masters
Middleweight Champion. *Ht* 5'10"
Manager J. Bishop
06.02.05 Jed Tytler W RSC 4 Southampton
26.06.05 Mark Wall W PTS 6 Southampton
25.09.05 Rocky Muscus W PTS 6 Southampton
16.12.05 Lee Hodgson W PTS 4 Bracknell
05.03.06 Anthony Young W RSC 3 Southampton
26.05.06 Jake Guntert W RSC 2 Bethnal Green
24.09.06 Lee Hodgson W RSC 3 Southampton
25.02.07 Conroy McIntosh W PTS 10 Southampton
(Vacant British Masters Middleweight Title)
16.09.07 Cello Renda L RSC 2 Southampton
(Vacant British Masters Middleweight Title)
02.03.08 Sherman Alleyne W PTS 6 Portsmouth
22.11.08 Max Maxwell L PTS 3 Bethnal Green
19.01.09 Anthony Young W RSC 8 Mayfair
(Vacant Southern Area Middleweight Title)
27.06.09 Duncan Cottier W PTS 6 Portsmouth
Career: 13 contests, won 11, lost 2.

Matthew Edmonds

Newport. *Born* Newport, 12 February, 1984
International Masters Bantamweight
Champion. *Ht* 5'6"
Manager C. Sanigar

15.09.06 Delroy Spencer W PTS 4 Newport
07.10.06 Colin Moffett W PTS 4 Belfast
10.11.06 Mo Khaled W PTS 6 Newport
03.03.07 Sumaila Badu W PTS 6 Newport
16.06.07 Jamil Hussain W RTD 3 Newport
(Vacant International Masters Bantamweight Title)
05.10.07 Kris Hughes L PTS 6 Newport
08.12.07 Jason Booth L RSC 9 Wigan
(Vacant Commonwealth Bantamweight Title)
05.04.08 Sumaila Badu W PTS 10 Newport
(International Masters Bantamweight Title Defence)
24.05.08 Herbert Quartey W RSC 6 Cardiff
12.07.08 Ayittey Mettle W PTS 6 Newport
24.10.08 Gheorghe Ghiompirica W PTS 6 Newport
06.03.09 Kakhaber Avetisian W PTS 6 Wigan
03.04.09 Gary Davies L RSC 7 Bethnal Green
(Vacant British Bantamweight Title)
Career: 13 contests, won 10, lost 3.

Chris Edwards

Stoke. *Born* Stoke, 6 May, 1976
British & Commonwealth Flyweight
Champion. Former British S.Flyweight
Champion. Former Undefeated English
Flyweight Champion. Former Undefeated
British Masters S.Bantamweight Champion.
Ht 5'3"
Manager M. Carney
03.04.98 Chris Thomas W RSC 2 Ebbw Vale
21.09.98 Russell Laing L PTS 6 Glasgow
26.02.99 Delroy Spencer L PTS 6 West Bromwich
17.04.99 Stevie Quinn L RSC 4 Dublin
19.10.99 Lee Georgiou L RSC 2 Bethnal Green
03.12.99 Daniel Ring L PTS 4 Peterborough
15.05.00 Paddy Folan L PTS 6 Bradford
07.10.00 Andy Roberts W PTS 4 Doncaster
27.11.00 Levi Pattison W PTS 4 Birmingham
16.03.01 Jamie Evans L PTS 6 Portsmouth
03.06.01 Darren Taylor DREW 6 Hanley
08.10.01 Levi Pattison L PTS 4 Barnsley
06.12.01 Neil Read W PTS 8 Stoke
10.10.02 Neil Read W PTS 6 Stoke
13.06.03 Lee Haskins L PTS 6 Bristol
23.04.04 Delroy Spencer DREW 6 Leicester
26.09.04 Neil Read W RSC 2 Stoke
(Vacant British Masters S.Bantamweight Title)
28.10.04 Colin Moffett L PTS 4 Belfast
12.11.05 Delroy Spencer W PTS 4 Stoke
18.02.06 Gary Ford L PTS 6 Stoke
10.03.06 Andrea Sarritzu L CO 4 Bergamo, Italy
06.05.06 Gary Sheil W PTS 6 Stoke
30.09.06 Usman Ahmed W PTS 6 Stoke
24.11.06 Dale Robinson W RSC 8 Stoke
(Vacant English Flyweight Title)
13.04.07 Dale Robinson DREW 12 Altrincham
(Vacant British & Commonwealth Flyweight Titles)
08.12.07 Jamie McDonnell W PTS 12 Wigan
(Vacant British S.Flyweight Title)
28.03.08 Andy Bell L PTS 12 Barnsley
(British S.Flyweight Title Defence)
23.01.09 Wayne Bloy W RTD 4 Stoke
(Vacant British & Commonwealth Flyweight Titles)

29.05.09 Usman Ahmed W PTS 12 Stoke
(British & Commonwealth Flyweight Title Defences)
Career: 29 contests, won 13, drew 3, lost 13..

Lee Edwards

Sheffield. *Born* Huntingdon, 25 May, 1984
Former Undefeated British Masters L.
Middleweight Champion. *Ht* 5'11"
Manager Self
08.05.05 Sergey Haritonov W PTS 6 Sheffield
24.07.05 Lee Williamson W PTS 6 Sheffield
30.10.05 Joe Mitchell L RSC 2 Sheffield
17.02.06 Malik Khan W RSC 2 Sheffield
20.04.07 Howard Clarke W PTS 6 Sheffield
16.09.07 Jon Musgrave W PTS 6 Sheffield
23.11.07 Paul Royston W PTS 6 Sheffield
15.02.08 Matt Scriven W PTS 6 Sheffield
14.09.08 Alex Matvienko W PTS 10 Wigan
(Vacant British Masters L. Middleweight Title)
10.10.08 David Kirk W PTS 4 Sheffield
05.12.08 Lee Murtagh W PTS 10 Sheffield
(British Masters L. Middleweight Title Defence)
Career: 11 contests, won 10, lost 1.

Mene Edwards   Philip Sharkey

Mene Edwards

Plumstead. *Born* Greenwich, 30 September, 1983
L.Heavyweight. *Ht* 6'3"
Manager M. Roe
30.06.09 Lee Nicholson W RTD 1 Bethnal Green
Career: 1 contest, won 1.

Paul Edwards

Liverpool. *Born* Liverpool, 1 October, 1986
Flyweight. *Ht* 5'5"
Manager F. Maloney
19.07.08 Robert Palmer W PTS 4 Liverpool
07.11.08 Delroy Spencer W PTS 4 Wigan
23.01.09 Elemir Rafael W PTS 4 Stoke

17.04.09 Itsko Veselinov W RSC 2 Leigh
29.05.09 Francis Croes W PTS 6 Stoke
Career: 5 contests, won 5.

Wayne Elcock

Birmingham. *Born* Birmingham, 12 February, 1974
Former British & WBU Middleweight Champion. Former Undefeated English Middleweight Champion. *Ht* 5'9½"
Manager Self
02.12.99 William Webster W PTS 6 Peterborough
04.03.00 Sonny Pollard W RSC 3 Peterborough
07.07.01 Darren Rhodes W PTS 4 Manchester
09.10.01 Valery Odin W PTS 4 Cardiff
02.03.02 Charles Shodiya W RSC 1 Bethnal Green
20.04.02 Howard Clarke W PTS 4 Cardiff
01.06.02 Jason Collins W RSC 2 Manchester
17.08.02 Ojay Abrahams W PTS 4 Cardiff
23.11.02 Jason Collins W RSC 1 Derby
15.02.03 Yuri Tsarenko W PTS 10 Wembley
05.04.03 Anthony Farnell W PTS 12 Manchester
   (WBU Middleweight Title Challenge)
29.11.03 Lawrence Murphy L CO 1 Renfrew
   (WBU Middleweight Title Defence)
07.02.04 Farai Musiiwa W PTS 6 Bethnal Green
05.06.04 Michael Monaghan W PTS 4 Bethnal Green
07.04.05 Darren Rhodes W CO 1 Birmingham
16.09.05 Scott Dann L PTS 12 Plymouth
   (British Middleweight Title Challenge)
06.05.06 Lawrence Murphy W RSC 5 Birmingham
   (Elim. British Middleweight Title)
08.09.06 Vince Baldassara W CO 6 Birmingham
   (Vacant WBF Inter-Continental Middleweight Title)
01.12.06 Steven Bendall W RSC 8 Birmingham
   (English Middleweight Title Challenge)
28.09.07 Howard Eastman W PTS 12 Coventry
   (British Middleweight Title Challenge)
08.12.07 Arthur Abraham L RSC 5 Basle, Switzerland
   (IBF Middleweight Title Challenge)
20.06.08 Darren McDermott W RSC 2 Wolverhampton
   (British Middleweight Title Defence)
14.03.09 Matthew Macklin L RSC 3 Birmingham
   (British Middleweight Title Defence)
Career: 23 contests, won 19, lost 4.

Joe Elfidh

Doncaster. *Born* Doncaster, 5 April, 1980
L.Welterweight. *Ht* 5'7¼"
Manager D. Hobson
23.11.07 Darren Askew W PTS 6 Rotherham
22.03.08 Karl Taylor W PTS 6 Sheffield
21.06.08 Abdul Rashid W PTS 6 Sheffield
19.09.08 Pete Buckley W PTS 6 Doncaster
14.02.09 Marian Cazacu W PTS 6 St Helier
Career: 5 contests, won 5.

Matthew Ellis

Blackpool. *Born* Oldham, 12 April, 1974
Heavyweight. *Ht* 5'11¾"
Manager Self
03.02.96 Laurent Rouze W CO 1 Liverpool

01.04.96 Ladislav Husarik W RTD 4 Den Bosch, Holland
06.09.96 Darren Fearn W RSC 6 Liverpool
26.10.96 Daniel Beun W RSC 1 Liverpool
01.03.97 Yuri Yelistratov L RSC 5 Liverpool
20.07.97 Ricardo Philips W PTS 4 California, USA
26.09.97 Albert Call DREW 6 Liverpool
12.03.98 Yuri Yelistratov W RSC 1 Liverpool
21.07.98 Chris Woollas W RSC 5 Widnes
24.10.98 Peter Hrivnak W RSC 1 Liverpool
12.12.98 Harry Senior W PTS 8 Southwark
27.02.99 Michael Murray W PTS 8 Bethnal Green
15.05.99 Biko Botowamungu W PTS 8 Blackpool
27.05.00 Alex Vasiliev W CO 4 Southwark
16.09.00 Dimitri Bakhtov W PTS 4 Bethnal Green
18.11.00 Chris Woollas W PTS 4 Dagenham
17.02.01 Alexei Osokin W PTS 8 Bethnal Green
12.07.01 Ronnie Smith W PTS 6 Houston, Texas, USA
22.09.01 Colin Abelson W CO 1 Bethnal Green
02.03.02 Dennis Bakhtov L RSC 5 Bethnal Green
   (WBC International Heavyweight Title Challenge)
29.03.03 Derek McCafferty W PTS 4 Wembley
31.05.03 Audley Harrison L RSC 2 Bethnal Green
27.10.03 Tony Moran L RSC 4 Glasgow
26.10.06 Chris Woollas W PTS 4 Dudley
08.02.08 Chris Burton L RTD 2 Peterlee
22.11.08 Luke Simpkin W PTS 4 Blackpool
06.12.08 Enzo Maccarinelli L RSC 2 Canning Town
11.04.09 Tyson Fury L CO 1 Bethnal Green
15.05.09 Tony Bellew L RSC 4 Belfast
Career: 29 contests, won 20, drew 1, lost 8.

Yassine El Maachi

Balham. *Born* Morocco, 19 September, 1979
L.Middleweight. *Ht* 5'7¼"
Manager J. Gill
02.09.01 Rudolf Murko W PTS 4 Den Haag, Netherlands
20.12.01 Anthony Armstead W PTS 6 Rotterdam, Netherlands
20.05.02 Jackson Osei Bonsu L CO 3 Roeselare, Belgium
21.06.03 Alex Solcsanyi W RSC 3 Den Haag, Netherlands
06.07.07 Brett Flournoy L RSC 4 Wigan
21.09.07 Scott Woolford W PTS 4 Bethnal Green
08.12.07 Denton Vassell L PTS 4 Bolton
30.03.08 Thomas McDonagh L PTS 6 Colne
10.10.08 Eamonn Goodbrand W PTS 6 Motherwell
15.11.08 Kevin Concepcion W RSC 2 Bethnal Green
21.12.08 Jamie Ambler W RSC 3 Motherwell
27.03.09 Arturs Jaskuls W PTS 4 Kensington
Career: 12 contests, won 8, lost 4.

Stuart Elwell

Darlaston. *Born* Walsall, 14 December, 1977

L.Middleweight. Former Undefeated Midlands Area Welterweight Champion. *Ht* 5'9"
Manager E. Johnson
06.11.00 Ernie Smith W PTS 6 Wolverhampton
28.01.01 Arv Mittoo W PTS 6 Wolverhampton
01.04.01 Richard Inquieti W PTS 6 Wolverhampton
06.10.05 Ernie Smith W PTS 6 Dudley
25.11.05 Ben Hudson W PTS 4 Walsall
10.03.06 David Kirk W PTS 10 Walsall
   (Vacant Midlands Area Welterweight Title)
18.05.06 Peter Dunn W PTS 6 Walsall
23.06.06 Franny Jones W RSC 1 Blackpool
10.11.06 Ben Hudson W PTS 4 Telford
23.03.07 John O'Donnell L PTS 10 Nottingham
   (Vacant English Welterweight Title)
20.07.07 Alexander Matviechuk W PTS 6 Wolverhampton
18.02.08 Chris Brophy W PTS 6 Glasgow
25.03.08 Vyacheslav Senchenko L RSC 2 Donetsk, Ukraine
   (WBA Inter-Continental Welterweight Title Challenge)
04.07.08 Ted Bami L RSC 7 Liverpool
28.11.08 Paul Burns W PTS 6 Glasgow
30.01.09 Kell Brook L RSC 2 Bethnal Green
   (British Welterweight Title Challenge)
Career: 16 contests, won 12, lost 4.

Bradley Evans

Royston. *Born* Cambridge, 3 May, 1989
Lightweight. *Ht* 5'6"
Manager T. Sims
28.02.09 Sid Razak W PTS 4 Norwich
23.05.09 Jevgenijs Kirillovs DREW 4 Watford
Career: 2 contests, won 1, drew 1.

Ryan Evans

Merthyr Tydfil. *Born* Merthyr Tydfil, 16 August, 1987
Welterweight. *Ht* 5'10"
Manager G. Lockett
30.06.09 Johnny Greaves W PTS 4 Bethnal Green
Career: 1 contest, won 1.

Scott Evans

Stourbridge. *Born* Wordsley, 1 March, 1988
British Masters Lightweight Champion. *Ht* 5'8¾"
Manager P. Rowson
25.10.07 Amir Nadi W PTS 4 Wolverhampton
28.11.07 Karl Taylor W RSC 3 Walsall
28.02.08 Kristian Laight W PTS 6 Wolverhampton
30.04.08 Amir Nadi W RSC 3 Wolverhampton
24.07.08 Pete Buckley W PTS 4 Wolverhampton
26.09.08 Peter Dunn W PTS 4 Wolverhampton
17.01.09 Matt Seawright W PTS 4 Wigan
27.02.09 Chris Long W PTS 10 Wolverhampton
   (Vacant British Masters Lightweight Title)
10.05.09 Dave Ryan L RSC 2 Derby
   (Vacant Midlands Area Welterweight Title)
Career: 9 contests, won 8, lost 1.

Andrew Facey

Sheffield. *Born* Wolverhampton, 20 May, 1972
English L.Middleweight Champion. Former Undefeated Central Area Middleweight Champion. *Ht* 6'0"
Manager D. Ingle

06.12.99 Peter McCormack W CO 2 Birmingham
09.06.00 Matthew Pepper W RSC 1 Hull
04.11.00 Earl Ling W PTS 6 Derby
11.12.00 Gary Jones W PTS 6 Cleethorpes
10.02.01 Louis Swales W RSC 3 Widnes
17.03.01 Darren Rhodes L PTS 4 Manchester
24.03.01 Matthew Tait W PTS 4 Chigwell
16.06.01 Earl Ling DREW 6 Derby
09.12.01 Michael Pinnock W PTS 6 Shaw
02.03.02 Darren Rhodes W RSC 6 Wakefield
(*Vacant Central Area Middleweight Title*)
20.04.02 Darren Ashton W PTS 6 Derby
13.04.02 Leigh Wicks W PTS 6 Norwich
03.08.02 Damon Hague L CO 5 Derby
(*Final Elim. WBF Middleweight Title*)
25.10.02 William Webster W PTS 4 Cotgrave
16.04.03 Gilbert Eastman W RSC 3 Nottingham
06.11.03 Matthew Macklin W PTS 10 Dagenham
(*Vacant English L.Middleweight Title*)
22.11.03 Jamie Moore L RSC 7 Belfast
(*British & Commonwealth L.Middleweight Title Challenges*)
04.06.04 Howard Clarke W PTS 6 Hull
17.09.04 Jason Collins W PTS 4 Sheffield
03.09.05 Jason Collins W PTS 4 Norwich
29.10.05 Howard Clarke W PTS 6 Aberdeen
27.05.06 Ojay Abrahams W PTS 6 Aberdeen
18.11.06 Bradley Pryce L PTS 12 Newport
(*Commonwealth L.Middleweight Title Challenge*)
26.01.07 Gary Woolcombe W RSC 5 Dagenham
(*English L.Middleweight Title Defence*)
26.10.07 Jamie Moore L RSC 11 Wigan
(*British L.Middleweight Title Challenge*)
24.05.08 Thomas McDonagh DREW 10 Manchester
(*English L.Middleweight Title Defence*)
28.03.09 Martins Kukuls W PTS 4 Liverpool
Career: 27 contests, won 20, drew 2, lost 5.

Shaun Farmer

Hartlepool. *Born* Hull, 7 March, 1977
L.Middleweight. *Ht* 6'0"
Manager O. Harrison

05.10.06 Lee Noble W PTS 6 Sunderland
17.12.06 Craig Bunn L PTS 6 Bolton
25.02.07 Alex Matvienko L PTS 6 Manchester
11.05.07 Matt Scriven W PTS 6 Sunderland
25.05.07 Paddy Pollock L PTS 6 Glasgow
24.06.07 Jon Foster W PTS 6 Sunderland
11.08.07 Paddy Pollock W PTS 6 Liverpool
19.10.07 Chris Black L CO 1 Motherwell
08.12.07 Brian Rose L RSC 3 Wigan

23.02.08 Paul Royston W PTS 6 Liverpool
20.03.08 Jon Musgrave W PTS 6 South Shields
15.05.08 Jon Musgrave L PTS 6 Sunderland
13.06.08 Ryan Ashworth L CO 3 Sunderland
03.10.08 Martyn King L PTS 6 Sunderland
08.11.08 Janos Fidel DREW 6 Wigan
04.12.08 Paul Royston W PTS 6 Sunderland
23.05.09 Chris Thompson L RSC 2 Queensferry
Career: 17 contests, won 7, drew 1, lost 9.

Adam Farrell

Swansea. *Born* Swansea, 8 June, 1986
L.Welterweight. *Ht* 5' 10"
Manager C. Sanigar
13.03.09 Ben Wakeham L RSC 3 Newport
05.06.09 James Todd L PTS 6 Newport
Career: 2 contests, lost 2.

Kieran Farrell

Heywood. Born Bury, 27 June, 1990
Flyweight. *Ht* 5' 6"
Manager S. Wood
24.01.09 Gary Sheil W RSC 3 Blackpool
29.03.09 Francis Croes W PTS 4 Bolton
17.05.09 Delroy Spencer W PTS 4 Bolton
Career: 3 contests, won 3.

Graham Fearn

York. *Born* York, 1 December, 1974
L.Welterweight. *Ht* 5'7¼"
Manager M. Marsden
10.12.07 Kristian Laight W PTS 6 Leicester
18.02.08 Brian Murphy W RSC 6 Glasgow
24.04.08 Bheki Moyo W PTS 6 Piccadilly
05.06.08 Karl Taylor W PTS 6 Leeds
11.07.08 Darren Askew L PTS 4 Wigan
03.04.09 Jonathan Hussey L PTS 6 Bethnal Green
Career: 6 contests, won 4, lost 2.

Femi Fehintola

Bradford. *Born* Bradford, 1 July, 1982
Former English Featherweight Champion. *Ht* 5'7"
Manager D. Hobson
26.09.03 John-Paul Ryan W PTS 6 Reading
07.11.03 Pete Buckley W PTS 6 Sheffield
10.12.03 Jason Nesbitt W PTS 6 Sheffield
06.02.04 Jason Nesbitt W PTS 6 Sheffield
20.04.04 Kristian Laight W PTS 6 Sheffield
17.06.04 Anthony Hanna W PTS 6 Sheffield
24.10.04 John-Paul Ryan W PTS 6 Sheffield
10.12.04 Philippe Meheust W PTS 6 Sheffield
04.03.05 Daniel Thorpe W PTS 6 Rotherham
24.07.05 Jason Nesbitt W PTS 6 Sheffield
14.10.05 Rakhim Mingaleev W PTS 8 Huddersfield
16.12.05 Frederic Gosset W PTS 8 Bracknell
18.03.06 Ivo Golakov W RSC 2 Monte Carlo, Monaco
13.05.06 Nikita Lukin W PTS 8 Sheffield
03.11.06 Carl Johanneson L RSC 6 Barnsley
(*British S.Featherweight Title Challenge*)
27.05.07 Carl Allen W PTS 6 Bradford
23.06.07 Barbaro Zepeda W PTS 4 Las Vegas, Nevada, USA
07.09.07 Karl Taylor W PTS 4 Doncaster

06.10.07 Steve Bell W PTS 10 Nottingham
(*Vacant English S.Featherweight Title*)
22.03.08 John Baguley W PTS 6 Sheffield
25.10.08 Ryan Barrett L CO 3 St Helier
(*English S.Featherweight Title Defence*)
Career: 21 contests, won 19, lost 2.

Dave Ferguson

Wallsend. *Born* North Shields, 28 February, 1976
Heavyweight. *Ht* 6'4"
Manager Self
16.02.07 David Ingleby W PTS 4 Sunderland
24.06.07 David Ingleby W PTS 4 Sunderland
23.09.07 Paul Malcolm W RTD 3 Hartlepool
06.12.07 Lee Mountford W PTS 6 Sunderland
20.03.08 Mark Walker W RSC 1 South Shields
11.04.08 Billy Bessey W PTS 3 Bethnal Green
11.04.08 Martin Rogan L PTS 3 Bethnal Green
13.06.08 Howard Daley W PTS 4 Sunderland
12.09.08 Luke Simpkin L PTS 3 Newcastle
28.02.09 Howard Daley W RSC 2 Newcastle
Career: 10 contests, won 8, lost 2.

Andrew Ferrans

New Cumnock. *Born* Irvine, 4 February, 1981
Welterweight. Former Undefeated British Masters S.Featherweight Champion. *Ht* 5'9"
Manager T. Gilmour
19.02.00 Chris Lyons W PTS 6 Prestwick
03.03.00 Gary Groves W RSC 1 Irvine
20.03.00 John Barnes DREW 6 Glasgow
06.06.00 Duncan Armstrong W PTS 6 Motherwell
18.09.00 Steve Brook W PTS 6 Glasgow
20.11.00 Duncan Armstrong W PTS 6 Glasgow
23.02.01 Dave Cotterill L RSC 2 Irvine
30.04.01 Dave Cotterill W RSC 1 Glasgow
04.06.01 Jason Nesbitt W RSC 2 Glasgow
17.09.01 Gary Flear W PTS 8 Glasgow
10.12.01 Jamie McKeever L PTS 6 Liverpool
21.01.02 Joel Viney W PTS 8 Glasgow
01.03.02 Peter Allen W PTS 8 Glasgow
13.04.02 Tony Mulholland L PTS 4 Liverpool
11.05.02 Marc Callaghan L PTS 6 Dagenham
23.09.02 Greg Edwards W RTD 4 Glasgow
08.10.02 Peter Allen W PTS 8 Glasgow
18.11.02 Joel Viney W PTS 6 Glasgow
30.11.02 Colin Toohey L PTS 6 Liverpool
28.02.03 Simon Chambers W RSC 7 Irvine
28.04.03 Craig Spacie L PTS 6 Nottingham
26.07.03 Baz Carey DREW 4 Plymouth
01.11.03 Anthony Hanna W PTS 4 Glasgow
19.01.04 Dariusz Snarski W PTS 6 Glasgow
15.03.04 Baz Carey W PTS 10 Glasgow
(*Vacant British Masters S.Featherweight Title*)
08.05.04 Carl Johanneson L RSC 6 Bristol
(*WBF S.Featherweight Title Challenge*)
26.02.05 Stephen Chinnock W RTD 5 Burton
24.10.05 Kristian Laight W PTS 8 Glasgow
23.02.06 Carl Johanneson L RSC 2 Leeds
(*Final Elim. British S.Featherweight Title*)
06.05.06 Sergii Tertii W PTS 6 Irvine
13.10.06 Frederic Gosset W PTS 6 Irvine
19.02.07 Billy Smith W PTS 6 Glasgow

111

05.06.07 Jay Morris W RSC 3 Glasgow
06.06.08 Simon Fleck W RSC 2 Glasgow
24.10.08 Ted Bami L RSC 1 Bethnal Green
Career: 35 contests, won 24, drew 2, lost 9.

John Fewkes

Sheffield. *Born* Sheffield, 16 July, 1985
Central Area L.Welterweight Champion.
Ht 5'8"
Manager G. Rhodes
17.09.04 Mark Dane W RSC 2 Sheffield
24.10.04 Lea Handley W PTS 6 Sheffield
10.12.04 Jason Nesbitt W PTS 6 Sheffield
04.03.05 Jason Nesbitt W PTS 6 Rotherham
08.05.05 Chris Long W PTS 8 Sheffield
25.06.05 Billy Smith W PTS 6 Wakefield
24.07.05 Karl Taylor W PTS 6 Sheffield
09.09.05 Rakhim Mingaleev W PTS 4 Sheffield
30.10.05 Tony Montana W PTS 6 Sheffield
17.02.06 Tony Montana W PTS 10 Sheffield
　　　(Central Area L.Welterweight Title Challenge)
21.07.06 Kristian Laight W RSC 5 Altrincham
29.09.06 Thomas Mazurkiewicz W PTS 4 Manchester
03.11.06 Scott Haywood W PTS 8 Barnsley
09.02.07 Craig Watson W PTS 8 Leeds
13.07.07 Tontcho Tontchev W PTS 8 Barnsley
19.10.07 Gary Reid W PTS 8 Doncaster
28.03.08 Frederic Gosset W PTS 4 Barnsley
05.09.08 Martin Gethin L RSC 4 Nottingham
　　　(Vacant English Lightweight Title)
Career: 18 contests, won 17, lost 1.

Janos Fidel

Warrington. *Born* Hungary, 13 March, 1978
Welterweight. *Ht* 6'0"
Manager O. Harrison
08.11.08 Shaun Farmer DREW 6 Wigan
27.11.08 Tommy Broadbent L RSC 2 Leeds
Career: 2 contests, drew 1, lost 1.

(John Joseph) Jonjo Finnegan

Burton on Trent. *Born* Burton on Trent, 25
April, 1980
S.Middleweight. *Ht* 6'1"
Manager E. Johnson
08.07.04 Paul Billington W PTS 6 Birmingham
25.11.04 Nick Okoth DREW 6 Birmingham
26.02.05 Arv Mittoo W PTS 4 Burton
07.04.05 Peter Dunn W PTS 6 Birmingham
24.04.05 Omid Bourzo L PTS 6 Derby
30.09.05 Robert Burton DREW 4 Burton
25.11.05 Paul Billington W PTS 6 Walsall
28.01.06 Dave Pearson W PTS 4 Nottingham
25.03.06 Dave Pearson W PTS 8 Burton
13.05.06 Ernie Smith W PTS 6 Sutton in Ashfield
01.06.06 Mark Phillips W PTS 4 Birmingham
16.09.06 Jamie Ambler W PTS 6 Burton
30.09.06 Dave Pearson W PTS 6 Middlesbrough
24.11.06 Dean Walker DREW 4 Nottingham
03.03.07 Neil Tidman L PTS 10 Burton
　　　(Vacant Midlands Area S.Middleweight Title)
21.09.07 Mark Phillips L PTS 10 Burton
　　　(Vacant British Masters L.Heavyweight Title)

16.05.08 Dave Pearson W PTS 4 Burton
12.07.08 Jim Rock L CO 7 Dublin
　　　(Vacant All-Ireland L.Heavyweight Title)
03.10.08 Adam Wilcox L RSC 3 Burton
31.05.09 Ernie Smith W PTS 4 Burton
Career: 20 contests, won 12, drew 3, lost 5.

Terry Flanagan

Manchester. *Born* Manchester, 11 June,
1989
Featherweight. *Ht* 5'9"
Manager S. Wood
24.01.09 Danny McDermid W PTS 6 Blackpool
29.03.09 Delroy Spencer W PTS 6 Bolton
Career: 2 contests, won 2.

Simon Fleck

Leicester. *Born* Leicester, 26 March, 1979
Middleweight. *Ht* 6'0"
Manager M. Shinfield
22.10.05 Simone Lucas W RSC 5 Mansfield
08.12.05 Tommy Jones W PTS 6 Derby
02.03.06 Mark Thompson L CO 3 Blackpool
24.04.06 Karl Taylor W PTS 6 Cleethorpes
14.12.06 Peter Dunn W PTS 6 Leicester
14.05.07 Rocky Muscas W PTS 6 Cleethorpes
06.10.07 Carl Drake DREW 8 Leicester
06.06.08 Andrew Ferrans L RSC 2 Glasgow
11.10.08 Harry Matthews L RTD 2 Hull
15.11.08 Carl Drake L RSC 3 Plymouth
17.05.09 Andrew Butlin L PTS 4 Bolton
25.06.09 Darryl Campbell L RTD 2 Glenrothes
Career: 12 contests, won 5, drew 1, lost 6.

James Flinn

Coventry. *Born* Coventry, 28 February,
1982
Welterweight. *Ht* 5'10¼"
Manager E. Johnson
16.05.08 Lance Verallo W RSC 3 Burton
20.06.08 Paddy Pollock W PTS 4 Wolverhampton
21.12.08 Bheki Moyo W PTS 6 Coventry
06.02.09 Jason Nesbitt W PTS 4 Birmingham
Career: 4 contests, won 4.

Steve Foster

Salford. *Born* Salford, 16 September, 1980
Featherweight. Former WBU Featherweight
Champion. Former Undefeated English
Featherweight Champion. *Ht* 5'6"
Manager F.Warren
15.09.01 Andy Greenaway W PTS 4 Manchester
27.10.01 Gareth Wiltshaw W PTS 4 Manchester
02.03.02 Andy Greenaway W RSC 1 Bethnal Green
04.05.02 Gareth Wiltshaw W PTS 4 Bethnal Green
08.07.02 Ian Turner W RSC 1 Mayfair
20.07.02 Paddy Folan W CO 1 Bethnal Green
28.09.02 Jason White W RSC 3 Manchester
14.12.02 Sean Green W RSC 3 Newcastle
22.03.03 David McIntyre W PTS 4 Renfrew
24.05.03 Henry Janes W PTS 6 Bethnal Green
12.07.03 David McIntyre W RTD 3 Renfrew

18.09.03 Alexander Abramenko W RTD 4 Dagenham
06.11.03 Vladimir Borov W RSC 8 Dagenham
13.12.03 Steve Gethin W RTD 3 Manchester
26.02.04 Sean Hughes W RSC 6 Widnes
　　　(Vacant English Featherweight Title)
30.07.04 Jean-Marie Codet W PTS 8 Bethnal Green
01.10.04 Gary Thornhill W RSC 9 Manchester
　　　(English Featherweight Title Defence)
11.02.05 Livinson Ruiz W CO 10 Manchester
　　　(Vacant WBU Featherweight Title)
16.07.05 Jim Betts W RTD 5 Bolton
10.12.05 Buster Dennis DREW 8 Canning Town
01.04.06 John Simpson W PTS 12 Bethnal Green
　　　(WBU Featherweight Title Defence)
08.07.06 Frederic Bonifai W RSC 2 Cardiff
14.10.06 Derry Matthews L PTS 12 Manchester
　　　(WBU Featherweight Title Defence)
14.07.07 Wladimir Borov W RSC 3 Greenwich
13.10.07 Jean-Marie Codet W CO 1 Bethnal Green
15.12.07 Alex Arthur L PTS 12 Edinburgh
　　　(WBO Interim S.Featherweight Title Challenge)
31.10.08 Jason Nesbitt W PTS 6 Birmingham
Career: 27 contests, won 24, drew 1, lost 2.

Carl Frampton

Belfast. *Born* Belfast, 21 February, 1987
Featherweight. *Ht* 5'4"
Manager B. Hearn
12.06.09 Sandor Szinavel W RSC 2 Liverpool
Career: 1 contest, won 1.

Dean Francis　　　　　Philip Sharkey

Dean Francis

Basingstoke. *Born* Basingstoke, 23 January,
1974
Former Undefeated British, Commonwealth
& IBO Inter-Continental L.Heavyweight
Champion. Former Undefeated English
Cruiserweight Champion. Former
Undefeated British, European & WBO
Inter-Continental S.Middleweight

Champion. *Ht* 5'10½"
Manager Self
28.05.94 Darren Littlewood W PTS 4 Queensway
17.06.94 Martin Jolley W PTS 6 Plymouth
21.07.94 Horace Fleary W RSC 4 Tooting
02.09.94 Steve Osborne W RTD 4 Spitalfields
27.10.94 Tony Booth W CO 1 Bayswater
22.11.94 Darron Griffiths W RTD 1 Bristol
30.03.95 Paul Murray W RSC 2 Bethnal Green
25.05.95 Hunter Clay W RSC 8 Reading
16.06.95 Paul Murray W RTD 3 Southwark
20.10.95 Zafarou Ballogou L RSC 10 Ipswich
 *(WBC International S. Middleweight
 Title Challenge)*
16.12.95 Kid Milo W RSC 3 Cardiff
13.02.96 Mike Bonislawski W RSC 2 Bethnal
 Green
26.04.96 Neil Simpson W RSC 3 Cardiff
08.06.96 John Marceta W RSC 8 Newcastle
14.09.96 Larry Kenny W RSC 2 Sheffield
19.10.96 Rolando Torres W RSC 4 Bristol
 *(Vacant WBO Inter-Continental
 S. Middleweight Title)*
14.03.97 Cornelius Carr W RSC 7 Reading
 *(WBO Inter-Continental
 S. Middleweight Title Defence)*
15.05.97 Kit Munro W RSC 2 Reading
 *(WBO Inter-Continental
 S. Middleweight Title Defence)*
19.07.97 David Starie W RSC 6 Wembley
 *(British S. Middleweight Title
 Challenge)*
19.12.97 Frederic Seillier W RSC 9 Millwall
 (Vacant European S. Middleweight Title)
07.03.98 Mark Baker W RSC 12 Reading
 *(British & WBO Inter-Continental
 S. Middleweight Title Defences)*
22.08.98 Xolani Ngemntu W CO 2
 Hammanskraal, South Africa
 *(WBO Inter-Continental
 S. Middleweight Title Defence)*
31.10.98 Undra White L RTD 4 Basingstoke
 *(Vacant IBO Inter-Continental
 S. Middleweight Title)*
20.04.02 Mondili Mbonambi W PTS 8 Wembley
29.03.03 Matthew Barney L PTS 12 Wembley
 (Vacant British S. Middleweight Title)
09.07.05 Paul Bonson W PTS 6 Bristol
12.11.05 Hastings Rasani W RSC 6 Bristol
25.02.06 Tommy Eastwood W PTS 10 Bristol
 (Vacant English Cruiserweight Title)
07.10.06 Hastings Rasani W CO 2 Weston super
 Mare
09.02.07 Ovill McKenzie W RSC 1 Bristol
 *(Commonwealth L.Heavyweight Title
 Challenge)*
02.06.07 Ayitey Powers W CO 9 Bristol
 *(Vacant IBO Inter-Continental
 L.Heavyweight Title)*
08.12.07 Michael Gbenga W PTS 12 Bolton
 *(Commonwealth L.Heavyweight Title
 Defence)*
13.06.08 Tony Oakey W RSC 9 Portsmouth
 *(Commonwealth L.Heavyweight Title
 Defence. British L.Heavyweight Title
 Challenge)*

13.02.09 Joey Vegas DREW 8 Swindon
19.05.09 Neil Simpson W RSC 3 Kensington
19.05.09 John Keeton L CO 1 Kensington
Career: 36 contests, won 31, drew 1, lost 4..

Carl Froch

Nottingham. *Born* Nottingham, 2 July, 1977
WBC S.Middleweight Champion. Former
Undefeated British, Commonwealth &
English S.Middleweight Champion. *Ht* 6'4"
Manager Self
16.03.02 Michael Pinnock W RSC 4 Bethnal
 Green
10.05.02 Ojay Abrahams W RSC 1 Bethnal Green
23.08.02 Darren Covill W RSC 1 Bethnal Green
25.10.02 Paul Bonson W PTS 6 Bethnal Green
21.12.02 Mike Duffield W RSC 1 Dagenham
28.01.03 Valery Odin W RSC 6 Nottingham
05.03.03 Varuzhan Davtyan W RSC 5 Bethnal
 Green
16.04.03 Michael Monaghan W RSC 3
 Nottingham
04.10.03 Vage Kocharyan W PTS 8 Muswell Hill
28.11.03 Alan Page W RSC 7 Derby
 *(Vacant English S.Middleweight Title.
 Elim. British S.Middleweight Title)*
30.01.04 Dmitri Adamovich W RSC 2 Dagenham
12.03.04 Charles Adamu W PTS 12 Nottingham
 *(Commonwealth S.Middleweight Title
 Challenge)*
02.06.04 Mark Woolnough W RSC 11
 Nottingham
 *(Commonwealth S.Middleweight Title
 Defence)*
24.09.04 Damon Hague W RSC 1 Nottingham
 *(Vacant British S.Middleweight Title.
 Commonwealth S.Middleweight Title
 Defence)*
21.04.05 Henry Porras W RSC 8 Hollywood,
 California, USA
09.07.05 Matthew Barney W PTS 12 Nottingham
 *(British & Commonwealth
 S.Middleweight Title Defences)*
02.12.05 Ruben Groenewald W RSC 5
 Nottingham
 *(Commonwealth S.Middleweight Title
 Defence)*
17.02.06 Dale Westerman W RSC 9 Bethnal
 Green
 *(Commonwealth S.Middleweight Title
 Defence)*
26.05.06 Brian Magee W RSC 11 Bethnal Green
 *(British & Commonwealth
 S.Middleweight Title Defences)*
24.11.06 Tony Dodson W CO 3 Nottingham
 *(British & Commonwealth
 S.Middleweight Title Defences)*
23.03.07 Sergei Tatevosyan W RSC 2 Nottingham
09.11.07 Robin Reid W RTD 5 Nottingham
 *(British S.Middleweight Title
 Defence)*
10.05.08 Albert Rybacki W RSC 4 Nottingham
06.12.08 Jean Pascal W PTS 12 Nottingham
 (Vacant WBC S.Middleweight Title)
25.04.09 Jermain Taylor W RSC 12
 Mashantucket, Connecticut, USA
 (WBC S.Middleweight Title Defence)
Career: 25 contests, won 25.

Michael Frontin

Edmonton. *Born* Mauritius, 25 November,
1977
L.Welterweight. *Ht* 5'6¼"
Manager C. Sanigar
01.12.07 Ben Murphy W PTS 4 Bethnal Green
10.12.07 Alexander Spitjo L PTS 6 Birmingham
01.03.08 Scott Lawton L PTS 6 Stoke
22.03.08 Nicki Smedley L PTS 6 Sheffield
13.09.08 Ryan Barrett DREW 4 Bethnal Green
17.10.08 Ajose Olusegun L PTS 6 Bethnal Green
15.11.08 Ben Murphy L PTS 6 Bethnal Green
29.05.09 Scott Haywood W PTS 6 Stoke
12.06.09 Nathan Brough L PTS 6 Liverpool
Career: 9 contests, won 2, drew 1, lost 6.

Courtney Fry

Wood Green. *Born* Enfield, 19 May, 1975
L.Heavyweight. *Ht* 6'1¼"
Manager J. Feld
29.03.03 Harry Butler W RSC 3 Wembley
31.05.03 Darren Ashton W PTS 4 Bethnal Green
24.10.03 Ovill McKenzie W PTS 4 Bethnal
 Green
20.03.04 Clint Johnson W RSC 2 Wembley
02.04.04 Paulino Da Silva W PTS 4 Plymouth
08.05.04 Radcliffe Green W PTS 6 Bristol
19.06.04 Valery Odin W PTS 8 Muswell Hill
17.12.04 Varuzhan Davtyan W RTD 2 Liverpool
13.05.05 Ovill McKenzie L PTS 4 Liverpool
07.04.06 Vasyl Kondor W PTS 6 Bristol
21.09.07 Nick Okoth W RSC 1 Bethnal Green
01.02.08 Tony Salam W CO 6 Bethnal Green
02.10.08 Jevgenijs Andrejevs W PTS 6
 Piccadilly
20.02.09 Shon Davies W PTS 3 Bethnal Green
20.02.09 Tony Oakey L PTS 3 Bethnal Green
Career: 15 contests, won 13, lost 2.

Nicky Furness

Kimberley. *Born* Nottingham, 13
September, 1983
L.Middleweight. *Ht* 5' 10"
Manager J. Tugby
05.10.08 Dennis Corpe W PTS 4 Nottingham
Career: 1 contest, won 1.

Phil Fury

Lancaster. *Born* Lancaster, 25 April, 1991
L.Middleweight. *Ht* 6' 0"
Manager R. McCracken
23.05.09 Lewis Byrne W PTS 4 Watford
13.06.09 Matt Seawright W RSC 2 Wigan
Career: 2 contests, won 2.

Tyson Fury

Wilmslow. *Born* Manchester, 1 June, 1988
Heavyweight. *Ht* 6' 7"
Manager R. McCracken
06.12.08 Bela Gyongyosi W RSC 1 Nottingham
17.01.09 Marcel Zeller W RSC 3 Wigan
28.02.09 Daniil Peretyatko W RTD 2 Norwich
14.03.09 Lee Swaby W RTD 4 Birmingham
11.04.09 Matthew Ellis W CO 1 Bethnal Green
23.05.09 Scott Belshaw W RSC 2 Watford
Career: 6 contests, won 6.

Luke Gallear

Derby. *Born* Derby, 20 December, 1984
L.Middleweight. *Ht* 5'9"
Manager M. Shinfield
31.03.07 Surinder Sekhon L PTS 6 Derby
10.12.07 John Wainwright L RSC 3 Cleethorpes
16.05.08 Kevin McCauley W PTS 6 Burton
08.12.08 Nick Coret DREW 6 Cleethorpes
31.05.09 Duane Parker L PTS 6 Burton
Career: 5 contests, won 1, drew 1, lost 3.

Scott Gammer

Pembroke Dock. *Born* Pembroke Dock, 24
October, 1976
Heavyweight. Former British Heavyweight
Champion. *Ht* 6'2"
Manager P. Boyce
15.09.02 Leighton Morgan W RSC 1 Swansea
26.10.02 James Gilbert W RSC 1 Maesteg
08.01.03 Dave Clarke W PTS 4 Aberdare
25.01.03 Ahmad Cheleh W CO 1 Bridgend
28.06.03 Dave Clarke W RSC 1 Cardiff
13.09.03 Derek McCafferty W PTS 6 Newport
08.11.03 Mendauga Kulikauskas DREW 6
 Bridgend
28.02.04 James Zikic W PTS 6 Bridgend
01.05.04 Paul Buttery W CO 1 Bridgend
02.06.04 Paul King W RSC 3 Hereford
17.09.04 Carl Baker W PTS 4 Plymouth
05.11.04 Roman Bugaj W RSC 2 Hereford
18.02.05 Micky Steeds W PTS 6 Brighton
15.05.05 Mark Krence W RSC 8 Sheffield
 (Elim. British Heavyweight Title)
30.09.05 Julius Francis W PTS 8 Carmarthen
10.12.05 Suren Kalachyan W PTS 6 Canning
 Town
16.06.06 Mark Krence W RSC 9 Carmarthen
 (Vacant British Heavyweight Title)
13.10.06 Micky Steeds W PTS 12 Aberavon
 (British Heavyweight Title Defence)
02.03.07 Danny Williams L CO 9 Neath
 (British Heavyweight Title Defence)
10.06.07 Paul King W PTS 6 Neath
29.09.07 John McDermott L PTS 10 Sheffield
 (Elim. British Heavyweight Title)
30.08.08 Francesco Pianeta L RTD 8 Prenzlauer
 Berg, Germany
 *(Vacant European Union Heavyweight
 Title)*
30.05.09 Robert Helenius L CO 6 Helsinki,
 Finland
Career: 23 contests, won 18, drew 1, lost 4.

Frankie Gavin

Birmingham. *Born* Birmingham, 28
September, 1985
L.Welterweight. *Ht* 5' 10"
Manager F. Warren
28.02.09 George Kadaria W RSC 4 Birmingham
15.05.09 Mourad Frarema W RSC 3 Belfast
Career: 2 contests, won 2.

Frankie Gavin   Philip Sharkey

(Boris) Bobby George (Georgiev)

London. *Born* Bulgaria, 5 December, 1982
Welterweight. *Ht* 5' 9"
Manager J. Eames
27.06.09 Lanquaye Wilson W RSC 1 Portsmouth
Career: 1 contest, won 1.

Darren Gethin

Walsall. *Born* Walsall, 19 August, 1976
Former Midlands Area Welterweight
Champion. Former Undefeated British
Masters L.Middleweight Champion. *Ht*
5'8"
Manager E. Johnson
08.07.04 Joe Mitchell DREW 6 Birmingham
12.09.04 Joe Mitchell W PTS 6 Shrewsbury
12.11.04 Tyrone McInerney L PTS 4 Halifax
26.02.05 Tye Williams DREW 4 Burton
18.04.05 Joe Mitchell W PTS 6 Bradford
25.04.05 Terry Carruthers L RSC 3 Cleethorpes
02.06.05 Franny Jones L PTS 8 Yarm
02.09.05 Scott Conway W RSC 1 Derby
10.09.05 Nathan Cleverly L PTS 4 Cardiff
01.10.05 Jonathan Hussey L PTS 6 Wigan
22.10.05 Joe McCluskey DREW 6 Coventry
12.02.06 Mark Thompson L PTS 4 Manchester
23.02.06 Khurram Hussain DREW 4 Leeds
03.03.06 Jason Rushton W PTS 6 Doncaster
24.04.06 Gary McArthur L PTS 6 Glasgow
09.05.06 Danny Reynolds DREW 4 Leeds
18.05.06 Lance Hall W PTS 6 Walsall
01.06.06 Craig Dickson W PTS 6 Birmingham
12.07.06 John O'Donnell L PTS 8 Bethnal Green
11.12.06 Simon Sherrington W PTS 10
 Birmingham
 *(Vacant British Masters L.Middleweight
 Title)*
19.02.07 Lee Noble L PTS 6 Glasgow
23.03.07 Tyan Booth W RSC 10 Nottingham
 *(Vacant Midlands Area Welterweight
 Title)*
10.09.07 Craig Dickson L PTS 6 Glasgow
09.11.07 Adnan Amar L RSC 10 Nottingham
 *(Midlands Area Welterweight Title
 Defence)*
01.02.08 Mark Thompson L RTD 2 Bethnal
 Green
22.03.08 Kell Brook L RTD 3 Cardiff

16.05.08 Chris Black L PTS 6 Motherwell
23.05.08 Chris Johnson L RSC 5 Wigan
12.06.09 Vince Baldassara L RSC 4 Clydebank
Career: 29 contests, won 8, drew 5, lost 16.

Martin Gethin
Walsall. *Born* Walsall, 16 November, 1983
Former English Lightweight Champion.
Former Undefeated Midlands Area
Lightweight Champion. Former Undefeated
British Masters L.Welterweight Champion.
Ht 5'6"
Manager E. Johnson
18.11.04 Kristian Laight W RSC 4 Shrewsbury
15.04.05 Jason Nesbitt W PTS 6 Shrewsbury
06.10.05 John-Paul Ryan W RSC 2 Dudley
25.11.05 Michael Medor W PTS 4 Walsall
10.03.06 Carl Allen W PTS 4 Walsall
01.06.06 Baz Carey W PTS 4 Birmingham
07.11.06 Kristian Laight W PTS 6 Leeds
05.12.06 Judex Meemea W RSC 3
    Wolverhampton
    (Vacant British Masters L.Welterweight
    Title)
20.04.07 Carl Allen DREW 6 Dudley
15.09.07 Craig Johnson W PTS 10 Birmingham
    (Vacant Midlands Area Lightweight
    Title)
08.10.07 Darren Broomhall W RSC 3
    Birmingham
07.12.07 Fabian Luque W RSC 4 Las Vegas,
    Nevada, USA
25.01.08 Carl Allen W PTS 6 Dagenham
25.02.08 Ali Wyatt W PTS 8 Birmingham
11.07.08 Nadeem Siddique W RSC 7 Wigan
05.09.08 John Fewkes W RSC 4 Nottingham
    (Vacant English Lightweight Title)
06.12.08 Scott Lawton L RSC 9 Nottingham
    (English Lightweight Title Defence)
28.03.09 John Watson L PTS 10 Liverpool
    (Elim. British Lightweight Title)
18.05.09 Chris Long L PTS 4 Birmingham
28.06.09 Jason Nesbitt W PTS 4 Luton
Career: 20 contests, won 16, drew 1, lost 3.

Martin Gethin   Philip Sharkey

Steve Gethin   Philip Sharkey

Steve Gethin
Walsall. *Born* Walsall, 30 July, 1978
Lightweight. *Ht* 5'9"
Manager E. Johnson
03.09.99 Ike Halls W RSC 3 West Bromwich
24.10.99 Ricky Bishop W RSC 4 Wolverhampton
22.01.00 Sebastian Hart L PTS 4 Birmingham
10.09.00 Nigel Senior DREW 6 Walsall
03.06.01 Richmond Asante L PTS 4 Southwark
28.11.01 Mickey Coveney L PTS 4 Bethnal
    Green
09.12.01 Gary Groves W PTS 6 Shaw
17.02.02 Gary Groves W PTS 6 Wolverhampton
01.06.02 Gary Davies W RSC 2 Manchester
21.09.02 Marc Callaghan L PTS 6 Brentwood
02.12.02 Neil Read W RTD 3 Leicester
14.12.02 Isaac Ward L PTS 4 Newcastle
08.02.03 Rocky Dean DREW 4 Norwich
15.02.03 Anthony Hanna W PTS 6
    Wolverhampton
08.05.03 Derry Matthews L RSC 3 Widnes
07.09.03 Henry Janes L PTS 4 Shrewsbury
02.10.03 Mark Moran L PTS 4 Liverpool
20.10.03 John Simpson L PTS 8 Glasgow
30.10.03 Gareth Payne W PTS 6 Dudley
13.12.03 Steve Foster L RTD 3 Manchester
05.03.04 Isaac Ward L PTS 6 Darlington
27.05.04 Marc Callaghan L PTS 6 Huddersfield
30.07.04 Chris Hooper L PTS 4 Bethnal Green
08.10.04 Ian Napa L PTS 6 Brentwood
22.10.04 Andy Bell L RSC 5 Mansfield
17.12.04 Mark Moran L PTS 4 Liverpool
13.02.05 Patrick Hyland L PTS 4 Brentwood
24.04.05 Darren Broomhall W CO 5 Derby
09.07.05 Billy Corcoran L PTS 6 Nottingham
05.11.05 Amir Khan L RSC 3 Renfrew
24.03.06 Ian Wilson L PTS 4 Bethnal Green
06.05.06 Paul Newby L PTS 4 Birmingham
13.05.06 Andy Bell W RSC 2 Sutton in Ashfield
21.05.06 Mark Alexander L PTS 4 Bethnal Green
30.09.06 Paul Truscott L PTS 4 Middlesbrough
13.10.06 Gary McArthur L PTS 6 Irvine
21.10.06 Ryan Barrett L PTS 6 Glasgow
28.10.06 Steve Bell L RTD 5 Bethnal Green
02.12.06 Mitch Prince L PTS 6 Clydebank
15.12.06 Ben Jones L PTS 4 Bethnal Green

22.01.07 Darren Johnstone L PTS 10 Glasgow
    (British Masters S.Featherweight Title
    Challenge)
30.03.07 David Mulholland L PTS 4 Crawley
20.04.07 Billy Corcoran L PTS 8 Dudley
13.07.07 Akaash Bhatia L RSC 5 Barnsley
13.10.07 Esham Pickering L RTD 3 Newark
01.12.07 Rocky Dean L RSC 5 Bethnal Green
25.01.08 Ben Jones L PTS 4 Dagenham
16.02.08 Jon Kays L PTS 6 Blackpool
23.02.08 Robin Deakin W PTS 4 Crawley
14.03.08 Anthony Crolla L PTS 6 Manchester
16.11.08 Anser Hussein L PTS 6 Shaw
26.11.08 Jamie Arthur L PTS 4 Piccadilly
13.12.08 Gareth Couch L PTS 4 Brentwood
20.12.08 Alfonso Vieyra L PTS 4 Bristol
23.01.09 Samir Mouneimne DREW 4 Stoke
16.02.09 Richard Barclay L PTS 6 Glasgow
28.02.09 Stephen Smith L RTD 1 Birmingham
17.04.09 Dean Mills L RSC 2 Bristol
17.05.09 Jon Kays L PTS 4 Bolton
24.05.09 Alan Winterbottom L PTS 6 Shaw
Career: 60 contests, won 11, drew 3, lost 46.

Richard Ghent
Coseley. *Born* West Bromwich, 23
November, 1987
L.Welterweight. *Ht* 5' 8"
Manager P. Rowson
09.11.08 Kristian Laight W PTS 4
    Wolverhampton
27.02.09 Craig Dyer W PTS 4 Wolverhampton
29.05.09 Jason Thompson W RSC 3 Dudley
Career: 3 contests, won 3.

Phil Gill   Philip Sharkey

Phil Gill
Waltham Abbey. *Born* Epping, 6 May,
1982
Welterweight. *Ht* 5' 6"
Manager M. Helliet
05.03.09 Johnny Greaves W PTS 4 Limehouse
12.06.09 Craig Dyer W PTS 4 Bethnal Green
Career: 2 contests, won 2.

Bobby Gladman   Philip Sharkey

Bobby Gladman

Ware. *Born* Edgware, 17 May, 1986
Welterweight. *Ht* 5' 11"
Manager M. Helliet
23.04.09 Karl Taylor W PTS 6 Mayfair
12.06.09 William Warburton W PTS 4 Bethnal
Green
Career: 2 contests, won 2.

Tom Glover   Philip Sharkey

Tom Glover

Maldon, Essex. *Born* Maldon, 21 June,
1981
Southern Area Welterweight Champion.
Former Undefeated British Masters
Lightweight Champion. *Ht* 5'6½"
Manager A. Sims
11.02.06 Billy Smith W PTS 4 Bethnal Green
24.03.06 Gavin Tait L PTS 4 Bethnal Green
03.06.06 Ben Hudson W PTS 4 Chigwell
26.10.06 James Gorman DREW 6 Belfast
09.12.06 Rocky Muscas W PTS 4 Chigwell
26.01.07 Nathan Weise DREW 4 Dagenham

01.07.07 John Baguley W PTS 10 Colchester
*(Vacant British Masters Lightweight
Title)*
07.09.07 Nadeem Siddique L PTS 6 Doncaster
05.10.07 Leonard Lothian L PTS 4 Bethnal
Green
25.11.07 Gavin Deacon W PTS 6 Colchester
04.04.08 Gareth Couch L PTS 6 Bethnal Green
10.05.08 Jack Perry DREW 4 Nottingham
03.10.08 Tristan Davies L PTS 6 Burton
15.11.08 Scott Woolford W PTS 10 Bethnal
Green
*(Vacant Southern Area Welterweight
Title)*
14.03.09 Chas Symonds W PTS 8 Birmingham
13.06.09 Nadeem Siddique W DIS 9 Wigan
Career: 16 contests, won 8, drew 3, lost 5.

Rick Godding

Bolton. *Born* Bolton, 18 February, 1985
L.Welterweight. *Ht* 5'10¼"
Manager S. Wood
23.12.07 Kristian Laight W PTS 6 Bolton
16.02.08 Senol Dervis W PTS 6 Blackpool
15.06.08 Carl Allen W PTS 6 St Helens
14.09.08 Johnny Greaves W PTS 4 Wigan
22.11.08 Daniel Thorpe W PTS 4 Blackpool
06.03.09 Kristian Laight W PTS 4 Wigan
29.03.09 Russell Pearce W RTD 2 Bolton
17.05.09 Carl Allen W PTS 4 Bolton
Career: 8 contests, won 8..

Michael Gomez (Armstrong)

Manchester. *Born* Dublin, 21 June, 1977
Lightweight. Former WBU S.Featherweight
Champion. Former Undefeated WBO Inter-
Continental & British S.Featherweight
Champion. Former WBO Inter-Continental
S.Featherweight Champion. Former
Undefeated Central Area & IBF Inter-
Continental Featherweight Champion.
Ht 5'5"
Manager S. Wood
10.06.95 Danny Ruegg W PTS 6 Manchester
15.09.95 Greg Upton L PTS 4 Mansfield
24.11.95 Danny Ruegg L PTS 4 Manchester
19.09.96 Martin Evans W RSC 1 Manchester
09.11.96 David Morris W PTS 4 Manchester
22.03.97 John Farrell W RSC 2 Wythenshawe
03.05.97 Chris Williams L PTS 4 Manchester
11.09.97 Wayne Jones W RSC 2 Widnes
18.04.98 Benny Jones W PTS 4 Manchester
16.05.98 Craig Spacie W RSC 3 Bethnal Green
05.09.98 Pete Buckley W PTS 6 Telford
14.11.98 David Jeffrey W RSC 1 Cheshunt
19.12.98 Kevin Sheil W RSC 4 Liverpool
13.02.99 Dave Hinds W PTS 6 Newcastle
27.02.99 Chris Jickells W RSC 5 Oldham
*(Vacant Central Area Featherweight
Title)*
29.05.99 Nigel Leake W RSC 2 Halifax
*(Vacant IBF Inter-Continental
Featherweight Title)*
07.08.99 William Alverzo W PTS 6 Atlantic City,
New Jersey, USA
04.09.99 Gary Thornhill W RSC 2 Bethnal Green
(Vacant British S. Featherweight Title)

06.11.99 Jose Juan Manjarrez W PTS 12 Widnes
*(WBO Inter-Continental
S. Featherweight Title Defence)*
11.12.99 Oscar Galindo W RSC 11 Liverpool
*(WBO Inter-Continental
S. Featherweight Title Defence)*
29.01.00 Chris Jickells W RSC 4 Manchester
29.02.00 Dean Pithie W PTS 12 Widnes
(British S. Featherweight Title Defence)
24.06.00 Carl Allen W CO 2 Glasgow
08.07.00 Carl Greaves W CO 2 Widnes
(British S. Featherweight Title Defence)
19.10.00 Awel Abdulai W PTS 8 Harrisburg,
USA
11.12.00 Ian McLeod W PTS 12 Widnes
(British S.Featherweight Title Defence)
10.02.01 Laszlo Bognar L RSC 9 Widnes
*(WBO Inter-Continental
S. Featherweight Title Defence)*
07.07.01 Laszlo Bognar W RSC 3 Manchester
*(WBO Inter-Continental
S. Featherweight Title Challenge)*
27.10.01 Craig Docherty W RSC 2 Manchester
(British S.Featherweight Title Defence)
01.06.02 Kevin Lear L RTD 8 Manchester
(Vacant WBU S. Featherweight Title)
28.09.02 Jimmy Beech W RSC 4 Manchester
18.01.03 Rakhim Mingaleev W RTD 4 Preston
05.04.03 Vladimir Borov W RSC 3 Manchester
25.10.03 Alex Arthur W RSC 5 Edinburgh
*(British S.Featherweight Title
Challenge)*
03.04.04 Ben Odamattey W RSC 3 Manchester
(Vacant WBU S.Featherweight Title)
22.05.04 Justin Juuko W RSC 2 Widnes
(WBU S.Featherweight Title Defence)
01.10.04 Leva Kirakosyan W RTD 6 Manchester
(WBU S.Featherweight Title Defence)
11.02.05 Javier Osvaldo Alvarez L RSC 6
Manchester
(WBU S.Featherweight Title Defence)
28.01.06 Peter McDonagh L RSC 5 Dublin
(Vacant All-Ireland Lightweight Title)
06.05.07 Daniel Thorpe W RSC 3 Altrincham
24.06.07 Youssef Al Hamidi W RTD 3 Wigan
19.10.07 Carl Johanneson L RSC 6 Doncaster
*(British S.Featherweight Title
Challenge)*
29.03.08 Baz Carey W PTS 6 Glasgow
21.06.08 Amir Khan L RSC 5 Birmingham
*(Commonwealth Lightweight Title
Challenge)*
28.09.08 Chris Brophy W RSC 2 Colne
10.10.08 Baz Carey W PTS 6 Motherwell
21.12.08 Chris Long W PTS 6 Motherwell
27.03.09 Ricky Burns L RSC 7 Glasgow
*(Commonwealth S.Featherweight Title
Challenge)*
Career: 48 contests, won 38, lost 10.

Adrian Gonzalez

Manchester. *Born* Riverside, California,
USA, 10 February, 1991
Featherweight. *Ht* 5' 11"
Manager R. Hatton
22.11.08 Jose Pacheco W PTS 4 Las Vegas,

Nevada, USA
14.03.09 Delroy Spencer W PTS 4 Bristol
28.03.09 Pavels Senkovs W PTS 4 Altrincham
Career: 3 contests, won 3.

Eamonn Goodbrand

Birkenshaw. *Born* Bellshill Scotalnd, 2
June, 1988
L.Middleweight. *Ht* 6' 1"
Manager R. Bannan
26.01.07 Rocky Muscas W PTS 6 Glasgow
16.03.07 Duncan Cottier W PTS 6 Glasgow
25.05.07 Steve Cooper W PTS 6 Glasgow
10.10.08 Yassine El Maachi L PTS 6 Motherwell
18.10.08 Kevin Lilley W PTS 6 Paisley
Career: 5 contests, won 4, lost 1.

Chris Goodwin

Chester. *Born* Chester, 31 October, 1988
Welterweight. *Ht* 5'7½"
Manager S. Goodwin
07.12.06 Chris Mullen L PTS 6 Sunderland
24.02.07 Kristian Laight W PTS 6 Stoke
12.05.07 James Lilley W PTS 4 Stoke
17.11.07 Pete Buckley W PTS 4 Stoke
01.03.08 Johnny Greaves W PTS 6 Stoke
17.05.08 Baz Carey W PTS 4 Stoke
06.06.08 Carl Allen W PTS 4 Stoke
13.09.08 Karl Taylor W PTS 4 Stoke
06.12.08 Scott Sandmann DREW 6 Wigan
17.01.09 Jon Baguley W PTS 4 Wigan
13.02.09 Daniel Thorpe W PTS 6 Wigan
07.03.09 Jimmy Briggs W PTS 6 Chester
23.05.09 Lester Walsh W PTS 6 Queensferry
Career: 13 contests, won 11, drew 1, lost 1.

Phil Goodwin

Hull. *Born* Hull, 2 May, 1980
L.Heavyweight. *Ht* 5'10"
Manager Self
25.09.07 Philip Callaghan W PTS 6 Hull
30.11.07 James Tucker W PTS 6 Hull
07.03.08 Rasham Sohi L RSC 3 Nottingham
21.06.08 Dave Pearson W RSC 2 Hull
11.10.08 Robert Burton W PTS 6 Hull
12.12.08 Tony Bellew L CO 2 Widnes
13.03.09 Justyn Hugh L PTS 6 Newport
Career: 7 contests, won 4, lost 3.

Martin Gordon   Philip Sharkey

Martin Gordon

Brierley Hill. *Born* Wordsley, 23 July, 1982
Welterweight. *Ht* 5'9"
Manager E. Johnson
26.10.06 Bheki Moyo DREW 6 Dudley
17.11.06 Billy Smith L PTS 6 Brierley Hill
06.12.06 Wayne Downing L PTS 6 Stoke
20.04.07 Kristian Laight L PTS 4 Dudley
28.11.07 Wayne Downing L PTS 4 Walsall
28.02.08 Matt Seawright L PTS 4
            Wolverhampton
24.07.08 Chris Thompson DREW 4
            Wolverhampton
09.11.08 Matt Seawright L PTS 4 Wolverhampton
29.05.09 Jason Nesbitt W PTS 4 Dudley
Career: 9 contests, won 1, drew 2, lost 6.

Billy Graham

Sutton in Ashfield. *Born* Falkirk, 2
September, 1983
Welterweight. *Ht* 6' 0"
Manager M. Shinfield
08.12.08 Jimmy Briggs W PTS 6 Cleethorpes
Career: 1 contest, won 1.

Nathan Graham   Philip Sharkey

Nathan Graham

Aylesbury. *Born* Aylesbury, 21 September,
1982
L.Middleweight. *Ht* 5' 9"
Manager Self
24.04.04 Tom Price W RSC 2 Reading
02.12.04 David Payne W RSC 3 Crystal Palace
26.03.05 Gatis Skuja W RSC 1 Hackney
19.11.05 Geraint Harvey W PTS 4 Southwark
26.02.06 Duncan Cottier W PTS 4 Dagenham
21.10.06 Imad Khamis W RSC 2 Southwark
02.12.06 Tyan Booth L PTS 6 Southwark
05.10.08 Geraint Harvey W PTS 4 Watford
27.03.09 JJ Bird W PTS 4 Kensington
Career: 9 contests, won 8, lost 1.

Martyn Grainger

Rochdale. *Born* Thorne, 8 July, 1984
Heavyweight. *Ht* 6' 3"
Manager O. Harrison

06.12.08 Paul Bonson L RSC 3 Wigan
13.02.09 Jason Callum W PTS 4 Wigan
03.04.09 Hastings Rasani W RSC 1 Leigh
Career: 3 contests, won 2, lost 1.

Michael Grant   Philip Sharkey

Michael Grant

Tottenham. *Born* London, 2 November,
1983
L.Welterweight. *Ht* 5' 7"
Manager J. Eames
24.07.05 David Kehoe W PTS 4 Leicester Square
16.09.05 Judex Meemea W RSC 3 Plymouth
09.10.05 Ali Wyatt DREW 4 Hammersmith
13.01.06 Patrik Prokopecz W PTS 4 Torrevieja,
            Spain
02.02.06 Peter Buckley W PTS 4 Piccadilly
30.03.06 Franck Aiello W PTS 4 Piccadilly
19.05.06 Lubos Priehradnik W PTS 6 Torrevieja,
            Spain
03.06.06 Ali Wyatt W PTS 4 Chigwell
24.09.06 Jav Jerome W PTS 4 Bethnal Green
13.10.06 Ceri Hall W PTS 6 Port Talbot
27.09.08 Jay Morris W DIS 6 Bethnal Green
15.11.08 Gary Reid W PTS 6 Greenwich
01.02.09 Christopher Sebire W PTS 6 Bethnal
            Green
Career: 13 contests, won 12, drew 1.

Keiron Gray   Philip Sharkey

Keiron Gray

Telford. *Born* West Bromwich, 8 January, 1978
Middleweight. *Ht* 5'10¼"
Manager E. Johnson
10.05.08 Lee Duncan W RSC 3 Nottingham
20.06.08 Tony Stones W PTS 4 Wolverhampton
12.09.08 Davey Jones W PTS 4 Wolverhampton
09.11.08 Matt Scriven W PTS 4 Wolverhampton
01.02.09 Paul Royston W PTS 6 Edgbaston
Career: 5 contests, won 5.

Johnny Greaves

East Ham. *Born* Forest Gate, 4 March, 1979
L.Welterweight. *Ht* 5'9"
Manager C. Greaves
09.06.07 Rob Hunt L PTS 6 Middlesbrough
28.06.07 Dean Harrison L PTS 6 Dudley
14.07.07 Jamie Cox L PTS 4 Greenwich
11.08.07 John Watson L PTS 4 Liverpool
16.09.07 Dwayne Hill L PTS 6 Sheffield
06.10.07 Anthony Crolla L RSC 3 Nottingham
25.11.07 Lee Purdy L PTS 6 Colchester
10.12.07 Darren Hamilton L RSC 3 Peterborough
01.02.08 Jamie Radford L PTS 4 Bethnal Green
15.02.08 Paul Holborn L PTS 6 Sunderland
23.02.08 Sergei Rozhakmens W RSC 1 Newark
01.03.08 Chris Goodwin L PTS 6 Stoke
08.03.08 Eddie Corcoran L PTS 4 Greenwich
17.03.08 Stuart Green L PTS 8 Glasgow
18.04.08 Scott Woolford L RSC 3 Bethnal Green
14.06.08 Liam Walsh L CO 4 Bethnal Green
14.09.08 Rick Godding L PTS 4 Wigan
27.09.08 Mark McCullough L PTS 6 Bracknell
04.10.08 Lee Purdy L RSC 3 Norwich
07.11.08 Peter Jones L PTS 4 Wigan
15.11.08 Ben Wakeham L PTS 6 Plymouth
29.11.08 Jamie Spence L PTS 4 Sleaford
06.12.08 Ryan Walsh L PTS 4 Canning Town
21.12.08 Karl Place L PTS 4 Bolton
23.01.09 Scott Lawton L PTS 6 Stoke
13.02.09 Danny Stewart L PTS 4 Swindon
05.03.09 Phil Gill L PTS 4 Limehouse
13.03.09 Lee Selby L PTS 6 Newport
20.03.09 Liam Shinkwin L PTS 6 Newham
29.03.09 Gary Sykes L PTS 4 Bolton
10.04.09 Richie Wyatt L PTS 4 Birmingham
17.04.09 Tyrone Nurse L PTS 4 Leigh
14.05.09 Adil Anwar L RSC 4 Leeds
12.06.09 Gavin Tait L PTS 4 Bethnal Green
19.06.09 Santino Caruana L PTS 4 Glasgow
30.06.09 Ryan Evans L PTS 4 Bethnal Green
Career: 36 contests, won 1, lost 35.

Stuart Green

Glenrothes. *Born* Kirkcaldy, 13 December, 1984
L.Welterweight. *Ht* 5'6"
Manager T. Gilmour
17.11.03 Chris Long W PTS 6 Glasgow
12.03.04 Jason Nesbitt W PTS 8 Irvine
07.06.04 Gavin Tait W PTS 6 Glasgow
11.10.04 Paul Holborn L PTS 6 Glasgow
21.02.05 Pete Buckley W PTS 6 Glasgow
11.06.05 Dave Hinds W PTS 6 Kirkcaldy
30.09.05 Fred Janes W PTS 4 Kirkcaldy
17.03.06 Adam Kelly W PTS 4 Kirkcaldy
21.04.06 Michael Kelly L PTS 4 Belfast
27.05.06 Lee McAllister L RSC 8 Aberdeen
(Vacant Scottish Area Lightweight Title)
09.09.06 Pete Buckley W PTS 8 Inverurie
18.09.06 Pete Buckley W PTS 6 Glasgow
06.10.06 Dean Hickman L PTS 6 Wolverhampton
03.11.06 Martin Kristjansen L PTS 6 Skive, Denmark
13.12.06 Chris Long W PTS 6 Strand
01.02.07 Sam Rukundo L PTS 6 Piccadilly
02.03.07 Ceri Hall L RSC 9 Neath
(Vacant Celtic L.Welterweight Title)
17.03.08 Johnny Greaves W PTS 8 Glasgow
10.11.08 Steve Williams L PTS 8 Glasgow
19.01.09 Charles Paul King L PTS 10 Glasgow
(Vacant Scottish Area Lightweight Title)
24.03.09 Stephen Burke L PTS 3 Glasgow
Career: 21 contests, won 11, lost 10.

Carl Griffiths

Oakham. *Born* Leicester, 4 July, 1984
Lightweight. *Ht* 5'5¾"
Manager D. Cowland
30.03.07 Tony McQuade L PTS 6 Peterborough
21.06.07 Sergei Rozhakmens W PTS 6 Peterborough
21.09.07 Sebastian Hart L CO 2 Peterborough
10.12.07 Leroy Smedley W RSC 2 Leicester
16.02.08 Dean Mills L RSC 6 Leicester
20.06.08 Dezzie O'Connor L PTS 6 Plymouth
23.06.09 Ibrar Riyaz L RTD 3 Longford
Career: 7 contests, won 2, lost 5.

George Groves　　　　Philip Sharkey

George Groves

Hammersmith. *Born* Hammersmith, 26 March, 1988
S.Middleweight. *Ht* 5'11"
Manager A. Booth

15.11.08 Kirill Pshonko W PTS 6 Greenwich
01.02.09 Romaric Hignard W RSC 3 Bethnal Green
28.03.09 Paul Samuels W RSC 1 Liverpool
25.04.09 Sandor Polgar W RSC 1 Belfast
Career: 4 contests, won 4.

Tomas Grublys

Hounslow. *Born* Lithuania, 11 February, 1978
L.Middleweight. *Ht* 5'8"
Manager M. Roe
13.09.08 Nick Coret W RSC 2 Bethnal Green
15.11.08 Chas Symonds W PTS 4 Bethnal Green
20.03.09 Paul Dyer W RSC 4 Newham
30.06.09 Alex Spitjo W RSC 4 Bethnal Green
Career: 4 contests, won 4.

Omar Gumati

Chester. *Born* Chester, 18 May, 1984
Middleweight. *Ht* 5'9¼"
Manager S. Goodwin
07.05.03 Craig Goodman W PTS 6 Ellesmere Port
02.10.03 Danny Moir L PTS 6 Sunderland
01.12.03 Ojay Abrahams W PTS 6 Leeds
05.12.05 Ryan Ashworth L PTS 6 Leeds
15.12.05 Davey Jones L PTS 6 Cleethorpes
11.02.06 Paul Porter W RSC 3 Bethnal Green
09.03.06 Martin Marshall DREW 6 Sunderland
20.03.06 Mark Franks W RTD 4 Leeds
23.04.06 Joe Mitchell W PTS 4 Chester
26.05.06 Wayne Goddard L PTS 4 Bethnal Green
17.05.08 Davey Jones W PTS 6 Stoke
13.09.08 Peter Dunn W PTS 6 Stoke
07.03.09 Lester Walsh W PTS 4 Chester
23.05.09 Paul Royston W PTS 6 Queensferry
Career: 14 contests, won 9, drew 1, lost 4..

Danny Gwilym

Bristol. *Born* Bristol, 15 January, 1975
L.Middleweight. *Ht* 5'7"
Manager T. Woodward
16.12.01 Wayne Wheeler L RSC 2 Bristol
11.02.02 James Lee L PTS 6 Southampton
12.07.02 Mo W PTS 6 Southampton
26.02.03 Wasim Hussain W PTS 6 Bristol
17.03.03 Danny Cooper L PTS 6 Southampton
16.04.03 Lenny Daws L RSC 2 Nottingham
26.09.03 Darren Covill W PTS 6 Millwall
12.10.03 Mo L PTS 6 Sheffield
06.12.03 Martin Concepcion L RSC 2 Cardiff
09.07.05 Arv Mittoo W RSC 4 Bristol
24.07.05 Garry Buckland L RSC 2 Leicester Square
12.11.05 Kristian Laight W PTS 6 Bristol
28.04.07 Paul Burns L PTS 6 Clydebank
06.05.07 Chris Johnson L RSC 4 Altrincham
21.10.07 Adam Wilcox W PTS 6 Swansea
23.02.09 Joel Walton W RSC 5 Birmingham
14.03.09 Jamie Ambler W PTS 4 Bristol
28.03.09 Prince Arron L PTS 4 Altrincham
Career: 18 contests, won 8, lost 10.

Saud Hafiz

Watford. *Born* Watford, 20 August, 1979
S.Featherweight. *Ht* 5'7¼"
Manager Self
31.01.08 Shaun Walton W PTS 4 Piccadilly
10.04.08 Shaun Walton W RSC 3 Piccadilly
01.08.08 Amir Nadi W RSC 3 Watford
Career: 3 contests, won 3.

Matthew Hainy

Derby. *Born* Dewsbury, 29 September, 1981
S.Middleweight. *Ht* 5'11¼"
Manager C. Mitchell
18.01.08 James Tucker W PTS 4 Burton
16.02.08 Ricky Strike W PTS 4 Leicester
22.06.08 Manoocha Salari W PTS 6 Derby
16.11.08 Anthony Young W PTS 6 Derby
10.05.09 Sam Horton L PTS 10 Derby
    (Vacant Midlands Area S.Middleweight Title)
Career: 5 contests, won 4, lost 1.

Matthew Hall

Manchester. *Born* Manchester, 5 July, 1984
Commonwealth L. Middleweight
Champion. *Ht* 5'7¾"
Manager F. Warren/B. Hughes
28.09.02 Pedro Thompson W RSC 1 Manchester
14.12.02 Pedro Thompson W PTS 4 Newcastle
18.01.03 Clive Johnson W PTS 4 Preston
05.04.03 Brian Coleman W RSC 1 Manchester
08.05.03 Patrick Cito W PTS 4 Widnes
06.05.04 Craig Lynch W PTS 6 Barnsley
12.06.04 Isidro Gonzalez W RSC 3 Manchester
01.10.04 Howard Clarke W RSC 3 Manchester
12.11.04 Ojay Abrahams W RSC 1 Halifax
03.12.04 Jason Collins W PTS 6 Edinburgh
21.01.05 Leigh Wicks W PTS 4 Bridgend
11.02.05 Sylvestre Marianini W CO 1 Manchester
04.06.05 Matt Scriven W RSC 2 Manchester
28.01.06 Jon Foster W RSC 3 Nottingham
11.03.06 Robert Burton W CO 1 Newport
08.07.06 Kevin Phelan W RSC 1 Cardiff
14.07.07 Martin Concepcion L RSC 1 Greenwich
03.12.07 Tyan Booth W PTS 8 Manchester
22.03.08 Kerry Hope W RSC 8 Cardiff
06.09.08 Taz Jones W RSC 5 Manchester
10.10.08 Ciaran Healy W RSC 3 Liverpool
12.12.08 Jason Rushton W RSC 6 Widnes
14.03.09 Bradley Pryce W RSC 2 Manchester
    (Commonwealth L.Middleweight Title Challenge)
Career: 23 contests, won 22, lost 1.

Stuart Hall

Darlington. *Born* Darlington, 24 February, 1980
S.Bantamweight. *Ht* 5'8¼"
Manager M. Marsden
26.04.08 Abdul Mougharbel W PTS 6 Darlington

06.10.08 Dougie Walton W RSC 6 Birmingham
16.01.09 Nick Seager W RSC 2 Middlesbrough
29.03.09 Stuart McFadyen DREW 6 Bolton
01.05.09 Anthony Hanna W PTS 4 Hartlepool
Career: 5 contests, won 4, drew 1.

Kevin Hammond

Lincoln. *Born* Lincoln, 8 November, 1980
Middleweight. *Ht* 5'9¼"
Manager C. Greaves
01.12.07 David Kirk W PTS 4 Nottingham
02.05.08 Gavin Brook W RTD 1 Nottingham
31.05.08 Lester Walsh DREW 4 Newark
05.09.08 Lester Walsh W PTS 6 Nottingham
29.11.08 Duncan Cottier W PTS 4 Sleaford
23.01.09 Jimmy Doherty W PTS 8 Stoke
28.03.09 Jon Musgrave L PTS 6 Lincoln
23.05.09 Paul Brown W RSC 2 Sleaford
Career: 8 contests, won 6, drew 1, lost 1.

Anthony Hanna

Birmingham. *Born* Birmingham, 22 September, 1974
Former Undefeated British Masters Featherweight Champion. Former Undefeated Midlands Area Flyweight Champion. *Ht* 5'6"
Manager Self
19.11.92 Nick Tooley L PTS 6 Evesham
10.12.92 Daren Fifield L RSC 6 Bethnal Green
11.05.93 Tiger Singh W PTS 6 Norwich
24.05.93 Lyndon Kershaw L PTS 6 Bradford
16.09.93 Chris Lyons W PTS 6 Southwark
06.10.93 Tiger Singh W PTS 6 Solihull
03.11.93 Mickey Cantwell L PTS 8 Bristol
25.01.94 Marty Chestnut W PTS 4 Picadilly
10.02.94 Allan Mooney W RTD 1 Glasgow
13.04.94 Allan Mooney L PTS 6 Glasgow
22.04.94 Jesper Jensen L PTS 6 Aalborg, Denmark
03.08.94 Paul Ingle L PTS 6 Bristol
01.10.94 Mark Hughes L PTS 4 Cardiff
30.11.94 Shaun Norman W PTS 10 Solihull
    (Vacant Midlands Area Flyweight Title)
24.02.95 Darren Greaves W RSC 5 Weston super Mare
06.03.95 Mark Hughes L PTS 6 Mayfair
27.04.95 Mickey Cantwell L PTS 6 Bethnal Green
05.05.95 Mark Cokely W RSC 4 Swansea
04.06.95 Mark Reynolds L PTS 10 Bethnal Green
    (Elim. British Flyweight Title)
02.07.95 Mickey Cantwell L PTS 6 Dublin
02.11.95 Shaun Norman W PTS 10 Mayfair
    (Midlands Area Flyweight Title Defence)
31.01.96 Marty Chestnut DREW 6 Stoke
20.03.96 Harry Woods L PTS 6 Cardiff
22.04.96 Neil Parry W PTS 6 Manchester
14.05.96 Dharmendra Singh Yadav L PTS 4 Dagenham
08.10.96 Marty Chestnut W PTS 6 Battersea
11.12.96 Mark Reynolds DREW 8 Southwark
28.01.97 Colin Moffett L PTS 4 Belfast
28.02.97 Paul Weir L PTS 8 Kilmarnock
14.03.97 Jesper Jensen L PTS 6 Odense, Denmark
30.04.97 Clinton Beeby DREW 6 Acton
10.05.97 Jason Booth L PTS 6 Nottingham
02.06.97 Keith Knox L PTS 6 Glasgow

14.10.97 Louis Veitch L PTS 6 Kilmarnock
27.10.97 Russell Laing W PTS 4 Musselburgh
13.11.97 Noel Wilders L PTS 6 Bradford
24.11.97 Shaun Anderson L PTS 8 Glasgow
20.12.97 Damaen Kelly L PTS 4 Belfast
31.01.98 Jason Booth L PTS 6 Edmonton
23.02.98 David Coldwell W PTS 6 Salford
19.03.98 Andy Roberts L PTS 6 Doncaster
18.05.98 Chris Emanuele W RSC 3 Cleethorpes
11.09.98 Nicky Booth DREW 6 Cleethorpes
18.09.98 Colin Moffett DREW 4 Belfast
29.10.98 Nick Tooley W RTD 6 Bayswater
25.11.98 Nicky Booth W PTS 6 Clydach
21.01.99 Ola Dali W PTS 6 Piccadilly
13.03.99 Damaen Kelly L PTS 12 Manchester
    (Vacant British Flyweight Title. Commonwealth Flyweight Title Challenge)
24.04.99 Noel Wilders L PTS 6 Peterborough
07.06.99 Alston Buchanan W RSC 3 Glasgow
29.06.99 Tommy Waite L PTS 4 Bethnal Green
16.10.99 Stevie Quinn W PTS 4 Belfast
22.11.99 Frankie DeMilo L PTS 6 Piccadilly
04.12.99 Ady Lewis L PTS 6 Manchester
19.02.00 Ian Napa L PTS 6 Dagenham
13.03.00 Mzukisi Sikali L PTS 6 Bethnal Green
27.05.00 Nicky Cook L PTS 6 Mayfair
25.07.00 David Lowry L PTS 4 Southwark
19.08.00 Marc Callaghan L PTS 4 Brentwood
29.09.00 Rocky Dean L PTS 4 Bethnal Green
07.10.00 Oleg Kiryukhin L PTS 6 Doncaster
14.10.00 Danny Costello DREW 4 Wembley
31.10.00 Dmitri Kirilov L PTS 6 Hammersmith
10.02.01 Tony Mulholland L PTS 4 Widnes
19.02.01 Alex Moon L PTS 6 Glasgow
03.03.01 Marc Callaghan L PTS 6 Wembley
24.04.01 Silence Mabuza L PTS 6 Liverpool
06.05.01 Michael Hunter L PTS 4 Hartlepool
26.05.01 Mickey Bowden L PTS 4 Bethnal Green
04.06.01 Michael Hunter L PTS 4 Hartlepool
01.11.01 Nigel Senior L PTS 6 Hull
24.11.01 Martin Power L PTS 4 Bethnal Green
08.12.01 Faprakob Rakkiatgym L PTS 8 Dagenham
24.03.02 Mickey Coveney L PTS 4 Streatham
23.06.02 Johannes Maisa L PTS 4 Southwark
30.10.02 Mickey Bowden L PTS 4 Leicester Square
08.11.02 Sean Green L PTS 6 Doncaster
17.11.02 Shinny Bayaar L PTS 6 Shaw
14.12.02 Michael Hunter L PTS 8 Newcastle
15.02.03 Steve Gethin L PTS 6 Wolverhampton
24.02.03 Jackson Williams W PTS 6 Birmingham
08.06.03 Darryn Walton L PTS 6 Shaw
25.09.03 Rob Jeffries L PTS 6 Bethnal Green
01.11.03 Andrew Ferrans L PTS 4 Glasgow
14.11.03 Mickey Bowden L PTS 4 Bethnal Green
21.11.03 Buster Dennis L PTS 6 Millwall
29.11.03 Willie Limond L PTS 4 Renfrew
09.04.04 Rendall Munroe L PTS 6 Rugby
16.04.04 Billy Corcoran L PTS 4 Bradford
24.04.04 Lee Beavis L PTS 4 Reading
12.05.04 Chris McDonagh L PTS 4 Reading
02.06.04 John Murray L PTS 4 Nottingham
17.06.04 Femi Fehintola L PTS 6 Sheffield
03.07.04 Jeff Thomas L PTS 6 Blackpool
12.11.06 Stuart McFadyen L PTS 6 Manchester
07.12.06 Shaun Doherty L PTS 6 Bradford
15.04.07 Josh Wale L PTS 6 Barnsley
02.06.07 Darryl Mitchell W RTD 5 Bristol
20.07.07 Ricky Owen L RSC 5 Wolverhampton

09.06.08 Furhan Rafiq W RSC 10 Glasgow
(Vacant British Masters Featherweight Title)
06.09.08 Steve Bell L PTS 8 Manchester
19.09.08 Jamie McDonnell L RSC 5 Doncaster
25.10.08 Sandy Bartlett W CO 4 Aberdeen
(British Masters Featherweight Title Defence)
09.11.08 Chris Male L PTS 4 Wolverhampton
22.11.08 Stuart McFadyen L PTS 4 Blackpool
12.12.08 Stephen Smith L PTS 4 Widnes
13.03.09 Martin Ward L PTS 4 Widnes
03.04.09 Craig Lyon L PTS 4 Leigh
01.05.09 Stuart Hall L PTS 4 Hartlepool
24.05.09 Robert Nelson L PTS 6 Bradford
12.06.09 Daniel Walton DREW 4 Wolverhampton
26.06.09 Liam Richards L PTS 6 Melksham
Career: 112 contests, won 22, drew 8, lost 82.

Ben Harding   Philip Sharkey

Ben Harding

Fowey. *Born* Amersham, 28 September, 1971
Heavyweight. *Ht* 6'3¼"
Manager N. Christian
09.11.07 Tony Booth W PTS 4 Plymouth
29.02.08 Howard Daley DREW 4 Plymouth
14.09.08 Scott Mitchell L PTS 6 Wigan
13.02.09 Howard Daley W PTS 4 Swindon
20.03.09 Tom Dallas L RSC 1 Newham
Career: 5 contests, won 2, drew 1, lost 2.

Audley Harrison

Wembley. *Born* Park Royal, 26 October, 1971
Heavyweight. Former Undefeated WBF Heavyweight Champion. *Ht* 6'4¾"
Manager Self
19.05.01 Michael Middleton W RSC 1 Wembley
22.09.01 Derek McCafferty W PTS 6 Newcastle
20.10.01 Piotr Jurczyk W RSC 2 Glasgow
20.04.02 Julius Long W CO 2 Wembley
21.05.02 Mark Krence W PTS 6 Custom House
10.07.02 Dominic Negus W PTS 6 Wembley
05.10.02 Wade Lewis W RSC 2 Liverpool
23.11.02 Shawn Robinson W RSC 1 Atlantic City, New Jersey, USA

08.02.03 Rob Calloway W RSC 5 Brentford
29.03.03 Ratko Draskovic W PTS 8 Wembley
31.05.03 Matthew Ellis W RSC 2 Bethnal Green
09.09.03 Quinn Navarre W RSC 3 Miami, Florida, USA
03.10.03 Lisandro Diaz W RSC 4 Las Vegas, Nevada, USA
12.12.03 Brian Nix W RSC 3 Laughlin, Nevada, USA
20.03.04 Richel Hersisia W CO 4 Wembley
(WBF Heavyweight Title Challenge)
08.05.04 Julius Francis W PTS 12 Bristol
(WBF Heavyweight Title Defence)
19.06.04 Tomasz Bonin W RSC 9 Muswell Hill
(WBF Heavyweight Title Defence)
09.06.05 Robert Davis W RSC 7 Temecula, California, USA
18.08.05 Robert Wiggins W RTD 4 San Jose, California, USA
10.12.05 Danny Williams L PTS 12 Canning Town
(Vacant Commonwealth Heavyweight Title)
14.04.06 Dominick Guinn L PTS 10 Rancho Mirage, California, USA
09.06.06 Andrew Greeley W CO 3 Atlantic City, New Jersey, USA
09.12.06 Danny Williams W RSC 3 Canning Town
17.02.07 Michael Sprott L RSC 3 Wembley
(European Union Heavyweight Title Challenge.Vacant English Heavyweight Title)
19.04.08 Jason Barnett W RSC 5 Las Vegas, Nevada, USA
06.09.08 George Arias W PTS 10 Manchester
06.12.08 Martin Rogan L PTS 10 Canning Town
Career: 27 contests, won 23, lost 4.

Audley Harrison   Philip Sharkey

Dean Harrison

Wolverhampton. *Born* Wolverhampton, 9 August, 1983
Welterweight. *Ht* 5'8"
Manager E. Johnson
06.10.06 Joe Mitchell W PTS 4 Wolverhampton
26.10.06 Kristian Laight W PTS 4 Dudley
05.12.06 Baz Carey W PTS 4 Wolverhampton

15.02.07 Daniel Thorpe W PTS 4 Dudley
23.03.07 Kristian Laight W PTS 4 Nottingham
20.04.07 Judex Meemea W RSC 6 Dudley
28.06.07 Johnny Greaves W PTS 6 Dudley
21.09.07 Jason Nesbitt W PTS 6 Burton
25.10.07 Rakhim Mingaleev W PTS 6 Wolverhampton
07.12.07 Ramon Guevara W RSC 5 Las Vegas, Nevada, USA
28.02.08 Alex Brew W RSC 7 Wolverhampton
30.04.08 Gary Reid W PTS 8 Wolverhampton
05.09.08 Scott Haywood L PTS 10 Nottingham
(Vacant English L.Welterweight Title)
09.11.08 Chris Long W RTD 8 Wolverhampton
06.02.09 Laszlo Komjathi W PTS 8 Birmingham
13.03.09 Paul McCloskey L RSC 4 Widnes
(British L.Welterweight Title Challenge)
12.06.09 Ali Wyatt W PTS 6 Wolverhampton
Career: 17 contests, won 15, lost 2.

Jon Harrison

Plymouth. *Born* Scunthorpe, 18 March, 1977
Former Undefeated International Masters L. Middleweight Champion. *Ht* 5'11½"
Manager N. Christian
13.01.96 Mark Haslam L PTS 6 Manchester
13.02.96 Paul Samuels L CO 1 Cardiff
16.05.96 Dave Fallon W RSC 4 Dunstable
03.07.96 Allan Gray L PTS 6 Wembley
01.10.96 Cam Raeside L PTS 6 Birmingham
07.11.96 Nicky Bardle L PTS 6 Battersea
14.12.96 James Hare L PTS 4 Sheffield
19.04.97 Jason Williams W PTS 6 Plymouth
11.07.97 Pat Larner L PTS 6 Brighton
07.10.97 Paul Salmon L PTS 6 Plymouth
23.02.98 Alan Gilbert L PTS 6 Windsor
24.03.98 Brian Coleman DREW 6 Wolverhampton
14.07.98 Jason Williams L RTD 2 Reading
12.05.01 Ernie Smith W PTS 4 Plymouth
15.09.01 Darren Williams L PTS 6 Swansea
02.04.04 Nathan Wyatt W PTS 6 Plymouth
27.05.04 Ady Clegg W PTS 4 Huddersfield
17.09.04 Geraint Harvey W PTS 6 Plymouth
13.12.04 Simon Sherrington L RSC 5 Birmingham
04.02.05 Joe Mitchell W PTS 6 Plymouth
29.04.05 Neil Jarmolinski W PTS 6 Plymouth
10.02.06 Jamie Ambler W PTS 4 Plymouth
15.09.06 Taz Jones L PTS 6 Newport
09.11.07 Gatis Skuja W PTS 10 Plymouth
(Vacant International Masters L.Middleweight Title)
29.02.08 Carl Drake L RSC 7 Plymouth
(Vacant Western Area L.Middleweight Title)
14.09.08 Jack Arnfield L PTS 4 Wigan
24.01.09 Brian Rose L RSC 2 Blackpool
Career: 27 contests, won 10, drew 1, lost 16.

Geraint Harvey

Mountain Ash. *Born* Church Village, 1 September, 1979
L.Middleweight. *Ht* 5'10"
Manager B. Coleman
22.09.03 Steve Scott W PTS 6 Cleethorpes
29.10.03 Darren Covill W PTS 4 Leicester Square
21.12.03 Danny Moir L PTS 6 Bolton

Geraint Harvey   Philip Sharkey

14.02.04 Arek Malek L PTS 4 Nottingham
28.02.04 Jamie Coyle L PTS 4 Bridgend
15.04.04 Terry Adams L PTS 6 Dudley
24.04.04 Chas Symonds L PTS 4 Reading
08.07.04 Terry Adams L RSC 6 Birmingham
17.09.04 Jon Harrison L PTS 6 Plymouth
24.09.04 Gary Woolcombe L PTS 4 Bethnal
　　　　　Green
16.10.04 Danny Goode L PTS 4 Dagenham
23.10.04 Peter Dunn W PTS 6 Wakefield
21.11.04 Robert Lloyd Taylor L PTS 4 Bracknell
03.12.04 Colin McNeil L PTS 6 Edinburgh
28.01.05 Chris Black L PTS 4 Glasgow
17.02.05 Young Mutley L PTS 6 Dudley
05.03.05 Duncan Cottier L PTS 4 Dagenham
29.04.05 Courtney Thomas L PTS 6 Plymouth
15.05.05 Stuart Brookes L PTS 6 Sheffield
01.06.05 Mark Franks L PTS 6 Leeds
16.06.05 George Hillyard L RSC 1 Dagenham
23.09.05 Mark Thompson L PTS 4 Manchester
07.10.05 Sam Webb L CO 1 Bethnal Green
19.11.05 Nathan Graham L PTS 4 Southwark
14.12.05 Brian Rose L PTS 6 Blackpool
20.03.06 Danny Reynolds L RTD 2 Leeds
06.05.06 Jonathan Hussey L PTS 6 Blackpool
13.05.06 Grant Skehill L PTS 4 Bethnal Green
21.05.06 Jamal Morrison L PTS 4 Bethnal Green
01.06.06 Kell Brook L RSC 3 Barnsley
10.07.06 Prince Arron L PTS 6 Manchester
11.09.06 George Katsimpas L RTD 2 Manchester
25.11.06 Scott Jordan L PTS 4 Belfast
02.12.06 Mark Hastie L PTS 6 Clydebank
17.12.06 Chris Johnson L PTS 6 Bolton
23.02.07 Dee Mitchell L PTS 6 Birmingham
03.03.07 Jamie Way L PTS 6 Newport
05.10.08 Nathan Graham L PTS 4 Watford
12.10.08 Brian Rose L PTS 4 Leigh
31.10.08 Thomas Costello L PTS 4 Birmingham
15.11.08 Gavin Brook W RSC 1 Plymouth
04.12.08 Andrew Butlin L PTS 6 Bradford
16.01.09 Mark Clauzel L PTS 4 Middlesbrough
24.01.09 Chris Johnson W PTS 4 Blackpool
21.02.09 Fred Janes L PTS 6 Merthyr Tydfil
27.03.09 Craig Windsor L PTS 4 Glasgow
24.04.09 Sam Sheedy L PTS 6 Sheffield
17.05.09 Trevor Crewe L RSC 4 Bolton
Career: 48 contests, won 5, lost 43.

Michael Harvey

Belfast. *Born* Rinteln, Germany, 23
October, 1985
Lightweight. *Ht* 5' 10"
Manager A. Wilton
28.06.09 Michael Devine L RSC 3 Luton
Career: 1 contest, lost 1.

Michael Harvey   Philip Sharkey

Lee Haskins

Bristol. *Born* Bristol, 29 November, 1983
Bantamweight. Former Undefeated
Commonwealth & English Flyweight
Champion. *Ht* 5'5"
Manager C. Sanigar
06.03.03 Ankar Miah W RSC 1 Bristol
13.06.03 Chris Edwards W PTS 6 Bristol
09.10.03 Neil Read W PTS 4 Bristol
05.12.03 Jason Thomas W PTS 6 Bristol
13.02.04 Marty Kayes W PTS 6 Bristol
08.05.04 Colin Moffett W RSC 2 Bristol
03.07.04 Sergei Tasimov W RSC 5 Bristol
01.10.04 Junior Anderson W CO 3 Bristol
03.12.04 Delroy Spencer W RTD 3 Bristol
　　　　　(Vacant English Flyweight Title)
18.02.05 Hugo Cardinale W CO 1 Torrevieja,
　　　　　Spain
08.04.05 Moses Kinyua W PTS 10 Bristol
29.04.05 Andrzej Ziora W RSC 1 Plymouth
16.09.05 Delroy Spencer W RTD 2 Plymouth
10.02.06 Anthony Mathias W RSC 2 Plymouth
　　　　　(Vacant Commonwealth Flyweight Title)
07.04.06 Zolile Mbityi W PTS 12 Bristol
　　　　　*(Commonwealth Flyweight Title
　　　　　Defence)*
06.10.06 Tshifhiwa Munyai L RSC 6 Bethnal
　　　　　Green
　　　　　*(Commonwealth Bantamweight Title
　　　　　Challenge)*
24.02.07 Sumaila Badu W PTS 6 Bristol
21.09.07 Ian Napa L RTD 7 Bethnal Green
　　　　　(British Bantamweight Title Challenge)
28.03.08 Jamie McDonnell W PTS 8 Barnsley
07.11.08 Andy Bell W PTS 12 Wigan
　　　　　(British S.Flyweight Title Challenge)
Career: 20 contests, won 18, lost 2.

Jason Hastie

Edinburgh. *Born* Edinburgh, 24 October,
1986
Featherweight. *Ht* 5'8¼"
Manager Self
17.11.07 Michael Crossan W PTS 4 Glasgow
15.12.07 Shaun Walton W PTS 4 Edinburgh
29.03.08 Robin Deakin W PTS 4 Glasgow
18.10.08 Mark Bett W PTS 4 Paisley
27.02.09 Robin Deakin W PTS 4 Paisley
Career: 5 contests, won 5.

Matthew Hatton   Philip Sharkey

Matthew Hatton

Manchester. *Born* Stockport, 15 May, 1981
Former Undefeated IBF Inter-Continental
Welterweight Champion. Former
Undefeated Central Area Welterweight
Champion. Former Undefeated Central
Area L.Middleweight Champion. *Ht* 5'8½"
Manager R. Hatton
23.09.00 David White W PTS 4 Bethnal Green
25.11.00 David White W PTS 4 Manchester
11.12.00 Danny Connelly W PTS 4 Widnes
15.01.01 Keith Jones W PTS 4 Manchester
10.02.01 Karl Taylor W PTS 4 Widnes
17.03.01 Assen Vassilev W RSC 5 Manchester
09.06.01 Brian Coleman W RTD 2 Bethnal Green
21.07.01 Ram Singh W RSC 2 Sheffield
15.09.01 Marcus Portman W RSC 3 Manchester
15.12.01 Dafydd Carlin W PTS 6 Wembley
09.02.02 Paul Denton W PTS 6 Manchester
04.05.02 Karl Taylor W RSC 3 Bethnal Green
20.07.02 Karl Taylor W RTD 2 Bethnal Green
28.09.02 David Kirk L PTS 6 Manchester
14.12.02 Paul Denton W PTS 6 Newcastle
15.02.03 David Keir L RSC 4 Wembley
08.05.03 Jay Mahoney W PTS 6 Widnes
17.07.03 Jay Mahoney W RSC 1 Dagenham
27.09.03 Taz Jones W PTS 6 Manchester
13.12.03 Franny Jones DREW 6 Manchester
26.02.04 Peter Dunn W PTS 6 Widnes
06.05.04 Robert Burton W PTS 10 Barnsley
　　　　　*(Central Area Welterweight Title
　　　　　Challenge)*
12.06.04 Matt Scriven W RSC 4 Manchester
01.10.04 Lee Armstrong W PTS 8 Manchester

121

12.11.04 Robert Burton W PTS 10 Halifax
(*Central Area L.Middleweight Title Challenge*)
11.03.05 Franny Jones W RTD 6 Doncaster
03.06.05 Adnan Hadoui W PTS 8 Manchester
09.09.05 Dmitry Yanushevich W RSC 4 Sheffield
26.11.05 Sergey Starkov W PTS 10 Sheffield
18.03.06 Alexander Abramenko W RTD 6 Monte Carlo, Monaco
13.05.06 Jose Medina W PTS 8 Boston, Massachusetts, USA
20.10.06 Alan Bosworth L DIS 10 Sheffield
(*Elim. British Welterweight Title*)
10.12.06 Vladimir Borovski W PTS 6 Sheffield
20.01.07 Frank Houghtaling W RTD 7 Las Vegas, Nevada, USA
(*Vacant IBF Inter-Continental Welterweight Title*)
23.06.07 Edwin Vazquez W PTS 12 Las Vegas, Nevada, USA
(*IBF Inter-Continental Welterweight Title Defence*)
20.10.07 Samuli Leppiaho W RSC 6 Dublin
08.12.07 Frankie Santos W PTS 8 Las Vegas, Nevada, USA
24.05.08 Craig Watson L PTS 12 Manchester
(*Commonwealth Welterweight Title Challenge*)
05.09.08 Scott Woolford W PTS 8 Nottingham
22.11.08 Ben Tackie W PTS 10 Las Vegas, Nevada, USA
28.03.09 Ted Bami W RSC 6 Altrincham
(*Elim. IBO Welterweight Title*)
02.05.09 Ernesto Zepeda W PTS 8 Las Vegas, Nevada, USA
Career: 42 contests, won 37, drew 1, lost 4.

Ricky Hatton

Manchester. *Born* Stockport, 6 October, 1978
Former IBO L.Welterweight Champion. Former Undefeated WBC International L.Welterweight Champion. Former Undefeated WBA Welterweight Champion. Former Undefeated WBA, IBF & WBU L.Welterweight Champion. Former Undefeated British, WBO Inter-Continental & Central Area L.Welterweight Champion. *Ht* 5'7½"
Manager Self
11.09.97 Kid McAuley W RTD 1 Widnes
19.12.97 Robert Alvarez W PTS 4 NYC, New York, USA
17.01.98 David Thompson W RSC 1 Bristol
27.03.98 Paul Salmon W RSC 1 Telford
18.04.98 Karl Taylor W RSC 1 Manchester
30.05.98 Mark Ramsey W PTS 6 Bristol
18.07.98 Anthony Campbell W PTS 6 Sheffield
19.09.98 Pascal Montulet W CO 2 Oberhausen, Germany
31.10.98 Kevin Carter W RSC 1 Atlantic City, New Jersey, USA
19.12.98 Paul Denton W RSC 6 Liverpool
27.02.99 Tommy Peacock W RSC 2 Oldham
(*Vacant Central Area L.Welterweight Title*)
03.04.99 Brian Coleman W CO 2 Kensington
29.05.99 Dillon Carew W RSC 5 Halifax
(*Vacant WBO Inter-Continental L. Welterweight Title*)

17.07.99 Mark Ramsey W PTS 6 Doncaster
09.10.99 Bernard Paul W RTD 4 Manchester
(*WBO Inter-Continental L. Welterweight Title Defence*)
11.12.99 Mark Winters W RSC 4 Liverpool
(*WBO Inter-Continental L. Welterweight Title Defence*)
29.01.00 Leoncio Garces W RSC 3 Manchester
25.03.00 Pedro Teran W RSC 4 Liverpool
(*WBO Inter-Continental L. Welterweight Title Defence*)
16.05.00 Ambioris Figuero W RSC 4 Warrington
(*WBO Inter-Continental L. Welterweight Title Defence*)
10.06.00 Gilbert Quiros W CO 2 Detroit, Michigan, USA
(*WBO Inter-Continental L. Welterweight Title Defence*)
23.09.00 Giuseppe Lauri W RSC 5 Bethnal Green
(*WBO Inter-Continental L.Welterweight Title Defence. WBA Inter-Continental L.Welterweight Title Challenge*)
21.10.00 Jonathan Thaxton W PTS 12 Wembley
(*Vacant British L.Welterweight Title*)
26.03.01 Tony Pep W CO 4 Wembley
(*Vacant WBU L. Welterweight Title*)
07.07.01 Jason Rowland W CO 4 Manchester
(*WBU L.Welterweight Title Defence*)
15.09.01 John Bailey W RSC 5 Manchester
(*WBU L.Welterweight Title Defence*)
27.10.01 Fred Pendleton W CO 2 Manchester
(*WBU L.Welterweight Title Defence*)
15.12.01 Justin Rowsell W RSC 2 Wembley
(*WBU L.Welterweight Title Defence*)
09.02.02 Mikhail Krivolapov W RSC 9 Manchester
(*WBU L. Welterweight Title Defence*)
01.06.02 Eamonn Magee W PTS 12 Manchester
(*WBU L. Welterweight Title Defence*)
28.09.02 Stephen Smith W DIS 2 Manchester
(*WBU L.Welterweight Title Defence*)
14.12.02 Joe Hutchinson W CO 4 Newcastle
(*WBU L. Welterweight Title Defence*)
05.04.03 Vince Philips W PTS 12 Manchester
(*WBU L.Welterweight Title Defence*)
27.09.03 Aldi Rios W RTD 9 Manchester
(*WBU L.Welterweight Title Defence*)
13.12.03 Ben Tackie W PTS 12 Manchester
(*WBU L.Welterweight Title Defence*)
03.04.04 Dennis Holbaek Pedersen W RSC 6 Manchester
(*WBU L.Welterweight Title Defence*)
12.06.04 Wilfredo Carlos Vilches W PTS 12 Manchester
(*WBU L.Welterweight Title Defence*)
01.10.04 Michael Stewart W RSC 5 Manchester
(*WBU L.Welterweight Title Defence. Final Elim. IBF L.Welterweight Title*)
11.12.04 Ray Oliveira W CO 10 Canning Town
(*WBU L.Welterweight Title Defence*)
04.06.05 Kostya Tszyu W RSC 11 Manchester
(*IBF L.Welterweight Title Challenge*)
26.11.05 Carlos Maussa W CO 9 Sheffield
(*IBF L.Welterweight Title Challenge. WBA L.Welterweight Title Defence*)
13.05.06 Luis Collazo W PTS 12 Boston, Massachusetts, USA
(*WBA Welterweight Title Challenge*)
20.01.07 Juan Urango W PTS 12 Las Vegas, Nevada, USA
(*IBF L.Welterweight Title Challenge. Vacant IBO L.Welterweight Title*)
23.06.07 Jose Luis Castillo W CO 4 Las Vegas, Nevada, USA

(*IBO L.Welterweight Title Defence. Vacant WBC International L.Welterweight Title*)
08.12.07 Floyd Mayweather L RSC 10 Las Vegas, Nevada, USA
(*WBC Welterweight Title Challenge*)
24.05.08 Juan Lazcano W PTS 12 Manchester
(*IBO L.Welterweight Title Defence*)
22.11.08 Paul Malignaggi W RSC 11 Las Vegas, Nevada, USA
(*IBO L.Welterweight Title Defence*)
02.05.09 Manny Pacquiao L CO 2 Las Vegas, Nevada, USA
(*IBO L.Welterweight Title Defence*)
Career: 47 contests, won 45, lost 2.

Stephen Haughian

Lurgan Co. Armagh. *Born* Craigavon, 20 November, 1984
All-Ireland Welterweight Champion. *Ht* 5'10½"
Manager J. Breen
18.03.05 James Gorman W PTS 4 Belfast
14.10.05 Imad Khamis W RSC 4 Dublin
24.11.05 James Gorman W PTS 6 Lurgan
28.01.06 Duncan Cottier W PTS 4 Dublin
20.05.06 Pete Buckley W PTS 4 Belfast
26.10.06 Denis Alekseevs W RSC 1 Belfast
11.11.06 Silence Saheed W PTS 6 Dublin
17.02.07 Dwayne Hill W RSC 2 Cork
25.03.07 Chill John W PTS 6 Dublin
14.07.07 Gary O'Connor W RSC 6 Dublin
20.10.07 Thomas Hengstberger W RSC 1 Dublin
11.11.07 Tye Williams W PTS 8 Dunshaughlin
08.12.07 Giammario Grassellini L PTS 12 Belfast
(*IBF Inter-Continental Welterweight Title Challenge*)
15.12.07 Artur Jashkul W PTS 6 Dublin
20.06.08 Raul Saiz W RSC 2 Wolverhampton
19.07.08 Giuseppe Langella W PTS 8 Limerick
15.11.08 Giammario Grassellini W PTS 8 Castlebar
07.02.09 Billy Walsh W RSC 3 Craigavon
(*Vacant All-Ireland Welterweight Title*)
11.04.09 Drew Campbell W RSC 1 Bethnal Green
Career: 19 contests, won 18, lost 1.

David Haye   Philip Sharkey

David Haye

Bermondsey. *Born* London, 13 October, 1980
Former Undefeated WBC, WBA & WBO Cruiserweight Champion. Former Undefeated European & English Cruiserweight Champion. *Ht* 6'3"
Manager Self
08.12.02 Tony Booth W RTD 2 Bethnal Green
24.01.03 Saber Zairi W RSC 4 Sheffield
04.03.03 Roger Bowden W RSC 2 Miami, Florida, USA
18.03.03 Phill Day W RSC 2 Reading
15.07.03 Vance Wynn W RSC 1 Los Angeles, California, USA
01.08.03 Greg Scott-Briggs W CO 1 Bethnal Green
26.09.03 Lolenga Mock W RSC 4 Reading
14.11.03 Tony Dowling W RSC 1 Bethnal Green
(Vacant English Cruiserweight Title)
20.03.04 Hastings Rasani W RSC 1 Wembley
12.05.04 Arthur Williams W RSC 3 Reading
10.09.04 Carl Thompson L RSC 5 Wembley
(IBO Cruiserweight Title Challenge)
10.12.04 Valery Semishkur W RSC 1 Sheffield
21.01.05 Garry Delaney W RTD 3 Brentford
04.03.05 Glen Kelly W CO 2 Rotherham
14.10.05 Vincenzo Rossitto W RSC 2 Huddersfield
16.12.05 Alexander Gurov W CO 1 Bracknell
(European Cruiserweight Title Challenge)
24.03.06 Lasse Johansen W RSC 8 Bethnal Green
(European Cruiserweight Title Defence)
21.07.06 Ismail Abdoul W PTS 12 Altrincham
(European Cruiserweight Title Defence)
17.11.06 Giacobbe Fragomeni W RSC 9 Bethnal Green
(European Cruiserweight Title Defence)
27.04.07 Tomasz Bonin W RSC 1 Wembley
10.11.07 Jean Marc Mormeck W RSC 7 Paris, France
(WBC & WBA Cruiserweight Title Challenges)
08.03.08 Enzo Maccarinelli W RSC 2 Greenwich
(WBC & WBA Cruiserweight Title Defences. WBO Cruiserweight Title Challenge)
15.11.08 Monte Barrett W RSC 5 Greenwich
(Elim. WBC Heavyweight Title)
Career: 23 contests, won 22, lost 1..

Peter Haymer

Enfield. *Born* London, 10 July, 1978
Former Undefeated English L.Heavyweight Champion.
Ht 6'1¼"
Manager Self
25.11.00 Adam Cale W RSC 1 Manchester
27.01.01 Darren Ashton W PTS 4 Bethnal Green
10.03.01 Daniel Ivanov W CO 2 Bethnal Green
26.03.01 Radcliffe Green W PTS 4 Wembley
05.05.01 Terry Morrill W PTS 4 Edmonton
22.09.01 Tony Booth W PTS 4 Bethnal Green
24.11.01 Nathan King L PTS 4 Bethnal Green
12.02.02 Nathan King L PTS 4 Bethnal Green
09.05.02 Mark Snipe W PTS 4 Leicester Square
15.06.02 Paul Bonson W PTS 4 Tottenham
30.10.02 Jimmy Steel W PTS 4 Leicester Square
18.03.03 Mark Brookes W PTS 6 Reading
18.09.03 Ovill McKenzie W PTS 4 Mayfair
10.12.03 Mark Brookes DREW 6 Sheffield
12.11.04 Steven Spartacus W PTS 10 Wembley
(English L.Heavyweight Title Challenge)
10.12.04 Mark Brookes W RSC 10 Sheffield
(English L.Heavyweight Title Defence)
24.04.05 Ryan Walls W PTS 6 Leicester Square
19.06.05 Tony Oakey W PTS 10 Bethnal Green
(English L.Heavyweight Title Defence)
07.04.06 Leigh Alliss W RSC 9 Bristol
(English L.Heavyweight Title Defence)
21.05.06 Varuzhan Davtyan W RSC 4 Bethnal Green
24.09.06 Ovill McKenzie L RSC 2 Bethnal Green
(Vacant Commonwealth L.Heavyweight Title)
18.05.07 Paul David L PTS 8 Canning Town
01.02.08 Tony Oakey L CO 9 Bethnal Green
(British L.Heavyweight Title Challenge)
27.09.08 Shon Davies L PTS 6 Bethnal Green
27.06.09 Danny Couzens DREW 4 Portsmouth
Career: 25 contests, won 17, drew 2, lost 6.

Scott Haywood

Derby. *Born* Derby, 5 June, 1981
Former Undefeated English L.Welterweight Champion. *Ht* 6'0"
Manager M. Shinfield
06.10.03 Pete Buckley W PTS 6 Barnsley
23.11.03 Arv Mittoo W PTS 6 Rotherham
16.02.04 Pete Buckley W PTS 6 Scunthorpe
26.04.04 Chris Brophy W RSC 5 Cleethorpes
27.09.04 Judex Meemea W PTS 6 Cleethorpes
16.12.04 Tony Montana L PTS 6 Cleethorpes
26.02.05 Jimmy Beech W PTS 6 Burton
24.04.05 Chris Long W PTS 6 Derby
02.09.05 Kristian Laight W PTS 6 Derby
08.12.05 Dave Hinds W RTD 3 Derby
28.01.06 Jus Wallie W PTS 4 Nottingham
25.03.06 Billy Smith W PTS 6 Burton
14.05.06 Surinder Sekhon W RSC 1 Derby
03.11.06 John Fewkes L PTS 8 Barnsley
09.02.07 Billy Smith W PTS 4 Leeds
13.04.07 Gary O'Connor W PTS 6 Altrincham
11.05.07 Billy Smith W PTS 4 Motherwell
08.12.07 Gavin Tait W PTS 6 Wigan
07.03.08 Gary Reid W PTS 6 Nottingham
02.05.08 Frederic Gosset W RSC 2 Nottingham
05.09.08 Dean Harrison W PTS 10 Nottingham
(Vacant English L.Welterweight Title)
27.02.09 Ajose Olusegun L RSC 7 Barnsley
(Commonwealth L.Welterweight Title Challenge)
29.05.09 Michael Frontin L PTS 6 Stoke
Career: 23 contests, won 19, lost 4.

Eugene Heagney

Huddersfield. *Born* Dublin, 4 April, 1983
Featherweight. *Ht* 5'8"
Manager M. Marsden
29.06.06 Neil Marston W PTS 6 Dudley
11.06.06 Delroy Spencer W PTS 4 Dublin
03.12.06 Neil Read W PTS 6 Wakefield
14.04.07 Delroy Spencer W PTS 6 Wakefield
14.06.07 Shaun Walton W PTS 6 Leeds
14.07.07 Colin Moffett W PTS 8 Dublin
15.12.07 Colin Moffett L RSC 8 Dublin
(Vacant All-Ireland Bantamweight Title)
12.07.08 Kemal Plavci W PTS 4 Dublin
18.12.08 Paul Hyland L PTS 6 Dublin
27.02.09 Jeremy Parodi L PTS 8 Toulon, France
Career: 10 contests, won 7, lost 3.

Ciaran Healy

Belfast. *Born* Belfast, 25 December, 1974
Former All-Ireland L.Middleweight Champion. *Ht* 5'11"
Manager Self
05.04.03 Tomas da Silva W PTS 4 Belfast
18.09.03 Patrick Cito W PTS 4 Mayfair
04.10.03 Joel Ani W PTS 4 Belfast
22.11.03 Neil Addis W RSC 1 Belfast
26.06.04 Jason McKay L PTS 6 Belfast
25.04.05 Vince Baldassara L RSC 4 Glasgow
17.06.05 Chris Black DREW 4 Glasgow
18.02.06 Karoly Domokos W PTS 4 Dublin
21.04.06 George Hillyard L CO 6 Belfast
18.11.06 Anthony Small L RSC 3 Newport
23.06.07 Lukasz Wawrzyczek L PTS 8 Dublin
18.08.07 Martins Kukuls W PTS 6 Cork
25.08.07 Andy Lee L RTD 4 Dublin
08.12.07 Lee Murtagh W CO 5 Belfast
(Vacant All-Ireland L.Middleweight Title Defence)
02.02.08 Pavel Lotah L PTS 6 Limerick
29.03.08 Pavel Lotah W PTS 8 Letterkenny
05.07.08 Jamie Moore L RSC 3 Dublin
(All-Ireland L.Middleweight Title Defence)
10.10.08 Matthew Hall L RSC 3 Liverpool
26.10.08 John Waldron W PTS 4 Killarney
12.12.08 Paul Smith L PTS 6 Widnes
15.05.09 Matt Scriven W PTS 4 Belfast
Career: 21 contests, won 10, drew 1, lost 10.

Ciaran Healy   Philip Sharkey

Suzanne Hemsley

Derby. *Born* Derby, 24 June, 1982
Lightweight. *Ht* 5'8"
Manager C. Mitchell
16.11.08 Lana Cooper W PTS 4 Derby
10.05.09 Kristine Shergold W PTS 6 Derby

13.06.09 Leticia Candal L PTS 4 Las Palmas, Spain
Career: 3 contests, won 2, lost 1.

John Wayne Hibbert   Philip Sharkey

John Wayne Hibbert
Stanford Le Hope. *Born* Orsett, 12 December, 1984
L.Welterweight. *Ht* 5' 8"
Manager R. Clark
21.06.09 Damien Jeffries W CO 1 Bethnal Green
Career: 1 contest, won 1.

Dean Hickman
West Bromwich. *Born* West Bromwich, 24 November, 1979
L.Welterweight. Former Undefeated Midlands Area L.Welterweight Champion.
Ht 5'7"
Manager E. Johnson
17.02.02 Wayne Wheeler DREW 6 Wolverhampton
13.04.02 Wayne Wheeler W PTS 6 Wolverhampton
13.07.02 Dai Bando W RSC 1 Wolverhampton
02.11.02 Darren Goode W RSC 2 Wolverhampton
15.02.03 Gareth Wiltshaw W PTS 6 Wolverhampton
21.03.03 David Vaughan W PTS 6 West Bromwich
30.06.03 Dave Hinds W RSC 4 Shrewsbury
17.07.03 Lee McAllister W PTS 6 Walsall
30.10.03 John-Paul Ryan W PTS 6 Dudley
15.04.04 Tony Montana W PTS 6 Dudley
04.06.04 Adnan Amar W RSC 8 Dudley
(Vacant Midlands Area L.Welterweight Title)
25.11.04 Ceri Hall W PTS 4 Birmingham
17.02.05 Gary Reid W PTS 10 Dudley
(Midlands Area L.Welterweight Title Defence)
11.03.05 Nigel Wright L CO 7 Doncaster
(Vacant English L.Welterweight Title)
16.02.06 Ernie Smith W PTS 4 Dudley
17.03.06 Barry Morrison L RSC 1 Kirkcaldy
(Elim. British L.Welterweight Title)
29.06.06 Tom Hogan W RSC 2 Dudley

06.10.06 Stuart Green W PTS 6 Wolverhampton
20.04.07 Gary Reid L RSC 5 Dudley
(Vacant Midlands Area L.Welterweight Title)
09.11.07 John Murray L RSC 4 Nottingham
(Vacant English Lightweight Title)
21.12.08 Steve Williams L RSC 2 Motherwell
Career: 21 contests, won 15, drew 1, lost 5.

Herbie Hide
Norwich. *Born* Nigeria, 27 August, 1971
WBC International Cruiserweight Champion. Former WBO Heavyweight Champion. Former Undefeated British, WBC International & Penta-Continental Heavyweight Champion. *Ht* 6'1½"
Manager Self
24.10.89 L. A. Williams W CO 2 Bethnal Green
05.11.89 Gary McCrory W RTD 1 Kensington
19.12.89 Steve Osborne W RSC 6 Bethnal Green
27.06.90 Alek Penarski W RSC 3 Kensington
05.09.90 Steve Lewsam W RSC 4 Brighton
26.09.90 Jonjo Greene W RSC 1 Manchester
17.10.90 Gus Mendes W RSC 2 Bethnal Green
18.11.90 Steve Lewsam W RSC 1 Birmingham
29.01.91 Lennie Howard W RSC 1 Wisbech
09.04.91 David Jules W RSC 1 Mayfair
14.05.91 John Westgarth W RTD 4 Dudley
03.07.91 Tucker Richards W RSC 3 Brentwood
15.10.91 Eddie Gonzalez W CO 2 Hamburg, Germany
29.10.91 Chris Jacobs W RSC 1 Cardiff
21.01.92 Conroy Nelson W RSC 2 Norwich
(Vacant WBC International Heavyweight Title)
03.03.92 Percell Davis W CO 1 Amsterdam, Holland
08.09.92 Jean Chanet W RSC 7 Norwich
06.10.92 Craig Peterson W RSC 7 Antwerp, Belgium
(WBC International Heavyweight Title Defence)
12.12.92 James Pritchard W RSC 2 Muswell Hill
30.01.93 Juan Antonio Diaz W RSC 3 Brentwood
(Vacant Penta-Continental Heavyweight Title)
27.02.93 Michael Murray W RSC 5 Dagenham
(Vacant British Heavyweight Title)
11.05.93 Jerry Halstead W RSC 4 Norwich
(Penta-Continental Heavyweight Title Defence)
18.09.93 Everett Martin W PTS 10 Leicester
06.11.93 Mike Dixon W RSC 9 Bethnal Green
(Penta-Continental Heavyweight Title Defence)
04.12.93 Jeff Lampkin W RSC 2 Sun City, South Africa
(WBC International Heavyweight Title Defence)
19.03.94 Michael Bentt W CO 7 Millwall
(WBO Heavyweight Title Challenge)
11.03.95 Riddick Bowe L CO 6 Las Vegas, Nevada, USA
(WBO Heavyweight Title Defence)
06.07.96 Michael Murray W RSC 6 Manchester
09.11.96 Frankie Swindell W CO 1 Manchester

28.06.97 Tony Tucker W RSC 2 Norwich
(Vacant WBO Heavyweight Title)
18.04.98 Damon Reed W RSC 1 Manchester
(WBO Heavyweight Title Defence)
26.09.98 Willi Fischer W RSC 2 Norwich
(WBO Heavyweight Title Defence)
26.06.99 Vitali Klitschko L CO 2 Millwall
(WBO Heavyweight Title Defence)
14.07.01 Alexei Osokin W RSC 3 Liverpool
22.09.01 Joseph Chingangu L RSC 2 Newcastle
16.04.03 Derek McCafferty W RSC 7 Nottingham
27.05.03 Joseph Chingangu W CO 1 Dagenham
04.10.03 Alex Vasiliev W RSC 5 Muswell Hill
12.03.04 Mendauga Kulikauskas L RSC 4 Nottingham
23.09.06 Mitch Hicks W RSC 1 Fort Smith, Arkansas, USA
24.03.07 Valery Semishkur W CO 1 Hamburg, Germany
27.04.07 Pavol Polakovic W CO 6 Hamburg, Germany
16.06.07 Aleh Dubiaha W CO 1 Ankara, Turkey
21.09.07 Mircea Telecan W RSC 1 Luebeck, Germany
23.12.07 Mikhail Nasyrov W RSC 6 Halle, Germany
(Vacant WBC International Cruiserweight Title)
11.03.08 Ruediger May W RSC 2 Halle, Germany
(WBC International Cruiserweight Title Defence)
30.05.08 Ehinomen Ehikhamenor W PTS 12 Baracaldo, Spain
(WBC International Cruiserweight Title Defence)
04.07.08 Nuri Seferi W PTS 12 Ankara, Turkey
(WBC International Cruiserweight Title Defence)
04.10.08 Aleksejs Kosobokovs W RTD 3 Norwich
18.11.08 Lukasz Rusiewicz W PTS 6 Cuxhaven, Germany
06.03.09 Sandro Siproshvili W PTS 8 Cuxhaven, Germany
26.06.09 Gabor Halasz W RSC 3 Voelklingen, Germany
Career: 52 contests, won 48, lost 4.

Graeme Higginson
Blackburn. *Born* Blackburn, 31 July, 1982
British Masters L.Welterweight Champion.
Ht 5'8¼"
Manager Self
14.10.05 Darren Johnstone L PTS 6 Motherwell
03.11.05 Tom Hogan L PTS 6 Sunderland
19.11.05 Mark Alexander L PTS 4 Southwark
23.01.06 Paul Appleby L RTD 3 Glasgow
04.03.06 Dougie Walton DREW 6 Coventry
27.05.06 Omar Akram W RSC 2 Glasgow
01.06.06 Paul Appleby L RSC 2 Birmingham
21.07.06 James Brown W PTS 4 Altrincham
06.12.06 Andrew Ward W PTS 6 Rotherham
28.01.07 Paul Truscott L PTS 4 Yarm
15.11.07 Adil Anwar W PTS 6 Leeds
01.12.07 Tristan Davies W RSC 5 Telford
(Vacant British Masters L.Welterweight Title)

124

06.06.08 Gary Reid W RSC 10 Stoke
    (British Masters L.Welterweight Title
    Defence)
19.09.08 Stefy Bull W PTS 10 Doncaster
    (British Masters L. Welterweight Title
    Defence)
13.03.09 Steve Williams L RSC 4 Widnes
24.05.09 Carl Allen W PTS 6 Shaw
Career: 16 contests, won 8, drew 1, lost 7.

Chris Higgs

Lydney. *Born* Bristol, 28 September, 1987
Lightweight. *Ht* 5' 8"
Manager J. Field
17.10.08 Daniel Thorpe W PTS 6 Swindon
13.02.09 Sid Razak W PTS 4 Swindon
10.04.09 Robin Deakin W RSC 3 Cheltenham
Career: 3 contests, won 3.

Chris Higgs   Philip Sharkey

Dwayne Hill

Sheffield. *Born* Sheffield, 31 January, 1986
Lightweight. *Ht* 5'8"
Manager Self
08.05.05 Anthony Christopher W PTS 6 Sheffield
24.07.05 Gary Coombes W RSC 3 Sheffield
30.10.05 Gavin Tait W PTS 6 Sheffield
12.11.05 Lance Verallo W PTS 6 Sheffield
17.02.06 Carl Allen W PTS 6 Sheffield
16.06.06 Daniel Thorpe W PTS 4 Liverpool
28.10.06 Youssef Al Hamidi L RSC 3 Sheffield
17.02.07 Stephen Haughian L RSC 2 Cork
13.07.07 Danny Wallace L RTD 3 Barnsley
16.09.07 Johnny Greaves W PTS 6 Sheffield
29.09.07 Vadzim Astapuk W PTS 4 Sheffield
19.10.07 Gary Sykes L RSC 4 Doncaster
06.12.07 George Watson L PTS 6 Sunderland
15.02.08 Carl Allen W PTS 6 Sheffield
01.03.08 Kevin Buckley L PTS 6 Stoke
20.03.08 Paul Holborn L PTS 6 South Shields
13.06.08 Paul Holborn L PTS 10 Sunderland
    (Vacant International Masters
    Lightweight Title)
12.09.08 Jon Baguley L RSC 3 Sheffield
    (Vacant Central Area Lightweight Title)
Career: 18 contests, won 9, lost 9.

Quinton Hillocks

Brierley Hill. *Born* Miami, Florida, USA,
16 August, 1984
S.Middleweight. *Ht* 6' 4"
Manager E. Johnson
01.02.09 Davey Jones W PTS 4 Edgbaston,
    Birmingham
14.03.09 Lee Duncan W PTS 4 Birmingham
Career: 2 contests, won 2.

George Hillyard

Canning Town. *Born* Forest Gate, 19
November, 1984
Former Undefeated British Masters
L.Middleweight Champion. *Ht* 5'9¼"
Manager A. Sims
16.06.05 Geraint Harvey W RSC 1 Dagenham
30.09.05 James Gorman W RSC 1 Kirkcaldy
21.10.05 Ernie Smith L PTS 4 Bethnal Green
18.11.05 Richard Mazurek W PTS 6 Dagenham
24.02.06 Gary Harrison W RTD 4 Dagenham
21.04.06 Ciaran Healy W CO 6 Belfast
22.09.06 Tyan Booth L PTS 6 Bethnal Green
15.12.06 Marcus Portman L PTS 8 Bethnal Green
20.01.07 Tony Randell DREW 4 Muswell Hill
18.05.07 Matt Scriven W PTS 4 Canning Town
16.06.07 Dave Wakefield W PTS 10 Chigwell
    (Vacant British Masters L.Middleweight
    Title)
05.10.07 Lee Noble W PTS 6 Bethnal Green
27.06.08 Danny Goode W RSC 2 Bethnal Green
23.05.09 Matthew Thirlwall L RTD 4 Watford
Career: 14 contests, won 9, drew 1, lost 4.

Paul Holborn

Sunderland. *Born* Sunderland, 1 March,
1984
International Masters Lightweight
Champion. *Ht* 5'8½"
Manager Self
11.10.04 Stuart Green W PTS 6 Glasgow
15.12.04 Amir Ali L PTS 6 Sheffield
06.10.05 Daniel Thorpe W PTS 6 Sunderland
03.11.05 Haroon Din DREW 6 Sunderland
28.04.06 Billy Smith W PTS 4 Hartlepool
11.05.06 Kristian Laight W PTS 6 Sunderland
05.10.06 Youssef Al Hamidi W PTS 6 Sunderland
15.02.08 Johnny Greaves W PTS 6 Sunderland
20.03.08 Dwayne Hill W PTS 6 South Shields
13.06.08 Dwayne Hill W PTS 10 Sunderland
    (Vacant International Masters
    Lightweight Title)
29.11.08 Amir Unsworth W PTS 10 Sleaford
    (International Masters Lightweight Title
    Defence)
24.03.09 Charles Paul King W PTS 3 Glasgow
24.03.09 Ryan Brawley L PTS 3 Glasgow
02.05.09 Youssef Al Hamidi W PTS 6 Sunderland
Career: 14 contests, won 11, drew 1, lost 2.

Myles Holder

Portobello. *Born* Wolverhampton, 6 March,
1989
Middleweight. *Ht* 5' 9"
Manager E. Johnson
29.05.09 Matt Seawright W PTS 4 Dudley
26.06.09 Gary Cooper W PTS 6 Melksham
Career: 2 contests, won 2.

Mike Holloway

Leeds. *Born* Leeds, 22 December, 1982
S.Bantamweight. *Ht* 5'7¼"
Manager D. Roche
28.03.08 Delroy Spencer W PTS 4 Barnsley
23.05.08 Mike Robinson L PTS 4 Wigan
06.06.08 Davey Savage L RSC 4 Glasgow
10.10.08 Ross Burkinshaw L RSC 1 Sheffield
08.11.08 Craig Lyon L RSC 5 Wigan
Career: 5 contests, won 1, lost 4.

Kerry Hope

Merthyr Tydfil. *Born* Merthyr Tydfil, 21
October, 1981
Middleweight. *Ht* 5'10"
Manager Self
21.01.05 Brian Coleman W PTS 4 Bridgend
08.04.05 Ernie Smith W PTS 4 Edinburgh
27.05.05 Lee Williamson W PTS 4 Spennymoor
10.09.05 John-Paul Temple W PTS 4 Cardiff
04.03.06 Matt Scriven W PTS 4 Manchester
01.06.06 Joe Mitchell W PTS 4 Barnsley
08.07.06 Ryan Rowlinson W PTS 4 Cardiff
18.11.06 Manoocha Salari W RSC 2 Newport
07.04.07 Jamie Ambler W PTS 6 Cardiff
21.07.07 Sherman Alleyne W PTS 6 Cardiff
03.11.07 Ernie Smith W PTS 4 Cardiff
22.03.08 Matthew Hall L RSC 8 Cardiff
21.02.09 Taz Jones L RSC 4 Merthyr Tydfil
    (Vacant Welsh Area L.Middleweight
    Title)
Career: 13 contests, won 11, lost 2.

Richard Horton

Romford. *Born* Romford, 12 November,
1981
S.Middleweight. *Ht* 6'0¾"
Manager D. Powell
25.02.06 Nick Okoth W CO 3 Canning Town
01.04.06 Ojay Abrahams W PTS 4 Bethnal Green
13.05.06 Mark Phillips W PTS 4 Bethnal Green
23.07.06 Shon Davies L RSC 1 Dagenham
24.09.06 Mark Phillips W PTS 4 Bethnal Green
01.12.07 Michael Banbula W PTS 4 Bethnal
    Green
04.04.08 Ruben Groenewald W PTS 6 Bethnal
    Green
30.01.09 Tony Salam L RSC 4 Bethnal Green
    (Vacant Southern Area S.Middleweight
    Title)
Career: 8 contests, won 6, lost 2.

Sam Horton

Stourbridge. *Born* Wordsley, 20 August,
1985
Midlands Area S.Middleweight Champion.
Ht 5'11"
Manager E. Johnson
07.10.06 Tony Randell W PTS 6 Walsall
17.11.06 Jon Foster W PTS 6 Brierley Hill
15.02.07 Dave Pearson W RSC 4 Dudley
20.04.07 Tony Stones W PTS 4 Dudley
28.06.07 Ernie Smith W PTS 4 Dudley
26.10.07 Davey Jones W PTS 6 Birmingham
18.01.08 Lee Noble W PTS 4 Burton
10.04.08 Tony Stones W PTS 6 Piccadilly
12.05.08 Lee Noble W PTS 8 Birmingham

02.10.08 Sherman Alleyne W RSC 4 Piccadilly
26.11.08 Vepkhia Tchilaia W PTS 6 Piccadilly
03.04.09 Jamie Ambler W PTS 6 Wolverhampton
10.05.09 Matthew Hainy W PTS 10 Derby
　　　　*(Vacant Midlands Area S.Middleweight
　　　　Title)*
Career: 13 contests, won 13.

Sam Horton 　　　　　　　Philip Sharkey

Matthew Hough

Walsall. *Born* Walsall, 5 January, 1977
L.Heavyweight. *Ht* 6'2"
Manager E. Johnson
17.02.05 Paddy Ryan W PTS 6 Dudley
21.04.05 Mark Phillips W PTS 4 Dudley
25.11.05 Robert Burton W PTS 4 Walsall
10.03.06 John Ruddock W PTS 6 Walsall
18.05.06 Dean Walker W PTS 6 Walsall
07.10.06 Danny McIntosh L RSC 6 Walsall
15.02.07 Nicki Taylor L RSC 2 Dudley
28.09.07 John Ruddock W RSC 3 Coventry
08.10.07 Mark Phillips W PTS 6 Birmingham
28.11.07 Jamie Ambler DREW 4 Walsall
28.02.08 Max Maxwell L RSC 3 Wolverhampton
　　　　*(Vacant Midlands Area Middleweight
　　　　Title)*
04.09.08 Danny Butler L RSC 5 Edgbaston
　　　　*(Vacant British Masters S. Middleweight
　　　　Title)*
Career: 12 contests, won 7, drew 1, lost 4.

Matthew Hough 　　　　　Philip Sharkey

Dave Howe

Sheffield. *Born* Sheffield, 18 August, 1980
Heavyweight. *Ht* 6' 8"
Manager G. Rhodes
12.09.08 Howard Daley W RSC 1 Sheffield
17.10.08 David Ingleby L CO 1 Bethnal Green
Career: 2 contests, won 1, lost 1.

Mark Hudson

Bradford. *Born* Bradford, 18 April, 1975
Featherweight. *Ht* 5' 7"
Manager M. Marsden
21.02.99 Gary Groves W RSC 3 Bradford
18.10.99 Peter Allen W PTS 6 Bradford
29.04.02 Dave Curran L RSC 1 Bradford
24.05.09 Masoor Walli L CO 1 Bradford
Career: 4 contests, won 2, lost 2.

Justyn Hugh

Newport. *Born* Newport, 13 February, 1984
L.Heavyweight. *Ht* 5' 11"
Manager C. Sanigar
12.07.08 Pawel Trebinski W PTS 6 Newport
24.10.08 Michael Banbula W PTS 6 Newport
13.03.09 Phil Goodwin W PTS 6 Newport
05.06.09 Michael Banbula W PTS 6 Newport
Career: 4 contests, won 4.

Danny Hughes

Sunderland. *Born* Sunderland, 3 March,
1986
Heavyweight. *Ht* 6'5¼"
Manager T. Conroy
24.06.07 Lee Webb W RSC 4 Sunderland
05.10.07 David Ingleby DREW 6 Sunderland
15.02.08 Lee Mountford W PTS 6 Sunderland
15.05.08 Steve Bodger W PTS 6 Sunderland
13.06.08 David Ingleby W PTS 4 Sunderland
28.02.09 Chris Woollas W PTS 6 Newcastle
02.05.09 Howard Daley W PTS 6 Sunderland
Career: 7 contests, won 6, drew 1.

Kris Hughes

Bellshill. *Born* Bellshill, 23 November,
1987
Bantamweight. *Ht* 5'11¼"
Manager A. Morrison
27.10.06 Delroy Spencer W PTS 6 Glasgow
26.01.07 Robert Bunford W PTS 6 Glasgow
05.10.07 Matthew Edmonds W PTS 6 Newport
27.02.09 Delroy Spencer W PTS 4 Paisley
06.03.09 Chris Riley W PTS 6 Glasgow
27.03.09 James Ancliff W PTS 4 Glasgow
29.05.09 Michael Crossan W PTS 6 Glasgow
19.06.09 James Ancliff W PTS 6 Glasgow
Career: 8 contests, won 8.

Sean Hughes

Pontefract. *Born* Pontefract, 5 June, 1982
S.Featherweight. Former Undefeated
Central Area S.Bantamweight Champion.
Ht 5'9"
Manager Self
02.03.02 Paddy Folan W PTS 6 Wakefield
25.06.02 John Paul Ryan W PTS 6 Rugby
05.10.02 Paddy Folan W PTS 4 Huddersfield

10.02.03 Neil Read W PTS 6 Sheffield
24.05.03 John-Paul Ryan W PTS 6 Sheffield
13.09.03 Daniel Thorpe W PTS 6 Wakefield
05.10.03 Paddy Folan W RSC 4 Bradford
　　　　*(Vacant Central Area S.Bantamweight
　　　　Title)*
07.12.03 Marty Kayes W PTS 6 Bradford
26.02.04 Steve Foster L RSC 6 Widnes
　　　　(Vacant English Featherweight Title)
23.10.04 Kristian Laight W PTS 6 Wakefield
04.03.05 Michael Hunter L RSC 6 Hartlepool
　　　　*(British S.Bantamweight Title
　　　　Challenge)*
08.05.05 Billy Smith W PTS 6 Bradford
25.06.05 Pete Buckley DREW 6 Wakefield
14.10.05 Bernard Dunne L RSC 2 Dublin
　　　　(Vacant IBC S.Bantamweight Title)
03.03.06 Marc Callaghan L PTS 10 Hartlepool
　　　　(Vacant English S.Bantamweight Title)
28.05.06 Shaun Walton W PTS 6 Wakefield
10.11.06 Riaz Durgahed L PTS 6 Hartlepool
24.11.06 Billy Corcoran L RSC 8 Nottingham
14.04.07 Sergei Rozhakmens W PTS 6 Wakefield
05.10.07 Sergei Rozhakmens W PTS 6
　　　　Sunderland
09.11.07 Esham Pickering W PTS 8 Nottingham
18.01.08 Esham Pickering L RSC 9 Burton
　　　　*(British S.Bantamweight Title
　　　　Challenge)*
18.07.08 Delroy Spencer W PTS 4 Dagenham
18.12.08 Jason Booth L RTD 10 Dublin
　　　　*(Commonwealth Bantamweight Title
　　　　Challenge)*
24.01.09 Mahyar Monshipour L RSC 8 Pau,
　　　　France
Career: 25 contests, won 15, drew 1, lost 9.

Sean Hughes 　　　　　　Philip Sharkey

Rob Hunt

Stafford. *Born* Stafford, 9 November, 1985
Welterweight. *Ht* 6'0"
Manager P. Dykes
18.05.06 Ian Clyde W RSC 1 Walsall
29.06.06 Pete Buckley W PTS 6 Dudley
07.10.06 Karl Taylor W PTS 6 Walsall
15.02.07 Kristian Laight W PTS 6 Dudley
09.06.07 Johnny Greaves W PTS 6
　　　　Middlesbrough

20.07.07 Karl Taylor W PTS 4 Wolverhampton
25.10.07 Leonard Lothian W PTS 4
Wolverhampton
28.02.08 Senol Dervis W PTS 4 Wolverhampton
30.04.08 Baz Carey W PTS 6 Wolverhampton
20.06.08 Alex Brew W PTS 6 Wolverhampton
26.09.08 Jason Nesbitt W PTS 8 Wolverhampton
06.02.09 Carl Allen W PTS 4 Birmingham
24.04.09 Chris Long DREW 4 Wolverhampton
Career: 13 contests, won 12, drew 1.

Rob Hunt   Philip Sharkey

Michael Hunter

Hartlepool. *Born* Hartlepool, 5 May, 1978
Featherweight. Former Undefeated British,
European, Commonwealth, WBF &
Northern Area S.Bantamweight Champion.
Ht 5'7½"
Manager Self
23.07.00 Sean Grant W PTS 6 Hartlepool
01.10.00 Chris Emanuele W PTS 6 Hartlepool
24.11.00 Gary Groves W RSC 2 Darlington
09.12.00 Chris Jickells W PTS 4 Southwark
11.02.01 Paddy Folan W RSC 6 Hartlepool
06.05.01 Anthony Hanna W PTS 4 Hartlepool
04.06.01 Anthony Hanna W PTS 4 Hartlepool
09.09.01 John Barnes W RSC 8 Hartlepool
*(Vacant Northern Area S.Bantamweight
Title)*
29.11.01 Joel Viney W PTS 6 Hartlepool
26.01.02 Stevie Quinn W CO 2 Dagenham
18.03.02 Marc Callaghan DREW 6 Crawley
18.05.02 Mark Payne W PTS 8 Millwall
18.10.02 Frankie DeMilo W PTS 12 Hartlepool
(Vacant WBF S. Bantamweight Title)
14.12.02 Anthony Hanna W PTS 8 Newcastle
07.06.03 Afrim Mustafa W RSC 5 Trieste, Italy
26.07.03 Rocky Dean W RSC 1 Plymouth
04.10.03 Nikolai Eremeev W PTS 6 Belfast
08.11.03 Gennadiy Delisandru W PTS 6 Bridgend
16.04.04 Mark Payne W RSC 7 Hartlepool
(Vacant British S.Bantamweight Title)
02.06.04 Vladimir Borov W PTS 6 Hereford
19.11.04 Marc Callaghan W RSC 10 Hartlepool
(British S.Bantamweight Title Defence)
04.03.05 Sean Hughes W RSC 6 Hartlepool
(British S.Bantamweight Title Defence)

27.05.05 Kamel Guerfi W RSC 6 Spennymoor
28.10.05 Esham Pickering W PTS 12 Hartlepool
*(European & Commonwealth
S.Bantamweight Title Challenges.
British S.Bantamweight Title Defence)*
03.03.06 Yersin Jailauov W RSC 2 Hartlepool
*(European S.Bantamweight Title
Defence)*
28.04.06 German Guartos W RTD 3 Hartlepool
*(European S.Bantamweight Title
Defence)*
23.06.06 Tuncay Kaya W CO 9 Blackpool
*(European S.Bantamweight Title
Defence)*
10.11.06 Steve Molitor L CO 5 Hartlepool
(Vacant IBF S.Bantamweight Title)
30.03.07 Ben Odamattey W PTS 8 Crawley
08.02.08 Youssef Al Hamidi W PTS 6 Peterlee
05.12.08 Osman Aktas W PTS 8 Dagenham
Career: 31 contests, won 29, drew 1, lost 1.

Michael Hunter   Philip Sharkey

Khurram Hussain

Bradford. *Born* Bradford, 11 August, 1980
Welterweight. *Ht* 5' 10"
Manager Self
13.11.05 Peter Dunn W PTS 4 Leeds
03.12.05 Kyle Taylor W PTS 6 Coventry
23.02.06 Darren Gethin DREW 4 Leeds
04.03.06 Joe McCluskey W PTS 6 Coventry
28.05.06 Tye Williams W PTS 6 Wakefield
24.02.07 Jonathan Hussey L PTS 6 Manchester
06.05.07 Karl Taylor W PTS 4 Leeds
27.05.07 Peter Dunn W PTS 4 Bradford
11.07.08 Paddy Pollock W PTS 4 Wigan
Career: 9 contests, won 7, drew 1, lost 1.

Anser Hussein

Rochdale. *Born* Dewsbury, 18 May, 1979
S.Featherweight. *Ht* 5' 10"
Manager J. Doughty
16.11.08 Steve Gethin W PTS 6 Shaw
24.05.09 Mo Khaled L PTS 6 Shaw
Career: 2 contests, won 1, lost 1.

Jonathan Hussey

Manchester. *Born* Manchester, 18 August,
1982
Welterweight. *Ht* 6'0"
Manager T. Gilmour
08.07.05 Joe Mitchell W PTS 4 Altrincham
01.10.05 Darren Gethin W PTS 6 Wigan
18.12.05 Karl Taylor W PTS 6 Bolton
12.02.06 Tye Williams W PTS 6 Manchester
06.05.06 Geraint Harvey W PTS 6 Blackpool
18.06.06 Barry Downes W PTS 6 Manchester
10.07.06 Imad Khamis W PTS 6 Manchester
26.10.06 Billy Smith L PTS 6 Dudley
24.02.07 Khurram Hussain W PTS 6 Manchester
28.09.07 Jason Nesbitt W PTS 6 Preston
14.03.08 Chris Brophy W RSC 6 Manchester
07.06.08 Russell Pearce W PTS 4 Wigan
28.11.08 Arek Malek W RTD 2 Glasgow
03.04.09 Graham Fearn W PTS 6 Bethnal Green
08.06.09 Charles Paul King L PTS 6 Glasgow
Career: 15 contests, won 13, lost 2.

Jonathan Hussey   Philip Sharkey

Paul Hyland

Hornchurch. *Born* Dublin, 19 November,
1984
All-Ireland S.Bantamweight Champion.
Ht 5' 7"
Manager J. Harding
05.11.04 Janos Garai W RSC 2 Hereford
19.02.05 Vladimir Bukovy W RSC 3 Dublin
04.06.05 Ferenc Szabo W PTS 6 Dublin
17.09.05 Andrej Surina W RTD 3 Dublin
14.10.05 Peter Feher W PTS 4 Dublin
18.11.05 Rakhim Mingaleev W PTS 4 Dagenham
24.02.06 Dariusz Snarski W PTS 6 Dagenham
11.03.06 Sandor Paska W RSC 3 Dublin
27.07.07 Arthur Parker W PTS 4 Saratoga
Springs, New York, USA
19.04.08 Ayittey Mettle W PTS 8 Dublin
05.07.08 Marc Callaghan W PTS 10 Dublin
*(Vacant All-Ireland S.Bantamweight
Title)*
06.09.08 Cristian Nicolae W PTS 6 Dublin
04.10.08 Lucian Gonzalez L PTS 4 Philadelphia,
Pennsylvania, USA
18.12.08 Eugene Heagney W PTS 6 Dublin
27.02.09 Nikita Lukin W PTS 6 Barnsley
Career: 15 contests, won 14, lost 1.

Jon Ibbotson

Sheffield. *Born* Sheffield, 2 September, 1982
L.Heavyweight. *Ht* 6'3½"
Manager Self
15.12.04 Paul Billington W PTS 4 Sheffield
20.02.05 Nick Okoth W PTS 6 Sheffield
22.04.05 Daniel Teasdale W RSC 1 Barnsley
18.06.05 Ojay Abrahams W PTS 4 Barnsley
05.03.06 Tony Booth W PTS 4 Sheffield
13.05.06 Magid Ben Driss W RSC 2 Sheffield
22.06.06 Robert Burton DREW 6 Sheffield
20.10.06 Robert Burton W CO 2 Sheffield
20.01.07 Shannon Anderson W RSC 1 Las Vegas, Nevada, USA
03.05.07 Darren Stubbs L RSC 4 Sheffield
22.03.08 Ayitey Powers W PTS 6 Sheffield
21.06.08 Simeon Cover W PTS 6 Sheffield
19.09.08 Paul Bonson W PTS 4 Doncaster
Career: 13 contests, won 11, drew 1, lost 1.

Alex Ibbs

Stoke. *Born* Stoke, 17 August, 1985
Heavyweight. *Ht* 6'4"
Manager M. Carney
01.12.06 Istvan Kecskes W PTS 4 Birmingham
12.05.07 David Ingleby W PTS 6 Stoke
17.11.07 Lee Mountford W PTS 6 Stoke
01.03.08 David Ingleby L RSC 4 Stoke
11.04.08 Martin Rogan L RSC 2 Bethnal Green
23.01.09 Steve Bodger W PTS 4 Stoke
Career: 6 contests, won 4, lost 2.

David Ingleby

Lancaster. *Born* Lancaster, 14 June, 1980
Heavyweight. *Ht* 6'3"
Manager Self
09.06.03 Costi Marin L RSC 1 Bradford
01.12.03 Paul Bonson L PTS 6 Leeds
28.02.04 Paul King L RSC 3 Manchester
01.05.04 Jason Callum L PTS 6 Coventry
10.07.04 Scott Lansdowne L RSC 4 Coventry
20.09.04 Dave Clarke W RTD 5 Glasgow
06.12.04 Paul Butlin L CO 5 Leicester
30.04.05 Paul Butlin W PTS 6 Coventry
02.06.05 Chris Burton L RSC 3 Yarm
12.12.05 Scott Lansdowne L RSC 1 Leicester
18.03.06 Paul Butlin W PTS 6 Coventry
06.04.06 Matt Paice L PTS 4 Piccadilly
13.05.06 Carl Baker L RSC 4 Sheffield
07.10.06 Henry Smith W PTS 6 Weston super Mare
16.02.07 Dave Ferguson L PTS 4 Sunderland
20.04.07 Billy Boyle L PTS 4 Sheffield
03.05.07 Scott Brookes L PTS 6 Sheffield
12.05.07 Alex Ibbs L PTS 6 Stoke
24.06.07 Dave Ferguson L PTS 4 Sunderland
06.07.07 Scott Mitchell L PTS 4 Wigan
15.07.07 Paul Malcolm L PTS 6 Hartlepool

27.07.07 James Dolan L PTS 4 Houghton le Spring
28.09.07 Howard Daley L PTS 6 Preston
05.10.07 Danny Hughes DREW 6 Sunderland
19.10.07 Dean O'Loughlin W RSC 5 Doncaster
01.03.08 Alex Ibbs W RSC 4 Stoke
13.06.08 Danny Hughes L PTS 4 Sunderland
12.09.08 Chris Burton L PTS 3 Newcastle
17.10.08 Dave Howe W CO 1 Bethnal Green
15.11.08 Larry Olubamiwo L RSC 2 Bethnal Green
07.03.09 Pele Reid L PTS 10 Birmingham
  (*Vacant British Masters Heavyweight Title*)
28.03.09 David Price L RSC 3 Liverpool
23.06.09 Coleman Barrett L PTS 6 Longford
Career: 33 contests, won 6, drew 1, lost 26.

Matt Jack   Philip Sharkey

Matt Jack

Newmarket. *Born* London, 25 August, 1981
S.Middleweight. *Ht* 6'1"
Manager J. Eames
22.03.09 Patrick Mendy L PTS 4 Bethnal Green
Career: 1 contest, lost 1.

Hamed Jamali

Birmingham. *Born* Iran, 23 November, 1973
S.Middleweight. *Ht* 5'9"
Manager Self
09.12.02 Dale Nixon W CO 1 Birmingham
24.02.03 Harry Butler W PTS 6 Birmingham
06.10.03 Simeon Cover W PTS 6 Birmingham
08.12.03 JJ Ojuederie W PTS 6 Birmingham
08.03.04 Ojay Abrahams W PTS 8 Birmingham
10.05.04 Jason Collins W PTS 8 Birmingham
11.10.04 Hastings Rasani W PTS 8 Birmingham
13.12.04 Simeon Cover L PTS 10 Birmingham
  (*Vacant British Masters S.Middleweight Title*)
21.02.05 Michael Pinnock W PTS 8 Birmingham
02.03.06 Lee Blundell L PTS 6 Blackpool
07.04.06 Dan Guthrie L RSC 3 Bristol
08.09.06 Cello Renda L RSC 1 Birmingham

25.01.08 Mark Nilsen W PTS 4 Birmingham
07.03.08 Adie Whitmore L PTS 4 Nottingham
16.05.08 Rod Anderton L PTS 10 Burton
  (*Vacant International Masters L.Heavyweight Title*)
Career: 15 contests, won 9, lost 6.

Troy James

Coventry. *Born* Coventry, 18 September, 1983
S.Featherweight. *Ht* 5'4"
Manager B. Hearn
16.01.09 Frederic Gosset W PTS 4 Middlesbrough
13.03.09 Ibrar Riyaz W PTS 4 Widnes
12.06.09 Chris Riley DREW 4 Liverpool
Career: 3 contests, won 2, drew 1.

Fred Janes

Cardiff. *Born* Cardiff, 17 December, 1984
Welterweight. *Ht* 5'9"
Manager B. Coleman
23.11.03 Paddy Folan W RSC 5 Rotherham
13.12.03 Stevie Bell L PTS 4 Manchester
13.02.04 Michael Graydon DREW 6 Bristol
06.03.04 John Bothwell DREW 4 Glasgow
01.04.04 Martin Power L RSC 2 Bethnal Green
02.06.04 John Simpson L PTS 6 Hereford
10.09.04 Matthew Marsh L PTS 4 Bethnal Green
16.10.04 Warren Dunkley L PTS 4 Dagenham
06.12.04 Danny Wallace L RSC 2 Leeds
29.04.05 Paul Buckley L PTS 4 Southwark
30.09.05 Stuart Green L PTS 4 Kirkcaldy
04.12.08 Tyrone Nurse L PTS 4 Bradford
21.02.09 Geraint Harvey W PTS 6 Merthyr Tydfil
Career: 13 contests, won 2, drew 2, lost 9.

Damien Jeffries   Philip Sharkey

Damien Jeffries

Manchester. *Born* Manchester, 6 September, 1982
Welterweight. *Ht* 5'6"
Manager G. Hunter
23.05.09 Ben Lawler L PTS 6 Sleaford
21.06.09 John Wayne Hibbert L CO 1 Bethnal Green
Career: 2 contests, lost 2.

Tony Jeffries

Sunderland. *Born* Sunderland, 2 March, 1985
L.Heavyweight. *Ht* 6' 2"
Manager P. Jeffries
27.02.09 Aliaksandr Vayavoda W RSC 1 Barnsley
02.05.09 Roy Meissner W RSC 2 Sunderland
Career: 2 contests, won 2.

Lee Jennings

Liverpool. *Born* Liverpool, 14 July, 1981
Lightweight. *Ht* 5'2¼"
Manager S. Wood
15.06.08 Kristian Laight W PTS 6 St Helens
14.09.08 John Vanemmenis W CO 2 Wigan
21.12.08 Youssef Al Hamidi L PTS 6 Bolton
28.03.09 Karl Taylor W PTS 4 Liverpool
Career: 4 contests, won 3, lost 1.

Michael Jennings

Chorley. *Born* Preston, 9 September, 1977
WBU Welterweight Champion. Former
British Welterweight Champion. Former
Undefeated English Welterweight
Champion. Former Undefeated WBU Inter-
Continental Welterweight Champion.
Ht 5'9¼"
Manager F. Warren/B.Hughes
15.05.99 Tony Smith W RSC 1 Blackpool
11.12.99 Lee Molyneux W PTS 4 Liverpool
29.02.00 Lee Molyneux W PTS 6 Widnes
25.03.00 Brian Coleman W PTS 6 Liverpool
16.05.00 Brian Coleman W PTS 6 Warrington
29.05.00 William Webster W PTS 6 Manchester
08.07.00 Paul Denton W PTS 6 Widnes
04.09.00 Mark Ramsey W PTS 6 Manchester
25.11.00 Ernie Smith W PTS 4 Manchester
11.12.00 Paul Denton W PTS 4 Widnes
10.02.01 Mark Haslam W RSC 2 Widnes
07.07.01 David Kirk W PTS 6 Manchester
15.09.01 Gary Harrison W PTS 6 Manchester
09.02.02 James Paisley W RSC 3 Manchester
01.06.02 Lee Williamson W PTS 4 Manchester
28.09.02 Karl Taylor W RSC 4 Manchester
01.11.02 Richard Inquieti W RSC 2 Preston
18.01.03 Lee Williamson W RTD 4 Preston
08.05.03 Jimmy Gould W RTD 6 Widnes
　　　　　(Vacant WBU Inter-Continental
　　　　　Welterweight Title)
27.09.03 Sammy Smith W RTD 4 Manchester
　　　　　(WBU Inter-Continental Welterweight
　　　　　Title Defence)
13.12.03 Peter Dunn W PTS 6 Manchester
01.04.04 Brett James W RTD 5 Bethnal Green
　　　　　(WBU Inter-Continental Welterweight
　　　　　Title Defence)
22.05.04 Rafal Jackiewicz W PTS 8 Widnes
01.10.04 Chris Saunders W RTD 5 Manchester
　　　　　(English Welterweight Title Challenge)
11.02.05 Vasile Dragomir W CO 3 Manchester
03.06.05 Gavin Down W RSC 9 Manchester
　　　　　(English Welterweight Title Defence)
16.07.05 Jimmy Vincent W CO 1 Bolton
　　　　　(Vacant British Welterweight Title)
25.10.05 Bradley Pryce W PTS 12 Preston
　　　　　(British Welterweight Title Defence)
28.01.06 Young Muttley L PTS 12 Nottingham
　　　　　(British Welterweight Title Defence)
02.09.06 Rastislav Kovac W CO 3 Bolton
07.04.07 Takaloo W PTS 12 Cardiff
　　　　　(WBU Welterweight Title Challenge)
28.09.07 Vladimir Khodokovski W PTS 8
　　　　　Preston
02.02.08 Ross Minter W RSC 9 Canning Town
　　　　　(WBU Welterweight Title Defence)
05.04.08 George Ungiadze W RSC 7 Bolton
14.11.08 Jason Rushton W PTS 8 Glasgow
21.02.09 Miguel Cotto L RSC 5 NYC, New York,
　　　　　USA
　　　　　(Vacant WBO Welterweight Title)
15.05.09 Willie Thompson W RSC 4 Belfast
Career: 37 contests, won 35, lost 2.

Michael Jennings　　　　　Philip Sharkey

Mick Jenno

Liverpool. *Born* Liverpool, 16 July, 1977
S.Middleweight. *Ht* 5'11"
Manager Self
30.06.07 Martin Gillick W RSC 1 Manchester
01.12.07 Gary Cooper W PTS 4 Liverpool
29.03.09 Mark Phillips W PTS 4 Bolton
17.05.09 Jamie Ambler W PTS 4 Bolton
Career: 4 contests, won 4.

Steve Jevons

Swanwick. *Born* Mansfield, 8 June, 1988
Welterweight. *Ht* 6'0¼"
Manager M. Shinfield
02.05.08 Bheki Moyo W PTS 4 Nottingham
05.10.08 Sergei Rozhakmens W PTS 4
　　　　　Nottingham
31.05.09 Daniel Thorpe W PTS 6 Burton
Career: 3 contests, won 3.

Chris Johnson

Manchester. *Born* Chorley, 8 March, 1981
L.Middleweight. *Ht* 5'10"
Manager S. Wood
29.09.06 Paul Porter L RSC 2 Manchester
17.12.06 Geraint Harvey W PTS 6 Bolton
11.03.07 Karl Taylor W RTD 3 Shaw
06.05.07 Danny Gwilym W RSC 4 Altrincham
24.06.07 David Kirk W PTS 4 Wigan
25.11.07 Peter Dunn W PTS 6 Colne
23.12.07 Steve Cooper W RSC 4 Bolton
16.02.08 Dave Murray W RSC 4 Blackpool
23.05.08 Darren Gethin W RSC 5 Wigan
14.09.08 David Kirk W PTS 4 Wigan
24.01.09 Geraint Harvey L PTS 4 Blackpool
17.05.09 Martyn King W PTS 4 Bolton
Career: 12 contests, won 10, lost 2.

Craig Johnson

Clay Cross. *Born* Chesterfield, 10
November, 1980
Lightweight. *Ht* 5'7"
Manager M. Shinfield
25.04.04 Peter Allen W PTS 6 Nottingham
18.09.04 David Bailey L PTS 6 Newark
22.10.04 Carl Allen W PTS 6 Mansfield
10.12.04 Pete Buckley W PTS 6 Mansfield
06.03.05 Ian Reid W PTS 6 Mansfield
11.09.05 Billy Smith W PTS 4 Kirkby in
　　　　　Ashfield
12.11.05 Jason Nesbitt W PTS 6 Sheffield
29.04.07 Sergei Rozhakmens W PTS 6
　　　　　Birmingham
15.09.07 Martin Gethin L PTS 10 Birmingham
　　　　　(Vacant Midlands Area Lightweight
　　　　　Title)
10.12.07 Gavin Deacon W PTS 6 Cleethorpes
22.09.08 Charles Paul King L PTS 8 Glasgow
22.11.08 Jon Kays W PTS 6 Blackpool
27.02.09 Lee Selby L PTS 4 Barnsley
Career: 13 contests, won 9, lost 4.

Danny Johnston

Stoke. *Born* Stoke, 19 May, 1981
L.Middleweight. *Ht* 5'10"
Manager P. Dykes
26.09.04 Karl Taylor W PTS 6 Stoke
12.11.05 Manoocha Salari L RSC 5 Stoke
18.02.06 Terry Carruthers L PTS 6 Stoke
06.05.06 Derek Greave W RSC 3 Stoke
24.11.06 Martin Marshall W PTS 6 Stoke
24.02.07 Howard Clarke W PTS 6 Stoke
12.05.07 Tomasz Mazurkiewicz L PTS 6 Stoke
27.02.09 Matt Seawright W PTS 4
　　　　　Wolverhampton
Career: 8 contests, won 5, lost 3.

Barrie Jones

Rhondda. *Born* Tylorstown, South Wales, 1
March, 1985
Welterweight. *Ht* 5'11¼"
Manager D. Powell/F. Warren
03.07.04 Pete Buckley W PTS 4 Newport
03.09.04 Dave Hinds W PTS 4 Newport
21.01.05 Lea Handley W PTS 4 Bridgend

17.06.05 Marco Cittadini W RSC 2 Glasgow
10.09.05 Jas Malik W RSC 1 Cardiff
11.03.06 Terry Carruthers W RSC 1 Newport
29.04.06 David Kehoe W RTD 2 Edinburgh
08.07.06 James Paisley W RSC 2 Cardiff
18.11.06 Ernie Smith W PTS 4 Newport
16.02.07 Chris Brophy W PTS 4 Merthyr Tydfil
07.04.07 Daniel Thorpe W RSC 2 Cardiff
05.05.07 Rocky Muscas W PTS 6 Glasgow
21.07.07 Billy Smith W PTS 4 Cardiff
07.09.07 Jay Morris W RTD 4 Mayfair
03.11.07 Silence Saheed W PTS 4 Cardiff
22.03.08 Tony Doherty L PTS 10 Cardiff
        (Vacant Welsh Area Welterweight Title)
14.06.08 Kell Brook L RSC 7 Bethnal Green
        (Vacant British Welterweight Title)
06.12.08 Souleymane M'Baye L PTS 8 Canning
        Town
13.02.09 Jay Morris W PTS 4 Swindon
Career: 19 contests, won 16, lost 3.

Ben Jones

Crawley. *Born*: Crawley, 12 June, 1982
Lightweight. *Ht* 5'8"
Manager Self
22.09.06 Carl Allen W PTS 4 Bethnal Green
15.12.06 Steve Gethin W PTS 4 Bethnal Green
30.03.07 Rom Krauklis L RSC 1 Crawley
25.01.08 Steve Gethin W PTS 4 Dagenham
23.02.08 Shaun Walton W RSC 4 Crawley
27.09.08 Cristian Nicolae W RSC 4 Bethnal
        Green
05.12.08 Sid Razak W PTS 6 Dagenham
03.04.09 Riaz Durgahed W PTS 6 Bethnal Green
Career: 8 contests, won 7, lost 1.

Davey Jones

Epworth. *Born* Grimsby, 30 May, 1977
S.Middleweight. *Ht* 5'11"
Manager M. Shinfield
23.09.02 William Webster W PTS 6 Cleethorpes
08.11.02 William Webster W PTS 6 Doncaster
30.11.02 Matt Scriven W PTS 6 Newark
16.12.02 Gary Jones W PTS 6 Cleethorpes
21.02.03 Jimi Hendricks W PTS 6 Doncaster
09.05.03 Wayne Shepherd W PTS 6 Doncaster
22.09.03 Steve Brumant L PTS 6 Cleethorpes
26.02.04 Paul Smith L PTS 4 Widnes
06.03.04 Paul Buchanan L PTS 4 Renfrew
23.05.05 Ernie Smith DREW 6 Cleethorpes
15.12.05 Omar Gumati W PTS 6 Cleethorpes
16.02.06 Mark Lloyd L PTS 6 Dudley
04.11.06 Jon Foster L DIS 6 Mansfield
11.12.06 Terry Adams W PTS 6 Cleethorpes
23.02.07 Jason Rushton L CO 7 Doncaster
        *(Vacant Central Area L.Middleweight
        Title)*
24.03.07 Kevin Concepcion L RSC 1 Coventry
28.06.07 Rob Kenney L PTS 4 Dudley
20.07.07 Steven Bendall L RTD 2
        Wolverhampton
13.10.07 Charlie Chiverton L PTS 4 Newark
26.10.07 Sam Horton L PTS 6 Birmingham
16.02.08 Alex Matvienko L RSC 2 Blackpool
17.05.08 Omar Gumati L PTS 6 Stoke
04.09.08 Philip Dowse DREW 6 Edgbaston

12.09.08 Keiron Gray L PTS 4 Wolverhampton
11.10.08 Sonny Pollard W PTS 6 Hull
14.11.08 Nasser Al Harbi L PTS 6 Birmingham
01.02.09 Quinton Hillocks L PTS 4 Edgbaston
03.04.09 Ben Wilkes L PTS 6 Wolverhampton
12.06.09 Ben Wilkes L CO 5 Wolverhampton
Career: 29 contests, won 9, drew 2, lost 18.

Justin Jones

Burslem. *Born* Burslem, 5 April, 1982
L.Heavyweight. *Ht* 6'3"
Manager O. Harrison
24.02.07 Richard Collins DREW 6 Stoke
14.03.08 Tony Stones W PTS 4 Manchester
23.05.09 James Tucker W RSC 1 Queensferry
Career: 3 contests, won 2, drew 1.

Peter Jones

Liverpool. *Born* Liverpool, 24 February, 1980
L.Welterweight. *Ht* 5'10"
Manager M. Scriven
07.11.08 Johnny Greaves W PTS 4 Wigan
08.06.09 Eddie Doyle L PTS 6 Glasgow
Career: 2 contests, won 1, lost 1.

Taz Jones   Philip Sharkey

(Lee) Taz Jones

Abercynon. *Born* Aberdare, 24 August, 1982
Welsh Area & International Masters L.Middleweight Champion. Former Undefeated British Masters L.Middleweight Champion.
Ht 5'11"
Manager B. Coleman
15.09.02 David White DREW 4 Swansea
02.11.02 Gerard McAuley DREW 4 Belfast

21.12.02 Luke Rudd W RTD 1 Millwall
08.01.03 Elroy Edwards W PTS 6 Aberdare
27.09.03 Matthew Hatton L PTS 6 Manchester
06.12.03 Ernie Smith W PTS 4 Cardiff
21.02.04 Craig Lynch W PTS 4 Cardiff
17.04.04 Andy Gibson W PTS 6 Belfast
03.09.04 Karl Taylor W PTS 4 Newport
30.09.04 Craig Dickson DREW 6 Glasgow
08.12.04 Kevin Phelan W PTS 10 Longford
        *(British Masters L.Middleweight Title
        Challenge)*
18.03.05 Neil Sinclair W RSC 1 Belfast
23.07.05 Colin McNeil L PTS 10 Edinburgh
        (Vacant Celtic L.Middleweight Title)
10.09.05 Tony Doherty L PTS 10 Cardiff
        (Vacant Celtic Welterweight Title)
28.04.06 Graham Delehedy W CO 6 Hartlepool
15.09.06 Jon Harrison W PTS 6 Newport
07.04.07 Tony Doherty L RSC 7 Cardiff
        (Celtic Welterweight Title Challenge)
20.06.08 Carl Drake W RSC 1 Plymouth
        *(Vacant International Masters
        L.Middleweight Title)*
06.09.08 Matthew Hall L RSC 5 Manchester
05.12.08 Grzegorz Proksa L RSC 4 Dagenham
21.02.09 Kerry Hope W RSC 4 Merthyr Tydfil
        *(Vacant Welsh Area L.Middleweight
        Title)*
Career: 21 contests, won 12, drew 3, lost 6.

Scott Jordan

Belfast. *Born* Dundonald, 22 April, 1984
L.Middleweight. *Ht* 5'9¼"
Manager Self
21.04.06 Jamie Ambler W PTS 4 Belfast
25.11.06 Geraint Harvey W PTS 4 Belfast
15.12.06 Greg Barton W PTS 4 Bethnal Green
25.03.07 Duncan Cottier W PTS 6 Dublin
30.06.07 Alexander Spitjo L RSC 5 Belfast
13.10.07 Denis Alekseevs W RSC 1 Belfast
05.12.08 Kevin McCauley W PTS 4 Dagenham
03.04.09 Lukasz Wawrzyczek L PTS 6 Bethnal
        Green
Career: 8 contests, won 6, lost 2.

Scott Jordan   Philip Sharkey

Zahir Kahut

Batley. *Born* Pakistan, 25 September, 1973
Heavyweight. *Ht* 6'6"
Manager Self
16.06.07 Scott Mitchell W PTS 6 Bolton
29.11.07 Lee Mountford W PTS 6 Bradford
17.01.09 Howard Daley W PTS 4 Wigan
28.02.09 Earl Ling L PTS 4 Norwich
24.05.09 Howard Daley W PTS 6 Bradford
Career: 5 contests, won 4, lost 1.

Jon Kays

Ashton under Lyne. *Born* Tameside, 24
May, 1983
Welterweight. *Ht* 5'8½"
Manager S. Wood
24.06.07 Pete Buckley W PTS 6 Wigan
12.10.07 Sergei Rozhakmens W RSC 4 Leeds
23.12.07 Craig O'Neile W RSC 2 Bolton
16.02.08 Steve Gethin W RSC 6 Blackpool
26.04.08 Robin Deakin W PTS 4 Wigan
12.10.08 Sid Razak W PTS 4 Leigh
22.11.08 Craig Johnson L PTS 6 Blackpool
06.03.09 Barrington Brown W PTS 6 Wigan
17.05.09 Steve Gethin W PTS 4 Bolton
Career: 9 contests, won 8, lost 1.

John Keeton

Sheffield. *Born* Sheffield, 19 May, 1972
Former British Cruiserweight Champion.
Former Undefeated WBF & WBO Inter-
Continental Cruiserweight Champion. *Ht*
6'0"
Manager D. Ingle
11.08.93 Tony Colclough W RSC 1 Mansfield
15.09.93 Val Golding L PTS 6 Ashford
27.10.93 Darren McKenna W RSC 3 Stoke
01.12.93 Julius Francis L PTS 4 Bethnal Green
19.01.94 Dennis Bailey W RTD 2 Stoke
17.02.94 Dermot Gascoyne L RSC 1 Dagenham
09.04.94 Eddie Knight W RTD 5 Mansfield
11.05.94 John Rice W RSC 5 Sheffield
02.06.94 Devon Rhooms W RSC 2 Tooting
06.09.94 Mark Walker W RSC 5 Stoke
24.09.94 Dirk Wallyn L CO 3 Middlekerke,
Belgium
26.10.94 Lee Archer W PTS 6 Stoke
09.12.94 Bruce Scott L CO 2 Bethnal Green
11.02.95 Rudiger May L PTS 6 Frankfurt,
Germany
06.03.95 Simon McDougall W RSC 5 Mayfair
07.07.95 Nicky Piper L RTD 2 Cardiff
15.09.95 Steve Osborne W RSC 4 Mansfield
27.10.95 Nicky Wadman W RSC 1 Brighton
03.11.95 Monty Wright W RSC 4 Dudley
11.11.95 Denzil Browne W RSC 4 Halifax
30.01.96 Cesar Kazadi W RSC 3 Lille, France
11.05.96 Terry Dunstan L RSC 1 Bethnal Green
(British Cruiserweight Title Challenge)
14.09.96 John Pierre W PTS 4 Sheffield
14.12.96 Nigel Rafferty W RTD 3 Sheffield
12.04.97 Nigel Rafferty W RSC 6 Sheffield

11.10.97 Kelly Oliver L RSC 8 Sheffield
*(Vacant WBO Inter-Continental
Cruiserweight Title)*
16.05.98 Jacob Mofokeng L RTD 4
Hammanskraal, South Africa
18.07.98 Kelly Oliver W RSC 2 Sheffield
23.01.99 Garry Delaney W PTS 12 Cheshunt
*(Vacant WBO Inter-Continental
Cruiserweight Title)*
15.05.99 William Barima W RTD 3 Sheffield
29.02.00 Tony Booth W RSC 2 Widnes
16.12.00 Bruce Scott L CO 6 Sheffield
(Vacant British Cruiserweight Title)
21.07.01 Radcliffe Green W PTS 4 Sheffield
19.03.02 Butch Lesley W PTS 12 Slough
(Vacant WBF Cruiserweight Title)
16.04.04 Paul Bonson W PTS 4 Bradford
14.05.05 Paul Bonson W PTS 4 Aberdeen
11.06.05 Krzysztof Wlodarczyk L RTD 3 Gorzow
Wielkopolski, Poland
*(WBC Youth Cruiserweight Title
Challenge)*
10.09.05 Don Diego Poeder L CO 1 Rotterdam,
Netherlands
01.06.06 Mark Hobson L RSC 4 Barnsley
*(British & Commonwealth
Cruiserweight Title Challenges)*
20.10.06 Lee Swaby W RSC 7 Sheffield
(Vacant British Cruiserweight Title)
19.03.07 Troy Ross L CO 2 Montreal, Canada
*(Vacant Commonwealth Cruiserweight
Title)*
29.09.07 Mark Hobson L RSC 4 Sheffield
(British Cruiserweight Title Defence)
19.05.09 Bruce Scott W PTS 3 Kensington
19.05.09 Ovill McKenzie L PTS 3 Kensington
19.05.09 Dean Francis W CO 1 Kensington
Career: 45 contests, won 28, lost 17.

John Keeton   Philip Sharkey

Lee Kellett

Barrow. *Born* Barrow, 28 September, 1978
Cruiserweight. *Ht* 6'2"
Manager T. Schofield
12.02.06 John Anthony L RSC 1 Manchester
23.06.06 Gary Thompson L PTS 4 Blackpool
13.10.06 Gary Neville W RSC 1 Irvine
25.02.07 Mervyn Langdale W RSC 1
Southampton

05.10.07 Victor Smith W PTS 4 Bethnal Green
01.08.08 Joe Smyth L RSC 1 Watford
16.11.08 Mervyn Langdale W RSC 6
Southampton
03.04.09 Jason Callum DREW 6 Leigh
Career: 8 contests, won 4, drew 1, lost 3.

Adam Kelly

Sheffield. *Born* Sheffield, 8 August, 1987
L.Welterweight. *Ht* 5'8"
Manager J. Ingle
08.12.05 Tom Hogan L PTS 6 Sunderland
05.03.06 Tye Williams W PTS 4 Sheffield
17.03.06 Stuart Green L PTS 4 Kirkcaldy
27.05.06 Mike Reid DREW 6 Aberdeen
20.10.06 Tye Williams W PTS 4 Sheffield
24.11.06 Pete Buckley W PTS 6 Hull
06.12.06 Rom Krauklis W PTS 6 Stoke
03.05.07 Matt Seawright W PTS 4 Sheffield
07.09.07 Matthew Martin Lewis W PTS 4
Doncaster
29.09.07 Matt Seawright W PTS 4 Sheffield
06.10.07 Mark Bett L RTD 3 Aberdeen
29.03.08 Mark Bett W PTS 6 Aberdeen
21.06.08 Amir Nadi W PTS 6 Sheffield
08.11.08 Lee Purdy L RSC 5 Bethnal Green
14.03.09 Chris Lewis L PTS 4 Birmingham
Career: 15 contests, won 9, drew 1, lost 5.

Joe Kelso

Muirkirk. *Born* Irvine, 7 September, 1986
L.Welterweight. *Ht* 5'10"
Manager T. Gilmour
27.04.09 Shaun Walton W PTS 6 Glasgow
19.06.09 Leon Dean L RSC 2 Aberdeen
Career: 2 contests, won 1, lost 1.

Colin Kenna

Southampton. *Born* Dublin, 28 July, 1976
Heavyweight. Former Southern Area
Heavyweight Champion. *Ht* 6'1"
Manager J. Bishop
25.02.01 Slick Miller W RSC 3 Streatham
22.04.01 Eamonn Glennon W PTS 4 Streatham
15.10.01 Tony Booth W PTS 6 Southampton
11.02.02 Dave Clarke W RSC 4 Southampton
08.04.02 James Gilbert W RSC 1 Southampton
12.07.02 Gary Williams W RSC 3 Southampton
01.11.02 Paul Buttery DREW 6 Preston
17.03.03 Derek McCafferty W PTS 6
Southampton
12.05.03 Paul Bonson W PTS 6 Southampton
01.08.03 Michael Sprott L RSC 1 Bethnal Green
*(Southern Area Heavyweight Title
Challenge)*
26.10.03 Darren Ashton W CO 1 Longford
20.02.04 Paul Bonson W PTS 6 Southampton
30.03.04 Chris Woollas W PTS 6 Southampton
12.05.04 Mark Krence L RTD 3 Reading
06.02.05 Oneal Murray W RTD 3 Southampton
19.02.05 Paul King DREW 6 Dublin
26.06.05 Julius Francis W PTS 4 Southampton
04.12.05 Wayne Llewelyn W CO 2 Portsmouth
*(Vacant Southern Area Heavyweight
Title)*
28.01.06 Luke Simpkin W PTS 8 Dublin
05.03.06 Micky Steeds L PTS 10 Southampton
*(Southern Area Heavyweight Title
Defence)*

22.04.06 Oleg Platov L RSC 5 Mannheim, Germany
25.02.07 Keith Long W PTS 8 Southampton
31.10.07 Roman Greenberg L PTS 8 Bayswater
25.01.08 Albert Sosnowski L PTS 10 Dagenham
11.04.08 Paul Butlin L RSC 2 Bethnal Green
27.09.08 Gurcharan Singh L CO 4 Bracknell
21.11.08 Sam Sexton L RSC 6 Bethnal Green
(Vacant Southern Area Heavyweight Title)
Career: 27 contests, won 16, drew 2, lost 9.

Rob Kenney

Wolverhampton. *Born* Wolverhampton, 1 August, 1977
Former Undefeated Midlands Area Middleweight Champion. *Ht* 5'9"
Manager E. Johnson
05.12.06 Peter Dunn DREW 4 Wolverhampton
15.02.07 Peter Dunn W PTS 4 Dudley
14.04.07 Peter Dunn W PTS 4 Wakefield
28.06.07 Davey Jones W PTS 4 Dudley
25.10.07 Paul Royston W PTS 6 Wolverhampton
28.02.08 Lance Verallo W PTS 4 Wolverhampton
30.04.08 Paul Royston W PTS 6 Wolverhampton
20.06.08 Drew Campbell W PTS 4 Wolverhampton
14.09.08 Max Maxwell W PTS 10 Edgbaston
(Midlands Area Middleweight Title Challenge)
24.04.09 JJ Bird DREW 4 Wolverhampton
31.05.09 Dale Miles L RSC 7 Burton
(Vacant British Masters Welterweight Title)
Career: 11 contests, won 8, drew 2, lost 1.

David Keogan

Liverpool. *Born* Liverpool, 1 May, 1987
Flyweight. *Ht* 5'5¼"
Manager S. Goodwin
01.12.07 John Donnelly L RSC 1 Liverpool
15.06.08 Najah Ali L RSC 1 Bethnal Green
24.07.08 James Mulhern L PTS 4 Wolverhampton
01.08.08 Ashley Sexton L PTS 4 Watford
16.11.08 Usman Ahmed L PTS 6 Derby
Career: 5 contests, lost 5.

Mark Ketnor

Whetstone. *Born* Leicester, 1 August, 1979
Middleweight. *Ht* 5' 8"
Manager L. Allen
04.04.09 Alastair Warren L RSC 5 Coventry
Career: 1 contest, lost 1.

Mo Khaled (Al Saroodi)

Sheffield. *Born* Doha, Qatar, 19 January, 1988
S.Bantamweight. *Ht* 5'4"
Manager J. Ingle
26.05.06 Neil Marston L DIS 5 Hull
12.07.06 Neil Marston W PTS 4 Bethnal Green
29.09.06 Danny Wallace L RSC 1 Manchester
10.11.06 Matthew Edmonds L PTS 6 Newport
11.03.07 Stuart McFadyen L PTS 6 Shaw
27.05.07 Robert Nelson DREW 6 Bradford

17.06.07 Andy Bell L PTS 10 Mansfield
(Vacant British Masters Bantamweight Title)
05.12.07 Josh Wale L RSC 4 Sheffield
(Vacant Central Area S.Bantamweight Title)
16.11.08 Alan Winterbottom W PTS 6 Shaw
17.01.09 Kevin Buckley L PTS 4 Wigan
24.05.09 Anser Hussein W PTS 6 Shaw
13.06.09 Bobby Ward DREW 4 Wigan
Career: 12 contests, won 3, drew 2, lost 7.

Amir Khan　　　　　　　Philip Sharkey

Amir Khan

Bolton. *Born* Bolton, 8 December, 1986
Former Undefeated WBA International Lightweight Champion. Former Undefeated WBO Inter-Continental Lightweight Champion. Former Undefeated Commonwealth Lightweight Champion. *Ht* 5'10"
Manager Self
16.07.05 David Bailey W RSC 1 Bolton
10.09.05 Baz Carey W PTS 4 Cardiff
05.11.05 Steve Gethin W RSC 3 Renfrew
10.12.05 Daniel Thorpe W RSC 2 Canning Town
28.01.06 Vitali Martynov W RSC 1 Nottingham
25.02.06 Jackson Williams W RSC 3 Canning Town
20.05.06 Laszlo Komjathi W PTS 6 Belfast
08.07.06 Colin Bain W RSC 2 Cardiff
02.09.06 Ryan Barrett W RSC 1 Bolton
09.12.06 Rachid Drilzane W PTS 10 Canning Town
(Vacant IBF Inter-Continental L.Welterweight Title)
17.02.07 Mohammed Medjadji W RSC 1 Wembley
07.04.07 Stefy Bull W RSC 3 Cardiff
14.07.07 Willie Limond W RTD 8 Greenwich
(Commonwealth Lightweight Title Challenge)
06.10.07 Scott Lawton W RSC 4 Nottingham
(Commonwealth Lightweight Title Defence)

08.12.07 Graham Earl W RSC 1 Bolton
(Commonwealth Lightweight Title Defence)
02.02.08 Gairy St Clair W PTS 12 Canning Town
(Commonwealth Lightweight Title Defence)
05.04.08 Martin Kristjansen W RSC 7 Bolton
(Vacant WBO Inter-Continental Lightweight Title)
21.06.08 Michael Gomez W RSC 5 Birmingham
(Commonwealth Lightweight Title Defence)
06.09.08 Breidis Prescott L CO 1 Manchester
(WBO Inter-Continental Lightweight Title Defence)
06.12.08 Oisin Fagan W RSC 2 Canning Town
(Vacant WBA International Lightweight Title)
14.03.09 Marco Antonio Barrera W TD 5 Manchester
(WBA International Lightweight Title Defence. Vacant WBO Inter-Continental Lightweight Title)
Career: 21 contests, won 20, lost 1.

Tasif Khan

Bradford. *Born* Bradford, 29 December, 1982
S.Bantamweight. *Ht* 5'7"
Manager J. Ingle/R. Margel
20.11.05 Gary Ford DREW 6 Shaw
23.02.06 Neil Read W RSC 6 Leeds
28.05.06 Delroy Spencer W PTS 6 Wakefield
06.07.07 Stuart McFadyen L PTS 4 Wigan
24.05.09 Anwar Alfadi DREW 4 Bradford
Career: 5 contests, won 2, drew 2, lost 1.

Charles Paul King

Motherwell. *Born* Bellshill, 26 October, 1982
Scottish Lightweight Champion. *Ht* 5'10"
Manager T. Gilmour
22.01.07 Rom Krauklis W PTS 6 Glasgow
26.03.07 Pete Buckley W PTS 6 Glasgow
28.04.07 Amir Nadi W PTS 6 Clydebank
08.06.07 Gavin Deacon W PTS 4 Motherwell
08.10.07 Karl Taylor W PTS 6 Glasgow
19.10.07 Matt Seawright W PTS 6 Motherwell
29.02.08 Abdul Rashid W PTS 4 Glasgow
17.03.08 Peter Dunn W PTS 6 Glasgow
28.04.08 Karl Taylor W PTS 6 Glasgow
16.05.08 Mark Bett W PTS 6 Motherwell
22.09.08 Craig Johnson W PTS 8 Glasgow
25.10.08 Daniel Thorpe W PTS 6 Aberdeen
28.11.08 Craig Dyer W PTS 4 Glasgow
19.01.09 Stuart Green W PTS 10 Glasgow
(Vacant Scottish Area Lightweight Title)
24.03.09 Paul Holborn L PTS 3 Glasgow
08.06.09 Jonathan Hussey W PTS 6 Glasgow
Career: 16 contests, won 15, lost 1.

Martyn King

Cleator Moor. *Born* Winchester, 26 April, 1985
L.Middleweight. *Ht* 6' 0"
Manager C. Aston

03.10.08 Shaun Farmer W PTS 6 Sunderland
04.12.08 Chris Brophy W PTS 6 Bradford
08.03.09 Sam Sheedy L PTS 6 Sheffield
17.05.09 Chris Johnson L PTS 4 Bolton
06.06.09 Harry Matthews L PTS 4 Beverley
Career: 5 contests, won 2, lost 3.

Nathan King

Mountain Ash. *Born* Aberdare, 19 March,
1981
L.Heavyweight. *Ht* 6'3"
Manager B. Coleman
27.01.01 Tony Oakey L PTS 6 Bethnal Green
28.04.01 Pinky Burton W PTS 4 Cardiff
09.06.01 Michael Pinnock W PTS 4 Bethnal
Green
09.10.01 Darren Ashton W PTS 6 Cardiff
24.11.01 Peter Haymer W PTS 4 Bethnal Green
12.02.02 Peter Haymer W PTS 4 Bethnal Green
20.04.02 Radcliffe Green W PTS 6 Cardiff
17.08.02 Valery Odin L PTS 6 Cardiff
14.12.02 Paul Bonson L PTS 4 Newcastle
10.04.03 Ovill McKenzie L PTS 4 Clydach
28.06.03 Varuzhan Davtyan W PTS 4 Cardiff
21.02.04 Daniel Sackey L PTS 4 Cardiff
12.03.04 Elvis Michailenko L PTS 6 Millwall
03.07.04 Nick Okoth W PTS 4 Newport
22.10.04 Hastings Rasani W PTS 6 Edinburgh
24.11.04 Eric Teymour L PTS 12 Mayfair
(*Vacant WBU S.Middleweight Title*)
13.02.05 Malik Dziarra W PTS 6 Brentwood
28.06.05 Malik Dziarra L PTS 8 Cuaxhaven,
Germany
13.05.06 Tony Oakey L PTS 6 Bethnal Green
15.09.06 Tyrone Wright W RTD 3 Newport
10.11.06 Neil Tidman W PTS 6 Newport
14.09.07 Steve McGuire L PTS 10 Kirkcaldy
(*Vacant Celtic S.Middleweight Title*)
20.09.08 Tony Dodson L PTS 6 Sheffield
07.11.08 Tony Quigley L RSC Wigan
27.03.09 Kenny Anderson L PTS 10 Glasgow
(*Vacant Celtic S.Middleweight Title*)
Career: 25 contests, won 12, lost 13.

David Kirk

Sutton in Ashfield. *Born* Mansfield, 5
October, 1974
Middleweight. Former Undefeated WBF
European Welterweight Champion. *Ht* 5'8"
Manager Self
01.11.96 Arv Mittoo W PTS 6 Mansfield
04.12.96 Stuart Rimmer W PTS 6 Stoke
20.02.97 Chris Price W PTS 6 Mansfield
16.03.97 Gary Hibbert L PTS 6 Shaw
25.03.97 Miguel Matthews W PTS 6
Wolverhampton
28.04.97 Mark Breslin L PTS 8 Glasgow
06.10.97 Christian Brady L PTS 6 Birmingham
30.10.97 Trevor Tacy L PTS 6 Newark
08.12.97 Nick Hall L PTS 6 Nottingham
12.01.98 Juha Temonen DREW 6 Helsinki,
Finland
24.01.98 Jason Cook L RSC 3 Cardiff
24.02.98 Roy Rutherford L PTS 6 Edgbaston
11.03.98 Patrick Gallagher L PTS 6 Bethnal
Green
27.04.98 Tommy Peacock L PTS 6 Manchester
08.05.98 Chris Barnett L PTS 6 Manchester

23.05.98 Graham Earl L PTS 4 Bethnal Green
04.06.98 Mark Richards L PTS 6 Dudley
21.09.98 Steve McLevy L PTS 8 Glasgow
12.10.98 Malcolm Melvin L PTS 10 Birmingham
(*Midlands Area L. Welterweight Title
Challenge*)
31.10.98 Bernard Paul L PTS 6 Southend
28.11.98 Glenn McClarnon L PTS 4 Belfast
11.12.98 Charlie Kane L PTS 8 Prestwick
20.02.99 Dennis Berry L PTS 10 Thornaby
(*Vacant Continental European
Welterweight Title*)
09.05.99 Sammy Smith L PTS 6 Bracknell
20.05.99 Steve Brumant W PTS 4 Kensington
05.06.99 Neil Sinclair L PTS 8 Cardiff
11.09.99 Glenn McClarnon L PTS 6 Sheffield
20.10.99 Dave Gibson W PTS 6 Stoke
18.11.99 Adrian Chase W PTS 10 Mayfair
(*Vacant WBF European Welterweight
Title*)
26.11.99 Gerard Murphy L RTD 3 Hull
25.03.00 Jacek Bielski L PTS 6 Liverpool
29.04.00 Eamonn Magee L RSC 8 Wembley
13.08.00 Ram Singh W PTS 6 Nottingham
09.09.00 Mally McIver L PTS 6 Newark
23.09.00 Steve Murray L PTS 4 Bethnal Green
09.10.00 Steve Saville W PTS 8 Birmingham
19.11.00 Gavin Down L PTS 10 Chesterfield
(*Vacant British Masters L.Welterweight
Title*)
01.12.00 Alan Bosworth DREW 8 Peterborough
04.02.01 Mark Winters L PTS 6 Queensferry
28.02.01 Ossie Duran L PTS 8 Kensington
(*Vacant WBF European Welterweight
Title*)
10.03.01 Junior Witter L RSC 2 Bethnal Green
10.04.01 Colin Lynes L PTS 6 Wembley
20.04.01 Mark Winters L PTS 6 Dublin
16.06.01 Oscar Hall L PTS 6 Derby
07.07.01 Michael Jennings L PTS 6 Manchester
28.07.01 Jonathan Thaxton L PTS 4 Wembley
13.09.01 David Walker DREW 8 Sheffield
17.11.01 Kevin McIntyre L PTS 4 Glasgow
24.11.01 Ivan Kirpa L PTS 4 Bethnal Green
08.12.01 Chris Saunders L CO 2 Chesterfield
26.01.02 Colin Lynes L PTS 6 Dagenham
09.02.02 David Barnes L RTD 1 Manchester
11.03.02 Matthew Macklin L PTS 4 Glasgow
25.05.02 Francis Barrett L PTS 6 Portsmouth
08.06.02 Kevin McIntyre L RTD 4 Renfrew
28.09.02 Matthew Hatton W PTS 6 Manchester
22.03.03 Kevin McIntyre L RSC 1 Renfrew
24.05.03 Nigel Wright L PTS 4 Bethnal Green
31.05.03 Sammy Smith L PTS 4 Bethnal Green
08.06.03 Adnan Amar L PTS 6 Nottingham
04.10.03 Francis Barrett L PTS 6 Muswell Hill
10.04.04 Albert Sosnowski L PTS 4 Manchester
07.05.04 Gary Woolcombe L PTS 4 Bethnal
Green
19.06.04 Gary Young L PTS 4 Renfrew
03.07.04 Tony Doherty L PTS 4 Newport
19.11.04 Ross Minter L PTS 6 Bethnal Green
03.12.04 Martin Concepcion L PTS 4 Edinburgh
11.09.05 Gatis Skuja L PTS 6 Kirkby in Ashfield
12.11.05 Joe Mitchell W PTS 6 Sheffield
10.03.06 Stuart Elwell L PTS 10 Walsall
(*Vacant Midlands Area Welterweight
Title*)
04.11.06 Colin McNeil L PTS 6 Glasgow
17.11.06 Sam Webb L PTS 4 Bethnal Green
09.12.06 Kell Brook L RSC 1 Canning Town

06.05.07 Brian Rose L PTS 6 Altrincham
18.05.07 Matthew Thirlwall L PTS 4 Canning
Town
24.06.07 Chris Johnson L PTS 4 Wigan
15.09.07 Gary Young L PTS 6 Paisley
06.10.07 Kevin Concepcion L PTS 6 Leicester
13.10.07 Billy Saunders L PTS 4 Bethnal
Green
03.11.07 Jamie Cox L PTS 4 Cardiff
01.12.07 Kevin Hammond L PTS 4 Nottingham
16.02.08 Jack Arnfield L PTS 6 Blackpool
01.03.08 Joe McCluskey L RSC 3 Coventry
05.04.08 Thomas Costello L PTS 4 Bolton
02.05.08 Sam Webb L PTS 6 Nottingham
14.09.08 Chris Johnson L PTS 4 Wigan
10.10.08 Lee Edwards L PTS 4 Sheffield
17.10.08 Danny Stewart L PTS 4 Swindon
22.11.08 Alex Matvienko L PTS 4 Blackpool
Career: 89 contests, won 11, drew 3, lost 75.

Chris Kitson

Kettering. *Born* Shefield, 5 June, 1988
Lightweight. *Ht* 5'6¼"
Manager G. Rhodes
23.11.07 Senol Dervis W PTS 6 Sheffield
12.10.08 Karl Place L RSC 2 Leigh
Career: 2 contests, won 1, lost 1.

Eder Kurti

Kennington. *Born* Albania, 29 August, 1984
S.Middleweight. *Ht* 5'10¾"
Manager M. Helliet
04.11.04 Cafu Santos W RSC 1 Piccadilly
02.12.04 Craig Lynch W DIS 4 Crystal Palace
27.01.05 Ojay Abrahams W PTS 6 Piccadilly
19.11.05 JJ Ojuederie L RSC 4 Southwark
06.10.06 Stuart Brookes L PTS 6 Mexborough
02.12.06 Dave Pearson W PTS 6 Southwark
18.02.07 Greg Barton L PTS 4 Bethnal Green
18.11.07 Craig Denton L PTS 4 Tooting
29.01.09 Kenroy Lambert W PTS 6 Holborn
23.04.09 Mark Phillips W PTS 6 Mayfair
12.06.09 Luke Osman W PTS 4 Bethnal Green
Career: 11 contests, won 7, lost 4.

Eder Kurti   Philip Sharkey

Kristian Laight

Nuneaton. *Born* Nuneaton, 15 June, 1980
Welterweight. *Ht* 5'10"
Manager J. Gill
26.09.03 James Paisley L PTS 6 Millwall
14.11.03 Matt Teague L PTS 6 Hull
05.12.03 Justin Hicks L PTS 6 Bristol
07.02.04 Kevin Mitchell L PTS 4 Bethnal Green
30.03.04 Chris McDonagh L PTS 6 Southampton
08.04.04 Jaz Virdee W PTS 6 Peterborough
20.04.04 Femi Fehintola L PTS 6 Sheffield
04.06.04 Gary Coombes DREW 6 Dudley
19.06.04 Ryan Barrett L PTS 4 Muswell Hill
23.10.04 Sean Hughes L PTS 6 Wakefield
18.11.04 Martin Gethin L RSC 4 Shrewsbury
17.12.04 Baz Carey L PTS 6 Coventry
08.05.05 Nadeem Siddique L RSC 7 Bradford
25.06.05 John-Paul Ryan DREW 6 Melton
  Mowbray
09.07.05 Chris Long L PTS 6 Bristol
02.09.05 Scott Haywood L PTS 6 Derby
06.10.05 Tom Hogan L PTS 6 Sunderland
24.10.05 Andrew Ferrans L PTS 8 Glasgow
12.11.05 Danny Gwilym L PTS 6 Bristol
20.11.05 Barry Downes DREW 6 Shaw
02.12.05 Charlie Thompson DREW 6 Doncaster
18.12.05 Gary O'Connor L PTS 6 Bolton
16.02.06 Haider Ali L PTS 4 Dudley
02.03.06 Jeff Thomas L PTS 6 Blackpool
30.03.06 Jaz Virdee L PTS 6 Peterborough
14.04.06 Tristan Davies L PTS 6 Telford
21.04.06 Wez Miller W PTS 6 Doncaster
11.05.06 Paul Holborn L PTS 6 Sunderland
21.05.06 Chris Long L PTS 6 Bristol
30.05.06 Akaash Bhatia L PTS 4 Bethnal Green
15.06.06 Neal McQuade W PTS 6 Peterborough
21.07.06 John Fewkes L RSC 5 Altrincham
09.10.06 Baz Carey DREW 6 Bedworth
26.10.06 Dean Harrison L PTS 4 Dudley
07.11.06 Martin Gethin L PTS 6 Leeds
24.11.06 Jack Perry L PTS 4 Nottingham
07.12.06 Ali Hussain W PTS 6 Bradford
15.02.07 Rob Hunt L PTS 6 Dudley
24.02.07 Chris Goodwin L PTS 6 Stoke
16.03.07 Lee Purdy L PTS 4 Norwich
23.03.07 Dean Harrison L PTS 4 Nottingham
13.04.07 Gary Sykes L PTS 4 Altrincham
20.04.07 Martin Gordon W PTS 4 Dudley
27.04.07 Ruben Giles L PTS 4 Wembley
05.10.07 George Watson L PTS 6 Sunderland
19.10.07 Stefy Bull L PTS 4 Doncaster
23.11.07 Stuart Kennedy L PTS 6 Houghton le
  Spring
30.11.07 Ross Hewitt L PTS 4 Newham
10.12.07 Graham Fearn L PTS 6 Leicester
23.12.07 Rick Godding L PTS 6 Bolton
18.01.08 Jack Perry L PTS 6 Burton
15.02.08 John Wainwright L PTS 6 Sheffield
28.02.08 Scott Evans L PTS 6 Wolverhampton
28.03.08 Tyrone Nurse L PTS 4 Barnsley

20.04.08 Darren Askew L PTS 6 Shaw
02.05.08 Chris Long L PTS 4 Bristol
12.05.08 Dean Arnold L PTS 6 Birmingham
23.05.08 Chris O'Brien L PTS 6 Wigan
15.06.08 Lee Jennings L PTS 6 St Helens
22.06.08 Jack Perry L PTS 6 Derby
06.10.08 Chris Lewis L PTS 6 Birmingham
09.11.08 Richard Ghent L PTS 4 Wolverhampton
29.11.08 Ben Lawler L PTS 6 Sleaford
06.12.08 Nathan McIntosh L PTS 6 Nottingham
21.12.08 Danny Coyle W PTS 6 Coventry
06.03.09 Rick Godding L PTS 4 Wigan
20.03.09 Henry Castle L PTS 6 Newham
03.04.09 Rob Doody L PTS 6 Wolverhampton
17.04.09 Nick Quigley L PTS 4 Leigh
23.05.09 Mark Walsh L PTS 4 Sleaford
06.06.09 Glen Matsell L PTS 6 Beverley
30.06.09 Martin Welsh L PTS 4 Bethnal Green
Career: 72 contests, won 6, drew 5, lost 61

Kenroy Lambert   Philip Sharkey

Kenroy Lambert

Luton. *Born* Grenada, WI, 14 March, 1972
Middleweight. *Ht* 5'9¼"
Manager M. Helliet
17.02.02 Mark Nilsen L PTS 6 Salford
27.03.02 Freddie Yemofio W PTS 6 Mayfair
17.09.02 Leigh Wicks W PTS 6 Bethnal Green
10.10.02 William Webster L PTS 6 Piccadilly
16.09.07 Paul Dyer L PTS 6 Southampton
07.10.07 Tommy Heffron L RSC 3 Shaw
29.02.08 Paul Brown L RSC 6 Plymouth
05.10.08 Daley Ojuederie L PTS 4 Watford
29.01.09 Eder Kurti L PTS 6 Holborn
05.03.09 Jack Morris L RSC 4 Limehouse
Career: 10 contests, won 2, lost 8.

Mervyn Langdale

Southampton. *Born* Hythe, Hull, 11 May,
1977
Heavyweight. *Ht* 6' 4"
Manager J. Bishop
06.02.05 Nick Okoth DREW 6 Southampton

24.09.06 Tony Booth L RSC 1 Southampton
25.02.07 Lee Kellett L RSC 1 Southampton
16.11.08 Lee Kellett L RSC 6 Southampton
Career: 4 contests, drew 1, lost 3.

Ben Lawler   Philip Sharkey

Ben Lawler

Skegness. *Born* Boston, 24 November, 1984
L.Welterweight. *Ht* 5'10¼"
Manager C. Greaves
31.05.08 Sid Razak W PTS 6 Newark
20.09.08 Karl Taylor W PTS 6 Newark
29.11.08 Kristian Laight W PTS 6 Sleaford
28.03.09 Carl Allen W PTS 4 Lincoln
23.05.09 Damien Jeffries W PTS 6 Sleaford
Career: 5 contests, won 5.

Scott Lawton

Stoke. *Born* Stoke, 23 September, 1976
English Lightweight Champion. Former
Undefeated Midlands Area Lightweight
Champion. *Ht* 5'10"
Manager M. Carney
29.09.01 Dave Hinds W RSC 2 Southwark
08.12.01 Ilias Miah W PTS 4 Dagenham
26.01.02 Pete Buckley W PTS 4 Bethnal Green
26.04.02 Pete Buckley W PTS 4 Coventry
06.09.02 Ben Hudson W PTS 4 Bethnal Green
30.01.03 Dave Stewart L PTS 6 Piccadilly
26.04.03 Chris McDonagh W RSC 2 Brentford
13.06.03 Jason Nesbitt W PTS 6 Queensway
14.11.03 Jimmy Beech W RSC 5 Bethnal Green
20.04.04 Henry Jones W PTS 6 Sheffield
17.06.04 Carl Allen W PTS 10 Sheffield
  *(Vacant Midlands Area Lightweight
  Title)*
17.09.04 Silence Saheed W PTS 6 Sheffield
10.12.04 Roger Sampson W PTS 6 Sheffield
04.03.05 Peter McDonagh W PTS 6 Rotherham
15.05.05 Carl Allen W PTS 6 Sheffield
24.07.05 Pete Buckley W PTS 6 Sheffield
09.09.05 Alan Temple L PTS 6 Sheffield
12.11.05 Ben Hudson W PTS 6 Stoke
18.02.06 Surinder Sekhon DREW 8 Stoke

06.05.06 Baz Carey W PTS 10 Stoke
    (Midlands Area Lightweight Title
    Defence)
09.06.06 Stefy Bull W RSC 8 Doncaster
    (Vacant English Lightweight Title)
30.09.06 Judex Meemea W DIS 7 Stoke
24.11.06 Karl Taylor W PTS 4 Stoke
16.03.07 Jonathan Thaxton L RSC 7 Norwich
    (British Lightweight Title Challenge)
06.10.07 Amir Khan L RSC 4 Nottingham
    (Commonwealth Lightweight Title
    Challenge)
17.11.07 Carl Allen W PTS 6 Stoke
01.03.08 Michael Frontin W PTS 6 Stoke
17.05.08 Youssef Al Hamidi W PTS 6 Stoke
13.09.08 Ali Wyatt W PTS 6 Stoke
06.12.08 Martin Gethin W RSC 9 Nottingham
    (English Lightweight Title Challenge)
23.01.09 Johnny Greaves W PTS 6 Stoke
13.06.09 John Murray L RSC 6 Wigan
Career: 32 contests, won 26, drew 1, lost 5

Matt Legg   Philip Sharkey

Matt Legg
Milton Keynes. *Born* Northampton, 17
April, 1976
Heavyweight. *Ht* 6' 2"
Manager Self
28.07.01 Mal Rice W PTS 4 Wembley
24.11.01 Tony Booth W PTS 4 Bethnal Green
20.07.02 Dave Clarke W RSC 2 Bethnal Green
12.10.02 Alvin Miller L RSC 2 Bethnal Green
01.08.08 Howard Daley W RSC 2 Watford
05.10.08 Jevgenijs Stamburskis W PTS 4 Watford
Career: 6 contests, won 5, lost 1.

Chris Lewis
Wolverhampton. *Born* Wolverhampton, 2
August, 1987
L.Welterweight. *Ht* 5' 8"
Manager E. Johnson
12.09.08 Pete Buckley W PTS 4 Wolverhampton
06.10.08 Kristian Laight W PTS 6 Birmingham
09.11.08 Bheki Moyo W PTS 6 Wolverhampton

08.12.08 Jason Nesbitt W PTS 6 Birmingham
27.02.09 Daniel Thorpe W PTS 4 Wolverhampton
14.03.09 Adam Kelly W PTS 4 Birmingham
12.06.09 Carl Allen W PTS 4 Wolverhampton
Career: 7 contests, won 7.

Dwayne Lewis
Canning Town. *Born* London, 12 June,
1979
S.Middleweight. *Ht* 5'11¼"
Manager Self
18.02.07 Nick Okoth DREW 4 Bethnal Green
21.09.07 Michael Banbula W PTS 4 Bethnal
    Green
30.11.07 Lee Nicholson W RTD 2 Newham
27.06.08 Jamie Ambler W RSC 2 Bethnal Green
04.10.08 Pawel Trebinski W RSC 3 Norwich
08.11.08 Dean Walker W RSC 1 Bethnal Green
13.12.08 Ryan Walls W PTS 6 Brentwood
Career: 7 contests, won 6, drew 1.

Dwayne Lewis   Philip Sharkey

Mark Lewis
Mansfield. *Born* Nottingham, 20 May, 1983
L.Heavyweight. *Ht* 5' 11"
Manager C. Greaves
16.03.09 Yanko Pavlov L PTS 6 Glasgow
Career: 1 contest, lost 1.

Ian Lewison
London. *Born* London, 24 September, 1981
Heavyweight. *Ht* 6' 1"
Manager B. Baker
20.03.09 Jason Callum W PTS 6 Bethnal Green
Career: 1 contest, won 1.

Pete Leworthy
Bristol. *Born* Bristol, 7 March, 1984
S.Featherweight. *Ht* 5' 10"
Manager T. Woodward
04.09.08 Sid Razak W PTS 4 Birmingham
12.10.08 Pete Buckley W PTS 6 Bristol
20.12.08 Shaun Walton W PTS 6 Bristol
14.03.09 Craig Dyer W PTS 4 Bristol
13.06.09 Pavels Senkovs L RSC 1 Bristol
Career: 5 contests, won 4, lost 1.

James Lilley
Swansea. *Born* Swansea, 14 November,
1986
Welterweight. *Ht* 5'10"
Manager C. Sanigar
08.10.06 Anthony Christopher W RSC 1 Swansea
24.02.07 Darren Hamilton L PTS 6 Bristol
12.05.07 Chris Goodwin L PTS 4 Stoke
21.10.07 Chris Brophy W PTS 4 Swansea
29.02.08 Ben Wakeham L PTS 6 Plymouth
30.03.08 Russell Pearce W PTS 6 Port Talbot
05.06.09 Rocky Chakir W PTS 6 Newport
Career: 7 contests, won 4, lost 3.

Kevin Lilley   Philip Sharkey

Kevin Lilley
Romford. *Born* Barking, 22 August, 1978
Middleweight. *Ht* 6' 0"
Manager C. Greaves
27.09.08 Duncan Cottier W PTS 4 Bethnal Green
18.10.08 Eamonn Goodbrand L PTS 6 Paisley
21.06.09 Ryan Toms L RSC 4 Bethnal Green
Career: 3 contests, won 1, lost 2.

Willie Limond
Glasgow. *Born* Glasgow, 2 February, 1979
WBU & IBO Inter-Continental Lightweight
Champion. Former Commonwealth
Lightweight Champion. Former Undefeated
Celtic & European Union S.Featherweight
Champion. *Ht* 5'7"
Manager A, Morrison
12.11.99 Lennie Hodgkins W RTD 1 Glasgow
13.12.99 Steve Hanley W PTS 6 Glasgow
24.02.00 Nigel Senior W RSC 6 Glasgow
18.03.00 Phil Lashley W RSC 1 Glasgow
07.04.00 Jimmy Beech W RSC 2 Glasgow
26.05.00 Billy Smith W PTS 4 Glasgow
24.06.00 Haroon Din W PTS 4 Glasgow
10.11.00 Danny Connelly W PTS 6 Glasgow
17.12.00 Billy Smith W PTS 6 Glasgow
15.02.01 Marcus Portman W PTS 6 Glasgow

135

03.04.01 Trevor Smith W PTS 4 Bethnal Green
27.04.01 Choi Tseveenpurev W PTS 6 Glasgow
07.09.01 Gary Reid W PTS 8 Glasgow
03.11.01 Rakhim Mingaleev W PTS 6 Glasgow
17.11.01 Keith Jones W PTS 4 Glasgow
11.03.02 Dave Hinds W PTS 6 Glasgow
06.09.02 Assen Vassilev W RSC 3 Glasgow
22.03.03 Jimmy Beech W CO 4 Renfrew
12.07.03 Alex Arthur L RSC 8 Renfrew
　　　　　(*British S.Featherweight Title*
　　　　　Challenge)
01.11.03 Dariusz Snarski W RSC 1 Glasgow
29.11.03 Anthony Hanna W PTS 4 Renfrew
06.03.04 Dafydd Carlin W RSC 1 Renfrew
19.06.04 Youssouf Djibaba W PTS 10 Renfrew
　　　　　(*Vacant European Union*
　　　　　S.Featherweight Title)
29.10.04 Frederic Bonifai W PTS 8 Glasgow
03.12.04 Alberto Lopez W PTS 10 Edinburgh
　　　　　(*European Union S.Featherweight Title*
　　　　　Defence)
20.05.05 John Mackay W RSC 5 Glasgow
17.06.05 Kevin O'Hara W PTS 10 Glasgow
　　　　　(*Vacant Celtic S.Featherweight Title*)
05.11.05 Jus Wallie W PTS 6 Renfrew
04.11.06 Kpakpo Allotey W PTS 12 Glasgow
　　　　　(*Vacant Commonwealth Lightweight*
　　　　　Title)
14.07.07 Amir Khan L RTD 8 Greenwich
　　　　　(*Commonwealth Lightweight Title*
　　　　　Defence)
29.03.08 Martin Watson W PTS 12 Glasgow
　　　　　(*Vacant IBO Inter-Continental*
　　　　　Lightweight Title)
18.10.08 Matt Scriven W PTS 8 Paisley
27.02.09 Harry Ramogoadi W PTS 8 Paisley
29.05.09 Ryan Barrett W PTS 12 Glasgow
　　　　　(*Vacant WBU Lightweight Title*)
Career: 34 contests, won 32, lost 2.

Martin Lindsay

Belfast. *Born* Belfast, 10 May, 1982
British Featherweight Champion. Former
Undefeated IBF Youth Featherweight
Champion. *Ht* 5'7"
Manager J. Rooney
02.12.04 Dai Davies W RSC 1 Crystal Palace
24.04.05 Rakhim Mingaleev W PTS 4 Leicester
　　　　　Square
02.07.05 Henry Janes W RSC 2 Dundalk
17.09.05 Peter Feher W PTS 4 Dublin
21.04.06 Chris Hooper W RSC 1 Belfast
13.10.06 Nikita Lukin W PTS 6 Aberavon
30.03.07 Buster Dennis W PTS 6 Crawley
14.07.07 Jose Silveira W PTS 6 Rama, Canada
27.10.07 Uriel Barrera W PTS 10 Rama, Canada
　　　　　(*Vacant IBF Youth Featherweight Title*)
08.12.07 Edison Torres W PTS 8 Belfast
19.01.08 Jason Hayward W CO 1 Rama, Canada
16.05.08 Marc Callaghan W PTS 8 Turin, Italy
20.09.08 Derry Matthews W CO 9 Sheffield
　　　　　(*Final Elim. British Featherweight Title*)
25.04.09 Paul Appleby W RSC 6 Belfast
　　　　　(*British Featherweight Title Challenge*)
Career: 14 contests, won 14.

Earl Ling

Norwich. *Born* Kings Lynn, 9 March, 1972
Cruiserweight. *Ht* 5' 10"
Manager G. Everett
08.09.92 Eddie Collins W PTS 6 Norwich
11.05.93 Mark Hale L RSC 2 Norwich
12.12.94 Clinton Woods L RSC 5 Cleethorpes
04.12.95 Jeff Finlayson L PTS 6 Manchester
26.02.96 Peter Waudby L PTS 6 Hull
19.03.96 James Lowther L RSC 4 Leeds
16.05.98 Dean Ashton DREW 6 Chigwell
02.07.98 Dean Ashton L RSC 2 Ipswich
17.09.98 Jimmy Steel DREW 6 Hove
19.01.99 Israel Khumalo L RSC 1 Ipswich
15.07.00 Mike Duffield W PTS 6 Norwich
04.11.00 Andrew Facey L PTS 6 Derby
16.06.01 Andrew Facey DREW 6 Derby
04.07.01 Calvin Stonestreet L PTS 4 Bloomsbury
13.04.02 Simeon Cover W CO 4 Norwich
25.04.02 Lee Whitehead W PTS 6 Hull
21.11.02 Michael Pinnock W PTS 6 Hull
12.04.03 Ryan Walls L RSC 4 Norwich
07.12.03 Nathan Joseph DREW 6 Bradford
21.02.04 Hastings Rasani DREW 6 Norwich
09.10.04 Nathan Joseph W PTS 6 Norwich
11.12.05 O'Neil Murray L RSC 3 Norwich
28.02.09 Zahid Kahut W PTS 4 Norwich
Career: 23 contests, won 7, drew 5, lost 11.

Mark Lloyd

Telford. *Born* Walsall, 21 October, 1975
Former Undefeated Midlands Area
Welterweight Champion. Former
Undefeated International & British Masters
L.Middleweight Champion.
Ht 5'10"
Manager Self
16.09.05 Dennis Corpe W PTS 6 Telford
04.12.05 Gatis Skuja W PTS 4 Telford
16.02.06 Davey Jones W PTS 6 Dudley
14.04.06 Ben Hudson W PTS 4 Telford
13.05.06 Tommy Jones W PTS 6 Sutton in
　　　　　Ashfield
29.06.06 Tommy Jones W PTS 6 Dudley
06.10.06 Terry Adams W RSC 7 Wolverhampton
　　　　　(*Vacant British Masters L.Middleweight*
　　　　　Title)
28.06.07 Neil Bonner W PTS 4 Dudley
15.09.07 Vladimir Borovski W PTS 10
　　　　　Birmingham
　　　　　(*Vacant International Masters*
　　　　　L.Middleweight Title)
1.12.07 Martin Marshall W RTD 8 Telford
　　　　　(*International Masters L.Middleweight*
　　　　　Title Defence)
10.05.08 Adnan Amar L PTS 10 Nottingham
　　　　　(*Vacant English Welterweight Title*)
20.06.08 Andrew Alan Lowe W RSC 8
　　　　　Wolverhampton
　　　　　(*Vacant Midlands Area Welterweight*
　　　　　Title)
24.10.08 Steve Conway W PTS 3 Bethnal Green
24.10.08 Ted Bami L PTS 3 Bethnal Green
24.04.09 Jamie Cox L RSC 8 Wolverhampton
Career: 15 contests, won 12, lost 3..

Michael Lomax

Chingford. *Born* London, 25 September,
1978
Welterweight. *Ht* 6'0"
Manager Self
05.07.03 Ernie Smith W PTS 4 Brentwood
20.09.03 Peter Dunn W PTS 4 Nottingham
14.11.03 Robert Lloyd-Taylor W PTS 6 Bethnal
　　　　　Green
16.01.04 Craig Lynch W PTS 6 Bradford
31.01.04 Steve Brumant W PTS 6 Bethnal Green
08.05.04 David Keir W RTD 4 Dagenham
13.02.05 Terry Adams W RSC 1 Brentwood
16.06.05 Jamie Coyle W PTS 6 Dagenham
18.11.05 Kevin Phelan W PTS 8 Dagenham
15.12.06 Billy Smith W PTS 6 Bethnal Green
30.03.07 Silence Saheed DREW 6 Crawley
06.07.07 Craig Watson L PTS 8 Wigan
25.01.08 Craig Dickson W PTS 6 Dagenham
24.10.08 Craig Dickson W PTS 3 Bethnal Green
24.10.08 Nigel Wright W PTS 3 Bethnal Green
24.10.08 Ted Bami W PTS 3 Bethnal Green
03.04.09 Yoann Camonin W PTS 8 Bethnal Green
Career: 17 contests, won 15, drew 1, lost 1.

Michael Lomax　　　　　　Philip Sharkey

Chris Long

Calne. *Born* Gloucester, 5 March, 1980
L.Welterweight. *Ht* 5'9"
Manager T. Woodward
15.05.03 Darren Goode W RSC 1 Clevedon
21.09.03 Daniel Thorpe L PTS 6 Bristol
17.11.03 Stuart Green L PTS 6 Glasgow
13.02.04 Justin Hicks W RSC 4 Bristol
29.02.04 Gareth Perkins L PTS 6 Bristol
12.03.04 Ivor Bonavic W PTS 6 Millwall
01.05.04 Stuart Philips W RSC 1 Bridgend
19.06.04 Ceri Hall L PTS 4 Muswell Hill
12.09.04 Ernie Smith DREW 6 Shrewsbury
24.09.04 John O'Donnell L RSC 4 Nottingham
02.12.04 Gavin Tait W PTS 6 Bristol
27.01.05 Sam Rukundo L PTS 4 Piccadilly
24.04.05 Scott Haywood L PTS 6 Derby
08.05.05 John Fewkes L PTS 8 Sheffield
09.07.05 Kristian Laight W PTS 6 Bristol
25.02.06 Muhsen Nasser L PTS 4 Bristol

05.03.06 Shane Watson L PTS 4 Southampton
25.03.06 Ryan Brawley L PTS 8 Irvine
21.05.06 Kristian Laight W PTS 6 Bristol
08.10.06 Stuart Philips L PTS 4 Swansea
03.12.06 Rocky Chakir W PTS 6 Bristol
13.12.06 Stuart Green L PTS 6 Strand
17.02.07 James Gorman L RSC 3 Cork
18.03.07 Chris Brophy DREW 6 Bristol
30.03.07 Tibor Dudas L PTS 4 Crawley
28.04.07 Gary McArthur L PTS 10 Clydebank
(*Vacant British Masters Lightweight Title*)
21.10.07 Damian Owen L PTS 4 Swansea
02.12.07 Russell Pearce DREW 6 Bristol
03.02.08 Billy Smith L PTS 6 Bristol
02.05.08 Kristian Laight W PTS 4 Bristol
16.05.08 Martin Watson L PTS 10 Motherwell
(*Vacant International Masters Lightweight Title*)
12.09.08 Steve Saville L PTS 4 Wolverhampton
09.11.08 Dean Harrison L RTD 8 , Wolverhampton
21.12.08 Michael Gomez L PTS 6 Motherwell
27.02.09 Scott Evans L PTS 10 Wolverhampton
(*Vacant British Masters Lightweight Title*)
24.04.09 Rob Hunt DREW 4 Wolverhampton
18.05.09 Martin Gethin W PTS 4 Birmingham
Career: 37 contests, won 10, drew 4, lost 23.

Chris Long   Philip Sharkey

Leonard Lothian

Sheffield. *Born* Northampton, 11 February, 1988
Welterweight. *Ht* 5'6"
Manager J. Ingle
16.03.07 Matthew Martin Lewis DREW 4 Norwich
19.05.07 Dave Ryan L PTS 6 Nottingham
26.05.07 Mike Reid W PTS 6 Aberdeen

01.07.07 Matthew Martin Lewis W PTS 4 Colchester
15.09.07 Marco Cittadini DREW 6 Paisley
25.09.07 Andy Cox W PTS 6 Hull
05.10.07 Tom Glover W PTS 4 Bethnal Green
12.10.07 Scott Sandmann L PTS 4 Peterlee
25.10.07 Rob Hunt L PTS 4 Wolverhampton
09.11.07 Amir Unsworth L PTS 4 Nottingham
30.11.07 Daniel Thorpe W PTS 6 Hull
10.12.07 Pete Buckley W PTS 6 Leicester
15.02.08 George Watson L PTS 6 Sunderland
14.03.08 Nathan Brough L PTS 6 Manchester
22.03.08 Andrew Murray L RSC 3 Dublin
14.02.09 Matt Seawright W PTS 4 St Helier
28.02.09 Lee Purdy L PTS 4 Norwich
Career: 17 contests, won 7, drew 2, lost 8..

Arnold Lydekaitis

Coventry. *Born* Lithuania,19 March, 1986
L.Middleweight. *Ht* 6' 1"
Manager E. Singh
27.02.09 Joel Ryan L PTS 4 Wolverhampton
Career: 1 contest, lost 1.

Colin Lynes

Hornchurch. *Born* Whitechapel, 26 November, 1977
Former European & British L.Welterweight Champion. Former Undefeated IBO L.Welterweight Champion. Former IBO Inter-Continental L.Welterweight Champion. *Ht* 5'7½"
Manager Self
04.06.98 Les Frost W CO 1 Barking
23.07.98 Ram Singh W CO 1 Barking
22.10.98 Brian Coleman W RSC 2 Barking
31.10.98 Marc Smith W PTS 4 Basingstoke
10.12.98 Trevor Smith W RSC 1 Barking
25.02.99 Dennis Griffin W PTS 6 Kentish Town
20.05.99 Mark Haslam W PTS 4 Barking
18.05.00 Jason Vlasman W RSC 2 Bethnal Green
16.09.00 Karl Taylor W PTS 6 Bethnal Green
14.10.00 Brian Coleman W PTS 6 Wembley
09.12.00 Jimmy Phelan W PTS 6 Southwark
17.02.01 Mark Ramsey W PTS 6 Bethnal Green
10.04.01 David Kirk W PTS 6 Wembley
10.11.01 Keith Jones W PTS 6 Wembley
01.12.01 Leonti Voronchuk W PTS 6 Bethnal Green
26.01.02 David Kirk W PTS 6 Dagenham
23.03.02 Peter Dunn W PTS 4 Southwark
18.05.02 Kevin Bennett W RSC 4 Millwall
29.06.02 Ian Smith W RSC 7 Brentwood
21.09.02 Abdelilah Touil W CO 7 Brentwood
07.12.02 Richard Kiley W RSC 9 Brentwood
(*Vacant IBO Inter-Continental L.Welterweight Title*)
08.03.03 Samuel Malinga L RTD 8 Bethnal Green
(*IBO Inter-Continental L.Welterweight Title Defence*)
18.10.03 Brian Coleman W PTS 4 Manchester
22.11.03 Fabrice Colombel W PTS 6 Belfast
31.01.04 Cesar Levia W PTS 8 Bethnal Green
08.05.04 Pablo Sarmiento W PTS 12 Dagenham
(*IBO L.Welterweight Title Challenge*)

13.02.05 Juaquin Gallardo W PTS 12 Brentwood
(*IBO L.Welterweight Title Defence*)
21.10.05 Junior Witter L PTS 12 Bethnal Green
(*British, Commonwealth & European L.Welterweight Title Challenges*)
20.01.06 Lenny Daws L RTD 9 Bethnal Green
(*Elim. British L.Welterweight Title. Vacant Southern Area L.Welterweight Title*)
15.12.06 Janos Petrovics W RSC 6 Bethnal Green
30.03.07 Arek Malek W RTD 2 Crawley
08.06.07 Barry Morrison W PTS 12 Motherwell
(*British L.Welterweight Title Challenge*)
20.07.07 Young Muttley W RSC 8 Wolverhampton
(*Vacant European L.Welterweight Title. British L.Welterweight Title Defence*)
25.01.08 Juho Tolppola W PTS 12 Dagenham
(*European L.Welterweight Title Defence*)
16.05.08 Gianluca Branco L PTS 12 Turin, Italy
(*European L.Welterweight Title Defence*)
05.12.08 Paul McCloskey L RTD 9 Dagenham
(*Vacant British L.Welterweight Title*)
Career: 36 contests, won 31, lost 5.

Colin Lynes   Philip Sharkey

Craig Lyon

St Helens. *Born* Whiston, 3 February, 1982
Bantamweight. *Ht* 5'3¼"
Manager O. Harrison
07.06.08 Delroy Spencer W PTS 6 Wigan
10.10.08 Delroy Spencer W PTS 4 Liverpool
08.11.08 Mike Holloway W RSC 5 Wigan
06.12.08 Juris Ivanovs W RSC 2 Wigan
14.03.09 Anwar Alfadi W PTS 4 Manchester
03.04.09 Anthony Hanna W PTS 4 Leigh
Career: 6 contests, won 6.

Pat McAleese

Newmarket. *Born* Newmarket, 27 June, 1986
L.Middleweight. *Ht* 5'10¼"
Manager J. Eames
15.06.08 Steve Cooper W RSC 4 Bethnal Green
27.09.08 John-Paul Temple W PTS 4 Bethnal Green
06.12.08 Duncan Cottier W PTS 4 Bethnal Green
01.02.09 Byron Vince W PTS 4 Bethnal Green
22.03.09 Lester Walsh W PTS 4 Bethnal Green
27.06.09 Paul Morby W PTS 6 Portsmouth
Career: 6 contests, won 6.

Lee McAllister

Aberdeen. *Born* Aberdeen, 5 October, 1982
Commonwealth Lightweight Champion.
WBU L.Welterweight Champion. Former
Undefeated WBU, Scottish Area & WBF
Inter-Continental Lightweight Champion.
Former Undefeated British Masters
L.Welterweight Champion. *Ht* 5'9"
Manager T. Gilmour
19.10.02 Baz Carey W PTS 4 Renfrew
17.11.02 Arv Mittoo W PTS 6 Bradford
23.02.03 Lee Williamson W PTS 6 Shrewsbury
13.04.03 Ernie Smith W PTS 4 Bradford
12.05.03 Ernie Smith W PTS 6 Birmingham
15.06.03 Brian Coleman W PTS 6 Bradford
11.07.03 John-Paul Ryan W RTD 2 Darlington
17.07.03 Dean Hickman L PTS 6 Walsall
03.08.03 Brian Coleman W PTS 4 Stalybridge
06.09.03 Jeff Thomas W PTS 10 Aberdeen
    *(Vacant British Masters L.Welterweight
    Title)*
28.11.03 Ernie Smith W PTS 6 Hull
30.01.04 Karl Taylor W PTS 4 Dagenham
08.03.04 Lee Williamson W PTS 6 Birmingham
15.05.04 Martin Hardcastle W PTS 8 Aberdeen
13.02.05 Daniel Thorpe W PTS 4 Bradford
26.04.05 Mark Wall W PTS 6 Leeds
14.05.05 Karl Taylor W RTD 3 Aberdeen
23.07.05 Billy Smith W PTS 4 Edinburgh
29.10.05 Jackson Williams W RSC 5 Aberdeen
18.02.06 Silence Saheed W PTS 4 Edinburgh
29.04.06 Peter Dunn W PTS 6 Edinburgh
12.05.06 Billy Smith W PTS 4 Bethnal Green
27.05.06 Stuart Green W RSC 8 Aberdeen
    *(Vacant Scottish Area Lightweight
    Title)*
28.10.06 Ben Hudson W PTS 8 Aberdeen
26.05.07 Ben Odamattey W PTS 10 Aberdeen
    *(Vacant WBF Inter-Continental
    Lightweight Title)*
06.10.07 Craig Docherty W RSC 9 Aberdeen
    (Vacant WBU Lightweight Title)
29.03.08 Mihaita Mutu W PTS 12 Aberdeen
    (Vacant WBU L.Welterweight Title)
25.10.08 Arek Malek W PTS 8 Aberdeen

17.01.09 John Murray L RSC 8 Wigan
    (British Lightweight Title Challenge)
14.03.09 Abdoulaye Soukouna W PTS 8
    Aberdeen
19.06.09 Godfriend Sowah W RSC 3 Aberdeen
    *(Vacant Commonwealth Lightweight
    Title)*
Career: 31 contests, won 29, lost 2.

Gary McArthur

Clydebank. *Born* Glasgow, 27 July, 1982
Former Undefeated British Masters
Lightweight Champion. *Ht* 5'9"
Manager T. Gilmour
23.01.06 Lance Verallo W PTS 6 Glasgow
13.03.06 Pete Buckley W PTS 6 Glasgow
24.04.06 Darren Gethin W PTS 6 Glasgow
18.09.06 Billy Smith W PTS 8 Glasgow
13.10.06 Steve Gethin W PTS 6 Irvine
02.12.06 Frederic Gosset W PTS 6 Clydebank
28.04.07 Chris Long W PTS 10 Clydebank
    *(Vacant British Masters Lightweight
    Title)*
08.06.07 Egon Szabo W PTS 6 Motherwell
14.09.07 Dariusz Snarski W PTS 6 Kirkcaldy
24.11.07 Henry Jones W RSC 7 Clydebank
    *(British Masters Lightweight
    Title Defence)*
21.01.08 Billy Smith W PTS 8 Glasgow
24.03.09 Steve Saville W PTS 3 Glasgow
24.03.09 Stephen Burke L RSC 1 Glasgow
12.06.09 Arek Malek W PTS 6 Clydebank
Career: 14 contests, won 13, lost 1.

Enzo Maccarinelli   Philip Sharkey

Enzo Maccarinelli

Swansea. *Born* Swansea, 20 August, 1980
Former WBO Cruiserweight Champion.
Former Undefeated WBU Cruiserweight
Champion. *Ht* 6'4"
Manager F. Warren
02.10.99 Paul Bonson W PTS 4 Cardiff
11.12.99 Mark Williams W RSC 1 Merthyr
26.02.00 Nigel Rafferty W RSC 3 Swansea
12.05.00 Lee Swaby L CO 3 Swansea
11.12.00 Chris Woollas W PTS 4 Widnes
28.04.01 Darren Ashton W CO 1 Cardiff

09.10.01 Eamonn Glennon W RSC 2 Cardiff
15.12.01 Kevin Barrett W RSC 2 Wembley
12.02.02 James Gilbert W RSC 2 Bethnal Green
20.04.02 Tony Booth W PTS 4 Cardiff
17.08.02 Tony Booth W RTD 2 Cardiff
12.10.02 Dave Clarke W RSC 2 Bethnal Green
18.01.03 Paul Bonson W PTS 4 Preston
29.03.03 Valery Shemishkur W RSC 1
    Portsmouth
28.06.03 Bruce Scott W RSC 4 Cardiff
    (Vacant WBU Cruiserweight Title)
13.09.03 Andrei Kiarsten W CO 1 Newport
    (WBU Cruiserweight Title Defence)
06.12.03 Earl Morais W RSC 1 Cardiff
    (WBU Cruiserweight Title Defence)
21.02.04 Garry Delaney W RSC 8 Cardiff
    (WBU Cruiserweight Title Defence)
03.07.04 Ismail Abdoul W PTS 12 Newport
    (WBU Cruiserweight Title Defence)
03.09.04 Jesper Kristiansen W CO 3 Newport
    (WBU Cruiserweight Title Defence)
21.01.05 Rich LaMontagne W RSC 4 Bridgend
    (WBU Cruiserweight Title Defence)
04.06.05 Roman Bugaj W RSC 1 Manchester
26.11.05 Marco Heinichen W RSC 1 Rome, Italy
04.03.06 Mark Hobson W PTS 12 Manchester
    (WBU Cruiserweight Title Defence)
08.07.06 Marcelo Dominguez W RSC 9 Cardiff
    *(Vacant WBO Interim Cruiserweight
    Title)*
14.10.06 Mark Hobson W RSC 1 Manchester
    (WBO Cruiserweight Title Defence)
07.04.07 Bobby Gunn W RSC 1 Cardiff
    (WBO Cruiserweight Title Defence)
21.07.07 Wayne Braithwaite W PTS 12 Cardiff
    (WBO Cruiserweight Title Defence)
03.11.07 Mohamed Azzaoui W RSC 4 Cardiff
    (WBO Cruiserweight Title Defence)
08.03.08 David Haye L RSC 2 Greenwich
    *(WBA & WBC Cruiserweight
    Title Challenges.WBO Cruiserweight
    Title Defence)*
06.12.08 Matthew Ellis W RSC 2 Canning Town
14.03.09 Ola Afolabi L RSC 9 Manchester
    *(Vacant WBO Interim Cruiserweight
    Title)*
Career: 32 contests, won 29, lost 3.

Kevin McCauley   Philip Sharkey

Kevin McCauley
Stourbridge. *Born* Stourbridge, 21 September, 1979
L.Welterweight. *Ht* 5'9¼"
Manager P. Rowson
16.05.08 Luke Gallear L PTS 6 Burton
24.07.08 Steve Cooper W PTS 4 Wolverhampton
26.09.08 Matt Seawright W PTS 4 Wolverhampton
14.11.08 Gary McMillan L PTS 4 Glasgow
05.12.08 Scott Jordan L PTS 4 Dagenham
19.01.09 Vince Baldassara L PTS 6 Glasgow
21.02.09 Luke Osman W PTS 6 Merthyr Tydfil
14.03.09 Liam Smith L PTS 4 Manchester
24.04.09 Jason Welborn L PTS 4 Wolverhampton
18.05.09 Callum Archer L PTS 8 Birmingham
29.05.09 Nasser Al Harbi L PTS 6 Dudley
13.06.09 Brock Cato W PTS 6 Bristol
26.06.09 Vatche Wartanian DREW 4 Melksham
Career: 13 contests, won 4, drew 1, lost 8.

Paul McCloskey　　　Philip Sharkey

Paul McCloskey
Dungiven. *Born* Londonderry, 3 August, 1979
British L. Welterweight Champion. Former Undefeated IBF International L.Welterweight Champion. *Ht* 5'8½"
Manager J. Breen
18.03.05 David Kehoe W RSC 3 Belfast
17.06.05 Oscar Milkitas W PTS 4 Glasgow
05.11.05 Billy Smith W PTS 4 Renfrew
24.11.05 Henry Janes W RSC 3 Lurgan
18.02.06 Duncan Cottier W PTS 6 Edinburgh
11.03.06 Surinder Sekhon W RSC 1 Newport
04.11.06 Daniel Thorpe W RTD 3 Glasgow
09.12.06 Silence Saheed W PTS 4 Canning Town
10.02.07 Eugen Stan W PTS 6 Letterkenny
17.02.07 Chill John W PTS 6 Cork
14.07.07 Ivan Orlando Bustos W CO 4 Dublin
25.08.07 Alfredo Di Feto W PTS 8 Dublin
20.10.07 Dariusz Snarski W RTD 6 Dublin
08.12.07 Tontcho Tontchev W RSC 4 Belfast
(Vacant IBF International L.Welterweight Title)
02.02.08 Manuel Garnica W PTS 10 Limerick
29.03.08 Cesar Bazan W PTS 10 Letterkenny
19.07.08 Nigel Wright W PTS 10 Limerick
05.12.08 Colin Lynes W RTD 9 Dagenham
(Vacant British L.Welterweight Title)
13.03.09 Dean Harrison W RSC 4 Widnes
(British L.Welterweight Title Defence)
Career: 19 contests, won 19.

Mark McCullough
High Wycombe. *Born* High Wycombe, 10 February, 1983
L.Welterweight. *Ht* 5'8¼"
Manager J. Evans
16.09.07 Darryl Still L PTS 4 Southampton
31.10.07 Daniel Thorpe W PTS 6 Bayswater
28.03.08 Lloyd Smith W RSC 3 Piccadilly
01.05.08 Dezzie O'Connor W CO 1 Piccadilly
15.06.08 Silence Saheed L PTS 4 Bethnal Green
29.07.08 Bronislav Kubin L PTS 6 Brno, Czech Republic
27.09.08 Johnny Greaves W PTS 6 Bracknell
06.12.08 Darryl Still W PTS 4 Bethnal Green
21.06.09 Lee Cook L PTS 6 Bethnal Green
Career: 9 contests, won 5, lost 4.

Danny McDermid
Leeds. *Born* Leeds, 4 August, 1986
Featherweight. *Ht* 5'6"
Manager D. Roche
24.01.09 Terry Flanagan L PTS 6 Blackpool
Career: 1 contest, lost 1.

Darren McDermott
Dudley. *Born* Dudley, 17 July, 1978
Former Undefeated Midlands Area Middleweight Champion. Former Undefeated British Masters Middleweight Champion. *Ht* 6'1"
Manager D. Powell
26.04.03 Leigh Wicks W PTS 4 Brentford
13.06.03 Gary Jones W RSC 1 Queensway
30.10.03 Harry Butler W PTS 4 Dudley
21.02.04 Freddie Yemofio W RSC 3 Cardiff
15.04.04 Mark Phillips W PTS 4 Dudley
03.07.04 Neil Addis W PTS 4 Newport
11.12.04 Gokhan Kazaz DREW 4 Canning Town
21.04.05 Howard Clarke W RTD 1 Dudley
06.10.05 Andy Halder W RTD 5 Dudley
(Midlands Area Middleweight Title Challenge)
16.02.06 Michael Monaghan W RTD 9 Dudley
(Midlands Area Middleweight Title Defence)
29.06.06 Andrzej Butowicz W RSC 3 Dudley
26.10.06 Hussain Osman W PTS 10 Dudley
(Vacant British Masters Middleweight Title)
15.02.07 Darren Rhodes W RSC 5 Dudley
(Elim.British Middleweight Title)
28.06.07 Conroy McIntosh W RSC 2 Dudley
(Midlands Area Middleweight Title Defence)
25.10.07 Kai Kauramaki W RSC 4 Wolverhampton
20.06.08 Wayne Elcock L RSC 2 Wolverhampton
(British Middleweight Title Challenge)
28.02.09 Steven Bendall W PTS 10 Birmingham
(English Middleweight Title Challenge)
24.04.09 Jamie Ambler W PTS 6 Wolverhampton
23.05.09 Darren Barker L RSC 4 Watford
(Commonwealth Middleweight Title Challenge)
Career: 19 contests, won 16, drew 1, lost 2.

John McDermott
Horndon. *Born* Basildon, 26 February, 1980
English Heavyweight Champion. *Ht* 6'3"
Manager J. Branch
23.09.00 Slick Miller W RSC 1 Bethnal Green
21.10.00 Gary Williams W PTS 4 Wembley
13.11.00 Geoff Hunter W RSC 1 Bethnal Green
27.01.01 Eamonn Glennon W RSC 1 Bethnal Green
24.02.01 Alexei Osokin W PTS 4 Bethnal Green
26.03.01 Mal Rice W RSC 2 Wembley
09.06.01 Luke Simpkin W PTS 6 Bethnal Green
22.09.01 Gary Williams W RSC 4 Bethnal Green
24.11.01 Gordon Minors W RSC 3 Bethnal Green
19.01.02 Tony Booth W RSC 1 Bethnal Green
04.05.02 Martin Roothman W RSC 1 Bethnal Green
14.09.02 Alexander Mileiko W RSC 2 Bethnal Green
12.10.02 Mendauga Kulikauskas W PTS 6 Bethnal Green
14.12.02 Jason Brewster W RSC 1 Newcastle
15.02.03 Derek McCafferty W PTS 4 Wembley
08.05.03 Konstantin Prizyuk W PTS 8 Widnes
18.09.03 Nicolai Popov L RSC 2 Dagenham
13.05.04 James Zikic W RSC 4 Bethnal Green
30.07.04 Suren Kalachyan W CO 7 Bethnal Green
11.12.04 Mark Krence L PTS 10 Canning Town
(Vacant English Heavyweight Title)
08.04.05 Slick Miller W RSC 1 Edinburgh
10.12.05 Matt Skelton L RSC 1 Canning Town
(British Heavyweight Title Challenge)
26.01.07 Vitaly Shkraba W RSC 1 Dagenham
02.03.07 Paul King W PTS 6 Neath
15.06.07 Luke Simpkin W RSC 2 Crystal Palace
29.09.07 Scott Gammer W PTS 10 Sheffield
(Elim. British Heavyweight Title)
01.02.08 Daniel Peret W PTS 6 Bethnal Green
18.04.08 Pele Reid W RSC 2 Bethnal Green
(Vacant English Heavyweight Title)
18.07.08 Danny Williams L PTS 12 Dagenham
(British Heavyweight Title Challenge)
02.05.09 Danny Williams L PTS 12 Sunderland
(British Heavyweight Title Challenge)
Career: 30 contests, won 25, lost 5.

Peter McDonagh
Bermondsey. *Born* Galway, 21 December, 1977
Southern Area L.Welterweight Champion. Former All-Ireland Lightweight Champion. Former Southern Area Lightweight Champion. *Ht* 5'9"
Manager M. Helliet
28.04.02 Arv Mittoo W PTS 6 Southwark
23.06.02 Dave Hinds W PTS 6 Southwark
14.09.02 Pete Buckley W PTS 4 Bethnal Green
27.10.02 Ben Hudson L PTS 6 Southwark
18.02.03 Daffyd Carlin L PTS 4 Bethnal Green
08.04.03 Ben Hudson W PTS 4 Bethnal Green
08.11.03 Ceri Hall L PTS 4 Bridgend
22.11.03 James Gorman L PTS 4 Belfast

139

21.02.04 Chill John W RTD 2 Brighton
06.03.04 Barry Hughes L PTS 6 Renfrew
07.04.04 Jon Honney W PTS 10 Leicester Square
(Vacant Southern Area Lightweight Title)
19.11.04 David Burke L PTS 8 Bethnal Green
21.01.05 Ryan Barrett L PTS 8 Brentford
04.03.05 Scott Lawton L PTS 6 Rotherham
30.04.05 Rob Jeffries L PTS 10 Dagenham
(Southern Area Lightweight Title Defence)
14.05.05 Robbie Murray L PTS 10 Dublin
(Vacant All-Ireland L.Welterweight Title)
07.08.05 Brunet Zamora L PTS 6 Rimini, Italy
04.11.05 Anthony Christopher W PTS 4 Bethnal Green
28.01.06 Michael Gomez W RSC 5 Dublin
(Vacant All-Ireland Lightweight Title)
24.09.06 Jason Nesbitt W PTS 4 Bethnal Green
01.12.06 Karl Taylor W PTS 4 Tower Hill
05.10.07 Duncan Cottier W PTS 4 Bethnal Green
29.02.08 Giuseppe Lauri L RSC 6 Milan, Italy
(European Union L.Welterweight Title Challenge)
12.07.08 Andrew Murray L PTS 10 Dublin
(All-Ireland Lightweight Title Defence)
27.09.08 Constantin Florescu W PTS 6 Brampton, Canada
13.12.08 Lee Purdy W PTS 10 Brentwood
(Vacant Southern Area L.Welterweight Title)
11.04.09 Lenny Daws L PTS 10 Bethnal Green
(Vacant English L.Welterweight Title)
12.06.09 Jimmy Briggs W PTS 4 Bethnal Green
Career: 28 contests, won 14, lost 14.

Peter McDonagh   Philip Sharkey

Thomas McDonagh

Manchester. *Born* Manchester, 8 December, 1980
Middleweight. Former Undefeated WBU Inter-Continental L.Middleweight Champion. *Ht* 6'0"
Manager B. Hughes
09.10.99 Lee Molyneux W PTS 4 Manchester
06.11.99 Lee Molyneux W PTS 4 Widnes
11.12.99 Arv Mittoo W RSC 2 Liverpool
29.01.00 Emmanuel Marcos W PTS 4 Manchester

29.02.00 William Webster W RTD 2 Widnes
25.03.00 Lee Molyneux W PTS 6 Liverpool
16.05.00 Richie Murray W PTS 4 Warrington
29.05.00 David Baptiste W PTS 6 Manchester
04.09.00 Colin Vidler W PTS 6 Manchester
11.12.00 Richie Murray W PTS 6 Widnes
15.01.01 Kid Halls W RSC 4 Manchester
10.02.01 Harry Butler W PTS 6 Widnes
17.03.01 David Baptiste W PTS 4 Manchester
07.07.01 Paul Denton W PTS 6 Manchester
15.09.01 Howard Clarke W PTS 6 Manchester
27.10.01 Mark Richards DREW 4 Manchester
09.02.02 Tomas da Silva W PTS 6 Manchester
01.06.02 Delroy Mellis W PTS 4 Manchester
28.09.02 Brian Coleman W RSC 1 Manchester
18.01.03 Tomas da Silva W PTS 4 Preston
05.04.03 Paul Wesley W PTS 6 Manchester
08.05.03 Marcus Portman W PTS 6 Widnes
27.09.03 Eugenio Monteiro W PTS 12 Manchester
(Vacant WBU Inter-Continental L.Middleweight Title)
26.02.04 Bobby Banghar W CO 2 Widnes
(WBU Inter-Continental L.Middleweight Title Defence)
03.04.04 Craig Lynch W PTS 6 Manchester
06.05.04 Bradley Pryce W PTS 12 Barnsley
(WBU Inter-Continental L.Middleweight Title Defence)
12.11.04 Darren Rhodes W PTS 10 Halifax
(Elim. British L.Middleweight Title)
03.06.05 Barrie Lee W RSC 7 Manchester
(WBU Inter-Continental L.Middleweight Title Defence)
25.10.05 Dean Walker W PTS 6 Preston
04.03.06 Wayne Alexander L PTS 12 Manchester
(WBU L.Middleweight Title Challenge)
14.10.06 Martin Concepcion W PTS 6 Manchester
21.04.07 Vladimir Borovski W PTS 6 Manchester
30.06.07 Alexander Matviechuk W PTS 6 Manchester
30.03.08 Yassine El Maachi W PTS 6 Colne
24.05.08 Andrew Facey DREW 10 Manchester
(English L.Middleweight Title Challenge)
12.10.08 Jason Rushton W PTS 6 Leigh
07.11.08 Michael Monaghan W PTS 6 Wigan
28.03.09 Max Maxwell W RSC 1 Altrincham
02.05.09 Sam Webb L PTS 10 Sunderland
(Elim. British L. Middleweight Title)
Career: 39 contests, won 34, drew 3, lost 2.

Nick MacDonald

Moreton. *Born* Birkenhead, 24 February 1984
S. Featherweight. *Ht* 5'6"
Manager T. Gilmour
16.10.06 Nikita Lukin L RSC 2 Bethnal Green
05.12.08 Nick Seagar W RSC 1 Dagenham
13.03.09 Ian Bailey W RTD 3 Widnes
03.04.09 Andrey Kostin W PTS 6 Bethnal Green
Career: 4 contests, won 3, lost 1.

Jamie McDonnell

Doncaster. *Born* Doncaster, 3 March, 1986
English Bantamweight Champion. *Ht* 5'8"
Manager D. Hobson
16.09.05 Neil Read W PTS 6 Doncaster

02.12.05 Delroy Spencer W PTS 6 Doncaster
03.03.06 Gary Sheil W PTS 6 Doncaster
21.04.06 Neil Marston W PTS 4 Doncaster
09.06.06 Dai Davies DREW 4 Doncaster
13.10.06 Wayne Bloy W PTS 4 Doncaster
01.12.06 Andy Bell W RSC 3 Doncaster
23.02.07 Wayne Bloy W RSC 3 Doncaster
(Vacant English Bantamweight Title)
21.09.07 Nikita Lukin W PTS 8 Bethnal Green
08.12.07 Chris Edwards L PTS 12 Wigan
(Vacant British S.Flyweight Title)
28.03.08 Lee Haskins L PTS 8 Barnsley
19.09.08 Anthony Hanna W RSC 5 Doncaster
25.10.08 Alain Bonnel W PTS 6 St Helier
14.02.09 Krastan Krastanov W RSC 3 St Helier
Career: 14 contests, won 11, drew 1, lost 2.

Paul McElhinney

Glasgow. *Born* Glasgow, 9 July, 1988
Featherweight. *Ht* 5'5"
Manager T. Gilmour
16.02.09 Nick Seager W PTS 6 Glasgow
12.06.09 Michael O'Gara W PTS 6 Clydebank
Career: 2 contests, won 2.

Stuart McFadyen

Colne. *Born* Burnley, 27 January, 1982
S.Bantamweight. *Ht* 5'4"
Manager S. Wood
21.07.06 Neil Read W RSC 1 Altrincham
29.09.06 Abdul Mougharbel W PTS 4 Manchester
12.11.06 Anthony Hanna W PTS 6 Manchester
09.02.07 John Baguley W PTS 4 Leeds
11.03.07 Mo Khaled W PTS 6 Shaw
06.07.07 Tasif Khan W PTS 4 Wigan
22.09.07 Delroy Spencer W PTS 6 Wigan
25.11.07 Gavin Reid L RSC 5 Colne
30.03.08 Abdul Mougharbel W PTS 6 Colne
15.06.08 Senol Dervis W PTS 6 St Helens
28.09.08 Delroy Spencer W PTS 4 Colne
22.11.08 Anthony Hanna W PTS 4 Blackpool
29.03.09 Stuart Hall DREW 6 Bolton
Career: 13 contests, won 11, drew 1, lost 1.

Steve McGuire   Philip Sharkey

Steve McGuire

Glenrothes. *Born* Kirkcaldy, 1 June, 1981
Former Undefeated Celtic S.Middleweight
Champion. *Ht* 6'2¼"
Manager T. Gilmour
17.11.03 Shane White W CO 2 Glasgow
22.04.04 Paul Billington W RTD 3 Glasgow
15.10.04 Karl Wheeler W PTS 4 Glasgow
11.06.05 Varuzhan Davtyan W PTS 6 Kirkcaldy
30.09.05 Marcin Radola W RSC 1 Kirkcaldy
17.03.06 Paul David W PTS 6 Kirkcaldy
28.04.06 Valery Odin W PTS 6 Hartlepool
16.06.06 Simeon Cover W PTS 6 Liverpool
10.11.06 Richard Turba DREW 6 Hartlepool
16.02.07 Roman Vanicky W RSC 1 Kirkcaldy
11.05.07 Neil Tidman W PTS 8 Motherwell
14.09.07 Nathan King W PTS 10 Kirkcaldy
(Vacant Celtic S.Middleweight Title)
29.02.08 Jamie Ambler W PTS 6 Glasgow
06.06.08 Anthony Young W PTS 6 Glasgow
20.10.08 Hastings Rasani W PTS 8 Glasgow
13.12.08 Brian Magee L CO 8 Brentwood
(Vacant British S.Middleweight Title)
Career: 16 contests, won 14, drew 1, lost 1.

Danny McIntosh

Norwich. *Born* Norwich, 1 March, 1980
English L. Heavyweight Champion. *Ht* 6'2"
Manager J. Ingle
09.04.05 Omid Bourzo W PTS 6 Norwich
03.09.05 Howard Clarke W PTS 4 Norwich
06.10.05 Michael Banbula W PTS 6 Longford
07.10.06 Matthew Hough W RSC 6 Walsall
16.03.07 Robert Burton W PTS 4 Norwich
04.10.07 Joey Vegas W PTS 6 Piccadilly
22.02.08 Nick Okoth W RSC 3 Bethnal Green
04.10.08 Steven Spartacus W RSC 7 Norwich
(Vacant English L.Heavyweight Title)
06.12.08 Rod Anderton W RSC 1 Nottingham
(English L.Heavyweight Title Defence)
28.02.09 Matthew Barney W DIS 5 Norwich
(English L.Heavyweight Title Defence)
Career: 10 contests, won 10.

Eddie McIntosh

Birmingham. *Born* Birmingham, 21
September, 1982
S.Middleweight. *Ht* 6'0¼"
Manager R. Woodhall
28.09.07 Nicki Taylor W CO 2 Birmingham
18.11.07 Mark Phillips W PTS 4 Birmingham
25.01.08 Philip Callaghan W PTS 4
Birmingham
13.04.08 Dave Pearson W PTS 4 Edgbaston
30.05.08 James Tucker W PTS 4 Birmingham
14.09.08 Robert Burton W PTS 4 Birmingham
14.11.08 Mark Phillips W PTS 4 Birmingham
10.04.09 Lee Nicholson W RSC 2 Birmingham
Career: 8 contests, won 8.

Nathan McIntosh

Nottingham. *Born* Nottingham, 2 February,
1988
L.Welterweight. *Ht* 5'8¼"
Manager J. Ingle
10.05.08 Danny Stewart W PTS 4 Nottingham

05.10.08 Peter Dunn W PTS 4 Nottingham
06.12.08 Kristian Laight W PTS 6 Nottingham
31.05.09 Chris Brophy W PTS 6 Burton
Career: 4 contests, won 4.

Kevin McIntyre

Paisley. *Born* Paisley, 5 May, 1978
Former Undefeated British, Celtic &
Scottish Area Welterweight Champion.
Ht 5'10½"
Manager B. Hughes
13.11.98 Ray Wood W RSC 4 Glasgow
18.02.99 Gareth Dooley W RSC 3 Glasgow
21.05.99 Mohamed Helel W PTS 6 Glasgow
26.06.99 Karim Bouali L RTD 1 Glasgow
18.03.00 Chris Hall W RSC 3 Glasgow
07.04.00 Dave Travers W RSC 4 Glasgow
26.05.00 Tommy Peacock W RSC 5 Glasgow
24.06.00 Lee Williamson W PTS 4 Glasgow
02.10.00 Paul Denton W PTS 6 Glasgow
10.11.00 Mark Ramsey W RSC 4 Glasgow
17.12.00 Ernie Smith W PTS 6 Glasgow
15.02.01 John Humphrey L RSC 4 Glasgow
27.04.01 Michael Smyth W PTS 6 Glasgow
17.11.01 David Kirk W PTS 4 Glasgow
16.12.01 Manzo Smith W PTS 6 Glasgow
11.03.02 Karl Taylor W PTS 4 Glasgow
26.04.02 Craig Lynch W PTS 10 Glasgow
*(Vacant Scottish Area Welterweight
Title)*
08.06.02 David Kirk W RTD 5 Renfrew
19.10.02 Nigel Wright W PTS 6 Renfrew
22.03.03 David Kirk W RSC 1 Renfrew
12.07.03 Paul Denton W PTS 4 Renfrew
25.10.03 Karim Hussine W PTS 6 Edinburgh
13.12.03 David Barnes L RTD 8 Manchester
(British Welterweight Title Challenge)
02.06.04 Keith Jones W PTS 6 Hereford
17.12.04 Sergey Starkov W PTS 6 Huddersfield
05.11.05 Nigel Wright L RSC 1 Renfrew
*(Final Elim. British L.Welterweight
Title)*
06.05.06 Gary Reid L RSC 6 Stoke
*(Vacant British Masters L.Welterweight
Title)*
05.05.07 Dave Wakefield W PTS 6 Glasgow
21.07.07 Tony Doherty W PTS 10 Cardiff
(Celtic Welterweight Title Challenge)
02.11.07 Kevin Anderson W PTS 12 Irvine
(British Welterweight Title Challenge)
29.02.08 Kevin Anderson W PTS 12 Glasgow
(British Welterweight Title Defence)
14.11.08 Kell Brook L RSC 1 Glasgow
(British Welterweight Title Challenge)
27.02.09 Jay Morris W RSC 2 Paisley
Career: 33 contests, won 27, lost 6.

Jason McKay

Banbridge. *Born* Craigavon, NI, 11
October, 1977
S.Middleweight. Former Undefeated All-
Ireland L.Heavyweight Champion. *Ht* 6'1"
Manager F. Warren/J. Breen
18.02.02 Jimmy Steel W PTS 4 Glasgow
11.05.02 Harry Butler W PTS 4 Dagenham
27.07.02 Simon Andrews W RSC 3 Nottingham
08.10.02 Dean Cockburn W PTS 4 Glasgow
08.02.03 William Webster W RSC 1 Liverpool
12.04.03 Marcin Radola W RSC 1 Bethnal Green

17.05.03 Varuzhan Davtyan W PTS 6 Liverpool
04.10.03 Jamie Hearn W PTS 8 Belfast
22.11.03 Ojay Abrahams W PTS 4 Belfast
17.04.04 Alan Gilbert W PTS 6 Belfast
26.06.04 Ciaran Healy W PTS 6 Belfast
05.11.04 Paul Buchanan L PTS 6 Hereford
24.11.05 Ojay Abrahams W PTS 4 Lurgan
18.02.06 Dean Walker W RTD 1 Edinburgh
20.05.06 Conroy McIntosh W PTS 6 Belfast
26.10.06 Sandris Tomson W RSC 6 Belfast
11.11.06 Michael Monaghan W PTS 10 Dublin
(Vacant All-Ireland L.Heavyweight Title)
25.03.07 Darren Rhodes W PTS 6 Dublin
18.08.07 Mugurel Sebe W PTS 8 Cork
15.12.07 Andy Lee L RTD 6 Dublin
*(Vacant All-Ireland S.Middleweight
Title)*
02.02.08 Martins Kukuls W PTS 6 Limerick
19.07.08 Marcin Piatkowski W RSC 3 Limerick
13.12.08 Darren Barker L RTD 6 Brentwood
*(Commonwealth Middleweight Title
Challenge)*
Career: 23 contests, won 20, lost 3.

Jason McKay   Philip Sharkey

(Helen) Angel McKenzie (Hobbs)

Thornton Heath. *Born* Russia, 10 June,
1973
L.Welterweight. *Ht* 5'7"
Manager Self
26.02.06 Alena Kokavcova W PTS 4 Dagenham
01.10.06 Elena Schmitt W PTS 4 Bruchsal,
Germany
11.11.06 Galina Gumliiska L PTS 4 Rheinstetten,
Germany
31.03.07 Ramona Kuehne L PTS 6 Berlin,
Germany
23.06.07 Jill Emery L PTS 8 Dublin
14.09.07 Vinni Skovgaard L PTS 6 Horsens,
Denmark
03.11.07 Sara Davies L PTS 4 Derby
01.12.07 Anna Ingman L PTS 4 Tidaholm,
Sweden
22.12.07 Nathalie Toro L PTS 6 Beyne, Belgium
03.05.08 Myriam Lamare L RSC 6 Marseille,
France
27.06.08 Myriam Lamare L RTD 3 Toulon,
France

11.07.08 Olga Bojare L PTS 8 Riga, Latvia
(Vacant Latvian female Lightweight Title)
08.11.08 Leticia Candal L PTS 8 Tenerife, Spain
16.11.08 Sara Davis L PTS 6 Derby
06.03.09 Lidia Andreeva L PTS 6 Yakutsk, Russia
24.04.09 Myriam Chomaz L PTS 6 Condom, France
08.05.09 Juliane Koffnit L PTS 4 Berlin, Germany
Career: 17 contests, won 2, lost 15.

Ovill McKenzie

Canning Town. *Born* Jamaica, 26 November, 1979
L.Heavyweight. Former Commonwealth L.Heavyweight Champion. *Ht* 5'9"
Manager M. Shinfield
06.03.03 Leigh Alliss W PTS 4 Bristol
10.04.03 Nathan King W PTS 4 Clydach
02.06.03 Pinky Burton L PTS 8 Glasgow
18.09.03 Peter Haymer L PTS 4 Mayfair
24.10.03 Courtney Fry L PTS 4 Bethnal Green
15.11.03 Edwin Cleary W PTS 4 Coventry
30.01.04 Steven Spartacus W PTS 6 Dagenham
12.03.04 Harry Butler W RSC 2 Millwall
03.04.04 Denis Inkin L PTS 8 Manchester
10.09.04 Tommy Eastwood L PTS 8 Wembley
04.12.04 Stipe Drews L PTS 8 Berlin, Germany
06.02.05 Paul Bonson W PTS 4 Southampton
13.02.05 Gyorgy Hidvegi W RSC 3 Brentwood
13.05.05 Courtney Fry W PTS 4 Liverpool
01.07.05 Hastings Rasani W PTS 6 Fulham
26.02.06 Tony Booth W PTS 4 Dagenham
23.03.06 Paul Bonson W PTS 6 The Strand
30.03.06 Paul Bonson W RSC 3 Bloomsbury
24.09.06 Peter Haymer W RSC 2 Bethnal Green
(Vacant Commonwealth L.Heavyweight Title)
09.02.07 Dean Francis L RSC 1 Bristol
(Commonwealth L.Heavyweight Title Defence)
16.09.07 Mark Nilsen W RSC 1 Derby
19.10.07 Tony Salam L PTS 6 Doncaster
17.04.09 Bob Ajisafe L PTS 8 Leigh
19.05.09 Darren Corbett W RSC 2 Kensington
19.05.09 Terry Dunstan W PTS 3 Kensington
19.05.09 John Keeton W PTS 3 Kensington
Career: 26 contests, won 17, lost 9.

Matthew Macklin

Birmingham. *Born* Birmingham, 14 May, 1982
British Middleweight Champion. Former Undefeated All-Ireland Middleweight Champion. *Ht* 5'10"
Manager Self
17.11.01 Ram Singh W RSC 1 Glasgow
15.12.01 Christian Hodorogea W CO 1 Wembley
09.02.02 Dimitri Protkunas W RTD 3 Manchester
11.03.02 David Kirk W PTS 4 Glasgow
20.04.02 Illia Spassov W CO 3 Cardiff
01.06.02 Guy Alton W RSC 3 Manchester
28.09.02 Leonti Voronchuk W RSC 5 Manchester
15.02.03 Ruslan Yakupov W PTS 6 Wembley
24.05.03 Paul Denton W PTS 6 Bethnal Green
06.11.03 Andrew Facey L PTS 10 Dagenham
(Vacant English L.Middleweight Title)
21.02.04 Dean Walker W CO 1 Cardiff
24.04.04 Scott Dixon W RTD 5 Reading

12.06.04 Ojay Abrahams W PTS 4 Manchester
14.05.05 Michael Monaghan W CO 5 Dublin
(Vacant All-Ireland Middleweight Title)
04.08.05 Leo Laudat W RSC 3 Atlantic City, New Jersey, USA
28.10.05 Anthony Little W RSC 2 Philadelphia, Pennsylvania, USA
26.11.05 Alexey Chirkov W CO 1 Sheffield
01.06.06 Marcin Piatkowski W RSC 4 Birmingham
29.09.06 Jamie Moore L RSC 10 Manchester
(British L.Middleweight Title Challenge)
20.07.07 Anatoliy Udalov W CO 1 Wolverhampton
25.08.07 Darren Rhodes W CO 4 Dublin
20.10.07 Alessio Furlan W RSC 8 Dublin
22.03.08 Luis Ramon Campas W PTS 10 Dublin
06.09.08 Francis Cheka W PTS 10 Manchester
31.10.08 Geard Ajetovic W PTS 10 Birmingham
14.03.09 Wayne Elcock W RSC 3 Birmingham
(British Middleweight Title Challenge)
Career: 26 contests, won 24, lost 2

Jamie McLevy

Glasgow. *Born* Glasgow, 5 September, 1985
Welterweight. *Ht* 6' 0"
Manager T. Gilmour
20.10.08 Steve Cooper W PTS 6 Glasgow
28.11.08 Gavin Deacon W RSC 2 Glasgow
27.04.09 Chris Brophy W PTS 8 Glasgow
Career: 3 contests, won 3.

Gary McMillan

Edinburgh. *Born* Edinburgh, 12 January, 1987
Welterweight. *Ht* 5'10"
Manager A. Morrison
17.11.06 Scott Woolford L PTS 4 Bethnal Green
16.02.07 Thomas Mazurkiewicz DREW 4 Kirkcaldy
26.10.07 Craig Tomes W PTS 6 Glasgow
09.12.07 Mark Bett W RSC 1 Glasgow
14.03.08 Duncan Cottier W PTS 6 Glasgow
17.05.08 Danny Goode W PTS 6 Glasgow
01.11.08 Matt Scriven W PTS 6 Glasgow
14.11.08 Kevin McCauley W PTS 4 Glasgow
27.02.09 Alex Spitjo W PTS 4 Paisley
06.03.09 Badru Lusambya W PTS 4 Glasgow
19.06.09 Alex Spitjo W PTS 6 Glasgow
Career: 11 contests, won 9, drew 1, lost 1.

Joe McNally

Liverpool. *Born* Liverpool, 30 October, 1984
Middleweight. *Ht* 5'9¾"
Manager Self
10.03.07 Rocky Muscas W PTS 4 Liverpool
23.02.08 Drew Campbell W PTS 4 Liverpool
16.03.08 Mark Phillips W RTD 2 Liverpool
07.06.08 Paul Royston W PTS 4 Wigan
19.07.08 James Tucker W PTS 6 Liverpool
15.11.08 Lester Walsh W RSC 3 Greenwich
28.03.09 Graham Delehedy W RTD 3 Liverpool
Career: 7 contests, won 7.

Shane McPhilbin

Nottingham. *Born* Nottingham, 10 January, 1986

Cruiserweight. *Ht* 6' 0"
Manager S. Calow
10.05.09 Michal Skierniewski W RSC 4 Derby
Career: 1 contest, won 1.

Tony McQuade

Peterborough. *Born* Peterborough, 2 June, 1988
S.Featherweight. *Ht* 5'5½"
Manager I. Pauly
07.12.06 Gavin Deacon DREW 6 Peterborough
30.03.07 Carl Griffiths W PTS 6 Peterborough
18.04.07 Leroy Smedley L PTS 6 Strand
21.06.07 Shaun Walton W PTS 6 Peterborough
20.07.07 Kevin Buckley L PTS 4 Wolverhampton
10.12.07 John Vanemmenis DREW 6 Peterborough
08.02.08 Gavin Reid L PTS 4 Peterlee
29.02.08 Davey Savage L PTS 4 Glasgow
14.03.08 John Donnelly L PTS 6 Manchester
05.04.08 Rob Turley L PTS 6 Newport
13.06.08 Billy Bell L PTS 6 Sunderland
13.09.08 Paul Economides L PTS 6 Stoke
06.12.08 Paul Economides L PTS 4 Wigan
Career: 13 contests, won 2, drew 2, lost 9.

Brian Magee

Belfast. *Born* Lisburn, 9 June, 1975
L.Heavyweight. Former Undefeated IBO S.Middleweight Champion. Former Undefeated IBO Inter-Continental S.Middleweight Champion. *Ht* 6'0"
Manager Self
13.03.99 Dean Ashton W RSC 2 Manchester
22.05.99 Richard Glaysher W RSC 1 Belfast
22.06.99 Chris Howarth W RSC 1 Ipswich
13.09.99 Dennis Doyley W RSC 3 Bethnal Green
16.10.99 Michael Pinnock W RSC 3 Belfast
12.02.00 Terry Morrill W RTD 4 Sheffield
21.02.00 Rob Stevenson W RSC 5 Southwark
20.03.00 Darren Ashton W RTD 5 Mansfield
15.04.00 Pedro Carragher W CO 2 Bethnal Green
12.06.00 Jason Barker W PTS 8 Belfast
11.11.00 Teimouraz Kikelidze W RSC 4 Belfast
29.01.01 Neil Linford W PTS 12 Peterborough
(Vacant IBO Inter-Continental S. Middleweight Title)
31.07.01 Chris Nembhard W RSC 6 Bethnal Green
10.12.01 Ramon Britez W CO 1 Liverpool
(IBO S.Middleweight Title Challenge)
18.03.02 Vage Kocharyan W PTS 8 Crawley
15.06.02 Mpush Makambi W RSC 7 Leeds
(IBO S. Middleweight Title Defence)
09.11.02 Jose Spearman W PTS 12 Altrincham
(IBO S. Middleweight Title Defence)
22.02.03 Miguel Jimenez W PTS 12 Huddersfield
(IBO S. Middleweight Title Defence)
21.06.03 Andre Thysse W RSC 10 Manchester
(IBO S.Middleweight Title Defence)
04.10.03 Omar Eduardo Gonzalez W RSC 1 Belfast
(IBO S.Middleweight Title Defence)
22.11.03 Hacine Cherifi W RTD 8 Belfast
(IBO S.Middleweight Title Defence)

17.04.04 Jerry Elliott W PTS 12 Belfast
(IBO S.Middleweight Title Defence)
26.06.04 Robin Reid L PTS 12 Belfast
(IBO S.Middleweight Title Defence)
26.11.04 Neil Linford W RSC 7 Altrincham
16.07.05 Vitali Tsypko L PTS 12 Nurnberg,
Germany
(Vacant European S.Middleweight Title)
14.10.05 Varuzhan Davtyan W RSC 2 Dublin
28.01.06 Daniil Prakapsou W RSC 2 Dublin
26.05.06 Carl Froch L RSC 11 Bethnal Green
*(British & Commonwealth
S.Middleweight Title Challenges)*
03.11.06 Paul David W PTS 6 Barnsley
26.01.07 Andrew Lowe W PTS 10 Dagenham
(Final Elim.British L.Heavyweight Title)
08.06.07 Danny Thornton W RTD 2 Motherwell
25.08.07 Tony Oakey DREW 12 Dublin
*(British L.Heavyweight Title
Challenge)*
08.02.08 Mark Nilsen W PTS 4 Peterlee
07.03.08 Tyrone Wright W PTS 6 Nottingham
11.07.08 Simeon Cover W RSC 4 Wigan
13.12.08 Steve McGuire W CO 8 Brentwood
(Vacant British S.Middleweight Title)
Career: 36 contests, won 32, drew 1, lost 3.

Michael Maguire
Peterborough. *Born* Peterborough, 1 March, 1989
S.Bantamweight. *Ht* 5' 3"
Manager A. Booth
20.09.08 Delroy Spencer W PTS 4 Sheffield
15.11.08 Yordan Vasilev W CO 1 Greenwich
01.02.09 Faycal Messaoudene W PTS 4 Bethnal Green
25.04.09 James Ancliff W PTS 4 Belfast
Career: 4 contests, won 4.

Tahir Majid
Manchester. *Born* Manchester, 14 July, 1983
S.Bantamweight. *Ht* 5' 3"
Manager B. Hughes
06.12.08 Rhys Roberts L RSC 2 Wigan
Career: 1 contest, lost 1.

Danny Maka
Maidenhead. *Born* Jersey, 29 July, 1980
L.Middleweight. *Ht* 6' 0"
Manager J. Evans
25.10.08 Peter Dunn W PTS 6 St Helier
19.11.08 Duncan Cottier W PTS 6 Bayswater
27.11.08 Luke Robinson L PTS 6 Leeds
07.03.09 Nasser Al Harbi L PTS 6 Birmingham
Career: 4 contests, won 2, lost 2.

Chris Male
Dudley. *Born* Dudley, 5 September, 1982
S.Featherweight. *Ht* 5' 6"
Manager E. Johnson
12.09.08 Shaun Walton W PTS 4 Wolverhampton
09.11.08 Anthony Hanna W PTS 4 Wolverhampton
01.02.09 Delroy Spencer W PTS 4 Birmingham
14.03.09 Pavels Senkovs W PTS 4 Birmingham
29.05.09 Shaun Walton W PTS 4 Dudley
Career: 5 contests, won 5.

Matthew Marsh
West Ham. *Born* Sidcup, 1 August, 1982
Former Undefeated British S.Bantamweight Champion. Former Undefeated Southern Area Featherweight & S.Bantamweight Champion. *Ht* 5'5¾"
Manager F. Warren/J. Eames
10.09.04 Fred Janes W PTS 4 Bethnal Green
19.11.04 Dean Ward W PTS 4 Bethnal Green
11.12.04 Abdul Mougharbel W PTS 4 Canning Town
25.02.05 Dai Davies W PTS 4 Wembley
10.12.05 Darren Cleary W PTS 4 Canning Town
29.06.06 Frederic Gosset W PTS 6 Bethnal Green
09.12.06 Rocky Dean W PTS 10 Canning Town
*(Southern Area Featherweight Title
Challenge)*
14.07.07 Rocky Dean W PTS 10 Greenwich
*(Vacant Southern Area S.Bantamweight
Title)*
13.10.07 Derry Matthews L RSC 11 Bethnal Green
(WBU Featherweight Title Challenge)
02.02.08 Ajibu Salum W CO 1 Canning Town
27.06.08 Esham Pickering W PTS 12 Bethnal Green
*(British S.Bantamweight Title
Challenge)*
21.11.08 Rocky Dean W PTS 12 Bethnal Green
(British S.Bantamweight Title Defence)
Career: 12 contests, won 11, lost 1.

Shanee Martin
Colchester. *Born* Dagenham, 31 January, 1982
Bantamweight. *Ht* 5'2"
Manager Self
16.10.04 Iliana Boneva W RSC 4 Dagenham
05.03.05 Svetla Taskova W PTS 6 Dagenham
18.09.05 Albena Atseva W RSC 3 Bethnal Green
19.11.05 Valerie Rangeard W PTS 6 Southwark
26.02.06 Maya Frenzel W RSC 5 Dagenham
23.07.06 Juliette Winter L PTS 8 Dagenham
21.10.06 Tatiana Puchkova W RSC 2 Southwark
03.12.06 Rebekka Herrmann W PTS 8 Bethnal Green
18.02.07 Oksana Romanova L RSC 7 Bethnal Green
04.05.07 Viktoria Milo L PTS 10 Szombathely, Hungary
*(Womens IBF-GBU Flyweight Title
Challenge)*
29.06.07 Svetla Taskova W PTS 6 Manchester
07.09.07 Susi Kentikian L RSC 3 Dusseldorf, Germany
*(Womens WBA Flyweight Title
Challenge)*
01.12.07 Juliette Winter DREW 6 Bethnal Green
27.09.08 Roxana Tenea W RSC 1 Bethnal Green
Career: 14 contests, won 9, drew 1, lost 4.

Glen Matsell
Hull. *Born* Hull, 24 March, 1975
L.Middleweight. *Ht* 5'9"
Manager J. Phelan
26.11.04 Ali Mateen W RTD 3 Hull
27.04.07 Ben Hudson W PTS 6 Hull
25.09.07 Alex Stoda W PTS 6 Hull

11.10.08 Jimmy Briggs W PTS 6 Hull
06.06.09 Kristian Laight W PTS 6 Beverley
Career: 5 contests, won 5.

Derry Matthews
Liverpool. *Born* Liverpool, 23 September, 1983
Former WBU Featherweight Champion. Former Undefeated English Featherweight Champion. *Ht* 5'8½"
Manager D. Coldwell
18.01.03 Sergei Tasimov W CO 1 Preston
05.04.03 Jus Wallie W PTS 4 Manchester
08.05.03 Steve Gethin W RSC 3 Widnes
20.06.03 Henry Janes W RSC 1 Liverpool
29.08.03 Marty Kayes W RTD 2 Liverpool
02.10.03 Alexei Volchan W RSC 2 Liverpool
13.12.03 Pete Buckley W PTS 4 Manchester
26.02.04 Gareth Payne W RSC 4 Widnes
03.04.04 Henry Janes W PTS 4 Manchester
10.09.04 Buster Dennis W PTS 6 Liverpool
17.12.04 Dean Ward W RSC 1 Liverpool
13.05.05 John Mackay W PTS 6 Liverpool
16.07.05 Dai Davies W RSC 2 Bolton
25.10.05 Frederic Bonifai W PTS 6 Preston
28.01.06 Stephen Chinnock W RTD 6 Nottingham
(Vacant English Featherweight Title)
01.06.06 Mickey Coveney W PTS 8 Barnsley
14.10.06 Steve Foster W PTS 12 Manchester
(WBU Featherweight Title Challenge)
10.03.07 John Simpson W PTS 12 Liverpool
(WBU Featherweight Title Defence)
13.10.07 Matthew Marsh W RSC 11 Bethnal Green
(WBU Featherweight Title Defence)
02.02.08 Nikoloz Berkatsashvili W CO 1 Canning Town
05.04.08 Choi Tseveenpurev L CO 5 Bolton
(WBU Featherweight Title Defence)
19.07.08 John Gicharu W PTS 8 Liverpool
20.09.08 Martin Lindsay L CO 9 Sheffield
(Final Elim. British Featherweight Title)
28.03.09 Harry Ramogoadi L CO 4 Liverpool
Career: 24 contests, won 21, lost 3..

Harry Matthews
York. *Born* Beverley, 21 February, 1988
Middleweight. *Ht* 5'9¼"
Manager J. Phelan
21.06.08 Jason Smith W PTS 6 Hull
11.10.08 Simon Fleck W RTD 2 Hull
29.11.08 Jon Musgrave W PTS 4 Sleaford
21.02.09 Paul Royston W PTS 4 Hull
04.04.09 Lester Walsh W PTS 4 Coventry
06.06.09 Martyn King W PTS 4 Beverley
Career: 6 contests, won 6.

Alex Matvienko
Bolton. *Born* Bolton, 9 May, 1978
British Masters L. Middleweight Champion. *Ht* 5'11"
Manager S. Wood
18.12.05 Tommy Jones W PTS 6 Bolton
02.04.06 Tony Randell W PTS 6 Shaw
21.07.06 Simone Lucas W PTS 4 Altrincham
29.09.06 Jon Foster W RTD 3 Manchester
12.11.06 Thomas Flynn W RSC 5 Manchester

ACTIVE BRITISH-BASED BOXERS: CAREER RECORDS

25.02.07 Shaun Farmer W PTS 6 Manchester
13.04.07 Ryan Ashworth DREW 4 Altrincham
24.06.07 Ronnie Daniels W PTS 6 Wigan
06.07.07 Martin Marshall DREW 4 Wigan
22.09.07 Martin Marshall W PTS 6 Wigan
08.12.07 Jamie Ambler W PTS 4 Wigan
16.02.08 Davey Jones W RSC 2 Blackpool
26.04.08 Drew Campbell W RSC 4 Wigan
14.09.08 Lee Edwards L PTS 10 Wigan
(Vacant British Masters L. Middleweight Title)
22.11.08 David Kirk W PTS 4 Blackpool
06.03.09 Paul Royston W PTS 6 Wigan
17.05.09 Jon Musgrave W PTS 10 Bolton
(Vacant British Masters L. Middleweight Title)
Career: 17 contests, won 14, drew 2, lost 1.

Kevin Maxwell
Belfast. *Born* Belfast, 4 April, 1984
Lightweight. *Ht* 5' 6"
Manager Self
30.06.07 Denis Sirjatovs W PTS 4 Belfast
03.04.09 Ibrar Riyaz L PTS 4 Bethnal Green
Career: 2 contests, won 1, lost 1.

Max Maxwell   Philip Sharkey

Max Maxwell
Birmingham. *Born* Jamaica, 26 July, 1979
Former Midlands Area Middleweight
Champion. *Ht* 5'10"
Manager R. Woodhall
26.10.06 Anthony Young L PTS 4 Wolverhampton
01.12.06 Ernie Smith W PTS 6 Birmingham
23.02.07 Peter Dunn W PTS 6 Birmingham
17.03.07 Sherman Alleyne W PTS 6 Birmingham
29.04.07 Matt Scriven W PTS 4 Birmingham
28.09.07 Duncan Cottier W PTS 6 Birmingham
25.01.08 Johnny Enigma W RSC 2 Birmingham
28.02.08 Matthew Hough W RSC 3 Wolverhampton
(Vacant Midlands Area Middleweight Title)
14.09.08 Rob Kenney L PTS 10 Birmingham
(Midlands Area Middleweight Title Defence)

22.11.08 Steve Ede W PTS 3 Bethnal Green
22.11.08 Cello Renda L PTS 3 Bethnal Green
01.02.09 Tony Randell L PTS 10 Birmingham
(Vacant Midlands Area Middleweight Title)
16.02.09 Chris Black DREW 6 Glasgow
07.03.09 Alex Spitjo W PTS 4 Birmingham
20.03.09 Sam Webb L PTS 8 Newham
28.03.09 Thomas McDonagh L RSC 1 Altrincham
Career: 16 contests, won 9, drew 1, lost 6.

Patrick J. Maxwell
Sheffield. *Born* USA, 20 March, 1979
S.Middleweight. *Ht* 5'8¼"
Manager Self
17.03.98 Danny Thornton W PTS 6 Sheffield
12.08.00 Matthew Ashmole W RSC 3 Wembley
26.03.01 Jason Collins L PTS 4 Wembley
27.10.01 Prince Kasi Kaihau W CO 4 Manchester
09.02.02 Leigh Wicks W PTS 4 Manchester
09.03.03 Surinder Sekhon W RSC 1 Shaw
10.06.03 Andy Halder W RSC 1 Sheffield
05.09.03 Isidro Gonzalez W RSC 6 Sheffield
07.11.03 Conroy McIntosh W RSC 4 Sheffield
17.06.04 Howard Clarke W RSC 1 Sheffield
21.09.05 Conroy McIntosh W RSC 2 Bradford
14.10.06 Anthony Little W RSC 3 Philadelphia, Pennsylvania, USA
17.11.06 Charden Ansoula W PTS 6 Cabazon, California, USA
09.03.07 Kevin Phelan W RSC 2 Dagenham
27.04.07 Geard Ajetovic DREW 6 Wembley
13.07.07 Geard Ajetovic L RSC 3 Barnsley
08.03.08 Anthony Young W RTD 4 Greenwich
30.11.08 Paul Samuels W PTS 6 Rotherham
29.03.09 Nick Okoth L RSC 1 Sheffield
Career: 19 contests, won 15, drew 1, lost 3.

Thomas Mazurkiewicz
Manchester. *Born* Poland, 11 May, 1984
Welterweight. *Ht* 5' 9"
Manager Self
11.09.06 Imad Khamis DREW 6 Manchester
23.09.06 Joe McCluskey W RSC 2 Coventry
29.09.06 John Fewkes L PTS 4 Manchester
23.11.06 Imad Khamis W PTS 6 Manchester
07.12.06 Martin Marshall L PTS 4 Sunderland
16.02.07 Gary McMillan DREW 4 Kirkcaldy
09.03.07 Paul Porter W PTS 4 Dagenham
12.05.07 Danny Johnston W PTS 6 Stoke
08.11.08 Jimmy Briggs W PTS 6 Wigan
23.01.09 Scott Miller L PTS 6 Stoke
Career: 10 contests, won 5, drew 2, lost 3.

Lee Meager
Salford. *Born* Salford, 18 January, 1978
Lightweight. Former British Lightweight
Champion. *Ht* 5'8"
Manager Self
16.09.00 Pete Buckley W PTS 4 Bethnal Green
14.10.00 Chris Jickells W PTS 4 Wembley
18.11.00 Billy Smith W RSC 1 Dagenham
09.12.00 Jason Nesbitt W RSC 2 Southwark
05.02.01 Carl Allen DREW 6 Hull
13.03.01 Lennie Hodgkins W RSC 3 Plymouth
12.05.01 Jason White W PTS 4 Plymouth
31.07.01 Steve Hanley W PTS 6 Bethnal Green
13.09.01 Arv Mittoo W PTS 6 Sheffield
16.03.02 Jason Nesbitt W PTS 6 Bethnal Green

10.05.02 Pete Buckley W PTS 6 Bethnal Green
25.10.02 Iain Eldridge W RSC 5 Bethnal Green
21.12.02 Chill John W RSC 5 Dagenham
28.01.03 Carl Allen W PTS 8 Nottingham
28.11.03 Pete Buckley W PTS 4 Derby
11.12.03 Charles Shepherd W RTD 7 Bethnal Green
02.06.04 Michael Muya W PTS 8 Nottingham
19.11.04 Danny Hunt L PTS 10 Bethnal Green
(English Lightweight Title Challenge)
09.07.05 Martin Watson W PTS 10 Nottingham
02.12.05 Tony Montana W PTS 8 Nottingham
17.02.06 Ben Hudson W PTS 4 Bethnal Green
12.05.06 Dave Stewart W RSC 6 Bethnal Green
(Vacant British Lightweight Title)
08.12.06 Jonathan Thaxton L PTS 12 Dagenham
(British Lightweight Title Defence)
07.09.07 Laszlo Komjathi W RTD 4 Doncaster
07.12.07 Jose Alberto Gonzalez DREW 8 Las Vegas, Nevada, USA
11.07.08 John Murray L RSC 5 Wigan
(Vacant British Lightweight Title)
Career: 26 contests, won 21, drew 2, lost 3.

Patrick Mendy
Reading. *Born* Reading, 26 September, 1990
Middleweight. *Ht* 5' 8"
Manager J. Evans
06.03.09 Travis Dickinson L PTS 4 Wigan
14.03.09 Tobias Webb L PTS 4 Manchester
22.03.09 Matt Jack W PTS 4 Bethnal Green
06.06.09 Luke Allon W PTS 6 Beverley
Career: 4 contests, won 2, lost 2.

Patrick Mendy   Philip Sharkey

Dale Miles
Alfreton. *Born* Mansfield, 19 November, 1984
British Masters Welterweight Champion.
Ht 5'11"
Manager M. Shinfield
13.05.06 Karl Taylor W RSC 3 Sutton in Ashfield
16.09.06 Steve Cooper W PTS 6 Burton
11.11.06 Jimmy Maile W RSC 5 Sutton in Ashfield
17.05.08 Jimmy Doherty W PTS 6 Stoke

20.09.08 JJ Bird W PTS 4 Newark
31.05.09 Rob Kenney W RSC 7 Burton
(Vacant British Masters Welterweight Title)
Career: 6 contests, won 6.

Harry Miles

Blackwood. *Born* Hereford, 18 November, 1985
L.Heavyweight. *Ht* 6'4¼"
Manager E. Calzaghe/F. Warren
21.07.07 Matthew Lloyd W CO 4 Cardiff
03.11.07 Mark Phillips W PTS 4 Cardiff
22.03.08 Jamie Norkett W PTS 4 Cardiff
05.06.09 Wayne Brooks L PTS 4 Newport
Career: 4 contests, won 3, lost 1.

Scott Miller

Stoke. *Born* Stoke, 7 July, 1982
Welterweight. *Ht* 5'11¼"
Manager M. Carney
17.11.07 Karl Taylor W PTS 6 Stoke
01.03.08 Craig Tomes W RSC 6 Stoke
20.03.08 Chris Mullen W PTS 6 South Shields
17.05.08 Jimmy Beech W RTD 2 Stoke
06.06.08 Ade Adebolu W RSC 2 Stoke
13.09.08 Billy Smith W PTS 4 Stoke
23.01.09 Thomas Mazurkiewicz W PTS 6 Stoke
Career: 7 contests, won 7.

Dean Mills   Philip Sharkey

Dean Mills

Bridgewater. *Born* Bridgewater, 13 October, 1987
S.Featherweight. *Ht* 5'5¾"
Manager N. Christian
09.11.07 Dezzie O'Connor L PTS 6 Plymouth
16.02.08 Carl Griffiths W RSC 6 Leicester
18.04.08 Billy Bell W PTS 6 Houghton le Spring
02.05.08 Barrington Brown DREW 4 Nottingham
07.03.09 Kevin Buckley DREW 4 Chester
17.04.09 Steve Gethin W RSC 2 Bristol
Career: 6 contests, won 3, drew 2, lost 1.

Ross Minter

Crawley. *Born* Crawley, 10 November, 1978
Welterweight. Former Undefeated Southern Area & English Welterweight Champion.
Ht 5'7¾"
Manager F. Warren
26.03.01 Brian Coleman W PTS 4 Wembley
05.05.01 Trevor Smith W RTD 3 Edmonton
28.07.01 Lee Williamson W PTS 4 Wembley
24.11.01 Karl Taylor W PTS 4 Bethnal Green
15.12.01 Ernie Smith W RSC 2 Wembley
02.03.02 Paul Denton W PTS 6 Bethnal Green
25.05.02 Howard Clarke L RSC 2 Portsmouth
12.10.02 Dafydd Carlin W RSC 1 Bethnal Green
15.02.03 Karl Taylor W PTS 6 Wembley
29.03.03 Jay Mahoney W RSC 2 Portsmouth
24.05.03 Jay Mahoney W PTS 6 Bethnal Green
18.09.03 John Marshall DREW 6 Dagenham
19.11.04 David Kirk W PTS 6 Bethnal Green
25.02.05 Ernie Smith W PTS 4 Wembley
29.04.05 Chas Symonds W RSC 3 Southwark
(Southern Area Welterweight Title Challenge)
23.09.05 Sammy Smith W RSC 3 Mayfair
(Southern Area Welterweight Title Defence)
10.12.05 Brett James W RSC 4 Canning Town
(Vacant English Welterweight Title. Southern Area Welterweight Title Defence)
08.07.06 Duncan Cottier W PTS 6 Cardiff
17.02.07 Sasha Shnip W RSC 2 Wembley
30.03.07 Freddy Curiel L RSC 8 Newcastle
02.02.08 Michael Jennings L RSC 9 Canning Town
(WBU Welterweight Title Challenge)
24.10.08 Nigel Wright L PTS 3 Bethnal Green
Career: 22 contests, won 17, drew 1, lost 4.

(Delroy) Dee Mitchell

Birmingham. *Born* Birmingham, 16 November, 1976
L.Middleweight. *Ht* 5'9"
Manager R. Woodhall
08.09.06 Chris Brophy W RSC 2 Birmingham
26.10.06 Tony Randell W PTS 4 Wolverhampton
01.12.06 Billy Smith W PTS 4 Birmingham
23.02.07 Geraint Harvey W PTS 4 Birmingham
17.03.07 Matt Scriven W RSC 2 Birmingham
29.04.07 Tye Williams W PTS 8 Birmingham
13.07.07 Gatis Skuja L RSC 5 Birmingham
18.11.07 Peter Dunn W PTS 6 Birmingham
21.06.08 Martin Concepcion L PTS 4 Birmingham
14.09.08 Gatis Skuja W PTS 4 Birmingham
06.02.09 Prince Arron L PTS 6 Birmingham
06.03.09 Jack Arnfield L PTS 4 Wigan
Career: 12 contests, won 8, lost 4.

Kevin Mitchell

Dagenham. *Born* Dagenham, 29 October, 1984
British, WBO & IBF Inter-Continental S.Featherweight Champion. Former Undefeated Commonwealth S..
Featherweight Champion. *Ht* 5'8"
Manager F. Warren

17.07.03 Stevie Quinn W CO 1 Dagenham
18.09.03 Csabi Ladanyi W RSC 1 Dagenham
06.11.03 Vlado Varhegyi W RSC 3 Dagenham
24.01.04 Jaz Virdee W RSC 1 Wembley
07.02.04 Kristian Laight W PTS 4 Bethnal Green
24.04.04 Eric Patrac W RSC 1 Reading
13.05.04 Slimane Kebaili W RSC 1 Bethnal Green
05.06.04 Jason Nesbitt W RSC 3 Bethnal Green
10.09.04 Arpad Toth W RSC 3 Bethnal Green
22.10.04 Mounir Guebbas W PTS 6 Edinburgh
19.11.04 Alain Rakow W CO 1 Bethnal Green
11.12.04 Henry Janes W PTS 4 Canning Town
08.04.05 Frederic Bonifai W PTS 6 Edinburgh
29.04.05 Karim Chakim W PTS 8 Southwark
23.09.05 Wladimir Borov W RSC 2 Mayfair
25.10.05 Daniel Thorpe W RSC 4 Preston
10.12.05 Mohammed Medjadji W RSC 6 Canning Town
(Vacant IBF Inter-Continental S.Featherweight Title)
25.02.06 Youssef Djibaba W PTS 12 Canning Town
(IBF Inter-Continental S.Featherweight Title Defence)
13.05.06 Kirkor Kirkorov W RTD 2 Bethnal Green
(IBF Inter-Continental S.Featherweight Title Defence)
08.07.06 Imad Ben Khalifa W RSC 2 Cardiff
08.09.06 Andrey Isaev W RSC 11 Mayfair
(IBF Inter-Continental S.Featherweight Title Defence)
28.10.06 George Ashie W PTS 12 Bethnal Green
(Vacant Commonwealth S.Featherweight Title)
10.03.07 Harry Ramogoadi W RSC 6 Liverpool
(Commonwealth S.Featherweight Title Defence)
14.07.07 Alexander Hrulev W CO 2 Greenwich
(Vacant WBO Inter-Continental S.Featherweight Title. IBF Inter-Continental S.Featherweight Title Defence)
12.01.08 Edison Torres W RSC 3 Bethnal Green
08.03.08 Carl Johanneson W RSC 9 Greenwich
(British S.Featherweight Title Challenge. Commonwealth S.Featherweight Title Defence)
07.06.08 Walter Estrada W RSC 5 Atlantic City, New Jersey, USA
(Vacant WBO Inter-Continental S.Featherweight Title)
22.05.09 Lanquaye Wilson W RSC 3 Bethnal Green
Career: 28 contests, won 28.

Scott Mitchell

Bolton. *Born* Bolton, 3 February, 1979
Heavyweight. *Ht* 6'3"
Manager O. Harrison
16.06.07 Zahir Kahut L PTS 6 Bolton
06.07.07 David Ingleby W PTS 4 Wigan
23.05.08 Paul Bonson W PTS 6 Wigan
14.09.08 Ben Harding W PTS 6 Wigan
08.11.08 Lee Mountford W PTS 6 Wigan
Career: 5 contests, won 4, lost 1.

145

Vinny Mitchell

Dagenham. *Born* Dagenham, 1 May, 1987
Lightweight. *Ht* 5'7¼"
Manager F. Warren
17.02.07 Shaun Walton W PTS 4 Wembley
14.07.07 Sergei Rozhakmens W RSC 3 Greenwich
12.01.08 Robin Deakin W PTS 4 Bethnal Green
08.03.08 John Baguley W PTS 4 Greenwich
14.06.08 Wladimir Borov W PTS 4 Bethnal Green
26.09.08 Shaun Walton W PTS 4 Bethnal Green
21.11.08 Riaz Durgahed W RSC 1 Bethnal Green
30.01.09 Robin Deakin W PTS 4 Bethnal Green
22.05.09 Youssef Al Hamidi W PTS 4 Bethnal Green
Career: 9 contests, won 9.

Matin Mohammed

Nottingham. *Born* Pakistan, 30 October, 1981
S.Featherweight. *Ht* 5' 9"
Manager Self
05.10.08 Pete Buckley DREW 4 Nottingham
31.10.08 Pete Buckley L PTS 4 Birmingham
Career: 2 contests, drew 1, lost 1.

Michael Monaghan

Lincoln. *Born* Nottingham, 31 May, 1976
L.Heavyweight. Former Midlands Area L.Heavyweight Champion. *Ht* 5'10¾"
Manager Self
23.09.96 Lee Simpkin W PTS 6 Cleethorpes
24.10.96 Lee Bird W RSC 6 Lincoln
09.12.96 Lee Simpkin W PTS 6 Chesterfield
16.12.96 Carlton Williams W PTS 6 Cleethorpes
20.03.97 Paul Miles W PTS 6 Newark
26.04.97 Paul Ryan L RSC 2 Swadlincote
05.07.97 Ali Khattab W PTS 4 Glasgow
18.08.97 Trevor Meikle W PTS 6 Nottingham
12.09.97 Willie Quinn L PTS 6 Glasgow
19.09.97 Roy Chipperfield W PTS 6 Salford
30.09.97 George Richards L PTS 6 Edgbaston
10.03.98 Anthony van Niekirk L RTD 6 Hammanskraal, South Africa
23.04.98 Darren Sweeney L PTS 10 Edgbaston
(Midlands Area Middleweight Title Challenge)
19.09.98 Jim Rock L PTS 12 Dublin
(Vacant WAA Inter-Continental S. Middleweight Title)
27.11.98 Mark Dawson W PTS 6 Nottingham
07.12.98 Mike Whittaker L PTS 6 Manchester
14.09.02 Paul Billington W RSC 4 Newark
30.11.02 Gary Beardsley W PTS 6 Newark
24.02.03 Jason Collins W PTS 8 Birmingham
16.04.03 Carl Froch L RSC 3 Nottingham
28.06.03 Gary Lockett L PTS 10 Cardiff
13.09.03 Tomas da Silva W PTS 6 Newport
25.04.04 Jason Collins W PTS 6 Nottingham
05.06.04 Wayne Elcock W PTS 4 Bethnal Green
03.09.04 Gary Lockett L RSC 3 Newport
29.10.04 Lawrence Murphy L PTS 6 Renfrew
20.02.05 Howard Clarke W PTS 6 Sheffield
18.03.05 Jim Rock L PTS 8 Belfast
27.03.05 Michal Bilak W PTS 6 Prague, Czech Republic
30.04.05 John Humphrey L PTS 6 Dagenham

14.05.05 Matthew Macklin L CO 5 Dublin
(Vacant All-Ireland Middleweight Title)
16.02.06 Darren McDermott L RTD 9 Dudley
(Midlands Area Middleweight Title Challenge)
06.10.06 Simeon Cover L PTS 6 Mansfield
11.11.06 Jason McKay L PTS 10 Dublin
(Vacant All-Ireland L.Heavyweight Title)
30.11.06 Joey Vegas L PTS 10 Piccadilly
(British Masters S.Middleweight Title Challenge)
03.03.07 Rod Anderton W PTS 10 Alfreton
(Vacant Midlands Area L.Heavyweight Title)
19.05.07 Tyrone Wright L RSC 10 Nottingham
(Midlands Area L.Heavyweight Defence. Vacant British Masters L.Heavyweight Title)
06.10.07 Neil Tidman L PTS 6 Leicester
09.11.07 Paul David L PTS 10 Nottingham
(Vacant Midlands Area S.Middleweight Title)
05.10.08 Cello Renda L PTS 4 Nottingham
07.11.08 Thomas McDonagh L PTS 6 Wigan
28.03.09 Jason Smith W PTS 6 Lincoln
28.05.09 Hassan N'Dam N'Jikam L RSC 7 Paris, France
Career: 43 contests, won 18, lost 25.

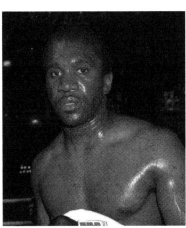

Sabie Montieth   Philip Sharkey

Sabie Montieth

Romford. *Born* Ilford, 3 December, 1973
L.Heavyweight. *Ht* 6' 0"
Manager M. Helliet
02.10.08 Jack Morris L PTS 4 Piccadilly
Career: 1 contest, lost 1.

Jamie Moore

Salford. *Born* Salford, 4 November, 1978
European & All-Ireland L. Middleweight Champion. Former Undefeated British L.Middleweight Champion. Former Commonwealth L.Middleweight Champion. *Ht* 5'8"
Manager S. Wood
09.10.99 Clive Johnson W RSC 3 Manchester
13.11.99 Peter Nightingale W PTS 4 Hull
19.12.99 Paul King W PTS 6 Salford

29.02.00 David Baptiste W RSC 3 Manchester
20.03.00 Harry Butler W RSC 2 Mansfield
14.04.00 Jimmy Steel W PTS 6 Manchester
27.05.00 Koba Kulu W RTD 3 Southwark
07.10.00 Leigh Wicks W PTS 4 Doncaster
12.11.00 Prince Kasi Kaihau W RSC 2 Manchester
25.11.00 Wayne Shepherd W RSC 3 Manchester
17.03.01 Richie Murray W RSC 1 Manchester
27.05.01 Paul Denton W RSC 3 Manchester
07.07.01 Scott Dixon L CO 5 Manchester
(Vacant WBO Inter-Continental L.Middleweight Title)
26.01.02 Harry Butler W RSC 3 Dagenham
09.03.02 Andrzej Butowicz W RSC 5 Manchester
07.09.02 Delroy Mellis W CO 6 Liverpool
08.02.03 Akhmed Oligov W PTS 6 Liverpool
19.04.03 Michael Jones W PTS 12 Liverpool
(Vacant British L. Middleweight Title. Commonwealth L. Middleweight Title Challenge)
18.10.03 Gary Logan W CO 5 Manchester
(British & Commonwealth L.Middleweight Title Defences)
22.11.03 Andrew Facey W RSC 7 Belfast
(British & Commonwealth L.Middleweight Title Defences)
10.04.04 Adam Katumwa W RSC 5 Manchester
(Vacant Commonwealth L.Middleweight Title)
26.06.04 Ossie Duran L RSC 3 Belfast
(Commonwealth L.Middleweight Title Defence)
26.11.04 Michael Jones L DIS 3 Altrincham
(British L.Middleweight Title Defence)
08.07.05 Michael Jones W RSC 6 Altrincham
(British L.Middleweight Title Challenge)
23.09.05 David Walker W RSC 4 Manchester
(British L.Middleweight Title Defence)
27.01.06 Vladimir Borovski W RSC 3 Dagenham
21.07.06 Mike Algoet W RSC 5 Altrincham
29.09.06 Matthew Macklin W RSC 10 Manchester
(British L.Middleweight Title Defence)
09.03.07 Mugurel Sebe W PTS 8 Dagenham
13.04.07 Sebastian Andres Lujan W PTS 12 Altrincham
26.10.07 Andrew Facey W RSC 11 Wigan
(British L.Middleweight Title Defence)
24.05.08 Esau Herrera W RSC 5 Manchester
05.07.08 Ciaran Healy W RSC 3 Dublin
(Vacant All-Ireland L.Middleweight Title)
06.03.09 Michele Piccirillo W CO 3 Wigan
(Vacant European L.Middleweight Title)
02.05.09 Roman Dzuman W RSC 2 Sunderland
(European L.Middleweight Title Defence)
Career: 35 contests, won 32, lost 3.

Mark Moran

Liverpool. *Born* Liverpool, 16 February, 1982
English S.Bantamweight Champion. *Ht* 5'5"
Manager S. Wood
02.10.03 Steve Gethin W PTS 4 Liverpool
13.12.03 Delroy Spencer W PTS 4 Manchester
26.02.04 Darren Cleary W PTS 4 Widnes
03.04.04 Neil Read W RSC 2 Manchester

22.05.04 Darren Cleary DREW 4 Widnes
17.12.04 Steve Gethin W PTS 4 Liverpool
22.09.07 John Baguley W PTS 4 Wigan
26.10.07 Gavin Reid W PTS 4 Wigan
08.12.07 Iordan Vasilev W CO 3 Wigan
16.03.08 Abdul Mougharbel W PTS 4 Liverpool
24.05.08 Danny Wallace W RSC 9 Manchester
    (Vacant English S.Bantamweight Title)
07.11.08 Youssef Al Hamidi W PTS 6 Wigan
17.04.09 Jason Booth L RSC 6 Leigh
    (Vacant British S.Bantamweight Title)
Career: 13 contests, won 11, drew 1, lost 1.

Paul Morby
Portsmouth. *Born* Portsmouth, 15 October, 1979
Middleweight. *Ht* 5'11"
Manager R. Davies
24.09.06 Jamie Ambler W PTS 4 Southampton
25.02.07 Dave Wakefield W PTS 6 Southampton
10.06.07 Philip Dowse L RSC 4 Neath
16.09.07 John-Paul Temple W PTS 4 Southampton
10.11.07 JJ Bird W PTS 6 Portsmouth
02.03.08 John-Paul Temple W PTS 4 Portsmouth
13.06.08 Chas Symonds L PTS 6 Portsmouth
17.04.09 Jack Arnfield L PTS 4 Leigh
27.06.09 Pat McAleese L PTS 6 Portsmouth
Career: 9 contests, won 5, lost 4.

Darren Morgan
Swansea. *Born* Swansea, 26 October, 1976
Heavyweight. *Ht* 6'1¼"
Manager Self
21.01.05 Ebrima Secka W RSC 1 Bridgend
04.06.05 Dave Clarke W RSC 1 Manchester
10.09.05 Tony Booth W PTS 4 Cardiff
25.02.06 Radcliffe Green W RSC 3 Canning Town
11.03.06 Istvan Kecskes W PTS 4 Newport
20.05.06 Martin Rogan L PTS 4 Belfast
13.10.07 Derek Chisora L PTS 4 Bethnal Green
12.01.08 Sam Sexton L PTS 6 Bethnal Green
11.04.08 David Dolan L PTS 3 Bethnal Green
12.09.08 Lee Swaby L PTS 3 Newcastle
Career: 10 contests, won 5, lost 5.

Simon Morgan
Llanelli. *Born* Swansea, 10 June, 1977
Welterweight. *Ht* 5' 7"
Manager N. Hodges
28.09.08 Chris O'Brien L RSC 2 Colne
Career: 1 contest, lost 1.

Andy Morris
Wythenshawe. *Born* Manchester, 10 March, 1983
Featherweight. Former British Featherweight Champion. Former Undefeated English Featherweight Champion. *Ht* 5'6½"
Manager F. Warren
18.01.03 Jason Nesbitt W PTS 4 Preston
05.04.03 Haroon Din W RSC 1 Manchester
08.05.03 Daniel Thorpe W PTS 4 Widnes
06.11.03 Dave Hinds W PTS 4 Dagenham

13.12.03 Henry Janes W PTS 4 Manchester
26.02.04 Daniel Thorpe W RSC 3 Widnes
03.04.04 Carl Allen W PTS 4 Manchester
12.06.04 Jus Wallie W PTS 6 Manchester
01.10.04 Chris Hooper W RSC 3 Manchester
11.02.05 Buster Dennis W PTS 6 Manchester
20.05.05 Rocky Dean W PTS 10 Southwark
    (Vacant English Featherweight Title)
23.09.05 Mickey Coveney W RSC 4 Mayfair
05.11.05 John Simpson W PTS 12 Renfrew
    (Vacant British Featherweight Title)
29.04.06 Rendall Munroe W PTS 12 Edinburgh
    (British Featherweight Title Defence)
09.12.06 John Simpson L RSC 5 Canning Town
    (British Featherweight Title Defence)
21.07.07 Daniel Thorpe W RSC 2 Cardiff
07.09.07 John Simpson L RSC 7 Mayfair
    (British Featherweight Title Challenge)
27.03.09 Youssef Al Hamidi W PTS 4 Glasgow
Career: 18 contests, won 16, lost 2.

Jack Morris
Margate. *Born* Greenwich, 15 August, 1982
L.Heavyweight. *Ht* 5'11½"
Manager M. Helliet
09.10.07 Michael Banbula L PTS 6 Tower Hamlets
28.03.08 Ricky Strike W PTS 4 Piccadilly
02.10.08 Sabie Montieth W PTS 4 Piccadilly
05.03.09 Kenroy Lambert W RSC 4 Limehouse
12.06.09 Jamie Ambler W PTS 4 Bethnal Green
Career: 5 contests, won 4, lost 1.

Jay Morris
Newport, IoW. *Born* Newport, IoW, 8 May, 1978
Welterweight. *Ht* 5'7"
Manager G. Earl
21.02.04 Judex Meemea DREW 4 Brighton
30.03.04 Casey Brooke W RSC 1 Southampton
21.11.04 Chris Brophy W RSC 1 Bracknell
12.02.05 Pete Buckley W PTS 6 Portsmouth
26.06.05 David Kehoe W PTS 4 Southampton
25.09.05 Ivor Bonavic L PTS 6 Southampton
04.12.05 Ivor Bonavic W PTS 6 Portsmouth
05.03.06 Duncan Cottier L RSC 2 Southampton
24.09.06 Duncan Cottier W PTS 4 Southampton
02.12.06 Alex Stoda L RSC 4 Southwark
03.05.07 David Barnes L RSC 1 Sheffield
05.06.07 Andrew Ferrans L RSC 3 Glasgow
07.09.07 Barrie Jones L RTD 4 Mayfair
01.12.07 Danny Goode W PTS 4 Bethnal Green
09.12.07 Paddy Pollock W PTS 6 Glasgow
23.02.08 Terry Adams W RSC 2 Crawley
14.03.08 Craig Docherty L PTS 6 Glasgow
13.06.08 Jason Rushton L PTS 6 Portsmouth
27.06.08 John O'Donnell L RSC 6 Bethnal Green
27.09.08 Michael Grant L DIS 6 Bethnal Green
08.11.08 Lenny Daws L PTS 6 Bethnal Green
21.11.08 Eddie Corcoran L RTD 4 Bethnal Green
13.02.09 Barrie Jones L PTS 4 Swindon
27.02.09 Kevin McIntyre L RSC 2 Paisley
25.04.09 Curtis Woodhouse W PTS 6 Belfast
27.06.09 Johnny Creamer W PTS 4 Portsmouth
Career: 26 contests, won 11, drew 1, lost 14.

Ally Morrison
Penrith. *Born* Penrith, 26 October, 1977
S.Middleweight. *Ht* 5' 11¼"
Manager Self
26.04.08 Dave Pearson W PTS 6 Wigan
28.09.08 Jamie Ambler W PTS 6 Colne
08.03.09 Carl Wild DREW 6 Sheffield
Career: 3 contests, won 2, drew 1.

Barry Morrison
Motherwell. *Born* Bellshill, 8 May, 1980
L.Welterweight. Former British L.Welterweight Champion. Former Undefeated British Masters L.Welterweight Champion. *Ht* 5'7"
Manager T. Gilmour
12.04.03 Keith Jones W PTS 4 Bethnal Green
28.04.03 Arv Mittoo W RSC 3 Nottingham
05.07.03 Cristian Hodorogea W RSC 3 Brentwood
06.09.03 Jay Mahoney W RSC 2 Huddersfield
04.10.03 Sergei Starkov W PTS 6 Belfast
01.11.03 Tarik Amrous W PTS 8 Glasgow
28.02.04 Zoltan Surman W RSC 3 Bridgend
22.04.04 Andrei Devyataykin W PTS 8 Glasgow
15.10.04 Adam Zadworny W RSC 2 Glasgow
27.05.05 Gary Reid W RTD 8 Motherwell
    (British Masters L.Welterweight Title Challenge)
14.10.05 Tony Montana W PTS 10 Motherwell
    (British Masters L.Welterweight Title Defence)
17.03.06 Dean Hickman W RSC 1 Kirkcaldy
    (Elim. British L.Welterweight Title)
21.04.06 Mihaita Mutu L PTS 8 Belfast
22.09.06 Mounir Guebbas W PTS 6 Bethnal Green
20.01.07 Lenny Daws W PTS 12 Muswell Hill
    (British L.Welterweight Title Challenge)
08.06.07 Colin Lynes L PTS 12 Motherwell
    (British L.Welterweight Title Defence)
19.10.07 Arek Malek W PTS 6 Motherwell
29.02.08 Billy Smith W PTS 6 Glasgow
04.07.08 David Barnes L PTS 12 Liverpool
    (British L.Welterweight Title Challenge)
19.01.09 Jason Nesbitt W PTS 6 Glasgow
Career: 20 contests, won 17, lost 3.

Samir Mouneimne
Newark. *Born* Newark, 13 June, 1987
Featherweight. *Ht* 5' 6"
Manager C. Greaves
23.01.09 Steve Gethin DREW 4 Stoke
28.03.09 Craig Dyer W PTS 4 Lincoln
29.05.09 Lee Selby W PTS 4 Stoke
Career: 3 contests, won 2, drew 1.

Lee Mountford
Pudsey. *Born* Leeds, 1 September, 1972
Heavyweight. *Ht* 6'2"
Manager Self
19.04.02 Gary Thompson DREW 4 Darlington
24.06.02 Eamonn Glennon L PTS 6 Bradford
20.11.02 Nate Joseph W PTS 6 Leeds
03.02.03 Eamonn Glennon DREW 6 Bradford
28.02.03 Gary Thompson W PTS 6 Irvine
13.05.03 Nate Joseph L PTS 6 Leeds
01.12.03 Dave Clarke W PTS 6 Bradford

15.03.04 Greg Scott-Briggs DREW 6 Bradford
09.04.04 Carl Wright L PTS 4 Rugby
20.04.04 Lee Swaby L RSC 1 Sheffield
26.09.04 Paul Butlin L PTS 6 Stoke
28.10.04 Martin Rogan L RSC 1 Belfast
13.02.05 Nate Joseph L PTS 6 Bradford
13.05.05 Tony Moran L RSC 1 Liverpool
18.06.05 John Anthony L RSC 5 Barnsley
25.09.05 Dave Clarke W PTS 4 Leeds
22.10.05 Tyrone Wright L CO 3 Mansfield
03.03.06 Stewart Mitchell L PTS 4 Doncaster
26.05.06 Tony Booth L PTS 6 Hull
15.10.06 Sam Sexton L RSC 2 Norwich
25.09.07 Dean O'Loughlin L PTS 6 Hull
19.10.07 Billy Boyle L PTS 6 Doncaster
17.11.07 Alex Ibbs L PTS 6 Stoke
29.11.07 Zahir Kahut L PTS 6 Bradford
06.12.07 Dave Ferguson L PTS 6 Sunderland
25.01.08 Tom Owens L PTS 6 Birmingham
15.02.08 Danny Hughes L PTS 6 Sunderland
28.02.08 Neil Perkins L PTS 4 Wolverhampton
29.03.08 Dave McKenna L PTS 6 Glasgow
08.11.08 Scott Mitchell L PTS 6 Wigan
19.11.08 Ali Adams L RSC 3 Bayswater
13.02.09 Rob Beech L PTS 4 Wigan
14.03.09 Andrew Young L RSC 2 Aberdeen
Career: 33 contests, won 4, drew 3, lost 26.

Bheki Moyo

Earls Court. *Born* Pretoria, South Africa, 6 October, 1974
L.Welterweight. *Ht* 5'7"
Manager Self
24.07.05 Judex Meemea L PTS 4 Leicester Square
28.10.05 Damian Owen L PTS 6 Hartlepool
17.11.05 Garry Buckland L RSC 3 Bristol
21.05.06 Ali Wyatt L RSC 3 Bristol
29.06.06 Nathan Weise L PTS 4 Bethnal Green
26.10.06 Martin Gordon DREW 6 Dudley
17.11.06 Ruben Giles L RSC 4 Bethnal Green
24.04.08 Graham Fearn L PTS 6 Piccadilly
02.05.08 Steve Jevons L PTS 4 Nottingham
20.06.08 Jimmy Briggs L PTS 6 Plymouth
09.11.08 Chris Lewis L PTS 6 Wolverhampton
26.11.08 Dean Arnold L PTS 6 Piccadilly
21.12.08 James Flinn L PTS 6 Coventry
05.03.09 Vinny Woolford L PTS 6 Limehouse
Career: 14 contests, drew 1, lost 13.

James Mulhern

Coventry. *Born* Coventry, 10 June, 1981
Flyweight. *Ht* 5' 2"
Manager E. Johnson
24.07.08 David Keogan W PTS 4 Wolverhampton
12.06.09 Francis Croes W PTS 4 Wolverhampton
Career: 2 contests, won 2.

Chris Mullen

South Shields. *Born* South Shields, 24 May, 1986
Welterweight. *Ht* 5'9"
Manager M. Gates
07.12.06 Chris Goodwin W PTS 6 Sunderland
13.04.07 Martin Sweeney W RSC 6 Houghton le Spring
23.11.07 Scott Sandmann W PTS 6 Houghton le Spring

20.03.08 Scott Miller L PTS 6 South Shields
25.07.08 Matt Seawright W RTD 2 Houghton le Spring
Career: 5 contests, won 4, lost 1.

Rendall Munroe   Philip Sharkey

Rendall Munroe

Leicester. *Born* Leicester, 1 June, 1980
European & Commonwealth
S.Bantamweight Champion. Former
Undefeated English S.Bantamweight
Champion. *Ht* 5'7"
Manager M. Shinfield
20.09.03 Joel Viney W RTD 3 Nottingham
23.11.03 John-Paul Ryan W PTS 6 Rotherham
14.02.04 Neil Read W RSC 1 Nottingham
09.04.04 Anthony Hanna W PTS 6 Rugby
26.04.04 Baz Carey W PTS 6 Cleethorpes
27.09.04 David Bailey W PTS 6 Cleethorpes
08.10.04 David Killu W PTS 6 Brentwood
18.06.05 Darren Broomhall W RSC 3 Barnsley
02.09.05 Riaz Durgahed W PTS 6 Derby
28.01.06 Jonathan Whiteman W RSC 2 Nottingham
29.04.06 Andy Morris L PTS 12 Edinburgh
(*British Featherweight Title Challenge*)
13.04.07 Gavin Deacon W PTS 6 Altrincham
13.07.07 Dai Davies W RSC 5 Barnsley
12.10.07 Marc Callaghan W RTD 6 Peterlee
(*English S.Bantamweight Title Challenge*)
07.03.08 Kiko Martinez W PTS 12 Nottingham
(*European S.Bantamweight Title Challenge*)
02.05.08 Salem Bouaita W RTD 7 Nottingham
(*European S.Bantamweight Title Defence*)
05.09.08 Arsen Martirosyan W PTS 12 Nottingham
(*European S.Bantamweight Title Defence*)
18.12.08 Fabrizio Trotta W RSC 5 Dublin
(*European S.Bantamweight Title Defence*)
27.02.09 Kiko Martinez W PTS 12 Barnsley
(*European S.Bantamweight Title Defence*)

02.05.09 Isaac Nettey W PTS 12 Sunderland
(*Vacant Commonwealth S.Bantamweight Title*)
Career: 20 contests, won 19, lost 1.

Ben Murphy

Hove. *Born* Hove, 11 March, 1980
L.Welterweight. *Ht* 5'3¾"
Manager B. Lawrence
17.03.07 Deniss Sirjatovs W PTS 4 Birmingham
29.04.07 Barry Downes W RSC 1 Birmingham
13.07.07 Neal McQuade W RSC 2 Birmingham
21.09.07 Lewis Smith W RSC 4 Peterborough
01.12.07 Michael Frontin L PTS 4 Bethnal Green
13.06.08 Garry Buckland W PTS 6 Portsmouth
15.11.08 Michael Frontin W PTS 6 Bethnal Green
24.03.09 Ryan Brawley L PTS 3 Glasgow
Career: 8 contests, won 6, lost 2.

Andrew Murray

St Albans. *Born* Cavan, 10 September, 1982
European Union Lightweight Champion.
All-Ireland Lightweight & L.Welterweight
Champion. *Ht* 5'10¼"
Manager Self
18.03.05 Jonathan Jones W RSC 4 Belfast
09.10.05 Billy Smith W PTS 4 Hammersmith
17.11.05 Silence Saheed W PTS 4 Piccadilly
02.02.06 Ian Reid W RSC 4 Holborn
30.03.06 Frederic Gosset W PTS 6 Piccadilly
21.05.06 Carl Allen W PTS 4 Bethnal Green
03.06.06 Tony Jourda W RSC 3 Dublin
04.10.07 Billy Smith W PTS 8 Piccadilly
08.12.07 James Gorman W TD 4 Belfast
(*Vacant All-Ireland L.Welterweight Title*)
22.03.08 Leonard Lothian W RSC 3 Dublin
29.03.08 Juris Ivanovs W RSC 3 Letterkenny
12.04.08 Wellington De Jesus W CO 1 Castlebar
12.07.08 Peter McDonagh W PTS 10 Dublin
(*Vacant All-Ireland Lightweight Title*)
07.02.09 Ali Wyatt W RSC 3 Craigavon
21.03.09 Daniel Rasilla W PTS 12 Dublin
(*Vacant European Union Lightweight Title*)
Career: 15 contests, won 15.

Joe Murray

Manchester. *Born* Manchester, 13 January, 1987
Featherweight. *Ht* 5' 8"
Manager J. Gallagher
28.03.09 Sid Razak W PTS 6 Altrincham
02.05.09 Missael Nunez W PTS 4 Las Vegas, Nevada, USA
Career: 2 contests, won 2.

John Murray

Manchester. *Born* Manchester, 20 December, 1984
Former Undefeated British & English
Lightweight Champion. Former Undefeated
WBC Youth Lightweight Champion.
Ht 5'8"
Manager M. Marsden
06.09.03 Pete Buckley W PTS 4 Huddersfield
18.10.03 Matthew Burke W RSC 1 Manchester

21.12.03 Jason Nesbitt W PTS 6 Bolton
30.01.04 Norman Dhalie W CO 2 Dagenham
12.03.04 John-Paul Ryan W RSC 1 Nottingham
02.06.04 Anthony Hanna W PTS 4 Nottingham
24.09.04 Dariusz Snarski W RSC 2 Nottingham
31.10.04 Ernie Smith W PTS 4 Shaw
26.11.04 Daniel Thorpe W RSC 2 Altrincham
09.12.04 Harry Ramogoadi W RSC 4 Stockport
06.03.05 Karl Taylor W PTS 6 Shaw
08.07.05 Mounir Guebbas W PTS 8 Altrincham
06.08.05 Johnny Walker W PTS 6 Tampa, Florida, USA
23.09.05 Azad Azizov W RSC 3 Manchester
29.10.05 Tyrone Wiggins W RSC 4 Gatineau, Canada
02.12.05 Nacho Mendoza W TD 8 Nottingham
(Vacant WBC Youth Lightweight Title)
12.07.06 Billy Smith W RSC 6 Bethnal Green
15.09.06 Moebi Sarouna W PTS 10 Muswell Hill
(WBC Youth Lightweight Title Defence)
08.12.06 Billy Smith W PTS 6 Dagenham
20.01.07 Ben Odamattey W RSC 5 Muswell Hill
05.05.07 Lorenzo Bethea W RSC 7 Las Vegas, Nevada, USA
09.11.07 Dean Hickman W RSC 4 Nottingham
(Vacant English Lightweight Title)
07.12.07 Miguel Angel Munguia W PTS 10 Las Vegas, Nevada, USA
10.05.08 Youssef Al Hamidi W PTS 8 Nottingham
11.07.08 Lee Meager W RSC 5 Wigan
(Vacant British Lightweight Title)
17.01.09 Lee McAllister W RSC 8 Wigan
(British Lightweight Title Defence)
13.06.09 Scott Lawton W RSC 6 Wigan
Career: 27 contests, won 27.

Martin Murray

Manchester. *Born* Knowsley, 27 September, 1982
S.Middleweight. *Ht* 6'0¼"
Manager O. Harrison
22.09.07 Jamie Ambler W PTS 6 Wigan
26.10.07 Philip Callaghan W RSC 1 Wigan
16.02.08 Dean Walker W PTS 6 Blackpool
16.03.08 Michael Banbula W PTS 6 Liverpool
18.04.08 James Tucker W PTS 4 Bethnal Green
23.05.08 Dean Walker W PTS 6 Wigan
15.06.08 Michael Recloux W PTS 6 St Helens
14.09.08 Carl Wild W RSC 2 Wigan
12.10.08 Joseph Sovijus W CO 1 Leigh
22.11.08 Danny Butler W PTS 3 Bethnal Green
22.11.08 Cello Renda W PTS 3 Bethnal Green
22.11.08 Joe Rea W PTS 3 Bethnal Green
06.03.09 Mikheil Khucishvili W RSC 4 Wigan
17.04.09 Kevin Concepcion W RSC 3 Leigh
Career: 14 contests, won 14.

Lee Murtagh

Leeds. *Born* Leeds, 30 September, 1973
Middleweight. Former Undefeated Central Area L.Middleweight Champion. Former Undefeated Central Area Middleweight Champion. Former British Masters Middleweight Champion. Former British Masters L.Middleweight Champion.
Ht 5'9¼"
Manager Self
12.06.95 Dave Curtis W PTS 6 Bradford

25.09.95 Roy Gbasai W PTS 6 Bradford
30.10.95 Cam Raeside L PTS 6 Bradford
11.12.95 Donovan Davey W PTS 6 Bradford
13.01.96 Peter Varnavas W PTS 6 Halifax
05.02.96 Shamus Casey W PTS 6 Bradford
20.05.96 Shaun O'Neill W PTS 6 Bradford
24.06.96 Michael Alexander W PTS 6 Bradford
28.10.96 Jimmy Vincent L RSC 2 Bradford
14.04.97 Lee Simpkin W PTS 6 Bradford
09.10.97 Brian Dunn W PTS 6 Leeds
05.03.98 Wayne Shepherd W PTS 6 Leeds
08.08.98 Alan Gilbert W PTS 4 Scarborough
13.03.99 Keith Palmer DREW 6 Manchester
27.09.99 Jawaid Khaliq L RSC 5 Leeds
(Vacant WBF European L. Middleweight Title)
27.02.00 Gareth Lovell W PTS 6 Leeds
24.09.00 Jon Foster W PTS 6 Shaw
03.12.00 Michael Alexander W PTS 6 Shaw
17.05.01 Ojay Abrahams L RSC 2 Leeds
(Vacant British Masters L. Middleweight Title)
03.03.02 Howard Clarke NC 2 Shaw
19.04.02 Neil Bonner W PTS 6 Darlington
21.06.02 Wayne Shepherd W PTS 10 Leeds
(Vacant British Masters Middleweight Title)
02.12.02 Martyn Bailey L RSC 6 Leeds
(British Masters Middleweight Title Defence)
10.05.03 Darren Rhodes L PTS 6 Huddersfield
15.09.03 Matt Scriven W DIS 9 Leeds
(British Masters L.Middleweight Title Challenge)
01.12.03 Gary Beardsley L RSC 6 Leeds
(British Masters L.Middleweight Title Defence)
08.06.04 Robert Burton L CO 3 Sheffield
(Vacant Central Area L.Middleweight Title)
15.12.04 Dean Walker W PTS 10 Sheffield
(Vacant Central Area Middleweight Title)
20.05.05 Jason Rushton W PTS 10 Doncaster
(Central Area L.Middleweight Title Challenge)
27.01.06 Gary Woolcombe L RSC 4 Dagenham
03.06.07 John Musgrave W PTS 6 Barnsley
30.06.07 Peter Dunn W PTS 6 Belfast
11.08.07 Graham Delehedy W PTS 6 Liverpool
13.10.07 Tye Williams W PTS 6 Belfast
08.12.07 Ciaran Healy L CO 5 Belfast
(Vacant All-Ireland L.Middleweight Title)
05.12.08 Lee Edwards L PTS 10 Sheffield
(British Masters L. Middleweight Title Challenge)
18.04.09 Carl Drake W PTS 6 Galway
Career: 37 contests, won 24, drew 1, lost 11, no contest 1.

Jon Musgrave

Barnsley. *Born* Barnsley, 26 July, 1982
L.Middleweight. *Ht* 5'11"
Manager T. Schofield
30.09.06 Andrew Alan Lowe W PTS 6 Stoke
01.12.06 James McKinley L PTS 4 Birmingham
26.03.07 Paul Royston W PTS 6 Glasgow
15.04.07 Sherman Alleyne W PTS 6 Barnsley
03.06.07 Lee Murtagh L PTS 6 Barnsley

16.09.07 Lee Edwards L PTS 6 Sheffield
13.10.07 Steve Cooper W PTS 6 Barnsley
23.02.08 Andrew Alan Lowe L PTS 6 Newark
20.03.08 Shaun Farmer L PTS 6 South Shields
15.05.08 Shaun Farmer W PTS 6 Sunderland
29.11.08 Harry Matthews L PTS 4 Sleaford
28.03.09 Kevin Hammond W PTS 6 Lincoln
17.05.09 Alex Matvienko L PTS 10 Bolton
(Vacant British Masters L. Middleweight Title)
Career: 13 contests, won 6, lost 7.

(Lee) Young Muttley (Woodley)

West Bromwich. *Born* West Bromwich, 17 May, 1976
L.Welterweight. Former British Welterweight Champion. Former Undefeated WBF Inter-Continental, English & Midlands Area L.Welterweight Champion. *Ht* 5'8½"
Manager E. Johnson
03.09.99 Dave Hinds W RSC 4 West Bromwich
24.10.99 David Kehoe W RTD 1 Wolverhampton
22.01.00 Wahid Fats L PTS 4 Birmingham
18.02.00 Stuart Rimmer W RSC 1 West Bromwich
27.11.00 Peter Dunn W RSC 3 Birmingham
07.09.01 Jon Honney W RSC 1 West Bromwich
16.11.01 Tony Montana W PTS 6 West Bromwich
26.11.01 Lee Byrne W RSC 1 Manchester
23.02.02 Brian Coleman W PTS 4 Nottingham
23.03.02 Adam Zadworny W RSC 3 Southwark
02.11.02 Tony Montana W PTS 4 Wolverhampton
21.03.03 Gary Reid W RSC 7 West Bromwich
(Vacant Midlands Area L.Welterweight Title)
28.04.03 John Marshall W RSC 5 Nottingham
17.07.03 Tony Montana W PTS 4 Walsall
19.02.04 Peter Dunn W PTS 4 Dudley
08.05.04 Sammy Smith W RSC 1 Bristol
(Vacant English L.Welterweight Title)
05.10.04 Gavin Down W RSC 6 Dudley
(English L.Welterweight Title Defence. Vacant WBF Inter-Continental L.Welterweight Title)
17.02.05 Geraint Harvey W PTS 6 Dudley
21.04.05 Oscar Hall W PTS 10 Dudley
(WBF Inter-Continental L.Welterweight Title Defence)
30.09.05 Surinder Sekhon W PTS 4 Burton
28.01.06 Michael Jennings W PTS 12 Nottingham
(British Welterweight Title Challenge)
01.06.06 Kevin Anderson L RSC 10 Birmingham
(British Welterweight Title Defence. Commonwealth Welterweight Title Challenge)
22.09.06 Alexander Abramenko W CO 1 Bethnal Green
25.01.07 Arek Malek W PTS 6 Milan, Italy
20.07.07 Colin Lynes L RSC 3 Wolverhampton
(Vacant European L.Welterweight Title. British L.Welterweight Title Challenge)
28.11.07 Vladimir Borovski W PTS 6 Walsall
14.03.08 Kevin Placide W RSC 4 Manchester
04.07.08 Sergej Savrinovics W PTS 6 Wolverhampton
06.02.09 Gatis Skuja W PTS 6 Birmingham
Career: 29 contests, won 26, lost 3.

Amir Nadi

Birmingham. *Born* Iraq, 21 November, 1981
L.Welterweight. *Ht* 5'10"
Manager M. Helliet
16.02.07 Steve Anning L PTS 4 Merthyr Tydfil
02.03.07 Abul Taher L PTS 6 Coventry
28.04.07 Charles Paul King L PTS 6 Clydebank
14.05.07 Andy Cox L PTS 6 Cleethorpes
16.09.07 Jack Perry L PTS 4 Derby
25.10.07 Scott Evans L PTS 4 Wolverhampton
10.11.07 Darren Askew L PTS 6 Stalybridge
20.04.08 Ali Shah L PTS 4 Shaw
30.04.08 Scott Evans L RSC 3 Wolverhampton
21.06.08 Adam Kelly L PTS 6 Sheffield
01.08.08 Saud Hafiz L RSC 3 Watford
Career: 11 contests, lost 11.

Amir Nadi   Philip Sharkey

Ian Napa

Hackney. *Born* Zimbabwe, 14 March, 1978
Former European Bantamweight Champion.
Former Undefeated British Bantamweight
Champion. Former Undefeated Southern
Area Flyweight Champion.
Ht 5'1"
Manager B. Lawrence
06.06.98 Nick Tooley W PTS 6 Liverpool
14.07.98 Nicky Booth W PTS 6 Reading
10.10.98 Sean Green W PTS 6 Bethnal Green
30.01.99 Delroy Spencer W PTS 6 Bethnal Green
15.11.99 Mark Reynolds W PTS 10 Bethnal
Green
(*Southern Area Flyweight Title
Challenge*)

19.02.00 Anthony Hanna W PTS 6 Dagenham
08.04.00 Delroy Spencer W PTS 8 Bethnal Green
15.07.00 Jamie Evans W PTS 4 Millwall
13.11.00 Jason Booth L PTS 12 Bethnal Green
(*British & Commonwealth Flyweight
Title Challenges*)
24.02.01 Oleg Kiryukhin W PTS 6 Bethnal Green
09.06.01 Peter Culshaw L RSC 8 Bethnal Green
(*WBU Flyweight Title Challenge*)
08.05.04 Danny Costello W PTS 4 Dagenham
08.10.04 Steve Gethin W PTS 6 Brentwood
13.02.05 Alexey Volchan W PTS 4 Brentwood
16.06.05 Marc Callaghan L PTS 10 Dagenham
(*Vacant Southern Area S.Bantamweight
Title*)
04.11.05 Martin Power L PTS 12 Bethnal Green
(*British Bantamweight Title Challenge*)
25.11.05 Damaen Kelly L PTS 10 Liverpool
06.10.06 Delroy Spencer W PTS 6 Bethnal Green
09.03.07 Simone Maludrottu L PTS 12 Dagenham
(*European Bantamweight Title
Challenge*)
06.07.07 Jason Booth W PTS 12 Wigan
(*Vacant British Bantamweight Title*)
21.09.07 Lee Haskins W RTD 7 Bethnal Green
(*British Bantamweight Title Defence*)
30.11.07 Martin Power W PTS 12 Newham
(*British Bantamweight Title Defence*)
02.05.08 Colin Moffett W PTS 12 Nottingham
(*British Bantamweight Title Defence*)
17.10.08 Carmelo Ballone W PTS 12 Bethnal
Green
(*European Bantamweight Title
Challenge*)
20.03.09 Malik Bouziane L PTS 12 Newham
(*European Bantamweight Title Defence*)
Career: 25 contests, won 18, lost 7.

Ian Napa   Philip Sharkey

Muhsen Nasser

Sheffield. *Born* Yemen, 10 April, 1986
L.Middleweight. *Ht* 5'11"
Manager J. Ingle
11.10.04 Andy Cosnett W PTS 6 Birmingham
26.11.04 Rocky Flanagan W PTS 6 Hull
27.01.05 Ernie Smith W PTS 6 Piccadilly
12.05.05 Martin Marshall W PTS 6 Sunderland
30.10.05 Lance Verallo W PTS 6 Sheffield
12.11.05 Dave Hinds W PTS 6 Sheffield
21.11.05 Peter Dunn W RSC 4 Glasgow
25.02.06 Chris Long W PTS 4 Bristol
05.03.06 Peter Dunn W PTS 4 Sheffield
06.10.06 Thomas Flynn W PTS 4 Mexborough
10.12.06 Karl Taylor W PTS 6 Sheffield
27.07.07 Peter Dunn W PTS 6 Houghton le
Spring
06.10.07 James Barker W RSC 1 Aberdeen
14.11.07 Billy Smith DREW 4 Bethnal Green
29.11.07 Ryan Ashworth W PTS 4 Bradford
18.01.08 Tye Williams W PTS 4 Burton
20.04.08 Jimmy Beech W PTS 6 Shaw
17.05.08 Paul Royston W PTS 4 Sheffield
05.12.08 Oliver Guettel L PTS 10 Halle an der
Saale, Germany
(*Vacant WBC Youth Welterweight Title*)
Career: 19 contests, won 17, drew 1, lost 1.

Robert Nelson   Philip Sharkey

Robert Nelson

Bradford. *Born* Bradford, 15 January, 1980
S.Bantamweight. *Ht* 5'5"
Manager M. Marsden
27.05.05 Delroy Spencer W PTS 4 Spennymoor
25.06.05 Delroy Spencer W PTS 6 Wakefield

13.11.05 Neil Marston W PTS 6 Leeds
09.05.06 Delroy Spencer DREW 6 Leeds
28.05.06 Neil Read W PTS 6 Wakefield
03.12.06 Robert Bunford W PTS 4 Wakefield
14.04.07 Shaun Walton W PTS 8 Wakefield
27.05.07 Mo Khaled DREW 6 Bradford
07.09.07 Andy Bell L RSC 7 Doncaster
(Vacant English S.Flyweight Title)
20.03.09 Ashley Sexton L RSC 6 Newham
24.05.09 Anthony Hanna W PTS 6 Bradford
Career: 11 contests, won 7, drew 2, lost 2.

Jason Nesbitt   Philip Sharkey

Jason Nesbitt

Nuneaton. *Born* Birmingham, 15
December, 1973
Welterweight. *Ht* 5'9"
Manager Self
06.11.00 Stephen Chinnock L PTS 6
Wolverhampton
09.12.00 Lee Meager L RSC 2 Southwark
29.01.01 Henry Castle L CO 6 Peterborough
27.03.01 Billy Smith W PTS 6 Brierley Hill
21.05.01 Sid Razak L PTS 6 Birmingham
04.06.01 Andrew Ferrans L RSC 2 Glasgow
07.07.01 Colin Toohey L PTS 4 Manchester
15.09.01 Colin Toohey L PTS 4 Manchester
22.09.01 John Mackay L PTS 4 Canning Town
01.11.01 Chris Hooper L RSC 6 Hull
16.03.02 Lee Meager L PTS 6 Bethnal Green
27.03.02 Greg Edwards W RSC 5 Mayfair
20.04.02 Henry Castle L PTS 4 Cardiff
04.05.02 Danny Hunt L PTS 4 Bethnal Green
15.06.02 Jesse James Daniel L PTS 4 Leeds
27.07.02 Craig Spacie L PTS 4 Nottingham
23.08.02 Billy Corcoran L PTS 4 Bethnal Green
25.10.02 Billy Corcoran L RSC 2 Bethnal Green
03.12.02 Mark Bowen L PTS 6 Shrewsbury
11.12.02 Matt Teague L PTS 6 Hull
20.12.02 Chris McDonagh L PTS 6 Bracknell
18.01.03 Andy Morris L PTS 4 Preston

09.02.03 Mally McIver L PTS 6 Bradford
09.03.03 Choi Tseveenpurev L PTS 8 Shaw
29.03.03 Kevin O'Hara L RSC 3 Portsmouth
07.05.03 Henry Jones L PTS 6 Ellesmere Port
02.06.03 Stefy Bull L PTS 6 Cleethorpes
13.06.03 Scott Lawton L PTS 6 Queensway
17.07.03 Haider Ali L PTS 4 Dagenham
29.08.03 Gary Thornhill L CO 1 Liverpool
05.10.03 Nadeem Siddique L PTS 6 Bradford
08.11.03 Harry Ramogoadi L PTS 6 Coventry
23.11.03 Amir Ali L PTS 6 Rotherham
10.12.03 Femi Fehintola L PTS 6 Sheffield
21.12.03 John Murray L PTS 6 Bolton
06.02.04 Femi Fehintola L PTS 6 Sheffield
23.02.04 Carl Greaves L PTS 6 Nottingham
05.03.04 Haroon Din L PTS 6 Darlington
12.03.04 Stuart Green L PTS 8 Irvine
03.04.04 Daniel Thorpe L PTS 6 Sheffield
16.04.04 John O'Donnell L PTS 4 Bradford
27.04.04 Jim Betts L PTS 6 Leeds
07.05.04 Jus Wallie L PTS 6 Bethnal Green
28.05.04 John Bothwell W RSC 3 Glasgow
05.06.04 Kevin Mitchell L RSC 3 Bethnal Green
30.07.04 Lee Beavis L PTS 4 Bethnal Green
20.09.04 Matt Teague L PTS 6 Cleethorpes
30.09.04 Eddie Nevins L PTS 6 Hull
18.11.04 Joel Viney W PTS 6 Blackpool
26.11.04 John Davidson W RSC 1 Altrincham
10.12.04 John Fewkes L PTS 6 Sheffield
17.12.04 Gwyn Wale L PTS 4 Huddersfield
13.02.05 Nadeem Siddique L PTS 6 Bradford
04.03.05 John Fewkes L PTS 6 Rotherham
01.04.05 Martin McDonagh L PTS 6 Glasgow
15.04.05 Martin Gethin L PTS 6 Shrewsbury
28.04.05 Ceri Hall L RTD 2 Clydach
02.06.05 Riaz Durgahed L PTS 6 Peterborough
24.07.05 Femi Fehintola L PTS 6 Sheffield
09.09.05 Nicki Smedley L PTS 4 Sheffield
30.09.05 Henry Jones L PTS 6 Carmarthen
16.10.05 Michael Medor L PTS 6 Peterborough
12.11.05 Craig Johnson L PTS 6 Sheffield
25.11.05 Nadeem Siddique L RSC 6 Hull
17.02.06 Dave Stewart L PTS 4 Bethnal Green
04.03.06 Tony Delaney L PTS 4 Manchester
01.04.06 Steve Bell L PTS 6 Bethnal Green
28.04.06 Davis Kamara L PTS 6 Manchester
06.05.06 Jimmy Doherty L PTS 6 Stoke
20.05.06 Anthony Christopher W RSC 4 Bristol
05.06.06 Mitch Prince L PTS 6 Glasgow
24.09.06 Peter McDonagh L PTS 4 Bethnal Green
01.10.06 Andrew Ward DREW 6 Rotherham
24.11.06 Chris Hooper DREW 6 Hull
02.12.06 Shane Watson L PTS 6 Longford
25.02.07 Danny Harding L PTS 6 Manchester
10.03.07 John Watson L PTS 4 Liverpool
28.04.07 Jonathan Whiteman W RTD 5 Newark
18.05.07 Dave Stewart L PTS 4 Canning Town
09.06.07 Davey Watson L PTS 6 Middlesbrough
13.07.07 Thomas Costello L PTS 4 Birmingham
21.09.07 Dean Harrison L PTS 6 Burton
28.09.07 Jonathan Hussey L PTS 6 Preston
26.09.08 Rob Hunt L PTS 8 Wolverhampton
20.10.08 Mitch Prince L PTS 6 Glasgow
31.10.08 Steve Foster L PTS 6 Birmingham
16.11.08 Dave Ryan L PTS 4 Derby
08.12.08 Chris Lewis L PTS 6 Birmingham

21.12.08 Gary Sykes L RSC 4 Bolton
19.01.09 Barry Morrison L PTS 6 Glasgow
06.02.09 James Flinn L PTS 4 Birmingham
21.02.09 James Todd L PTS 6 Merthyr Tydfil
05.03.09 Wayne Alwan-Arab L PTS 6 Limehouse
14.03.09 Callum Archer L PTS 4 Birmingham
03.04.09 Tristan Davies L PTS 4 Wolverhampton
10.04.09 Duane Parker L PTS 6 Cheltenham
17.04.09 Danny Stewart NC 3 Bristol
29.05.09 Martin Gordon L PTS 4 Dudley
13.06.09 Damian Owen L PTS 4 Bristol
28.06.09 Martin Gethin L PTS 4 Luton
Career: 100 contests, won 7, drew 2, lost 90, no
contest 1.

Ollie Newham

Nottingham. *Born* Nottingham, 8 October,
1986
Middleweight. *Ht* 6'2"
Manager M. Shinfield
08.09.07 Peter Dunn W PTS 6 Sutton in Ashfield
01.12.07 Jon Foster W RSC 2 Nottingham
02.05.08 Paul Brown W RSC 4 Nottingham
31.05.09 Paul Royston W PTS 6 Burton
Career: 4 contests, won 4.

Lee Nicholson

Doncaster. *Born* Mexborough, 10
November, 1976
Cruiserweight. *Ht* 5'11"
Manager C. Greaves
24.09.01 Jason Brewster L PTS 6 Cleethorpes
17.02.02 Jason Brewster L PTS 6 Wolverhampton
11.05.02 Fola Okesola L RSC 1 Dagenham
07.09.03 Stewart West L RSC 2 Shrewsbury
01.12.03 Mike Duffield W PTS 6 Barnsley
15.12.03 Simeon Cover L RSC 4 Cleethorpes
29.10.04 Dean Cockburn L RSC 2 Doncaster
13.12.04 Dean Cockburn L RSC 3 Cleethorpes
23.05.05 Slick Miller W PTS 6 Cleethorpes
03.03.06 Jimmy Harrington DREW 4 Doncaster
21.04.06 Jimmy Harrington L RTD 3 Doncaster
13.10.06 Billy Wilson L RSC 5 Doncaster
19.10.07 Ryan Rowlinson W PTS 4 Doncaster
26.10.07 Carl Dilks L RSC 4 Wigan
30.11.07 Dwayne Lewis L RTD 2 Newham
08.11.08 Stephen Birch L CO 1 Wigan
08.12.08 Dave Pearson DREW 6 Cleethorpes
01.02.09 Caine Brodie L RSC 1 Bethnal Green
10.04.09 Eddie McIntosh L RSC 2 Birmingham
30.06.09 Mene Edwards L RTD 1 Bethnal
Green
Career: 20 contests, won 3, drew 2, lost 15.

Mark Nilsen

Sale. *Born* Manchester, 26 July, 1978
L.Heavyweight. *Ht* 6'0"
Manager R. Woodhall
17.02.02 Kenroy Lambert W PTS 6 Salford
26.10.06 Chris Harman W PTS 6 Dudley
06.12.06 Simon Wood W PTS 4 Stoke
24.02.07 Carl Wild W PTS 6 Manchester
21.04.07 Tomas Da Silva W RSC 5 Manchester
30.06.07 Nicki Taylor W CO 4 Manchester
16.09.07 Ovill McKenzie L RSC 1 Derby

28.11.07 Ruben Groenewald L PTS 6 Piccadilly
25.01.08 Hamed Jamali L PTS 4 Birmingham
08.02.08 Brian Magee L PTS 4 Peterlee
23.02.08 Joey Ainscough L PTS 4 Liverpool
07.03.08 Rod Anderton L PTS 4 Nottingham
28.03.08 Billy Boyle L RTD 1 Barnsley
31.05.08 Jamie Norkett L PTS 4 Newark
12.07.08 Paul Samuels L RSC 1 Newport
14.09.08 Mark Regan L PTS 6 Birmingham
16.11.08 Darren Stubbs L PTS 10 Shaw
(Vacant British Masters L. Heavyweight Title)
24.01.09 Carl Dilks L RSC 4 Blackpool
18.04.09 Colm Keane L PTS 6 Galway
23.05.09 Michael Sweeney L PTS 6 Castlebar
12.06.09 JJ Ojuederie L PTS 6 Bethnal Green
21.06.09 Leon Williams L PTS 6 Bethnal Green
Career: 22 contests, won 6, lost 16.

Lee Noble

Sheffield. *Born* Barnsley, 23 April, 1987
Middleweight. Former Undefeated British
Masters Middleweight Champion. *Ht* 6'0"
Manager Self
05.10.06 Shaun Farmer L PTS 6 Sunderland
13.10.06 Jason Rushton W PTS 6 Doncaster
20.10.06 Jak Hibbert W RSC 6 Sheffield
27.10.06 Peter Dunn W PTS 6 Glasgow
10.12.06 Jak Hibbert W PTS 6 Sheffield
09.02.07 Mark Thompson L PTS 6 Leeds
19.02.07 Darren Gethin W PTS 6 Glasgow
11.03.07 Magic Kidem W PTS 4 Shaw
03.05.07 Stuart Brookes L PTS 10 Sheffield
(Vacant British Masters L.Heavyweight Title)
17.06.07 Alexander Spitjo W PTS 4 Mansfield
22.09.07 Brian Rose L PTS 4 Wigan
05.10.07 George Hillyard L PTS 6 Bethnal Green
03.11.07 Thomas Povlsen L PTS 6 Cardiff
20.11.07 William Ruiz W RSC 4 Vilamoura, Portugal
02.12.07 Drew Campbell W PTS 6 Oldham
18.01.08 Sam Horton L PTS 4 Burton
23.02.08 Anthony Young W PTS 10 Crawley
(Vacant British Masters Middleweight Title)
12.05.08 Sam Horton L PTS 8 Birmingham
13.03.09 Grzegorz Proksa L RSC 3 Widnes
Career: 19 contests, won 10, lost 9.

Jamie Norkett

Newark. *Born* Harpenden, 15 February, 1977
L.Heavyweight. *Ht* 6'3¼"
Manager C. Greaves
08.09.07 Carl Wild L PTS 4 Sutton in Ashfield
13.10.07 Magic Kidem W CO 3 Newark
14.11.07 Victor Smith L PTS 4 Bethnal Green
23.02.08 Dave Pearson W PTS 6 Newark
22.03.08 Harry Miles L PTS 4 Cardiff
26.04.08 Bob Ajisafe L PTS 4 Darlington
31.05.08 Mark Nilsen W PTS 4 Newark
25.07.08 Bob Ajisafe L PTS 4 Houghton le Spring
01.08.08 Caine Brodie L PTS 4 Watford

22.09.08 Yanko Pavlov L RSC 4 Glasgow
06.06.09 Sonny Pollard L PTS 4 Beverley
21.06.09 Scott Douglas L PTS 4 Bethnal Green
Career: 12 contests, won 3, lost 9.

Jamie Norkett   Philip Sharkey

Robert Norton

Stourbridge. *Born* Dudley, 20 January, 1972
British & Commonwealth Creuiserweight
Champion. Former Undefeated English
Cruiserweight Champion. Former
Undefeated British Masters Cruiserweight
Champion. Former WBU Cruiserweight
Champion. *Ht* 6'2"
Manager P. Rowson
30.09.93 Stuart Fleet W CO 2 Walsall
27.10.93 Kent Davis W PTS 6 West Bromwich
02.12.93 Eddie Pyatt W RSC 2 Walsall
26.01.94 Lennie Howard W PTS 6 Birmingham
17.05.94 Steve Osborne W PTS 6 Kettering
05.10.94 Chris Woollas DREW 6 Wolverhampton
30.11.94 L. A. Williams W RSC 2 Wolverhampton
10.02.95 Newby Stevens W RSC 3 Birmingham
22.02.95 Steve Osborne W PTS 6 Telford
21.04.95 Cordwell Hylton W PTS 6 Dudley
25.10.95 Nigel Rafferty W RSC 6 Telford
31.01.96 Gary Williams W RSC 2 Birmingham
25.04.96 Steve Osborne W RSC 5 Mayfair
01.10.96 Andrew Benson W RSC 6 Birmingham
12.11.96 Nigel Rafferty W PTS 8 Dudley
11.02.97 Touami Benhamed W RSC 5 Bethnal Green
16.04.97 Tony Booth W RSC 4 Bethnal Green
20.12.97 Darren Corbett L PTS 12 Belfast
(Commonwealth Cruiserweight Title Challenge)
03.04.98 Adrian Nicolai W RSC 2 West Bromwich
03.10.98 Tim Brown W CO 3 West Bromwich
01.04.99 Jacob Mofokeng W PTS 12 Birmingham
(WBU Cruiserweight Title Challenge)
24.09.99 Sebastiaan Rothmann L RSC 8 Merthyr
(WBU Cruiserweight Title Defence)

30.09.00 Tony Booth W RSC 3 Peterborough
18.11.00 Darron Griffiths W PTS 10 Dagenham
(Elim. British Cruiserweight Title)
05.02.01 Lee Swaby W PTS 8 Hull
30.11.02 Paul Bonson W PTS 6 Coventry
05.09.03 Mark Hobson L PTS 12 Sheffield
(Commonwealth Cruiserweight Title Challenge. Vacant British Cruiserweight Title)
09.04.04 Greg Scott-Briggs W CO 1 Rugby
10.07.04 Chris Woollas W RSC 4 Coventry
06.12.04 Paul Bonson W CO 6 Leicester
(Vacant British Masters Cruiserweight Title)
22.10.05 Dmitry Adamovich W CO 2 Coventry
09.10.06 Roland Horvath W RSC 3 Bedworth
02.03.07 Tommy Eastwood W RSC 8 Coventry
(Vacant English Cruiserweight Title)
08.12.07 Enad Licina L PTS 8 Basle, Switzerland
03.10.08 Micky Steeds W PTS 12 Burton
(Vacant British Cruiserweight Title)
06.02.09 David Dolan W PTS 12 Birmingham
(British Cruiserweight Title Defence. Vacant Commonwealth Cruiserweight Title)
Career: 36 contests, won 31, drew 1, lost 4.

Robert Norton   Philip Sharkey

Tyrone Nurse

Huddersfield. *Born* Huddersfield, 4 January, 1990
L.Welterweight. *Ht* 5'11¼"
Manager S. Wood/C. Aston
28.03.08 Kristian Laight W PTS 4 Barnsley
05.09.08 Carl Allen W PTS 4 Nottingham
28.09.08 Carl Allen W PTS 4 Colne
04.12.08 Fred Janes W PTS 4 Bradford
21.12.08 Sid Razak W PTS 4 Bolton
27.02.09 Baz Carey W PTS 4 Barnsley
17.04.09 Johnny Greaves W PTS 4 Leigh
24.05.09 Ibrar Riyaz W PTS 4 Shaw
Career: 8 contests, won 8.

Tony Oakey

Havant. *Born* Portsmouth, 2 January, 1976
International Masters L. Heavyweight
Champion. Former British & WBU
L. Heavyweight Champion. Former
Undefeated Commonwealth & Southern
Area L. Heavyweight Champion *Ht* 5'8"
Manager J. Eames
12.09.98 Smokey Enison W RSC 2 Bethnal Green
21.11.98 Zak Chelli W RSC 1 Southwark
16.01.99 Jimmy Steel W PTS 4 Bethnal Green
06.03.99 Mark Dawson W PTS 4 Southwark
10.07.99 Jimmy Steel W PTS 4 Southwark
01.10.99 Michael Pinnock W PTS 4 Bethnal
Green
21.02.00 Darren Ashton W PTS 4 Southwark
13.03.00 Martin Jolley W PTS 6 Bethnal Green
21.10.00 Darren Ashton W PTS 4 Wembley
27.01.01 Nathan King W PTS 6 Bethnal Green
26.03.01 Butch Lesley W PTS 10 Wembley
 *(Southern Area L. Heavyweight Title
 Challenge)*
08.05.01 Hastings Rasani W RSC 10 Barnsley
 *(Vacant Commonwealth L. Heavyweight
 Title)*
09.09.01 Konstantin Ochrej W RSC 4 Southwark
20.10.01 Chris Davies W PTS 12 Portsmouth
 *(Commonwealth L. Heavyweight Title
 Defence)*
02.03.02 Konstantin Shvets W PTS 12 Bethnal
Green
 (Vacant WBU L. Heavyweight Title)
25.05.02 Neil Simpson W PTS 12 Portsmouth
 (WBU L. Heavyweight Title Defence)
12.10.02 Andrei Kaersten W PTS 12 Bethnal
Green
 (WBU L. Heavyweight Title Defence)
29.03.03 Neil Linford W PTS 12 Portsmouth
 (WBU L. Heavyweight Title Defence)
11.10.03 Matthew Barney L PTS 12 Portsmouth
 (WBU L. Heavyweight Title Defence)
12.02.05 Varuzhan Davtyan W RTD 5 Portsmouth
19.06.05 Peter Haymer L PTS 10 Bethnal Green
 *(English L. Heavyweight Title
 Challenge)*
01.04.06 Radek Seman W PTS 8 Bethnal Green
13.05.06 Nathan King W PTS 6 Bethnal Green
28.10.06 Simeon Cover W PTS 6 Bethnal Green
09.03.07 Josip Jalusic W PTS 6 Dagenham
18.05.07 Steven Spartacus W RSC 12 Canning
Town
 (Vacant British L. Heavyweight Title)
25.08.07 Brian Magee DREW 12 Dublin
 (British L. Heavyweight Title Defence)
01.02.08 Peter Haymer W CO 9 Bethnal Green
 (British L. Heavyweight Title Defence)
13.06.08 Dean Francis L RSC 9 Portsmouth
 *(British L. Heavyweight Title Defence.
 Commonwealth L. Heavyweight Title
 Challenge)*
10.10.08 Nathan Cleverly L PTS 12 Liverpool
 *(Vacant Commonwealth L.Heavyweight
 Title)*

20.02.09 Billy Boyle W PTS 3 Bethnal Green
20.02.09 Darren Stubbs W PTS 3 Bethnal Green
20.02.09 Courtney Fry W PTS 3 Bethnal Green
27.06.09 Shon Davies W RSC 4 Portsmouth
 *(International Masters L. Heavyweight
 Title)*
Career: 34 contests, won 29, drew 1, lost 4.

Chris O'Brien

Nelson. *Born* Burnley, 24 September, 1981
Welterweight. *Ht* 6'0¼"
Manager S. Wood
26.04.08 Russell Pearce W PTS 6 Wigan
23.05.08 Kristian Laight W PTS 6 Wigan
28.09.08 Simon Morgan W RSC 2 Colne
22.11.08 Peter Dunn W PTS 6 Blackpool
29.03.09 Chris Brophy W PTS 6 Bolton
Career: 5 contests, won 5.

Dezzie O'Connor   Philip Sharkey

(David) Dezzie O'Connor

Plymouth. *Born* Plymouth, 26 September,
1984
L.Welterweight. *Ht* 5'6"
Manager C. Sanigar
23.02.07 Jamie Spence L RSC 3 Peterborough
09.11.07 Dean Mills W PTS 6 Plymouth
29.02.08 John Vanemmenis W RSC 5 Plymouth
01.05.08 Mark McCullough L CO 1 Piccadilly
20.06.08 Carl Griffiths W PTS 6 Plymouth
15.11.08 Ibrar Riyaz W PTS 6 Plymouth
Career: 6 contests, won 4, lost 2.

John O'Donnell

Shepherds Bush. *Born* Croydon, 13
November, 1985
Commonwealth Welterweight Champion.
Former Undefeated English Welterweight
Champion. *Ht* 5'11"
Manager Self
16.04.04 Jason Nesbitt W PTS 4 Bradford
02.06.04 Dave Hinds W PTS 4 Nottingham
24.09.04 Chris Long W RSC 4 Nottingham
12.11.04 Ernie Smith W PTS 6 Wembley
10.04.05 Duncan Cottier W PTS 4 Brentwood
09.07.05 Ben Hudson W RTD 3 Nottingham

21.10.05 Ben Hudson W PTS 4 Bethnal Green
20.01.06 Matt Scriven W RSC 4 Bethnal Green
28.01.06 Zaid Bediouri W PTS 6 Dublin
17.02.06 Karl Taylor W PTS 4 Bethnal Green
12.05.06 Duncan Cottier W RTD 3 Bethnal Green
12.07.06 Darren Gethin W PTS 8 Bethnal Green
15.09.06 Silence Saheed W PTS 6 Muswell Hill
08.12.06 Ernie Smith W CO 2 Dagenham
23.03.07 Stuart Elwell W PTS 10 Nottingham
 (Vacant English Welterweight Title)
05.05.07 Christian Solano L RSC 2 Las Vegas,
Nevada, USA
10.05.08 Billy Smith W PTS 4 Nottingham
27.06.08 Jay Morris W RSC 6 Bethnal Green
19.07.08 Sergejs Volodins W RSC 5 Limerick
04.10.08 Sergej Savrinovics W RTD 3 Norwich
15.11.08 Suleyman Dag W RSC 3 Castlebar
11.04.09 Craig Watson W PTS 12 Bethnal Green
 *(Commonwealth Welterweight Title
 Challenge)*
Career: 22 contests, won 21, lost 1.

Michael O'Gara

Middlesbrough. *Born* Middlesbrough, 6
June, 1977
Featherweight. *Ht* 5' 5"
Manager G. Robinson
12.06.09 Paul McElhinney L PTS 6 Clydebank
Career: 1 contest, lost 1.

Kevin O'Hara   Philip Sharkey

Kevin O'Hara

Belfast. *Born* Belfast, 21 September, 1981
Welterweight. *Ht* 5'6"
Manager J.Breen/F.Warren
02.11.02 Mike Harrington W RSC 1 Belfast
01.02.03 Jus Wallie W RSC 2 Belfast
29.03.03 Jason Nesbitt W RSC 3 Portsmouth
14.06.03 Piotr Niesporek W PTS 4 Magdeburg,
Germany
02.10.03 Vladimir Borov W PTS 6 Liverpool
30.10.03 Henry Janes W PTS 6 Belfast
29.11.03 Gareth Payne W PTS 4 Renfrew
06.03.04 Henry Janes W PTS 6 Renfrew
01.04.04 Buster Dennis W PTS 4 Bethnal Green
06.05.04 Choi Tsveenpurev L PTS 8 Barnsley
28.10.04 Jean-Marie Codet W PTS 8 Belfast

17.06.05 Willie Limond L PTS 10 Glasgow
    (Vacant Celtic S.Featherweight Title)
24.11.05 Damian Owen W PTS 6 Lurgan
20.05.06 Daniel Thorpe W PTS 6 Belfast
26.10.06 Eric Patrac W PTS 6 Belfast
30.11.07 Henry Castle L PTS 8 Newham
19.04.08 Eddie Hyland L PTS 10 Dublin
    (Vacant All-Ireland S.Featherweight
    Title)
08.11.08 Robin Deakin W RSC 1 Bethnal Green
07.02.09 Silence Saheed W RSC 3 Craigavon
15.05.09 Jon Baguley W PTS 6 Belfast
19.06.09 Ricky Burns L PTS 12 Glasgow
    (Commonwealth S.Featherweight Title
    Challenge)
Career: 21 contests, won 16, lost 5.

Daley Ojuederie

Watford. *Born* Watford, 13 September, 1979
Middleweight. *Ht* 6' 0"
Manager S. Fearon
03.12.06 Gatis Skuja DREW 4 Bethnal Green
01.08.08 Anthony Young W RSC 4 Watford
05.10.08 Kenroy Lambert W PTS 4 Watford
Career: 3 contests, won 2, drew 1.

JJ Ojuederie   Philip Sharkey

(Gary) JJ Ojuederie

Watford. *Born* Watford, 13 September, 1979
Southern Area L.Heavyweight Champion.
International Masters Cruiserweight
Champion. *Ht* 6'0"
Manager M. Helliet
29.09.00 Chris Nembhard L RSC 1 Bethnal Green
08.12.03 Hamid Jamali L PTS 6 Birmingham
13.02.04 Jason Samuels L DIS 3 Bristol
28.02.04 Mike Allen W RSC 1 Bridgend
16.10.05 Karl Wheeler DREW 4 Peterborough
19.11.05 Eder Kurti W RSC 4 Southwark
16.12.05 Sam Price W PTS 6 Bracknell
26.02.06 Simeon Cover W PTS 4 Dagenham
23.07.06 Carl Wright W PTS 4 Dagenham
03.12.06 Tony Booth W PTS 4 Bethnal Green
15.04.07 John Anthony W PTS 6 Barnsley
19.10.07 Ayitey Powers W PTS 10 Mayfair
    (Vacant International Masters
    Cruiserweight Title)

01.12.07 Hastings Rasani W PTS 6 Bethnal
    Green
16.05.08 Andrew Lowe W PTS 10 Holborn
    (Southern Area L.Heavyweight
    Title Challenge)
01.08.08 Joey Vegas L RSC 7 Watford
05.10.08 Joey Vegas W PTS 10 Watford
    (Southern Area L.Heavyweight Title
    Defence)
12.06.09 Mark Nilsen W PTS 6 Bethnal Green
Career: 17 contests, won 12, drew 1, lost 4

Nick Okoth   Philip Sharkey

Nick Okoth

Battersea. *Born* Camden Town, 19 July,
1973
L. Heavyweight. *Ht* 5'11"
Manager Self
18.09.03 Mark Phillips W PTS 4 Mayfair
28.02.04 Paulino Da Silva L PTS 6 Manchester
08.04.04 Karl Wheeler L PTS 6 Peterborough
24.04.04 Daniel Sackey L RSC 2 Reading
03.07.04 Nathan King L PTS 4 Newport
31.10.04 Darren Stubbs L PTS 6 Shaw
25.11.04 Jonjo Finnegan DREW 6 Birmingham
03.12.04 Paul Henry W RSC 5 Bristol
21.01.05 Sam Price L PTS 6 Brentford
06.02.05 Mervyn Langdale DREW 6
    Southampton
20.02.05 Jon Ibbotson L PTS 6 Sheffield
08.04.05 Dan Guthrie L RSC 2 Bristol
09.09.05 Steven Birch W PTS 4 Sheffield
28.01.06 Rod Anderton L PTS 4 Nottingham
25.02.06 Richard Horton L CO 3 Canning Town
29.09.06 Chris Harman W PTS 4 Cardiff
14.10.06 Kenny Anderson L RSC 4 Manchester
18.02.07 Dwayne Lewis DREW 4 Bethnal Green
02.03.07 Wayne Brooks DREW 4 Neath
07.04.07 Nathan Cleverly L PTS 8 Cardiff
15.06.07 Tony Salam L PTS 4 Crystal Palace
06.07.07 Tony Dodson L PTS 4 Wigan
14.09.07 Gordon Brennan W PTS 4 Kirkcaldy
21.09.07 Courtney Fry L RSC 1 Bethnal Green
27.10.07 Ladislav Kutil W RSC 4 Prague, Czech
    Republic
21.12.07 Roman Kracik L PTS 6 Brno, Czech
    Republic
15.02.08 Billy Boyle L PTS 4 Sheffield

22.02.08 Danny McIntosh L RSC 3 Bethnal
    Green
01.05.08 Neil Simpson L RSC 10 Piccadilly
    (British Masters Cruiserweight Title
    Challenge)
06.09.08 Denis Lebedev L RSC 2 Manchester
24.01.09 Matty Askin L PTS 4 Blackpool
22.03.09 Bobby Scott W PTS 4 Bethnal Green
29.03.09 Patrick J. Maxwell W RSC 1 Sheffield
24.04.09 Danny Tombs DREW 4 Sheffield
02.05.09 Jon-Lewis Dickinson L PTS 4
    Sunderland
25.06.09 Matthew Barr L PTS 4 Mayfair
Career: 36 contests, won 8, drew 5, lost 23.

Dean O'Loughlin

Hull. *Born* Beverley, 25 September, 1982
Heavyweight. *Ht* 6'5"
Manager J. Rushton
01.12.06 Lee Webb W RSC 3 Doncaster
23.02.07 Lee Webb W RSC 2 Doncaster
25.09.07 Lee Mountford W PTS 6 Hull
19.10.07 David Ingleby L RSC 5 Doncaster
21.06.08 Howard Daley W PTS 6 Hull
21.02.09 Chris Woollas NC 1 Hull
Career: 6 contests, won 4, lost 1, no contest 1.

Larry Olubamiwo

London. *Born* Lambeth, 18 October, 1978
Heavyweight. *Ht* 6' 4"
Manager F. Maloney
17.10.08 Vlado Szabo W RSC 1 Bethnal Green
15.11.08 David Ingleby W RSC 2 Bethnal Green
23.01.09 Mihai Iftode W CO 2 Stoke
20.03.09 Michal Skierniewski W CO 1 Newham
02.05.09 Daniil Peretyatko L PTS 6 Sunderland
Career: 5 contests, won 4, lost 1.

Ajose Olusegun

Kentish Town. *Born* Nigeria, 6 December,
1979
British & Commonwealth L.Welterweight
Champion. Former Undefeated ABU
L.Welterweight Champion. *Ht* 5'9"
Manager Self
24.05.01 Tony Montana W RSC 1 Kensington
21.06.01 Woody Greenaway W RSC 1 Earls
    Court
09.09.01 Sunni Ajayi W PTS 6 Lagos, Nigeria
04.10.01 Stuart Rimmer W RTD 2 Finsbury
13.03.02 Gary Flear W PTS 4 Mayfair
13.06.02 Keith Jones W PTS 6 Leicester Square
30.10.02 Martin Holgate W RSC 7 Leicester
    Square
27.11.02 Vladimir Kortovski W RSC 1 Tel Aviv,
    Israel
15.12.02 Adewale Adegbusi W RSC 6 Lagos,
    Nigeria
20.03.03 Cristian Hodorogea W PTS 4
    Queensway
26.04.03 Keith Jones W PTS 6 Brentford
29.10.03 Karl Taylor W PTS 6 Leicester Square
10.04.04 Victor Kpadenue W PTS 12 Carabas,
    Nigeria
    (ABU L.Welterweight Title Challenge)
03.09.04 Bradley Pryce W RSC 4 Newport
26.03.05 Vasile Dragomir W PTS 8 Hackney
26.05.06 Alexander Abramenko W RSC 2
    Bethnal Green

29.06.06 Ali Nuumbembe W CO 6 Bethnal Green
17.11.06 Franck Aiello W RSC 2 Bethnal Green
09.03.07 Vladimir Khodokovski W PTS 6
Dagenham
15.06.07 Gary Reid W PTS 12 Crystal Palace
*(Vacant Commonwealth L.Welterweight
Title)*
26.10.07 Armando Candel W RSC 3 Wigan
08.02.08 Nigel Wright W PTS 12 Peterlee
*(Commonwealth L.Welterweight Title
Defence)*
18.04.08 Alexander Spitjo W RSC 3 Bethnal
Green
18.07.08 Mihaita Mutu W PTS 6 Dagenham
17.10.08 Michael Frontin W PTS 6 Bethnal Green
27.02.09 Scott Haywood W RSC 7 Barnsley
*(Commonwealth L.Welterweight Title
Defence)*
12.06.09 Nigel Wright W PTS 12 Liverpool
*(Vacant British L.Welterweight Title.
Commonwealth L.Welterweight Title
Defence)*
Career: 27 contests, won 27.

Ajose Olusegun　　　　Philip Sharkey

Steve O'Meara

West Drayton. *Born* West Drayton, 31
December, 1983
L.Middleweight. *Ht* 5'11¼"
Manager T. Sims
04.04.08 Ben Hudson W PTS 4 Bethnal Green
06.06.08 Dontre King W RSC 2 Philadelphia,
Pennsylvania, USA
11.07.08 Billy Smith W PTS 4 Wigan
08.11.08 JJ Bird W PTS 4 Bethnal Green
13.12.08 Matt Scriven W PTS 4 Brentwood
28.02.09 Drew Campbell W PTS 4 Norwich
11.04.09 Lewis Byrne W RTD 2 Bethnal Green
23.05.09 Drew Campbell W PTS 6 Watford
Career: 8 contests, won 8.

Eddie O'Rourke

Newark. *Born* Nottingham, 20 October,
1989
Lightweight. *Ht* 5'8¼"
Manager C. Greaves
31.05.08 Senol Dervis W PTS 6 Newark
20.09.08 Sid Razak W PTS 6 Newark
Career: 2 contests, won 2.

Eddie O'Rourke　　　　Philip Sharkey

Luke Osman

Merthyr. *Born* Merthyr, 10 March, 1986
Middleweight. *Ht* 6'1"
Manager C, Sanigar
28.06.08 Lester Walsh L PTS 6 Leicester
21.02.09 Kevin McCauley L PTS 6 Merthyr
Tydfil
05.06.09 Lee Churcher L PTS 6 Newport
12.06.09 Eder Kurti L PTS 4 Bethnal Green
Career: 4 contests, lost 4.

Damian Owen

Swansea. *Born* Swansea, 7 May, 1985
Welsh Area Lightweight Champion. *Ht* 5'7"
Manager T. Gilmour
01.10.04 Darren Payne W RSC 4 Bristol
05.11.04 Peter Allen W RSC 1 Hereford
08.04.05 Jus Wallie W PTS 4 Bristol
28.10.05 Bheki Moyo W PTS 6 Hartlepool
24.11.05 Kevin O'Hara L PTS 6 Lurgan
25.02.06 Carl Allen W PTS 6 Bristol
21.04.06 Steve Mullin W RSC 6 Belfast
13.10.06 Yauhen Kruhlik W PTS 6 Aberavon
02.03.07 Dean Philips W CO 4 Neath
(Vacant Welsh Area Lightweight Title)
08.06.07 Pedro Verdu L RSC 3 Motherwell
21.10.07 Chris Long W PTS 4 Swansea
13.06.09 Jason Nesbitt W PTS 4 Bristol
Career: 12 contests, won 10, lost 2.

Ricky Owen

Swansea. *Born* Swansea, 10 May, 1985
Featherweight. *Ht* 5'6"
Manager B. Hearn
05.11.04 Sandy Bartlett W RSC 2 Hereford
16.06.05 Billy Smith W PTS 4 Dagenham
30.09.05 Rakhim Mingaleev W PTS 4
Carmarthen
03.03.06 Alexander Vladimirov W PTS 6
Hartlepool
02.03.07 Egon Szabo W PTS 6 Neath
20.07.07 Anthony Hanna W RSC 5
Wolverhampton
02.11.07 Robin Deakin W RSC 2 Irvine
25.01.08 Frederic Gosset W PTS 6 Dagenham

30.03.08 Dai Davies W CO 5 Port Talbot
06.06.08 Sumaila Badu W PTS 6 Glasgow
03.04.09 James Ancliff W PTS 6 Bethnal Green
Career: 11 contests, won 11.

Ricky Owen　　　　Philip Sharkey

Tony Owen

Carshalton. *Born* Sutton, 18 February, 1987
Lightweight. *Ht* 5' 10"
Manager D. Cowland
20.03.09 Darryl Still W PTS 4 Bethnal Green
12.06.09 Youssef Al Hamidi W PTS 4 Bethnal
Green
Career: 2 contests, won 2.

Karol Ozimkowski

London. *Born* Poland, 10 May, 1986
L.Welterweight. *Ht* 6' 0"
Manager J. Rooney
27.09.08 Badru Lusambya L PTS 4 Bethnal Green
06.12.08 Johnny Creamer L PTS 4 Bethnal Green
Career: 2 contests, lost 2.

Karol Ozimkowski　　　　Philip Sharkey

Sam Padgett
Dudley. *Born* Worsley, 15 June, 1987
Middleweight. *Ht* 5' 8"
Manager E. Johnson
29.05.09 Steve Spence W CO 4 Dudley
Career: 1 contest, won 1.

Robert Palmer
Barnstaple. *Born* Barnstaple, 10 April, 1986
Flyweight. *Ht* 5' 5"
Manager N. Christian
19.07.08 Paul Edwards L PTS 4 Liverpool
Career: 1 contest, lost 1.

Duane Parker
Swadlincote. *Born* Burton, 14 September, 1987
L.Middleweight. *Ht* 5'11¼"
M*anager* E. Johnson
21.09.07 Peter Dunn W PTS 6 Burton
18.01.08 Lance Verallo W PTS 4 Burton
16.05.08 Peter Dunn W PTS 6 Burton
22.06.08 Chris Thompson W PTS 4 Derby
03.10.08 Paul Royston W PTS 6 Burton
23.02.09 Chris Brophy W PTS 6 Birmingham
10.04.09 Jason Nesbitt W PTS 6 Cheltenham
31.05.09 Luke Gallear W PTS 6 Burton
Career: 8 contests, won 8.

Duane Parker   Philip Sharkey

(Rasab) Raz Parnez
Glasgow. *Born* Rutherglen, 6 March, 1982
Heavyweight. *Ht* 6' 4"
Manager L. Murphy
01.11.08 Tony Booth L RTD 4 Glasgow
Career: 1 contest, lost 1.

Yanko Pavlov
Fife. *Born* Bulgaria, 27 July, 1982
Cruiserweight. *Ht* 6'0¼"
Manager T. Gilmour
09.05.08 Bob Ajisafe L PTS 4 Middlesbrough
22.09.08 Jamie Norkett W RSC 4 Glasgow
16.03.09 Mark Lewis W PTS 6 Glasgow
Career: 3 contests, won 2, lost 1.

Russell Pearce
Welshpool. *Born* Shrewsbury, 28 October, 1986
Welterweight. *Ht* 5'10¼"
Manager N. Hodges
21.10.07 Steve Cooper W PTS 4 Swansea
02.12.07 Chris Long DREW 6 Bristol
30.03.08 James Lilley L PTS 6 Port Talbot
26.04.08 Chris O'Brien L PTS 6 Wigan
12.05.08 Callum Archer DREW 6 Birmingham
07.06.08 Jonathan Hussey L PTS 4 Wigan
27.06.08 Daniel Herdman L RTD 2 Bethnal Green
12.09.08 Sam Sheedy L RTD 2 Sheffield
16.11.08 Darryl Still W PTS 6 Southampton
28.11.08 Nathan Brough L RSC 1 Glasgow
14.03.09 Martin Robins L PTS 4 Bristol
29.03.09 Rick Godding L RTD 2 Bolton
Career: 12 contests, won 2, drew 2, lost 8.

Dave Pearson
Middlesbrough. *Born* Middlesbrough, 1 April, 1974
L.Heavyweight. *Ht* 6'2¾"
Manager Self
15.04.02 Ian Thomas L CO 3 Shrewsbury
03.10.02 Gary Firby W CO 3 Sunderland
21.10.02 Gary Jones L RSC 3 Cleethorpes
05.12.02 Chris Steele W PTS 6 Sunderland
24.03.03 Reagan Denton L PTS 6 Barnsley
31.05.03 Gary Jones L RSC 2 Barnsley
11.07.03 Ben Coward L PTS 6 Darlington
16.02.04 Brian Coleman L PTS 6 Scunthorpe
26.02.04 Tony Quigley L RSC 1 Widnes
26.04.04 Mark Phillips L RSC 6 Cleethorpes
25.06.04 Gerard London L PTS 4 Bethnal Green
06.11.04 Brian Coleman W PTS 6 Coventry
16.12.04 Peter McCormack W PTS 6 Cleethorpes
25.04.05 Peter McCormack W PTS 6 Cleethorpes
02.09.05 Mark Phillips L PTS 6 Derby
15.12.05 Ryan Rowlinson L PTS 6 Cleethorpes
28.01.06 Jonjo Finnegan L PTS 4 Nottingham
25.03.06 Jonjo Finnegan L PTS 8 Burton
24.04.06 Magic Kidem W PTS 6 Cleethorpes
30.09.06 Jonjo Finnegan L PTS 6 Middlesbrough
08.10.06 Leon Owen L PTS 4 Swansea
02.12.06 Eder Kurti L PTS 6 Southwark
15.02.07 Sam Horton L RSC 4 Dudley
14.05.07 Tony Stones DREW 6 Cleethorpes
25.10.07 Richard Collins L RSC 3 Wolverhampton
23.02.08 Jamie Norkett L PTS 6 Newark
13.04.08 Eddie McIntosh L PTS 4 Edgbaston
26.04.08 Ally Morrison L PTS 6 Wigan
16.05.08 Jonjo Finnegan W PTS 4 Burton
21.06.08 Phil Goodwin L RSC 2 Hull

03.10.08 James Tucker L PTS 6 Sunderland
11.10.08 Luke Allon L RTD 2 Hull
08.12.08 Lee Nicholson DREW 6 Cleethorpes
Career: 33 contests, won 6, drew 2, lost 25.

Neil Perkins
Birmingham. *Born* Shrewsbury, 2 October, 1981
Heavyweight. *Ht* 6'5¼"
Manager P. Rowson
28.02.08 Lee Mountford W PTS 4 Wolverhampton
30.04.08 Paul Bonson W PTS 6 Wolverhampton
24.07.08 Howard Daley W PTS 4 Wolverhampton
12.06.09 Jason Callum W RSC 3 Wolverhampton
Career: 4 contests, won 4.

Jack Perry
Derby. *Born* Derby, 20 June, 1987
L.Welterweight. *Ht* 6'1"
Manager J. Ingle
16.09.06 Deniss Sirjatovs W PTS 6 Burton
24.11.06 Kristian Laight W PTS 4 Nottingham
03.03.07 Matt Seawright W RSC 2 Burton
16.09.07 Amir Nadi W PTS 4 Derby
03.11.07 Peter Dunn W PTS 6 Derby
18.01.08 Kristian Laight W PTS 4 Burton
10.05.08 Tom Glover DREW 4 Nottingham
22.06.08 Kristian Laight W PTS 6 Derby
06.12.08 Karl Taylor W PTS 4 Nottingham
31.05.09 Carl Allen W PTS 4 Burton
Career: 10 contests, won 9, drew 1.

Mark Phillips
St Clare's. *Born* Carmarthen, 28 April, 1975
L.Heavyweight. Former Undefeated British Masters L.Heavyweight Champion. *Ht* 6'0"
Manager Self
26.10.00 Shayne Webb W PTS 6 Clydach
12.12.00 Tommy Matthews W PTS 6 Clydach
13.03.01 William Webster W RTD 1 Plymouth
07.10.01 Danny Norton W PTS 6 Wolverhampton
12.12.01 Simon Andrews W PTS 6 Clydach
25.04.02 Mark Ellwood L PTS 6 Hull
10.05.02 Scott Dann L PTS 6 Bethnal Green
23.06.02 Gareth Hogg L PTS 4 Southwark
10.07.02 Scott Dann L PTS 4 Wembley
03.12.02 Jamie Hearn L PTS 4 Bethnal Green
20.12.02 Ryan Walls L PTS 4 Bracknell
06.03.03 Darren Dorrington L PTS 8 Bristol
21.03.03 Steve Timms L PTS 6 West Bromwich
05.04.03 Dale Nixon L PTS 6 Coventry
13.04.03 Donovan Smillie L PTS 6 Bradford
12.05.03 Leigh Alliss L PTS 6 Southampton
27.05.03 Steven Spartacus L RSC 2 Dagenham
30.06.03 Roddy Doran L PTS 6 Shrewsbury
06.09.03 Alan Page L PTS 6 Huddersfield
18.09.03 Nick Okoth L PTS 4 Mayfair
09.10.03 Leigh Alliss L PTS 4 Bristol
30.11.03 Jimi Hendricks W PTS 6 Swansea
16.01.04 Donovan Smillie L PTS 4 Bradford
07.04.04 Christian Imaga L PTS 6 Leicester Square
15.04.04 Darren McDermott L PTS 4 Dudley
26.04.04 Dave Pearson W RSC 6 Cleethorpes
04.06.04 Steve Timms L PTS 6 Dudley
03.12.04 Dan Guthrie L RSC 1 Bristol
26.02.05 Matt Galer L PTS 6 Burton

21.04.05 Matthew Hough L PTS 4 Dudley
09.07.05 Liam Stinchcombe L PTS 4 Bristol
02.09.05 Dave Pearson W PTS 6 Derby
25.09.05 Lee Hodgson L PTS 6 Southampton
10.10.05 Peter McCormack W PTS 6 Birmingham
04.11.05 Gary Woolcombe L PTS 4 Bethnal Green
24.11.05 Glenn McClarnon L PTS 4 Lurgan
04.03.06 James Davenport L PTS 4 Manchester
30.03.06 Danny Tombs L PTS 4 Bloomsbury
13.05.06 Richard Horton L PTS 4 Bethnal Green
01.06.06 Jonjo Finnegan L PTS 4 Birmingham
09.06.06 Jason Rushton L PTS 6 Doncaster
08.07.06 Nathan Cleverly L PTS 4 Cardiff
08.09.06 James McKinley L PTS 4 Birmingham
24.09.06 Richard Horton L PTS 4 Bethnal Green
08.10.06 Shon Davies L PTS 4 Swansea
28.10.06 Carl Wild L PTS 6 Sheffield
02.12.06 Neil Tidman L PTS 6 Coventry
17.12.06 Robin White L PTS 4 Bolton
23.04.07 Kenny Davidson L PTS 6 Glasgow
06.05.07 Joey Ainscough L PTS 6 Altrincham
13.05.07 Kevin Concepcion L PTS 6 Birmingham
02.06.07 Robert Boardman L PTS 6 Bristol
28.06.07 Richard Collins L PTS 4 Dudley
21.09.07 Jonjo Finnegan W PTS 10 Burton
(Vacant British Masters L.Heavyweight Title)
08.10.07 Matthew Hough L PTS 6 Birmingham
03.11.07 Harry Miles L PTS 4 Cardiff
18.11.07 Eddie McIntosh L PTS 4 Birmingham
28.11.07 Wayne Alwan Arab L PTS 4 Piccadilly
16.02.08 Rasham Sohi L PTS 6 Leicester
16.03.08 Joe McNally L RTD 2 Liverpool
12.09.08 Joe Skeldon L PTS 4 Wolverhampton
12.10.08 Danny Butler L PTS 4 Bristol
14.11.08 Eddie McIntosh L PTS 4 Birmingham
08.12.08 Joel Walton L PTS 6 Birmingham
01.02.09 Mark Regan L PTS 6 Birmingham
27.02.09 Ben Wilkes L PTS 4 Wolverhampton
29.03.09 Mick Jenno L PTS 4 Bolton
23.04.09 Eder Kurti L PTS 6 Mayfair
29.05.09 Llewellyn Davies L PTS 4 Dudley
Career: 69 contests, won 9, lost 60.

Esham Pickering

Newark. *Born* Newark, 7 August, 1976
Former British, European & Commonwealth S.Bantamweight Champion. Former Undefeated British Masters Bantamweight Champion. *Ht* 5'5"
Manager C. Greaves
23.09.96 Brendan Bryce W RSC 5 Cleethorpes
24.10.96 Kevin Sheil W PTS 6 Lincoln
22.11.96 Amjid Mahmood W RSC 2 Hull
09.12.96 Des Gargano W RTD 2 Chesterfield
16.12.96 Graham McGrath W PTS 6 Cleethorpes
20.03.97 Robert Braddock W RSC 6 Newark
12.04.97 Graham McGrath W PTS 4 Sheffield
26.04.97 Mike Deveney W PTS 4 Swadlincote
16.05.97 Chris Price W PTS 6 Hull
26.06.97 Graham McGrath W PTS 6 Salford
01.11.97 Mike Deveney W RSC 8 Glasgow
(Elim. British Featherweight Title)
09.05.98 Jonjo Irwin L PTS 12 Sheffield
(Vacant British Featherweight Title)
11.09.98 Louis Veitch W PTS 6 Newark

15.08.99 Chris Lyons W RSC 2 Derby
23.10.99 Ian Turner W PTS 6 Telford
20.11.99 Marc Smith W PTS 6 Grantham
19.02.00 Kevin Gerowski W PTS 10 Newark
(Vacant British Masters Bantamweight Title. Elim. British Bantamweight Title)
13.08.00 Lee Williamson W PTS 6 Nottingham
16.12.00 Mauricio Martinez L RSC 1 Sheffield
(WBO Bantamweight Title Challenge)
15.09.01 Carl Allen W PTS 6 Derby
08.12.01 Carl Allen W PTS 8 Chesterfield
20.04.02 Carl Allen W PTS 6 Derby
24.09.02 Alejandro Monzon L PTS 12 Gran Canaria, Spain
(Vacant WBA Inter-Continental S.Featherweight Title)
02.12.02 Carl Allen W PTS 6 Leicester
08.02.03 Duncan Karanja W CO 5 Brentford
(Vacant Commonwealth S.Bantamweight Title)
12.07.03 Brian Carr W RSC 4 Renfrew
(Vacant British S.Bantamweight Title. Commonwealth S.Bantamweight Title Defence)
24.10.03 Alfred Tetteh W RSC 7 Bethnal Green
(Commonwealth S.Bantamweight Title Defence)
16.01.04 Vincenzo Gigliotti W CO 10 Bradford
(Vacant European S.Bantamweight Title)
12.05.04 Juan Garcia Martin W RSC 8 Reading
(European S.Bantamweight Title Defence)
08.05.05 Noel Wilders W PTS 8 Bradford
09.06.05 Miguel Mallon W RSC 10 Alcobendas, Madrid, Spain
(European S.Bantamweight Title Defence)
28.10.05 Michael Hunter L PTS 12 Hartlepool
(European & Commonwealth S.Bantamweight Title Defences. British S.Bantamweight Title Challenge)
02.12.05 Frederic Bonifai W PTS 6 Nottingham
11.11.06 Bernard Dunne L PTS 12 Dublin
(Vacant European S.Bantamweight Title)
20.01.07 Frederic Gosset W PTS 6 Muswell Hill
16.03.07 Marc Callaghan W PTS 12 Norwich
(Vacant British S.Bantamweight Title)
13.10.07 Steve Gethin W RTD 3 Newark
09.11.07 Sean Hughes L PTS 8 Nottingham
18.01.08 Sean Hughes W RSC 9 Burton
(British S.Bantamweight Title Defence)
27.06.08 Matthew Marsh L PTS 12 Bethnal Green
(British S.Bantamweight Title Defence)
28.11.08 Paul Appleby L PTS 12 Glasgow
(British Featherweight Title Challenge)
23.05.09 Sid Razak W PTS 6 Sleaford
Career: 42 contests, won 34, lost 8.

Karl Place

Manchester. *Born* Manchester, 26 September, 1988
L.Welterweight. *Ht* 5' 11"
Manager S. Wood
12.10.08 Chris Kitson W RSC 2 Leigh
07.11.08 Carl Allen W PTS 4 Wigan
21.12.08 Johnny Greaves L PTS 4 Bolton
06.03.09 Baz Carey W PTS 4 Wigan
17.04.09 Jamie Spence W RSC 2 Leigh
Career: 5 contests, won 5.

Sonny Pollard

Hull. *Born* Hull, 3 November, 1976
S.Middleweight. *Ht* 5' 9"
Manager J. Phelan
09.06.98 Seamus Casey W PTS 4 Hull
08.08.98 Harry Butler L RSC 4 Scarborough
04.03.00 Wayne Elcock L RSC 3 Peterborough
26.09.02 Gary Jones W PTS 6 Hull
11.12.02 Martin Scotland W RSC 2 Hull
03.04.03 Wayne Shepherd W PTS 6 Hull
17.04.03 Andrey Ivanov W PTS 6 Hull
25.09.03 Patrick Cito W PTS 6 Hull
14.11.03 Howard Clarke W PTS 6 Hull
11.10.08 Davey Jones L PTS 6 Hull
06.06.09 Jamie Norkett W PTS 4 Beverley
Career: 11 contests, won 8, lost 3.

(Patrick) Paddy Pollock

Wishaw. *Born* Bellshill, 10 October, 1985
L.Middleweight. *Ht* 5'10½"
Manager A. Morrison
22.04.06 Duncan Cottier W PTS 6 Glasgow
21.10.06 Tyrone McInerney DREW 6 Glasgow
10.12.06 Ciaran Duffy W PTS 6 Glasgow
26.01.07 Dave Wakefield L PTS 6 Glasgow
16.02.07 Martin Marshall L PTS 4 Sunderland
16.03.07 Tom Hogan W RSC 3 Glasgow
25.05.07 Shaun Farmer W PTS 6 Glasgow
11.08.07 Shaun Farmer L PTS 6 Liverpool
26.10.07 Mark Bett DREW 6 Glasgow
09.12.07 Jay Morris L PTS 6 Glasgow
17.05.08 Duncan Cottier W PTS 6 Glasgow
20.06.08 James Flinn L PTS 4 Wolverhampton
11.07.08 Khurram Hussain L PTS 4 Wigan
01.11.08 Ben Deghani W CO 1 Glasgow
28.11.08 Jamie Coyle L RSC 3 Glasgow
06.03.09 Ciaran Duffy L PTS 10 Glasgow
(Vacant Scottish Area L.Middleweight Title)
Career: 16 contests, won 6, drew 2, lost 8.

Marcus Portman

West Bromwich. *Born* West Bromwich, 26 September, 1980
L.Middleweight. Former Undefeated WBF L.Middleweight Champion. Former Undefeated British Masters Welterweight Champion. *Ht* 6'0"
Manager Self
18.02.00 Ray Wood W PTS 6 West Bromwich
28.03.00 Billy Smith W PTS 6 Wolverhampton
10.09.00 Alan Kershaw W RSC 2 Walsall
15.02.01 Willie Limond L PTS 6 Glasgow
01.04.01 Tony Smith W PTS 6 Wolverhampton
20.04.01 Darren Melville L RSC 3 Millwall
07.09.01 Tony Smith W PTS 6 West Bromwich
15.09.01 Matthew Hatton L RSC 3 Manchester
12.12.01 Ross McCord DREW 4 Clydach
18.01.02 Andy Egan W PTS 4 Coventry
25.02.02 Sammy Smith W PTS 6 Slough
27.04.02 Gavin Wake W PTS 4 Huddersfield
08.05.03 Thomas McDonagh L PTS 6 Widnes
17.05.03 Scott Dixon W PTS 6 Liverpool
30.06.03 Wayne Wheeler W RSC 3 Shrewsbury
07.09.03 Jason Williams W PTS 6 Shrewsbury
19.02.04 Richard Swallow W PTS 10 Dudley
(British Masters Welterweight Title Challenge)

157

03.04.04 Chris Saunders L RSC 1 Sheffield
(Vacant English Welterweight Title)
29.06.06 Peter Dunn W PTS 6 Dudley
18.09.06 Peter Dunn W PTS 6 Glasgow
07.10.06 Ben Hudson W PTS 6 Walsall
15.12.06 George Hillyard W PTS 8 Bethnal Green
20.07.07 Jozsef Matolcsi W RSC 6 Wolverhampton
(WBF L.Middleweight Title Challenge)
12.10.07 Jozsef Matolcsi W PTS 12 Peterlee
(WBF L.Middleweight Title Defence)
08.12.07 Gary Woolcombe L RTD 8 Wigan
(Vacant British L.Middleweight Title)
28.04.08 Dean Walker W PTS 6 Glasgow
21.06.08 Bradley Pryce L RSC 6 Birmingham
(Commonwealth L.Middleweight Title Challenge)
24.04.09 Alex Spitjo W PTS 4 Wolverhampton
Career: 28 contests, won 20, drew 1, lost 7.

Martin Power

St Pancras. *Born* London, 14 February, 1980
Bantamweight. Former Undefeated British Bantamweight Champion. *Ht* 5'6"
Manager F. Maloney
09.06.01 Sean Grant W PTS 4 Bethnal Green
28.07.01 Andrew Greenaway W RSC 3 Wembley
22.09.01 Stevie Quinn W RSC 2 Bethnal Green
24.11.01 Anthony Hanna W PTS 4 Bethnal Green
19.01.02 Gareth Wiltshaw W PTS 4 Bethnal Green
08.07.02 Darren Cleary W PTS 4 Mayfair
12.10.02 Stevie Quinn W RSC 4 Bethnal Green
15.02.03 Stevie Quinn W RTD 1 Wembley
29.03.03 Dave Hinds W PTS 4 Portsmouth
17.07.03 Darren Cleary W PTS 6 Dagenham
06.11.03 Rocky Dean W PTS 6 Dagenham
24.01.04 Delroy Spencer W RTD 1 Wembley
01.04.04 Fred Janes W RSC 2 Bethnal Green
13.05.04 Jean-Marie Codet W PTS 8 Bethnal Green
30.07.04 Delroy Spencer W CO 2 Bethnal Green
11.12.04 Shinny Bayaar W PTS 10 Canning Town
20.05.05 Dale Robinson W PTS 12 Southwark
(Vacant British Bantamweight Title)
04.11.05 Ian Napa W PTS 12 Bethnal Green
(British Bantamweight Title Defence)
30.05.06 Isaac Ward W RSC 8 Bethnal Green
(British Bantamweight Title Defence)
29.06.06 Tshifhiwa Munyai L RSC 9 Bethnal Green
(Vacant Commonwealth Bantamweight Title)
26.01.07 Tshifhiwa Munyai L RTD 5 Dagenham
(Commonwealth Bantamweight Title Challenge)
30.11.07 Ian Napa L PTS 12 Newham
(British Bantamweight Title Challenge)
18.12.08 Gary Davies L RSC 2 Dublin
30.06.09 Sid Razak W PTS 6 Bethnal Green
Career: 24 contests, won 20, lost 4.

Ayitey Powers

Edmonton. *Born* Mamprobi, Ghana, 3 July, 1980
L.Heavyweight. Former Undefeated

Ghanian & West African Middleweight & S.Middleweight Champion. *Ht* 5'10¼"
Manager J. Feld
30.09.00 Joshua Okine W RSC 4 Kaneshie, Ghana
26.01.01 Ashiaquaye Aryee DREW 8 Kaneshie, Ghana
12.10.01 George Amuzu W PTS 6 Kaneshie, Ghana
03.05.02 Akeem Alarape W RSC 8 Accra, Ghana
02.06.02 Marciano Commey W RSC 6 Kaneshie, Ghana
(Vacant Ghanaian & West African Middleweight Titles)
02.11.02 Victor Kpadenue W PTS 8 Accra, Ghana
(Ghanaian & West African Middleweight Title Defences)
06.12.02 Joshua Clottey L PTS 10 Accra, Ghana
27.12.02 Kojo Adaho W RSC 6 Cotonou, Benin
(Ghanaian & West African Middleweight Title Defences)
20.01.03 Dornu Kwame W RSC 4 Lome, Togo
(Ghanaian & West African Middleweight Title Defences)
06.03.03 Samuel Shegu W PTS 10 Accra, Ghana
(Ghanaian & West African Middleweight Title Defences)
28.06.03 Madaga Solomon W CO 1 Accra, Ghana
15.08.03 Osumanu Adama L PTS 12 Kaneshie, Ghana
(Ghanaian & West African L.Middleweight Title Challenges)
31.01.04 Richard Williams L RSC 7 Bethnal Green
(Vacant Commonwealth L.Middleweight Title)
03.07.04 James Obede Toney L PTS 12 Accra, Ghana
(Vacant WBC International & Commonwealth Middleweight Titles)
18.12.04 Mohammed Konde W CO 12 Accra, Ghana
(Vacant Ghanaian & West African S.Middleweight Titles)
26.08.05 Flash Issaka W RSC 4 Kaneshie, Ghana
(Vacant Ghanaian S.Middleweight Title)
18.11.06 Gary Lockett L PTS 10 Newport
08.12.06 Steven Spartacus W PTS 6 Dagenham
23.02.07 Matthew Barney L PTS 6 Peterborough
23.03.07 Amer Khan L PTS 6 Nottingham
30.03.07 Cello Renda W RSC 2 Peterborough
02.06.07 Dean Francis L CO 9 Bristol
(Vacant IBO Inter-Continental L.Heavyweight Title)
21.07.07 Nathan Cleverly L CO 6 Cardiff
19.10.07 JJ Ojuederie L PTS 10 Mayfair
(Vacant International Masters Cruiserweight Title)
22.03.08 Jon Ibbotson L PTS 6 Sheffield
29.03.08 Paul David L PTS 6 Aberdeen
16.05.08 Matthew Barney L PTS 6 Holborn
15.06.08 Tony Quigley L PTS 6 St Helens
18.07.08 Tony Bellew L PTS 4 Dagenham
Career: 29 contests, won 13, drew 1, lost 15.

David Price

Liverpool. *Born* Liverpool 6 July, 1983
Heavyweight. *Ht* 6'8"
Manager A. Booth
28.03.09 David Ingleby W RSC 3 Liverpool
Career: 1 contest, won 1.

Mitch Prince

Cumbernauld. *Born* Johannesburg, South Africa, 15 March, 1984
Lightweight. *Ht* 5'5"
Manager Self
05.06.06 Jason Nesbitt W PTS 6 Glasgow
29.09.06 Peter Buckley W PTS 6 Motherwell
03.11.06 Peter Buckley W PTS 6 Glasgow
02.12.06 Steve Gethin W PTS 6 Clydebank
16.02.07 Dariusz Snarski DREW 6 Kirkcaldy
20.10.08 Jason Nesbitt W PTS 6 Glasgow
Career: 6 contests, won 5, drew 1.

Bradley Pryce   Philip Sharkey

Bradley Pryce (Price)

Newbridge. *Born* Newport, 15 March, 1981
Former Commonwealth L.Middleweight Champion. Former Undefeated Welsh Welterweight Champion. Former Undefeated IBF Inter-Continental L.Welterweight Champion. Former Undefeated WBO Inter-Continental Lightweight Champion. *Ht* 5'11"
Manager E. Calzaghe
17.07.99 Dave Hinds W PTS 4 Doncaster
23.10.99 David Jeffrey W RSC 3 Telford
06.11.99 Eddie Nevins W RSC 2 Widnes
29.01.00 Pete Buckley W PTS 4 Manchester
29.02.00 Carl Allen W PTS 4 Widnes
16.05.00 Carl Allen W RSC 3 Warrington
15.07.00 Gary Flear W RSC 1 Millwall
07.10.00 Gary Reid W RSC 5 Doncaster
27.01.01 Joel Viney W RSC 3 Bethnal Green
17.03.01 Brian Coleman W PTS 4 Manchester
28.04.01 Jason Hall W PTS 12 Cardiff
(Vacant WBO Inter-Continental Lightweight Title)
21.07.01 Stuart Patterson W RSC 5 Sheffield

09.10.01 Lucky Sambo W PTS 12 Cardiff
(WBO Inter-Continental Lightweight Title Defence)
12.02.02 Gavin Down W RSC 9 Bethnal Green
(Vacant IBF Inter-Continental L.Welterweight Title)
20.04.02 Dafydd Carlin W RSC 8 Cardiff
08.06.02 Pete Buckley W RSC 1 Renfrew
17.08.02 Ted Bami L RSC 6 Cardiff
23.11.02 Craig Lynch W CO 4 Derby
01.02.03 Neil Sinclair L RSC 8 Belfast
(British Welterweight Title Challenge)
08.05.03 Ivan Kirpa W PTS 10 Widnes
21.02.04 Farai Musiiwa L PTS 6 Cardiff
06.05.04 Thomas McDonagh L PTS 12 Barnsley
(WBU International L.Middleweight Title Challenge)
03.07.04 Keith Jones W RSC 8 Newport
(Vacant Welsh Area Welterweight Title)
03.09.04 Ajose Olusegun L RSC 4 Newport
11.12.04 Sergey Styopkin W RSC 10 Canning Town
25.10.05 Michael Jennings L PTS 12 Preston
(British Welterweight Title Challenge)
11.03.06 Ossie Duran W PTS 12 Newport
(Commonwealth L.Middleweight Title Challenge)
08.07.06 Hassan Matumla W RSC 4 Cardiff
(Commonwealth L.Middleweight Title Defence)
18.11.06 Andrew Facey W PTS 12 Newport
(Commonwealth L.Middleweight Title Defence)
07.04.07 Thomas Awinbono W PTS 12 Cardiff
(Commonwealth L.Middleweight Title Defence)
14.07.07 Anthony Small W RSC 7 Greenwich
(Commonwealth L.Middleweight Title Defence)
06.10.07 Martin Concepcion W RSC 3 Nottingham
(Commonwealth L.Middleweight Title Defence)
21.06.08 Marcus Portman W RSC 6 Birmingham
(Commonwealth L.Middleweight Title Defence)
14.03.09 Matthew Hall L RSC 2 Manchester
(Commonwealth L.Middleweight Title Defence)
Career: 34 contests, won 27, lost 7.

Lee Purdy

Colchester. *Born* Colchester, 29 May, 1987
Welterweight. *Ht* 5'7"
Manager Self
08.12.06 Deniss Sirjatovs W RSC 3 Dagenham
16.03.07 Kristian Laight W PTS 4 Norwich
16.06.07 Duncan Cottier W PTS 4 Chigwell
01.07.07 Ben Hudson W PTS 6 Colchester
25.11.07 Johnny Greaves W PTS 6 Colchester
25.01.08 Craig Dyer W RSC 1 Dagenham
04.04.08 Jamie Spence W RSC 1 Bethnal Green
27.06.08 Geoffrey Munika DREW 6 Bethnal Green
04.10.08 Johnny Greaves W RSC 3 Norwich
08.11.08 Adam Kelly W RSC 5 Bethnal Green
13.12.08 Peter McDonagh L PTS 10 Brentwood
(Vacant Southern Area L.Welterweight Title)
28.02.09 Leonard Lothian W PTS 4 Norwich
Career: 12 contests, won 10, drew 1, lost 1.

Kreshnik Qato   Philip Sharkey

Kreshnik Qato

Wembley. *Born* Albania, 13 August, 1978
WBF Middleweight Champion. Former Undefeated European Union EE & Southern Area S.Middleweight Champion. Former Undefeated Eastern European Boxing Association S.Middleweight Champion.
Ht 5'9½"
Manager P. Fondu
28.09.01 Erik Teymour L PTS 6 Millwall
16.12.01 Lawrence Murphy L PTS 6 Glasgow
08.04.02 Ty Browne W PTS 4 Southampton
10.05.02 Paul Jones L PTS 6 Millwall
20.03.03 Jason Collins W PTS 4 Queensway
13.04.03 Mark Thornton W RSC 3 Streatham
13.05.03 Danny Thornton W PTS 6 Leeds
26.07.03 Scott Dann L RSC 2 Plymouth
26.09.03 Joel Ani W PTS 6 Millwall
14.11.03 Steven Bendall L PTS 8 Bethnal Green
21.02.04 Gary Lockett L RSC 2 Cardiff
16.10.04 Vladimir Zavgorodniy W PTS 10 Yalta, Ukraine
(Vacant Eastern European Boxing Association S.Middleweight Title)
05.03.05 Rizvan Magomedov W PTS 12 Durres, Albania
(Eastern European Boxing Association S.Middleweight Title Defence)
12.06.05 Dmitry Donetskiy W RSC 6 Leicester Square
09.10.05 Daniil Prakapsou W PTS 8 Hammersmith
02.04.06 Laurent Goury W PTS 6 Bethnal Green
26.05.06 Simone Lucas W PTS 4 Bethnal Green
15.07.06 Sylvain Touzet W PTS 6 Tirana, Albania
15.09.06 Simeon Cover W PTS 6 Muswell Hill
08.12.06 Simeon Cover W PTS 10 Dagenham
(Vacant Southern Area S.Middleweight Title)
03.03.07 Alexander Zaitsev W PTS 12 Tirana, Albania
(Vacant European Union-EE S.Middleweight Title)
14.11.07 Ernie Smith W PTS 6 Bethnal Green

04.04.08 Vitor Sa W PTS 12 Tirana, Albania
(Vacant WBF Middleweight Title)
20.12.08 David Estrada W RSC 6 Washington DC, USA
(WBF Middleweight Title Defence)
27.03.09 Jurijs Boreiko W PTS 6 Kensington
Career: 25 contests, won 19, lost 6.

Tariq Quaddas

Peterborough. *Born* Peterborough, 6 July, 1990
S.Middleweight. *Ht* 5'11"
Manager D. Powell
31.10.08 Jamie Ambler W PTS 4 Birmingham
21.11.08 Tony Randell L CO 3 Bethnal Green
Career: 2 contests, won 1, lost 1.

Scott Quigg

Bury. *Born* Bury, 9 October, 1988
S.Bantamweight. *Ht* 5'8"
Manager B. Hughes
21.04.07 Gary Sheil W PTS 6 Manchester
30.06.07 Shaun Walton W RSC 1 Manchester
11.08.07 Shaun Walton W PTS 6 Liverpool
28.09.07 Sandy Bartlett W RSC 3 Preston
03.12.07 Delroy Spencer W PTS 6 Manchester
14.03.08 Gheorghe Ghiompirica W PTS 4 Manchester
07.06.08 Sid Razak W RSC 2 Wigan
04.07.08 Angelo Villani W RSC 2 Liverpool
19.07.08 Peter Allen W RSC 1 Liverpool
07.11.08 Sumaila Badu W RSC 1 Wigan
06.12.08 Gheorghe Ghiompirica W PTS 4 Wigan
24.01.09 Carl Allen W PTS 4 Blackpool
28.03.09 Faycal Messaoudene W RSC 5 Altrincham
Career: 13 contests, won 13.

Nick Quigley

Melling Mount. *Born* Melling Mount, 20 September, 1988
Welterweight. *Ht* 6'1"
Manager S. Wood
24.01.09 Jimmy Briggs W PTS 6 Blackpool
17.04.09 Kristian Laight W PTS 4 Leigh
Career: 2 contests, won 2.

Tony Quigley

Liverpool. *Born* Liverpool, 1 October, 1984
L.Heavyweight. *Ht* 5'10"
Manager S. Wood
26.02.04 Dave Pearson W RSC 1 Widnes
22.05.04 Patrick Cito W PTS 4 Widnes
01.10.04 Leigh Wicks W PTS 4 Manchester
11.02.05 Shpetim Hoti W CO 1 Manchester
03.06.05 Varuzhan Davtyan W PTS 4 Manchester
04.03.06 Ojay Abrahams W PTS 4 Manchester
01.06.06 Simeon Cover W PTS 4 Barnsley
14.10.06 Nathan Cleverly L RSC 5 Manchester
10.03.07 Dean Walker W RSC 2 Liverpool
26.04.07 Ricky Strike W RSC 3 Manchester
11.08.07 Jevgenijs Andrejevs W PTS 4 Liverpool
15.06.08 Ayitey Powers W PTS 6 St Helens
07.11.08 Nathan King W RSC 5 Wigan
28.03.09 Tony Dodson W RSC 12 Liverpool
(Vacant British S.Middleweight Title)
Career: 14 contests, won 13, lost 1.

Harry Ramogoadi   Philip Sharkey

Harry Ramogoadi

Rugby. *Born* Johannesburg, South Africa,
21 March, 1976
Featherweight. *Ht* 5' 6"
Manager J. Gill
20.11.98 Dan Ngweyna W PTS 4 Thembisa,
South Africa
24.01.99 Zachariah Mudau W PTS 4
Johannesburg, South Africa
26.03.99 Jan van Rooyen DREW 4 TWitbank,
South Africa
27.06.99 Kenneth Buhlalu W PTS 4 Durban,
South Africa
23.07.99 Bethule Machedi W PTS 4
Johannesburg, South Africa
25.09.99 Malepa Levi W PTS 6 Nelspruit, South
Africa
01.12.99 Mandla Mashiane L PTS 6
Johannesburg, South Africa
13.07.00 Martin Mnyandu L PTS 6 Johannesburg,
South Africa
28.10.00 Trevor Gouws W PTS 6 Johannesburg,
South Africa
18.02.01 Thomas Mashaba DREW 6
Johannesburg, South Africa
15.04.01 Malepa Levi W PTS 8 Johannesburg,
South Africa
02.11.01 Malcolm Klassen W PTS 6 Benoni,
South Africa
08.02.02 Takalani Kwinda W PTS 8
Johannesburg, South Africa
09.10.02 Ariel Mathebula W PTS 6 Sandton,
South Africa
24.10.03 Stephen Oates W PTS 6 Bethnal Green
08.11.03 Jason Nesbitt W PTS 6 Coventry
09.04.04 Nigel Senior W CO 1 Rugby
10.07.04 Choi Tseveenpurev L RSC 6 Coventry
(*British Masters Featherweight Title
Challenge*)
09.12.04 John Murray L RSC 4 Stockport

06.03.05 Choi Tseveenpurev L RSC 5 Shaw
(*British Masters Featherweight Title
Challenge*)
01.06.05 Danny Wallace W PTS 6 Leeds
23.07.05 Jamie Arthur W RSC 5 Edinburgh
18.10.06 Buster Dennis W RSC 9 Bayswater
(*Vacant British Masters Featherweight
Title*)
09.12.06 Nicky Cook L PTS 8 Canning Town
22.12.06 Daniel Thorpe W PTS 6 Coventry
10.03.07 Kevin Mitchell L RSC 6 Liverpool
(*Commonwealth S.Featherweight Title
Challenge*)
13.04.07 Ferenc Szabo W RSC 4 Rugby
15.06.07 Tshifhiwa Munyai L PTS 8 Crystal
Palace
18.07.08 Gary Sykes L PTS 6 Dagenham
20.09.08 Josh Wale W RTD 3 Sheffield
27.02.09 Willie Limond L PTS 8 Paisley
28.03.09 Derry Matthews W CO 4 Liverpool
Career: 32 contests, won 20, drew 2, lost 10.

Stewart Ramplin

Manchester. *Born* Manchester, 14
September, 1981
Lightweight. *Ht* 5' 10"
Manager J. Pennington
08.11.08 Daniel Thorpe L RSC 5 Wigan
Career: 1 contest, lost 1.

Tony Randell (Webster)

Birmingham. *Born* Peterborough, 11 April,
1982
Midlands Area Middleweight Champion.
Ht 5'11½"
Manager E. Johnson
16.12.04 Scott Conway W PTS 6 Cleethorpes
13.02.05 Gavin Smith L PTS 6 Bradford
23.03.05 Danny Goode L PTS 6 Leicester Square
01.04.05 Chris Black L PTS 6 Glasgow
16.05.05 Sergey Haritonov W RSC 4 Birmingham
24.07.05 Stuart Brookes L PTS 6 Sheffield
09.09.05 Stuart Brookes L RSC 3 Sheffield
10.10.05 Simon Sherrington L PTS 6 Birmingham
30.10.05 Jake Guntert L PTS 4 Bethnal Green
18.12.05 Mark Thompson L RSC 2 Bolton
17.02.06 Reagan Denton L PTS 6 Sheffield
18.03.06 Sam Gorman W PTS 6 Coventry
02.04.06 Alex Matvienko L PTS 6 Shaw
13.04.06 Danny Wright L PTS 6 Leeds
20.05.06 George Katsimpas L RSC 1 Bristol
16.09.06 Karl Chiverton L PTS 6 Burton
07.10.06 Sam Horton L PTS 6 Walsall
26.10.06 Dee Mitchell L PTS 4 Wolverhampton
06.12.06 Ryan Rowlinson DREW 6 Rotherham
20.01.07 George Hillyard DREW 4 Muswell Hill
31.05.07 Brian Rose L PTS 6 Manchester
24.06.07 Johnny Enigma W RSC 5 Wigan
08.10.07 Graham Delehedy W PTS 10 Glasgow
(*Vacant International Masters
Middleweight Title*)
22.02.08 Chris Black L PTS 6 Motherwell
28.04.08 Jamie Coyle L PTS 8 Glasgow
03.10.08 Prince Arron L RSC 4 Burton
21.11.08 Tariq Quaddas W CO 3 Bethnal Green
20.12.08 Danny Butler L PTS 6 Bristol
01.02.09 Max Maxwell W PTS 10 Birmingham
(*Vacant Midlands Area Middleweight
Title*)

05.03.09 Wayne Downing W RSC 2 Limehouse
25.06.09 Matt Scriven W PTS 4 Mayfair
Career: 31 contests, won 9, drew 2, lost 20.

Tony Randell   Philip Sharkey

Hastings Rasani

Birmingham. *Born* Zimbabwe, 16 April,
1974
Cruiserweight. *Ht* 6'2"
Manager Self
21.12.97 Elias Chikwanda W RSC 4 Harare,
Zimbabwe
28.02.98 Victor Ndebele W CO 1 Harare,
Zimbabwe
04.04.98 William Mpoku W PTS 8 Harare,
Zimbabwe
03.05.98 Nightshow Mafukidze W CO 3 Harare,
Zimbabwe
30.05.98 Frank Mutiyaya W RSC 4 Harare,
Zimbabwe
24.07.98 Ambrose Mlilo L RSC 9 Harare,
Zimbabwe
13.01.99 Tobia Wede W RSC 4 Harare,
Zimbabwe
27.02.99 Ambrose Mlilo L CO 9 Harare,
Zimbabwe
27.03.99 Gibson Mapfumo W CO 1 Harare,
Zimbabwe
17.04.99 Eric Sauti W RSC 2 Harare, Zimbabwe
05.06.99 Gibson Mapfumo W RSC 2 Harare,
Zimbabwe
18.12.99 Gibson Mapfumo W RSC 3 Harare,
Zimbabwe
02.01.01 Neil Simpson L CO 4 Coventry
(*Vacant Commonwealth L.Heavyweight
Title*)
24.03.01 Gibson Mapfumo W CO 3 Harare,
Zimbabwe
28.04.01 Arigoma Chiponda W DIS Harare,
Zimbabwe
08.05.01 Tony Oakey L RSC 10 Barnsley
(*Vacant Commonwealth L.Heavyweight
Title*)
06.10.01 Sipho Moyo L CO 9 Harare, Zimbabwe
15.03.02 Elvis Michailenko L RSC 5 Millwall
24.05.03 Elvis Michailenko L RSC 4 Bethnal
Green
31.07.03 Mark Brookes L PTS 6 Sheffield

05.09.03 Carl Thompson L RSC 1 Sheffield
04.10.03 Steven Spartacus L RSC 1 Muswell Hill
11.11.03 Denzil Browne L PTS 6 Leeds
13.02.04 Leigh Alliss L PTS 6 Bristol
21.02.04 Earl Ling DREW 6 Norwich
12.03.04 Simeon Cover W CO 6 Irvine
20.03.04 David Haye L RSC 1 Wembley
12.05.04 Jamie Hearn L RSC 4 Reading
17.06.04 Amer Khan L PTS 6 Sheffield
17.09.04 Mark Brookes L PTS 6 Sheffield
11.10.04 Hamed Jamali L PTS 8 Birmingham
22.10.04 Nathan King L PTS 6 Edinburgh
08.12.04 Sam Price L PTS 6 Longford
17.12.04 Neil Simpson L PTS 6 Coventry
21.02.05 Karl Wheeler L PTS 6 Peterborough
24.04.05 Nicki Taylor W RTD 4 Askern
08.05.05 Nate Joseph W RSC 4 Bradford
15.05.05 Danny Grainger W RSC 5 Sheffield
02.06.05 Karl Wheeler W RSC 5 Peterborough
01.07.05 Ovill McKenzie L PTS 6 Fulham
09.09.05 Lee Swaby L PTS 4 Sheffield
24.09.05 Neil Linford W RSC 5 Coventry
12.11.05 Dean Francis L RSC 6 Bristol
19.12.05 Valery Odin W PTS 4 Longford
11.03.06 Bruce Scott W PTS 8 Newport
07.10.06 Dean Francis L CO 2 Weston super Mare
02.12.06 Tommy Eastwood L PTS 6 Longford
20.01.07 Troy Ross L CO 3 Muswell Hill
11.03.07 Darren Stubbs L RSC 5 Shaw
29.09.07 Scott Brookes L PTS 4 Sheffield
07.10.07 Darren Stubbs L PTS 6 Shaw
03.11.07 Anders Hugger L PTS 6 Cardiff
01.12.07 JJ Ojuederie L PTS 6 Bethnal Green
23.02.08 Kelly Oliver L PTS 4 Newark
22.03.08 Mark Krence L PTS 4 Sheffield
24.04.08 Egbui Ikeagwu DREW 4 Piccadilly
15.06.08 Paul Keir L PTS 4 St Helens
06.09.08 Tony Bellew L RSC 1 Manchester
20.10.08 Steve McGuire L PTS 8 Glasgow
14.11.08 Kenny Anderson L RSC 3 Glasgow
01.02.09 Rhys Davies DREW 4 Birmingham
14.03.09 Dyah Davis L PTS 6 Bristol
03.04.09 Martyn Grainger L RSC 1 Leigh
12.06.09 Joe Smyth L RSC 2 Bethnal Green
Career: 64 contests, won 20, drew 3, lost 41.

Sid Razak   Philip Sharkey

(Shahid) Sid Razak
Birmingham. *Born* Birmingham, 9 March, 1973
Lightweight. *Ht* 5'7"
Manager R. Woodhall
13.02.01 Neil Read W PTS 6 Brierley Hill
27.03.01 Tommy Thomas W RSC 2 Brierley Hill
21.05.01 Jason Nesbitt W PTS 6 Birmingham
08.10.01 Gareth Wiltshaw L PTS 6 Birmingham
14.09.02 J.J.Moore L PTS 6 Newark
26.09.02 Chris Hooper L PTS 6 Hull
08.12.03 Steve Mullin L PTS 6 Birmingham
08.03.04 Steve Mullin L PTS 6 Birmingham
01.06.07 Sergei Rozhakmens L PTS 6 Birmingham
31.05.08 Ben Lawler L PTS 6 Newark
07.06.08 Scott Quigg L RSC 2 Wigan
12.07.08 Lee Selby L PTS 6 Newport
19.07.08 Rhys Roberts L PTS 4 Liverpool
04.09.08 Pete Leworthy L PTS 4 Birmingham
12.09.08 Craig Bromley L PTS 4 Sheffield
20.09.08 Eddie O'Rourke L PTS 6 Newark
04.10.08 Logan McGuinness L PTS 4 Norwich
12.10.08 Jon Kays L PTS 4 Leigh
24.10.08 Rob Turley L PTS 4 Newport
31.10.08 Stephen Smith L RSC 3 Birmingham
05.12.08 Ben Jones L PTS 6 Dagenham
21.12.08 Tyrone Nurse L PTS 4 Bolton
16.01.09 Dougie Curran L PTS 4 Middlesbrough
30.01.09 Ryan Walsh L PTS 4 Bethnal Green
13.02.09 Chris Higgs L PTS 4 Swindon
28.02.09 Bradley Evans L PTS 4 Norwich
16.03.09 Davey Savage L PTS 10 Glasgow
(Vacant British Masters Featherweight Title)
28.03.09 Joe Murray L PTS 6 Altrincham
01.05.09 Martin Ward L PTS 4 Hartlepool
23.05.09 Esham Pickering L PTS 6 Sleaford
30.06.09 Martin Power L PTS 6 Bethnal Green
Career: 31 contests, won 3, lost 28.

Joe Rea   Philip Sharkey

Joe Rea
Birmingham. *Born* Ballymena, 24 July, 1983
S.Middleweight. *Ht* 6'0¼"
Manager R. Woodhall
11.06.04 Devin Womack W RSC 1 Plymouth, Mass, USA

10.08.04 Henry Dukes ND 2 Hyannis, Mass, USA
01.10.04 Robert Muhammad W PTS 4 Boston, Mass, USA
25.03.05 Jerald Lowe W RSC 3 Dorchester, Mass, USA
01.04.05 Cory Phelps W RSC 2 New Haven, Connecticut, USA
19.11.05 Michael Rayner W RSC 1 Dorchester, USA
07.07.06 Valentino Jalomo DREW 4 Hyannis, Mass, USA
13.04.08 Jamie Ambler W PTS 4 Edgbaston
22.11.08 Martin Murray L PTS 3 Bethnal Green
Career: 9 contests, won 6, drew 1, lost 1, no decision 1.

Wayne Reed
Sheffield. *Born* Sheffield, 5 August, 1987
L.Middleweight. *Ht* 5' 10"
Manager G. Rhodes
10.10.08 Paul Royston W PTS 6 Sheffield
14.05.09 Kurt Bromberg W PTS 6 Leeds
Career: 2 contests, won 2.

Mark Regan
Birmingham. *Born* Birmingham, 23 July, 1983
L.Heavyweight. *Ht* 5' 11"
Manager R. Woodhall
14.09.08 Mark Nilsen W PTS 6 Birmingham
14.11.08 Robert Burton W RSC 5 Birmingham
01.02.09 Mark Phillips W PTS 6 Birmingham
07.03.09 Michael Banbula W PTS 4 Birmingham
10.04.09 James Tucker W PTS 4 Birmingham
Career: 5 contests, won 5.

Gary Reid
Stoke. *Born* Jamaica, 20 November, 1972
L.Welterweight. Former Undefeated Midlands Area & British Masters L.Welterweight Champion. *Ht* 5'5½"
Manager Self
09.12.98 Carl Tilley W CO 1 Stoke
11.02.99 Ted Bami L RSC 2 Dudley
23.03.99 Lee Williamson W PTS 6 Wolverhampton
07.10.99 Stuart Rimmer W RSC 2 Mere
19.12.99 No No Junior L PTS 6 Salford
14.04.00 Lee Molyneux W PTS 6 Manchester
18.05.00 Sammy Smith W RSC 1 Bethnal Green
23.07.00 Kevin Bennett L RSC 4 Hartlepool
21.09.00 Karim Bouali L PTS 4 Bloomsbury
07.10.00 Bradley Pryce L RSC 5 Doncaster
07.09.01 Willie Limond L PTS 8 Glasgow
22.09.01 Francis Barrett L PTS 4 Bethnal Green
17.02.02 Richie Caparelli W PTS 6 Salford
02.03.02 Paul Halpin L RSC 3 Bethnal Green
26.04.02 Martin Watson L PTS 6 Glasgow
28.05.02 Gareth Jordan DREW 6 Liverpool
13.07.02 Gary Greenwood L RSC 5 Coventry
05.10.02 Joel Viney W CO 2 Coventry
18.11.02 Martin Watson L RSC 4 Glasgow
21.03.03 Young Muttley L RSC 7 West Bromwich
(Vacant Midlands Area L.Welterweight Title)
10.10.03 Oscar Hall W RSC 2 Darlington

26.09.04 Tony Montana W PTS 10 Stoke
(Vacant British Masters L.Welterweight Title)
17.02.05 Dean Hickman L PTS 10 Dudley
(Midlands Area L.Welterweight Title Challenge)
27.05.05 Barry Morrison L RTD 8 Motherwell
(British Masters L.Welterweight Title Defence)
25.11.05 Jason Cook L DIS 2 Liverpool
18.02.06 Davis Kamara W PTS 6 Stoke
06.05.06 Kevin McIntyre W RSC 6 Stoke
(Vacant British Masters L.Welterweight Title)
26.05.06 Leo O'Reilly W RSC 2 Bethnal Green
04.11.06 Nigel Wright L PTS 10 Glasgow
(English L.Welterweight Title Challenge)
20.04.07 Dean Hickman W RSC 5 Dudley
(Vacant Midlands Area L.Welterweight Title)
15.06.07 Ajose Olusegun L PTS 12 Crystal Palace
(Vacant Commonwealth L.Welterweight Title)
19.10.07 John Fewkes L PTS 8 Doncaster
07.03.08 Scott Haywood L PTS 6 Nottingham
30.04.08 Dean Harrison L PTS 8 Wolverhampton
06.06.08 Graeme Higginson L RSC 10 Stoke
(British Masters L.Welterweight Title Challenge)
15.11.08 Michael Grant L PTS 6 O2 Greenwich
Career: 36 contests, won 13, drew 1, lost 22.

Gavin Reid

Redcar. *Born* Aberdeen, 17 November, 1978
S.Bantamweight. *Ht* 5'8½"
Manager M. Marsden
09.06.07 Neil Marston W CO 2 Middlesbrough
15.07.07 Delroy Spencer W PTS 6 Hartlepool
26.10.07 Mark Moran L PTS 4 Wigan
25.11.07 Stuart McFadyen W RSC 5 Colne
08.02.08 Tony McQuade W PTS 4 Peterlee
22.02.08 Andrew Kooner L RSC 8 Bethnal Green
09.05.08 John Donnelly W CO 4 Middlesbrough
16.01.09 Bismarck Alfaro L PTS 8 Middlesbrough
Career: 8 contests, won 5, lost 3.

Marlon Reid Philip Sharkey

Marlon Reid

Swindon. *Born* Swindon, 17 April, 1982
Middleweight. *Ht* 6' 2"
Manager J. Feld
17.10.08 Gary Cooper W PTS 4 Swindon
14.12.08 James Tucker W PTS 4 Bristol
13.02.09 Sherman Alleyne W RSC 3 Swindon
Career: 3 contests, won 3.

Mike Reid

Aberdeen. *Born* Inverurie, 4 November, 1983
Welterweight. *Ht* 5' 8"
Manager G. Jeans
15.11.04 Willie Valentine W PTS 6 Glasgow
21.02.05 Tom Hogan W PTS 6 Glasgow
11.06.05 Lance Verallo W PTS 6 Kirkcaldy
30.09.05 Ben Hudson W PTS 4 Kirkcaldy
24.10.05 Chris Brophy W RSC 2 Glasgow
31.03.06 Tom Hogan L PTS 6 Inverurie
27.05.06 Adam Kelly DREW 6 Aberdeen
09.09.06 Billy Smith L PTS 8 Inverurie
03.11.06 Tye Williams L RSC 6 Glasgow
26.05.07 Leonard Lothian L PTS 6 Aberdeen
29.05.09 Ben Deghani L RSC 2 Glasgow
Career: 11 contests, won 5, drew 1, lost 5.

Pele Reid

Birmingham. *Born* Birmingham, 11 January, 1973
British Masters Heavyweight Champion. Former Undefeated WBO Inter-Continental Heavyweight Champion. *Ht* 6'3"
Manager Self
24.11.95 Gary Williams W RSC 1 Manchester
20.01.96 Joey Paladino W RSC 1 Mansfield
26.01.96 Vance Idiens W RSC 1 Brighton
11.05.96 Keith Fletcher W CO 1 Bethnal Green
25.06.96 Andy Lambert W CO 1 Mansfield
12.10.96 Eduardo Carranza W CO 2 Milan, Italy
02.11.96 Ricky Sullivan W RSC 2 Garmisch, Germany
25.02.97 Michael Murray W RSC 1 Sheffield
28.06.97 Ricardo Kennedy W RSC 1 Norwich
(Vacant WBO Inter-Continental Heavyweight Title)
11.10.97 Eli Dixon W CO 9 Sheffield
(WBO Inter-Continental Heavyweight Title Defence)
15.11.97 Albert Call W RSC 2 Bristol
06.06.98 Wayne Llewelyn W CO 1 Liverpool
(Elim. British Heavyweight Title)
19.09.98 Biko Botowamungo W RTD 3 Oberhausen, Germany
30.01.99 Julius Francis L RSC 3 Bethnal Green
(British & Commonwealth Heavyweight Title Challenges)
26.06.99 Orlin Norris L RSC 1 Millwall
22.01.00 Jacklord Jacobs L RSC 2 Birmingham
04.10.01 Mal Rice W PTS 4 Finsbury
13.12.01 Derek McCafferty W RSC 3 Leicester Square
27.01.02 Luke Simpkin DREW 4 Streatham
09.05.02 Michael Sprott L RSC 7 Leicester Square
(Vacant WBF European Heavyweight Title)
06.09.02 Derek McCafferty DREW 4 Bethnal Green

15.10.02 Joseph Chingangu W RSC 3 Bethnal Green
01.12.06 Paul King W RSC 6 Birmingham
17.03.07 Roman Suchoterin W PTS 6 Birmingham
01.06.07 Chris Woollas W CO 1 Birmingham
18.04.08 John McDermott L RSC 2 Bethnal Green
(Vacant English Heavyweight Title)
12.09.08 Sam Sexton L PTS 3 Newcastle
07.03.09 David Ingleby W PTS 10 Birmingham
(Vacant Brithish Masters Heavyweight Title)
Career: 28 contests, won 20, drew 2, lost 6

Cello Renda Philip Sharkey

(Marcello) Cello Renda

Peterborough. *Born* Peterborough, 4 June, 1985
Middleweight. Former Undefeated British Masters Middleweight Champion. *Ht* 5'11"
Manager I. Pauly
30.09.04 Mark Ellwood W RSC 2 Hull
04.11.04 Joey Vegas L RSC 3 Piccadilly
12.12.04 Scott Forsyth W RSC 1 Glasgow
21.02.05 Tom Cannon W PTS 6 Peterborough
11.03.05 Ricardo Samms L PTS 4 Doncaster
02.06.05 Michael Banbula DREW 6 Peterborough
16.10.05 Howard Clarke W PTS 4 Peterborough
12.12.05 Robert Burton W CO 1 Peterborough
10.02.06 Conroy McIntosh W RSC 1 Plymouth
30.03.06 Terry Adams W PTS 4 Peterborough
15.06.06 Gatis Skuja W PTS 4 Peterborough
23.06.06 Howard Clarke W PTS 8 Birmingham
08.09.06 Hamed Jamali W RSC 1 Birmingham
26.10.06 George Katsimpas L RSC 2 Wolverhampton
07.12.06 Hussain Osman W RSC 4 Peterborough
23.02.07 Vince Baldassara W CO 3 Birmingham
30.03.07 Ayitey Powers L RSC 2 Peterborough
29.06.07 Prince Arron L PTS 10 Manchester
(Vacant British Masters Middleweight Title)
16.09.07 Steve Ede W RSC 2 Southampton
(Vacant British Masters Middleweight Title)

10.12.07 Ryan Rowlinson W RTD 4 Peterborough
(British Masters Middleweight Title Defence)
08.03.08 Paul Smith L RSC 6 Greenwich
(Vacant English Middleweight Title)
05.10.08 Michael Monaghan W PTS 4 Nottingham
22.11.08 Danny Thornton W RSC 2 Bethnal Green
22.11.08 Max Maxwell W PTS 3 Bethnal Green
22.11.08 Martin Murray L PTS 3 Bethnal Green
Career: 25 contests, won 17, drew 1, lost 7.

Darren Rhodes

Leeds. *Born* Leeds, 16 September, 1975
S.Middleweight. *Ht* 5'11"
Manager Self
18.07.98 Andy Kemp W RSC 1 Sheffield
10.10.98 Perry Ayres W CO 2 Bethnal Green
27.02.99 Gareth Lovell W PTS 4 Oldham
01.05.99 Carlton Williams W RSC 4 Crystal Palace
29.05.99 Sean Pritchard DREW 4 Halifax
09.10.99 Leigh Wicks W PTS 4 Manchester
11.12.99 Leigh Wicks W PTS 4 Liverpool
25.03.00 Leigh Wicks W PTS 4 Liverpool
29.05.00 Dean Ashton W RSC 3 Manchester
08.07.00 Jason Collins DREW 4 Widnes
04.09.00 Jason Collins L PTS 4 Manchester
11.12.00 Paul Wesley W PTS 4 Widnes
17.03.01 Andrew Facey W PTS 4 Manchester
07.07.01 Wayne Elcock L PTS 4 Manchester
24.11.01 Simeon Cover W RSC 5 Wakefield
02.03.02 Andrew Facey L RSC 6 Wakefield
(Vacant Central Area Middleweight Title)
21.05.02 Hussain Osman L PTS 10 Custom House
15.06.02 Harry Butler W PTS 4 Leeds
28.09.02 Martin Thompson W PTS 8 Wakefield
09.11.02 Wayne Pinder L RSC 4 Altrincham
12.04.03 Mihaly Kotai L PTS 10 Bethnal Green
10.05.03 Lee Murtagh W PTS 6 Huddersfield
05.07.03 Darren Bruce W RSC 3 Brentwood
06.09.03 Scott Dixon DREW 6 Huddersfield
04.12.03 Steve Roberts W CO 6 Huddersfield
10.04.04 Michael Jones L RSC 3 Manchester
(Final Elim. British L.Middleweight Title)
12.11.04 Thomas McDonagh L PTS 10 Halifax
(Elim. British L.Middleweight Title)
07.04.05 Wayne Elcock L CO 1 Birmingham
25.09.05 Howard Clarke W PTS 6 Leeds
13.11.05 Ernie Smith W PTS 6 Leeds
23.02.06 Peter Dunn W PTS 6 Leeds
09.09.06 Jozsef Nagy L PTS 12 Szentes, Hungary
(Vacant IBF Inter-Continental S.Middleweight Title)
03.12.06 Robert Burton W PTS 6 Wakefield
15.02.07 Darren McDermott L RSC 5 Dudley
(Elim.British Middleweight Title)
25.03.07 Jason McKay L PTS 6 Dublin
06.05.07 Dean Walker W PTS 4 Leeds
25.08.07 Matthew Macklin L CO 4 Dublin
01.12.07 Kevin Concepcion L RSC 5 Coventry
28.03.08 Kevin Concepcion L CO 4 Barnsley
Career: 39 contests, won 21, drew 3, lost 15

Ryan Rhodes

Sheffield. *Born* Sheffield, 20 November, 1976
WBC International L. Middleweight Champion. Former Undefeated British L.Middleweight Champion. Former Undefeated WBO Inter-Continental Middleweight Champion. Former Undefeated IBF Inter-Continental L.Middleweight Champion.
Ht 5'8½"
Manager F. Warren/D. Coldwell
04.02.95 Lee Crocker W RSC 2 Cardiff
04.03.95 Shamus Casey W CO 1 Livingston
06.05.95 Chris Richards W PTS 6 Shepton Mallet
15.09.95 John Rice W RSC 2 Mansfield
10.11.95 Mark Dawson W PTS 6 Derby
20.01.96 John Duckworth W RSC 2 Mansfield
26.01.96 Martin Jolley W CO 3 Brighton
11.05.96 Martin Jolley W RSC 2 Bethnal Green
25.06.96 Roy Chipperfield W RSC 1 Mansfield
14.09.96 Del Bryan W PTS 6 Sheffield
14.12.96 Paul Jones W RSC 8 Sheffield
(Vacant British L. Middleweight Title)
25.02.97 Peter Waudby W CO 1 Sheffield
(British L. Middleweight Title Defence)
14.03.97 Del Bryan W RSC 7 Reading
(British L. Middleweight Title Defence)
12.04.97 Lindon Scarlett W RSC 1 Sheffield
(Vacant IBF Inter-Continental L. Middleweight Title)
02.08.97 Ed Griffin W RSC 2 Barnsley
(IBF Inter-Continental L. Middleweight Title Defence. Vacant WBO L. Middleweight Title)
11.10.97 Yuri Epifantsev W RSC 2 Sheffield
(Final Elim. WBO Middleweight Title)
13.12.97 Otis Grant L PTS 12 Sheffield
(Vacant WBO Middleweight Title)
18.07.98 Lorant Szabo W RSC 8 Sheffield
(WBO Inter-Continental Middleweight Title Challenge)
28.11.98 Fidel Avendano W RSC 1 Sheffield
(WBO Inter-Continental Middleweight Title Defence)
27.03.99 Peter Mason W RSC 1 Derby
17.07.99 Jason Matthews L CO 2 Doncaster
(Vacant WBO Middleweight Title)
15.01.00 Eddie Haley W RSC 5 Doncaster
16.05.00 Ojay Abrahams W PTS 6 Warrington
21.10.00 Michael Alexander W PTS 6 Wembley
16.12.00 Howard Clarke W PTS 6 Sheffield
21.07.01 Youri Tsarenko W PTS 6 Sheffield
27.10.01 Jason Collins W PTS 4 Manchester
16.03.02 Lee Blundell L RSC 3 Bethnal Green
(Vacant WBF Inter-Continental Middleweight Title)
16.04.03 Paul Wesley W CO 3 Nottingham
25.07.03 Alan Gilbert W RSC 5 Norwich
11.12.03 Peter Jackson W PTS 6 Bethnal Green
12.03.04 Scott Dixon W PTS 8 Nottingham
16.04.04 Tomas da Silva W RSC 4 Bradford
22.04.05 Peter Jackson W PTS 6 Barnsley
03.06.05 Craig Lynch W RSC 3 Manchester
16.07.05 Alan Gilbert W RSC 2 Bolton
25.10.05 Hussain Osman W RTD 4 Preston
01.06.06 Jevgenijs Andrejevs W PTS 8 Barnsley
08.07.06 Gary Lockett L PTS 12 Cardiff
(WBU Middleweight Title Challenge)

03.06.07 Paul Buchanan W RSC 1 Barnsley
13.10.07 Olufemi Moses W RSC 2 Barnsley
05.12.07 Manoocha Salari W RSC 4 Sheffield
18.04.08 Gary Woolcombe W CO 9 Bethnal Green
(British L.Middleweight Title Challenge)
20.09.08 Jamie Coyle W PTS 12 Sheffield
(British L.Middleweight Title Defence)
15.11.08 Vincent Vuma W PTS 12 Greenwich
(WBC International L.Middleweight Title Challenge)
25.04.09 Janos Petrovics W RSC 7 Belfast
Career: 46 contests, won 42, lost 4.

Liam Richards

Melksham. *Born* Swindon, 3 July, 1986
S.Featherweight. *Ht* 5'4"
Manager P. Rowson
26.06.09 Anthony Hanna W PTS 6 Melksham
Career: 1 contest, won 1.

Chris Riley

Middlesbrough. *Born* Middlesbrough, 29 March, 1988
Featherweight. *Ht* 5'8"
Manager P. Fondu
07.10.08 Alexander Litva DREW 6 Minsk, Belarus
06.03.09 Kris Hughes L PTS 6 Glasgow
29.05.09 Youssef Al Hamidi W PTS 4 Stoke
12.06.09 Troy James DREW 4 Liverpool
Career: 4 contests, won 1, drew 2, lost 1.

Ibrar Riyaz   Philip Sharkey

Ibrar Riyaz

Reading. *Born* Blackburn, 27 June, 1985
Featherweight. *Ht* 5'4"
Manager J. Evans
27.09.08 Ian Bailey L PTS 6 Bracknell
12.10.08 Mike Robinson L PTS 4 Leigh
15.11.08 Dezzie O'Connor L PTS 6 Plymouth
13.03.09 Troy James L PTS 4 Widnes
03.04.09 Kevin Maxwell W PTS 4 Bethnal Green
18.04.09 Gavin Prunty W PTS 4 Galway, Ireland

24.05.09 Tyrone Nurse L PTS 4 Shaw
23.06.09 Carl Griffiths W RTD 3 Heathrow
30.06.09 Liam Shinkwin DREW 6 Bethnal Green
Career: 9 contests, won 3, drew 1, lost 5.

Daniel Roberts

Bristol. *Born* Croydon, 14 July, 1987
L.Heavyweight. *Ht* 6' 0"
Manager C. Sanigar
24.10.08 James Tucker W PTS 6 Newport
16.11.08 Sammy Couzens L PTS 4 Southampton
13.03.09 Elvis Dube W CO 6 Newport
05.06.09 Dave Sadler W PTS 6 Newport
Career: 4 contests, won 3, lost 1.

Rhys Roberts

Manchester. *Born* Manchester, 3 June, 1989
S.Bantamweight. *Ht* 5'6"
Manager B. Hughes
30.06.07 Delroy Spencer W PTS 6 Manchester
11.08.07 Delroy Spencer W PTS 6 Liverpool
07.06.08 Shaun Walton W PTS 4 Wigan
04.07.08 Delroy Spencer W PTS 4 Liverpool
19.07.08 Sid Razak W PTS 4 Liverpool
06.12.08 Tahir Majid W RSC 2 Wigan
28.03.09 Jason Thomas W PTS 4 Altrincham
Career: 7 contests, won 7.

Martin Robins

Bristol. *Born* Bristol, 14 July, 1987
L.Middleweight. *Ht* 5' 11"
Manager T. Woodward
14.03.09 Russell Pearce W PTS 4 Bristol
13.06.09 Chris Brophy W PTS 6 Bristol
Career: 2 contests, won 2.

John Robinson

Washington. *Born* Sunderland, 18 March, 1977
L.Heavyweight. *Ht* 5' 10"
Manager Self
25.07.08 Michael Banbula L PTS 6 Houghton le Spring
Career: 1 contest, lost 1.

Luke Robinson   Philip Sharkey

Luke Robinson

Castleford. *Born* Pontefract, 1 May, 1988
L.Middleweight. *Ht* 5' 11"
Manager M. Bateson
27.11.08 Danny Maka W PTS 6 Leeds
Career: 1 contest, won 1.

Mike Robinson   Philip Sharkey

Mike Robinson

Liverpool. *Born* Liverpool, 30 April, 1985
S.Bantamweight. *Ht* 5'5¼"
Manager S. Wood
26.04.08 Delroy Spencer W PTS 6 Wigan
23.05.08 Mike Holloway W PTS 4 Wigan
12.10.08 Ibrar Riyaz W PTS 4 Leigh
29.01.09 Gheorghe Ghiompirica W PTS 4 Holborn
27.02.09 Ross Burkinshaw DREW 4 Barnsley
23.04.09 Ross Burkinshaw L RSC 7 Limehouse
          (Vacant English S.Flyweight Title)
Career: 6 contests, won 4, drew 1, lost 1.

Martin Rogan

Belfast. *Born* Belfast, 1 May, 1971
Former Commonwealth Heavyweight Champion. *Ht* 6'3"
Manager J. Breen
28.10.04 Lee Mountford W RSC 1 Belfast
18.03.05 Billy Bessey W PTS 4 Belfast
04.06.05 Tony Booth W RSC 2 Manchester
20.05.06 Darren Morgan W PTS 4 Belfast
07.10.06 Paul King W PTS 6 Belfast
26.10.06 Jevgenijs Stamburskis W RSC 3 Belfast
13.10.07 Radcliffe Green W RSC 2 Belfast
11.04.08 Alex Ibbs W RSC 2 Bethnal Green
11.04.08 Dave Ferguson W PTS 3 Bethnal Green
11.04.08 David Dolan W PTS 3 Bethnal Green
06.12.08 Audley Harrison W PTS 10 Canning Town
28.02.09 Matt Skelton W RSC 11 Birmingham
          (Commonwealth Heavyweight Title Challenge)
15.05.09 Sam Sexton L RSC 8 Belfast
          (Commonwealth Heavyweight Title Defence)
Career: 13 contests, won 12, lost 1.

Del Rogers

Lutterworth. *Born* Northampton, 20 November, 1987
Featherweight. *Ht* 5' 7"
Manager P. Lynch
11.04.09 Mariusz Bak W PTS 4 Bethnal Green
18.05.09 Shaun Walton W PTS 6 Birmingham
Career: 2 contests, won 2.

Brian Rose

Blackpool. *Born* Birmingham, 2 February, 1985
Middleweight. *Ht* 6'0"
Manager S. Wood
14.12.05 Geraint Harvey W PTS 6 Blackpool
25.02.07 Ernie Smith W PTS 6 Manchester
06.05.07 David Kirk W PTS 6 Altrincham
31.05.07 Tony Randell W PTS 6 Manchester
24.06.07 Justin Barnes W RSC 2 Wigan
22.09.07 Lee Noble W PTS 4 Wigan
08.12.07 Shaun Farmer W RSC 3 Wigan
16.02.08 Manoocha Salari DREW 6 Blackpool
26.04.08 Ernie Smith W PTS 4 Wigan
15.06.08 Kobe Vandekerkhove W PTS 6 St Helens
12.10.08 Geraint Harvey W PTS 4 Leigh
24.01.09 Jon Harrison W RSC 2 Blackpool
02.05.09 Matt Scriven W PTS 4 Sunderland
Career: 13 contests, won 12, drew 1.

Ryan Rowlinson

Rotherham. *Born* Mexborough, 4 June, 1979
S.Middleweight. *Ht* 6'0"
Manager Self
15.12.05 Dave Pearson W PTS 6 Cleethorpes
18.02.06 Craig Lynch DREW 4 Edinburgh
01.06.06 Robert Burton LPTS 4 Barnsley
18.06.06 Craig Bunn L PTS 6 Manchester
08.07.06 Kerry Hope L PTS 4 Cardiff
01.10.06 Ernie Smith W PTS 6 Rotherham
09.10.06 Kevin Concepcion L PTS 6 Bedworth
06.12.06 Tony Randell DREW 6 Rotherham
16.06.07 Nigel Travis L PTS 6 Bolton
19.10.07 Lee Nicholson L PTS 4 Doncaster
10.12.07 Cello Renda L RTD 4 Peterborough
          (British Masters Middleweight Title Challenge)
19.09.08 Jason Smith W RSC 1 Doncaster
Career: 12 contests, won 3, drew 2, lost 7.

Paul Royston

Sheffield. *Born* Rotherham, 16 January, 1985
L.Middleweight. *Ht* 5'10"
Manager D. Coldwell
24.02.07 Stuart Jeffrey L PTS 6 Manchester
26.03.07 Jon Musgrave L PTS 6 Glasgow
15.04.07 Thomas Flynn W RSC 3 Barnsley
06.05.07 Johnny Enigma L PTS 6 Altrincham
03.06.07 Steve Cooper L PTS 6 Barnsley
30.06.07 Willie Thompson L PTS 4 Belfast
08.09.07 Danny Connors L PTS 4 Sutton in Ashfield
15.09.07 Stevie Weir L PTS 6 Paisley
28.09.07 Leigh Hallet W RSC 3 Birmingham

13.10.07 Craig Tomes L PTS 6 Barnsley
25.10.07 Rob Kenney L PTS 6 Wolverhampton
10.11.07 Tommy Heffron L PTS 6 Stalybridge
23.11.07 Lee Edwards L PTS 6 Sheffield
15.12.07 Kris Carslaw L PTS 4 Edinburgh
02.02.08 Sam Webb L PTS 6 Canning Town
16.02.08 Lester Walsh L PTS 6 Leicester
23.02.08 Shaun Farmer L PTS 6 Liverpool
16.03.08 Chris Thompson W PTS 6 Sheffield
30.03.08 Peter Dunn L PTS 4 Colne
18.04.08 Ryan Ashworth L PTS 6 Houghton le
Spring
30.04.08 Rob Kenney L PTS 6 Wolverhampton
17.05.08 Muhsen Nasser L PTS 4 Sheffield
30.05.08 Nasser Al Harbi L PTS 6 Birmingham
07.06.08 Joe McNally L PTS 4 Wigan
20.06.08 Jamie Ball L PTS 4 Wolverhampton
22.09.08 Chris Black L PTS 6 Glasgow
03.10.08 Duane Parker L PTS 6 Burton
10.10.08 Wayne Reed L PTS 6 Sheffield
22.11.08 Jack Arnfield L PTS 4 Blackpool
04.12.08 Shaun Farmer L PTS 6 Sunderland
01.02.09 Keiron Gray L PTS 6 Birmingham
21.02.09 Harry Matthews L PTS 4 Hull
06.03.09 Alex Matvienko L PTS 6 Wigan
14.03.09 Willie Bilan W PTS 6 Aberdeen
23.04.09 Wayne Alwan-Arab L PTS 6 Mayfair
23.05.09 Omar Gumati L PTS 6 Queensferry
31.05.09 Ollie Newham L PTS 6 Burton
Career: 37 contests, won 4, lost 33.

Sergei Rozhakmens

Sutton in Ashfield. *Born* Riga, Latvia, 6
May, 1979
Lightweight. *Ht* 5'7"
Manager M. Scriven
13.11.02 Sergei Lazarenko W RSC 1 Tallin,
Estonia
22.02.03 Leonti Voronchuk L RSC 3 Narva,
Estonia
20.02.06 Jimmy Gilhaney L PTS 6 Glasgow
06.05.06 Jamie McIlroy L PTS 6 Irvine
18.06.06 Abdul Rashid L PTS 6 Manchester
15.09.06 Andy Davis L RSC 4 Newport
10.11.06 Shaun Walton L PTS 6 Telford
20.11.06 Brian Murphy L PTS 6 Glasgow
30.11.06 Neil Marston L PTS 6 Piccadilly
01.02.07 Kim Poulsen L RSC 5 Piccadilly
01.04.07 Shaun Walton DREW 6 Shrewsbury
14.04.07 Sean Hughes L PTS 6 Wakefield
29.04.07 Craig Johnson L PTS 6 Birmingham
06.05.07 Davey Watson L PTS 6 Darlington
01.06.07 Sid Razak W PTS 6 Birmingham
09.06.07 James McElvaney L PTS 6
Middlesbrough
21.06.07 Carl Griffiths L PTS 6 Peterborough
30.06.07 Amir Unsworth L PTS 6 Manchester
14.07.07 Vinny Mitchell L RSC 3 Greenwich
14.09.07 John Donnelly L PTS 4 Kirkcaldy
23.09.07 Mark Dawes L PTS 6 Hartlepool
05.10.07 Sean Hughes L PTS 6 Sunderland
12.10.07 Jon Kays L RSC 4 Leeds
15.11.07 Craig O'Neile L RSC 2 Leeds
23.02.08 Johnny Greaves L RSC 1 Newark
05.10.08 Steve Jevons L PTS 4 Nottingham
Career: 26 contests, won 2, drew 1, lost 23.

Jason Rushton

Doncaster. *Born* Doncaster, 15 February,
1983
Former Central Area L.Middleweight
Champion. *Ht* 5'10"
Manager Self
27.10.01 Ram Singh W PTS 6 Manchester
09.02.02 Brian Gifford W RSC 1 Manchester
01.06.02 Tony Smith W PTS 4 Manchester
08.11.02 Gary Hadwin W CO 4 Doncaster
21.02.03 Wayne Shepherd W PTS 6 Doncaster
05.09.03 Harry Butler W PTS 4 Doncaster
27.09.03 Jimi Hendricks W PTS 4 Manchester
06.03.04 Peter Dunn W PTS 6 Renfrew
06.05.04 Peter Dunn W PTS 4 Barnsley
03.09.04 Ernie Smith W PTS 4 Doncaster
29.10.04 Brian Coleman W PTS 6 Doncaster
04.02.05 Howard Clarke W PTS 4 Doncaster
11.03.05 Lee Armstrong W PTS 10 Doncaster
*(Vacant Central Area L.Middleweight
Title)*
20.05.05 Lee Murtagh L PTS 10 Doncaster
*(Central Area L.Middleweight Title
Defence)*
02.12.05 Joe Mitchell W PTS 6 Doncaster
03.03.06 Darren Gethin L PTS 6 Doncaster
21.04.06 Peter Dunn W PTS 6 Doncaster
09.06.06 Mark Phillips W PTS 6 Doncaster
13.10.06 Lee Noble L PTS 6 Doncaster
23.02.07 Davey Jones W CO 7 Doncaster
*(Vacant Central Area L.Middleweight
Title)*
21.09.07 Gary Woolcombe L RSC 7 Bethnal
Green
28.03.08 Danny Reynolds L RSC 1 Barnsley
*(Central Area L.Middleweight Title
Defence)*
13.06.08 Jay Morris W PTS 6 Portsmouth
12.10.08 Thomas McDonagh L PTS 6 Leigh
14.11.08 Michael Jennings L PTS 8 Glasgow
12.12.08 Matthew Hall L RSC 6 Widnes
13.02.09 Jamie Cox L RSC 1 Swindon
Career: 27 contests, won 18, lost 9.

Jason Rushton   Philip Sharkey

Stephen Russell

Paisley. *Born* Paisley, 29 December, 1987
Featherweight. *Ht* 5'6"
Manager Self
27.10.06 Shaun Doherty W PTS 6 Glasgow
26.01.07 Abdul Mougharbel W PTS 6 Glasgow
05.05.07 Delroy Spencer W PTS 4 Glasgow
15.09.07 Robert Bunford W PTS 6 Paisley
29.03.08 Shaun Walton W PTS 4 Glasgow
18.10.08 Sumaila Badu W PTS 6 Paisley
Career: 6 contests, won 6.

Dave Ryan   Philip Sharkey

Dave Ryan

Derby. *Born* Derby, 6 May, 1988
Midlands Area Welterweight Champion.
Ht 5'10"
Manager C. Mitchell
31.03.07 Deniss Sirjatovs W PTS 6 Derby
19.05.07 Leonard Lothian W PTS 6 Nottingham
16.09.07 Albi Hunt W RSC 2 Derby
03.11.07 Baz Carey W PTS 6 Derby
30.11.07 Scott Woolford L PTS 4 Newham
10.05.08 Carl Allen W PTS 4 Nottingham
22.06.08 Carl Allen W PTS 8 Derby
16.11.08 Jason Nesbitt W PTS 4 Derby
27.02.09 Jamie Way W PTS 4 Barnsley
10.05.09 Scott Evans W RSC 2 Derby
*(Vacant Midlands Area Welterweight
Title)*
Career: 10 contests, won 9, lost 1.

Joel Ryan

Walsall. *Born* Walsall, 31 March, 1990
L.Middleweight. *Ht* 5'9"
Manager E. Johnson
27.02.09 Arnold Lydekaitis W PTS 4
Wolverhampton
Career: 1 contest, won 1.

Dave Sadler

Leeds. *Born* Leeds, 14 December, 1980
S.Middleweight. *Ht* 5' 11"
Manager M. Marsden
06.05.07 Jeff Hamilton L PTS 6 Leeds
05.06.09 Daniel Roberts L PTS 6 Newport
26.06.09 Nick Blackwell L RSC 3 Melksham
Career: 3 contests, lost 3.

(Saheed) Silence Saheed (Salawu)

Canning Town. *Born* Ibadan, Nigeria, 1
January, 1978
L.Welterweight. *Ht* 5'6"
Manager D. Lutaaya
28.03.03 Martin Hardcastle W PTS 4 Millwall
10.04.03 Ceri Hall DREW 4 Clydach
27.05.03 Francis Barrett W RSC 1 Dagenham
11.10.03 Wayne Wheeler W RSC 1 Portsmouth
15.11.03 Gary Greenwood W RTD 1 Coventry
21.11.03 Jaz Virdee W RSC 2 Millwall
01.05.04 Alan Temple L DIS 8 Gravesend
    *(Vacant British Masters Lightweight
    Title)*
17.09.04 Scott Lawton L PTS 6 Sheffield
24.09.04 James Gorman W PTS 6 Millwall
09.10.04 Jonathan Thaxton L PTS 6 Norwich
22.10.04 Nigel Wright L PTS 8 Edinburgh
10.04.05 Lenny Daws L PTS 6 Brentwood
01.07.05 Gareth Couch L PTS 4 Fulham
30.09.05 Karl David W PTS 6 Carmarthen
21.10.05 Ted Bami L PTS 6 Bethnal Green
17.11.05 Andrew Murray L PTS 4 Piccadilly
24.11.05 Ceri Hall L PTS 6 Clydach
02.02.06 Sam Rukundo L PTS 10 Holborn
    *(Vacant British Masters Lightweight
    Title)*
18.02.06 Lee McAllister L PTS 4 Edinburgh
04.03.06 David Barnes L PTS 4 Manchester
23.03.06 Imad Khamis W RSC 5 The Strand
02.04.06 Leo O'Reilly DREW 6 Bethnal Green
10.07.06 Gary O'Connor L PTS 6 Manchester
15.09.06 John O'Donnell L PTS 6 Muswell Hill
11.11.06 Stephen Haughian L PTS 6 Dublin
01.12.06 Anthony Maynard L PTS 6 Birmingham
09.12.06 Paul McCloskey L PTS 4 Canning Town
23.02.07 Olufemi Moses L PTS 4 Manchester
30.03.07 Michael Lomax DREW 6 Crawley
03.11.07 Barrie Jones L PTS 4 Cardiff
09.12.07 Craig Docherty L PTS 6 Glasgow
22.02.08 Ricky Burns L RSC 3 Motherwell
15.06.08 Mark McCullough W PTS 4 Bethnal
    Green
15.11.08 John Watson L PTS 4 Greenwich
07.02.09 Kevin O'Hara L RSC 3 Craigavon
Career: 35 contests, won 9, drew 3, lost 23.

Tony Salam

Romford. *Born* Nigeria, 24 September,
1983
Southern Area S. Middleweight Champion.
Ht 6'0"
Manager D. Powell

03.11.06 Csaba Andras W RSC 2 Barnsley
26.01.07 Paul David W PTS 4 Dagenham
09.03.07 Nicki Taylor W RSC 1 Dagenham
27.04.07 John Anthony W PTS 4 Wembley
15.06.07 Nick Okoth W PTS 4 Crystal Palace
19.10.07 Ovill McKenzie W PTS 6 Doncaster
30.11.07 Carl Wild W RTD 4 Newham
01.02.08 Courtney Fry L CO 6 Bethnal Green
30.01.09 Richard Horton W RSC 4 Bethnal Green
    *(Vacant Southern Area S.Middleweight
    Title)*
Career: 9 contests, won 8, lost 1.

Tony Salam   Philip Sharkey

Manoocha Salari

Worksop. *Born* Iran, 25 May, 1974
Midlands Area L.Middleweight Champion.
Ht 5'9½"
Manager Self
12.11.05 Danny Johnston W RSC 5 Stoke
25.11.05 Paul McInnes W PTS 6 Walsall
12.12.05 Simon Sherrington DREW 6
    Birmingham
28.01.06 Martin Concepcion W RSC 2
    Nottingham
26.02.06 Gokhan Kazaz DREW 4 Dagenham
13.05.06 Geard Ajetovic L RSC 4 Sheffield
18.11.06 Kerry Hope L RSC 2 Newport
03.03.07 Matt Galer W RSC 8 Burton
    *(Midlands Area L.Middleweight Title
    Challenge)*
13.04.07 Mark Thompson L RSC 1 Altrincham
23.11.07 Stuart Brookes L PTS 6 Rotherham
05.12.07 Ryan Rhodes L RSC 5 Sheffield
16.02.08 Brian Rose DREW 6 Blackpool
05.04.08 Denton Vassell L PTS 4 Bolton
22.06.08 Matthew Hainy L PTS 6 Derby
12.09.08 Jezz Wilson L RSC 2 Sheffield
25.10.08 Gavin Smith L PTS 6 St Helier
Career: 16 contests, won 4, drew 3, lost 9.

Paul Samuels

Newport. *Born* Newport, 23 March, 1973
S. Middleweight. Former Undefeated IBF
Inter-Continental & Welsh L. Middleweight
Champion. *Ht* 6' 0"
Manager Self

11.11.95 Wayne Windle W RSC 2 Halifax
13.02.96 Jon Harrison W RSC 1 Cardiff
05.03.96 Tom Welsh W RSC 3 Bethnal Green
13.03.96 Brian Coleman W PTS 6 Wembley
15.05.96 Gary Hiscox W RSC 3 Cardiff
12.11.96 Mark Ramsey W RSC 4 Dudley
21.06.97 Howard Clarke W PTS 8 Cardiff
15.11.97 Justin Simmons W CO 1 Bristol
24.01.98 Kasi Kaihau W CO 3 Cardiff
25.04.98 Del Bryan W PTS 8 Cardiff
05.09.98 Spencer McCracken W PTS 8 Telford
05.12.98 Craig Winter W CO 2 Bristol
    (Vacant Welsh L. Middleweight Title)
27.03.99 Pedro Carragher W RSC 3 Derby
05.06.99 Eric Holland W RSC 9 Cardiff
    *(Vacant IBF Inter-Continental
    L.Middleweight Title)*
23.10.99 Ojay Abrahams W PTS 8 Telford
19.02.00 Wayne Alexander L RSC 3 Dagenham
    (Vacant British L.Middleweight Title)
23.01.01 Roberto Dellapenna DREW 6 Crawley
27.01.02 Howard Clarke W PTS 8 Streatham
29.06.02 Richard Williams T DRAW 3 Brentwood
    (IBO L.Middleweight Title Challenge)
07.12.02 Richard Williams L RSC 10 Brentwood
    (IBO L.Middleweight Title Challenge)
25.01.03 Howard Clarke W PTS 6 Bridgend
08.12.06 Darren Barker L CO 1 Dagenham
12.07.08 Mark Nilsen W RSC 1 Newport
22.11.08 Danny Butler L PTS 3 Bethnal Green
30.11.08 Patrick J. Maxwell L PTS 6 Rotherham
21.02.09 Jamie Ambler W PTS 4 Merthyr Tydfil
28.03.09 George Groves L RSC 1 Liverpool
Career: 27 contests, won 19, drew 2, lost 6.

Scott Sandmann

Manchester. *Born* London, 4 October, 1981
L.Welterweight. *Ht* 5'10¼"
Manager J. Gallagher
28.09.07 Craig Tomes W PTS 6 Preston
12.10.07 Leonard Lothian W PTS 4 Peterlee
23.11.07 Chris Mullen L PTS 6 Houghton le
    Spring
05.06.08 Adil Anwar L RSC 1 Leeds
06.12.08 Chris Goodwin DREW 6 Wigan
Career: 5 contests, won 2, drew 1, lost 2.

Laura Saperstein

Tottenham. *Born* Australia, 29 August, 1971
Lightweight. *Ht* 5'6¼"
Manager C. Hall
18.11.07 Borislava Goranova W PTS 4 Tooting
01.02.08 Olga Varchenko W PTS 4 Bethnal
    Green
18.04.08 Kristine Shergold W PTS 4 Bethnal
    Green
07.08.08 Nongmawe Sitphuton W RSC 1 Phuket,
    Thailand
30.08.08 Ploysuay Sakrungruang W PTS 4
    Bangkok, Thailand
15.09.08 Nong Tak Sakrungruang W PTS 4
    Phuket, Thailand
22.03.09 Galina Gumliiska W PTS 4 Bethnal
    Green
Career: 7 contests, won 7.

Billy Joe Saunders

Welwyn Garden City. *Born* Welwyn Garden City, 30 August, 1989
S.Middleweight. *Ht* 5' 10"
Manager F. Warren
28.02.09 Attila Molnar W RSC 2 Birmingham
15.05.09 Ronny Gabel W RSC 2 Belfast
Career: 2 contests, won 2.

Davey Savage

Glasgow. *Born* Glasgow, 2 July, 1986
British Masters Featherweight Champion. *Ht* 5'9¼"
Manager T. Gilmour
08.10.07 Delroy Spencer W PTS 6 Glasgow
24.11.07 Shaun Walton W PTS 6 Clydebank
21.01.08 Shaun Walton W PTS 6 Glasgow
29.02.08 Tony McQuade W PTS 4 Glasgow
06.06.08 Mike Holloway W RSC 4 Glasgow
10.10.08 Shaun Walton W PTS 6 Motherwell
28.11.08 Billy Bell W RSC 1 Glasgow
16.03.09 Sid Razak W PTS 10 Glasgow
  (Vacant British Masters Featherweight Title)
12.06.09 Jason Thomas W PTS 8 Clydebank
Career: 9 contests, won 9.

Steve Saville

Wolverhampton. *Born* Wolverhampton, 29 September, 1976
Midlands Area Lightweight Champion. *Ht* 5'4¼"
Manager E. Johnson
08.06.98 Simon Chambers W RSC 2 Birmingham
07.10.98 Dave Hinds W PTS 6 Stoke
26.11.98 Dave Hinds W PTS 6 Edgbaston
14.12.98 Woody Greenaway L PTS 6 Birmingham
27.01.99 Darren Woodley W PTS 6 Stoke
23.03.99 Benny Jones W PTS 6 Wolverhampton
14.06.99 Trevor Tacy L PTS 8 Birmingham
12.10.99 Gary Flear W RSC 6 Wolverhampton
20.10.99 Arv Mittoo W PTS 8 Stoke
08.02.00 Marc Smith W PTS 6 Wolverhampton
13.03.00 Dave Gibson W RSC 6 Birmingham
09.10.00 David Kirk L PTS 8 Birmingham
06.11.00 Woody Greenaway W CO 5 Wolverhampton
28.11.00 Danny Connelly W PTS 8 Brierley Hill
11.12.00 Keith Jones W PTS 8 Birmingham
01.04.01 Gavin Down L RSC 3 Alfreton
  (Vacant Midlands Area L.Welterweight Title)
13.07.02 Wayne Wheeler W CO 2 Wolverhampton
07.10.02 Gareth Wiltshaw W RSC 3 Birmingham
09.12.02 Keith Jones W PTS 8 Birmingham
20.06.08 Baz Carey W PTS 4 Wolverhampton
11.07.08 Mark Bett W RSC 4 Wigan
12.09.08 Chris Long W PTS 4 Wolverhampton
09.11.08 Baz Carey W RSC 7 Wolverhampton
  (Vacant Midlands Area Lightweight Title)
24.03.09 Gary McArthur L PTS 3 Glasgow
Career: 24 contests, won 19, lost 5.

Bobby Scott (Hayes-Scott)

Thamesmead. *Born* Lambeth, 4 January, 1976
Cruiserweight. *Ht* 6' 0"
Manager F. Barrett
18.02.01 Kevin Burton W RSC 1 Southwark
07.04.01 Paul Bonson W PTS 4 Wembley
03.06.01 Radcliffe Green L CO 4 Southwark
09.09.01 Adam Cale W RSC 1 Southwark
06.12.08 Danny Couzens DREW 4 Bethnal Green
22.03.09 Nick Okoth L PTS 4 Bethnal Green
10.04.09 Leon Williams L RSC 1 Cheltenham
Career: 7 contests, won 3, drew 1, lost 3.

Bobby Scott   Philip Sharkey

Bruce Scott

Hackney. *Born* Jamaica, 16 August, 1969
Cruiserweight. Former Undefeated British, Commonwealth, WBU & Southern Area Cruiserweight Champion. *Ht* 5' 9"
Manager J. Rooney
25.04.91 Mark Bowen L PTS 6 Mayfair
16.09.91 Randy B Powell W RSC 5 Mayfair
21.11.91 Steve Osborne W PTS 6 Burton
27.04.92 John Kaighin W CO 4 Mayfair
07.09.92 Lee Prudden W PTS 6 Bethnal Green
03.12.92 Mark Pain W RSC 5 Lewisham
15.02.93 Paul McCarthy W PTS 6 Mayfair
22.04.93 Sean O'Phoenix W RSC 3 Mayfair
14.06.93 John Oxenham W RSC 1 Bayswater
04.10.93 Simon McDougall W PTS 6 Mayfair
16.12.93 Bobby Mack W RSC 4 Newport
05.04.94 Steve Osborne W RSC 5 Bethnal Green
17.10.94 Bobbie Joe Edwards W PTS 8 Mayfair
09.12.94 John Keeton W CO 2 Bethnal Green
19.04.95 Nigel Rafferty W RSC 2 Bethnal Green
19.05.95 Cordwell Hylton W RSC 1 Southwark
11.11.95 Tony Booth W RSC 3 Halifax
05.03.96 Nick Manners W RSC 5 Bethnal Green
13.07.96 Tony Booth W PTS 8 Bethnal Green
30.11.96 Nicky Piper L RSC 7 Tylorstown
  (Commonwealth L.Heavyweight Title Challenge)
15.05.97 Grant Briggs W RSC 2 Reading
04.10.97 Tony Booth L PTS 8 Muswell Hill

21.04.98 Dominic Negus W RSC 9 Picketts Lock
  (Southern Area Cruiserweight Title Challenge)
28.11.98 Darren Corbett W RSC 10 Belfast
  (Commonwealth Cruiserweight Title Challenge. Vacant British Cruiserweight Title)
15.05.99 Johnny Nelson L PTS 12 Sheffield
  (WBO Cruiserweight Title Challenge)
17.07.99 Juan Carlos Gomez L RSC 6 Düsseldorf, Germany
  (WBC Cruiserweight Title Challenge)
08.04.00 Chris Woollas W RSC 2 YBethnal Green
24.06.00 Adam Watt L RSC 4 Glasgow
  (Vacant Commonwealth Cruiserweight Title)
16.12.00 John Keeton W CO 6 Sheffield
  (Vacant British Cruiserweight Title)
10.03.01 Garry Delaney W RSC 3 Bethnal Green
  (British Cruiserweight Title Defence. Vacant Commonwealth Cruiserweight Title)
28.07.01 Rene Janvier W PTS 12 Wembley
28.06.03 Enzo Maccarinelli L RSC 4 Cardiff
  (Vacant WBU Cruiserweight Title)
07.02.04 Radcliffe Green W PTS 6 Bethnal Green
17.12.04 Mark Hobson L PTS 12 Huddersfield
  (British & Commonwealth Cruiserweight Title Challenges)
10.12.05 Paul Bonson W PTS 4 Canning Town
11.03.06 Hastings Rasani L PTS 8 Newport
19.05.09 John Keeton L PTS 3 Kensington
Career: 37 contests, won 27, lost 10.

Bruce Scott   Philip Sharkey

Ryan Scott

Wishaw. *Born* Lanark, 8 November, 1983
Welterweight. *Ht* 5' 10"
Manager L. Murphy
14.11.08 Mark Bett W RSC 1 Glasgow
Career: 1 contest, won 1.

Lindsay Scragg

Wolverhampton. *Born* Wolverhampton, 19 April, 1979
Global Boxing Council Female S.Featherweight Champion. *Ht* 5'3¼"
Manager E. Johnson

15.02.07 Valerie Rangeard W RSC 2 Dudley
28.06.07 Yarkor Chavez Annan W PTS 4 Dudley
25.10.07 Olga Michenko W RSC 2
Wolverhampton
28.02.08 Yarkor Chavez Annan W RSC 6
Wolverhampton
30.04.08 Viktoria Oleynik W PTS 6
Wolverhampton
20.06.08 Galina Gumliiska W PTS 4
Wolverhampton
12.09.08 Galina Gumliiska W PTS 6
Wolverhampton
07.11.08 Jelena Mrdjenovich L PTS 10
Edmonton, Canada
(Vacant WBC female S.Featherweight Title)
27.02.09 Lana Cooper W PTS 6 Wolverhampton
12.06.09 Kristine Shergold W PTS 10
Wolverhampton
(Vacant Global Boxing Council Female S.Featherweight Title)
Career: 10 contests, won 9, lost 1.

Matt Scriven

Nottingham. *Born* Nottingham, 1
September, 1973
Middleweight. Former Undefeated
Midlands Area L.Middleweight Champion.
Former British Masters L.Middleweight
Champion. *Ht* 5'10"
Manager Self
26.11.97 Shamus Casey W PTS 6 Stoke
08.12.97 Shane Thomas W PTS 6 Bradford
20.03.98 C. J. Jackson L PTS 6 Ilkeston
15.05.98 Lee Bird W RSC 5 Nottingham
08.10.98 Stevie McCready L RTD 3 Sunderland
01.04.99 Adrian Houldey W PTS 6 Birmingham
25.04.99 Danny Thornton L RSC 4 Leeds
27.06.99 Shane Junior L RSC 2 Alfreton
11.09.99 David Arundel L RTD 1 Sheffield
20.03.00 James Docherty L PTS 8 Glasgow
27.03.00 Matt Mowatt L PTS 4 Barnsley
09.04.00 David Matthews W PTS 6 Alfreton
06.06.00 Jackie Townsley L RSC 3 Motherwell
04.11.00 Brett James L RTD 1 Bethnal Green
04.02.01 Mark Paxford L PTS 6 Queensferry
26.02.01 Pedro Thompson W RTD 1 Nottingham
12.03.01 Ernie Smith W PTS 6 Birmingham
20.03.01 James Docherty L RSC 1 Glasgow
21.05.01 Christian Brady L RSC 5 Birmingham
(Vacant Midlands Area Welterweight Title)
21.10.01 Neil Bonner NC 1 Glasgow
04.03.02 Danny Parkinson L PTS 6 Bradford
22.04.02 Gary Porter L PTS 6 Glasgow
28.05.02 Peter Dunn W PTS 8 Leeds
14.09.02 Ernie Smith W PTS 6 Newark
29.09.02 James Lee L RTD 4 Shrewsbury
30.11.02 Davey Jones L PTS 6 Newark
16.03.03 Lee Williamson W PTS 10 Nottingham
(Vacant Midlands Area & British Masters L. Middleweight Titles)
08.06.03 Wayne Shepherd W PTS 10 Nottingham
(British Masters L.Middleweight Title Defence)
15.09.03 Lee Murtagh L DIS 9 Leeds
(British Masters L.Middleweight Title Defence)
12.03.04 David Walker L RSC 3 Nottingham

12.06.04 Matthew Hatton L RSC 4 Manchester
18.09.04 Robert Lloyd-Taylor L RTD 4 Newark
28.01.05 Colin McNeil L PTS 4 Renfrew
06.03.05 Mark Wall W PTS 4 Mansfield
29.04.05 Gary Woolcombe L RSC 4 Southwark
04.06.05 Matthew Hall L RSC 2 Manchester
20.01.06 John O'Donnell L RSC 4 Bethnal Green
04.03.06 Kerry Hope L PTS 4 Manchester
04.11.06 Peter Dunn W PTS 6 Mansfield
23.02.07 James McKinley L PTS 6 Birmingham
17.03.07 Dee Mitchell L RSC 2 Birmingham
29.04.07 Max Maxwell L PTS 4 Birmingham
11.05.07 Shaun Farmer L PTS 6 Sunderland
18.05.07 George Hillyard L PTS 4 Canning Town
31.05.07 Dave Wakefield L PTS 6 Manchester
24.06.07 Martin Marshall L PTS 6 Sunderland
15.07.07 Craig Denton L PTS 6 Hartlepool
15.02.08 Lee Edwards L PTS 6 Sheffield
22.02.08 Paul Burns L PTS 6 Motherwell
21.06.08 Joe Selkirk L PTS 4 Birmingham
14.09.08 Nasser Al Harbi L PTS 4 Birmingham
02.10.08 Wayne Alwan-Arab L PTS 5 Piccadilly
18.10.08 Willie Limond L PTS 8 Paisley
01.11.08 Gary McMillan L PTS 6 Glasgow
09.11.08 Keiron Gray L PTS 4 Wolverhampton
06.12.08 Ashley Theophane L PTS 6 Bethnal
Green
13.12.08 Steve O'Meara L PTS 4 Brentwood
30.01.09 Denton Vassell L RSC 3 Bethnal Green
28.02.09 Thomas Costello L PTS 4 Birmingham
14.03.09 Brock Cato L PTS 6 Bristol
29.03.09 Curtis Woodhouse L PTS 6 Sheffield
24.04.09 Jamie Ball L PTS 4 Wolverhampton
02.05.09 Brian Rose L PTS 4 Sunderland
15.05.09 Ciaran Healy L PTS 4 Belfast
13.06.09 Danny Butler L PTS 4 Bristol
25.06.09 Tony Randell L PTS 4 Mayfair
Career: 66 contests, won 13, lost 52, no contest 1.

Matt Scriven   Philip Sharkey

Nick Seager

Snodland. *Born* Chatham, 23 September,
1983
S.Bantamweight. *Ht* 5' 6"
Manager M. Stone
05.12.08 Nick MacDonald L RSC 1 Dagenham
16.01.09 Stuart Hall L RSC 2 Middlesbrough

16.02.09 Paul McElhinney L PTS 6 Glasgow
23.05.09 Steve Barnes L RSC 1 Watford
Career: 4 contests, lost 4.

Matt Seawright

Tamworth. *Born* Bathgate, 8 February, 1978
Welterweight. *Ht* 5'7"
Manager E. Johnson
03.03.07 Jack Perry L RSC 2 Burton
03.05.07 Adam Kelly L PTS 4 Sheffield
29.09.07 Adam Kelly L PTS 4 Sheffield
19.10.07 Charles Paul King L PTS 6 Motherwell
17.11.07 Jimmy Doherty L PTS 4 Stoke
28.02.08 Martin Gordon W PTS 4
Wolverhampton
16.03.08 Curtis Woodhouse L RTD 3 Sheffield
09.06.08 Mark Bett L RSC 5 Glasgow
25.07.08 Chris Mullen L RTD 2 Houghton le
Spring
26.09.08 Kevin McCauley L PTS 4
Wolverhampton
10.10.08 Willie Bilan L PTS 6 Motherwell
09.11.08 Martin Gordon W PTS 4 Wolverhampton
16.11.08 Ali Shah L RSC 3 Shaw
21.12.08 Eddie Doyle L PTS 6 Motherwell
17.01.09 Scott Evans L PTS 4 Wigan
14.02.09 Leonard Lothian L PTS 4 St Helier
27.02.09 Danny Johnston L PTS 4
Wolverhampton
08.03.09 Masoor Walli W PTS 4 Sheffield
17.04.09 Adam Cummings L PTS 6 Bristol
29.05.09 Myles Holder L PTS 4 Dudley
13.06.09 Phil Fury L RSC 2 Wigan
Career: 21 contests, won 3, lost 18.

Arturs Selaves

Coventry. *Born* Latvia, 12 February, 1988
L.Middleweight. *Ht* 5' 8"
Manager C. Singh
06.02.09 Jamie Ball L RSC 3 Birmingham
Career: 1 contest, lost 1.

Lee Selby

Barry. *Born* Cardiff, 14 January, 1987
S.Featherweight. *Ht* 5' 5"
Manager C. Sanigar
12.07.08 Sid Razak W PTS 6 Newport
24.10.08 Pete Buckley W PTS 6 Newport
27.02.09 Craig Johnson W PTS 4 Barnsley
13.03.09 Johnny Greaves W PTS 6 Newport
29.05.09 Samir Mouneimne L PTS 4 Stoke
Career: 5 contests, won 4, lost 1.

Joe Selkirk

Liverpool. *Born* Liverpool, 2 August, 1985
Middleweight. *Ht* 6'0¾"
Manager F. Warren
21.06.08 Matt Scriven W PTS 4 Birmingham
10.10.08 Ernie Smith W PTS 4 Liverpool
Career: 2 contests, won 2.

Pavels Senkovs

Mansfield. *Born* Latvia, 18 August, 1989
Featherweight. *Ht* 5' 8"
Manager M. Scriven
14.03.09 Chris Male L PTS 4 Birmingham
28.03.09 Adrian Gonzalez L PTS 4 Altrincham

17.04.09 Jamie Speight L PTS 4 Bristol
23.05.09 Paul Economides L PTS 6 Queensferry
13.06.09 Pete Leworthy W RSC 1 Bristol
28.06.09 Blaine Courtney L PTS 6 Luton
Career: 6 contests, won 1, lost 5.

Pavels Senkovs   Philip Sharkey

Ashley Sexton

Cheshunt. *Born* London, 21 October, 1987
Flyweight. *Ht* 5' 5"
Manager M. Helliet
01.08.08 David Keogan W PTS 4 Watford
17.10.08 Delroy Spencer W PTS 4 Bethnal Green
06.12.08 Levan Garibashvili W RSC 3 Bethnal
    Green
23.01.09 Fikret Remziev W RSC 2 Stoke
20.03.09 Robert Nelson W RSC 6 Newham
29.05.09 Delroy Spencer W PTS 6 Stoke
30.06.09 Kemal Plavci W PTS 6 Bethnal Green
Career: 7 contests, won 7.

Sam Sexton

Norwich. *Born* Norwich, 18 July, 1984
Commonwealth Heavyweight Champion.
Former Undefeated Southern Area
Heavyweight Champion. *Ht* 6'2"
Manager G. Everett
03.09.05 Paul Bonson W PTS 6 Norwich
11.12.05 Jason Callum W PTS 6 Norwich
12.05.06 Istvan Kecskes W PTS 4 Bethnal Green
15.10.06 Lee Mountford W RSC 2 Norwich
16.03.07 Paul King W PTS 6 Norwich
13.10.07 Luke Simpkin W RSC 5 Bethnal Green
12.01.08 Darren Morgan W PTS 6 Bethnal
    Green
14.06.08 Derek Chisora L RSC 6 Bethnal Green
12.09.08 Pele Reid W PTS 3 Newcastle
12.09.08 Luke Simpkin W PTS 3 Newcastle
12.09.08 Chris Burton W RSC 3 Newcastle
21.11.08 Colin Kenna W RSC 6 Bethnal Green
    (Vacant Southern Area Heavyweight
    Title)
15.05.09 Martin Rogan W RSC 8 Belfast
    (Commonwealth Heavyweight Title
    Challenge)
Career: 13 contests, won 12, lost 1.

Ali Shah

Sheffield. *Born* Blackburn, 16 October,
1986
Welterweight. *Ht* 6'2¼"
Manager J. Ingle
20.04.08 Amir Nadi W PTS 4 Shaw
1.07.08 Pete Buckley W PTS 4 Wigan
16.11.08 Matt Seawright W RSC 3 Shaw
17.01.09 Karl Taylor W PTS 4 Wigan
Career: 4 contests, won 4.

Sam Sheedy

Sheffield. *Born* Sheffield, 2 May, 1988
L.Middleweight. *Ht* 5' 11"
Manager G. Rhodes
12.09.08 Russell Pearce W RTD 2 Sheffield
08.03.09 Martyn King W PTS 6 Sheffield
24.04.09 Geraint Harvey W PTS 6 Sheffield
Career: 3 contests, won 3.

Keith Sheen

Birmingham. *Born* Moseley, 26 July, 1979
Welterweight. *Ht* 5' 8"
Manager E. Johnson
14.09.08 Danny Coyle W PTS 6 Birmingham
27.02.09 Karl Taylor W PTS 6 Wolverhampton
Career: 2 contests, won 2.

Gary Sheil

Chester. *Born* Chester, 29 June, 1983
Bantamweight. *Ht* 5'2¾"
Manager Self
03.03.06 Jamie McDonnell L PTS 6 Doncaster
23.04.06 Delroy Spencer L PTS 6 Chester
06.05.06 Chris Edwards L PTS 6 Stoke
03.03.07 Usman Ahmed L PTS 6 Alfreton
21.04.07 Scott Quigg L PTS 6 Manchester
16.09.07 Usman Ahmed L PTS 6 Derby
06.10.07 Don Broadhurst L PTS 6 Nottingham
24.01.09 Kieran Farrell L RSC 3 Blackpool
Career: 8 contests, lost 8.

Kristine Shergold   Philip Sharkey

Kristine Shergold

Paignton. *Born* Torquay, 2 March, 1981
S.Featherweight. *Ht* 5'1¼"
Manager E. Johnson
18.04.08 Laura Saperstein L PTS 4 Bethnal
    Green
10.05.09 Suzanne Hemsley L PTS 6 Derby
12.06.09 Lyndsay Scragg L PTS 10
    Wolverhampton
    (Vacant Global Boxing Council Female
    S. Featherweight Title)
26.06.09 Lana Cooper W PTS 6 Melksham
Career: 5 contests, won 2, lost 3.

Liam Shinkwin

Bushey Heath. *Born* Watford, 28
September, 1985
Lightweight. *Ht* 5' 9"
Manager R. Clark
13.09.08 Robin Deakin W PTS 4 Bethnal Green
20.03.09 Johnny Greaves W PTS 6 Newham
30.06.09 Ibrar Riyaz DREW 6 Bethnal Green
Career: 3 contests, won 2, drew 1.

Nadeem Siddique

Bradford. *Born* Bradford, 28 October, 1977
Former Undefeated Central Area
Welterweight Champion. Former
Undefeated British Masters Welterweight
Champion. *Ht* 5'8"
Manager J. Ingle
17.11.02 Daniel Thorpe W PTS 4 Bradford
09.02.03 Norman Dhalie W PTS 4 Bradford
13.04.03 Dave Hinds W PTS 4 Bradford
15.06.03 Nigel Senior W PTS 6 Bradford
05.10.03 Jason Nesbitt W PTS 6 Bradford
27.10.03 Daniel Thorpe W PTS 6 Glasgow
07.12.03 Chris Duggan W RSC 2 Bradford
16.01.04 Pete Buckley W PTS 4 Bradford
16.04.04 Arv Mittoo W PTS 6 Bradford
15.05.04 Joel Viney W PTS 6 Aberdeen
24.09.04 Dave Hinds W PTS 4 Nottingham
13.02.05 Jason Nesbitt W PTS 6 Bradford
09.04.05 Pete Buckley W PTS 6 Norwich
08.05.05 Kristian Laight W RSC 7 Bradford
03.06.05 Daniel Thorpe W PTS 6 Hull
13.11.05 Billy Smith W PTS 6 Leeds
25.11.05 Jason Nesbitt W RSC 6 Hull
13.04.06 David Kehoe W PTS 6 Leeds
27.05.07 Tye Williams W RSC 4 Bradford
    (Vacant Central Area & British Masters
    Welterweight Titles)
07.09.07 Tom Glover W PTS 6 Doncaster
29.03.08 Salaheddine Sarhani W RSC 4
    Aberdeen
10.05.08 Alex Brew W CO 2 Nottingham
11.07.08 Martin Gethin L RSC 7 Wigan
13.06.09 Tom Glover L DIS 9 Wigan
Career: 24 contests, won 22, lost 2.

Luke Simpkin

Swadlincote. *Born* Derby, 5 May, 1979
Heavyweight. *Ht* 6'2"
Manager Self
24.09.98 Simon Taylor W CO 3 Edgbaston
16.10.98 Chris P. Bacon L PTS 6 Salford

10.12.98 Jason Flisher W RSC 5 Barking
04.02.99 Danny Watts L CO 3 Lewisham
28.05.99 Tommy Bannister W RSC 4 Liverpool
07.08.99 Owen Beck L PTS 4 Dagenham
11.09.99 Scott Lansdowne L PTS 4 Sheffield
11.03.00 Albert Sosnowski L PTS 4 Kensington
27.03.00 Mark Hobson L PTS 4 Barnsley
29.04.00 Johan Thorbjoernsson L PTS 4
          Wembley
23.09.00 Mark Potter L PTS 6 Bethnal Green
30.09.00 Gordon Minors DREW 4 Peterborough
18.11.00 Keith Long L RSC 3 Dagenham
03.02.01 Paul Buttery W RSC 1 Manchester
01.04.01 Wayne Llewelyn L PTS 6 Southwark
24.04.01 Darren Chubbs L PTS 4 Liverpool
06.05.01 Billy Bessey L PTS 6 Hartlepool
09.06.01 John McDermott L PTS 6 Bethnal
          Green
13.09.01 Mark Krence L PTS 4 Sheffield
10.12.01 Mark Hobson L RTD 3 Liverpool
27.01.02 Pele Reid DREW 4 Streatham
15.03.02 Mike Holden L PTS 6 Millwall
13.04.02 Fola Okesola W PTS 4 Liverpool
10.05.02 Julius Francis DREW 6 Millwall
23.08.02 Mark Potter L PTS 6 Bethnal Green
10.06.03 Mark Krence L RTD 8 Sheffield
          *(Vacant Midlands Area Heavyweight
          Title)*
05.09.03 Roman Greenberg L RTD 4 Sheffield
25.04.04 Dave Clarke W RSC 2 Nottingham
18.09.04 Paul King L PTS 6 Newark
02.12.04 Micky Steeds L RSC 3 Crystal Palace
21.02.05 Ian Millarvie L PTS 6 Glasgow
26.04.05 Carl Baker W RSC 4 Leeds
09.07.05 Henry Smith W RSC 3 Bristol
11.09.05 Carl Baker L PTS 10 Kirkby in
          Ashfield
          *(British Masters Heavyweight Title
          Challenge)*
28.01.06 Colin Kenna L PTS 8 Dublin
25.03.06 Istvan Kecskes W PTS 4 Burton
02.12.06 Micky Steeds L PTS 6 Southwark
03.03.07 Paul Butlin L PTS 4 Burton
15.06.07 John McDermott L RSC 2 Crystal
          Palace
27.07.07 David Dolan L RSC 6 Houghton le
          Spring
16.09.07 Billy Bessey W CO 6 Southampton
13.10.07 Sam Sexton L RSC 5 Bethnal Green
12.09.08 Dave Ferguson W PTS 3 Newcastle
12.09.08 Sam Sexton L PTS 3 Newcastle
22.11.08 Mathew Ellis L PTS 4 Blackpool
Career: 45 contests, won 11, drew 3, lost 31.

John Simpson

Greenock. *Born* Greenock, 26 July, 1983
Commonwealth Featherweight Champion.
Former British Featherweight Champion.
Ht 5'7"
Manager A. Morrison
23.09.02 Simon Chambers W RSC 1 Glasgow
06.10.02 Lee Holmes L PTS 6 Rhyl
07.12.02 Matthew Burke W PTS 4 Brentwood
20.01.03 John-Paul Ryan W PTS 6 Glasgow
17.02.03 Joel Viney W RTD 1 Glasgow
14.04.03 Simon Chambers W PTS 6 Glasgow
20.10.03 Steve Gethin W PTS 8 Glasgow
01.11.03 Mark Alexander W PTS 4 Glasgow
19.01.04 Henry Janes W PTS 8 Glasgow

31.01.04 Gennadiy Delisandru W PTS 4 Bethnal
          Green
22.04.04 Jus Wallie W PTS 6 Glasgow
02.06.04 Fred Janes W PTS 6 Hereford
20.09.04 Marc Callaghan W PTS 8 Glasgow
05.11.04 Dazzo Williams L PTS 12 Hereford
          (British Featherweight Title Challenge)
06.06.05 Dariusz Snarski W RSC 3 Glasgow
05.11.05 Andy Morris L PTS 12 Renfrew
          (Vacant British Featherweight Title)
01.04.06 Steve Foster L PTS 12 Bethnal Green
          (WBU Featherweight Title Challenge)
09.12.06 Andy Morris W RSC 5 Canning Town
          (British Featherweight Title Challenge)
10.03.07 Derry Matthews L PTS 12 Liverpool
          (WBU Featherweight Title Challenge)
08.06.07 Ryan Barrett W CO 5 Mayfair
          (British Featherweight Title Defence)
07.09.07 Andy Morris W RSC 7 Mayfair
          (British Featherweight Title Defence)
15.12.07 Youssef Al Hamidi W PTS 8 Edinburgh
06.06.08 Paul Appleby L PTS 12 Glasgow
          (British Featherweight Title Defence)
28.11.08 John Gicharu W PTS 8 Glasgow
16.01.09 Paul Truscott W RSC 8 Middlesbrough
          *(Commonwealth Featherweight Title
          Challenge)*
Career: 25 contests, won 19, lost 6.

Neil Simpson

Coventry. *Born* London, 5 July, 1970
British Masters Cruiserweight
Champion. Former Undefeated British &
Commonwealth L.Heavyweight Champion.
Former Midlands Area L.Heavyweight
Champion. *Ht* 6'2¼"
Manager Self
04.10.94 Kenny Nevers W PTS 4 Mayfair
20.10.94 Johnny Hooks W RSC 2 Walsall
05.12.94 Chris Woollas L PTS 6 Cleethorpes
15.12.94 Paul Murray W PTS 6 Walsall
06.03.95 Greg Scott-Briggs W RTD 5 Leicester
17.03.95 Thomas Hansvoll L PTS 4
          Copenhagen, Denmark
26.04.95 Craig Joseph L PTS 6 Solihull
11.05.95 Andy McVeigh L CO 2 Dudley
24.06.95 Dave Owens W RSC 1 Cleethorpes
25.09.95 Tony Booth L PTS 8 Cleethorpes
11.10.95 Darren Ashton W RSC 3 Solihull
29.11.95 Greg Scott-Briggs W DIS 7 Solihull
          *(Vacant Midlands Area L.Heavyweight
          Title)*
19.02.96 Stephen Wilson L PTS 6 Glasgow
27.03.96 Tony Booth W PTS 6 Whitwick
26.04.96 Dean Francis L RSC 3 Cardiff
02.10.96 Chris Davies W PTS 4 Cardiff
28.10.96 Nigel Rafferty W PTS 8 Leicester
03.12.96 Danny Peters L PTS 6 Liverpool
03.02.97 Michael Pinnock W PTS 6 Leicester
25.04.97 Stuart Fleet L PTS 10 Cleethorpes
          *(Midlands Area L.Heavyweight Title
          Defence)*
20.10.97 Slick Miller W RTD 1 Leicester
15.12.97 Chris Woollas L PTS 6 Cleethorpes
11.05.98 Greg Scott-Briggs W PTS 6 Leicester

30.11.98 Slick Miller W CO 3 Leicester
26.02.99 Adam Cale W RSC 3 Coventry
12.07.99 Tony Booth W PTS 10 Coventry
          (Elim. British L.Heavyweight Title)
14.12.99 Darren Corbett L PTS 12 Coventry
          *(Vacant IBO Inter-Continental
          L.Heavyweight Title)*
22.05.00 Mark Baker W PTS 12 Coventry
          (Vacant British L.Heavyweight Title)
18.11.00 Mark Delaney W RSC 1 Dagenham
          (British L.Heavyweight Title Defence)
02.01.01 Hastings Rasani W RSC 4 Coventry
          *(Vacant Commonwealth
          L.Heavyweight Title)*
06.04.01 Yawe Davis L RSC 3 Grosseto, Italy
          (Vacant European L.Heavyweight Title)
25.05.02 Tony Oakey L PTS 12 Portsmouth
          (WBU L.Heavyweight Title Challenge)
08.03.03 Peter Oboh L RSC 11 Coventry
          *(Vacant British L.Heavyweight
          Title Commonwealth L.Heavyweight
          Title Challenge)*
20.04.04 Mark Brookes L PTS 10 Sheffield
          (Elim. British L.Heavyweight Title)
17.12.04 Hastings Rasani W PTS 6 Coventry
18.06.05 Paul Bonson W PTS 6 Coventry
16.09.05 Leigh Alliss L RSC 3 Plymouth
10.02.06 Gareth Hogg L PTS 6 Plymouth
18.03.06 Varuzhan Davtyan W RSC 1 Coventry
25.09.07 Tony Booth W PTS 10 Hull
          *(Vacant British Masters Cruiserweight
          Title)*
01.12.07 John Anthony W PTS 4 Coventry
01.03.08 Tony Booth W PTS 4 Coventry
01.05.08 Nick Okoth W RSC 10 Piccadilly
          *(British Masters Cruiserweight Title
          Defence)*
03.10.08 Paul Bonson DREW 4 Burton
06.12.08 Derek Chisora L RTD 2 Canning Town
19.05.09 Dean Francis L RSC 3 Kensington
Career: 46 contests, won 26, drew 1, lost 19.

Neil Sinclair

Belfast. *Born* Belfast, 23 February, 1974
All-Ireland L.Middleweight Champion.
Former Undefeated British Welterweight
Champion. *Ht* 5'10½"
Manager Self
14.04.95 Marty Duke W RSC 2 Belfast
27.05.95 Andrew Jervis L RSC 3 Belfast
17.07.95 Andy Peach W RSC 1 Mayfair
26.08.95 George Wilson W PTS 4 Belfast
07.10.95 Wayne Shepherd W PTS 6 Belfast
02.12.95 Brian Coleman W RTD 1 Belfast
13.04.96 Hughie Davey W PTS 6 Liverpool
28.05.96 Prince Kasi Kaihau W RSC 2 Belfast
03.09.96 Dennis Berry L PTS 6 Belfast
27.09.97 Trevor Meikle W RSC 5 Belfast
20.12.97 Chris Pollock W RTD 3 Belfast
21.02.98 Leigh Wicks W RSC 1 Belfast
19.09.98 Paul Denton W RSC 1 Dublin
07.12.98 Michael Smyth W CO 1 Acton
22.01.99 Mark Ramsey W CO 3 Dublin
05.06.99 David Kirk W PTS 8 Cardiff
16.10.99 Paul Dyer W RSC 6 Belfast
18.03.00 Dennis Berry W RSC 2 Glasgow
16.05.00 Paul Dyer W RSC 6 Warrington
24.06.00 Chris Henry W RSC 1 Glasgow
12.08.00 Adrian Chase W RSC 2 Wembley

16.12.00 Daniel Santos L CO 2 Sheffield
(WBO Welterweight Title Challenge)
28.04.01 Zoltan Szilii W CO 2 Cardiff
22.09.01 Viktor Fesetchko W PTS 6 Bethnal
Green
19.11.01 Harry Dhami W RSC 5 Glasgow
(British Welterweight Title Challenge)
20.04.02 Leonti Voronchuk W RSC 4 Cardiff
15.06.02 Derek Roche W CO 1 Leeds
(British Welterweight Title Defence)
17.08.02 Dmitri Kashkan W RSC 4 Cardiff
02.11.02 Paul Knights W RSC 2 Belfast
(British Welterweight Title Defence)
01.02.03 Bradley Pryce W RSC 8 Belfast
(British Welterweight Title Defence)
30.07.04 Craig Lynch W PTS 6 Bethnal Green
18.03.05 Taz Jones L RSC 1 Belfast
05.07.06 Jerome Ellis L CO 6 Colorado Springs,
Colorado, USA
17.02.07 Arek Malek W RSC 4 Cork
23.06.07 Franny Jones L CO 5 Dublin
18.08.07 Sergejs Savrinovics W PTS 6 Cork
29.03.08 Juan Martinez Bas W PTS 8
Letterkenny
07.06.08 Daniele Petrucci L PTS 12 Rome, Italy
*(European Union Welterweight Title
Challenge)*
15.05.09 Henry Coyle W RSC 3 Belfast
*(Vacant All-Ireland L.Middleweight
Title)*
Career: 39 contests, won 32, lost 7.

Grant Skehill

Wanstead. *Born* London, 1 October, 1985
L.Middleweight. *Ht* 5'11¼"
Manager F. Warren
13.05.06 Geraint Harvey W PTS 4 Bethnal Green
28.10.06 Ernie Smith W PTS 4 Bethnal Green
17.02.07 Duncan Cottier W PTS 4 Wembley
13.10.07 Rocky Muscus W PTS 4 Bethnal Green
12.01.08 Ben Hudson W PTS 4 Bethnal Green
14.06.08 Duncan Cottier W PTS 4 Bethnal
Green
26.09.08 Billy Smith W PTS 4 Bethnal Green
21.11.08 JJ Bird W PTS 4 Bethnal Green
Career: 8 contests, won 8.

Joe Skeldon

Tipton. *Born* Dudley, 14 December, 1971
L.Middleweight. *Ht* 5' 7"
Manager E. Johnson
03.10.98 Pedro Thompson L RSC 5 West
Bromwich
01.04.99 Kevin Laing W PTS 6 Birmingham
20.05.99 Clive Johnson L PTS 6 Barking
24.07.08 Jason Smith W RSC 6 Wolverhampton
12.09.08 Mark Phillips W PTS 4 Wolverhampton
10.04.09 Jamie Ambler L PTS 4 Cheltenham
Career: 6 contests, won 3, lost 3.

Matt Skelton

Bedford. *Born* Bedford, 23 January, 1968
Former Undefeated European Heavyweight
Champion. Former Commonwealth
Heavyweight Champion. Former
Undefeated British, WBU & English
Heavyweight Champion. *Ht* 6'3"
Manager Self

22.09.02 Gifford Shillingford W RSC 2
Southwark
27.10.02 Slick Miller W CO 1 Southwark
08.12.02 Neil Kirkwood W RSC 1 Bethnal Green
18.02.03 Jacklord Jacobs W RSC 4 Bethnal Green
08.04.03 Alexei Varakin W CO 2 Bethnal Green
15.05.03 Dave Clarke W RSC 1 Mayfair
17.07.03 Antoine Palatis W RSC 4 Dagenham
18.09.03 Mike Holden W RSC 6 Dagenham
(Vacant English Heavyweight Title)
11.10.03 Costi Marin W RSC 1 Portsmouth
25.10.03 Ratko Draskovic W RSC 3 Edinburgh
15.11.03 Patriche Costel W CO 1 Bayreuth,
Germany
07.02.04 Julius Francis W PTS 10 Bethnal Green
(English Heavyweight Title Defence)
24.04.04 Michael Sprott W CO 12 Reading
*(British & Commonwealth Heavyweight
Title Challenges)*
05.06.04 Bob Mirovic W RTD 4 Bethnal Green
*(Commonwealth Heavyweight Title
Defence)*
19.11.04 Keith Long W RSC 11 Bethnal Green
*(British & Commonwealth Heavyweight
Title Defences)*
25.02.05 Fabio Eduardo Moli W RSC 6 Wembley
(Vacant WBU Heavyweight Title)
16.07.05 Mark Krence W RTD 7 Bolton
(British Heavyweight Title Defence)
10.12.05 John McDermott W RSC 9 Canning Town
(British Heavyweight Title Defence)
25.02.06 Danny Williams L PTS 12 Canning
Town
*(Commonwealth Heavyweight Title
Challenge)*
01.04.06 Suren Kalachyan W CO 4 Bethnal
Green
08.07.06 Danny Williams W PTS 12 Cardiff
*(Commonwealth Heavyweight Title
Challenge)*
14.07.07 Michael Sprott W PTS 12 Greenwich
*(Commonwealth Heavyweight Title
Defence)*
19.01.08 Ruslan Chagaev L PTS 12 Dusseldorf,
Germany
(WBA Heavyweight Title Challenge)
19.12.08 Paolo Vidoz W RTD 9 Milan, Italy
(Vacant European Heavyweight Title)
28.02.09 Martin Rogan L RSC 11 Birmingham
*(Commonwealth Heavyweight Title
Defence)*
Career: 25 contests, won 22, lost 3.

Michal Skierniewski

Crewe. *Born* Gdynia, Poland, 11 October,
1976
Heavyweight. *Ht* 6' 3"
Manager K. Stubbs
21.01.06 Imrich Borka W CO 1 Busko Zdroj,
Poland
25.02.06 Tomas Mrazek DREW 4 Wolow,
Poland
21.12.07 Andrej Puchalski W PTS 4 Bialystok,
Poland
29.02.08 Ryszard Raszkiewicz L PTS 4
Piaseczno, Poland

20.04.08 Aleksandrs Selezens L PTS 4 Radom,
Poland
01.06.08 Andrej Puchalski W PTS 4 Jozefow,
Poland
28.06.08 Tomasz Zeprzalka L RSC 4 Sanok,
Poland
20.03.09 Larry Olubamiwo L CO 1 Newham
10.05.09 Shane McPhilbin L RSC 4 Derby
Career: 9 contests, won 3, drew 1, lost 5.

Michal Skierniewski   Philip Sharkey

Gatis Skuja

Bethnal Green. *Born* Latvia, 23 June, 1982
L.Middleweight. *Ht* 5'9"
Manager Self
26.03.05 Nathan Graham L RSC 1 Hackney
11.09.05 David Kirk W PTS 6 Kirkby in
Ashfield
04.12.05 Mark Lloyd L PTS 4 Telford
24.02.06 Terry Adams DREW 4 Birmingham
24.03.06 Sam Webb L PTS 4 Bethnal Green
22.05.06 Simon Sherrington DREW 8
Birmingham
15.06.06 Cello Renda L PTS 4 Peterborough
14.07.06 Laurent Gomis L RSC 2 Alicante, Spain
29.09.06 Brett Flournoy L PTS 4 Manchester
03.11.06 Gavin Smith DREW 6 Barnsley
03.12.06 Daley Oujederie DREW 4 Bethnal
Green
03.03.07 Robbie James L PTS 6 Newport
13.07.07 Dee Mitchell W RSC 5 Birmingham
11.08.07 Denton Vassell L PTS 4 Liverpool
23.09.07 Fred Smith W RSC 1 Longford
05.10.07 Daniel Herdman W PTS 4 Bethnal
Green
19.10.07 Danny Reynolds L PTS 6 Doncaster
09.11.07 Jon Harrison L PTS 10 Plymouth
*(Vacant International Masters
L.Middleweight Title)*
14.09.08 Dee Mitchell W PTS 4 Birmingham
17.10.08 Mark Thompson L PTS 6 Bethnal Green
15.11.08 Paul Brown W PTS 6 Plymouth
06.02.09 Young Muttley L PTS 6 Birmingham
Career: 22 contests, won 5, drew 4, lost 13.

Scott Slater

Nottingham. *Born* Nottingham, 28
December, 1989
Lightweight. *Ht* 5' 9"
Manager M. Shinfield
12.06.09 Richard Barclay W CO 1 Clydebank
Career: 1 contest, won 1.

Anthony Small

Deptford. *Born* London, 28 June, 1981
Southern Area L.Middleweight Champion.
Ht 5'9"
Manager F. Warren
12.05.04 Lance Hall W RSC 1 Reading
10.09.04 Emmanuel Marcos W RSC 1 Wembley
10.12.04 Howard Clarke W PTS 4 Sheffield
21.01.05 Andrei Sherel W RSC 3 Brentford
24.04.05 Dmitry Donetskiy W PTS 4 Leicester
Square
16.06.05 Howard Clarke W PTS 6 Mayfair
20.07.05 David le Franc W RSC 1 Monte Carlo,
Monaco
14.10.05 Ismael Kerzazi W RSC 1 Huddersfield
23.11.05 Ernie Smith W PTS 6 Mayfair
24.03.06 Kai Kauramaki W CO 3 Bethnal Green
30.05.06 Alexander Matviechuk W RSC 6
Bethnal Green
21.07.06 Vladimir Borovski W PTS 6 Altrincham
21.10.06 Prince Arron W RSC 2 Southwark
18.11.06 Ciaran Healy W RSC 3 Newport
09.12.06 Kevin Phelan W RSC 1 Canning Town
17.02.07 Sergey Starkov W RSC 4 Wembley
30.03.07 Walter Wright W PTS 8 Newcastle
14.07.07 Bradley Pryce L RSC 7 Greenwich
*(Commonwealth L.Middleweight Title
Challenge)*
12.01.08 Takaloo W RSC 7 Bethnal Green
*(Vacant Southern Area L.Middleweight
Title)*
14.06.08 George Katsimpas W RSC 8 Bethnal
Green
*(Southern Area L.Middleweight Title
Defence)*
12.09.08 Freddy Curiel W RSC 10 Mayfair
*(Vacant WBA International
L.Middleweight Title. Vacant EBA
L.Middleweight Title)*
06.12.08 Steve Conway W RSC 2 Canning Town
Career: 22 contests, won 21, lost 1.

Billy Smith

Stourport. *Born* Kidderminster, 10 June,
1978
Welterweight. Former Undefeated Midlands
Area L.Welterweight Champion. *Ht* 5'7"
Manager Self
28.03.00 Marcus Portman L PTS 6
Wolverhampton
07.04.00 Barry Hughes L PTS 6 Glasgow
18.05.00 Manzo Smith L PTS 4 Bethnal Green
26.05.00 Willie Limond L PTS 4 Glasgow
07.07.00 Gareth Jordan L PTS 6 Chigwell
15.07.00 David Walker L RTD 2 Millwall
09.09.00 Ricky Eccleston L PTS 4 Manchester
24.09.00 Choi Tsveenpurev L RTD 2 Shaw
18.11.00 Lee Meager L RSC 1 Dagenham
17.12.00 Willie Limond L PTS 6 Glasgow
03.02.01 Scott Spencer L PTS 6 Brighton

09.03.01 Darren Melville L PTS 4 Millwall
27.03.01 Jason Nesbitt L PTS 6 Brierley Hill
05.03.05 Lee Cook L PTS 4 Southwark
23.03.05 Sam Rukundo L RSC 3 Leicester Square
30.04.05 Baz Carey L PTS 6 Coventry
08.05.05 Sean Hughes L PTS 6 Bradford
20.05.05 Stefy Bull L PTS 6 Doncaster
02.06.05 Isaac Ward L PTS 8 Yarm
16.06.05 Ricky Owen L PTS 4 Dagenham
25.06.05 John Fewkes L PTS 6 Wakefield
16.07.05 Craig Watson L PTS 4 Bolton
23.07.05 Lee McAllister L PTS 4 Edinburgh
11.09.05 Craig Johnson L PTS 4 Kirkby in
Ashfield
24.09.05 Baz Carey NC 5 Coventry
01.10.05 John Davidson W PTS 6 Wigan
09.10.05 Andrew Murray L PTS 4 Hammersmith
22.10.05 Jonathan Whiteman L PTS 6 Mansfield
05.11.05 Paul McCloskey L PTS 4 Renfrew
13.11.05 Nadeem Siddique L PTS 6 Leeds
25.11.05 Steve Mullin L PTS 4 Liverpool
03.12.05 Baz Carey L PTS 6 Coventry
12.12.05 Judex Meemea L PTS 6 Peterborough
11.02.06 Tom Glover L PTS 4 Bethnal Green
24.02.06 Lance Hall W PTS 6 Birmingham
25.03.06 Scott Haywood L PTS 6 Burton
07.04.06 Michael Graydon W PTS 4 Bristol
28.04.06 Paul Holborn L PTS 4 Hartlepool
12.05.06 Lee McAllister L PTS 4 Bethnal Green
21.05.06 Ashley Theophane L PTS 4 Bethnal
Green
30.05.06 Chris Pacy L PTS 4 Bethnal Green
16.06.06 Ceri Hall L PTS 6 Carmarthen
23.06.06 Paul Truscott L PTS 4 Blackpool
12.07.06 John Murray L RSC 6 Bethnal Green
02.09.06 Stephen Burke L PTS 4 Bolton
09.09.06 Mike Reid W PTS 8 Inverurie
18.09.06 Gary McArthur L PTS 8 Glasgow
29.09.06 Gwyn Wale W PTS 6 Motherwell
26.10.06 Jonathan Hussey W PTS 6 Dudley
04.11.06 Jonathan Whiteman W PTS 6 Mansfield
17.11.06 Martin Gordon W PTS 6 Brierley Hill
01.12.06 Dee Mitchell L PTS 4 Birmingham
08.12.06 John Murray L PTS 6 Dagenham
15.12.06 Michael Lomax L PTS 6 Bethnal Green
09.02.07 Scott Haywood L PTS 4 Leeds
19.02.07 Andrew Ferrans L PTS 6 Glasgow
24.03.07 Baz Carey W PTS 10 Coventry
*(Vacant Midlands Area L.Welterweight
Title)*
07.04.07 Gavin Rees L PTS 6 Cardiff
11.05.07 Scott Haywood L PTS 4 Motherwell
18.05.07 Lenny Daws L PTS 6 Canning Town
25.05.07 Craig Docherty L PTS 6 Glasgow
08.06.07 Nathan Brough L PTS 4 Motherwell
21.07.07 Barrie Jones L PTS 4 Cardiff
15.09.07 Carl Allen W PTS 10 Birmingham
*(Vacant Midlands Area L.Welterweight
Title)*
04.10.07 Andrew Murray L PTS 8 Piccadilly
13.10.07 Eddie Corcoran L PTS 4 Bethnal Green
25.10.07 Tristan Davies L PTS 4 Wolverhampton
02.11.07 George McIlroy W PTS 6 Irvine
14.11.07 Muhsen Nasser DREW 4 Bethnal
Green
24.11.07 Craig Dickson L PTS 6 Clydebank
01.12.07 Stephen Burke L PTS 6 Liverpool
15.12.07 Ricky Burns L PTS 6 Edinburgh
21.01.08 Gary McArthur L PTS 8 Glasgow
03.02.08 Chris Long W PTS 6 Bristol
22.02.08 Dave Stewart L PTS 6 Bethnal Green

29.02.08 Barry Morrison L PTS 6 Glasgow
08.03.08 Christopher Sebire L PTS 4 Greenwich
22.03.08 Ricky Burns L PTS 4 Cardiff
30.03.08 Jack Arnfield L PTS 6 Colne
18.04.08 Stuart Kennedy L PTS 6 Houghton le
Spring
02.05.08 Kevin Concepcion L PTS 6 Nottingham
10.05.08 John O'Donnell L PTS 4 Nottingham
21.06.08 Jamie Cox L PTS 6 Birmingham
28.06.08 Liam Anthony L PTS 6 Leicester
11.07.08 Steve O'Meara L PTS 4 Wigan
18.07.08 Gavin Tait L PTS 4 Dagenham
05.09.08 Karl Chiverton L PTS 4 Nottingham
13.09.08 Scott Miller L PTS 4 Stoke
26.09.08 Grant Skehill L PTS 4 Bethnal Green
17.10.08 Jamie Cox L RSC 5 Swindon
Career: 90 contests, won 12, drew 1, lost 76, no
contest 1.

Ernie Smith

Stourport. *Born* Kidderminster, 10 June,
1978
S.Middleweight. *Ht* 5'8"
Manager Self
24.11.98 Woody Greenaway L PTS 6
Wolverhampton
05.12.98 Gavin Rees L PTS 4 Bristol
27.01.99 Arv Mittoo DREW 6 Stoke
11.02.99 Tony Smith W PTS 6 Dudley
22.02.99 Liam Maltby W PTS 4 Peterborough
08.03.99 Wayne Jones W PTS 6 Birmingham
18.03.99 Carl Greaves L PTS 6 Doncaster
25.03.99 Brian Coleman L PTS 6 Edgbaston
27.05.99 Brian Coleman W PTS 6 Edgbaston
14.06.99 Dave Gibson W PTS 6 Birmingham
22.06.99 Koba Gogoladze L RSC 1 Ipswich
03.10.99 Gavin Down L RSC 1 Chesterfield
30.11.99 Brian Coleman L PTS 8 Wolverhampton
13.12.99 Richie Murray L RSC 5 Cleethorpes
24.02.00 Brian Coleman L PTS 6 Edgbaston
02.03.00 Oscar Hall L PTS 6 Birkenhead
10.03.00 John Tiftik L PTS 4 Chigwell
18.03.00 Biagio Falcone L PTS 4 Glasgow
07.04.00 Barry Connell L PTS 6 Glasgow
14.04.00 Jose Luis Castro L PTS 6 Madrid, Spain
06.05.00 Matthew Barr L PTS 4 Southwark
15.05.00 Harry Butler L PTS 6 Birmingham
26.05.00 Biagio Falcone L PTS 4 Glasgow
06.06.00 Chris Henry L PTS 8 Brierley Hill
08.07.00 Takaloo L RSC 4 Widnes
13.08.00 Jawaid Khaliq L RSC 4 Nottingham
*(Vacant Midlands Area Welterweight
Title)*
24.09.00 Shaun Horsfall L PTS 6 Shaw
09.10.00 Dave Gibson W PTS 6 Birmingham
22.10.00 Matthew Barr L PTS 4 Streatham
06.11.00 Stuart Elwell L PTS 6 Wolverhampton
25.11.00 Michael Jennings L PTS 4 Manchester
03.12.00 Shaun Horsfall L PTS 6 Shaw
17.12.00 Kevin McIntyre L PTS 6 Glasgow
20.01.01 David Walker L RTD 1 Bethnal Green
12.03.01 Matt Scriven L PTS 6 Birmingham
24.03.01 Bobby Banghar L PTS 4 Chigwell
12.05.01 Jon Harrison L PTS 4 Plymouth
21.05.01 Brian Coleman W PTS 6 Birmingham
03.06.01 Babatunde Ajayi L PTS 4 Southwark
16.06.01 Bobby Banghar L PTS 6 Dagenham
26.07.01 Andy Abrol L PTS 6 Blackpool
13.09.01 Leo O'Reilly L PTS 6 Sheffield
29.09.01 Brett James L PTS 6 Southwark

01.11.01 Lance Crosby L PTS 6 Hull
17.11.01 Nigel Wright L PTS 4 Glasgow
15.12.01 Ross Minter L RSC 2 Wembley
11.02.02 Tony Montana L PTS 6 Shrewsbury
13.05.02 Martin Scotland W RTD 2 Birmingham
15.06.02 Gavin Wake L PTS 4 Leeds
08.07.02 Gavin Rees L RSC 5 Mayfair
06.09.02 Ricky Burns L PTS 6 Glasgow
14.09.02 Matt Scriven L PTS 6 Newark
29.09.02 Anthony Christopher L PTS 6 Shrewsbury
18.11.02 Craig Dickson L PTS 6 Glasgow
03.12.02 Anthony Christopher W PTS 6 Shrewsbury
23.02.03 Gary Greenwood L PTS 4 Shrewsbury
24.03.03 Darrell Grafton L PTS 6 Barnsley
13.04.03 Lee McAllister L PTS 4 Bradford
28.04.03 Adnan Amar L PTS 6 Cleethorpes
12.05.03 Lee McAllister L PTS 6 Birmingham
31.05.03 Robbie Sivyer L PTS 6 Barnsley
08.06.03 Jonathan Woollins W PTS 4 Nottingham
15.06.03 Ali Nuumembe L PTS 4 Bradford
05.07.03 Michael Lomax L PTS 4 Brentwood
29.08.03 Ali Nuumembe L PTS 6 Liverpool
04.10.03 Lenny Daws L PTS 4 Muswell Hill
18.11.03 Chas Symonds L PTS 6 Bethnal Green
28.11.03 Lee McAllister L PTS 6 Hull
06.12.03 Taz Jones L PTS 4 Cardiff
07.02.04 Gary Woolcombe L PTS 4 Bethnal Green
09.04.04 Richard Swallow L PTS 4 Rugby
19.04.04 Craig Dickson L PTS 6 Glasgow
10.05.04 Adnan Amar L PTS 6 Birmingham
27.05.04 Graham Delehedy L RSC 3 Huddersfield
08.07.04 Steve Brumant L PTS 8 Birmingham
30.07.04 Tony Doherty L PTS 6 Bethnal Green
03.09.04 Jason Rushton L PTS 6 Doncaster
12.09.04 Chris Long DREW 6 Shrewsbury
24.09.04 Lenny Daws L PTS 6 Nottingham
23.10.04 Steve Conway L PTS 6 Wakefield
31.10.04 John Murray L PTS 4 Shaw
12.11.04 John O'Donnell L PTS 6 Wembley
25.11.04 Joe Mitchell W PTS 6 Birmingham
03.12.04 George Telfer L PTS 4 Edinburgh
13.12.04 Luke Teague L PTS 6 Cleethorpes
27.01.05 Muhsen Nasser L PTS 6 Piccadilly
12.02.05 Nathan Ward L PTS 6 Portsmouth
25.02.05 Ross Minter L PTS 4 Wembley
05.03.05 Gary Woolcombe L PTS 6 Southwark
23.03.05 Delroy Mellis L PTS 6 Leicester Square
08.04.05 Kerry Hope L PTS 4 Edinburgh
21.04.05 Jimmy Gould L PTS 4 Dudley
30.04.05 Andy Egan DREW 6 Coventry
08.05.05 Danny Parkinson L PTS 6 Bradford
15.05.05 Kell Brook L PTS 6 Sheffield
23.05.05 Davey Jones DREW 6 Cleethorpes
03.06.05 Martin Concepcion L PTS 4 Manchester
18.06.05 Richard Mazurek W PTS 6 Coventry
25.06.05 Adnan Amar L PTS 6 Melton Mowbray
09.07.05 Darren Barker L PTS 6 Nottingham
16.07.05 Tony Doherty NC 2 Bolton
23.07.05 Nathan Cleverly L PTS 4 Edinburgh
10.09.05 Kell Brook L PTS 4 Cardiff
25.09.05 Gavin Smith DREW 6 Leeds
06.10.05 Stuart Elwell L PTS 6 Dudley
21.10.05 George Hillyard W PTS 4 Bethnal Green
28.10.05 Franny Jones L PTS 4 Hartlepool
13.11.05 Darren Rhodes L PTS 6 Leeds
23.11.05 Anthony Small L PTS 6 Mayfair
02.12.05 Matthew Thirlwall L PTS 4 Nottingham

18.12.05 Ali Nuumbembe L CO 4 Bolton
28.01.06 Tony Doherty L PTS 6 Nottingham
16.02.06 Dean Hickman L PTS 4 Dudley
24.02.06 Joe Mitchell L PTS 6 Birmingham
04.03.06 Sean McKervey L PTS 6 Coventry
02.04.06 Mark Thompson L PTS 6 Shaw
29.04.06 Kell Brook L PTS 6 Edinburgh
06.05.06 Terry Adams L PTS 6 Birmingham
13.05.06 Jonjo Finnegan L PTS 6 Sutton in Ashfield
01.06.06 James Hare L CO 5 Barnsley
21.07.06 Mark Thompson L RSC 3 Altrincham
02.09.06 Denton Vassell L RSC 3 Bolton
01.10.06 Ryan Rowlinson L PTS 6 Rotherham
28.10.06 Grant Skehill L PTS 4 Bethnal Green
04.11.06 Gary Young L PTS 6 Glasgow
11.11.06 Karl Chiverton L PTS 6 Sutton in Ashfield
18.11.06 Barrie Jones L PTS 4 Newport
01.12.06 Max Maxwell L PTS 6 Birmingham
08.12.06 John O'Donnell L CO 2 Dagenham
09.02.07 Brett Flournoy L PTS 4 Leeds
16.02.07 Philip Dowse L PTS 6 Merthyr Tydfil
25.02.07 Brian Rose L PTS 6 Manchester
16.06.07 Sean Crompton L PTS 6 Bolton
28.06.07 Sam Horton L PTS 4 Dudley
13.07.07 James McKinley L PTS 6 Birmingham
11.08.07 Joey Ainscough L PTS 6 Liverpool
15.09.07 Ricky Burns L PTS 6 Paisley
23.09.07 Craig Denton L PTS 8 Hartlepool
06.10.07 Adnan Amar L PTS 4 Nottingham
13.10.07 Andrew Alan Lowe L PTS 6 Newark
03.11.07 Kerry Hope L PTS 4 Cardiff
14.11.07 Kreshnik Qato L PTS 6 Bethnal Green
24.11.07 Jamie Coyle L PTS 6 Clydebank
01.12.07 Greg Barton L PTS 4 Bethnal Green
29.03.08 Stevie Weir L PTS 4 Glasgow
13.04.08 Nasser Al Harbi L PTS 4 Edgbaston
26.04.08 Brian Rose L PTS 4 Wigan
09.05.08 Craig Denton L RSC 2 Middlesbrough
26.09.08 Jamie Ball L PTS 6 Wolverhampton
10.10.08 Joe Selkirk L PTS 4 Liverpool
18.10.08 Kris Carslaw L PTS 4 Paisley
14.11.08 Ciaran Duffy L PTS 4 Glasgow
27.11.08 Adil Anwar L PTS 6 Leeds
06.12.08 Jamie Cox L CO 1 Canning Town
27.02.09 Russ Colley L PTS 4 Wolverhampton
16.03.09 Vince Baldassara L RSC 2 Glasgow
27.04.09 Darryl Campbell L RSC 5 Glasgow
31.05.09 Jonjo Finnegan L PTS 4 Burton
12.06.09 Bobby Wood L PTS 4 Wolverhampton
Career: 159 contests, won 13, drew 5, lost 140, no contest 1.

Gavin Smith

Bradford. *Born* Bradford, 16 December, 1981
L.Middleweight. *Ht* 5'7¾"
Manager D. Hobson
23.10.04 Mark Wall W PTS 6 Wakefield
10.12.04 Mark Wall W PTS 4 Sheffield
13.02.05 Tony Randell W PTS 6 Bradford
24.07.05 Terry Adams L PTS 6 Sheffield
25.09.05 Ernie Smith DREW 6 Leeds
23.02.06 Jav Jerome W RSC 5 Leeds
13.05.06 Aleksandr Zhuk W RSC 3 Sheffield
03.11.06 Gatis Skuja DREW 6 Barnsley

22.03.08 Drew Campbell W PTS 6 Sheffield
19.09.08 Alex Spitjo W PTS 6 Doncaster
25.10.08 Manoocha Salari W PTS 6 St Helier
Career: 11 contests, won 8, drew 2, lost 1.

Henry Smith

Bristol. *Born* Bristol, 24 September, 1978
Heavyweight. *Ht* 5' 11"
Manager J. Feld
20.02.05 Radcliffe Green W PTS 6 Bristol
21.03.05 Billy McClung L PTS 6 Glasgow
09.07.05 Luke Simpkin L RSC 3 Bristol
07.10.06 David Ingleby L PTS 6 Weston super Mare
14.12.08 Paul Bonson W PTS 4 Bristol
Career: 5 contests, won 2, lost 3.

Jason Smith

Barnsley. *Born* Sheffield, 9 January, 1979
S.Middleweight. *Ht* 5'11¼"
Manager T. Schofield
09.11.07 Paul Brown L PTS 6 Plymouth
21.02.08 Kurt Bromberg L PTS 6 Leeds
21.06.08 Harry Matthews L PTS 6 Hull
24.07.08 Joe Skeldon L RSC 6 Wolverhampton
19.09.08 Ryan Rowlinson L RSC 1 Doncaster
04.12.08 Elvis Dube W PTS 6 Sunderland
28.03.09 Michael Monaghan L PTS 6 Lincoln
Career: 7 contests, won 1, lost 6.

Liam Smith

Liverpool. *Born* Liverpool, 28 July, 1988
Welterweight. *Ht* 5' 9"
Manager F. Warren
10.10.08 Duncan Cottier W PTS 4 Liverpool
12.12.08 John Vanemmenis W RSC 1 Widnes
14.03.09 Kevin McCauley W PTS 4 Manchester
Career: 3 contests, won 3.

Lloyd Smith

Portsmouth. *Born* Portsmouth, 18 November, 1988
Welterweight. *Ht* 5'9¼"
Manager J. Bishop
10.11.07 Rory Malone L PTS 6 Portsmouth
02.03.08 Jimmy Briggs L PTS 6 Portsmouth
28.03.08 Mark McCullough L RSC 3 Piccadilly
16.11.08 Chris Brophy W PTS 6 Southampton
27.06.09 Nathan Weise L CO 2 Portsmouth
Career: 5 contests, won 1, lost 4.

Paul Smith

Liverpool. *Born* Liverpool, 6 October, 1982
WBA International S. Middleweight Champion. Former Undefeated Central Area Middleweight Champion. Former English Middleweight Champion.
Ht 5'11"
Manager F. Warren
05.04.03 Howard Clarke W PTS 4 Manchester
08.05.03 Andrei Ivanov W RSC 2 Widnes
20.06.03 Elroy Edwards W PTS 4 Liverpool
29.08.03 Patrick Cito W PTS 4 Liverpool
02.10.03 Mike Duffield W RSC 1 Liverpool
13.12.03 Joel Ani W PTS 4 Manchester
26.02.04 Davey Jones W PTS 4 Widnes

03.04.04 Howard Clarke W PTS 4 Manchester
12.06.04 Steve Timms W RSC 1 Manchester
10.09.04 Ojay Abrahams W PTS 4 Liverpool
01.10.04 Jason Collins W RSC 1 Manchester
17.12.04 Howard Clarke W CO 1 Liverpool
11.02.05 Robert Burton W CO 1 Manchester
03.06.05 Simeon Cover W PTS 6 Manchester
11.03.06 Hussain Osman W RSC 4 Newport
01.06.06 Conroy McIntosh W PTS 8 Barnsley
14.10.06 Dean Walker W RSC 3 Manchester
(Vacant Central Area Middleweight Title)
18.11.06 Ryan Walls W RSC 4 Newport
10.03.07 Alexander Polizzi W RSC 8 Liverpool
30.03.07 Jonathan Reid W RSC 7 Newcastle
09.10.07 David Banks W PTS 5 Los Angeles, Calfornia, USA
08.12.07 Francis Cheka W PTS 8 Bolton
08.03.08 Cello Renda W RSC 6 Greenwich
(Vacant English Middleweight Title)
21.06.08 Steven Bendall L PTS 10 Birmingham
(English Middleweight Title Defence)
06.09.08 Danny Thornton W CO 6 Manchester
12.12.08 Ciaran Healy W PTS 6 Widnes
14.03.09 Rashid Matumla W RSC 2 Manchester
(Vacant WBA International S.Middleweight Title)
Career: 27 contests, won 26, lost 1.

Joe Smyth   Philip Sharkey

Stephen Smith

Liverpool. *Born* Liverpool, 22 July, 1985
Featherweight. *Ht* 5'6½"
Manager F. Warren
21.06.08 Shaun Walton W CO 3 Birmingham
06.09.08 Wladimir Borov W RSC 1 Manchester
10.10.08 Robin Deakin W RSC 2 Liverpool
31.10.08 Sid Razak W RSC 3 Birmingham
12.12.08 Anthony Hanna W PTS 4 Widnes
28.02.09 Steve Gethin W RTD 1 Birmingham
22.05.09 Zsolt Nagy W PTS 6 Bethnal Green
Career: 7 contests, won 7.

Joe Smyth

Potters Bar. Born Edgware, 5 June, 1985
L.Heavyweight. *Ht* 6' 1"
Manager J. Harding
04.07.08 Paul Bonson W PTS 4 Liverpool

01.08.08 Lee Kellett W RSC 1 Watford
05.10.08 Andrejs Tolstihs W PTS 4 Watford
05.12.08 Gordon Brennan W RSC 2 Dagenham
12.06.09 Hastings Rasani W RSC 2 Bethnal Green
Career: 5 contests, won 5.

Albert Sosnowski

Brentwood. *Born* Warsaw, Poland, 7 March, 1979
Former Undefeated WBF Heavyweight Champion. *Ht* 6'3½"
Manager B. Hearn
22.07.98 Jan Drobena W RSC 1 Outrup, Denmark
25.09.98 Andrzej Dziewulski W RSC 4 Poznan, Poland
02.10.98 Rene Hanl W PTS 4 Wroclaw, Poland
13.02.99 Viktor Juhasz W RSC 1 Jastrzebie Zdroj, Poland
12.03.99 Chris Woollas W PTS 4 Bethnal Green
17.04.99 Stipe Balic W PTS 4 Warsaw, Poland
28.05.99 Gary Williams W RSC 4 Liverpool
26.06.99 Biko Botowamungu W PTS 4 Wroclaw, Poland
17.07.99 Bruno Foster W RSC 6 Gdansk, Poland
18.09.99 Ignacio Orsola W CO 1 Gdansk, Poland
22.10.99 Jeff Lally W RSC 3 Detroit, Michigan, USA
20.11.99 Henry Kolle Njume W PTS 6 Gliwice, Poland
11.03.00 Luke Simpkin W PTS 4 Kensington
08.04.00 Slobodan Popovic W CO 1 Gdansk, Poland
27.05.00 Neil Kirkwood W RSC 1 Mayfair
24.06.00 Clarence Goins W RSC 2 Torun, Poland
19.08.00 Dan Conway W PTS 4 Mashantucket, Connecticut, USA
30.09.00 Everett Martin W RSC 7 Rotterdam, Holland
27.11.00 Michael Murray W RSC 5 Birmingham
17.03.01 Arthur Cook L CO 9 Budapest, Hungary
(Vacant WBC World Youth Heavyweight Title)
07.07.01 Dirk Wallyn W PTS 6 Amsterdam, Holland
13.10.01 Stanislav Tomkatchov W RSC 3 Budapest, Hungary
27.10.01 Robert Magureanu W RSC 4 Kolobrzeg, Poland
22.01.02 Catalin Zmarandescu W CO 1 Gdynia, Poland
09.03.02 Jacob Odhiambo W CO 1 Budapest, Hungary
27.07.02 Paul Bonson W PTS 4 Nottingham
07.12.02 Jacklord Jacobs W PTS 6 Brentwood
08.03.03 Mindaugas Kulikauskas W RSC 2 Bethnal Green
12.04.03 Mike Holden W PTS 6 Bethnal Green
05.07.03 Jason Brewster W RSC 2 Brentwood
22.11.03 Chris Woollas W RSC 1 Belfast
31.01.04 Greg Scott-Briggs W CO 2 Bethnal Green
10.04.04 Paul King W PTS 4 Manchester
26.06.04 Wojciech Bartnik W PTS 6 Belfast
11.09.04 Kenny Craven W CO 2 Budapest, Hungary

22.01.05 Tommy Connelly W RSC 2 Miami, Florida, USA
19.03.05 Travis Fulton W RSC 2 Las Vegas, Nevada, USA
28.05.05 Orlin Norris W PTS 6 Los Angeles, California, USA
25.05.06 Osborne Machimana W PTS 10 Brakpan, South Africa
04.11.06 Lawrence Tauasa W PTS 12 Kempton Park, South Africa
(Vacant WBF Heavyweight Title)
08.06.07 Steve Herelius W RSC 9 Motherwell
14.09.07 Manuel Alberto Pucheta W CO 2 Kirkcaldy
(WBF Heavyweight Title Defence)
25.01.08 Colin Kenna W PTS 10 Dagenham
25.04.08 Terrell Nelson W RSC 5 NYC, New York, USA
06.08.08 Zuri Lawrence L PTS 8 NYC, New York, USA
08.11.08 Danny Williams W RSC 8 Bethnal Green
04.04.09 Francesco Pianeta DREW 12 Düsseldorf, Germany
(Vacant European Union Heavyweight Title)
Career: 47 contests, won 44, drew 1, lost 2.

Steven Spartacus   Philip Sharkey

Steven Spartacus

Ipswich. *Born* Bury St.Edmunds, 3 November, 1976
L.Heavyweight. Former Undefeated British Masters L. Heavyweight Champion. Former English L. Heavyweight Champion.
Ht 5' 10"
Manager T. Sims
08.09.00 Michael Pinnock W PTS 4 Hammersmith
30.09.00 Martin Jolley W PTS 6 Chigwell
24.03.01 Calvin Stonestreet W PTS 4 Chigwell
16.06.01 Kevin Burton W RSC 1 Dagenham
07.09.01 Rob Stevenson W RSC 4 Bethnal Green
27.10.01 Darren Ashton W PTS 4 Manchester
24.11.01 Michael Pinnock W PTS 4 Bethnal Green

15.12.01 O'Neil Murray W RSC 4 Chigwell
19.01.02 Darren Ashton W PTS 4 Bethnal Green
14.09.02 Calvin Stonestreet W RSC 3 Bethnal Green
08.02.03 Paul Bonson W PTS 6 Norwich
27.05.03 Mark Phillips W RSC 2 Dagenham
25.07.03 Simeon Cover W CO 3 Norwich
(Vacant British Masters L. Heavyweight Title)
04.10.03 Hastings Rasani W RSC 1 Wood Green
11.12.03 Scott Lansdowne W RSC 3 Bethnal Green
(Vacant English L.Heavyweight Title)
30.01.04 Ovill McKenzie L PTS 6 Dagenham
02.06.04 Varuzhan Davtyan W RSC 1 Nottingham
12.11.04 Peter Haymer L PTS 10 Wembley
(English L.Heavyweight Title Defence)
10.04.05 Sam Price W RSC 6 Brentwood
(British Masters L. Heavyweight Title Defence)
11.12.05 Varuzhan Davtyan W CO 1 Chigwell
17.02.06 Karim Bennama W PTS 6 Bethnal Green
08.12.06 Ayitey Powers L PTS 6 Dagenham
18.05.07 Tony Oakey L RSC 12 Canning Town
(Vacant British L.Heavyweight Title)
04.10.08 Danny McIntosh L RSC 7 Norwich
(Vacant English L.Heavyweight Title)
20.02.09 Darren Stubbs L RSC 2 Bethnal Green
Career: 25 contests, won 19, lost 6.

Jamie Speight

Newton Abbott. Born Torquay, 9
September, 1988
Featherweight. *Ht* 5' 6"
Manager J. Feld
17.04.09 Pavels Senkovs W PTS 4 Bristol
Career: 1 contest, won 1.

Jamie Speight   Philip Sharkey

Jamie Spence

Northampton. *Born* Northampton, 9 June,
1984
L.Welterweight. *Ht* 5'7¼"
Manager Self
03.12.06 Gavin Tait L RSC 4 Bethnal Green
23.02.07 Dezzie O'Connor W RSC 3
Peterborough
01.06.07 Deniss Sirjatovs W RSC 3 Peterborough
21.09.07 Craig Dyer W PTS 6 Peterborough
22.02.08 Baz Carey W PTS 4 Bethnal Green
04.04.08 Lee Purdy L RSC 1 Bethnal Green
29.11.08 Johnny Greaves W PTS 4 Sleaford
17.04.09 Karl Place L RSC 2 Leigh
Career: 8 contests, won 5, lost 3.

Steve Spence

Scunthorpe. *Born* Scunthorpe, 15 June,
1987
Middleweight. *Ht* 5' 7"
Manager C. Greaves
29.05.09 Sam Padgett L CO 4 Dudley
Career: 1 contest, lost 1.

Delroy Spencer

Walsall. *Born* Walsall, 25 July, 1968
Bantamweight. Former Undefeated British
Masters Flyweight Champion. *Ht* 5'4"
Manager Self
30.10.98 Gwyn Evans L PTS 4 Peterborough
21.11.98 Jamie Evans W PTS 4 Southwark
30.01.99 Ian Napa L PTS 6 Bethnal Green
26.02.99 Chris Edwards W PTS 6 West Bromwich
30.04.99 Nicky Booth L PTS 6 Scunthorpe
06.06.99 Nicky Booth L PTS 6 Nottingham
19.06.99 Willie Valentine L PTS 4 Dublin
16.10.99 Colin Moffett W PTS 4 Bethnal Green
31.10.99 Shane Mallon W PTS 6 Raynes Park
29.11.99 Lee Georgiou L PTS 4 Wembley
19.02.00 Steffen Norskov L PTS 4 Aalborg,
Denmark
08.04.00 Ian Napa L PTS 8 Bethnal Green
15.04.00 Lee Georgiou L PTS 4 Bethnal Green
04.07.00 Ankar Miah W RSC 3 Tooting
13.07.00 Darren Hayde W PTS 4 Bethnal Green
30.09.00 Paul Weir L PTS 8 Chigwell
28.10.00 Dale Robinson L RSC 4 Coventry
02.12.00 Keith Knox W PTS 6 Bethnal Green
08.05.01 Levi Pattison L PTS 4 Barnsley
22.05.01 Mimoun Chent L DIS 5 Telde, Gran
Canaria
16.06.01 Sunkanmi Ogunbiyi L PTS 4 Wembley
22.11.01 Darren Taylor W PTS 8 Paddington
(Vacant British Masters Flyweight Title)
09.12.01 Shinny Bayaar L PTS 4 Shaw
19.12.01 Gareth Payne L PTS 4 Coventry
18.01.02 Gareth Payne W PTS 4 Coventry
28.01.02 Levi Pattison L RSC 5 Barnsley
19.10.03 Shinny Bayaar L PTS 6 Shaw
13.12.03 Mark Moran L PTS 4 Manchester
24.01.04 Martin Power L RTD 1 Wembley
23.04.04 Chris Edwards DREW 6 Leicester
26.06.04 Damaen Kelly L RSC 4 Belfast
30.07.04 Martin Power L CO 2 Bethnal Green
31.10.04 Shinny Bayaar L PTS 6 Shaw
12.11.04 Stevie Quinn L PTS 6 Belfast
03.12.04 Lee Haskins L RTD 3 Bristol
(Vacant English Flyweight Title)
27.05.05 Robert Nelson L PTS 4 Spennymoor
25.06.05 Robert Nelson L PTS 6 Wakefield
16.09.05 Lee Haskins L RTD 5 Plymouth
16.10.05 Moses Kinyua L PTS 6 Peterborough
30.10.05 Lee Fortt L PTS 4 Bethnal Green
12.11.05 Chris Edwards L PTS 4 Stoke
02.12.05 Jamie McDonnell L PTS 6 Doncaster
11.02.06 John Armour L PTS 6 Bethnal Green
04.03.06 Dale Robinson L RSC 3 Manchester
02.04.06 Shinny Bayaar L PTS 6 Shaw
23.04.06 Gary Sheil W PTS 6 Chester
09.05.06 Robert Nelson DREW 6 Leeds
20.05.06 Colin Moffett L PTS 4 Belfast
28.05.06 Tasif Khan L PTS 6 Wakefield
02.09.06 Don Broadhurst L PTS 4 Bolton
15.09.06 Matthew Edmonds L PTS 4 Newport
06.10.06 Ian Napa L PTS 6 Bethnal Green

27.10.06 Kris Hughes L PTS 6 Glasgow
11.11.06 Eugene Heagney L PTS 4 Dublin
11.12.06 Usman Ahmed DREW 6 Cleethorpes
09.02.07 Ross Burkinshaw L PTS 4 Leeds
26.02.07 Dougie Walton L PTS 6 Birmingham
07.04.07 Don Broadhurst L PTS 4 Cardiff
14.04.07 Eugene Heagney L PTS 6 Wakefield
05.05.07 Stephen Russell L PTS 4 Glasgow
19.05.07 Andy Bell L PTS 4 Nottingham
03.06.07 Josh Wale L PTS 6 Barnsley
16.06.07 Rob Turley L PTS 6 Newport
30.06.07 Rhys Roberts L PTS 4 Manchester
15.07.07 Gavin Reid L PTS 6 Hartlepool
22.07.07 Andy Bell L PTS 6 Mansfield
11.08.07 Rhys Roberts L PTS 6 Liverpool
08.09.07 Wayne Bloy L PTS 4 Sutton in Ashfield
22.09.07 Stuart McFadyen L PTS 6 Wigan
08.10.07 Davey Savage L PTS 6 Glasgow
26.10.07 Dougie Walton L PTS 6 Birmingham
05.11.07 John Donnelly L PTS 6 Glasgow
03.12.07 Scott Quigg L PTS 6 Manchester
02.02.08 Michael Walsh L RSC 3 Canning Town
14.03.08 Kallum De'Ath L PTS 6 Manchester
28.03.08 Mike Holloway L PTS 4 Barnsley
19.04.08 Luke Wilton L PTS 4 Dublin
26.04.08 Mike Robinson L PTS 6 Wigan
17.05.08 Paul Economides L PTS 6 Stoke
07.06.08 Craig Lyon L PTS 6 Wigan
15.06.08 Ian Bailey L PTS 6 Bethnal Green
04.07.08 Rhys Roberts L PTS 4 Liverpool
18.07.08 Sean Hughes L PTS 4 Dagenham
20.09.08 Michael Maguire L PTS 6 Sheffield
28.09.08 Stuart McFadyen L PTS 4 Colne
10.10.08 Craig Lyon L PTS 4 Liverpool
17.10.08 Ashley Sexton L PTS 4 Bethnal Green
07.11.08 Paul Edwards L PTS 4 Wigan
06.12.08 Michael Walsh L RTD 2 Canning Town
19.01.09 Najah Ali L PTS 4 Mayfair
01.02.09 Chris Male L PTS 4 Birmingham
13.02.09 Paul Economides L PTS 4 Wigan
27.02.09 Kris Hughes L PTS 4 Paisley
07.03.09 Daniel Walton L PTS 4 Birmingham
14.03.09 Adrian Gonzalez L PTS 4 Bristol
29.03.09 Terry Flanagan L PTS 6 Bolton
25.04.09 Luke Wilton L PTS 4 Belfast
17.05.09 Kieran Farrell L PTS 6 Bolton
29.05.09 Ashley Sexton L PTS 6 Stoke
28.06.09 Luke Wilton W PTS 4 Luton
Career: 100 contests, won 11, drew 3, lost 86.

Alexander Spitjo

Mansfield. *Born* Riga, Latvia, 21 February,
1986
L.Middleweight. *Ht* 5'10½"
Manager M. Scriven/J.Gill
13.04.07 Brett Flournoy L PTS 4 Altrincham
27.04.07 Sam Webb L RSC 1 Wembley
17.06.07 Lee Noble L PTS 4 Mansfield
30.06.07 Scott Jordan W RSC 5 Belfast
14.09.07 Willie Bilan W CO 1 Kirkcaldy
08.10.07 Ali Wyatt W RTD 5 Birmingham
10.12.07 Michael Frontin W PTS 6 Birmingham
07.03.08 Garry Buckland L RSC 3 Nottingham
18.04.08 Ajose Olusegun L RSC 3 Bethnal
Green
18.07.08 Chas Symonds L RSC 3 Dagenham
19.09.08 Gavin Smith L PTS 6 Doncaster
10.10.08 Denton Vassell L CO 3 Liverpool
06.12.08 Mark Douglas W RSC 1 Bethnal Green
27.02.09 Gary McMillan L PTS 4 Paisley

07.03.09 Max Maxwell L PTS 4 Birmingham
24.04.09 Marcus Portman L PTS 4
Wolverhampton
23.05.09 Tom Doran L PTS 4 Queensferry
08.06.09 Chris Black W PTS 6 Glasgow
19.06.09 Gary McMillan L PTS 6 Glasgow
30.06.09 Tomas Grublys L RSC 4 Bethnal Green
Career: 20 contests, won 6, lost 14.

Michael Sprott

Reading. *Born* Reading, 16 January, 1975
Former Undefeated European Union
Heavyweight Champion. Former
Undefeated English Heavyweight
Champion. Former British &
Commonwealth Heavyweight Champion.
Former Undefeated Southern Area & WBF
European Heavyweight Champion.
Ht 6'0¾"
Manager J. Evans
20.11.96 Geoff Hunter W RSC 1 Wembley
19.02.97 Johnny Davison W CO 2 Acton
17.03.97 Slick Miller W CO 1 Mayfair
16.04.97 Tim Redman W CO 2 Bethnal Green
20.05.97 Waldeck Fransas W PTS 6 Edmonton
02.09.97 Gary Williams W PTS 6 Southwark
08.11.97 Darren Fearn W PTS 6 Southwark
06.12.97 Nick Howard W RSC 1 Wembley
10.01.98 Johnny Davison W RSC 2 Bethnal
Green
14.02.98 Ray Kane W RTD 1 Southwark
14.03.98 Michael Murray W PTS 6 Bethnal
Green
12.09.98 Harry Senior L RSC 6 Bethnal Green
*(Vacant Southern Area Heavyweight
Title)*
16.01.99 Gary Williams W PTS 6 Bethnal Green
10.07.99 Chris Woollas W RTD 4 Southwark
18.01.00 Tony Booth W PTS 6 Mansfield
14.10.00 Wayne Llewelyn L PTS 3 Wembley
17.02.01 Timo Hoffmann W PTS 8 Bethnal Green
24.03.01 Timo Hoffmann L PTS 8 Magdeburg,
Germany
03.11.01 Corrie Sanders L RSC 1 Brakpan, South
Africa
20.12.01 Jermell Lamar Barnes W PTS 8
Rotterdam, Holland
12.02.02 Danny Williams L RTD 8 Bethnal Green
*(British & Commonwealth Heavyweight
Title Challenges)*
09.05.02 Pele Reid W RSC 7 Leicester Square
*(Vacant WBF European Heavyweight
Title)*
10.07.02 Garing Lane W PTS 6 Wembley
17.09.02 Derek McCafferty W PTS 8 Bethnal
Green
12.12.02 Tamas Feheri W RSC 2 Leicester Square
24.01.03 Mike Holden W RSC 4 Sheffield
18.03.03 Mark Potter W RSC 3 Reading
*(Southern Area Heavyweight Title
Challenge. Elim. British Heavyweight
Title)*
10.06.03 Petr Horacek W CO 1 Sheffield
01.08.03 Colin Kenna W RSC 1 Bethnal Green
*(Southern Area Heavyweight Title
Defence)*
26.09.03 Danny Williams L RSC 5 Reading
*(British & Commonwealth Heavyweight
Title Challenges)*

24.01.04 Danny Williams W PTS 12 Wembley
*(British & Commonwealth Heavyweight
Title Challenges)*
24.04.04 Matt Skelton L CO 12 Reading
*(British & Commonwealth Heavyweight
Title Defences)*
10.09.04 Robert Sulgan W RSC 1 Bethnal Green
23.04.05 Cengiz Koc W PTS 10 Dortmund,
Germany
*(Vacant European Union Heavyweight
Title)*
01.10.05 Paolo Vidoz L PTS 12 Oldenburg,
Germany
(European Heavyweight Title Challenge)
13.12.05 Vladimir Virchis L PTS 12 Solden,
Austria
*(WBO Inter-Continental Heavyweight
Title Challenge)*
18.02.06 Antoine Palatis W PTS 10 Edinburgh
*(Vacant European Union Heavyweight
Title)*
15.07.06 Ruslan Chagaev L RSC 8 Hamburg,
Germany
*(Vacant WBO Asia-Pacific Heavyweight
Title)*
04.11.06 Rene Dettweiler W PTS 12 Mülheim an
der Ruhr, Germany
*(European Union Heavyweight Title
Defence)*
17.02.07 Audley Harrison W RSC 3 Wembley
*(European Union Heavyweight Title
Defence. Vacant English Heavyweight
Title)*
14.07.07 Matt Skelton L PTS 12 Greenwich
*(Commonwealth Heavyweight Title
Challenge)*
31.05.08 Taras Bidenko L PTS 10 Dusseldorf,
Germany
19.11.08 Zack Page W PTS 6 Bayswater
14.03.09 Lamon Brewster L PTS 8 Kiel, Germany
20.06.09 Alexander Ustinov L PTS 10
Gelsenkirchen, Germany
Career: 45 contests, won 31, lost 14.

Mike Stanton

Liverpool. *Born* Liverpool, 27 January,
1987
S.Middleweight. *Ht* 5' 11"
Manager T. Gilmour
05.12.08 Jamie Ambler W PTS 4 Dagenham
12.06.09 Kurt Bromberg L RSC 3 Liverpool
Career: 2 contests, won 1, lost 1.

Micky Steeds

Isle of Dogs. *Born* London, 14 September,
1983
Cruiserweight. Former Undefeated
Southern Area Heavyweight Champion.
Ht 6'0"
Manager M. Roe
18.09.03 Slick Miller W PTS 4 Mayfair
21.02.04 Brodie Pearmaine W RSC 1 Brighton
12.03.04 Paul King W PTS 6 Millwall
02.12.04 Luke Simpkin W RSC 3 Crystal Palace
18.02.05 Scott Gammer L PTS 6 Brighton
24.04.05 Julius Francis W PTS 8 Leicester Square
12.06.05 Mal Rice W PTS 6 Leicester Square
24.07.05 Garry Delaney W PTS 6 Leicester
Square

05.03.06 Colin Kenna W PTS 10 Southampton
*(Southern Area Heavyweight Title
Challenge)*
13.10.06 Scott Gammer L PTS 12 Aberavon
(British Heavyweight Title Challenge)
02.12.06 Luke Simpkin W PTS 6 Southwark
18.05.07 John Anthony W PTS 6 Canning Town
18.04.08 Paul Bonson W PTS 8 Bethnal Green
13.06.08 Radcliffe Green W RTD 4 Portsmouth
03.10.08 Robert Norton L PTS 12 Burton
(Vacant British Cruiserweight Title)
28.02.09 Yoan Pablo Hernandez L CO 5
Neubrandenburg, Germany
19.05.09 Darren Corbett L PTS 3 Kensington
Career: 17 contests, won 12, lost 5.

Danny Stewart

Bristol. *Born* Bristol, 3 January, 1986
L.Welterweight. *Ht* 5'11¼"
Manager J. Feld
23.02.08 John Baguley L RSC 2 Crawley
30.03.08 Craig Dyer W PTS 4 Port Talbot
10.05.08 Nathan McIntosh L PTS 4 Nottingham
17.10.08 David Kirk W PTS 4 Swindon
14.12.08 Robin Deakin W RSC 3 Bristol
13.02.09 Johnny Greaves W PTS 4 Swindon
17.04.09 Jason Nesbitt NC 3 Bristol
Career: 7 contests, won 4, lost 2, no contest 1.

Darryl Still

Basingstoke. *Born* Basingstoke, 26
November, 1980
Welterweight. *Ht* 5'8¼"
Manager J. Bishop
16.09.07 Mark McCullough W PTS 4
Southampton
10.11.07 Craig Dyer W PTS 6 Portsmouth
02.03.08 David Kehoe W PTS 4 Portsmouth
16.11.08 Russell Pearce L PTS 6 Southampton
06.12.08 Mark McCullough L PTS 4 Bethnal
Green
20.03.09 Tony Owen L PTS 4 Bethnal Green
Career: 6 contests, won 3, lost 3.

Alex Strutt

Ombersley. *Born* Banbury, 9 April, 1982
Middleweight. *Ht* 5'11¼"
Manager R. Woodhall
28.09.07 Lance Verallo W RSC 2 Birmingham
13.04.08 Ben Hudson W PTS 4 Edgbaston
14.11.08 Pawel Trebinski DREW 6 Birmingham
Career: 3 contests, won 2, drew 1.

Darren Stubbs

Oldham. *Born* Manchester, 16 October,
1971
Central Area & British Masters
L.Heavyweight Champion. *Ht* 5'10"
Manager J. Doughty
02.06.02 Adam Cale W RSC 6 Shaw
21.06.02 Dean Cockburn L RSC 1 Leeds
17.11.02 Shpetim Hoti W RTD 2 Shaw
29.11.02 Jamie Wilson W PTS 6 Hull
09.03.03 Martin Thompson W RSC 3 Shaw
18.03.03 Jamie Hearn W RSC 3 Reading
08.06.03 Danny Grainger L RSC 2 Shaw
19.10.03 Paul Wesley W PTS 6 Shaw

29.02.04 Patrick Cito W PTS 6 Shaw
10.04.04 Alan Page L PTS 4 Manchester
20.04.04 Paul Owen W PTS 6 Sheffield
31.10.04 Nick Okoth W PTS 6 Shaw
20.11.05 Paul Bonson W PTS 6 Shaw
02.04.06 Howard Clarke W PTS 6 Shaw
18.06.06 Amer Khan L PTS 10 Manchester
   (Vacant Central Area L.Heavyweight
   Title)
11.03.07 Hastings Rasani W RSC 5 Shaw
03.05.07 Jon Ibbotson W RSC 4 Sheffield
07.10.07 Hastings Rasani W PTS 6 Shaw
02.12.07 Simeon Cover W PTS 6 Oldham
20.04.08 Simeon Cover W RTD 7 Shaw
   (Vacant British Masters L.Heavyweight
   Title)
16.11.08 Mark Nilsen W PTS 10 Shaw
20.02.09 Steven Spartacus W RSC 2 Bethnal
   Green
20.02.09 Tony Oakey L PTS 3 Bethnal Green
20.02.09 Carl Dilks W PTS 3 Bethnal Green
24.05.09 Carl Wild W PTS 10 Shaw
   (Vacant Central Area L.Heavyweight
   Title)
Career: 25 contests, won 20, lost 5.

Darren Stubbs   Philip Sharkey

Mark Stupple

Thamesmead. *Born* Bermondsey, 23
September, 1970
L.Middleweight. *Ht* 5' 8"
Manager F. Maloney
28.04.02 Pedro Thompson L RSC 4 Southwark
23.06.02 Arv Mittoo W PTS 6 Southwark
18.11.03 Brian Coleman W PTS 6 Bethnal Green
15.11.08 Peter Dunn W PTS 6 Bethnal Green
Career: 4 contests, won 3, lost 1.

Darren Sutherland

Chislehurst. *Born* Dublin, 18 April, 1982
S.Middleweight. *Ht* 5' 9"
Manager F. Maloney
18.12.08 Georgi Iliev W RSC 1 Dublin
06.03.09 Siarhei Navarka W RSC 3 Wigan
29.05.09 Vepkhia Tchilaia W RSC 4 Stoke
30.06.09 Gennadiy Rasalev W RSC 4 Bethnal
   Green
Career: 4 contests, won 4.

Lee Swaby

Lincoln. *Born* Lincoln, 14 May, 1976
Midlands Area Heavyweight Champion.
Former Undefeated British Masters
Cruiserweight Champion. *Ht* 6'2"
Manager D. Hobson
29.04.97 Naveed Anwar W PTS 6 Manchester
19.06.97 Liam Richardson W RSC 4 Scunthorpe
30.10.97 Phil Ball W RSC 3 Newark
17.11.97 L. A. Williams W PTS 6 Manchester
02.02.98 Tim Redman L PTS 6 Manchester
27.02.98 John Wilson W CO 3 Glasgow
07.03.98 Phill Day L PTS 4 Reading
08.05.98 Chris P. Bacon L RSC 3 Manchester
17.07.98 Chris P. Bacon L PTS 6 Mere
19.09.98 Cathal O'Grady L RSC 1 Dublin
20.12.98 Mark Levy L RTD 5 Salford
23.06.99 Lee Archer W PTS 6 West Bromwich
04.09.99 Garry Delaney L PTS 8 Bethnal
   Green
03.10.99 Brian Gascoigne DREW 6 Chesterfield
11.12.99 Owen Beck L PTS 4 Liverpool
05.03.00 Kelly Oliver L PTS 10 Peterborough
   (Vacant British Masters Cruiserweight
   Title)
15.04.00 Mark Levy W PTS 4 Bethnal Green
12.05.00 Enzo Maccarinelli W CO 3 Swansea
26.05.00 Steffen Nielsen L PTS 4 Holbaek,
   Denmark
09.09.00 Tony Dowling W RSC 9 Newark
   (Vacant British Masters Cruiserweight
   Title)
05.02.01 Robert Norton L PTS 8 Hull
24.03.01 Crawford Ashley L PTS 8 Sheffield
30.04.01 Eamonn Glennon W PTS 6 Glasgow
02.06.01 Denzil Browne DREW 8 Wakefield
31.07.01 Stephane Allouane W PTS 4 Bethnal
   Green
13.09.01 Kevin Barrett W PTS 4 Sheffield
15.12.01 Chris Woollas W RSC 4 Sheffield
27.04.02 Mark Hobson L PTS 10 Huddersfield
   (Final Elim. British Cruiserweight Title)
03.08.02 Greg Scott-Briggs W RSC 4 Derby
05.12.02 Eamonn Glennon W PTS 4 Sheffield
24.01.03 Tommy Eastwood W PTS 6 Sheffield
10.06.03 Paul Bonson W PTS 4 Sheffield
05.09.03 Brodie Pearmaine W RTD 4 Sheffield
20.04.04 Lee Mountford W RSC 1 Sheffield
27.05.04 Mark Hobson L RSC 6 Huddersfield
   (British & Commonwealth
   Cruiserweight Title Challenges)
24.10.04 Denzil Browne W RSC 7 Sheffield
   (Elim. British Cruiserweight Title)
09.09.05 Hastings Rasani W PTS 4 Sheffield
26.11.05 Vitaly Shkraba W RSC 3 Sheffield
04.03.06 Marco Huck L RTD 6 Oldenburg,
   Germany
20.10.06 John Keeton L RSC 7 Sheffield
   (Vacant British Cruiserweight Title)
02.12.06 Alexander Alexeev L RSC 5 Berlin,
   Germany
07.12.07 Sebastian Koeber L PTS 6 Alsterdorf,
   Germany
08.02.08 David Dolan L PTS 6 Peterlee
09.05.08 Chris Burton L PTS 8 Middlesbrough
12.09.08 Darren Morgan W PTS 3 Newcastle

12.09.08 Chris Burton L PTS 3 Newcastle
26.09.08 Derek Chisora L RSC 3 Bethnal Green
14.03.09 Tyson Fury L RTD 4 Birmingham
09.05.09 Paul Butlin W PTS 10 Lincoln
   (Vacant Midlands Area Heavyweight
   Title)
Career: 49 contests, won 24, drew 2, lost 23.

Gary Sykes

Dewsbury. *Born* Dewsbury, 13 February,
1984
Lightweight. *Ht* 5'8"
Manager C. Aston/S. Wood
23.02.06 Dave Hinds W PTS 6 Leeds
13.04.06 Dai Davies W CO 3 Leeds
13.04.07 Kristian Laight W PTS 4 Altrincham
24.06.07 Rom Krauklis W PTS 4 Wigan
13.07.07 Deniss Sirjatovs W RSC 2 Barnsley
19.10.07 Dwayne Hill W RSC 4 Doncaster
08.12.07 Carl Allen W PTS 6 Wigan
28.03.08 Peter Allen W PTS 6 Barnsley
18.07.08 Harry Ramogoadi W PTS 6 Dagenham
21.12.08 Jason Nesbitt W RSC 4 Bolton
29.03.09 Johnny Greaves W PTS 4 Bolton
29.05.09 Anthony Crolla W PTS 10 Stoke
   (Elim. British S. Featherweight Title)
Career: 12 contests, won 12.

Chas Symonds

Croydon *Born* Croydon, 8 July, 1982
Welterweight. Former Undefeated British
Masters Welterweight Champion. Former
Southern Area Welterweight Champion. *Ht*
5'6¼"
Manager S. Barrett
18.02.03 Darren Goode W RSC 2 Bethnal Green
08.04.03 Lee Bedell W PTS 4 Bethnal Green
03.06.03 Arv Mittoo W PTS 6 Bethnal Green
22.07.03 Pete Buckley W PTS 6 Bethnal Green
25.09.03 Ben Hudson W PTS 6 Bethnal Green
18.11.03 Ernie Smith W PTS 6 Bethnal Green
20.02.04 Dave Wakefield W RSC 5 Bethnal
   Green
24.04.04 Geraint Harvey W PTS 4 Reading
07.05.04 Robert Lloyd-Taylor W RTD 5 Bethnal
   Green
25.06.04 Brett James W RSC 4 Bethnal Green
   (Southern Area Welterweight Title
   Challenge)
24.09.04 Keith Jones W PTS 10 Bethnal Green
   (Vacant British Masters Welterweight
   Title)
25.02.05 Peter Dunn W PTS 4 Wembley
29.04.05 Ross Minter L RSC 3 Southwark
   (Southern Area Welterweight Title
   Defence)
13.06.08 Paul Morby W PTS 6 Portsmouth
18.07.08 Alex Spitjo W RSC 3 Dagenham
15.11.08 Tomas Grublys L PTS 4 Bethnal Green
14.03.09 Tom Glover L PTS 8 Birmingham
22.03.09 Badru Lusamba L RSC 3 Bethnal
   Green
Career: 18 contests, won 14, lost 4.

Gavin Tait

Carmarthen. *Born* Carmarthen, 2 March, 1976
Welterweight. *Ht* 5'7"
Manager Self
07.06.04 Stuart Green L PTS 6 Glasgow
03.07.04 Justin Hicks W RSC 5 Bristol
05.10.04 Tristan Davies L PTS 6 Dudley
24.11.04 David Pereira L PTS 6 Mayfair
02.12.04 Chris Long L PTS 6 Bristol
07.04.05 Gary Coombes W RSC 3 Birmingham
27.05.05 Darren Johnstone L PTS 6 Motherwell
30.10.05 Dwayne Hill L PTS 6 Sheffield
24.03.06 Tom Glover W PTS 4 Bethnal Green
21.10.06 Calvin White W PTS 4 Southwark
03.12.06 Jamie Spence W RSC 4 Bethnal Green
08.12.07 Scott Haywood L PTS 6 Wigan
16.05.08 Paul Burns L PTS 10 Motherwell
 (Vacant International Masters Welterweight Title)
18.07.08 Billy Smith W PTS 4 Dagenham
13.09.08 Baz Carey W PTS 4 Bethnal Green
12.06.09 Johnny Greaves W PTS 4 Bethnal Green
Career: 16 contests, won 8, lost 8.

Gavin Tait   Philip Sharkey

Karl Taylor

Birmingham. *Born* Birmingham, 5 January, 1966
Welterweight. Former Undefeated Midlands Area Lightweight Champion. *Ht* 5'5"
Manager E. Johnson
18.03.87 Steve Brown W PTS 6 Stoke
06.04.87 Paul Taylor L PTS 6 Southampton
12.06.87 Mark Begley W RSC 1 Leamington
18.11.87 Colin Lynch W RSC 4 Solihull
29.02.88 Peter Bradley L PTS 8 Birmingham
04.10.89 Mark Antony W CO 2 Stafford
30.10.89 Tony Feliciello L PTS 8 Birmingham
06.12.89 John Davison L PTS 8 Leicester

23.12.89 Regilio Tuur L RTD 1 Hoogvliet, Holland
22.02.90 Mark Ramsey L RSC 4 Hull
29.10.90 Steve Walker DREW 6 Birmingham
10.12.90 Elvis Parsley L PTS 6 Birmingham
16.01.91 Wayne Windle W PTS 8 Stoke
02.05.91 Billy Schwer L RSC 2 Northampton
25.07.91 Peter Till L RSC 4 Dudley
 (Midlands Area Lightweight Title Challenge)
24.02.92 Charlie Kane L PTS 8 Glasgow
28.04.92 Richard Woolgar W PTS 6 Wolverhampton
29.05.92 Alan McDowall L PTS 6 Glasgow
25.07.92 Michael Armstrong L RSC 3 Manchester
02.11.92 Hugh Forde L PTS 6 Wolverhampton
23.11.92 Dave McHale L PTS 8 Glasgow
22.12.92 Patrick Gallagher L RSC 3 Mayfair
13.02.93 Craig Dermody L RSC 5 Manchester
31.03.93 Craig Dermody W PTS 6 Barking
07.06.93 Mark Geraghty W PTS 8 Glasgow
13.08.93 Giorgio Campanella L CO 6 Arezzo, Italy
05.10.93 Paul Harvey W PTS 6 Mayfair
21.10.93 Charles Shepherd L RTD 5 Bayswater
21.12.93 Patrick Gallagher L PTS 6 Mayfair
09.02.94 Alan Levene W RSC 2 Brentwood
01.03.94 Shaun Cogan L PTS 6 Dudley
15.03.94 Patrick Gallagher L PTS 6 Mayfair
18.04.94 Peter Till W PTS 10 Walsall
 (Midlands Area Lightweight Title Challenge)
24.05.94 Michael Ayers DREW 8 Sunderland
12.11.94 P. J. Gallagher L PTS 6 Dublin
29.11.94 Dingaan Thobela W PTS 8 Cannock
31.03.95 Michael Ayers L RSC 8 Crystal Palace
 (British Lightweight Title Challenge)
06.05.95 Cham Joof W PTS 8 Shepton Mallet
23.06.95 Poli Diaz L PTS 8 Madrid, Spain
02.09.95 Paul Ryan L RSC 3 Wembley
04.11.95 Carl Wright L PTS 6 Liverpool
15.12.95 Peter Richardson L PTS 8 Bethnal Green
23.01.96 Paul Knights DREW 6 Bethnal Green
05.03.96 Andy Holligan L PTS 6 Barrow
20.03.96 Mervyn Bennett W PTS 8 Cardiff
21.05.96 Malcolm Melvin L PTS 10 Edgbaston
 (Midlands Area L. Welterweight Title Challenge)
07.10.96 Joshua Clottey L RSC 2 Lewisham
20.12.96 Anatoly Alexandrov L RSC 7 Bilbao, Spain
28.01.97 Eamonn Magee L PTS 6 Belfast
28.02.97 Mark Breslin L RSC 6 Kilmarnock
30.08.97 Gilbert Eastman L PTS 4 Cheshunt
25.10.97 Tontcho Tontchev L PTS 4 Queensferry
22.11.97 Bobby Vanzie L PTS 6 Manchester
18.04.98 Ricky Hatton L RSC 1 Manchester
18.07.98 James Hare L PTS 4 Sheffield
26.09.98 Oktay Urkal L PTS 8 Norwich
28.11.98 Junior Witter L PTS 4 Sheffield
06.03.99 George Scott L RSC 4 Southwark
15.05.99 Jon Thaxton L PTS 6 Sheffield
10.07.99 Eamonn Magee L RTD 3 Southwark
06.11.99 Alan Sebire W PTS 6 Widnes
15.11.99 Steve Murray L RSC 1 Bethnal Green
19.08.00 Iain Eldridge L PTS 4 Brentwood
04.09.00 Tomas Jansson L PTS 6 Manchester
16.09.00 Colin Lynes L PTS 6 Bethnal Green
09.12.00 David Walker L PTS 6 Southwark
10.02.01 Matthew Hatton L PTS 4 Widnes

10.03.01 Francis Barrett L RSC 3 Bethnal Green
10.04.01 Costas Katsantonis L PTS 4 Wembley
16.06.01 Brett James DREW 4 Wembley
15.09.01 David Barnes L PTS 4 Manchester
28.10.01 Babatunde Ajayi L PTS 4 Southwark
24.11.01 Ross Minter L PTS 4 Bethnal Green
15.12.01 Alexandra Vetoux L PTS 4 Wembley
12.02.02 Brett James DREW 4 Bethnal Green
11.03.02 Kevin McIntyre L PTS 4 Glasgow
04.05.02 Matthew Hatton L RSC 3 Bethnal Green
25.06.02 Rimell Taylor DREW 6 Rugby
20.07.02 Matthew Hatton L RTD 2 Bethnal Green
28.09.02 Michael Jennings L RSC 4 Manchester
16.11.02 Gavin Wake L PTS 4 Nottingham
30.11.02 Tony Conroy L PTS 4 Coventry
14.12.02 Alexander Vetoux L RTD 3 Newcastle
15.02.03 Ross Minter L PTS 6 Wembley
29.03.03 Alexander Vetoux L RSC 1 Portsmouth
08.05.03 Tony Doherty L PTS 4 Widnes
25.07.03 Lenny Daws L RTD 2 Norwich
06.10.03 Jonathan Woollins W PTS 6 Birmingham
29.10.03 Ajose Olusegun L PTS 6 Leicester Square
29.11.03 Gary Young L RSC 3 Renfrew
30.01.04 Lee McAllister L PTS 4 Dagenham
05.03.04 Oscar Hall L PTS 6 Darlington
27.03.04 Jamie Arthur L PTS 6 Edinburgh
06.05.04 Ashley Theophane L PTS 4 Barnsley
22.05.04 Tony Doherty L RTD 2 Widnes
03.09.04 Taz Jones L PTS 4 Newport
18.09.04 Karl Chiverton L PTS 6 Newark
26.09.04 Danny Johnston L PTS 6 Stoke
19.11.04 Tony Doherty L RSC 2 Bethnal Green
19.12.04 Kell Brook L PTS 6 Bolton
06.03.05 John Murray L PTS 6 Shaw
14.05.05 Lee McAllister L RTD 3 Aberdeen
26.06.05 Henry Castle L PTS 6 Southampton
24.07.05 John Fewkes L PTS 6 Sheffield
16.09.05 Tristan Davies L PTS 4 Telford
08.11.05 Danny Reynolds L RSC 4 Leeds
11.12.05 Paul Halpin L PTS 4 Chigwell
18.12.05 Jonathan Hussey L PTS 6 Bolton
17.02.06 John O'Donnell L PTS 4 Bethnal Green
01.04.06 Ashley Theophane L PTS 4 Bethnal Green
24.04.06 Simon Fleck L PTS 6 Cleethorpes
13.05.06 Dale Miles L RSC 3 Sutton in Ashfield
18.06.06 Prince Arron L PTS 6 Manchester
15.09.06 Garry Buckland L PTS 6 Newport
07.10.06 Rob Hunt L PTS 6 Walsall
24.11.06 Scott Lawton L PTS 6 Stoke
01.12.06 Peter McDonagh L PTS 4 Tower Hill
10.12.06 Muhsen Nasser L PTS 6 Sheffield
17.02.07 Eddie Corcoran L PTS 4 Wembley
11.03.07 Chris Johnson L RTD 3 Shaw
06.05.07 Khurram Hussain L PTS 4 Leeds
09.06.07 Mark Dawes L PTS 6 Middlesbrough
20.07.07 Rob Hunt L PTS 4 Wolverhampton
07.09.07 Femi Fehintola L PTS 4 Doncaster
23.09.07 Ruben Giles L PTS 6 Longford
08.10.07 Charles Paul King L PTS 6 Glasgow
19.10.07 Mark Hastie L PTS 6 Motherwell
17.11.07 Scott Miller L PTS 6 Stoke
28.11.07 Scott Evans L RSC 3 Walsall
22.03.08 Joe Elfidh L PTS 6 Sheffield
28.04.08 Charles Paul King L PTS 6 Glasgow
05.06.08 Graham Fearn L PTS 6 Leeds
15.06.08 Danny Chamberlain L PTS 6 Bethnal Green
04.07.08 Steve Williams L PTS 4 Liverpool

25.07.08 Mark Dawes L PTS 6 Houghton le
Spring
13.09.08 Chris Goodwin L PTS 4 Stoke
20.09.08 Ben Lawler L PTS 6 Newark
24.10.08 Eisa Al Dah L PTS 6 Newport
06.12.08 Jack Perry L PTS 4 Nottingham
17.01.09 Ali Shah L PTS 4 Wigan
13.02.09 Adam Cummings DREW 4 Swindon
27.02.09 Keith Sheen L PTS 6 Wolverhampton
28.03.09 Lee Jennings L PTS 4 Liverpool
10.04.09 Adam Cummings L PTS 4 Cheltenham
23.04.09 Bobby Gladman L PTS 6 Mayfair
10.05.09 Scott Conway L PTS 6 Derby
17.05.09 Tony Aitcheson L PTS 6 Bolton
12.06.09 Rob Doody L PTS 6 Wolverhampton
28.06.09 Graham Earl L PTS 6 Luton
Career: 149 contests, won 16, drew 7, lost 126.

Karl Taylor   Philip Sharkey

John-Paul Temple
Brighton. *Born* London, 30 May, 1973
L.Middleweight. *Ht* 5'11"
Manager R. Davies
11.02.97 Mark O'Callaghan W PTS 6 Bethnal
Green
17.03.97 Les Frost W CO 4 Mayfair
24.04.97 Chris Lyons W PTS 6 Mayfair
23.10.97 Chris Lyons W PTS 8 Mayfair
26.03.98 Trevor Smith L RSC 5 Piccadilly
28.04.98 Chris Price L PTS 6 Brentford
05.10.99 Jason Hall L PTS 6 Bloomsbury
25.02.00 Daniel James L PTS 10 Newmarket
*(Vacant Southern Area L.Welterweight
Title)*
21.11.04 Neil Jarmolinski DREW 4 Bracknell
03.12.04 Barrie Lee L PTS 4 Edinburgh
30.04.05 Danny Goode L PTS 4 Dagenham
26.06.05 Danny Goode L PTS 4 Southampton
10.09.05 Kerry Hope L PTS 4 Cardiff
06.10.05 Kevin Phelan L PTS 6 Longford
02.12.05 Darren Barker L RSC 6 Nottingham
29.06.06 Karl David L PTS 6 Cardiff
16.09.07 Paul Morby L PTS 4 Southampton
02.03.08 Paul Morby L PTS 4 Portsmouth
27.09.08 Pat McAleese L PTS 4 Bethnal Green
Career: 19 contests, won 4, drew 1, lost 14.

John-Paul Temple   Philip Sharkey

Jonathan Thaxton
Norwich. *Born* Norwich, 10 September,
1974
Former European Lightweight Champion.
Former Undefeated British & WBF
Lightweight Champion. Former Southern
Area, IBF & WBO Inter-Continental
L.Welterweight Champion.
Ht 5'6"
Manager J. Ingle
09.12.92 Scott Smith W PTS 6 Stoke
03.03.93 Dean Hiscox W PTS 6 Solihull
17.03.93 John O. Johnson W PTS 6 Stoke
23.06.93 Brian Coleman W PTS 8 Gorleston
22.09.93 John Smith W PTS 6 Wembley
07.12.93 Dean Hollington W RSC 3 Bethnal
Green
10.03.94 B. F. Williams W RSC 4 Watford
*(Vacant Southern Area L.Welterweight
Title)*
18.11.94 Keith Marner L PTS 10 Bracknell
*(Southern Area L.Welterweight Title
Defence)*
26.05.95 David Thompson W RSC 6 Norwich
23.06.95 Delroy Leslie W PTS 6 Bethnal Green
12.08.95 Rene Prins L PTS 8 Zaandam, Holland
08.12.95 Colin Dunne L RSC 5 Bethnal Green
*(Vacant Southern Area Lightweight
Title)*
20.01.96 John O. Johnson W RSC 4 Mansfield
13.02.96 Paul Ryan W RSC 1 Bethnal Green
25.06.96 Mark Elliot W CO 5 Mansfield
*(Vacant IBF Inter-Continental
L.Welterweight Title)*
14.09.96 Bernard Paul W PTS 12 Sheffield
*(Vacant WBO Inter-Continental
L.Welterweight Title)*
27.03.97 Paul Burke W RSC 9 Norwich
*(IBF & WBO Inter-Continental
L.Welterweight Title Defences)*
28.06.97 Gagik Chachatrian W RSC 2 Norwich
*(IBF & WBO Inter-Continental
L.Welterweight Title Defences)*

29.11.97 Rimvidas Billius W PTS 12 Norwich
*(IBF & WBO Inter-Continental
L.Welterweight Title Defences)*
26.09.98 Emanuel Burton L RSC 7 Norwich
*(IBF & WBO Inter-Continental
L.Welterweight Title Defences)*
15.05.99 Karl Taylor W PTS 6 Sheffield
07.08.99 Brian Coleman W PTS 6 Dagenham
15.11.99 Jason Rowland L RSC 5 Bethnal Green
(British L.Welterweight Title Challenge)
15.07.00 Kimoun Kouassi W RSC 3 Norwich
21.10.00 Ricky Hatton L PTS 12 Wembley
(Vacant British L.Welterweight Title)
26.03.01 Alan Temple W PTS 4 Wembley
28.07.01 David Kirk W PTS 4 Wembley
09.02.02 Eamonn Magee L RSC 6 Manchester
*(Commonwealth L.Welterweight Title
Challenge)*
13.04.02 Chill John W RSC 2 Norwich
15.06.02 Marc Waelkens W RSC 7 Norwich
21.09.02 Viktor Baranov W RSC 1 Norwich
09.10.04 Silence Saheed W PTS 6 Norwich
13.12.04 Carl Allen W RSC 1 Birmingham
09.04.05 Christophe de Busillet W CO 4 Norwich
(Vacant WBF Lightweight Title)
03.09.05 Vasile Dragomir W CO 4 Norwich
(WBF Lightweight Title Defence)
17.02.06 Alan Temple W RSC 5 Bethnal Green
13.05.06 Jorge Daniel Miranda W PTS 10
Sheffield
08.12.06 Lee Meager W PTS 12 Dagenham
(British Lightweight Title Challenge)
16.03.07 Scott Lawton W RSC 7 Norwich
(British Lightweight Title Defence)
05.10.07 Dave Stewart W RSC 12 Bethnal Green
(British Lightweight Title Defence
04.04.08 Yuri Romanov L RSC 6 Bethnal Green
*(European) Lightweight Title
Challenge)*
04.10.08 Juan Carlos Diaz Melero W CO 3
Norwich
(Vacant European Lightweight Title)
28.02.09 Anthony Mezaache L PTS 12 Norwich
(European Lightweight Title Defence)
Career: 43 contests, won 34, lost 9.

Ashley Theophane   Philip Sharkey

179

Ashley Theophane

Kilburn. *Born* London, 20 August, 1980
L.Welterweight. Former Undeeated Global
Boxing Council Welterweight Champion.
Ht 5'7"
Manager Self
03.06.03 Lee Bedell W RSC 4 Bethnal Green
22.07.03 Brian Coleman W PTS 6 Bethnal Green
25.04.04 David Kirk W PTS 6 Nottingham
06.05.04 Karl Taylor W PTS 4 Barnsley
05.06.04 Chris Brophy W RSC 3 Bethnal Green
19.06.04 Arv Mittoo W PTS 4 Muswell Hill
02.12.04 Keith Jones W PTS 6 Crystal Palace
26.03.05 Judex Meemea L PTS 6 Hackney
24.04.05 David Kehoe W PTS 4 Leicester Square
12.06.05 Jus Wallie W PTS 4 Leicester Square
18.09.05 Oscar Milkitas L PTS 4 Bethnal Green
09.10.05 David Kehoe W PTS 4 Hammersmith
19.11.05 Duncan Cottier W PTS 6 Southwark
25.02.06 Daniel Thorpe DREW 4 Canning Town
17.03.06 Josef Holub W CO 3 Horka, Germany
01.04.06 Karl Taylor W PTS 4 Bethnal Green
21.05.06 Billy Smith W PTS 4 Bethnal Green
24.09.06 Jon Honney W PTS 6 Bethnal Green
07.10.06 Ibrahim Barakat W PTS 6 Horka,
Germany
02.12.06 Omar Siala W RSC 11 Berlin, Germany
(Vacant GBC Welterweight Title)
20.01.07 Alan Bosworth W RSC 7 Muswell Hill
(Elim. British L.Welterweight Title)
16.11.07 Marcos Hernandez W RSC 3 Gros Islet,
Saint Lucia
01.12.07 Rocky Muscus W RSC 1 Bethnal
Green
15.02.08 Ali Oubaali L PTS 10 Uncasville,
Connecticut, USA
15.06.08 Geoffrey Munika W PTS 6 Bethnal
Green
31.07.08 DeMarcus Corley W PTS 8 Rochester,
New York, USA
06.12.08 Matt Scriven W PTS 6 Bethnal Green
22.03.09 Craig Docherty W PTS 6 Bethnal Green
21.06.09 Mark Douglas W PTS 8 Bethnal Green
Career: 29 contests, won 25, drew 1, lost 3.

Matthew Thirlwall

Bermondsey. *Born* Middlesbrough, 28
November, 1980
S.Middleweight. *Ht* 5'9½"
Manager R. McCracken
16.03.02 William Webster W RSC 1 Bethnal
Green
10.05.02 Leigh Wicks W PTS 4 Bethnal Green
23.08.02 Harry Butler W RSC 3 Bethnal Green
25.10.02 Jason Collins W RSC 5 Bethnal Green
21.12.02 Howard Clarke W PTS 6 Dagenham
28.01.03 Gary Beardsley L PTS 6 Nottingham
16.04.03 Gary Beardsley W PTS 6 Nottingham
27.05.03 Leigh Wicks W PTS 6 Dagenham
04.10.03 Dean Powell W RSC 2 Muswell Hill
11.12.03 Harry Butler W PTS 6 Bethnal Green
12.03.04 Patrick Cito W RSC 3 Nottingham
24.09.04 Jason Collins L PTS 6 Nottingham
02.12.05 Ernie Smith W PTS 4 Nottingham
20.01.06 Donovan Smillie W CO 6 Bethnal Green
*(Final Elim. English S.Middleweight
Title)*
24.03.06 Moises Martinez W RSC 6 Hollywood,
Florida, USA

08.12.06 Howard Clarke W PTS 4 Dagenham
20.01.07 Hussain Osman W RSC 5 Muswell Hill
18.05.07 David Kirk W PTS 4 Canning Town
14.11.07 Danny Thornton L RSC 3 Bethnal
Green
13.12.08 Sherman Alleyne W RSC 4 Brentwood
28.02.09 James Tucker W PTS 6 Norwich
23.05.09 George Hillyard W RTD 4 Watford
Career: 22 contests, won 19, lost 3.

Matthew Thirwall   Philip Sharkey

Aaron Thomas

Stoke. *Born* St Asaph, 11 April, 1980
Welterweight. *Ht* 5'8"
Manager C. Sanigar
30.09.06 Martin Sweeney W CO 2 Stoke
24.11.06 Ben Hudson W PTS 6 Stoke
12.05.07 Surinder Sekhon W PTS 4 Stoke
23.05.09 William Warburton W PTS 4
Queensferry
Career: 4 contests, won 4.

Jason Thomas

Merthyr Tydfil. *Born* Pontypridd, 7
October, 1976
S.Featherweight. *Ht* 5'6"
Manager B. Coleman
28.11.95 Henry Jones W PTS 4 Cardiff
08.12.95 John Sillo L PTS 6 Liverpool
13.01.96 Paul Griffin L RSC 2 Manchester
02.10.96 Henry Jones L PTS 6 Cardiff
23.10.96 Noel Wilders L PTS 6 Halifax
27.11.96 Jason Booth L PTS 4 Swansea
02.06.97 Colin Moffett W RSC 3 Belfast
02.08.97 Peter Culshaw L PTS 8 Barnsley
14.10.97 Graham McGrath W PTS 6
Wolverhampton
25.10.97 Keith Knox L PTS 8 Queensferry
04.12.97 Sean Green DREW 4 Doncaster
13.02.98 Nick Tooley W PTS 6 Weston super
Mare
18.04.98 Hector Orozco DREW 4 Manchester
14.05.98 John Matthews L PTS 6 Acton
03.10.98 Michael Alldis L PTS 6 Crawley
06.02.99 Noel Wilders L PTS 10 Halifax
(Elim. British Bantamweight Title)

15.05.99 Alex Moon L PTS 8 Blackpool
24.09.99 Frankie De Milo W RSC 2 Merthyr
Tydfil
15.11.99 Stephen Oates L PTS 6 Bethnal Green
19.02.00 Stephen Oates L PTS 6 Dagenham
29.03.00 Frankie De Milo L RSC 8 Piccadilly
*(Vacant British Masters S.Bantamweight
Title)*
06.10.00 Takalani Ndlovu L RSC 2 Maidstone
05.12.00 Kevin Gerowski L PTS 8 Nottingham
24.05.01 Stewart Sanderson DREW 6 Glasgow
08.06.01 Karim Quibir Lopez L CO 4 Orense,
Spain
17.11.01 Chris Emanuele L RSC 1 Coventry
23.02.02 Jason Booth L PTS 6 Nottingham
27.04.02 Dale Robinson L RSC 4 Huddersfield
05.10.02 Gary Davies L RSC 5 Liverpool
24.03.03 Chris Emanuele W PTS 4 Barnsley
05.12.03 Lee Haskins L PTS 6 Bristol
29.02.04 Riaz Durgahed L RSC 1 Bristol
28.03.09 Rhys Roberts L PTS 4 Altrincham
12.06.09 Davey Savage L PTS 8 Clydebank
Career: 34 contests, won 7, drew 3, lost 24.

Chris Thompson

Leeds. *Born* Leeds, 5 April, 1984
L.Middleweight. *Ht* 5'11¼"
Manager D. Roche
31.01.08 Steve Cooper L RSC 2 Piccadilly
16.03.08 Paul Royston L PTS 6 Sheffield
22.06.08 Duane Parker L PTS 4 Derby
24.07.08 Martin Gordon DREW 4
Wolverhampton
23.05.09 Shaun Farmer W RSC 2 Queensferry
12.06.09 Wayne Alwan-Arab L PTS 6 Bethnal
Green
Career: 6 contests, won 1, drew 1, lost 4.

Jason Thompson

Huddersfield. *Born* Huddersfield, 1 June,
1982
Lightweight. *Ht* 5'10"
Manager C. Aston
08.03.09 Jason Carr DREW 4 Sheffield
29.05.09 Richard Ghent L RSC 3 Dudley
Career: 2 contests, drew 1, lost 1.

Mark Thompson

Heywood. *Born* Rochdale, 28 May, 1981
L.Middleweight. Former Undefeated
International Masters Welterweight
Champion. *Ht* 5'11"
Manager S. Wood
23.09.05 Geraint Harvey W PTS 4 Manchester
20.11.05 Danny Moir W RSC 2 Shaw
18.12.05 Tony Randell W RSC 2 Bolton
12.02.06 Darren Gethin W PTS 4 Manchester
02.03.06 Simon Fleck W CO 3 Blackpool
02.04.06 Ernie Smith W PTS 6 Shaw
18.06.06 Alex Stoda W RSC 1 Manchester
21.07.06 Ernie Smith W RSC 3 Altrincham
29.09.06 Alexander Matviechuk W PTS 8
Manchester
09.02.07 Lee Noble W PTS 6 Leeds
13.04.07 Manoocha Salari W RSC 1 Altrincham
06.07.07 Vincent Vuma L RSC 8 Wigan
*(Vacant WBC International
L.Middleweight Title)*

22.09.07 Ronny Daniels W RSC 1 Wigan
26.10.07 Frank Harroche Horta W PTS 8 Wigan
01.02.08 Darren Gethin W RTD 2 Bethnal Green
26.04.08 Maurycy Gojko W RSC 1 Wigan
(Vacant International Masters
Welterweight Title)
13.06.08 Artur Jashkul W CO 1 Portsmouth
17.10.08 Gatis Skuja W PTS 6 Bethnal Green
07.11.08 Craig Dickson W RSC 7 Wigan
03.04.09 Johannes Fabrizius W PTS 6 Leigh
Career: 20 contests, won 19, lost 1.

Willie Thompson

Ballyclare. Born Larne, 2 January, 1980
L.Middleweight. Ht 6'0"
Manager A. Wilton
30.06.07 Paul Royston W PTS 4 Belfast
25.08.07 Artur Jashkul W PTS 4 Dublin
13.10.07 Peter Dunn W PTS 6 Belfast
08.12.07 Duncan Cottier W PTS 4 Belfast
22.03.08 Semens Moroshek W PTS 4 Dublin
31.05.08 Janis Chernouskis W PTS 6 Belfast
18.12.08 Karl Chiverton DREW 4 Dublin
15.05.09 Michael Jennings L RSC 4 Belfast
Career: 8 contests, won 6, drew 1, lost 1.

Danny Thornton

Leeds. Born Leeds, 20 July, 1978
Cruiserweight. Former Undefeated Central
Area Middleweight Champion. Ht 5'10"
Manager Self
06.10.97 Pedro Carragher L PTS 6 Bradford
13.11.97 Shaun O'Neill DREW 6 Bradford
08.12.97 Shaun O'Neill DREW 6 Bradford
09.02.98 Roy Chipperfield W RSC 4 Bradford
17.03.98 Patrick J. Maxwell L PTS 6 Sheffield
30.03.98 Mark Owens W PTS 6 Bradford
15.05.98 Danny Bell W PTS 6 Nottingham
15.06.98 Jimmy Hawk W PTS 6 Bradford
12.10.98 Wayne Shepherd W PTS 6 Bradford
21.02.99 Shaun O'Neill W RSC 5 Bradford
25.04.99 Matt Scriven W RSC 4 Leeds
14.06.99 Martin Thompson W PTS 6 Bradford
18.10.99 Paul Henry W PTS 4 Bradford
14.11.99 Dean Ashton W PTS 4 Bradford
06.12.99 Lee Blundell L PTS 6 Bradford
05.02.00 Steve Roberts L PTS 6 Bethnal Green
25.03.00 Lee Molloy W RSC 2 Liverpool
06.06.00 Joe Townsley L RSC 7 Motherwell
(IBO Inter-Continental
L. Middleweight Title Challenge)
30.11.00 Lee Blundell L RSC 8 Blackpool
(Vacant Central Area L. Middleweight
Title)
20.03.01 Ian Toby W PTS 8 Leeds
13.11.01 Matt Galer L RSC 4 Leeds
02.12.02 Gary Thompson W PTS 6 Leeds
13.05.03 Kreshnik Qato L PTS 6 Leeds
06.06.03 Jason Collins W PTS 10 Hull
(Vacant Central Area Middleweight
Title)
28.11.03 Jason Collins W PTS 10 Hull
(Central Area Middleweight Title
Defence)
10.02.04 Mo W PTS 6 Barnsley
08.05.04 Scott Dann L RSC 3 Bristol
(Vacant English Middleweight Title)
14.05.05 Simeon Cover DREW 6 Aberdeen
01.06.05 Gary Thompson W PTS 4 Leeds

25.09.05 Simeon Cover W PTS 6 Leeds
29.10.05 Jozsef Nagy L PTS 12 Szentes, Hungary
(Vacant EBA S.Middleweight Title)
23.02.06 Howard Clarke W PTS 6 Leeds
20.03.06 Ojay Abrahams W PTS 6 Leeds
12.05.06 Darren Barker L RSC 6 Bethnal Green
01.06.07 Jorge Gomez W PTS 4 Peterborough
08.06.07 Brian Magee L RTD 2 Motherwell
07.09.07 Danny Grainger W PTS 4 Doncaster
12.10.07 Carl Wild W PTS 6 Leeds
14.11.07 Matthew Thirlwall W RSC 3 Bethnal
Green
08.02.08 Martin Marshall W PTS 4 Peterlee
06.09.08 Paul Smith L CO 6 Manchester
22.11.08 Cello Renda L RSC 2 Bethnal Green
Career: 42 contests, won 25, drew 3, lost 14.

Danny Thornton   Philip Sharkey

Daniel Thorpe

Sheffield. Born Sheffield, 24 September,
1977
Lightweight. Former Central Area
Lightweight Champion. Ht 5'7½"
Manager Self
07.09.01 Brian Gifford DREW 4 Bethnal Green
24.09.01 Ram Singh W RSC 4 Cleethorpes
17.11.01 Mally McIver L PTS 6 Dewsbury
10.12.01 Jason Gonzales W RSC 2 Birmingham
17.12.01 Joel Viney L RSC 2 Cleethorpes
11.02.02 Gareth Wiltshaw L PTS 6 Shrewsbury
04.03.02 Dave Travers W PTS 6 Birmingham
13.04.02 Jackson Williams L PTS 6 Norwich
11.05.02 Dean Scott W RSC 1 Chesterfield
21.05.02 Chris McDonagh L PTS 6 Custom
House
08.06.02 Gary Young L RSC 1 Renfrew
12.07.02 Chill John L PTS 4 Southampton
21.07.02 John Marshall L RSC 1 Salford
22.09.02 Albi Hunt L PTS 6 Southwark
05.10.02 Gavin Down L RSC 2 Chesterfield
17.11.02 Nadeem Siddique L PTS 4 Bradford
29.11.02 Pete Buckley W PTS 6 Hull
21.12.02 Billy Corcoran L CO 2 Dagenham
16.02.03 Eddie Nevins L RSC 8 Salford
(Vacant Central Area S.Featherweight
Title)
22.03.03 Jamie Arthur L PTS 4 Renfrew

29.03.03 Danny Hunt L PTS 6 Portsmouth
12.04.03 Jackson Williams L PTS 6 Norwich
19.04.03 Steve Mullin W RSC 1 Liverpool
28.04.03 Jeff Thomas L PTS 6 Cleethorpes
08.05.03 Andy Morris L PTS 4 Widnes
08.06.03 Choi Tsveenpurev L PTS 8 Shaw
20.06.03 Colin Toohey L PTS 6 Liverpool
28.06.03 Gavin Rees L RSC 1 Cardiff
03.08.03 Joel Viney L PTS 6 Stalybridge
06.09.03 Joel Viney W PTS 6 Aberdeen
13.09.03 Sean Hughes L PTS 6 Wakefield
21.09.03 Chris Long W PTS 6 Bristol
12.10.03 Baz Carey DREW 6 Sheffield
19.10.03 Charles Shepherd L PTS 6 Shaw
27.10.03 Nadeem Siddique L PTS 6 Glasgow
06.11.03 Lee Beavis L PTS 4 Dagenham
07.12.03 Mally McIver W PTS 10 Bradford
(Vacant Central Area Lightweight Title)
21.12.03 Pete Buckley W PTS 6 Bolton
26.02.04 Andy Morris L RSC 3 Widnes
03.04.04 Jason Nesbitt W PTS 6 Sheffield
23.04.04 Dave Hinds W PTS 6 Leicester
07.05.04 Stefy Bull L PTS 10 Doncaster
(Central Area Lightweight Title
Defence)
22.05.04 Gary Thornhill L RSC 4 Manchester
03.07.04 Joel Viney W RSC 1 Blackpool
10.09.04 Mickey Bowden W PTS 6 Wembley
18.09.04 Carl Greaves L PTS 6 Newark
01.10.04 Steve Bell L PTS 6 Manchester
08.10.04 Ricky Burns L PTS 6 Glasgow
16.10.04 Ryan Barrett L PTS 4 Dagenham
29.10.04 Adnan Amar L PTS 4 Worksop
06.11.04 Baz Carey W PTS 6 Coventry
26.11.04 John Murray L RSC 2 Altrincham
13.02.05 Lee McAllister L PTS 4 Bradford
04.03.05 Femi Fehintola L PTS 6 Rotherham
10.04.05 Dave Stewart L RSC 3 Brentwood
14.05.05 Tye Williams W RSC 3 Aberdeen
26.05.05 Baz Carey L PTS 6 Mayfair
03.06.05 Nadeem Siddique L PTS 6 Hull
24.06.05 James Gorman L PTS 6 Belfast
02.07.05 Michael Kelly L PTS 4 Dundalk
09.07.05 Carl Johanneson L RSC 3 Bristol
25.09.05 Jon Honney W PTS 4 Southampton
06.10.05 Paul Holborn L PTS 6 Sunderland
25.10.05 Kevin Mitchell L RSC 4 Preston
25.11.05 Haider Ali W RTD 4 Walsall
10.12.05 Amir Khan L RSC 2 Canning Town
27.01.06 Ian Wilson L PTS 4 Dagenham
25.02.06 Ashley Theophane DREW 4 Canning
Town
11.03.06 Gavin Rees L RSC 5 Newport
13.05.06 Dean Smith L PTS 4 Bethnal Green
20.05.06 Kevin O'Hara L PTS 6 Belfast
28.05.06 Shane Watson L PTS 6 Longford
16.06.06 Dwayne Hill L PTS 4 Liverpool
23.06.06 Anthony Maynard L PTS 4 Birmingham
02.09.06 Steve Bell L RTD 4 Bolton
06.10.06 Jonathan Whiteman L PTS 6 Mansfield
18.10.06 Gareth Couch L PTS 4 Bayswater
04.11.06 Paul McCloskey L RTD 3 Glasgow
06.12.06 Pete Buckley W PTS 6 Rotherham
14.12.06 Gavin Deacon W PTS 6 Leicester
22.12.06 Harry Ramogoadi L PTS 6 Coventry
15.02.07 Dean Harrison L PTS 4 Dudley
10.03.07 Stephen Burke L PTS 4 Liverpool
07.04.07 Barrie Jones L RSC 2 Cardiff
06.05.07 Michael Gomez L RSC 3 Altrincham
08.06.07 Albi Hunt L PTS 4 Mayfair
30.06.07 Eddie Hyland L PTS 4 Belfast

21.07.07 Andy Morris L RSC 2 Cardiff
09.10.07 Giovanni Kopogo W RSC 2 Tower Hamlets
12.10.07 Paul Truscott L PTS 4 Peterlee
31.10.07 Mark McCullough L PTS 6 Bayswater
17.11.07 Marco Cittadini L PTS 4 Glasgow
30.11.07 Leonard Lothian L PTS 6 Hull
08.12.07 Anthony Crolla L RTD 2 Bolton
02.02.08 Liam Walsh L CO 1 Canning Town
17.10.08 Chris Higgs L PTS 6 Swindon
25.10.08 Charles Paul King L PTS 6 Aberdeen
08.11.08 Stewart Ramplin W RSC 5 Wigan
22.11.08 Rick Godding L PTS 4 Blackpool
01.02.09 Lee Cook L PTS 4 Bethnal Green
13.02.09 Chris Goodwin L PTS 6 Wigan
27.02.09 Chris Lewis L PTS 4 Wolverhampton
14.03.09 Eddie Doyle L PTS 6 Aberdeen
03.04.09 Darren Askew L PTS 6 Leigh
24.05.09 Shinny Bayaar L PTS 4 Shaw
31.05.09 Steve Jevons L PTS 6 Burton
12.06.09 Ryan Brawley L PTS 6 Clydebank
Career: 107 contests, won 23, drew 3, lost 81.

James Todd

Swansea. *Born* Swansea, 4 March, 1988
L.Welterweight. *Ht* 5' 9"
Manager E. Calzaghe
14.12.08 Adam Cummings DREW 4 Bristol
21.02.09 Jason Nesbitt W PTS 6 Merthyr Tydfil
05.06.09 Adam Farrell W PTS 6 Newport
Career: 3 contests, won 2, drew 1.

Danny Tombs

Sheffield. *Born* London, 26 May, 1986
L.Heavyweight. *Ht* 5'10½"
Manager Self
12.11.05 Nicki Taylor DREW 4 Sheffield
19.11.05 Michael Banbula W RSC 2 Southwark
30.03.06 Mark Phillips W PTS 4 Bloomsbury
21.10.06 Tony Booth L PTS 4 Southwark
10.11.07 David Gentles W PTS 4 Stalybridge
08.03.09 Adam Wilcox W RSC 2 Sheffield
24.04.09 Nick Okoth DREW 4 Sheffield
Career: 7 contests, won 4, drew 2, lost 1.

Craig Tomes

Barnsley. *Born* Barnsley, 22 November, 1980
Welterweight. *Ht* 5'7"
Manager Self
14.06.07 Adil Anwar L PTS 6 Leeds
11.08.07 Stephen Burke L RSC 1 Liverpool
28.09.07 Scott Sandmann L PTS 6 Preston
13.10.07 Paul Royston W PTS 6 Barnsley
26.10.07 Gary McMillan L PTS 6 Glasgow
05.12.07 Curtis Woodhouse L RSC 1 Sheffield
01.03.08 Scott Miller L RSC 6 Stoke
13.04.08 Danny Coyle L PTS 6 Edgbaston
03.04.09 William Warburton L PTS 6 Leigh
Career: 9 contests, won 1, lost 8.

Ryan Toms

Ruislip. *Born* Perrivale, 16 December, 1981
L.Middleweight. *Ht* 5' 10"
Manager D. Currivan
21.06.09 Kevin Lilley W RSC 4 Bethnal Green
Career: 1 contest, won 1.

Ryan Toms   Philip Sharkey

Pawel Trebinski

Tooting. *Born* Poland, 21 October, 1983
L.Heavyweight. *Ht* 5'10¼"
Manager D. Cowland
01.05.08 Michael Banbula W PTS 6 Piccadilly
25.05.08 Mark Denton L RSC 3 Hartlepool
12.07.08 Justyn Hugh L PTS 6 Newport
04.10.08 Dwayne Lewis L RSC 3 Norwich
14.11.08 Alex Strutt DREW 6 Birmingham
02.05.09 Travis Dickinson L RSC 1 Sunderland
Career: 6 contests, won 1, drew 1, lost 4.

Paul Truscott

Middlesbrough. *Born* Middlesbrough, 1 May, 1986
Former Commonwealth Featherweight Champion. *Ht* 5'9"
Manager M. Marsden
23.06.06 Billy Smith W PTS 4 Blackpool
30.09.06 Steve Gethin W PTS 4 Middlesbrough
10.11.06 Rakhim Mingaleev W PTS 4 Hartlepool
28.01.07 Graeme Higginson W PTS 4 Yarm
25.03.07 Peter Feher W RSC 1 Dublin
20.04.07 Riaz Durgahed W PTS 4 Dudley
09.06.07 Ben Odamattey W PTS 6 Middlesbrough
12.10.07 Daniel Thorpe W PTS 4 Peterlee
15.12.07 Nikita Lukin W PTS 6 Dublin
08.02.08 Samir Kasmi W PTS 8 Peterlee

Paul Truscott   Philip Sharkey

182

09.05.08 Osumanu Akaba W PTS 12
Middlesbrough
*(Vacant Commonwealth Featherweight
Title)*
03.10.08 Alex Miskirtchian W PTS 8 Burton
16.01.09 John Simpson L RSC 8 Middlesbrough
*(Commonwealth Featherweight Title
Defence)*
12.06.09 Andrey Kostin W PTS 6 Liverpool
Career: 14 contests, won 13, lost 1.

James Tucker

Doncaster. *Born* Doncaster, 8 February,
1985
S.Middleweight. *Ht* 5'10¼"
Manager D. Coldwell
30.11.07 Phil Goodwin L PTS 6 Hull
18.01.08 Matthew Hainy L PTS 4 Burton
02.02.08 Tommy Saunders L PTS 4 Canning
Town
16.03.08 Carl Wild L PTS 6 Sheffield
28.03.08 Michael Banbula L PTS 4 Piccadilly
18.04.08 Martin Murray L PTS 4 Bethnal Green
15.05.08 Martin Marshall L PTS 6 Sunderland
30.05.08 Eddie McIntosh L PTS 4 Birmingham
09.06.08 Graham Delehedy DREW 6 Glasgow
21.06.08 Richard Collins L PTS 4 Birmingham
19.07.08 Joe McNally L PTS 6 Liverpool
03.10.08 Dave Pearson W PTS 6 Sunderland
24.10.08 Daniel Roberts L PTS 6 Newport
10.11.08 Kenny Davidson DREW 6 Glasgow
05.12.08 Carl Wild L PTS 6 Sheffield
14.12.08 Marlon Reid L PTS 4 Bristol
30.01.09 John Waldron L PTS 4 Dublin
21.02.09 Luke Allon L PTS 6 Hull
28.02.09 Matthew Thirlwall L PTS 6 Norwich
03.04.09 Paulino Da Silva L PTS 6 Leigh
10.04.09 Mark Regan L PTS 4 Birmingham
17.04.09 Carl Dilks L PTS 4 Leigh
23.05.09 Justin Jones L RSC 1 Queensferry
Career: 23 contests, won 1, drew 2, lost 20.

Rob Turley

Cefn Fforest. *Born* Newport, 24 November,
1986
S.Featherweight. *Ht* 5'7"
Manager C. Sanigar
16.06.07 Delroy Spencer W PTS 6 Newport
05.10.07 John Vanemmenis W RSC 3 Newport
05.04.08 Tony McQuade W PTS 6 Newport
24.05.08 Riaz Durgahed L PTS 6 Cardiff
12.07.08 Geoffrey Munika W PTS 6 Newport
24.10.08 Sid Razak W PTS 4 Newport
13.03.09 Robin Deakin W PTS 6 Newport
05.06.09 Dai Davies L RSC 9 Newport
(Vacant Welsh Area Featherweight Title)
Career: 8 contests, won 6, lost 2.

Amir Unsworth (Morshedi)

Sleaford. *Born* Warrington, 12 January,
1981
L.Welterweight. *Ht* 5'7"
Manager C. Greaves
30.06.07 Sergei Rozhakmens W PTS 6
Manchester
11.08.07 Mark Bett W RSC 4 Liverpool
09.11.07 Leonard Lothian W PTS 4 Nottingham

23.02.08 Carl Allen W PTS 4 Newark
31.05.08 Baz Carey W PTS 4 Newark
19.07.08 Senol Dervis W PTS 4 Liverpool
20.09.08 Ali Wyatt W PTS 6 Newark
29.11.08 Paul Holborn L PTS 10 Sleaford
*(International Masters Lightweight Title
Challenge)*
07.03.09 Gavin Deacon W PTS 6 Chester
23.05.09 Gavin Deacon L PTS 10 Sleaford
*(Vacant Midlands Area L.Welterweight
Title)*
Career: 10 contests, won 8, lost 2.

Amir Unsworth   Philip Sharkey

John Vanemmenis

Bideford. *Born* Barnstaple, 17 September,
1981
Lightweight. *Ht* 5'6¼"
Manager N. Christian
05.10.07 Rob Turley L RSC 3 Newport
01.12.07 Shaun Walton W PTS 6 Telford
10.12.07 Tony McQuade DREW 6 Peterborough
29.02.08 Dezzie O'Connor L RSC 5 Plymouth
20.06.08 Ali Wyatt L PTS 4 Plymouth
18.07.08 Akaash Bhatia L RSC 3 Dagenham
14.09.08 Lee Jennings L CO 2 Wigan
12.12.08 Liam Smith L RSC 1 Widnes
07.03.09 Paul Economides L PTS 4 Chester
Career: 9 contests, won 1, drew 1, lost 7.

Denton Vassell

Manchester. *Born* Manchester, 13
September, 1984
L.Middleweight. *Ht* 5'9¾"
Manager F. Warren
02.09.06 Ernie Smith W RSC 3 Bolton
09.12.06 Duncan Cottier W PTS 4 Canning Town
10.03.07 Steve Cooper W RSC 2 Liverpool
11.08.07 Gatis Skuja W PTS 4 Liverpool
07.09.07 Sherman Alleyne W RSC 1 Mayfair
08.12.07 Yassine El Maachi W PTS 4 Bolton
05.04.08 Manoocha Salari W PTS 4 Bolton
06.09.08 Jimmy Beech W PTS 6 Manchester
10.10.08 Alex Spitjo W CO 3 Liverpool
30.01.09 Matt Scriven W RSC 3 Bethnal Green
14.03.09 Eddie Corcoran W PTS 6 Manchester
Career: 11 contests, won 11.

Joey Vegas (Lubega)

Tottenham. *Born* Namirembe Uganda, 1
January, 1982
Cruiserweight. Former Undefeated British
Masters S.Middleweight Champion. *Ht* 5'8½"
Manager M. Helliet
04.11.04 Cello Renda W RSC 3 Piccadilly
27.01.05 Egbui Ikeagwo W PTS 4 Piccadilly
26.03.05 Egbui Ikeagwo W PTS 4 Hackney
26.05.05 Gareth Lawrence W PTS 4 Mayfair
17.11.05 Conroy McIntosh W RSC 3 Piccadilly
30.03.06 Simeon Cover W PTS 10 Piccadilly
*(British Masters S.Middleweight Title
Challenge)*
12.07.06 Simeon Cover W PTS 4 Bethnal Green
30.11.06 Michael Monaghan W PTS 10 Piccadilly
*(British Masters S.Middleweight Title
Defence)*
13.12.06 Varuzhan Davtyan W RSC 1 Strand
18.04.07 Neil Tidman W PTS 4 Strand
04.10.07 Danny McIntosh L PTS 6 Piccadilly
03.11.07 Nathan Cleverly L PTS 8 Cardiff
14.11.07 Geard Ajetovic L RSC 4 Bethnal Green
01.08.08 JJ Ojuederie W RSC 7 Watford
05.10.08 JJ Ojuederie W PTS 10 Watford
*(Southern Area L.Heavyweight Title
Challenge)*
13.02.09 Dean Francis DREW 8 Swindon
20.03.09 Edison Miranda L RSC 5 Bethnal Green
Career: 17 contests, won 11, drew 1, lost 5.

Joey Vegas   Philip Sharkey

Alfonso Vieyra

Denton. Born Santa Ana, California, USA,
15 November, 1989
S.Featherweight. *Ht* 5'5"
Manager R. Hatton
20.12.08 Steve Gethin W PTS 4 Bristol
28.03.09 Shaun Walton W RSC 1 Altrincham
Career: 2 contests, won 2.

Byron Vince

Northampton. *Born* Bury St Edmunds, 3
March, 1984
Welterweight. *Ht* 5'10¼"
Manager J. Cox
18.11.07 Charlie Collins W RSC 3 Tooting
28.11.07 Darren Hamilton L PTS 6 Piccadilly
10.12.07 Richard Hall L PTS 6 Cleethorpes
08.12.08 Callum Archer L RSC 1 Birmingham
01.02.09 Pat McAleese L PTS 4 Bethnal Green
Career: 5 contests, won 1, lost 4.

Ben Wakeham

Torquay. *Born* Torquay, 3 December, 1988
Welterweight. *Ht* 5'10¼"
Manager Self
09.11.07 Jimmy Briggs W PTS 6 Plymouth
29.02.08 James Lilley W PTS 6 Plymouth
15.11.08 Johnny Greaves W PTS 6 Plymouth
13.03.09 Adam Farrell W RSC 3 Newport
Career: 4 contests, won 4.

Josh Wale

Brampton. *Born* Barnsley, 8 April, 1988
Central Area S.Bantamweight Champion.
Ht 5'7"
Manager T. Gilmour
13.10.06 Neil Read W RSC 1 Doncaster
15.04.07 Anthony Hanna W PTS 6 Barnsley
03.06.07 Delroy Spencer W PTS 6 Barnsley
13.10.07 Shaun Walton W PTS 4 Barnsley
05.12.07 Mo Khaled W RSC 4 Sheffield
　　　　　 (Vacant Central Area S.Bantamweight
　　　　　 Title)
16.03.08 Robin Deakin W PTS 6 Sheffield
17.05.08 Ayittey Mettle W RSC 1 Sheffield
20.09.08 Harry Ramogoadi L RTD 3 Sheffield
19.06.09 Wladimir Borov W RSC 4 Aberdeen
Career: 9 contests, won 8, lost 1.

Dean Walker　　　　　　　Philip Sharkey

Dean Walker

Sheffield. *Born* Sheffield, 25 April, 1979
L.Heavyweight. *Ht* 5'11"
Manager D. Coldwell
21.10.00 Colin McCash DREW 6 Sheffield
11.12.00 James Lee L PTS 6 Sheffield
27.07.01 Chris Duggan W RSC 4 Sheffield
15.12.01 William Webster W PTS 6 Sheffield
03.03.02 Shaun Horsfall W PTS 6 Shaw
02.06.02 Wayne Shepherd W PTS 6 Shaw

03.08.02 Richard Inquieti W PTS 6 Derby
05.10.02 Martin Scotland W PTS 6 Chesterfield
24.05.03 Neil Bonner W PTS 6 Sheffield
12.10.03 Paul Lomax W PTS 6 Sheffield
10.02.04 Neil Addis W PTS 6 Barnsley
21.02.04 Matthew Macklin L CO 1 Cardiff
08.06.04 Andrei Ivanov W PTS 6 Sheffield
03.09.04 Dean Cockburn L PTS 10 Doncaster
　　　　　 (Vacant Central Area S.Middleweight
　　　　　 Title)
15.12.04 Lee Murtagh L PTS 10 Sheffield
　　　　　 (Vacant Central Central Area
　　　　　 Middleweight Title)
20.02.05 Mo W PTS 6 Sheffield
19.03.05 Jozsef Nagy L RTD 8 Tapolca, Hungary
　　　　　 (IBF Inter-Continental Middleweight
　　　　　 Title Challenge)
16.07.05 Darren Barker L PTS 6 Chigwell
25.10.05 Thomas McDonagh L PTS 6 Preston
18.02.06 Jason McKay L RTD 1 Edinburgh
18.05.06 Matthew Hough L PTS 6 Walsall
14.10.06 Paul Smith L RSC 3 Manchester
　　　　　 (Vacant Central Area Middleweight
　　　　　 Title)
12.11.06 Craig Bunn DREW 6 Manchester
24.11.06 Jonjo Finnegan DREW 4 Nottingham
11.12.06 Tyrone Wright L PTS 6 Cleethorpes
10.03.07 Tony Quigley L RSC 2 Liverpool
15.04.07 Robert Burton L PTS 6 Barnsley
06.05.07 Darren Rhodes L PTS 4 Leeds
21.07.07 Kenny Anderson L RSC 2 Cardiff
08.09.07 Brian Wood W PTS 6 Sutton in
　　　　　 Ashfield
21.09.07 Rod Anderton L PTS 6 Burton
16.02.08 Martin Murray L PTS 6 Blackpool
16.03.08 Carl Dilks L PTS 6 Liverpool
29.03.08 Kenny Anderson L RTD 4 Glasgow
28.04.08 Marcus Portman L PTS 6 Glasgow
23.05.08 Martin Murray L PTS 6 Wigan
08.11.08 Dwayne Lewis L RSC 1 Bethnal Green
Career: 37 contests, won 12, drew 3, lost 22.

Masoor Walli

Sheffield. *Born* Afganistan, 1 January, 1987
Welterweight. *Ht* 5'10"
Manager G. Rhodes
08.03.09 Matt Seawright L PTS 4 Sheffield
24.05.09 Mark Hudson W CO 1 Bradford
Career: 2 contests, won 1, lost 1.

Ryan Walls

Slough. *Born* Reading, 29 January, 1979
L.Heavyweight. *Ht* 6'0"
Manager M. Helliet
20.12.02 Mark Phillips W PTS 6 Bracknell
23.02.03 Michael Pinnock W PTS 6 Streatham
21.03.03 Jimmy Steel W PTS 6 Longford
12.04.03 Earl Ling W RSC 4 Norwich
09.05.03 Darren Ashton W PTS 6 Longford
01.08.03 Darren Ashton W PTS 4 Bethnal Green
26.10.03 Michael Pinnock W PTS 10 Longford
25.03.04 Pinky Burton L PTS 10 Longford
08.05.04 Toks Owoh W PTS 6 Bristol
08.12.04 Varuzhan Davtyan W PTS 4 Longford
24.02.05 Ryan Kerr L PTS 10 Sunderland
　　　　　 (Vacant English S.Middleweight Title)
24.04.05 Peter Haymer L PTS 6 Leicester Square
08.05.05 Donovan Smillie W PTS 6 Bradford
20.06.05 Simeon Cover W RSC 8 Longford

19.12.05 Gareth Lawrence W RSC 6 Longford
06.10.06 Hussain Osman L RSC 2 Bethnal Green
18.11.06 Paul Smith L RSC 4 Newport
24.02.07 Tomas Da Silva W RSC 2 Bracknell
05.10.08 Anthony Young W PTS 4 Watford
13.12.08 Dwayne Lewis L PTS 6 Brentwood
Career: 20 contests, won 14, lost 6.

Ryan Walls　　　　　　　Philip Sharkey

Lester Walsh　　　　　　　Philip Sharkey

Lester Walsh

Leicester. *Born* Greenock, 26 January, 1976
Middleweight. *Ht* 5'8"
Manager Self
01.12.07 Rocky Chakir L PTS 6 Coventry
16.02.08 Paul Royston W PTS 6 Leicester
31.05.08 Kevin Hammond DREW 4 Newark
28.06.08 Luke Osman W PTS 6 Leicester
05.09.08 Kevin Hammond L PTS 6 Nottingham
15.11.08 Joe McNally L RSC 3 Greenwich
07.03.09 Omar Gumati L PTS 4 Chester
22.03.09 Pat McAleese L PTS 4 Bethnal Green
04.04.09 Harry Matthews L PTS 4 Coventry
23.05.09 Chris Goodwin L PTS 6 Queensferry
Career: 10 contests, won 2, drew 1, lost 7.

Liam Walsh

Cromer. *Born* Rochdale, 18 May, 1986
Lightweight. *Ht* 5'7¼"
Manager G. Everett
02.02.08 Daniel Thorpe W CO 1 Canning Town
14.06.08 Johnny Greaves W CO 4 Bethnal Green
06.12.08 Youssef Al Hamidi W PTS 4 Canning Town
30.01.09 Shaun Walton W RSC 1 Bethnal Green
22.05.09 Baz Carey W RSC 3 Bethnal Green
Career: 5 contests, won 5.

Mark Walsh

Leicester. *Born* Greenock, 25 August, 1977
Welterweight. *Ht* 5' 9"
Manager C. Greaves
20.09.08 Syed Ali DREW 6 Newark
29.11.08 Jimmy Briggs W PTS 6 Sleaford
23.05.09 Kristian Laight W PTS 4 Sleaford
Career: 3 contests, won 2, drew 1.

Mark Walsh   Philip Sharkey

Michael Walsh

Cromer. *Born* Rochdale, 4 August, 1984
S.Bantamweight. *Ht* 5'5¼"
Manager G. Everett
02.02.08 Delroy Spencer W RSC 3 Canning Town
08.03.08 Khvicha Papiashvili W RSC 4 Greenwich
14.06.08 Fouad El Bahji W RSC 3 Bethnal Green
06.12.08 Delroy Spencer W RTD 2 Canning Town
22.05.09 Isaac Owusu W RSC 4 Bethnal Green
Career: 5 contests, won 5.

Ryan Walsh

Cromer. *Born* Rochdale, 18 May, 1986
Featherweight. *Ht* 5'4¼"
Manager G. Everett
02.02.08 Riaz Durgahed W CO 1 Canning Town
08.03.08 Robin Deakin W PTS 4 Greenwich
14.06.08 Gheorghe Ghiompirica W PTS 4 Bethnal Green
26.09.08 Robin Deakin W PTS 4 Bethnal Green
06.12.08 Johnny Greaves W PTS 4 Canning Town

30.01.09 Sid Razak W PTS 4 Bethnal Green
22.05.09 Marc Callaghan W RTD 3 Bethnal Green
Career: 7 contests, won 7.

Daniel Walton

Birmingham. *Born* Birmingham, 11 November, 1989
Featherweight. *Ht* 5' 4"
Manager P. Rowson
07.03.09 Delroy Spencer W PTS 4 Birmingham
12.06.09 Anthony Hanna DREW 4 Wolverhampton
Career: 2 contests, won 1, drew 1.

Dougie Walton

Coventry. *Born* Coventry, 9 August, 1981
Featherweight. *Ht* 5'4"
Manager Self
04.03.06 Graeme Higginson DREW 6 Coventry
09.10.06 Neil Marston W PTS 6 Birmingham
11.12.06 Neil Read W RSC 5 Birmingham
26.02.07 Delroy Spencer W PTS 6 Birmingham
13.05.07 Shaun Walton W PTS 4 Birmingham
28.09.07 Shaun Walton W PTS 6 Coventry
26.10.07 Delroy Spencer W PTS 6 Birmingham
06.10.08 Stuart Hall L RSC 6 Birmingham
Career: 8 contests, won 6, drew 1, lost 1.

Joel Walton

Birmingham. *Born* Solihull, 15 August, 1987
S.Middleweight. *Ht* 5' 10"
Manager P. Lynch
08.12.08 Mark Phillips W PTS 6 Birmingham
23.02.09 Danny Gwilym L RSC 5 Birmingham
Career: 2 contests, won 1, lost 1.

Shaun Walton

Telford. *Born* West Bromwich, 2 January, 1975
Lightweight. *Ht* 5'10"
Manager E. Johnson
15.04.05 Dave Hinds W PTS 6 Shrewsbury
16.09.05 Abdul Mougharbel W PTS 6 Telford
14.10.05 Craig Bromley L PTS 4 Huddersfield
04.12.05 Abdul Mougharbel DREW 6 Telford
10.03.06 Andy Davis L PTS 6 Walsall
28.05.06 Sean Hughes L PTS 6 Wakefield
05.06.06 Furhan Rafiq L PTS 6 Glasgow
09.09.06 Furhan Rafiq L PTS 6 Inverurie
06.10.06 Andy Bell L PTS 6 Mansfield
13.10.06 Jamie McIlroy L PTS 6 Irvine
21.10.06 Mark Alexander L PTS 6 Southwark
28.10.06 Robin Deakin L PTS 4 Bethnal Green
10.11.06 Sergei Rozhakmens W PTS 6 Telford
30.11.06 Kim Poulsen L PTS 6 Piccadilly
13.12.06 Darryl Mitchell L PTS 4 Strand
22.01.07 Furhan Rafiq L PTS 6 Glasgow
17.02.07 Vinny Mitchell L PTS 4 Wembley
03.03.07 Kevin Buckley L PTS 6 Burton
01.04.07 Sergei Rozhakmens DREW 6 Shrewsbury
14.04.07 Robert Nelson L PTS 8 Wakefield
23.04.07 Brian Murphy W RSC 5 Glasgow
06.05.07 James McElvaney L PTS 6 Darlington
13.05.07 Dougie Walton L PTS 4 Birmingham
05.06.07 John Donnelly L PTS 6 Glasgow
14.06.07 Eugene Heagney L PTS 6 Leeds

21.06.07 Tony McQuade L PTS 6 Peterborough
30.06.07 Scott Quigg L RSC 1 Manchester
11.08.07 Scott Quigg L PTS 6 Liverpool
10.09.07 John Bothwell W PTS 6 Glasgow
28.09.07 Dougie Walton L PTS 6 Coventry
13.10.07 Josh Wale L PTS 4 Barnsley
24.11.07 Davey Savage L PTS 6 Clydebank
01.12.07 John Vanemmenis L PTS 6 Telford
15.12.07 Jason Hastie L PTS 4 Edinburgh
21.01.08 Davey Savage L PTS 6 Glasgow
31.01.08 Saud Hafiz L PTS 4 Piccadilly
23.02.08 Ben Jones L RSC 4 Crawley
29.03.08 Stephen Russell L PTS 4 Glasgow
10.04.08 Saud Hafiz L RSC 4 Piccadilly
07.06.08 Rhys Roberts L PTS 4 Wigan
21.06.08 Stephen Smith L CO 3 Birmingham
12.09.08 Chris Male L PTS 4 Wolverhampton
26.09.08 Vinny Mitchell L PTS 4 Bethnal Green
10.10.08 Davey Savage L PTS 6 Motherwell
25.10.08 James Ancliff L PTS 6 Aberdeen
08.11.08 Gareth Couch L RSC 1 Bethnal Green
12.12.08 Steve Bell L PTS 6 Widnes
20.12.08 Pete Leworthy L PTS 6 Bristol
30.01.09 Liam Walsh L RSC 1 Bethnal Green
20.03.09 Najah Ali L PTS 4 Bethnal Green
28.03.09 Alfonso Vieyra L RSC 1 Altrincham
27.04.09 Joe Kelso L PTS 6 Glasgow
18.05.09 Del Rogers L PTS 6 Birmingham
29.05.09 Chris Male L PTS 4 Dudley
Career: 54 contests, won 4, drew 3, lost 47.

William Warburton   Philip Sharkey

William Warburton

Atherton. *Born* Bolton, 6 April, 1987
Welterweight. *Ht* 5' 11"
Manager J. Pennington
03.04.09 Craig Tomes W PTS 6 Leigh
23.05.09 Aaron Thomas L PTS 4 Queensferry
12.06.09 Bobby Gladman L PTS 4 Bethnal Green
25.06.09 Willie Bilan L PTS 6 Glenrothes
Career: 4 contests, won 1, lost 3.

Bobby Ward

Romford. *Born* London, 26 November, 1986
Lightweight. *Ht* 5' 7"
Manager T. Sims
13.06.09 Mo Khaled DREW 4 Wigan
Career: 1 contest, drew 1.

Martin Ward

West Rainton. *Born* Durham, 11 March, 1988
Featherweight. *Ht* 5' 8"
Manager D. Garside
13.03.09 Anthony Hanna W PTS 4 Widnes
01.05.09 Sid Razak W PTS 4 Hartlepool
12.06.09 Ignac Kassai W PTS 4 Liverpool
Career: 3 contests, won 3.

Alastair Warren

Huddersfield. *Born* Barnsley, 27 May, 1987
S.Middleweight. *Ht* 6' 0"
Manager C. Aston
04.04.09 Mark Ketnor W RSC 5 Coventry
Career: 1 contest, won 1.

Craig Watson

Manchester. *Born* Oldham, 7 February, 1983
Former Commonwealth Welterweight Champion. *Ht* 5'10"
Manager Self
20.05.05 Willie Valentine W RTD 2 Southwark
19.06.05 Jus Wallie W PTS 4 Bethnal Green
16.07.05 Billy Smith W PTS 4 Bolton
07.10.05 Ben Hudson W PTS 4 Bethnal Green
04.11.05 Sergii Tertii W PTS 6 Bethnal Green
29.09.06 Michael Medor W RSC 1 Manchester
25.11.06 Rakhim Mingaleev W PTS 6 Belfast
09.02.07 John Fewkes L PTS 8 Leeds
27.04.07 Robert Lloyd-Taylor W PTS 8 Wembley
06.07.07 Michael Lomax W PTS 8 Wigan
21.09.07 Robert Lloyd-Taylor W RSC 1 Bethnal Green
26.10.07 Frederic Gosset W PTS 6 Wigan
08.12.07 Ali Nuumbembe W RSC 8 Wigan
(Commonwealth Welterweight Title Challenge)
08.03.08 Daniele Petrucci L RSC 3 Rome, Italy
(Vacant European Union Welterweight Title)
24.05.08 Matthew Hatton W PTS 12 Manchester
(Commonwealth Welterweight Title Defence)
11.04.09 John O'Donnell L PTS 12 Bethnal Green
(Commonwealth Welterweight Title Defence)
Career: 16 contests, won 13, lost 3.

George Watson

Newcastle. *Born* Newcastle, 13 December, 1983
Lightweight. *Ht* 6'0"
Manager T. Conroy
11.05.07 Gavin Deacon W PTS 6 Sunderland
05.10.07 Kristian Laight W PTS 6 Sunderland
02.11.07 Ryan Brawley L PTS 6 Irvine
06.12.07 Dwayne Hill W PTS 6 Sunderland
15.02.08 Leonard Lothian W PTS 6 Sunderland
20.03.08 Youssef Al Hamidi W PTS 6 South Shields
14.11.08 Jon Baguley DREW 4 Glasgow
28.02.09 Lubos Priehradnik W RSC 3 Newcastle
Career: 8 contests, won 6, drew 1, lost 1.

John Watson

Liverpool. *Born* Whiston, 9 June, 1983
L.Welterweight. *Ht* 5'9¾"
Manager Self
10.03.07 Jason Nesbitt W PTS 4 Liverpool
11.08.07 Johnny Greaves W PTS 4 Liverpool
01.12.07 Ade Adebolu W RSC 4 Liverpool
23.02.08 Darren Broomhall W CO 1 Liverpool
16.03.08 Baz Carey W PTS 4 Liverpool
07.06.08 John Baguley W PTS 4 Wigan
19.07.08 Ali Wyatt W RTD 4 Liverpool
20.09.08 Geoffrey Munika W RSC 1 Sheffield
15.11.08 Silence Saheed W PTS 4 Greenwich
28.03.09 Martin Gethin W PTS 10 Liverpool
(Elim. British Lightweight Title)
Career: 10 contests, won 10.

John Watson   Philip Sharkey

Shane Watson

Ruislip. *Born* Hillingdon, 12 August, 1984
L.Welterweight. *Ht* 5'9½"
Manager J. Evans
23.11.05 Pete Buckley W PTS 6 Mayfair
04.12.05 Duncan Cottier W PTS 4 Portsmouth
05.03.06 Chris Long W PTS 4 Southampton
07.04.06 Anthony Christopher W RSC 1 Longford
28.05.06 Daniel Thorpe W PTS 6 Longford
02.12.06 Jason Nesbitt W PTS 6 Longford
23.09.07 Pete Buckley W PTS 6 Longford
16.11.08 Craig Dyer W PTS 4 Southampton
20.03.09 Lee Cook L PTS 10 Bethnal Green
(Vacant Southern Area Lightweight Title)
Career: 9 contests, won 8, lost 1.

Jamie Way

Abercarn. *Born* Newport, 11 December, 1981
International Masters L. Welterweight Champion. *Ht* 5'7"
Manager B. Powell
15.09.06 Jimmy Maile W RSC 4 Newport
10.11.06 Pawel Jas W PTS 6 Newport
03.03.07 Geraint Harvey W PTS 6 Newport
16.06.07 Steve Cooper W PTS 6 Newport
05.10.07 Lewis Byrne W PTS 4 Newport
05.04.08 Jimmy Briggs W PTS 6 Newport
24.05.08 Rocky Chakir W PTS 6 Cardiff
24.10.08 Ali Wyatt W PTS 10 Newport
(Vacant International Masters L. Welterweight Title)
27.02.09 Dave Ryan L PTS 4 Barnsley
Career: 9 contests, won 8, lost 1.

Sam Webb   Philip Sharkey

Sam Webb

Chislehurst. *Born* Sidcup, 11 April, 1981
Middleweight. *Ht* 5'8¾"
Manager Self
07.10.05 Geraint Harvey W CO 1 Bethnal Green
04.11.05 Vadzim Astapuk W RSC 2 Bethnal Green
27.01.06 Aleksandr Zhuk W PTS 4 Dagenham
24.03.06 Gatis Skuja W PTS 4 Bethnal Green
30.05.06 Alex Stoda L RSC 3 Bethnal Green
17.11.06 David Kirk W PTS 4 Bethnal Green
27.04.07 Alexander Spitjo W RSC 1 Wembley
15.06.07 Ben Hudson W PTS 4 Crystal Palace
12.01.08 Duncan Cottier W PTS 4 Bethnal Green
02.02.08 Paul Royston W PTS 6 Canning Town
02.05.08 David Kirk W PTS 6 Nottingham
13.06.08 Paul Dyer W PTS 6 Portsmouth
17.10.08 Gilbert Eastman W RSC 8 Bethnal Green
20.03.09 Max Maxwell W PTS 8 Newham
02.05.09 Thomas McDonagh W PTS 10 Sunderland
(Elim. British L. Middleweight Title)
Career: 15 contests, won 14, lost 1.

Tobias Webb

Swansea. *Born* Swansea, 25 August, 1988
S.Middleweight. *Ht* 6' 0"
Manager F. Warren
14.03.09 Patrick Mendy W PTS 4 Manchester
19.06.09 Michael Banbula W PTS 4 Glasgow
Career: 2 contests, won 2.

Stevie Weir

Paisley. *Born* Paisley, 7 July, 1982
L.Middleweight. *Ht* 5'10¼"
Manager J. McIntyre

15.09.07 Paul Royston W PTS 6 Paisley
29.03.08 Ernie Smith W PTS 4 Glasgow
18.10.08 Duncan Cottier W PTS 4 Paisley
Career: 3 contests, won 3.

Nathan Weise

Thameside. *Born* Bath, 7 July, 1984
Welterweight. *Ht* 5'11½"
Manager Self
29.06.06 Bheki Moyo W PTS 4 Bethnal Green
26.01.07 Tom Glover DREW 4 Dagenham
15.06.08 Mark Douglas L PTS 4 Bethnal Green
22.03.09 Lewis Byrne W PTS 4 Bethnal Green
27.06.09 Lloyd Smith W CO 2 Portsmouth
Career: 5 contests, won 3, drew 1, lost 1.

Jason Welborn   Philip Sharkey

Jason Welborn

Warley. *Born* Sandwell, 9 May, 1986
Welterweight. *Ht* 5' 10"
Manager D. Powell
12.12.05 Jamie Ambler W RSC 1 Birmingham
27.02.06 Tyan Booth L CO 3 Birmingham
05.12.06 Aldon Stewart W RSC 3 Wolverhampton
24.04.09 Kevin McCauley W PTS 4
        Wolverhampton
Career: 4 contests, won 3, lost 1.

Martin Welsh   Philip Sharkey

Martin Welsh

Swanley. *Born* Dartford, 27 November,
1980
Welterweight. *Ht* 5' 10"
Manager F. Maloney
30.06.09 Kristian Laight W PTS 4 Bethnal Green
Career: 1 contest, won 1.

Adie Whitmore

Derby. *Born* Alfreton, 28 July, 1987
S.Middleweight. *Ht* 6'2"
Manager Self
08.12.05 Jimi Hendricks W RSC 1 Derby
14.05.06 Jon Foster W RSC 6 Derby
11.11.06 Ojay Abrahams W PTS 6 Sutton in
        Ashfield
23.03.07 Jon Foster W RTD 4 Nottingham
21.09.07 Robert Burton W PTS 6 Burton
01.12.07 Nicki Taylor W CO 1 Nottingham
07.03.08 Hamed Jamali W PTS 4 Nottingham
02.05.08 Carl Wild W CO 1 Nottingham
05.09.08 Bob Ajisafe L RSC 4 Nottingham
Career: 9 contests, won 8, lost 1.

Adam Wilcox

Cross Hands. *Born* Blacktown, Australia, 1
June, 1979
L.Heavyweight. *Ht* 5'8¼"
Manager Self
21.10.07 Danny Gwilym L PTS 6 Swansea
03.11.07 Tony Bellew L RSC 3 Cardiff
02.12.07 Robert Boardman L PTS 4 Bristol
15.06.08 Carl Dilks L RSC 3 St Helens
03.10.08 Jonjo Finnegan W RSC 3 Burton
08.03.09 Danny Tombs L RSC 2 Sheffield
Career: 6 contests, won 1, lost 5.

Adam Wilcox   Philip Sharkey

Carl Wild

Sheffield. *Born* Sheffield, 3 April, 1986
L.Heavyweight. *Ht* 6'2"
Manager Self
28.10.06 Mark Phillips W PTS 6 Sheffield
24.02.07 Mark Nilsen L PTS 6 Manchester
20.04.07 Philip Callaghan W RSC 1 Sheffield
06.05.07 Carl Dilks L PTS 6 Altrincham

16.06.07 Carl Dilks L PTS 6 Bolton
13.07.07 Rod Anderton L PTS 4 Barnsley
08.09.07 Jamie Norkett W PTS 4 Sutton in
        Ashfield
16.09.07 Nicki Taylor W PTS 6 Sheffield
12.10.07 Danny Thornton L PTS 6 Leeds
15.11.07 Clint Johnson W PTS 6 Leeds
23.11.07 Scott Brookes L PTS 4 Rotherham
30.11.07 Tony Salam L RTD 4 Newham
16.03.08 James Tucker W PTS 6 Sheffield
02.05.08 Adie Whitmore L CO 1 Nottingham
14.09.08 Martin Murray L RSC 2 Wigan
05.12.08 James Tucker W PTS 6 Sheffield
08.03.09 Ally Morrison DREW 4 Sheffield
29.03.09 Joey Ainscough DREW 4 Bolton
24.04.09 Michael Banbula L PTS 4 Sheffield
24.05.09 Darren Stubbs L PTS 10 Shaw
        *(Vacant Central Area L.Heavyweight
        Title)*
Career: 20 contests, won 7, drew 2, lost 11.

Ben Wilkes

Wolverhampton. *Born* Wolverhampton, 7
October, 1986
S.Middleweight. *Ht* 5' 9"
Manager E. Johnson
27.02.09 Mark Phillips W PTS 4 Wolverhampton
03.04.09 Davey Jones W PTS 6 Wolverhampton
12.06.09 Davey Jones W CO 5 Wolverhampton
Career: 3 contests, won 3.

Danny Williams

Brixton. *Born* London, 13 July, 1973
British Heavyweight Champion. Former
Commonwealth Heavyweight Champion.
Former Undefeated WBO & WBU Inter-
Continental Heavyweight Champion.
Ht 6'3"
Manager Self
21.10.95 Vance Idiens W CO 2 Bethnal Green
09.12.95 Joey Paladino W RSC 1 Bethnal Green
13.02.96 Slick Miller W RSC 1 Bethnal Green
09.03.96 James Wilder W PTS 4 Millstreet
13.07.96 John Pierre W PTS 4 Bethnal Green
31.08.96 Andy Lambert W RSC 2 Dublin
09.11.96 Michael Murray W CO 1 Manchester
08.02.97 Shane Woollas W RSC 2 Millwall
03.05.97 Albert Call W RSC 4 Manchester
19.07.97 R. F. McKenzie W RSC 2 Wembley
15.11.97 Bruce Douglas W RSC 2 Bristol
19.12.97 Derek Amos W RSC 4 NYC, New York,
        USA
21.02.98 Shane Woollas W RSC 2 Belfast
16.05.98 Antonio Diaz W CO 3 Bethnal Green
10.10.98 Antoine Palatis W PTS 12 Bethnal
        Green
        *(Vacant WBO Inter-Continental
        Heavyweight Title)*
03.04.99 Julius Francis L PTS 12 Kensington
        *(British & Commonwealth Heavyweight
        Title Challenges)*
02.10.99 Ferenc Deak W RTD 1 Namur, Belgium
18.12.99 Harry Senior W PTS 12 Southwark
        *(Vacant Commonwealth Heavyweight
        Title)*
19.02.00 Anton Nel W CO 5 Dagenham
06.05.00 Michael Murray W RSC 6 Frankfurt,
        Germany

24.06.00 Craig Bowen-Price W CO 1 Glasgow
23.09.00 Quinn Navarre W RSC 6 Bethnal Green
21.10.00 Mark Potter W RSC 6 Wembley
(Commonwealth & WBO Inter-Continental Heavyweight Title Defences. Vacant British Heavyweight Title)
09.06.01 Kali Meehan W RSC 1 Bethnal Green
(Commonwealth Heavyweight Title Defence)
28.07.01 Julius Francis W CO 4 Wembley
(British & Commonwealth Heavyweight Title Defences)
15.12.01 Shawn Robinson W RSC 2 Mashantucket Connecticut, USA
12.02.02 Michael Sprott W RTD 7 Bethnal Green
(British & Commonwealth Heavyweight Title Defences)
17.09.02 Keith Long W PTS 12 Bethnal Green
(British & Commonwealth Heavyweight Title Defences)
08.02.03 Sinan Samil Sam L RSC 6 Berlin, Germany
(European Heavyweight Title Challenge)
26.04.03 Bob Mirovic W RSC 4 Brentford
(Commonwealth Heavyweight Title Defence)
26.09.03 Michael Sprott W RSC 5 Reading
(British & Commonwealth Heavyweight Title Defences)
24.01.04 Michael Sprott L PTS 12 Wembley
(British & Commonwealth Heavyweight Title Defences)
01.04.04 Ratko Draskovic W RSC 1 Bethnal Green
13.05.04 Augustin N'Gou W RTD 3 Bethnal Green
(Vacant WBU Inter-Continental Heavyweight Title)
30.07.04 Mike Tyson W CO 4 Louisville, Kentucky, USA
11.12.04 Vitali Klitschko L RSC 8 Las Vegas, USA
(WBC Heavyweight Title Challenge)
04.06.05 Zoltan Petranyi W RSC 3 Manchester
10.12.05 Audley Harrison W PTS 12 Canning Town
(Vacant Commonwealth Heavyweight Title)
25.02.06 Matt Skelton W PTS 12 Canning Town
(Commonwealth Heavyweight Title Defence)
20.05.06 Adnan Serin W RTD 3 Belfast
08.07.06 Matt Skelton L PTS 12 Cardiff
(Commonwealth Heavyweight Title Defence)
09.12.06 Audley Harrison L RSC 3 Canning Town
02.03.07 Scott Gammer W CO 9 Neath
(British Heavyweight Title Challenge)
08.12.07 Oleg Platov NC 4 Basle, Switzerland
(IBF Inter-Continental Heavyweight Title Challenge)
12.04.08 Marcus McGee W PTS 6 Tampa, Florida, USA
30.05.08 Konstantin Airich W RSC 7 Baracaldo, Spain
18.07.08 John McDermott W PTS 12 Dagenham
(British Heavyweight Title Defence)
08.11.08 Albert Sosnowski L RSC 8 Bethnal Green

02.05.09 John McDermott W PTS 12 Sunderland
(British Heavyweight Title Defence)
Career: 49 contests, won 41, lost 7, no contest 1.

Leon Williams

Streatham. *Born* London, 6 November, 1983
Cruiserweight. *Ht* 5' 11"
Manager J. Feld
10.04.09 Bobby Scott W RSC 1 Cheltenham
21.06.09 Mark Nilsen W PTS 6 Bethnal Green
Career: 2 contests, won 2.

Steve Williams

Wallasey. *Born* Wallasey, 29 February, 1984
Welterweight. *Ht* 5'8¼"
Manager T. Gilmour
23.02.08 Martin Sweeney W PTS 6 Liverpool
17.03.08 Steve Cooper W PTS 6 Glasgow
07.06.08 David Kehoe W RSC 1 Wigan
04.07.08 Karl Taylor W PTS 4 Liverpool
10.11.08 Stuart Green W PTS 8 Glasgow
21.12.08 Dean Hickman W RSC 2 Motherwell
13.03.09 Graeme Higginson W RSC 4 Widnes
12.06.09 Slawomir Ziemlewicz W PTS 8 Liverpool
Career: 8 contests, won 8.

Tye Williams   Philip Sharkey

Tye Williams

Dewsbury. *Born* London, 9 June, 1976
Welterweight. *Ht* 5'9"
Manager Self
23.10.04 Rocky Muscus W PTS 6 Wakefield
09.11.04 Lea Handley L RSC 1 Leeds
26.02.05 Darren Gethin DREW 4 Burton
14.05.05 Daniel Thorpe L RSC 3 Aberdeen
25.06.05 Gary Connolly W CO 4 Wakefield
11.12.05 Jackson Williams L PTS 6 Norwich
12.02.06 Jonathan Hussey L PTS 6 Manchester
05.03.06 Adam Kelly L PTS 4 Sheffield
25.03.06 Scott Conway DREW 4 Burton
14.05.06 Scott Conway W RSC 5 Derby
28.05.06 Khurram Hussain L PTS 6 Wakefield
18.09.06 Wayne Downing W RSC 2 Glasgow
20.10.06 Adam Kelly L PTS 4 Sheffield

03.11.06 Mike Reid W RSC 6 Glasgow
15.04.07 Chris Saunders L PTS 6 Barnsley
29.04.07 Dee Mitchell L PTS 8 Birmingham
27.05.07 Nadeem Siddique L RSC 4 Bradford
(Vacant Central Area & British Masters Welterweight Titles)
13.10.07 Lee Murtagh L PTS 6 Belfast
11.11.07 Stephen Haughian L PTS 8 Dunshaughlin
18.01.08 Muhsen Nasser L PTS 4 Burton
29.02.08 Jamie Coyle L RSC 2 Glasgow
19.04.08 Gary O'Sullivan L RSC 1 Dublin
13.09.08 Jimmy Doherty L PTS 8 Stoke
26.09.08 Russ Colley L PTS 4 Wolverhampton
09.11.08 Jamie Ball L PTS 4 Wolverhampton
29.01.09 Wayne Alwan-Arab L RSC 4 Holborn
Career: 26 contests, won 5, drew 2, lost 19.

(Jeremy) Jezz Wilson

Sheffield. *Born* Wolverhampton, 22 June, 1979
S.Middleweight. *Ht* 5'9"
Manager G. Rhodes
20.04.07 Peter Cannon W RSC 5 Sheffield
16.09.07 Jon Foster W RSC 1 Sheffield
23.11.07 Nigel Travis W RSC 4 Sheffield
15.02.08 Jamie Ambler W PTS 6 Sheffield
12.09.08 Manoocha Salari W RSC 2 Sheffield
Career: 5 contests, won 5.

Luke Wilton

Crossgar. *Born* Barking, 12 May, 1988
Bantamweight. *Ht* 5'5¼"
Manager A. Wilton
29.03.08 Istvan Ajtai W RSC 1 Letterkenny
19.04.08 Delroy Spencer W PTS 4 Dublin
31.05.08 Kemal Plavci W PTS 4 Belfast
18.12.08 Usman Ahmed L PTS 4 Dublin
25.04.09 Delroy Spencer W PTS 4 Belfast
15.05.09 Anwar Alfadi DREW 6 Belfast
28.06.09 Delroy Spencer L PTS 4 Luton
Career: 7 contests, won 4, drew 1, lost 2.

Craig Windsor

Coatbridge. *Born* Bellshill, 17 June, 1982
Welterweight. *Ht* 5' 6"
Manager A. Morrison
06.03.09 Ben Deghani W RSC 3 Glasgow
27.03.09 Geraint Harvey W PTS 4 Glasgow
19.06.09 Ben Deghani W RSC 3 Glasgow
Career: 3 contests, won 3.

Juliette Winter

Derby. *Born* Whitehaven, 21 February, 1973
Bantamweight. *Ht* 5'6"
Manager Self
16.06.01 Sara Hall L RTD 4 Derby
20.09.01 Claire Cooper L RSC 4 Blackfriars
20.03.03 Cathy Brown W PTS 4 Queensway
24.01.04 Esther Schouten L RTD 3 Amsterdam, Holland
23.07.06 Shanee Martin W PTS 8 Dagenham
24.09.06 Cathy Brown L PTS 10 Bethnal Green
(Vacant Womens English Bantamweight Title)
12.05.07 Yarkor Chavez Annan W PTS 4 Stoke

17.11.07 Nadia Raoui L PTS 10 Schwedt, Germany
(Vacant Womens IBF Inter-Continental Flyweight Title)
01.12.07 Shanee Martin DREW 6 Bethnal Green
19.04.08 Magdalena Dahlen L PTS 6 Magdeburg, Germany
16.11.08 Zsofia Bedo W PTS 6 Derby
Career: 11 contests, won 4, drew 1, lost 6.

Alan Winterbottom
Oldham. *Born* Oldham, 1 July, 1978
S.Featherweight. *Ht* 5' 8"
Manager J. Doughty
16.11.08 Mo Khaled L PTS 6 Shaw
24.05.09 Steve Gethin W PTS 6 Shaw
Career: 2 contests, won 1, lost 1.

Junior Witter
Bradford. *Born* Bradford, 10 March, 1974
Former WBC L.Welterweight Champion. Former Undefeated British, Commonwealth, European, European Union, WBU Inter-Continental & WBF L.Welterweight Champion. *Ht* 5'7"
Manager D. Ingle
18.01.97 Cam Raeside DREW 6 Swadlincote
04.03.97 John Green W PTS 6 Yarm
20.03.97 Lee Molyneux W RSC 6 Salford
25.04.97 Trevor Meikle W PTS 6 Mere
15.05.97 Andreas Panayi W RSC 5 Reading
02.08.97 Brian Coleman W PTS 4 Barnsley
04.10.97 Michael Alexander W PTS 4 Hannover, Germany
07.02.98 Mark Ramsey DREW 6 Cheshunt
05.03.98 Brian Coleman W PTS 6 Leeds
18.04.98 Jan Bergman W PTS 6 Manchester
05.09.98 Mark Winters W PTS 8 Telford
28.11.98 Karl Taylor W PTS 4 Sheffield
13.02.99 Malcolm Melvin W RSC 2 Newcastle
(Vacant WBF L. Welterweight Title)
17.07.99 Isaac Cruz W PTS 8 Doncaster
06.11.99 Harry Butler W PTS 6 Widnes
21.03.00 Mrhai Iourgh W RSC 1 Telde, Gran Canaria
08.04.00 Arv Mittoo W PTS 4 Bethnal Green
24.06.00 Zab Judah L PTS 12 Glasgow
(IBF L. Welterweight Title Challenge)
20.10.00 Steve Conway W RTD 4 Belfast
25.11.00 Chris Henry W RSC 3 Manchester
10.03.01 David Kirk W RSC 2 Bethnal Green
22.05.01 Fabrice Faradji W RSC 1 Telde, Gran Canaria
21.07.01 Alan Temple W CO 5 Sheffield
27.10.01 Colin Mayisela W RSC 2 Manchester
(Vacant WBU Inter-Continental L.Welterweight Title)
16.03.02 Alan Bosworth W RSC 3 Northampton
(Vacant British L.Welterweight Title)
08.07.02 Laatekwi Hammond W RSC 2 Mayfair
(Vacant Commonwealth L.Welterweight Title)
19.10.02 Lucky Samba W RSC 2 Renfrew
23.11.02 Giuseppe Lauri W RSC 2 Derby
(Final Elim. WBO L. Welterweight Title)
05.04.03 Jurgen Haeck W RTD 4 Manchester
(Vacant European Union L.Welterweight Title)

27.09.03 Fred Kinuthia W RSC 2 Manchester
(Commonwealth L.Welterweight Title Defence)
16.04.04 Oscar Hall W RSC 3 Bradford
02.06.04 Salvatore Battaglia W RSC 2 Nottingham
(Vacant European L.Welterweight Title)
12.11.04 Krzysztof Bienias W RSC 2 Wembley
(European L.Welterweight Title Defence)
19.02.05 Lovemore N'Dou W PTS 12 Los Angeles, California, USA
(Commonwealth L.Welterweight Title Defence)
09.07.05 Andreas Kotelnik W PTS 12 Nottingham
(European L.Welterweight Title Defence)
21.10.05 Colin Lynes W PTS 12 Bethnal Green
(British, Commonwealth & European L.Welterweight Title Defences)
15.09.06 DeMarcus Corley W PTS 12 Muswell Hill
(Vacant WBC L.Welterweight Title)
20.01.07 Arturo Morua W RSC 9 Muswell Hill
(WBC L.Welterweight Title Defence)
07.09.07 Vivian Harris W CO 7 Doncaster
(WBC L.Welterweight Title Defence)
10.05.08 Tim Bradley L PTS 12 Nottingham
(WBC L.Welterweight Title Defence)
08.11.08 Victor Hugo Castro W CO 3 Bethnal Green
Career: 41 contests, won 37, drew 2, lost 2.

Junior Witter   Philip Sharkey

Bobby Wood
Walsall. *Born* Walsall, 29 April, 1981
Middleweight. *Ht* 5' 10"
Manager E. Johnson
03.04.09 Gavin Brook W PTS 4 Wolverhampton
12.06.09 Ernie Smith W PTS 4 Wolverhampton
Career: 2 contests, won 2.

Curtis Woodhouse
Hull. *Born* Beverley, 17 April, 1980
L.Middleweight. *Ht* 5'8¼"
Manager D. Coldwell
08.09.06 Dean Marcantonio W PTS 4 Mayfair

15.04.07 Duncan Cottier W PTS 4 Barnsley
03.06.07 Peter Dunn W PTS 4 Barnsley
05.12.07 Craig Tomes W RSC 1 Sheffield
16.03.08 Matt Seawright W RTD 3 Sheffield
17.05.08 Dave Murray W RSC 2 Sheffield
21.06.08 Wayne Downing W CO 1 Birmingham
20.09.08 Jimmy Beech W PTS 4 Sheffield
30.11.08 Peter Dunn W RSC 6 Rotherham
29.03.09 Matt Scriven W PTS 6 Sheffield
25.04.09 Jay Morris L PTS 6 Belfast
Career: 11 contests, won 10, lost 1.

Clinton Woods
Sheffield. *Born* Sheffield, 1 May, 1972
Former IBF L.Heavyweight Champion. Former Undefeated British, European, WBC International & Commonwealth L.Heavyweight Champion. Former Commonwealth S.Middleweight Champion. Former Undefeated Central Area S.Middleweight Champion. *Ht* 6'2"
Manager Self
17.11.94 Dave Proctor W PTS 6 Sheffield
12.12.94 Earl Ling W RSC 5 Cleethorpes
23.02.95 Paul Clarkson W RSC 1 Hull
06.04.95 Japhet Hans W RSC 3 Sheffield
16.05.95 Kevin Burton W PTS 6 Cleethorpes
14.06.95 Kevin Burton W RSC 6 Batley
21.09.95 Paul Murray W PTS 6 Sheffield
20.10.95 Phil Ball W RSC 4 Mansfield
22.11.95 Andy Ewen W RSC 3 Sheffield
05.02.96 Chris Walker W RSC 6 Bradford
16.03.96 John Duckworth W PTS 8 Sheffield
13.06.96 Ernie Loveridge W PTS 6 Sheffield
14.11.96 Craig Joseph W PTS 10 Sheffield
(Vacant Central Area S. Middleweight Title)
20.02.97 Rocky Shelly W RSC 2 Mansfield
10.04.97 Darren Littlewood W RSC 6 Sheffield
(Central Area S. Middleweight Title Defence)
26.06.97 Darren Ashton W PTS 6 Sheffield
25.10.97 Danny Juma W PTS 8 Queensferry
26.11.97 Jeff Finlayson W PTS 8 Sheffield
06.12.97 Mark Baker W PTS 12 Wembley
(Vacant Commonwealth S.Middleweight Title)
28.03.98 David Starie L PTS 12 Hull
(Commonwealth S. Middleweight Title Defence)
18.06.98 Peter Mason W RTD 4 Sheffield
30.11.98 Mark Smallwood W RSC 7 Manchester
13.03.99 Crawford Ashley W RSC 8 Manchester
(British, Commonwealth & European L. Heavyweight Title Challenges)
10.07.99 Sam Leuii W RSC 6 Southwark
(Commonwealth L. Heavyweight Title Defence)
11.09.99 Lenox Lewis W RSC 10 Sheffield
(Commonwealth L. Heavyweight Title Defence)
10.12.99 Terry Ford W RTD 4 Warsaw, Poland
12.02.00 Juan Perez Nelongo W PTS 12 Sheffield
(European L. Heavyweight Title Defence)
29.04.00 Ole Klemetsen W RSC 9 Wembley
(European L. Heavyweight Title Defence)
15.07.00 Greg Scott-Briggs W RSC 3 Millwall

24.03.01 Ali Forbes W RTD 10 Sheffield
*(Vacant WBC International
L. Heavyweight Title)*
27.07.01 Paul Bonson W PTS 6 Sheffield
13.09.01 Yawe Davis W PTS 12 Sheffield
(Final Elim.WBC L.Heavyweight Title)
16.03.02 Clint Johnson W RSC 3 Bethnal Green
07.09.02 Roy Jones L RSC 6 Portland, Oregon,
USA
*(WBC, WBA & IBF L.Heavyweight Title
Challenges)*
24.01.03 Sergio Martin Beaz W RSC 3 Sheffield
18.03.03 Arturo Rivera W RSC 2 Reading
10.06.03 Demetrius Jenkins W RSC 7 Sheffield
07.11.03 Glengoffe Johnson DREW 12 Sheffield
(Vacant IBF L.Heavyweight Title)
06.02.04 Glengoffe Johnson L PTS 12 Sheffield
(Vacant IBF L.Heavyweight Title)
24.10.04 Jason DeLisle W RSC 12 Sheffield
(Elim. IBF L.Heavyweight Title)
04.03.05 Rico Hoye W RSC 5 Rotherham
(Vacant IBF L.Heavyweight Title)
09.09.05 Julio Gonzalez W PTS 12 Sheffield
(IBF L.Heavyweight Title Defence)
13.05.06 Jason DeLisle W RSC 6 Sheffield
(IBF L.Heavyweight Title Defence)
02.09.06 Glengoffe Johnson W PTS 12 Bolton
(IBF L.Heavyweight Title Defence)
29.09.07 Julio Cesar Gonzalez W PTS 12
Sheffield
(IBF L.Heavyweight Title Defence)
12.04.08 Antonio Tarver L PTS 12 Tampa,
Florida, USA
*(IBF L.Heavyweight Title Defence. IBO
L.Heavyweight Title Challenge)*
14.02.09 Elvir Muriqi W PTS 12 St Helier
(Elim. IBF L.Heavyweight Title)
Career: 47 contests, won 42, drew 1, lost 4.

Gary Woolcombe

Welling. *Born* London, 4 August, 1982
Former British L.Middleweight Champion.
Former Undefeated Southern Area &
British Masters L.Middleweight Champion.
Ht 5'10¾"
Manager Self
15.05.03 Paul McIlwaine W RSC 2 Mayfair
22.07.03 Arv Mittoo W PTS 6 Bethnal Green
25.09.03 Pete Buckley W PTS 6 Bethnal Green
18.11.03 John Butler W PTS 4 Bethnal Green
07.02.04 Ernie Smith W PTS 4 Bethnal Green
14.02.04 Lee Williamson W PTS 6 Holborn
07.05.04 David Kirk W PTS 4 Bethnal Green
05.06.04 Ivor Bonavic W PTS 4 Bethnal Green
24.09.04 Geraint Harvey W PTS 4 Bethnal Green
19.11.04 Keith Jones W PTS 4 Bethnal Green
11.12.04 Peter Dunn W PTS 4 Canning Town
12.02.05 Howard Clarke W PTS 6 Portsmouth
05.03.05 Ernie Smith W PTS 6 Southwark
29.04.05 Matt Scriven W RSC 4 Southwark
20.05.05 Danny Parkinson W RSC 3 Southwark
19.06.05 Peter Dunn W RSC 6 Bethnal Green
07.10.05 Delroy Mellis W RTD 8 Bethnal Green
*(Vacant British Masters L.Middleweight
Title)*
04.11.05 Mark Phillips W PTS 4 Bethnal Green
27.01.06 Lee Murtagh W RSC 4 Dagenham
24.03.06 Eugenio Monteiro W PTS 8 Bethnal
Green

26.05.06 Gilbert Eastman W RSC 7 Bethnal
Green
*(Southern Area L.Middleweight Title
Challenge)*
03.11.06 Alex Stoda W DIS 4 Barnsley
26.01.07 Andrew Facey L RSC 5 Dagenham
*(English L.Middleweight Title
Challenge)*
15.06.07 Anthony Young W RSC 4 Crystal Palace
21.09.07 Jason Rushton W RSC 7 Bethnal Green
08.12.07 Marcus Portman W RTD 8 Wigan
(Vacant British L.Middleweight Title)
18.04.08 Ryan Rhodes L CO 9 Bethnal Green
(British L.Middleweight Title Defence)
15.11.08 Janis Chernouskis W PTS 6 Bethnal
Green
23.04.09 Vladimir Borovski W PTS 6 Limehouse
Career: 29 contests, won 27, lost 2.

Scott Woolford

Ramsgate. *Born* Rush Green, 6 September,
1983
L.Middleweight. *Ht* 5'7"
Manager Self
30.05.06 David Kehoe W PTS 4 Bethnal Green
06.10.06 Tommy Jones W PTS 4 Bethnal Green
17.11.06 Gary McMillan W PTS 4 Bethnal Green
15.06.07 Tyrone McInerney W PTS 4 Crystal
Palace
21.09.07 Yassine El Maachi L PTS 4 Bethnal
Green
30.11.07 Dave Ryan W PTS 4 Newham
01.02.08 Terry Adams W PTS 4 Bethnal Green
18.04.08 Johnny Greaves W RSC 3 Bethnal
Green
18.07.08 Jimmy Beech W PTS 4 Dagenham
05.09.08 Matthew Hatton L PTS 8 Nottingham
15.11.08 Tom Glover L PTS 10 Bethnal Green
*(Vacant Southern Area Welterweight
Title)*
20.03.09 Mark Douglas L RSC 3 Bethnal Green
Career: 12 contests, won 8, lost 4.

Vinny Woolford   Philip Sharkey

Vinny Woolford

Ramsgate. *Born* Dagenham, 14 October,
1981
L.Welterweight. *Ht* 5' 7"
Manager F. Maloney
13.09.08 Gavin Deacon W RTD 2 Bethnal Green
05.03.09 Bheki Moyo W PTS 6 Limehouse
Career: 2 contests, won 2.

Chris Woollas

Epworth. *Born* Scunthorpe, 22 November,
1973
Heavyweight. Former Undefeated Midlands
Area Cruiserweight Champion. *Ht* 5'11"
Manager M. Shinfield
17.08.94 Darren Littlewood W RSC 4 Sheffield
05.10.94 Robert Norton DREW 6 Wolverhampton
05.12.94 Neil Simpson W PTS 6 Cleethorpes
10.02.95 Monty Wright L RSC 4 Birmingham
30.06.95 Kenny Nevers L RSC 2 Doncaster
25.09.95 Cliff Elden DREW 6 Cleethorpes
08.11.95 Stevie Pettit W PTS 6 Walsall
17.11.95 Markku Salminen L PTS 6 Helsinki,
Finland
11.12.95 Cliff Elden DREW 6 Cleethorpes
15.02.96 Pele Lawrence W RSC 6 Sheffield
29.02.96 John Pierre DREW 6 Scunthorpe
16.03.96 David Jules W PTS 6 Sheffield
22.04.96 Jacklord Jacobs DREW 4 Crystal Palace
30.05.96 Martin Langtry L RSC 6 Lincoln
*(Midlands Area Cruiserweight Title
Challenge)*
03.09.96 Darren Corbett L RSC 7 Belfast
02.10.96 Rocky Shelly W RSC 6 Stoke
09.10.96 Nigel Rafferty W PTS 6 Stoke
28.10.96 Colin Brown L PTS 8 Glasgow
10.11.96 Michael Gale DREW 6 Glasgow
25.11.96 Albert Call L PTS 6 Cleethorpes
17.12.96 Darren Corbett L RSC 1 Doncaster
16.01.97 Mark Smallwood L PTS 8 Solihull
31.01.97 Tim Redman L PTS 6 Pentre Halkyn
14.03.97 Kelly Oliver L PTS 6 Reading
24.03.97 Mikael Lindblad L RSC 7 Helsinki,
Finland
19.06.97 Ian Henry W PTS 6 Scunthorpe
02.08.97 Kelly Oliver L RSC 3 Barnsley
15.12.97 Neil Simpson W PTS 6 Cleethorpes
26.01.98 Colin Brown W PTS 6 Glasgow
26.03.98 Cliff Elden L PTS 4 Scunthorpe
06.05.98 Simon McDougall W PTS 6 Blackpool
21.07.98 Matthew Ellis L RSC 5 Widnes
11.09.98 Lennox Williams W PTS 6 Cleethorpes
12.03.99 Albert Sosnowski L PTS 4 Bethnal
Green
27.05.99 Nigel Rafferty W PTS 10 Edgbaston
*(Midlands Area Cruiserweight Title
Challenge)*
10.07.99 Michael Sprott L RTD 4 Southwark
13.09.99 Dominic Negus L PTS 10 Bethnal Green
(Elim. British Cruiserweight Title)
09.10.99 Chris P. Bacon L PTS 4 Manchester
30.10.99 Terry Dunstan L RSC 1 Southwark
08.04.00 Bruce Scott L RSC 2 Bethnal Green
13.07.00 Firat Aslan L RSC 2 Bethnal Green
08.09.00 Petr Horacek L PTS 4 Hammersmith

21.10.00 Danny Percival L PTS 4 Wembley
18.11.00 Matthew Ellis L PTS 4 Dagenham
11.12.00 Enzo Maccarinelli L PTS 4 Widnes
15.12.01 Lee Swaby L RSC 4 Sheffield
21.10.02 Greg Scott-Briggs W PTS 6 Cleethorpes
01.11.02 Spencer Wilding DREW 6 Preston
28.04.03 Eamonn Glennon W PTS 6 Cleethorpes
22.11.03 Albert Sosnowski L RSC 1 Belfast
16.02.04 Dave Clarke W PTS 6 Scunthorpe
30.03.04 Colin Kenna L PTS 6 Southampton
10.07.04 Robert Norton L RSC 4 Coventry
30.09.04 Paul King L PTS 4 Glasgow
06.11.04 Carl Wright L RSC 1 Coventry
16.12.04 Billy Wilson W PTS 6 Cleethorpes
26.10.06 Matthew Ellis L PTS 4 Dudley
04.11.06 Mark Walker DREW 4 Glasgow
11.12.06 Istvan Kecskes W PTS 6 Cleethorpes
28.01.07 Chris Burton L RSC 3 Yarm
01.06.07 Pele Reid L CO 1 Birmingham
30.06.07 Scott Belshaw L CO 1 Belfast
14.09.07 Ian Millarvie L RSC 2 Kirkcaldy
21.02.09 Dean O'Loughlin NC 1 Hull
28.02.09 Danny Hughes L PTS 6 Newcastle
09.05.09 Carl Baker L PTS 6 Lincoln
13.06.09 Richard Towers L PTS 4 Wigan
25.06.09 Ali Adams L PTS 6 Mayfair
Career: 68 contests, won 18, drew 8, lost 41, no contest 1.

Chris Woollas   Philip Sharkey

Nigel Wright

Crook. *Born* Bishop Auckland, 22 June, 1979
Former Undefeated English L.Welterweight Champion. *Ht* 5'9"
Manager G. Robinson
10.02.01 Keith Jones W PTS 4 Widnes
15.09.01 Tommy Peacock W RSC 1 Manchester
17.11.01 Ernie Smith W PTS 4 Glasgow
19.01.02 Woody Greenaway W CO 2 Bethnal Green
11.03.02 James Paisley W PTS 4 Glasgow
19.10.02 Kevin McIntyre L PTS 6 Renfrew
29.03.03 Darren Melville W PTS 6 Portsmouth

24.05.03 David Kirk W PTS 4 Bethnal Green
02.10.03 Nigel Senior W RSC 5 Liverpool
29.11.03 Jason Hall W PTS 6 Renfrew
06.03.04 George Telfer W RSC 3 Renfrew
22.05.04 Jon Honney W RSC 2 Widnes
22.10.04 Silence Saheed W PTS 8 Edinburgh
11.03.05 Dean Hickman W CO 7 Doncaster
(*Vacant English L.Welterweight Title*)
27.05.05 Alan Bosworth W PTS 10 Spennymoor
(*English L.Welterweight Title Defence*)
05.11.05 Kevin McIntyre W RSC 1 Renfrew
(*Final Elim. British L.Welterweight Title*)
18.02.06 Valery Kharyanov W CO 4 Edinburgh
12.05.06 Lenny Daws L PTS 12 Bethnal Green
(*Vacant British L.Welterweight Title*)
04.11.06 Gary Reid W PTS 10 Glasgow
(*English L.Welterweight Title Defence*)
30.03.07 Jonathan Nelson W RTD 2 Newcastle
14.11.07 Lenny Daws DREW 10 Bethnal Green
(*English L.Welterweight Title Defence*)
08.02.08 Ajose Olusegun L PTS 12 Peterlee
(*Commonwealth L.Welterweight Title Challenge*)
19.07.08 Paul McCloskey L PTS 10 Limerick
24.10.08 Ross Minter W PTS 3 Bethnal Green
24.10.08 Michael Lomax L PTS 3 Bethnal Green
03.04.09 Arek Malek W PTS 6 Bethnal Green
12.06.09 Ajose Olusegun L PTS 12 Liverpool
(*Vacant British L.Welterweight Title. Commonwealth L.Welterweight Title Challenge*)
Career: 27 contests, won 20, drew 1, lost 6.

Tyrone Wright

Nottingham. *Born* Nottingham, 7 September, 1978
Midlands Area L.Heavyweight Champion. Former Undefeated British Masters L.Heavyweight Champion. *Ht* 6'2"
Manager J. Gill
22.10.05 Lee Mountford W CO 3 Mansfield
15.12.05 Gary Thompson DREW 6 Cleethorpes
24.04.06 Csaba Andras W CO 2 Cleethorpes
15.09.06 Nathan King L RTD 3 Newport
11.11.06 Gordon Brennan W PTS 6 Sutton in Ashfield
11.12.06 Dean Walker W PTS 6 Cleethorpes
03.03.07 Shon Davies W PTS 6 Alfreton
19.05.07 Michael Monaghan W RSC 10 Nottingham
(*Midlands Area L.Heavyweight Title Challenge. Vacant British Masters L.Heavyweight Title*)
09.11.07 Simeon Cover W PTS 4 Nottingham
07.03.08 Brian Magee L PTS 6 Nottingham
10.05.08 Paul David W PTS 10 Nottingham
(*Midlands Area L.Heavyweight Title Defence*)
06.12.08 Paul David L CO 7 Nottingham
(*Vacant English S.Middleweight Title*)
Career: 12 contests, won 8, drew 1, lost 3.

Ali Wyatt

Torquay. *Born* Iran, 15 May, 1977
Welterweight. *Ht* 5'5¾"
Manager C. Sanigar

09.10.05 Michael Grant DREW 4 Hammersmith
17.11.05 Stuart Philips L PTS 4 Bristol
21.05.06 Bheki Moyo W RSC 3 Bristol
03.06.06 Michael Grant L PTS 4 Chigwell
23.06.06 Lance Hall W RSC 5 Birmingham
26.02.07 Joe McCluskey W RSC 5 Birmingham
13.05.07 Joe McCluskey DREW 8 Birmingham
08.10.07 Alexander Spitjo L RTD 5 Birmingham
25.02.08 Martin Gethin L PTS 8 Birmingham
05.04.08 Garry Buckland L PTS 6 Newport
20.06.08 John Vanemmenis W PTS 4 Plymouth
19.07.08 John Watson L RTD 4 Liverpool
13.09.08 Scott Lawton L PTS 6 Stoke
20.09.08 Amir Unsworth L PTS 6 Newark
24.10.08 Jamie Way L PTS 10 Newport
(*Vacant International Masters Lightweight Title*)
07.02.09 Andrew Murray L RSC 3 Craigavon
12.06.09 Dean Harrison L PTS 6 Wolverhampton
Career: 17 contests, won 4, drew 2, lost 11.

Richie Wyatt

Stourbridge. *Born* Wordsley, 1 April, 1981
L.Welterweight. *Ht* 5' 9"
Manager R. Woodhall
10.04.09 Johnny Greaves W PTS 4 Birmingham
Career: 1 contest, won 1.

Andrew Young

Inverness. *Born* Inverness, 6 May, 1980
Cruiserweight. *Ht* 6' 2"
Manager T. Gilmour
02.03.07 John Anthony L CO 1 Irvine
05.06.07 James Swindells W RSC 2 Glasgow
14.03.09 Lee Mountford W RSC 2 Aberdeen
Career: 3 contests, won 2, lost 1.

Anthony Young

Crawley. *Born* Crawley, 10 April, 1984
S.Middleweight. *Ht* 5'11¼"
Manager J. Evans
30.10.05 Alex Stoda W PTS 6 Bethnal Green
05.03.06 Steve Ede L RSC 3 Southampton
18.10.06 Rocky Muscas W PTS 4 Bayswater
26.10.06 Max Maxwell W PTS 4 Wolverhampton
22.02.07 Danny Reynolds L RSC 4 Leeds
08.06.07 Greg Barton W PTS 4 Mayfair
15.06.07 Gary Woolcombe L RSC 4 Crystal Palace
23.09.07 Simon O'Donnell L PTS 6 Longford
27.10.07 Pavel Dostal L PTS 6 Prague, Czech Republic
21.12.07 Tomas Kugler L PTS 6 Brno, Czech Republic
23.02.08 Lee Noble L PTS 10 Crawley
(*Vacant British Masters Middleweight Title*)
08.03.08 Patrick J. Maxwell L RTD 4 Greenwich
06.06.08 Steve McGuire L PTS 6 Glasgow
15.06.08 Gokhan Kazaz L PTS 6 Bethnal Green
01.08.08 Daley Ojuederie L RSC 4 Watford
27.09.08 Danny Couzens L PTS 4 Bracknell
05.10.08 Ryan Walls L PTS 4 Watford
16.11.08 Matthew Hainy L PTS 6 Derby
19.01.09 Steve Ede L RSC 8 Mayfair
(*Vacant Southern Area Middleweight Title*)
Career: 19 contests, won 4, lost 15.

PROFESSIONAL BOXING PROMOTERS' ASSOCIATION

PRESENTS

THE BRITISH AND INTERNATIONAL MASTERS CHAMPIONS

UNDER BBB OF C RULES

	BRITISH	INTERNATIONAL
HEAVY	PELE REID	VACANT
CRUISER	NEIL SIMPSON	JJ OJUEDERIE
LIGHT-HEAVY	DARREN STUBBS	TONY OAKEY
SUPER-MIDDLE	VACANT	VACANT
MIDDLE	DANNY BUTLER	VACANT
LIGHT-MIDDLE	ALEX MATVIENKO	TAZ JONES
WELTER	DALE MILES	VACANT
LIGHT-WELTER	GRAEME HIGGINSON	JAMIE WAY
LIGHT	SCOTT EVANS	PAUL HOLBORN
SUPER FEATHER	DARREN JOHNSTONE	VACANT
FEATHER	DAVEY SAVAGE	BEN JONES
SUPER-BANTAM	VACANT	VACANT
BANTAM	VACANT	MATTHEW EDMONDS
SUPER-FLY	VACANT	SHINNY BAYAAR
FLY	VACANT	VACANT

THE ONLY ALL-COMERS TITLE OPERATING IN BRITISH BOXING. OUR CHAMPIONS HAVE TO DEFEND WHEN A VALID CHALLENGE IS MADE WITH MORE THAN 30 DAYS NOTICE. TO CHALLENGE FOR OUR TITLE, PROMOTORS SHOULD APPLY TO:

THE PBPA   TEL: 01797 260616
UNIT 2   FAX: 01797 260642
SIX ACRES   EMAIL: info@pbpauk.com
STODDARDS LANE
BECKLEY
EAST SUSSEX TN31 6UG

PRESIDENT: Keith Walker
CHAIRMAN: Bruce Baker
GENERAL SECRETARY: Greg Steene
DIRECTORS: B. Baker, G. Steene, J. Gill, J. Evans, T. Brogan

MEMBERSHIP IS OPEN TO PROMOTERS AND MANAGERS. THOSE INTERESTED PLEASE APPLY

British Area Title Bouts, 2008-2009

Please note that BBBoC Regulations state that any Area champion who wins English, Celtic, British, Commonwealth, European and World championships have to automatically relinquish their titles.

Central Area

Title holders at 30 June 2009

Fly: *vacant*. **S.Fly**: *vacant*. **Bantam**: *vacant*. **S.Bantam**: Josh Wale. **Feather**: *vacant*. **S.Feather**: Steve Bell. **Light**: Jon Baguley. **L.Welter**: John Fewkes. **Welter**: *vacant*. **L.Middle**: *vacant*. **Middle**: *vacant*. **S.Middle**: Paulino Da Silva. **L.Heavy**: Darren Stubbs. **Cruiser**: vacant. **Heavy**: *vacant*.

Title bouts held between 1 July 2008 and 30 June 2009

12 September	Jon Baguley W RSC 3 Dwayne Hill, Sheffield (Vacant Lightweight Title)
24 May	Darren Stubbs W PTS 10 Carl Wild, Shaw (Vacant L.Heavyweight Title)
Between 1 July	2008 and 30 June 2009, Stefy Bull (Light), Nadeem Sidique (Welter) and Paul Smith (Middle) relinquished their titles, while Danny Reynolds (L.Middle) and Amer Khan (L.Heavy) forfeited their titles.

Midlands Area

Titleholders at 30 June 2009

Fly: *vacant*. **S.Fly**: *vacant*. **Bantam**: *vacant*. **S.Bantam**: *vacant*. **Feather**: *vacant*. **S.Feather**: *vacant*. **Light**: Steve Saville. **L.Welter**: Gavin Deacon. **Welter**: Dave Ryan. **L.Middle**: Manoocha Salari. **Middle**: Tony Randell. **S.Middle**: Sam Horton. **L.Heavy**: Tyrone Wright. **Cruiser**: *vacant*. **Heavy**: Lee Swaby.

Title bouts held between 1 July 2008 and 30 June 2009

14 September	Max Maxwell L PTS 10 Rob Kenney, Edgbaston (Middleweight Title Defence)
9 November	Steve Saville W RSC 7 Baz Carey, Wolverhampton (Vacant Lightweight Title)
1 February	Tony Randell W PTS 10 Max Maxwell, Edgbaston (Vacant Middleweight Title)
9 May	Lee Swaby W PTS 10 Paul Butlin, Lincoln (Vacant Heavyweight Title)
10 May	Dave Ryan W RSC 2 Scott Evans, Derby (Vacant Welterweight Title)
10 May	Sam Horton W PTS 10 Matt Hainy, Derby (Vacant S.Middleweight Title)
23 May	Gavin Deacon W PTS 10 Amir Unsworth, Sleaford (Vacant L.Welterweight Title)

Between 1 July 2008 and 30 June 2009, Martin Gethin (Light), Mark Lloyd (Welter), Rob Kenney (Middle) and Paul David (S.Middle) relinquished their titles, while Carl Wright (Cruiser) was asked to hand over his belt.

Northern Area

Titleholders at 30 June 2009

Fly: *vacant*. **S.Fly**: *vacant*. **Bantam**: *vacant*. **S.Bantam**: *vacant*. **Feather**: *vacant*. **S.Feather**: *vacant*. **Light**: *vacant*. **L.Welter**: *vacant*. **Welter**: *vacant*. **L.Middle**: *vacant*. **Middle**: *vacant*. **S.Middle**: *vacant*. **L.Heavy**: *vacant*. **Cruiser**: *vacant*. **Heavy**: *vacant*.

Title bouts held between 1 July 2008 and 30 June 2009

None

Northern Ireland Area

Titleholders at 30 June 2009

Fly: *vacant*. **S.Fly**: *vacant*. **Bantam**: *vacant*. **S.Bantam**: *vacant*. **Feather**: *vacant*. **S.Feather**: *vacant*. **Light**: *vacant*. **L.Welter**: James Gorman. **Welter**: *vacant*. **L.Middle**: *vacant*. **Middle**: *vacant*. **S.Middle**: *vacant*. **L.Heavy**: *vacant*. **Cruiser**: *vacant*. **Heavy**: *vacant*.

Title bouts held between 1 July 2008 and 30 June 2009

None

Scottish Area

Titleholders at 30 June 2009

Fly: vacant. **S.Fly**: vacant. **Bantam**: vacant. **S.Bantam**: vacant. **Feather**: Furhan Rafiq. **S.Feather**: *vacant*. **Light**: Charles Paul King. **L.Welter**: vacant. **Welter**: vacant. **L.Middle**: Ciaran Duffy. **Middle**: Vince Baldassara. **S.Middle**: Tom Cannon. **L.Heavy**: vacant. **Cruiser**: vacant. **Heavy**: vacant.

Title bouts held between 1 July 2008 and 30 June 2009

| 19 January | Charles Paul King W PTS 10 Stuart Green, Glasgow (Vacant Lightweight Title) |
| 6 March | Ciaran Duffy W PTS 10 Paddy Pollock, Glasgow (Vacant L.Middleweight Title) |

Between 1 July 2008 and 30 June 2009, Colin McNeil (L.Middle) retired.

Southern Area

Titleholders at 30 June 2009

Fly: *vacant*. **S.Fly**: *vacant*. **Bantam**: *vacant*. **S.Bantam**: *vacant*. **Feather**: Akaash Bhatia. **S.Feather**: *vacant*. **Light**: Lee Cook. **L.Welter**: Peter McDonagh. **Welter**: Tom Glover. **L.Middle**: *vacant*.

Middle: Steve Ede. **S.Middle**: Tony Salam. **L.Heavy**: JJ Ojuderie. **Cruiser**: *vacant*. **Heavy**: *vacant*.

Title bouts held between 1 July 2008 and 30 June 2009

5 October	JJ Ojuederie W PTS 10 Joey Vegas, Watford (L.Heavyweight Title Defence)
7 November	Akaash Bhatia W CO 2 Marc Callaghan, Wigan (Vacant Featherweight Title)
15 November	Tom Glover W PTS 10 Scott Woolford, Bethnal Green (Vacant Welterweight Title)
21 November	Sam Sexton W RSC 6 Colin Kenna, Bethnal Green (Vacant Heavyweight Title)
13 December	Peter McDonagh W PTS 10 Lee Purdy, Brentwood (Vacant L.Welterweight Title)
19 January	Steve Ede W RSC 8 Anthony Young, Mayfair (Vacant Middleweight Title)
30 January	Tony Salam W RSC 4 Richard Horton, Bethnal Green (Vacant S.Middleweight Title)
20 March	Lee Cook W PTS 10 Shane Watson, Bethnal Green (Vacant Lightweight Title)

Between 1 July 2008 and 30 June 2009, Jon Honey (L.Welter), Anthony Small (L.Middle), Tommy Eastwood (Cruiser) and Sam Sexton (Heavy) all relinquished their titles.

Welsh Area

Titleholders at 30 June 2009

Fly: *vacant*. **S.Fly**: *vacant*. **Bantam**: *vacant*. **S.Bantam**: *vacant*.

Feather: Dai Davies. **S.Feather**: Jamie Arthur. **Light**: Damian Owen. **L.Welter**: *vacant*. **Welter**: Tony Doherty. **L.Middle**: Taz Jones. **Middle**: *vacant*. **S.Middle**: *vacant*. **L.Heavy**: Shon Davies. **Cruiser**: *vacant*. **Heavy**: *vacant*.

Title bouts held between 1 July 2008 and 30 June 2009

12 July	Dai Davies L CO 2 Jamie Arthur, Newport (S.Featherweight Title Defence)
21 February	Taz Jones W RSC 4 Kerry Hope, Merthyr (Vacant L.Middleweight Title)
5 June	Dai Davies W RSC 9 Rob Turley, Newport (Vacant Featherweight Title)

Western Area

Titleholders at 30 June 2009

Fly: *vacant*. **S.Fly**: *vacant*. **Bantam**: *vacant*. **S.Bantam**: *vacant*. **Feather**: *vacant*. **S.Feather**: *vacant*. **Light**: *vacant*. **L.Welter**: *vacant*. **Welter**: *vacant*. **L.Middle**: Carl Drake. **Middle**: Danny Butler. **S.Middle**: *vacant*. **L.Heavy**: *vacant*. **Cruiser**: *vacant*. **Heavy**: *vacant*.

Title bouts held between 1 July 2008 and 30 June 2009

| 14 March | Danny Butler W PTS 10 Carl Drake, Bristol (Vacant Middleweight Title) |

Sam Sexton (left) shown probing Colin Kenna's defences during their contest for the vacant Southern Area heavyweight title. Sexton won in the sixth round

Philip Sharkey

English and Celtic Title Bouts, 2008-2009

English Championships

Titleholders at 30 June 2009

Fly: *vacant*. **S.Fly**: Ross Burkinshaw. **Bantam**: Jamie McDonnell. **S.Bantam**: Mark Moran. **Feather**: *vacant*. **S.Feather**: Ryan Barrett. **Light**: Scott Lawton. **L.Welter**: Lenny Daws. **Welter**: Adnan Amar. **L.Middle**: Andrew Facey. **Middle**: Darren McDermott. **S.Middle**: Paul David. **L.Heavy**: Danny McIntosh. **Cruiser**: *vacant*. **Heavy**: John McDermott.

Title bouts held between 1 July 2008 and 30 June 2009

5 September	Martin Gethin W RSC 4 John Fewkes, Nottingham (Vacant Lightweight Title)
5 September	Scott Haywood W PTS 10 Dean Harrison, Nottingham (Vacant L.Welterweight Title)
4 October	Danny McIntosh W RSC 7 Steven Spartacus, Norwich (Vacant L.Heavyweight Title)
25 October	Femi Fehintola L CO 3 Ryan Barrett, St Helier (S.Featherweight Title Defence)
6 December	Danny McIntosh W RSC 1 Rod Anderton, Nottingham (L.Heavyweight Title Defence)
6 December	Martin Gethin L RSC 9 Scott Lawton, Nottingham (Lightweight Title Defence)
6 December	Paul David W CO 7 Tyrone Wright, Nottingham (Vacant S.Middleweight Title)
28 February	Steven Bendall L PTS 10 Darren McDermott, Birmingham (Middleweight Title Defence)
28 February	Danny McIntosh W DIS 5 Matthew Barney, Norwich (L.Heavyweight Title Defence)
11 April	Lenny Daws W PTS 10 Peter McDonagh, Bethnal Green (Vacant L.Welterweight Title)
23 April	Ross Burkinshaw W RSC 7 Mike Robinson, Limehouse (Vacant S.Flyweight Title)

Between 1 July 2008 and 30 June 2009, Nigel Wright (L.Welter) and Robert Norton (Cruiser) relinquished their titles.

Celtic Championships

Titleholders at 30 June 2009

Fly: *vacant*. **S.Fly**: *vacant*. **Bantam**: *vacant*. **S.Bantam**: *vacant*. **Feather**: *vacant*. **S.Feather**: *vacant*. **Light**: Garry Buckland. **L.Welter**: Stuart Phillips. **Welter**: *vacant*. **L.Middle**: *vacant*. **Middle**: *vacant*. **S.Middle**: Kenny Anderson. **L.Heavy**: *vacant*. **Cruiser**: *vacant*. **Heavy**: *vacant*.

Title bouts held between 1 July 2008 and 30 June 2009

27 February	Garry Buckland W PTS 10 Craig Docherty, Barnsley (Lightweight Title Defence)
27 March	Kenny Anderson W PTS 10 Nathan King, Glasgow (Vacant S.Middleweight Title)

Between 1 July 2008 and 30 June 2009, Steve McGuire (S.Middle) relinquished his title.

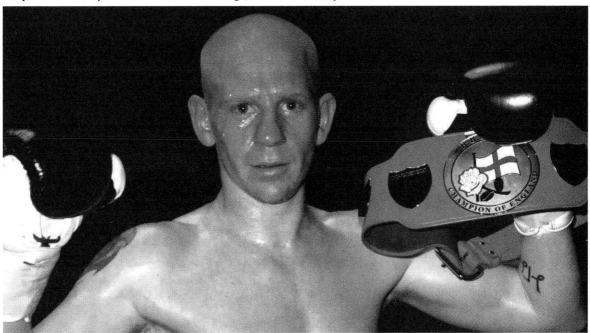

Ryan Barrett proudly displays the English Championship Belt after knocking out Femi Fehintola in St Helier   Philip Sharkey

British Title Bouts, 2008-2009

All of last season's title bouts are shown in date order within their weight divisions and give the boxers' respective weights, the names of the referees and judges involved, and the scorecards if going to a decision. Foreign-born boxers who contest a British title, having been qualified by being British citizens for more than five years, are shown by domicile/country of birth.

Flyweight
23 January Chris Edwards 109 (England) W RTD 4 Wayne Bloy 110 (England), Fenton Manor Sports Complex, Stoke. Referee: Mark Green. Judges: John Keane, Terry O'Connor, Richie Davies. Having drawn against Dale Robinson in a title fight on 13 April 2007, Edwards became the first champion since England's Jason Booth handed back the belt in December 2003. The vacant Commonwealth title was also on the line.
29 May Chris Edwards 110 (England) W PTS 12 Usman Ahmed 108 (England), Fenton Manor Sports Complex, Stoke. Referee: Phil Edwards. Judges: Richie Davies 118-109, John Keane 117-111, Ian John-Lewis 118-109. Edwards was also defending the Commonwealth crown.

S.Flyweight
7 November Andy Bell 115 (England) L PTS 12 Lee Haskins 114 (England), Robin Park Centre, Wigan. Referee: Phil Edwards. Judges: Howard Foster 113-116, Victor Loughlin 114-115, Dave Parris 113-116.

Bantamweight
3 April Gary Davies 117 (England) W RSC 7 Matthew Edmonds 117 (Wales), York Hall, Bethnal Green, London. Referee: Dave Parris. Judges: Mark Green, Ian John-Lewis, Marcus McDonnell. Contested for the championship after Ian Napa (England) had decided to relinquish the title on 19 March to concentrate on defending his European crown and aim for a world championship opportunity.

S.Bantamweight
21 November Matthew Marsh 122 (England) W PTS 12 Rocky Dean 121 (England), York Hall, Bethnal Green, London. Referee: Phil Edwards. Judges: Howard Foster 116-112, Richie Davies 116-113, Ian John-Lewis 114-114. Marsh relinquished the title in mid-April when unable to make the weight for a defence against Mark Moran and Jason Booth stepped in at short notice.
17 April Jason Booth 121 (England) W RSC 6 Mark Moran 121 (England), Indoor Sports Centre, Leigh. Referee: Howard Foster. Judges: Victor Loughlin, Phil Edwards, Dave Parris.
30 June Jason Booth 121 (England) W PTS 12 Rocky Dean 121 (England), York Hall, Bethnal Green, London. Referee: Richie Davies. Judges: Dave Parris 120-108, Ian John-Lewis 119-109, Mark Green 119-109.

Featherweight
28 November Paul Appleby 125 (Scotland) W PTS 12 Esham Pickering 125 (England), Bellahouston Sports Centre,

Contested for the vacant British bantamweight title, Gary Davies (left) sets about Mathew Edmonds prior to stopping him in the seventh round
Philip Sharkey

Glasgow. Referee: John Keane. Judges: Phil Edwards 116-113, Victor Loughlin 117-112, Terry O'Connor 117-111.
25 April Paul Appleby 125 (Scotland) L RSC 6 Martin Lindsay 125 (Northern Ireland), Ulster Hall, Belfast. Referee: Howard Foster. Judges: Dave Parris, Richie Davies, Ian John-Lewis.

S.Featherweight
There were no championship defences made by Kevin Mitchell (England) between 1 July 2008 and 30 June 2009.

Lightweight
11 July John Murray 134 (England) W RSC 5 Lee Meager 134 (England), Robin Park Centre, Wigan. Referee: Howard Foster. Judges: Phil Edwards, Terry O'Connor, Mickey Vann. Contested for the vacant title after Jonathan Thaxton (England) had handed back the belt on 17 June.
17 January John Murray 134 (England) W RSC 8 Lee McAllister 134 (Scotland), Robin Park Centre, Wigan. Referee: John Keane. Judges: Terry O'Connor, Phil Edwards, Ian John-Lewis. Murray forfeited the title when coming in over the weight for a defence against Scott Lawton (England) at the Robin Park Centre on 13 June. The fight went ahead with Lawton, who still had an opportunity of winning the title, being stopped in the sixth. Victor Loughlin refereed and the three judges were Phil Edwards, Dave Parris and Howard Foster.

L.Welterweight
4 July David Barnes 140 (England) W PTS 12 Barry Morrison 139 (Scotland), Everton Park Sports Centre, Liverpool. Referee: Mark Green. Judges: Mickey Vann 116-113, Phil Edwards 116-113, Ian John-Lewis 116-112. Barnes relinquished the title on 1 December after damaging his left hand in preparation for a defence against Colin Lynes on 5 December. Paul McCloskey stepped in at short notice to face Lynes.
5 December Paul McCloskey 138 (Northern Ireland) W RTD 9 Colin Lynes 139 (England), Goresbrook Leisure Centre, Dagenham. Referee: Mickey Vann. Judges: Mark Green, Richie Davies, Victor Loughlin.
13 March Paul McCloskey 139 (Northern Ireland) W RSC 4 Dean Harrison 140 (England), Kingsway Leisure Centre, Widnes. Referee: Marcus McDonnell. Judges: Phil Edwards, Mark Green, John Keane. McCloskey relinquished the title in mid-May to concentrate on a contest against France's Souleymane Mbaye for the European championship.
12 June Ajose Olusegun 139 (England/Nigeria) W PTS 12 Nigel Wright 139 (England), Olympia, Liverpool. Referee: Mark Green. Judges: Phil Edwards 117-112, Howard Foster 117-111, John Keane 116-113. Billed for the vacant title, Olusegun's Commonwealth crown was also at stake.

Welterweight
14 November Kell Brook 146 (England) W RSC 1 Kevin McIntyre 146 (Scotland), Kelvin Hall, Glasgow. Referee: Victor Loughlin. Judges: Ian John-Lewis, John Keane. Marcus McDonnell.
30 January Kell Brook 146 (England) W RSC 2 Stuart Elwell 146 (England), York Hall, Bethnal Green, London. Referee: Marcus McDonnell. Judges: Richie Davies, Mark Green, Ian John-Lewis.

L.Middleweight
20 September Ryan Rhodes 153 (England) W PTS 12 Jamie Coyle 153 (Scotland), Hillsborough Leisure Centre, Sheffield. Referee: Ian John-Lewis. Judges: Phil Edwards 120-109, Victor Loughlin 118-111, Marcus McDonnell 120-110. Rhodes relinquished the title in mid-April due to a managerial dispute.

Middleweight
14 March Wayne Elcock 159 (England) L RSC 3 Matthew Macklin 159 (England), Aston Events Centre, Birmingham. Referee: Victor Loughlin. Judges: Mark Green, John Keane, Marcus McDonnell.

S.Middleweight
13 December Brian Magee 166 (Northern Ireland) W CO 8 Steve McGuire 166 (Scotland), International Centre, Brentwood. Referee: Richie Davies. Judges: Marcus McDonnell, Dave Parris, Mickey Vann. Contested for the vacant title after England's Carl Froch decided to give up his crown in order to concentrate on a contest against Canada's Jean Pascal for the vacant WBA championship. Having put his first notch on the Lonsdale Belt, Magee was forced to relinquish the title two weeks before making his first defence on 28 March, against Tony Dodson, due to a persistent back injury. Dodson would still get a crack at the title after Tony Quigley stepped in at short notice.
28 March Tony Quigley 167 (England) W RSC 12 Tony Dodson 167 (England), Echo Arena, Liverpool. Referee: Victor Loughlin. Judges: Howard Foster, Richie Davies, Marcus McDonnell.

L.Heavyweight
Dean Francis (England) failed to make a defence during the period and relinquished the title in mid-April when struggling to make the weight.

Cruiserweight
3 October Robert Norton 200 (England) W PTS 12 Micky Steeds 196 (England), Meadowside Leisure Centre, Burton. Referee: Howard Foster. Judges: John Keane 119-108, Victor Loughlin 118-110, Marcus McDonnell 118-109. Contested for the vacant title after Mark Hobson (England) announced his retirement on 25 April.
6 February Robert Norton 198 (England) W PTS 12 David Dolan 198 (England), Aston Events Centre, Birmingham. Referee: Dave Parris. Judges: John Keane 116-109, Terry O'Connor 115-110, Howard Foster 114-111. The vacant Commonwealth title was also at stake in this contest.

Heavyweight
18 July Danny Williams 265 (England) W PTS 12 John McDermott 252 (England), Goresbrook Leisure Centre, Dagenham. Referee: Dave Parris. Judges: Marcus McDonnell 114-113, Mark Green 114-111, Richie Davies 113-113.
2 May Danny Williams 262 (England) W PTS 12 John McDermott 256 (England), Crowtree Leisure Centre, Sunderland. Referee: Terry O'Connor. Judges: John Keane 116-111, Victor Loughlin 116-111, Richie Davies 113-115.

Lord Lonsdale Challenge Belts: Outright Winners

Outright Winners of the National Sporting Club's Challenge Belt, 1909-1935 (21)

Under pressure from other promoters with bigger venues, and in an effort to sustain their monopoly – having controlled championship fights in Britain up until that point in time – the National Sporting Club launched the belt in 1909. They did so on the proviso that there should be eight weight divisions – fly, bantam, feather, light, welter, middle, light-heavy, and heavy – and that to win a belt outright a champion must score three title-match victories at the same weight, but not necessarily consecutively. Worth a substantial amount of money, and carrying a £1 a week pension from the age of 50, the President of the NSC, Lord Lonsdale, donated the first of 22 belts struck. Known as the Lonsdale Belt, despite the inscription reading: 'The National Sporting Club's Challenge Belt', the first man to put a notch on a belt was Freddie Welsh, who outpointed Johnny Summers for the lightweight title on 8 November 1909, while Jim Driscoll became the first man to win one outright. The record time for winning the belt is held by Jim Higgins (279 days).

FLYWEIGHT	Jimmy Wilde; Jackie Brown
BANTAMWEIGHT	Digger Stanley; Joe Fox; Jim Higgins; Johnny Brown; Dick Corbett; Johnny King
FEATHERWEIGHT	Jim Driscoll; Tancy Lee; Johnny Cuthbert; Nel Tarleton
LIGHTWEIGHT	Freddie Welsh
WELTERWEIGHT	Johnny Basham; Jack Hood
MIDDLEWEIGHT	Pat O'Keefe; Len Harvey; Jock McAvoy
L. HEAVYWEIGHT	Dick Smith
HEAVYWEIGHT	Bombardier Billy Wells; Jack Petersen

Note: Both Dick Corbett and Johnny King – with one notch apiece on the 'special' British Empire Lonsdale Belt that was struck in 1933 and later presented to the winner of the Tommy Farr v Joe Louis fight – were allowed to keep their Lonsdale Belts with just two notches secured; Freddie Welsh, also with two notches, was awarded a belt due to his inability to defend because of the First World War; the first bantam belt came back into circulation and was awarded to Johnny Brown; Al Foreman, with just one notch on the second lightweight belt, took it back to Canada with him without the consent of the BBBoC; while the second light-heavy belt was awarded to Jack Smith of Worcester for winning a novices heavyweight competition. Having emigrated to New Zealand, Smith later presented the visiting Her Majesty The Queen with the belt and it now hangs in the BBBoC's offices.

Outright Winners of the BBBoC Lord Lonsdale Challenge Belt, 1936-2009 (124)

Re-introduced by the British Boxing Board of Control as the Lord Lonsdale Challenge Belt, but of less intrinsic value, Benny Lynch's eight-round win over Pat Palmer (16 September 1936 at Shawfield Park, Glasgow) got the new version underway, while Eric Boon became the first man to win one outright, in 1939, following victories over Dave Crowley (2) and Arthur Danahar. Since those early days, six further weight divisions have been added and, following on from Henry Cooper's feat of winning three Lonsdale Belts outright, on 10 June 1981 the BBBoC's rules and regulations were amended to read that no boxer shall receive more than one belt as his own property, in any one weight division. A later amendment stated that from 1 September 1999, any boxer putting a notch on a Lonsdale Belt for the first time would require three more notches at the same weight before he could call the belt his own. However, men who already had a notch on the Lonsdale Belt prior to 1 September 1999 could contest it under the former ruling of three winning championship contests at the same weight. Incidentally, the fastest of the modern belt winners is Ryan Rhodes (90 days), while Chris and Kevin Finnegan are the only brothers to have each won a belt outright.

FLYWEIGHT	Jackie Paterson; Terry Allen; Walter McGowan; John McCluskey; Hugh Russell; Charlie Magri; Pat Clinton; Robbie Regan; Francis Ampofo; Ady Lewis
BANTAMWEIGHT	Johnny King; Peter Keenan (2); Freddie Gilroy; Alan Rudkin; Johnny Owen; Billy Hardy; Drew Docherty; Nicky Booth; Ian Napa
S. BANTAMWEIGHT	Richie Wenton; Michael Brodie; Michael Alldis; Michael Hunter
FEATHERWEIGHT	Nel Tarleton; Ronnie Clayton (2); Charlie Hill; Howard Winstone (2); Evan Armstrong; Pat Cowdell; Robert Dickie; Paul Hodkinson; Colin McMillan; Sean Murphy; Paul Ingle; Jonjo Irwin; Dazzo Williams
S. FEATHERWEIGHT	Jimmy Anderson; John Doherty; Floyd Havard; Charles Shepherd; Michael Gomez; Alex Arthur;

	Carl Johanneson
LIGHTWEIGHT	Eric Boon; Billy Thompson; Joe Lucy; Dave Charnley; Maurice Cullen; Ken Buchanan; Jim Watt; George Feeney; Tony Willis; Carl Crook; Billy Schwer; Michael Ayers; Bobby Vanzie; Graham Earl
L. WELTERWEIGHT	Joey Singleton; Colin Power; Clinton McKenzie; Lloyd Christie; Andy Holligan; Ross Hale; Junior Witter
WELTERWEIGHT	Ernie Roderick; Wally Thom; Brian Curvis (2); Ralph Charles; Colin Jones; Lloyd Honeyghan; Kirkland Laing; Del Bryan; Geoff McCreesh; Derek Roche; Neil Sinclair; David Barnes
L. MIDDLEWEIGHT	Maurice Hope; Jimmy Batten; Pat Thomas; Prince Rodney; Andy Till; Robert McCracken; Ryan Rhodes; Ensley Bingham; Jamie Moore
MIDDLEWEIGHT	Pat McAteer; Terry Downes; Johnny Pritchett; Bunny Sterling; Alan Minter; Kevin Finnegan; Roy Gumbs; Tony Sibson; Herol Graham; Neville Brown; Howard Eastman; Scott Dann
S. MIDDLEWEIGHT	Sammy Storey; David Starie; Carl Froch
L. HEAVYWEIGHT	Randy Turpin; Chic Calderwood; Chris Finnegan; Bunny Johnson; Tom Collins; Dennis Andries; Tony Wilson; Crawford Ashley
CRUISERWEIGHT	Johnny Nelson; Terry Dunstan; Bruce Scott; Mark Hobson
HEAVYWEIGHT	Henry Cooper (3); Horace Notice; Lennox Lewis; Julius Francis; Danny Williams; Matt Skelton

Note: Walter McGowan, Charlie Magri and Junior Witter, with one notch apiece, kept their belts under the three years/no available challengers' ruling, while Johnny King, with two notches, was awarded the belt on the grounds that the Second World War stopped him from making further defences. Incidentally, King and Nel Tarleton are the only men to have won both the NSC and BBBoC belts outright.

Ryan Rhodes (right), seen here taking the WBC International title from Vincent Vuma last November, won a Lonsdale Belt outright in a record time of 90 days

Philip Sharkey

British Champions Since Gloves, 1878-2009

The listings below show the tenure of all British champions at each weight since gloves (two ounces or more) were introduced to British rings under Queensberry Rules. Although Charley Davis (147 lbs) had beaten Ted Napper (140 lbs) with gloves in 1873, we start with Denny Harrington, who defeated George Rooke for both the English and world middleweight titles in London on 12 March 1878. We also make a point of ignoring competition winners, apart from Anthony Diamond who beat Dido Plumb for the middles title over 12 rounds, basically because full championship conditions or finish fights of three-minute rounds were not applied. Another point worth bearing in mind, is that prior to the 1880s there were only five weights – heavy, middle, light, feather and bantam. Anything above 154 lbs, the middleweight limit, was classified a heavyweight contest, whereas lightweight, feather and bantamweight poundages were much looser. Therefore, to put things into current perspective, in many cases we have had to ascertain the actual poundage of fighters concerned and relate them to the modern weight classes. Another point worth remembering is that men born outside Britain who won international titles in this country, are not recorded for fear of added confusion and, although many of the champions or claimants listed before 1909 were no more than English titleholders, having fought for the 'championship of England', for our purposes they carry the 'British' label.

Prior to 1909, the year that the Lord Lonsdale Challenge Belt was introduced and weight classes subsequently standardised, poundages within divisions could vary quite substantially, thus enabling men fighting at different weights to claim the same 'title' at the same time. A brief history of the weight fluctuations between 1891 and 1909, shows:

Bantamweight   With the coming of gloves, the division did not really take off until Nunc Wallace established himself at 112 lbs on beating (small) Bill Goode after nine rounds in London on 12 March 1889. Later, with Wallace fighting above the weight, Billy Plimmer was generally recognised as the country's leading eight stoner, following victories over Charles Mansford and Jem Stevens, and became accepted as world champion when George Dixon, the number one in America's eyes, gradually increased his weight. In 1895, Pedlar Palmer took the British title at 112 lbs, but by 1900 he had developed into a 114 pounder. Between 1902 and 1904, Joe Bowker defended regularly at 116 lbs and in 1909 the NSC standardised the weight at 118 lbs, even though the USA continued for a short while to accept only 116 lbs.

Featherweight   Between 1886 and 1895, one of the most prestigious championship belts in this country was fought for at 126 lbs and, although George Dixon was recognised in the USA as world featherweight champion – gradually moving from 114 to 122 lbs – no major international contests took place in Britain during the above period at his weight. It was only in 1895, when Fred Johnson took the British title at 120 lbs, losing it to Ben Jordan two years later, that we came into line with the USA. Ben Jordan became an outstanding champion who, between 1898 and 1899, was seen by the NSC as world champion at 120 lbs. However, first Harry Greenfield, then Jabez White and Will Curley, continued to claim the 126 lbs version of the British title and it was only in 1900, when Jack Roberts beat Curley, that the weight limit was finally standardised at nine stone.

Lightweight   Outstanding champions often carried their weights as they grew in size. A perfect example of this was Dick Burge, the British lightweight champion from 1891-1901, who gradually increased from 134 to 144 lbs, while still maintaining his right to the title. It was not until 1902 that Jabez White brought the division into line with the USA. Later, both White, and then Goldswain, carried their weight up to 140 lbs and it was left to Johnny Summers to set the current limit of 135 lbs.

Welterweight   The presence of Dick Burge fighting from 134 to 144 lbs plus up until 1900, explains quite adequately why the welterweight division, although very popular in the USA, did not take off in this country until 1902. The championship was contested between 142 and 146 lbs in those days and was not really supported by the NSC, but by 1909 with their backing it finally became established at 147 lbs.

Before the Second World War, Ben Foord (South Africa) became the first foreign-born British Champion when beating Jack Petersen for the heavyweight title on 17 August 1936, having been domiciled in Britain for more than two years. Under the same scheme Australians George Cook (1934) and Al Bourke (1935) contested the British title at heavyweight and middleweight, respectively. Later, on 8 September 1970, Bunny Sterling became the first immigrant to win a British title under the ten-year residential ruling, while on 28 June 1948, Dick Turpin had won the British middleweight title and, in doing so, became the first coloured fighter to win the title, thus breaking down the so-called 'colour bar'. On 20 May 1998, the BBBoC passed a ruling allowing fighters from abroad, who take out British citizenship, the opportunity to fight for the British title after five years residency instead of ten.

Note that the Lonsdale Belt notches (title bout wins) relate to NSC, 1909-1935, and BBBoC, 1936-2009.

Champions in **bold** are accorded national recognition.

*Undefeated champions (Does not include men who forfeited titles).

Title Holder	Lonsdale Belt Notches	Tenure	Title Holder	Lonsdale Belt Notches	Tenure	Title Holder	Lonsdale Belt Notches	Tenure
Flyweight (112 lbs)			**Joe Symonds**	1	1915-1916	**Jackie Paterson**	4	1939-1948
Sid Smith		1911	**Jimmy Wilde***	3	1916-1923	**Rinty Monaghan***	1	1948-1950
Sid Smith	1	1911-1913	**Elky Clark***	2	1924-1927	**Terry Allen**	1	1951-1952
Bill Ladbury		1913-1914	**Johnny Hill***	1	1927-1929	**Teddy Gardner***	1	1952
Percy Jones	1	1914	**Jackie Brown**		1929-1930	**Terry Allen***	2	1952-1954
Joe Symonds		1914	**Bert Kirby**	1	1930-1931	**Dai Dower***	1	1955-1957
Tancy Lee	1	1914-1915	**Jackie Brown**	3	1931-1935	**Frankie Jones**	2	1957-1960
Jimmy Wilde		1914-1915	**Benny Lynch***	2	1935-1938	**Johnny Caldwell***	1	1960-1961

BRITISH CHAMPIONS SINCE GLOVES, 1878-2009

Title Holder	Lonsdale Belt Notches	Tenure
Jackie Brown	1	1962-1963
Walter McGowan*	1	1963-1966
John McCluskey*	3	1967-1977
Charlie Magri*	1	1977-1981
Kelvin Smart	1	1982-1984
Hugh Russell*	3	1984-1985
Duke McKenzie*	2	1985-1986
Dave Boy McAuley*	1	1986-1988
Pat Clinton*	3	1988-1991
Robbie Regan	1	1991
Francis Ampofo	1	1991
Robbie Regan*	2	1991-1992
Francis Ampofo	3	1992-1996
Mickey Cantwell*	1	1996-1997
Ady Lewis*	3	1997-1998
Damaen Kelly	1	1999
Keith Knox	1	1999
Jason Booth*	2	1999-2003
Chris Edwards	2	2009-

S. Flyweight (115 lbs)

Title Holder	Lonsdale Belt Notches	Tenure
Chris Edwards	1	2007-2008
Andy Bell	1	2008
Lee Haskins	1	2008-

Bantamweight (118 lbs)

Title Holder	Lonsdale Belt Notches	Tenure
Nunc Wallace*		1889-1891
Billy Plimmer		1891-1895
Tom Gardner		1892
Willie Smith		1892-1896
Nunc Wallace		1893-1895
George Corfield		1893-1896
Pedlar Palmer		1895-1900
Billy Plimmer		1896-1898
Harry Ware		1899-1900
Harry Ware		1900-1902
Andrew Tokell		1901-1902
Jim Williams		1902
Andrew Tokell		1902
Harry Ware		1902
Joe Bowker		1902-1910
Owen Moran		1905-1907
Digger Stanley		1906-1910
Digger Stanley	2	1910-1913
Bill Beynon	1	1913
Digger Stanley	1	1913-1914
Curley Walker*	1	1914-1915
Joe Fox*	3	1915-1917
Tommy Noble	1	1918-1919
Walter Ross*	1	1919-1920
Jim Higgins	3	1920-1922
Tommy Harrison		1922-1923
Bugler Harry Lake	1	1923
Johnny Brown	3	1923-1928
Alf Pattenden	2	1928-1929
Johnny Brown		1928
Teddy Baldock		1928-1929
Teddy Baldock*	1	1929-1931
Dick Corbett	1	1931-1932
Johnny King	1	1932-1934
Dick Corbett*	1	1934
Johnny King	1+2	1935-1947
Jackie Paterson	2	1947-1949
Stan Rowan*	1	1949
Danny O'Sullivan	1	1949-1951
Peter Keenan	3	1951-1953
John Kelly	1	1953-1954
Peter Keenan	3	1954-1959
Freddie Gilroy*	4	1959-1963
Johnny Caldwell	1	1964-1965
Alan Rudkin	1	1965-1966
Walter McGowan	1	1966-1968
Alan Rudkin*	4	1968-1972
Johnny Clark*	1	1973-1974
Dave Needham	1	1974-1975
Paddy Maguire	1	1975-1977
Johnny Owen*	4	1977-1980
John Feeney	1	1981-1983
Hugh Russell	1	1983
Davy Larmour	1	1983
John Feeney	1	1983-1985
Ray Gilbody	2	1985-1987
Billy Hardy*	5	1987-1991
Joe Kelly	1	1992
Drew Docherty	4	1992-1997
Paul Lloyd	2	1997-1999
Noel Wilders*	2	1999-2000
Ady Lewis	1	2000
Tommy Waite	1	2000
Nicky Booth	5	2000-2004
Martin Power*	3	2005-2007
Ian Napa*	4	2007-2009
Gary Davies	1	2009-

S. Bantamweight (122 lbs)

Title Holder	Lonsdale Belt Notches	Tenure
Richie Wenton*	3	1994-1996
Michael Brodie*	3	1997-1999
Patrick Mullings	1	1999
Drew Docherty*	1	1999
Michael Alldis	3	1999-2001
Patrick Mullings	1	2001
Michael Alldis*	1	2002
Esham Pickering*	1	2003-2004
Michael Hunter*	4	2004-2006
Esham Pickering	2	2006-2008
Matthew Marsh*	2	2008-2009
Jason Booth	2	2009-

Featherweight (126 lbs)

Title Holder	Lonsdale Belt Notches	Tenure
Bill Baxter		1884-1891
Harry Overton		1890-1891
Billy Reader		1891-1892
Fred Johnson		1891-1895
Harry Spurden		1892-1895
Jack Fitzpatrick		1895-1897
Fred Johnson		1895-1897
Harry Greenfield		1896-1899
Ben Jordan*		1897-1900
Jabez White		1899-1900
Will Curley		1900-1901
Jack Roberts		1901-1902
Will Curley		1902-1903
Ben Jordan*		1902-1905
Joe Bowker		1905
Johnny Summers		1906
Joe Bowker		1905-1906
Jim Driscoll		1906-1907
Spike Robson		1906-1907
Jim Driscoll*	3	1907-1913
Spike Robson		1907-1910
Ted Kid Lewis*	1	1913-1914
Llew Edwards*	1	1915-1917
Charlie Hardcastle	1	1917
Tancy Lee*	3	1917-1919
Mike Honeyman	2	1920-1921
Joe Fox*	1	1921-1922
George McKenzie	2	1924-1925
Johnny Curley	2	1925-1927
Johnny Cuthbert	1	1927-1928
Harry Corbett	1	1928-1929
Johnny Cuthbert	2	1929-1931
Nel Tarleton	1	1931-1932
Seaman Tommy Watson	2	1932-1934
Nel Tarleton	2	1934-1936
Johnny McGrory	1	1936-1938
Jim Spider Kelly	1	1938-1939
Johnny Cusick	1	1939-1940
Nel Tarleton*	3	1940-1947
Ronnie Clayton	6	1947-1954
Sammy McCarthy	1	1954-1955
Billy Spider Kelly	1	1955-1956
Charlie Hill	3	1956-1959
Bobby Neill	1	1959-1960
Terry Spinks	2	1960-1961
Howard Winstone*	7	1961-1969
Jimmy Revie	2	1969-1971
Evan Armstrong	2	1971-1972
Tommy Glencross	1	1972-1973
Evan Armstrong*	2	1973-1975
Vernon Sollas	1	1975-1977
Alan Richardson	2	1977-1978
Dave Needham	2	1978-1979
Pat Cowdell*	3	1979-1982
Steve Sims*	1	1982-1983
Barry McGuigan*	2	1983-1986
Robert Dickie	3	1986-1988
Peter Harris	1	1988
Paul Hodkinson*	3	1988-1990
Sean Murphy	2	1990-1991
Gary de Roux	1	1991
Colin McMillan*	3	1991-1992
John Davison*	1	1992-1993
Sean Murphy	1	1993
Duke McKenzie*	1	1993-1994
Billy Hardy*	1	1994
Michael Deveney	1	1995
Jonjo Irwin	2	1995-1996
Colin McMillan	1	1996-1997
Paul Ingle*	3	1997-1998
Jonjo Irwin*	2	1998-1999
Gary Thornhill	1	2000
Scott Harrison*	3	2001-2002
Jamie McKeever	1	2003
Roy Rutherford	1	2003
Dazzo Williams	4	2003-2005
Nicky Cook*	1	2005
Andy Morris	2	2005-2006
John Simpson	3	2006-2008
Paul Appleby	2	2008-2009
Martin Lindsay	1	2009-

S. Featherweight (130 lbs)

Title Holder	Lonsdale Belt Notches	Tenure
Jimmy Anderson*	3	1968-1970
John Doherty	1	1986
Pat Cowdell	1	1986
Najib Daho	1	1986-1987
Pat Cowdell	1	1987-1988
Floyd Havard	1	1988-1989
John Doherty	1	1989-1990
Joey Jacobs	1	1990
Hugh Forde	1	1990
Kevin Pritchard	1	1990-1991
Robert Dickie	1	1991
Sugar Gibiliru	1	1991

Title Holder	Lonsdale Belt Notches	Tenure
John Doherty	1	1991-1992
Michael Armstrong	1	1992
Neil Haddock	2	1992-1994
Floyd Havard*	3	1994-1995
P. J. Gallagher	2	1996-1997
Charles Shepherd	3	1997-1999
Michael Gomez*	5	1999-2002
Alex Arthur	3	2002-2003
Michael Gomez	1	2003-2004
Alex Arthur*	2	2005-2006
Carl Johanneson	4	2006-2008
Kevin Mitchell	1	2008-

Lightweight (135 lbs)

Title Holder	Lonsdale Belt Notches	Tenure
Dick Burge		1891-1897
Harry Nickless		1891-1894
Tom Causer		1894-1897
Tom Causer		1897
Dick Burge*		1897-1901
Jabez White		1902-1906
Jack Goldswain		1906-1908
Johnny Summers		1908-1909
Freddie Welsh	1	1909-1911
Matt Wells	1	1911-1912
Freddie Welsh*	1	1912-1919
Bob Marriott*	1	1919-1920
Ernie Rice	1	1921-1922
Seaman Nobby Hall		1922-1923
Harry Mason		1923-1924
Ernie Izzard	2	1924-1925
Harry Mason		1924-1925
Harry Mason*	1	1925-1928
Sam Steward		1928-1929
Fred Webster		1929-1930
Al Foreman*	1	1930-1932
Johnny Cuthbert		1932-1934
Harry Mizler		1934
Jackie Kid Berg		1934-1936
Jimmy Walsh	1	1936-1938
Dave Crowley	1	1938
Eric Boon	3	1938-1944
Ronnie James*	1	1944-1947
Billy Thompson	3	1947-1951
Tommy McGovern	1	1951-1952
Frank Johnson	1	1952-1953
Joe Lucy	1	1953-1955
Frank Johnson	1	1955-1956
Joe Lucy	2	1956-1957
Dave Charnley*	3	1957-1965
Maurice Cullen	4	1965-1968
Ken Buchanan*	2	1968-1971
Willie Reilly*	1	1972
Jim Watt	1	1972-1973
Ken Buchanan*	1	1973-1974
Jim Watt*	2	1975-1977
Charlie Nash*	1	1978-1979
Ray Cattouse	2	1980-1982
George Feeney*	3	1982-1985
Tony Willis	3	1985-1987
Alex Dickson	1	1987-1988
Steve Boyle	2	1988-1990
Carl Crook	5	1990-1992
Billy Schwer	1	1992-1993
Paul Burke	1	1993
Billy Schwer*	2	1993-1995
Michael Ayers*	5	1995-1997
Wayne Rigby	2	1998
Bobby Vanzie	5	1998-2003
Graham Earl	1	2003-2004
Graham Earl*	3	2004-2006
Lee Meager	1	2006
Jonathan Thaxton*	3	2006-2008
John Murray	2	2008-2009

L. Welterweight (140 lbs)

Title Holder	Lonsdale Belt Notches	Tenure
Des Rea	1	1968-1969
Vic Andreetti*	2	1969-1970
Des Morrison	1	1973-1974
Pat McCormack	1	1974
Joey Singleton	3	1974-1976
Dave Boy Green*	1	1976-1977
Colin Power*	2	1977-1978
Clinton McKenzie	1	1978-1979
Colin Power	1	1979
Clinton McKenzie	5	1979-1984
Terry Marsh*	1	1984-1986
Tony Laing*	1	1986
Tony McKenzie	2	1986-1987
Lloyd Christie	3	1987-1989
Clinton McKenzie*	1	1989
Pat Barrett*	2	1989-1990
Tony Ekubia	1	1990-1991
Andy Holligan	3	1991-1994
Ross Hale	4	1994-1995
Paul Ryan	1	1995-1996
Andy Holligan*	1	1996-1997
Mark Winters	2	1997-1998
Jason Rowland*	2	1998-2000
Ricky Hatton*	1	2000-2001
Junior Witter*	2	2002-2006
Lenny Daws	1	2006-2007
Barry Morrison	1	2007
Colin Lynes*	2	2007-2008
David Barnes*	2	2008
Paul McCloskey*	2	2008-2009
Ajose Olusegun	1	2009-

Welterweight (147 lbs)

Title Holder	Lonsdale Belt Notches	Tenure
Charlie Allum		1903-1904
Charlie Knock		1904-1906
Curly Watson		1906-1910
Young Joseph		1908-1910
Young Joseph	1	1910-1911
Arthur Evernden		1911-1912
Johnny Summers		1912
Johnny Summers	2	1912-1914
Tom McCormick		1914
Matt Wells		1914
Johnny Basham	3	1914-1920
Matt Wells		1914-1919
Ted Kid Lewis		1920-1924
Tommy Milligan*		1924-1925
Hamilton Johnny Brown		1925
Harry Mason		1925-1926
Jack Hood*	3	1926-1934
Harry Mason		1934
Pat Butler*		1934-1936
Dave McCleave		1936
Jake Kilrain	1	1936-1939
Ernie Roderick	5	1939-1948
Henry Hall	1	1948-1949
Eddie Thomas	2	1949-1951
Wally Thom	1	1951-1952
Cliff Curvis*	1	1952-1953
Wally Thom	1	1953-1956
Peter Waterman*	2	1956-1958
Tommy Molloy	2	1958-1960
Wally Swift	1	1960
Brian Curvis*	7	1960-1966
Johnny Cooke	2	1967-1968
Ralph Charles*	3	1968-1972
Bobby Arthur	1	1972-1973
John H. Stracey*	1	1973-1975
Pat Thomas	1	1975-1976
Henry Rhiney	2	1976-1979
Kirkland Laing	1	1979-1980
Colin Jones	3	1980-1982
Lloyd Honeyghan*	2	1983-1985
Kostas Petrou	1	1985
Sylvester Mittee	1	1985
Lloyd Honeyghan*	1	1985-1986
Kirkland Laing	4	1987-1991
Del Bryan	2	1991-1992
Gary Jacobs*	2	1992-1993
Del Bryan	4	1993-1995
Chris Saunders	1	1995-1996
Kevin Lueshing	1	1996-1997
Geoff McCreesh*	4	1997-1999
Derek Roche	3	1999-2000
Harry Dhami	3	2000-2001
Neil Sinclair*	4	2001-2003
David Barnes	4	2003-2005
Michael Jennings	2	2005-2006
Young Muttley	1	2006
Kevin Anderson	3	2006-2007
Kevin McIntyre	1	2008
Kell Brook	3	2008-

L. Middleweight (154 lbs)

Title Holder	Lonsdale Belt Notches	Tenure
Larry Paul	2	1973-1974
Maurice Hope*	3	1974-1977
Jimmy Batten	3	1977-1979
Pat Thomas	3	1979-1981
Herol Graham*	2	1981-1983
Prince Rodney*	1	1983-1984
Jimmy Cable	2	1984-1985
Prince Rodney	2	1985-1986
Chris Pyatt*	1	1986
Lloyd Hibbert*	1	1987
Gary Cooper	1	1988
Gary Stretch	2	1988-1990
Wally Swift Jnr	2	1991-1992
Andy Till	3	1992-1994
Robert McCracken*	3	1994-1995
Ensley Bingham*	2	1996
Ryan Rhodes*	3	1996-1997
Ensley Bingham	3	1997-1999
Wayne Alexander*	2	2000-2003
Jamie Moore	3	2003-2004
Michael Jones	1	2004-2005
Jamie Moore	4	2005-2007
Gary Woolcombe	1	2007-2008
Ryan Rhodes*	2	2008-2009

Middleweight (160 lbs)

Title Holder	Lonsdale Belt Notches	Tenure
Denny Harrington		1878-1880
William Sheriff*		1880-1883
Bill Goode		1887-1890
Toff Wall*		1890
Ted Pritchard		1890-1895
Ted White		1893-1895
Ted White*		1895-1896
Anthony Diamond*		1898
Dick Burge*		1898-1900
Jack Palmer		1902-1903
Charlie Allum		1905-1906
Pat O'Keefe		1906

BRITISH CHAMPIONS SINCE GLOVES, 1878-2009

Title Holder	Lonsdale Belt Notches	Tenure
Tom Thomas	1	1906-1910
Jim Sullivan*	1	1910-1912
Jack Harrison*	1	1912-1913
Pat O'Keefe	2	1914-1916
Bandsman Jack Blake	1	1916-1918
Pat O'Keefe*	1	1918-1919
Ted Kid Lewis		1920-1921
Tom Gummer	1	1920-1921
Gus Platts		1921
Johnny Basham		1921
Ted Kid Lewis	2	1921-1923
Johnny Basham		1921
Roland Todd		1923-1925
Roland Todd		1925-1927
Tommy Milligan	1	1926-1928
Frank Moody		1927-1928
Alex Ireland		1928-1929
Len Harvey	5	1929-1933
Jock McAvoy	3+2	1933-1944
Ernie Roderick	1	1945-1946
Vince Hawkins	1	1946-1948
Dick Turpin	2	1948-1950
Albert Finch	1	1950
Randy Turpin*	1	1950-1954
Johnny Sullivan	1	1954-1955
Pat McAteer*	3	1955-1958
Terry Downes	1	1958-1959
John Cowboy McCormack	1	1959
Terry Downes	2	1959-1962
George Aldridge	1	1962-1963
Mick Leahy	1	1963-1964
Wally Swift	1	1964-1965
Johnny Pritchett*	4	1965-1969
Les McAteer	1	1969-1970
Mark Rowe	1	1970
Bunny Sterling	4	1970-1974
Kevin Finnegan*	1	1974
Bunny Sterling*	1	1975
Alan Minter	3	1975-1977
Kevin Finnegan	1	1977
Alan Minter*	1	1977-1978
Tony Sibson	1	1979
Kevin Finnegan*	1	1979-1980
Roy Gumbs	3	1981-1983
Mark Kaylor	1	1983-1984
Tony Sibson*	1	1984
Herol Graham*	1	1985-1986
Brian Anderson	1	1986-1987
Tony Sibson*	1	1987-1988
Herol Graham	4	1988-1992
Frank Grant	2	1992-1993
Neville Brown	6	1993-1998
Glenn Catley*	1	1998
Howard Eastman*	4	1998-2004
Scott Dann*	4	2004-2006
Howard Eastman	1	2006-2007
Wayne Elcock	2	2007-2009
Matthew Macklin	1	2009-

S. Middleweight (168 lbs)

Title Holder	Lonsdale Belt Notches	Tenure
Sammy Storey	2	1989-1990
James Cook*	1	1990-1991
Fidel Castro	2	1991-1992
Henry Wharton*	1	1992-1993
James Cook	1	1993-1994
Cornelius Carr*	1	1994
Ali Forbes	1	1995
Sammy Storey*	1	1995
Joe Calzaghe*	2	1995-1997
David Starie	1	1997
Dean Francis*	2	1997-1998
David Starie*	5	1998-2003
Matthew Barney*	1	2003
Tony Dodson*	1	2003-2004
Carl Froch*	5	2004-2008
Brian Magee*	1	2008-2009
Tony Quigley	1	2009-

L. Heavyweight (175lbs)

Title Holder	Lonsdale Belt Notches	Tenure
Dennis Haugh		1913-1914
Dick Smith	2	1914-1916
Harry Reeve*	1	1916-1917
Dick Smith*	1	1918-1919
Boy McCormick*	1	1919-1921
Jack Bloomfield*	1	1922-1924
Tom Berry	1	1925-1927
Gipsy Daniels*	1	1927
Frank Moody	1	1927-1929
Harry Crossley	1	1929-1932
Jack Petersen*	1	1932
Len Harvey*	1	1933-1934
Eddie Phillips		1935-1937
Jock McAvoy	1	1937-1938
Len Harvey	2	1938-1942
Freddie Mills*	1	1942-1950
Don Cockell	2	1950-1952
Randy Turpin*	1	1952
Dennis Powell	1	1953
Alex Buxton	2	1953-1955
Randy Turpin*	1	1955
Ron Barton*	1	1956
Randy Turpin*	2	1956-1958
Chic Calderwood	3	1960-1963
Chic Calderwood*	1	1964-1966
Young John McCormack	2	1967-1969
Eddie Avoth	2	1969-1971
Chris Finnegan	2	1971-1973
John Conteh*	2	1973-1974
Johnny Frankham	1	1975
Chris Finnegan*	1	1975-1976
Tim Wood	1	1976-1977
Bunny Johnson*	3	1977-1981
Tom Collins	3	1982-1984
Dennis Andries*	5	1984-1986
Tom Collins*	1	1987
Tony Wilson	3	1987-1989
Tom Collins*	1	1989-1990
Steve McCarthy	1	1990-1991
Crawford Ashley*	3	1991-1992
Maurice Core*	2	1992-1994
Crawford Ashley	3	1994-1999
Clinton Woods*	1	1999-2000
Neil Simpson*	2	2000-2002
Peter Oboh	2	2003-2007
Tony Oakey	3	2007-2008
Dean Francis*	1	2008-2009

Cruiserweight (200 lbs)

Title Holder	Lonsdale Belt Notches	Tenure
Sam Reeson*	1	1985-1986
Andy Straughn	1	1986-1987
Roy Smith	1	1987
Tee Jay	1	1987-1988
Glenn McCrory*	2	1988
Andy Straughn	1	1988-1989
Johnny Nelson*	3	1989-1991
Derek Angol*	2	1991-1992
Carl Thompson*	1	1992-1994
Dennis Andries	1	1995
Terry Dunstan*	3	1995-1996
Johnny Nelson*	1	1996-1998
Bruce Scott	1	1998-1999
Carl Thompson*	1	1999-2000
Bruce Scott	2	2000-2003
Mark Hobson*	5	2003-2006
John Keeton	1	2006-2007
Mark Hobson*	1	2008
Robert Norton	2	2008-

Heavyweight (200 lbs +)

Title Holder	Lonsdale Belt Notches	Tenure
Tom Allen*		1878-1882
Charlie Mitchell*		1882-1894
Jem Smith		1889-1891
Ted Pritchard		1891-1895
Jem Smith		1895-1896
George Chrisp		1901
Jack Scales		1901-1902
Jack Palmer		1903-1906
Gunner Moir		1906-1909
Iron Hague		1909-1910
P.O. Curran		1910-1911
Iron Hague		1910-1911
Bombardier Billy Wells	3	1911-1919
Joe Beckett		1919
Frank Goddard	1	1919
Joe Beckett*	1	1919-1923
Frank Goddard		1923-1926
Phil Scott*		1926-1931
Reggie Meen		1931-1932
Jack Petersen	3	1932-1933
Len Harvey		1933-1934
Jack Petersen		1934-1936
Ben Foord		1936-1937
Tommy Farr*	1	1937-1938
Len Harvey*	1	1938-1942
Jack London	1	1944-1945
Bruce Woodcock	2	1945-1950
Jack Gardner	1	1950-1952
Johnny Williams	1	1952-1953
Don Cockell*	1	1953-1956
Joe Erskine	2	1956-1958
Brian London	1	1958-1959
Henry Cooper*	9	1959-1969
Jack Bodell	1	1969-1970
Henry Cooper	1	1970-1971
Joe Bugner	1	1971
Jack Bodell	1	1971-1972
Danny McAlinden	1	1972-1975
Bunny Johnson	1	1975
Richard Dunn	2	1975-1976
Joe Bugner*	1	1976-1977
John L. Gardner*	2	1978-1980
Gordon Ferris	1	1981
Neville Meade	1	1981-1983
David Pearce*	1	1983-1985
Hughroy Currie	1	1985-1986
Horace Notice*	4	1986-1988
Gary Mason	2	1989-1991
Lennox Lewis*	3	1991-1993
Herbie Hide*	1	1993-1994
James Oyebola	1	1994-1995
Scott Welch*	1	1995-1996
Julius Francis	4	1997-2000
Mike Holden*	1	2000
Danny Williams	5	2000-2004
Michael Sprott	1	2004
Matt Skelton	4	2004-2006
Scott Gammer	2	2006-2007
Danny Williams	3	2007-

Commonwealth Title Bouts, 2008-2009

All of last season's title bouts are shown in date order within their weight divisions and give the boxers' respective weights, the names of all referees and British judges where applicable, along with the scorecards if going to a decision. Boxers are denoted by their country of citizenship/birthplace. All venues, unless stated otherwise, are British.

Flyweight
23 January Chris Edwards 109 (England) W RTD 4 Wayne Bloy 110 (England), Fenton Manor Sports Complex, Stoke. Referee: Mark Green. Judges: John Keane, Terry O'Connor, Richie Davies. Billed for the vacant title, Lee Haskins having returned his belt on 28 March 2007. The vacant British title was also on the line.
29 May Chris Edwards 110 (England) W PTS 12 Usman Ahmed 108 (England), Fenton Manor Sports Complex, Stoke. Referee: Phil Edwards. Judges: Richie Davies 118-109, John Keane 117-111, Ian John-Lewis 118-119. Edwards was also defending his British title.

S.Flyweight
31 October Don Broadhurst 114 (England) W PTS 12 Isaac Quaye 112½ (Ghana), Aston Villa Leisure Centre, Birmingham. Referee: Richie Davies. Judges: Victor Loughlin 120-108, Mickey Vann 120-108, John Keane 119-109. Billed for the vacant title, this was the inaugural contest at the weight.
28 February Don Broadhurst 114¾ (England) W RSC 11 Isaac Owusu 114½ (Ghana), National Indoor Arena, Birmingham. Referee: Ian John-Lewis. Judges: Howard Foster, John Keane, Victor Loughlin.

24 April Don Broadhurst 114 (England) W RSC 6 Asamoah Wilson 112½ (Ghana), Civic Centre, Wolverhampton. Referee: Mark Green. Judges: Terry O'Connor, Victor Loughlin, John Keane.

Bantamweight
18 December Jason Booth 116 (England) W RTD 10 Sean Hughes 116 (England), City University, Dublin, Ireland. Referee: Mickey Vann. Judges: Phil Edwards, Victor Loughlin, John Keane.

S.Bantamweight
2 May Rendall Munroe 122 (England) W PTS 12 Isaac Nettey 120½ (Ghana), Crowtree Leisure Centre, Sunderland. Referee: Richie Davies. Judges: John Keane 120-109, Victor Loughlin 119-110, Terry O'Connor 119-110. Billed for the vacant title after Anyetei Laryea (Ghana) announced on 3 April that he would not be making a defence.

Featherweight
16 January Paul Truscott 125¾ (England) L RSC 8 John Simpson 125 (Scotland), Eston Sports Academy, Middlesbrough. Referee: Howard Foster. Judges: Victor Loughlin, Marcus McDonnell, Dave Parris.

Making his second defence of the Commonwealth super-flyweight title, Don Broadhurst (left) slams in a left hook to the head of Asamoah Wilson shortly before stopping the Ghanaian in the sixth

Philip Sharkey

S.Featherweight

26 September Ricky Burns 128¼ (Scotland) W PTS 12 Osumanu Akaba 128 (Ghana), York Hall, Bethnal Green, London. Referee: Marcus McDonnell. Judges: Richie Davies 116-113, Dave Parris 117-112, Mark Green 116-112. Billed for the vacant title after England's Kevin Mitchell, still recovering from a hand injury, handed in his belt two weeks earlier on the basis that he would be the number-one challenger when fit again.

14 November Ricky Burns 130 (Scotland) W RSC 7 Yakubu Amidu 129¾ (Ghana), Kelvin Hall, Glasgow. Referee: Ian John-Lewis. Judges: John Keane, Victor Loughlin, Marcus McDonnell.

27 March Ricky Burns 129½ (Scotland) W RSC 7 Michael Gomez 129¼ (England), Bellahouston Sports Centre, Glasgow. Referee: Howard Foster. Judges: Richie Davies, Victor Loughlin, Marcus McDonnell.

19 June Ricky Burns 130 (Scotland) W PTS 12 Kevin O'Hara 129½ (Northern Ireland), Bellahouston Sports Centre, Glasgow. Referee: Terry O'Connor. Judges: Dave Parris 117-110, Howard Foster 115-113, Victor Loughlin 117-111.

Lightweight

19 June Lee McAllister 134¾ (Scotland) W RSC 3 Godfriend Sowah 134¼ (Ghana), Beach Ballroom, Aberdeen. Referee: Marcus McDonnell. Judges: Dave Parris, Howard Foster, Victor Loughlin. Billed for the vacant title after it was announced at the end of April that Amir Khan (England) had handed his belt in to concentrate on a world title opportunity.

L.Welterweight

27 February Ajose Olusegun 139¾ (England/Nigeria) W RSC 7 Scott Heywood 139½ (England), The Metrodome, Barnsley. Referee: John Keane. Judges: Richie Davies, Howard Foster, Ian John-Lewis.

12 June Ajose Olusegun 139¼ (England/Nigeria) W PTS 12 Nigel Wright 139½ (England), Olympia, Liverpool. Referee: Mark Green. Judges: Phil Edwards 117-112, Howard Foster 117-111, John Keane 116-113. Having qualified for British citizenship under the five-year ruling, Olusegun was also contesting the vacant British title as well as defending his Commonwealth crown.

Welterweight

11 April Craig Watson 146½ (England) L PTS 12 John O'Donnell 146 (England), York Hall, Bethnal Green, London. Referee: Victor Loughlin. Judges: Richie Davies 114-115, Dave Parris 114-115, John Keane 116-113.

L.Middleweight

14 March Bradley Pryce 152½ (Wales) L RSC 2 Matthew Hall 153 (England), MEN Arena, Manchester. Referee: Ian John-Lewis. Judges: Phil Edwards, Dave Parris, Terry O'Connor.

Middleweight

13 December Darren Barker 159½ (England) W RTD 6 Jason McKay 158 (Northern Ireland), International Centre, Brentwood. Referee: Mickey Vann. Judges: Dave Parris, Marcus McDonnell, Richie Davies.

23 May Darren Barker 159¾ (England) W RSC 4 Darren McDermott 159¾ (England), The Colosseum, Watford. Referee: Dave Parris. Judges: Richie Davies, Mark Green, Terry O'Connor.

S.Middleweight

19 July Jermaine Mackey 167 (Bahamas) W PTS 12 Michael Gbenga 166 (Ghana), Kendel GL Isaac's National Gymnasium, Nassau, Bahamas. Referee: Matthew Nixon. Scorecards: 115-113, 117-111, 118-113. The title had been vacant ever since England's Carl Froch had handed in his belt on 12 June 2007 in order to concentrate on a world title shot.

L.Heavyweight

10 October Nathan Cleverly 173½ (Wales) W PTS 12 Tony Oakey 174½ (England), Everton Park Sports Centre, Liverpool. Referee: Victor Loughlin. Judges: Phil Edwards 119-110, Howard Foster 117-111, Mickey Vann 116-112. Contested for the vacant title after Dean Francis (England), who had been due to defend against Cleverly, handed in his belt on the premise that he would not be ready in time. Oakey was quickly drafted in to keep the show alive.

12 December Nathan Cleverly 174¾ (Wales) W CO 4 Douglas Otieno 174 (Kenya), Kingsway Leisure Centre, Widnes. Referee: Phil Edwards. Judges: Howard Foster, Dave Parris, Mickey Vann.

13 February Nathan Cleverly 174 (Wales) W RSC 1 Samson Onyango 174½ (Kenya), Oasis Leisure Centre, Swindon. Referee: Mark Green. Judges: Phil Edwards, John Keane, Terry O'Connor.

22 May Nathan Cleverly 174 (Wales) W RSC 2 Billy Boyle 172½ (England), York Hall, Bethnal Green, London. Referee: Marcus McDonnell. Judges: Howard Foster, Ian John-Lewis, Dave Parris.

Cruiserweight

6 February Robert Norton 198 (England) W PTS 12 David Dolan 198 (England), Aston Events Centre, Birmingham. Referee: Dave Parris. Judges: John Keane 116-109, Howard Foster 114-111, Terry O'Connor 115-110. Contested for the vacant title after Canada's Troy Ross was stripped of the belt in November for failing to make a defence within the allotted time scale. Norton's British title was also at stake.

Heavyweight

28 February Matt Skelton 247½ (England) L RSC 11 Martin Rogan 225 (Northern Ireland), National Indoor Arena, Birmingham. Referee: John Keane. Judges: Howard Foster, Ian John-Lewis, Victor Loughlin.

15 May Martin Rogan 228 (Northern Ireland) L RSC 8 Sam Sexton 241 (England), Odyssey Arena, Belfast. Referee: Dave Parris. Judges: Mark Green, Victor Loughlin, Terry O'Connor.

Commonwealth Champions, 1887-2009

Since the 1997 edition, Harold Alderman's magnificent research into Imperial British Empire title fights has introduced many more claimants/champions than were shown previously. Prior to 12 October 1954, the date that the British Commonwealth and Empire Boxing Championships Committee was formed, there was no official body as such and the Australian and British promoters virtually ran the show, with other members of the British Empire mainly out in the cold. We have also listed Canadian representatives, despite championship boxing in that country being contested over ten or 12 rounds at most, but they are not accorded the same kind of recognition that their British and Australian counterparts are. Boxers who became Commonwealth champions while being licensed and qualified to contest national titles outside of their country of birth are recorded by domicile/birthplace. Reconstituted as the British Commonwealth Boxing Championships Committee on 22 November 1972, and with a current membership that includes Australia, Bahamas, Barbados, Canada, Ghana, Guyana, Jamaica, Kenya, Namibia, New Zealand, Nigeria, South Africa, Tanzania, Trinidad &Tobago, Uganda and Zambia, in 1989 the 'British' tag was dropped.

COMMONWEALTH COUNTRY CODE
A = Australia; ANT = Antigua; BAH = Bahamas; BAR = Barbados; BER = Bermuda; C = Canada; E = England; F = Fiji; GH = Ghana; GU = Guyana; I = Ireland; J = Jamaica; K = Kenya; MAU = Mauritius; N = Nigeria; NAM = Namibia; NZ = New Zealand; NI = Northern Ireland; PNG = Papua New Guinea; SA = South Africa; SAM = Samoa; S = Scotland; SK = St Kitts; SL = St Lucia; T = Tonga; TR = Trinidad; U = Uganda; W = Wales; ZA = Zambia; ZI = Zimbabwe.

Champions in **bold** denote those recognised by the British Commonwealth and Empire Boxing Championships Committee (1954 to date) and, prior to that, those with the best claims

*Undefeated champions (Does not include men who forfeited titles)

Flyweight (112 lbs)

Name	Code	Years
Elky Clark*	S	1924-1927
Harry Hill	E	1929
Frenchy Belanger	C	1929
Vic White	A	1929-1930
Teddy Green	A	1930-1931
Jackie Paterson	S	1940-1948
Rinty Monaghan*	NI	1948-1950
Teddy Gardner	E	1952
Jake Tuli	SA	1952-1954
Dai Dower*	W	1954-1957
Frankie Jones	S	1957
Dennis Adams*	SA	1957-1962
Jackie Brown	S	1962-1963
Walter McGowan*	S	1963-1969
John McCluskey	S	1970-1971
Henry Nissen	A	1971-1974
Big Jim West*	A	1974-1975
Patrick Mambwe	ZA	1976-1979
Ray Amoo	N	1980
Steve Muchoki	K	1980-1983
Keith Wallace*	E	1983-1984
Richard Clarke	J	1986-1987
Nana Yaw Konadu*	GH	1987-1989
Alfred Kotey*	GH	1989-1993
Francis Ampofo*	E/GH	1993
Daren Fifield	E	1993-1994
Francis Ampofo	E/GH	1994-1995
Danny Ward	SA	1995-1996
Peter Culshaw	E	1996-1997
Ady Lewis*	E	1997-1998
Alfonso Zvenyika	ZI	1998
Damaen Kelly	NI	1998-1999
Keith Knox	S	1999
Jason Booth*	E	1999-2003
Dale Robinson	E	2003-2004
Lee Haskins*	E	2006-2007
Chris Edwards	E	2009-

S. Flyweight (115 lbs)

Name	Code	Years
Don Broadhurst	E	2008-

Bantamweight (118 lbs)

Name	Code	Years
Digger Stanley	E	1904-1905
Owen Moran	E	1905
Ted Green	A	1905-1911
Charlie Simpson*	A	1911-1912
Jim Higgins	S	1920-1922
Tommy Harrison	E	1922-1923
Bugler Harry Lake	E	1923
Johnny Brown	E	1923-1928
Billy McAllister	A	1928-1930
Teddy Baldock*	E	1928-1930
Johnny Peters	E	1930
Dick Corbett	E	1930-1932
Johnny King	E	1932-1934
Dick Corbett	E	1934
Frankie Martin	C	1935-1937
Baby Yack	C	1937
Johnny Gaudes	C	1937-1939
Lefty Gwynn	C	1939
Baby Yack	C	1939-1940
Jim Brady	S	1941-1945
Jackie Paterson	S	1945-1949
Stan Rowan	E	1949
Vic Toweel	SA	1949-1952
Jimmy Carruthers*	A	1952-1954
Peter Keenan	S	1955-1959
Freddie Gilroy*	NI	1959-1963
Johnny Caldwell	NI	1964-1965
Alan Rudkin	E	1965-1966
Walter McGowan	S	1966-1968
Alan Rudkin	E	1968-1969
Lionel Rose*	A	1969
Alan Rudkin*	E	1970-1972
Paul Ferreri	A	1972-1977
Sulley Shittu	GH	1977-1978
Johnny Owen*	W	1978-1980
Paul Ferreri	A	1981-1986
Ray Minus*	BAH	1986-1991
John Armour*	E	1992-1996
Paul Lloyd*	E	1996-2000
Ady Lewis	E	2000
Tommy Waite	NI	2000
Nicky Booth	E	2000-2002
Steve Molitor	C	2002-2004
Joseph Agbeko	GH	2004-2006
Tshifhiwa Munyai*	SA	2006-2007
Jason Booth	E	2007-

S. Bantamweight (122 lbs)

Name	Code	Years
Neil Swain	W	1995
Neil Swain	W	1996-1997
Michael Brodie	E	1997-1999
Nedal Hussein*	A	2000-2001
Brian Carr	S	2001-2002
Michael Alldis	E	2002
Esham Pickering	E	2003-2005
Michael Hunter*	E	2005-2006
Isaac Ward	E	2007
Anyetei Laryea*	GH	2007-2009
Rendall Munroe	E	2009-

Featherweight (126 lbs)

Name	Code	Years
Jim Driscoll*	W	1908-1913
Llew Edwards	W	1915-1916
Charlie Simpson*	A	1916
Tommy Noble	E	1919-1921
Bert Spargo	A	1921-1922
Bert McCarthy	A	1922
Bert Spargo	A	1922-1923

Title Holder	Domicile/Birthplace	Tenure
Billy Grime	A	1923
Ernie Baxter	A	1923
Leo Kid Roy	C	1923
Bert Ristuccia	A	1923-1924
Barney Wilshur	C	1923
Benny Gould	C	1923-1924
Billy Grime	A	1924
Leo Kid Roy	C	1924-1932
Johnny McGrory	S	1936-1938
Jim Spider Kelly	NI	1938-1939
Johnny Cusick	E	1939-1940
Nel Tarleton	E	1940-1947
Tiger Al Phillips	E	1947
Ronnie Clayton	E	1947-1951
Roy Ankrah	GH	1951-1954
Billy Spider Kelly	NI	1954-1955
Hogan Kid Bassey*	N	1955-1957
Percy Lewis	TR	1957-1960
Floyd Robertson	GH	1960-1967
John O'Brien	S	1967
Johnny Famechon*	A	1967-1969
Toro George	NZ	1970-1972
Bobby Dunne	A	1972-1974
Evan Armstrong	S	1974
David Kotey*	GH	1974-1975
Eddie Ndukwu	N	1977-1980
Pat Ford*	GU	1980-1981
Azumah Nelson*	GH	1981-1985
Tyrone Downes	BAR	1986-1988
Thunder Aryeh	GH	1988-1989
Oblitey Commey	GH	1989-1990
Modest Napunyi	K	1990-1991
Barrington Francis*	C	1991
Colin McMillan*	E	1992
Billy Hardy*	E	1992-1996
Jonjo Irwin	E	1996-1997
Paul Ingle*	E	1997-1999
Patrick Mullings	E	1999-2000
Scott Harrison*	S	2000-2002
Nicky Cook*	E	2003-2005
Jackson Asiku*	A/U	2005-2008
Paul Truscott	E	2008-2009
John Simpson	S	2009-

S. Featherweight (130 lbs)

Title Holder	Domicile/Birthplace	Tenure
Billy Moeller	A	1975-1977
Johnny Aba*	PNG	1977-1982
Langton Tinago	ZI	1983-1984
John Sichula	ZA	1984
Lester Ellis*	A/E	1984-1985
John Sichula	ZA	1985-1986
Sam Akromah	GH	1986-1987
John Sichula	ZA	1987-1989
Mark Reefer*	E	1989-1990
Thunder Aryeh	GH	1990-1991
Hugh Forde	E	1991
Paul Harvey	E	1991-1992
Tony Pep	C	1992-1995
Justin Juuko*	U	1995-1998
Charles Shepherd*	E	1999
Mick O'Malley	A	1999-2000
Ian McLeod*	S	2000
James Armah*	GH	2000-2001
Alex Moon	E	2001-2002
Dean Pithie	E	2002-2003
Craig Docherty	S	2003-2004
Alex Arthur*	S	2004-2006
Kevin Mitchell*	E	2006-2008
Ricky Burns	S	2008-

Lightweight (135 lbs)

Title Holder	Domicile/Birthplace	Tenure
Jim Burge	A	1890
George Dawson*	A	1890
Harry Nickless	E	1892-1894
Arthur Valentine	E	1894-1895
Dick Burge*	E	1894-1895
Jim Murphy*	NZ	1894-1897
Eddie Connolly*	C	1896-1897
Jack Goldswain	E	1906-1908
Jack McGowan	A	1909
Hughie Mehegan	A	1909-1910
Johnny Summers*	E	1910
Hughie Mehegan	A	1911
Freddie Welsh*	W	1912-1914
Ernie Izzard	E	1928
Tommy Fairhall	A	1928-1930
Al Foreman	E	1930-1933
Jimmy Kelso	A	1933
Al Foreman*	E	1933-1934
Laurie Stevens*	SA	1936-1937
Dave Crowley	E	1938
Eric Boon	E	1938-1944
Ronnie James*	W	1944-1947
Arthur King	C	1948-1951
Frank Johnson	E	1953
Pat Ford	A	1953-1954
Ivor Germain	BAR	1954
Pat Ford	A	1954-1955
Johnny van Rensburg	SA	1955-1956
Willie Toweel	SA	1956-1959
Dave Charnley	E	1959-1962
Bunny Grant	J	1962-1967
Manny Santos*	NZ	1967
Love Allotey	GH	1967-1968
Percy Hayles	J	1968-1975
Jonathan Dele	N	1975-1977
Lennox Blackmore	GU	1977-1978
Hogan Jimoh	N	1978-1980
Langton Tinago	ZI	1980-1981
Barry Michael	A/E	1981-1982
Claude Noel	T	1982-1984
Graeme Brooke	A	1984-1985
Barry Michael*	A/E	1985-1986
Langton Tinago	ZI	1986-1987
Mo Hussein	E	1987-1989
Pat Doherty	E	1989
Najib Daho	E	1989-1990
Carl Crook	E	1990-1992
Billy Schwer	E	1992-1993
Paul Burke	E	1993
Billy Schwer	E	1993-1995
David Tetteh	GH	1995-1997
Billy Irwin	C	1997
David Tetteh	GH	1997-1999
Bobby Vanzie	E	1999-2001
James Armah*	GH	2001-2002
David Burke*	E	2002
Michael Muya	K	2003
Kevin Bennett	E	2003-2005
Graham Earl*	E	2005-2006
Willie Limond	S	2006-2007
Amir Khan*	E	2007-2009
Lee McAllister	S	2009-

L. Welterweight (140 lbs)

Title Holder	Domicile/Birthplace	Tenure
Joe Tetteh	GH	1972-1973
Hector Thompson	A	1973-1977
Baby Cassius Austin	A	1977-1978
Jeff Malcolm	A	1978-1979
Obisia Nwankpa	N	1979-1983
Billy Famous	N	1983-1986
Tony Laing	E	1987-1988
Lester Ellis	A/E	1988-1989
Steve Larrimore	BAH	1989
Tony Ekubia	E/N	1989-1991
Andy Holligan	E	1991-1994
Ross Hale	E	1994-1995
Paul Ryan	E	1995-1996
Andy Holligan	E	1996-1997
Bernard Paul	E/MAU	1997-1999
Eamonn Magee	NI	1999-
Paul Burke	E	1997
Felix Bwalya*	ZA	1997
Paul Burke	E	1998-1999
Eamonn Magee*	NI	1999-2002
Junior Witter*	E	2002-2006
Ajose Olusegun	E/N	2007-

Welterweight (147 lbs)

Title Holder	Domicile/Birthplace	Tenure
Tom Williams	A	1892-1895
Dick Burge	E	1895-1897
Eddie Connolly*	C	1903-1905
Joe White*	C	1907-1909
Johnny Summers	E	1912-1914
Tom McCormick	I	1914
Matt Wells	E	1914-1919
Fred Kay	A	1915
Tommy Uren	A	1915-1916
Fritz Holland	A	1916
Tommy Uren	A	1916-1919
Fred Kay	A	1919-1920
Johnny Basham	W	1919-1920
Bermondsey Billy Wells	E	1922
Ted Kid Lewis	E	1920-1924
Tommy Milligan*	S	1924-1925
Jack Carroll	A	1928
Charlie Purdie	A	1928-1929
Wally Hancock	A	1929-1930
Tommy Fairhall*	A	1930
Jack Carroll	A	1934-1938

Title Holder	Domicile/ Birthplace	Tenure
Eddie Thomas	W	1951
Wally Thom	E	1951-1952
Cliff Curvis	W	1952
Gerald Dreyer	SA	1952-1954
Barry Brown	NZ	1954
George Barnes	A	1954-1956
Darby Brown	A	1956
George Barnes	A	1956-1958
Johnny van Rensburg	SA	1958
George Barnes	A	1958-1960
Brian Curvis*	W	1960-1966
Johnny Cooke	E	1967-1968
Ralph Charles*	E	1968-1972
Clyde Gray	C	1973-1979
Chris Clarke	C	1979
Clyde Gray*	C	1979-1980
Colin Jones*	W	1981-1984
Sylvester Mittee	E/SL	1984-1985
Lloyd Honeyghan*	E/J	1985-1986
Brian Janssen	A	1987
Wilf Gentzen	A	1987-1988
Gary Jacobs	S	1988-1989
Donovan Boucher	C	1989-1992
Eamonn Loughran*	NI	1992-1993
Andrew Murray*	GU	1993-1997
Kofi Jantuah*	GH	1997-2000

Title Holder	Domicile/ Birthplace	Tenure
Scott Dixon*	S	2000
Jawaid Khaliq*	E	2000-2001
Julian Holland	A	2001-2002
James Hare*	E	2002-2003
Ossie Duran*	GH	2003-2004
Fatai Onikeke	NI	2004-2005
Joshua Okine	GH	2005
Kevin Anderson	S	2005-2007
Ali Nuumbembe	NAM	2007-2007
Craig Watson	E	2007-2009
John O'Donnell	E	2009-

L. Middleweight (154 lbs)

Title Holder	Domicile/ Birthplace	Tenure
Charkey Ramon*	A	1972-1975
Maurice Hope*	E/ANT	1976-1979
Kenny Bristol	GU	1979-1981
Herol Graham*	E	1981-1984
Ken Salisbury	A/E	1984-1985
Nick Wilshire	E	1985-1987
Lloyd Hibbert	E	1987
Troy Waters*	A/E	1987-1991
Chris Pyatt*	E	1991-1992
Mickey Hughes	E	1992-1993
Lloyd Honeyghan	E/J	1993-1994
Leo Young	A	1994-1995
Kevin Kelly	A	1995

Title Holder	Domicile/ Birthplace	Tenure
Chris Pyatt	E	1995-1996
Steve Foster	E	1996-1997
Kevin Kelly	A	1997-1999
Tony Badea	C	1999-2001
Richard Williams*	E	2001
Joshua Onyango	K	2002
Michael Jones	E	2002-2003
Jamie Moore*	E	2003-2004
Richard Williams*	E	2004
Jamie Moore	E	2004
Ossie Duran	GH	2004-2006
Bradley Pryce	W	2006-2009
Matthew Hall	E	2009-

Middleweight (160 lbs)

Title Holder	Domicile/ Birthplace	Tenure
Chesterfield Goode	E	1887-1890
Toff Wall	E	1890-1891
Jim Hall	A	1892-1893
Bill Heffernan	NZ	1894-1896
Bill Doherty	A	1896-1897
Billy Edwards	A	1897-1898
Dido Plumb*	E	1898-1901
Tom Duggan	A	1901-1903
Jack Palmer*	E	1902-1904
Jewey Cooke	E	1903-1904
Tom Dingey	C	1904-1905

England's Darren Barker (right) forced Northern Ireland's Jason McKay to retire at the end of the sixth round when defending his Commonwealth middleweight title at Brentwood's International Centre last December

Philip Sharkey

Title Holder	Domicile/ Birthplace	Tenure
Jack Lalor	SA	1905
Ted Nelson	A	1905
Tom Dingey	C	1905
Sam Langford*	C	1907-1911
Ed Williams	A	1908-1910
Arthur Cripps	A	1910
Dave Smith	A	1910-1911
Jerry Jerome	A	1913
Arthur Evernden	E	1913-1914
Mick King	A	1914-1915
Les Darcy*	A	1915-1917
Ted Kid Lewis	E	1922-1923
Roland Todd	E	1923-1926
Len Johnson	E	1926-1928
Tommy Milligan	S	1926-1928
Alex Ireland	S	1928-1929
Len Harvey	E	1929-1933
Del Fontaine	C	1931
Ted Moore	E	1931
Jock McAvoy	E	1933-1939
Ron Richards*	A	1940
Ron Richards*	A	1941-1942
Bos Murphy	NZ	1948
Dick Turpin	E	1948-1949
Dave Sands*	A	1949-1952
Randy Turpin	E	1952-1954
Al Bourke	A	1952-1954
Johnny Sullivan	E	1954-1955
Pat McAteer	E	1955-1958
Dick Tiger	N	1958-1960
Wilf Greaves	C	1960
Dick Tiger*	N	1960-1962
Gomeo Brennan	BAH	1963-1964
Tuna Scanlon*	NZ	1964
Gomeo Brennan	BAH	1964-1966
Blair Richardson*	C	1966-1967
Milo Calhoun	J	1967
Johnny Pritchett*	E	1967-1969
Les McAteer	E	1969-1970
Mark Rowe	E	1970
Bunny Sterling	E/J	1970-1972
Tony Mundine*	A	1972-1975
Monty Betham	NZ	1975-1978
Al Korovou	A	1978
Ayub Kalule	U	1978-1980
Tony Sibson*	E	1980-1983
Roy Gumbs	E/SK	1983
Mark Kaylor	E	1983-1984
Tony Sibson*	E	1984-1988
Nigel Benn	E	1988-1989
Michael Watson*	E	1989-1991
Richie Woodhall	E	1992-1995
Robert McCracken	E	1995-1997
Johnson Tshuma	SA	1997-1998
Paul Jones	E	1998-1999
Jason Matthews*	E	1999
Alain Bonnamie*	C	1999-2000
Sam Soliman	A	2000
Howard Eastman*	E/GU	2000-2004

Title Holder	Domicile/ Birthplace	Tenure
James Obede Toney	GH	2004-2006
Scott Dann*	E	2006-2007
Howard Eastman*	E/GU	2007
Darren Barker	E	2007-

S. Middleweight (168 lbs)

Title Holder	Domicile/ Birthplace	Tenure
Rod Carr	A	1989-1990
Lou Cafaro	A	1990-1991
Henry Wharton*	E	1991-1997
Clinton Woods	E	1997-1998
David Starie	E	1998-2003
Andre Thysse	SA	2003
Charles Adamu	GH	2003-2004
Carl Froch*	E	2004-2007
Jermaine Mackey	BAH	2008-

L. Heavyweight (175 lbs)

Title Holder	Domicile/ Birthplace	Tenure
Dave Smith*	A	1911-1915
Jack Bloomfield*	E	1923-1924
Tom Berry	E	1927
Gipsy Daniels*	W	1927
Len Harvey	E	1939-1942
Freddie Mills*	E	1942-1950
Randy Turpin*	E	1952-1955
Gordon Wallace	C	1956-1957
Yvon Durelle*	C	1957-1959
Chic Calderwood	S	1960-1963
Bob Dunlop*	A	1968-1970
Eddie Avoth	W	1970-1971
Chris Finnegan	E	1971-1973
John Conteh*	E	1973-1974
Steve Aczel	A	1975
Tony Mundine	A	1975-1978
Gary Summerhays	C	1978-1979
Lottie Mwale	ZA	1979-1985
Leslie Stewart*	TR	1985-1987
Willie Featherstone	C	1987-1989
Guy Waters*	A/E	1989-1993
Brent Kosolofski	C	1993-1994
Garry Delaney	E	1994-1995
Noel Magee	I	1995
Nicky Piper*	W	1995-1997
Crawford Ashley	E	1998-1999
Clinton Woods*	E	1999-2000
Neil Simpson	E	2001
Tony Oakey*	E	2001-2002
Peter Oboh*	E/N	2002-2006
Ovill McKenzie	J	2006-2007
Dean Francis*	E	2007-2008
Nathan Cleverly	W	2008-

Cruiserweight (200 lbs)

Title Holder	Domicile/ Birthplace	Tenure
Stewart Lithgo	E	1984
Chisanda Mutti	ZA	1984-1987
Glenn McCrory*	E	1987-1989
Apollo Sweet	A	1989
Derek Angol*	E	1989-1993
Francis Wanyama	U	1994-1995
Chris Okoh	E	1995-1997

Title Holder	Domicile/ Birthplace	Tenure
Darren Corbett	NI	1997-1998
Bruce Scott	E/J	1998-1999
Adam Watt*	A	2000-2001
Bruce Scott*	E/J	2001-2003
Mark Hobson*	E	2003-2006
Troy Ross	C	2007-2008
Robert Norton	E	2009-

Heavyweight (200 lbs +)

Title Holder	Domicile/ Birthplace	Tenure
Peter Jackson*	A	1889-1901
Dan Creedon	NZ	1896-1903
Billy McColl	A	1902-1905
Tim Murphy	A	1905-1906
Bill Squires	A	1906-1909
Bill Lang	A	1909-1910
Tommy Burns*	C	1910-1911
P.O. Curran	I	1911
Dan Flynn	I	1911
Bombardier Billy Wells	E	1911-1919
Bill Lang	A	1911-1913
Dave Smith	A	1913-1917
Joe Beckett*	E	1919-1923
Phil Scott	E	1926-1931
Larry Gains	C	1931-1934
Len Harvey	E	1934
Jack Petersen	W	1934-1936
Ben Foord	SA	1936-1937
Tommy Farr	W	1937
Len Harvey*	E	1939-1942
Jack London	E	1944-1945
Bruce Woodcock	E	1945-1950
Jack Gardner	E	1950-1952
Johnny Williams	W	1952-1953
Don Cockell	E	1953-1956
Joe Bygraves	J	1956-1957
Joe Erskine	W	1957-1958
Brian London	E	1958-1959
Henry Cooper	E	1959-1971
Joe Bugner	E	1971
Jack Bodell	E	1971-1972
Danny McAlinden	NI	1972-1975
Bunny Johnson	E/J	1975
Richard Dunn	E	1975-1976
Joe Bugner*	E	1976-1977
John L. Gardner*	E	1978-1981
Trevor Berbick	C/J	1981-1986
Horace Notice*	E	1986-1988
Derek Williams	E	1988-1992
Lennox Lewis*	E	1992-1993
Henry Akinwande	E	1993-1995
Scott Welch	E	1995-1997
Julius Francis*	E	1997-1999
Danny Williams	E	1999-2004
Michael Sprott	E	2004
Matt Skelton*	E	2004-2005
Danny Williams	E	2005-2006
Matt Skelton	E	2006-2009
Martin Rogan	NI	2009
Sam Sexton	E	2009

European Title Bouts, 2008-2009

All of last season's title bouts are shown in date order within their weight divisions and give the boxers' respective weights, along with the scorecards if going to a decision. Referees are named, as are British judges where applicable.

Flyweight
16 January Ivan Pozo 111½ (Spain) W TD 9 Christophe Rodrigues 109½ (France), Travesa Pavilion, Vigo, Spain. Referee: Adrio Zannoni. Contested for the vacant title after Bernard Inom (France) announced that he was retiring from boxing on 26 September 2008. Booked for a return against Rodrigues due to the unsatisfactory ending. Pozo relinquished the title on 30 April due having difficulty in making the weight.

Bantamweight
17 October Carmelo Ballone 117½ (Belgium) L PTS 12 Ian Napa 117½ (England), York Hall, Bethnal Green, London, England. Referee: Erkki Meronen. Scorecards: 113-114, 113-114, 114-114.
20 March Ian Napa 118 (England) L PTS 12 Malik Bouziane 118 (France), Leisure Centre, Newham, London, England. Referee: Giuseppe Quartarone. Scorecards: 113-115, 110-118, 111-117.
19 June Malik Bouziane 117¼ (France) W PTS 12 Carmelo Ballone 118 (Belgium), Sports Centre, Massy, France. Referee: Guido Cavalieri. Scorecards: 115-112, 115-112, 114-113.

S.Bantamweight
5 September Rendall Munroe 121¾ (England) W PTS 12 Arsen Martirosyan 121½ (Armenia), Harvey Hadden Leisure Centre, Nottingham. Referee: Adrio Zannoni. Scorecards: 115-113, 115-113, 117-112.
18 October Rendall Munroe 121 (England) W RSC 5 Fabrizio Trotta 121 (Italy), City University, Dublin, Ireland. Referee: Erkki Meronen.
27 February Rendall Munroe 121¾ (England) W PTS 12 Kiko Martinez 120½ (Spain), The Metrodome, Barnsley, England. Referee: Daniel van der Wiele. Scorecards: 116-113, 116-112, 118-110.

Featherweight
8 July Oleg Yefimovych 124 (Ukraine) W PTS 12 Sergio Blanco 125½ (Spain), Drusba Sports Palace, Donetsk, Ukraine. Referee: Massimo Barrovecchio. Scorecards: Mickey Vann 119-108, 118-110, 119-109. Contested for the vacant title, Alberto Servidei (Italy) having forfeited the championship on 4 April after pulling out of a title defence against Blanco.
29 November Oleg Yefimovych 124½ (Ukraine) W RSC 1 Luca Maggio 123¼ (Italy), Drusba Sports Palace, Donetsk, Ukraine. Referee: Mickey Vann.

France's Malik Bouziane (right) slams in a right to the head on his way to picking up Ian Napa's European bantamweight title

Philip Sharkey

10 April Oleg Yefimovych 126 (Ukraine) W PTS 12 Osman Aktas 125¼ (France), Drusba Sports Palace, Donetsk, Ukraine. Referee: Erkki Meronen. Scorecards: Terry O'Connor 119-109, 119-109, 120-108.

S.Featherweight
5 December Sergei Gulyakevich 128½ (Belarus) W PTS 12 Vitali Tajbert 129¾ (Kazakhstan), Brandberge Sports Hall, Halle, Germany. Referee: Giuseppe Quartarone. Scorecards: Terry O'Connor 117-112, 117-112, 115-113.

Lightweight
4 October Jonathan Thaxton 134½ (England) W CO 3 Juan Carlos Diaz Melero 134¾ (Spain), The Showgrounds, Norwich, England. Referee: Robin Dolpierre. Billed for the vacant title, Belarus'Yuri Romanov having relinquished the title on 23 April in order to concentrate on getting a world championship opportunity.
28 February Jonathan Thaxton 134½ (England) L PTS 12 Anthony Mezaache 134½ (France), The Showgrounds, Norwich, England. Referee: Massimo Barrovecchio. Scorecards: 112-115, 111-115, 113-114.

L.Welterweight
19 December Gianluca Branco 138¾ (Italy) W RSC 9 Juho Tolppola 138½ (Finland), The Palalido, Milan, Italy. Referee: Ian John-Lewis. Having difficulty in being comfortable at the weight, Branco relinquished the title on 31 March 2009.

Welterweight
14 September Jackson Osei-Bonsu 146 (Belgium/Ghana) L PTS 12 Rafel Jackiewicz 147 (Poland), Hala MOSiR Indoor Arena, Lodz, Poland. Referee: Guido Cavalieri. Scorecards: 112-116, 110-117, 113-114.
29 November Rafel Jackiewicz 147 (Poland) W PTS 12 Jan Zaveck 146½ (Slovenia), Municipal Sports & Recreation Centre, Katowice, Poland. Referee: Esa Lehtossari. Scorecards: 116-113, 115-114, 113-116.
28 February Rafel Jackiewicz 147 (Poland) W PTS 12 Luciano Abis 145½ (Italy), Global Municipal Sports Hall, Lublin, Poland. Referee: Terry O'Connor. Scorecards: 118-112, 116-112, 117-111. Jackiewicz relinquished the title on 20 April to concentrate on a possible IBF eliminator.

L.Middleweight
12 July Zaurbek Baysangurov 153½ (Russia) W RTD 7 Ivan Grontsa 153½ (Moldova), Color Line Arena, Hamburg, Germany. Referee: Dave Parris. Baysangurov relinquished the title on 30 September to get in line for a crack at the world title.
6 March Jamie Moore 154 (England) W CO 3 Michele Piccirillo 153 (Italy), Robin Park Centre, Wigan, England. Referee: Robin Dolpierre.

2 May Jamie Moore 154 (England) W RSC 2 Roman Dzuman 153½ (Ukraine), Crowtree Leisure Centre, Sunderland, England. Referee: Adrio Zannoni.

Middleweight
28 November Khoren Gevor 159¼ (Armenia) W RSC 7 Amin Asikainen 159½ (Finland), Hartwall Arena, Helsinki, Finland. Referee: Mark Green. Judge: Richie Davies. Billed for the vacant title after Sebastian Sylvester (Germany) handed in his belt on 17 July to prepare for a WBA championship bout against Felix Sturm, Gevor also went down the same road when relinquishing on 25 May to concentrate on his upcoming crack at Sturm on 11 July.

S.Middleweight
20 September Karo Murat 166 (Germany) W PTS 12 Gabriel Campillo 167¾ (Spain), Seidensticker Hall, Bielfeld, Germany. Referee: Massimo Barrovecchio. Scorecards: Howard Foster 115-113, 115-113, 115-115.
28 February Karo Mura 166¾ (Germany) W RSC 10 Cristian Sanavia 166½ (Italy), Jahn Sports Arena, Neubrandenburg, Germany. Referee: Erkki Meronen.

L.Heavyweight
7 March Juergen Braehmer 174¾ (Germany) W RSC 1 Rachid Kanfouah 173¾ (France), Freiberger Arena, Dresden, Germany. Richie Davies. Judge: John Keane. Billed for the vacant title after Yuri Barashian (Armenia) handed back his belt in May 2008 to prepare for a vacant WBA championship fight against Hugo Garay on 3 July 2008.
6 June Juergen Braehmer 174½ (Germany) W RSC 1 Antonio Brancalion 174½ (Italy), Koenig Pilsener Arena, Oberhausen, Germany. Referee: Terry O'Connor.

Cruiserweight
20 September Jean-Marc Monrose 197¼ (France) L RSC 12 Marco Huck 197¼ (Yugoslavia), Seidensticker Hall, Bielfeld, Germany. Referee: Terry O'Connor. Judge: Howard Foster.
25 October Marco Huck 198 (Yugoslavia) W RSC 2 Fabio Tuiach 198¾ (Italy), Weser-Ems Hall, Oldenburg, Germany. Referee: Dave Parris. Judge: Howard Foster.
24 January Marco Huck 196 (Yugoslavia) W RSC 3 Geoffrey Battalo 197 (Belgium), Erdgas Arena, Riesa, Germany. Referee: Guido Cavalieri. Judge: Howard Foster.
9 May Marco Huck 199½ (Yugoslavia) W RSC 5 Vitali Rusal 191½ (Ukraine), Jako Arena, Bamberg, Germany. Referee: Guido Cavalieri. Judge: Richie Davies.

Heavyweight
4 July Sinan Samil Sam 252½ (Turkey) W PTS 12 Paolo Vidoz 250 (Italy), Bueyeuk Anadolu Hotel, Ankara, Turkey. Referee: Erkki Meronen. Scorecards: 115-113, 115-114, 114-114. The fight came about after Vladimir Virchis (Ukraine) handed in his belt on 8 October to concentrate on securing a world title shot. Following a decision that left a bad taste, Sam was told that his first defence would be against Vidoz, but rather than go through all that again he relinquished the title on 28 July.
19 December Matt Skelton 250¼ (England) W RTD 9 Paolo Vidoz 238 (Italy), The Palalido, Milan, Italy. Referee: Robin Dolpierre. Skelton forfeited the title on 2 March after losing his Commonwealth crown to Martin Rogan on 28 February.

European Champions, 1909-2009

Prior to 1946, the championship was contested under the auspices of the International Boxing Union, re-named that year as the European Boxing Union (EBU). The IBU had come into being when Victor Breyer, a Paris-based journalist and boxing referee who later edited the Annuaire du Ring (first edition in 1910), warmed to the idea of an organisation that controlled boxing right across Europe, regarding rules and championship fights between the champions of the respective countries. He first came to London at the end of 1909 to discuss the subject with the NSC, but went away disappointed. However, at a meeting between officials from Switzerland and France in March 1912, the IBU was initially formed and, by June of that year, had published their first ratings. By April 1914, Belgium had also joined the organisation, although it would not be until the war was over that the IBU really took off. Many of the early champions shown on the listings were the result of promoters, especially the NSC, billing their own championship fights. Although the (French dominated) IBU recognised certain champions, prior to being re-formed in May 1920, they did not find their administrative 'feet' fully until other countries such as Italy (1922), Holland (1923), and Spain (1924), produced challengers for titles. Later in the 1920s, Germany (1926), Denmark (1928), Portugal (1929) and Romania (1929) also joined the fold. Unfortunately, for Britain, its representatives (Although the BBBoC, as we know it today, was formed in 1929, an earlier attempt to form a Board of Control had been initiated in April 1918 by the NSC and it was that body who were involved here) failed to reach agreement on the three judges' ruling, following several meetings with the IBU early in 1920 and, apart from Elky Clark (fly), Ernie Rice and Alf Howard (light), and Jack Hood (welter), who conformed to that stipulation, fighters from these shores would not be officially recognised as champions until the EBU was formed in 1946. This led to British fighters claiming the title after beating IBU titleholders, or their successors, under championship conditions in this country. The only men who did not come into this category were Kid Nicholson (bantam), and Ted Kid Lewis and Tommy Milligan (welter), who defeated men not recognised by the IBU.

EUROPEAN COUNTRY CODE
ARM = Armenia; AU = Austria; BE = Belarus; BEL = Belgium; BUL = Bulgaria; CRO = Croatia; CZ = Czechoslovakia; DEN = Denmark; E = England; FIN = Finland; FR = France; GEO = Georgia; GER = Germany; GRE = Greece; HOL = Holland; HUN = Hungary; ITA = Italy; KAZ = Kazakhstan; LUX = Luxembourg; NI= Northern Ireland; NOR = Norway; POL = Poland; POR = Portugal; RoI = Republic of Ireland; ROM = Romania; RUS = Russia; S = Scotland; SP = Spain; SWE = Sweden; SWI = Switzerland; TU = Turkey; UK = Ukraine; W= Wales; YUG = Yugoslavia.

Champions in **bold** denote those recognised by the IBU/EBU

*Undefeated champions (Does not include men who may have forfeited titles)

Title Holder	Birthplace/ Domicile	Tenure	Title Holder	Birthplace/ Domicile	Tenure	Title Holder	Birthplace/ Domicile	Tenure
Flyweight (112 lbs)			Fernando Atzori	ITA	1973	Kid Nicholson	E	1928
Sid Smith	E	1913	**Fritz Chervet***	SWI	1973-1974	Teddy Baldock	E	1928-1931
Bill Ladbury	E	1913-1914	**Franco Udella**	ITA	1974-1979	**Domenico Bernasconi**	ITA	1929
Percy Jones	W	1914	**Charlie Magri***	E	1979-1983	**Carlos Flix**	SP	1929-1931
Joe Symonds	E	1914	**Antoine Montero**	FR	1983-1984	**Lucien Popescu**	ROM	1931-1932
Tancy Lee	S	1914-1916	**Charlie Magri***	E	1984-1985	**Domenico Bernasconi**	ITA	1932
Jimmy Wilde	W	1914-1915	**Franco Cherchi**	ITA	1985	**Nicholas Biquet**	BEL	1932-1935
Jimmy Wilde*	W	1916-1923	**Charlie Magri**	E	1985-1986	**Maurice Dubois**	SWI	1935-1936
Michel Montreuil	BEL	1923-1925	**Duke McKenzie***	E	1986-1988	**Joseph Decico**	FR	1936
Elky Clark*	S	1925-1927	**Eyup Can***	TU	1989-1990	**Aurel Toma**	ROM	1936-1937
Victor Ferrand	SP	1927	**Pat Clinton***	S	1990-1991	**Nicholas Biquet**	BEL	1937-1938
Emile Pladner	FR	1928-1929	**Salvatore Fanni**	ITA	1991-1992	**Aurel Toma**	ROM	1938-1939
Johnny Hill	S	1928-1929	**Robbie Regan***	W	1992-1993	**Ernst Weiss**	AU	1939
Eugene Huat	FR	1929	**Luigi Camputaro**	ITA	1993-1994	**Gino Cattaneo**	ITA	1939-1941
Emile Degand	BEL	1929-1930	**Robbie Regan***	W	1994-1995	**Gino Bondavilli***	ITA	1941-1943
Kid Oliva	FR	1930	**Luigi Camputaro***	ITA	1995-1996	**Jackie Paterson**	S	1946
Lucien Popescu	ROM	1930-1931	**Jesper Jensen**	DEN	1996-1997	**Theo Medina**	FR	1946-1947
Jackie Brown	E	1931-1935	**David Guerault***	FR	1997-1999	**Peter Kane**	E	1947-1948
Praxile Gyde	FR	1932-1935	**Alexander Mahmutov**	RUS	1999-2000	**Guido Ferracin**	ITA	1948-1949
Benny Lynch	S	1935-1938	**Damaen Kelly***	NI	2000	**Luis Romero**	SP	1949-1951
Kid David*	BEL	1935-1936	**Alexander Mahmutov**	RUS	2000-2002	**Peter Keenan**	S	1951-1952
Ernst Weiss	AU	1936	**Mimoun Chent**	FR	2002-2003	**Jean Sneyers***	BEL	1952-1953
Valentin Angelmann*	FR	1936-1938	**Alexander Mahmutov***	RUS	2003	**Peter Keenan**	S	1953
Enrico Urbinati*	ITA	1938-1943	**Brahim Asloum***	FR	2003-2005	**John Kelly**	NI	1953-1954
Raoul Degryse	BEL	1946-1947	**Ivan Pozo**	SP	2005-2006	**Robert Cohen***	FR	1954-1955
Maurice Sandeyron	FR	1947-1949	**Andrea Sarritzu**	ITA	2006-2008	**Mario D'Agata**	ITA	1955-1958
Rinty Monaghan*	NI	1949-1950	**Bernard Inom***	FR	2008	**Piero Rollo**	ITA	1958-1959
Terry Allen	E	1950	**Ivan Pozo***	SP	2009	**Freddie Gilroy**	NI	1959-1960
Jean Sneyers*	BEL	1950-1951				**Pierre Cossemyns**	BEL	1961-1962
Teddy Gardner*	E	1952	**Bantamweight (118 lbs)**			**Piero Rollo**	ITA	1962
Louis Skena*	FR	1953-1954	Joe Bowker	E	1910	**Alphonse Halimi**	FR	1962
Nazzareno Giannelli	ITA	1954-1955	Digger Stanley	E	1910-1912	**Piero Rollo**	ITA	1962-1963
Dai Dower	W	1955	**Charles Ledoux**	FR	1912-1921	**Mimoun Ben Ali**	SP	1963
Young Martin	SP	1955-1959	Bill Beynon	W	1913	**Risto Luukkonen**	FIN	1963-1964
Risto Luukkonen	FIN	1959-1961	Tommy Harrison	E	1921-1922	**Mimoun Ben Ali**	SP	1965
Salvatore Burruni*	ITA	1961-1965	**Charles Ledoux**	FR	1922-1923	**Tommaso Galli**	ITA	1965-1966
Rene Libeer	FR	1965-1966	Bugler Harry Lake	E	1923	**Mimoun Ben Ali**	SP	1966-1968
Fernando Atzori	ITA	1967-1972	Johnny Brown	E	1923-1928	**Salvatore Burruni***	ITA	1968-1969
Fritz Chervet	SWI	1972-1973	**Henry Scillie***	BEL	1925-1928	**Franco Zurlo**	ITA	1969-1971

Title Holder	Birthplace/Domicile	Tenure
Alan Rudkin	E	1971
Agustin Senin*	SP	1971-1973
Johnny Clark*	E	1973-1974
Bob Allotey	SP	1974-1975
Daniel Trioulaire	FR	1975-1976
Salvatore Fabrizio	ITA	1976-1977
Franco Zurlo	ITA	1977-1978
Juan Francisco Rodriguez	SP	1978-1980
Johnny Owen*	W	1980
Valerio Nati	ITA	1980-1982
Giuseppe Fossati	ITA	1982-1983
Walter Giorgetti	ITA	1983-1984
Ciro de Leva*	ITA	1984-1986
Antoine Montero	FR	1986-1987
Louis Gomis*	FR	1987-1988
Fabrice Benichou	FR	1988
Vincenzo Belcastro*	ITA	1988-1990
Thierry Jacob*	FR	1990-1992
Johnny Bredahl*	DEN	1992
Vincenzo Belcastro	ITA	1993-1994
Prince Naseem Hamed*	E	1994-1995
John Armour*	E	1995-1996
Johnny Bredahl	DEN	1996-1998
Paul Lloyd*	E	1998-1999
Johnny Bredahl*	DEN	1999-2000
Luigi Castiglione	ITA	2000-2001
Fabien Guillerme	FR	2001
Alex Yagupov	RUS	2001
Spend Abazi	SWE	2001-2002
Noel Wilders	E	2003
David Guerault	FR	2003-2004
Frederic Patrac	FR	2004
Simone Maludrottu*	ITA	2004-2007
Carmelo Ballone	BEL	2008
Ian Napa	E	2008-2009
Malik Bouziane	FR	2009-

S. Bantamweight (122 lbs)

Title Holder	Birthplace/Domicile	Tenure
Vincenzo Belcastro	ITA	1995-1996
Salim Medjkoune	FR	1996
Martin Krastev	BUL	1996-1997
Spencer Oliver	E	1997-1998
Sergei Devakov	UK	1998-1999
Michael Brodie*	E	1999-2000
Vladislav Antonov	RUS	2000-2001
Salim Medjkoune*	FR	2001-2002
Mahyar Monshipour*	FR	2002-2003
Esham Pickering	E	2003-2005
Michael Hunter*	E	2005-2006
Bernard Dunne	RoI	2006-2007
Kiko Martinez	SP	2007-2008
Rendall Munroe	E	2008-

Featherweight (126 lbs)

Title Holder	Birthplace/Domicile	Tenure
Young Joey Smith	E	1911
Jean Poesy	FR	1911-1912
Jim Driscoll*	W	1912-1913
Ted Kid Lewis*	E	1913-1914
Louis de Ponthieu*	FR	1919-1920
Arthur Wyns	BEL	1920-1922
Billy Matthews	E	1922
Eugene Criqui*	FR	1922-1923
Edouard Mascart	FR	1923-1924
Charles Ledoux	FR	1924
Henri Hebrans	BEL	1924-1925
Antonio Ruiz	SP	1925-1928
Luigi Quadrini	ITA	1928-1929
Knud Larsen	DEN	1929
Jose Girones	SP	1929-1934
Maurice Holtzer*	FR	1935-1938
Phil Dolhem	BEL	1938-1939
Lucien Popescu	ROM	1939-1941
Ernst Weiss	AU	1941
Gino Bondavilli	ITA	1941-1945
Ermanno Bonetti*	ITA	1945-1946
Tiger Al Phillips	E	1947
Ronnie Clayton	E	1947-1948
Ray Famechon	FR	1948-1953

Title Holder	Birthplace/Domicile	Tenure
Jean Sneyers	BEL	1953-1954
Ray Famechon	FR	1954-1955
Fred Galiana*	SP	1955-1956
Cherif Hamia	FR	1957-1958
Sergio Caprari	ITA	1958-1959
Gracieux Lamperti	FR	1959-1962
Alberto Serti	ITA	1962-1963
Howard Winstone	W	1963-1967
Jose Legra*	SP	1967-1968
Manuel Calvo	SP	1968-1969
Tommaso Galli	ITA	1969-1970
Jose Legra*	SP	1970-1972
Gitano Jiminez	SP	1973-1975
Elio Cotena	ITA	1975-1976
Nino Jimenez	SP	1976-1977
Manuel Masso	SP	1977
Roberto Castanon*	SP	1977-1981
Salvatore Melluzzo	ITA	1981-1982
Pat Cowdell*	E	1982-1983
Loris Stecca*	ITA	1983
Barry McGuigan*	NI	1983-1985
Jim McDonnell*	E	1985-1987
Valerio Nati*	ITA	1987
Jean-Marc Renard*	BEL	1988-1989
Paul Hodkinson*	E	1989-1991
Fabrice Benichou	FR	1991-1992
Maurizio Stecca	ITA	1992-1993
Herve Jacob	FR	1993
Maurizio Stecca	ITA	1993
Stephane Haccoun	FR	1993-1994
Stefano Zoff	ITA	1994
Medhi Labdouni	FR	1994-1995
Billy Hardy	E	1995-1998
Paul Ingle*	E	1998-1999
Steve Robinson	W	1999-2000
Istvan Kovacs*	HUN	2000-2001
Manuel Calvo*	SP	2001-2002
Cyril Thomas	FR	2002-2004
Nicky Cook*	E	2004-2006
Cyril Thomas*	FR	2006-2007
Alberto Servidei	ITA	2007-2008
Olrg Yefimovych	UK	2008-

S. Featherweight (130 lbs)

Title Holder	Birthplace/Domicile	Tenure
Tommaso Galli	ITA	1971-1972
Domenico Chiloiro	ITA	1972
Lothar Abend	GER	1972-1974
Sven-Erik Paulsen*	NOR	1974-1976
Roland Cazeaux	FR	1976
Natale Vezzoli	ITA	1976-1979
Carlos Hernandez	SP	1979
Rodolfo Sanchez	SP	1979
Carlos Hernandez	SP	1979-1982
Cornelius Boza-Edwards*	E	1982
Roberto Castanon	SP	1982-1983
Alfredo Raininger	ITA	1983-1984
Jean-Marc Renard	BEL	1984
Pat Cowdell	E	1984-1985
Jean-Marc Renard*	BEL	1986-1987
Salvatore Curcetti	ITA	1987-1988
Piero Morello	ITA	1988
Lars Lund Jensen	DEN	1988
Racheed Lawal	DEN	1988-1989
Daniel Londas*	FR	1989-1991
Jimmy Bredahl*	DEN	1992
Regilio Tuur	HOL	1992-1993
Jacobin Yoma	FR	1993-1995
Anatoly Alexandrov*	KAZ	1995-1996
Julian Lorcy*	FR	1996
Djamel Lifa	FR	1997-1998
Anatoly Alexandrov*	RUS	1998
Dennis Holbaek Pedersen	DEN	1999-2000
Boris Sinitsin	RUS	2000
Dennis Holbaek Pedersen	DEN	2000
Tontcho Tontchev*	BUL	2001
Boris Sinitsin	RUS	2001-2002
Pedro Oscar Miranda	SP	2002
Affif Djelti	FR	2002-2003

Title Holder	Birthplace/Domicile	Tenure
Boris Sinitsin	RUS	2003-2005
Alex Arthur*	S	2005-2006
Leva Kirakosyan	ARM	2007-2008
Sergei Gulyakevich	BE	2008-

Lightweight (135 lbs)

Title Holder	Birthplace/Domicile	Tenure
Freddie Welsh	W	1909-1911
Matt Wells	E	1911-1912
Freddie Welsh*	W	1912-1914
Georges Papin	FR	1920-1921
Ernie Rice	E	1921-1922
Seaman Nobby Hall	E	1922-1923
Harry Mason	E	1923-1926
Fred Bretonnel	FR	1924
Lucien Vinez	FR	1924-1927
Luis Rayo*	SP	1927-1928
Aime Raphael	FR	1928-1929
Francois Sybille	BEL	1929-1930
Alf Howard	E	1930
Harry Corbett	E	1930-1931
Francois Sybille	BEL	1930-1931
Bep van Klaveren	HOL	1931-1932
Cleto Locatelli	ITA	1932
Francois Sybille	BEL	1932-1933
Cleto Locatelli*	ITA	1933
Francois Sybille	BEL	1934
Carlo Orlandi*	ITA	1934-1935
Enrico Venturi*	ITA	1935-1936
Vittorio Tamagnini	ITA	1936-1937
Maurice Arnault	FR	1937
Gustave Humery	FR	1937-1938
Aldo Spoldi*	ITA	1938-1939
Karl Blaho	AU	1940-1941
Bruno Bisterzo	ITA	1941
Ascenzo Botta	ITA	1941
Bruno Bisterzo	ITA	1941-1942
Ascenzo Botta	ITA	1942
Roberto Proietti	ITA	1942-1943
Bruno Bisterzo	ITA	1943-1946
Roberto Proietti*	ITA	1946
Emile Dicristo	FR	1946-1947
Kid Dussart	BEL	1947
Roberto Proietti	ITA	1947-1948
Billy Thompson	E	1948-1949
Kid Dussart	BEL	1949
Roberto Proietti*	ITA	1949-1950
Pierre Montane	FR	1951
Elis Ask	FIN	1951-1952
Jorgen Johansen	DEN	1952-1954
Duilio Loi*	ITA	1954-1959
Mario Vecchiatto	ITA	1959-1960
Dave Charnley	E	1960-1963
Conny Rudhof*	GER	1963-1964
Willi Quatuor*	GER	1964-1965
Franco Brondi	ITA	1965
Maurice Tavant	FR	1965-1966
Borge Krogh	DEN	1966-1967
Pedro Carrasco*	SP	1967-1969
Miguel Velazquez	SP	1970-1971
Antonio Puddu	ITA	1971-1974
Ken Buchanan*	S	1974-1975
Fernand Roelandts	BEL	1976
Perico Fernandez*	SP	1976-1977
Jim Watt*	S	1977-1979
Charlie Nash*	NI	1979-1980
Francisco Leon	SP	1980
Charlie Nash	NI	1980-1981
Joey Gibilisco	ITA	1981-1983
Lucio Cusma	ITA	1983-1984
Rene Weller	GER	1984-1986
Gert Bo Jacobsen	DEN	1986-1988
Rene Weller*	GER	1988
Policarpo Diaz*	SP	1988-1990
Antonio Renzo	ITA	1991-1992
Jean-Baptiste Mendy*	FR	1992-1994
Racheed Lawal	DEN	1994
Jean-Baptiste Mendy*	FR	1994-1995
Angel Mona	FR	1995-1997
Manuel Carlos Fernandes	FR	1997

Title Holder	Birthplace/Domicile	Tenure
Oscar Garcia Cano	SP	1997
Billy Schwer*	E	1997-1999
Oscar Garcia Cano	SP	1999-2000
Lucien Lorcy*	FR	2000-2001
Stefano Zoff*	ITA	2001-2002
Jason Cook	W	2002-2003
Stefano Zoff*	ITA	2003-2005
Juan Carlos Diaz Melero	SP	2005-2006
Yuri Romanov*	BE	2006-2008
Jonathan Thaxton	E	2008-2009
Anthony Mezaache	FR	2009-

L. Welterweight (140 lbs)

Title Holder	Birthplace/Domicile	Tenure
Olli Maki	FIN	1964-1965
Juan Sombrita-Albornoz	SP	1965
Willi Quatuor*	GER	1965-1966
Conny Rudhof	GER	1967
Johann Orsolics	AU	1967-1968
Bruno Arcari*	ITA	1968-1970
Rene Roque	FR	1970-1971
Pedro Carrasco*	SP	1971-1972
Roger Zami	FR	1972
Cemal Kamaci	TU	1972-1973
Toni Ortiz	SP	1973-1974
Perico Fernandez*	SP	1974
Jose Ramon Gomez-Fouz	SP	1975
Cemal Kamaci*	TU	1975-1976
Dave Boy Green*	E	1976-1977
Primo Bandini	ITA	1977
Jean-Baptiste Piedvache	FR	1977-1978
Colin Power	E	1978
Fernando Sanchez	SP	1978-1979
Jose Luis Heredia	SP	1979
Jo Kimpuani	FR	1979-1980
Giuseppe Martinese	ITA	1980
Antonio Guinaldo	SP	1980-1981
Clinton McKenzie	E	1981-1982
Robert Gambini	FR	1982-1983
Patrizio Oliva*	ITA	1983-1985
Terry Marsh	E	1985-1986
Tusikoleta Nkalankete	FR	1987-1989
Efren Calamati	ITA	1989-1990
Pat Barrett	E	1990-1992
Valery Kayumba	ITA	1992-1993
Christian Merle	FR	1993-1994
Valery Kayumba	FR	1994
Khalid Rahilou*	FR	1994-1996
Soren Sondergaard*	DEN	1996-1998
Thomas Damgaard*	DEN	1998-2000
Oktay Urkal*	GER	2000-2001
Gianluca Branco*	ITA	2001-2002
Oktay Urkal*	GER	2002-2003
Junior Witter*	E	2004-2006
Ted Bami*	E	2006-2007
Colin Lynes	E	2007-2008
Gianluca Branco*	ITA	2008-2009

Welterweight (147 lbs)

Title Holder	Birthplace/Domicile	Tenure
Young Joseph	E	1910-1911
Georges Carpentier*	FR	1911-1912
Albert Badoud*	SWI	1915-1921
Johnny Basham	W	1919-1920
Ted Kid Lewis	E	1920-1924
Piet Hobin	BEL	1921-1925
Billy Mack	E	1923
Tommy Milligan	S	1924-1925
Mario Bosisio*	ITA	1925-1928
Leo Darton	BEL	1928
Alf Genon	BEL	1928-1929
Gustave Roth	BEL	1929-1932
Adrien Aneet	BEL	1932-1933
Jack Hood*	E	1933
Gustav Eder	GER	1934-1936
Felix Wouters	BEL	1936-1938
Saverio Turiello	ITA	1938-1939
Marcel Cerdan*	FR	1939-1942
Ernie Roderick	E	1946-1947
Robert Villemain*	FR	1947-1948
Livio Minelli	ITA	1949-1950

Title Holder	Birthplace/Domicile	Tenure
Michele Palermo	ITA	1950-1951
Eddie Thomas	W	1951
Charles Humez*	FR	1951-1952
Gilbert Lavoine	FR	1953-1954
Wally Thom	E	1954-1955
Idrissa Dione	FR	1955-1956
Emilio Marconi	ITA	1956-1958
Peter Waterman*	E	1958
Emilio Marconi	ITA	1958-1959
Duilio Loi*	ITA	1959-1963
Fortunato Manca*	ITA	1964-1965
Jean Josselin	FR	1966-1967
Carmelo Bossi	ITA	1967-1968
Fighting Mack	HOL	1968-1969
Silvano Bertini	ITA	1969
Jean Josselin	FR	1969
Johann Orsolics	AU	1969-1970
Ralph Charles	E	1970-1971
Roger Menetrey	FR	1971-1974
John H. Stracey*	E	1974-1975
Marco Scano	ITA	1976-1977
Jorgen Hansen	DEN	1977
Jorg Eipel	GER	1977
Alain Marion	FR	1977-1978
Jorgen Hansen	DEN	1978
Josef Pachler	AU	1978
Henry Rhiney	E	1978-1979
Dave Boy Green	E	1979
Jorgen Hansen*	DEN	1979-1981
Hans-Henrik Palm	DEN	1982
Colin Jones*	W	1982-1983
Gilles Elbilia	FR	1983-1984
Gianfranco Rosi	ITA	1984-1985
Lloyd Honeyghan*	E	1985-1986
Jose Varela	GER	1986-1987
Alfonso Redondo	SP	1987
Mauro Martelli*	SWI	1987-1988
Nino la Rocca	ITA	1989
Antoine Fernandez	FR	1989-1990
Kirkland Laing	E	1990
Patrizio Oliva*	ITA	1990-1992
Ludovic Proto	FR	1992-1993
Gary Jacobs*	S	1993-1994
Jose Luis Navarro	SP	1994-1995
Valery Kayumba	FR	1995
Patrick Charpentier*	FR	1995-1996
Andrei Pestriaev*	RUS	1997
Michele Piccirillo*	ITA	1997-1998
Maxim Nesterenko	RUS	1998-1999
Alessandro Duran	ITA	1999
Andrei Pestriaev	RUS	1999-2000
Alessandro Duran	ITA	2000
Thomas Damgaard	DEN	2000-2001
Alessandro Duran	ITA	2001-2002
Christian Bladt	DEN	2002
Michel Trabant*	GER	2002-2003
Frederic Klose	FR	2003-2005
Oktay Urkal*	GER	2005
Frederic Klose*	FR	2006
Jackson Osei Bonsu	BEL	2007-2008
Rafel Jackiewicz*	POL	2008-2009

L. Middleweight (154 lbs)

Title Holder	Birthplace/Domicile	Tenure
Bruno Visintin	ITA	1964-1966
Bo Hogberg	SWE	1966
Yolande Leveque	FR	1966
Sandro Mazzinghi*	ITA	1966-1968
Remo Golfarini	ITA	1968-1969
Gerhard Piaskowy	GER	1969-1970
Jose Hernandez	SP	1970-1972
Juan Carlos Duran	ITA	1972-1973
Jacques Kechichian	FR	1973-1974
Jose Duran	SP	1974-1975
Eckhard Dagge	GER	1975-1976
Vito Antuofermo	ITA	1976
Maurice Hope*	E	1976-1978
Gilbert Cohen	FR	1978-1979
Marijan Benes	YUG	1979-1981
Louis Acaries	FR	1981

Title Holder	Birthplace/Domicile	Tenure
Luigi Minchillo*	ITA	1981-1983
Herol Graham*	E	1983-1984
Jimmy Cable	E	1984
Georg Steinherr	GER	1984-1985
Said Skouma*	FR	1985-1986
Chris Pyatt	E	1986-1987
Gianfranco Rosi*	ITA	1987
Rene Jacquot*	FR	1988-1989
Edip Secovic	AU	1989
Giuseppe Leto	ITA	1989
Gilbert Dele*	FR	1989-1990
Said Skouma	FR	1991
Mourad Louati	HOL	1991
Jean-Claude Fontana	FR	1991-1992
Laurent Boudouani	FR	1992-1993
Bernard Razzano	FR	1993-1994
Javier Castillejos	SP	1994-1995
Laurent Boudouani*	FR	1995-1996
Faouzi Hattab	FR	1996
Davide Ciarlante*	ITA	1996-1997
Javier Castillejo*	SP	1998
Mamadou Thiam*	FR	1998-2000
Roman Karmazin*	RUS	2000
Mamadou Thiam*	FR	2001
Wayne Alexander*	E	2002
Roman Karmazin*	RUS	2003-2004
Sergei Dzindziruk*	UK	2004-2005
Michele Piccirillo*	ITA	2006-2007
Zaurbek Baysangurov*	RUS	2007-2008
Jamie Moore	E	2009-

Middleweight (160 lbs)

Title Holder	Birthplace/Domicile	Tenure
Georges Carpentier*	FR	1912-1918
Ercole Balzac	FR	1920-1921
Gus Platts	E	1921
Willem Westbroek	HOL	1921
Johnny Basham	W	1921
Ted Kid Lewis	E	1921-1923
Roland Todd	E	1923-1924
Ted Kid Lewis	E	1924-1925
Bruno Frattini	ITA	1924-1925
Tommy Milligan	S	1925-1928
Rene Devos	BEL	1926-1927
Barthelemy Molina	FR	1928
Alex Ireland	S	1928-1929
Mario Bosisio	ITA	1928
Leone Jacovacci	ITA	1928-1929
Len Johnson	E	1928-1929
Marcel Thil	FR	1929-1930
Mario Bosisio	ITA	1930-1931
Poldi Steinbach	AU	1931
Hein Domgoergen	GER	1931-1932
Ignacio Ara	SP	1932-1933
Gustave Roth	BEL	1933-1934
Marcel Thil*	FR	1934-1938
Edouard Tenet	FR	1938
Bep van Klaveren	HOL	1938
Anton Christoforidis	GRE	1938-1939
Edouard Tenet	FR	1939
Josef Besselmann*	GER	1942-1943
Marcel Cerdan	FR	1947-1948
Cyrille Delannoit	BEL	1948
Marcel Cerdan*	FR	1948
Cyrille Delannoit	BEL	1948-1949
Tiberio Mitri*	ITA	1949-1950
Randy Turpin	E	1951-1954
Tiberio Mitri	ITA	1954
Charles Humez	FR	1954-1958
Gustav Scholz*	GER	1958-1961
John Cowboy McCormack	S	1961-1962
Chris Christensen	DEN	1962
Laszlo Papp*	HUN	1962-1965
Nino Benvenuti*	ITA	1965-1967
Juan Carlos Duran	ITA	1967-1969
Tom Bogs	DEN	1969-1970
Juan Carlos Duran	ITA	1970-1971
Jean-Claude Bouttier	FR	1971-1972
Tom Bogs*	DEN	1973

EUROPEAN CHAMPIONS, 1909-2009

Title Holder	Birthplace/Domicile	Tenure
Elio Calcabrini	ITA	1973-1974
Jean-Claude Bouttier	FR	1974
Kevin Finnegan	E	1974-1975
Gratien Tonna*	FR	1975
Bunny Sterling	E	1976
Angelo Jacopucci	ITA	1976
Germano Valsecchi	ITA	1976-1977
Alan Minter	E	1977
Gratien Tonna	FR	1977-1978
Alan Minter*	E	1978-1979
Kevin Finnegan	E	1980
Matteo Salvemini	ITA	1980
Tony Sibson*	E	1980-1982
Louis Acaries	FR	1982-1984
Tony Sibson	E	1984-1985
Ayub Kalule	DEN	1985-1986
Herol Graham	E	1986-1987
Sumbu Kalambay*	ITA	1987
Pierre Joly	FR	1987-1988
Christophe Tiozzo*	FR	1988-1989
Francesco dell' Aquila	ITA	1989-1990
Sumbu Kalambay*	ITA	1990-1993
Agostino Cardamone*	ITA	1993-1994
Richie Woodhall*	E	1995-1996
Alexandre Zaitsev	RUS	1996
Hassine Cherifi*	FR	1996-1998
Agostino Cardamone*	ITA	1998
Erland Betare*	FR	1999-2000
Howard Eastman*	E	2001
Cristian Sanavia	ITA	2001-2002
Morrade Hakkar*	FR	2002
Howard Eastman*	E	2003-2004
Morrade Hakkar*	FR	2005
Sebastian Sylvester	GER	2005-2006
Amin Asikainen	FIN	2006-2007
Sebastian Sylvester*	GER	2007-2008
Khoren Gevor*	ARM	2008-2009

S. Middleweight (168 lbs)

Title Holder	Birthplace/Domicile	Tenure
Mauro Galvano*	ITA	1990-1991
James Cook	E	1991-1992
Franck Nicotra*	FR	1992
Vincenzo Nardiello	ITA	1992-1993
Ray Close*	NI	1993
Vinzenzo Nardiello	ITA	1993-1994
Frederic Seillier*	FR	1994-1995
Henry Wharton*	E	1995-1996
Frederic Seillier*	FR	1996
Andrei Shkalikov*	RUS	1997
Dean Francis*	E	1997-1998
Bruno Girard*	FR	1999
Andrei Shkalikov	RUS	2000-2001
Danilo Haeussler	GER	2001-2003
Mads Larsen*	DEN	2003-2004
Rudy Markussen*	DEN	2004-2005
Vitali Tsypko	UK	2005
Jackson Chanet	FR	2005-2006
Mger Mkrtchian	ARM	2006
David Gogoya	GEO	2006-2007
Cristian Sanavia	ITA	2007-2008
Karo Murat	GER	2008-

L. Heavyweight (175 lbs)

Title Holder	Birthplace/Domicile	Tenure
Georges Carpentier	FR	1913-1922
Battling Siki	FR	1922-1923
Emile Morelle	FR	1923
Raymond Bonnel	FR	1923-1924
Louis Clement	SWI	1924-1926
Herman van T'Hof	HOL	1926
Fernand Delarge	BEL	1926-1927
Max Schmeling*	GER	1927-1928
Michele Bonaglia*	ITA	1929-1930
Ernst Pistulla*	GER	1931-1932
Adolf Heuser*	GER	1932
John Andersson	SWE	1933
Martinez de Alfara	SP	1934
Marcel Thil	FR	1934-1935
Merlo Preciso	ITA	1935
Hein Lazek	AU	1935-1936

Title Holder	Birthplace/Domicile	Tenure
Gustave Roth	BEL	1936-1938
Adolf Heuser*	GER	1938-1939
Luigi Musina*	ITA	1942-1943
Freddie Mills*	E	1947-1950
Albert Yvel	FR	1950-1951
Don Cockell*	E	1951-1952
Conny Rux*	GER	1952
Jacques Hairabedian	FR	1953-1954
Gerhard Hecht	GER	1954-1955
Willi Hoepner	GER	1955
Gerhard Hecht	GER	1955-1957
Artemio Calzavara	ITA	1957-1958
Willi Hoepner	GER	1958
Erich Schoeppner	GER	1958-1962
Giulio Rinaldi	ITA	1962-1964
Gustav Scholz*	GER	1964-1965
Giulio Rinaldi	ITA	1965-1966
Piero del Papa	ITA	1966-1967
Lothar Stengel	GER	1967-1968
Tom Bogs*	DEN	1968-1969
Yvan Prebeg	YUG	1969-1970
Piero del Papa	ITA	1970-1971
Conny Velensek	GER	1971-1972
Chris Finnegan	E	1972
Rudiger Schmidtke	GER	1972-1973
John Conteh*	E	1973-1974
Domenico Adinolfi	ITA	1974-1976
Mate Parlov*	YUG	1976-1977
Aldo Traversaro	ITA	1977-1979
Rudi Koopmans	HOL	1979-1984
Richard Caramonolis	FR	1984
Alex Blanchard	HOL	1984-1987
Tom Collins	E	1987-1988
Pedro van Raamsdonk	HOL	1988
Jan Lefeber	HOL	1988-1989
Eric Nicoletta	FR	1989-1990
Tom Collins	E	1990-1991
Graciano Rocchigiani*	GER	1991-1992
Eddie Smulders	HOL	1993-1994
Fabrice Tiozzo*	FR	1994-1995
Eddy Smulders	HOL	1995-1996
Crawford Ashley	E	1997
Ole Klemetsen*	NOR	1997-1998
Crawford Ashley	E	1998-1999
Clinton Woods*	E	1999-2000
Yawe Davis	ITA	2001-2002
Thomas Ulrich*	GER	2002-2003
Stipe Drews*	CRO	2003-2004
Thomas Ulrich*	GER	2004-2005
Stipe Drews*	CRO	2006
Thomas Ulrich	GER	2007-2008
Yuri Barashian*	ARM	2008
Juergen Braehmer	GER	2009-

Cruiserweight (200 lbs)

Title Holder	Birthplace/Domicile	Tenure
Sam Reeson*	E	1987-1988
Angelo Rottoli	ITA	1989
Anaclet Wamba*	FR	1989-1990
Johnny Nelson*	E	1990-1992
Akim Tafer*	FR	1992-1993
Massimiliano Duran	ITA	1993-1994
Carl Thompson	E	1994
Alexander Gurov	UK	1995
Patrice Aouissi	FR	1995
Alexander Gurov*	UK	1995-1996
Akim Tafer*	FR	1996-1997
Johnny Nelson	E	1997-1998
Terry Dunstan*	E	1998
Alexei Iliin	RUS	1999
Torsten May*	GER	1999-2000
Carl Thompson*	E	2000-2001
Alexander Gurov*	UK	2001-2002
Pietro Aurino*	ITA	2002-2003
Vincenzo Cantatore	ITA	2004
Alexander Gurov	UK	2004-2005
David Haye*	E	2005-2007
Vincenzo Cantatore	ITA	2007
Johny Jensen	DEN	2007-2008

Title Holder	Birthplace/Domicile	Tenure
Jean-Marc Monrose	FR	2008
Marco Huck	YUG	2008-

Heavyweight (200 lbs +)

Title Holder	Birthplace/Domicile	Tenure
Georges Carpentier	FR	1913-1922
Battling Siki	FR	1922-1923
Erminio Spalla	ITA	1923-1926
Paolino Uzcudun	SP	1926-1928
Harry Persson	SWE	1926
Phil Scott	E	1927
Pierre Charles	BEL	1929-1931
Hein Muller	GER	1931-1932
Pierre Charles	BEL	1932-1933
Paolino Uzcudun	SP	1933
Primo Carnera	ITA	1933-1935
Pierre Charles	BEL	1935-1937
Arno Kolblin	GER	1937-1938
Hein Lazek	AU	1938-1939
Adolf Heuser	GER	1939
Max Schmeling*	GER	1939-1941
Olle Tandberg	SWE	1943
Karel Sys*	BEL	1943-1946
Bruce Woodcock	E	1946-1949
Joe Weidin	AU	1950-1951
Jack Gardner	E	1951
Hein Ten Hoff	GER	1951-1952
Karel Sys	BEL	1952
Heinz Neuhaus	GER	1952-1955
Franco Cavicchi	ITA	1955-1956
Ingemar Johansson*	SWE	1956-1959
Dick Richardson	W	1960-1962
Ingemar Johansson*	SWE	1962-1963
Henry Cooper*	E	1964
Karl Mildenberger	GER	1964-1968
Henry Cooper*	E	1968-1969
Peter Weiland	GER	1969-1970
Jose Urtain	SP	1970
Henry Cooper	E	1970-1971
Joe Bugner	E	1971
Jack Bodell	E	1971
Jose Urtain	SP	1971-1972
Jurgen Blin	GER	1972
Joe Bugner*	E	1972-1975
Richard Dunn	E	1976
Joe Bugner	E	1976-1977
Jean-Pierre Coopman	BEL	1977
Lucien Rodriguez	FR	1977
Alfredo Evangelista	SP	1977-1979
Lorenzo Zanon*	SP	1979-1980
John L. Gardner*	E	1980-1981
Lucien Rodriguez	FR	1981-1984
Steffen Tangstad	NOR	1984-1985
Anders Eklund	SWE	1985
Frank Bruno*	E	1985-1986
Steffen Tangstad	NOR	1986
Alfredo Evangelista	SP	1987
Anders Eklund	SWE	1987
Francesco Damiani	ITA	1987-1989
Derek Williams	E	1989-1990
Jean Chanet	FR	1990
Lennox Lewis*	E	1990-1992
Henry Akinwande*	E	1993-1995
Zeljko Mavrovic*	CRO	1995-1998
Vitali Klitschko*	UK	1998-1999
Vladimir Klitschko*	UK	1999-2000
Vitali Klitschko*	UK	2000-2001
Luan Krasniqi	GER	2002
Przemyslaw Saleta	POL	2002
Sinan Samil Sam	TU	2002-2004
Luan Krasniqi	GER	2004-2005
Paolo Vidoz	ITA	2005-2006
Vladimir Virchis*	UK	2006-2007
Sinan Samil Sam*	TU	2008
Matt Skelton	E	2008-2009

A-Z of Current World Champions

by Eric Armit

Shows the record since 1 July 2008, plus career summary and pen portrait, of all men holding IBF, WBA, WBC and WBO titles as at 30 June 2009. The author has also produced the same data for those who first won titles during that period but were no longer champions on 30 June 2009. World champions belonging to other bodies are shown if they are considered to be the best men at the weight, such as Manny Pacquiao. Incidentally, the place name given is the respective boxer's domicile and may not necessarily be his birthplace, while all nicknames are shown where applicable in brackets. Not included are British fighters, Nicky Cook (former WBO super-featherweight champion) and Carl Froch (WBC super-middleweight champion). Their full records can be found among the Active British-Based Boxers: Career Records section.

Arthur (King Arthur) Abraham

Berlin, Germany. *Born* Yerevan, Armenia, 20 February, 1980
IBF Middleweight Champion
Major Amateur Honours: Competed in the 2000 European Olympic qualifiers
Turned Pro: August 2003
Significant Results: Cristian Zanabria W CO 5, Nader Hamdan W RSC 12, Ian Gardner W PTS 12, Hector Velazco W CO 5, Howard Eastman W PTS 12, Kingsley Ikeke W CO 5, Shannon Taylor W PTS 12, Kofi Jantuah W PTS 12, Edison Miranda W PTS 12 and W RSC 4, Sebastien Demers W CO 3, Khoren Gevor W CO 11, Wayne Elcock W RSC 5, Elvin Ayala W CO 12
Type/Style: Slow starter, but a tough, strong and aggressive fighter
Points of Interest: 5' 10 " tall. Arthur's real name is Avetik Abrahamyan and although born in Armenia he received German citizenship in 2006. He is with the Sauerland Group, as is his brother Alex who boxes as a pro at light-middleweight. Has 24 wins by stoppage or kayo after winning his first 14 bouts inside the distance. Won the vacant IBF title by beating Kingsley Ikeke in December 2005 and has made 11 defences, being played into the ring by the Smurf Song from the TV programme, which featured a Father Abraham. Had to survive a fractured jaw when beating Edison Miranda in 2006, and their return fight in June 2008 was a catchweight contest that did not involve the IBF title
08.11.08 Raul Martinez W RTD 6 Bamberg
(IBF Middleweight Title Defence)
14.03.09 Lajuan Simon W PTS 12 Kiel
(IBF Middleweight Title Defence)
27.06.09 Mahir Oral W RSC 10 Berlin
(IBF Middleweight Title Defence)
Career: 30 contests, won 30.

Tomasz (Goral) Adamek

Zywiec, Poland. *Born* 1 December, 1976
IBF Cruiserweight Champion.
Former WBC L.Heavyweight Champion
Major Amateur Honours: Won bronze medals in the 1996 Copenhagen Cup, Acropolis Tournament and the 1998 European Championships
Turned Pro: March 1999
Significant Results: Rudi Lupo W PTS 10, Zdravko Kostic W PTS 10, Sergei Karanevich W PTS 10, Roberto Coelho W PTS 8, Jabrail Jabrailov W CO 5, Ismail Abdoul W PTS 8, Paul Briggs W PTS 12 (twice), Thomas Ulrich W CO 6, Chad Dawson L PTS 12, Luis Pineda W RSC 7, O'Neil Bell W RSC 8
Type/Style: An upright, tough battler with a good jab and a hard right-hand punch
Points of Interest: 6' 1½" tall. Turned pro in Manchester and had his first two fights in England. He has 25 wins by stoppage or kayo and suffered a broken nose whilst preparing to fight Paul Briggs for the vacant WBC light-heavyweight title in May 2005, but concealed it and then had it broken again during the fight. Made three defences of the WBC title before losing it to Chad Dawson in February 2007. Moved up to cruiserweight in 2008 and is now based in Newark, New Jersey
11.07.08 Gary Gomez W RTD 7 Chicago
11.12.08 Steve Cunningham W PTS 12 Newark
(IBF Cruiserweight Title Challenge)
27.02.09 Johnathon Banks W RSC 8 Newark
(IBF Cruiserweight Title Defence)
Career: 38 contests, won 37, lost 1.

Joseph (King Kong) Agbeko

Accra, Ghana. *Born* 22 March, 1980
IBF Bantamweight Champion.
Former Undefeated Commonwealth and African Boxing Union Bantamweight Champion
Major Amateur Honours: As the champion of Ghana in 1998, he competed in the Commonwealth Games in the same year
Turned Pro: December 1998
Significant Results: Johannes Maisa W PTS 12, Michael Kizza W RSC 2, Wladimir Sidorenko L PTS 12, Sumaila Badu W PTS 12, Luis Alberto Perez W RSC 7
Type/Style: Upright, orthodox fighter with a strong jab and a hard punch
Points of Interest: 5' 6" tall. Was inactive from October 2004, when he won the vacant Commonwealth bantamweight title, until March 2007, due to contractual problems. This is something that has marked his career and continues to do so, as he has made only one title defence since September 2007. Showed his potential in taking Wladimir Sidorenko to a majority verdict when losing to the future WBA super-bantamweight champion in Germany in 2004 and then won the IBF title by halting Luis Alberto Perez in September 2007. Having held on to his title with a majority verdict against William Gonzalez, he is now based in New York and has 22 wins inside the distance
11.12.08 William Gonzalez W PTS 12 Newark
(IBF Bantamweight Title Defence)
Career: 27 contests, won 26, lost 1.

Takahiro Aoh

Ichihara, Japan. *Born* 6 April, 1984
WBC Featherweight Champion
& Former Undefeated Japanese
Featherweight Champion
Major Amateur Honours: Six times
Japanese High Schools champion
with a record of 76 wins and three
losses
Turned Pro: September 2003
Significant Results: Richard Carrillo
W PTS 10, Francisco Dianzo W PTS
10, Hiroyuki Enoki DREW 12
Type/Style: Is a fast punching and
aggressive southpaw
Points of Interest: 5'6" tall with a 68
½" reach, he is managed by leading
Japanese fight figure, Akihiko Honda.
His first fight with Oscar Larios
resulted in a very hotly disputed split
decision win for Larios and the WBC
ordered a return. Only eight of his
wins have come by kayo or stoppage
16.10.08 Oscar Larios L PTS 12 Tokyo
    (WBC Featherweight Title Challenge)
12.03.09 Oscar Larios W PTS 12 Tokyo
    (WBC Featherweight Title Challenge)
Career: 19 contests, won 17, drew 1, lost 1.

Brahim Asloum

Bourgoin Jaillieu, France. *Born* 31
January, 1979
WBA L.Flyweight Champion.
Former Undefeated European and
French Flyweight Champion
Major Amateur Honours: Competed
in the 1997 European Junior
Championships held in Birmingham;
reached the quarter-finals of the
1999 World Championships, losing
to Brian Viloria; won a silver medal
in the 1999 French Championships;
won gold medals in the 2000 French
Championships and in the 2000
Acropolis Cup before taking the gold
medal in the 2000 Olympics at 106lbs,
beating Viloria in the early rounds
Turned Pro: January 2001
Significant Results: Zolile Mbityi W
PTS 8, Jose Lopez Bueno W PTS
12 & W PTS 12, Ivan Pozo W PTS
12, Alex Mahmutov W PTS 12,
Nohel Arambulet W PTS 12, Edgar
Velasquez W TD 8, Lorenzo Parra
L PTS 12, Jose Jimenez W PTS 12,
Omar Narvaez L PTS 12, Juan Carlos

Reveco W PTS 12
Type/Style: Busy, southpaw
combination puncher who often
switches to a right-handed stance
Points of Interest: 5' 5" tall. His
Olympic gold was the first won by
a Frenchman since 1936. Lost to
Lorenzo Parra in a challenge for the
WBA flyweight title in December
2005 and to Omar Narvaez for
the WBO flyweight title in March
2007, before moving down to
light-flyweight. Won the WBA title
by beating Juan Carlos Reveco
in December 2007, but has yet to
defend the title. His brother Redouane
competed in the 2004 Olympics and
is now unbeaten as a pro. Brahim has
ten wins by stoppage or kayo
27.04.09 Humberto Pool W CO 3 Le Cannet
Career: 26 contests, won 24, lost 2.

Karoly (Hitter) Balzsay

Kecskemet, Hungary. *Born* 23 July,
1979
WBO S.Middleweight Champion
Major Amateur Honours: A silver
medallist at the 1997 European Junior
Championships, he competed in the
1997 World Junior Championships,
the 1999 World Championships
and the 2000 Olympic Games
before winning a silver medal in
the 2002 European Championships.
He then competed in the 2003
World Championships and the 2004
Olympic Games, having won gold
medals in the 2000 Chemie Pokal,
2001 Acropolis, 2003 Bocskei Cup
and 2003 Green Hill Tournaments.
Seven times a Hungarian champion,
he claims 231 wins in 260 fights
Turned Pro: September 2004
Significant Results: Etienne Whitaker
W RSC 4, Soon Botes W CO 2,
Ruben Acosta W PTS 12
Type/Style: Tall, sharp, fast-punching
southpaw
Points of Interest: 6'0" tall. Now lives
in Germany and is part of the Klaus-
Peter Kohl's Universum-Spotlight
stable, as is Denis Inkin from whom
he won the WBO title. He has a
qualification in Sports Management
and his hobbies include sailing
and motor sports. Has 15 wins by

stoppage or kayo
05.07.08 Jose Alberto Clavero W CO 5 Halle
10.01.09 Denis Inkin W PTS 12 Magdeburg
    (WBO S.Middleweight Title
    Challenge)
25.04.09 Maselino Masoe W RSC 11 Krefeld
    (WBO S.Middleweight Title Defence)
Career: 21 contests, won 21.

Andre Berto

Miami, Florida, USA. *Born* 7
September, 1983
WBC Welterweight Champion
Major Amateur Honours: Won a
gold medal in the Police Athletic
League Championships, a silver
medal in the 2000 USA Junior
National Championships and a gold
medal in the 2001 National Golden
Gloves. In 2002 he won a gold
medal in the Police Athletic League
Championships, a silver medal in the
USA Championships, a bronze medal
in the USA Under-19 Championships
and represented the USA in the World
Cup. The following year saw him
winning a gold medal in the National
Golden Gloves, a silver medal in the
USA championships and a bronze
medal in the World Championships,
where he beat Darren Barker.
Although disqualified in the USA
Olympic trials, as he had dual USA
and Haitian citizenship he re-entered
the Olympic qualifiers representing
Haiti and won a berth in Athens by
finishing as runner-up in the Americas
qualifiers in Tijuana. Was eliminated
by France's Xavier Noel in the
Olympics
Turned Pro: December 2004
Significant Results: Sam Sparkman
W RSC 2, James Crayton W CO 5,
Miguel Figueroa W RSC 6, Norberto
Bravo W RSC 1, Cosme Rivera W
PTS 10, David Estrada W RSC 11,
Michael Trabant W RTD 6, Miguel
Angel Rodriguez W RSC 7
Type/Style: Has an excellent jab and
is a strong body puncher with fast
hands
Points of Interest: 5' 9" tall. Although
Andre was born in Miami, his parents
were both born in Haiti. His father,
who first took problem child Andre
to the gym at the age of ten, fought
in ultimate fighting contests, while a

brother is a State champion wrestler and one of his sisters also boxes. His loss in the Olympic trials was a disqualification for wrestling his opponent to the canvas. This decision was overturned by a committee, but re-instated by another committee. Although he represented Haiti in the Olympics, he had never set foot in the country before doing so. Won the WBC title by halting Miguel Angel Rodriguez in June 2008 and has made three defences. Has 19 wins by stoppage or kayo

27.09.08 Steve Forbes W PTS 12 Los Angeles
(WBC Welterweight Title Defence)
17.01.09 Luis Collazo W PTS 12 Biloxi
(WBC Welterweight Title Defence)
30.05.09 Juan Urango W PTS 12 Hollywood
(WBC Welterweight Title Defence)
Career: 25 contests, won 25.

Tim (Desert Storm) Bradley

Palm Springs, California, USA. *Born* 29 August, 1983
WBO L.Welterweight Champion. Former Undefeated WBC L.Welterweight Champion
Major Amateur Honours: Won a silver medal in the Police Athletic League Championships in 2000, took gold in 2001 and bronze in 2002. Was the 2001 United States Under-19 champion, won a bronze medal in the 2002 USA Championships and a silver medal in the 2002 National Golden Gloves
Turned Pro: August 2004
Significant Results: Francisco Rincon W PTS 10, Rafael Ortiz W RTD 2, Arturo Urena W RSC 3, Alfonso Sanchez W CO 1, Manuel Garnica W PTS 8, Donald Camarena W PTS 10, Junior Witter W PTS 12
Type/Style: Compact fighter with a busy, aggressive style, who is a good right hand puncher. Tends to wear down his opponents rather than kayo them. Has a good chin
Points of Interest: 5' 6" tall. The 'Desert Storm' nickname relates to his Palm Springs residency and not the military campaign of that name. He is jointly trained by his father, Tim, and Joel Diaz, a former IBF lightweight title challenger. The May 2008 title-winning fight with Junior Witter

was his first fight outside California. When the WBC ordered that the winner of his unification fight with Kendall Holt must decide which title they wish to retain, Tim relinquished the WBC title on 28 April. Has 11 wins by stoppage or kayo

13.09.08 Edner Cherry W PTS 12 Biloxi
(WBC L.Welterweight Title Defence)
04.04.09 Kendall Holt W PTS 12 Montreal
(WBC L.Welterweight Title Defence.
WBO L.Welterweight Title Challenge)
Career: 24 contests, won 24.

Tim Bradley   Philip Sharkey

Lucian (Le Tombeur) Bute

Galati, Romania. *Born* 28 February, 1980
IBF S. Middleweight Champion
Major Amateur Honours: Took a silver medal in the first European Cadets Championships in 1996, won bronze medals at both the 1998 World Junior Championships and 1999 World Senior Championships and competed in the 2003 World Championships. Earlier, he had won gold medals in the 2001 Francophone Games and the Ahmet Comert Tournament, but was eliminated in the quarter-finals of the 2002 European Championships by Karoly Balzsay
Turned Pro: November 2003
Significant Results: Dingaan Thobela W RSC 4, Jose Spearman W CO 8, Kabary Salem W RSC 8, Andre

Thysse W PTS 12, Lolenga Mock W PTS 12, James Obede Toney W RSC 8, Sergey Tatesvoyan W PTS 12, Sakio Bika W PTS 12, Alejandro Berrio W RSC 11, William Joppy W RSC 10
Type/Style: Stylish southpaw, who is a sound technician boxer with good hand and foot speed
Points of Interest: 6'2" tall, he is based in Montreal and has only fought back home in Romania once. Has also campaigned as a light-heavyweight, but has no problems with the super-middleweight limit. Won the IBF title by stopping Alejandro Berrio in October 2007 and has made three defences, but only the bell ending the fight saved him against Librado Andrade, when he was out on his feet and helpless. Has won 19 bouts by stoppage or kayo

24.10.08 Librado Andrade W PTS 12 Montreal
(IBF S.Middleweight Title Defence)
13.03.09 Fulgencio Zuniga W RSC 4 Montreal
(IBF S.Middleweight Title Defence)
Career: 24 contests, won 24.

Celestino (Pelenchin) Caballero

Colon, Panama. *Born* 21 June, 1976
WBA & IBF S.Bantamweight Champion
Major Amateur Honours: None known
Turned Pro: November 1998
Significant Results: Jose Rojas L CO 3, Giovanni Andrade W DIS 10, Ricardo Cordoba L PTS 12, Daniel Ponce de Leon W PTS 12, Yober Ortega W PTS 12, Roberto Bonilla W RSC 7, Somsak Sithchatchawal W RSC 3, Ricardo Castillo W DIS 9, Jorge Lacierva W PTS 12, Mauricio Pastrana W RSC 8, Lorenzo Parra W RSC 12
Type/Style: Is a tall, rangy southpaw
Points of Interest: He is 5'11" tall and is also known as 'The Towering Inferno'. Wanted to be a footballer, but took up boxing instead for financial reasons and started boxing at the age of 14. First won the interim WBA title by beating Yober Ortega in October 2005 and became the full champion with his crushing victory over Somsak Sithchatchawal in

Thailand in October 2006. Promoted by Sycuan Ringside promotions, a native American promotions group, he has 22 wins by stoppage or kayo. His title-winning fight with Somsak Sithchatchawal was staged at an ancient Temple and has since defended his title seven times, including the victory over Steve Molitor which also gave him the IBF title. Weight making problems are catching up with him and he looked lucky to retain his titles against Jeffrey Mathebula on a split decision.Celestino is trained by Francisco Arroyo, who had fights in England in 1988, 1990 and 1991

18.09.08 Elvis Mejia W RSC 1 Panama City
(WBA S.Bantamweight Title Defence)
21.11.08 Steve Molitor W RSC 4 Orillia
(WBA S.Bantamweight Title Defence. IBF S.Bantamweight Title Challenge)
30.04.09 Jeffrey Mathebula W PTS 12 Panama City
(WBA & IBF S.Bantamweight Title Defences)
Career: 34 contests, won 32, lost 2.

Ivan (Iron Boy) Calderon

Guaynabo, Puerto Rico. *Born* 7 January, 1975
WBO L.Flyweight Champion.
Former Undefeated WBO
M.Flyweight Champion
Major Amateur Honours: A bronze medallist in the 1999 Pan-American Games, he competed in the World Championships that year and won a silver medal in the 1999 Central American Games before being selected for the 2000 Olympic Games. Claims 110 wins in 130 bouts
Turned Pro: February 2001
Significant Results: Eduardo Marquez W TD 9, Lorenzo Trejo W PTS 12, Alex Sanchez W PTS 12, Edgar Cardenas W CO 11, Roberto Leyva W PTS 12, Carlos Fajardo W PTS 12, Noel Tunacao W RSC 8, Gerard Verde W PTS 12, Daniel Reyes W PTS 12, Isaac Bustos W PTS 12, Miguel Tellez W RSC 9, Jose Luis Valera W PTS 12, Ronald Barrera W PTS 12, Hugo Cazares W PTS 12, Juan Esquer W PTS 12, Nelson Dieppa W PTS 12

Type/Style: Southpaw. Although an excellent technical boxer and good counter-puncher, he lacks power
Points of Interest: 5' 0" tall. Won the WBO mini-flyweight title with a technical verdict over Eduardo Marquez in May 2003 and made 11 defences before moving up to win the light-flyweight title by beating Hugo Cazares in August 2007. He has defended the title four times. An extrovert who is tremendously popular in Puerto Rico, being voted 'Boxer of the Year' there in 2002, he has only six wins by stoppage or kayo. Revenged an amateur defeat when beating Jose Luis Varela. Head clashes abound in his fights, with Ivan always being the one cut, which is why there have been four technical decisions in his contests

30.08.08 Hugo Cazares W TD 7 Bayamon
(WBO L.Flyweight Title Defence)
13.06.09 Rodel Mayol TECH DRAW 6 New York City
(WBO L.Flyweight Title Defence)
Career: 33 contests won 32, drew 1.

Gabriel (Chico Guapo) Campillo

Madrid, Spain. *Born* 19 December, 1978
WBA L.Heavyweight Champion.
Former Undefeated Spanish
L.Heavyweight Champion
Major Amateur Honours: Won the Spanish Championship at 81kgs in 2002
Turned Pro: February 2002
Significant Results: Juan Nelongo Perez W PTS 10 & W RSC 5, Vyacheslav Uzelkov L CO 6
Type/Style: Tall, tough southpaw with an excellent jab
Points of Interest: 6'2" tall. He is the 13th Spanish fighter to win a version of a world title. Moved down to super-middleweight to challenge Karo Murat for the European title and stayed there to win the European Union crown by beating Lolenga Mock. Has only six wins inside the distance

20.09.08 Karo Murat L PTS 12 Bielefeld
(EBU S Middleweight Title Challenge)
08.03.09 Lolenga Mock W PTS 12 Kokkedal
20.06.09 Hugo Garay W PTS 12 Sunchales
(WBA L.Heavyweight Title Challenge)
Career: 20 contests, won 18, lost 2.

Joshua (Grand Master) Clottey

Accra, Ghana. *Born* 16 March, 1977
Former Undefeated IBF
Welterweight Champion.
Former Undefeated Ghanaian
L.Welterweight and African Boxing Union Welterweight Champion
Major Amateur Honours: Competed in the 1994 Commonwealth Games
Turned Pro: March 1995
Significant Results Sam Akromah W PTS 8, Mark Ramsey W PTS 8, Carlos Baldomir L DIS 11, Steve Martinez NC 2, Richard Gutierrez W PTS 12, Antonio Margarito L PTS 12, Diego Corrales W PTS 10, Shamone Alvarez W PTS 12, Jose Luis Cruz W RSC 5
Type/Style: Strong, tough with an excellent jab, plenty of stamina and a good chin
Points of Interest: 5'8" tall with a 70" reach. Although based in Britain in the late 1990s, he is now based in New York. Failed in a challenge for the WBO title in 2006, being outpointed by Antonio Margarito. He was stripped of the IBF title after signing to fight Miguel Cotto for the WBO title, then climbed off the floor in the first round to take Cotto to a disputed split decision. Has 20 wins by stoppage or kayo

02.08.08 Zab Judah W TD 9 Las Vegas
(Vacant IBF Welterweight Title)
13.06.09 Miguel Cotto L PTS 12 New York City
(WBO Welterweight Title Challenge)
Career: 39 contests, won 35, lost 3, no contest 1.

Miguel Cotto

Caguas, Puerto Rico. *Born* 29 October, 1980
WBO Welterweight Champion.
Former WBA Welterweight
Champion & Former Undefeated
WBO L.Welterweight Champion
Major Amateur Honours: Won a gold medal in the 1997 Pan-American Championships, a bronze medal in the 1997 Central American Games, silver medals in the 1997 and 1998 World Junior Championships, won silver medals in the Pan-American Cadet Championships and the Central American Games in 1998, but competed without success in both the

World Championships and the Pan-American Games in 1999. After being eliminated by Mohamed Abdulaev in the 2000 Olympics, he won a gold medal in the 2000 Central American Games

Turned Pro: February 2001

Significant Results: Justin Juuko W RSC 5, John Brown W PTS 10, Cesar Bazan W RSC 11, Joel Perez W CO 4, Demetrio Ceballos W RSC 7, Charles Maussa W RSC 8, Victoriano Sosa W RSC 4, Lovemore Ndou W PTS 12, Kelson Pinto W RSC 6, Randall Bailey W RSC 6, DeMarcus Corley W RSC 5, Mohamad Abdulaev W RSC 9, Ricardo Torres W CO 7, Gianluca Branco W RSC 8, Paulie Malignaggi W PTS 12, Carlos Quintana W RTD 5, Oktay Urkal W RSC 11, Zab Judah W RSC 11, Shane Mosley W PTS 12, Alfonso Gomez W RTD 5

Type/Style: Miguel is a classy hard-hitting box puncher with an exciting style, but lacking sound defensive qualities

Points of Interest: 5'8" tall with a 67" reach. His father, uncle and cousin all boxed and his brother, Jose Miguel Cotto, lost to Juan Diaz in a fight for the IBF lightweight title in April 2006. Was trained by his uncle Evangelista, but a gym brawl between the two ended the relationship in April this year. Won the WBO light-welterweight title in September 2004 by beating Kelson Pinto and made six title defences before moving up to win the WBA welterweight title. Lost the title in his fifth defence, being stopped by Antonio Margarito. He went on to win the vacant WBO crown by beating Michael Jennings and had to overcome a bad cut to retain the title on a split decision against Joshua Clottey. Miguel has 27 wins inside the distance

26.07.08 Antonio Margarito L RSC 11 Las Vegas
(WBA Welterweight Title Defence)
21.02.09 Michael Jennings W RSC 5 New York City
(Vacant WBO Welterweight Title)
13.06.09 Joshua Clottey W PTS 12 New York City
(WBO Welterweight Title Defence)
Career: 35 contests, won 34, lost 1.

Cristobal (Lacandon) Cruz

Chiapas, Mexico. *Born* 19 May, 1977
IBF Featherweight Champion

Major Amateur Honours: None known

Turned Pro: January 1992

Significant Results: Francisco Dianzo W RSC 11 & W RSC 6, Martin Honorio L CO 1, Heriberto Ruiz L PTS 10, Jorge Solis L PTS 10, Juan Ruiz L PTS 12, Cornelius Lock W RSC 8, Luisito Espinosa W CO 3, Steve Luevano L PTS 12, Francisco Lorenzo L PTS 8 & L PTS 12, Zahir Raheem L PTS 10, Thomas Mashaba W PTS 12

Type/Style: Aggressive, tough infighter who takes a punch well and wears his opponents down with his body attacks and high work rate

Points of Interest: 5'7" tall with a 68" reach. Turned pro at the age of 14. nicknamed 'Lacandon' which means 'strong Indian'. Was looked upon as just a tough, durable journeymen until he beat Thomas Mashaba for the IBO title in March 2008, a fight that earned him a shot at the vacant IBF title. Has 23 wins by stoppage or kayo and has only failed to last the distance twice in 51 fights

23.10.08 Orlando Salido W PTS 12 Airways Heights
(Vacant IBF Featherweight Title)
14.02.09 Cyril Thomas W PTS 12 St Quentin
(IBF Featherweight Title Defence)
Career: 51 contests, won 38, drew 1, lost 11, no contest 1.

Vic (Raging Bull) Darchinyan

Australia. *Born* Vanadvor, Armenia, 7 January, 1976
IBF, WBA & WBC S.Flyweight Champion. Former IBF Flyweight Champion. Former Undefeated Australian Flyweight Champion

Major Amateur Honours: Competed in the 1997 World Championships, won a bronze medal in the 1998 European Championships and was selected for the 2000 European Championships. Was a quarter-finalist in the 2000 Olympics

Turned Pro: November 2000

Significant Results: Raul Medina W TD 8, Wandee Chor Chareon W CO 4 & W CO 5, Alejandro Montiel W PTS 10, Irene Pacheco W RSC 11, Mzukisi Sikali W RSC 8, Jair Jimenez W RSC 5, Diosdado Gabi W RSC 8, Luis Maldonado W RSC 8, Glenn Donaire W TD 6, Victor Burgos W RSC 12, Nonito Donaire L RSC 5, Z Gorres DREW 12

Type/Style: A strong, aggressive southpaw, who is a good boxer with a hard punch in both hands

Points of Interest: 5'5" tall. His real christian name is Vakhtang, and he stayed and settled in Australia after representing Armenia in the Sydney Olympics. Originally trained by Jeff Fenech, but now by Billy Hussein, he won the Australian flyweight title in only his seventh fight and the IBF title in December 2004 when stopping the previously unbeaten Irene Pacheco, going on to make seven defences. Lost the title to Nonito Donaire in July 2007, after which he moved up to super-flyweight. Has stopped or kayoed 26 opponents

02.08.08 Dimitri Kirilov W CO 5 Tacoma
(IBF S.Flyweight Title Challenge)
01.11.08 Cristian Mijares W CO 9 Los Angeles
(IBF S.Flyweight Title Defence. WBA & WBC S.Flyweight Title Challenges)
07.02.09 Jorge Arce W RTD 11 Anaheim
(IBF, WBA & WBC S.Flyweight Title Defences)
Career: 34 contests, won 32, drew 1, lost 1.

Chad (Bad) Dawson

Hartsville, South Carolina, USA.
Born 13 July, 1982
Former Undefeated IBF, IBO & WBC L.Heavyweight Champion.

Major Amateur Honours: Finished as runner up in the 1998 United States Junior Championships, collected a bronze medal in the 2000 World Junior Championships and took the gold medal in the United States Under-19 Championships. Claims a 67-13 amateur record

Turned Pro: August 2001

Significant Results: Brett Lally W RSC 4, Darnell Wilson W PTS 10, Carl Daniels W RTD 7, Ian Gardner W RSC 11, Eric Harding W PTS 12, Tomasz Adamek W PTS 12, Jesus Ruiz W RSC 6, Epifanio Mendoza W RSC 4, Glen Johnson W PTS 12

Type/Style: Tall southpaw who has a

fast, hard jab and a big right cross
Points of Interest: 6'3" tall. He has four brothers and two sisters. Chad's father was a pro boxer back in the 1980s, winning only one of his six bouts, and Chad started boxing at the age of 11. He works as a volunteer at the local YMCA and brings his son into the ring before and after each fight. Has 17 wins by stoppage or kayo, but had to climb off the floor to beat Tomasz Adamek for the WBC title in February 2007. Made three title defences and was then stripped of the title for preferring to fight Antonio Tarver for the IBF title. Relinquished the IBF title in May to move down to super-middleweight
11.10.08 Antonio Tarver W PTS 12 Las Vegas
(IBF L.Heavyweight Title Challenge)
09.05.09 Antonio Tarver W PTS 12 Las Vegas
(IBF L.Heavyweight Title Defence)
Career: 29 contests, won 28, no contest 1.

Adrian (The Shark) Diaconu
Ploesti-Prahova, Romania. *Born* 9 June, 1978
Former WBC L.Heavyweight Champion. Former Undefeated Canadian L.Heavyweight Champion
Major Amateur Honours: A bronze medallist in both the 1997 World Junior Championships and the 1998 European Championships, he won a silver medal in the 1999 World Championships and was a quarter-finalist in the 2000 Olympics
Turned Pro: March 2001
Significant Results: Roberto Coehlo W PTS 10, Max Hyman W RSC 4, Andre Thysse W PTS 12, Rico Hoye W RSC 3, Chris Henry W PTS 12
Type/Style: Methodical, strong and rugged with a heavy punch, but with questionable stamina
Points of Interest: 5' 9" tall. As an amateur he beat Carl Froch in England. Turned pro in Canada and has only fought in Romania twice. Won the WBC 'interim' title in April 2008 when beating Chris Henry and was recognized as full champion in July 2008 after Chad Dawson was stripped of the title. Has 15 wins inside the distance.
04.04 09 David Whittom W PTS 8 Montreal

19.06.09 Jean Pascal L PTS 12 Montreal
(WBC L.Heavyweight Title Defence)
Career: 27 contests, won 26, lost 1.

Nonito (The Filipino Flash) Donaire
Talibon, Philippines. *Born* 16 November, 1982
IBF Flyweight Champion
Major Amateur Honours: Won gold medals in the 1998 USA National Silver Gloves, in both the 1999 and 2000 USA Junior Olympics at 106lbs and in the USA Championships in 2000. There he lost to Brian Viloria, as did his brother Glenn, before being beaten by Karoz Norman in the Olympic trials. He claims a 68-8 amateur record
Turned Pro: February 2001
Significant Results: Rosendo Sanchez L PTS 5, Kaichon Sorvorapin W CO 2, Paulino Villalobos W RSC 6, Ildo Julio W PTS 8, Oscar Andrade W PTS 12, Vic Darchinyan W RSC 5, Luis Maldonado W RSC 8
Type/Style: Sharp, fast boxer who has a dangerous left hook, but hits hard with both hands
Points of Interest: 5' 7" tall. Trained by his father, his elder brother Glenn was also a successful amateur and is a world-rated flyweight. In addition, two of Nonito's cousins work his corner and his girlfriend is a martial arts expert. Brother Glenn lost on a technical decision to Vic Darchinyan for the IBF flyweight title in October 2006, while Nonito's win over Darchinyan in July 2007 for the IBF title was a massive upset. He has made three defences and has 12 wins inside the distance
01.11.08 Moruti Mthalane W RSC 6 Las Vegas
(IBF Flyweight Title Defence)
19.04.09 Raul Martinez W RSC 4 Quezon City
(IBF Flyweight Title Defence)
Career: 22 contests, won 21, lost 1.

Sergei (Razor) Dzindziruk
Nozewska, Ukraine. *Born* 1 March, 1976
WBO L.Middleweight Champion. Former Undefeated European L.Middleweight Champion
Major Amateur Honours: Competed in the 1993 European, 1994 World

Junior Championships and the 1996 Olympics. Won a bronze medal in the 1996 European Championships, silver medals in the 1997 World Championships and 1998 European Championships, and competed in the 1998 Goodwill Games. He claims 195 wins in 220 fights
Turned Pro: February 1999
Significant Results: Ariel Chavez W RSC 7, Andrei Pestriaev W RSC 5, Mamadou Thiam W RTD 3, Hussein Bayram W CO 11, Jimmy Colas W PTS 12, Daniel Santos W PTS 12, Sebastian Lujan W PTS 12, Alisultan Nadirbegov W PTS 12, Carlos Nascimento W RSC 11, Lukas Konecny W PTS 12
Type/Style: Tall, lean southpaw who is a good boxer with a hard right hook
Points of Interest: 6'0" tall. He started boxing in 1985 and is based in Germany but three of his first four pro fights were in Britain. However, his first fight in Poland was not sanctioned by the Polish federation and so is not included on the record given below. He won the European title by beating Mamadou Thiam in July 2004 and made two defences. Won the WBO title in December 2005 when beating Daniel Santos. Has 22 wins inside the distance and has made just five defences in 42 months
01.11.08 Joel Julio W PTS 12 Oberhausen
(WBO L.Middleweight Title Defence)
Career: 35 contests, won 35.

Zsolt (Firebird) Erdei
Budapest, Hungary. *Born* 31 May, 1974
WBO L.Heavyweight Champion
Major Amateur Honours: Won a gold medal at the 1992 European Junior Championship, before competing in the 1995 World Championships and 1996 Olympics. Having won a silver medal in the 1996 European Championships, he picked up gold in the 1997 World Championships and the 1998 and 2000 European Championships. He followed that up with a bronze medal in the 2000 Olympics
Turned Pro: December 2000
Significant Results: Jim Murray W

CO 5, Juan Carlos Gimenez W RSC 8, Massimiliano Saiani W RSC 7, Julio Gonzalez W PTS 12, Hugo Garay W PTS 12 & W PTS 12, Alejandro Lakatus W PTS 12, Mehdi Sahnoune W RSC 12, Paul Murdoch W RSC 10, Thomas Ulrich W PTS 12, Danny Santiago W RSC 8, Tito Mendoza W PTS 12, DeAndre Abron W PTS 12

Type/Style: He is a clever, technical craftsman with a strong, accurate jab, but despite having 17 wins inside the distance he is not a puncher

Points of Interest: 5' 10" tall with a 72" reach. Floored twice in early fights, he is based in Germany and in beating Julio Gonzalez in January 2004 he brought the WBO title back to his stable after fellow Universum fighter, Dariusz Michalczewski, had lost it to the same fighter. Has 17 wins inside the distance and has made 13 defences, although the opposition has generally been mediocre. Yuri Barashian failed to make the weight for his challenge, but Zsolt could have lost the title if he had been beaten

10.01.09 Yuri Barashian W PTS 12 Magdeburg
Career: 30 contests, won 30.

Vernon (The Viper) Forrest

Augusta, Georgia, USA. *Born* 21 February, 1971
Former Undefeated WBC L.Middleweight Champion.
Former WBC Welterweight Champion. Former Undefeated IBF Welterweight Champion

Major Amateur Honours: Was a silver medallist in the 1991 World Championships, losing to Kostya Tszyu in the final. A year later he beat Shane Mosley and Steve Johnston in the USA Olympic trials and then competed in the 1992 Olympics, where he was eliminated by Britain's Peter Richardson

Turned pro: November 1992

Significant Results: Adrian Stone W RSC 11, Steve Martinez W RSC 1, Santiago Samaniego W CO 7, Vince Phillips W PTS 12, Raul Frank NC 3 and W PTS 12, Shane Mosley W PTS 12, Ricardo Mayorga L RSC 3 & L PTS 12, Ike Quartey W PTS 10,

Carlos Baldomir W PTS 12, Michele Piccirillo W RSC 11, Sergio Mora L PTS 12

Type/Style: Tall, quick boxer with a long reach and a strong jab

Points of Interest: 6' 0" tall. Attended College under a boxing scholarship. His first fight with Raul Frank in May 2001 for the vacant IBF welterweight title was declared a no-contest when Frank was cut. Won the vacant IBF crown by outpointing Frank in return in May 2001, but relinquished the title to challenge Shane Mosley successfully for the WBC title in July 2002. Lost the WBC title in a unification bout against the WBA champion, Ricardo Mayorga, in January 2003 and failed in a challenge for the same titles against Mayorga in July 2003. Moved up and won the WBC light-middleweight title when beating Carlos Baldomir for the vacant crown in July 2007, but lost the title to Sergio Mora in his second defence in June 2008. Regained the title from Mora, but was stripped of the WBC title in May due to ongoing injury problems. Has 29 wins by stoppage or knockout. Stop Press: Was murdered on 26 July (see Obituaries)

13.09.08 Sergio Mora W PTS 12 Las Vegas
(WBC L.Middleweight Title Challenge)

Career: 45 contests, won 41, lost 3, no contest 1.

Giacobbe Fragomeni

Milan, Italy. *Born* 13 August, 1969
WBC Cruiserweight Champion.
Former Undefeated European Cruiserweight Champion

Major Amateur Honours: Won a bronze medal in the 1997 World Championships, before collecting silver in the 1998 World Cup and gold in the 1998 European Championships. Was a quarter-finalist in the 1999 World Championships, going on to compete in the 2000 Olympics before turning pro

Turned Pro: May 2001

Significant Results: Ismail Abdoul W PTS 8, Frederic Serrat W PTS 12, Daniel Bispo W PTS 12, David Haye L RSC 9, Vincenzo Rossitto W PTS 12, Rachid Hadak W PTS 12

Type/Style: Solidly built, rugged pressure fighter who likes to work inside. Has a good chin and plenty of guts

Points of Interest: 5'9½" tall. Lost in the quarter-finals of the 1997 World Championships to Ruslan Chagaev, but was upgraded to bronze medalist when Chagaev was disqualified for having fought as a professional. Lost to Kevin Evans in the 1999 World Championships, but beat David Haye in the 2000 Olympic qualifiers. From one of Milan's roughest areas, he had

Giacobbe Fragomeni   Philip Sharkey

a tough background, including a fight against drugs and did not turn pro until he was 31. Trained by former world champion, Patrizio Oliva, he had to climb off the floor to retain his title against Krzysztof Wlodarczyk. Has ten wins inside the distance

24.10.08 Rudolf Kraj W T D 8 Milan
(Vacant WBC Cruiserweight Title)
16.05.09 Krzysztof Wlodarczyk DREW 12 Rome
(WBC Cruiserweight Title Defence)
Career: 28 contests, won 26, drew 1, lost 1.

Hugo (Pigu) Garay

Tigre, Argentina. *Born* 27 November, 1980
Former WBA L.Heavyweight Champion. Former Undefeated South American & Argentinian L.Heavyweight Champion
Major Amateur Honours: An Argentinian Junior and Senior Championship winner, he won a silver medal at the 1998 World Junior Championships and followed it up with a bronze medal at the 1999 Pan-American Games. He also competed in the 2000 Olympics
Turned Pro: July 2001
Significant Results: Hector Sotelo W PTS 8 & W RSC 1, Alejandro Lakatus W RSC 12, Zsolt Erdei L PTS 12 & L PTS 12
Type/Style: Strong if crude, with a tough chin, a dangerous left uppercut and excellent stamina
Points of Interest: 6' 0" tall. Had to climb off the floor twice before stopping Alejandro Lakatus. The fights with Zsolt Erdei were challenges for the WBO light-heavyweight title, with the first being a majority verdict and the second a split decision. With 17 wins by stoppage or kayo, seven in the first round, the loss to Gabriel Campillo was a huge upset

03.07.08 Yuri Barashian W PTS 12 Buenos Aires
(Vacant WBA L.Heavyweight Title)
22.11.08 Juergen Braehmer W PTS 12 Rostock
(WBA L.Heavyweight Title Defence)
20.06.09 Gabriel Campillo L PTS 12 Sunchales
(WBA L.Heavyweight Title Defence)
Career: 36 contests, won 33, lost 3.

Raul (Rayito) Garcia

La Paz, Mexico. *Born* 10 September, 1982
IBF M.Flyweight Champion. Former Undefeated Mexican M.Flyweight Champion
Major Amateur Honours: None known
Turned Pro: July 2004
Significant Results: Jesus Iribe W RSC 8, Sammy Gutierrez DREW 12 & W PTS 12, Ronald Barrera W PTS 12, Florante Condes W PTS 12
Type/Style: Southpaw. Is a good, classy, stylish boxer who is a sharp puncher
Points of Interest: Is the first boxer from Baja California to win a world title and has never boxed outside of the Mexican State. He is one of five children and is a keen fisherman. Started boxing when he was 17 and won the Mexican title in June 2007, beating Sammy Gutierrez, but made only one defence before winning the IBF title in June 2008 when climbing off the floor to outpoint Florante Condes. Has made three defences and has 16 wins by stoppage or kayo

13.09.08 Jose Luis Varela W PTS 12 La Paz
(IBF M.Flyweight Title Defence)
13.12.08 Jose Luis Varela W PTS 12 Loreto
(IBF M.Flyweight Title Defence)
11.04.09 Ronald Barrera W RSC 6 La Paz
(IBF M.Flyweight Title Defence)
Career: 27 contests, won 26, drew 1.

Roman (Little Chocolate) Gonzalez

Managua, Nicaragua. *Born* 17 June, 1987
WBA M.Flyweight Champion
Major Amateur Honours: Won a gold medal in the 2004 Central American Championships and claims 74 wins in 75 fights
Turned Pro: July 2005
Significant Results: Vicente Hernandez W RSC 2, Jose Luis Varela W RSC 1, Eriberto Gejon W CO 1, Hiroshi Matsumoto W PTS 10, Javier Murillo W PTS 10
Type/Style: Is fast-handed and hard punching with a wicked body attack
Points of Interest: 5' 3" tall. Also nicknamed 'The Explosive Thin Man' in honour of Alexis Arguello. Started boxing as a kid to win food baskets as prizes as sometimes the family could only afford to eat once a day. Signed up by Japanese promoter, Akihiko Honda. Won his first 16 bouts by stoppage or kayo and has 20 wins inside the distance, but only beat Francisco Rosas on a majority decision

12.07.08 Abraham Irias W RSC 2 Managua
15.09.08 Yutaka Niida W RSC 4 Yokohama
(WBA M.Flyweight Title Challenge)
13.12.08 Miguel Tellez W RTD 3 Managua
28.02.09 Francisco Rosas W PTS 12 Oaxaca
(WBA M.Flyweight Title Defence)
Career: 23 contests, won 23.

Hozumi Hasegawa

Nishiwaki City, Japan. *Born* 16 December, 1980
WBC Bantamweight Champion
Major Amateur Honours: None known
Turned Pro: November 1999
Significant Results: Jess Maca W PTS 12, Gunao Uno W PTS 12, Alvin Felisilda W CO 10, Jun Toriumi W PTS 10, Veerapol Sahaprom W PTS 12 & W PTS 12, Gerard Martinez W RSC 7, Genaro Garcia W PTS 12, Simpiwe Vetyeka W PTS 12, Simone Maludrotto W PTS 12, Cristian Faccio W RSC 2
Type/Style: Is a tall, fast and stylish southpaw who utilises a counter-punching style
Points of Interest: 5'6" tall. With only ten wins inside the distance, he was once known as the 'Japanese Pernell Whittaker' due to his boxing skills. Lost two of his first five fights, but is now unbeaten in 23 bouts. Veerapol had not tasted defeat in his last 45 fights before Hozumi beat him for the WBC title in April 2005. Has since made eight defences

16.10.08 Alejandro Valdez W RSC 2 Tokyo
(WBC Bantamweight Title Defence)
12.03.09 Vusi Malinga W RSC 1 Kobe
(WBC Bantamweight Title Defence)
Career: 28 contests, won 26, lost 2.

Kendall (Rated R) Holt

Patterson, New Jersey, USA. *Born* 14 June, 1981
Former WBO L.Welterweight Champion
Major Amateur Honours: A quarter-finalist in the 1999 National Golden

Gloves, prior to winning the bronze medal a year later, he also competed in the 2000 Eastern Olympic trials
Turned Pro: March 2001
Significant Results: David Diaz W RSC 8, Isaac Hlatshwayo W PTS 12, Mike Aranoutis W PTS 12, Ricardo Torres L RSC 11
Type/Style: A fast-handed, hard puncher, who is slick and versatile, but has also been on the floor a few times.
Points of Interest: 5' 9" tall with a 74" reach. In April 2009 Kendall pleaded guilty to a charge of money laundering arising from drug deals made by his manager. He admitted that on several occasions he collected bags of money and delivered them to his manager and is currently in a pre-trial intervention programme which may allow him to avoid imprisonment. Lost on a very controversial stoppage to Ricardo Torres for the WBO title in 2007, but climbed off the floor twice when kayoing Torres in just 61 seconds in a return match. Has 13 wins inside the distance

05.07.08 Ricardo Torres W CO 1 Las Vegas
(WBO L.Welterweight Title Challenge)
13.12.08 Demetrius Hopkins W PTS 12 Atlantic City
(WBO L.Welterweight Title Defence)
04.04.09 Tim Bradley L PTS 12 Montreal
(WBO L.Welterweight Title Defence.
WBC L.Welterweight Title Challenge)
Career: 28 contests, won 25, lost 3.

Denis (Technician) Inkin

Novosibirsk, Russia. *Born* 7 January, 1978
WBO S.Middleweight Champion
Major Amateur Honours: Won the Russian Cadet Championship (1994) and Junior Championship (1996), prior to winning a gold medal in the 1994 European Cadet Championships. He then competed in the 1997 Ali Cup, losing to Jeff Lacy, and was a quarter-finalist in the 1997 World Junior Championships. Having won gold medals in the 1997 and 1999 World Military Championships, he won a gold medal in the 1998 Felix Stamm Tournament and competed in the 1998 Goodwill Games
Turned Pro: June 2001

Significant Results: Yuri Tsarenko W PTS 8, Ovill McKenzie W PTS 8, Julio Cesar Vasquez W RTD 7, Peter Mashamite W PTS 10, Konni Konrad W PTS 8, Mario Veit W CO 7, Joszef Nagy W RSC 5, Martin Bruer W PTS 12
Type/Style: 5' 11½" tall. Is a crafty, tactically astute fighter with an excellent jab
Points of Interest: Starting boxing at the age of ten, he is a former tank captain in the Russian army. Originally turned pro in Russia, but then signed for Universum Box-Promotion in 2005 and relocated to Germany. Injury twice forced him to pull out of WBC eliminators against Carl Froch. Has 24 wins inside the distance

24.07.08 Sergey Beloshapkin W PTS 6 Ekaterinburg
27.09.08 Fulgencio Zuniga W PTS 12 Hamburg
(Vacant WBO S.Middleweight Title)
10.01.09 Karoly Balzsay L PTS 12 Magdeburg
(WBO S.Middleweight Title Defence)
Career: 35 contests, won 34, lost 1.

Chris (The Dragon) John

Semarang, Indonesia. *Born* 4 September, 1981
WBA Featherweight Champion. Former Undefeated Indonesian Featherweight Champion
Major Amateur Honours: None known
Turned Pro: June 1998
Significant Results: Ratanchai Sorvorapin W PTS 10, Oscar Leon W PTS 10, Osamu Sato W PTS 12, Jose Rojas T DRAW 4 & W PTS 12, Derrick Gainer W PTS 12, Tommy Browne W RTD 9, Juan Manuel Marquez W PTS 12, Renan Acosta W PTS 12, Zaiki Takemoto W RTD 9, Roinet Caballero W RTD 7
Type/Style: He is a tall switch-hitting, counter-puncher with good footwork
Points of Interest: 5' 7½" tall with a 65" reach. Christened Johannes Christian John, his original nickname was 'Thin Man', which he took as a tribute to Alexis Arguello, before eventually deciding that it was no longer suitable for his improved muscular build. His father was a former amateur boxer and Chris

has been boxing since he was six, originally training in a garage before being based in a gym in Australia. He is also an international standard competitor at martial arts, winning a gold medal in the South-East Asia Games in 1997. He won the vacant 'interim' WBA title in September 2003 by beating Oscar Leon and made three defences until being recognised as the full champion when Juan Manuel Marquez was stripped of the title in 2005. Has made seven defences of the full title and has 22 wins inside the distance. Was lucky not to be stripped of his title when he failed to turn up at the weigh-in for a 2008 defence against Jackson Asiku due to a purse dispute. The bout was then cancelled

24.10.08 Hiroyuki Enoki W PTS 12 Tokyo
(WBA Featherweight Title Defence)
28.02.09 Rocky Juarez DREW 12 Houston
(WBA Featherweight Title Defence)
Career: 44 contests, won 42, drew 2.

Guillermo (The Cat) Jones

Colon, Panama. *Born* 5 May, 1972
WBA Cruiserweight Champion
Major Amateur Honours: A Panamanian Championship winner, he competed in the North American qualifiers for the 1992 Olympics and had a record of 22 wins and two losses
Turned Pro: July 1993
Significant Results: Gilberto Barreto W CO 1, David Noel L CO 2 & W RSC 1, Laurent Boudouani DREW 12 & L PTS 12, Jaffa Ballagou W PTS 6, Tim Williamson W PTS 10, Johnny Nelson DREW 12, Luciano Torres W RSC 1, Steve Cunningham L PTS 10, Kelvin Davis W RSC 4, Wayne Braithwaite W RSC 4
Type/Style: Is freakishly tall and a hard puncher
Points of Interest: Although 6'4" tall, he started out as a welterweight. Won his first 21 fights, including 11 first-round victories. The two fights with Laurent Boudouani in 1998 were both challenges for the WBA light-middleweight title, and the 2002 draw with Johnny Nelson was a challenge for the WBO cruiserweight title. Has

28 wins by stoppage or kayo and his two decision losses were both split decisions

27.09.08 Firat Arslan W RSC 10 Hamburg
(WBC Cruiserweight Title Challenge)
Career: 41 contests, won 36, drew 2, lost 3.

Denkaosan Kaowichit

Samui, Thailand. *Born* 23 August, 1976

WBA Flyweight Champion

Major Amateur Honours: None. Was a champion in Thai kick-boxing

Turned Pro: November 1996

Significant Results: Melvin Magramo W PTS 12 (twice), Eric Morel L RSC 11, Celso Danggod W PTS 12, Randy Mangubat W RSC 7, Richie Mepranum W PTS 12, Takefumi Sakata DREW 12

Type/Style: Is a solid boxer with plenty of power in his right hand

Points of Interest: 5' 3½" tall. His real name is Sutep Wangmuk but he has also fought as Denkaosan Singwangcha and Denkaosaen Kratindaengym. Denkaosin's first fight was a 12-round contest for a local title and all of his first 17 fights were scheduled for 12 rounds. His loss to Eric Morel in 2002 was a challenge for the WBA flyweight title, as was his 2007 draw with Takefumi Sakata, a fight in which he fractured his thumb. Has 20 wins by knockout or stoppage and is unbeaten in his last 28 fights, but only beat Hiroyuki Hisataka on a split decision

29.08.08 Falazona Fidal W PTS 6 Patumthanee
17.10.08 Dennis Juntillano W CO 2 Bangkok
31.12.08 Takefumi Sakata W CO 2 Hiroshima
(WBA Flyweight Title Challenge)
26.05.09 Hiroyuki Hisataka W PTS 12 Uttaradit
(WBA Flyweight Title Defence)
Career: 49 contests, won 47, drew 1, lost 1.

Mikkel (Viking Warrior) Kessler

Copenhagen, Denmark. *Born* 1 March, 1979

WBA S.Middleweight Champion. Former WBA & WBC S.Middleweight Champion

Major Amateur Honours: Won the European Junior Championship in 1996 and the Danish Junior Championships in 1996 and 1997

Turned Pro: March 1998

Significant Results: Elicier Julio W CO 3, Manny Sobral W RTD 5, Dingaan Thobela W PTS 12, Henry Porras W RSC 9, Julio Cesar Green W CO 1, Andre Thysse W PTS 12, Manny Siaca W RTD 7, Anthony Mundine W PTS 12, Eric Lucas W RSC 10, Markus Beyer W CO 3, Librado Andrade W PTS 12, Joe Calzaghe L PTS 12, Dimitri Sartison W CO 12

Type/Style: A tall, strong, quality box fighter with a good jab, he has been unfortunate to have suffered from hand injuries in the past

Points of Interest: 6'1" tall with a 73" reach. Heavily tattooed, he came in against Manny Siaca in November 2004 for the title as a late substitute, when Mads Larsen dropped out, and made the most of his opportunity. He made two defences of his WBA title before adding the WBC title to his tally. Lost both titles in a unification fight with WBO champion Joe Calzaghe in 2007, but regained the WBA title by beating Dimitri Sartison for the vacant crown in June 2008. Has 31 wins by stoppage or kayo

25.10.08 Danilo Haussler W CO 3 Oldenburg
(WBA S.Middleweight Title Defence)
Career: 42 contests, won 41, lost 1.

Malcolm (Stone) Klassen

Toekumsrus, South Africa. *Born* 12 March, 1981

IBF S.Featherweight Champion. Former Undefeated South African Featherweight Champion

Major Amateur Honours: None known

Turned Pro: May 1999

Significant Results: Takalani Ndlovu L PTS 6, Harry Ramogoadi L PTS 6, Jeff Mathebula DREW 6, Edward Mpofu W PTS 12, Lindile Tyhali W RSC 3, Willie Mabasa W PTS 12, Gairy St Clair W PTS 12, Mzonke Fana L PTS 12

Type/Style: Relentlessly aggressive two-fisted fighter with outstanding hand speed

Points of Interest: 5' 4" tall. When he started out as a pro he won only three of his first six fights. Originally fought at super-featherweight but then boxed as low as super- bantamweight.

Won the South African featherweight title by beating Edward Mpofu in August 2005 and made three defences before moving up a weight to win the IBF title in the higher division when beating Gairy St Clair in November 2006. Lost the title in his first defence to Mzonke Fana in April 2007. He and Cassius Baloyi were both from the same stable with the same manager and trainer, which is the first time in South African boxing history that two such fighters have fought for a version of a world title. His record sports 15 wins inside the distance

29.08.08 Manuel Medina W RSC 2 Temba
18.04.09 Cassius Baloyi W RSC 7 Mafikeng
(IBF S.Featherweight Title Challenge)
Career: 30 contests, won 24, drew 2, lost 4.

Vitali (Iron Fist) Klitschko

Belovodsk, Ukraine. *Born* Belovodsk, Kyrgyzstan, 19 February, 1971

WBC Heavyweight Champion. Former WBO Heavyweight Champion. Former Undefeated European Heavyweight Champion

Major Amateur Honours: Won the gold medal at the European Junior Championships in 1993 and silver medals in the 1995 World Championships and World Military Championships. Claims 195 wins in 210 fights

Turned Pro: November 1996

Significant Results: Julius Francis W RSC 2, Mario Schiesser W CO 2, Herbie Hide W CO 2, Obed Sullivan W RSC 9, Chris Byrd L RTD 9, Timo Hoffmann W PTS 12, Orlin Norris W RTD 1, Ross Puritty W RSC 11, Vaughan Bean W RSC 11, Larry Donald W RSC 10, Lennox Lewis L RSC 6, Kirk Johnson W RSC 2, Corrie Sanders W RSC 8, Danny Williams W RSC 8

Type/Style: Tall and upright fighter with a heavy punch in his right hand

Points of Interest: 6' 7" tall with an 80" reach. Son of an Air Force Colonel and brother of Olympic gold medal winner and current IBF and WBO champion, Vladimir, he was originally a kick-boxing world champion. Won the WBO title in

Vitali Klitschko   Les Clark

June 1999 by beating Herbie Hide and made three defences before losing to Chris Byrd in April 2000, when he suffered a torn rotator cuff. Apart from the Timo Hoffman bout every other fight has ended inside the distance. Judges had him ahead against Lennox Lewis when cuts forced the stoppage. Won the vacant WBC title by beating Corrie Sanders in April 2004, but made only one defence, against Danny Williams in December 2004, and then retired. Entered politics and ran for mayor of Kiev and for parliament, but was unsuccessful in both. Returned after almost four years and regained the WBC crown by beating Samuel Peter. Recently won a court case against the WBC, which allowed him to ignore their instructions to defend the title against Oleg Maskaev. Has 36 wins inside the distance

11.10.08 Samuel Peter W RTD 8 Berlin
(WBC Heavyweight Title Challenge)
21.03.09 Juan Carlos Gomez W RSC 9 Stuttgart
(WBC Heavyweight Title Defence)
Career: 39 contests, won 37, lost 2.

Vladimir (Steel Hammer) Klitschko

Kiev, Ukraine. *Born* Semipatalatinsk, Kazakhstan, 25 March, 1976
IBF & WBO Heavyweight

Champion. Former Undefeated European Heavyweight Champion
Major Amateur Honours: Having won a gold medal in the 1993 European Junior Championships and silver medals in the 1994 World Junior Championships and World Military Championships, he won the gold medal at the 1995 World Military Championships. This was followed by a silver medal win in the 1996 European Championships, prior to picking up a gold medal in the 1996 Olympics
Turned Pro: November 1996
Significant Results: Ross Puritty L RSC 11, Axel Schulz W RSC 8, Chris Byrd W PTS 12 & W RSC 7, Frans Botha W RSC 8, Ray Mercer W RSC 6, Jameel McCline W RSC 10, Corrie Sanders L RSC 2, Lamon Brewster L RSC 5 & W RTD 6, DaVarryl Williamson W TD 5, Eliseo Castillo W RSC 4, Samuel Peter W PTS 12, Calvin Brock W RSC 7, Ray Austin W RSC 2, Sultan Ibragimov W PTS 12
Type/Style: Although he has a mechanical jab and cross approach his reach and punching power makes him a dangerous, if unpredictable, opponent. However, despite being a double champion there are still some

questions over his stamina and chin
Points of Interest: 6' 6" tall. Is the son of an Air Force Colonel and brother of current WBC heavyweight champion, Vitali. Despite losing his first amateur fight he was not deterred and went on to become Olympic champion in Atlanta. After winning the European title by beating Axel Schulz in September 1999 he made only one defence before relinquishing it and going on to win the WBO title when outpointing Chris Byrd in October 2000. He made five defences before dropping the title in a shock stoppage loss to Corrie Sanders in March 2003. Was then stopped by Lamon Brewster in a fight for the vacant WBO title in April 2004. Now self managed, he won the IBF title by beating Chris Byrd in April 2006 and the WBO title by outpointing Sultan Ibragimov in February 2008. The WBA refused to sanction his fight with Ruslan Chagaev as being for their title, which stopped the brothers from owning the top four belts. He has 47 wins inside the distance and all three of his losses have also ended inside the distance

12.07.08 Tony Thompson W CO 11 Hamburg
(IBF & WBO Heavyweight Title Defences)
13.12.08 Hasim Rahman W RSC 7 Mannheim
(IBF & WBO Heavyweight Title Defences)
20.06.09 Ruslan Chagaev W RTD 10 Gelsenkirchen
(IBF & WBO Heavyweight Title Defences)
Career: 56 contests, won 53, lost 3.

Andrej (Andreas) Kotelnik

Lvov, Ukraine. *Born* 29 December, 1977
WBA L.Welterweight Champion
Major Amateur Honours: Although he won gold medals in the 1995 European Junior Championships and the 1999 European Senior Championships, he then competed without success in the 1997 World Championships. Before turning over, he won a silver medal in the 2000 Olympics and claims 135 wins in 150 amateur bouts
Turned Pro: December 2000
Significant Results: Fabrice Colombel W PTS 12, Arturo Urena W RSC

10, Sayan Sanchat W PTS 8, Gabriel Mapouka W PTS 12, Souleymane M'baye L PTS 12, Junior Witter L PTS 12, Mohamad Abdulla W PTS 12, William Gonzalez W RSC 8, Souleymane M'Baye DREW 12, Gavin Rees W RSC 12

Type/Style: An upright and stylish boxer with a good defence, who can be one-paced at times

Points of Interest: 5'7½" tall. Trained by the former European amateur champion, Michael Trimm, he was unsuccessful in his first challenge for the WBA title, being held to a draw by Souleymane M'baye in March 2007, but won the title by halting Gavin Rees in March last year. Has made two defences and has 13 wins inside the distance

13.09.08 Norio Kimura W PTS 12 Lviv
    (WBA L.Welterweight Title Defence)
07.02.09 Marcos Maidana W PTS 12 Rostock
    (WBA L.Welterweight Title Defence)
Career: 34 contests, won 31, drew 1, lost 2.

Jorge (Golden Boy) Linares

Barinitas, Venezuela. *Born* 22 August, 1985
WBA S.Featherweight Champion. Former Undefeated WBC Featherweight Champion
Major Amateur Honours: Won the Venezuelan Junior Championship four times and was the silver medallist in the 2001 Venezuelan Senior Championships
Turned Pro: December 2002
Significant Results: Pedrito Laurente W PTS 10, Hugo Soto W PTS 10, Mike Domingo W PTS 10, Renan Acosta W PTS 10, Saohin Condo W PTS 10, Pedro Navarrete W PTS 10, Oscar Larios W RSC 10, Gamaliel Diaz W CO 8
Type/Style: Classy combination puncher, who is fast with real power in both hands
Points of Interest: 5' 8" tall. Turned pro as a super bantamweight at the age of 17 under the Akihiko Honda banner in Japan and is still based there. Won the vacant WBC featherweight title by halting Oscar Larios in July 2007 and made one defence before relinquishing the title to move up

to super-featherweight. A scheduled title defence in May was cancelled due to concerns over the outbreak of swine flu. His brother, Nelson, is also unbeaten as a pro. Jorge has 18 wins by stoppage or kayo

28.11.08 Whyber Garcia W RSC 5 Panama City
    (Vacant WBA S.Featherweight Title)
27.06.09 Josafat Perez W RSC 8 Nuevo Laredo
    (WBA S.Featherweight Title Defence)
Career: 27 contests, won 27.

Jose (Carita) Lopez

Trujillo, Alto, Puerto Rico. *Born* 29 March, 1972
WBO S.Flyweight Champion. Former Undefeated Puerto Rican Flyweight Champion
Major Amateur Honours: An amateur international and gold medallist at the 1991 Copa Games
Turned pro: November 1991
Significant Results: Alberto Jimenez L PTS 12, Jose Luis Zepeda W RSC 4, Carlos Salazar L PTS 12, Isidro Garcia W PTS 12, Mauricio Pastrana L PTS 12, Fernando Montiel L PTS 12, Everardo Morales W PTS 12, Omar Soto W CO 2, Juan Keb Baas W RSC 11, Kermin Guardia W PTS 10, Juan Rosas W PTS 12
Type/Style: Is a tough and aggressive boxer with a solid chin
Points of Interest: 5' 5" tall. Was unsuccessful in four shots at the WBO flyweight title before moving up and winning the super-flyweight title. Has never been stopped and has 32 wins by stoppage or kayo. Had Fernando Montiel on the canvas when challenging for the WBO flyweight title in 2001 and Isidro Garcia, who beat Jose for the vacant WBO flyweight title in 1999, actually climbed out of the audience as a late substitute to take part in the fight. Finally succeeded in his fifth attempt at the age of 37

07.08.08 Oscar Andrade W RTD 7 Toa Baja
04.10.08 Jonathan Perez W RSC 7 Hato Rey
28.03.09 Pramuansak Posuwan W PTS 12 Bayamon
    (Vacant WBO S.Flyweight Title)
Career: 48 contests, won 39, drew 2, lost 7.

Juan Manuel (Juanma) López

Rio Piedras, Puerto Rica. *Born* 30 June, 1983

WBO S.Bantamweight Champion
Major Amateur Honours: Was a five-time Puerto Rican Championship winner and won gold medals in the 2001 and 2004 Jose Che Aponte Tournament. Earlier, he had won a silver medal in the 2001 Pan-American Championships and a bronze medal in the 2002 Central American Games, before losing to Abner Mares in the quarter-finals of the 2003 Pan-American Games. Won a place at the 2004 Olympics by finishing runner-up in the Tijuana qualifier, but lost in the first series in Athens
Turned Pro: January 2005
Significant Results: Luis Bolano W RTD 2, Edel Ruiz W RTD 6, Jose Alonso W RSC 3, Cuauhtemoc Vargas W RTD 6, Giovanni Andrade W RSC 1, Hugo Dianzo W RSC 10, Jonathan Oquendo W RSC 3, Daniel Ponce de Leon W RSC 1
Type/Style: This strong, smart, hard-punching southpaw, who can box or brawl, has real kayo power in both hands
Points of Interest: 5' 7" tall. His father was tired of him fighting in the street so took him to the gym when Juan was just ten years old. One of his brothers fought as an amateur. Is a stable mate of Miguel Cotto and always has his partner, Barbara de Jesus, as part of his corner team when he fights. Won the WBO title in June last year by stopping Daniel Ponce de Leon and has made four defences. Has won 24 of his 26 fights by stoppage or kayo

04.10.08 Cesar Figueroa W CO 1 Hato Rey
    (WBO S.Bantamweight Title Defence)
06.12.08 Sergio Medina W RSC 1 Las Vegas
    (WBO S.Bantamweight Title Defence)
25.04.09 Gerry Penalosa W RTD 9 Bayamon
    (WBO S.Bantamweight Title Defence)
27.06.09 Olivier Lontchi W RTD 9 Atlantic City
    (WBO S.Bantamweight Title Defence)
Career: 26 contests, won 26.

Steve Luevano

Los Angeles, California, USA. *Born* 3 March, 1981
WBO Featherweight Champion
Major Amateur Honours: Won the Californian Junior Silver Gloves in 1996, the USA Junior Olympics

Steve Luevano   Les Clark

Championship in 1997, the gold medal in the 1998 USA Under-19 Championships and competed in the 1998 Under-19 World Championships. Having won silver medals in both the 1999 USA Senior Championships and the National Golden Gloves, he lost to Rocky Juarez in the Olympic trials. Claims 187 wins in 205 amateur and junior contests

Turned Pro: June 2000

Significant Results: Freddie Neal W RTD 9, Aldo Valtierra W PTS 10, Genaro Trazancos W RSC 5, Ruben Estanislao W PTS 12, Jorge Martinez W PTS 10, Martin Honorio L PTS 10, Cristobal Cruz W PTS 12, Nicky Cook W CO 11, Terdsak Jandaeng W PTS 12, Mario Santiago DREW 12

Type/Style: A Southpaw, he is a good technical fighter with an excellent jab and solid defence

Points of Interest: 5' 7" tall. Started boxing in 1998 and is trained by the former IBF super-featherweight champion, Roberto Garcia. Married with two children, he plans to join the police force when he retires. Won the vacant WBO title by kayoing Nicky Cook in July 2007 and has made three

defences. Has 15 wins by stoppage or kayo

18.10.08 Billy Dib W PTS 12 Atlantic City
(WBO Featherweight Title Defence)
Career: 38 contests, won 36, drew 1, lost 1.

Antonio Margarito
Tijuana, Mexico. *Born* 18 March, 1978
Former WBA & WBO Welterweight Champion. Former Undefeated IBF Welterweight Champion

Major Amateur Honours: None known, but he claims 18 wins in 23 contests

Turned Pro: January 1994

Significant Results: Larry Dixon L PTS 10, Rodney Jones L PTS 10, Alfred Ankamah W CO 4, Danny Perez W PTS 8, David Kamau W CO 2, Frankie Randall W RSC 4, Daniel Santos NC 1 & L TD 9, Antonio Diaz W RSC 10, Danny Perez W PTS 12, Andrew Lewis W RSC 2, Hercules Kyvelos W RSC 2, Sebastien Lujan W RSC 10, Kermit Cintron W RSC 5, Paul Williams L PTS 12, Golden Johnson W RSC 1, Kermit Cintron W CO 6

Type/Style: Is a tall, strong, aggressive banger. Although a bit a bit one-paced he has a good jab and a strong chin

Points of Interest: 6'0" tall. Turned pro at the age of 15 and suffered three early defeats. His first fight with Daniel Santos for the WBO welterweight title in July 2001 was stopped and declared a no-contest, due to Antonio suffering a bad cut, and when Santos handed in the belt Antonio won the vacant title by beating Antonio Diaz in March 2002. His challenge against Santos for the WBO light-middleweight title in September 2004 also went to a technical decision due to a cut. Made seven defences and then lost his title to Paul Williams, but bounced back to kayo previous victim, Kermit Cintron, for the IBF title. Stripped for choosing to fight Miguel Cotto for the WBA crown, he has been suspended for one year by the Californian Commission after it was found that an illegal substance was being applied to his hand bandages for the fight with

Shane Mosley. Has 27 wins inside the distance

26.07.08 Miguel Cotto W RSC 11 Las Vegas
(WBA Welterweight Title Challenge)
24.01.09 Shane Mosley L RSC 9 Los Angeles
(WBA Welterweight Title Defence)
Career: 44 contests, won 37, lost 6, no contests 1.

Juan Manuel (Dinamita) Marquez
Mexico City, Mexico. *Born* 23 August, 1973
WBA & WBO Lightweight Champion. WBC S.Featherweight Champion. Former Undefeated IBF, WBA & WBO Featherweight Champion

Major Amateur Honours: None known, but claims 32 wins in 33 bouts

Turned Pro: May 1993

Significant Results: Julian Wheeler W RSC 10, Julio Gervacio W CO 10, Agapito Sanchez W PTS 12, Alfred Kotey W PTS 12, Freddy Norwood L PTS 12, Daniel Jimenez W RTD 7, Julio Gamboa W RTD 6, Robbie Peden W RSC 10, Manuel Medina W RSC 7, Derrick Gainer W TD 7, Manny Pacquiao DREW 12 & L PTS 12, Orlando Salido W PTS 12, Victor Polo W PTS 12, Chris John L PTS 12, Terdsak Jandaeng W RSC 7, Marco Antonio Barrera W PTS 12, Rocky Juarez W PTS 12

Type/Style: Solid and compact stylist with power in either hand

Points of Interest: 5' 7" tall. Juan Manuel originally studied to be an accountant, but the lure of the ring was too great. His Father boxed as a pro and he is the elder brother of the former undefeated IBF bantamweight and WBC super bantamweight champion, Rafael. Juan Manuel started boxing at the age of 12 and lost his first pro fight on a disqualification. Was defeated by Freddy Norwood in a challenge for the WBA featherweight title in September 1999, but then won the IBF title by beating Manuel Medina in February 2003. Never lost either title in the ring, being stripped of the IBF title and then losing WBA recognition because he was no longer a double or 'super' champion. Failed in a challenge for his old WBA title when losing on points to Chris John in Indonesia in March 2006 and then won the 'interim' WBO featherweight title by beating Terdsak Jandaeng. He eventually became the full champion when Scott Harrison was stripped off the title. Moved up to super-featherweight and won the WBC title by beating Marco Antonio Barrera in March 2007, making one defence before losing the title to Manny Pacquiao in March last year. He then moved up to lightweight. Was floored three times in the first round of his first fight with Manny Pacquiao in May 2004. Has 33 wins on stoppage or kayo

13.09.08 Joel Casamayor W RSC 11 Las Vegas
28.02.09 Juan Diaz W RSC 9 Houston
(Vacant WBA & WBO Lightweight Titles)
Career: 55 contests, won 50, drew 1, lost 4.

Roman (Rocky) Martinez

Vega Baja, Puerto Rico. *Born* 31 January, 1983
WBO S.Featherweight Champion
Major Amateur Honours: Competed in the 1999 Jose 'Cheo' Aponte Tournament and claims 61 fights with only 16 losses
Turned Pro: December 2001
Significant Results: Wilfredo Vargas W CO 3, Francisco Lorenzo W PTS 12, Cristian Favela W PTS 10, Daniel Jimenez W RSC 12
Type/Style: Orthodox with a high guard, he has a good jab and is both fast and strong. He also is a hard body puncher, with power in both hands and good chin
Points of Interest: He has six sisters and three brothers and is married with one son Started boxing in 1995. 5'8" tall with 67" reach, he has 13 wins inside the distance
30.08.08 Santos Benavides W RSC 6 Bayamon
13.12.08 Walter Estrada W PTS 10 Hato Rey
14.03.09 Nicky Cook W RSC 4 Manchester
(WBO S.Featherweight Title Challenge)
Career: 23 contests, won 22, drew 1.

Sergio (Maravilla) Martinez

Quilmes, Argentina. Born 21 February, 1975
WBC L.Middleweight Champion.
Former Undefeated Argentinian

Welterweight Champion
Major Amateur Honours: As the winner of the Argentinian Championship in 1997, he competed in the World Championships in the same year
Turned Pro: December 1997
Significant Results: Antonio Margarito L RSC 7, Enrique Areco W RSC 8, Francisco Mora W PTS 10, Richard Williams W PTS 12 & W RTD 9, Adrian Stone W RSC 12, Saul Roman W CO 4, Archak TerMeliksetian W RSC 7
Type/Style: Is a southpaw with a hands down slick style
Points of Interest: 5' 11" tall. The wins over Richard Williams and Adrian Stone were for the IBO title. Martinez was floored twice in the first Williams fight. Won the vacant WBC 'interim' title when beating Alex Bunema and defended it against Kermit Cintron. Was elevated to full championship status when Vernon Forrest was stripped of the title in May 2009. Has 24 wins by stoppage or kayo
04.10.08 Alex Bunema W RTD 8 Temecula
14.02.09 Kermit Cintron DREW 12 Sunrise
(WBC 'Interim' L.Middleweight Title Defence)
Career: 47 contests, won 44, drew 1, lost 2.

Fernando (Cochulito) Montiel

Los Mochis, Mexico. *Born* 1 March, 1979
WBO Bantamweight Champion.
Former Undefeated WBO S. Flyweight and Flyweight Champion
Major Amateur Honours: Claiming 33 wins in 36 fights, he was a local Golden Gloves champion.
Turned Pro: December 1996
Significant Results: Paulino Villalobos DREW 10 & W PTS 10, Sergio Millan W PTS 10, Cruz Carbajal W RSC 4, Isidro Garcia W RSC 7, Zoltan Lunka W RSC 7, Juan Domingo Cordoba W CO 1, Jose Lopez W PTS 12, Pedro Alcazar W RSC 6, Roy Doliguez W RSC 3, Mark Johnson L PTS 12, Reynaldo Hurtado W CO 7, Ivan Hernandez W RSC 7, Evert Briceno W PTS 12, Pramuansak Posuwan W PTS 12, Jhonny Gonzalez L PTS 12, Z Gorres W PTS 12, Cecilio Santos W RSC 10, Luis Melendez W RSC

12, Martin Castillo W CO 4, Luis Maldonado W RSC 3
Type/Style: Clever and stylish, he has a good uppercut
Points of Interest: 5'4" tall. The youngest of a fighting family, his father and four brothers all being boxers, he won his first 11 bouts inside the distance. Jointly trained by his father Manuel and a Japanese trainer based in Mexico, Fernando has 29 wins by knockout or stoppage. He won the WBO flyweight title, stopping Isidro Garcia in December 2000, and made three defences before moving up to win the super- flyweight title by beating Pedro Alcazar in June 2002. Sadly, Alcazar collapsed and died after the fight. Having lost the title in his second defence to Mark Johnson in August 2003, Fernando came back to regain the title when stopping Ivan Hernandez in April 2005 and made two defences. He made an unsuccessful challenge to Jhonny Gonzales for the WBO bantamweight title in May 2006, and then made five more defences of his super-flyweight title before moving up to bantamweight. Won the vacant WBO title when beating Diego Silva after Gerry Penalosa had handed in his belt in February
02.11.08 Juan Alberto Rosas W PTS 10 Aguscalientes
28.03.09 Diego Silva W CO 3 Tijuana
(WBO Bantamweight Title Defence)
Career: 42 contests, won 39, drew 1, lost 2.

Anselmo (Chemito) Moreno

San Miguel, Panama. *Born* 28 June, 1985
WBA Bantamweight Champion
Major Amateur Honours: Was the Panamanian Champion at mini-flyweight in 2001
Turned Pro: March 2002
Significant Results: David Arosemena W PTS 6, Felix Machado W PTS 10, Jose de Jesus Lopez W RSC 5, Nestor Paniagua W PTS 10, Luis Benavidez W CO 2, Tomas Rojas W PTS 10, Ricardo Vargas W RSC 1, Wladimir Sidorenko W PTS 12
Type/Style: Fast, lanky, slick counter-punching southpaw

Points of Interest: 5' 7" tall. Turned pro as a flyweight and even fought at light-flyweight, but made so little money early in his career that he took a job as a house painter. Things looked up after his 2006 win over former super-flyweight champion, Felix Machado, and he won the WBA title by beating Wladimir Sidorenko in May 2008. As Panama's 25th world champion, he has made three defences. He is Panama's 25th "world" champion. Has eight wins by stoppage or kayo

18.09.08 Cecilio Santos W TD 7 Panama City
(WBA Bantamweight Title Defence)
30.10.08 Rolly Lunas W PTS 12 Panama City
(WBA Bantamweight Title Defence)
02.05.09 Wladimir Sidorenko W PTS 12 Bremen
(WBA Bantamweight Title Defence)
Career: 27 contests, won 25, drew 1, lost 1.

Shane (Sugar) Mosley
Lynwood, California, USA. *Born* 7 September, 1971
WBA Welterweight Champion. Former WBC & WBA L.Middleweight Champion. Former WBC Welterweight Champion. Former Undefeated IBF Lightweight Champion
Major Amateur Honours: Won a silver medal in the 1989 World Junior Championships and was a gold medallist in the 1990 and 1992 United States Championships, but lost in the finals of the USA Olympic trials to Vernon Forrest
Turned Pro: February 1993
Significant Results: Philip Holiday W PTS 12, John John Molina W RSC 8, James Leija W RTD 9, Golden Johnson W CO 7, John Brown W RSC 8, Oscar de la Hoya W PTS 12 & W PTS 12, Antonio Diaz W RSC 6, Shannan Taylor W RTD 5, Adrian Stone W RSC 3, Vernon Forrest L PTS 12 & L PTS 12, Raul Marquez T Draw 3, Ronald Wright L PTS 12 & L PTS 12, Fernando Vargas W RSC 10, Luis Collazo W PTS 12, Miguel Cotto L PTS 12
Type/Style: Is a slick, smooth, fast-handed stylist with quick reflexes and good mobility who can also punch with power

Shane Mosley   Les Clark

Points of Interest: 5' 9" tall with a 74" reach. Having started boxing at eight years of age, he is now trained by his father. Also beat Oscar de la Hoya as an amateur. Made eight defences of the IBF lightweight title before moving up to win the welterweight crown when defeating de la Hoya in June 2000. He then made three defences of the WBC welterweight title before losing it to Vernon Forrest in January 2002. Moved up again to light-middleweight and beat de la Hoya again in 2003 to win the WBA and WBC titles, but lost them in his first defence to Ronald Wright. Moved back down to welterweight in 2007, losing in a challenge to Miguel Cotto for the WBA title, but won the title when stopping Antonio Margarito. Has 39 wins inside the distance
27.09.08 Ricardo Mayorga W CO 12 Carson
24.01.09 Antonio Margarito W RSC 9 Los Angeles
(WBA Welterweight Title Challenge)
Career: 52 contests, won 46, lost 5, no contest 1.

Daisuke Naito
Hokkaido, Japan. *Born* 30 August, 1974
WBC Flyweight Champion. Former Undefeated Japanese Flyweight Champion
Major Amateur Honours: None known
Turned Pro: October 1996
Significant Results: Takefumi Sakata DREW 10, Pongsaklek Wonjongkam L CO 1, L TD 7, W PTS 12 & DREW 12, Teppei Kikui W PTS 10, Hiroshi Nakano W TD 6, Daigo Nakahiro W PTS 10, Noriyuki Komatsu W RSC 6, Daiki Kameda W PTS 12
Type/Style: Unorthodox, aggressive swinger
Points of Interest: 5' 4" tall. His first-round kayo loss to Pongsaklek Wonjongkam in a challenge for the WBC title in April 2002 took just 34 seconds, making it the fastest finish in a flyweight title bout. Daisuke had been unbeaten in 21 bouts up to that time. Their second fight went to the cards after he had been badly cut. He finally beat Wonjongkam in July 2007 to win the WBC title and drew with same opponent in a title defence in March last year. Was voted 'Fighter of the Year' in Japan in 2007. Has 20 wins inside the distance, but had to climb off the floor to beat Xiong Zhao

Zhong in his fifth title defence
30.07.08 Tomonobu Shimizu W CO 10 Tokyo
(WBC Flyweight Title Defence)
23.12.08 Shingo Yamaguchi W RSC 11 Tokyo
(WBC Flyweight Title Defence)
26.05.09 Xiong Zhao Zhong W PTS 12 Tokyo
(WBC Flyweight Title Defence)
Career: 40 contests, won 35, drew 3, lost 2.

Omar (Huracan) Narvaez

Trelew, Argentina. *Born* 7 October, 1975
WBO Flyweight Champion
Major Amateur Honours: Won a bronze medal in the 1997 World Championships and a silver in the 1999 Championships before striking gold in the 1999 Pan-American Games and South American Championships. Earlier he had competed in the 1996 Olympics, where he beat the future double WBO champion, Joan Guzman. He also competed in the 2000 Olympics
Turned Pro: December 2000
Significant Results: Carlos Montiveros DREW 4, Wellington Vicente W PTS 10, Marcos Obregon W PTS 10, Adonis Rivas W PTS 12, Luis Lazarate W DIS 10, Andrea Sarritzu W PTS 12 & DREW 12, Everardo Morales W RSC 5, Alexander Mahmutov W RSC 10, Bernard Inom W RSC 11, Dario Azuaga W RSC 6, Rexon Flores W PTS 12, Walberto Ramos W PTS 12, Brahim Asloum W PTS 12, Marlon Marques W RSC 4, Carlos Tamara W PTS 12, Ivan Pozo W RTD 7
Type/Style: A stocky, tough and aggressive southpaw with fast hands
Points of Interest: 5'3" tall. Became the first of the 2000 Olympians to win a version of a world title when he beat Adolfo Rivas in only his 12th paid fight in July 2002. Was originally trained by Cuba's Sarbelio Fuentes but now has a local trainer. Has made 19 title defences, passing the record for world title defences for an Argentinian previously held by Carlos Monzon. Has 18 wins by stoppage or kayo
20.09.08 Alejandro Hernandez W PTS 12 Puerto Madryn
(WBO Flyweight Title Defence)
07.02.09 Rayonta Whitfield W RSC 10 Puerto Madryn

(WBO Flyweight Title Defence)
26.06.09 Omar Soto W RSC 11 Buenos Aires
(WBO Flyweight Title Defence)
Career: 32 contests, won 30, drew 2.

Donnie (Ahas) Nietes

Bacolod City, Philippines. *Born* 13 May, 1982
WBO M.Flyweight Champion
Major Amateur Honours: None known
Turned Pro: April 2003
Significant Results: Abrin Matta W RSC 5, Angky Angkota L PTS 10, Ricardo Albia W RSC 7, Henri Amol W CO 2, Saengpetch Sor Sakulphan W CO 7, Pornsuwan Kratingdaenggym W PTS 12
Type/Style: Skilful boxer who can also punch a bit
Points of Interest: 5' 3" tall. When he won the vacant WBO title by beating Pornsuwan Kratingdaenggym in September 2007 he became the first world champion for the Antonio Aldeguer stable after they had lost in three attempts in the previous 12 months. After winning the title contract problems kept him inactive for 11 months, but has now made two defences. Has 14 wins inside the distance
30.08.08 Eddy Castro W RSC 2 Cebu City
(WBO M.Flyweight Title Defence)
28.02.09 Erik Ramirez W PTS 12 Oaxaca
(WBO M.Flyweight Title Defence)
Career: 28 contests, won 24, drew 3, lost 1.

Toshiaki Nishioka

Kakogawa, Japan. *Born* 27 July, 1976
WBC S.Bantamweight Champion. Former Undefeated Japanese Bantamweight Champion
Major Amateur Honours: None known
Turned Pro: December 1994
Significant Results: Junichi Watanabe W CO 2, Veeraphol Sahaprom L PTS 12 & DREW 12, Gerardo Martinez W PTS 10, Evangelio Perez W CO 1, Pedrito Laurente W PTS 10 & W CO 9, Hugo Vargas W PTS 10
Type/Style: Is a hard-punching southpaw, but a bit mechanical
Points of Interest: All four fights with Veeraphol Sahaprom were challenges

for the WBC bantamweight title. Won the vacant WBC 'interim' title when beating Napapol Kiatisakchokchai and became full champion when Israel Vasquez relinquished the title in December 2008. Has 20 wins by stoppage or kayo and has made two defences
15.09.08 Napapol Kiatisakchokchai W PTS 12 Yokohama
03.01.09 Genaro Garcia W RSC 12 Yokohama
(WBC S.Bantamweight Title Defence)
23.05.09 Jhonny Gonzalez W RSC 3 Monterrey
(WBC S.Bantamweight Title Defence)
Career: 41 contests, won 34, drew 3, lost 4.

Manny Pacquiao

Bukidnon, Philippines. *Born* 17 December, 1976
Former Undefeated WBC Lightweight Champion. Former Undefeated WBC S.Featherweight Champion. Former Undefeated IBF S.Bantamweight Champion. Former WBC Flyweight Champion
Major Amateur Honours: None, but started at 13 and won 60 of 64 fights
Turned Pro: January 1995
Significant Results: Rostico Torrecampo L CO 3, Chockchai Chokwiwat W CO 5, Chatchai Sasakul W CO 8, Medgoen Singsurat L CO 3, Nedal Hussein W RSC 10, Lehlohonolo Ledwaba W RSC 6, Agapito Sanchez T DRAW 6, Jorge Julio W RSC 2, Emmanuel Lucero W RSC 3, Marco Antonio Barrera W RSC 11 & W PTS 12, Juan Manuel Marquez DREW 12 & W PTS 12, Oscar Larios W PTS 12, Erik Morales L PTS 10, W RSC 10 & W CO 3, Jorge Solis W CO 8, David Diaz W RSC 9
Type/Style: Stocky, aggressive, exciting and hard-punching southpaw
Points of Interest: Known as 'Pac Man'. Turning pro at the age of 18 as a mini-flyweight, he won the WBC flyweight title by knocking out Chatchai Sasakul in December 1998. Made one defence and then, when struggling to make the weight, lost the title on a kayo to Medgoen Singsurat in September 1999. Promptly moved straight up to super-bantamweight. Won the IBF title in June 2001 with an upset stoppage victory over Lehlohonolo Ledwaba

when coming in as a substitute at two weeks notice. Made six defences and then drew in a dramatic battle with Juan Manuel Marquez in a challenge for the IBF and WBA featherweight titles. Moved up again to super-featherweight to add the WBC title to his list of honours and won two out of three dramatic battles against Erik Morales. Added a fourth division title by beating David Diaz and is the only fighter to have spanned from flyweight to lightweight in winning world titles. Trained by Freddie Roach, he has 37 wins by stoppage or kayo. His brother Bobby is also a pro. Vacated the WBC lightweight title in February 2009 to fight Ricky Hatton and, on winning, cemented his place as *The Ring* magazine's best pound-for-pound fighter
06.12.08 Oscar de la Hoya W RTD 8 Las Vegas
02.05.09 Ricky Hatton W CO 2 Las Vegas
     (IBO L.Welterweight Title Challenge)
Career: 54 contests, won 49, drew 2, lost 3.

Jean Pascal

Laval, Canada. *Born* Haiti, 28 October, 1982
WBC L.Heavyweight Champion. Former Undefeated Canadian S.Middleweight Champion
Major Amateur Honours: A gold medallist in the 2001 Francophile Games, he competed in the 2001 World Championships and won a silver medal in the 2002 Chowdhry Cup. Having won the gold medal at the 2002 Commonwealth Games, he went on to win a gold medal in the 2003 Jose Cheo Aponte Tournament, a bronze medal in the 2003 Pan-American Games and a bronze medal in the 2003 Copenhagen Cup before competing in the 2004 Olympics. Won the Canadian championship seven times
Turned Pro: February 2005
Significant Results: Jermain Mackey W PTS 12, Lafarrell Bunting W PTS 12, Kingsley Ikeke W PTS 12, Esteban Camou W CO 3, Omar Pittman W PTS 10
Type/Style: Tough, aggressive banger with an excellent chin
Points of Interest: 5' 11" tall. Beat Paul

Smith in the 2002 Commonwealth Games and won and lost against Craig McEwan in international matches. Having moved with his family to Canada in the 1980s, he started going to the gym at the age of 15. Has 15 wins by stoppage or kayo
06.12.08 Carl Froch L PTS 12 Nottingham
     (Vacant WBC S. Middleweight Title)
04.04.09 Pablo Nievas W CO 5 Montreal
19.06.09 Adrian Diaconu W PTS 12 Montreal
     (WBC L.Heavyweight Title Challenge)
Career: 24 contests, won 23, lost 1.

Kelly (Ghost) Pavlik

Youngstown, Ohio, USA. *Born* 4 April, 1982
WBC & WBO Middleweight Champion
Major Amateur Honours: Having won the National Police Athletic League Junior Championship, the National Golden Gloves Junior Championship in 1998 and the United States Under-19 championship in 1999, he was a bronze medallist in the 2000 USA Championships. Claims 89 wins in 98 contests
Turned Pro: June 2000
Significant Results: Ross Thompson W PTS 8, Fulgencio Zuniga W RTD 9, Bronco McKart W RSC 6, Lenord Pierre W RSC 4, Jose Luis Zertuche W CO 8, Edison Miranda W RSC 7, Jermain Taylor W RSC 7 & W PTS 12, Gary Lockett W RSC 3
Type/Style: Skilled and polished, he is a pressure fighter with a hard jab, a big right hand punch and a strong chin
Points of Interest: 6'2 ½" tall with a 75" reach. His father, Michael, is his joint manager and trainer and he had two brothers who boxed as amateurs. After flirting with martial arts Kelly was inspired to take up boxing by former IBF lightweight champion, Harry Arroyo, who also hails from Youngstown. He lost to Jermain Taylor in the 2000 Olympic trials but gained revenge by beating Taylor in September 2007 to win the WBC and WBO titles. Has made two defences, the return match with Taylor in February 2008 being a non-title bout. A college student, he graduated in computer graphics. Has stopped or

kayoed 31 opponents
18.10.08 Bernard Hopkins L PTS 12 Atlantic City
21.02.09 Marco Antonio Rubio W RTD 9 Youngstown
     (WBC & WBO Middleweight Title Defences)
Career: 36 contests, won 35, lost 1.

Victor Ramirez

Buenos Aires, Argentina. *Born* 30 March, 1984
WBO Cruiserweight Champion. Former Undefeated South American Cruiserweight Champion
Major Amateur Honours: Won the Argentinian Championship in 2003 and 2005 and was a silver medallist in the 2005 Pan-American Championships
Turned Pro: April 2006
Significant Results: Sebastian Ceballos L PTS 6, Mario Ordales W PTS 6
Type/Style: Is a strong, tough relentless battler and heavy hooker
Points of Interest: Won his amateur titles as a super-heavyweight, and lost to Olympic gold medallist, Odlanier Solis, in the finals of the South American Championships. He turned professional as a heavyweight, having 12 wins inside the distance, but has only had four fights at cruiserweight. Nickname 'El Tyson de Abasto', he won the 'interim' WBO title when beating Alex Alexeev and received full status as WBO champion when David Haye relinquished the title in February 2009
30.08.08 Mauro Ordiales W RTD 11 Caseros
     (Vacant South American Cruiserweight Title)
04.12.08 Hector Sotelo W RSC 2 Buenos Aires
     (South American Cruiserweight Title Defence)
17.01.09 Alexander Alexeev W RTD 9 Dusseldorf
16.05.09 Ali Ismailov W PTS 12 Buenos Aires
     (WBO Cruiserweight Title Defence)
Career: 17 contests, won 15, lost 1, no contest 1.

Daniel Santos

San Juan, Puerto Rico. *Born* 10 October, 1975
WBA L.Middleweight Champion. Former WBO L.Middleweight Champion. Former Undefeated WBO Welterweight Champion
Major Amateur Honours: Won a

bronze medal in the 1992 World Junior Championships before competing in the 1993 World Championships and the 1994 Goodwill Games. At senior level he won a silver medal in the 1995 Pan-American Games, competed in the 1995 World Championships and was a bronze medallist in the 1996 Olympic Games

Turned Pro: September 1996

Significant Results: Ray Lovato W RSC 2, Kofi Jantuah L RSC 5, Ahmed Katajev L PTS 12 & W CO 5, Giovanni Parisi W RSC 4, Neil Sinclair W CO 2, Antonio Margarito NC 1 & W TD 9, Luis Ramon Campas W RSC 11, Mehrdud Takaloo W PTS 12, Fulgencio Zuniga W PTS 12, Michael Lerma W PTS 12, Sergei Dzindziruk L PTS 12, Jose Antonio Rivera W RSC 8

Type/Style: Fast, clever and flashy, the southpaw is a heavy left-hand puncher whose chin and stamina is questionable

Points of Interest: 6' 0" tall. Lost to David Reid in the Pan-American Games. Unbeaten in his first 21 fights, he lost a disputed decision to Ahmed Kotiev in his first challenge for the WBO welterweight title in 1999. The WBO ordered a rematch, which Santos won in May 2000. Made three defences of his welterweight title before winning the vacant light-middleweight crown, beating Luis Ramon Campas in March 2002, and making five defences before losing the title to Sergei Dzindziruk in December 2005. Not very active, he has had only one fight in the past 20 months and only two in the last three years

11.07.08 Joachim Alcine W CO 6 Montreal
(WBA L.Middleweight Title Challenge)

Career: 37 contests, won 32, drew 1, lost 3, no contest 1.

Olyedong Sithsamerchai

Bangkok, Thailand. *Born* 17 July, 1985

WBC M.Flyweight Champion

Major Amateur Honours: None, but was a star in Muay Thai contests

Turned Pro: September 2002

Significant Results: Arman del a Cruz W PTS 10, Alex Aroy W PTS 10, Rollen Del Castillo W PTS 10, Omar Soto W PTS 12, Eagle Den Junlaphan W PTS 12, Junichi Ebisuoka W CO 9

Type/Style: Is a fast moving, counter-punching southpaw with good stamina

Points of Interest: 5' 2" tall. His real name is Kittipong Jaikajang. He has never fought outside Thailand and was fighting ten round bouts after only three contests. Won the WBC title in November 2007, beating Eagle Den Junlaphan, and has made three defences. Has 12 wins by stoppage or kayo

25.09.08 John Cut Siregar W CO 4 Bangkok
27.11.08 Pornsawan Porpramook W PTS 12 Phitsanulok
(WBC M.FlyweightTitle Defence)
27.03.09 Darmea Jordan w pts 6 Nakhon Ratchasima
29.05.09 Muhammad Rachman W TD 11 Patong Phuket
(WBC M Flyweight Title Defence)

Career: 30 contests, won 30.

Edgar Sosa

Mexico City, Mexico. *Born* 23 August, 1979

WBC L.Flyweight Champion

Major Amateur Honours: None known

Turned Pro: April 2002

Significant Results: Ulises Solis L PTS 6 & L PTS 12, Manuel Vargas L RSC 8, Omar Nino Romero L PTS 10, Isaac Bustos L PTS 12, Domingo Guillen W RSC 6, Francisco Rosas W PTS 12, Gilberto Keb Baas W PTS 12, Nohel Aramabulet W TD 10, Brian Viloria W PTS 12, Luis Lazarte W DIS 10, Lorenzo Trejo W RSC 9, Roberto Leyva W RSC 4, Jesus Iribe W PTS 12, Takashi Kunishige W RSC 8

Type/Style: A good tactical boxer with a strong jab and plenty of movement, he has a tough chin and packs real punching power

Points of Interest: A couple of his uncles were boxers and he started boxing at the age of ten. Trained by Miguel "Raton" Gonzalez, who is the father of the former WBO bantamweight champion, Jhonny

Gonzalez, and managed by Haitian businessman, Jacques Deschamps, he has become one of the most popular boxers in Mexico. In late 2003 his record was a mediocre 12-5, but four of the losses were close decisions to fighters who went on to win versions of world titles and Edgar is unbeaten in his last 24 contests, winning the vacant WBC title with a victory over Brian Viloria in April 2007. Has made nine defences of his title in two years and has 20 wins by stoppage or kayo

27.09.08 Sonny Boy Jaro W PTS 12 Mexico City
(WBC L.Flyweight Title Defence)
29.11.08 Juanito Rubillar W RSC 7 Mexico City
(WBC L.Flyweight Title Defence)
04.04.09 Porsawan Porpramook W RSC 4 Ciudad Victoria
(WBC L.Flyweight Title Defence)
20.06.09 Carlos Melo W RSC 5 Mexico City
(WBC L.Flyweight Title Defence)

Career: 41 contests, won 36, lost 5.

Humberto (Zorrita) Soto

Los Mochis, Mexico. *Born* 11 May, 1980

WBC S.Featherweight Champion

Major Amateur Honours: None known, but claims 60 fights with only eight losses

Turned Pro: September 1997

Significant Results: Hector Marquez L RTD 11, Mark Burse W PTS 10, Kevin Kelley L PTS 12, Cesar Figueroa W RSC 7, Jorge Solis NC 3, Ricardo Juarez W PTS 12, Oscar Leon W RSC 9, Bobby Pacquiao W CO 7, Joan Guzman L PTS 12, Francisco Lorenzo L DIS 4

Type/Style: Is an exciting, aggressive and hard-hitting box-puncher

Points of Interest: 5' 7½" tall. Turned pro at 18 and fought in Britain in November 1999, beating Dave Hinds on points in Hull. Real christian name is Armando. Born and brought up in a cardboard house, his manager, Nacho Huizar, bought his contract for just $200. Won the WBC 'interim' featherweight title by beating Ricardo Juarez in August 2005, but never won the full title. Moved up to super-featherweight but lost to Joan Guzman for the WBO title in November 2007. Lost a controversial disqualification against Francisco Lorenzo for the 'interim' WBC title in

June 2008. However, the WBC refused to accept the result and Humberto won the 'interim' title when forcing Gamaliel Diaz to retire in the 11th round. He then went on to beat Lorenzo for the vacant title and has now defended the championship twice. Has 31 wins by kayo or stoppage

11.10.08 Gamaliel Diaz W RTD 11 Torreon
(Vacant WBC 'Interim' S.Featherweight Title)
20.12.08 Francisco Lorenzo W PTS 12 Cozumel
(Vacant WBC S.Featherweight Title)
28.03.09 Antonio Davis W RSC 4 Tijuana
(WBC S.Featherweight Title Defence)
02.05.09 Benoit Gaudet W RSC 9 Las Vegas
(WBC S.Featherweight Title Defence)
Career: 58 contests, won 48, drew 2, lost 7, no contest 1.

Cory (The Next Generation) Spinks

St Louis, Missouri, USA. *Born* 20 February, 1978
IBF L.Middleweight Champion. Former WBA, WBC and IBF Welterweight Champion
Major Amateur Honours: Won the 1997 Police Athletic League Championships and claims 78 wins in 81 contests.
Turned Pro: November 1997
Significant Results: Antonio Diaz L PTS 12, Jorge Vaca W RSC 7, Edgar Ruiz W PTS 10, Larry Marks W PTS 12, Michele Piccirillo L PTS 12 & W PTS 12, Rafael Pineda W TD 7, Ricardo Mayorga W PTS 12, Zab Judah W PTS 12 & L RSC 9, Miguel Gonzalez W PTS 12, Roman Karmazin W PTS 12, Rodney Jones W PTS 12, Jermain Taylor L PTS 12, Verno Phillips L PTS 12
Type/Style: A tall, upright southpaw with good speed, who is a fine combination puncher
Points of Interest: 5'10" tall. He is the son of former world heavyweight champion, Leon, and nephew of Mike. Lost to Michele Piccirillo on a disputed decision in his challenge for the IBF welterweight title in 2002 but then beat the Italian in a return in March 2003 and added the WBA and WBC titles when outscoring Ricardo Mayorga in December 2003. Made successful defences against Zab Judah and Miguel Gonzalez, only to lose the

titles to Judah in February 2005. He was then inactive until beating Roman Karmazin to win the IBF light-middleweight title in July 2006. Made an unsuccessful challenge to Jermain Taylor for the WBC and WBO middleweight titles in May 2007 and lost the IBF title to Verno Phillips in March 2008. Was then inactive until regaining the IBF title with his win over Deandre Latimore. Has only 11 wins by stoppage or kayo

24.04.09 DeAndre Latimore W PTS 12 St Louis
(Vacant IBF L.Middleweight Title)
Career: 42 contests, won 37, lost 5.

Felix (Storm) Sturm

Leverkusen, Germany. *Born* 31 January, 1979
WBA Middleweight Champion. Former WBO Middleweight Champion
Major Amateur Honours: The winner of a gold medal in the 1997 European Junior Championships, he won the German championship in 1995, 1998 and 1999, was a quarter-finalist in both the 1999 World Championships and 2000 Olympics, and won a gold medal in the European Championships in 2000. Claims 113 wins in 122 fights
Turned Pro: January 2001
Significant Results: Hector Velazco W PTS 12, Ruben Varon W PTS 12, Oscar de la Hoya L PTS 12, Robert Frazier W PTS 10, Hassine Cherifi W CO 3, Bert Schenk W CO 2, Jorge Sendra W PTS 12, Maselino Maseo W PTS 12, Javier Castillejo L RSC 10 & W PTS 12, Noe Gonzalez W PTS 12, Randy Griffin DREW 12, Jamie Pittman W RSC 7
Type/Style: Is a tall, strong, technically sound, box-puncher with a solid jab
Points of Interest: 5'11" tall. Fought in the amateurs under his real name Adnan Catic, but took the name Sturm, which means 'storm' in German, as a pro. Won the WBO middleweight crown by beating Hector Velazco in September 2003 and made one defence before losing the title on a close decision to Oscar de la Hoya in June 2004. Won the WBA 'secondary' title when beating Maselino Maseo in March 2006 and was recognised as

a full WBA champion when Jermain Taylor was stripped of the 'super' title in 2006. Lost the title to Javier Castillejo in July 2006, but regained it when beating Castillejo in April 2007 and has made six defences since then. Has only 14 wins inside the distance

05.07.08 Randy Griffin W PTS 12 Halle
(WBA Middleweight Title Defence)
01.11.08 Sebastian Sylvester W PTS 12 Oberhausen
(WBA Middleweight Title Defence)
25.04.09 Koji Sato W RSC 7 Krefeld
(WBA Middleweight Title Defence)
Career: 35 contests, won 32, drew 1, lost 2.

Juan Francisco (Iron Twin) Urango

Monteria, Colombia. *Born* 4 October, 1980
IBF L.Welterweight Champion
Major Amateur Honours: Competed in the 1998 World Junior Championships and won Colombian National Championships from 1997 to 2001. Claiming to have had 160 amateur fights, he lost to Miguel Cotto in the Americas qualifiers for the 2000 Olympics
Turned Pro: April 2004
Significant Results: Leva Kirakosyan W PTS 8, Sergey Sorokin W PTS 6, Mike Aranoutis DREW 12, Francisco Campos W CO 5, Andre Eason W RSC 7, Naoufel Ben Rabah W PTS 12, Ricky Hatton L PTS 12, Carlos Vilches W CO 4
Type/Style: A strong southpaw, who is a fast-handed and smooth boxer with a big left hook. Also has a good chin
Points of Interest: 5' 8" tall. He has six children, three sisters and four brothers, one of whom is his identical twin, Pedro, who is also a professional, which is where Juan's nickname comes from. Wanted to be a baseball player, but was introduced to boxing by his cousins when he was ten and had his first fight at the age of 14. Trained by the uncle of Miguel Cotto, he won the IBF title for the first time by beating Naoufel Ben Rabah in June 2006, but lost it in his first defence to Ricky Hatton in January 2007. Failed in a challenge to Andre Berto for the WBC welterweight title. Has 16 wins by stoppage or kayo

30.01.09 Herman Ngoudjo W PTS 12 Montreal
(Vacant IBF L.Welterweight Title)
30.05.09 Andre Berto L PTS 12 Hollywood
(WBC Welterweight Title Challenge)
Career: 24 contests, won 21, drew 1, lost 2.

Edwin (Dinamita) Valero

Merida, Venezuela. *Born* 3 December, 1981
WBC Lightweight Champion. Former Undefeated WBA S.Featherweight Champion
Major Amateur Honours: Three times a winner of the Venezuelan championship, he won a gold medal in the 2000 Central American Games and competed in the 2000 Olympics qualifiers. Claims only six losses in 92 fights
Turned Pro: July 2002
Significant Results: Roque Cassiani W CO 1, Esteban Morales W CO 1, Aram Ramazyan W CO 1, Whyber Garcia W CO 1, Genaro Trazancos W RSC 2, Vicente Mosquera W RSC 10, Miguel Lozada W RSC 1, Nobuhito Honmo W RSC 8, Zaid Zavaleta W RSC 3, Takehiro Shimada W RSC 7
Type/Style: Loose-limbed, wide open, aggressive southpaw banger with a devastating punch in both hands
Points of Interest: 5' 7" tall. Having started boxing at the age of 12, he set a record by winning all of his first 18 pro bouts inside the first round. Based in Japan, he was banned from fighting in the United States after failing an MRI Scan in New York in 2004. This was due to a brain injury suffered in a motor cycle accident in Venezuela, but has since fought in Argentina, Panama, Venezuela, Japan, France and Mexico and Texas. Won the WBA super-featherweight title by halting Vicente Mosquera in August 2006 and made four defences before moving up to lightweight. All of his fights have ended inside the distance and only six have lasted more than one round
04.04.09 Antonio Pitalua W RSC 2 Austin
(Vacant WBC Lightweight Title)
Career: 25 contests, won 25.

Nikolai (The Beast from the East) Valuev

St Petersburg, Russia. *Born* 21 August, 1973

WBA Heavyweight Champion
Major Amateur Honours: Had only 15 amateur fights, including participation in the 1994 Goodwill Games
Turned Pro: October 1993
Significant Results: Andreas Sidon W RSC 4, Taras Bidenko W PTS 12, Bob Mirovic W PTS 8, Dick Ryan W RSC 1, Marcelo Dominguez W PTS 8, Richard Bango W RSC 6, Paolo Vidoz W RSC 9, Gerald Nobles W DIS 4, Attila Levin W RSC 3, Cliff Etienne W CO 3, John Ruiz W PTS 12, Owen Beck W RSC 3, Monte Barrett W RSC 11, Jameel McCline W RTD 3, Ruslan Chagaev L PTS 12, Sergey Lyakhovich W PTS 12
Type/Style: He is slow but very strong and uses his height and weight effectively
Points of Interest: Although both of his parents were only 5'5" tall, Nikolai, at 7'2", is the tallest and heaviest fighter to ever win a version of the heavyweight title, when he beat John Ruiz in December 2005. As a youth he won national junior championships at basketball and discus before taking up boxing at the age of 20. He lost the WBA title in his fourth defence when he was outpointed by Ruslan Chagaev in April 2007, but due to injury problems the WBA relegated Chagaev to 'Champion in Recess' in 2008 and Valuev won the 'secondary' title with his 2008 win over Ruiz. He then made a successful defence, outpointing Evander Holyfield. A return bout with Chagaev had to be cancelled after the latter failed the medical tests and when the man from Uzbekistan decided to take a fight with Vladimir Klitschko for the IBF/WBO versions of the title without having permission from the WBA he was stripped. At that point, Valuev, who is now based in Germany, was fully recognised by the WBA as being their champion. Has scored 34 wins by stoppage or knockout
30.08.08 John Ruiz W PTS 12 Berlin
(Vacant WBA 'Secondary' Heavyweight Title)
20.12.08 Evander Holyfield W PTS 12 Zurich
(WBA 'Secondary' Heavyweight Title Defence)
Career: 52 contests, won 50, lost 1, no contest 1.

Brian (The Hawaiian Punch) Viloria

Waipahu, Hawaii, USA. *Born* 24 November, 1980
IBF L.Flyweight Champion. Former WBC L.Flyweight Champion
Major Amateur Honours: Won United States Junior Championships in 1995 and 1996 at 100lbs and followed it up with gold medals in the World Championships, the United States Championships and the National Golden Gloves Championships in 1999. He competed in the 2000 Olympics before going pro
Turned Pro: May 2001
Significant Results: Sandro Oviedo W CO 1, Alberto Rossel NC 3 and W PTS 12, Juan Javier Lagos W PTS 12, Valentin Leon W RSC 8, Luis Doria W RSC 1, Juan Alfonso Keb Baas W PTS 12, Gilberto Keb Baas W CO 11, Angel Priolo W CO 7, Eric Ortiz W CO 1, Jose Antonio Aguirre W PTS 12, Omar Romero L PTS 12, Omar Romero DREW 12, Edgar Sosa L PTS 12
Type/Style: Is a stylish, sharp-punching little fighter, who is a good body puncher but sometimes makes hard work of what should be easy fights
Points of Interest: 5' 4" tall. Although born in Hawaii, Brian is of Filipino parentage and was raised there. He won a scholarship to the United States Olympic Education Centre. Won the WBC light-flyweight title by kayoing Eric Ortiz in September 2005, but lost the title in his second defence, to Omar Nino, in August 2006. In their return match, Nino won again but the result was ruled a no-contest after Romero failed a drugs test. Failed in an attempt to win the WBC title when he was outpointed by Edgar Sosa in April 2007. Has 15 wins inside the distance
25.09.08 Juan Javier Lagos W PTS 8 El Cajon
12.12.08 Benjamin Garcia W CO 2 Los Angeles
19.04.09 Ulises Solis W CO 11 Quezon City
(IBF L.Flyweight Title Challenge)
Career: 29 contests, won 25, lost 2, no contest 2.

World Title Bouts, 2008-2009

by Bob Yalen

All of last season's title bouts for the IBF, WBA, WBC and WBO are shown in date order within their weight division and give the boxers' respective weights as well as the scorecards if going to a decision. British officials, where applicable, are also listed. Yet again there were no WORLD TITLE FIGHTS as such, just a proliferation of champions recognised by the above four commissions and spread over 17 weight divisions. Below the premier league, come other commissions such as the WBU, IBO, IBC and WBF, etc, etc, which would devalue the world championships even further if one recognised their champions as being the best in the world. Despite that, we have recorded fights involving the Philippines' Manny Pacquiao (IBO light-welterweight champion) as he is unarguably the top man at the weight. Right now, the WBA have decided to continue recognising their champions who move on to claim other commissions' titles as super champions – despite vacating the title and creating a new champion, who, for our purposes, is classified as a 'secondary' champion – which if taken up in general could eventually lead to the best man at his weight being recognised universally as a world champion if the fights can be made..

M. Flyweight

30 August Donnie Nietes 105 (Philippines) W RSC 2 Eddy Castro 103½ (Nicaragua), Waterfront Hotel, Cebu City, Philippines - WBO. Referee: Raul Caiz (junior). On 26 September at the Municipal Sports Hall (no 2), Caseros, Buenos Aires, Argentina, Daniel Reyes (Colombia) outpointed Luis Alberto Lazarte (Argentina) over 12 rounds to win the vacant WBO 'interim' title, but lost it on 6 December when knocked out in the fourth round by Manuel Vargas (Mexico) at the Fair Auditorium, Lagos de Moreno, Jalisco, Mexico. Vargas went on to retain the 'interim' title when outpointing Panama's Walter Tello over 12 rounds at the Expo Forum, Hermosillo, Sonora, Mexico on 12 February 2009.

13 September Raul Garcia 105 (Mexico) W PTS 12 Jose Luis Varela 104 (Venezuela), Arturo C. Nahl Stadium, La Paz, Baja, Mexico - IBF. Referee: Jack Reiss. Scorecards: 118-110, 118-110, 118-110.

15 September Yutaka Niida 104¼ (Japan) L RSC 4 Roman Gonzalez 104½ (Nicaragua), The Pacifico, Yokohama, Japan - WBA. Referee: Mark Nelson.

27 November Oleydong Sithsamerchai 105 (Thailand) W PTS 12 Pornsawan Porpramook 105 (Thailand), City Hall Ground Arena, Phitsanulok, Thailand - WBC. Referee: Jae-Bong Kim. Scorecards: 118-110, 117-113, 120-108. Earlier, on 2 August, in Ponce, Puerto Rico, Nicaragua's Juan Palacios won the vacant WBC 'interim' title when knocking out Omar Soto (Puerto Rico) inside ten rounds and then successfully defended it on 7 November when stopping Teruo Misawa (Japan) inside seven rounds at the Sichuan Gymnasium, Chengdu, China.

13 December Raul Garcia 105 (Mexico) W PTS 12 Jose Luis Varela 105 (Venezuela), Medrano Meza Gymnasium, Loreto, Baja California, Mexico - IBF. Referee: Wayne Hedgepeth. Scorecards: 120-107, 120-107, 119-108.

28 February Donnie Nietes 104½ (Philippines) W PTS 12 Erik Ramirez 105 (Mexico), Guelaguetza Auditorium, Oaxaca, Mexico - WBO. Referee: Luis Pabon. Scorecards: 113-111, 116-108, 115-109.

28 February Roman Gonzalez 104½ (Nicaragua) W PTS 12 Francisco Rosas 105 (Mexico), Guelaguetza Auditorium, Oaxaca, Mexico - WBA. Referee: Russell Mora. Scorecards: 115-113, 116-112, 114-114.

11 April Raul Garcia 105 (Mexico) W RSC 6 Ronald Barrera 104¾ (Colombia), Arturo C. Nahl Stadium, La Paz, Baja California, Mexico - IBF. Referee: Rafael Ramos.

29 May Oleydong Sithsamerchai 105 (Thailand) W TD 11 Muhammad Rachman 105 (Indonesia), Bangla Boxing Stadium, Patong, Phuket, Thailand - WBC. Referee: Malcolm Bulner. Scorecards: 106-101, 105-103, 105-103. Juan Palacios (Nicaragua) defended the WBC 'interim' title when stopping Mexico's Erik Ramirez inside ten rounds at the Banamex Exhibition Centre, Mexico City, Mexico on 13 June.

L. Flyweight

12 July Ulises Solis 107¾ (Mexico) W PTS 12 Glenn Donaire 107¾ (Philippines), Exhibition Centre, Hermosilla, Mexico - IBF. Referee: Pat Russell. Scorecards: 120-108, 120-108, 120-107.

30 August Ivan Calderon 107½ (Puerto Rico) W TD 7 Hugo Cazares 108 (Mexico), Ruben Rodriguez Coliseum, Bayamon, Puerto Rico - WBO. Referee: Luis Pabon. Scorecards: 68-65, 68-65, 67-66.

27 September Edgar Sosa 107 (Mexico) W PTS 12 Sonny Boy Jaro 108 (Philippines), The Arena, Mexico City, Mexico - WBC. Referee: Hector Afu. Scorecards: 118-110, 117-110, 117-110.

2 November Ulises Solis 108 (Mexico) W PTS 12 Nerys Espinoza 108 (Nicaragua), San Marcos National Fair Auditorium, Aguascalientes, Mexico - IBF. Referee: Robert Byrd. Scorecards: 115-109, 117-107, 118-107.

29 November Edgar Sosa 108 (Mexico) W RSC 7 Juanito Rubillar 106 (Philippines), The Arena, Mexico City - WBC. Referee: Harold Laurens.

4 April Edgar Sosa 108 (Mexico) W RSC 4 Pornsawan Porpramook 107¾ (Thailand), Entertainment Centre, Ciudad Victoria, Mexico - WBC. Referee: Hector Afu.

19 April Ulises Solis 107 (Mexico) L CO 11 Brian Viloria 108 (USA), Araneta Coliseum, Quezon City, Manila,

WORLD TITLE BOUTS, 2008-2009

Philippines - IBF. Referee: Bruce McTavish.

13 June Ivan Calderon 106¼ (Puerto Rico) TECH DRAW 6 Rodel Mayol 106 (Philippines), Madison Square Garden, NYC, New York, USA - WBO. Referee: Benji Estevez. Scorecards: 58-56, 57-57, 56-58.

20 June Edgar Sosa 108 (Mexico) W RSC 5 Carlos Melo 107¾ (Panama), The Arena, Mexico City, Mexico - WBC. Referee: Frank Garza.

Note: There were no defences made by France's Brahim Asloum, the WBA champion, during the period. However, on 26 July 2008 at the MGM Grand, Las Vegas, Nevada, USA, Mexico's Giovanni Segura outpointed Cesar Canchila (Colombia) over 12 rounds to win the vacant WBA 'interim' title and successfully defended it against the same opponent in Mexicali, Baja California, Mexico, on 14 March 2009, when winning by a fourth-round stoppage. After Asloum pulled out of a proposed title defence in July against Segura, at the time of going to press it was expected that he would be stripped.

Flyweight

30 July Takefumi Sakata 112 (Japan) W PTS 12 Hiroyuki Hisataka 111¾ (Japan), Korakuen Hall, Tokyo, Japan - WBA. Referee: Kazunobu Asao. Scorecards: 117-111, 118-111, 116-112.

30 July Daisuke Naito 112 (Japan) W CO 10 Tomonobu Shimizu 112 (Japan), Korakuen Hall, Tokyo, Japan - WBC. Referee: Frank Garza.

20 September Omar Narvaez 112 (Argentina) W PTS 12 Alejandro Hernandez 111½ (Mexico), New Aurinegro Sports Palace, Puerto Madryn, Chubut, Argentina - WBO. Referee: Luis Pabon. Scorecards: 117-111, 116-112, 119-110.

1 November Nonito Donaire 112 (Philippines) W RSC 6 Moruti Mthalane 111 (South Africa), Mandalay Bay Resort & Casino, Las Vegas, Nevada, USA - IBF. Referee: Joe Cortez.

23 December Daisuke Naito 112 (Japan) W RSC 11 Shingo Yamaguchi 111¾ (Japan), Kokugikan Sumo Arena, Tokyo, Japan - WBC. Referee: Yuji Fukuchi. On 24 April 2009, fighting in a makeshift outdoor arena in Chachoengsao, Thailand, Pongsaklek Wonjongkam (Thailand) beat Mexico's Julio Cesar Miranda on points over 12 rounds to win the vacant WBC 'interim' title.

31 December Takefumi Sakata 112 (Japan) L CO 2 Denkaosan Kaovichit 111¾ (Thailand), Sun Plaza Hall, Hiroshima, Japan - WBA. Referee: Roberto Ramirez.

7 February Omar Narvaez 111½ (Argentina) W RSC 10 Rayonta Whitfield 111¾ (USA), New Aurinegro Sports Palace, Puerto Madryn, Chabut, Argentina - WBO. Referee: Damuel Viruet.

19 April Nonito Donaire 111½ (Philippines) W RSC 4 Raul Martinez 112 (USA), Araneta Coliseum, Quezon City, Manila, Philippines - IBF. Referee: Pete Podgorski.

26 May Daisuke Naito 112 (Japan) W PTS 12 Xiong Zhao Zhong 112 (China), Differ-Ariake Arena, Tokyo, Japan - WBC. Referee: Bruce McTavish. Scorecards: 114-110, 114-111, 113-111.

26 May Denkaosan Kaovichit 112 (Thailand) W PTS 12 Hiroyuki Hisataka 112 (Japan), Central Sports Stadium, Uttaradit, Thailand - WBA. Referee: Lahcen Oumghar. Scorecards: 116-112, 115-112, 114-115.

26 June Omar Narvaez 112 (Argentina) W RSC 11 Omar Soto 111 (Mexico), Luna Park Stadium, Buenos Aires, Argentina - WBO. Referee: Roberto Ramirez (junior).

S. Flyweight

2 August Dimitri Kirilov 114½ (Russia) L CO 5 Vic Darchinyan 114 (Armenia), Emerald Queen Casino, Tacoma, Washington, USA - IBF. Referee: Earl Brown.

30 August Cristian Mijares 115 (Mexico) W RSC 3 Chatchai Sasakul 115 (Thailand), The Arena, Monterrey, Mexico - WBC/WBA. Referee: Toby Gibson. With Mijares recognized as a 'super' champion by the WBA, Rafael Concepcion (Panama) and AJ Banal (Philippines) contested the 'secondary' championship on 26 July in Cebu City, Philippines. The fight ended by way of a tenth-round count-out in favour of Concepcion. On 15 September, Concepcion lost the WBA 'secondary' title when retiring at the end of the ninth round against Jorge Arce (Mexico) at the Mexico City Arena, Mexico.

1 November Vic Darchinyan 115 (Armenia) W CO 9 Cristian Mijares 115 (Mexico), Home Depot Centre, Carson, California, USA - WBA/WBC/IBF. Referee: Lou Moret. On the same day at the Mandalay Bay Resort & Casino, Nevada, Jorge Arce (Mexico) stopped Isidro Garcia (USA) inside four rounds to successfully defend his WBA 'secondary' title.

7 February Vic Darchinyan 115 (Armenia) W RTD 11 Jorge Arce 115 (Mexico), The Pond, Anaheim, California, USA - WBA/WBC/IBF. Referee: Lou Moret. On 11 April at the Prefectural Gymnasium, Osaka, Japan, in an all-Japanese fight, Nobuo Nashiro stopped Konosuke Tomiyama in the eighth round to take the WBA 'secondary' title.

28 March Jose Lopez 115 (Puerto Rico) W PTS 12 Pramuansak Posuwan 114¼ (Thailand), Ruben Rodriguez Coliseum, Bayamon, Puerto Rico - WBO. Contested for the vacant title after Mexico's Fernando Montiel relinquished the WBO title in February 2009 in order to fight for the organisation's bantamweight crown.

Bantamweight

18 September Anselmo Moreno 118 (Panama) W TD 7 Cecilio Santos 117 (Mexico), Figali Convention Centre, Panama City, Panama - WBA. Referee: Roberto Ramirez. Scorecards: 70-63, 70-63, 70-63.

16 October Hozumi Hasegawa 118 (Japan) W RSC 2 Alejandro Valdez 117½ (Mexico), Yoyogi 1 National Gymnasium, Tokyo, Japan - WBC. Referee: Mike Griffin.

30 October Anselmo Moreno 117¾ (Panama) W PTS 12

Rolly Lunas 117¾ (Philippines), Figali Convention Centre, Panama City, Panama - WBA. Referee: Manuel Rodriguez. Scorecards: 120-108, 118-110, 119-109.

11 December Joseph Agbeko 118 (Ghana) W PTS 12 William Gonzalez 117 (Nicaragua), Prudential Centre, Newark, New Jersey, USA - IBF. Referee: Earl Brown. Scorecards: 116-112, 116-112, 114-114.

12 March Hozumi Hasegawa 117¾ (Japan) W RSC 1 Vusi Malinga 115½ (South Africa), World Memorial Hall, Kobe, Japan - WBC. Referee: Laurence Cole.

28 March Fernando Montiel 118 (Mexico) W CO 3 Diego Silva 117 (Argentina), The Bullring, Tijuana, Baja California, Mexico - WBO. Contested for the vacant title after Gerry Penalosa (Philippines) had handed over the WBO belt in February 2009 in order to fight for the organisation's super-featherweight crown.

2 May Anselmo Moreno 117½ (Panama) W PTS 12 Wladimir Sidorenko 117¾ (Ukraine), Exhibition Hall, Bremen, Germany - WBA. Referee: Benji Esteves (junior). Scorecards: 115-113, 115-113, 113-115.

S. Bantamweight

29 August Steve Molitor 121½ (Canada) W RSC 10 Ceferino Dario Labarda 121¼ (Argentina), Rama Casino, Orillia, Ontario, Canada - IBF. Referee: Charlie Fitch.

18 September Celestino Caballero 122 (Panama) W RSC 1 Elvis Mejia 122 (Colombia), Figali Convention Centre, Panama City, Panama - WBA. Referee: Luis Pabon. On the same show, Ricardo Cordoba (Panama) won the vacant WBA 'interim' title when outpointing Luis Alberto Perez (Nicaragua) over 12 rounds.

4 October Juan Manuel Lopez 121 (Puerto Rico) W CO 1 Cesar Figueroa 121½ (Mexico), Jose Miguel Agrelot Coliseum, Hato Rey, Puerto Rico - WBO. Referee: Roberto Ramirez.

21 November Celestino Caballero 121¾ (Panama) W RSC 4 Steve Molitor 121¾ (Canada), Rama Casino, Orillia, Ontario, Canada - WBA/IBF. Referee: Luis Pabon. After beating Molitor, the WBA moved Caballero into the position of 'super' champion to enable a 'secondary' title fight to take place between Panama's Ricardo Cordoba and Bernard Dunne (Ireland) at the O2 Arena, Dublin, Ireland on 21 March. Taking full advantage of being given the chance to fight on home turf, Dunne won by an 11th-round stoppage.

6 December Juan Manuel Lopez 122 (Puerto Rico) W RSC 1 Sergio Medina 122 (Argentina), MGM Grand Garden Arena, Las Vegas, Nevada, USA - WBO. Referee: Joe Cortez.

3 January Toshiaki Nishioka 121½ (Japan) w rsc 12 Genaro Garcia 122 (Mexico), The Pacifico, Yokohama, Japan - WBC. Referee: Bruce McTavish. Having outpointed Thailand's Napapol Kiatisakchokchai over 12 rounds at the Pacifico on 15 September 2008 to win the vacant WBC 'interim' title, when Israel Vazquez (Mexico) was stripped on the day of the Nishioka v Garcia fight, following retina

surgery, the man from Japan was handed full championship status.

25 April Juan Manuel Lopez 121¾ (Puerto Rico) W RTD 9 Gerry Penalosa 121½ (Philippines), Ruben Rodriguez Coliseum, Bayamon, Puerto Rico - WBO. Referee: Jose Rivera.

30 April Celestino Caballero 121¼ (Panama) W PTS 12 Jeffrey Mathebula 120 (South Africa), Roberto Duran Arena, Panama City, Panama - WBA/IBF. Referee: Ernie Sharif. Scorecards: 116-112, 116-112, 112-116. On the same day at a makeshift outdoor arena in Rangsit, Thailand, Poonsawat Kratingdaeng (Thailand) stopped Venezuela's Rafael Hernandez in nine rounds to win the vacant WBA 'interim' title.

23 May Toshiaki Nishioka 122 (Japan) W RSC 3 Jhonny Gonzalez 122 (Mexico), The Arena, Monterrey, Mexico - WBC. Referee: Kenny Bayless.

27 June Juan Manuel Lopez 121½ (Puerto Rico) W RTD 9 Olivier Lontchi 120 (Cameroon), Boardwalk Hall, Atlantic City, New Jersey, USA - WBO. Referee: Allan Huggins.

Featherweight

16 October Oscar Larios 126 (Mexico) W PTS 12 Takahiro Aoh 126 (Japan), Yoyogi 1 National Gymnasium, Tokyo, Japan - WBC. Referee: Vic Drakulich. Scorecards: 114-112, 115-111, 112-114. Earlier, on 2 August 2008, Larios had successfully defended his WBC 'interim' title when stopping Nicaragua's Marlon Aguilar inside seven rounds at the Benito Juarez Auditorium in Zapapan, Jalisco, Mexoco and when Jorge Linares (Venezuela) relinquished the WBC title on 13 August 2008 in order to fight at a higher weight he was appointed as champion.

18 October Steve Luevano 126 (USA) W PTS 12 Billy Dib 126 (Australia), Boardwalk Hall, Atlantic City, New Jersey, USA - WBO. Referee: Steve Smoger. Scorecards: 115-113, 117-111, 116-112.

23 October Cristobal Cruz 126 (Mexico) W PTS 12 Orlando Salido 126 (Mexico), Northern Quest Casino, Airway Heights, Washington, USA - IBF. Referee: Jack Reiss. Scorecards: 116-112, 116-112, 113-115. Billed for the vacant title after Robert Guerrero (USA) had decided to move up a weight in June.

24 October Chris John 125½ (Indonesia) W PTS 12 Hiroyuki Enoki 126 (Japan), Korakuen Hall, Tokyo, Japan - WBA. Referee: Silvestre Abainza. Scorecards: 118-110, 118-110, 117-111.

14 February Cristobal Cruz 125 (Mexico) W PTS 12 Cyril Thomas 125 (France), Sports Palace, St Quentin, France - IBF. Referee: Roberto Ramirez. Scorecards: 116-112, 115-113, 115-113.

28 February Chris John 125¼ (Indonesia) DREW 12 Rocky Juarez 125½ (USA), Toyota Centre, Houston, Texas, USA - WBA. Referee: Laurence Cole. Scorecards: 114-114, 114-114, 114-114. On 17 April at Buffalo Bill's Star Arena, Primm, Nevada, USA, Cuba's Yuriorkis Gamboa stopped

Jose Rojas (Venezuela) inside ten rounds to win the vacant WBA 'interim' title.

12 March Oscar Larios (126 Mexico) L PTS 12 Takahiro Aoh 126 (Japan), Korakuen Hall, Tokyo, Japan - WBC. Referee: Kenny Bayless. Scorecards: 107-119, 109-118, 111-116. Although not in this time frame, Aoh would lose his title to the Dominican Republic's Elio Rojas on 14 July.

S. Featherweight

6 September Alex Arthur 130 (Scotland) L PTS 12 Nicky Cook 129½ (England), MEN Arena, Manchester, England - WBO. Referee: Mickey Vann. Scorecards: Roy Francis 112-117, Dave Parris 111-117, Terry O'Connor 114-115.

13 September Cassius Baloyi 129 (South Africa) W RSC 3 Javier Osvaldo Alvarez 129¾ (Argentina), Emperor's Palace, Kempton Park, South Africa - IBF. Referee: Sparkle Lee.

28 November Jorge Linares 129 (Venezuela) W RSC 5 Whyber Garcia 129½ (Panama), ATLAPA Convention Centre, Panama City, Panama - WBA. Referee: Steve Smoger. Contested for the vacant title after Venezuela's Edwin Valero returned his WBA belt on 3 September when moving up a division.

20 December Humberto Soto 130 (Mexico) W PTS 15 Francisco Lorenzo 129 (Dominican Republic), Andres Quintana Roo Park Arena, Cozumel, Mexico - WBC. Referee: Jay Nady. Scorecards: 117-109, 118-108, 117-109. Contested for the vacant title after Manny Pacquiao (Philippines) had handed back his belt in early June to challenge David Diaz (USA) for the WBC lightweight crown and Soto and Gamaliel Diaz (Mexico) had contested the vacant 'interim' championship at the Bullring in Coahuila, Mexico on 11 October, the latter retiring at the end of the tenth round.

14 March Nicky Cook 130 (England) L RSC 4 Roman Martinez 129 (Puerto Rico), MEN Arena, Manchester, England - WBO. Referee: Dave Parris. Judge: Mickey Vann.

28 March Humberto Soto 130 (Mexico) W RSC 4 Antonio Davis 130 (USA), The Bullring, Tijuana, Baja California, Mexico - WBC. Referee: Roberto Ramirez (junior).

18 April Cassius Baloyi 129¼ (South Africa) L RSC 7 Malcolm Klassen 128¾ (South Africa), North-West University Arena, Mafikeng, South Africa - IBF. Referee: Sam Williams.

2 May Humberto Soto 130 (Mexico) W RSC 9 Benoit Gaudet 129 (Canada), MGM Grand Garden Arena, Las Vegas, Nevada, USA - WBC. Referee: Jay Nady.

27 June Jorge Linares 130 (Venezuela) W RSC 8 Josafat Perez 130 (Mexico), Lauro Luis Longoria Bullring, Nuevo Laredo, Tamaulipas, Mexico - WBA. Referee: Luis Pabon.

Lightweight

28 February Juan Manuel Marquez 134¼ (Mexico) W RSC 9 Juan Diaz 134½ (USA), Toyota Centre, Houston, Texas,

USA - WBA/WBO. Referee: Rafael Ramos. Contested for the vacant titles after Nate Campbell (USA) forfeited when coming in over the weight for a defence against South Africa's Ali Funeka at the Bank Atlanta Centre, Sunrise, Florida, USA on 14 February. Earlier, when Yusuk Kobori (Japan) defended the WBA 'secondary' title on 3 January 2009, he was outpointed over 12 rounds by Namibia's Paulus Moses at the Pacifico, Yokohama, Japan. At the time it was thought that the Namibian would be upgraded to full championship honours, only for the WBA to announce that Diaz and Marquez would be contesting their 'super' title.

4 April Edwin Valero 134½ (Venezuela) W RSC 2 Antonio Pitalua 135 (Colombia), Frank Erwin Centre, Austin, Texas, USA - WBC. Referee: Laurence Cole. Contested for the vacant title after Manny Pacquiao (Philippines) handed in his WBC championship belt on 28 February, having decided to challenge Ricky Hatton for the IBO light-welter crown.

Note: There were no IBF title fights during the period, Nate Campbell (USA) being stripped of his belt on 14 February.

L. Welterweight

5 July Ricardo Torres 139 (Colombia) L CO 1 Kendall Holt 139 (USA), Planet Holywood Resort & Casino, Las Vegas, Nevada, USA - WBO. Referee: Jay Nady.

13 September Tim Bradley 139¾ (USA) W PTS 12 Edner Cherry 139¼ (Bahamas), Beau Rivage Resort & Casino, Biloxi, Mississippi, USA - WBC. Referee: Gary Ritter. Scorecards: 118-109, 119-109, 117-110.

13 September Andreas Kotelnik 140 (Ukraine) W PTS 12 Norio Kimura 140 (Japan), Sports Palace, Lviv, Ukraine - WBA. Referee: Stan Christodoulou. Scorecards: 119-109, 118-110, 119-109.

22 November Ricky Hatton 140 (England) W RTD 11 Paul Malignaggi 139 (USA), MGM Grand Garden Arena, Las Vegas, Nevada, USA - IBO. Referee: Kenny Bayless.

13 December Kendall Holt 140 (USA) W PTS 12 Demetrius Hopkins 140 (USA), Boardwalk Hall, Atlantic City, New Jersey, USA - WBO. Referee: Allen Huggins. Scorecards: 117-111, 116-112, 113-115.

30 January Juan Urango 139 (Colombia) W PTS 12 Herman Ngoudjo 139¼ (Cameroon), Bell Centre, Montreal, Canada - IBF. Referee: Marlon Wright. Scorecards: 118-108, 116-110, 120-106. Billed for the vacant title after Paul Malignaggi (USA) was stripped of the IBF title in September, having signed to meet England's Ricky Hatton for the IBO crown rather than agreeing to make a defence against the number-one challenger, Ngoudjo.

7 February Andreas Kotelnik 139½ (Ukraine) W PTS 12 Marcos Maidana 140 (Argentina), Stadium Hall, Rostock, Germany - WBA. Referee: Hector Afu. Scorecards: 115-114, 115-113, 113-115. On 27 June, Maidana won the vacant WBA 'interim' title when he stopped Victor Ortiz (USA) in the sixth round at the Staples Centre, Los Angeles, California, USA.

4 April Tim Bradley 138¾ (USA) W PTS 12 Kendall Holt

140 (USA), Bell Centre, Montreal, Canada - WBC/WBO. Referee: Michael Griffin. Scorecards: 114-112, 115-111, 115-111. On 25 April at the Ruben Rodriguez Coliseum, Bayamon, Puerto Rico, Lamont Peterson (USA) won the vacant WBO 'interim' title when stopping France's Willy Blain in the seventh round. Bradley was stripped of the WBC title in April when unable to agree terms to meet their number one challenger, Devon Alexander (USA). Alexander had been due to meet England's Junior Witter for the WBC 'interim' belt, a contest that was re-billed as being for the vacant title.

2 May Ricky Hatton 140 (England) L CO 2 Manny Pacquiao 138 (Philippines), MGM Grand Garden Arena, Las Vegas, Nevada, USA - IBO. Referee: Kenny Bayless.

Welterweight

26 July Miguel Cotto 147 (Puerto Rico) L RSC 11 Antonio Margarito 147 (Mexico), MGM Grand Garden Arena, Las Vegas, Nevada, USA - WBA. Referee: Kenny Bayless.

2 August Joshua Clottey 147 (Ghana) W TD 9 Zab Judah 143 (USA), Palms Hotel & Casino, Las Vegas, Nevada, USA - IBF. Referee: Robert Byrd. Scorecards: 87-84, 86-85, 86-85. Contested for the vacant title after Antonio Margarito (Mexico) had handed his belt in during May in order to make a match with Miguel Cotto (Puerto Rico) for the latter's WBA crown. Clottey was stripped of the belt on 16 April after also signing to meet Cotto.

27 September Andre Berto 145½ (USA) W PTS 12 Steve Forbes 147 (USA), Staples Centre, Los Angeles, California, USA - WBC. Referee: James Jen-Kin. Scorecards: 116-111, 118-109, 118-109.

17 January Andre Berto 146 (USA) W PTS 12 Luis Collazo 145¾ (USA), Beau Rivage Resort & Casino, Biloxi, Mississippi, USA - WBC. Referee: Keith Hughes. Scorecards: 116-111, 114-113, 114-113.

24 January Antonio Margarito 145¾ (Mexico) L RSC 9 Shane Mosley 147 (USA), Staples Centre, Los Angeles, California, USA - WBA. Referee: Raul Caiz. After Mosley was promoted to 'super' champion status by the WBA, Yuri Nuzhnenko, the 'interim' titleholder, was stopped in the 11th round by Vyacheslav Senchenko at the Sports Palace, Donetsk, Ukraine on 10 April. In a battle between Ukranians, Senchenko would be seen as the new 'secondary' champion.

21 February Miguel Cotto 146 (Puerto Rico) W RSC 5 Michael Jennings 146½ (England), Madison Square Garden, NYC, New York, USA - WBO. Referee: Benji Esteves. Billed for the vacant title after Paul Williams (USA) handed back his belt in November to contest the WBO 'interim' light-middleweight championship.

30 May Andre Berto 145¼ (USA) W PTS 12 Juan Urango 146½ (Colombia), Seminole Hard Rock Arena, Hollywood, Florida, USA - WBC. Referee: Tommy Kimmons. Scorecards: 118-110, 118-110, 117-111.

13 June Miguel Cotto 146 (Puerto Rico) W PTS 12 Joshua Clottey 147 (Ghana), Madison Square Garden, NYC, New York, USA - WBO. Referee: Arthur Mercante (junior). Scorecards: 116-111, 115-112, 113-114.

L. Middleweight

11 July Joachim Alcine 153 (Haiti) L CO 6 Daniel Santos 153 (Puerto Rico), Uniprix Stadium, Montreal, Canada - WBA. Referee: Marlon Wright.

13 September Sergio Mora 154 (Mexico) L PTS 12 Vernon Forrest 154 (USA), MGM Grand, Las Vegas, Nevada, USA - WBC. Referee: Vic Drakulich. Scorecards: 109-118, 110-117, 108-119. On 4 October at the Pechanga Resort & Casino, Temecula, California, USA, Sergio Martinez (Argentina) forced Alex Bunema (Congo) to retire at the end of the eighth round of a contest to decide the vacant WBO 'interim' title. Martinez successfully defended the WBC 'interim' title when drawing over 12 rounds Kermit Cintron (USA) at the Bank Atlantic Centre, Sunrise, Florida, USA on 14 February. After being out of the ring since his win over Mora due to a persistent rib injury, Forrest was stripped of the title on 21 May 2009, the WBC announcing that the 'interim' champion, Martinez, had been upgraded to full championship status.

Cory Spinks, IBF light-middleweight champion.   Les Clark

1 November Sergei Dzindziruk 153¼ (Ukraine) W PTS 12 Joel Julio 154 (Colombia), Koenig Pilsener Arena, Oberhausen, Germany - WBO. Referee: Genaro Rodriguez. Scorecards: 116-112, 117-111, 116-112. On 29 November at the Citizens' Business Bank Arena, Ontario, California, USA, Paul Williams (USA) forced Verno Phillips (Belize) to retire at the end of the eighth round of their fight for the vacant WBO 'interim' title.

24 April Cory Spinks 152¾ (USA) W PTS 12 DeAndre Latimore 153½ (USA), Scot Trade Centre, St Louis, Missouri, USA - IBF. Referee: Earl Morton. Scorecards: 114-113, 115-112, 112-115. Billed for the vacant title following Belize's Verno Phillips' decision to hand back his belt on 19 November 2008.

Middleweight

5 July Felix Sturm 159½ (Germany) W PTS 12 Randy Griffin 159¾ (USA), Gerry Weber Stadium, Halle, Germany - WBA. Referee: Guillermo Perez Pineda. Scorecards: 116-112, 116-113, 118-110.

1 November Felix Sturm 159½ (Germany) W PTS 12 Sebastian Sylvester 159½ (Germany), Koenig Pilsener Arena, Oberhausen, Germany - WBA. Referee: Guillermo Perez Pineda. Scorecards: 118-110, 118-110, 119-109.

8 November Arthur Abraham 159¾ (Armenia) W RTD 6 Raul Marquez 160 (Mexico), Jako Arena, Bamberg, Germany - IBF. Referee: Wayne Kelly. Judge: Mickey Vann.

21 February Kelly Pavlik 159 (USA) W RTD 9 Marco Antonio Rubio 160 (Mexico), Chevrolet Centre, Youngstown, Ohio, USA - WBO/WBC. Referee: Frank Garza. On 11 July at the Nuerburg Ring, Germany, Sebastian Zbik (Germany) outpointed Italy's Domenico Spada over 12 rounds to win the vacant WBC 'interim' title.

14 March Arthur Abraham 159¾ (Armenia) W PTS 12 Lajuan Simon 157¼ (USA), Osteeee Hall, Kiel, Germany – IBF. Referee: Benji Esteves. Scorecards: Howard Foster 117-110, 118-109, 117-110.

25 April Felix Sturm 159 (Germany) W RSC 7 Koji Sato 159¾ (Japan), Konig Sports Palace, Krefeld, Germany - WBA. Referee: Luis Pabon.

27 June Arthur Abraham 159¾ (Armenia) W RSC 10 Mahir Oral 158¾ (Germany), Max Schmeling Hall, Berlin, Germany - IBF. Referee: Earl Brown. Judge: Howard Foster.

S. Middleweight

27 September Denis Inkin 167¼ (Russia) W PTS 12 Fulgencio Zuniga 166¼ (Colombia), Color Line Arena, Hamburg, Germany - WBO. Referee: Mark Nelson. Scorecards: 117-111, 116-112, 118-110. When Joe Calzaghe (Wales) decided to hand back his WBO belt on 26 September, his decision allowed the WBO 'interim' title fight scheduled for the next day between Inkin and Zuniga to go ahead for the full title.

24 October Lucian Bute 168 (Romania) W PTS 12 Librado Andrade 167¾ (Mexico), Bell Centre, Montreal, Quebec, Canada - IBF. Referee: Marion Wright. Scorecards: 117-109, Mickey Vann 115-111, 115-110.

25 October Mikkel Kessler 167¼ (Denmark) W CO 3 Danilo Haussler 167¼ (Germany), Weser-Ems Hall, Oldenburg, Germany - WBA. Referee: Stan Christodoulou. Judge: John Coyle. Billed for the vacant title after Joe Calzaghe (Wales) handed in his belt on 26 September.

6 December Carl Froch 166½ (England) W PTS 12 Jean Pascal 167¾ (Canada), Trent FM Arena, Nottingham, England - WBC. Referee: Guido Cavalieri. Scorecards: 116-112, 117-111, 118-110. After Joe Calzaghe (Wales) relinquished the WBC title at the end of June to pursue a fight at the light-heavyweight limit against Roy Jones, England's Carl Froch would eventually meet Canada's Jean Pascal to decide the vacant crown.

10 January Denis Inkin 167¼ (Russia) L PTS 12 Karoly Balzsay 167¼ (Hungary), Borderland Hall, Magdeburg, Germany - WBO. Referee: Jose Rivera. Scorecards: 115-113, 116-112, 116-112.

13 March Lucien Bute 167½ (Romania) W RSC 4 Fulgencio Zuniga 167¾ (Colombia), Bell Centre, Montreal, Quebec, Canada - IBF. Referee: Lindsay Page.

25 April Karoly Balzsay 167½ (Hungary) W RSC 11 Maselino Masoe 167¼ (Western Samoa), Konig Sports Palace, Krefeld, Germany - WBO. Referee: Mark Nelson.

25 April Carl Froch 167 (England) W RSC 12 Jermain Taylor 166 (USA), Foxwoods Resort & Casino, Mashantucket, Connecticut, USA - WBC. Referee: Michael Ortega.

L. Heavyweight

3 July Hugo Garay 174¾ (Argentina) W PTS 12 Yuri Barashian 175 (Armenia), Luna Park Stadium, Buenos Aires, Argentina - WBA. Referee: Roberto Ramirez. Scorecards: 118-111, 120-108, 118-110. Contested for the vacant title after Australia's Danny Green retired at the end of March.

11 October Antonio Tarver 174 (USA) L PTS 12 Chad Dawson 174 (USA), Palms Casino, Las Vegas, Nevada, USA - IBF/IBO. Referee: Jay Nady. Scorecards: 109-118, 110-117, 110-117.

22 November Hugo Garay 175 (Argentina) W PTS 12 Juergen Braehmer 174¼ (Germany), Stadium Hall, Rostock, Germany - WBA. Referee: Stan Christodoulou. Scorecards: 118-110, 117-112, 116-115.

9 May Chad Dawson 175 (USA) W PTS 12 Antonio Tarver 172 (USA), Hard Rock Hotel & Casino, Las Vegas, Nevada, USA IBF/IBO. Referee: Robert Byrd. Scorecards: 116-112, 117-111, 117-111. Dawson relinquished the title on 27 May to negotiate a match against Glen Johnson.

19 June Adrian Diaconu 173¼ (Romania) L PTS 12 Jean Pascal 174¼ (Canada), Bell Centre, Montreal, Quebec, Canada - WBC. Referee: Frank Garza. Scorecards: John Keane 112-116, 111-116, 112-115. This was the first

Nikolai Valuev, the WBA heavyweight champion

Les Clark

defence for Diaconu who, as the WBC 'interim' champion, was upgraded in July 2008 after Chad Dawson (USA) had handed his WBC belt back in order to challenge Antonio Tarver (USA) for the IBO/IBF titles rather than be forced into a defence against the Romanian.

20 June Hugo Garay 175 (Argentina) L PTS 12 Gabriel Campillo 174¼ (Spain), Freedom Club Stadium, Sunchales, Santa Fe, Argentina - WBA. Referee: Steve Smoger. Scorecards: 114-115, 113-114, 114-114.

Note: There were no defences for Zsolt Erdei (Hungary), the WBO champion, during the period. Although he had been due to defend his title against Armenia's Yuri Barashian at the Borderland Hall, Magedeburg, Germany on 10 January 2009, the Armenian came in over the weight. Erdei kept his part of the bargain, despite the fight having no championship status, winning on points over 12 rounds.

Cruiserweight

27 September Firat Arslan 198¼ (Germany) L RSC 10 Guillermo Jones 199½ (Panama), Color Line Arena, Hamburg, Germany - WBA. Referee: Luis Pabon. Judge: Paul Thomas. Arslan, the WBA 'interim' champion had been upgraded to full championship status on 16 June after England's David Haye decided to move up to the heavyweight division on 12 May.

24 October Giacobbe Fragomeni 194½ (Italy) W TD 8 Rudolf Kraj 198½ (Czech Republic), Sports Palace, Milan, Italy - WBC. Referee: Yuji Fukuchi. Scorecards: Richie Davies 77-74, 76-75, 77-74. Billed for the vacant title following David Haye's decision on 12 May to move up among the heavyweights.

11 December Steve Cunningham 197 (USA) L PTS 12 Tomasz Adamek 198 (Poland), Prudential Centre, Newark, New Jersey, USA - IBF. Referee: Earl Morton. Scorecards: 112-115, 110-116, 114-112.

27 February Tomasz Adamek 199 (Poland) W RSC 8 Jonathan Banks 200 (USA), Prudential Centre, Newark, New Jersey, USA - IBF. Referee: Eddie Cotton.

16 May Victor Ramirez 198½ (Argentina) W PTS 12 Ali Ismailov 197½ (Ukraine), Luna Park Stadium, Buenos Aires, Argentina - WBO. Referee: Michael Ortega. Scorecards: 116-112, 115-113, 113-115. Following the decision by David Haye (England) to return his WBO belt on 22 July, Ramirez won the vacant WBO 'interim' title when forcing Alexander Alekseev (Uzbekhistan) to retire after nine rounds at the Castle Guard Arena, Dusseldorf, Germany on 17 January 2009, before being promoted to full championship status a few days later. Following that, Ola Afolabi (England) knocked out Enzo Maccarinelli (Wales) in the ninth round to win the vacant WBO 'interim' title at the MEN Arena, Manchester, England on 14 March. Paul Thomas was one of the judges. Originally, Maccarinelli was matched against Jonathan Banks (USA) but when he pulled out Afolabi stepped in at relavely short notice.

16 May Giacobbe Fragomeni 197¼ (Italy) DREW 12 Krzysztof Wlodarczyk 198½ (Poland), Grand Theatre, Rome, Italy - WBC. Referee: Ian-John Lewis. Scorecards: 114-113, Richie Davies 116-112, 114-114.

Heavyweight

12 July Vladimir Klitschko 241 (Ukraine) W CO 11 Tony Thompson 247½ (USA), Color Line Arena, Hamburg, Germany - IBF/WBO. Referee: Joe Cortez.

11 October Samuel Peter 253½ (Nigeria) L RTD 8 Vitali Klitschko 247 (Ukraine), O2 World Arena, Berlin, Germany - WBC. Referee: Massimo Barrovecchio. Judge: John Keane.

13 December Vladimir Klitschko 244¾ (Ukraine) W RSC 7 Hasim Rahman 253½ (USA), SAP Arena, Mannheim, Germany - IBF/WBO. Referee: Tony Weeks.

7 February Ruslan Chagaev 227 (Uzbekistan) W TD 6 Carl Davis Drumond 229 (Costa Rica), Stadium Hall, Rostock, Germany - WBA. Referee: Gustavo Padilla. Scorecards: 60-54, 58-56, Paul Thomas 58-56. Earlier, whilst in training for a defence against Russia's Nikolai Valuev on 5 July 2008, the fight was cancelled when Chagaev suffered a complete tear of an Achilles tendon in the final week of training. With Chagaev given the title of 'Champion in Recess', the two leading contenders, Valuev and John Ruiz (Puerto Rico), were selected to meet for the vacant 'secondary' title in the Max Schmeling Hall, Berlin, Germany on 30 August, the former winning on points over 12 rounds. At the end of the year, on 20 December, Valuev held on to his 'secondary' title when outscoring Evander Holyfield (USA) over 12 rounds at the Stadium Hall, Zurich, Switzerland. Finally getting back in action, Chagaev was given a reasonable opponent by the WBA to feel his way back. It did not quite go to plan. Having been badly cut over the left eye in the third round the fight was eventually called off at the end of the sixth when the doctor decided that Chagaev was in no position to continue, with the injury rapidly worsening. With the cut-eye ruling coming into play, the champion was declared the winner due to him being ahead on all three cards. On 20 June, Chagaev took on Vladimir Klitschko (Ukraine) for the IBF/WBO versions of the title without being given permission by the WBA and, on losing, he was stripped of the title, which was then handed to Valuev, the 'secondary' champion.

21 March Vitali Klitschko 249¼ (Ukraine) W RSC 9 Juan Carlos Gomez 230½ (Cuba), Hanns Martin Schleyer Hall, Stuttgart, Germany - WBC. Referee: Daniel van der Wiele. Judge: John Keane.

20 June Vladimir Klitschko 240½ (Ukraine) W RTD 10 Ruslan Chagaev 225 (Uzbekistan), Veltins Arena, Gelsenkirchen, Germany – IBF/WBO. Referee: Eddie Cotton.

Note: Although Vladimir (Kazakhstan) and Vitali Klitschko (Kyrgyzstan) were born outside of the Ukraine they both see themselves as Ukrainians, having arrived there as very young children, and that is the country I have recorded them under.

World Champions Since Gloves, 1889-2009

Since I began to carry out extensive research into world championship boxing from the very beginnings of gloved action, I discovered much that needed to be amended regarding the historical listings as we know them, especially prior to the 1920s. Although yet to finalise my researches, despite making considerable changes, the listings are the most comprehensive ever published. Bearing all that in mind, and using a wide range of American newspapers, the aim has been to discover just who had claims, valid or otherwise. Studying the records of all the recognised champions, supplied by Professor Luckett Davis and his team, fights against all opposition have been analysed to produce the ultimate data. Because there were no boxing commissions as such in America prior to the 1920s, the yardstick used to determine valid claims were victories over the leading fighters of the day and recognition given within the newspapers. Only where that criteria has been met have I adjusted previous information. Please note that weight limits for the bantam (1919), feather (1921), light (1913), welter (1921) and middleweight (1921) divisions were only universally recognised in the years stated in brackets. Prior to that the champions shown would have won title claims at varying weights, which were massaged in later years to fit the modern weight classes.

Championship Status Code:

AU = Austria; AUST = Australia; CALIF = California; CAN = Canada; CLE = Cleveland Boxing Commission; EBU = European Boxing Union; FL = Florida; FR = France; GB = Great Britain; GEO = Georgia; H = Hawaii; IBF = International Boxing Federation; IBU = International Boxing Union; ILL = Illinois; LOUIS = Louisiana; MARY = Maryland; MASS = Massachusetts; MICH = Michigan; NBA = National Boxing Association; NC = North Carolina; NY = New York; PEN = Pennsylvania; SA = South Africa; TBC = Territorial Boxing Commission; USA = United States; WBA = World Boxing Association; WBC = World Boxing Council; WBO = World Boxing Organisation.

Champions in **bold** are accorded universal recognition.

*Undefeated champions (Only relates to universally recognised champions prior to 1962 and thereafter WBA/WBC/IBF/ WBO champions, apart from the odd occasion. Does not include men who forfeited titles).

Title Holder	Birthplace	Tenure	Status	Title Holder	Birthplace	Tenure	Status
M. Flyweight (105 lbs)				Miguel Barrera	Colombia	2002-2003	IBF
Kyung-Yung Lee*	S Korea	1987	IBF	Eduardo Marquez	Nicaragua	2003	WBO
Hiroki Ioka	Japan	1987-1988	WBC	Ivan Calderon*	Puerto Rico	2003-2007	WBO
Silvio Gamez*	Venezuela	1988-1989	WBA	Edgar Cardenas	Mexico	2003	IBF
Samuth Sithnaruepol	Thailand	1988-1989	IBF	Daniel Reyes	Colombia	2003-2004	IBF
Napa Kiatwanchai	Thailand	1988-1989	WBC	Eagle Kyowa	Thailand	2004	WBC
Bong-Jun Kim	S Korea	1989-1991	WBA	Muhammad Rachman	Indonesia	2004-2007	IBF
Nico Thomas	Indonesia	1989	IBF	Yutaka Niida	Japan	2004-2008	WBA
Rafael Torres	Dom Republic	1989-1992	WBO	Isaac Bustos	Mexico	2004-2005	WBC
Eric Chavez	Philippines	1989-1990	IBF	Katsunari Takayama	Japan	2005	WBC
Jum-Hwan Choi	S Korea	1989-1990	WBC	Eagle Kyowa	Thailand	2005-2007	WBC
Hideyuki Ohashi	Japan	1990	WBC	Florante Condes	Philippines	2007-2008	IBF
Fahlan Lukmingkwan	Thailand	1990-1992	IBF	Donnie Nietes	Philippines	2007-	WBO
Ricardo Lopez*	Mexico	1990-1997	WBC	Oleydong Sithsamerchai	Thailand	2007-	WBC
Hi-Yon Choi	S Korea	1991-1992	WBA	Raul Garcia	Mexico	2008-	IBF
Manny Melchor	Philippines	1992	IBF	Roman Gonzalez	Nicaragua	2009-	WBA
Hideyuki Ohashi	Japan	1992-1993	WBA				
Ratanapol Sowvoraphin	Thailand	1992-1996	IBF	**L. Flyweight (108 lbs)**			
Chana Porpaoin	Thailand	1993-1995	WBA	Franco Udella	Italy	1975	WBC
Paul Weir*	Scotland	1993-1994	WBO	Jaime Rios	Panama	1975-1976	WBA
Alex Sanchez	Puerto Rico	1993-1997	WBO	Luis Estaba	Venezuela	1975-1978	WBC
Rosendo Alvarez	Nicaragua	1995-1998	WBA	Juan Guzman	Dom Republic	1976	WBA
Ratanapol Sowvoraphin	Thailand	1996-1997	IBF	Yoko Gushiken	Japan	1976-1981	WBA
Ricardo Lopez*	Mexico	1997-1998	WBC/WBO	Freddie Castillo	Mexico	1978	WBC
Zolani Petelo*	S Africa	1997-2000	IBF	Sor Vorasingh	Thailand	1978	WBC
Ricardo Lopez*	Mexico	1998	WBC	Sun-Jun Kim	S Korea	1978-1980	WBC
Eric Jamili	Philippines	1998	WBO	Shigeo Nakajima	Japan	1980	WBC
Kermin Guardia*	Colombia	1998-2002	WBO	Hilario Zapata	Panama	1980-1982	WBC
Ricardo Lopez*	Mexico	1998-1999	WBA/WBC	Pedro Flores	Mexico	1981	WBA
Wandee Chor Chareon	Thailand	1999-2000	WBC	Hwan-Jin Kim	S Korea	1981	WBA
Nohel Arambulet	Venezuela	1999-2000	WBA	Katsuo Tokashiki	Japan	1981-1983	WBA
Jose Antonio Aguirre	Mexico	2000-2004	WBC	Amado Ursua	Mexico	1982	WBC
Jomo Gamboa	Philippines	2000	WBA	Tadashi Tomori	Japan	1982	WBC
Keitaro Hoshino	Japan	2000-2001	WBA	Hilario Zapata	Panama	1982-1983	WBC
Chana Porpaoin	Thailand	2001	WBA	Jung-Koo Chang*	S Korea	1983-1988	WBC
Roberto Levya	Mexico	2001-2003	IBF	Lupe Madera	Mexico	1983-1984	WBA
Yutaka Niida*	Japan	2001	WBA	Dodie Penalosa	Philippines	1983-1986	IBF
Keitaro Hoshino	Japan	2002	WBA	Francisco Quiroz	Dom Republic	1984-1985	WBA
Jorge Mata	Spain	2002-2003	WBO	Joey Olivo	USA	1985	WBA
Nohel Arambulet	Venezuela	2002-2004	WBA	Myung-Woo Yuh	S Korea	1985-1991	WBA

Title Holder	Birthplace	Tenure	Status
Jum-Hwan Choi	S Korea	1986-1988	IBF
Tacy Macalos	Philippines	1988-1989	IBF
German Torres	Mexico	1988-1989	WBC
Yul-Woo Lee	S Korea	1989	WBC
Muangchai Kitikasem	Thailand	1989-1990	IBF
Jose de Jesus	Puerto Rico	1989-1992	WBO
Humberto Gonzalez	Mexico	1989-1990	WBC
Michael Carbajal*	USA	1990-1993	IBF
Rolando Pascua	Philippines	1990-1991	WBC
Melchor Cob Castro	Mexico	1991	WBC
Humberto Gonzalez	Mexico	1991-1993	WBC
Hiroki Ioka	Japan	1991-1992	WBA
Josue Camacho	Puerto Rico	1992-1994	WBO
Myung-Woo Yuh*	S Korea	1992-1993	WBA
Michael Carbajal	USA	1993-1994	IBF/WBC
Silvio Gamez	Venezuela	1993-1995	WBA
Humberto Gonzalez	Mexico	1994-1995	WBC/IBF
Michael Carbajal*	USA	1994	WBO
Paul Weir	Scotland	1994-1995	WBO
Hi-Yong Choi	S Korea	1995-1996	WBA
Saman Sorjaturong*	Thailand	1995	WBC/IBF
Jacob Matlala*	South Africa	1995-1997	WBO
Saman Sorjaturong	Thailand	1995-1999	WBC
Carlos Murillo	Panama	1996	WBA
Michael Carbajal	USA	1996-1997	IBF
Keiji Yamaguchi	Japan	1996	WBA
Pichitnoi Chor Siriwat	Thailand	1996-2000	WBA
Mauricio Pastrana	Colombia	1997-1998	IBF
Jesus Chong	Mexico	1997	WBO
Melchor Cob Castro	Mexico	1997-1998	WBO
Mauricio Pastrana	Colombia	1997-1998	IBF
Juan Domingo Cordoba	Argentina	1998	WBO
Jorge Arce	Mexico	1998-1999	WBO
Will Grigsby	USA	1998-1999	IBF
Michael Carbajal*	USA	1999-2000	WBO
Ricardo Lopez*	Mexico	1999-2002	IBF
Yo-Sam Choi	S Korea	1999-2002	WBC
Masibuleke Makepula*	S Africa	2000	WBO
Will Grigsby	USA	2000	WBO
Beibis Mendoza	Colombia	2000-2001	WBA
Rosendo Alvarez	Nicaragua	2001-2004	WBA
Nelson Dieppa	Puerto Rico	2001-2005	WBO
Jorge Arce*	Mexico	2002-2005	WBC
Jose Victor Burgos	Mexico	2003-2004	IBF
Erick Ortiz	Mexico	2005	WBC
Roberto Vasquez*	Panama	2005-2006	WBA
Hugo Cazares	Mexico	2005-2007	WBO
Will Grigsby	USA	2005-2006	IBF
Brian Viloria	USA	2005-2006	WBC
Ulises Solis	Mexico	2006-2009	IBF
Koki Kameda*	Japan	2006-2007	WBA
Omar Nino	Mexico	2006-2007	WBC
Edgar Sosa	Mexico	2007-	WBC
Juan Carlos Reveco	Argentina	2007	WBA
Ivan Calderon	Puerto Rico	2007-	WBO
Brahim Asloum	France	2007-	WBA
Brian Viloria	USA	2009-	IBF

Flyweight (112 lbs)

Title Holder	Birthplace	Tenure	Status
Johnny Coulon	Canada	1910	USA
Sid Smith	England	1911-1913	GB
Sid Smith	England	1913	GB/IBU
Bill Ladbury	England	1913-1914	GB/IBU
Percy Jones	Wales	1914	GB/IBU
Tancy Lee	Scotland	1915	GB/IBU
Joe Symonds	England	1915-1916	GB/IBU
Jimmy Wilde	Wales	1916	GB/IBU
Jimmy Wilde	Wales	1916-1923	
Pancho Villa*	Philippines	1923-1925	
Fidel la Barba	USA	1925-1927	NBA/CALIF
Fidel la Barba*	USA	1927	
Pinky Silverberg	USA	1927	NBA

Title Holder	Birthplace	Tenure	Status
Johnny McCoy	USA	1927-1928	CALIF
Izzy Schwartz	USA	1927-1929	NY
Frenchy Belanger	Canada	1927-1928	NBA
Newsboy Brown	Russia	1928	CALIF
Johnny Hill	Scotland	1928-1929	GB
Frankie Genaro	USA	1928-1929	NBA
Emile Pladner	France	1929	NBA/IBU
Frankie Genaro	USA	1929-1931	NBA/IBU
Midget Wolgast	USA	1930-1935	NY
Young Perez	Tunisia	1931-1932	NBA/IBU
Jackie Brown	England	1932-1935	NBA/IBU
Jackie Brown	England	1935	GB/NBA
Benny Lynch	Scotland	1935-1937	GB/NBA
Small Montana	Philippines	1935-1937	NY/CALIF
Valentin Angelmann	France	1936-1938	IBU
Peter Kane*	England	1938-1939	NBA/NY/GB/IBU
Little Dado	Philippines	1938-1939	CALIF
Little Dado	Philippines	1939-1943	NBA/CALIF
Jackie Paterson	Scotland	1943-1947	
Jackie Paterson	Scotland	1947-1948	GB/NY
Rinty Monaghan	Ireland	1947-1948	NBA
Rinty Monaghan*	Ireland	1948-1950	
Terry Allen	England	1950	
Dado Marino	Hawaii	1950-1952	
Yoshio Shirai	Japan	1952-1954	
Pascual Perez	Argentina	1954-1960	
Pone Kingpetch	Thailand	1960-1962	

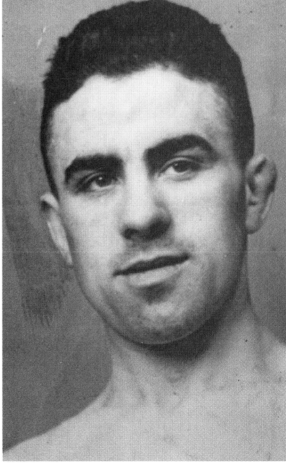

Jackie Brown

246

Title Holder	Birthplace	Tenure	Status
Fighting Harada	Japan	1962-1963	
Pone Kingpetch	Thailand	1963	
Hiroyuki Ebihara	Japan	1963-1964	
Pone Kingpetch	Thailand	1964-1965	
Salvatore Burruni	Italy	1965	
Salvatore Burruni	Italy	1965-1966	WBC
Horacio Accavallo*	Argentina	1966-1968	WBA
Walter McGowan	Scotland	1966	WBC
Chartchai Chionoi	Thailand	1966-1969	WBC
Efren Torres	Mexico	1969-1970	WBC
Hiroyuki Ebihara	Japan	1969	WBA
Bernabe Villacampo	Philippines	1969-1970	WBA
Chartchai Chionoi	Thailand	1970	WBC
Berkrerk Chartvanchai	Thailand	1970	WBA
Masao Ohba*	Japan	1970-1973	WBA
Erbito Salavarria	Philippines	1970-1971	WBC
Betulio Gonzalez	Venezuela	1971-1972	WBC
Venice Borkorsor*	Thailand	1972-1973	WBC
Chartchai Chionoi	Thailand	1973-1974	WBA
Betulio Gonzalez	Venezuela	1973-1974	WBC
Shoji Oguma	Japan	1974-1975	WBC
Susumu Hanagata	Japan	1974-1975	WBA
Miguel Canto	Mexico	1975-1979	WBC
Erbito Salavarria	Philippines	1975-1976	WBA
Alfonso Lopez	Panama	1976	WBA
Guty Espadas	Mexico	1976-1978	WBA
Betulio Gonzalez	Venezuela	1978-1979	WBA
Chan-Hee Park	S Korea	1979-1980	WBC
Luis Ibarra	Panama	1979-1980	WBA
Tae-Shik Kim	S Korea	1980	WBA
Shoji Oguma	Japan	1980-1981	WBC
Peter Mathebula	S Africa	1980-1981	WBA
Santos Laciar	Argentina	1981	WBA
Antonio Avelar	Mexico	1981-1982	WBC
Luis Ibarra	Panama	1981	WBA
Juan Herrera	Mexico	1981-1982	WBA
Prudencio Cardona	Colombia	1982	WBC
Santos Laciar*	Argentina	1982-1985	WBA
Freddie Castillo	Mexico	1982	WBC
Eleonicio Mercedes	Dom Republic	1982-1983	WBC
Charlie Magri	Tunisia	1983	WBC
Frank Cedeno	Philippines	1983-1984	WBC
Soon-Chun Kwon	S Korea	1983-1985	IBF
Koji Kobayashi	Japan	1984	WBC
Gabriel Bernal	Mexico	1984	WBC
Sot Chitalada	Thailand	1984-1988	WBC
Hilario Zapata	Panama	1985-1987	WBA
Chong-Kwan Chung	S Korea	1985-1986	IBF
Bi-Won Chung	S Korea	1986	IBF
Hi-Sup Shin	S Korea	1986-1987	IBF
Fidel Bassa	Colombia	1987-1989	WBA
Dodie Penalosa	Philippines	1987	IBF
Chang-Ho Choi	S Korea	1987-1988	IBF
Rolando Bohol	Philippines	1988	IBF
Yong-Kang Kim	S Korea	1988-1989	WBC
Duke McKenzie	England	1988-1989	IBF
Elvis Alvarez*	Colombia	1989	WBO
Sot Chitalada	Thailand	1989-1991	WBC
Dave McAuley	Ireland	1989-1992	IBF
Jesus Rojas	Venezuela	1989-1900	WBA
Yukihito Tamakuma	Japan	1990-1991	WBA
Isidro Perez	Mexico	1990-1992	WBO
Yul-Woo Lee	S Korea	1990	WBA
Muangchai Kitikasem	Thailand	1991-1992	WBC
Elvis Alvarez	Colombia	1991	WBA
Yong-Kang Kim	S Korea	1991-1992	WBA
Pat Clinton	Scotland	1992-1993	WBO
Rodolfo Blanco	Colombia	1992	IBF
Yuri Arbachakov	Russia	1992-1997	WBC
Aquiles Guzman	Venezuela	1992	WBA
Pichit Sitbangprachan*	Thailand	1992-1994	IBF
David Griman	Venezuela	1992-1994	WBA

Title Holder	Birthplace	Tenure	Status
Jacob Matlala	S Africa	1993-1995	WBO
Saen Sorploenchit	Thailand	1994-1996	WBA
Alberto Jimenez	Mexico	1995-1996	WBO
Francisco Tejedor	Colombia	1995	IBF
Danny Romero*	USA	1995-1996	IBF
Mark Johnson*	USA	1996-1998	IBF
Jose Bonilla	Venezuela	1996-1998	WBA
Carlos Salazar	Argentina	1996-1998	WBO
Chatchai Sasakul	Thailand	1997-1998	WBC
Hugo Soto	Argentina	1998-1999	WBA
Ruben Sanchez	Mexico	1998-1999	WBO
Manny Pacquiao	Philippines	1998-1999	WBC
Silvio Gamez	Venezuela	1999	WBA
Irene Pacheco	Colombia	1999-2004	IBF
Jose Antonio Lopez	Spain	1999	WBO
Sornpichai Pisanurachan	Thailand	1999-2000	WBA
Medgoen Singsurat	Thailand	1999-2000	WBC
Isidro Garcia	Mexico	1999-2000	WBO
Malcolm Tunacao	Philippines	2000-2001	WBC
Eric Morel	USA	2000-2003	WBA
Fernando Montiel*	Mexico	2000-2002	WBO
Pongsaklek Wonjongkam	Thailand	2001-2007	WBC
Adonis Rivas	Nicaragua	2002	WBO
Omar Narvaez	Argentina	2002-	WBO
Lorenzo Parra	Venezuela	2003-2007	WBA
Vic Darchinyan	Armenia	2004-2007	IBF
Takefumi Sakata	Japan	2007-2008	WBA
Nonito Donaire	Philippines	2007-	IBF
Daisuke Naito	Japan	2007-	WBC
Denkaosan Kaovichit	Thailand	2009-	WBA

S. Flyweight (115 lbs)

Title Holder	Birthplace	Tenure	Status
Rafael Orono	Venezuela	1980-1981	WBC
Chul-Ho Kim	S Korea	1981-1982	WBC
Gustavo Ballas	Argentina	1981	WBA
Rafael Pedroza	Panama	1981-1982	WBA
Jiro Watanabe	Japan	1982-1984	WBA
Rafael Orono	Venezuela	1982-1983	WBC
Payao Poontarat	Thailand	1983-1984	WBC
Joo-Do Chun	S Korea	1983-1985	IBF
Jiro Watanabe	Japan	1984-1986	WBC
Kaosai Galaxy*	Thailand	1984-1992	WBA
Elly Pical	Indonesia	1985-1986	IBF
Cesar Polanco	Dom Republic	1986	IBF
Gilberto Roman	Mexico	1986-1987	WBC
Elly Pical	Indonesia	1986-1987	IBF
Santos Laciar	Argentina	1987	WBC
Tae-Il Chang	S Korea	1987	IBF
Jesus Rojas	Colombia	1987-1988	WBC
Elly Pical	Indonesia	1987-1989	IBF
Gilberto Roman	Mexico	1988-1989	WBC
Jose Ruiz	Puerto Rico	1989-1992	WBO
Juan Polo Perez	Colombia	1989-1990	IBF
Nana Yaw Konadu	Ghana	1989-1990	WBC
Sung-Il Moon	S Korea	1990-1993	WBC
Robert Quiroga	USA	1990-1993	IBF
Jose Quirino	Mexico	1992	WBO
Katsuya Onizuka	Japan	1992-1994	WBA
Johnny Bredahl	Denmark	1992-1994	WBO
Julio Cesar Borboa	Mexico	1993-1994	IBF
Jose Luis Bueno	Mexico	1993-1994	WBC
Hiroshi Kawashima	Japan	1994-1997	WBC
Harold Grey	Colombia	1994-1995	IBF
Hyung-Chul Lee	S Korea	1994-1995	WBA
Johnny Tapia*	USA	1994-1997	WBO
Alimi Goitia	Venezuela	1995-1996	WBA
Carlos Salazar	Argentina	1995-1996	IBF
Harold Grey	Colombia	1996	IBF
Yokthai Sith-Oar	Thailand	1996-1997	WBA
Danny Romero	USA	1996-1997	IBF
Gerry Penalosa	Philippines	1997-1998	WBC
Johnny Tapia*	USA	1997-1998	IBF/WBO

WORLD CHAMPIONS SINCE GLOVES, 1889-2009

Title Holder	Birthplace	Tenure	Status
Satoshi Iida	Japan	1997-1998	WBA
In-Joo Cho	S Korea	1998-2000	WBC
Victor Godoi	Argentina	1998-1999	WBO
Jesus Rojas	Venezuela	1998-1999	WBA
Mark Johnson	USA	1999-2000	IBF
Diego Morales	Mexico	1999	WBO
Hideki Todaka	Japan	1999-2000	WBA
Adonis Rivas	Nicaragua	1999-2001	WBO
Felix Machado	Venezuela	2000-2003	IBF
Masamori Tokuyama	Japan	2000-2004	WBC
Silvio Gamez	Venezuela	2000-2001	WBA
Celes Kobayashi	Japan	2001-2002	WBA
Pedro Alcazar	Panama	2001-2002	WBO
Alexander Munoz	Venezuela	2002-2004	WBA
Fernando Montiel	Mexico	2002-2003	WBO
Luis Perez	Nicaragua	2003-2006	IBF
Mark Johnson	USA	2003-2004	WBO
Katsushige Kawashima	Japan	2004-2005	WBC
Ivan Hernandez	Mexico	2004-2005	WBO
Martin Castillo	Mexico	2004-2006	WBA
Fernando Montiel*	Mexico	2005-2009	WBO
Masamori Tokuyama*	Japan	2005-2006	WBC
Nobuo Nashiro	Japan	2006-2007	WBA
Cristian Mijares	Mexico	2007-2008	WBC
Alexander Munoz	Venezuela	2007	WBA
Dimitri Kirilov	Russia	2007-2008	IBF
Vic Darchinyan*	Armenia	2008	IBF
Vic Darchinyan	Armenia	2008-	WBA/WBC/IBF
Jose Lopez	Puerto Rico	2009-	WBO

Bantamweight (118 lbs)

Title Holder	Birthplace	Tenure	Status
Tommy Kelly	USA	1889	
George Dixon	Canada	1889-1890	
Chappie Moran	England	1889-1890	
Tommy Kelly	USA	1890-1892	
Billy Plimmer	England	1892-1895	
Pedlar Palmer	England	1895-1899	
Terry McGovern	USA	1899	USA
Pedlar Palmer	England	1899-1900	GB
Terry McGovern*	USA	1899-1900	
Clarence Forbes	USA	1900	
Johnny Reagan	USA	1900-1902	
Harry Ware	England	1900-1902	GB
Harry Harris	USA	1901	
Harry Forbes	USA	1901-1902	
Kid McFadden	USA	1901	
Dan Dougherty	USA	1901	
Andrew Tokell	England	1902	GB
Harry Ware	England	1902	GB
Harry Forbes	USA	1902-1903	USA
Joe Bowker	England	1902-1904	GB
Frankie Neil	USA	1903-1904	USA
Joe Bowker*	England	1904-1905	
Frankie Neil	USA	1905	USA
Digger Stanley	England	1905-1907	
Owen Moran	England	1905-1907	
Jimmy Walsh	USA	1905-1908	USA
Owen Moran	England	1907	GB
Monte Attell	USA	1908-1910	
Jimmy Walsh	USA	1908-1911	
Digger Stanley	England	1909-1912	GB
Frankie Conley	Italy	1910-1911	
Johnny Coulon	Canada	1910-1911	
Monte Attell	USA	1910-1911	
Johnny Coulon	Canada	1911-1913	USA
Charles Ledoux	France	1912-1913	GB/IBU
Eddie Campi	USA	1913-1914	
Johnny Coulon	Canada	1913-1914	
Kid Williams	Denmark	1913-1914	
Kid Williams	Denmark	1914-1915	
Kid Williams	Denmark	1915-1917	
Johnny Ertle	USA	1915-1918	

Title Holder	Birthplace	Tenure	Status
Pete Herman	USA	1917-1919	
Pal Moore	USA	1918-1919	
Pete Herman	USA	1919-1920	
Joe Lynch	USA	1920-1921	
Pete Herman	USA	1921	
Johnny Buff	USA	1921-1922	
Joe Lynch	USA	1922-1923	
Joe Lynch	USA	1923-1924	NBA
Joe Burman	England	1923	NY
Abe Goldstein	USA	1923-1924	NY
Joe Lynch	USA	1924	
Abe Goldstein	USA	1924	
Eddie Martin	USA	1924-1925	
Charley Rosenberg	USA	1925-1926	
Charley Rosenberg	USA	1926-1927	NY
Bud Taylor*	USA	1926-1928	NBA
Teddy Baldock	England	1927-1928	GB
Bushy Graham*	Italy	1928-1929	NY
Al Brown	Panama	1929-1931	
Al Brown	Panama	1931	NY/IBU
Pete Sanstol	Norway	1931	CAN
Al Brown	Panama	1931-1933	
Al Brown	Panama	1933-1934	NY/NBA/IBU
Speedy Dado	Philippines	1933	CALIF
Baby Casanova	Mexico	1933-1934	CALIF
Sixto Escobar	Puerto Rico	1934	CAN
Sixto Escobar	Puerto Rico	1934-1935	NBA
Al Brown	Panama	1934-1935	NY/IBU
Lou Salica	USA	1935	CALIF
Baltazar Sangchilli	Spain	1935-1938	IBU
Lou Salica	USA	1935	NBA/NY
Sixto Escobar	Puerto Rico	1935-1937	NBA/NY
Harry Jeffra	USA	1937-1938	NY/NBA
Sixto Escobar	Puerto Rico	1938-1939	NY/NBA
Al Brown	Panama	1938	IBU
Sixto Escobar	Puerto Rico	1939	
George Pace	USA	1939-1940	NBA
Lou Salica	USA	1939	CALIF
Tony Olivera	USA	1939-1940	CALIF
Little Dado	Philippines	1940	CALIF
Lou Salica	USA	1940-1941	
Kenny Lindsay	Canada	1941	CAN
Lou Salica	USA	1942	NY
David Kui Kong Young	Hawaii	1941-1943	TBC
Lou Salica	USA	1941-1942	NY/NBA
Manuel Ortiz	USA	1942-1943	NBA
Manuel Ortiz	USA	1943-1945	NY/NBA
David Kui Kong Young	Hawaii	1943	TBC
Rush Dalma	Philippines	1943-1945	TBC
Manuel Ortiz	USA	1945-1947	
Harold Dade	USA	1947	
Manuel Ortiz	USA	1947-1950	
Vic Toweel	S Africa	1950-1952	
Jimmy Carruthers*	Australia	1952-1954	
Robert Cohen	Algeria	1954	
Robert Cohen	Algeria	1954-1956	NY/EBU
Raton Macias	Mexico	1955-1957	NBA
Mario D'Agata	Italy	1956-1957	NY/EBU
Alphonse Halimi	Algeria	1957	NY/EBU
Alphonse Halimi	Algeria	1957-1959	
Joe Becerra*	Mexico	1959-1960	
Alphonse Halimi	Algeria	1960-1961	EBU
Eder Jofre	Brazil	1960-1962	NBA
Johnny Caldwell	Ireland	1961-1962	EBU
Eder Jofre	Brazil	1962-1965	
Fighting Harada	Japan	1965-1968	
Lionel Rose	Australia	1968-1969	
Ruben Olivares	Mexico	1969-1970	
Chuchu Castillo	Mexico	1970-1971	
Ruben Olivares	Mexico	1971-1972	
Rafael Herrera	Mexico	1972	
Enrique Pinder	Panama	1972	

Title Holder	Birthplace	Tenure	Status
Enrique Pinder	Panama	1972-1973	WBC
Romeo Anaya	Mexico	1973	WBA
Rafael Herrera	Mexico	1973-1974	WBC
Arnold Taylor	S Africa	1973-1974	WBA
Soo-Hwan Hong	S Korea	1974-1975	WBA
Rodolfo Martinez	Mexico	1974-1976	WBC
Alfonso Zamora	Mexico	1975-1977	WBA
Carlos Zarate	Mexico	1976-1979	WBC
Jorge Lujan	Panama	1977-1980	WBA
Lupe Pintor*	Mexico	1979-1983	WBC
Julian Solis	Puerto Rico	1980	WBA
Jeff Chandler	USA	1980-1984	WBA
Albert Davila	USA	1983-1985	WBC
Richard Sandoval	USA	1984-1986	WBA
Satoshi Shingaki	Japan	1984-1985	IBF
Jeff Fenech*	Australia	1985-1987	IBF
Daniel Zaragoza	Mexico	1985	WBC
Miguel Lora	Colombia	1985-1988	WBC
Gaby Canizales	USA	1986	WBA
Bernardo Pinango*	Venezuela	1986-1987	WBA
Takuya Muguruma	Japan	1987	WBA
Kelvin Seabrooks	USA	1987-1988	IBF
Chang-Yung Park	S Korea	1987	WBA
Wilfredo Vasquez	Puerto Rico	1987-1988	WBA
Kaokor Galaxy	Thailand	1988	WBA
Orlando Canizales*	USA	1988-1994	IBF
Sung-Il Moon	S Korea	1988-1989	WBA
Raul Perez	Mexico	1988-1991	WBC
Israel Contrerras*	Venezuela	1989-1991	WBO
Kaokor Galaxy	Thailand	1989	WBA
Luisito Espinosa	Philippines	1989-1991	WBA
Greg Richardson	USA	1991	WBC
Gaby Canizales	USA	1991	WBO
Duke McKenzie	England	1991-1992	WBO
Joichiro Tatsuyushi*	Japan	1991-1992	WBC
Israel Contrerras	Venezuela	1991-1992	WBA
Eddie Cook	USA	1992	WBA
Victor Rabanales	Mexico	1992-1993	WBC
Rafael del Valle	Puerto Rico	1992-1994	WBO
Jorge Elicier Julio	Colombia	1992-1993	WBA
Il-Jung Byun	S Korea	1993	WBC
Junior Jones	USA	1993-1994	WBA
Yasuei Yakushiji	Japan	1993-1995	WBC
John Michael Johnson	USA	1994	WBA
Daorung Chuwatana	Thailand	1994-1995	WBA
Alfred Kotey	Ghana	1994-1995	WBO
Harold Mestre	Colombia	1995	IBF
Mbulelo Botile	S Africa	1995-1997	IBF
Wayne McCullough	Ireland	1995-1997	WBC
Veeraphol Sahaprom	Thailand	1995-1996	WBA
Daniel Jimenez	Puerto Rico	1995-1996	WBO
Nana Yaw Konadu	Ghana	1996	WBA
Robbie Regan*	Wales	1996-1998	WBO
Daorung Chuwatana	Thailand	1996-1997	WBA
Sirimongkol Singmanassak	Thailand	1997	WBC
Nana Yaw Konadu	Ghana	1997-1998	WBA
Tim Austin	USA	1997-2003	IBF
Joichiro Tatsuyoshi	Japan	1997-1998	WBC
Jorge Elicier Julio	Colombia	1998-2000	WBO
Johnny Tapia	USA	1998-1999	WBA
Veeraphol Sahaprom	Thailand	1998-2005	WBC
Paulie Ayala	USA	1999-2001	WBA
Johnny Tapia*	USA	2000	WBO
Mauricio Martinez	Panama	2000-2002	WBO
Eidy Moya	Venezuela	2001-2002	WBA
Cruz Carbajal	Mexico	2002-2004	WBO
Johnny Bredahl*	Denmark	2002-2004	WBA
Rafael Marquez*	Mexico	2003-2007	IBF
Ratanchai Sowvoraphin	Thailand	2004-2005	WBO
Julio Zarate	Mexico	2004-2005	WBO
Wladimir Sidorenko	Ukraine	2005-2008	WBA
Hozumi Hasegawa	Japan	2005-	WBC

Title Holder	Birthplace	Tenure	Status
Jhonny Gonzalez	Mexico	2005-2007	WBO
Luis Perez	Nicaragua	2007	IBF
Gerry Penalosa*	Philippines	2007-2009	WBO
Joseph Agbeko	Ghana	2007-	IBF
Anselmo Moreno	Panama	2008-	WBA
Fernando Montiel	Mexico	2009-	WBO

S. Bantamweight (122 lbs)

Title Holder	Birthplace	Tenure	Status
Rigoberto Riasco	Panama	1976	WBC
Royal Kobayashi	Japan	1976	WBC
Dong-Kyun Yum	S Korea	1976-1977	WBC
Wilfredo Gomez*	Puerto Rico	1977-1983	WBC
Soo-Hwan Hong	S Korea	1977-1978	WBA
Ricardo Cardona	Colombia	1978-1980	WBA
Leo Randolph	USA	1980	WBA
Sergio Palma	Argentina	1980-1982	WBA
Leonardo Cruz	Dom Republic	1982-1984	WBA
Jaime Garza	USA	1983-1984	WBC
Bobby Berna	Philippines	1983-1984	IBF
Loris Stecca	Italy	1984	WBA
Seung-In Suh	S Korea	1984-1985	IBF
Victor Callejas	Puerto Rico	1984-1986	WBA
Juan Meza	Mexico	1984-1985	WBC
Ji-Won Kim*	S Korea	1985-1986	IBF
Lupe Pintor	Mexico	1985-1986	WBC
Samart Payakarun	Thailand	1986-1987	WBC
Louie Espinosa	USA	1987	WBA
Seung-Hoon Lee*	S Korea	1987-1988	IBF
Jeff Fenech*	Australia	1987-1988	WBC
Julio Gervacio	Dom Republic	1987-1988	WBA
Bernardo Pinango	Venezuela	1988	WBA
Daniel Zaragoza	Mexico	1988-1990	WBC
Jose Sanabria	Venezuela	1988-1989	IBF
Juan J. Estrada	Mexico	1988-1989	WBA
Fabrice Benichou	Spain	1989-1990	IBF
Kenny Mitchell	USA	1989	WBO
Valerio Nati	Italy	1989-1990	WBO
Jesus Salud	USA	1989-1990	WBA
Welcome Ncita	S Africa	1990-1992	IBF
Paul Banke	USA	1990	WBC
Orlando Fernandez	Puerto Rico	1990-1991	WBO
Luis Mendoza	Colombia	1990-1991	WBA
Pedro Decima	Argentina	1990-1991	WBC
Kiyoshi Hatanaka	Japan	1991	WBC
Jesse Benavides	USA	1991-1992	WBO
Daniel Zaragoza	Mexico	1991-1992	WBC
Raul Perez	Mexico	1991-1992	WBA
Thierry Jacob	France	1992	WBC
Wilfredo Vasquez	Puerto Rico	1992-1995	WBA
Tracy Harris Patterson	USA	1992-1994	WBC
Duke McKenzie	England	1992-1993	WBO
Kennedy McKinney	USA	1992-1994	IBF
Daniel Jimenez	Puerto Rico	1993-1995	WBO
Vuyani Bungu *	S Africa	1994-1999	IBF
Hector Acero-Sanchez	Dom Republic	1994-1995	WBC
Marco Antonio Barrera	Mexico	1995-1996	WBO
Antonio Cermeno *	Venezuela	1995-1997	WBA
Daniel Zaragoza	Mexico	1995-1997	WBC
Junior Jones	USA	1996-1997	WBO
Erik Morales	Mexico	1997-2000	WBC
Kennedy McKinney*	USA	1997-1998	WBO
Enrique Sanchez	Mexico	1998	WBA
Marco Antonio Barrera	Mexico	1998-2000	WBO
Nestor Garza	Mexico	1998-2000	WBA
Lehlohonolo Ledwaba	S Africa	1999-2001	IBF
Erik Morales	Mexico	2000	WBC/WBO
Erik Morales*	Mexico	2000	WBC
Marco Antonio Barrera*	Mexico	2000-2001	WBO
Clarence Adams	USA	2000-2001	WBA
Willie Jorrin	USA	2000-2002	WBC
Manny Pacquiao*	Philippines	2001-2003	IBF
Agapito Sanchez*	Dom Republic	2001-2002	WBO

WORLD CHAMPIONS SINCE GLOVES, 1889-2009

Title Holder	Birthplace	Tenure	Status	Title Holder	Birthplace	Tenure	Status
Yober Ortega	Venezuela	2001-2002	WBA	Henry Armstrong	USA	1936-1937	CALIF/MEX
Yoddamrong Sithyodthong	Thailand	2002	WBA	Mike Belloise	USA	1936	NY
Osamu Sato	Japan	2002	WBA	Maurice Holtzer	France	1937-1938	IBU
Joan Guzman*	Dom Republic	2002-2005	WBO	Henry Armstrong*	USA	1937-1938	NBA/NY
Salim Medjkoune	France	2002-2003	WBA	Leo Rodak	USA	1938	MARY
Oscar Larios	Mexico	2002-2005	WBC	Joey Archibald	USA	1938-1939	NY
Mahyar Monshipour	Iran	2003-2006	WBA	Leo Rodak	USA	1938-1939	NBA
Israel Vazquez*	Mexico	2004-2005	IBF	**Joey Archibald**	USA	1939-1940	
Daniel Ponce de Leon	Mexico	2005-2008	WBO	Joey Archibald	USA	1940	NY
Israel Vazquez	Mexico	2005-2006	IBF/WBC	Petey Scalzo	USA	1940-1941	NBA
Somsak Sithchatchawal	Thailand	2006	WBA	Jimmy Perrin	USA	1940	LOUIS
Israel Vazquez	Mexico	2006-2007	WBC	Harry Jeffra	USA	1940-1941	NY/MARY
Celestino Caballero*	Panama	2006-2008	WBA	Joey Archibald	USA	1941	NY/MARY
Steve Molitor	Canada	2006-2008	IBF	Richie Lemos	USA	1941	NBA
Rafael Marquez	Mexico	2007	WBC	Chalky Wright	Mexico	1941-1942	NY/MARY
Israel Vazquez	Mexico	2007-2009	WBC	Jackie Wilson	USA	1941-1943	NBA
Juan Manuel Lopez	Puerto Rico	2008-	WBO	Willie Pep	USA	1942-1946	NY
Celestino Caballero	Panama	2008-	WBA/IBF	Jackie Callura	Canada	1943	NBA
Toshiaki Nishioka	Japan	2009-	WBC	Phil Terranova	USA	1943-1944	NBA
				Sal Bartolo	USA	1944-1946	NBA
Featherweight (126 lbs)				**Willie Pep**	USA	1946-1948	
Ike Weir	Ireland	1889-1890		**Sandy Saddler**	USA	1948-1949	
Billy Murphy	New Zealand	1890-1893		**Willie Pep**	USA	1949-1950	
George Dixon	Canada	1890-1893		**Sandy Saddler***	USA	1950-1957	
Young Griffo	Australia	1890-1893		**Hogan Kid Bassey**	Nigeria	1957-1959	
Johnny Griffin	USA	1891-1893		**Davey Moore**	USA	1959-1963	
Solly Smith	USA	1893		**Sugar Ramos**	Cuba	1963-1964	
George Dixon	Canada	1893-1896		**Vicente Saldivar***	Mexico	1964-1967	
Solly Smith	USA	1896-1898		Raul Rojas	USA	1967	CALIF
Frank Erne	USA	1896-1897		Howard Winstone	Wales	1968	WBC
George Dixon	Canada	1896-1900		Raul Rojas	USA	1968	WBA
Harry Greenfield	England	1897-1899		Johnny Famechon	France	1968-1969	AUST
Ben Jordan	England	1897-1899		Jose Legra	Cuba	1968-1969	WBC
Will Curley	England	1897-1899		Shozo Saijyo	Japan	1968-1971	WBA
Dave Sullivan	Ireland	1898		Johnny Famechon	France	1969-1970	WBC
Ben Jordan	England	1899-1905	GB	Vicente Saldivar	Mexico	1970	WBC
Eddie Santry	USA	1899-1900		Kuniaki Shibata	Japan	1970-1972	WBC
Terry McGovern	USA	1900		Antonio Gomez	Venezuela	1971-1972	WBA
Terry McGovern	USA	1900-1901	USA	Clemente Sanchez	Mexico	1972	WBC
Young Corbett II	USA	1901-1903	USA	Ernesto Marcel*	Panama	1972-1974	WBA
Eddie Hanlon	USA	1903		Jose Legra	Cuba	1972-1973	WBC
Young Corbett II	USA	1903-1904		Eder Jofre	Brazil	1973-1974	WBC
Abe Attell	USA	1903-1904		Ruben Olivares	Mexico	1974	WBA
Abe Attell	USA	1904-1911	USA	Bobby Chacon	USA	1974-1975	WBC
Joe Bowker	England	1905-1907	GB	Alexis Arguello*	Nicaragua	1974-1977	WBA
Jim Driscoll	Wales	1907-1912	GB	Ruben Olivares	Mexico	1975	WBC
Abe Attell	USA	1911-1912		David Kotey	Ghana	1975-1976	WBC
Joe Coster	USA	1911		Danny Lopez	USA	1976-1980	WBC
Joe Rivers	Mexico	1911		Rafael Ortega	Panama	1977	WBA
Johnny Kilbane	USA	1911-1912		Cecilio Lastra	Spain	1977-1978	WBA
Jim Driscoll*	Wales	1912-1913	GB/IBU	Eusebio Pedroza	Panama	1978-1985	WBA
Johnny Kilbane	USA	1912-1922	USA	Salvador Sanchez*	Mexico	1980-1982	WBC
Johnny Kilbane	USA	1922-1923	NBA	Juan Laporte	Puerto Rico	1982-1984	WBC
Johnny Dundee	Italy	1922-1923	NY	Min-Keun Oh	S Korea	1984-1985	IBF
Eugene Criqui	France	1923		Wilfredo Gomez	Puerto Rico	1984	WBC
Johnny Dundee*	Italy	1923-1924		Azumah Nelson*	Ghana	1984-1988	WBC
Kid Kaplan	Russia	1925	NY	Barry McGuigan	Ireland	1985-1986	WBA
Kid Kaplan*	Russia	1925-1926		Ki-Yung Chung	S Korea	1985-1986	IBF
Honeyboy Finnegan	USA	1926-1927	MASS	Steve Cruz	USA	1986-1987	WBA
Benny Bass	Russia	1927-1928	NBA	Antonio Rivera	Puerto Rico	1986-1988	IBF
Tony Canzoneri	USA	1928		Antonio Esparragoza	Venezuela	1987-1991	WBA
Andre Routis	France	1928-1929		Calvin Grove	USA	1988	IBF
Bat Battalino	USA	1929-1932		Jeff Fenech*	Australia	1988-1989	WBC
Bat Battalino	USA	1932	NBA	Jorge Paez*	Mexico	1988-1990	IBF
Tommy Paul	USA	1932-1933	NBA	Maurizio Stecca	Italy	1989	WBO
Kid Chocolate*	Cuba	1932-1934	NY	Louie Espinosa	USA	1989-1990	WBO
Baby Arizmendi	Mexico	1932-1933	CALIF	Jorge Paez*	Mexico	1990-1991	IBF/WBO
Freddie Miller	USA	1933-1936	NBA	Marcos Villasana	Mexico	1990-1991	WBC
Baby Arizmendi	Mexico	1934-1935	NY	Kyun-Yung Park	S Korea	1991-1993	WBA
Baby Arizmendi	Mexico	1935-1936	NY/MEX	Troy Dorsey	USA	1991	IBF
Baby Arizmendi	Mexico	1936	MEX	Maurizio Stecca	Italy	1991-1992	WBO
Petey Sarron	USA	1936-1937	NBA	Manuel Medina	Mexico	1991-1993	IBF

Title Holder	Birthplace	Tenure	Status
Paul Hodkinson	England	1991-1993	WBC
Colin McMillan	England	1992	WBO
Ruben Palacio	Colombia	1992-1993	WBO
Tom Johnson	USA	1993-1997	IBF
Steve Robinson	Wales	1993-1995	WBO
Gregorio Vargas	Mexico	1993	WBC
Kevin Kelley	USA	1993-1995	WBC
Eloy Rojas	Venezuela	1993-1996	WBA
Alejandro Gonzalez	Mexico	1995	WBC
Manuel Medina	Mexico	1995	WBC
Prince Naseem Hamed*	England	1995-1997	WBO
Luisito Espinosa	Philippines	1995-1999	WBC
Wilfredo Vasquez	Puerto Rico	1996-1998	WBA
Prince Naseem Hamed *	England	1997	WBO/IBF
Prince Naseem Hamed*	England	1997-1999	WBO
Hector Lizarraga	Mexico	1997-1998	IBF
Freddie Norwood	USA	1998	WBA
Manuel Medina	Mexico	1998-1999	IBF
Antonio Cermeno	Venezuela	1998-1999	WBA
Cesar Soto	Mexico	1999	WBC
Freddie Norwood	USA	1999-2000	WBA
Prince Naseem Hamed	England	1999-2000	WBC/WBO
Paul Ingle	England	1999-2000	IBF
Prince Naseem Hamed*	England	2000	WBO
Gustavo Espadas	Mexico	2000-2001	WBC
Derrick Gainer	USA	2000-2003	WBA
Mbulelo Botile	S Africa	2000-2001	IBF
Istvan Kovacs	Hungary	2001	WBO
Erik Morales	Mexico	2001-2002	WBC
Frankie Toledo	USA	2001	IBF
Julio Pablo Chacon	Argentina	2001-2002	WBO
Manuel Medina	Mexico	2001-2002	IBF
Johnny Tapia	USA	2002	IBF
Marco Antonio Barrera*	Mexico	2002	WBC
Scott Harrison	Scotland	2002-2003	WBO
Erik Morales*	Mexico	2002-2003	WBC
Juan Manuel Marquez*	Mexico	2003	IBF
Manuel Medina	Mexico	2003	WBO
Juan Manuel Marquez	Mexico	2003-2005	IBF/WBA
Scott Harrison	Scotland	2003-2006	WBO
In-Jin Chi	S Korea	2004-2006	WBC
Juan Manuel Marquez	Mexico	2005-2006	WBA
Valdemir Pereira	Brazil	2005-2006	IBF
Takashi Koshimoto	Japan	2006	WBC
Chris John	Indonesia	2006-	WBA
Eric Aiken	USA	2006	IBF
Rodolfo Lopez	Mexico	2006	WBC
Robert Guerrero	USA	2006	IBF
Orlando Salido	Mexico	2006	IBF
Juan Manuel Marquez*	Mexico	2006-2007	WBO
In-Jin Chi*	S Korea	2006-2007	WBC
Robert Guerrero*	USA	2007-2008	IBF
Steve Luevano	USA	2007-	WBO
Jorge Linares*	Venezuela	2007-2008	WBC
Oscar Larios	Mexico	2008-2009	WBC
Cristobal Cruz	Mexico	2008-	IBF
Takahiro Aoh	Japan	2009-	WBC

S. Featherweight (130 lbs)

Title Holder	Birthplace	Tenure	Status
Johnny Dundee	Italy	1921-1923	NY
Jack Bernstein	USA	1923	NY
Jack Bernstein	USA	1923	NBA/NY
Johnny Dundee	Italy	1923-1924	NBA/NY
Kid Sullivan	USA	1924-1925	NBA/NY
Mike Ballerino	USA	1925	NBA/NY
Tod Morgan	USA	1925-1929	NBA/NY
Benny Bass	Russia	1929-1930	NBA/NY
Benny Bass	Russia	1930-1931	NBA
Kid Chocolate	Cuba	1931-1933	NBA
Frankie Klick	USA	1933-1934	NBA
Sandy Saddler	USA	1949-1950	NBA
Sandy Saddler	USA	1950-1951	CLE

Title Holder	Birthplace	Tenure	Status
Harold Gomes	USA	1959-1960	NBA
Flash Elorde	Philippines	1960-1962	NBA
Flash Elorde	Philippines	1962-1967	WBA
Raul Rojas	USA	1967	CALIF
Yoshiaki Numata	Japan	1967	WBA
Hiroshi Kobayashi	Japan	1967-1971	WBA
Rene Barrientos	Philippines	1969-1970	WBC
Yoshiaki Numata	Japan	1970-1971	WBC
Alfredo Marcano	Venezuela	1971-1972	WBA
Ricardo Arredondo	Mexico	1971-1974	WBC
Ben Villaflor	Philippines	1972-1973	WBA
Kuniaki Shibata	Japan	1973	WBA
Ben Villaflor	Philippines	1973-1976	WBA
Kuniaki Shibata	Japan	1974-1975	WBC
Alfredo Escalera	Puerto Rico	1975-1978	WBC
Sam Serrano	Puerto Rico	1976-1980	WBA
Alexis Arguello*	Nicaragua	1978-1980	WBC
Yasutsune Uehara	Japan	1980-1981	WBA
Rafael Limon	Mexico	1980-1981	WBC
Cornelius Boza-Edwards	Uganda	1981	WBC
Sam Serrano	Puerto Rico	1981-1983	WBA
Rolando Navarrete	Philippines	1981-1982	WBC
Rafael Limon	Mexico	1982	WBC
Bobby Chacon	USA	1982-1983	WBC
Roger Mayweather	USA	1983-1984	WBA
Hector Camacho*	Puerto Rico	1983-1984	WBC
Rocky Lockridge	USA	1984-1985	WBA
Hwan-Kil Yuh	S Korea	1984-1985	IBF
Julio Cesar Chavez*	Mexico	1984-1987	WBC
Lester Ellis	England	1985	IBF
Wilfredo Gomez	Puerto Rico	1985-1986	WBA
Barry Michael	England	1985-1987	IBF
Alfredo Layne	Panama	1986	WBA
Brian Mitchell*	S Africa	1986-1991	WBA
Rocky Lockridge	USA	1987-1988	IBF
Azumah Nelson	Ghana	1988-1994	WBC
Tony Lopez	USA	1988-1989	IBF
Juan Molina*	Puerto Rico	1989	WBO
Juan Molina	Puerto Rico	1989-1990	IBF
Kamel Bou Ali	Tunisia	1989-1992	WBO
Tony Lopez	USA	1990-1991	IBF
Joey Gamache*	USA	1991	WBA
Brian Mitchell*	S Africa	1991-1992	IBF
Genaro Hernandez	USA	1991-1995	WBA
Juan Molina*	Puerto Rico	1992-1995	IBF
Daniel Londas	France	1992	WBO
Jimmy Bredahl	Denmark	1992-1994	WBO
Oscar de la Hoya*	USA	1994	WBO
James Leija	USA	1994	WBC
Gabriel Ruelas	USA	1994-1995	WBC
Regilio Tuur*	Surinam	1994-1997	WBO
Eddie Hopson	USA	1995	IBF
Tracy Harris Patterson	USA	1995	IBF
Yong-Soo Choi	S Korea	1995-1998	WBA
Arturo Gatti*	Canada	1995-1997	IBF
Azumah Nelson	Ghana	1996-1997	WBC
Genaro Hernandez	USA	1997-1998	WBC
Barry Jones*	Wales	1997-1998	WBO
Roberto Garcia	USA	1998-1999	IBF
Anatoly Alexandrov	Kazakhstan	1998-1999	WBO
Takenori Hatakeyama	Japan	1998-1999	WBA
Floyd Mayweather*	USA	1998-2002	WBC
Lakva Sim	Mongolia	1999	WBA
Acelino Freitas*	Brazil	1999-2002	WBO
Diego Corrales*	USA	1999-2000	IBF
Jong-Kwon Baek	S Korea	1999-2000	WBA
Joel Casamayor	Cuba	2000-2002	WBA
Steve Forbes	USA	2000-2002	IBF
Acelino Freitas*	Brazil	2002-2004	WBO/WBA
Sirimongkol Singmanassak	Thailand	2002-2003	WBC
Carlos Hernandez	El Salvador	2003-2004	IBF
Jesus Chavez	Mexico	2003-2004	WBC

Title Holder	Birthplace	Tenure	Status		Title Holder	Birthplace	Tenure	Status
Yodesnan Sornontachai	Thailand	2004-2005	WBA		**Ike Williams**	USA	1947-1951	
Erik Morales	Mexico	2004	WBC		**Jimmy Carter**	USA	1951-1952	
Diego Corrales*	USA	2004	WBO		**Lauro Salas**	Mexico	1952	
Erik Morales	Mexico	2004	IBF		**Jimmy Carter**	USA	1952-1954	
Mike Anchondo	USA	2004-2005	WBO		**Paddy de Marco**	USA	1954	
Marco Antonio Barrera*	Mexico	2004-2005	WBC		**Jimmy Carter**	USA	1954-1955	
Robbie Peden	Australia	2005	IBF		**Wallace Bud Smith**	USA	1955-1956	
Jorge Barrios	Argentina	2005-2006	WBO		**Joe Brown**	USA	1956-1962	
Vincente Mosquera	Panama	2005-2006	WBA		**Carlos Ortiz**	Puerto Rico	1962-1963	
Marco Antonio Barrera*	Mexico	2005-2006	WBC/IBF		Carlos Ortiz*	Puerto Rico	1963-1964	WBA/WBC
Marco Antonio Barrera	Mexico	2006-2007	WBC		Kenny Lane	USA	1963-1964	MICH
Cassius Baloyi	South Africa	2006	IBF		**Carlos Ortiz**	Puerto Rico	1964-1965	
Gairy St Clair	Guyana	2006	IBF		**Ismael Laguna**	Panama	1965	
Edwin Valero*	Venezuela	2006-2008	WBA		**Carlos Ortiz**	Puerto Rico	1965-1966	
Malcolm Klassen	S Africa	2006-2007	IBF		Carlos Ortiz*	Puerto Rico	1966-1967	WBA
Joan Guzman*	Dom Republic	2006-2008	WBO		**Carlos Ortiz**	Puerto Rico	1967-1968	
Juan Manuel Marquez	Mexico	2007-2008	WBC		**Carlos Teo Cruz**	Dom Republic	1968-1969	
Mzonke Fana	S Africa	2007-2008	IBF		**Mando Ramos**	USA	1969-1970	
Manny Pacquiao*	Philippines	2008	WBC		**Ismael Laguna**	Panama	1970	
Cassius Baloyi	South Africa	2008-2009	IBF		Ismael Laguna	Panama	1970	WBA
Alex Arthur	Scotland	2008	WBO		Ken Buchanan*	Scotland	1970-1971	WBA
Nicky Cook	England	2008-2009	WBO		**Ken Buchanan**	Scotland	1971	
Roman Martinez	Puerto Rico	2009-	WBO		Ken Buchanan	Scotland	1971-1972	WBA
Jorge Linares	Venezuela	2008-	WBA		Pedro Carrasco	Spain	1971-1972	WBC
Humberto Soto	Mexico	2008-	WBC		Mando Ramos	USA	1972	WBC
Malcolm Klassen	South Africa	2009-	IBF		Roberto Duran*	Panama	1972-1978	WBA
					Chango Carmona	Mexico	1972	WBC
Lightweight (135 lbs)					Rodolfo Gonzalez	Mexico	1972-1974	WBC
Jack McAuliffe	Ireland	1889-1894	USA		Guts Ishimatsu	Japan	1974-1976	WBC
Jem Carney	England	1889-1891			Esteban de Jesus	Puerto Rico	1976-1978	WBC
Jimmy Carroll	England	1889-1891			**Roberto Duran***	Panama	1978-1979	
Dick Burge	England	1891-1896	GB		Jim Watt	Scotland	1979-1981	WBC
George Lavigne	USA	1894-1896	USA		Ernesto Espana	Venezuela	1979-1980	WBA
George Lavigne	USA	1896			Hilmer Kenty	USA	1980-1981	WBA
George Lavigne	USA	1896-1897			Sean O'Grady	USA	1981	WBA
Eddie Connolly	Canada	1896-1897			Alexis Arguello*	Nicaragua	1981-1983	WBC
George Lavigne	USA	1897-1899			Claude Noel	Trinidad	1981	WBA
Frank Erne	Switzerland	1899-1902			Arturo Frias	USA	1981-1982	WBA
Joe Gans	USA	1902			Ray Mancini	USA	1982-1984	WBA
Joe Gans	USA	1902-1906			Edwin Rosario	Puerto Rico	1983-1984	WBC
Jabez White	England	1902-1905	GB		Charlie Choo Choo Brown	USA	1984	IBF
Jimmy Britt	USA	1902-1905			Harry Arroyo	USA	1984-1985	IBF
Battling Nelson	Denmark	1905-1907			Livingstone Bramble	USA	1984-1986	WBA
Joe Gans	USA	1906-1908			Jose Luis Ramirez	Mexico	1984-1985	WBC
Battling Nelson	Denmark	1908-1910			Jimmy Paul	USA	1985-1986	IBF
Ad Wolgast	USA	1910-1912			Hector Camacho*	Puerto Rico	1985-1987	WBC
Willie Ritchie	USA	1912			Edwin Rosario	Puerto Rico	1986-1987	WBA
Freddie Welsh	Wales	1912-1914	GB		Greg Haugen	USA	1986-1987	IBF
Willie Ritchie	USA	1912-1914	USA		Vinny Pazienza	USA	1987-1988	IBF
Freddie Welsh	Wales	1914-1917			Jose Luis Ramirez	Mexico	1987-1988	WBC
Benny Leonard*	USA	1917-1925			Julio Cesar Chavez*	Mexico	1987-1988	WBA
Jimmy Goodrich	USA	1925	NY		Greg Haugen	USA	1988-1989	IBF
Rocky Kansas	USA	1925-1926			Julio Cesar Chavez*	Mexico	1988-1989	WBA/WBC
Sammy Mandell	USA	1926-1930			Mauricio Aceves	Mexico	1989-1990	WBO
Al Singer	USA	1930			Pernell Whitaker*	USA	1989	IBF
Tony Canzoneri	USA	1930-1933			Edwin Rosario	Puerto Rico	1989-1990	WBA
Barney Ross*	USA	1933-1935			Pernell Whitaker*	USA	1989-1990	IBF/WBC
Tony Canzoneri	USA	1935-1936			Juan Nazario	Puerto Rico	1990	WBA
Lou Ambers	USA	1936-1938			Pernell Whitaker*	USA	1990-1992	IBF/WBC/WBA
Henry Armstrong	USA	1938-1939			Dingaan Thobela*	S Africa	1990-1992	WBO
Lou Ambers	USA	1939-1940			Joey Gamache	USA	1992	WBA
Sammy Angott	USA	1940-1941	NBA		Miguel Gonzalez*	Mexico	1992-1996	WBC
Lew Jenkins	USA	1940-1941	NY		Giovanni Parisi	Italy	1992-1994	WBO
Sammy Angott*	USA	1941-1942			Tony Lopez	USA	1992-1993	WBA
Beau Jack	USA	1942-1943	NY		Fred Pendleton	USA	1993-1994	IBF
Slugger White	USA	1943	MARY		Dingaan Thobela	S Africa	1993	WBA
Bob Montgomery	USA	1943	NY		Orzubek Nazarov	Kyrghyzstan	1993-1998	WBA
Sammy Angott	USA	1943-1944	NBA		Rafael Ruelas	USA	1994-1995	IBF
Beau Jack	USA	1943-1944	NY		Oscar de la Hoya*	USA	1994-1995	WBO
Bob Montgomery	USA	1944-1947	NY		Oscar de la Hoya*	USA	1995	WBO/IBF
Juan Zurita	Mexico	1944-1945	NBA		Oscar de la Hoya*	USA	1995-1996	WBO
Ike Williams	USA	1945-1947	NBA		Phillip Holiday	S Africa	1995-1997	IBF

Title Holder	Birthplace	Tenure	Status	Title Holder	Birthplace	Tenure	Status
Jean-Baptiste Mendy	France	1996-1997	WBC	Miguel Velasquez	Spain	1976	WBC
Artur Grigorian	Uzbekistan	1996-2004	WBO	Saensak Muangsurin	Thailand	1976-1978	WBC
Steve Johnston	USA	1997-1998	WBC	Antonio Cervantes	Colombia	1977-1980	WBA
Shane Mosley*	USA	1997-1999	IBF	Wilfred Benitez*	USA	1977-1978	NY
Jean-Baptiste Mendy	France	1998-1999	WBA	Sang-Hyun Kim	S Korea	1978-1980	WBC
Cesar Bazan	Mexico	1998-1999	WBC	Saoul Mamby	USA	1980-1982	WBC
Steve Johnston	USA	1999-2000	WBC	Aaron Pryor*	USA	1980-1984	WBA
Julien Lorcy	France	1999	WBA	Leroy Haley	USA	1982-1983	WBC
Stefano Zoff	Italy	1999	WBA	Bruce Curry	USA	1983-1984	WBC
Paul Spadafora*	USA	1999-2003	IBF	Johnny Bumphus	USA	1984	WBA
Gilberto Serrano	Venezuela	1999-2000	WBA	Bill Costello	USA	1984-1985	WBC
Takanori Hatakeyama	Japan	2000-2001	WBA	Gene Hatcher	USA	1984-1985	WBA
Jose Luis Castillo	Mexico	2000-2002	WBC	Aaron Pryor	USA	1984-1985	IBF
Julien Lorcy	France	2001	WBA	Ubaldo Sacco	Argentina	1985-1986	WBA
Raul Balbi	Argentina	2001-2002	WBA	Lonnie Smith	USA	1985-1986	WBC
Leonardo Dorin	Romania	2002-2003	WBA	Patrizio Oliva	Italy	1986-1987	WBA
Floyd Mayweather*	USA	2002-2004	WBC	Gary Hinton	USA	1986	IBF
Javier Jauregui	Mexico	2003-2004	IBF	Rene Arredondo	Mexico	1986	WBC
Acelino Freitas	Brazil	2004	WBO	Tsuyoshi Hamada	Japan	1986-1987	WBC
Lakva Sim	Mongolia	2004	WBA	Joe Manley	USA	1986-1987	IBF
Julio Diaz*	Mexico	2004-2005	IBF	Terry Marsh*	England	1987	IBF
Jose Luis Castillo	Mexico	2004-2005	WBC	Juan M. Coggi	Argentina	1987-1990	WBA
Juan Diaz*	USA	2004-2007	WBA	Rene Arredondo	Mexico	1987	WBC
Diego Corrales*	USA	2004-2005	WBO	Roger Mayweather	USA	1987-1989	WBC
Diego Corrales	USA	2005-2006	WBC/WBO	James McGirt	USA	1988	IBF
Leavander Johnson	USA	2005	IBF	Meldrick Taylor	USA	1988-1990	IBF
Jesus Chavez	Mexico	2005-2007	IBF	Hector Camacho	Puerto Rico	1989-1991	WBO
Diego Corrales	USA	2006	WBC	Julio Cesar Chavez*	Mexico	1989-1990	WBC
Acelino Freitas	Brazil	2006-2007	WBO	Julio Cesar Chavez*	Mexico	1990-1991	IBF/WBC
Joel Casamayor	Cuba	2006-2007	WBC	Loreto Garza	USA	1990-1991	WBA
Julio Diaz	USA	2007	IBF	Greg Haugen	USA	1991	WBO
David Diaz	USA	2007-2008	WBC	Hector Camacho	Puerto Rico	1991-1992	WBO
Juan Diaz*	USA	2007	WBA/WBO	Edwin Rosario	Puerto Rico	1991-1992	WBA
Juan Diaz	USA	2007-2008	WBA/WBO/IBF	Julio Cesar Chavez	Mexico	1991-1994	WBC
Nate Campbell	USA	2008-2009	WBA/WBO/IBF	Rafael Pineda	Colombia	1991-1992	IBF
Manny Pacquiao	Philippines	2008-	WBC	Akinobu Hiranaka	Japan	1992	WBA
Juan Manuel Marquez	Mexico	2009-	WBA/WBO	Carlos Gonzalez	Mexico	1992-1993	WBO
Edwin Valero	Venezuela	2009-	WBC	Pernell Whitaker*	USA	1992-1993	IBF
				Morris East	Philippines	1992-1993	WBA
L. Welterweight (140 lbs)				Juan M. Coggi	Argentina	1993-1994	WBA
Pinkey Mitchell	USA	1922-1926	NBA	Charles Murray	USA	1993-1994	IBF
Mushy Callahan	USA	1926-1927	NBA	Zack Padilla*	USA	1993-1994	WBO
Mushy Callahan	USA	1927-1930	NBA/NY	Frankie Randall	USA	1994	WBA
Mushy Callahan	USA	1930	NBA	Jake Rodriguez	USA	1994-1995	IBF
Jackie Kid Berg	England	1930-1931	NBA	Julio Cesar Chavez	Mexico	1994-1996	WBC
Tony Canzoneri	USA	1931-1932	NBA	Frankie Randall	USA	1994-1996	WBA
Johnny Jadick	USA	1932	NBA	Konstantin Tszyu	Russia	1995-1997	IBF
Johnny Jadick	USA	1932-1933	PEN	Sammy Fuentes	Puerto Rico	1995-1996	WBO
Battling Shaw	Mexico	1933	LOUIS	Juan M. Coggi	Argentina	1996	WBA
Tony Canzoneri	USA	1933	LOUIS	Giovanni Parisi	Italy	1996-1998	WBO
Barney Ross*	USA	1933-1935	ILL	Oscar de la Hoya*	USA	1996-1997	WBC
Maxie Berger	Canada	1939	CAN	Frankie Randall	USA	1996-1997	WBA
Harry Weekly	USA	1941-1942	LOUIS	Khalid Rahilou	France	1997-1998	WBA
Tippy Larkin	USA	1946-1947	NY/NBA	Vince Phillips	USA	1997-1999	IBF
Carlos Ortiz	Puerto Rico	1959-1960	NBA	Carlos Gonzalez	Mexico	1998-1999	WBO
Duilio Loi	Italy	1960-1962	NBA	Sharmba Mitchell	USA	1998-2001	WBA
Duilio Loi	Italy	1962	WBA	Terron Millett	USA	1999	IBF
Eddie Perkins	USA	1962	WBA	Randall Bailey	USA	1999-2000	WBO
Duilio Loi*	Italy	1962-1963	WBA	Kostya Tszyu*	Russia	1999-2001	WBC
Roberto Cruz	Philippines	1963	WBA	Zab Judah	USA	2000-2001	IBF
Eddie Perkins	USA	1963-1965	WBA	Ener Julio	Colombia	2000-2001	WBO
Carlos Hernandez	Venezuela	1965-1966	WBA	Kostya Tszyu*	Russia	2001	WBA/WBC
Sandro Lopopolo	Italy	1966-1967	WBA	DeMarcus Corley	USA	2001-2003	WBO
Paul Fujii	Hawaii	1967-1968	WBA	Kostya Tszyu*	Russia	2001-2004	WBA/WBC/IBF
Nicolino Loche	Argentina	1968-1972	WBA	Zab Judah*	USA	2003-2004	WBO
Pedro Adigue	Philippines	1968-1970	WBC	Kostya Tszyu	Russia	2004-2005	IBF
Bruno Arcari*	Italy	1970-1974	WBC	Arturo Gatti	Canada	2004-2005	WBC
Alfonso Frazer	Panama	1972	WBA	Vivien Harris	Guyana	2004-2005	WBA
Antonio Cervantes	Colombia	1972-1976	WBA	Miguel Cotto*	Puerto Rico	2004-2006	WBA
Perico Fernandez	Spain	1974-1975	WBC	Ricky Hatton*	England	2005	IBF
Saensak Muangsurin	Thailand	1975-1976	WBC	Carlos Maussa	Colombia	2005	WBA
Wilfred Benitez	USA	1976	WBA	Floyd Mayweather*	USA	2005-2006	WBC

WORLD CHAMPIONS SINCE GLOVES, 1889-2009

Title Holder	Birthplace	Tenure	Status
Ricky Hatton*	England	2005-2006	IBF/WBA
Juan Urango	Colombia	2006-2007	IBF
Souleymane M'Baye	France	2006-2007	WBA
Junior Witter	England	2006-2008	WBC
Ricardo Torres	Colombia	2006-2008	WBO
Ricky Hatton*	England	2007	IBF
Lovemore Ndou	S Africa	2007	IBF
Paul Malignaggi	USA	2007-2008	IBF
Ricky Hatton	England	2007-2009	IBO
Gavin Rees	Wales	2007-2008	WBA
Andreas Kotelnik	Ukraine	2008-	WBA
Tim Bradley*	USA	2008-2009	WBC
Kendall Holt	USA	2008-2009	WBO
Juan Urango	Colombia	2009-	IBF
Tim Bradley	USA	2009	WBC/WBO
Tim Bradley	USA	2009-	WBO
Manny Pacquiao	Philippines	2009-	IBO

Welterweight (147 lbs)

Title Holder	Birthplace	Tenure	Status
Paddy Duffy	USA	1889-1890	
Tommy Ryan	USA	1891-1894	
Mysterious Billy Smith	USA	1892-1894	
Tommy Ryan	USA	1894-1897	USA
Tommy Ryan	USA	1897-1899	
Dick Burge	GB	1897	
George Green	USA	1897	
Tom Causer	GB	1897	
Joe Walcott	Barbados	1897	
George Lavigne	USA	1897-1899	
Dick Burge	GB	1897-1898	
Mysterious Billy Smith	USA	1898-1900	
Bobby Dobbs	USA	1898-1902	
Rube Ferns	USA	1900	
Matty Matthews	USA	1900	
Eddie Connolly	Canada	1900	
Matty Matthews	USA	1900-1901	
Rube Ferns	USA	1901	
Joe Walcott	Barbados	1901-1906	
Eddie Connolly	Canada	1902-1903	GB
Matty Matthews	USA	1902-1903	
Rube Ferns	USA	1903	
Martin Duffy	USA	1903-1904	
Honey Mellody	USA	1904	
Jack Clancy	USA	1904-1905	GB
Dixie Kid	USA	1904-1905	
Buddy Ryan	USA	1904-1905	
Sam Langford	Canada	1904-1905	
George Petersen	USA	1905	
Jimmy Gardner	USA	1905	
Mike Twin Sullivan	USA	1905-1906	
Joe Gans	USA	1906	
Joe Walcott	Barbados	1906	USA
Honey Mellody	USA	1906	USA
Honey Mellody	USA	1906-1907	
Joe Thomas	USA	1906-1907	
Mike Twin Sullivan	USA	1907-1911	
Jimmy Gardner	USA	1907-1908	
Frank Mantell	USA	1907-1908	
Harry Lewis	USA	1908-1910	
Jack Blackburn	USA	1908	
Jimmy Gardner	USA	1908-1909	
Willie Lewis	USA	1909-1910	
Harry Lewis	USA	1910-1911	GB/FR
Jimmy Clabby	USA	1910-1911	
Dixie Kid	USA	1911-1912	GB/FR
Ray Bronson	USA	1911-1914	
Marcel Thomas	France	1912-1913	FR
Wildcat Ferns	USA	1912-1913	
Spike Kelly	USA	1913-1914	
Mike Glover	USA	1913-1915	
Mike Gibbons	USA	1913-1914	
Waldemar Holberg	Denmark	1914	

Title Holder	Birthplace	Tenure	Status
Tom McCormick	Ireland	1914	
Matt Wells	England	1914-1915	AUSTR
Kid Graves	USA	1914-1917	
Jack Britton	USA	1915	
Ted Kid Lewis	England	1915-1916	
Jack Britton	USA	1916-1917	
Ted Kid Lewis	England	1917	
Ted Kid Lewis	England	1917-1919	
Jack Britton	USA	1919-1922	
Mickey Walker	USA	1922-1923	
Mickey Walker	USA	1923-1924	NBA
Dave Shade	USA	1923	NY
Jimmy Jones	USA	1923	NY/MASS
Mickey Walker	USA	1924-1926	
Pete Latzo	USA	1926-1927	
Joe Dundee	Italy	1927-1928	
Joe Dundee	Italy	1928-1929	NY
Jackie Fields	USA	1929	NBA
Jackie Fields	USA	1929-1930	
Young Jack Thompson	USA	1930	
Tommy Freeman	USA	1930-1931	
Young Jack Thompson	USA	1930	
Lou Brouillard	Canada	1931-1932	
Jackie Fields	USA	1932-1933	
Young Corbett III	Italy	1933	
Jimmy McLarnin	Ireland	1933-1934	

Don Curry

Title Holder	Birthplace	Tenure	Status	Title Holder	Birthplace	Tenure	Status
Barney Ross	USA	1934		Simon Brown	Jamaica	1991	WBC
Jimmy McLarnin	Ireland	1934-1935		Maurice Blocker	USA	1991-1993	IBF
Barney Ross	USA	1935-1938		James McGirt	USA	1991-1993	WBC
Barney Ross	USA	1938	NY/NBA	Crisanto Espana	Venezuela	1992-1994	WBA
Felix Wouters	Belgium	1938	IBU	Gert Bo Jacobsen*	Denmark	1993	WBO
Henry Armstrong	USA	1938-1940		Pernell Whitaker	USA	1993-1997	WBC
Fritzie Zivic	USA	1940		Felix Trinidad*	Puerto Rico	1993-2000	IBF
Fritzie Zivic	USA	1940-1941	NY/NBA	Eamonn Loughran	Ireland	1993-1996	WBO
Izzy Jannazzo	USA	1940-1942	MARY	Ike Quartey	Ghana	1994-1998	WBA
Red Cochrane	USA	1941-1942	NY/NBA	Jose Luis Lopez	Mexico	1996-1997	WBO
Red Cochrane	USA	1942-1946		Michael Loewe*	Romania	1997-1998	WBO
Marty Servo	USA	1946		Oscar de la Hoya	USA	1997-1999	WBC
Sugar Ray Robinson*	USA	1946-1951		Ahmed Kotiev	Russia	1998-2000	WBO
Johnny Bratton	USA	1951	NBA	James Page	USA	1998-2000	WBA
Kid Gavilan	Cuba	1951-1952	NBA/NY	Oscar de la Hoya	USA	2000	WBC
Kid Gavilan	Cuba	1952-1954		Daniel Santos*	Puerto Rico	2000-2002	WBO
Johnny Saxton	USA	1954-1955		Shane Mosley	USA	2000-2002	WBC
Tony de Marco	USA	1955		Andrew Lewis	Guyana	2001-2002	WBA
Carmen Basilio	USA	1955-1956		Vernon Forrest	USA	2001	IBF
Johnny Saxton	USA	1956		Vernon Forrest	USA	2002-2003	WBC
Carmen Basilio*	USA	1956-1957		Antonio Margarito	Mexico	2002-2007	WBO
Virgil Akins	USA	1957-1958	MASS	Ricardo Mayorga*	Nicaragua	2002-2003	WBA
Virgil Akins	USA	1958		Michele Piccirillo	Italy	2002-2003	IBF
Don Jordan	Dom Republic	1958-1960		Ricardo Mayorga	Nicaragua	2003	WBA/WBC
Benny Kid Paret	Cuba	1960-1961		Cory Spinks*	USA	2003	IBF
Emile Griffith	Virgin Islands	1961		Cory Spinks	USA	2003-2005	IBF/WBA/WBC
Benny Kid Paret	Cuba	1961-1962		Zab Judah	USA	2005-2006	IBF/WBA/WBC
Emile Griffith	Virgin Islands	1962-1963		Carlos Baldomir	Argentina	2006	WBC
Luis Rodriguez	Cuba	1963		Zab Judah	USA	2006	IBF
Emile Griffith*	Virgin Islands	1963-1966		Luis Collazo	USA	2006	WBA
Willie Ludick	S Africa	1966-1968	SA	Floyd Mayweather*	USA	2006	IBF
Curtis Cokes*	USA	1966	WBA	Ricky Hatton*	England	2006	WBA
Curtis Cokes*	USA	1966-1967	WBA/WBC	Kermin Cintron	Puerto Rico	2006-2008	IBF
Charley Shipes	USA	1966-1967	CALIF	Floyd Mayweather*	USA	2006-2008	WBC
Curtis Cokes	USA	1968-1969		Miguel Cotto	Puerto Rico	2006-2008	WBA
Jose Napoles	Cuba	1969-1970		Paul WIlliams	USA	2007-2008	WBO
Billy Backus	USA	1970-1971		Carlos Quintana	Puerto Rico	2008	WBO
Jose Napoles	Cuba	1971-1972		Antonio Margarito*	Mexico	2008	IBF
Jose Napoles*	Cuba	1972-1974	WBA/WBC	Paul Williams*	USA	2008	WBO
Hedgemon Lewis	USA	1972-1974	NY	Andre Berto	USA	2008-	WBC
Jose Napoles	Cuba	1974-1975		Antonio Margarito	Mexico	2008-2009	WBA
Jose Napoles	Cuba	1975	WBC	Joshua Clottey	Ghana	2008-2009	IBF
Angel Espada	Puerto Rico	1975-1976	WBA	Shane Mosley	USA	2009-	WBA
John H. Stracey	England	1975-1976	WBC	Miguel Cotto	Puerto Rico	2009-	WBO
Carlos Palomino	Mexico	1976-1979	WBC				
Pipino Cuevas	Mexico	1976-1980	WBA	**L. Middleweight (154 lbs)**			
Wilfred Benitez	USA	1979	WBC	Emile Griffith*	USA	1962-1963	AU
Sugar Ray Leonard	USA	1979-1980	WBC	Denny Moyer	USA	1962-1963	WBA
Roberto Duran	Panama	1980	WBC	Ralph Dupas	USA	1963	WBA
Thomas Hearns	USA	1980-1981	WBA	Sandro Mazzinghi	Italy	1963-1965	WBA
Sugar Ray Leonard	USA	1980-1981	WBC	Nino Benvenuti	Italy	1965-1966	WBA
Sugar Ray Leonard*	USA	1981-1982		Ki-Soo Kim	S Korea	1966-1968	WBA
Don Curry*	USA	1983-1984	WBA	Sandro Mazzinghi	Italy	1968-1969	WBA
Milton McCrory	USA	1983-1985	WBC	Freddie Little	USA	1969-1970	WBA
Don Curry*	USA	1984-1985	WBA/IBF	Carmelo Bossi	Italy	1970-1971	WBA
Don Curry	USA	1985-1986		Koichi Wajima	Japan	1971-1974	WBA
Lloyd Honeyghan	Jamaica	1986		Oscar Albarado	USA	1974-1975	WBA
Lloyd Honeyghan	Jamaica	1986-1987	WBC/IBF	Koichi Wajima	Japan	1975	WBA
Mark Breland	USA	1987	WBA	Miguel de Oliveira	Brazil	1975	WBC
Marlon Starling	USA	1987-1988	WBA	Jae-Do Yuh	S Korea	1975-1976	WBA
Jorge Vaca	Mexico	1987-1988	WBC	Elisha Obed	Bahamas	1975-1976	WBC
Lloyd Honeyghan	Jamaica	1988-1989	WBC	Koichi Wajima	Japan	1976	WBA
Simon Brown*	Jamaica	1988-1991	IBF	Jose Duran	Spain	1976	WBA
Tomas Molinares*	Colombia	1988-1989	WBA	Eckhard Dagge	Germany	1976-1977	WBC
Mark Breland	USA	1989-1990	WBA	Miguel Castellini	Argentina	1976-1977	WBA
Marlon Starling	USA	1989-1990	WBC	Eddie Gazo	Nicaragua	1977-1978	WBA
Genaro Leon*	Mexico	1989	WBO	Rocky Mattioli	Italy	1977-1979	WBC
Manning Galloway	USA	1989-1993	WBO	Masashi Kudo	Japan	1978-1979	WBA
Aaron Davis	USA	1990-1991	WBA	Maurice Hope	Antigua	1979-1981	WBC
Maurice Blocker	USA	1990-1991	WBC	Ayub Kalule	Uganda	1979-1981	WBA
Meldrick Taylor	USA	1991-1992	WBA	Wilfred Benitez	USA	1981-1982	WBC
Simon Brown*	Jamaica	1991	WBC/IBF	Sugar Ray Leonard*	USA	1981	WBA

255

Title Holder	Birthplace	Tenure	Status
Tadashi Mihara	Japan	1981-1982	WBA
Davey Moore	USA	1982-1983	WBA
Thomas Hearns*	USA	1982-1986	WBC
Roberto Duran*	Panama	1983-1984	WBA
Mark Medal	USA	1984	IBF
Mike McCallum*	Jamaica	1984-1987	WBA
Carlos Santos	Puerto Rico	1984-1986	IBF
Buster Drayton	USA	1986-1987	IBF
Duane Thomas	USA	1986-1987	WBC
Matthew Hilton	Canada	1987-1988	IBF
Lupe Aquino	Mexico	1987	WBC
Gianfranco Rosi	Italy	1987-1988	WBC
Julian Jackson*	Virgin Islands	1987-1990	WBA
Don Curry	USA	1988-1989	WBC
Robert Hines	USA	1988-1989	IBF
John David Jackson*	USA	1988-1993	WBO
Darrin van Horn	USA	1989	IBF
Rene Jacqot	France	1989	WBC
John Mugabi	Uganda	1989-1990	WBC
Gianfranco Rosi	Italy	1989-1994	IBF
Terry Norris	USA	1990-1993	WBC
Gilbert Dele	France	1991	WBA
Vinny Pazienza*	USA	1991-1992	WBA
Julio Cesar Vasquez	Argentina	1992-1995	WBA
Verno Phillips	USA	1993-1995	WBO
Simon Brown	USA	1993-1994	WBC
Terry Norris	USA	1994	WBC
Vince Pettway	USA	1994-1995	IBF
Luis Santana	Dom Republic	1994-1995	WBC
Pernell Whitaker*	USA	1995	WBA
Gianfranco Rosi	Italy	1995	WBO
Carl Daniels	USA	1995	WBA
Verno Phillips	USA	1995	WBO
Paul Vaden	USA	1995	IBF
Terry Norris*	USA	1995	WBC
Paul Jones	England	1995-1996	WBO
Terry Norris	USA	1995-1997	IBF/WBC
Julio Cesar Vasquez	Argentina	1995-1996	WBA
Bronco McKart	USA	1996	WBO
Ronald Wright	USA	1996-1998	WBO
Laurent Boudouani	France	1996-1999	WBA
Terry Norris	USA	1997	WBC
Raul Marquez	USA	1997	IBF
Luis Campas	Mexico	1997-1998	IBF
Keith Mullings	USA	1997-1999	WBC
Harry Simon*	Namibia	1998-2001	WBO
Fernando Vargas	USA	1998-2000	IBF
Javier Castillejo	Spain	1999-2001	WBC
David Reid	USA	1999-2000	WBA
Felix Trinidad*	Puerto Rico	2000	WBA
Felix Trinidad*	Puerto Rico	2000-2001	IBF/WBA
Oscar de la Hoya*	USA	2001-2002	WBC
Fernando Vargas	USA	2001-2002	WBA
Ronald Wright*	USA	2001-2004	IBF
Daniel Santos	Puerto Rico	2002-2005	WBO
Oscar de la Hoya	USA	2002-2003	WBA/WBC
Shane Mosley	USA	2003-2004	WBA/WBC
Ronald Wright	USA	2004	IBF/WBA/WBC
Ronald Wright	USA	2004-2005	WBA/WBC
Verno Phillips	USA	2004	IBF
Kassim Ouma	Uganda	2004-2005	IBF
Ronald Wright*	USA	2005	WBC
Travis Simms	USA	2005	WBA
Javier Castillejo	Spain	2005	WBC
Alejandro Garcia	Mexico	2005-2006	WBA
Roman Karmazin	Russia	2005-2006	IBF
Ricardo Mayorga	Nicaragua	2005-2006	WBC
Sergei Dzindziruk	Ukraine	2005-	WBO
Jose Antonio Rivera	USA	2006-2007	WBA
Oscar de la Hoya	USA	2006-2007	WBC
Cory Spinks	USA	2006-2008	IBF
Travis Simms	USA	2007	WBA

Title Holder	Birthplace	Tenure	Status
Floyd Mayweather*	USA	2007	WBC
Joachim Alcine	Haiti	2007-2008	WBA
Vernon Forrest	USA	2007-2008	WBC
Verno Phillips*	Belize	2008	IBF
Sergio Mora	Mexico	2008	WBC
Daniel Santos	Puerto Rico	2008-	WBA
Vernon Forrest	USA	2008-2009	WBC
Cory Spinks	USA	2009-	IBF
Sergio Martinez	Argentina	2009-	WBC

Middleweight (160 lbs)

Title Holder	Birthplace	Tenure	Status
Nonpareil Jack Dempsey	Ireland	1889-1891	USA
Bob Fitzsimmons	England	1891-1893	USA
Jim Hall	Australia	1892-1893	GB
Bob Fitzsimmons	England	1893-1894	
Bob Fitzsimmons	England	1894-1899	
Frank Craig	USA	1894-1895	GB
Dan Creedon	New Zealand	1895-1897	GB
Tommy Ryan	USA	1895-1896	
Kid McCoy	USA	1896-1898	
Tommy Ryan	USA	1898-1905	
Charley McKeever	USA	1900-1902	
George Gardner	USA	1901-1902	
Jack O'Brien	USA	1901-1905	
George Green	USA	1901-1902	
Jack Palmer	England	1902-1903	GB
Hugo Kelly	USA	1905-1908	
Jack Twin Sullivan	USA	1905-1908	
Sam Langford	Canada	1907-1911	
Billy Papke	USA	1908	
Stanley Ketchel	USA	1908	
Billy Papke	USA	1908	
Stanley Ketchel	USA	1908-1910	
Billy Papke	USA	1910-1913	
Stanley Ketchel*	USA	1910	
Hugo Kelly	USA	1910-1912	
Cyclone Johnny Thompson	USA	1911-1912	
Harry Lewis	USA	1911	
Leo Houck	USA	1911-1912	
Georges Carpentier	France	1911-1912	
Jack Dillon	USA	1912	
Frank Mantell	USA	1912-1913	
Frank Klaus	USA	1912-1913	
Georges Carpentier	France	1912	IBU
Jack Dillon	USA	1912-1915	
Eddie McGoorty	USA	1912-1913	
Frank Klaus	USA	1913	IBU
Jimmy Clabby	USA	1913-1914	
George Chip	USA	1913-1914	
Joe Borrell	USA	1913-1914	
Jeff Smith	USA	1913-1914	
Eddie McGoorty	USA	1914	AUSTR
Jeff Smith	USA	1914	AUSTR
Al McCoy	USA	1914-1917	
Jimmy Clabby	USA	1914-1915	
Mick King	Australia	1914	AUSTR
Jeff Smith	USA	1914-1915	AUSTR
Young Ahearn	England	1915-1916	
Les Darcy*	Australia	1915-1917	AUSTR
Mike Gibbons	USA	1916-1917	
Mike O'Dowd	USA	1917-1920	
Johnny Wilson	USA	1920-1921	
Johnny Wilson	USA	1921-1922	NBA/NY
Bryan Downey	USA	1921-1922	OHIO
Johnny Wilson	USA	1922-1923	NBA
Dave Rosenberg	USA	1922	NY
Jock Malone	USA	1922-1923	OHIO
Mike O'Dowd	USA	1922-1923	NY
Johnny Wilson	USA	1923	
Harry Greb	USA	1923-1926	
Tiger Flowers	USA	1926	
Mickey Walker	USA	1926-1931	

Title Holder	Birthplace	Tenure	Status	Title Holder	Birthplace	Tenure	Status
Gorilla Jones	USA	1932	NBA	Mike McCallum	Jamaica	1989-1991	WBA
Marcel Thil	France	1932-1933	NBA/IBU	Nigel Benn	England	1990	WBO
Marcel Thil	France	1933-1937	IBU	Chris Eubank*	England	1990-1991	WBO
Ben Jeby	USA	1933	NY	Julian Jackson	Virgin Islands	1990-1993	WBC
Lou Brouillard	Canada	1933	NY	James Toney*	USA	1991-1993	IBF
Lou Brouillard	Canada	1933	NY/NBA	Gerald McClellan*	USA	1991-1993	WBO
Vearl Whitehead	USA	1933	CALIF	Reggie Johnson	USA	1992-1993	WBA
Teddy Yarosz	USA	1933-1934	PEN	Gerald McClellan*	USA	1993-1995	WBC
Vince Dundee	USA	1933-1934	NY/NBA	Chris Pyatt	England	1993-1994	WBO
Teddy Yarosz	USA	1934-1935	NY/NBA	Roy Jones*	USA	1993-1994	IBF
Babe Risko	USA	1935-1936	NY/NBA	John David Jackson	USA	1993-1994	WBA
Freddie Steele	USA	1936-1938	NY/NBA	Steve Collins*	Ireland	1994-1995	WBO
Fred Apostoli	USA	1937-1938	IBU	Jorge Castro	Argentina	1994	WBA
Edouard Tenet	France	1938	IBU	Julian Jackson	Virgin Islands	1995	WBC
Young Corbett III	Italy	1938	CALIF	Bernard Hopkins*	USA	1995-2001	IBF
Freddie Steele	USA	1938	NBA	Lonnie Bradley*	USA	1995-1998	WBO
Al Hostak	USA	1938	NBA	Quincy Taylor	USA	1995-1996	WBC
Solly Krieger	USA	1938-1939	NBA	Shinji Takehara	Japan	1995-1996	WBA
Fred Apostoli	USA	1938-1939	NY	Keith Holmes	USA	1996-1998	WBC
Al Hostak	USA	1939-1940	NBA	William Joppy	USA	1996-1997	WBA
Ceferino Garcia	Philippines	1939-1940	NY	Julio Cesar Green	Dom Republic	1997-1998	WBA
Ken Overlin	USA	1940-1941	NY	William Joppy	USA	1998-2001	WBA
Tony Zale	USA	1940-1941	NBA	Hassine Cherifi	France	1998-1999	WBC
Billy Soose	USA	1941	NY	Otis Grant*	Canada	1998	WBO
Tony Zale	USA	1941-1947		Bert Schenk	Germany	1999	WBO
Rocky Graziano	USA	1947-1948		Keith Holmes	USA	1999-2001	WBC
Tony Zale	USA	1948		Jason Matthews	England	1999	WBO
Marcel Cerdan	Algeria	1948-1949		Armand Krajnc	Slovenia	1999-2002	WBO
Jake la Motta	USA	1949-1950		Bernard Hopkins*	USA	2001	WBC/IBF
Jake la Motta	USA	1950-1951	NY/NBA	Felix Trinidad	Puerto Rico	2001	WBA
Sugar Ray Robinson	USA	1950-1951	PEN	Bernard Hopkins*	USA	2001-2004	WBC/WBA/IBF
Sugar Ray Robinson	USA	1951		Harry Simon	Namibia	2002-2003	WBO
Randy Turpin	England	1951		Hector Javier Velazco	Argentina	2003	WBO
Sugar Ray Robinson*	USA	1951-1952		Felix Sturm	Germany	2003-2004	WBO
Randy Turpin	England	1953	GB/EBU	Oscar de la Hoya	USA	2004	WBO
Carl Bobo Olson	Hawaii	1953-1955		Bernard Hopkins	USA	2004-2005	IBF/WBA/WBC/WBO
Sugar Ray Robinson	USA	1955-1957					
Gene Fullmer	USA	1957		Jermain Taylor*	USA	2005	IBF/WBA/WBC/WBO
Sugar Ray Robinson	USA	1957					
Carmen Basilio	USA	1957-1958		Jermain Taylor*	USA	2005	WBA/WBC/WBO
Sugar Ray Robinson	USA	1958-1959		Arthur Abraham	Armenia	2005-	IBF
Sugar Ray Robinson	USA	1959-1960	NY/EBU	Jermain Taylor	USA	2006-2007	WBC/WBO
Gene Fullmer	USA	1959-1962	NBA	Javier Castillejo	Spain	2006	WBA
Paul Pender	USA	1960-1961	NY/EBU	Mariano Carrera	Argentina	2006-2007	WBA
Terry Downes	England	1961-1962	NY/EBU	Javier Castillejo	Spain	2007	WBA
Paul Pender	USA	1962	NY/EBU	Felix Sturm	Germany	2007-	WBA
Dick Tiger	Nigeria	1962-1963	NBA	Kelly Pavlik	USA	2007-	WBC/WBO
Dick Tiger	Nigeria	1963					
Joey Giardello	USA	1963-1965		**S. Middleweight (168 lbs)**			
Dick Tiger	Nigeria	1965-1966		Murray Sutherland	Scotland	1984	IBF
Emile Griffith	Virgin Islands	1966-1967		Chong-Pal Park*	S Korea	1984-1987	IBF
Nino Benvenuti	Italy	1967		Chong-Pal Park*	S Korea	1987-1988	WBA
Emile Griffith	Virgin Islands	1967-1968		Graciano Rocchigiani*	Germany	1988-1989	IBF
Nino Benvenuti	Italy	1968-1970		Fully Obelmejias	Venezuela	1988-1989	WBA
Carlos Monzon	Argentina	1970-1974		Sugar Ray Leonard*	USA	1988-1990	WBC
Carlos Monzon*	Argentina	1974-1976	WBA	Thomas Hearns*	USA	1988-1991	WBO
Rodrigo Valdez	Colombia	1974-1976	WBC	In-Chul Baek	S Korea	1989-1990	WBA
Carlos Monzon*	Argentina	1976-1977		Lindell Holmes	USA	1990-1991	IBF
Rodrigo Valdez	Colombia	1977-1978		Christophe Tiozzo	France	1990-1991	WBA
Hugo Corro	Argentina	1978-1979		Mauro Galvano	Italy	1990-1992	WBC
Vito Antuofermo	Italy	1979-1980		Victor Cordoba	Panama	1991-1992	WBA
Alan Minter	England	1980		Darrin van Horn	USA	1991-1992	IBF
Marvin Hagler	USA	1980-1987		Chris Eubank	England	1991-1995	WBO
Marvin Hagler	USA	1987	WBC/IBF	Iran Barkley	USA	1992-1993	IBF
Sugar Ray Leonard	USA	1987	WBC	Michael Nunn	USA	1992-1994	WBA
Frank Tate	USA	1987-1988	IBF	Nigel Benn	England	1992-1996	WBC
Sumbu Kalambay	Zaire	1987-1989	WBA	James Toney	USA	1993-1994	IBF
Thomas Hearns	USA	1987-1988	WBC	Steve Little	USA	1994	WBA
Iran Barkley	USA	1988-1989	WBC	Frank Liles	USA	1994-1999	WBA
Michael Nunn	USA	1988-1991	IBF	Roy Jones*	USA	1994-1997	IBF
Roberto Duran	Panama	1989-1990	WBC	Steve Collins*	Ireland	1995-1997	WBO
Doug de Witt	USA	1989-1990	WBO	Thulani Malinga	S Africa	1996	WBC

257

Title Holder	Birthplace	Tenure	Status
Vincenzo Nardiello	Italy	1996	WBC
Robin Reid	England	1996-1997	WBC
Charles Brewer	USA	1997-1998	IBF
Joe Calzaghe*	Wales	1997-2006	WBO
Thulani Malinga	S Africa	1997-1998	WBC
Richie Woodhall	England	1998-1999	WBC
Sven Ottke*	Germany	1998-2003	IBF
Byron Mitchell	USA	1999-2000	WBA
Markus Beyer	Germany	1999-2000	WBC
Bruno Girard	France	2000-2001	WBA
Glenn Catley	England	2000	WBC
Dingaan Thobela	S Africa	2000	WBC
Dave Hilton	Canada	2000-2001	WBC
Byron Mitchell	USA	2001-2003	WBA
Eric Lucas	Canada	2001-2003	WBC
Sven Ottke*	Germany	2003-2004	IBF/WBA
Markus Beyer	Germany	2003-2004	WBC
Anthony Mundine	Australia	2004	WBA
Manny Sica	Puerto Rico	2004	WBA
Cristian Sanavia	Italy	2004	WBC
Jeff Lacy	USA	2004-2006	IBF
Markus Beyer	Germany	2004-2006	WBC
Mikkel Kessler*	Denmark	2004-2006	WBA
Joe Calzaghe*	Wales	2006	WBO/IBF
Mikkel Kessler	Denmark	2006-2007	WBC/WBA
Joe Calzaghe*	Wales	2006-2007	WBO
Alejandro Berrio	Colombia	2007	IBF
Lucien Bute	Romania	2007-	IBF
Joe Calzaghe*	Wales	2007-2008	WBA/WBC/WBO
Joe Calzaghe*	Wales	2008	WBA/WBO
Denis Inkin	Russia	2008-2009	WBO
Mikkel Kessler	Denmark	2008-	WBA
Carl Froch	England	2008-	WBC
Karoly Balzsay	Hungary	2009-	WBO

L. Heavyweight (175 lbs)

Title Holder	Birthplace	Tenure	Status
Jack Root	Austria	1903	
George Gardner	Ireland	1903	
George Gardner	Ireland	1903	USA
Bob Fitzsimmons	England	1903-1905	USA
Jack O'Brien	USA	1905-1911	
Sam Langford	Canada	1911-1913	
Georges Carpentier	France	1913-1920	IBU
Jack Dillon	USA	1914-1916	USA
Battling Levinsky	USA	1916-1920	USA
Georges Carpentier	France	1920-1922	
Battling Siki	Senegal	1922-1923	
Mike McTigue	Ireland	1923-1925	
Paul Berlenbach	USA	1925-1926	
Jack Delaney*	Canada	1926-1927	
Jimmy Slattery	USA	1927	NBA
Tommy Loughran	USA	1927	NY
Tommy Loughran*	USA	1927-1929	
Jimmy Slattery	USA	1930	NY
Maxie Rosenbloom	USA	1930-1931	
Maxie Rosenbloom	USA	1931-1933	NY
George Nichols	USA	1932	NBA
Bob Godwin	USA	1933	NBA
Maxie Rosenbloom	USA	1933-1934	
Maxie Rosenbloom	USA	1934	NY
Joe Knight	USA	1934-1935	FL/NC/GEO
Bob Olin	USA	1934-1935	NY
Al McCoy	Canada	1935	CAN
Bob Olin	USA	1935	NY/NBA
John Henry Lewis	USA	1935-1938	NY/NBA
Gustav Roth	Belgium	1936-1938	IBU
Ad Heuser	Germany	1938	IBU
John Henry Lewis	USA	1938	
John Henry Lewis	USA	1938-1939	NBA
Melio Bettina	USA	1939	NY
Len Harvey	England	1939-1942	GB
Billy Conn	USA	1939-1940	NY/NBA

Title Holder	Birthplace	Tenure	Status
Anton Christoforidis	Greece	1941	NBA
Gus Lesnevich	USA	1941	NBA
Gus Lesnevich	USA	1941-1946	NY/NBA
Freddie Mills	England	1942-1946	GB
Gus Lesnevich	USA	1946-1948	
Freddie Mills	England	1948-1950	
Joey Maxim	USA	1950-1952	
Archie Moore	USA	1952-1960	
Archie Moore	USA	1960-1962	NY/EBU
Harold Johnson	USA	1961-1962	NBA
Harold Johnson	USA	1962-1963	
Willie Pastrano	USA	1963	
Willie Pastrano*	USA	1963-1964	WBA/WBC
Eddie Cotton	USA	1963-1964	MICH
Willie Pastrano	USA	1964-1965	
Jose Torres	Puerto Rico	1965-1966	
Dick Tiger	Nigeria	1966-1968	
Bob Foster	USA	1968-1970	
Bob Foster*	USA	1970-1972	WBC
Vicente Rondon	Venezuela	1971-1972	WBA
Bob Foster*	USA	1972-1974	
John Conteh	England	1974-1977	WBC
Victor Galindez	Argentina	1974-1978	WBA
Miguel Cuello	Argentina	1977-1978	WBC
Mate Parlov	Yugoslavia	1978	WBC

Willie Pastrano

Title Holder	Birthplace	Tenure	Status
Mike Rossman	USA	1978-1979	WBA
Marvin Johnson	USA	1978-1979	WBC
Victor Galindez	Argentina	1979	WBA
Matt Saad Muhammad	USA	1979-1981	WBC
Marvin Johnson	USA	1979-1980	WBA
Mustafa Muhammad	USA	1980-1981	WBA
Michael Spinks*	USA	1981-1983	WBA
Dwight Muhammad Qawi	USA	1981-1983	WBC
Michael Spinks*	USA	1983-1985	
J. B. Williamson	USA	1985-1986	WBC
Slobodan Kacar	Yugoslavia	1985-1986	IBF
Marvin Johnson	USA	1986-1987	WBA
Dennis Andries	Guyana	1986-1987	WBC
Bobby Czyz	USA	1986-1987	IBF
Thomas Hearns*	USA	1987	WBC
Leslie Stewart	Trinidad	1987	WBA
Virgil Hill	USA	1987-1991	WBA
Charles Williams	USA	1987-1993	IBF
Don Lalonde	Canada	1987-1988	WBC
Sugar Ray Leonard*	USA	1988	WBC
Michael Moorer*	USA	1988-1991	WBO
Dennis Andries	Guyana	1989	WBC
Jeff Harding	Australia	1989-1990	WBC
Dennis Andries	Guyana	1990-1991	WBC
Leonzer Barber	USA	1991-1994	WBO
Thomas Hearns	USA	1991-1992	WBA
Jeff Harding	Australia	1991-1994	WBC
Iran Barkley*	USA	1992	WBA
Virgil Hill*	USA	1992-1996	WBA
Henry Maske	Germany	1993-1996	IBF
Mike McCallum	Jamaica	1994-1995	WBC
Dariusz Michalczewski*	Poland	1994-1997	WBO
Fabrice Tiozzo	France	1995-1997	WBC
Virgil Hill	USA	1996-1997	IBF/WBA
Roy Jones	USA	1997	WBC
Montell Griffin	USA	1997	WBC
Dariusz Michalczewski*	Poland	1997	WBO/IBF/WBA
Dariusz Michalczewski	Poland	1997-2003	WBO
William Guthrie	USA	1997-1998	IBF
Roy Jones*	USA	1997-1998	WBC
Lou del Valle	USA	1997-1998	WBA
Reggie Johnson	USA	1998-1999	IBF
Roy Jones*	USA	1998-1999	WBC/WBA
Roy Jones*	USA	1999-2002	WBC/WBA/IBF
Roy Jones*	USA	2002-2003	WBA/WBC
Mehdi Sahnoune	France	2003	WBA
Antonio Tarver*	USA	2003	IBF/WBC
Silvio Branco	Italy	2003-2004	WBA
Julio Gonzalez	Mexico	2003-2004	WBO
Antonio Tarver*	USA	2003-2004	WBC
Zsolt Erdei	Hungary	2004-	WBO
Glengoffe Johnson*	Jamaica	2004	IBF
Antoine Tarver	USA	2004-2006	IBO
Fabrice Tiozzo*	France	2004-2006	WBA
Clinton Woods	England	2005-2008	IBF
Tomasz Adamek	Poland	2005-2007	WBC
Bernard Hopkins*	USA	2006	IBO
Silvio Branco	Italy	2006-2007	WBA
Chad Dawson*	USA	2006-2008	WBC
Stipe Drews	Croatia	2007	WBA
Antonio Tarver*	USA	2007-2008	IBO
Danny Green*	Australia	2007-2008	WBA
Antonio Tarver	USA	2008	IBO/IBF
Hugo Garay	Argentina	2008-2009	WBA
Adrian Diaconu	Romania	2008-2009	WBC
Chad Dawson*	USA	2008-2009	IBF/IBO
Jean Pascal	Canada	2009-	WBC
Gabriel Campillo	Spain	2009-	WBA

Cruiserweight (200 lbs)

Title Holder	Birthplace	Tenure	Status
Marvin Camel	USA	1979-1980	WBC
Carlos de Leon	Puerto Rico	1980-1982	WBC
Ossie Ocasio	Puerto Rico	1982-1984	WBA
S. T. Gordon	USA	1982-1983	WBC
Marvin Camel	USA	1983-1984	IBF
Carlos de Leon	Puerto Rico	1983-1985	WBC
Lee Roy Murphy	USA	1984-1986	IBF
Piet Crous	S Africa	1984-1985	WBA
Alfonso Ratliff	USA	1985	WBC
Dwight Muhammad Qawi	USA	1985-1986	WBA
Bernard Benton	USA	1985-1986	WBC
Carlos de Leon	Puerto Rico	1986-1988	WBC
Evander Holyfield*	USA	1986-1987	WBA
Rickey Parkey	USA	1986-1987	IBF
Evander Holyfield*	USA	1987-1988	WBA/IBF
Evander Holyfield*	USA	1988	
Taoufik Belbouli*	France	1989	WBA
Carlos de Leon	Puerto Rico	1989-1990	WBC
Glenn McCrory	England	1989-1990	IBF
Robert Daniels	USA	1989-1991	WBA
Boone Pultz	USA	1989-1990	WBO
Jeff Lampkin*	USA	1990-1991	IBF
Magne Havnaa*	Norway	1990-1992	WBO
Masimilliano Duran	Italy	1990-1991	WBC
Bobby Czyz	USA	1991-1993	WBA
Anaclet Wamba	Congo	1991-1995	WBC
James Warring	USA	1991-1992	IBF
Tyrone Booze	USA	1992-1993	WBO
Al Cole*	USA	1992-1996	IBF
Marcus Bott	Germany	1993	WBO
Nestor Giovannini	Argentina	1993-1994	WBO
Orlin Norris	USA	1993-1995	WBA
Dariusz Michalczewski*	Poland	1994-1995	WBO
Ralf Rocchigiani	Germany	1995-1997	WBO
Nate Miller	USA	1995-1997	WBA
Marcelo Dominguez	Argentina	1995-1998	WBC
Adolpho Washington	USA	1996-1997	IBF
Uriah Grant	USA	1997	IBF
Carl Thompson	England	1997-1999	WBO
Imamu Mayfield	USA	1997-1998	IBF
Fabrice Tiozzo	France	1997-2000	WBA
Juan Carlos Gomez*	Cuba	1998-2002	WBC
Arthur Williams	USA	1998-1999	IBF
Johnny Nelson*	England	1999-2006	WBO
Vassily Jirov	Kazakhstan	1999-2003	IBF
Virgil Hill	USA	2000-2002	WBA
Jean-Marc Mormeck*	Guadeloupe	2002-2005	WBA
Wayne Braithwaite	Guyana	2002-2005	WBC
James Toney*	USA	2003-2004	IBF
Kelvin Davis	USA	2004-2005	IBF
Jean-Marc Mormeck	Guadaloupe	2005-2006	WBA/WBC
O'Neil Bell*	USA	2005-2006	IBF
O'Neil Bell	USA	2006	IBF/WBA/WBC
O'Neil Bell	USA	2006-2007	WBA/WBC
Enzo Maccarinelli	Wales	2006-2008	WBO
Krzysztof Wlodarczyk	Poland	2006-2007	IBF
Jean-Marc Mormeck	Guadaloupe	2007	WBA/WBC
Steve Cunningham	USA	2007-2008	IBF
David Haye*	England	2007-2008	WBC/WBA
David Haye*	England	2008	WBC/WBA/WBO
Firat Arslan	Germany	2008	WBA
David Haye*	England	2008	WBO
Guillermo Jones	Panama	2008-	WBA
Giacobbe Fragomeni	Italy	2008-	WBC
Tomasz Adamek	Poland	2008-	IBF
Victor Ramirez	Argentina	2009-	WBO

Heavyweight (200 lbs+)

Title Holder	Birthplace	Tenure	Status
John L. Sullivan	USA	1889-1892	USA
Peter Jackson	Australia	1889-1892	
Frank Slavin	Australia	1890-1892	GB/AUST
Peter Jackson	Australia	1892-1893	GB/AUST
James J. Corbett	USA	1892-1894	USA
James J. Corbett	USA	1894-1895	

WORLD CHAMPIONS SINCE GLOVES, 1889-2009

Title Holder	Birthplace	Tenure	Status	Title Holder	Birthplace	Tenure	Status
James J. Corbett	USA	1895-1897		Larry Holmes	USA	1983-1985	IBF
Peter Maher	Ireland	1895-1896		Tim Witherspoon	USA	1984	WBC
Bob Fitzsimmons	England	1896-1897		Pinklon Thomas	USA	1984-1986	WBC
Bob Fitzsimmons	England	1897-1899		Greg Page	USA	1984-1985	WBA
James J. Jeffries	USA	1899-1902		Tony Tubbs	USA	1985-1986	WBA
James J. Jeffries	USA	1902-1905		Michael Spinks	USA	1985-1987	IBF
Denver Ed Martin	USA	1902-1903		Tim Witherspoon	USA	1986	WBA
Jack Johnson	USA	1902-1908		Trevor Berbick	Jamaica	1986	WBC
Bob Fitzsimmons	England	1905		Mike Tyson*	USA	1986-1987	WBC
Marvin Hart	USA	1905-1906		James Smith	USA	1986-1987	WBA
Jack O'Brien	USA	1905-1906		Mike Tyson*	USA	1987	WBA/WBC
Tommy Burns	Canada	1906-1908		Tony Tucker	USA	1987	IBF
Jack Johnson	USA	1908-1909		**Mike Tyson**	USA	1987-1989	
Jack Johnson	USA	1909-1915		Mike Tyson	USA	1989-1990	IBF/WBA/WBC
Sam Langford	USA	1909-1911		Francesco Damiani	Italy	1989-1991	WBO
Sam McVey	USA	1911-1912		James Douglas	USA	1990	IBF/WBA/WBC
Sam Langford	USA	1912-1914		Evander Holyfield	USA	1990-1992	IBF/WBA/WBC
Luther McCarty	USA	1913		Ray Mercer	USA	1991-1992	WBO
Arthur Pelkey	Canada	1913-1914		Michael Moorer*	USA	1992-1993	WBO
Gunboat Smith	USA	1914		Riddick Bowe	USA	1992	IBF/WBA/WBC
Harry Wills	USA	1914		Riddick Bowe	USA	1992-1993	IBF/WBA
Georges Carpentier	France	1914		Lennox Lewis	England	1992-1994	WBC
Sam Langford	USA	1914-1915		Tommy Morrison	USA	1993	WBO
Jess Willard	USA	1915-1919		Michael Bentt	England	1993-1994	WBO
Joe Jeannette	USA	1915		Evander Holyfield	USA	1993-1994	WBA/IBF
Sam McVey	USA	1915		Herbie Hide	England	1994-1995	WBO
Harry Wills	USA	1915-1916		Michael Moorer	USA	1994	WBA/IBF
Sam Langford	USA	1916-1917		Oliver McCall	USA	1994-1995	WBC
Bill Tate	USA	1917		George Foreman	USA	1994-1995	WBA/IBF
Sam Langford	USA	1917-1918		Riddick Bowe*	USA	1995-1996	WBO
Harry Wills	USA	1918-1926		George Foreman*	USA	1995	IBF
Jack Dempsey	USA	1919-1926		Bruce Seldon	USA	1995-1996	WBA
Gene Tunney*	USA	1926-1928		Frank Bruno	England	1995-1996	WBC
Max Schmeling	Germany	1930-1932		Frans Botha	S Africa	1995-1996	IBF
Jack Sharkey	USA	1932-1933		Mike Tyson	USA	1996	WBC
Primo Carnera	Italy	1933-1934		Michael Moorer	USA	1996-1997	IBF
Max Baer	USA	1934-1935		Henry Akinwande*	England	1996-1997	WBO
James J. Braddock	USA	1935		Mike Tyson	USA	1996	WBA
James J. Braddock	USA	1935-1936	NY/NBA	Evander Holyfield*	USA	1996-1997	WBA
George Godfrey	USA	1935-1936	IBU	Lennox Lewis*	England	1997-1999	WBC
James J. Braddock	USA	1936-1937		Herbie Hide	England	1997-1999	WBO
Joe Louis*	USA	1937-1949		Evander Holyfield	USA	1997-1999	IBF/WBA
Ezzard Charles	USA	1949-1950	NBA	Vitali Klitschko	Ukraine	1999-2000	WBO
Lee Savold	USA	1950-1951	GB/EBU	Lennox Lewis*	England	1999-2000	IBF/WBA/WBC
Ezzard Charles	USA	1950-1951	NY/NBA	Chris Byrd	USA	2000	WBO
Joe Louis	USA	1951	GB/EBU	Lennox Lewis	England	2000-2001	IBF/WBC
Jersey Joe Walcott	USA	1951	NY/NBA	Evander Holyfield	USA	2000-2001	WBA
Jersey Joe Walcott	USA	1951-1952		Vladimir Klitschko	Ukraine	2000-2003	WBO
Rocky Marciano*	USA	1952-1956		John Ruiz	USA	2001-2003	WBA
Floyd Patterson	USA	1956-1959		Hasim Rahman	USA	2001	WBC/IBF
Ingemar Johansson	Sweden	1959-1960		Lennox Lewis*	England	2001-2002	WBC/IBF
Floyd Patterson	USA	1960-1962		Lennox Lewis*	England	2002-2004	WBC
Sonny Liston	USA	1962-1964		Chris Byrd	USA	2002-2006	IBF
Muhammad Ali	USA	1964		Roy Jones*	USA	2003	WBA
Muhammad Ali*	USA	1964-1967	WBC	Corrie Sanders*	S Africa	2003	WBO
Ernie Terrell	USA	1965-1967	WBA	Lamon Brewster	USA	2004-2006	WBO
Muhammad Ali	USA	1967		John Ruiz	Puerto Rico	2004-2005	WBA
Muhammad Ali	USA	1967-1968	WBC	Vitali Klitschko*	Ukraine	2004-2005	WBC
Joe Frazier*	USA	1968-1970	NY/MASS	James Toney	USA	2005	WBA
Jimmy Ellis	USA	1968-1970	WBA	John Ruiz	Puerto Rico	2005	WBA
Joe Frazier	USA	1970-1973		Nikolai Valuev	Russia	2005-2007	WBA
George Foreman	USA	1973-1974		Hasim Rahman	USA	2005-2006	WBC
Muhammad Ali	USA	1974-1978		Sergei Lyakhovich	Belarus	2006	WBO
Leon Spinks	USA	1978		Vladimir Klitschko*	Ukraine	2006-2008	IBF
Leon Spinks	USA	1978	WBA	Oleg Maskaev	Kazakhstan	2006-2008	WBC
Ken Norton	USA	1978	WBC	Shannon Briggs	USA	2006-2007	WBO
Larry Holmes*	USA	1978-1983	WBC	Ruslan Chagaev	Uzbekistan	2007-2009	WBA
Muhammad Ali*	USA	1978-1979	WBA	Sultan Ibragimov	Russia	2007-2008	WBO
John Tate	USA	1979-1980	WBA	Samuel Peter	Nigeria	2008	WBC
Mike Weaver	USA	1980-1982	WBA	Vladimir Klitschko	Ukraine	2008-	IBF/WBO
Michael Dokes	USA	1982-1983	WBA	Vitali Klitschko	Ukraine	2008-	WBC
Gerrie Coetzee	S Africa	1983-1984	WBA	Nikolai Valuev	Russia	2009-	WBA

ABA National Championships, 2008-2009

Note: Only men who fought at some stage of the competition are included

Home Counties v Eastern Counties

Home Counties   The Irish Centre, Slough – 27 March & Wycombe Wanderers FC – 3 April
L.Fly: *final*: B. Fowl (Hoddesdon) wo. **Fly**: *final*: D. Culling (Stevenage) wo. **Bantam**: *final*: L. Lewis (Oxford BA) wo. **Feather**: *final*: J. Mason (Welwyn Garden City) wo. **Light**: *semi-finals*: R. O'Brien (Reading) wo, A. Lever (Bedford) w pts D. Leo (Cheshunt); *final*: A. Lever w pts R. O'Brien. **L.Welter**: *semi-finals*: D. Docherty (Bushey) wo, B. Crotty (Stevenage) w pts D. Phillips (Luton Shamrock); *final*: D. Docherty w pts B. Crotty. **Welter**: *final*: J. Perry (Stevenage) w pts J. Hill (Blackbird Leys). **Middle**: *final*: A. Dennis (Welwyn Garden City) wo. **L.Heavy**: *final*: M. Shinkwin (Bushey) w pts D. Colquhoun (Lewsey). **Cruiser**: *final*: R. Evans (Banbury) w pts S. Jury (Thames Valley). **Heavy**: *final*: D. Gardener (Hoddesdon) w pts M. Churcher (Thames Valley). **S.Heavy**: *final*: S. Parsons (Milton Keynes) wo.

Eastern Counties   Rayleigh Mill ABC – 7 March, Lea Valley High School, Enfield – 21 March & Eastgate ABC, Debenham – 27 March
L.Fly: no entries. **Fly**: no entries. **Bantam**: *final*: D. Perry (Norwich Lads) wo. **Feather**: *final*: J. Taylor (Brentwood) wo. **Light**: *final*: J. Homer (Rayleigh) w pts M. Poston (Harwich). **L.Welter**: *semi-finals*: J. Payne (Chatteris) wo, B. Savva (Kingfisher) w pts K. Allen (Eastgate); *final*: J. Payne (Chatteris) w rsc 3 K. Allen – replaced B. Savva. **Welter**: *semi-finals*: J. Powell (Clacton) wo, P. Smith (New Astley) w pts S. Moise (Aylesham); *final*: P. Smith w pts J. Powell. **Middle**: *semi-finals*: B. Harris (Berry Boys) w rsc 2 Y. Mehmet (Chalvedon), A. Ogogo (Triple A) w rsc F. Sictorness (Norwich Lads); *final*: A. Ogogo w rtd 3 B. Harris. **L.Heavy**: *final*: C. Brown (Chatteris) wo. **Cruiser**: no entries. **Heavy**: no entries. **S.Heavy**: no entries.

Home Counties v Eastern Counties   The Auction House, Luton – 17 April
L.Fly: B. Fowl (Hoddesdon) wo. **Fly**: D. Culling (Stevenage) wo. **Bantam**: D. Perry (Norwich Lads) w pts L. Lewis (Oxford BA). **Feather**: J. Taylor (Brentwood) w pts J. Mason (Welwyn Garden City). **Light**: J. Homer (Rayleigh) w pts A. Lever (Bedford). **L.Welter**: D. Docherty (Bushey) w pts J. Payne (Chatteris). **Welter**: J. Perry (Stevenage) w pts P. Smith (New Astley). **Middle**: A. Ogogo (Triple A) w pts A. Dennis (Welwyn Garden City). **L.Heavy**: M. Shinkwin (Bushey) w pts C. Brown (Chatteris). **Cruiser**: R. Evans (Banbury) wo. **Heavy**: D. Gardener (Hoddesdon) wo. **S.Heavy**: S. Parsons (Milton Keynes) wo.

London

North-East Division   Dukes Hall, Hornchurch – 20 March
L.Fly: no entries. **Fly**: no entries. **Bantam**: *final*: M. Ward (Repton) w pts M. Chanda (Crown & Manor). **Feather**: *final*: B. Morgan (West Ham) w pts D. Burrell (Peacock). **Light**: *final*: M. McCarthy (Repton) w pts S. Burrell (Peacock). **L.Welter**: *final*: L. Turner (Repton) wo. **Welter**: *semi-finals*: G. Thomas (Peacock) wo, D. O'Shaughnessy (West Ham) w rsc 1 J. Anthony (Newham); *final*: D. O'Shaughnessy w rsc 1 G. Thomas. **Middle**: *semi-finals*: I. Kinisona (Peacock) w pts L. Markham (Five Star), F. Buglioni (Repton); *final*: F. Buglioni w rsc I. Kinisona. **L.Heavy**: *semi-finals*: J. Gosling (Barking) w pts R. Russell (Broad Street), J. Summers (Peacock) w pts R. Shagouri (Repton); *final*: J. Summers w pts J. Gosling. **Cruiser**: *final*: T. Conquest (Dagenham) w pts T. Lohdi (Repton). **Heavy**: *final*: R. Newland (Peacock) wo. **S.Heavy**: *final*: W. Camacho (Peacock) w pts D. Campbell (Repton).

North-West Division   Brent Town Hall, Wembley – 19 March & Lea Valley High School, Enfield – 21 March
L.Fly: no entries. **Fly**: no entries. **Bantam**: no entries. **Feather**: *final*: S. Ojomoh (Haringey) w pts D. Rowe (Dale Youth). **Light**: *semi-finals*: M. McKray (Haringey) wo, A. O'Neil (Hayes) w pts K. Barnes (Tottenham & Enfield); *final*: M. McKray w rsc 1 A. O'Neil. **L.Welter**: *quarter-finals*: M. Mellish (Times) wo, C. Madoni (Dale Yourh) wo, R. Taylor (Haringey) w rsc 3 C. Moreno (Islington), T. Tear (Dale Youth) w pts B. Zarakani (Haringey); *semi-finals*: R. Taylor w pts M. Mellish, T. Tear w pts C. Madoni; *final*: R. Taylor w pts T. Tear. **Welter**: *semi-finals*: E. Ochieng (Haringey) w pts J. Brennan (Dale Youth), M. Lothian (Northolt) w pts H. Sidiqzai (Dale Youth); *final*: E. Ochieng w pts H. Sidiqzai. **Middle**: *quarter-finals*: L. Reid (Dale Youth) wo, J. Easy (Haringey) wo, B. Faywaz (Hanwell) wo, A. Higgins (St Pancras) w pts J. Ryder (Angel); *semi-finals*: L. Reid w pts J. Easy, A. Higgins w pts B. Faywaz; *final*: L. Reid w pts A. Higgins. **L.Heavy**: *final*: R. McCauley (St Pancras) wo. **Cruiser**: *final*: R. Ali (Dale Youth) wo. **Heavy**: *final*: M. Khamula (All Stars) wo. **S.Heavy**: no entries.

South-East Division   Fairfield Hall, Croydon – 19 March
L.Fly: *final*: D. Langley (Hollington) wo. **Fly**: no entries. **Bantam**: no entries: **Feather**: *final*: L. Pettitt (Nemesis) wo. **Light**: *semi-finals*: M. White-Dowe (Eltham) wo, L. Gibb (Nemesis) w pts C. Whyatt (Fitzroy Lodge); *final*: L. Gibb w pts M. White-Dowe. **L.Welter**: no entries. **Welter**: *semi-finals*: J. Ejapovi (Lynn) wo, A. Patterson (Fitzroy Lodge) w pts D. Setterfield (New Addington); *final*: A. Patterson w pts J. Egapovi. **Middle**: *semi-finals*: D. Burton (Honor Oak) wo, F. Mankenda (Hollington) w pts C. Esiaka (Fitzroy Lodge); *final*: F. Mankenda w pts D. Burton. **L.Heavy**: *final*: O. Mbwakongo (Lynn) wo. **Cruiser**: *final*: J. Haye (Fitzroy Lodge) wo. **Heavy**: *final*: W. Byrne (Fitzroy Lodge) wo. **S.Heavy**: *semi-finals*: A. Isa (Miguels) wo, H-M Kwok (Samuel Montague) w pts D. Akinlade (Fitzroy Lodge); final: A. Isa w pts H-M Kwok.

South-West Division   Fairfield Hall, Croydon – 19 March
L.Fly: no entries. **Fly**: no entries. **Bantam**: no entries. **Feather**: no entries. **Light**: *final*: R. Boylan (Earlsfield) wo. **L.Welter**: *final*: B. Skeete (Earlsfield) wo. **Welter**: *final*: R. Garvey (Earlsfield) wo. **Middle**: *final*: K. Garvey (Earlsfield) wo. **L.Heavy**: no entries. **Cruiser**: no entries. **Heavy**: no entries. **S.Heavy**: no entries.

London Semi-Finals & Finals   York Hall, Bethnal Green – 26 March & 5 April
L.Fly: *final*: D. Langley (Hollington) wo. **Fly**: no entries. **Bantam**: *final*: M. Ward (Repton) wo. **Feather**: *semi-finals*: L. Pettitt (Nemesis) wo, B. Morgan (West Ham) w pts S. Ojomo (Haringey); *final*: L. Pettitt w pts B. Morgan. **Light**: *semi-finals*: M. McCarthy (Repton) w pts M. McKray (Haringey), L. Gibb (Nemesis) w pts R. Boylan (Earlsfield); *final*: M. McCarthy w pts L. Gibb. **L.Welter**: *semi-finals*: R. Taylor (Haringey) wo, B. Skeete (Earlsfield) w pts L. Turner (Repton); *final*: B. Skeete w pts R. Taylor. **Welter**: *semi-finals*: A. Patterson (Fitzroy Lodge) w pts E. Ochieng (Haringey), D. O'Shaughnessy (West Ham) w rsc 1 R. Garvey (Earlsfield); *final*: D. O'Shaughnessy w pts E. Ochieng. **Middle**: *semi-finals*: K. Garvey (Earlsfield) w pts F. Makenda (Hollington), F. Buglioni (Repton) w rsc 1 L. Reid (Dale Youth); *final*: K. Garvey w pts F. Buglioni. **L.Heavy**: *semi-finals*: J. Summers (Peacock) wo, O. Mbwakongo (Lynn) w rsc 2 R. McCauley (St Pancras); *final*: O. Mbwakongo w rsc 2 J. Summers. **Cruiser**: *semi-finals*: J. Haye (Fitzroy Lodge) wo, T. Conquest (Dagenham) w pts R. Ali (Dale Youth); *final*: T. Conquest w pts J. Haye. **Heavy**: *semi-finals*: M. Khamula (All Stars) wo, R. Newland (Peacock) w pts W. Byrne (Fitzroy Lodge); *final*: R. Newland w pts M. Khamula. **S.Heavy**: *final*: A. Isa (Miguels) w rsc 3 W. Camacho (Peacock).

Midland Counties

Standard Triumph Club – 22 March & 5 April & The Sports & Social Club, Donnington – 1 April
L.Fly: *final*: S. Smith (Kings Heath) wo. **Fly**: *final*: G. Yafai (Birmingham) w pts U. Malik (Merlin Youth). **Bantam**: *final*: Y. Nasseer (Donnington) w pts J. Fletcher (Donnington). **Feather**: *semi-finals*: L. Wood (Phoenix) wo, L. Glover (William Perry) w rsc 3 A. Hale (Kettering); *final*: L. Glover w pts L. Wood. **Light**: *semi-finals*: R. Bennett (Kettering) wo, J. Mason (Kings Heath) w pts N. Rafiq (Queensberry Police) *final*: J. Mason w rsc 1 R. Bennett. **L.Welter**: *quarter-finals*: C. Truman (Aston) wo, N. Heaney (Hulton Abbey) w pts D. Jones (Kettering), S. Morrison (Birmingham) w pts I. Kiyimba (Belgrave), D. Baptiste (Bracebridge) w rsc 3 C. Speed (Triumph); *semi-finals*: D. Baptiste w pts S. Morrison, C. Truman (Aston) w pts N. Heaney; *final*: D. Baptiste w pts C. Truman. **Welter**: *prelims*: J. McGough (Triumph) wo, D. Singleton (South Normanton) wo, T. Hadtistyllis (Leicester) wo, S. Cooper (Pleck) wo, K. Hooper (Grimsby) wo, M. Pardoe (Droitwich) wo, J. Thompson (Belgrave) wo, T. Langford (Hall Green) w rsc 1 N. Hill (Trinity); *quarter-finals*: J. Thompson w pts J. McGough, T. Langford w pts S. Cooper, K. Hooper w pts T. Hadtistyllis, M. Pardoe w pts D. Singleton; *semi-finals*: T. Langford w pts J. Thompson, M. Pardoe w pts K. Hooper; *final*: T. Langford w pts M. Pardoe. **Middle**: *quarter-finals*: B. Binch (Bingham) wo, E. Essuman (Bilborough) wo, C. Cunningham (Warley) wo,

C. Valentine (Benny's) w rsc 1 L. Morris (Terry Allen Unique); *semi-finals*: B. Binch w pts E. Essuman, C. Valentine w rsc 4 C. Cunningham; *final*: C. Valentine w rsc 3 B. Binch. **L.Heavy**: *quarter-finals*: A. Johnson (St George's) wo, C. Delve (Droitwich) wo, L. Daly (Kings Heath) w pts T. Staples (Grimsby), J. Smyle (Leicester) w pts J. Jones (Terry Allen Unique); *semi-finals*: A. Johnson w pts C. Delve, J. Smyle w pts L. Daly; *final*: A. Johnson w pts J. Smyle. **Cruiser**: *semi-finals*: D. Jenvey (Droitwich) wo, S. Barclay (Corby) w pts D. Smith (Donnington); *final*: S. Barclay w rsc 1 D. Jenvey. **Heavy**: *semi-finals*: P. Stepien (Birmingham) w pts D. Davis (Trinity), C. Keane (Pleck) w pts E. Clayton; *final*: C. Keane w rsc 3 P. Stepien (Birmingham). **S.Heavy**: *semi-finals*: P. Mytych (Birmingham) wo, D. Ward (Belgrave) w pts L. Frater (Phoenix); *final*: P. Mytych w rsc 2 D. Ward.

North-West Counties

Merseyside & Cheshire Region – Austin Rawlinson Leisure Centre, Speke – 5 April & Alsop High School, Walton – 9 April
L.Fly: *final*: P. Butler (Vauxhall Motors) wo. **Fly**: *final*: P. Smith (Stockbridge) w pts I. Halsall (Lowe House). **Bantam**: *final*: K. Satchell (Everton Red Triangle) w pts A. Bridge (Croxteth). **Feather**: *final*: R. Farrag (Everton Red Triangle) w pts J. Quigley (Tower Hill). **Light**: *final*: T. Stalker (St Aloysius) w pts S. Maxwell (Higherside). **L.Welter**: *semi-finals*: C. Callaghan (Sefton) w rsc 2 C. Kelly (Kirkdale), S. Jennings (Tower Hill) w rsc 1 J. Tonks (Salisbury); *final*: S. Jennings w pts C. Callaghan. **Welter**: *final*: G. Ormrod (Lowe House) w pts A. Ismail (Salisbury). **Middle**: *semi-finals*: A. Farrell (Salisbury) w rsc 1 B. Rennie (Lowe House), T. Jones (Skelmersdale) w pts J. Seddon (Transport); *final*: A. Farrell w rtd 3 T. Jones. **L.Heavy**: *final*: M. Fielding (Rotunda) w co 1 A. Davies (Skelmersdale). **Cruiser**: *final*: W. Adenyi (Vauxhall Motors) wo. **Heavy**: *final*: R. Stainton (North Mersey) wo. **S.Heavy**: *final*: J. Winters (Kirkby) wo.

North-West Region   Audley Community Centre, Blackburn – 27 March, Citizen Suite, City of Manchester Stadium, Manchester – 28 March & Rumworth Hall, Bolton – 1 April
L.Fly: *final*: T. Stubbs (Northside) wo. **Fly**: *final*: Y. Arif (Elite) wo. **Bantam**: no entries. **Feather**: *final*: B. Younis (Bridgewater Salford) w pts L. Gillespie (Bridgewater Salford). **Light**: *semi-finals*: D. Boswell (Withins School Police) wo, M. Glen (Leigh) w pts P. Coleman (Shannon's); *final*: D. Boswell w pts M. Glen. **L.Welter**: *quarter-finals*: S. Singleton (Elite) w pts T. Bradford (Paramount), R. Heffron (Boarshaw) w pts A. Apergis (Moss Side), J. Bailie (Whitehaven) w pts A. Hollerhan (Roche), J. McCardle (Middleton) w pts J. Donald (Shannon's); *semi-finals*: R. Heffron w pts S. Singleton, J. McCardle w pts J. Bailie; *final*: R. Heffron w pts J. McCardle. **Welter**: *quarter-finals*: K. Grieve (Blackburn) wo, M. Ryan (Middleton) w rsc 1 S. Aluko (Northside), J. Brown (Boarshaw) w pts D. Coyle (Moss Side), S. Cardle (Kirkham & Fylde) w pts A. Mushtaq (Roche); *semi-finals*: M. Ryan wo K. Grieve, S. Cardle w pts J. Brown; *final*: S. Cardle w pts M. Ryan. **Middle**: *quarter-finals*: L. Brewster (Ashton) wo, K. Kirkham (Northside) wo, M. Hall (Larches) wo, H. Burton (Jimmy Egan's) w rsc 3 J. Burke (Pool of Life);

semi-finals: K. Kirkham w pts L. Brewster, H. Burton w pts M. Hall; *final*: H. Burton w pts K. Kirkham. **L.Heavy**: *semi-finals*: K. Borucki (Manx) w pts L. Holland (Jimmy Egan's), P. Bebbington (Macclesfield) w pts K. Debanks (Jimmy Egan's); *final*: K. Borucki wo P. Bebbington. **Cruiser**: *semi-finals:* D. Winrow (Manx) w pts P. Morris (Larches), C. Healey (Bredbury) w pts W. Pridding (Droylsden); *final*: C. Healey w pts D. Winrow. Heavy: no entries. S.Heavy: no entries.

North-West Counties Finals   Everton Park Sports Centre, Liverpool – 17 April
L. Fly: T. Stubbs (Northside) w pts P. Butler (Vauxhall Motors). **Fly**: P. Smith (Stockbridge) w rsc 3 Y. Arif (Elite). **Bantam**: K. Satchell (Everton Red Triangle) wo. **Feather**: B. Younis (Northside) w pts R. Farrag (Everton Red Triangle). **Light**: T. Stalker (St Aloysius) w pts D. Boswell (Withins School Police). **L.Welter**: R. Heffron (Boarshaw) w rsc 3 S. Jennings (Tower Hill). **Welter**: S. Cardle (Kirkham) w rtd 3 G. Ormrod (Lowe House). **Middle**: H. Burton (Jimmy Egan's) w pts A. Farrell (Salisbury). **L.Heavy**: M. Fielding (Rotunda) w pts K. Borucki (Manx). **Cruiser**: W. Adenyi (Vauxhall Motors) w pts C. Healey (Bredbury). **Heavy**: R. Stainton (North Mersey) wo. **S.Heavy**: J. Winters (Kirkby) wo.

Southern Counties v Combined Services

Southern Counties   Esso Waterside Sports Club, Fawley – 29 March & 5 April
L.Fly: *final*: B. Brazil (Aldershot) wo. **Fly**: no entries. **Bantam**: *final*: A. Cutler (Golden Ring) wo. **Feather**: *final*: I. Weaver (Golden Ring) wo. **Light**: *final*: J. Fernandes (Golden Ring) w pts S. Attrell (West Hill). **L.Welter**: *quarter-finals*: F. Moore (Titchfield) wo, R. Payne (Crawley) w pts R. Goodfellow (Whitstable), S. Ellis (Foley) w pts S. Ayres (Guildford), A. Dingsdale (Brompton) w pts R. Matthews (Stacey); *semi-finals*: R. Payne w pts S. Ellis, A. Dingsdale w pts F. Moore; *final*: A. Dingsdale w pts R. Payne. **Welter**: *semi-finals*: L. Ellet (Hove) w pts A. Swan (Faversham), A. Grigg (Golden Ring) w pts S. Sadler (Guildford); *final*: A. Grigg w pts L. Ellet. **Middle**: *semi-finals*: M. Coombes (Portsmouth University) w pts M. O'Sullivan (Portsmouth University), T. Hill (Golden Ring) w pts J. Lawrence (Isle of Thanet); *final*: T. Hill w pts M. Coombes. **L.Heavy**: *semi-finals*: A. Gibbens (Bognor) w rsc 2 R. Moore (Waterlooville), M. Atkins (Golden Ring) w rsc 2 D. Hendy (Potsmouth University); *final*: M. Atkins w rsc 2 A. Gibbens. **Cruiser**: *final*: D. Woodgate (Isle of Thanet) w pts S. Hopkins (Horsham). **Heavy**: *final*: M. Matthewsian (Golden Ring) wo. **S.Heavy**: *final*: D. Taylor (Golden Ring) w pts N. Baker (Hove).

Combined Services   HMS Nelson, Portsmouth – 18 March
L.Fly: *final*: K. Subhan (Army) wo. **Fly**: *final*: A. Whitfield (Army) wo. **Bantam**: *final*: J. Allen (Army) w rtd 3 R. Murray (RN). **Feather**: *final*: A. Downes (Army) wo. **Light**: *final*: M. Stead (Army) wo. **L.Welter**: *final*: S. Turner (Army) w pts M. Flowers (RN). **Welter**: *semi-finals*: M. Todd (RAF) wo, P. Ferguson (RN) w pts G. McGee; *final*: P. Ferguson w pts M. Todd. **Middle**: *final*:

N. Gittus (Army) wo. **L.Heavy**: *final*: P. Ormston (RN) w pts G. Jones (Army). **Cruiser**: *final*: N. McGarry (RN) w disq 3 L. John (Army). **Heavy**: *final*: E. Izonritei (Army) wo. **S.Heavy**: *final*: J. Harvey (RN) w rtd 2 W. Robanakadavu (Army).

Southern Counties v Combined Services   Esso Waterside Sports Club, Fawley 17 April
L.Fly: B. Brazil (Aldershot) w pts K. Subhan (Army). **Fly**: A. Whitfield (Army) wo. **Bantam**: J. Allen (Army) w pts A. Cutler (Golden Ring). **Feather**: I. Weaver (Golden Ring) w rtd 3 A. Downes (Army). **Light**: M. Stead (Army) w pts J. Fernandes (Golden Ring). **L.Welter**: A. Dingsdale (Brompton) w pts S. Sweeney (Army) – replaced S. Turner (Army). **Welter**: A. Grigg (Golden Ring) w pts G. McGee (Army) - replaced P. Ferguson (RN). **Middle**: T. Hill (Golden Ring) w pts N. Gittus (Army). **L.Heavy**: M. Atkins (Golden Ring) w pts G. Jones (Army) – replaced P. Ormston (RN). **Cruiser**: D. Woodgate (Isle of Thanet) w co 1 N. McGarry (RN). **Heavy**: E. Izonritei (Army) w pts M. Matthewsian (Golden Ring). **S.Heavy**: J. Harvey (RN) w co 2 D. Taylor (Golden Ring).

Tyne, Tees & Wear

Seaham Leisure Centre – 29 March, Hartlepool Borough Hall – 2 April & Peterlee Leisure Centre – 5 April
L.Fly: *final*: A. Dillon (North Benwell) wo. **Fly**: *final*: J. Spragg (Spennymoor) w pts D. Candish (Empire SoB). **Bantam**: *final*: P. Gidney (Boldon) wo. **Feather**: *semi-finals*: M. Hadfield (Headland) wo, A. Nelson (Horsley Hill) w pts R. Jameson (South Bank); *final*: M. Hadfield w rsc 3 A. Nelson. **Light**: *semi-finals*: D. Phillips (South Bank) wo, G. Reay (East Durham College) w pts K. Goodings (Sunderland); *final*: D. Phillips w pts G. Reay. **L.Welter**: *semi-finals*: S. Buckley (Hartlepool Catholic) w pts P. Robinson (Hartlepool Catholic), D. Ferguson (Newcastle East End) w pts M. Robinson (Sunderland); *final*: S. Buckley w pts D. Ferguson. **Welter**: *quarter-finals*: B. Falaja (Phil Thomas SoB) wo, G. Dodds (Spennymoor) wo, C. Dixon (Birtley) wo, G. Foot (Sunderland) w rsc 2 C. Wallace (East Durham); *semi-finals*: B. Falaja w pts G. Dodds, G. Foot w pts C. Dixon; *final*: G. Foot w pts B. Falaja. **Middle**: *semi-finals*: R. Ismay (Birtley) wo, M. Watson (Sunderland) w pts I. Turnbull (Romany Way); *final*: R. Ismay w pts M. Watson. **L.Heavy**: *semi-finals*: L. Osueke (Northumbria BA) wo, S. McCrone (Spennymoor) w pts K. Thompson (South Durham); *final*: S. McCrone w pts L. Osueke. **Cruiser**: *final*: D. Cullerton (Sunderland) w pts N. Wiley (Redcar). **Heavy**: S. Denham (Aycliffe) wo. **S.Heavy**: *semi-finals*: B. Ellsworthy (Bishop Auckland) wo, S. Vallily (South Bank) w pts M. Smith; *final*: S. Vallily w pts B. Ellsworthy.

Western Counties

Lister Social Club, Dursley – 21 March, The Leisure Centre, Newquay – 28 March & Hutton Moor Leisure Centre, Weston super Mare – 4 April

L.Fly: no entries. **Fly**: *final*: B. Watson (Amalgamated) wo. **Bantam**: no entries. **Feather**: *final*: D. Webb (Empire) wo. **Light**: *semi-finals*: B. Murray (Leonis) w pts B. Zacharhin (Pilgrim), D. Bharj (Walcot) w pts W. Lily (Sydenham); *final*: D. Bharj w pts B. Murray. **L.Welter**: *semi-finals*: R. Powell (Pisces) w pts R. Grigg (Bideford), J. Hughes (Malmesbury) w pts J. Hicks (Yeovil); *final*: J. Hughes w pts R. Powell. **Welter**: *semi-finals*: J. Jameson (Yeovil) wo, D. Kennedy (Leonis) w pts A. Khan (Exeter); *final*: D. Kennedy w rsc 3 J. Jameson. **Middle**: *semi-finals*: K. Young (Penhill) wo, S. Smart (Camborne & Redruth) w pts L. Whane (Apollo); *final*: S. Smart w pts K. Young. **L.Heavy**: *semi-finals*: C. Pearson (Amalgamated) wo, D. Dungay (Devonport) w D. McNally (Newquay); *final*: C. Pearson w pts D. Dungay. **Cruiser**: *final*: M. Jennings (Amalgamated) wo. **Heavy**: *final*: M. Reynolds (Walcott) w pts R. Pow (Empire). **S.Heavy**: no entries.

Yorkshire

Havercroft Sports Centre, Wakefield – 18 & 25 April

L.Fly: *final*: R. Downie (Scarborough) wo. **Fly**: no entries. **Bantam**: *final*: J. Cunningham (Doncaster Plant) wo. **Feather**: *final*: S. Marcus (Sheffield Boxing Centre) wo. **Light**: *semi-finals*: J. Warrington (Locky's) wo, J. Rodgers (Parsons Cross) w pts S. Gladwin (Rawthorpe); *final*: J. Warrington w pts J. Rodgers. **L.Welter**: *semi-finals*: L. Powell (Sharkeys) w pts K. Headbah (Unity), A. Townend (Hard & Fast) w pts S. Newlove (St Paul's); *final*: A. Townend w co 3 L. Powell (Sharkeys). **Welter**: *final*: L. Cameron (Steel City) w pts L. Walsh (Cleckheaton). **Middle**: *semi-finals*: J. Scotter (Scarborough) wo, L. Taylor (Hillsborough) w pts D. Slaney (Conisbrough); *final*: J. Scotter w pts L. Taylor. **L.Heavy**: *semi-finals*: L. Atkin (York) wo, J. McCalman (Rawthorpe) w rsc 3 V. Collingwood (St Paul's); *final*: J. McCalman w pts L. Atkin. **Cruiser**: *final*: S. Askham (Hard & Fast) wo. **Heavy**: *final*: K. Bell (Unity) wo. **S.Heavy**: *final*: R. Hayles (Unity) w rtd 2 J. Radford (Hard & Fast).

English ABA Quarter-Finals, Semi-Finals & Finals

English Institute of Sport's Badminton Hall, Sheffield – 1, 2 & 8 May

L. Fly: *quarter-finals*: D. Langley (Hollington) wo, S. Smith (Kings Heath) w pts R. Downie (Scarborough), T. Stubbs (Northside) w pts A. Dillon (North Benwell), B. Fowl (Hoddesdon) w pts B. Brazil (Aldershot); *semi-finals*: T. Stubbs w pts S. Smith, D. Langley w rsc 2 B. Fowl; *final*: T. Stubbs w pts D. Langley. **Fly**: *quarter-finals*: G. Yafai (Birmingham) wo, B. Watson (Amalgamated) wo, P. Smith (Stockbridge) w pts J. Spragg (Spennymoor), A. Whitfield (Army) w pts D. Culling (Stevenage); *semi-finals*: A. Whitfield w pts B. Watson, G. Yafai w pts P. Smith; *final*: G. Yafai w pts A. Whitfield. **Bantam**: *quarter-finals*: M. Ward (Repton) wo, J. Allen (Army) w pts D. Perry (Norwich Lads), J. Cunningham (Doncaster Plant) w pts Y. Nasseer (Donnington), P. Gidney (Boldon) w pts K.

Satchell (Everton Red Triangle); *semi-finals*: J. Cunningham w pts P. Gidney, J. Allen w disq 3 M. Ward; *final*: J. Allen w pts J. Cunningham. **Feather**: *quarter-finals*: L. Glover (William Perry) w rsc 2 S. Marcus (Sheffield Boxing Centre), B. Younis (Northside) w pts M. Hadfield (Headland), L. Pettitt (Nemesis) w pts D. Webb (Empire), I. Weaver (Golden Ring) w rsc 2 J. Mason (Welwyn Garden City) – replaced J. Taylor (Brentwood); *semi-finals*: B. Younis w disq 3 L. Glover, I. Weaver w pts L. Pettitt; *final*: I. Weaver w pts B. Younis. **Light**: *quarter-finals*: J. Warrington (Locky's) w pts J. Mason (Kings Heath), T. Stalker (St Aloysius) w pts D. Phillips (South Bank), D. Bharj (Walcot) w pts M. McCarthy (Repton), M. Stead (Army) w pts J. Homer (Rayleigh); *semi-finals*: T. Stalker w pts J. Warrington, M. Stead w pts D. Bharj; *final*: M. Stead w pts T. Stalker. **L.Welter**: *quarter-finals*: A. Townend (Hard & Fast) w co 3 D. Baptiste (Bracebridge), R. Heffron (Boarshaw) w pts S. Buckley (Hartlepool Catholic), B. Skeete (Earlsfield) w pts J. Hughes (Malmesbury), D. Docherty (Bushey) w pts A. Dingsdale (Brompton); *semi-finals*: R. Heffron w pts A. Townend, B. Skeete w pts D. Docherty; *final*: R. Heffron w rsc 2 B. Skeete. **Welter**: *quarter-finals*: L. Cameron (Steel City) w rsc 3 T. Langford (Hall Green), S. Cardle (Kirkham) w pts G. Foot (Sunderland), D. O'Shaughnessy (West Ham) w pts D. Kennedy (Leonis), J. Perry (Stevenage) w pts A. Grigg (Golden Ring); *semi-finals*: L. Cameron w pts S. Cardle, D. O'Shaughnessy w rsc 2 J. Perry; *final*: L. Cameron w pts D. O'Shaughnessy. **Middle**: *quarter-finals*: J. Scotter (Scarborough) w pts C. Valentine (Benny's), H. Burton (Jimmy Egan's) w pts R. Ismay (Birtley), K. Garvey (Earlsfield) w pts S. Smart (Camborne & Redruth), A. Ogogo (Triple A) w pts T. Hill (Golden Ring); *semi-finals*: H. Burton w pts J. Scotter, K. Garvey w pts A. Ogogo; *final*: H. Burton w pts K. Garvey. **L.Heavy**: *quarter-finals*: A. Johnson (St George's) w pts J. McCalman (Rawthorpe), L. Osueke (Northumbria BA) - replaced S. McCrone (Spennymoor) - w pts M. Fielding (Rotunda), O. Mbwakongo (Lynn) w rsc 2 C. Pearson (Amalgamated), M. Shinkwin (Bushey) w pts M. Atkins (Golden Ring); *semi-finals*: O. Mbwakongo w pts M. Shinkwin, L. Osueke w pts A. Johnson; *final*: O. Mbwakongo w pts L. Osueke. **Cruiser**: *quarter-finals*: S. Barclay (Corby) w pts S. Askham (Hard & Fast), W. Adenyi (Vauxhall Motors) w pts D. Cullerton (Sunderland), T. Conquest (Dagenham) w rsc 3 M. Jennings (Amalgamated), R. Evans (Banbury) w pts D. Woodgate (Isle of Thanet); *semi-finals:* W. Adenyi w pts S. Barclay, R. Evans w pts T. Conquest; *final*: R. Evans w pts W. Adenyi. **Heavy**: *quarter-finals*: D. Gardener (Hoddesdon) w pts M. Matthewsian (Golden Ring) – replaced E. Izonritei (Army), C. Keane (Pleck) w pts K. Bell (Unity), R. Stainton (North Mersey) w rtd 2 S. Denham (Aycliffe), M. Reynolds (Walcot) w rsc 3 M. Khamula (All Stars) – replaced R. Newland (Peacock); *semi-finals*: C. Keane w rsc 2 R. Stainton, D. Gardener wo M. Reynolds; *final*: C. Keane w co 2 D. Gardener. **S.Heavy**: *quarter-finals*: A. Isa (Miguels) wo, R. Hayles (Unity) wo P. Mytych (Birmingham), S. Vallily (South Bank) w pts J. Winters (Kirkby), J. Harvey (RN) w rsc 3 S. Parsons (Milton Keynes); *semi-finals*: S. Vallily w rsc 3 R. Hayles, A. Isa w rsc 3 J. Harvey; *final*: S. Vallily w pts A. Isa.

ABA Champions, 1881-2009

L. Flyweight
1971 M. Abrams
1972 M. Abrams
1973 M. Abrams
1974 C. Magri
1975 M. Lawless
1976 P. Fletcher
1977 P. Fletcher
1978 J. Dawson
1979 J. Dawson
1980 T. Barker
1981 J. Lyon
1982 J. Lyon
1983 J. Lyon
1984 J. Lyon
1985 M. Epton
1986 M. Epton
1987 M. Epton
1988 M. Cantwell
1989 M. Cantwell
1990 N. Tooley
1991 P. Culshaw
1992 D. Fifield
1993 M. Hughes
1994 G. Jones
1995 D. Fox
1996 R. Mercer
1997 I. Napa
1998 J. Evans
1999 G. Jones
2000 J. Mulherne
2001 C. Lyon
2002 D. Langley
2003 C. Lyon
2004 S. McDonald
2005 D. Langley
2006 J. Fowl
2007 K. Saeed
2008 T. Stubbs
2009 T. Stubbs

Flyweight
1920 H. Groves
1921 W. Cuthbertson
1922 E. Warwick
1923 L. Tarrant
1924 E. Warwick
1925 E. Warwick
1926 J. Hill
1927 J. Roland
1928 C. Taylor
1929 T. Pardoe
1930 T. Pardoe
1931 T. Pardoe
1932 T. Pardoe
1933 T. Pardoe
1934 P. Palmer
1935 G. Fayaud
1936 G. Fayaud
1937 P. O'Donaghue
1938 A. Russell
1939 D. McKay
1944 J. Clinton
1945 J. Bryce
1946 R. Gallacher
1947 J. Clinton
1948 H. Carpenter
1949 H. Riley
1950 A. Jones
1951 G. John
1952 D. Dower
1953 R. Currie
1954 R. Currie
1955 D. Lloyd
1956 T. Spinks
1957 R. Davies
1958 J. Brown
1959 M. Gushlow
1960 D. Lee
1961 W. McGowan
1962 M. Pye
1963 M. Laud
1964 J. McCluskey
1965 J. McCluskey
1966 P. Maguire
1967 S. Curtis
1968 J. McGonigle
1969 D. Needham
1970 D. Needham
1971 P. Wakefield
1972 M. O'Sullivan
1973 R. Hilton
1974 M. O'Sullivan
1975 C. Magri
1976 C. Magri
1977 C. Magri
1978 G. Nickels
1979 R. Gilbody
1980 K. Wallace
1981 K. Wallace
1982 J. Kelly
1983 S. Nolan
1984 P. Clinton
1985 P. Clinton
1986 J. Lyon
1987 J. Lyon
1988 J. Lyon
1989 J. Lyon
1990 J. Armour
1991 P. Ingle
1992 K. Knox
1993 P. Ingle
1994 D. Costello
1995 D. Costello
1996 D. Costello
1997 M. Hunter
1998 J. Hegney
1999 D. Robinson
2000 D. Robinson
2001 M. Marsh
2002 D. Barriball
2003 D. Broadhurst
2004 S. Langley
2005 S. Langley
2006 P. Edwards
2007 M. Walsh
2008 A. Whitfield
2009 G. Yafai

Bantamweight
1884 A. Woodward
1885 A. Woodward
1886 T. Isley
1887 T. Isley
1888 H. Oakman
1889 H. Brown
1890 J. Rowe
1891 E. Moore
1892 F. Godbold
1893 E. Watson
1894 P. Jones
1895 P. Jones
1896 P. Jones
1897 C. Lamb
1898 F. Herring
1899 A. Avent
1900 J. Freeman
1901 W. Morgan
1902 A. Miner
1903 H. Perry
1904 H. Perry
1905 W. Webb
1906 T. Ringer
1907 E. Adams
1908 H. Thomas
1909 J. Condon
1910 W. Webb
1911 W. Allen
1912 W. Allen
1913 A. Wye
1914 W. Allen
1919 W. Allen
1920 G. McKenzie
1921 L. Tarrant
1922 W. Boulding
1923 A. Smith
1924 L. Tarrant
1925 A. Goom
1926 F. Webster
1927 E. Warwick
1928 J. Garland
1929 F. Bennett
1930 H. Mizler
1931 F. Bennett
1932 J. Treadaway
1933 G. Johnston
1934 J. Barnes
1935 L. Case
1936 A. Barnes
1937 A. Barnes
1938 J. Pottinger
1939 R. Watson
1944 R. Bissell
1945 P. Brander
1946 C. Squire
1947 D. O'Sullivan
1948 T. Profitt
1949 T. Miller
1950 K. Lawrence
1951 T. Nicholls
1952 T. Nicholls
1953 J. Smillie
1954 J. Smillie
1955 G. Dormer
1956 O. Reilly
1957 J. Morrissey
1958 H. Winstone
1959 D. Weller
1960 F. Taylor
1961 P. Benneyworth
1962 P. Benneyworth
1963 B. Packer
1964 B. Packer
1965 R. Mallon
1966 J. Clark
1967 M. Carter
1968 M. Carter
1969 M. Piner
1970 A. Oxley
1971 G. Turpin
1972 G. Turpin
1973 P. Cowdell
1974 S. Ogilvie
1975 S. Ogilvie
1976 J. Bambrick
1977 J. Turner
1978 J. Turner
1979 R. Ashton
1980 R. Gilboy
1981 P. Jones
1982 R. Gilbody
1983 J. Hyland
1984 J. Hyland
1985 S. Murphy
1986 S. Murphy
1987 J. Sillitoe
1988 K. Howlett
1989 K. Howlett
1990 P. Lloyd
1991 D. Hardie
1992 P. Mullings
1993 R. Evatt
1994 S. Oliver
1995 N. Wilders
1996 L. Eedle
1997 S. Oates
1998 L. Pattison
1999 M. Hunter
2000 S. Foster
2001 S. Foster
2002 D. Matthews
2003 N. McDonald
2004 M. Marsh
2005 N. McDonald
2006 N. McDonald
2007 L. Campbell
2008 L. Campbell
2009 J. Allen

Featherweight
1881 T. Hill
1882 T. Hill
1883 T. Hill
1884 E. Hutchings
1885 J. Pennell
1886 T. McNeil
1887 J. Pennell
1888 J. Taylor
1889 G. Belsey
1890 G. Belsey
1891 F. Curtis
1892 F. Curtis
1893 T. Davidson
1894 R. Gunn
1895 R. Gunn
1896 R. Gunn
1897 N. Smith
1898 P. Lunn
1899 J. Scholes
1900 R. Lee
1901 C. Clarke
1902 C. Clarke
1903 J. Godfrey
1904 C. Morris
1905 H. Holmes
1906 A. Miner
1907 C. Morris
1908 T. Ringer
1909 A. Lambert
1910 C. Houghton
1911 H. Bowers
1912 G. Baker
1913 G. Baker
1914 G. Baker
1919 G. Baker
1920 J. Fleming
1921 G. Baker
1922 E. Swash
1923 E. Swash
1924 A. Beavis
1925 A. Beavis
1926 R. Minshull
1927 F. Webster
1928 F. Meachem
1929 F. Meachem
1930 J. Duffield
1931 B. Caplan
1932 H. Mizler
1933 J. Walters
1934 J. Treadaway
1935 E. Ryan
1936 J. Treadaway
1937 A. Harper
1938 C. Gallie
1939 C. Gallie
1944 D. Sullivan
1945 J. Carter
1946 P. Brander
1947 S. Evans
1948 P. Brander
1949 H. Gilliland
1950 P. Brander
1951 J. Travers
1952 P. Lewis
1953 P. Lewis
1954 D. Charnley
1955 T. Nicholls
1956 T. Nicholls
1957 M. Collins
1958 M. Collins
1959 G. Judge
1960 P. Lundgren
1961 P. Cheevers
1962 B. Wilson
1963 A. Riley
1964 R. Smith
1965 K. Buchanan
1966 H. Baxter
1967 K. Cooper
1968 J. Cheshire
1969 A. Richardson
1970 D. Polak
1971 T. Wright
1972 K. Laing
1973 J. Lynch
1974 G. Gilbody
1975 R. Beaumont
1976 P. Cowdell
1977 P. Cowdell
1978 M. O'Brien

1979 P. Hanlon
1980 M. Hanif
1981 P. Hanlon
1982 H. Henry
1983 P. Bradley
1984 K. Taylor
1985 F. Havard
1986 P. Hodkinson
1987 P. English
1988 D. Anderson
1989 P. Richardson
1990 B. Carr
1991 J. Irwin
1992 A. Temple
1993 J. Cook
1994 D. Pithie
1995 D. Burrows
1996 T. Mulholland
1997 S. Bell
1998 D. Williams
1999 S. Miller
2000 H. Castle
2001 S. Bell
2002 D. Mulholland
2003 K. Mitchell
2004 D. Mulholland
2005 G. Sykes
2006 S. Smith
2007 S. Smith
2008 B. Evans
2009 I. Weaver

Lightweight
1881 F. Hobday
1882 A. Bettinson
1883 A. Diamond
1884 A. Diamond
1885 A. Diamond
1886 G. Roberts
1887 J. Hair
1888 A. Newton
1889 W. Neale
1890 A. Newton
1891 E. Dettmer
1892 E. Dettmer
1893 W. Campbell
1894 W. Campbell
1895 A. Randall
1896 A. Vanderhout
1897 A. Vanderhout
1898 H. Marks
1899 H. Brewer
1900 G. Humphries
1901 A. Warner
1902 A. Warner
1903 H. Fergus
1904 M. Wells
1905 M. Wells
1906 M. Wells
1907 M. Wells
1908 H. Holmes
1909 F. Grace
1910 T. Tees
1911 A. Spenceley
1912 R. Marriott
1913 R. Grace
1914 R. Marriott
1919 F. Grace
1920 F. Grace
1921 G. Shorter
1922 G. Renouf
1923 G. Shorter
1924 W. White

1925 E. Viney
1926 T. Slater
1927 W. Hunt
1928 F. Webster
1929 W. Hunt
1930 J. Waples
1931 D. McCleave
1932 F. Meachem
1933 H. Mizler
1934 J. Rolland
1935 F. Frost
1936 F. Simpson
1937 A. Danahar
1938 T. McGrath
1939 H. Groves
1944 W. Thompson
1945 J. Williamson
1946 E. Thomas
1947 C. Morrissey
1948 R. Cooper
1949 A. Smith
1950 R. Latham
1951 R. Hinson
1952 F. Reardon
1953 D. Hinson
1954 G. Whelan
1955 S. Coffey
1956 R. McTaggart
1957 J. Kidd
1958 R. McTaggart
1959 P. Warwick
1960 R. McTaggart
1961 P. Warwick
1962 B. Whelan
1963 B. O'Sullivan
1964 J. Dunne
1965 A. White
1966 J. Head
1967 T. Waller
1968 J. Watt
1969 H. Hayes
1970 N. Cole
1971 J. Singleton
1972 N. Cole
1973 T. Dunn
1974 J. Lynch
1975 P. Cowdell
1976 S. Mittee
1977 G. Gilbody
1978 T. Marsh
1979 G. Gilbody
1980 G. Gilbody
1981 G. Gilbody
1982 J. McDonnell
1983 K. Willis
1984 A. Dickson
1985 E. McAuley
1986 J. Jacobs
1987 M. Ayers
1988 C. Kane
1989 M. Ramsey
1990 P. Gallagher
1991 P. Ramsey
1992 D. Amory
1993 B. Welsh
1994 A. Green
1995 R. Rutherford
1996 K. Wing
1997 M. Hawthorne
1998 A. McLean
1999 S. Burke
2000 A. McLean
2001 S. Burke

2002 A. Morris
2003 S. Burke
2004 C. Pacy
2005 F. Gavin
2006 A. Crolla
2007 F. Gavin
2008 M. Stead
2009 M. Stead

L. Welterweight
1951 W. Connor
1952 P. Waterman
1953 D. Hughes
1954 G. Martin
1955 F. McQuillan
1956 D. Stone
1957 D. Stone
1958 R. Kane
1959 R. Kane
1960 R. Day
1961 B. Brazier
1962 B. Brazier
1963 R. McTaggart
1964 R. Taylor
1965 R. McTaggart
1966 W. Hiatt
1967 B. Hudspeth
1968 E. Cole
1969 J. Stracey
1970 D. Davies
1971 M. Kingwell
1972 T. Waller
1973 N. Cole
1974 P. Kelly
1975 J. Zeraschi
1976 C. McKenzie
1977 J. Douglas
1978 D. Williams
1979 E. Copeland
1980 A. Willis
1981 A. Willis
1982 A. Adams
1983 D. Dent
1984 D. Griffiths
1985 I. Mustafa
1986 J. Alsop
1987 A. Holligan
1988 A. Hall
1989 A. Hall
1990 J. Pender
1991 J. Matthews
1992 D. McCarrick
1993 P. Richardson
1994 A. Temple
1995 A. Vaughan
1996 C. Wall
1997 R. Hatton
1998 N. Wright
1999 D. Happe
2000 N. Wright
2001 G. Smith
2002 L. Daws
2003 L. Beavis
2004 J. Watson
2005 M. Grant
2006 J. Cox
2007 B. Saunders
2008 L. Smith
2009 R. Heffron

Welterweight
1920 F. Whitbread
1921 A. Ireland

1922 E. White
1923 P. Green
1924 P. O'Hanrahan
1925 P. O'Hanrahan
1926 B. Marshall
1927 H. Dunn
1928 H. Bone
1929 T. Wigmore
1930 F. Brooman
1931 J. Barry
1932 D. McCleave
1933 P. Peters
1934 D. McCleave
1935 D. Lynch
1936 W. Pack
1937 D. Lynch
1938 C. Webster
1939 R. Thomas
1944 H. Hall
1945 R. Turpin
1946 J. Ryan
1947 J. Ryan
1948 M. Shacklady
1949 A. Buxton
1950 T. Ratcliffe
1951 J. Maloney
1952 J. Maloney
1953 L. Morgan
1954 N. Gargano
1955 N. Gargano
1956 N. Gargano
1957 R. Warnes
1958 B. Nancurvis
1959 J. McGrail
1960 C. Humphries
1961 A. Lewis
1962 J. Pritchett
1963 J. Pritchett
1964 M. Varley
1965 P. Henderson
1966 P. Cragg
1967 D. Cranswick
1968 A. Tottoh
1969 T. Henderson
1970 T. Waller
1971 D. Davies
1972 T. Francis
1973 T. Waller
1974 T. Waller
1975 W. Bennett
1976 C. Jones
1977 C. Jones
1978 E. Byrne
1979 J. Frost
1980 T. Marsh
1981 T. Marsh
1982 C. Pyatt
1983 R. McKenley
1984 M. Hughes
1985 E. McDonald
1986 D. Dyer
1987 M. Elliot
1988 M. McCreath
1989 M. Elliot
1990 A. Carew
1991 J. Calzaghe
1992 M. Santini
1993 C. Bessey
1994 K. Short
1995 M. Hall
1996 J. Khaliq
1997 F. Barrett
1998 D. Walker

1999 A. Cesay
2000 F. Doherty
2001 M. Macklin
2002 M. Lomax
2003 D. Happe
2004 M. Murray
2005 B. Flournoy
2006 D. Vassell
2007 J. Selkirk
2008 A. Ogogo
2009 L. Cameron

L. Middleweight
1951 A. Lay
1952 B. Foster
1953 B. Wells
1954 B. Wells
1955 B. Foster
1956 J. McCormack
1957 J. Cunningham
1958 S. Pearson
1959 S. Pearson
1960 W. Fisher
1961 J. Gamble
1962 J. Lloyd
1963 A. Wyper
1964 W. Robinson
1965 P. Dwyer
1966 T. Imrie
1967 A. Edwards
1968 E. Blake
1969 T. Imrie
1970 D. Simmonds
1971 A. Edwards
1972 L. Paul
1973 R. Maxwell
1974 R. Maxwell
1975 A. Harrison
1976 W. Lauder
1977 C. Malarkey
1978 E. Henderson
1979 D. Brewster
1980 J. Price
1981 E. Christie
1982 D. Milligan
1983 R. Douglas
1984 R. Douglas
1985 R. Douglas
1986 T. Velinor
1987 N. Brown
1988 W. Ellis
1989 N. Brown
1990 T. Taylor
1991 T. Taylor
1992 J. Calzaghe
1993 D. Starie
1994 W. Alexander
1995 C. Bessey
1996 S. Dann
1997 C. Bessey
1998 C. Bessey
1999 C. Bessey
2000 C. Bessey
2001 M. Thirwall
2002 P. Smith

Middleweight
1881 T. Bellhouse
1882 A. H. Curnick
1883 A. J. Curnick
1884 W. Brown
1885 M. Salmon
1886 W. King

1887 R. Hair
1888 R. Hair
1889 G. Sykes
1890 J. Hoare
1891 J. Steers
1892 J. Steers
1893 J. Steers
1894 W. Sykes
1895 G. Townsend
1896 W. Ross
1897 W. Dees
1898 G. Townsend
1899 R. Warnes
1900 E. Mann
1901 R. Warnes
1902 E. Mann
1903 R. Warnes
1904 E. Mann
1905 J. Douglas
1906 A. Murdock
1907 R. Warnes
1908 W. Child
1909 W. Child
1910 R. Warnes
1911 W. Child
1912 E. Chandler
1913 W. Bradley
1914 H. Brown
1919 H. Mallin
1920 H. Mallin
1921 H. Mallin
1922 H. Mallin
1923 H. Mallin
1924 J. Elliot
1925 J. Elliot
1926 F. P. Crawley
1927 F. P. Crawley
1928 F. Mallin
1929 F. Mallin
1930 F. Mallin
1931 F. Mallin
1932 F. Mallin
1933 A. Shawyer
1934 J. Magill
1935 J. Magill
1936 A. Harrington
1937 M. Dennis
1938 H. Tiller
1939 H. Davies
1944 J. Hockley
1945 R. Parker
1946 R. Turpin
1947 R. Agland
1948 J. Wright
1949 S. Lewis
1950 P. Longo
1951 E. Ludlam
1952 T. Gooding
1953 R. Barton
1954 K. Phillips
1955 F. Hope
1956 R. Redrup
1957 P. Burke
1958 P. Hill
1959 F. Elderfield
1960 R. Addison
1961 J. Caiger
1962 A. Matthews
1963 A. Matthews
1964 W. Stack
1965 W. Robinson
1966 C. Finnegan
1967 A. Ball

1968 P. McCann
1969 D. Wallington
1970 J. Conteh
1971 A. Minter
1972 F. Lucas
1973 F. Lucas
1974 D. Odwell
1975 D. Odwell
1976 E. Burke
1977 R. Davies
1978 H. Graham
1979 N. Wilshire
1980 M. Kaylor
1981 B. Schumacher
1982 J. Price
1983 T. Forbes
1984 B. Schumacher
1985 D. Cronin
1986 N. Benn
1987 R. Douglas
1988 M. Edwards
1989 S. Johnson
1990 S. Wilson
1991 M. Edwards
1992 L. Woolcock
1993 J. Calzaghe
1994 D. Starie
1995 J. Matthews
1996 J. Pearce
1997 I. Cooper
1998 J. Pearce
1999 C. Froch
2000 S. Swales
2001 C. Froch
2002 N. Perkins
2003 N. Perkins
2004 D. Guthrie
2005 J. Degale
2006 J. Degale
2007 G. Groves
2008 G. Groves
2009 H. Burton

L. Heavyweight
1920 H. Franks
1921 L. Collett
1922 H. Mitchell
1923 H. Mitchell
1924 H. Mitchell
1925 H. Mitchell
1926 D. McCorkindale
1927 A. Jackson
1928 A. Jackson
1929 J. Goyder
1930 J. Murphy
1931 J. Petersen
1932 J. Goyder
1933 G. Brennan
1934 G. Brennan
1935 R. Hearns
1936 J. Magill
1937 J. Wilby
1938 A. S. Brown
1939 B. Woodcock
1944 E. Shackleton
1945 A. Watson
1946 J. Taylor
1947 A. Watson
1948 D. Scott
1949 *Declared no contest*
1950 P. Messervy
1951 G. Walker
1952 H. Cooper

1953 H. Cooper
1954 A. Madigan
1955 D. Rent
1956 D. Mooney
1957 T. Green
1958 J. Leeming
1959 J. Ould
1960 J. Ould
1961 J. Bodell
1962 J. Hendrickson
1963 P. Murphy
1964 J. Fisher
1965 E. Whistler
1966 R. Tighe
1967 M. Smith
1968 R. Brittle
1969 J. Frankham
1970 J. Rafferty
1971 J. Conteh
1972 W. Knight
1973 W. Knight
1974 W. Knight
1975 M. Heath
1976 G. Evans
1977 C. Lawson
1978 V. Smith
1979 A. Straughn
1980 A. Straughn
1981 A. Straughn
1982 G. Crawford
1983 A. Wilson
1984 A. Wilson
1985 J. Beckles
1986 J. Moran
1987 J. Beckles
1988 H. Lawson
1989 N. Piper
1990 J. McCluskey
1991 A. Todd
1992 K. Oliver
1993 K. Oliver
1994 K. Oliver
1995 K. Oliver
1996 C. Fry
1997 P. Rogers
1998 C. Fry
1999 J. Ainscough
2000 P. Haymer
2001 C. Fry
2002 T. Marsden
2003 J. Boyd
2004 M. Abdusalem
2005 D. Pendleton
2006 T. Jeffries
2007 O. Mbwakongo
2008 I. Szucs
2009 O. Mbwakongo

Cruiserweight
1998 T. Oakey
1999 M. Krence
2000 J. Dolan
2001 J. Dolan
2002 J. Dolan
2007 J-L Dickinson
2008 M. Askin
2009 R. Evans

Heavyweight
1881 R. Frost-Smith
1882 H. Dearsley
1883 H. Dearsley
1884 H. Dearsley

1885 W. West
1886 A. Diamond
1887 E. White
1888 W. King
1889 A. Bowman
1890 J. Steers
1891 V. Barker
1892 J. Steers
1893 J. Steers
1894 H. King
1895 W. E. Johnstone
1896 W. E. Johnstone
1897 G. Townsend
1898 G. Townsend
1899 F. Parks
1900 W. Dees
1901 F. Parks
1902 F. Parks
1903 F. Dickson
1904 A. Horner
1905 F. Parks
1906 F. Parks
1907 H. Brewer
1908 S. Evans
1909 C. Brown
1910 F. Storbeck
1911 W. Hazell
1912 R. Smith
1913 R. Smith
1914 E. Chandler
1919 H. Brown
1920 R. Rawson
1921 R. Rawson
1922 T. Evans
1923 E. Eagan
1924 A. Clifton
1925 D. Lister
1926 T. Petersen
1927 C. Capper
1928 J. L. Driscoll
1929 P. Floyd
1930 V. Stuart
1931 M. Flanagan
1932 V. Stuart
1933 C. O'Grady
1934 P. Floyd
1935 P. Floyd
1936 V. Stuart
1937 V. Stuart
1938 G. Preston
1939 A. Porter
1944 M. Hart
1945 D. Scott
1946 P. Floyd
1947 G. Scriven
1948 J. Gardner
1949 A. Worrall
1950 P. Toch
1951 A. Halsey
1952 E. Hearn
1953 J. Erskine
1954 B. Harper
1955 D. Rowe
1956 D. Rent
1957 D. Thomas
1958 D. Thomas
1959 D. Thomas
1960 L. Hobbs
1961 W. Walker
1962 R. Dryden
1963 R. Sanders
1964 C. Woodhouse
1965 W. Wells
1966 A. Brogan

1967 P. Boddington
1968 W. Wells
1969 A. Burton
1970 J. Gilmour
1971 L. Stevens
1972 T. Wood
1973 G. McEwan
1974 N. Meade
1975 G. McEwan
1976 J. Rafferty
1977 G. Adair
1978 J. Awome
1979 A. Palmer
1980 F. Bruno
1981 A. Elliott
1982 H. Hylton
1983 H. Notice
1984 D. Young
1985 H. Hylton
1986 E. Cardouza
1987 J. Moran
1988 H. Akinwande
1989 H. Akinwande
1990 K. Inglis
1991 P. Lawson
1992 S. Welch
1993 P. Lawson
1994 S. Burford
1995 M. Ellis
1996 T. Oakey
1997 B. Stevens
1998 N. Hosking
1999 S. St John
2000 D. Dolan
2001 D. Dolan
2002 D. Dolan
2003 M. O'Connell
2004 T. Bellew
2005 T. Bellew
2006 T. Bellew
2007 Daniel Price
2008 W. Baister
2009 C. Keane

S. Heavyweight
1982 A. Elliott
1983 K. Ferdinand
1984 R. Wells
1985 G. Williamson
1986 J. Oyebola
1987 J. Oyebola
1988 K. McCormack
1989 P. Passley
1990 K. McCormack
1991 K. McCormack
1992 M. Hopper
1993 M. McKenzie
1994 D. Watts
1995 R. Allen
1996 D. Watts
1997 A. Harrison
1998 A. Harrison
1999 W. Bessey
2000 J. McDermott
2001 M. Grainger
2002 M. Grainger
2003 David Price
2004 J. Young
2005 David Price
2006 D. Chisora
2007 David Price
2008 T. Fury
2009 S. Valuly

Irish Championships, 2008-2009

Senior Tournament

The National Stadium, Dublin - 6, 7, 13, 14 & 20 February
L.Fly: *final*: P. Barnes (Holy Family GG, Belfast) wo. **Fly**: *quarter-finals*: C. Ahern (Baldoyle, Dublin) wo, N. Walker (Dockers, Belfast) wo, D. Geraghty (Dublin Docklands) wo, R. Dalton (St John's, Belfast) w pts J. Conlon (St John Bosco, Belfast); *semi-finals*: C. Ahern wo N. Walker, D. Geraghty w pts R. Dalton; *final*: D. Geraghty w pts C. Ahern. **Bantam**: *quarter-finals*: R. Lindberg (Immaculata, Belfast) wo, J.J. Nevin (Cavan) wo, T. McCullough (Illies Golden Gloves, Donegal) wo, D. Coughlan (St Anne's, Westport) w pts R. Sweetman (Blessington, Wicklow); *semi-finals*: J.J. Nevin w pts T. McCullough, R. Lindberg w pts D. Coughlan: *final*: J.J. Nevin w pts R. Lindberg. **Feather**: *quarter-finals*: D.O. Joyce (St Michael's, Athy) wo, D. Lawlor (Carlow), C. Frampton (Midland White City, Belfast) w pts. T. McKenna (Oliver Plunkett, Belfast), K. Fennessy (Clonmel) w pts S. Kilroy (Holy Family, Drogheda); *semi-finals*: D.O. Joyce w pts D Lawlor, C. Frampton w rtd 2 K. Fennessy; *final*: C. Frampton w pts D. O. Joyce. **Light**: *quarter-finals*: R. Hickey (Grangecon, Wicklow) wo, E. Donovan (St Michael's, Athy) wo, C. Bates (St Mary's, Dublin) w pts E. Touhy (Athlone), R. Moylett (St Anne's, Westport) w pts R. Gorman (Bracken, Dublin); *semi-finals*: R. Hickey w pts C. Bates, E Donovan w pts R. Moylett; *final*: E. Donovan w pts R. Hickey. **L.Welter**: *prelims*: J.J. Joyce (St Michael's. Athy) wo, M. McLoughlin (Camdonagh, Donegal) wo, J. McDonagh (Dockers, Belfast) wo, J. KAvanagh (Crumlin, Dublin) wo, S. Donnelly (All Saints, Ballymena) wo, P. Sutcliffe (Crumlin, Dublin) w0, P.J. Ward (Olympic, Galway) w ptd N. Murray (Gorey, Wexford), N. McGinley (Bishop Kelly, Omagh) w rsc 2 P. Barbour (Dromore, Tyrone); *quarter-finals*: J.J. Joyce w pts P.J. Ward, M. McLoughlin w pts J. McDonagh, J. Kavanagh w ptd S. Donnelly, P.Sutcliffe w rse 1 N. McGinley; *semi-finals*: J.J. Joyce w pts M. McLoughlin, P. Sutcliffe w rse 2 J. Kavanagh; *final*: P. Sutcliffe w rse 1 J.J. Joyce. **Welter**: *prelims*: W. McLoughlin (Illies Golden Gloves, Donegal) wo, T. Blaney (Westside, Dublin) wo, R. Sheahan (St Michael's, Athy) wo, J. Dowling (Paulstown, Kilkenny) w rse 3 R. Brennan (Dealgan, Dundalk), D. Walsh (St John's, Belfast) w rtd 3 N. Sommers (St Matthew's, Dublin). F. Redmond (Arklow, Wicklow) w pts S. Murtagh (Crumlin, Dublin), C. McAuley (Dealgan, Dundalk) w rsc 2 S. Hunt (St Matthew's, Dublin), M. McNamara (St Francis, Limerick) w pts Z. Buyaliskis (Arklow, Wicklow); *quarter-finals*: W. McLoughlin w pts T. Blaney, R. Sheahan w pts J. Dowling, F. Redmond w pts D. Walsh, C. McAuley w pts M. McNamara; *semi-finals*: W. McLoughlin w pts R. Sheahan, C. McAuley w pts F. Redmond; *final*: W. McLoughlin w rsc 2 C. McAuley. **Middle**: *prelims*: D. Joyce (St Michael's, Athy) wo, A. Soldra (Sacre Coeur, Wexford) wo, M. Collins (Darndale, Dublin) wo, E. O'Kane (Immaculata, Belfast) wo, S. O'Reilly (Twintowns, Donegal) w pts B. Brosnan (Olympic, Galway), D. O'Neill (Paulstown, Kilkenny) w pts E. Healy (Portlaoise, Laois), J. J. McDonagh (Brosna, Offaly) w pts M. Carlyle (Crumlin, Dublin), L. Keeler (St Matthew's, Dublin) w rsc 1 S. Shevlin (Dealgan, Dundalk); *quarter-finals*: D. Joyce w pts A. Soldra, S. O'Reilly w pts M. Collins, D. O'Neill w pts J. J. McDonagh, E. O'Kane w pts L. Keeler; *semi-finals*: S. O'Reilly w pts D. Joyce, D. O'Neill w pts E. O'Kane; *final*: D. O'Neill w pts S. O'Reilly. **L.Heavy**: *quarter-finals*: K. Egan (Neilstown, Dublin) wo, D. Hogan (Grangecon, Wicklow) wo, B. Fitzpatrick (West Finglas, Dublin) wo, T. McCarthy (Oliver Plunkett, Belfast) w pts T. Roohan (St Joseph's, Sligo); *semi-finals*: K. Egan w pts D. Hogan, T. McCarthy w pts B. Fitzpatrick; *final*: K. Egan T. McCarthy. **Heavy**: *prelims*: C. Sheehan (Clonmel, Tipperary) wo, D. Traynor (St Bronagh's, Newry) w rsc 3 M. Mullaney (Claremorris, Mayo), J. Sweeney (Drimnagh, Dublin) w rsc 2 S. Crudden (Enniskillen, Fermanagh), P. Corcoran (Galway) w rsc 1 P. Coyle (Geesala, Mayo), A. Reynolds (St Joseph's, Sligo) w pts W. Byrne (Knocknagoshel, Kerry), H. Joyce (St Michael's, Athy) w pts A. Griofa (Conamara, Galway), J. Sweeney (Dungloe, Donegal) w pts N. Kennedy (Gorey, Wexford), P. Kearns (Golden Cobra, Dublin) w pts M. McDonagh (Olympic, Galway); *quarter-finals*: C. Sheehan w pts D. Traynor, J.

Sweeney wo P. Corcoran, A. Reynolds w rtd 3 H. Joyce, J. Sweeney w pts P. Kearns; *semi-finals*: C. Sheehan w pts J. Sweeney, A. Reynolds w rsc 3 J. Sweeney; *final*: C. Sheehan w pts A. Reynolds. **S.Heavy**: *quarter-finals*: T. Crampton (St Bronagh's, Newry) wo, J. Joyce (Moate, Offaly/Wesmeath) wo, A. Crampton (St Bronagh's, Newry) wo, D. Joyce (Moate, Offaly/Westmeath) w rsc 2 G. Smith (Crumlin, Dublin); *semi-finals*: J. Joyce w pts A. Crampton, D. Joyce w pts T. Crampton; *final*: D. Joyce wo J. Joyce.

Intermediate Finals

The National Stadium, Dublin – 5 December
L.Fly: M. Lally (St Anne's, Westport) wo. **Fly:** D. Geraghty (Dublin Docklands) w pts G. Molloy (Moate, Westmeath). **Bantam:** G. Murray (St Saviour's, Dublin) w pts C. Fleming (Dromore, Tyrone). **Feather:** T. McKenna (Oliver Plunkett, Belfast) w rsc 1 G. Keating (St Saviour's, Dublin). **Light:** C. Haggarty (Golden Cobra, Dublin) w pts E. Finnegan (St Agnes, Belfast). **L.Welter:** R. Gorman (Bracken, Dublin) w pts N. McGinley (Bishop Kelly, Tyrone). **Welter:** J. Quigley (Finn Valley, Donegal) w pts P. J. Ward (Olympic, Galway). **Middle:** R. O'Donoghue (Riverstown, Cork) w pts J. J. Joyce (St Matthew's, Dublin). **L.Heavy:** J. Sweeney (St Joseph's, Sligo) w pts S. O'Reilly (Twintowns, Donegal). **Cruiser**: R. Barrett (Olympic, Galway) w pts D. Tourish (Twintowns, Donegal). **Heavy:** P. Coyle (Geesala, Mayo) w pts C. Barry (Dungarvin, Waterford). **S.Heavy:** J. Joyce (Moate, Westmeath) w rsc 4 P. Williams (Rathkeale, Limerick).

Under-21 Finals

National Stadium, Dublin – 7 November
L.Fly: M. Lally (St Anne's, Westport) wo. **Fly:** G. Molloy (Moate, Westmeath) w pts D. Geraghty (Dublin Docklands). **Bantam:** D. Coughlan (St Anne's, Westmeath) w rsc 2 J. Smith (Blessington, Wicklow). **Feather:** S. Kilroy (Holy Family, Drogheda) w pts Graham Keating (St Saviour's, Dublin). **Light:** Gavin Keating (St Saviour's, Dublin) w pts S. Upton (Holy Family GG, Belfast). **L.Welter:** J. Ferrin (Holy Family GG, Belfast) w pts L. Fryers (Clones). **Welter:** J. Quigley (Finn Valley, Donegal) w pts T. O'Donnell (Ballymun, Dublin). **L.Middle:** S. McGuigan (Clones) w pts J. J. Joyce (St Matthew's, Dublin). **Middle:** S. O'Reilly (Twintowns, Donegal) w pts B. Brosnan (Olympic, Galway). **L.Heavy:** S. Ward (Monkstown, Antrim) w pts M. Ward (Galway). **Cruiser:** C. McAuley (Holy Family GG, Belfast) w pts D. Trainor (St Bronagh's, Newry). **Heavy:** P. Corcoran (Galway) w pts M. Stokes (Letterkenny, Donegal). **S.Heavy:** J. Joyce (Moate, Westmeath) w pts A. O'Neill (Paulstown, Kilkenny).

Under-19 Finals

National Stadium, Dublin – 22 May
L.Fly: L. Lynch (Geesala, Mayo) w rsc 2 B. Dobbins (St Joseph's, Derry). **Fly:** G. Molloy (Moate, Offaly/Westmeath) w pts C. Phelan (Ryston, Kildare). **Bantam:** S. McComb (Holy Trinity, Belfast) w pts G. Holmes (Dublin Docklands). **Feather:** J. Fryers (Immaculata, Belfast) w pts J. O'Neill (St David's Naas, Kildare). **Light:** M. O'Hara (Holy Trinity, Belfast) w pts P. Kelly (Twintowns, Donegal). **L.Welter:** G. Moore (Oakleaf, Derry) w pts S. Duffy (Keady, Armagh). **Welter:** J. Quigley (Finn Valley, Donegal) w rsc 3 G. Murphy (Dublin Dockyards). **Middle:** C. Cummins (Clonoe, Tyrone) w pts B. Roe (Dublin Dockyards). **L.Heavy:** P. McDonagh (Brosna, Westmeath) w pts P. Ward (St Anthony's, Galway). **Heavy:** K. O'Griofa (Conamara, Galway) w pts P. Purcell Darndale, Dublin). **S.Heavy:** S. Turner (Drimnagh, Dublin) w pts J. Leahy (Bay City, Dublin).

Scottish and Welsh Senior Championships, 2008-2009

Scottish ABA

High School Gymnasium, Lasswade – 7 & 27 March, Auction Rooms, Lanark – 13 March & The Treetops Hilton Hotel, Aberdeen – 20 March

L.Fly: no entries. **Fly**: *final*: R. Wright (Clydeview) w pts J. Thomson (McNair/Dennistoun). **Bantam**: *quarter-finals*: G. Stemp (Holyrood) w pts B. Parker (Linwood), A. Bilan (Kingdom) w rsc 2 D. George (Aberdeen), D. Cowan (Craigmillar) w rsc 3 R. Warden (Kinross), A. Cuthbert (Granite City) w disq 3 D. Singh (Bellahouston); *semi-finals*: G. Stemp w pts A. Bilan, A. Cuthbert w pts D. Cowan; *final*: G. Stemp w pts A. Cuthbert. **Feather**: *quarter-finals*: S. Dick (Paisley) wo, J. Slowey (McNair/Dennistoun) wo, M. Roberts (Forgewood) w pts L. Moles (Denny), A. McKelvin (Glenrothes) w pts D. McInally (Doon Valley); *semi-finals*: A. McKelvie wo S. Dick, J. Slowey w pts M. Roberts; *final*: J. Slowey w pts A. McKelvie. **Light**: *prelims*: S. Watson (Fauldhouse) wo, D. Louden (Gilmerton) wo, T. James (Craigmillar) wo, R. Love (Holyrood) wo, R. Smith (Renfrewshire) wo, W. Marshall (Barn) wo, I. McDonald (Hillpark) wo, J. Downie (Newarthill) w pts A. Black (Kirkintilloch); *quarter-finals*: S. Watson w pts D. Louden, T. James w pts R. Love, R. Smith w pts W. Marshall, J. Downie w pts I. McDonald; *semi-finals*: R. Smith w pts J. Downie, S. Watson w pts T. James; *final*: R. Smith w pts S. Watson. **L.Welter**: *prelims*: E. Gear (Kingswells) wo, S. Sharoudi (Forgewood) wo, K. White (Alloa) wo, E. Finney (Kingdom) w rsc 3 I. Berganovic (Inverness), S. Hill (Bellahouston) w pts D. Foster (Arbroath), R. McMurdie (Newarthill) w rsc 1 R. Howie (Kinross), D. McGinn (Cleland) w pts J. Kerr (Irvine Vineborough), J. Thain (Lochend) w pts D. Brown (Port Glasgow); *quarter-finals*: S. Sharoudi w pts K. White, E. Finney w pts E. Gear, R. McMurdie w pts D. McGinn, S. Hill w rsc 3 J. Thain; *semi-finals*: R. McMurdie w pts S. Hill, S. Sharoudi w pts E. Finney; *final*: S. Sharoudi w pts R. McMurdie. **Welter**: *first series*: T. Philbin (Lochend) wo, J. McLaughlin (Hillpark) wo, C. McNeil (Blantyre Miners) wo, G. Thomson (Stirling) wo, J. Whyte (Alloa) wo, J. Slaven (Kilsyth) wo, A. Gonsalves (Kinross) wo, S. Freeman (Midlothian) wo, S. Finney (Kingdom) wo, A. Chisholm (Inverness) wo, L. Gallacher (Forgewood) w pts P. Allinson (Millenium), C. Steele (Cleland) w pts S. Ross (Inverness), A. Hardie (Leith Victoria) w pts D. Greig (Kincorth), M. McAllister (Granite City) w pts A. Smart (Arbroath), J. McCallum (Barn) w pts R. Singh (Bellahouston), S. Banks (Jervison) w pts K. Guthrie (Kingdom); *second series*: J. McLaughlin w pts T. Philbin, S. Banks w rsc 2 A. Hardie, G. Thomson w disq 2 J. Whyte, J. Slaven w rsc 3 C. McNeil, A. Gonsalves w pts S. Freeman, S. Finney w pts A. Chisholm, C. Gallacher w pts C. Steele, M. McAllister w pts J. McCallum; *quarter-finals*: G. Thomson w pts J. Slaven, J. McLaughlin w pts A. Gonsalves, S. Finney w pts L. Gallacher, M. McAllister w pts S. Banks; *semi-finals*: G. Thomson w pts J. McLaughlin, S. Finney w pts M. McAllister; *final*: S. Finney w pts G. Thomson. **Middle**: *prelims*: C. Cowan (Lochend) wo, D. Yorston (Leith Victoria) wo, D. Reid (Alloa) wo, R. Kaminski (Perth Railways) wo, P. Warner (Springhill) wo, K. McMurray (Larkhall) wo, S. Keane (Kingdom) w pts S. Morgan (Midlothian), P. Lee (Newarthill) w pts M. McGregor (Fauldhouse); *quarter-finals*: C. Cowan w rsc 3 D. Yorston, D. Reid w pts R. Kaminski, P. Warner w pts K. McMurray, P. Lee w pts S. Keane; *semi-finals*: C. Cowan w pts P. Warner, D. Reid w pts P. Lee; *final*: D. Reid w pts C. Cowan. **L.Heavy**: *quarter-finals*: J. Quigley (Port Glasgow) wo, E. Ahonso (Granite City) wo, M. Donald (Kincorth) w pts J. Thomson (Springhill), C. Johnson (Newarthill) w pts T. Carter (Leith Victoria); *semi-finals*: C. Johnson wo M. Donald, E. Ahonso

w pts J. Quigley; *final*: C. Johnson w rtd 2 E. Ahonso. **Heavy**: *semi-finals*: S. Allison (Hawick) wo, S. Simmons (Leith Victoria) w pts M. McDonough (Port Glasgow); *final*: S. Simmons w rsc 3 S. Allison. **S.Heavy**: *quarter-finals*: S. Finlay (Kincorth) wo, J. Perry (Larkhall) wo, R. Henderson (Springhill) wo, J. McAvoy (Stirling) w pts S. Palmer (Inverness); *semi-finals*: S. Finlay w pts J. Perry, R. Henderson w rsc 3 J. McAvoy; *final*: J. Perry w pts R. Henderson.

Wales ABA

Pill Millenium Centre, Newport – 14 February, Rhonda Fach Leisure Centre – 21 February & Welsh Institute of Sport, Cardiff – 6 March

L.Fly: *final*: J. Harris (Premier) wo. **Fly**: *final*: J. Gage (Penyrheol) w pts A. Perry (Colcot). **Bantam**: *semi-finals*: A. Selby (Splott Adventure) wo, J. Beasley (Aberystwyth) w pts N. Rees (Cwmcarn); *final*: A. Selby w pts J. Beasley. **Feather**: *quarter-finals*: L. Blaney (Newtown) wo, K. Jones (Ferndale) wo, S. Riva (Cardiff YMCA) wo, C. Evans (Pontypool) w co 1 G. Brewer (Trimsaran), *semi-finals*: C. Evans w rsc 1 L. Blaney, K. Jones w pts S. Riva; *final*: C. Evans w pts K. Jones. **Light**: *quarter-finals*: S. Brewer (Kyber Colts) wo, B. Gillen (Prince of Wales) wo, P. Davies (Diamond G) wo, L. Cooksey (Prince of Wales) w pts K. Wisniewski (Army); *semi-finals*: S. Brewer w pts L. Cooksey, B. Gillen w pts P. Davies; *final*: S. Brewer w pts B. Gillen. **L.Welter**: *quarter-finals*: L. Rees (Rhondda) wo, C. Jenkins (Cwmgors) wo, J. Davies (Newtown) w pts S. Punter (Dyffryn), L. Quinn (Dyffryn) w pts L. Harding (Newtown); *semi-finals*: L. Quinn w pts J. Davies, L. Rees w pts C. Jenkins; *final*: L. Rees w pts L. Quinn. **Welter**: *prelims*: A. Edwards (Pontypool) wo, S. Spooner (Ely Star) wo, Danny Jones (Kyber Colts) wo, Dave Jones (Fleur de Lys) wo, A. Farrell (Gwent) wo, J. Davies (Aberystwyth), A. Randall (Colcot) wo, R. Evans (Dowlais) w rsc 3 J. Palmer (Merlin's Bridge); *quarter-finals*: A. Edwards w pts S. Spooner, Danny Jones w pts Dave Jones, A. Farrell w pts J. Davies, R. Evans w rtd 1 A. Randall; *semi-finals*: Danny Jones w pts A. Edwards, R. Evans w pts A. Farrell; *final*: R. Evans w pts Danny Jones. **Middle**: *prelims*: S. Burnett (Tiger Bay) wo, G. Staddon (Trostre) wo, I. Jenkins (Bonymaen) wo, K. O'Sullivan (Merlin's Bridge) wo, M. Innes (Cwmbran) w pts E. Jodlowski (St Joseph's, Newport), T. Doran (Shotton) w rsc 1 J. Flower (Newtown), C. Harris (Dowlais) w pts J. Jones (Trimsaran), L. Bunce (Merthyr Ex-Servicemen) w pts M. Jones (AMA); *quarter-finals*: S. Burnett w pts G. Staddon, I. Jenkins w pts K. O'Sullivan, T. Doran w pts M. Innes, L. Bunce w rsc 3 C. Harris; *semi-finals*: T. Doran w pts L. Bunce, I. Jenkins w pts S. Burnett; *final*: T. Doran w pts I. Jenkins, **L.Heavy**: *prelims*: C. Ware (Bonymaen) wo, L. Davies (Merlin's Bridge) wo, F. Borg (Prince of Wales) wo, G. Butler (Crindau Harlequins) wo, L. Churcher (St Joseph's, Newport) wo, J. Evans (Pontypool) w co 1 M. Woodward (Tiger Bay), J. Asare (Merthyr Ex-Servicemen) w rsc 2 G. Millington (Shotton), J. M. Williams (ASC Llangefni) w pts K. Crowley (All Saints); *quarter-finals*: C. Ware w pts L. Davies, F. Borg w pts G. Butler, L. Churcher w pts J. Evans, J. M. Williams w pts J. Asare; *semi-finals*: L. Churcher w pts J. M. Williams, C. Ware w pts F. Borg; *final*: C. Ware w pts L. Churcher. **Heavy**: *quarter-finals*: J. O'Kelly (Barry East End) wo, R. Penn (Trostre) wo, L. Davies (Kyber Colts) wo, J. Bunce (Merthyr Ex-Servicemen) w pts G. Jones (Army); *semi-finals*: L. Davies w pts J. Bunce, J. O'Kelly wo R. Penn; *final*: J. O'Kelly w pts L. Davies. **S.Heavy**: *semi-finals*: A. W. Jones (Deva Police) wo, D. Darch (ANA) w pts C. Parfitt (Aberaman); *final*: A. W. Jones w pts D. Darch.

British Junior Championship Finals, 2008-2009

National Association of Clubs for Young People (NACYP)
The Festival Hall, Kirkby in Ashfield – 23 March
Class A: 46kg: C. Gibbs (Eastside) w pts C. Edwards (Newham). 48kg: C. Nixon (Wombwell & Dearne) w pts G. Ghani (Red Dragon). 50kg: A. Elder (Sefton) w pts L. Desmond (Newham). 52kg: A. Fleming (Bridgewater Salford) w pts L. Fleming (Red Dragon). 54kg: H. Thomas (Darlington) w pts M. Buckland (St Joseph's). 57kg: Z. Smith (Tower Hill) w pts J. Pigford (Golden Ring). 60kg: M. McDonnell (Northside) wo A. Doe (Repton). 63kg: D. Jones (West Leeds) w pts R. Rosser (Dale Youth). 63kg: F. Bennett (Eastside) w pts E. Matthews (Guildford). 70kg: Z. Burton (Jimmy Egan's) w pts M. Bull (Splott Adventure). 75kg: C. Gallant (Spennymoor) w pts N. Thorley (St Joseph's). 80kg: J. Massey (Buxton) w pts S. Smith (Pinewood Starr). 85kg: E. Frankham (Wisbech) w pts S. Rafferty (Stables).

Institute of Sport, Sheffield – 25 March
Class B: 48kg: R. Hamza (Aston) w pts M. Cleaver (Stables). 50kg: M. Smith (Bushey) w pts J. Dennard (Nemesis). 52kg: J. Beer (Five Star) w pts I. Lone (Burmantofts). 54kg: G. Veness (Newham) w pts D. Harker (Darlington). 57kg: A. Shafiq (South Bank) w rsc 3 L. Coppin (Brentwood). 60kg: L. Adolphe (Earlsfield) w pts A. Smith (All Comers). 63kg: S. McNess (Repton) w pts M. Cash (St Albans). 66kg: J. Saunders (St Mary's) w pts J. Turner (Wigan). 70kg: D. Dignum (Brentwood) w pts A. Carolan (Doncaster Plant). 75kg: N. Nichols (Cwmcarn) w pts M. Davis (Salisbury). 80kg: E. Duraku (Reading) w rsc 1 H. Amjad (Bury). 85kg: no entries. 91kg: W. Cassap (Lambton Street) wo.

The Troxy, Commercial Road, Limehouse, London – 26 March
Class C: 48kg: J. McCulley (Bexley) w pts A. Ghani (Red Dragon). 51kg: C. Hoy (West Ham) w pts B. Joyce (Kings Heath). 54kg: S. McGoldrick (St Joseph's) w rsc 1 P. Cope (Gus Robinson's). 57kg: B. Awad (Unity) w pts J. Smith (Hailsham). 60kg: S. Jenkins (St Michael's) w rsc P. Hyland (Immaculata). 64kg: M. Heffron (Boarshaw) w pts C. Brunning (Kingfisher). 69kg: T. Baker (Repton) w pts C. Smith (Rotunda). 75kg: C. Cotton (Parsons Cross) w rsc 1 M. Johnston (Abbey). 81kg: P. Bebbington (Macclesfield) w co 1 M. Toner (All Blacks). 86kg: M. Neilson (Tom Hill) w pts B. Manning (Clonard). 91kg: K. Skill (Woodseats) w pts G. Brided (Sweet Science Academy). 91+kg: J. Ducille (Aston) w pts S. Gunter (Stable).

Golden Gloves (Schools)
Goresbrook Leisure Centre, Dagenham – 7 & 8 March
Class 1: 30kg: S. Rankin (Knowsley Vale) w pts S. Edwards (Newham). 32kg: L. Milburn (South Durham) w pts E. Saunders (Farnham). 34kg: C. Jones (Lions) w pts L. Arnold (Bexley). 36kg: P. McGrail (Everton Red Triangle) w pts P. Ellis (West Ham). 38kg: M. Ali (Cleckheaton) w pts C. Crosby (March). 40kg: J. Smith (Eltham) w pts S. Iqbal (Bury). 42kg: J. Flynn (Berinsfield) w pts H. Rush (Retford). 44kg: E. Delaney (Finchley) w pts S. Smith (Droitwich). 46kg: J. Melvin (Hall Green) w pts B. Bendall (Woking). 48kg: R. Pettengell (Epsom & Ewell) w pts H. Mohammed (Donnington). 50kg: L. Dobson (St Aloysius) w pts D. Bell (Dagenham). 52kg: J. Stringer (Stacey) w pts K. Myers (Long Lane). 54kg: P. McCann (Kettering) w pts R. Connor (Gloucester). 60kg: W. Lee (Stevenage) w pts L. Claridge (Hull Saints).
Class 2: 34kg: R. Burrows (Pleck) w pts T. Kindon (Guildford). 36kg: A. Sharp (Eltham) w pts L. McCormack (Birtley). 38kg: J. Tokeley (West Ham) w pts A. Burnside (Darlington). 40kg: C. McKinnon (Woking) w pts J. Foster (Retford). 42kg: T. Aitchinson (Skelmersdale) w pts S. Robinson (Dale Youth). 44kg: T. Woledge (St Mary's) w disq 3 C. Parker (Royal Oak). 46kg: D. Johnson (Newham) w pts B. Jackson (Hard & Fast). 48kg: H. Mahmood (Bury) w pts C. Stevens (March). 50kg:

I. McLeod (Sunderland) w pts J. Weedon (Five Star). 52kg: D. Gardner (Birtley) w pts T. McDonagh (Walcot). 54kg: T. Matthews (Faversham) w pts I. Shah (Blackburn & Darwen). 57kg: S. Baker (Repton) w pts K. Mahmood (Capital). 60kg: G. Baker (Swanley) wo C. Hayes (Broughton). 63kg: A. Little (St Mary's) wo B. Ako (Salisbury). 66kg: D. Rooney (Furs) w pts G. Bacon (Hoddesdon).

Class 3: 38kg: J. Bateson (Burmantofts) w pts O. Acheampong (Peacock). 40kg: J. Smith (Bushey) w pts T. Wilson (Knowsley Vale). 42kg: M. Leech (Bridgewater Salford) wo P. Lovejoy (Repton). 44kg: K. Jones (Northside) w pts J. Pritchard (Portsmouth). 46kg: T. Beaney (West Ham) w pts T. Ward (Birtley). 48kg: S. Bezzina (Newham) w pts L. Etheridge (Pleck). 50kg: A. Price (West Ham) w pts R. Fillingham (Bracebridge). 52kg: R. Wallace (Repton) w pts J. Thompson (Kingston). 54kg: L. Saunders (West Ham) w pts S. Patterson (Sunderland). 57kg: C. Wells (Walcot) w pts J. Hughes (St Aloysius). 60kg: G. Crotty (Stevenage) w pts M. Johnson (Kirkby). 63kg: A. Smith (Dale Youth) w pts N. Pemberton (Bridgewater Salford). 66kg: R. Martin (Walcot) w rsc 2 P. Miller (Lancaster). 70kg: S. Woodall (Eastside) w pts T. Nejat (Waltham Forest). 75kg: T. Buckley (Repton) w pts O. Basara (Strood).

ABA Youth
Everton Park Sports Centre, Liverpool - 30 & 31 May
Class 4: 46kg: C. Gibbs (Eastside) w pts L. Patel (Repton). 48kg: C. Nixon (Wombwell & Dearne) w pts C. Ali (Repton). 50kg: J. Costello (Chelmsley Wood) w pts L. Desmond (Newham). 52kg: Q. Ashfaq (Burmantofts) w pts R. McNamara (Hoddesdon). 54kg: C. Smith (West Ham) w pts J. Roberts (Worcester). 57kg: Z. Smith (Tower Hill) w pts G. Moughton (Newham). 60kg: M. McDonnell (Northside) w pts F. Cash (Guildford). 63kg: D. Jones (West Leeds) w pts A. Hutchins (Basingstoke). 66kg: J. Coyle (Newham) w pts F. Bennett (Eastside). 70kg: W. Ingram (Gloucester) w pts J. Clayton (Chelmsley Wood). 75kg: C. Gallant (Spennymoor) w pts J. Peterson (Cheshunt). 80kg: J. Massey (Buxton) w pts S. Smith (Pinewood Starr). 85kg: E. Frankham (Wisbech) w pts K. Butler (William Perry).
Class 5: 48kg: R. Hamza (Aston) w pts H. Sweeney (New Addington). 50kg: P. Cawley (Chelmsley Wood) w pts G. Chapman (Crawley). 52kg: I. Lone (Burmantofts) w pts J. Cooper (Lawrence). 54kg: R. Walker (South Bank) w pts G. Veness (Newham). 57kg: S. Ali (South Bank) w pts B. Beadon (Repton). 60kg: S. Bowen (Earl Shilton) w pts A. Smith (Littleport). 63kg: S. Lewis (Long Lane) w pts S. McNess. 66kg: J. Kelly (Jimmy Egan's) w pts G. O'Mahoney (Repton). 70kg: D. Dignum (Brentwood) w pts A. Carolan (Doncaster Plant). 75kg: J. Steffe (Roche) w pts J. Ball (Sporting Ring). 80kg: M. Watson (South Durham) w pts E. Duraku (Reading). 85kg: W. Cassap (Lambton Street) w pts S. Delaney (Hornchurch & Elm Park). 91kg: A. Hussain (Northumbria) w pts L. Robinson (Haringey).
Class 6: 50kg: C. Blinkhorn (Withins Police School) w pts C. Hoy (West Ham). 52: H. Khan (Bury) w pts B. Truby (Bexley. 54: Peter Cope (Gus Robinson's) w pts A. Hussan (Walcott). 57: J. Kennedy (Folkestone) w pts Z. Khan (Karmand). 60kg: J. Saunders (South Durham) w pts J. Brayer (Earlsfield). 63kg: C. Brunning (Kingfisher) w pts M. Heffron (Boarshaw). 66kg: C. Gaynor (Millennium) w pts G. Carman (Guildford). 70kg: A. Fowler (Golden Ring) w co 2 T. Baker (Repton). 75kg: P. Macivilicuilius (Kingfisher) w pts C. Cotton (Parsons Cross). 80kg: R. Colquhoun (Lewsey) w pts D. Fusco (East Durham). 85kg: M. Joraat (Haringey) w pts M. Neilson. 91kg: D. Nelson (Tameside) w pts M. Raza (Repton). 91+kg: F. Clarke (Burton) wo S. Cleary (Finchley).

International Amateur Champions, 1904-2009

Shows all Olympic, World, European and Commonwealth Champions since 1904. All British and Irish silver and bronze medallists are shown throughout where applicable. It is worth noting that the 1924, 1928 and 1932 European Championship medals were given to those who went the furthest in the Olympic Games in those years. Recently, European and World Junior Championships have been renamed as Youth Championships and apply to lads under the age of 19 at a certain date. That said, the first three European Junior Championships were contested by under-21s.

Country Code ALG = Algeria; ARG = Argentina; ARM = Armenia; AUS = Australia; AUT = Austria; AZE = Azerbaijan; BE = Belarus; BEL= Belgium; BUL = Bulgaria; CAN = Canada; CEY = Ceylon (now Sri Lanka); CI = Channel Islands; CHI = China; CUB =Cuba; DEN = Denmark; DOM = Dominican Republic; ENG = England; ESP = Spain; EST = Estonia; FIJ = Fiji Islands; FIN= Finland; FRA = France; GBR = United Kingdom; GDR = German Democratic Republic; GEO = Georgia; GER = Germany(but West Germany only from 1968-1990); GHA = Ghana; GUY = Guyana; HOL = Netherlands; HUN = Hungary; IND =India; IRL = Ireland; ITA = Italy; JAM = Jamaica; JPN = Japan; KAZ = Kazakhstan; KEN = Kenya; LIT= Lithuania; MAS =Malaysia; MEX = Mexico; MON=Mongolia; MOR = Morocco; MRI = Mauritius; NAM = Nambia; NKO = North Korea; NIG= Nigeria; NIR = Northern Ireland; NOR = Norway; NZL = New Zealand; PAK = Pakistan; POL = Poland; PUR = Puerto Rico; ROM = Romania; RUS = Russia; SAF = South Africa; SCO = Scotland; SER = Serbia; SKO = South Korea; SR = SouthernRhodesia; STV = St Vincent; SWE = Sweden; TCH = Czechoslovakia; THA = Thailand; TUR = Turkey; UGA = Uganda; UKR = Ukraine; URS = USSR; USA = United States of America; UZB = Uzbekistan; VEN = Venezuela; WAL = Wales; YUG =Yugoslavia; ZAM = Zambia.

Olympic Champions, 1904-2008

St Louis, USA - 1904
Fly: G. Finnegan (USA). **Bantam:** O. Kirk (USA). **Feather:** O. Kirk (USA). **Light:** H. Spangler (USA). **Welter:** A. Young (USA). **Middle:** C. May (USA). **Heavy:** S. Berger (USA).

London, England - 1908
Bantam: H. Thomas (GBR). **Feather:** R. Gunn (GBR). **Light:** F. Grace (GBR). **Middle:** J.W.H.T. Douglas (GBR). **Heavy:** A. Oldman (GBR). **Silver medals:** J. Condon (GBR), C. Morris (GBR), F. Spiller (GBR), S. Evans (GBR). **Bronze medals:** W. Webb (GBR), H. Rodding (GBR), T. Ringer (GBR), H. Johnson (GBR), R. Warnes (GBR), W. Philo (GBR), F. Parks (GBR).

Antwerp, Belgium - 1920
Fly: F. Genaro (USA). **Bantam:** C. Walker (SAF). **Feather:** R. Fritsch (FRA). **Light:** S. Mossberg (USA). **Welter:** T. Schneider (CAN). **Middle:** H. Mallin (GBR). **L. Heavy:** E. Eagan (USA). **Heavy:** R. Rawson (GBR). **Silver medal:** A. Ireland (GBR). **Bronze medals:** W. Cuthbertson (GBR), G. McKenzie (GBR), H. Franks (GBR).

Paris, France - 1924
Fly: F. la Barba (USA). **Bantam:** W. Smith (SAF). **Feather:** J. Fields (USA). **Light:** H. Nielson (DEN). **Welter:** J. Delarge (BEL). **Middle:** H. Mallin (GBR). **L. Heavy:** H. Mitchell (GBR). **Heavy:** O. von Porat (NOR). **Silver medals:** J. McKenzie (GBR), J. Elliot (GBR).

Amsterdam, Holland - 1928
Fly: A. Kocsis (HUN). **Bantam:** V. Tamagnini (ITA). **Feather:** B. van Klaveren (HOL). **Light:** C. Orlando (ITA). **Welter:** E. Morgan (NZL). **Middle:** P. Toscani (ITA). **L. Heavy:** V. Avendano (ARG). **Heavy:** A. Rodriguez Jurado (ARG).

Los Angeles, USA - 1932
Fly: I. Enekes (HUN). **Bantam:** H. Gwynne (CAN). **Feather:** C. Robledo (ARG). **Light:** L. Stevens (SAF). **Welter:** E. Flynn (USA). **Middle:** C. Barth (USA). **L. Heavy:** D. Carstens (SAF). **Heavy:** A. Lovell (ARG).

Berlin, West Germany - 1936
Fly: W. Kaiser (GER). **Bantam:** U. Sergo (ITA). **Feather:** O. Casanova (ARG). **Light:** I. Harangi (HUN). **Welter:** S. Suvio (FIN). **Middle:** J. Despeaux (FRA). **L. Heavy:** R. Michelot (FRA). **Heavy:** H. Runge (GER).

London, England - 1948
Fly: P. Perez (ARG). **Bantam:** T. Csik (HUN). **Feather:** E. Formenti (ITA). **Light:** G. Dreyer (SAF). **Welter:** J. Torma (TCH). **Middle:** L. Papp (HUN). **L. Heavy:** G. Hunter (SAF). **Heavy:** R. Iglesas (ARG). **Silver medals:** J. Wright (GBR), D. Scott (GBR).

Helsinki, Finland - 1952
Fly: N. Brooks (USA). **Bantam:** P. Hamalainen (FIN). **Feather:** J. Zachara (TCH). **Light:** A. Bolognesi (ITA). **L. Welter:** C. Adkins (USA). **Welter:** Z. Chychla (POL). **L. Middle:** L. Papp (HUN). **Middle:** F. Patterson (USA). **L. Heavy:** N. Lee (USA). **Heavy:** E. Sanders (USA). **Silver medal:** J. McNally (IRL).

Melbourne, Australia - 1956
Fly: T. Spinks (GBR). **Bantam:** W. Behrendt (GER). **Feather:** V. Safronov (URS). **Light:** R. McTaggart (GBR). **L. Welter:** V. Jengibarian (URS). **Welter:** N. Linca (ROM). **L. Middle:** L. Papp (HUN). **Middle:** G. Schatkov (URS). **L. Heavy:** J. Boyd (USA). **Heavy:** P. Rademacher (USA). **Silver medals:** T. Nicholls (GBR), F. Tiedt (IRL). **Bronze medals:** J. Caldwell (IRL), F. Gilroy (IRL), A. Bryne (IRL), N. Gargano (GBR), J. McCormack (GBR).

Rome, Italy - 1960
Fly: G. Torok (HUN). **Bantam:** O. Grigoryev (URS). **Feather:** F. Musso (ITA). **Light:** K. Pazdzior (POL). **L. Welter:** B. Nemecek (TCH). **Welter:** N. Benvenuti (ITA). **L. Middle:** W. McClure (USA). **Middle:** E. Crook (USA). **L. Heavy:** C. Clay (USA). **Heavy:** F. de Piccoli (ITA). **Bronze medals:** R. McTaggart (GBR), J. Lloyd (GBR), W. Fisher (GBR).

Tokyo, Japan - 1964
Fly: F. Atzori (ITA). **Bantam:** T. Sakurai (JPN). **Feather:** S. Stepashkin (URS). **Light:** J. Grudzien (POL). **L. Welter:** J. Kulej (POL). **Welter:** M. Kasprzyk (POL). **L. Middle:** B. Lagutin (URS). **Middle:** V. Popenchenko (URS). **L. Heavy:** C. Pinto (ITA). **Heavy:** J. Frazier (USA). **Bronze medal:** J. McCourt (IRL).

Mexico City, Mexico - 1968
L. Fly: F. Rodriguez (VEN). **Fly:** R. Delgado (MEX). **Bantam:** V. Sokolov (URS). **Feather:** A. Roldan (MEX). **Light:** R. Harris (USA). **L. Welter:** J. Kulej (POL). **Welter:** M. Wolke (GDR). **L. Middle:** B. Lagutin (URS). **Middle:** C. Finnegan (GBR). **L. Heavy:** D. Poznyak (URS). **Heavy:** G. Foreman (USA).

Munich, West Germany - 1972
L. Fly: G. Gedo (HUN). **Fly:** G. Kostadinov (BUL). **Bantam:** O. Martinez (CUB). **Feather:** B. Kusnetsov (URS). **Light:** J. Szczepanski (POL). **L. Welter:** R. Seales (USA). **Welter:** E. Correa (CUB). **L. Middle:** D. Kottysch (GER). **Middle:** V. Lemeschev (URS). **L. Heavy:** M. Parlov (YUG). **Heavy:** T. Stevenson (CUB). **Bronze medals:** R. Evans (GBR), G. Turpin (GBR), A. Minter (GBR).

Montreal, Canada - 1976
L. Fly: J. Hernandez (CUB). **Fly:** L. Randolph (USA). **Bantam:** Y-J. Gu (NKO). **Feather:** A. Herrera (CUB). **Light:** H. Davis (USA). **L. Welter:** R. Leonard (USA). **Welter:** J. Bachfield (GDR). **L. Middle:** J. Rybicki (POL). **Middle:** M. Spinks (USA). **L. Heavy:** L. Spinks (USA). **Heavy:** T. Stevenson (CUB). **Bronze medal:** P. Cowdell (GBR).

Moscow, USSR - 1980
L. Fly: S. Sabirov (URS). **Fly:** P. Lessov (BUL). **Bantam:** J. Hernandez (CUB). **Feather:** R. Fink (GDR). **Light:** A. Herrera (CUB). **L. Welter:** P. Oliva (ITA). **Welter:** A. Aldama (CUB). **L. Middle:** A. Martinez (CUB). **Middle:** J. Gomez (CUB). **L. Heavy:** S. Kacar (YUG). **Heavy:** T. Stevenson (CUB). **Bronze medals:** H. Russell (IRL), A. Willis (GBR).

Los Angeles, USA - 1984
L. Fly: P. Gonzalez (USA). **Fly:** S. McCrory (USA). **Bantam:** M. Stecca (ITA). **Feather:** M. Taylor (USA). **Light:** P. Whitaker (USA). **L. Welter:** J. Page (USA). **Welter:** M. Breland (USA). **L. Middle:** F. Tate (USA). **Middle:** J-S. Shin (SKO). **L. Heavy:** A. Josipovic (YUG). **Heavy:** H. Tillman (USA). **S. Heavy:** T. Biggs (USA). **Bronze medal:** B. Wells (GBR).

Seoul, South Korea - 1988
L. Fly: I. Mustafov (BUL). **Fly:** H-S. Kim (SKO). **Bantam:** K. McKinney (USA). **Feather:** G. Parisi (ITA). **Light:** A. Zuelow (GDR). **L. Welter:** V. Yanovsky (URS). **Welter:** R. Wangila (KEN). **L. Middle:** S-H. Park (SKO). **Middle:** H. Maske (GDR). **L. Heavy:** A. Maynard (USA). **Heavy:** R. Mercer (USA). **S. Heavy:** L. Lewis (CAN). **Bronze medal:** R. Woodhall (GBR).

Barcelona, Spain - 1992
L. Fly: R. Marcelo (CUB). **Fly:** C-C. Su (NKO). **Bantam:** J. Casamayor (CUB). **Feather:** A. Tews (GER). **Light:** O. de la Hoya (USA). **L. Welter:** H. Vinent (CUB). **Welter:** M. Carruth (IRL). **L. Middle:** J. Lemus (CUB). **Middle:** A. Hernandez (CUB). **L. Heavy:** T. May (GER). **Heavy:** F. Savon (CUB). **S. Heavy:** R. Balado (CUB). **Silver medal:** W. McCullough (IRL). **Bronze medal:** R. Reid (GBR).

271

Atlanta, USA - 1996

L. Fly: D. Petrov (BUL). **Fly:** M. Romero (CUB). **Bantam:** I. Kovaks (HUN). **Feather:** S. Kamsing (THA). **Light:** H. Soltani (ALG). **L. Welter:** H. Vinent (CUB). **Welter:** O. Saitov (RUS). **L. Middle:** D. Reid (USA). **Middle:** A. Hernandez (CUB). **L. Heavy:** V. Jirov (KAZ). **Heavy:** F. Savon (CUB). **S. Heavy:** Vladimir Klitschko (UKR).

Sydney, Australia - 2000

L. Fly: B. Aslom (FRA). **Fly:** W. Ponlid (THA). **Bantam:** G. Rigondeaux (CUB). **Feather:** B. Sattarkhanov (KAZ). **Light:** M. Kindelan (CUB). **L. Welter:** M. Abdullaev (UZB). **Welter:** O. Saitov (RUS). **L. Middle:** Y. Ibraimov (KAZ). **Middle:** J. Gutierrez Espinosa (CUB). **L. Heavy:** A. Lebziak (RUS). **Heavy:** F. Savon (CUB). **S. Heavy:** A. Harrison (ENG).

Athens, Greece - 2004

L. Fly: Y. Bartelemi (CUB). **Fly:** Y. Gamboa (CUB). **Bantam:** G. Rigondeaux (CUB). **Feather:** A. Tischenko (RUS). **Light:** M. Kindelan (CUB). **L. Welter:** M. Boonjumnong (THA). **Welter:** B. Artayev (KAZ). **Middle:** G. Gaiderbekov (RUS). **L. Heavy:** A. Ward (USA). **Heavy:** O. Solis (CUB). **S. Heavy:** A. Povetkin (RUS). **Silver medal:** A. Khan (ENG).

Beijing, China - 2008

L. Fly: Zou Shiming (CHI). **Fly:** S. Jongjohor (THA). **Bantam:** B-U Enkhbat (MON). **Feather:** V.Lomachenko (UKR). **Light:** A.Tishchenko (RUS). **L. Welter:** F. Diaz (CUB). **Welter:** B. Sarsekbayev (KAZ). **Middle:** J. Degale (ENG). **L. Heavy:** Xiaoping Zhang (CHI). **Heavy:** R. Chakhiev (RUS). **S. Heavy:** R.Cammarelle (ITA). **Silver medal:** K.Egan (IRL). **Bronze medals:** P. Barnes (IRL), D. Sutherland (IRL), T. Jeffries (ENG), D. Price (ENG)

World Champions, 1974-2007

Havana, Cuba - 1974

L. Fly: J. Hernandez (CUB). **Fly:** D. Rodriguez (CUB). **Bantam:** W. Gomez (PUR). **Feather:** H. Davis (USA). **Light:** V. Solomin (URS). **L. Welter:** A. Kalule (UGA). **Welter:** E. Correa (CUB). **L. Middle:** R. Garbey (CUB). **Middle:** R. Riskiev (URS). **L. Heavy:** M. Parlov (YUG). **Heavy:** T. Stevenson (CUB).

Belgrade, Yugoslavia - 1978

L. Fly: S. Muchoki (KEN). **Fly:** H. Strednicki (POL). **Bantam:** A. Horta (CUB). **Feather:** A. Herrera (CUB). **Light:** D. Andeh (NIG). **L. Welter:** V. Lvov (URS). **Welter:** V. Rachkov (URS). **L. Middle:** V. Savchenko (URS). **Middle:** J. Gomez (CUB). **L. Heavy:** S. Soria (CUB). **Heavy:** T. Stevenson (CUB).

Munich, West Germany - 1982

L. Fly: I. Mustafov (BUL). **Fly:** Y. Alexandrov (URS). **Bantam:** F. Favors (USA). **Feather:** A. Horta (CUB). **Light:** A. Herrera (CUB). **L. Welter:** C. Garcia (CUB). **Welter:** M. Breland (USA). **L. Middle:** A. Koshkin (URS). **Middle:** B. Comas (CUB). **L. Heavy:** P. Romero (CUB). **Heavy:** A. Jagubkin (URS). **S. Heavy:** T. Biggs (USA). **Bronze medal:** T. Corr (IRL).

Reno, USA - 1986

L. Fly: J. Odelin (CUB). **Fly:** P. Reyes (CUB). **Bantam:** S-I. Moon (SKO). **Feather:** K. Banks (USA). **Light:** A. Horta (CUB). **L. Welter:** V. Shishov (URS). **Welter:** K. Gould (USA). **L. Middle:** A. Espinosa (CUB). **Middle:** D. Allen (USA). **L. Heavy:** P. Romero (CUB). **Heavy:** F. Savon (CUB). **S. Heavy:** T. Stevenson (CUB).

Moscow, USSR - 1989

L. Fly: E. Griffin (USA). **Fly:** Y. Arbachakov (URS). **Bantam:** E. Carrion (CUB). **Feather:** A. Khamatov (URS). **Light:** J. Gonzalez (CUB). **L. Welter:** I. Ruzinkov (URS). **Welter:** F. Vastag (Rom). **L. Middle:** I. Akopokhian (URS). **Middle:** A. Kurniavka (URS). **L. Heavy:** H. Maske (GDR). **Heavy:** F. Savon (CUB). **S. Heavy:** R. Balado (CUB). **Bronze medal:** M. Carruth (IRL).

Sydney, Australia - 1991

L. Fly: E. Griffin (USA). **Fly:** I. Kovacs (HUN). **Bantam:** S. Todorov (BUL). **Feather:** K. Kirkorov (BUL). **Light:** M. Rudolph (GER). **L. Welter:** K. Tszyu (URS). **Welter:** J. Hernandez (CUB). **L. Middle:** J. Lemus (CUB). **Middle:** T. Russo (ITA). **L. Heavy:** T. May (GER). **Heavy:** F. Savon (CUB). **S. Heavy:** R. Balado (CUB).

Tampere, Finland - 1993

L. Fly: N. Munchian (ARM). **Fly:** W. Font (CUB). **Bantam:** A. Christov (BUL). **Feather:** S. Todorov (BUL). **Light:** D. Austin (CUB). **L. Welter:** H. Vinent (CUB). **Welter:** J. Hernandez (CUB). **L. Middle:** F. Vastag (ROM). **Middle:** A. Hernandez (CUB). **L. Heavy:** R. Garbey (CUB). **Heavy:** F. Savon (CUB). **S. Heavy:** R. Balado (CUB). **Bronze medal:** D. Kelly (IRL).

Berlin, Germany - 1995

L. Fly: D. Petrov (BUL). **Fly:** Z. Lunka (GER). **Bantam:** R. Malachbekov (RUS). **Feather:** S. Todorov (BUL). **Light:** L. Doroftel (ROM). **L. Welter:** H. Vinent (CUB). **Welter:** J. Hernandez (CUB). **L. Middle:** F. Vastag (ROM). **Middle:** A. Hernandez (CUB). **L. Heavy:** A. Tarver (USA). **Heavy:** F. Savon (CUB). **S. Heavy:** A. Lezin (RUS).

Budapest, Hungary - 1997

L. Fly: M. Romero (CUB). **Fly:** M. Mantilla (CUB). **Bantam:** R Malakhbekov (RUS). **Feather:** I. Kovacs (HUN). **Light:** A. Maletin (RUS). **L. Welter:** D. Simion (ROM). **Welter:** O. Saitov (RUS). **L. Middle:** A. Duvergel (CUB). **Middle:** Z. Erdei (HUN). **L. Heavy:** A. Lebsiak (RUS). **Heavy:** F. Savon (CUB). **S. Heavy:** G. Kandelaki (GEO). **Bronze medal:** S. Kirk (IRL).

Houston, USA - 1999

L. Fly: B. Viloria (USA). **Fly:** B. Jumadilov (KAZ). **Bantam:** R. Crinu (ROM). **Feather:** R. Juarez (USA). **Light:** M. Kindelan (CUB). **L. Welter:** M. Abdullaev (UZB). **Welter:** J. Hernandez (CUB). **L. Middle:** M. Simion (ROM). **Middle:** U. Haydarov (UZB). **L. Heavy:** M. Simms (USA). **Heavy:** M. Bennett (USA). **S. Heavy:** S. Samilsan (TUR). **Bronze medal:** K. Evans (WAL).

Belfast, Northern Ireland - 2001

L. Fly: Y. Bartelemi (CUB). **Fly:** J. Thomas (FRA). **Bantam:** G. Rigondeaux (CUB). **Feather:** R. Palyani (TUR). **Light:** M. Kindelan (CUB). **L. Welter:** D. Luna Martinez (CUB). **Welter:** L. Aragon (CUB). **L. Middle:** D. Austin (CUB). **Middle:** A. Gogolev (RUS). **L. Heavy:** Y. Makarenko (RUS). **Heavy:** O. Solis (CUB). **S. Heavy:** R. Chagaev (UZB). **Silver medal:** D. Haye (ENG). **Bronze medals:** J. Moore (IRL), C. Froch (ENG).

Bangkok, Thailand - 2003

L. Fly: S. Karazov (RUS). **Fly:** S. Jongjohor (THA). **Bantam:** A. Mamedov (AZE). **Feather:** G. Jafarov (KAZ). **Light:** M. Kindelan (CUB). **L. Welter:** W. Blain (FRA). **Welter:** L. Aragon (CUB). **Middle:** G. Golovkin (KAZ). **L. Heavy:** Y. Makarenko (RUS). **Heavy:** O. Solis (CUB). **S. Heavy:** A. Povetkin (RUS).

Mianyang City, China - 2005

L. Fly: Zou Shiming (CHI). **Fly:** O-S Lee (SKO). **Bantam:** G. Rigondeaux (CUB). **Feather:** A. Tischenko (RUS). **Light:** Y. Ugas (CUB). **L. Welter:** S. Sapiyev (KAZ). **Welter:** E. Lara (CUB). **Middle:** M. Korobev (RUS). **L. Heavy:** Y. Dzhanabergenov (KAZ). **Heavy:** A. Alexeev (RUS). **S. Heavy:** O. Solis (CUB). **Bronze medal:** N. Perkins (ENG).

Chicago, USA - 2007

L. Fly: Zou Shiming (CHI). **Fly:** R. Warren (USA). **Bantam:** S.Vodopyanov (RUS). **Feather:** A. Selimov (RUS). **Light:** F. Gavin (ENG). **L. Welter:** S. Sapiyev (KAZ). **Welter:** D. Andrade (USA). **Middle:** M. Korobev (RUS). **L. Heavy:** A. Atoev (UZB). **Heavy:** C. Russo (ITA). **S. Heavy:** R. Cammarelle (ITA).

World Junior (Youth) Champions, 1979-2008

Yokohama, Japan - 1979

L. Fly: R. Shannon (USA). **Fly:** P. Lessov (BUL). **Bantam:** P-K. Choi (SKO). **Feather:** Y. Gladychev (URS). **Light:** R. Blake (USA). **L. Welter:** I. Akopokhian (URS). **Welter:** M. McCrory (USA). **L. Middle:** A. Mayes (USA). **Middle:** A. Milov (URS). **L. Heavy:** A. Lebedev (URS). **Heavy:** M. Frazier (USA). **Silver medals:** N. Wilshire (ENG), D. Cross (ENG). **Bronze medal:** I. Scott (SCO).

Santa Domingo, Dominican Republic - 1983

L. Fly: M. Herrera (DOM). **Fly:** J. Gonzalez (DOM). **Bantam:** J. Molina (PUR). **Feather:** A. Miesses (DOM). **Light:** A. Beltre (DOM). **L. Welter:** A. Espinoza (CUB). **Welter:** M. Watkins (USA). **L. Middle:** U. Castillo (CUB). **Middle:** R. Batista (CUB). **L. Heavy:** O. Pought (USA). **Heavy:** A. Williams (USA). **S. Heavy:** L. Lewis (CAN).

Bucharest, Romania - 1985

L. Fly: R-S. Hwang (SKO). **Fly:** T. Marcelica (ROM). **Bantam:** R. Diaz (CUB). **Feather:** D. Maeran (ROM). **Light:** J. Teiche (GDR). **L. Welter:** W. Saeger (GDR). **Welter:** A. Stoianov (BUL). **L. Middle:** M. Franek (TCH). **Middle:** O. Zahalotskih (URS). **L. Heavy:** B. Riddick (USA). **Heavy:** F. Savon (CUB). **S. Heavy:** A. Prianichnikov (URS).

Havana, Cuba - 1987

L. Fly: E. Paisan (CUB). **Fly:** C. Daniels (USA). **Bantam:** A. Moya (CUB). **Feather:** G. Iliyasov (URS). **Light:** J. Hernandez (CUB). **L. Welter:** L. Mihai (ROM). **Welter:** F. Vastag (ROM). **L. Middle:** A. Lobsyak (URS). **Middle:** W. Martinez (CUB). **L. Heavy:** D. Yeliseyev (URS). **Heavy:** R. Balado (CUB). **S. Heavy:** L. Martinez (CUB). **Silver medal:** E. Loughran (IRL). **Bronze medal:** D. Galvin (IRL).

San Juan, Puerto Rico - 1989

L. Fly: D. Petrov (BUL). **Fly:** N. Monchai (FRA). **Bantam:** J. Casamayor (CUB). **Feather:** C. Febres (PUR). **Light:** A. Acevedo (CUB). **L. Welter:** E. Berger (GDR). **Welter:** A. Hernandez (CUB). **L. Middle:** L. Bedey (CUB). **Middle:** R. Garbey (CUB). **L. Heavy:** R. Alvarez (CUB). **Heavy:** K. Johnson (CAN). **S. Heavy:** A. Burdiantz (URS). **Silver medals:** E. Magee (IRL), R. Reid (ENG), S. Wilson (SCO).

Lima, Peru - 1990

L. Fly: D. Alicea (PUR). **Fly:** K. Pielert (GDR). **Bantam:** K. Baravi (URS). **Feather:** A. Vaughan (ENG). **Light:** J. Mendez (CUB). **L. Welter:** H. Vinent (CUB). **Welter:** A. Hernandez (CUB). **L. Middle:** A. Kakauridze (URS). **Middle:**

J. Gomez (CUB). **L. Heavy:** B. Torsten (GDR). **Heavy:** I. Andreev (URS). **S. Heavy:** J. Quesada (CUB). **Bronze medal:** P. Ingle (ENG).

Montreal, Canada - 1992
L. Fly: W. Font (CUB). **Fly:** J. Oragon (CUB). **Bantam:** N. Machado (CUB). **Feather:** M. Stewart (CAN). **Light:** D. Austin (CUB). **L. Welter:** O. Saitov (RUS). **Welter:** L. Brors (GER). **L. Middle:** J. Acosta (CUB). **Middle:** I. Arsangaliev (RUS). **L. Heavy:** S. Samilsan (TUR). **Heavy:** G. Kandeliaki (GEO). **S. Heavy:** M. Porchnev (RUS). **Bronze medal:** N. Sinclair (IRL).

Istanbul, Turkey - 1994
L. Fly: J. Turunen (FIN). **Fly:** A. Jimenez (CUB). **Bantam:** J. Despaigne (CUB). **Feather:** D. Simion (ROM). **Light:** L. Diogenes (CUB). **L. Welter:** V. Romero (CUB). **Welter:** E. Aslan (TUR). **L. Middle:** G. Ledsvanys (CUB). **Middle:** M. Genc (TUR). **L. Heavy:** P. Aurino (ITA). **Heavy:** M. Lopez (CUB). **S. Heavy:** P. Carrion (CUB).

Havana, Cuba - 1996
L. Fly: L. Hernandez (CUB). **Fly:** L. Cabrera (CUB). **Bantam:** P. Miradal (CUB). **Feather:** E. Rodriguez (CUB). **Light:** R. Vaillan (CUB). **L. Welter:** T. Mergadze (RUS). **Welter:** J. Brahmer (GER). **L. Middle:** L. Mezquia (CUB). **Middle:** V. Pletniov (RUS). **L. Heavy:** O. Simon (CUB). **Heavy:** A. Yatsenko (UKR). **S. Heavy:** S. Fabre (CUB). **Bronze medal:** R. Hatton (ENG).

Buenos Aires, Argentina - 1998
L. Fly: S. Tanasie (ROM). **Fly:** S. Yeledov (KAZ). **Bantam:** S. Suleymanov (UKR). **Feather:** I. Perez (ARG). **Light:** A. Solopov (RUS). **L. Welter:** Y. Tomashov (UKR). **Welter:** K. Oustarkhanov (RUS). **L. Middle:** S. Kostenko (UKR). **Middle:** M. Kempe (GER). **L. Heavy:** H. Yohanson Martinez (CUB). **Heavy:** O. Solis Fonte (CUB). **S. Heavy:** B. Ohanyan (ARM). **Silver medal:** H. Cunningham (IRL). **Bronze medal:** D. Campbell (IRL).

Budapest, Hungary - 2000
L. Fly: Y. Leon Alarcon (CUB). **Fly:** O. Franco Vaszquez (CUB). **Bantam:** V. Tajbert (GER). **Feather:** G. Kate (HUN). **Light:** F. Adzsanalov (AZE). **L. Welter:** G. Galovkin (KAZ). **Welter:** S. Ustunel (TUR). **L. Middle:** D. Chernysh (RUS). **Middle:** F. Sullivan Barrera (CUB). **L. Heavy:** A. Shekmourov (RUS). **Heavy:** D. Medzhydov (UKR). **S. Heavy:** A. Dmitrienko (RUS). **Bronze medal:** C. Barrett (IRL).

Santiago, Cuba - 2002
L. Fly: D. Acripitian (RUS). **Fly:** Y. Fabregas (CUB). **Bantam:** S. Bahodirijan (UZB). **Feather:** A. Tichtchenko (RUS). **Light:** S. Mendez (CUB). **L. Welter:** K. Iliyasov (KAZ). **Welter:** J. McPherson (USA). **L. Middle:** V. Diaz (CUB). **Middle:** A. Duarte (CUB). **L. Heavy:** R. Zavalnyuyk (UKR). **Heavy:** Y. P. Hernandez (CUB). **S. Heavy:** P. Portal (CUB). **Silver medal:** A. Lee (IRL). **Bronze medal:** N. Brough (ENG).

Jeju Island, South Korea - 2004
L. Fly: P. Bedak (Hun). **Fly:** I. Rahimov (UZB). **Bantam:** A. Abdimomunov (KAZ). **Feather:** E. Ambartsumyan (RUS). **Light:** A. Khan (ENG). **L. Welter:** C. Banteur (CUB). **Welter:** E. Rasulov (UZB). **Middle:** D. Tchudinov (RUS). **L. Heavy:** I. Perez (CUB). **Heavy:** E. Romanov (RUS). **S.Heavy:** D. Boytsov (RUS). **Bronze medal:** D. Price (ENG).

Agadir, Morocco - 2006
L.Fly: A.Collado Acosta (CUB). **Fly:** V.Lomachenko (UKR). **Bantam:** M.Ouatine (MOR). **Feather:** Y.Frometa (CUB). **Light:** R.Iglesias (CUB). **L.Welter:** B.Backsai (HUN). **Welter:** J.Iglesias (CUB). **Middle:** L.Garcia (CUB). **L.Heavy:** I.Yandiev (RUS). **Heavy:** S.Kalchugin (RUS). **S.Heavy:** C.Ciocan (ROM). **Bronze medals:** O.Mbwakongo (ENG), T.Fury (ENG).

Guadalajara, Mexico - 2008
L.Fly: M. Thokchom (IND). **Fly:** J. Gonzalez (PUR). **Bantam:** M. Kurbanov (RUS). **Feather:** O.R. Valdez (MEX). **Light:** R. Moylett (IRL). **L.Welter:** F. Izla (CUB). **Welter:** O. Molina (MEX). **Middle:** R. Recio (CUB). **L.Heavy:** J.A. Larduet (CUB). **Heavy:** E. Savon (CUB). **S.Heavy:** J. Dawejko (USA). **Silver medal:** J. Kavanagh (IRL). **Bronze medals:** T. McCarthy (IRL), D. Joyce (IRL).

European Champions, 1924-2008
Paris, France - 1924
Fly: J. McKenzie (GBR). **Bantam:** J. Ces (FRA). **Feather:** R. de Vergnie (BEL). **Light:** N. Nielsen (DEN). **Welter:** J. Delarge (BEL). **Middle:** H. Mallin (GBR). **L. Heavy:** H. Mitchell (GBR). **Heavy:** O. von Porat (NOR).

Stockholm, Sweden - 1925
Fly: E. Pladner (FRA). **Bantam:** A. Rule (GBR). **Feather:** P. Andren (SWE). **Light:** S. Johanssen (SWE). **Welter:** H. Nielsen (DEN). **Middle:** F. Crawley (GBR). **L. Heavy:** T. Petersen (DEN). **Heavy:** B. Persson (SWE). **Silver medals:** J. James (GBR), E. Viney (GBR), D. Lister (GBR).

Berlin, Germany - 1927
Fly: L. Boman (SWE). **Bantam:** K. Dalchow (GER). **Feather:** F. Dubbers (GER).

Light: H. Domgoergen (GER). **Welter:** R. Caneva (ITA). **Middle:** J. Christensen (NOR). **L. Heavy:** H. Muller (GER). **Heavy:** N. Ramm (SWE).

Amsterdam, Holland - 1928
Fly: A. Kocsis (HUN). **Bantam:** V. Tamagnini (ITA). **Feather:** B. van Klaveren (HOL). **Light:** C. Orlandi (ITA). **Welter:** R. Galataud (FRA). **Middle:** P. Toscani (ITA). **L. Heavy:** E. Pistulla (GER). **Heavy:** N. Ramm (SWE).

Budapest, Hungary - 1930
Fly: I. Enekes (HUN). **Bantam:** J. Szeles (HUN). **Feather:** G. Szabo (HUN). **Light:** M. Bianchini (ITA). **Welter:** J. Besselmann (GER). **Middle:** C. Meroni (ITA). **L. Heavy:** T. Petersen (DEN). **Heavy:** J. Michaelson (DEN).

Los Angeles, USA - 1932
Fly: I. Enekes (HUN). **Bantam:** H. Ziglarski (GER). **Feather:** J. Schleinkofer (GER). **Light:** T. Ahlqvist (SWE). **Welter:** E. Campe (GER). **Middle:** R. Michelot (FRA). **L. Heavy:** G. Rossi (ITA). **Heavy:** L. Rovati (ITA).

Budapest, Hungary - 1934
Fly: P. Palmer (GBR). **Bantam:** I. Enekes (HUN). **Feather:** O. Kaestner (GER). **Light:** E. Facchini (ITA). **Welter:** D. McCleave (GBR). **Middle:** S. Szigetti (HUN). **L. Heavy:** P. Zehetmayer (AUT). **Heavy:** G. Baerlund (FIN). **Bronze medal:** P. Floyd (GBR).

Milan, Italy - 1937
Fly: I. Enekes (HUN). **Bantam:** U. Sergo (ITA). **Feather:** A. Polus (POL). **Light:** H. Nuremberg (GER). **Welter:** M. Murach (GER). **Middle:** H. Chmielewski (POL). **L. Heavy:** S. Szigetti (HUN). **Heavy:** O. Tandberg (SWE).

Dublin, Eire - 1939
Fly: J. Ingle (IRL). **Bantam:** U. Sergo (ITA). **Feather:** P. Dowdall (IRL). **Light:** H. Nuremberg (GER). **Welter:** A. Kolczyski (POL). **Middle:** A. Raadik (EST). **L. Heavy:** L. Musina (ITA). **Heavy:** O. Tandberg (SWE). **Bronze medal:** C. Evenden (IRL).

Dublin, Eire - 1947
Fly: L. Martinez (ESP). **Bantam:** L. Bogacs (HUN). **Feather:** K. Kreuger (SWE). **Light:** J. Vissers (BEL). **Welter:** J. Ryan (ENG). **Middle:** A. Escudie (FRA). **L. Heavy:** H. Quentemeyer (HOL). **Heavy:** G. O'Colmain (IRL). **Silver medals:** J. Clinton (SCO), P. Maguire (IRL), W. Thom (ENG), G. Scriven (ENG). **Bronze medals:** J. Dwyer (SCO), A. Sanderson (ENG), W. Frith (SCO), E. Cantwell (IRL), K. Wyatt (ENG).

Oslo, Norway - 1949
Fly: J. Kasperczak (POL). **Bantam:** G. Zuddas (ITA). **Feather:** J. Bataille (FRA). **Light:** M. McCullagh (IRL). **Welter:** J. Torma (TCH). **Middle:** L. Papp (HUN). **L. Heavy:** G. di Segni (ITA). **Heavy:** L. Bene (HUN). **Bronze medal:** D. Connell (IRL).

Milan, Italy - 1951
Fly: A. Pozzali (ITA). **Bantam:** V. Dall'Osso (ITA). **Feather:** J. Ventaja (FRA). **Light:** B. Visintin (ITA). **L. Welter:** H. Schelling (GER). **Welter:** Z. Chychla (POL). **L. Middle:** L. Papp (HUN). **Middle:** S. Sjolin (SWE). **L. Heavy:** M. Limage (BEL). **Heavy:** G. di Segni (ITA). **Silver medal:** J. Kelly (IRL). **Bronze medals:** D. Connell (IRL), T. Milligan (IRL), A. Lay (ENG).

Warsaw, Poland - 1953
Fly: H. Kukier (POL). **Bantam:** Z. Stefaniuk (POL). **Feather:** J. Kruza (POL). **Light:** V. Jengibarian (URS). **L. Welter:** L. Drogosz (POL). **Welter:** Z. Chychla (POL). **L. Middle:** B. Wells (ENG). **Middle:** D. Wemhoner (GER). **L. Heavy:** U. Nietchke (GER). **Heavy:** A. Schotzikas (URS). **Silver medal:** T. Milligan (IRL). **Bronze medals:** J. McNally (IRL), R. Barton (ENG).

Berlin, West Germany - 1955
Fly: E. Basel (GER). **Bantam:** Z. Stefaniuk (POL). **Feather:** T. Nicholls (ENG). **Light:** H. Kurschat (GER). **L. Welter:** L. Drogosz (POL). **Welter:** N. Gargano (ENG). **L. Middle:** Z. Pietrzykowski (POL). **Middle:** G. Schatkov (URS). **L. Heavy:** E. Schoeppner (GER). **Heavy:** A. Schotzikas (URS).

Prague, Czechoslovakia - 1957
Fly: M. Homberg (GER). **Bantam:** O. Grigoryev (URS). **Feather:** D. Venilov (BUL). **Light:** K. Pazdzior (POL). **L. Welter:** V. Jengibarian (URS). **Welter:** M. Graus (GER). **L. Middle:** N. Benvenuti (ITA). **Middle:** Z. Pietrzykowski (POL). **L. Heavy:** G. Negrea (ROM). **Heavy:** A. Abramov (URS). **Bronze medals:** R. Davies (WAL), J. Morrissey (SCO), J. Kidd (SCO), F. Teidt (IRL).

Lucerne, Switzerland - 1959
Fly: M. Homberg (GER). **Bantam:** H. Rascher (GER). **Feather:** J. Adamski (POL). **Light:** O. Maki (FIN). **L. Welter:** V. Jengibarian (URS). **Welter:** L. Drogosz (POL). **L. Middle:** N. Benvenuti (ITA). **Middle:** G. Schatkov (URS). **L. Heavy:** Z. Pietrzykowski (POL). **Heavy:** A. Abramov (URS). **Silver medal:** D. Thomas (ENG). **Bronze medals:** A. McClean (IRL), H. Perry (IRL), C. McCoy (IRL), H. Scott (ENG).

273

Belgrade, Yugoslavia - 1961

Fly: P. Vacca (ITA). **Bantam:** S. Sivko (URS). **Feather:** F. Taylor (ENG). **Light:** R. McTaggart (SCO). **L. Welter:** A. Tamulis (URS). **Welter:** R. Tamulis (URS). **L. Middle:** B. Lagutin (URS). **Middle:** T. Walasek (POL). **L. Heavy:** G. Saraudi (ITA). **Heavy:** A. Abramov (URS). **Bronze medals:** P. Warwick (ENG), I. McKenzie (SCO), J. Bodell (ENG).

Moscow, USSR - 1963

Fly: V. Bystrov (URS). **Bantam:** O. Grigoryev (URS). **Feather:** S. Stepashkin (URS). **Light:** J. Kajdi (HUN). **L. Welter:** J. Kulej (POL). **Welter:** R. Tamulis (URS). **L. Middle:** B. Lagutin (URS). **Middle:** V. Popenchenko (URS). **L. Heavy:** Z. Pietrzykowski (POL). **Heavy:** J. Nemec (TCH). **Silver medal:** A. Wyper (SCO).

Berlin, East Germany - 1965

Fly: H. Freisdadt (GER). **Bantam:** O. Grigoryev (URS). **Feather:** S. Stepashkin (URS). **Light:** V. Barranikov (URS). **L. Welter:** J. Kulej (POL). **Welter:** R. Tamulis (URS). **L. Middle:** V. Ageyev (URS). **Middle:** V. Popenchenko (URS). **L. Heavy:** D. Poznyak (URS). **Heavy:** A. Isosimov (URS). **Silver medal:** B. Robinson (ENG). **Bronze medals:** J. McCluskey (SCO), K. Buchanan (SCO), J. McCourt (IRL).

Rome, Italy - 1967

Fly: H. Skrzyczak (POL). **Bantam:** N. Giju (ROM). **Feather:** R. Petek (POL). **Light:** J. Grudzien (POL). **L. Welter:** V. Frolov (URS). **Welter:** B. Nemecek (TCH). **L. Middle:** V. Ageyev (URS). **Middle:** M. Casati (ITA). **L. Heavy:** D. Poznyak (URS). **Heavy:** M. Baruzzi (ITA). **Silver medal:** P. Boddington (ENG).

Bucharest, Romania - 1969

L. Fly: G. Gedo (HUN). **Fly:** C. Ciuca (ROM). **Bantam:** A. Dumitrescu (ROM). **Feather:** L. Orban (HUN). **Light:** S. Cutov (ROM). **L. Welter:** V. Frolov (URS). **Welter:** G. Meier (GER). **L. Middle:** V. Tregubov (URS). **Middle:** V. Tarasenkov (URS). **L. Heavy:** D. Poznyak (URS). **Heavy:** I. Alexe (ROM). **Bronze medals:** M. Dowling (IRL), M. Piner (ENG), A. Richardson (ENG), T. Imrie (SCO).

Madrid, Spain - 1971

L. Fly: G. Gedo (HUN). **Fly:** J. Rodriguez (ESP). **Bantam:** T. Badar (HUN). **Feather:** R. Tomczyk (POL). **Light:** J. Szczepanski (POL). **L. Welter:** U. Beyer (GDR). **Welter:** J. Kajdi (HUN). **L. Middle:** V. Tregubov (URS). **Middle:** J. Juotsiavitchus (URS). **L. Heavy:** M. Parlov (YUG). **Heavy:** V. Tchernishev (URS). **Bronze medals:** N. McLaughlin (IRL), M. Dowling (IRL), B. McCarthy (IRL), **M.** Kingwell (ENG), L. Stevens (ENG).

Belgrade, Yugoslavia - 1973

L. Fly: V. Zasypko (URS). **Fly:** C. Gruescu (ROM). **Bantam:** A. Cosentino (FRA). **Feather:** S. Forster (GDR). **Light:** S. Cutov (ROM). **L. Welter:** M. Benes (YUG). **Welter:** S. Csjef (HUN). **L. Middle:** A. Klimanov (URS). **Middle:** V. Lemechev (URS). **L. Heavy:** M. Parlov (YUG). **Heavy:** V. Ulyanich (URS). **Bronze medal:** J. Bambrick (SCO).

Katowice, Poland - 1975

L. Fly: A. Tkachenko (URS). **Fly:** V. Zasypko (URS). **Bantam:** V. Rybakov (URS). **Feather:** T. Badari (HUN). **Light:** S. Cutov (ROM). **L. Welter:** V. Limasov (URS). **Welter:** K. Marjaama (FIN). **L. Middle:** W. Rudnowski (POL). **Middle:** V. Lemechev (URS). **L. Heavy:** A. Klimanov (URS). **Heavy:** A. Biegalski (POL). **Bronze medals:** C. Magri (ENG), P. Cowdell (ENG), G. McEwan (ENG).

Halle, East Germany - 1977

L. Fly: H. Srednicki (POL). **Fly:** L. Blazynski (POL). **Bantam:** S. Forster (GDR). **Feather:** R. Nowakowski (GDR). **Light:** A. Rusevski (YUG). **L. Welter:** B. Gajda (POL). **Welter:** V. Limasov (URS). **L. Middle:** V. Saychenko (URS). **Middle:** I. Shaposhnikov (URS). **L. Heavy:** D. Kvachadze (URS). **Heavy:** E. Gorstkov (URS). **Bronze medal:** P. Sutcliffe (IRL).

Cologne, West Germany - 1979

L. Fly: S. Sabirov (URS). **Fly:** H. Srednicki (POL). **Bantam:** N. Khrapzov (URS). **Feather:** V. Rybakov(URS). **Light:** V. Demianenko (URS). **L. Welter:** S. Konakbaev (URS). **Welter:** E. Muller (GER). **L. Middle:** M. Perunovic (YUG). **Middle:** T. Uusiverta (FIN). **L. Heavy:** A. Nikolyan (URS). **Heavy:** E. Gorstkov (URS). **S. Heavy:** P. Hussing (GER). **Bronze medal:** P. Sutcliffe (IRL).

Tampere, Finland - 1981

L. Fly: I. Mustafov (BUL). **Fly:** P. Lessov (BUL). **Bantam:** V. Miroschnichenko (URS). **Feather:** R. Nowakowski (GDR). **Light:** V. Rybakov (URS). **L. Welter:** V. Shisov (URS). **Welter:** S. Konakvbaev (URS). **L. Middle:** A. Koshkin (URS). **Middle:** J. Torbek (URS). **L. Heavy:** A Krupin (URS). **Heavy:** A. Jagupkin (URS). **S. Heavy:** F. Damiani (ITA). **Bronze medal:** G. Hawkins (IRL).

Varna, Bulgaria - 1983

L. Fly: I. Mustafov (BUL). **Fly:** P. Lessov (BUL). **Bantam:** Y. Alexandrov (URS). **Feather:** S. Nurkazov (URS). **Light:** E. Chuprenski (BUL). **L. Welter:** V. Shishov (URS). **Welter:** P. Galkin (URS). **L. Middle:** V. Laptev (URS). **Middle:** V. Melnik (URS). **L. Heavy:** V. Kokhanovski (URS). **Heavy:** A. Jagubkin (URS). **S. Heavy:** F. Damiani (ITA). **Bronze medal:** K. Joyce (IRL).

Budapest, Hungary - 1985

L. Fly: R. Breitbarth (GDR). **Fly:** D. Berg (GDR). **Bantam:** L. Simic (YUG). **Feather:** S. Khachatrian (URS). **Light:** E. Chuprenski (BUL). **L. Welter:** S. Mehnert (GDR). **Welter:** I. Akopokhian (URS). **L. Middle:** M. Timm (GDR). **Middle:** H. Maske (GDR). **L. Heavy:** N. Shanavasov (URS). **Heavy:** A. Jagubkin (URS). **S. Heavy:** F. Somodi (HUN). **Bronze medals:** S. Casey(IRL), J. Beckles (ENG).

Turin, Italy - 1987

L. Fly: N. Munchyan (URS). **Fly:** A. Tews (GDR). **Bantam:** A. Hristov (BUL). **Feather:** M. Kazaryan (URS). **Light:** O. Nazarov (URS). **L. Welter:** B. Abadjier (BUL). **Welter:** V. Shishov (URS). **L. Middle:** E. Richter (GDR). **Middle:** H. Maske (GDR). **L. Heavy:** Y. Vaulin (URS). **Heavy:** A. Vanderlijde (HOL). **S. Heavy:** U. Kaden (GDR). **Bronze medal:** N. Brown (ENG).

Athens, Greece - 1989

L. Fly: I.Mustafov (BUL). **Fly:** Y. Arbachakov (URS). **Bantam:** S. Todorov (BUL). **Feather:** K. Kirkorov (BUL). **Light:** K. Tsziu (URS). **L. Welter:** I. Ruznikov (URS). **Welter:** S. Mehnert (GDR). **L. Middle:** I. Akopokhian (URS). **Middle:** H. Maske (GDR). **L. Heavy:** S. Lange (GDR). **Heavy:** A. Vanderlijde (HOL). **S. Heavy:** U. Kaden (GDR). **Bronze medal:** D. Anderson (SCO).

Gothenburg, Sweden - 1991

L. Fly: I. Marinov (BUL). **Fly:** I. Kovacs (HUN). **Bantam:** S. Todorov (BUL). **Feather:** P. Griffin (IRL). **Light:** V. Nistor (ROM). **L. Welter:** K. Tsziu (URS). **Welter:** R. Welin (SWE). **L. Middle:** I. Akopokhian (URS). **Middle:** S. Otke (GER). **L. Heavy:** D. Michalczewski (GER). **Heavy:** A. Vanderlijde (HOL). **S. Heavy:** E. Beloussov (URS). **Bronze medals:** P. Weir (SCO), A. Vaughan (ENG).

Bursa, Turkey - 1993

L. Fly: D. Petrov (BUL). **Fly:** R. Husseinov (AZE). **Bantam:** R. Malakhbetov (RUS). **Feather:** S. Todorov (BUL). **Light:** J. Bielski (POL). **L. Welter:** N. Suleymanogiu (TUR). **Welter:** V. Karpaclauskas (LIT). **L. Middle:** F. Vastag (ROM). **Middle:** D. Eigenbrodt (GER). **L. Heavy:** I. Kshinin (RUS). **Heavy:** G. Kandelaki (GEO). **S. Heavy:** S. Rusinov (BUL). **Bronze medals:** P. Griffin (IRL), D. Williams (ENG), K. McCormack (WAL).

Vejle, Denmark - 1996

L. Fly: D. Petrov (BUL). **Fly:** A. Pakeev (RUS). **Bantam:** I. Kovacs (HUN). **Feather:** R. Paliani (RUS). **Light:** L. Doroftei (ROM). **L. Welter:** O. Urkal (GER). **Welter:** H. Al (DEN). **L. Middle:** F. Vastag (ROM). **Middle:** S. Ottke (GER). **L. Heavy:** P. Aurino (ITA). **Heavy:** V. Krasniqi (GER). **S. Heavy:** A. Lezin (RUS). **Bronze medals:** S. Harrison (SCO), D. Burke (ENG), D. Kelly (IRL).

Minsk, Belarus - 1998

L. Fly: S. Kazakov (RUS). **Fly:** V. Sidorenko (UKR). **Bantam:** S. Danilchenko (UKR). **Feather:** R. Malakhbekov (RUS). **Light:** K. Huste (GER). **L. Welter:** D. Simion (ROM). **Welter:** O. Saitov (RUS). **L. Middle:** F. Esther (FRA). **Middle:** Z. Erdei (HUN). **L. Heavy:** A. Lebsiak (RUS). **Heavy:** G. Fragomeni (ITA). **S. Heavy:** A. Lezin (RUS). **Silver Medals:** B. Magee (IRL), C. Fry (ENG). **Bronze medal:** C. Bessey (ENG).

Tampere, Finland - 2000

L. Fly: Valeri Sidorenko (UKR). **Fly:** Vladimir Sidorenko (UKR). **Bantam:** A. Agagueloglu (TUR). **Feather:** R. Paliani (TUR). **Light:** A. Maletin (RUS). **L. Welter:** A. Leonev (RUS). **Welter:** B. Ueluesoy (TUR). **L. Middle:** A. Catic (GER). **Middle:** Z. Erdei (HUN). **L. Heavy:** A. Lebsiak (RUS). **Heavy:** J. Chanet (FRA). **S. Heavy:** A. Lezin (RUS).

Perm, Russia - 2002

L. Fly: S. Kazakov (RUS). **Fly:** G. Balakshin (RUS). **Bantam:** K. Khatsygov (BE). **Feather:** R. Malakhbekov (RUS). **Light:** A. Maletin (RUS). **L. Welter:** D. Panayotov (BUL). **Welter:** T. Gaidalov (RUS). **L. Middle:** A. Mishin (RUS). **Middle:** O. Mashkin (UKR). **L. Heavy:** M. Gala (RUS). **Heavy:** E. Makarenko (RUS). **S. Heavy:** A. Povetkin (RUS).

Pula, Croatia - 2004

L. Fly: S. Kazakov (RUS). **Fly:** G. Balakchine (RUS). **Bantam:** G. Kovalev (RUS). **Feather:** V. Tajbert (GER). **Light:** D. Stilianov (RUS). **L. Welter:** A. Maletin (RUS). **Welter:** O. Saitov (RUS). **Middle:** G. Gaiderbekov (RUS). **L. Heavy:** E. Makarenko (RUS). **Heavy:** A. Alekeevn (RUS). **S. Heavy:** A. Povertkin (RUS). **Bronze medals:** R. Davies (WAL), J. Morrissey (SCO), J. Kidd (SCO), F. Teidt (IRL).

Plovdiv, Bulgaria - 2006

L.Fly: D. Ayrapetyan (RUS). **Fly:** G. Balakshin (RUS). **Bantam:** A Aliev (RUS). **Feather:** A. Selminov (RUS). **Light:** A Tishchenko (RUS). **L.Welter:** B. Georgiev (BUL). **Welter:** A. Balanov (RUS). **Middle:** M. Korobov (RUS).

L.Heavy: A. Beterbiev (RUS). **Heavy:** D. Poyatsika (UKR). **S.Heavy:** I. Timurziev (RUS). **Bronze medals:** S. Smith (ENG), F. Mhura (SCO), K. Egan (IRL).

Liverpool, England - 2008
L.Fly: H. Danielyan (ARM). **Fly:** G. Chygayev (UKR). **Bantam:** L. Campbell (ENG). **Feather:** V. Lomachenko (UKR). **Light:** L. Kostylev (RUS). **L.Welter:** E. Hambartsumyan (ARM). **Welter:** M. Nurudzinau (BE). **Middle:** I. Senay (UKR). **L.Heavy:** O. Usyk (UKR). **Heavy:** E. Mekhontsev (RUS). **S.Heavy:** K. Pulev (BUL). **Bronze medals:** A. Selby (WAL), R. Hickey (IRL), J.J. Joyce (IRL), E. O'Kane (IRL).

European Junior (Youth) Champions, 1970-2009
Miskolc, Hungary - 1970
L. Fly: Gluck (HUN). **Fly:** Z. Kismeneth (HUN). **Bantam:** A. Levitschev (URS). **Feather:** Andrianov (URS). **Light:** L. Juhasz (HUN). **L. Welter:** K. Nemec (HUN). **Welter:** Davidov (URS). **L. Middle:** A. Lemeschuk (URS). **Middle:** N. Anfimov (URS). **L. Heavy:** O. Sasche (GDR). **Heavy:** J. Reder (HUN). **Bronze medals:** D. Needham (ENG), R. Barlow (ENG), L. Stevens (ENG).

Bucharest, Romania - 1972
L. Fly: A. Turei (ROM). **Fly:** Condurat (ROM). **Bantam:** V. Solomin (URS). **Feather:** V. Lvov (URS). **Light:** S. Cutov (ROM). **L. Welter:** K. Pierwieniecki (POL). **Welter:** Zorov (URS). **L. Middle:** Babescu (ROM). **Middle:** V. Lemeschev (URS). **L. Heavy:** Mirounik (URS). **Heavy:** Subutin (URS). **Bronze medals:** J. Gale (ENG), R. Maxwell (ENG), D. Odwell (ENG).

Kiev, Russia - 1974
L. Fly: A. Tkachenko (URS). **Fly:** V. Rybakov (URS). **Bantam:** C. Andreikovski (BUL). **Feather:** V. Sorokin (URS). **Light:** V. Limasov (URS). **L. Welter:** N. Sigov (URS). **Welter:** M. Bychkov (URS). **L. Middle:** V. Danshin (URS). **Middle:** D. Jende (GDR). **L. Heavy:** K. Dafinoiu (ROM). **Heavy:** K. Mashev (BUL). **Silver medal:** C. Magri (ENG). **Bronze medals:** G. Gilbody (ENG), K. Laing (ENG).

Izmir, Turkey - 1976
L. Fly: C. Seican (ROM). **Fly:** G. Khratsov (URS). **Bantam:** M. Navros (URS). **Feather:** V. Demoianeko (URS). **Light:** M. Puzovic (YUG). **L. Welter:** V. Zverev (URS). **Welter:** K. Ozoglouz (TUR). **L. Middle:** W. Lauder (SCO). **Middle:** H. Lenhart (GER). **L. Heavy:** I. Yantchauskas (URS). **Heavy:** B. Enjenyan (URS). **Silver medal:** J. Decker (ENG). **Bronze medals:** I. McLeod (SCO), N. Croombes (ENG).

Dublin, Ireland - 1978
L. Fly: R. Marx (GDR). **Fly:** D. Radu (ROM). **Bantam:** S. Khatchatrian (URS). **Feather:** H. Loukmanov (URS). **Light:** P. Oliva (ITA). **L. Welter:** V. Laptiev (URS). **Welter:** R. Filimanov (URS). **L. Middle:** A. Beliave (URS). **Middle:** G. Zinkovitch (URS). **L. Heavy:** I. Jolta (ROM). **Heavy:** P. Stoimenov (URS). Silver medals: M. Holmes (IRL), P. Hanlon (ENG), M. Courtney (ENG). **Bronze medals:** T. Thompson (IRL), J. Turner (ENG), M. Bennett (WAL), J. McAllister (SCO), C. Devine (ENG).

Rimini, Italy - 1980
L. Fly: A. Mikoulin (URS). **Fly:** J. Varadi (HUN). **Bantam:** F. Rauschning (GDR). **Feather:** J. Gladychev (URS). **Light:** V. Shishov (URS). **L. Welter:** R. Lomski (BUL). **Welter:** T. Holonics (GDR). **L. Middle:** N. Wilshire (ENG). **Middle:** S. Laptiev (URS). **L. Heavy:** V. Dolgoun (URS). **Heavy:** V. Tioumentsev (URS). **S. Heavy:** S. Kormihtsine (URS). **Bronze medals:** N. Potter (ENG), B. McGuigan (IRL), M. Brereton (IRL), D. Cross (ENG).

Schwerin, East Germany - 1982
L. Fly: R. Kabirov (URS). **Fly:** I. Filchev (BUL). **Bantam:** M. Stecca (ITA). **Feather:** B. Blagoev (BUL). **Light:** E. Chakimov (URS). **L. Welter:** S. Mehnert (GDR). **Welter:** T. Schmitz (GDR). **L. Middle:** B. Shararov (URS). **Middle:** E. Christie (ENG). **L. Heavy:** Y. Waulin (URS). **Heavy:** A. Popov (URS). **S. Heavy:** V. Aldoshin (URS). **Silver medal:** D. Kenny (ENG). **Bronze medal:** O. Jones (ENG).

Tampere, Finland - 1984
L. Fly: R. Breitbart (GDR). **Fly:** D. Berg (GDR). **Bantam:** K. Khdrian (URS). **Feather:** O. Nazarov (URS). **Light:** C. Furnikov (BUL). **L. Welter:** W. Schmidt (GDR). **Welter:** K. Doinov (BUL). **L. Middle:** O. Volkov (URS). **Middle:** R. Ryll (GDR). **L. Heavy:** G. Peskov (URS). **Heavy:** R. Draskovic (YUG). **S. Heavy:** L. Kamenov (BUL). **Bronze medals:** J. Lowey (IRL), F. Harding (ENG), N. Moore (ENG).

Copenhagen, Denmark - 1986
L. Fly: S. Todorov (BUL). **Fly:** S. Galotian (URS). **Bantam:** D. Drumm (GDR). **Feather:** K. Tsziu (URS). **Light:** G. Akopkhian (URS). **L. Welter:** F. Vastag (ROM). **Welter:** S. Karavayev (URS). **L. Middle:** E. Elibaev (URS). **Middle:** A. Kurnabka (URS). **L. Heavy:** A. Schultz (GDR). **Heavy:** A. Golota (POL). **S. Heavy:** A. Prianichnikov (URS).

Gdansk, Poland - 1988
L. Fly: I. Kovacs (HUN). **Fly:** M. Beyer (GDR). **Bantam:** M. Aitzanov (URS). **Feather:** M. Rudolph (GDR). **Light:** M. Shaburov (URS). **L. Welter:** G. Campanella (ITA). **Welter:** D. Konsun (URS). **L. Middle:** K. Kiselev (URS). **Middle:** A. Rudenko (URS). **L. Heavy:** O. Velikanov (URS). **Heavy:** A. Ter-Okopian (URS). **S. Heavy:** E. Belusov (URS). **Bronze medals:** P. Ramsey (ENG), M. Smyth (WAL).

Usti Nad Labem, Czechoslovakia - 1990
L. Fly: Z. Paliani (URS). **Fly:** K. Pielert (GDR). **Bantam:** K. Baravi (URS). **Feather:** P. Gvasalia (URS). **Light:** J. Hildenbrandt (GDR). **L. Welter:** N. Smanov (URS). **Welter:** A. Preda (ROM). **L. Middle:** A. Kakauridze (URS). **Middle:** J. Schwank (GDR). **L. Heavy:** Iljin (URS). **Heavy:** I. Andrejev (URS). **S. Heavy:** W. Fischer (GDR). **Silver medal:** A. Todd (ENG). **Bronze medal:** P. Craig (ENG).

Edinburgh, Scotland - 1992
L. Fly: M. Ismailov (URS). **Fly:** F. Brennfuhrer (GER). **Bantam:** S. Kuchler (GER). **Feather:** M. Silantiev (URS). **Light:** S. Shcherbakov (URS). **L. Welter:** O. Saitov (URS). **Welter:** H. Kurlumaz (TUR). **L. Middle:** Z. Erdie (HUN). **Middle:** V. Zhirov (URS). **L. Heavy:** D. Gorbachev (URS). **Heavy:** L. Achkasov (URS). **S. Heavy:** A. Mamedov (URS). Silver medals: M. Hall (ENG), B. Jones (WAL). **Bronze medals:** F. Slane (IRL), G. Stephens (IRL), C. Davies (WAL).

Salonika, Greece - 1993
L. Fly: O. Kiroukhine (UKR). **Fly:** R. Husseinov (AZE). **Bantam:** M. Kulbe (GER). **Feather:** E. Zakharov (RUS). **Light:** O. Sergeev (RUS). **L. Welter:** A. Selihanov (RUS). **Welter:** O. Kudinov (UKR). **L. Middle:** E. Makarenko (RUS). **Middle:** D. Droukovski (RUS). **L. Heavy:** A. Voida (RUS). **Heavy:** Vladimir Klitschko (UKR). **S. Heavy:** A. Moiseev (RUS). **Bronze medal:** D. Costello (ENG).

Sifok, Hungary - 1995
L. Fly: D. Gaissine (RUS). **Fly:** A. Kotelnik (UKR). **Bantam:** A. Loutsenko (UKR). **Feather:** S. Harrisson (SCO). **Light:** D. Simon (ROM). **L. Welter:** B. Ulusoy (TUR). **Welter:** O. Bouts (UKR). **L. Middle:** O. Bukalo (UKR). **Middle:** V. Plettnev (RUS). **L. Heavy:** A. Derevtsov (RUS). **Heavy:** C. O'Grady (IRL). **S. Heavy:** D. Savvine (RUS). **Silver medal:** G. Murphy (SCO). **Bronze medal:** N. Linford (ENG).

Birmingham, England - 1997
L. Fly: G. Balakshine (RUS). **Fly:** K. Dzhamoloudinov (RUS). **Bantam:** A. Shaiduline (RUS). **Feather:** D. Marciukaitis (LIT). **Light:** D. Baranov (RUS). **L. Welter:** A. Mishine (RUS). **Welter:** D. Yuldashev (UKR). **L. Middle:** A. Catic (GER). **Middle:** D. Lebedev (RUS). **L. Heavy:** V. Uzelkov (UKR). **Heavy:** S. Koeber (GER). **S. Heavy:** D. Pirozhenko (RUS). **Silver medal:** S. Miller (ENG). **Bronze medals:** S. Burke (ENG), M. Dean (ENG), P. Pierson (ENG), M. Lee (IRE).

Rijeka, Croatia - 1999
L. Fly: Kibalyuk (UKR). **Fly:** A. Bakhtin (RUS). **Bantam:** V. Simion (ROM). **Feather:** Kiutkhukow (BUL). **Light:** Pontilov (RUS). **L. Welter:** G. Ajetovic (YUG). **Welter:** S. Nouaouria (FRA). **L. Middle:** S. Kazantsev (RUS). **Middle:** D. Tsariouk (RUS). **L. Heavy:** Alexeev (RUS). **Heavy:** Alborov (RUS). **S. Heavy:** Soukhoverkov (RUS). **Bronze medal:** S. Birch (ENG).

Sarejevo, Croatia - 2001
L. Fly: A. Taratokin (RUS). **Fly:** E. Abzalimov (RUS). **Bantam:** G. Kovaljov (RUS). **Feather:** M. Hratchev (RUS). **Light:** S. Aydin (TUR). **L. Welter:** D. Mikulin (RUS). **Welter:** O. Bokalo (UKR). **L. Middle:** M. Korobov (RUS). **Middle:** I. Bogdanov (UKR). **L. Heavy:** R. Kahkijev (RUS). **Heavy:** V. Zuyev (BE). **S. Heavy:** I. Timurziejev (RUS). **Bronze medal:** K. Anderson (SCO).

Warsaw, Poland - 2003
L. Fly: P. Bedak (HUN). **Fly:** A. Ganev (RUS). **Bantam:** M. Tretiak (UKR). **Feather:** A. Alexandru (ROM). **Light:** A. Aleksiev (RUS). **L. Welter:** T. Tabotadze (GER). **Welter:** Z. Baisangurov (RUS). **Middle:** J. Machoncev (RUS). **L. Heavy:** I. Michalkin (RUS). **Heavy:** Y. Romanov (RUS). **S. Heavy:** D. Arshba (RUS). **Bronze medal:** S. Smith (ENG), F. Gavin (ENG), J. O'Donnell (ENG), T. Jeffries (ENG).

Tallinn, Estonia - 2005
L. Fly: S. Vodopyanov (RUS). **Fly:** S. Mamodov (AZE). **Bantam:** A. Akhba (RUS). **Feather:** M. Ignatev (RUS). **Light:** I. Iksanov (RUS). **L. Welter:** A.Zamkovoy (RUS). **Welter:** M. Koptyakov (RUS). **Middle:** N. Skiarov (RUS). **L.Heavy:** D. Chudinov (RUS). **Heavy:** S. Kalchugin (RUS). **S. Heavy:** A.Volkov (RUS). **Bronze medal:** J. Joyce (IRL).

Sombor, Serbia - 2007
L.Fly: M.Dvinskiy (RUS). **Fly:** M.Aloyan (RUS). **Bantam:** M.Maguire (ENG). **Feather:** B.Shelestyuk (UKR). **Light:** V.Shipunov (RUS). **L.Welter:** D.Lazarev (UKR). **Welter:** Y.Khytrov (UKR). **Middle:** N.Jovanovic (SER). **L.Heavy:**

E.Yakushev (RUS). **Heavy:** V.Kudukhov (RUS). **S.Heavy:** M.Babanin (RUS). Silver medals: K.Saeed (ENG), T.Fury (ENG).

Szczecin, Poland - 2009
L.Fly: E. Mamishzade (AZE). **Fly:** K. Aylazyan (ARM). **Bantam:** R. Abdurakhmanov (RUS). **Feather:** M. Ward (ENG). **Light:** E. Petrauskas (LIT). **L.Welter:** A. Besputin (RUS). **Welter:** J. Quigley (IRL). **Middle:** T. Zeuge (GER). **L.Heavy:** E. Tishchenko (RUS). **Heavy:** S. Varga (HUN). **S.Heavy:** D. Mansour (CRO). **Silver medal:** M. Heffron (ENG).

Commonwealth Champions, 1930-2006
Hamilton, Canada - 1930
Fly: W. Smith (SAF). **Bantam:** H. Mizler (ENG). **Feather:** F. Meacham (ENG). **Light:** J. Rolland (SCO). **Welter:** L. Hall (SAF). **Middle:** F. Mallin (ENG). **L. Heavy:** J. Goyder (ENG). **Heavy:** V. Stuart (ENG). **Silver medals:** T. Pardoe (ENG), T. Holt (SCO). **Bronze medals:** A. Lyons (SCO), A. Love (ENG), F. Breeman (ENG).

Wembley, England - 1934
Fly: P. Palmer (ENG). **Bantam:** F. Ryan (ENG). **Feather:** C. Cattarall (SAF). **Light:** L. Cook (AUS). **Welter:** D. McCleave (ENG). **Middle:** A. Shawyer (ENG). **L. Heavy:** G. Brennan (ENG). **Heavy:** P. Floyd (ENG). **Silver medals:** A. Barnes (WAL), J. Jones (WAL), F. Taylor (WAL), J. Holton (SCO). **Bronze medals:** J. Pottinger (WAL), T. Wells (SCO), H. Moy (ENG), W. Duncan (NIR), J. Magill (NIR), Lord D. Douglas-Hamilton (SCO).

Melbourne, Australia - 1938
Fly: J. Joubert (SAF). **Bantam:** W. Butler (ENG). **Feather:** A. Henricus (CEY). **Light:** H. Groves (ENG). **Welter:** W. Smith (AUS). **Middle:** D. Reardon (WAL). **L. Heavy:** N. Wolmarans (SAF). **Heavy:** T. Osborne (CAN). **Silver medals:** J. Watson (SCO), M. Dennis (ENG). **Bronze medals:** H. Cameron (SCO), J. Wilby (ENG).

Auckland, New Zealand - 1950
Fly: H. Riley (SCO). **Bantam:** J. van Rensburg (SAF). **Feather:** H. Gilliland (SCO). **Light:** R. Latham (ENG). **Welter:** T. Ratcliffe (ENG). **Middle:** T. van Schalkwyk (SAF). **L. Heavy:** D. Scott (ENG). **Heavy:** F. Creagh (NZL). **Bronze medal:** P. Brander (ENG).

Vancouver, Canada - 1954
Fly: R. Currie (SCO). **Bantam:** J. Smillie (SCO). **Feather:** L. Leisching (SAF). **Light:** P. van Staden (SR). **L. Welter:** M. Bergin (CAN). **Welter:** N. Gargano (ENG). **L. Middle:** W. Greaves (CAN). **Middle:** J. van de Kolff (SAF). **L. Heavy:** P. van Vuuren (SAF). **Heavy:** B. Harper (ENG). **Silver medals:** M. Collins (WAL), F. McQuillan (SCO). **Bronze medals:** D. Charnley (ENG), B. Wells (ENG).

Cardiff, Wales - 1958
Fly: J. Brown (SCO). **Bantam:** H. Winstone (WAL). **Feather:** W. Taylor (AUS). **Light:** R. McTaggart (SCO). **L. Welter:** H. Loubscher (SAF). **Welter:** J. Greyling (SAF). **L. Middle:** G. Webster (SAF). **Middle:** T. Milligan (NIR). **L. Heavy:** A. Madigan (AUS). **Heavy:** D. Bekker (SAF). **Silver medals:** T. Bache (ENG), M. Collins (WAL), J. Jordan (NIR), R. Kane (SCO), S. Pearson (ENG), A. Higgins (WAL), D. Thomas (ENG). **Bronze medals:** P. Lavery (NIR), D. Braithwaite (WAL), R. Hanna (NIR), A. Owen (SCO), J. McClory (NIR), J. Cooke (ENG), J. Jacobs (ENG), B. Nancurvis (ENG), R. Scott (SCO), W. Brown (WAL), J. Caiger (ENG), W. Bannon (SCO), R. Pleace (WAL).

Perth, Australia - 1962
Fly: R. Mallon (SCO). **Bantam:** J. Dynevor (AUS). **Feather:** J. McDermott (SCO). **Light:** E. Blay (GHA). **L. Welter:** C. Quartey (GHA). **Welter:** W. Coe (NZL). **L. Middle:** H. Mann (CAN). **Middle:** M. Calhoun (JAM). **L. Heavy:** A. Madigan (AUS). **Heavy:** G. Oywello (UGA). **Silver medals:** R. McTaggart (SCO), J. Pritchett (ENG). **Bronze medals:** M. Pye (ENG), P. Benneyworth (ENG), B. Whelan (ENG), B. Brazier (ENG), C. Rice (NIR), T. Menzies (SCO), H. Christie (NIR), A. Turmel (CI).

Kingston, Jamaica - 1966
Fly: S. Shittu (GHA). **Bantam:** E. Ndukwu (NIG). **Feather:** P. Waruinge (KEN). **Light:** A. Andeh (NIG). **L. Welter:** J. McCourt (NIR). **Welter:** E. Blay (GHA). **L. Middle:** M. Rowe (ENG). **Middle:** J. Darkey (GHA). **L. Heavy:** R. Tighe (ENG). **Heavy:** W. Kini (NZL). **Silver medals:** P. Maguire (NIR), R. Thurston (ENG), R. Arthur (ENG), T. Imrie (SCO). **Bronze medals:** S. Lockhart (NIR), A. Peace (SCO), F. Young (NIR), J. Turpin (ENG), D. McAlinden (NIR).

Edinburgh, Scotland - 1970
L. Fly: J. Odwori (UGA). **Fly:** D. Needham (ENG). **Bantam:** S. Shittu (GHA). **Feather:** P. Waruinge (KEN). **Light:** A. Adeyemi (NIG). **L. Welter:** M. Muruli (UGA). **Welter:** E. Ankudey (GHA). **L. Middle:** T. Imrie (SCO). **Middle:** J. Conteh (ENG). **L. Heavy:** F. Ayinla (NIG). **Heavy:** B. Masanda (UGA). **Silver medals:** T. Davies (WAL), J. Gillan (SCO), D. Davies (WAL), J. McKinty (NIR). **Bronze medals:** M. Abrams (ENG), A. McHugh (SCO), D. Larmour (NIR), S. Oglivie (SCO), A. Richardson (ENG), T. Joyce (SCO), P. Doherty (NIR), J. Rafferty (SCO), L. Stevens (ENG).

Christchurch, New Zealand - 1974
L. Fly: S. Muchoki (KEN). **Fly:** D. Larmour (NIR). **Bantam:** P. Cowdell (ENG). **Feather:** E. Ndukwu (NIG). **Light:** A. Kalule (UGA). **L. Welter:** O. Nwankpa (NIG). **Welter:** M. Muruli (UGA). **L. Middle:** L. Mwale (ZAM). **Middle:** F. Lucas (STV). **L. Heavy:** W. Knight (ENG). **Heavy:** N. Meade (ENG). **Silver medals:** E. McKenzie (WAL), A. Harrison (SCO). **Bronze medals:** J. Bambrick (SCO), J. Douglas (SCO), J. Rodgers (NIR), S. Cooney (SCO), R. Davies (ENG), C. Speare (ENG), G. Ferris (NIR).

Edmonton, Canada - 1978
L. Fly: S. Muchoki (KEN). **Fly:** M. Irungu (KEN). **Bantam:** B. McGuigan (NIR). **Feather:** A. Nelson (GHA). **Light:** G. Hamill (NIR). **L. Welter:** W. Braithwaite (GUY). **Welter:** M. McCallum (JAM). **L. Middle:** K. Perlette (CAN). **Middle:** P. McElwaine (AUS). **L. Heavy:** R. Fortin (CAN). **Heavy:** J. Awome (ENG). **Silver medals:** J. Douglas (SCO), K. Beattie (NIR), D. Parkes (ENG), V. Smith (ENG). **Bronze medals:** H. Russell (NIR), M. O'Brien (ENG), J. McAllister (SCO), T. Feal (WAL).

Brisbane, Australia - 1982
L. Fly: A. Wachire (KEN). **Fly:** M. Mutua (KEN). **Bantam:** J. Orewa (NIG). **Feather:** P. Konyegwachie (NIG). **Light:** H. Khalili (KEN). **L. Welter:** C. Ossai (NIG). **Welter:** C. Pyatt (ENG). **L. Middle:** S. O'Sullivan (CAN). **Middle:** J. Price (ENG). **L. Heavy:** F. Sani (FIJ). **Heavy:** W. de Wit (CAN). **Silver medals:** J. Lyon (ENG), J. Kelly (SCO), R. Webb (NIR), P. Hanlon (ENG), J. McDonnell (ENG), N. Croombes (ENG), H. Hylton (ENG). **Bronze medals:** R. Gilbody (ENG), C. McIntosh (ENG), R. Corr (NIR).

Edinburgh, Scotland - 1986
L. Fly: S. Olson (CAN). **Fly:** J. Lyon (ENG). **Bantam:** S. Murphy (ENG). **Feather:** B. Downey (CAN). **Light:** A. Dar (CAN). **L. Welter:** H. Grant (CAN). **Welter:** D. Dyer (ENG). **L. Middle:** D. Sherry (CAN). **Middle:** R. Douglas (ENG). **L. Heavy:** J. Moran (ENG). **Heavy:** J. Peau (NZL). **S. Heavy:** L. Lewis (CAN). **Silver medals:** M. Epton (ENG), R. Nash (NIR), P. English (ENG), N. Haddock (WAL), J. McAlister (SCO), H. Lawson (SCO), D. Young (SCO), A. Evans (WAL). **Bronze medals:** W. Docherty (SCO), J. Todd (NIR), K. Webber (WAL), G. Brooks (SCO), J. Wallace (SCO), C. Carleton (NIR), J. Jacobs (ENG), B. Lowe (NIR), D. Denny (NIR), G. Thomas (WAL), A. Mullen (SCO), G. Ferrie (SCO), P. Tinney (NIR), B. Pullen (WAL), E. Cardouza (ENG), J. Oyebola (ENG), J. Sillitoe (CI).

Auckland, New Zealand - 1990
L. Fly: J. Juuko (UGA). **Fly:** W. McCullough (NIR). **Bantam:** S. Mohammed (NIG). **Feather:** J. Irwin (ENG). **Light:** G. Nyakana (UGA). **L. Welter:** C. Kane (SCO). **Welter:** D. Defiagbon (NIG). **L. Middle:** R. Woodhall (ENG). **Middle:** C. Johnson (CAN). **L. Heavy:** J. Akhasamba (KEN). **Heavy:** G. Onyango (KEN). **S. Heavy:** M. Kenny (NZL). **Bronze medals:** D. Anderson (SCO), M. Edwards (ENG), P. Douglas (NIR).

Victoria, Canada - 1994
L. Fly: H. Ramadhani (KEN). **Fly:** P. Shepherd (SCO). **Bantam:** R. Peden (AUS). **Feather:** C. Patton (CAN). **Light:** M. Strange (CAN). **L. Welter:** P. Richardson (ENG). **Welter:** N. Sinclair (NIR). **L. Middle:** M. Renaghan (NIR), M. Winters (NIR), J. Wilson (SCO). **Middle:** R. Donaldson (CAN). **L. Heavy:** D. Brown (CAN). **Heavy:** O. Ahmed (KEN). **S. Heavy:** D. Dokiwari (NIG). **Silver medals:** S. Oliver (ENG), J. Cook (WAL), M. **Bronze medals:** D. Costello (ENG), J. Townsley (SCO), D. Williams (ENG).

Kuala Lumpar, Malaysia - 1998
L. Fly: S. Biki (MAS). **Fly:** R. Sunee (MRI). **Bantam:** M. Yomba (TAN). **Feather:** A. Arthur (SCO). **Light:** R. Narh (GHA). **L. Welter:** M. Strange (CAN). **Welter:** J. Molitor (CAN). **L. Middle:** C. Bessey (ENG). **Middle:** J. Pearce (ENG). **L. Heavy:** C. Fry (ENG). **Heavy:** M. Simmons (CAN). **S. Heavy:** A. Harrison (ENG). **Silver medal:** L. Cunningham (ENG). **Bronze medals:** G. Jones (ENG), A. McLean (ENG), C. McNeil (SCO), J. Townsley (SCO), B. Magee (NIR), K. Evans (WAL).

Manchester, England - 2002
L. Fly: M. Ali Qamar (IND). **Fly:** K. Kanyanta (ZAM). **Bantam:** J. Kane (AUS). **Feather:** H. Ali (PAK). **Light:** J. Arthur (WAL). **L. Welter:** D. Barker (ENG). **Welter:** D. Geale (AUS). **L. Middle:** J. Pascal (CAN). **Middle:** P. Miller (AUS). **L. Heavy:** J. Albert (NIG). **Heavy:** J. Douglas (CAN). **S. Heavy:** D. Dolan (ENG). **Silver medals:** D. Langley (ENG), P. Smith (ENG), S. Birch (ENG). **Bronze medals:** M. Moran (ENG), A. Morris (ENG), C. McEwan (SCO), A. Young (SCO), K. Evans (WAL).

Melbourne, Australia - 2006
L. Fly: J. Utoni (NAM). **Fly:** D. Broadhurst (ENG). **Bantam:** G. Kumar (FIJ). **Feather:** S. Smith (ENG). **Light:** F. Gavin (ENG). **L. Welter:** J. Cox (ENG). **Welter:** B. Mwelase (SA). **Middle:** J. Fletcher (AUS). **L. Heavy:** K. Anderson (SCO). **Heavy:** B. Pitt (AUS). **S. Heavy:** D. Price (ENG). **Silver medals:** D. Langley (ENG), K. Evans (WAL). **Bronze medals:** M. Nasir (WAL), D. Edwards (WAL), J. Crees (WAL), N. Perkins (ENG), J. Degale (ENG).

Directory of Ex-Boxers' Associations
by Ray Caulfield

BOURNEMOUTH Founded 1980. HQ: The Cricketers, Windham Road, off Ashley Road, Bournemouth. Dai Dower MBE (P); Dave Fry (C); Peter Judge (T & VC); Jack Streek (S), 38 St Leonard's Farm, Ringwood Road, Ferndown, Dorset BH22 0AG (0120 289 4647)

BRIGHTON Formed 2007. HQ: Southwick Football Club, Old Barn Way, off Manor Hall Way, Southwick, Sussex. Alan Minter (P); Ernie Price (C); John McNeil (VC); Mick Smith (PRO); Karen Knight (T & S), 1 Tall Trees, Penstone Park, Lancing, West Sussex BN15 9AG (0190 376 6893). E-mail: kazzie.knight@homecall.co.uk

CORNWALL Founded 1989. HQ: Upper Tolcarne House, Burras, Wendron, Helston. Salvo Nucciforo (VC); Eric Bradshaw (T); Stan Cullis (P & PRO), Upper Tolcarne House, Burras, Wendron, Helston, Cornwall TR13 0JD (0120 983 1463). E-mail: stan@cullis1.freeserve.co.uk

CROYDON Founded 1982. HQ: Ivy House Club, Campbell Road, West Croydon. Gilbert Allnutt (P); Barry Penny (C); vacant (VC); Simon Euan-Smith (S & PRO), 151 Upper Selsdon Road, Sanderstead, Surrey CR2 0DO (0208 407 0785)

EASTERN AREA Founded 1973. HQ: Coach & Horses, Union Street, Norwich. Mick Smith (P); Bill Smith (VC); Ron Springall (S & T); Clive Campling (C), 54 Robson Road, Norwich, Norfolk NR5 8NZ. (Mick Smith: 01760 720271)

HOME COUNTIES Founded 2005. HQ: Golden Lion Public House, High Street, London Colney, Herts. Terry Downes (P); Bob Williams (C); Ann Ayles (T); Dave Ayles (S), 3 Burgess Close, Dunstable, Beds LU6 3EU (01582 864274). E-mail: d.ayles@ntlworld.com

HULL & EAST YORKSHIRE Founded 1993. HQ: Crooked Billett, Holdens Road, Hull or Kings Arms, King Street, Bridlington. Charles McGhee (C); Johnny Borrill (P); Len Storey (T); Bert Smith (S), 54 St Aidan Road, Bridlington, E. Yorks (01262 672 573)

IPSWICH Founded 1970. HQ: Loco Club, Station Street, Stoke, Ipswich. Alby Kingham (P); Chris Collins (PRO); Vic Thurlow (C & T); Eric Roper (S); contact number (01473 712684)

IRISH Founded 1973. HQ: National Boxing Stadium, South Circular Road, Dublin. Val Harris (P); Martin Gannon (C); Tommy Butler (T); Paddy O'Reilly (VC); Willie Duggan (S), 175 Kimmage Road West, Dublin 6W

KENT Founded 1967. HQ: RAFA Club, Dock Road, Chatham. Harry Doherty (P); Bill Quinton (C); Paul Nihill MBE (S, PRO & T), Flat 20, Yeoman House, Princess Street, Rochester, Kent ME1 2LW (07984 531 828)

LEEDS Founded 1952. HQ: North Leeds WMC, Lincoln Green Road, Leeds. Alan Richardson (P); Kevin Cunningham (C); Peter Selby (S); Alan Alster (T); Frank Johnson (PRO), 82 Windmill Chase, Rothwell, Leeds, Yorks LS26 0XB (0113 288 7753)

LEICESTER Founded 1972. HQ: The Jungle Club, Checketts Road, Leicester. Mick Greaves (P & C); Fred Roberts (T), Alan Parr (S & PRO), 22 Hewes Close, Glen Parva, Leicester LE2 9NU (0116 277 9327/0791 332 3950). E-mail: alan.parr3@btinternet.com

LONDON Founded 1971. HQ; The Queen Mary College, Bancroft Road, Mile End, London E1. Stephen Powell (P); Micky O'Sullivan (C); Charlie Wright (VC); Ray Caulfield (T); Mrs Mary Powell (S), 36 St Peters Street, Islington, London N1 8JT (0207 226 9032). E-mail: marypowell@btconnect.com

MANCHESTER Founded 1968. HQ: The Crown & Cushion, Corporation Street, Manchester. Tommy Proffitt (LP); Jack Edwards (P); Neville Tetlow (VC); Kenny Baker (T); Eddie Sinclair (PRO); Jimmy Lewis (C); Eddie Copeland (S), 9 Lakeside, Hadfield, Glossop, Derbys SK13 1HW (0145 786 8142). E-mail: edwin@edwin8.wanadoo.co.uk

MERSEYSIDE Founded 1973. HQ: The Basement Club, Hockenhall Alley, Liverpool. Harry Scott (P); Tony Smith (VP); Terry Carson (C & PRO); Jim Jenkinson (S & T), 13 Brooklands Avenue, Waterloo, Liverpool, Merseyside L22 3XY (0151 928 0301). E-mail: mersey-wirralformerboxers @hotmail.com. Website: www.mfba.org.uk

MIDLANDS Founded 2002. HQ: The Portland Pavilion, Portland Road, Edgbaston, Birmingham. Bunny Johnson (P); Martin Florey (C); Paul Rowson (VC); Stephen Florey (T); Jerry Hjelter (S & PRO), 67 Abberley Avenue, Stourport on Severn, Warwicks DY13 0LY (0129 987 9907). E-mail: jerryhjboxing@hotmail. com. Website: www.midlandexboxersassociation.fortunecity.com/index.html

NORTHAMPTONSHIRE Founded 1981. HQ: Park Inn, Silver Street, Northampton. Dick Rogers (P); Mick Doran (VP); Gil Wilson (C); Brian Thomas (VC); George Ward (PRO); Mrs Pam Ward (S & T), 6 Derwent Close, Kings Heath, Northampton NN5 7JS (0160 458 3057)

NORTHERN FEDERATION Founded 1974. Several member EBAs. Annual Gala. Geoff Shaw (P); Terry Carson (C); Eddie Copeland (S & T), 9 Lakeside, Hadfield, Glossop, Derbys SK13 1HW

NORTHERN IRELAND Founded 1970. HQ: Ulster Sports Club, High Street, Belfast. Gerry Hassett (P); Cecil Martin (C); S.Thompson (T); Terry Milligan (S), 32 Rockdale Street, Belfast BT12 7PA

NORTH STAFFS & SOUTH CHESHIRE Founded 1969. HQ: The Roe Buck, Wedgwood Place, Burslem, Stoke on Trent. Roy Simms (C); Larry Parkes (VC); John Greatbach (T); Billy Tudor (P). Les Dean (S & PRO), Trees, Pinewood Drive, Ashley Heath, Market Drayton, Shropshire TF9 4PA (01630 672 484)

NORWICH Founded 1990. HQ: Wymondham Snooker Club, Town Green, Wymondham, Norfolk. Les King (P & C); Len Jarvis (T); Reg Harris (S), contact number (0195 360 3997)

NOTTINGHAM Founded 1979. HQ: The Duke of Cambridge, Carlton Road, Nottingham. Len Chorley (P); Walter Spencer (C); Mick Smith (VC); Gary Rooksby (T); John Kinsella (PRO); Graham Rooksby (S), 42 Spinney Road, Keyworth, Notts NG12 5LN (0115 937 5242). E-mail: nebsa@rooksby.com

PLYMOUTH Founded 1982. HQ: Stoke Social Club, Devonport Road, Plymouth. Tom Pryce-Davies (P); Jimmy Ryan (C); Jimmy Bevel (VC); Arthur Willis (T); Pat Crago (S & PRO), 8 Hawkinge Gardens, Ernsettle, Plymouth, Devon PL5 2RJ (0175 236 6339). E-mail: crago@blueyonder.co.uk

PRESTON Founded 1973. HQ: Barney's Piano Bar, Church Street, Preston. John Allen (C & S); Eddie Monahan (P); Bobby Rhodes (T), 1 Norris Street, Preston, Lancs PR1 7PX

ST HELENS Founded 1983. HQ: Royal Naval Association, Volunteer Street, St Helens. Ray Britch (C); Tommy McNamara (T); Paul Britch (S), 16 Oxley Street, Sutton, St Helens, Merseyside WA9 3PE

SCOTTISH Founded 1997. HQ: Iron Horse Public House, West Nile Street, Glasgow. John McCluskey (P); Frank O'Donnell (LP); Phil McIntyre (C); Bob Keddie (VC); Peter Baines (T), E-mail: p.baines20@ntlworld.com; Hugh Dickson (S), 3 Spring Bank Gardens, Falkirk FK2 7DE (01324 617303)

SHEFFIELD & SOUTH YORKSHIRE Founded 1974. Reformed 2002. HQ: Handsworth Social Club, 13 Hall Road, Handsworth, Sheffield (0114 269 3019). Billy Calvert (P & T); Harry Carnell (C); Eric Goodlad (VC). (Billy Calvert: 01909 568884)

SQUARE RING (TORBAY) Founded 1978. HQ: Snooty Fox Hotel, St Marychurch. Ken Wittey (C); Johnny Mudge (S); Jim Banks (T); Paul King (P & VC), 8 Winchester Avenue, Torquay, Devon TQ2 8AR

SUNDERLAND Founded 1959. HQ: Railway Club, Holmeside, Sunderland, Tyne & Wear. George Martin (P); Ted Lynn (C); Gordon (Pedro) Phillips (VC); Geoff Rushworth (PRO); Les Simm (T & S), 21 Orchard Street, Pallion, Sunderland, Tyne & Wear SR4 6QL (0191 514 1809)

SUSSEX Founded 1974. Reformed 2003. HQ: Hove Conservative Club, 102 Blatchington Road, Hove BN3 3DL. Tommy Mellis (P); Mick Smith (PRO); Steve Wood (C); Dennis Smith (VC); Rob Benson (S & T); contact number (077799 740 213). E-mail: HYPERLINK "mailto: peter.benson@730ntlworld.com" peter.benson@730ntlworld.com. Website: www.sussexexboxers.com

TYNESIDE Founded 1970. HQ: The Pelaw Social Club, Heworth House, Kirkstone Road, Pelaw, Gateshead. Maxie Walsh (P, PRO & C); Dave McCormick (VC); Malcolm Dinning (T); Maxie Walsh (P, C & S), c/o 9 Prendwick Court, Hebburn, Tyne & Wear NE31 2NQ (0191 483 4267)

WELSH Founded 1976. HQ: Rhydyfelin Labour Club, Pontypridd. Patron: Lord Brooks of Tremorfa. Wynford Jones (P); John Floyd (C); Danny Davies (VC); Mark Warner (T); Don James (S), 5 Aeron Terrace, Twynyroyn, Merthyr Tydfil, South Wales C47 0LN

WIRRAL Founded 1973. Reformed 2003. HQ: RNA Club, Thornbury Park Road East, Birkenhead. Frank Johnson (P); Pat Garry (T); Terry Carson (C); Pat McAteer (VC); Alan Crowther (S), 15 Scythia Close, New Ferry, Wirral, Merseyside CH62 1HH (0151 645 0466). Website: www.lmu.livjm.ac.uk/inmylife/channels/sport/1116.htm

The above information is set at the time of going to press and no responsibility can be taken for any changes in officers or addresses of HQs that may happen between then and publication or changes that have not been notified to me.

ABBREVIATIONS

P - President. HP - Honorary President. LP - Life President. AP - Acting President. C - Chairman. VC - Vice Chairman. T - Treasurer. S - Secretary. PRO - Public Relations Officer and/or Press Officer.

Midlands EBA and London EBA working together to raise funds for a British Boxing Hall of Fame: PJ Rowson presenting the cheque from the Hope and Glory Boxing Dinner sponsored by Speedy Hire PLC. Eighteen World champions, 33 British champions and two Olympic gold medallists were present in what was a large gathering of champions, who all came to give support for the Hall of Fame that will honour all our great champions. Left to right: PJ Rowson MEBA, Stephen Powell LEBA, Charlie Wright LEBA, Ray Caulfield LEBA and Martin Florey MEBA

Obituaries
by Derek O'Dell

It is impossible to list everyone, but I have again done my best to include final tributes for as many of the well-known boxers and other familiar names within the sport who have passed away since the 2009 *BBBoC British Boxing Yearbook* was published. We honour them and remember them.

ABBEY John Nii *From* Ghana. *Died* 1 February 2009, aged 26. John, residing in Croydon, Surrey, was fatally stabbed at a bus stop when accompanying his daughter. He represented Ghana as a featherweight in the 2002 Commonwealth Games in Manchester and was due to make his debut as a professional. A benefit night to raise money for his five children was held at Streatham. Three men were arrested and one charged with murder following this event.

A'COURT Clem *From* Morden. *Died* March 2009, aged 77. I remember Clem well when he was punching for pay under the management of Croydon's Alf Hart. Freddie March, an old friend sadly now deceased, was a regular sparring partner. Clem was a good amateur who won several bantamweight titles while boxing for Epsom and Ewell ABC and much was expected from him as a professional. He turned pro in 1953, starting with a loss to Fred Angel that he quickly avenged, and retired after Tommy Gillen of Hayes beat him in two rounds at Epsom Baths towards the end of 1954. Clem twice beat Johnny Barnham, a brother of the crack lightweight, Tommy, and drew with *Boxing News* office boy, Harry Alley. Although being too good for Jimmy Frew and George Connors, he could never get the decision over Cliff Giles in any of their three meetings. On retiring, Clem moved to Norfolk and worked for a removal firm. He was married with two children who, with his wife Joyce, survive him.

AGUILLON Daniel *From* Mexico City, Mexico. *Died* 18 October 2008, aged 24. There are no names in Daniel Aguillon's record to warrant a WBC Fecarbox super-featherweight title shot against unbeaten Alejandro Sanabria last October. Daniel had been matched with novices throughout his 17 previous outings but when his big opportunity arose he took it with both hands and, in a fight that had thrills and spills galore, he stumbled at the last hurdle. Sanabria, having his 16th fight against much better opposition than that of his challenger, was on the deck in the opening round but Daniel could not keep him there and was himself down in the fourth. Fortunes swayed to and fro. Going into the last session, Daniel needed to win it to force a draw on two of the judges' cards but he had given his all and ran out of steam. When Sanabria put him down again, that was it and after lapsing in to a coma he passed away five days later.

ALBERT Howie *From* Secacus, New Jersey, USA. *Died* January 2009, aged 86. The New Year was only hours old when the news arrived of Howie's death. He had been ailing for some time, being able to climb stairs with only the utmost difficulty. His primary role in boxing was that of a fighters' manager. From his New York office, in partnership with Gil Clancy, he handled the fight affairs of Rodrigo Valdez, George Foreman, Jerry Quarry, Juan LaPorte and Emile Griffith. In 1990 his services to boxing were recognised when he was inducted into the New Jersey Hall of Fame.

ALEXANDER Willie *From* Chester, Pennsylvania, USA. *Died* 13 October 2008, aged 81. Willie was a featherweight with a low percentage of wins in mainly eight-round fights. That he answered the opening bell 74 times speaks for his crowd-pleasing style and he was constantly in demand by local promoters and matchmakers. The lack of a heavy punch handicapped him, most of his 15 wins going the full distance. He turned pro in 1944 with scant success until the 1950s when experience gained from 70 odd fights enabled him to twice beat Filbertoi Osario and take 'name' fighters, Miguel Berrios and Fernando Gagnon, the distance.

AMBROSE Billy *From* Stepney. *Died* 23 April 2009, aged 79. It took a good'un to beat Jeff Tite in the early 1950s and Billy did it twice. The first time was a disqualification victory. A return over eight rounds at Manor Place Baths showed that victory was deserved in both cases. A one-punch knockout fighter, he turned pro in 1948 and scored three clean knockouts in his first four fights. Kay Kalio was the first man to beat him, but Billy bounced back with a points win over Frank Baldwin of British Honduras before upsetting the highly fancied Eric McQuade by a quick kayo. He also knocked out Bob Burniston, Bobby Baines and Johnny McLaren. Kit Pompey spoiled a winning streak in 1951 when he became only one of two men to beat Billy inside the distance. That was the last loss on his record that shows victories over Kit Pompey, Israel Boyle, Piet van Staden, Reg McMurdie and Pete Davis of Slough. As an amateur he lost to the great CSMI Johnny Ryan in an attempt to win an ABA title at welterweight. He turned professional under the management of Fred Govier and finished as a middleweight in 1952 with a win over the fighting fireman from the Borough, Bob Cleaver.

ANGELL Mick *From* Cricklewood. *Died* April 2009, aged 78. Mick was a busy prelim-fighter whose career was cut short by a back injury after his 28th fight. He was a middleweight and one of two fighting brothers. In more recent times, Mick's son, Steve, also donned the gloves for pay. My record for Mick shows 14 wins, two draws and 12 losses from July 1951 to November 1952. His best victories came against Arthur Garrett and Ken Tisor. He was beaten twice by that fine Eastern Counties' scrapper, Johnny Pipe and held Bobby Manito and Ronnie Davis to drawn decisions. Other notables he fought were Paul King, Jack Thornbury and Noel Sinfield.

ARBOLEDA Jose *From* Panama. *Died* 7 August 2009, aged 27. Jose died after a bus he was travelling in crashed and left him with terminal terminal head injuries as well as severe damage to his lungs and liver. He was a featherweight with a 29-fight record that shows four defeats. Turning professional in 2002, Jose won the WBA's Fedalatin super-bantamweight title in 2004 by beating Jose Francisco Mendoza. He had put his title on the line six times up to his death, with his last defence also being an eliminator for the more prestigious WBA bantamweight title. In the next series, he was eliminated by Fernando Beltram, but he was still hopeful of fighting for the IBF super-bantam title again after failing in his first crack at the title in 2007.

ARGUELLO Alexis *From* Managua, Nicaragua. *Died* July 2009, aged 57. This was one of the great champions of modern times – a title-holder at three weight divisions and the man who destroyed Ruben Olivares, Alfredo Escalara and Ruben Castillo. Alexis came from poor beginnings in Managua to fight his way to the top of his profession. A tall, power-punching boxer with a keen, analytical brain, he was first challenging for world honours at the age of 21. He found the WBA featherweight champion, Ernesto Marcel, too ring-wise and lost the decision, yet his day would come. By the following year he had matured into a formidable fighter with clear signs of approaching greatness. He took out Ruben Olivares with one punch to gain the title that the latter had won from Marcel. Later, Alexis fought for another three world championships, winning two of them and losing against Aaron Pryor in an attempt to secure the WBA light-welterweight crown. That was in 1982 and Pryor also won the return, which convinced man from Nicaragua that his best days had gone. Alexis defended the title he won from Olivares four times, then won the WBC super-featherweight title from Alfredo Escalera in 1978. It was a brutal fight in which the champion was stopped in the 13th round. He fared worse in the return, being dropped twice before losing on a knockout. In a defence against Bobby Chacon, Alexis came from behind to stop his man. He was one of the division's big hitters. He had made six defences before turning his attention to the lightweight division where Scotland's Jim

Watt held the WBC title. They fought in London and Alexis returned home with yet another title to his name. Defences followed against Ray Mancini, Roberto Elizondo, James Busceme and Andrew Ganigan. The Pryor fights followed in 1982 and in between those matches he stopped Claude Noel. Soon after which he announced his retirement having never lost any of his world titles. Political unrest at home when revolutionary forces seized his property and froze his savings, led him to make several comebacks in which he beat Billy Costello and Pat Jefferson. An eight-year gap and a couple of meaningless fights followed before final retirement came in 1995. He threw his hat into the political arena and was elected mayor of Managua in 2008, but his private life was in turmoil. He found it difficult to cope with life outside of boxing and took to drugs and drink and there were hints of suspected improprieties during his rise in politics. Several times he spoke of suicide and it seems that he did take his own life. When his body was found a gun was in his hand.

Alexis Arguello

BACALLAO Hiram *From* Camaguey, Cuba. *Died* 11 September 2008, aged 70. Starting in 1957 Hiram won eight fights before losing to Jose Oliva, who he beat in a return match. In so doing, he won the Cuban flyweight championship. Notable wins followed over Mario DeLeon, Ramon Calatayud and Oscar Suarez. For beating Calatayud he took over the number nine spot in the world ratings. He split two decisions with Pedro Ortiz in Panama City and got his best result in Mexico City where he drew with Joe Medel. Hiram lost to Felix Gutierrez in Havana and when he travelled to Caracas for a big match with Larry Pineda, he was left disappointed. After nine rounds it was declared as 'no contest'. He came back after being inactive in 1962-63 to lose a ten rounder to Eduardo Hernandez and his name disappeared from the record books after that.

BAHAMA Yama *From* Bimini, Bahamas. *Died* June 2009, aged 75. This popular middleweight, born William Hohalis Butler in 1933, threw his first professional punch under the nom-de-ring of Yama Bahama in 1954. After a so-so start he got into his stride by the end of the year and went through his next 33 fights without loss. Wins over Paolo Melis, Hardy Smallwood and Gil Turner put him on the fringe of world class before Ted Lowry edged him out on a split decision in Michigan. A couple of good victories over Tex Gonzalez and Jimmy Martinez got him a match with Isaac Logart who outpointed him. Yama returned to his home turf to beat Willie Johnson and then lost narrowly in a rematch with Gil Turner in Miami Beach. He could go in with the best men and hold his own, fighting Phil Moyer, Kid Gavilan, Joe Miceli, Arthur King, Wilf Greaves, Victor Zalazar, Giancarlo Garbelli, Stan Harrington, Del Flanagan, Ted Wright, Joey Giambra, Emile Griffith, Gaylord Barnes, Luis Rodriguez and Farid Salim. In 1962 he campaigned back home in the Bahamas where he won all his seven fights even though he was, by then, fading. A loss to little-known Linnes Johnson at Miami Beach was his last fight. His record is a respectable 76 victories in 93 fights and his best wins were against Giambra, Gavilan, Turner, Moyer, Flanagan and Miceli.

BANWELL Gerry *From* Tonyrefail, Wales. *Died* 28 December 2008, aged 66. Welsh middleweight Gerry Banwell had 23 fights between 1962 and 1966. He beat Joe Falcon, Steve Ellwood, Eric Young, Jack Burley and Steve Richards but would have been wise to quit after beating Willie Fisher. That was his last win and the following five defeats, culminating in a stoppage by Liam Mullen, spoiled his won-lost statistics. In 23 contests he won 14 and lost nine.

BARLOW Tony *From* Manchester. *Died* 4 June 2009, aged 67. When reviewing the complete record, both amateur and professional for Tony, the overall impression is that his achievements were outstanding. He was a small man, well under five feet, and a southpaw who was unfazed by having to ply some of his trade in hostile foreign rings. He twice challenged for the British flyweight championship coming up against one of the better post-war title-holders in John McCluskey. Tony could never beat the Scot in four attempts. His pro career began in 1963 and he was

a busy fighter for a man active in a division that was not exactly overcrowded. Up until drawing with Monty Laud in November 1964 he'd had 18 fights with three losses. He avenged two of them and forced a draw with Graham Price who had previously outpointed him. Cuts plagued Tony throughout his fighting life and scarcity of opposition forced him to seek fights overseas in Switzerland and Johannesburg. He returned from Switzerland in 1967 to beat competent men in Winston van Guylenburg, George Hind and Orizu Obilaso, with whom he had previously boxed a draw. Another win over Obilaso in a good fight brought about a third meeting which Barlow lost on cuts. That was his last fight. Injuries and weight disadvantages meant that he had not achieved what had been expected of him after his foray as an amateur. He was an ABA finalist in 1962, losing to Mickey Pye, and an England rep with some stunning knockout wins on his scoresheet. In the 1962 ABA quarter-finals he knocked out Alan Rudkin's conqueror, Bobby Mallon, and the ex-champion, Mick Gushlow. Tony boxed for his country against Russia, scoring a stoppage win, and was once again a winner when England met Wales. Cancer was the cause of death. He is survived by a daughter, Joanne.

BLACK Frank *From* Dagenham. *Died* 7 December 2008, aged 73. Hours after returning from an east-London promotion, Frank a cuts-man, trainer and cornerman - one of the indispensable, unsung, staples of the game - had a massive heart-attack and died at his Dagenham home. Frank's involvement in boxing goes back years. After quitting active boxing in the unpaid ranks, Frank was dormant for some time before emerging as trainer for Reg Gullefer who was married to his sister. When Reg retired, Frank was asked to assist Terry Lawless who ran one of the most successful post-war boxing stables. He was to become deeply involved in working with Jimmy Tibbs and to train stars such as Jim Watt, Jimmy Flint, Gary Mason, John Stracey, Maurice Hope, Jimmy Anderson, Frank Bruno, Charlie Magri, Lloyd Honeyghan, Kirkland Laing etc. When the Lawless empire split, Frank went it alone and ran the famous Peacock gym and developed his own fighters' stable. He was a modest, quiet man and very highly respected as shown by the numerous mourners at his funeral and the tributes that poured in following the sad news of his sudden death.

BODAK Chuck *From* Gary, Indiana, USA. *Died* 5 February 2009, aged 92. A boxing manager and cornerman, Chuck, who worked with close on 50 world champions was a larger-than-life character whose long connection to boxing goes back to the days of Rocky Marciano. He was devoted to boxing. Chuck's services were recognised officially when he was inducted into the WBC Legends of Boxing Museum.

BOZZANO Giacomo (Mino) *From* Sestri Levante, Italy. *Died* 21 November 2008, aged 74. After fighting his way to the 1956 Olympic heavyweight semi-finals, Mino put together a fine professional record that contains some notable wins. Surprisingly, in a six-year campaign he never won a title despite being one of the best big men in Europe. Having run up 25 consecutive victories his name was entered for an elimination series to challenge for the European title, but Hans Kalbfell knocked him out inside a round and thereby exposed the Italian's vulnerability to jaw punches. Until then, he had shown impressive form, beating Joe Bygraves, Hans Friedrich, Maurice Mols, Uber Bacilieri, Lucien Touzard, Marcel Limage, Robert Duquesne, Franco Cavicci, Jose Gonzalez, Alaine Cherville, Sifa Kavalu and the former light-heavyweight champion of the world, Joey Maxim. Following the loss to Kalbfell, Mino rested for ten months before outpointing the awkward American, Bert Whitehurst, before he was matched with an unknown and inexperienced German named Gerhardt Zech. Zech went on to have a successful career but it was a major upset when he scored a clean knockout victory over the ring-rusty Italian. To his credit, Mino picked up the pieces and enjoyed some of his best wins. He knocked out Spain's Jose Gonzalez for the second time, beat Alain Cherville, Jose Peyre and Horst Niche (twice), then got a long-awaited shot at the Italian championship held by Sante Amonte. Instead of using his reach advantage, Mino chose to slug it out at close quarters, a tactic that played into Amonte's hands. By round three he was groggy and forced to concede defeat. He never fought again, but his gameness did much to dispel the notion that he could not take it.

Cesar Brion

BRION Cesar *From* Cordoba, Argentina. *Died* 9 July 2009, aged 84. Veteran British fans will remember Cesar, an Argentinian heavyweight, who was brought here in 1951 to test the potentiality of Jack Gardner, the new British champion. Cesar was too busy for him and his points victory showed that future world-title plans for the ex-guardsman were far too ambitious. In the gym I thought that Cesar looked ordinary but he got his act together when he got in the ring with Gardner. Before coming here he had beaten Charlie Norkus, Bill Weinberg, Bernie Reynolds and, significantly, Tami Mauriello. There were losses to Roland LaStarza before Joe Louis, old as he was, beat him on points (and later would do so again). Over the next three years Cesar beat Abel Cestac, Wes Bascom, Joe Kahut, Johnny Holman and Dan Bucceroni. There were losses to Bob Dunlap, Ezzard Charles and Bob Baker before he returned to Argentina to run up a series of wins over very moderate opposition prior to retiring in 1955 with 58 wins and 11 losses on his record.

BURNEY Tiggy *From* Faversham. *Died* October 2008, aged 69. Tiggy was a good amateur flyweight and popular in his local area. He turned pro in 1959, losing to Davey Whittaker in his first contest, before reverting back to the Simon Pure ranks.

BUTLER George *From* Camberwell. *Died* December 2008. In last year's list of obituaries, I confidently stated that Phil Digby was, before his death, the last living boxer to have fought at the Ring. I should have known better. George outlived Phil and there could well be more out there who performed at the Blackfriars Road venue. It was there, in April 1938, that George twice beat Bob Ransford. Like all of his known fights, they were over six rounds. Another interesting fact is that the Devonshire Club and Holborn Stadium were other arenas where George performed. His is a short record of ten fights, yet it is important because of the connection with places steeped in boxing history and because some of the men he fought went on to build up fine career records.

BUTLER Jackie *From* Preston. *Died* January 2009, aged 73. Jackie's last good win came in 1957 when he beat Jimmy Croll. In retrospect he should not have continued boxing when Mick Leahy stopped him two weeks later. He had four more fights without a win against rated opposition. Those losing fights upped his total of losses to 16 out of a total of 37 fights. He began as a lightweight and finished as a welterweight and was not helped by the fact that there was no light-welter division in his day. Going up nine pounds in weight was a demanding leap, which is probably why he did not do so well at 135lbs. He began in 1952 and took his time in establishing himself as a useful pro. A winning three-fight series in Detroit, Michigan, USA must have given his confidence a boost because back home in English rings his career took off with wins over Johnny Miller, Vince Marshall, Gerry McStravick, Al Sharpe, Joe Rufus and Gordon Goodman (twice). There was a draw with Alby Tissong, soon after dropping a points decision to Leo Molloy. Jackie was one of Dave Charnley's victims during the Dartford Destroyer's rise to the top and later, over in Marseille, he was outpointed by Valere Benedetto after performing creditably. He was very popular at the Tower Circus, Blackpool, winning five fights out of five, and at the Liverpool Stadium where he fought 15 times, losing only four.

Alex Buxton

BUXTON Alex *From* Watford. *Died* 5 April 2008, aged 82. It is sad when an old champion's death is not recorded in national papers that lauded him when in his prime. We missed the passing of this former British light-heavyweight champion in our last issue. Had it not been for his sons returning a grant made to him, the sad news may have never been chronicled. Bernard Hart informed me of Alex's death. Bernard, who I have long considered deserves a major award

for his sevices to boxing, once employed Alex as manager of one of his 'Lonsdale' shops. Reviewing Alex's boxing career in the space available is not easy. His record can be split into five parts, beginning with his introduction into the game, then his time in Australia, his return to England, his rise to championship honours and the later years when he was used as a trial horse, especially in Continental rings. Even though he was then past his best and rarely won, he was no pushover. Albert Finch, who lost a challenge for Alex's title, once told me of how Alex often drew the short straw and got fights with big men like Karl Mildenberger, Willie Besmanhoff and Pierro Tomassoni. Some like Bruno Tripodi, Peter Muller and Max Resch underrated him and came unstuck. Although he was devoid of a win in his final 13 fights, Alex was still a good fighter with the experience to look after himself. When he was losing more than he won, he seldom failed to last the full course. He began in 1942 and up to 1945 had only a modest 50-50 record. Then he joined the Marines and travelled to Sydney a couple of years later. In Australia he won six fights via the short route before dropping a 12-round decision to Dave Sands, who was already showing signs of incipient greatness. Alex licked Dave's brother, Richie, three times and in a second campaign down-under, lost again to Dave and also to a top American, O'Neill Bell. Then he fought 13 times with just one loss. He beat the Alabama Kid twice and outpointed the Aussie light-heavyweight champion, Jack Johnson. Settling back in Watford in 1948, he fought through to 1953 before winning the British title from Dennis Powell. Alex had been boxing at that weight only a short while. His scoresheet at the middleweight limit is remarkable. He went in with top-notch fighters such as Johnny Barton, Ron Crookes, Henry Hall, Bert Sanders, Richard Armah, Jimmy Davis, Ron Pudney, Alby Hollister, Ron Grogan, Reg Hoblyn, George Dilkes, Joe Rood, Jimmy Davis, Des Jones, Jim Wellard, Chris Adcock, Vince Hawkins and his nemeses, Randolph Turpin. Imported fighters all came the same to Alex. He never picked an opponent, taking on Lucien Krawczyk, Billy Coloulias, Koffi Kiteman, Gaston Chambraud, Widmer Milandri, George Angelo, Kid Marcel, Jackie Marr, Burl Charity, Bobby Dawson, Hans Stretz and Peter Muller among others. I could go on but the above is ample evidence with which to judge his calibre. He lost his title to Turpin in 1955 and with it went the chance of picking up the Empire crown. Although past his peak he was still mixing it with Charles Humez, Gustav Scholz, Wim Snoek, Max Resch and Ollie Bengtsston etc. In his later years, he fought mostly overseas on his opponent's patch but the money was good even if he got few favours. His last contest was a points loss to Bob Nicholson in 1963. He had been fighting for 21 years. In his retirement years he was asked, together with other fighters, to appear on a television programme. The theme was supposed to be boxers discussing their experiences. In an underhand and discreditable way the show was presented by an unctious, snidey young man who chose the occasion to denigrate the game. He came unstuck when trying to put words in Alex's mouth. Alex knew the less savoury side of the game but he never forgot that boxing made him a somebody. The way he put down that presenter was a master-class performance. Years ago Alec Steen told me of Alex's health problems. In 2005, he was transferred to a home following the onset of Alzheimers' disease and it was in that home he breathed his last. He was one of five brothers, all of whom were to become boxers. Alex, who also had a passion for motor-cycle speedway, was the best of the lot and he outlived them all bar Allan.

BYRNE Steve *From* Birkenhead. *Died* 22 December 2008, aged 95. Harold Alderman MBE informs me of the death of old-timer Steve Kennedy, who boxed under the name of Steve Byrne from 1933 to 1936. He was a middleweight and as far as we can trace, had 18 fights of which he won 12. He was a boxer rather than a puncher, scoring all but one of his wins on points. Both Cock Moffatt and Tom Reddington beat him. Steve died in Arrol Park Hospital in his hometown of Birkenhead.

Johnny Caldwell

CALDWELL Johnny *From* Belfast. *Died* 10 July 2009, aged 71. Having won a bronze medal in the 1956 Olympics, early in his pro career he soon became referred to as 'the cold-eyed killer'. Johnny beat Dennis Adams, Michel Lamora, Risto Luukonnen and Rene Libeer before stopping

Frankie Jones in three rounds for the British flyweight crown. Four fights later he was sensational in outpointing Alphonse Halimi to claim EBU-recognised world championship tenure at bantamweight. Still unbeaten after another two fights, he again beat Halimi in defence of his title. On the other side of the Atlantic the great Brazilian bantamweight, Eder Jofre, also unbeaten, was recognised as champion. To clear up the mess, they were matched in Jofre's hometown of Sao Paulo and after a hard fight the Brazilian's heavy punching brought him victory in the tenth round. Confidence dented, Johnny returned home to be surprisingly stopped by Michel Atlan. He challenged fellow Irishman Freddie Gilroy for the British and Empire bantamweight titles but lost the fight in the tenth round. He was back to form in 1964 and showed that a year's rest had done him good. Gilroy had defected so Johnny was paired with that hard fighter from Hartlepool, George Bowes, for the vacant titles. Johnny was now British and Empire bantamweight champion and he held those crowns for just over a year, in which he had three fights. When Alan Rudkin took both titles off him in 1965, the end was near. A loss to Monty Laud prompted him to hang up the gloves. His was a fairly brief career, but in it he achieved much and made his fellow-countrymen proud.

CALLAGHAN Mike *From* Belfast. *Died* May 2009, aged 83. Mike dabbled in boxing in many capacities before settling down to assist Jack Solomons in some of his biggest promotions. Later, he worked with Barney Eastwood back in the days when Barney's stable contained some of the best fighters of the day. Mike or 'Mick' as he was affectionately known, took up the role of boxers' manager and was instrumental in guiding Eamonn Magee to the Commonwealth light-welterweight championship. He leaves his wife, Judy, five children and 13 grandchildren.

CARPENTER Frank *From* Coventry. *Died* 3 December 2008, aged 65. A former Midlands' heavyweight, Frank had a brief, nine-fight career that was confined to the year of 1972. His record is notable in that all his opponents were well-known during that period. He lost twice, both times to Guinea Roger who was a strong, power-punching fighter unconcerned with finesse. Frank twice beat Dave Parris, currently a top referee, along with Dennis Avoth (twice), John Cullen, Dave Roden and Paul Cassidy. He had it in him to get high up in the ratings but packed it in for an easier way of earning a living after Roger beat him for the second time.

CASTELLANI Rocky *From* Luzerne, Pennsylvania, USA. *Died* August 2008, aged 82. Glancing through Rocky's record, which spans over a decade from 1946 to 1957, I am reminded how privileged I have been to have lived through those times when men had long careers and fought regularly against the best around. Rocky was a prime example of that category of fighter. He is remembered in particular for putting Sugar Ray Robinson on the canvas during their 1955 fight. The Sugar man was but one of the world title holders who shared a ring with him, with Joey Giardello, Bobo Olson, Kid Gavilan, Gene Fullmer and Johnny Bratton being the others. Rocky won one out of three outings against Giardello, beat Johnny Bratton twice and lost to Gavilan, Fullmer and Olson, whose world middleweight title was at stake. Both men hit the deck in that fight. Rocky fought his first six fights as Rocky Wargo, his birthname being Attilio Castellani. He fought for three years before coming into prominence with victories over Lenny Mancini, Jimmy King, Harold Green, Walter Cartier and Sonny Horne. After that it was contenders and good ten-round fighters who shared a ring with him: Rory Calhoun, Lester Felton, Joey Giambra, Johnny Sullivan, Holly Mims, Ernie 'The Rock' Durando, Gil Turner, Pierre Langlois, Ralph 'Tiger' Jones, Jimmy Herring, Billy Graham, Ralph Zanelli, Chico Varona, Phil Burton, Tony Janiro and Charlie Fusari. He had 83 fights, of which he lost 14. A fine boxer and top contender for most of his career he retired when he still had it in him to hold his own with the best around before becoming a top referee and judge.

Rocky Castellani

CHADE Yamil *From* USA. *Died* April 2009, aged 79. The Lebanese-born manager is remembered for bringing Kid Gavilan to London for two fights against Peter Waterman. The first decision against Gavilan was one of the most controversial of any given within these shores. Referee Ben Green was 'retired' by the Board of Control and an age limit of 65 was introduced for all British referees. Yamil's vociferous reaction got a good deal of publicity and a return match, which Gavilan won, was hastily arranged. The next display of his histrionics came when Germinal Ballarin was adjudged to have beaten his man in Paris. The papers carried a picture of Yamil, as a corollary to strong verbal protests, lying face-down on the ring floor, head outside the ropes, remonstrating with an official. He was quite a character and boxing was his life. Years after Gavilan retired he was handling Wilfredo Gomez and more recently, Felix Trinidad, but by then he had mellowed. His contribution to the game was recognized in 2008 when, suffering from advanced Alzheimers, he received the WBC life-time achievement award.

CIDONE Vinnie *From* Brooklyn, NYC, New York, USA. *Died* 19 November 2008, aged 87. The New York suburb of Brooklyn has produced dozens of good and great fighters. Vinnie Cidone, who hailed from the Redwood area, fell short of championship standard yet he fought Rocky Graziano, Walter Cartier, Paddy Young, Georgie Small, Aldo Minelli, Ernie 'The Rock' Durando and Joey DeJohn. Although they all beat him, Vinnie was always in with a puncher's chance. He floored Graziano, only to be denied victory when a cut eye forced the referee to intervene. Cuts were again the cause of his loss when Young beat him. There was little between them on the points tally and both men hit the deck when he fought Durando, a fighter renowned for his toughness. Early in his career, Cidone broke Terry Wagner's jaw. He could certainly hit and that is one reason that his fight with Graziano had an attendance of 12,386, which is a record for an indoor sporting event in the State of Wisconsin. He boxed in that busy period from 1947 to 1951, losing only three of his first 30 fights. Half of his wins came inside the scheduled distance and nearly all his fights were held in the New York State. One month after losing to Cartier he got a 'name' fighter on his list of victims when he outpointed Herbie Kronowitz and followed it by knocking out Gene Boland and Lou Valles. He moved in with the rated middleweights in 1950 but could not match the power of Graziano, Durando and Young. After 1951 was over he called it a day. In five outings that year, he was successful only once, when stopping Milton Lattimore. He gave a decent account of himself against Aldo Minelli and Al 'Red' Priest but two-round losses to both Joey DeJohn and Gus Rubicini were his swan song.

COLE Neville *From* Stepney, London. *Died* 30 March 2009, aged 56. There were two fighting Cole brothers.

Eamonn, the elder, was ABA light-welterweight champion in 1968. In that same year, his brother Neville won the junior class 'A' title. Neville, like his brother, a southpaw, died suddenly last August. He was a multiple champion. Apart from a batch of schoolboy titles, he was ABA lightweight champion in his first senior year and again in 1972. Neville represented us in several international matches and also at the Munich Olympics, where he unfortunately fell victim to a hasty decision that ruled him out in the first series. He decided to try his luck as a light-welter from that point and fought in international bouts against Ireland (the country of his birth) and the USA. Selected to compete in the European championships, he was beaten by the eventual champion, Yugoslavia's Marijan Benes, in controversial circumstances. Benes landed a series of heavy punches, one of them after the bell. The facial injuries caused by that incident put Neville in hospital. He never fought again.

Hector Constance

CONSTANCE Hector *From* Trinidad. *Died* 3 April 2008, aged 75. Had it not been for the vigilance of Austrian Boxing Board official, Friedrich Muhlohcker, Hector Constance's death in Vienna may have gone unreported. I used the same gym as Hector back in the early 1950s and admired his smooth boxing skills. He could look after himself, as his American record against world-class performers shows very clearly. Over in the States he beat Kid Gavilan, Ralph 'Tiger' Jones and Chico Varona, but lost to a peak-form Virgil Akins. He began in his native Trinidad but the names

of his opponents mean little outside of the Caribbean. The exceptions being Boswell St Louis, against whom he twice drew, and Hugh Serville, who also later fought on these shores. He started his 1952 campaign in England by beating Wally Thom, Peter Fallon and Israel Boyle before drawing with and beating Jackie Braddock. He made frequent appearances in boxing booths and fought extensively in Europe: Germany, Denmark, Luxembourg, Italy, Spain, Austria, Finland, Turkey, Holland, France and Italy. During his 21-year-career he trod canvas in Venezuela, Singapore, Aruba, Guyana and Thailand. When his reflexes dimmed to only a shadow of what they once had been, he carried on plying his trade and took dubious decisions and bias in his stride as long as he could put food on the table. He fought Nino Benvenuti, Fred Galiana, Domenica Tiberia, Harko Kokmeyer, Stefan Redl, Jupp Elze, Mauri Backman, Heinz Freitag, Bruno Visintin, Luis Folledo, Chris Christensen, Albert Carroll etc, etc. Of his last 49 fights he won only nine with seven draws. An Austrian promoter befriended him and got him some fights, so he decided to settle there. In post-boxing years he helped to run a shop in Vienna where he was popular but never had savings. He was buried in a pauper's grave but the Austrian Federation is making arrangements to erect a headstone to commemorate Hector's remarkable contribution to the game.

Cliff Curvis

CURVIS Cliff *From* Swansea. *Died* 22 April 2009, aged 81. For many years the mantle of being oldest living British champion belonged to Vince Hawkins. This passed on to

Billy Thompson who died just a few weeks after usurping Vince. Cliff Curvis, who passed away in a nursing home last April, had a slightly longer tenure than Thompson but only just. He was a southpaw and proficient in boxing technique. Cliff started young, making his debut as a young lightweight in 1944 when he was 17. Under his father's management, he progressed well, beating Cliff Anderson in his sixth fight and outpointing Ben Duffy, Frank Williams and Bert Jackson before emerging as a title prospect when outscoring Sunderland's Tom Smith, who was an outstanding scrapper at European level. At this stage, the Curvis camp became too ambitious. Al Phillips was too ringwise and too fistically mature for Cliff, who lasted only two rounds. He bounced back to win all his fights in 1947. But by 1949 he was having trouble in meeting the weight limit and lost a final eliminator to Harry Hughes when injuries badly affected his vision. Moving up to the lightweight division, Cliff overcame a few setbacks to put himself in the challenger's role for Eddie Thomas's British title. After 15 rounds, Eddie kept his title by a narrow margin. When another opportunity came in 1951, Cliff knocked out the British and Empire champion, Wally Thom. He was champion at last. It had taken him eight years to get there. On the way he had accounted for Jim Brady, Ronnie James, Andre Famechon, Joseph Preys, Paddy Dowdall, Claude Dennington, Ernie Roderick, Ivor 'Kid' Germain, Gwyn Williams, Titi Clavel, Giel de Roode and Billy Rattray. He had lost to Charles Humez and Peter Fallon and later lost his Empire title to Gerald Dreyer when badly handicapped by a broken bone in his left hand. Dreyer survived a long count in the sixth round, but the punch that put him down was the one that broke the bone. A proposed title defence against Peter Fallon drew a measly offer of a £850 purse and that was a gross total. Cliff would have taken home £380 of that sum. "If that is all a British title is worth, I will retire", he said. He was adamant and Britain lost a fine boxer who, at 27, had plenty of good boxing left in him. Later, he renewed his interest in boxing and was a BBBof C Inspector and a familiar face at the big fights.

D'AGATA Mario *From* Arezzo, Italy. *Died* 4 April 2009, aged 82. The beautiful Tuscan town of Arezzo, 50 kilometres east of Sienna, once boasted of having a resident world champion. Little Mario had to depose a great fighter in Robert Cohen, who had beaten him once, to establish himself king of the world's bantamweights. He did it in style, flooring the champion in round six and forcing a stoppage soon after. It had taken him seven years of fighting to get there. He did so in stages. First winning the Italian title from Gianni Zuddas in 1953, the European championship from Andre Valignat two years later and emerging on the world scene with wins over Billy Peacock and Emile Chemama. Mario was a deaf mute and survived a shooting incident in 1955. He overcame those obstacles through sheer determination and that attribute was what got him to the top in his profession. Turning professional in 1950 after a fine career in the unpaid ranks, he is said to have engaged in 110 contests as an amateur. When Alphonse Halimi took his title in 1957, Mario rested for three months before stopping Federico Scarponi, Jean Renard and Michel Lamora. He was showing signs of slipping when Piero Rollo took his European title and subsequent defeats by Freddie Gilroy, Jackie Brown, Jose Becerra confirmed this. When old foe, Scarponi, beat him in 1962 it was the end.

DAK Steve *From* Sydney, Australia. *Died* April 2009, aged 44. Yet another Aussie scrapper died prematurely from gunshot wounds when former State middleweight champion, Steve, was found dead a few days following the shooting of Vince Cervi. He was a tough fighter who gave the WBC light-heavyweight title-holder, Jeff Harding, stiff opposition.

DALY John *From* Los Angeles, California, USA. *Died* November 2008, aged 71. London-born John was never far from boxing and boxers. He was son of Tommy Daly and nephew of George, both of whom were prominent lightweights in their day. John boxed but only as an amateur. Father Tommy saw that his son got a good education. After leaving St Joseph's Roman Catholic school, he worked at Covent Garden fruit market and had a spell as a silver service waiter in the Merchant Navy. That is where he met former amateur star, Bruce Wells. Because of his strong connection with the game, John was granted a manager's licence and, for a while, he handled Billy Aird, Terry Toole, and the Ould twins. John had always been interested in films and when working as an insurance salesman with Canada Life he met David Hemmings, his involvement in the industry beginning in 1967. He went on to produce *Platoon*, *The Terminator* and *The Last Emperor* and many more classic movies. His success was highlighted by Oscar awards in 1987 and 1988. In partnership with David Hemmings he formed Hemdale, which produced over 100 films, many of which were box-office hits that gathered Oscars galore. When Don King approached Jack Solomons in order to get Ali a shot at George Foreman in Zaire, Jolly Jack suggested Don should contact Hemdale for sponsorship. Hemdale raised the money and, as co-promoters with the President of Zaire, got a foothold into boxing in a big way. King was deeply involved but was never on record in an official capacity. Hemdale became a multi-million dollar concern and financed big fights for five years before folding with the death of David Hemmings. In 2003, John became Chief Director of the company, Film and Music Entertainment. Cancer was to take a hold of him in recent years and he finally lost a long battle against the disease. I am grateful to BBBof C Inspector, Billy Ball, whose wife Eileen is related to the Dalys, for so much of the above information.

DAW Les *From* Dagenham. *Died* 24 December 2008, aged 81. A flyweight-cum-bantamweight scrapper, Les began his pro career in the 'boom' year of 1948. Having won the RAF amateur flyweight title in 1947 and represented the ABA at the weight he could have expected to move up the ratings, but he never got beyond the six-round stage and met with mixed success in a 28-fight career. In his first year he got a draw with Ireland's Hughie Byrne, but went through another four losing fights before scoring a win over Harold Clark. There were further successes against Pat Roberts, Bernie Driscoll and Dickie Sullivan. Early in his career he met Jimmy Cardew and Tommy Bramble, both of whom outpointed him. Aylesham's Johnny Hughes beat him four times, each fight being a crowd-pleaser. Les boxed on to January 1952, fighting three times that month. He outpointed Albert Stokes and had his last contest at the NSC against Paddy Hyland. In retirement he worked as a van driver.

DELL Carl *From* Oneonta, New York, USA. *Died* 22 January 2009, aged 93. Carl J. Delberto, to give him his birthname, began boxing in 1937 as a prelim fighter. He had 50 contests with one loss before very ambitiously tangling with the fistic trio of Holman Williams, Cocoa Kid and Charley Burley, who spoiled his record. Each of those classy black fighters outpointed Carl, who by then was a ten-rounds, main-event performer. Then came a four fight series against Ernest 'Cat' Williams whose claws were at first too sharp for him. Carl squared the series two-all then turned up in Australia. It was 1943. He won a couple of fights in Brisbane, but then stepped way out of his class and suffered stoppage losses to Tommy Burns and Vic Patrick. That appeared to have been the end of his career until his name cropped up again in 1950 when he would have been 34. There are three fights, all prelims, recorded at the middleweight limit. Research has not yet definitely linked the two careers but the significance is obvious.

DEVINO Archie *From* Queens, NYC, New York, USA. *Died* 29 June 2009, aged 81. In 58 fights, this New York featherweight won 44 and drew three. He began punching for pay in 1944 and went through to the end of 1946 with only five losses in 33 fights. Archie had been fighting in the eight-round class for four years when wins over Bobby Bell and the previously unbeaten Luis Galvini got him an offer of a fight with highly-rated Frenchman, Ray Famechon. They fought in a scheduled ten-rounder at Madison Square Garden. The Frenchman was too strong for Archie, who was stopped in seven rounds. It was nearly a year before he boxed again but he could not beat Frankie Sodano so he quit boxing altogether. He had been in there with Leo LeBrun, Jimmy Callura, Eddie Compo, Johnny 'Red' DeFazio and Filberto Osario, among other good men.

DEVLIN Arthur *From* Millwall, London. *Died* December 2008, aged 73. When Isidore Green ran his shows at the Wembley Town Hall in the 1950s, he used Arthur Devlin's services on 12 of his promotions. Arthur was an archetypal small-halls fighter who lost only two of his first 20 fights, going through wins over Billy Graydon, Johnny Collier, Pat McCairn, Andy Doherty and Peter Sexton (twice) before coming unstuck against George Carroll. In their three fights he never could find a way to beat George. Their third meeting was for the vacant Southern Area featherweight title in 1958 at Shoreditch Town Hall. Arthur fell foul of Johnny Howard in his ninth fight but had a good sequence of wins after that. He beat Terry Rees, Terry Toole, Alan Branquet, Wallace Boodhoo, Alf Drew and Ron Jones before scoring his finest victory over Con Mount Bassie at the NSC. Unfortunately, it was all downhill after the title fight with Carroll. Losses to Bobby Neill and Robbie Wilson convinced him that it was time to go. He had been to the well 25 times and had 17 wins and a draw against Alf Drew, whom he beat in a rematch.

DOCUSEN Bernard *From* New Orleans, Louisiana, USA. *Died* 11 January 2009, aged 81. There were two fighting Docusen brothers, Maxie and Bernard, who were of French, Filipino extraction and active from the mid-1940s. Both were world class with superb records. Bernard, the elder by a couple of years, died last January after suffering a series of heart attacks. He was a welterweight, highly skilled, and a former AAU bantamweight champion who took to the ring professionally at the age of 17 and fought for four years before tasting defeat, which he quickly avenged. He was fighting amongst the best by that time, having earned his spurs by beating notable fighters like Phil Terranova, Lulu Constantino, Jackie Graves and Lefty LaChance. At 21 he challenged Sugar Ray Robinson for his world welterweight title and proved his claim to being in championship class when taking the fight to the Sugarman and edging ahead on the points tally. Robinson dropped him with a big left hook in the 11th round. Bernard still attacked and went the distance but history shows that the championship stayed in the Robinson camp. Bernard was 21 at that time, but had been fighting for four and a half years. He continued until 1952, beating good men like Johnny Bratton, Tippy Larkin and Ralph Zannelli. Freddie Dawson beat him in 1949 and losses to Gil Turner and Joey Giambra signalled the end. He retired at 26, having fought 88 times with ten losses. For a while he worked as a welder before moving to Detroit and taking up the position of a school caretaker. His wife, Ernestine, six children and 15 grandchildren survive him.

DORMER George *From* East Ham, London. *Died* December 2008, aged 73. As an amateur, George was ABA bantamweight champion in 1955 and twice Army and ISBA titleholder. It was no wonder that he was matched, right from the beginning of his career with established boxers.

There are no 'unknowns' in his record. He began in 1955 and ten months later was boxing eight-rounders. In his second outing, he impressively stopped Jimmy Brewer. who'd had 46 fights with 11 losses. Other wins came at the expense of Ron Johnson, Robert Meunier, George O'Neill, Jimmy Carson and Alan Sillett. John Smillie was the first to beat him and did it again in 1957. Another man he could not beat was Chic Brogan. On the credit side were some fine victories over Charlie Tucker, Malcom Ames, David Oved and John O'Brien. Bobby Neill started a run of bad luck that lasted throughout the remainder of George's career. He stopped George in five rounds and defeats followed against Billy Rafferty, Terry Toole, Terry Spinks, Con Mount Bassie, Paddy Kelly and finally, Danny O'Brien. He fought on the undercard of Dave Charnley v Joe Lucy lightweight title fight at Harringay against the unbeaten South African champion, Graham van der Walt, and won in the fourth round when referee Pat Floyd stopped the fight. George appeared six times at the Empress Hall, Earls Court and once at the Albert Hall. His best win was when he stopped Tucker at Streatham Ice Rink in 1957. He suffered from Alzheimer's disease.

George Dormer

DOUGLAS Lord Milo *From* Bayswater, London. *Died* 21 July 2009, aged 34. The tragic suicide of Lord Milo Douglas breaks a link in the chain that can be traced back to the promulgation of the Queensberry rules that, with few alterations from their original form, govern boxing today. Lord Milo Douglas was second in line to the title of Marquess of Queensberry. He was one of 12 children, his father, the Marquess, being twice married. Milo suffered from bi-polar disorder that for long periods caused severe depression. He was a teacher and also a tireless charity worker whose medication never seemed to completely negate his health problems. It was his ancestor, John Sholto Douglas, the ninth Marquess of Queensberry, who gave his name to the rules of boxing, devised by the lightweight champion boxer, Arthur Chambers, in 1872. Seven years ago, Lord Milo's half-sister, Lady Alice Douglas, said: "Through marriages, affairs and adoptions, we Queensberrys, with our family name Douglas, can boast links with everyone from boxers, bank robbers, Oscar Wilde and Osama Bin Laden. Despite this 700-year-old heritage, we are a proud, modern and gloriously dysfunctional family". Lord Milo's older brother, Viscount Drumlanrig, son of his father's second wife, as was Milo, now becomes heir to the title.

DUSGATE James *From* Costa Rica. *Died* April 2009, aged 64. When our editor, Barry Hugman, Fred Snelling and I were trying to get *Boxing Monthly* off the ground we were put in touch with James Dusgate by a mutual friend, Ricky Porter, who used to box out of Shepherds Bush. Ricky knew James from their amateur days when they were both quickly ascending in their respective weight divisions. Ricky, aware of James's writing abilities, got us a first class and prolific correspondent on Latin American boxing and boxers. James had moved from England when he met the girl who would become his wife. His reports were regular and in-depth and we always printed them in full. *Boxing News* also benefited from this reliable scribe who got to know the scene in Central America as few others had done before him. He had performed well as an amateur and was Porter's long-time friend, Ricky being one of those men who never neglects a friendship. The two always kept in touch by phone and by letter. James had two children who, with wife Theresa, survive him.

ELLIOTT Chris *From* Leicester. *Died* March 2009, aged 68. The Leicester lightweight was one of the most experienced men around in this country during his time, cramming in over 80 fights between 1958 and 1967. He fought Willi Quator, Ken Buchanan, John Smillie, Billy Calvert, Spike McCormick, Freddie King, Vic Andreeti, Johnny McKenna, Boswell St Louis, Winston and Mick Laud, Peter Cheevers, Al White, and won the Midlands Area title from Terry Edwards in 1962. It is a sign of the times he boxed in, that he had 43 fights before he got a shot at that title, which he held for three years. Chris lost his share of fights but he was a man who had learned his craft and could look after himself. In defeat he was usually there at the final bell. Only three of his losing fights ended early and neither Ken Buchanan nor Vic Andreeti could stop him. In both cases the points' deficit was narrow. Had he been active a decade earlier, he would have joined the ranks of the centurions.

FENTON Jack *From* Leicester. *Died* September 2008, aged 80. Jack was one of the Midlands' most successful amateur coaches of post-war years, having had a long experience as an army boxer before becoming a trainer at Belgrave and Old Robin Hood ABCs. Jack took Tim Wood to the ABA title, trained Tony Sibson, Rendall Munroe, the Concepcion brothers, Tony McKenzie and Chris Pyatt. Their subsequent success in the professional ranks can be attributed to Jack, who instilled in them sound boxing technique and the value of both fitness and dedication. Dedication is a factor that he possessed in abundance himself as his long connection with boxing indicates.

FINNEGAN Chris MBE From Iver Heath. Died 2 March 2009, aged 64. Five months separate the death of former British, European and Commonwealth light-heavyweight champion, Chris, with that of his younger brother, Kevin. At domestic and European level they were a formidable couple. Chris's challenge for the world title epitomised the gameness and never-give-up attitude that pervaded his career. Behind on points against Bob Foster going into the 14th round, his only chance of winning the title was via a stoppage. Finnegan was no knockout specialist, but even though physically drained he chose to slug it out and go for broke. What guts he had! He was a southpaw who returned from the Olympics in Mexico with a gold medal, a feat which gained him an MBE. He had gone as an underdog before returning triumphant but in debt, and a paid career was the obvious course to take. His manager Sam Burns and trainer, Freddie Hill, persuaded him to alter his style and become professional in his application to the game. When he beat Ronnie Hough and Harry Scott he was on his way to title contention. Chris's fights with Tom Bogs, John Conteh, Mike Quarry and Johnny Frankham have been well documented, his sportsmanship and dignity are what I will dwell on. For instance, there was not a hint of a complaint when cuts caused by a dubious head clash ended his challenge for John Conteh's titles in 1974. "Good luck to him" was his only comment to the press and his reaction was exemplary when Harry Gibbs raised Johnny Frankham's hand back in 1975 after Chris had seemed a clear winner. There he was, title gone, shaking his head in sheer disbelief. The crowd took it badly and trouble seemed imminent. A bottle was thrown from the balcony into the ring. The descent of crowd behaviour started then and continued its course to the gutter in modern times. Chris defused a nasty situation by walking over to Frankham to congratulate him. Next day, he and Johnny were seen together at the races both the worse for wear after a drink or two. Harry Gibbs was full of trepidation when he next met Finnegan. There was no need. Chris, being Chris, quickly offered his hand. He was the same in retirement when asked to attend a charity function. There was never a demand for payment unlike some of the so-called celebrities who demand sums like £500, charity or no charity. Chris was content with a free supply of his favourite tipple. Failing eyesight closed his career after he regained his British title. He lost his 46-year-old wife to cancer and did not have an easy life in retirement, but he was always cheerful and positive. In a tribute to Chris when he was forced to give up boxing, Frank Butler said that the fans loved him because he never once picked their pockets. He gave his all and never squealed at a bad decision. That says it all.

Chris Finnegan

FINNEGAN Kevin *From* Iver Heath. *Died* October 2008, aged 60. When deciding where to place Kevin Finnegan in the pantheon of British Middleweight champions, two fights against Marvin Hagler in 1978 must be considered. Both were ten-rounders and both were terminated because of cuts incurred by the Englishman, but in terms of how

Kevin Finnegan

each fight was progressing there is plenty of unbiased opinion that Hagler was having more than he could handle. Finnegan always seemed to raise his game when in there with the iron of the middleweight division. He was three times British champion, beating Bunny Sterling for the first notch in his Lonsdale Belt, regaining it from Frankie Lucas, losing it to Alan Minter, and then making the belt his own property by taking the same title from Tony Sibson. Kevin lost title fights to Alan Minter on three occasions. All were very disputed decisions of the wafer-thin variety. Following his first aquisition of the middleweight crown, he picked up the European version by beating Jean-Claude Bouttier in Paris. Kevin decided to relinquish his British title but the following year he lost his one title possession to Gratien Tonna in Monte Carlo and had to wait five years before he got Tonna back in the ring. Kevin's best days were then gone. He had only a couple more fights before calling time on his career, but he turned back the clock to earn one of the best wins of his career and, in so doing, he regained his old EBU title and he did it in France. European title fights were over 12 rounds at the time. He made two defences - one in Germany when he drew with Georg Steinherr and the next, his final fight when he lost to Matteo Salvamini in Rome. His rise up to title status was rapid, beating Harry Scott and Eric Blake in British title eliminators and picking up the Southern Area crown on the way. This was after only

a dozen fights. Kevin beat Pat McCann, Dick Duffy, Frank Reiche, Ronnie Hough, Carlos Marks and Lennie Gibbs. Only Minter, Tonna, Salvemini and Ayub Kalule beat him on points, all other losses came via injury. He retired to Spain in his post-boxing years and spent his leisure time either painting or drinking alcohol, having a penchant for both. Kevin was a talented painter, one good enough to have one of his works exhibited in National Portrait Gallery. As for drinking, it became such a temptation for him that he decided to return to England. He lived in Uxbridge and became friendly with an Asian family of butchers from whom he rented a room over the shop. His death was sudden and a complete surprise. Brother Chris said with customary modesty: "Of the two of us, I may have been the star but Kevin was the class-act".

FLORES Benjamin *From* Houston, Texas, USA. *Died* 5 May 2009, aged 24. The Texas-based Mexican died after being beaten by Al Seegar for the vacant NABF super-bantamweight title. With only 23 fights to his record and having fought just three ten round contests, of which he lost two, it was ambitious to catapult him into a world-title fight, despite him being a fighter of decent class. He paid for it with his life. Three fights previously, he had won what was termed as the Continental America's super-bantamweight championship and was showing promise, but was out of his depth at this level.

FORREST Vernon *From* Augusta, Georgia,. USA. *Died* 26 July 2009, aged 38. This three-time world champion and former Olympian will be missed not only by the boxing fraternity but also by the hundreds of beneficiaries of his wide charity work. Vernon came across as a genuine nice guy, immensely popular, and one of the better modern-day champions. His record speaks for itself: Just three losses in 45 contests, twice a winner over Shane Mosley and holder of world titles at light-welterweight, welterweight and light-middleweight (twice). He regained the light-middleweight championship from Sergio Mora in 2008, having originally won the title (WBC) from Carlos Baldomir before losing it to Mora in his second defence. Forrest made no mistake in the return. The only other losses were to Ricardo Mayorga, who beat him twice at a time when Forrest was suffering from painful arm and elbow injuries. Vince beat Ike Quartey, Santiago Samaniego, Vince Phillips, Ray Oliveira, Marlon Thomas and Adrian Stone. His death came in a shooting incident when two men attempted to steal his car and, at the time of going to press, one man has been charged for the offence.

FRATALA Francesco *From* Cavitavecchia, Italy. *Died* 8 December 2008, aged 81. One of Gustav Scholz's opponents has died in America where he settled after ending his second boxing campaign there in 1954. Francesco faced the unbeaten Scholz with only seven fights under his belt. He did well and took the German the distance. Francesco began and ended his short career in the USA. He had won three out of five fights before returning to the land of his birth to have a further six outings. He won half of them, which models his entire career: 15 contests, won seven, lost eight. In his hometown of Civitavecchia, he twice stopped Vittorio Fuino but decided to head back across the big pond after losing to Luigi Male in 1952. He fought on for another two years, beating Paul Nichols and closing his career after dropping a verdict to Eddie Andrews in Boston.

FUENTES Ramon *From* Los Angeles, California, USA. *Died* 20 July 2009, aged 83. Any welterweight who was active in the 1950s had to be pretty damned good to crash into the ratings. It was a division crammed with talented ringmen. Ramon was not quite good enough to challenge for the world title but he was Californian champion and that carried more prestige than many of today's world titles fabricated by the alphabet brigade. He won that title in 1952, defended it seven times and never lost it. His career was just into its second year when he shot out of the six-round class to beat the experienced Phil Burton. The sum total of Ramon's experience was 35 rounds at that time. Burton, who had been to the well 67 times, was floored in the last round but got up to go the distance. He then beat Charlie Salas and went on to 1953 before tasting defeat, Kid Gavilan and Gil Turner beating him. Ramon closed the year by beating 'Golden boy' Art Aragon, then Danny 'Bang Bang' Womber, who had eight fights in Britain, before successfully defending his State title against the 110-fight veteran, Mario Trigo. In 1956, he got his revenge over a fading Kid Gavilan. Three fights in Australia saw him beat George Barnes and Luigi Coluzzi, but a badly cut eye ruled him out against little-known Billy Hester. He was also one of the very few men to beat master-boxer Billy Graham. Johnny Saxton beat Ramon, as did Isaac Logart, Chico Vejar and Del Flanagan, all top men. There was a loss and a win against Joe Miceli and victories over Carmen Fiore and Hector Constance. His last win came in 1957 when he beat Stan Harrington in Hawaii. After that he lost them all but look at the opposition: Ralph Dupas, Phil Moyer, Tony Dupas and Jimmy Martinez. Participating in 57 fights against that class of talent is some achievement. I will leave the reader to name all the world titleholders in that list.

GALADA Ludumo *From* South Africa. *Died* 11 January 2009, aged 26. As the reigning WBF featherweight champion, Ludumo was one of the brightest stars of African boxing before losing his life tragically in a car accident early in January. He was unbeaten and set to defend his title against Takalani Ndlovu. Victory, which seemed likely, would have catapulted him into the front echelons of world's featherweights. Ludumo had been the South African champion since 2007. Quick victories over Pedro Navarette and David Kiilu, from whom he won his world title, emphasised the power and tremendous potential of a man yet to reach his prime.

GATTI Arturo *From* Montreal, Canada. *Died* 11 July 2009, aged 37. Arturo was the darling of boxing's television age. His uncompromising, exciting style and his seeming imperviousness to punishment provided some of the most exciting fights in recent times. Arturo was involved in contests that were named 'Fight of the Year' on four occasions and most of his other scraps kept people on the edge of their seats. He was a world champion at two weights, first at super-featherweight, a title he gained by beating Tracy Harris Patterson in a sensational battle, and the other at light-welter where he won the WBC version of the crown by trimming the previously unbeaten Italian, Gianluca Branco. He was of Italian birth himself and was based in Montreal as an amateur before taking up residence in Jersey City, USA when he turned professional. Arturo defended his IBF super-featherweight title three times, beating Gabriel Ruelas twice in terrific contests. His first step-up in weight saw him suffer a stoppage loss to Angel Manfredy in 1998, followed by two points losses to Ivan Robinson. On all occasions his never-say-die approach and his desire to always do his best, endeared him to the fans. Four straight wins then saw him in with Oscar de la Hoya who was too good for him but Arturo could turn things round with one punch and his popularity never waned. His trilogy with Mickey Ward, another man of similar style and sprit, were three of the most exciting fights of recent times. Such was the volume of punishment that each received in their first fight, which Ward won on a split vote, that I thought it unwise for a return to take place. For the last two fights, trainer Buddy McGirt instilled some boxing skills into him and he proved to be a surprisingly quick learner. He won both the last two of their meetings. Next time out he beat Branco for his second world title. He defended twice before losing it to Floyd Mayweather, who completely outboxed him. The signs were that he should quit but a chance to win the WBC welterweight title from Carlos Baldomir was too tempting. Arturo took heavy punishment before being stopped in the ninth round. Another painful loss followed to Alfonso Gomez and that was the end. He had won 31 of his victories by knockout with only nine defeats. Outside the ring his life was just as colourful. A partying type who lived life to the full, he married a young Brazilian girl, but their relationship was tempestuous. When he was found dead, whilst on holiday in Brazil with his wife and son, the police initially arrested his wife before concluding that the boxer had hung himself in the early hours of the morning. However, at the time of going to press it was still unclear as to whether it was a suicide or murder.

Joey Giardello

GIARDELLO Joey *From* Brooklyn, NYC, New York, USA. *Died* September 2008, aged 78. Carmen Orlando Tilelli used a friend's birth certificate to join the army. It got him into the para-troop division despite his own certificate showing him to be underage. He became Joey Giardello and retained the name when, without prior amateur experience, he took to fighting for pay. It was 19 years before he hung up his gloves, going out with a win over Jack Rogers in 1967. He had 133 contests and met six world champions, beating three of them and drawing once against Gene Fullmer in 1960, being outpointed by Ralph Dupas and Terry Downes. Joey won the world middleweight championship from Dick Tiger and defended it once against Rubin 'Hurricane' Carter. He and Tiger were great rivals, splitting four decisions between them at two apiece, but it was Tiger who won the last one and, in doing so, regained the title. Joey fought on for only two more years, but he was then a 37-year-old veteran. He had been in with the top men in Sugar Ray Robinson, Johnny Saxton, Rory Calhoun, Rocky Castellani, Joey Giambria, Ralph 'Tiger' Jones, Harold Green, Chico Vejar, Ernie Durando, Joe Miceli, Pierre Langlois, Bobby Dykes, Billy Graham, Gil Turner, Billy Kilgore, Randy Sandy, Spider Webb, Franz Szuzina, Charlie Cotton, Wilf Greaves, Walter Cartier, Holly Mims, Rocky Rivero, Del Flanagan and Henry Hank etc. The opposition was top-class. Perhaps that is why it took over a 100 fights for him to get his first title crack (a gruelling draw with Gene Fullmer) and win the championship in his 124th outing. As champion, Joey raised money to aid children with Downs Syndrome, a disability which afflicted his son, Carmen. He had three other sons, five grandchildren and is also survived by his wife, Rosalie. Joey's final years were tough. He suffered from all manner of ailments, but it was diabetes and heart failure that got him in the end.

GIBSON Toby *From* Youngstown, Ohio. *Died* 26 November 2008, aged 61. A Nevada State referee, Toby committed suicide in November by inhalation of carbon monoxide fumes from his car, whose engine he switched on while in a closed garage. He had been a referee for over 20 years, with many world-title matches to his credit. Toby was born in Ohio but moved to Las Vegas, Nevada where he established himself as an arbiter for the State Athletic Commission. The reason for his suicide has not officially been announced but a strong pointer is that he had recently lost his job with the Forestry Department. A few days earlier he had officiated on the Ricky Hatton v Paul Malignaggi undercard, when he was the referee for Hatton's brother, Matthew's win over Ben Tackie.

GIDNEY Len *From* Norwich. *Died* May 2009, aged 87. Len was a product of Norwich Lads' Club, which spawned many men who went on to become good professional fighters. He was active in the latter days of Ginger Sadd's career. Just 13 fights have been traced for him. He beat Herbie Beckett, Ivor Warren, George Garnham, Reg Williams, Johnny Fox and lost to rated men like Willie Whyte and Johnny Barton. His last fight, in 1948, was a loss to Pat Burke of Widnes.

GOODWIN Mickey *From* Detroit, Michigan, USA. *Died* 5 March 2009, aged 51. It was Mickey's punching power that attracted Emanuel Steward. The trainer thought, with good reason, that properly trained, a man with such natural assets could make it to the top. He was due for a big disappointment. What Mickey had in his fists was negated by a seeming lack of ambition. When he ran up a winning streak in 1993, it followed an absence of eight years! Mickey was a golden gloves champion in the amateurs and as a professional lost only two of 43 fights. He started in 1977 as a middleweight and increasing poundage eventually forced him to compete in the light-heavyweight division. Ted Sands became the first to beat him, before Mickey fought for and won the Michigan State title by beating Ken Ringo in three rounds. He defended once then lost to Darryl Spain in 1985. That was all until 1993. He won another seven fights and retired. A stroke followed by a fall on the stairs at home is what finished him. He went to bed and was later found to have died.

GUTTERIDGE Reg OBE *From* Islington, London.. *Died* 25 January 2009, aged 84. With a family history of boxing connections going back to the 1800s, Reg could figuratively be said to have been born wearing boxing gloves. It is said, and is probably correct, that his grandfather, Arthur, was the first man to box at the old National Sporting Club. His father and uncle, who were twins, were well-known cornermen of repute in the 1920s and 1930s and ran a gymnasium, through which passed many of the big names of the time. It was inevitable that Reg would take to the game. That was in his flyweight years. Army service put paid to his fistic ambitions when he trod on a mine during the Normandy landings and lost a leg. Those who met him in later years would never have realised about this affliction. I discovered that he served, as I did later, with the Third Infantry Division, which through the years seems to have been at the front of conflicts. We used to have an amusing repartee over our army experiences. Reg had a sharp cockney wit and could have a crowd in stitches of laughter when he took the microphone at ex-boxers' meetings. He could have earned a living as a stand-up comedian, but, instead, he became a journalist and for 30 years was boxing reporter for the *Evening News*. When the paper ceased, he became a television personality, taking up the position as boxing commentator for ITV. He was always more at home behind a microphone than he was in a Fleet Street office and in partnership with Jim Watt he covered all the big fights from the early 1980s. There was always an anecdote deriving from his experiences. Reg once spoke of the difficulty of getting a word in the ring from Mike Tyson after his fights. "You had to stick the microphone under his elbow if you could get space", he said. "It seemed as if the whole world wanted to interview him". There was an occasion when Reg beat the others to it and had a clear passage across the ring to Tyson's corner. Suddenly, someone 'in a suit' blocked the way and demanded: "Ask him about Nelson Mandela". Reg told him what is the anglo-saxon, cockney equivalent of 'Go away!', forgetting that the sound was still on and that his words had been heard by millions. "There were 13 letters sent in concerning that", Reg said "and not one complaint amongst them. Most of them were congratulatory for putting the guy in his place". The Sam Taub award for excellence in broadcast journalism followed by an OBE in 1995 were appropriate acknowledgements of Reg's contribution to the fight game. He also was an inductee into the Boxing Hall of Fame and later recorded his boxing experiences in book form with an autobiographical, *Uppercuts and Dazes*. A serious heart operation in recent years slowed him down and the death of a daughter at an early age shattered him. Through it all he maintained his old wit, being a born raconteur. He admitted to not having a memory for dates and sequence of events and some of his more amusing experiences have never been put into print. With his death an era dies. The game changes, as does everything, but boxing men will always be grateful that he brought the great fights into their living rooms. Reg, a one-off, is survived by his wife, Connie, a daughter and four grandchildren.

HANCOCK Taffy *From* Coledale, NSW, Australia. *Died* 9 November 2008, aged 81. Former Australian flyweight champion Taffy began boxing in 1945 at Thirrol where he won a competition held over three days. He was unbeaten until 1948 before he lost a challenge for the Australian title to Mick Hill, a man he had previously beaten and with whom he was to clash three more times. Taffy grabbed the title from him in1949, lost it in the return the following year and had to wait until 1951 before again getting the belt around his waist. On that occasion, the man in the opposite corner was Jimmy Laffin. Taffy stopped him in 13 rounds. The previous year Laffin had succumbed in 12, but there had been no title at stake. En route to his first championship, Taffy had beaten Emile Famechon, who had performed well in England in the mid-1940s. Famechon settled in Australia and saw his nephew, Johnny, rise to the pinnacle of his profession in the 1960s. The most prominent name on Taffy's record is that of Jimmy Carruthers, but the result of their fight was a predictable win for the latter. It lasted seven rounds. Soon afterwards Taffy defended his title against Jackie Burke but it was the last good win of his career. Bobby Sinn, Tanny Campo and Kid Dynamite beat him and Vince Blake took his title in 1954. The year 1955 saw the end. He lost to that colourful Aboriginal scrapper, Teddy Rainbow, and Frankie Bennett edged him out on points. At that stage Taffy decided to retire.

Vince Hawkins

HARRIS Basil *From* Oxford. *Died* 22 December 2008, aged 83. Basil, who was active right up to his death, succumbed to cancer just before last Christmas. His brief boxing career, which took place in 1947-1948, was confined to Oxford and Cheltenham venues apart from two contests at Islington's Caledonian Road Baths. The Baths are still there today but have for many years been out of use. Basil beat Frank Edwards there by a first-round stoppage. On his home patch, Oxford Town Hall, he knocked out Charlie Winters, but Swindon's Owen Randall twice beat him. No fights can be found for 1949 onwards.

HARRIS Sammy *From* Pakistan. *Died* October 2008. Sammy was Pakistan's flyweight hope in a five-man team competing at the Melbourne Olympics in November 1956. His division was the hardest one in which to compete. Among the entrants were Rene Libeer, Salvatore Burruni, Johnny Caldwell, Warner Batchelor, Kenji Yonekura and Terry Spinks. He and all his team-mates were eliminated in their first fights and in all cases but Sammy's, their opponents were beaten in the next series. Sammy had the misfortune to face the eventual gold-medallist, Terry Spinks. He went the distance but found Spinks too fast and too elusive. The trade paper reported that they met again socially in more recent years and, as is usual when former boxers meet, they greeted each other warmly and reminisced for hours.

HAWKINS Vince *From* Eastleigh. *Died* December 2008, aged 85. The ability and outstanding record of this former British middleweight champion was seldom appreciated during his boxing days. The emphasis always seemed to fall on his having a splendid physique but not punching power commensurate with it. Such views were harsh on a man who stopped many of his opponents, took on men that others avoided and had 62 fights before tasting a defeat that he subsequently avenged. In erasing that blot he won the vacant British championship. Vince lost only ten of his 87 contests and eight of those defeats came in the last three years of his career. I remember a time when Vince was going through a bad patch. He had been stopped by Dick Turpin, was narrowly outpointed by the celebrated Randolph, Dick's brother, lost an Empire title bid against New Zealand's Bos Murphy and in a second match with Turpin senior was outpointed and relieved of his title. At the end of that particularly bad year, he accepted a fight with top European fighter, Jean Stock. I did not expect him to win but he did. Boxing with all his old dash and aplomb, he got his career back on track, then proved that at domestic level he was a force still to be reckoned with by beating Alex Buxton. Apart from Buxton, Vince beat Albert Finch, Dave McCleave and Ernie Roderick, all of whom would win a British title, and there were title challengers and top contenders who failed to get the better of him: Mark Hart, Ginger Sadd, Bert Gilroy, Jack Lewis, Glen Moody and Pat O'Connor to quote just a few. His career started in 1940 when he was 17. Up to 1948 he had lost only three of 77 fights. I'm not trying to elevate Vince's status by saying that he was one of our great fighters but he does belong in the category occupied by men like Sadd and Finch as being a reliable professional who never picked or chose a foe. Vince won the Southern Area title, which then carried prestige, from McCleave in 1944. He lost a British title contest against Roderick the following year and with that, sustained his first loss. He got Roderick back in the ring the following year and took the title from him. Among the good European scrappers' names on his record are Cyrille Delannoit, Gus DeGouve, Augustin Mendicute, Widmer Milandri and Joe Brun. On the domestic front he beat Harry O'Grady, George Bennett, Jack Beech, Charlie Parkin, Paddy Roche, Tommy Davies, Lefty Flynn, Jimmy Ingle, George Dilkes and Jimmy Bray. Having incurred consecutive losses to George Angelo, Dick Turpin and George Casson in 1950, he chose that time to retire. From memory, I recall that he was a junior ABA champion as an amateur and an engine fireman on the old Southern Railway. In his day, Eastleigh was a railway depot. His manager was John Simpson of Basingstoke - a decent man who really cared for his fighters. After finishing with boxing, Vince worked for a firm in Winchester until he was 70. For many years he was our oldest living champion, a mantle that passed to Cliff Curvis, who also died recently. Vince was married to Marian and is survived by her, a son, a daughter, grandchildren and great grandchildren.

HOBY Alan OBE *From* London. *Died* November 2008, aged 94. The long journalistic career of Alan began as a 16-shillings-a-week reporter for the *Richmond and Twickenham News*, where his ambition to report various boxing and sporting events was nurtured. Eventually, he graduated on to *The People*. That was back in the days of Peter Kane, Nel Tarleton, Eric Boon, Dave Crowley and Benny Lynch, who he saw beat Small Montana in 1937. As a teenager in 1932, Alan had watched, Larry Gains trim the giant Primo Carnera at the White City. His love affair with boxing dated from then. He was in the Marines during the war when he read a story concerning the murder of Stanley Ketchel. Fascinated by this, he researched information on Ketchel and wrote an article on the boxer's life that was published by the *Sunday Express*, a paper for which he was to report on sport from 1949 to 1986. He saw six Olympic Games and was ringside at all the big fights of that period - the Turpin v Robinson fights, Ali's clashes with Frazier, Foreman, Norton, Liston and all three of Howard Winstone's encounters with Saldivar. Alan named Sugar Ray Robinson as the greaest fighter of his time. He had a remarkable memory for detail and a graphic style of reporting which gained him an OBE for services to sport in 1986.

HUNT Reg *From* Watford. *Died* February 2009, aged 91. Reg confined most of his boxing activity to the area within 30 miles' radius of Watford. Beginning in 1936, there are 14 fights on his record. He won half of them, yet was considered efficient enough to fight ten-rounders. Two local boys he fought were Billy Hawkins and Ted MacDonald.

Ingemar Johansson

JOHANSSON Ingemar *From* Gothenburg, Sweden. *Died* 30 January 2009, aged 76. Prior to Lennox Lewis, Sweden's Ingemar was the last European to annex the world heavyweight championship. He was also, up to his death, the oldest living former heavyweight champion. His disqualification in the 1952 Olympic final has been well documented. Seven years later he was his country's hero when he stopped Floyd Patterson and became undisputed champion. In those days, the best man at his weight was champion. Fragmented titles did not come along until Cassius Clay was stripped of his title after refusing induction into the armed services. The first inkling that the Swede could rise higher than champion at European level was when he beat Francesco Cavicchi for that title. Unfazed and still confident despite trailing on points, he took out the huge Italian with one punch, his right hand punch now being termed 'Ingo's Bingo'. He did much the same to Eddie Machen a couple of years later to find himself in line for a shot at the big prize. He had defended his European title twice against the British contenders, Joe Erskine and Henry Cooper. He had also broken Peter Bates' jaw when knocking him out. Despite his obvious punching powers, he was not expected to do the same against Floyd Patterson. After two quiet and dull rounds one solid dig put paid to the defending champion. Floyd got up in no condition to go on but shocking refereeing by Ruby Goldstein allowed the carnage

to continue. It was 1959. Over the next three years, Ingemar and Floyd monopolised the championship. Patterson regained the title in 1960 with an emphatic knockout and won the rubber match a year later. Both were on the deck in the first round but the Swede ran out of steam and took the full count on one knee in round six. Ingemar returned to the European circuit, fighting just four more times. He knocked out Dick Richardson, Wim Snoek and Joe Bygraves, but his last fight, a points win over Brian London, saw him saved him from a knockout by the final bell. He knew it was time to go, so he never fought again. The Swede was a good businessman who held on to his ring earnings, invested them wisely and died a rich man. Suffering from encroaching Alzheimer's disease over the past few years, he beat every man he fought, a record he shares with Gene Tunney, Rocky Marciano and Lennox Lewis.

Dick Johnson

JOHNSON Dick *From* Stanton Hill. *Died* 7 January 2009, aged 90. Old Dick followed the game for all his adult life. Long after he hung up his gloves he was churning out articles on boxing history for local papers and ex-boxers' newsletters. He specialised in bare-knuckle history and wrote a book on it, which is not easy to find nowadays and does not come cheap. Dick drew on gloves as a paid fighter back in 1938, losing to a Ginger Smith and then forcing him to a draw. Because it was wartime, his career never really got off the ground until 1943 when he had 12 fights, losing three. Many of these were against servicemen like L/Cpl Cooper, A/C Massey, Driver Langton etc; After hostilities ceased, familiar names like Billy Biddles, Dick Leivers, Leo

Phillips, Bob Barlow and Rugger North started to appear on his record. He lost to Jimmy Anderson (senior) and future champion Henry Hall in 1946, had a draw and two stoppage wins over Pat Magee and in 1947, drew with Phil Volante. From 1948 until retirement in 1954, he never lost a fight and there are 23 entries on his score sheet, compiled by the late Vic Hardwicke. Jim Cameron, Bobby Clarke, Bob Savage, Jack Russell, Teddy Parker, Frank Barron, Pat Markey and Frank Shannon were amongst those who never made it to the final bell and there were just three points wins and two draws. The last fight found for him was a seventh-round stoppage win over Manchester's Bobby Mann in January 1954. It is clear that Dick carried a hefty punch. He lived alone for the last years of his life, becoming house-bound in the end and lonely. Because of his age, most of his contemporaries had gone so he confined his boxing activities to journalism. The late Brian Daltrey used to keep in touch and, at his request, I dug out some of Dick's articles to replace those that Dick had lost. That pleased him no end. He was a friendly and kind man and one of the few of his era still around in the 21st Century.

JONI Simphiwe *From* East London, South Africa. *Died* 11 December 2008, aged 35. The sad saga of the early deaths of South African boxers continued when this lightweight was fatally wounded following a dispute outside his home. He fought from 1993 to 2006, winning 17 out of 25 contests and challenging twice for the South African title.

KOMATSU Noriyuki *From* Osaka, Japan. *Died* April 2009, aged 29. Noriyuki was a former OBPF flyweight champion before he challenged Thailand's more experienced Pongsaklek Wonjongkam for the WBC flyweight championship. He was stopped by the hard-punching champion, who had packed in over 50 fights, with 11 of them being for the world title. Noriyuki had 36 fights in all with 24 wins. He won the Oriental and Pacific title by beating Jung-Oh Sung in 2002 and held on to it until losing it to Trash Nakanuma in 2004. This was his fourth title defence, having retained against Nakanuma earlier. Later he was to win back that title by beating Federico Catabay, only to lose it again when fighting for the Japanese championship. Daisuke Naito grabbed both titles by stopping Komatsu in six rounds. The national title then passed to Kenji Yoshida and Noriyuki had a shot at winning it, in 2007, but without success. He fought on until February of this year, winning two and drawing one from four outings, his final fight being a loss to Ratanapol Sor Vorapin. His death was due extensive injuries following to fall from a waterfall.

LaROSA Tony *From* Chicago, Illinois, USA. *Died* 5 October 2008, aged 41. Tony started boxing in 1988 and had only two losses in 16 fights before venturing to Paris where he lost to Eric Nicoletta in1991. He did well up to

1996 when he lost to Denmark's Brian Nielsen. Following that he blew hot and cold until he became a trialhorse, albeit, a respectable one. A loss due to injuries against 'Buster' Douglas preceded a bad patch of seven defeats, Lamon Brewster and Courage Tchabalala being among his opponents. He regrouped to hammer out wins over Iran Barkley, Dwight Muhammad Qawi and Trevor Berbick, but those were his last successes of note. Francois Botha, Dominic Guinn, Donovan Ruddock and Vladimir Klitschko all stopped him. Taking a year's rest in 2003, he had no luck in a comeback, his last fight coming in 2004.

LEDUC Mark *From* Kingson, Ontario, Canada. *Died* 22 July 2009. aged 47. A long and successful amateur career brought fame to Mark when, at the age of 30, he emerged from the 1992 Barcelona Olympics with a siver medal. This was expected to launch him into success as a professional, but it was not to be. Mark won four fights then was narrowly beaten by Michel Galarneau. He never fought again, turning his attention to Toronto's Aids' Charity where he worked as a volunteer. His homosexual proclivities spurred him to devote his life to helping those unfortunate to be afflicted with this modern disease. His main income came from his work in the film industry. Having collapsed in a sauna and dying four days later, the possible cause of death was given as a 'heat stroke'.

LONGHURST Ernie *From* Dartford. *Died* July 2009, aged 69. A top amateur in the days of serious competition, Ernie first made his mark when eliminating the Olympic bronze medallist, Jim Lloyd, in the 1961 Army championships before going out in the final to Bob Keddie. Back in civvies, boxing for the Fitzroy Lodge, in 1963 he won the London middleweight title, beating Kevin O'Reilly and Alan Munro on the way before being eliminated in the ABA semis by Ernie Lofthouse. That season he was also selected for England in two matches against Russia. In 1964 he defeated his arch-rival, Stan Miles, to win the South-East Divisional title before being beaten by Tony Moore in the London finals. When he retired he helped run the Samuel Montagu ABC for a while and was always around the amateurs, never having gone pro. A plumber by trade, Ernie passed away after being diagnosed with cancer just two weeks earlier.

LOTTER Billy *From* Pretoria, Gauteng, South Africa. *Died* 13 February 2009, aged 71. Starting as a welterweight in 1956, Billy, a southpaw with fighting talent, went through four weight divisions before becoming heavyweight champion of his country in 1964. He challenged for national titles at welter, middle and light-heavy, giving Mike Holt an extremely hard fight before going up yet another division where he finally got a championship belt by easily beating Stoffel Willemse on points in Johannesburg. As a middleweight he twice beat that very good and very tough scrapper, Hottie van Heerden. Billy fought over here just once, beating Johnny Hendrickson in three rounds in 1965. He then beat the big Italian, Giorgio Masteghin, but it would be his last big win. Having lost his heavyweight title to Gerrie de Bruyn in 1966, Billy then retired to take out a trainer's licence, Charlie Weir and Kallie Knoetzee being his most successful fighters.

Pat McAteer

McATEER Pat *From* Birkenhead. *Died* 1 May 2009, aged 77. Going into his contest with Ellsworth 'Spider' Webb, Pat seemed destined to become a force at world level. He had convincingly beaten Jerry Luedee in his American debut and had a magnificent record of 47 fights with only two defeats. He was British and Empire middleweight champion, having taken those titles from Johnny Sullivan, and had defended the Empire crown against Mike Holt and both titles against Lew Lazar. At the time he fought Webb he was practically unbeatable in Europe and his win over Luedee suggested a bright future as a world contender. Our hopes for him were shattered when he lasted under six minutes. He continued his career and seemed most unfortunate to get only a draw with Dick Tiger. He was well ahead in the return match but at a late stage he decided to forgo his boxing for a fight and was stopped, thus losing his Empire title. He had also lost a fight for the European title against Charles Humez, cut eyes forcing his retirement when he was doing well. Previously, Pat had kayoed Jimmy Elliott in defence of his Empire diadem, the latter dying from injuries suffered during the contest. After that, Pat was never quite the same, although he was still a good champion and won the Lonsdale Belt outright by licking Martin Hansen. When Terry Downes took his title from him in 1958, Pat quit the game. He married an American girl and located to the States.

They had four children and, at the time of his death, eight grandchildren.

McMANUS Johnny *From* Twechar, Glasgow. *Died* January 2009, aged 88. A lot is expected of a prominent amateur when he turns pro. Such was the case with Canadian-born Johnny, who was a flyweight in the simon-pure ranks. He was in the army during the war and claimed to have boxed regularly for his ROAC unit. As a paid performer, he fought from bantam to lightweight, starting out in 1937 with a ten-round contest against Belfast's Al Sharpe. Johnny forced his man to retire in five rounds, which was a great result against an established fighter. His next was a ten-round points win over another good'un in Syd Parker, but his handlers were too ambitious. After only four fights he was thrown in against one of the world's leading bantamweights in Aurel Toma, the former European champion. Despite taking two counts, Johnny lasted nine rounds. It did not seem to do him any harm and he was back in action and in winning mode a week later. Johnny got into his stride in 1938 when he knocked out Pat Palmer and southpaw Jim Warnock before outscoring Len 'Nipper' Hampston. He got his first shot at Teddy O'Neill's Scottish title but spoiled his chances by coming in too light. Perhaps he had weakened himself because he took a battering and four counts before being pulled out in the 13th round. Nine days later an eye injury forced him to concede to Johnny King. The Scot seemed unaffected by his loss to O'Neill and had King in trouble several times, but his cuts were too severe to allow him to continue. There was not a lot of activity during the war years, yet it was towards the end of the conflict that he won the Scottish lightweight title by stopping Joe Kerr. He lost to Dave Crowley and beat Dennis Chadwick and Johnny Russell. Later, in peacetime he repeated his win over Russell and also beat George Daly and Phil Freeman. The year 1947 was his last in the ring, Army service overseas having hindered his progress at a time when he should have been at his peak. Consecutive losses to Stan Hawthorne and Eddie Miller told him that it was time to go.

MACIAS Raul (Raton) *From* Tepito, Mexico City, Mexico. *Died* 23 March 2009, aged 75. A hard-punching Mexican, Raton lost only twice in an outstanding career. He was unfortunate to meet Alphonse Halimi when the Frenchman was right at his peak, the Frenchman keeping winning a split decision and keeping his world bantamweight championship. Raton boxed on for another five years and never lost again. He had won the Mexican title in his first year as a paid fighter and considering the depth of talent in Mexico it was a remarkable achievement. He soon reached world class, beating Billy Peacock, Filberto Nava and Nate Brooks, the last fight being for the North-American title. This was in his second fighting year and at this point he developed a punch that was to gain him 22 wins within the scheduled distance.

By stopping Thailand's Chamrern Songkitrak he won the vacant NBA title in 1955 but was surprisingly knocked out by former victim Peacock, suffering a broken jaw which put him on the sidelines for five months. Raton was a proud fighter. He did not choose a patsy as his next opponent but fought and beat the experienced New York bantamweight, Cecil Schoonmaker. He defended his NBA championship against Leo Espinosa and Dommy Ursua, both of whom failed to last the distance. On the run-up to the loss to Halimi, he beat Tanny Campo, Larry Bataan, Gaetano Annaloro, Juan Cardenas and Hector Ceballos in a series of 17 impressive wins. He retired in 1959, but returned for one last fight, in 1963, beating Chocolate Zambrano in a charity event. The bantamweight division was saturated with class fighters during Raton's reign and his success is a mark of his stature as a fighter.

Freddie Mack

MACK Freddie *From* South Carolina, USA. *Died* 11 January 2009, aged 75. It was cancer that caused Freddie's death. He fought it for years and refused to let it rule his life, carrying on with his post-boxing interests as a musician and a band-leader. In the early 1990s he settled in Scotland where he later married and helped found the Scottish Boxing Hall of Fame, which is a steady, well-supported and strong organisation. In the beginning, the bulk of his boxing was done in the USA where he started out as a pro in 1954. By 1961 he had spread his fistic activities around the globe to Lima, Canada, Italy and eventually England, by which time he had put on poundage and was often boxing as a heavyweight. An interesting item in his record is a fourth-round stoppge defeat at the hands of Paul Pender, the winner being seven years into his pro career. Freddie never got into the big time in the States, losing to Yvon Durelle and Jerry Luedee. He was on firmer ground as a simon pure, when he was befriended by Floyd Patterson and, as a middleweight, accompanied Floyd to the Helsinki Olympics as a stand-by substitute. He beat a few fighters when in the six-round class and did better as his status improved. Arriving in Rome in 1961, he beat Sante Amonte, Ottavio Panunzi and Renato Moraes, losing to Jesse Bowdry and holding Piero Tomasoni to a ten-round draw. On England's shores he gave weight to Joe Erskine and lost on points, then beat Ray Shiel, Ron Gray, Joe Louis (Birkenhead) and stopped Jack Bodell. Interspersed with these fights were trips back to Italy where he enhanced his reputation with the Tomasoni fight. His best win came in 1965 when he stopped Chic Calderwood, but the same year saw him have his last fight when Bodell beat him in a return meeting. Freddie kept himself active in the capacity of a sparring partner to our top heavyweights, but his music interests soon took over. He had been in films too and also in a few television programmes. Freddie was a popular man and, as the above summary shows, he lived his life to the full. He leaves a wife, children and grandchildren.

MANCA Fortunato *From* Cagliari, Italy. *Died*: 16 December 2008, aged: 73. Back in the 1950s there was considerable boxing in Sardinia. Alas, it has now dried up to just a trickle. Fortunato was one of the island's busiest fighters, raking up 82 fights between 1957 and 1965. He had 30 fights before his first loss, which was by disqualification to Jean Hoeffler in Milan, and he boxed another 23 opponents before the great Dulio Loi beat him in a match for the European welterweight championship in 1962, Fortunato took him the full 15 rounds. Dismayed by the loss, he flew to Sweden and was outpointed by Jose Assumpcao before getting his enthusiasm back and picking up the Italian light-middleweight title from Ferdinando Proietti. On the way to the championship he had knocked out Harko Kokmeijer, Jean Hoeffler and Andre Mauguin, and had licked Wally Swift, Maurice Auzel, Johnny Melfah, Al Brown, Gunter Hase, Leo Maloney, Sani Armstrong, Jimmy Croll, Michel Lombardet, Al Sharpe, Chris Christensen and Ben Buker ll. There were draws with Attu Clottey and Bruno Visintin, plus stoppage wins over Tony Smith, Ben Moktar and Attu Clottey and he beat Ireland's Freddie Tiedt on a foul. Also, he avenged the earlier loss to Jean Hoeffler with an emphatic knockout and took care of Assumpcao after winning the title. Bob Cofie surprised him with a points win in 1963 and trips to Argentina and Denmark were unsuccessful, losing to Jorge Fernandez and Christensen, his old foe. Back home he relinquished his Italian crown to fight for the vacant EBU title, which he won by stopping Francois Pavilla. Ambitiously, he went in with Sandro Mazzinghi for the WBA and WBC light-middleweight belts but lost. With his career coming to an end, he lost to Curtis Cokes, defended his European title against Carmelo Garcia, beat Dramane Ouedrago and Apidej Sithiran before calling it quits. In what was a fine record, he had 82 fights, with just eight losses.

MARCANO Alfredo *From* Sucre, Venezuela. *Died* 5 April 2009, aged 62. It takes a good fighter to come from behind especially at world level. Alfredo had to do so when he challenged Hiroshi Kobayashi for the Jap's WBA super-featherweight title. Trailing on points, he stopped his man in the tenth round. He did not sit on his laurels and just four months later he defended against Kenji Iwata in Caracas before losing it to Ben Villaflor in 1972. There are some notable names on his record. Wins came over Richie Sue, Bernardo Caraballo, Jaime Perez, Miguel Herrara and Octavio Gomez. There is a draw with Cruz Marcano and losses to Ernesto Marcel and Ricardo Arredondo. A failed Challenge for Bobby Chacon's WBC featherweight title, followed by two further losses, signalled the end. He succumbed to cancer after a long battle with the dreaded disease.

MARIE Bobby *From* Miami, Florida, USA. *Died* 1 October 2008, aged 71. A popular supporting-bill fighter, active in Miami during the 1950s and '60s, lightweight Bobby twice lost to the local prospect, Tony Mamarelli, before scoring five victories over Sammy Seabrooke. He won four out of five fights with George Sawyer and ended a 51-fight career when losing to Johnny Bizzarro in Pennsylvania. It was the only time he plied his wares outside of Florida.

MORENO Santos (Apache) *From* Juarez, Mexico. *Died* 16 June 2009. Mexico's Santos had a very slow start to his professional career, with only ten fights between 1976 and 1980. The tenth was his first loss when Hector Cortez beat him for the NABF super-featherweight title, after which he started to fight in top company. Results were mixed but he took them all on and was considered to be no easy touch. He revenged an earlier loss to Nicky Perez, who had earlier beaten him in a match for the NABF super-bantamweight crown. Over here he lost to Mo Hussein and Pat Cowdell, then confined the remainder of his fights to Mexico and the USA. He took on Ruben Castillo, Juan Estrada, Rafael Limon, Oscar Bejines, Marcos Villasana, Vince Phillips, Calvin Grove and fought for the last time in 1990, losing to Roger Mayweather.

MUANGSURIN Saengsak *From* Bangkok, Thailand. *Died* April 2009, aged 58. In the record books as Thailand's former WBC light-welterweight champion, Saensak's

achievements were quite remarkable, inasmuch as he won his world title in his third professional fight. It was no fluke victory, beating the champion, Perico Fernandez of Spain, decisively via an eighth-round stoppage. He defended once before another Spaniard, Miguel Velasquez, relieved him of his crown in 1976. The Thai had been in command when accused of hitting after the bell and being disqualified, but got back his title in a rematch. He was a good champion who went through seven defences before losing to Sang-Hyun Kim. Knocked out by Tommy Hearns in 1979, by then his career was on the rocks, but he carried on with sparse success until 1981. Failing eyesight and financial difficulties forced him to depend on grants from sporting associations. He died in hospital from natural causes.

MUDGE Johnny *From* Torquay. *Died* May 2009, aged 81. Johnny, a Western Counties' middleweight champion as an amateur and later an experienced booth fighter, took out a professional licence in 1951 and boxed for five years, beating men like Johnny James, Eric Thomas, Steve Coombes, Don Desborough, Mick Endley, Alf Lay, Frank Bassenger, Bill Watkins and Mike Kelly. He also boxed Peter Longo to a draw. Most of Johnny's wins came inside the distance and he was known as a strong puncher. He retired to help run the Apollo ABC at Babbacombe. My thanks go to Harold Alderman MBE for this information.

MUHAMMAD Herbert *From* Chicago, Illinois, USA. *Died* 25 August 2008, aged 79. It was after beating Sonny Liston in 1964 that Cassius Clay announced that he was of Islamic faith and had changed his name to Muhammad Ali. Guiding him both spiritually and in business affairs was Herbert Muhammad. Whatever decisions the official management of Ali made, the final word came from his newly-found mentor, who died in 2008 after heart surgery.

MURPHY Arthur *From* Camden Town, London. *Died* December 2008, aged 72. There are 29 winning fights on Arthur's record and only five of them were via points decisions. At his own level, Arthur was a banger. There are five clean knockouts and eight stoppages recorded for 1955, the year he started out. He was a lightweight who travelled to Bournemouth for his fistic baptism, losing on points to Eddie Baker. Arthur finished the year with another points loss to Mickey Driscoll, who I later saw fight in Australia where I believe he settled. Sandwiched between those two losses are 13 inside-the-distance wins. Jackie Leonard, Oliver Paul and Maurice Mufitt are three of the names on the list. His best win was a knockout over Barney Beale at Wembley in 1956, but it pushed him up in class too soon. Three consecutive defeats, against Jimmy Tippett, Sammy Odell and Ray Akwei, followed before Arthur got back into winning mode. He had 39 contests in all, fighting Kenny Taylor, Ernie Fossey, Teddy Best, Bryn

Phillips (twice) and Andy Baird before closing with a win over Peter Anderson in January 1959.

Dave Needham

NEEDHAM Dave *From* Nottingham. *Died* September 2008, aged 57. One of 1979's most controversial decisions was that awarded to Dave over Pat Cowdell in a fight for his British featherweight championship. The furore that greeted the one-point margin on referee Sid Nathan's scorecard was mainly due to there being a huge contingent of Cowdell supporters in the Civic Hall, Wolverhampton. Had Cowdell not been guilty of incessant holding, for which he was constantly warned, the verdict may have been different, but Sid Nathan was not intimidated by partisan support and had the courage to score it in Needham's favour. A quick return followed with the margin between them so slight, but this time Cowdell made sure of the verdict. Pat won the rubber match too and, as is often the case with the passing of championships, the loser was at the tail-end of his career. By European standards, Dave was one of our better featherweights, having entered the pro ranks in 1971 following a fine amateur career in which he had twice won an ABA title at flyweight whilst in his teens. He was also a Commonwealth Games gold medallist. A southpaw by style and one with a good boxing brain, his main weakness was being prone to cuts. Many of Dave's defeats were caused by cut eyes and the sad thing is that he was often well in

the lead when having to bow out. He was into his 23rd fight without loss when he won the British bantamweight title from Paddy Maguire in a cracking contest. En-route to the title, his victims included John McClusky, John Kellie, Earl Large, Karim Young, Billy Hardacre, Paddy Graham, Colin Miles and South Africa's Bashew Sibaca. There was one draw of 'hometown' variety which occured against Daniel Triouliare in a fight following Dave's acquisition of the British title. In that one, the European title was at stake. Cuts were responsible for losing his British title back to Maguire and a following loss in South Africa to Arnold Taylor was his last at the bantamweight limit. At featherweight, he revenged a previous loss to Alan Richardson (cuts again) by beating Alan in a fight for the British title. A notable knockout win over Vernon Sollas put him in line for that title shot and soon his name was put forward to challenge for the European crown. Dave was past his best at this stage and was unsuccessful, Roberto Castanon beating him in Spain, and he next defended his national title against Cowdell. This is where we came in but there was another title challenge, for the Commonwealth title, squeezed between the last two fights with Cowdell. Dave lost this with a cut mouth against Charm Chituele then fought Cowdell three weeks later. That was his finale. The cause of his death at an early age has not been disclosed. He lived in Thailand for the last two years of his life but was not forgotten by his fans back home.

NEESON Charlie *From* Belfast, Northern Ireland. *Died* 3 March 2009, aged 84. Belfast boxing writer, Brian Madden, has informed me of the death of this former lightweight boxer, who passed away in the Royal Victoria Hospital. Fifteen of Charlie's 19 fights took place in Belfast's Ulster Hall where he beat Johnny Hazel, Roy MacGregor and Jackie Robinson amongst others. In 1949, he was outpointed by Frank Johnson at the Royal Hippodrome, the winner going on to win the British and British Empire titles. Charlie boxed on until 1951, taking on Tony McTigue, Black Bond, Paddy Dowdall etc, and retired with eight losses. Even in retirement he kept exceptionally fit, joining Beechmount Harriers Athletic Club long before jogging became a social activity and could often be seen pounding the street of Belfast.

NOGUCHI Kyo *From* Tokyo, Japan. *Died* 1 January 2009, aged 69. When former world flyweight challenger, Kyo, was active, the Far East and Mexico were teeming with good flyweights. In an eight-year career between 1955 and 1963 he had 52 fights, of which he won 37, drew five and lost ten. Kyo was a southpaw, born in Shanghai and of Japanese nationality. Of his first 17 fights it is interesting to see that all but two of his foes were debutants. There was a draw with Sadao Yaoita in his fifth outing and it was the same man who stopped his unbeaten streak in 1957. Another to beat him later was Takeshi Yamaguchi. That was in 1958, but from then on he fought mainly ten rounders in good company. He drew with Larry Pineda, which established him as being a fighter bordering world class. Then ran up seven wins before Yaoita beat him again in a fight for the Orient title. He won the Japanese title on the second attempt then travelled to Thailand where he beat Cherngchai Laemfapha by a knockout, but was outpointed by future world champion, Chartchai Chionoi. After beating Baby Espinoza he was ready to fight Pone Kingpetch for the Thailander's world title. Kingpetch had dethroned the great Pascual Perez and defended against both him and Mitsunori Seki. He was too good for the man from Japan and won by unanimous decision. There was not much more after that - four fights of which Kyo won only one, losing the national championship on the way. His last three fights took place in the same arena where he had started out in 1955.

Gerry O'Colmain

O'COLMAIN Gerry *From* Dublin, Ireland. *Died* November 2008, aged 88. Gerry was one of Ireland's very best post-war amateur boxers. As a member of the North City ABC he did the club proud when reaching the pinnacle of many notable achievements by winning the European heavyweight championship in Dublin. It was 1947 and in the opposite corner was George Scriven, who did well to go the full distance after taking two long counts. Gerry had been around for quite a few years at that stage. He started as a light-heavy, won two national titles in the early 1940s, before going up in weight and boxing at championship level well into the '50s. He represented his country in the 1948 Olympics, won seven national heavyweight titles and was

selected for the Europe versus the USA Golden Gloves' team in 1947. An eye injury, sustained in 1954 during his work as a blacksmith, forced him to retire from the game at the age of 30 when he was still a considerable force.

O'NEILL Gerry *From* Belfast. *Died* 3 August 2009, aged 77. A very late entry in this list of obits is Gerry O'Neill, whose demise was noted by the boxing writer, Brian Madden. Brian's observance allows us to record the death of a man who was very popular with Belfast boxing fans. The *Belfast Press* carried a notice in its births and deaths column without a mention of Gerry's involvement with boxing. He was a lightweight who first punched for pay in 1950 and who fought mostly against local men before retiring in 1959 with a 27-16-5 record, following a loss to Bobby Griffin. Gerry fought Paddy Graham, Tommy Lamour, Joe Sharpe (brother of Al), Pat O'Brien, Gerry Smythe's brother Billy and boxing record-compiler, Fred Heatley, whose deep knowledge of boxing matters has been vital to this publication. He and Fred were close neighbours. The only non-Belfast opponent that I can pick out in Gerry's account is Lulu Robinson of Nigeria who was stopped in five rounds midway through Gerry's career. He died peacefully at home following a long illness and leaves a wife, Pauline, and six children.

ORBAN Laszlo *From* Hungary. *Died* July 2009, aged 59. Having won the European Games featherweight title in 1969, beating England's Alan Richardson in the semi-finals, Laszlo was up at lightweight for the 1972 Olympics. A southpaw, he reached the final, only to lose to the very good Pole, Jan Szczepanski, by a narrow margin. In 1973 he represented Hungary in the European championships, but after winning his opening contest he was eliminated by Ryszard Tomczyk of Poland. He never turned pro.

PAGE Greg *From* Louisville, Kentucky, USA. *Died* 27 April 2009, aged 50. Brain injuries received in an ill-advised contest with Dale Crowe in 2001 hastened the death of this former WBA heavyweight champion. Greg, who was in a coma for a week following the fight, sued the Kentucky officials for poor medical control and was awarded over a million dollars. At 20, he was Golden gloves champion and quickly made an impression when he turned pro. He had been sparring with Muhammad Ali since he was 15 and many of the great man's skills rubbed off on him. His ascent to the WBA title was quick and impressive, beating Alfredo Evangelistic and clever Jimmy Young before sustaining his first loss when Trevor Berbick outpointed him. He came straight back with a win over James Tillis before going to South Africa and knocking out the title holder, Gerrie Coetzee, in 1984. His tenure was brief. Tony Tubbs took his title five months later but Greg was still a force and continued to box at top level, going in with 'Buster' Douglas and Joe Bugner. Donovan Ruddock, Francesco Damiani and Bruce Seldon all beat him and after losing to the latter he should have called it a day. Coming back three years later, he was no longer able to stay in contention with the top-rated men and could only win over obscure opponents. He managed to avenge a defeat by Tim Witherspoon but it was meaningless at that stage. It was a far cry from 1984 when he nearly beat Tim for the vacant WBC crown.

PARISI Giovanni *From* Voghera, Italy. *Died* March 2009, aged 42. As an amateur, Giovanni won the Italian light and featherweight titles and crowned his simon-pure career by winning the gold medal at featherweight in the 1988 Seoul Olympics. He turned professional in 1989 and had lost only one fight up to beating Stefano Cassi for the national lightweight title. The man who beat him was Antonio Rivera, but Giovanni would get his revenge later on when he was WBO champion. He was a strong puncher and most of his victories came inside the scheduled distance. Stoppage wins continued going into 1991, when he knocked out Javier Altamarino for the WBO title at lightweight. He defended twice, beating Michael Ayers and Rivera both of whom were amongst the few to go the full distance with him. In 1994, Giovanni campaigned successfully in the USA and retired as undefeated champion later in the year to throw his hat in with the light-welters. A series of wins put him in line for a shot at Julio Cesar Chavez's WBC championship but he lost on points. He had better luck the following year when he relieved Sammy Fuentes of his WBO light-welter title which, after four defences, he was to lose to Carlos Gonzalez in 1998. A failed bid for the WBO welterweight crown in July 2000 was his last bid for world honours and he had four more wins before retiring after Frederic Klose narrowly beat him for the European title. His death at 42 was the tragic result of a road accident.

PEACE Andy *From* Glenrothes, Fife. *Died* June 2009, aged 64. Boxing for the Lochore ABC in the 1960s, Andy was good enough to win a Scottish amateur welterweight title and a Commonwealth Games' bronze medal in 1966. He also represented Scotland many times. His all-action style was thought to be better suited to the pro ranks and at the beginning of 1969 he discarded his vest after moving down to Rugby to win the Midlands title before being disqualified in the 1968 ABA semis against Brian Whelan. He started well, winning his first five contests, but after being outpointed by Don McMillan for the Scottish middleweight title in May 1971 he called it a day. Andy had beaten Tommy Tiger, Panther Cyril, Clive Cook and Fred Powney, and shared the ring with good men such as Dave Cranswick, Ricky Porter, Bernie Terrell, Tommy Gray and Jan Kies before returning to Scotland to run the highly successful Exit ABC. Andy passed away after a long battle with ill health.

PERRYMENT Wally *From* Clapton, London. *Died* May 2009, aged 94. A real old-timer's death was recorded when 94-year-old Wally, who was boxing 75 years ago, passed away. Miles Templeton has traced only one fight for him so far, a loss to Chelmsford's Bill Bright on the latter's home patch. Other results will emerge later. Men like Wally received scant news coverage and many of their exploits are unrecorded except by their own memories. That he was a member of the London Ex-Boxers' Association from its early days indicates that he never lost his interest in the game. As a man who boxed so long ago, his passing deserves a respected mention.

POST Mike *From* Indianapolis, Indiana, USA. *Died* 28 November 2008, aged 28. A light-welterweight, Mike began boxing in 2004 and was active up to his death. His last recorded fight was a points win over Ruben Galvan in May 2008 which took place in Canada, the country of his birth. He had just one defeat, by Justin Danforth, in 19 fights, his best wins being stoppages against Brian Paul and John Hoffman. The autopsy was unable to determine the cause of death, but a police spokesman stated that there were no suspicious circumstances involved.

REDFERN John *From* Sheffield. *Died* 18 January 2009, aged 65. Mick Smith, the roving ambassador of the British ex -boxers' movement has informed me of the sudden passing of John, who was found dead in his armchair by his neighbour soon after complaining of not feeling well. He was secretary of Sheffield EBA, a post he had held for many years and must have attended a meeting at every EBA in the country sometime in his life. To journalists, record compilers and historians he was a source of help and information through his huge collection of books, magazines and photos which he would offer on loan to his many friends in the boxing world. The editor of this book was a recipient of John's kindness when working on the *World Championship Encyclopedia*, a future publication, and was shocked by his demise. There are many books and magazines on the game that have been enhanced by John's input. This applies to the book you are now reading. Help was always offered rather than our having to request it and his death leaves a gap that cannot be filled. John lived alone and had a son, who predeceased him, and one daughter who survives him.

RICCIO Tony *From* Bayonne, New Jersey, USA. *Died* 23 September 2008, aged 82 You will not find Tony's name amidst the middleweight champions and contenders of his day but there are names on his record of men who did make the grade: Harold Green, Danny Kapilow, Sonny Horne, Rocky Castellani, Lee Sala, Joe Miceli, Izzy Janazzo, Charlie Fusari, Pete Mead, Cecil Hudson, Tommy Bell, Rudy Zadell, Georgie Small and the celebrated Sugar Ray

Robinson. There is a win over Harold Anspatch in 1948 that intrigued me as I was unaware that the latter had boxed professionally. Anspatch came here in 1946 as a highly-touted star of an American team matched with the ABA and was sensationally beaten by Randolph Turpin, who then turned pro and got to the pinnacle of his division in 1951 when Tony was at the tail end of his career. Tony's career began in 1942 and by the time the war-torn years were over he was boxing ten-round, main-event bouts. His record, which up to then had been respectable, became spotty, but he was often in there with the iron of his division. Also, he did not find the transition from welter to middleweight an easy one. He drew with Harold Green in 1944, lost six out of 18 scraps in 1945 but in 1946 was beaten by Robinson, Joey LaMotta, Hudson and Mead. There was a good win on the credit side of his fistic account when he outpointed Sonny Horne. Against Castellani he lost two and then forced a draw. Another fine victory came against Sammy Angott, but this preceded losses to Miceli and Bell, both of them highly-rated men. Tony took a year's rest and came back in 1952 to beat LeRoy Tate before disappearing from the boxing scene. His known record is 105 fights, 55 wins, 13 draws and 37 losses.

RIX George *From* Dagenham. *Died* April 2009, aged 71. A former good-class amateur, George won the North-East Divisional bantam title in 1962 when outpointing Repton's Johnny Coats, a former opponent of the editor. Beaten in the London semis by Peter Bennyworth, who went on to retain his ABA title, George was Terry Spinks' first senior opponent back in 1955. He passed away after a long illness.

ROLLE Baby Boy *From* Nassau, Bahamas. *Died* 2009, aged 65. The death of Baby Boy Rolle early in 2009 passed almost unnoticed in the British press. Considering some of the names on his record and that he twice challenged for the Commonwealth light-heavyweight championship, this is a serious omission. The men who beat him for the aforementioned title were none other than John Conteh and Tony Mundine. The Baby fought from 1960 to 1982 and was pressing 40 when he had his last fight, a ten-round points win over Carl Baker. He fought some good men, many of them rated in the higher echelons of the world's light-heavies such as Pierre Fourie, Lonnie Bennett, James Scott, Gomeo Brennan, Jorge Ahumada as well as Conteh and Mundine. The only other British-based boxer's name to appear is that of Tim Wood, who outpointed him at the WSC Mayfair in 1975. For the first ten years of his career, he fought only in the Bahamas, being the Bahamian champion at heavy and light-heavyweight, but the opposition was not too demanding. It was only when he beat Brennan in 1972 that he got into the Commonwealth ratings. He had dropped a couple of decisions in 1970 to the Miami-based heavyweight, Eddie Talahami, who had

given Joe Bugner a boxing lesson before walking into a solid right. Although he was beginning to make a name for himself, his handlers pushed him into fights where he was meeting very experienced men. In other words, he was often an 'opponent', but one who could look after himself. Considering the calibre of opposition his overall record of 55 fights with 17 losses is a respectable one and he was certainly one of the best men to fight out of the Bahamas.

RWABWOGO Leo *From* Tororo, Uganda. *Died* 14 January 2009, aged 59. As one of his country's most successful amateur boxers, Leo would have been expected to turn professional, but after winning an Olympic Games' flyweight bronze medal in 1968 he decided to go for gold in the 1972 Games. Having put out the fancied David Vasquez (USA) and Tibor Badari (Hungary) in the early stages before losing to Poland's Artur Olech in the semis, there was plenty of ground for optimism. Although failing to win the Commonwealth Games title in 1970, losing to England's Dave Needham in the final, he went to Munich as one of the favourites. It was not to be though and after reaching the final, beating Maurice O'Sullivan (GB) and Neil McLaughlin (Ireland) on the way, he was outscored by Bulgaria's Gheorghi Kostadinov for the gold.

SALANDY Jisselle *From* Trinidad. *Died* 5 January 2009, aged 21. The undefeated female junior-middleweight champion was tragically killed in a car crash in Trinidad early in the New Year. She was holder of WBA, WBC and WIBA titles, all of which she won when stopping Liz Mooney. A tall woman, very powerful, and unbeaten in 17 outings, she had begun boxing at 16 with two knockout wins over Nimba Wahtuse, winning her first title two years later. In three of her fights, six titles were at stake. Her final contest took place eight days before her death.

SAXTON Johnny *From* Newark, New Jersey, USA. *Died* 4 October 2008, aged 78. A few days before hearing of Johnny Saxton's death, I was watching a DVD recording of his first fight with Carmen Basilio and was expecting his points victory to look controversial. Saxton was managed by Frank 'Blinky' Palermo who had close connections with what was euphemistically termed as 'the mob'. Saxton's record up to then was remarkable. He had cleaned up all the iron of the welterweight division, but I had a rather a cynical view of that because of Palermo's influence. I was wrong. The man could fight. There was no fluke victory over Basilio. On film it looked a close but clear win over one of the division's toughest performers. Notwithstanding his two subsequent losses to Basilio, that fight clearly emphasised Saxton's status as a class performer and, by his record, one of the greats of his era. On the way to the world welterweight title, which he held twice, he beat Joe Miceli, Lester Felton, Livio Minelli, Tony Pellone, Virgil Akins, Mario Trigo,

Ralph 'Tiger' Jones, Freddie Dawson, Danny 'Bang Bang' Womber, Luther Rawlings and drew with Wallace 'Bud' Smith. He was five years into his career before he lost for the first time, Gil Turner scoring a split-decision win over him in 1953. Later, when he was champion, Saxton avenged that loss. Although losing to Del Flanagan in that year, by virtue of victories over Joey Giardello and Johnny Bratton, Johnny got a successful shot at Kid Gavilan's crown. Then, after a shock loss to Ronnie Delaney, Johnny dropped a decision to Tony DeMarco and lost his championship. Four fights later he got the title back from Carmen Basilio, who had usurped DeMarco. By then he was showing signs of the hard fights in a notable career, and Basilio twice beat him in championship contests. It was no surprise when Johnny quit the following year after losing to Denny Moyer and Willie Green. He was living in dire poverty, handicapped by a leg injury, when he was moved to sheltered accommodation some year's back and after signs of dementia were apparent he was transferred to a hospice where he stayed up to his death.

Johnny Saxton

SCHULBERG Budd *From* Long Island, New York, USA. *Died* 5 August 2009, aged 95. To followers of boxing, Budd Wilson Schulberg will be remembered for his book, *The Harder they Fall*, which is a thinly-disguised story of the exploitation of Primo Carnera. It followed his first novel, *What Makes Sammy Run*, which became a best-seller. The Carnera-based story received even wider acclaim and was made into a film that starred Humphrey Bogart in his last role. Schulberg became boxing editor of the American

periodical, *Sports Illustrated*, and later wrote *Loser and Still Champion*, which is a commentary on the first Frazier v Ali contest in Madison Square Garden. In it, Schulberg shows his admiration of Ali but in an oblique way refers to Frazier as being just a 'slugger'. This bias in favour of the loser gives hardly any credit to Frazier, who was at one stage showing equal defensive skills as his opponent. It remains a brilliantly written book and did much to re-establish Ali as a peerless purveyor of boxing skills. Budd wrote the screenplay for his novel, *On the Waterfront*, which showed the corruption rampant in dockland trade unions while also having a strong boxing theme. It won eight Academy Awards. Like his father, he was a life-long boxing fan and his books based on the game, will always be considered as being some of the finest writing of its type. He was married four times and had five children.

SINN Bobby *From* Brisbane, Australia. *Died* 23 July 2009, aged 77. This aboriginal scrapper held the bantam and featherweight championships of Australia. Active in the 1950s, his 60-fight career peaked when he faced world bantamweight champion, Jimmy Carruthers, in a 12-round non-title affair in Sydney. Bobby was the underdog but he gave Carruthers a hard time of it and the decision in favour of the champion was not popular. Bobby seldom stopped his forward march and enticed Carruthers into toe-to-toe exchanges. That was Bobby's style and it made him a favourite with the fans. There are notable names on his fight record, such as Taffy Hancock, Sergio Caprari, Billy Peacock, Amleto Falcinelli, Pierre Cossemyns, Gianni Zuddas. He also challenged Peter Keenan in a bid for the Scot's Empire bantamweight title. Keenan was on his best form and retained his crown on points. Just before fighting Keenan, Bobby dropped a decision to Mario D'Agata, who was Italian champion and very much on the way up, becoming a world champion just 18 months later. Bobby came back from his loss to Keenan to take the Australian bantamweight championship. He was bang on form in beating Russell Sands but lost the title in his first defence and never regained the form he had shown at his peak. Regardless, he had enough left to wrest the national featherweight title from George Flemming in 1957 before trying his luck in the lightweight division. He was out of his depth and when Ollie Taylor beat him in 1958 he walked away from the game.

SKINKISS Stan *From* Manchester. *Died* 5 March 2009, aged 77. The death of Stan rekindles memories of the 1950s when the British feather and lightweight divisions oozed talent. A former Northern Counties' amateur champion, who was one of many good, solid performers around at the time, he began in 1951 after a long amateur career in which he boxed over a hundred bouts. Jack Bates, whose activities in boxing go back to the 1920s and '30s, was his mentor and he guided Stan through 15 fights in his first paid year. Stan beat Gene Caffrey in his third fight and by the end of the year had accounted for Hugh Mackie, Black Bond, Roy Groom, Billy Daniels and Johnny Haywood. Just two losses in such company was a good start, but he was forced to retire against Teddy Peckham in 1952 before coming back strongly to knockout Charlie Tucker and outpoint Freddie Hicks. It was in September of that year that he was matched with Hogan 'Kid' Bassey, who beat him. It was no disgrace, as Bassey would go on to become world featherweight champion. Stan was fighting the title contenders now, such as Freddie King, Johnny Butterworth, Sammy Bonnici, Denny Dawson, Tommy Miller, Ken Lawrence, Jim Kenny and Jackie Turpin et al. The year 1953 was his worst, with just one win in four outings. Alby Tissong and Laurie McShane beat him, but his victory over Freddie King was decisive and a shock for London fight-fans. The experienced, smooth-boxing Allan Tanner outpointed him and a following points win over Paddy Graham was his last notable victory. Losses to Gordon Goodman and the rising star, Dave Charnley indicated that Stan's best days were over. He was on business in London when he was taken ill and died.

Stan Skinkiss

SMITH Walter *From* Alabama, USA. *Died* February 2009, aged 94. Veteran trainer Walter was cut down by heart failure six years short of reaching his 100th birthday. He was a quiet man, never a self-publicist, but he knew boxing as few others did. He brought Emanuel Steward to the fore and joined him as a co-trainer to great fighters like Tommy Hearns and Hilmer Kenty. Dozens of champions and rated

fighters were handled by this successful team, who also worked with Britain's Dennis Andries during his American campaign. The Kronk gymnasium was part of Walter's life and his life was part of the Kronk. Men with his training skills are thin on the ground. His wife, Carrie survives him.

Gerry Smyth

SMYTH Gerry *From* Belfast, Northern Ireland. *Died* 10 Jan 2009, aged 85. A former Northern Ireland lightweight champion, Gerry was one of five boxing brothers, but the only one of them to have won a title. Gerry was All-Ireland champ as an amateur and the Northern Ireland lightweight titleholder as a professional. He boxed from 1946 to 1956, beginning in style by beating Harry Hughes in Glasgow before returning to his home turf to flatten John Ingle in 30 seconds. Too much was expected of him in his early career and he was thrown in with Stan Hawthorne, Bert Hornby, Paddy Dowdall, Dick Leivers, Tom Smith and Billy Thompson. He beat Hornby and knocked out Leivers but, not surprisingly, lost to the others. As his career settled down, he rose up in the ratings. In 1949 he lost a contest through cut eyes to Mickey O'Neill, but got Mickey back for a return and beat him. The championship came with the win. He later lost his title to Ricky McCullough, but regained it three months later and held on to the belt until he retired. Gerry was a crowd pleaser who drew large crowds to the Ulster Hall, his aggressive, action-packed style making him a favourite with the fans. His three fight series with Jim Keery were some of the best fights seen in Belfast in my time. One apiece going into the rubber meeting, it was excitement all the way as fortunes see-sawed until the old bug-bear of cuts forced Gerry's cornermen to throw in the towel in the 13th round. In a ten-year career, he went in with Ivor 'Kid' Germain, Peter Fallon, Kurt Ernest, Paddy Graham, Lahouri Godih, Roy Sharples, Al Brown, Santos Martins and Harry Warner. After losing a challenge for Roy Baird's welterweight championship Gerry called it a day. He ran a successful grocery business until he was 70 and joined the Northern Ireland Ex-Boxers' Association. Still remembered and a popular member, Gerry passed away in hospital following a short illness.

SPARKS Al *From* Winnepeg, Canada. *Died* October 2008, aged 70. A former British Empire light-heavyweight title challenger and twice holder of the Canadian title, Al was a southpaw with a record of 33 fights of which he won 20 and drew one. Boxing from 1956 to 1977, he quickly established himself as a force in Canadian boxing. Even so, it took until 1968 before he won the Canadian championship when beating Leslie Borden. He was quick to make a defence against Frank Bullard, then lost his title to Rene Durelle. Durelle gave him a return two months later and Al won on points. This time, he held on to his title for five years before losing it to Gary Summerhayes. In between those fights, he lost an Empire title challenge to Bob Dunlop in Australia, coming very close to winning in the 12th round when he twice dropped the Aussie for long counts. He was stopped by Carl 'Bobo' Olsen in 1960 and was inactive for two years from 1965. In a comeback fight he lost to Eddie Talhami, who I later saw outbox Joe Bugner before running in to one of Joe's right handers. Al then successfully defended his title against Bullard and Durelle. Having defended against Stewart Gray, Al was deeply affected when Gray died after being kayoed in seven rounds. It was following that fight that Al lost to Summerhayes and was then stopped by Len Hutchings. There was just one more outing, a win over George Jerome, before Al retired. He was 39 and went on to coach youngsters for years. Because of his gentlemanly demeanour and enthusiasm for boxing, he was always greeted warmly when at the ringside. A stroke was the main contributor to his death.

SPENCER Harry *From* Croydon. *Died* 30 December 2008, aged 99. Miles Templeton, who supplies me with so many fight results that are gleaned from local newspapers, is still uncovering reports of contests for Harry Spencer. Harry was brother to Herbie, against whom he fought three times. In their last fight, when they drew over six rounds, Harry adopted the monikker, 'Harry Marks' of Penge, which made the billing of Marks v Spencer. Their first match took place in 1922 and Miles has Harry boxing spasmodically up to the end of 1932. His most significant fights were wins over Arthur Eggleton, Fred Prior and Ted Vince.

SUAREZ Oscar *From* Puerto Rico. *Died* September 2008, aged 47. One of modern times' successful trainers, Oscar died of pancreatic cancer at his home in New Jersey. A transplanted Puerto Rican and a former pro fighter, he worked with three world champions in Jhonny Gonzalez, Naseem Hamed, following his split from Brendan Ingle, and Acelino Freitas. Others who benefited from Oscar's expertise were Omar Sheika, Aginaldo Nunes, Jose Reyes and Freddie Cardena. Freitas was inconsolable when he heard the news. "He was a great friend as well as being my trainer", he remarked.

Billy Taylor

TAYLOR Billy *From* Chiswick. *Died* December 2008. This old-timer boxed between 1944 and 1946, there being 16 contests traced for him, of which he won 12. He was a favourite at Caledonian Road Baths where he fought eight times. Billy beat Tommy Foxhall of Tipton, Phil Palmer, Jim Anderson (senior), Jimmy Jury, Jordan Tarone and Billy Cunningham and lost twice to Scotland's Harry Hughes, who later challenged for the British lightweight title. Billy's age has not been disclosed but a safe estimate is that he was in his early 80s.

THOMPSON Billy *From* Hickleton Main. *Died* 4 January 2009, aged 85. For a few days, after the death of Vince Hawkins, Billy Thompson was the oldest living British champion. Unfortunately, he never knew it because he was in a nursing home and ravaged with an illness that left him just a shell of the bright young man he had been in his prime. He held the lightweight title for four years, winning it by beating Stan Hawthorne, one of the hardest-punching lightweights of those times. Stan had previously beaten Billy for the vacant Northern Area title in 1946 and with the title in his hands, declared himself 'Cock of the North'. When Billy got him in the ring again, he gave Hawthorne a three round hammering and walked away as champion. Having won the ABA title in 1944, Billy turned professional the following year, being a well-muscled, stocky fighter, which was not surprising considering his interests in gymnastics. Conversely, he was one of the very few fighters of his time to wear glasses in private life and, despite his build, he was a damaging rather than powerful hitter. Benny Huntman managed him and it was really he who lost Billy's lightweight title when he brought his charge into the ring so drastically weakened by weight reduction that he was unable to take even the lightest of punches. Billy lost his crown to stable-mate Tommy McGovern, a man he had previously licked, and Huntman lost his licence and a huge stable of boxers with it. Billy had a three fight series with Andre Famechon, losing the first fight then trimming the Frenchman twice. Prior to their first meeting he got a shot at the European Championship and won it on points by trimming Roberto Proietti. He then lost a challenge to Arthur King for the British Empire crown, when cuts forced him to concede, and that fine boxer, Solly Cantor, took a narrow points victory over him at Harringay. Billy was soon back in winning form, defending the European title against Pierre Montane and Joseph Preys. He lost that prize when disqualified against Kid Dussart and was then surprisingly knocked out by old opponent, Pierre Montane. Weight problems were taking their toll and it was soon after that he lost his one remaining asset to McGovern. Although moving up a division the end was near and, following a few more wins, a loss to Roy Baird signalled the end. In a creditable career he'd made the Lonsdale Belt his own property and risen to the top of his profession within Europe. In later years he asked me if I could help him sell the belt. Billy stressed that he did not need the money but wanted to avoid any family financial squabbles over his estate when he died. I found a buyer for him, but am pleased that Billy ultimately decided not to sell. The next time I saw him he said that the matter had been discussed and the decided arrangements were satisfactory to all. What a pity that this approachable, friendly and well-mannered man should be afflicted with an incurable illness that tarnished his final years.

TOOMEY Mick *From* Kingston upon Hull. *Died* September 2008, aged 73. Mick boxed as an amateur for the St Mary's ABC and reached the Hull and East Riding finals. He was still in his teens then and as he progressed into manhood he played rugby league right through until his mid-30s. His enthusiasm for boxing had never waned and when his job as a docker folded, Mick set about organising gymnasium facilities where he trained and managed local boys, one of whom was his son, Kevin. After years of struggling his dedication paid off. Central Area lightweight champion, Kevin, fought for area titles five times and Chris Clarkson won Area titles at featherweight and bantamweight levels. Eventually, Mick had a nucleus of ambitious boxers in his stable and became general manager for Frank Maloney and Pat Brogan, who ran shows at the City Hall. In company with Brian Leven and Mike Ullyatt, the Hull and District Sporting Club was established. Mick wrote a history of Hull boxing which was published in soft-back form in 1996. When I read my copy, I was surprised at the good sentence construction and writing style that made it flow as a good book should. Mick was a Council member of the Central Area Board of Control and founder member of his local Ex-Boxers' Association. He was also very active in charity work, which involved looking after elderly people. His was a useful and full life and he put so much more into boxing, a sport he loved, than he ever got out of it.

TORRES Jose *From* Ponce, Puerto Rico. *Died* 19 January 2009, aged 72. Jose was a great fighter, an ex-world champion at light heavyweight and a man who again rose to prominence following his active career. He began boxing when in the US army, becoming a Golden Gloves champion and silver medallist in the Melbourne Olympics, losing to Laszlo Papp in the final. His professional debut came in1958 and he scored an impressive run of knockout wins until his 12th contest when he faced a peak-form Benny Paret, who held him to a draw. That result consolidated the obvious fact that Torres was world-championship material. He won another 13 before suffering his first defeat and only stoppage loss, against Cuba's Florentino Fernandez. Bouncing back with a win over Don Fullmer, the following year he added the names of Jose Gonzalez, Gomeo Brennan and ex-middleweight champion, Carl Bobo Olson, to his list of victims. The Olson victory came via a quick knockout that pushed him up to the leading light-heavyweight title challenger. Jose won the title the following year by flooring and stopping Willie Pastrano. Not many boxers put Willie on the deck but Jose did and increased his stoppage wins total, which eventually reached 29 out of 41 winning fights. He was a good champion, defending against Wayne Thornton, Eddie Cotton and finally Chic Calderwood, whom he knocked cold in round two. Dick Tiger took his title via a points win in 1966 and won the rematch too. That last decision caused a large-scale riot in Madison Square Garden as Jose appeared to be a clear winner. Wins over Bob Dunlap and Charlie Green followed, the latter putting Jose on the deck twice without being able to keep him there. Realising his best days were over he wisely decided to call an end to his gloved days. He became a representative of New York's

Puerto Rican community and went on the lecture circuit. Articulate, literate and politically astute, he became New York State Athletic Commissioner in 1984. He had written a biography of Muhammad Ali in 1971 and followed with one on Mike Tyson in 1987, both books receiving critical acclaim. In 1990 he took up the position of WBO President, a role he held for five years. 2007 saw him move back to Puerto Rico from New York in order to concentrate on writing on boxing and military history. 'Chegui' Torres as he was known, was elected into the Boxing Hall of Fame in 1997. He leaves a wife, Ramonita Ortiz.

TRISTRAM Lew *From* Derby. *Died* 11 March 2009, aged 78. A Midland Counties schoolboy champion, who as a naval airman became the Royal Navy amateur featherweight champion in 1954, Lew was competing with the likes of Dick McTaggart, Dave Charnley, Malcolm Collins and Tommy Nicholls in what was the number-one weight division in amateur boxing in this country at the time. Although hand injuries and illness eventually forced him out of competitive boxing he maintained his interest in the sport through the Merlin Youth Club that he set up in 1963 and, having put many lads on the straight and narrow through boxing, the club will be a lasting legacy to his memory.

TSUJI Masatate *From* Tokyo, Japan. *Died* 24 March 2009, aged 30. The death of this straw-weight boxer, following a loss to Yuji Kanemitsu in Tokyo, raises concerns over the medical administration of Oriental boxing. These concerns are largely based on the scene in Thailand where a spate of deaths points to the necessity of global medical procedures. Masatat was pushed into national contendership after an upset victory over a former world title challenger.

VARGAS Ronny *Born* New York, USA. *Died* 16 August 2008, aged 20. Up to the time he was fatally wounded by a gunman in the Bronx, Ronny, a middleweight, was unbeaten in eight fights. He was a three-time Golden Gloves champion and big things were expected of him as a professional. Only two of his eight fights went the scheduled distance, but he was untested against experienced opposition. His last fight, one month before he died, saw him knockout James Denson in three rounds.

WARBURTON Frankie *From* Chorley. *Died* 2 Feb 2009, aged 81. Frankie had 21 contests between 1948 and 1951. He and Colin Clough met four times, splitting the series at two wins each. His main success came in the middle part of his career when he beat Dennis Nagle, Johnny Black of Preston, Willie Thompson and knocked out Bobby Drake. He was out of luck at Belfast's Ulster Hall, where he fought twice, losing to Sammy Fisher and Joe McLaughlin, his only eight round fights. For the remaining 19, he was confined to a supporting role to the main event.

WASSAJA Mustafa *From* Copenhagen, Denmark. *Died* 27 April 2009, aged 55. There were times when Mustafa looked like getting to the very top of his profession after fleeing Idi Amin's war-torn Uganda to settle in Denmark, where all but three of his 28 fights took place. Mustafa had solid fistic credentials, being the middleweight winner of the 1975 pre-Olympic tournament in Montreal and quickly made his mark as a pro. As a southpaw and a talented fighter, his rise was rapid, beating Bunny Sterling in his fifth fight, then licking Tom Bethea, Roy John and Bobby Lloyd before ambitiously fighting and beating the great Bob Foster, albeit on a retirement. An arm injury had made Foster's task impossible. Up at light-heavyweight, his tally of wins continued, Tom Collins, Dennis Andries, Bunny Johnson, Jerry Celestine, Jesse Burnett and Victor Attivor all losing to him. He also avenged his only loss when beating the highly-regarded South-American, Avenamar Peralta. Back in 1977, Peralta, a veteran of 113 fights had outpointed him. Significantly, it was only Mustafa's third pro outing. In 1982, He stepped outside Denmark to challenge Michael Spinks for the WBA light-heavyweight title, but came unstuck when stopped in six rounds. Tony Mundine then outpointed him in Marseille and an unsuccessful bid to capture the Commonwealth title from Lotte Mwale in Lusaka was his last fight. Although he had a remarkable record I am left wondering how far he may have progressed had he not been brought up on a series of eight-round fights. He was not a heavy puncher and needed more ten and 12-round contests to realise his full potential.

WILSON Ossie *From* Northampton. *Died* October 2008, aged 80. Ten defeats in 16 fights between indicate that this Northampton welterweight Wilson was never a candidate for championship honours, yet he was much better than his record suggests. Having researched press reports of most of his fights and remembering so many of his opponents, I know that he was a respected small-halls' fighter who was popular at Hoxton Baths, Mile End Arena, Wembley Town Hall and Manor Place Baths. He fought just one eight-rounder, losing to Dagenham's Harry Warner at Watford, and the trade paper reports that he did well. There is a draw with Frank Priest midway through his short career and a notable victory over Ken Tizor. A late surge just failed to overhaul the points deficit against Ken Bebbington and another draw came against Bobby Callaghan. Ossie met Les Garbutt, Johnny Hunt, Johnny Fish and Tooting's Ron Kensington, so he was not in there with mugs. He fought from 1948 to 1952.

WILSON Willie *From* Nottingham. *Died* May 2009, aged 52. Peter 'Willie' Wilson had only brief exposure to boxing when in the army, but he was keen to continue when in civilian life and joined the Jimmy Gill stable in Nottingham. Starting in 1983, he boxed through to 1987 having 33 contests. He won only five but learned enough to become an eight-round fighter with some known names on his record. Prominent is that of Jim McDonnell, whom he fought twice. Ossie also mixed it with Glyn Rhodes, Andrew Furlong, Steve Boyle, Abdul Kareem, Mark Dinnage and Brian Roche.

WOODS Charles (Babe) *From* Boston, Mass, USA. *Died* November 2008, aged 93. The veteran manager and trainer guided Paul Pender to two separate terms as the world middleweight champion. Pender gained his first title in 1960, beating Sugar Ray Robinson, but lost it to Terry Downes the following year. Although Pender regained the title after outpointing Downes in Boston in 1962, he was stripped of it a year later and never fought again. Babe never found himself another fighter of world class.

YESIKO Gaybon *From* Transvaal, South Africa. *Died* November 2008, aged 52. Gaybon competed for national South African titles 12 times during his ten-year career. His first title came in 1981 when after five years of campaigning and one unsuccessful shot at the national bantamweight championship, he stopped Nkosinkulu Moss for the junior-featherweight crown. Dropping down a division, he won the Transvaal bantamweight title in his next fight and later won the junior featherweight crown, which he defended once before being usurped by Patrick Mbuma. Unfazed by that loss, he acquired the vacant Transvaal title in his next fight. Between these contests he outscored Jose Narvaez and drew with Kenny Mitchell. His tall and slight frame belied his amazing ability to jump back and forth between three weight divisions. After losing twice to Welile Nkosinkulu for the South African bantam championship, he lost to Bashew Sibaca at the featherweight limit. But just four months later he came back to beat Israel Papane in a junior featherweight contest. Each one was a title contest. He won and lost the South African junior featherweight championship in 1985, had five more fights and retired in 1987. The cause of death is reported as being due to a stomach complaint.

YUH Hwan-Kil *From* Kyongnam, South Korea. *Died* 21 April 2009, aged 46. This South Korean's career is a mirror on the state of boxing in recent times. He was a talented but inexperienced featherweight who acquired the vacant IBF super-featherweight championship in 1984. Up to that point he had beaten only one man of note in Koichi Matsushima. Of his earlier foes, 13 had only a single victory between them. Hyun Ahn, a fellow-countryman, with ten wins in 11 fights, became the first to beat Yuh, who then began to meet serious opposition. His latent talent then began to manifest. He won the OPBF featherweight title and defended it three times, but only against mediocre opposition. Stepping up in class he went from 1982 to 1984 unbeaten. During that time he beat Rod Sequenan for the IBF title, which he defended twice, losing on the last occasion to Australia's Lester Ellis. One win followed and then he quit boxing.

Other pro boxers who also passed away during the period, include **Walter Orlando Acosta** 31 (Argentinian light-welter, 1998 to 2007 – 22 contests), **Franco Antonini** 78 (Italian light, 1951 to 1958 - 41 contests), **Salamo Arouch** 86 (Israeli feather, 1955 - 1), **Johnny Azzard** (Australian welter, 1951 to 1957 - 25), **Faraji Badili** 26 (Tanzanian light-welter, 2000 to 2009 - 6 contests), **Lee Ballard** 76 (American middle, 1958 to 1963 - 36 contests), **Bluey Bostock** 75 (Australian light-welter, 1953 to 1959 - 11 contests), **Al Brooks** 64 (American heavy, 1966 to 1983 - 30 contests), **Billy Carabello** 57 (American middle, 1980 - 2 contests), **Brian Carden** 31 (American welter, 2005 to 2009 - 16 contests), **Vince Carlill** 73 (Australian welter, 1962 to 1965 - 17 contests), **Nicolas Cervera** 37 (Colombian light-welter, 1991 to 2005 - 41 contests), **Vince Cervi** 41 (Australian heavy, 1985 to 1997 - 18 contests), **Tommy Corrick** 78 (Canadian feather, 1950 to 1957 - 45 contests), **Dick Cotton** 75 (American middle, 1959 to 1962 - 16 contests), **Flavio DeBonis** 95 (American feather, 1933 to 1941 - 9 contests), **Elmo Mamede De Carvalho** 47 (Brazilian heavy, 1994 to 2000 - 16 contests), **Bert DeWitt** 76 (American welter, 1951 to 1956 - 10 contests), **Osmar Dias** 38 (Brazilian middle, 1997 to 2008 - 6 contests), **Bill Enright** 89 (New Zealand middle, 1940 to 1946 - 8 contests), **Joey Erskine** 78 (American welter, 1953 to 1954 - 11 contests), **Miguel Garcia** 63 (Argentinian feather, 1969 to 1972 - 23 contests), **Steve Garrett** 39 (American super-middle, 2000 to 2007 - 8 contests), **Joe Grubba** 82 (Australian light, 1943 to 1946 - 4 contests), **Joel Hayeu** (Papua New Guinea light-welter, 2009 - 1 contest), **Richard Hill** 76 (American middle, 1957 to 1963 - 14 contests), **Eddie Johnson** 64 (American middle, 1963 to 1971 - 31 contests), **Anatoly Klimanov** 59 (Ukranian heavy, 1992 - 1 contest), **Franklin Medina** 27 (Venezuelan bantam, 2004 to 2007 - 8 contests), **Francisco Moncivais** 21 (American heavy, 2009 - 2), **William Morelo** 26 (Colombian welter, 2000 to 2009 - 34 contests), **Andras Nagy** 23 (Hungarian cruiser, 2008 - 3 contests), **Marco Nazareth** (Mexican light-welter, 2005 to 2009 - 8 contests), **Nick Nichols** 72 (American feather, 1961 to 1967 - 16 contests), **Hipolito Segundo Nunez** 54 (Argentinian feather, 1974 to 1987 - 106 contests), **Scott Papasodora** 50 (American light-middle, 1980 to 1991 - 24 contests), **Joseph Phiri** 44 (Zambian heavy, 2001 to 2008 - 9 contests), **Rachel Purdy** 31 (Australian fly, 1997 to 2000 - 2 contests), **Bobo Renfrow** 59 (American heavy, 1968 to 1975 - 13 contests), **Ray Robinson** 60 (American light-heavy, 1976 to 1982 - 3 contests), **Freddy Sammons** 91 (American welter, 1943 to 1948 - 29 contests), **Bill Schellhas** 66 (American heavy, 1967 to 1971 - 17 contests), **Ben Skelton** 84 (American light-heavy, 1946 to 1955 - 28 contests), **Romolo Spila** 74 (Italian light-welter, 1957 to 1964 - 27 contests), **Jeff Stoudemire** 51 (American middle, 1980 to 1984 - 17 contests).

Leading BBBoC License Holders: Names and Addresses

Licensed Promoters

Michael Alldis
77 Buckswood Drive
Gossops Green
West Sussex RH11 8HU
01293 553 945

Mark Bateson
33 Springfield Road
Guisley
Leeds LS20 9AN
07778 601427

Jack Bishop
76 Gordon Road
Fareham
Hants PO16 7SS
01329 284708

Black Eye Promotions
Nick Hodges & Jane
Couch MBE
Llys y Deryn
Cilcennin
Lampeter
Ceredigion SA48 8RR
0157 047 0452

**Adam Booth
(Haymaker
Promotions)**
57 Jackson Road
Bromley
Kent BR2 8NT
07932 952666

Joe Calzaghe CBE
2 Manor Gardens
Maesrudded Lane
Blackwood
Gwent NP12 0AG
07841 039717

George Carman
17 Bodley House
Trewarden Avenue
Iver Heath
Bucks SL0 0SG
07881 415700

**Michael Carney
(Impact Boxing
Promotions)**
Bradley Arms Farm
Alton Road
Cheadle
Staffs ST10 4RA
07970 495597

Miranda Carter
86 Keslake Road
London NW6 6DG
07979 494950

**Dave Coldwell
(Koncrete Promotions)**
5 Penwood Walk
Bramley
Rotherham
Yorks S66 3XS
01709 701911

Patrick Connaughton
5th Floor, Harlech Court
Bute Terrace
Cardiff CF10 2FR

**Coventry Sporting
Club**
85 Lentons Lane
Aldermans Green
Coventry CV2 1NY
02476 614114

Pat Cowdell
129a Moat Road
Oldbury, Warley
West Midlands
01215 528082

Jim Curry
Ring Square
57 London Road
High Wycombe
Bucks HP11 1BS
07977 410648

**Jack Doughty
(Tara Promotions)**
Lane End Cottage
Golden Street
Off Buckstone Road
Shaw
Oldham OL1 8LY
01706 845753

Spencer Fearon
4 Curtain Road
Liverpool Street
London EC2A NQE
07957 921235

**Jonathan Feld
(World Sports
Organisation)**
Suite 6640
555 White Hart Lane
London N17 3RN
0208 888 5131

**Stephen Garber
(Premier SC)**
PO Box 704
Bradford
West Yorks
BD3 7WU
08703 505525

Dave Garside
33 Lowthian Road
Hartlepool
Cleveland
TS26 8AL
01429 291611
07973 792588

Christopher Gilmour
Platinum House
120 Carnegie Road
Hillington Park
Glasgow
G52 4JZ
07730 415036

**Tommy Gilmour MBE
(St Andrew's Sporting
Club)**
Platinum House
120 Carnegie Road
Hillington Park
Glasgow G52 4JZ
01418 105700

Carl Greaves
62 Nelson Road
Balderton
Newark
Notts NG24 3EL
01636 612320

Johnny Griffin
07989 215287
01162 629287

Oliver Harrison
Oliver's Gym
Charlestown Recreation
Centre
Holland Walk
Salford M6 6FW
07818 822522

Richard Hatton MBE
Hatton Health & Fitness
Hatton House
Market Street
Hyde
Cheshire SK14 1HE
07919 523859

Tony Hay
Romilly House
201 First Avenue
Central Park
Petherton Road
Hengrove
Bristol
BS14 9BZ
07974 662968

**Barry Hearn
(Matchroom)**
'Mascalls'
Mascalls Lane
Great Warley
Essex CM14 5LJ
01277 359900

**Michael Helliet
(Mayfair Sporting
Club)**
Flat 1
102 Whitfield Street
London W1T 5EB
0207 388 5999
07843 636920

**Mick Hennessy
(Hennessy Sports)**
Ravensbourne
Westerham Road
Keston
Kent BR2 6HE
08448 007138

Dennis Hobson
Apt 5 Cambrette
Le Grand Route de la
Cote
Jersey
Channel Islands JE2
6FF
07836 252429

**Dennis Hobson Snr
(DVSA Promotions)**
73 Darnall Road
Don Valley
Sheffield S9 5AH
01142 434700

Gary Hyde
18 Graystokes Park
Gosforth
Newcastle NE3 2DZ
07752 111621

Alma Ingle
26 Newman Road
Wincobank
Sheffield S9 1LP
01142 811277

**Philip Jeffries
(Bulldog Sports
Management Ltd)**
Silkworth Cottage
Warden Low Lane
Sunderland
SR3 2PD
01915 640202

**Lee McAllister
(Granite City Boxing
Promotions)**
Blairythan
Blairythan Terrace
Foveran
Aberdeen AB41 6AX
07912 626344

Malcolm McKillop
14 Springfield Road
Mangotsfield
Bristol
01179 573567

Patrick Magee
35 Deramore Park South
Belfast BT9 5BY
02890 748588

**Frank Maloney
(Maloney Promotions)**
33b High Street
Chiselhurst
Kent BR7 5AE
02084 677647

Rebecca Margel
10 Bentcliffe Lane
Leeds
LS17 6QF
01132 680681

Keith Mayo
1(a) The Openheimer
Centre
Greenbridge Road
Swindon
Wilts SN3 3LH
01793 618100

Clifton Mitchell
Newton House
1 Broadway Park Close
Derby DE22 1BU
01332 367453

Alex Morrison
197 Swanston Street
Laird Business Park
Dalmarnock
Glasgow
G40 4HW
01415 547777

Katherine Morrison
197 Swanston Street
Laird Business Park
Dalmarnock
Glasgow
G40 4HW
01415 547777

Jonathan Pegg
(Pugilist Promotions)
9 Finchmead Road
Tile Cross
Birmingham
01217 702214

Brian Peters
The County Club
Dunshaughlin
Co.Meath
Ireland
003 531 824 0724

Carlo Rea
15 Sandpiper Crescent
Coatbridge
ML5 4UW
07766 667660

Glyn Rhodes
166 Oldfield Road
Stannington
Sheffield S6 6DY
01142 326513

Gus Robinson MBE
Stranton House
West View Road
Hartlepool
Cleveland TS24 0BB
01429 234221

Paul Rowson
(PJ Promotions)
Roughstones
75 Catholic Lane
Sedgley
West Midlands
DY3 3YE
01902 670007

Chris Sanigar
Bristol Boxing Gym
40 Thomas Street
St Agnes
Bristol
Avon BS2 9LL
01179 496699

Jamie Sanigar
Bristol Boxing Gym
40 Thomas Street
St Agnes
Bristol
Avon BS2 9LL
01179 496699

Matt Scriven
(The Robin Hood
Executive Sporting
Club)
The Old One, Two
Fitness & Boxing Studio
2a Thoresby Street
Mansfield
Notts NG18 1QF
07833 995770

Kevin Spratt
8 Springfield Road
Guisley
Leeds LS20 8AL
01943 876229

Keith Walker
(Walkers Boxing
Promotions)
Headlands House
Business Centre
Suite 21-35
Spawd Bone Lane
Knottingley
West Yorks WF11 0HY
01977 662616

Frank Warren
(Sports Network)
Centurion House
Bircherley Green
Hertford
Herts SG14 1AP
01992 505550

Robert Waterman
7 Elmstead Close
Totteridge
London N20 8ER
0208 445 0257

Derek V Williams
1 Westwood Avenue
Upper Norwood
London SE19 3UD
07908 570354

Jane Wilton
(Belfast Boxing
Promotions)
The Bridge
42 Derryboy Road
Crossgar
Northern Ireland
BT30 9LH
02897 542195
01603 868606

Stephen Wood
(VIP Promotions)
Chaddock Lane
Astley
Manchester M29 7JT
07973 376796

Licensed Managers

Michael Alldis
77 Buckswood Drive
Gossops Green
Crawley
West Sussex RH11 8HU
0773 435 1966

Les Allen
85 Lentons Lane
Aldermans Green
Coventry CV2 1NY
07980 313414

Chris Aston
54/56 May Street
Crosland Moor
Huddersfield
West Yorks HD4 5DG
0148 432 9112

Andy Ayling
Centurion House
Bircherley Green
Hertford
Herts SG14 1AP
0199250 5550

Robert Bannan
1c Thornton Street
Townhead, Coatbridge
North Lanarkshire
ML5 2NZ
0123 660 6736

Bruce Baker
Unit 2, Six Acres
Stoddards Lane
Beckley, Nr Rye
East Sussex
TN31 6UG
01797 260 616

Wayne Barker
1 Manchester Road
Droylsden
Manchester M43 6EP
0161 301 3799

Steven Barrett
22 Drake Crescent
North Thamesmead
London SE28 8PZ
0208 473 0655

Mark Bateson
33 Springfield Road
Guiseley
Leeds LS20 9AN
0777 860 1427

Jack Bishop
76 Gordon Road
Fareham
Hants
PO16 7SS
0132 928 4708

Adam Booth
57 Jackson Road
Bromley
Kent BR2 8NT
07932 952666

Peter Bowen
50 Newman Avenue
Lanesfield
Wolverhampton
West Midlands
WV4 6BZ
0190 282 8159

Paul Boyce
Lodge Garage
Shelone Road
Briton Ferry
Neath
SA11 2NJ
0783 637 72702

David Bradley
The Dovecote
Aston Hall
Claverley
WV5 7DZ
0174 671 0287

John Branch
44 Hill Way
Holly Lodge Estate
London NE6 4EP

John Breen
Cedar Lodge
589 Antrim Road
Belfast BT15
0289 077 0238

Roy Callaghan
158 Harwich Road
Little Clacton
Essex
CO16 9NL
0793 994 7807

Scott Calow
18 Farnsworth Grove
Huthwaite
Notts
NG17 2NL
0787 664 1055

Enzo Calzaghe
51 Caerbryn
Pentwynmawr
Newbridge
Gwent
0149 524 8988

Michael Carney
Bradley Elms Farm
Alton Road
Threapwood
Cheadle
Stoke on Trent
Staffs
ST10 4RA
0797 049 5597

Richard Clark
17 Church Street
Milton Regis
Kent ME10 2JZ
07967 205476

Nigel Christian
22 Spire Court
Efford
Plymouth
PL3 6HP
0175 225 1136

Azumah Cofie
Suite 130
Dorset House
Duke Street
Chelmsford
Essex
CM1 1TB
0786 797 7406

David Coldwell
5 Penwood Park
Bramley
Rotherham
Yorks S66 3XS
0779 945 6400

Brian Coleman
31 Gwernifor Street
Mountain Ash
Mid Glamorgan
CF45 3NA
07816 084 838

Tommy Conroy
144 High Street East
Sunderland
Tyne and Wear
0191 567 6871

David Cowland
3 Linkfield Court
78 Auckland Road
London SE19 2DQ
0208 771 5974

John Cox
68 Chilton Way
Duston
Northants NN5 6AR
0781 499 2249

Dave Currivan
15 Northolt Avenue
South Ruislip
Middlesex
0208 841 9933

David Davies
10 Bryngelli
Carmel
Llanelli
Dyfed SA14 7TL
0126 984 3204

Ronnie Davies
3 Vallensdean Cottages
Hangleton Lane
Portslade
Sussex
0127 341 6497

Jack Doughty
Lane End Cottage
Golden Street
Off Buckstones Road
Shaw
Oldham OL2 8LY
0170 684 5753

Paul Dykes
7 Hadderidge
Burslem
Stoke on Trent
ST6 3ER
0783 177 7310

John Eames
83 Stokes Road
East Ham
London E6 3SF
0207 473 3173

Graham Earl
28 Talbot Road
Luton
Beds
LU2 7RW
0158 245 1117

Jim Evans
88 Windsor Road
Maidenhead
Berks SL6 2DJ
0162 862 3640

Graham Everett
7 Laud Close
Norwich NR7 0TN
0160 370 1484

Spencer Fearon
4 Curtain Road
Liverpool Street
London EC2A NQE
07957 921235

Neil Featherby
Mole Cottage
66 Chapel Lane
Felthorpe
Norwich NR10 4DN
01603 754 241

Jonathan Feld
Suite 6640
555 White Hart Lane
London N17 3RN
0208 888 3131

Chris Firth
10 Williams Street
Prescot
Meseyside L34 5SJ
0151 289 3579

Tania Follett
123 Calfridus Way
Bracknell
Berks
RG12 3HD
07930 904303

Philippe Fondu
1b Nursery Gardens
Birch Cottage
Chislehurst
Kent
BR7 5BW
0208 295 3598

Ali Forbes
196 Brampton Road
Bexleyheath
London DA7 4SY
0208 855 5292

Steve Foster
62 Overdale
Swinton
M27 3DL
0784 250 8193

Winston Fuller
271 Cavendish Road
Balham
London
SW12 0PH
0793 917 7929

Joseph Gallagher
0161 374 1683

Dai Gardiner
13 Hengoed Hall Drive
Cefn Hengoed
Mid Glamorgan
CF8 7JW
0144 381 2971

Dave Garside
33 Lowthian Road
Hartlepool
Cleveland
TS26 8AL
0142 929 1611

Malcolm Gates
78 Cedar Drive
Jarrow
Tyne &Wear
NE32 4BG
0191 537 2574

Jimmy Gill
5 Black Rod Close
Toten
Nottingham NG9 6GQ
0115 972 0433

Tommy Gilmour
Platinum House
120 Carnegie Road
Hillington Park
Glasgow
G52 4NY
0141 810 5700

Stephen Goodwin
Unit W1
Chester Enterprise
Centre
Hoole Bridge
Chester
0124 434 2012

Lee Graham
28 Smeaton Court
50 Rockingham Street
London SE1 6PF
0207 357 6648

Carl Greaves
62 Nelson Road
Balderton
Newark
Notts NG24 3EL
0163 661 2320

Christopher Hall
38 Fairley Way
Cheshunt
Herts
EN7 6LG
0783 813 2091

Jess Harding
c/o UK Industrial Pallets
Ltd
Travellers Lane
Industrial Estate
Travellers Lane
Welham Green
Hatfield
Herts
AL9 7HF
0170 727 0440

Tony Harris
Mir House
North Circus Street
Nottingham NG1 5AE
07749 442373

Oliver Harrison
Oliver's Gym
Charlestown Recreation
Centre
Holland Walk
Salford M6 6FW
07818 822522

Richard Hatton
25 Queens Drive
Gee Cross
Hyde
Cheshire
SK14 5LQ
0161 366 8133

Barry Hearn
'Mascalls'
Mascalls Lane
Great Warley
Brentwood
Essex CM14 5LJ
0127 735 9900

Michael Helliet
Flat 1
Lower Ground Floor
102 Whitfield Street
London W1T 5EB
0207 388 5999

Martin Herdman
24a Crown Road
St Margarets
Twickenham
Middlesex TW1 3EE
0208 891 6040

Dennis Hobson
Apt 5 Cambrette
Le Grande Route de la
Cote
Jersey
Channel Islands JE2
6FF
07836 252429

Dennis Hobson Snr
73 Darnall Road
Sheffield S9 5AH
0114 243 4700

Nicholas Hodges
Llys-y-Deryn
Cilcennin
Lampeter
Ceredigion
West Wales
SA48 8RR
0157 047 0452

Harry Holland
12 Kendall Close
Feltham
Middlesex
0208 867 0435

Lloyd Honeyghan
PO Box 17216
London SE17 1ZU
07956 405007

Brian Hughes MBE
41 Fold Green
Chadderton
Lancs OL9 9DX
0161 620 2916

Geoff Hunter
6 Hawkshead Way
Winsford
Cheshire CW7 2SZ
0160 686 2162

Dominic Ingle
5 Eccles Street
Sheffield
S9 1LN
0114 281 1277

John Ingle
24 Rockmount Road
Wincobank
Sheffield S9
07802 306 423

Grant Jeans
Flat 1/2
5 Walmer Crescent
Kinning Park
Glasgow G51 1AT
07810 496881

Philip Jeffries
Silksworth Cottage
Warden Law Lane
Sunderland
Tyne & Wear SR3 2PD
0191 564 0202

Errol Johnson
36 Newton Street
West Bromwich
West Midlands
B71 3RQ
0121 532 6118

Thomas Jones
13 Planetree Road
Hale
Cheshire
WA15 9JL
0161 980 2661

Frank Joseph
29 Arlington Road
Ealing
London W13 8PF
07789 136 682

Brian Lawrence
218 Millfields Road
London E5 0AR
0208 561 6736

Gary Lockett
32 Coed Mieri
Tyla Garw
Pontyclun CF72 9UW
07903 574100

Daniel Lutaaya
c/o Zaina Bukenya
41 Cresset House
Retreat Place
London E9 6RW
0795 162 7066

Pat Lynch
80 Broad Oaks Road
Solihull
West Midlands
B91 1HZ
01676 33374

Robert McCracken
16 Dugard Way
The Ridings
Droitwich WR9 8UX
0190 579 8976

Jim McDonnell
2 Meadway
Hillside Avenue
Woodford Green
Essex IG8 7RF
07860 770006

John McIntyre
123 Newton Avenue
Barrhead G78 2PS
0141 571 4393

Owen McMahon
3 Atlantic Avenue
Belfast BT15
0289 074 3535

Colin McMillan
60 Billet Road
Chadwell Heath
Romford
Essex RM6 5SU
0208 597 4464

Patrick Magee
35 Deramore Park South
Belfast BT9 5JY
07860 543 277
02890 758 588

Frank Maloney
33b High Street
Chislehurst
Kent BR7 5AE
0208 467 7647

Lee Maloney
4 St Pauls Cottages
Wentlock Court
Halewood Village
Liverpool
L26 0TA
0797 102 4704

Nick Manners
5 Foundry Avenue
Harehills
Leeds LS9 6BY
0793 296 5863

Rebecca Margel
10 Bentcliffe Lane
Leeds
LS17 6QF
0113 268 0681

Michael Marsden
1 North View
Roydes Lane
Rothwell
Leeds
LS26 0BQ
0113 282 5565

Clifton Mitchell
Newton House
1 Broadway Park Close
Derby DE22 1BU
01332 367453

Alex Morrison
197 Swanston Street
Laird Business Park
Dalmarnock
Glasgow G40 4HW
0141 554 7777

Lawrence Murphy
4 Dunblane Place
Kirkshaws
Coatbridge
North Lanarkshire ML5 5EQ
0123 642 7872

Trevor Nerwal
2 Canal Cottage
Old Warwick Road
Lapworth
Solihull B94 6BA
07748 244672

Chris Okoh
73 Purley Downs Road
Sanderstead
Surrey CR2 0RG
07799 510590

Ian Pauly
1202 Lincoln Road
Peterborough
PE4 6LA
0173 331 1266

Joseph Pennington
215 North Road
Clayton
Manchester
M11 4WQ
0161 223 4463

Jimmy Phelan
5 Farlington Close
Bilton Grange
Hull HU9 4AT
01482 789 959

Brian Powell
138 Laurel Road
Bassaleg
Newport
Gwent NP10 8PT
0163 389 2165

Dean Powell
Sports Network
Centurion House
Bircherley Green
Herts
07956 905741

Glyn Rhodes
166 Oldfield Road
Stannington
Sheffield S6 6DY
0114 232 6513

Gus Robinson MBE
Stranton House
Westview Road
Hartlepool
TS24 0BB
0142 923 4221

Steve Robinson
2 Whitehorn Way
Marshfield
Cardiff CF3 2TL
0163 368 1103

Derek Roche
29 Hazel Avenue
Skelton Woods
Leeds LS14 2HW
0113 265 2907

Mark Roe
48 Westbrooke Road
Sidcup
Kent DA15 7PH
0208 309 9396

John Rooney
11 Cedar House
Erlanger Road
London
SE14 5TB
0788 407 7024

Paul Rowson
Roughstones
75 Catholic Lane
Sedgley
West Midlands DY3 3YE
0190 267 0007

John Rushton
20 Alverley Lane
Balby
Doncaster
DN4 9AS
0130 231 0919

Chris Sanigar
Bristol Boxing Gym
40 Thomas Street
St Agnes
Bristol BS2 9LL
0117 949 6699

Trevor Schofield
234 Doncaster Road
Barnsley
South Yorks
S70 1UQ
0122 629 7376

Matthew Scriven
The Old One, Two
Fitness &Boxing Studio
2a Thoresby Street
Mansfield
Notts NG18 1QF
0783 399 5770

Mike Shinfield
126 Birchwood Lane
Somercotes
Derbys DE55 4NE
0177 360 3124

Tony Sims
67 Peel Place
Clayhall
Ilford
Essex IG5 0PT
0208 550 8911

Gurchuran Singh
Pro Gymnasium
Rear of 661 Foleshill Road
Coventry
CV6 5JQ
0777 576 7815

Les Southey
Oakhouse
Park Way
Hillingdon
Middlesex
0189 525 4719

Marvin Stone
4 Othello Court
3 Old Hospital Close
Tooting
London SW12 8SR
0208 767 1373

Karl Stubbs
56 Stubbs Gate
Newcastle
Staffordshire ST5 1LU
0178 266 1251

Glenroy Taylor
73 Aspen Lane
Northolt
Middlesex
U35 6XH
0795 645 3787

Jack Trickett
Blossom Barn
Blossom Lane
Woodford
Cheshire
SK7 1RE
0161 439 8943

James Tugby
5 Burnside Close
Kirby in Ashfield
Notts
NG17 8NX
0777 022 6656

Louis Veitch
The Victory Public
House
105 Caunce Street
Blackpool FY1 3NG
07843 250471

Keith Walker
Headland House
Suite 21-35
Spawd Bone Lane
Knottingley
West Yorks
WF11 0HY
0197 760 7888

Frank Warren
Centurion House
Bircherley Green
Hertford
Herts
SG14 1AP
0199 250 5550

Derek V Williams
1 Westwood Avenue
Upper Norwood
London SE19 3UD
0208 765 0492

Alan Wilton
The Bridge
42 Derryboy Road
Crossgar
BT30 9LH
0289 754 2195

Stephen Wood
Chaddock Lane
Astley
Manchester M29 7JT
0194 288 5700

Richie Woodhall
3 Leasowe Green
Lightmoor
Telford
Shropshire
TF4 3QX
0195 259 3886

Tex Woodward
Spaniorum Farm
Compton Greenfield
Bristol
BS12 3RX
0145 463 2448

Licensed Matchmakers

Neil Bowers
59 Carson Road
Canning Town
London
E16 4BD
0207 473 5631

Nigel Christian
22 Spire Court
Efford
Plymouth
PL3 6HP
0175 225 1136

Brian Coleman
31 Gwernifor Street
Mountain Ash
Mid-Glamorgan CF45
3NA
07816 084838

Jim Evans
88 Windsor Road
Bray
Maidenhead
Berks SL6 2DJ
0162 862 3640

Jonathan Feld
Suite 6640
555 White Hart Lane
London N17 7RN
0208 888 5131

Jimmy Gill
5 Black Rod Close
Toten
Nottingham NG9 6GQ
0115 972 0433

Tommy Gilmour MBE
Platinum House
120 Carnegie Road
Hillington Park
Glasgow
G52 4NY
0141 810 5700

Roy Hilder
2 Farrington Place
Chislehurst
Kent BR7 6BE
0208 325 6156

Nicholas Hodges
Llys y Deryn
Cilcennin
Lampeter
Ceredigion SA48 8RR
0157 047 0452

John Ingle
24 Rockmount Road
Wincobank
Sheffield S9 1LP
07802 306 423

Grant Jeans
Flat 1/2
5 Walmer Crescent
Kinning Park
Glasgow G51 1AT
07810 496881

Errol Johnson
36 Newton Street
West Bromwich
Birmingham
B71 3RQ
0121 532 6118

Michael Marsden
1 North View
Roydes Lane
Rothwell
Leeds LS26 0BQ
0113 282 2210

Ken Morton
3 St Quintin Mount
'Bradway'
Sheffield S17 4PQ
0114 262 1829

Dean Powell
Sports Network
Centurion House
Bircherley Green
Herts SG14 1AP
0199 250 5550

Richard Poxon
148 Cliffefield Road
Sheffield S8 9BS
0114 225 7856

Chris Sanigar
Bristol Boxing Gym
40 Thomas Street
St Agnes
Bristol
BS2 9LL
0117 949 6699

John Wilson
1 Shenley Hill
Radlett
Herts
WD7 3AS
01923 857874

The Editor and all members of the BBBoC *British Boxing Yearbook* would like to congratulate

Harold Alderman, MBE

On being awarded the Member of the British Empire medal for services to sports heritage

Harold received this prestigious award from Prince Charles at Buckingham Palace on 28 May

Boxing is Harold's life and he has helped countless family members throughout the country to find out more about their relatives' boxing careers. Since 1960, he has made regular pilgrimages from his home in Aylesham, Kent to the National Newspaper Library in Colindale, London in order to find and collate thousands of fight reports that would have remained undiscovered had it not been for his diligence

A former junior amateur boxer before eye trouble forced him to retire, Harold was a founder member of the Aylesham Amateur Boxing Club and is currently the club's President

Without Harold's expert help, the Editor, who is currently producing an extensive *World Championship Boxing Encyclopedia*, would not have been able to pin together the complete history of gloved boxing held in Britain since the 1870s.
Harold, who is admired by record compilers on both sides of the Atlantic, fully deserves this honour

Licensed BBBoC Referees, Timekeepers, Ringwhips and Inspectors

Licensed Referees

Class 'B'
Michael Alexander	Central Area
Reece Carter	Welsh Area
Robert Chalmers	Midlands Area
Nigel Gill	Midlands Area
Paul McCullagh	Northern Ireland
Kenneth Pringle	Scottish Area
Gary Williams	Northern Area
Graeme Williams	Northern Area

Class 'A'
Mark Curry	Northern Area
Kenneth Curtis	Southern Area
Roddy Evans	WelshArea
Paul Graham	Scottish Area
Stephen Gray	Central Area
Jeff Hinds	Southern Area
David Irving	Northern Ireland
Wynford Jones	Welsh Area
Shaun Messer	Midlands Area
Sean Russell	Northern Ireland
Grant Wallis	Western Area
Bob Williams	Southern Area
Andrew Wright	Northern Area

Class 'A' Star
Richie Davies	Southern Area
Phil Edwards	Central Area
Howard Foster	Central Area
Mark Green	Southern Area
Ian John-Lewis	Southern Area
John Keane	Midlands Area
Victor Loughlin	Scottish Area
Marcus McDonnell	Southern Area
Terry O'Connor	Midlands Area
Dave Parris	Southern Area

Licensed Timekeepers

Arnold Bryson	Northern Area
Neil Burder	Welsh Area
Anthony Dunkerley	Midlands Area
Andrew East	Central Area
Robert Edgeworth	Southern Area
Dale Elliott	Northern Ireland
Martin Fallon	Midlands Area
Harry Foxall	Midlands Area
Eric Gilmour	Scottish Area
Gary Grennan	Central Area
Brian Heath	Midlands Area
James Kirkwood	Scottish Area
Jon Lee	Western Area
Roddy McAllister	Scottish Area
Michael McCann	Southern Area
Peter McCann	Southern Area
Raymond Rice	Southern Area
Colin Roberts	Central Area

David Walters	Welsh Area
Kevin Walters	Northern Area
Nick White	Southern Area

Licensed Ringwhips

Jeremy Brown	Scottish Area
Michael Burke	Scottish Area
Stephen Bush	Western Area
Steve Butler	Central Area
Ernie Draper	Southern Area
Mark Elkin	Midlands Area
Simon Goodall	Midlands Area
Mark Currivan	Southern Area
David Hall	Central Area
Mervyn Lewis	Welsh Area
Stuart Lithgo	Northern Area
Tommy Miller (Jnr)	Central Area
Barry Pinder	Central Area
Tim Piper	Midlands Area
Sandy Risley	Southern Area
Tony Sarullo	Western Area
Stephen Sidebottom	Central Area

Inspectors

Herold Adams	Southern Area
Alan Alster	Central Area
William Ball	Southern Area
Richard Barber	Southern Area
Don Bartlett	Midlands Area
David Boulter	Central Area
Geoff Boulter	Midlands Area
Fred Breyer	Southern Area
Walter Campbell	Northern Ireland
Edward Cassidy	Northern Ireland
Michael Collier	Southern Area
Dai Corp	Welsh Area
Julian Courtney	Welsh Area
Maurice Cunningham	Northern Ireland
Robert Curry	Northern Area
Mark Davidson	Central Area
Jaswinder Dhaliwal	Midlands Area
Christopher Dolman	Midlands Area
Gordon Foulds	Scottish Area
Kevin Fulthorpe	Welsh Area
James Gamble	Northern Ireland
Paul Gooding	Welsh Area
Tony Hedges	Midlands Area
Michael Hills	Northern Area
Alan Honnibal	Western Area
Ben Hudson	Southern Area
Wayne Hutton	Northern Ireland
James Ivory	Central Area
Philip Jones	Midlands Area
Nicholas Laidman	Southern Area
John Latham	Central Area
Kevin Leafe	Central Area

Denzil Lewis	Central Area
Eddie Lillis	Central Area
Reginald Long	Northern Area
Bob Lonkhurst	Southern Area
Sam McAughtry	Northern Ireland
Dave McAuley	Northern Ireland
Liam McColgan	Scottish Area
Billy McCrory	Northern Ireland
Keith MacFarlane	Scottish Area
Gerry McGinley	Scottish Area
Paul McKeown	Northern Ireland
Neil McLean	Scottish Area
Michael Madden	Northern Ireland
Paddy Maguire	Northern Ireland
Andy Morris	Central Area
Daryl Neatis	Northern Area
Thomas Nichol	Northern Ireland
Phil O'Hare	Central Area
Richard Parsons	Western Area
Ron Pavett	Welsh Area
Richard Peers	Central Area
Dave Porter	Southern Area
Fred Potter	Northern Area
Suzanne Potts	Midlands Area
Martin Quinn	Northern Ireland
Steve Ray	Central Area
Hugh Russell	Northern Ireland
Charlie Sexton	Scottish Area
Glyn Thomas	Welsh Area
Nigel Underwood	Midlands Area
Richard Vaughan	Midlands Area
David Venn	Northern Area
Phil Waites	Midlands Area
Ron Warburton	Central Area
Mark Warner	Welsh Area
Craig Williams	Northern Area
Robert Wilson	Scottish Area
Fred Wright	Central Area

Grant Wallis: Class 'A' Western Area referee   Philip Sharkey

Boxers' Record Index

Advertisers